Birth, Marriage, Divorce, Bigamy, and Death Notices

From the Alcona County Review

Volume 1: 1877-1899

Alcona County, Michigan

Robert L. Ferrett

Donald A. Ferrett

Sturgeon Point Press

ISBN: 978-0-9744004-0-2

Published by Sturgeon Point Press

Birth, Marriage, Divorce, Bigamy, and Death Notices
From the Alcona County Review,
Volume 1: 1877-1899

Table of Contents

Birth, Marriage, Divorce, Bigamy, and Death Notices
From the Alcona County Review,
Volume 1: 1877-1899
Introduction

Series Introduction

Genealogists and family historians place great emphasis on the major life events of their ancestors. We, too, believe that the dates and locations of those events are important, but also see value in knowing the context in which they took place. Local newspapers often contain articles covering the lives of citizens from the entire community, rather than just the well-to-do, and are a rich source of information needed to understand the lives of one's ancestors. Much additional information can often (though not always) be obtained from vital record notices beyond the names, dates, and locations of the events. The diligent newspaper researcher can go beyond these vital records and find that their ancestor lost a valuable horse, opened a store, or went on a trip to a specific town in Ontario to visit relatives.

The State of Michigan passed laws requiring the recording of all births, marriages, and deaths occurring in the State beginning in 1867. Many such events went unrecorded in rural areas well into the twentieth century. That puts genealogists and family historians at a distinct disadvantage in these areas! An initial motivation for undertaking our transcription effort was this lack of official records for many of these vital events. We were also very interested in learning about life in Alcona County and along the Lake Huron Shore from the perspective of the local newspaper editor and the area correspondents.

The first newspaper to publish in Alcona County, *The Alcona County Review,* began publication in Harrisville, Michigan, on April 4, 1877, and continues to be the paper of record for the county to this day. The main source for the notices in this series is a set of microfilms of *The Review* that was filmed in the late 1990s by the current publisher, Ms. Cheryl Peterson, using donations solicited by the Alcona Historical Society. Some volumes also include articles from the *The Alcona County Herald,* which began publication in Lincoln, Michigan on January 1, 1908, initially as the *The Lincoln Herald.* We have included all of the notices that we could find in *The Review,* and a few from the *Herald,* including those of anyone from out of the area who had a connection to Alcona County or the Lake Huron Shore. The deaths of international, national, or state political figures were not included unless such a connection existed. Some issues of the newspaper were not available for filming and may not exist. Recently, both *The Review* and the *Herald* have been digitized. The microfilm and digitized versions (in PDF format) are available for searching at the Alcona County Library (Main library address: 312 W. Main, Harrisville, Michigan).

The notices are broken into seven volumes in an attempt to keep each volume down to a manageable size. Volume One covers a large time span, the years 1877-1899, since the county was small then and there were fewer events each year that were reported. Volumes Six and Seven cover only five years each due to the increasing activity in the county during and after World War II.

The volumes are divided into sections for each event type: Birth, Marriage, Divorce, Bigamy, and Death. Within each section, the articles are alphabetized by the names at the top of each article. For marriages, divorces, and bigamy notices, they are alphabetized by the surname of the male. A comprehensive index is included at the end for all names at the tops of the articles, including brides or wives. Maiden names, where known, are also included in the index for brides/wives who were previously married. The reader will undoubtedly notice the many occasions in which female given names or maiden names are unknown. We have used the term "Mrs." when we could not find the maiden name of a previously married bride, woman in a divorce case, or the wife of a bigamist. We have searched a variety of sources (see section on sources) to try to identify the full names of those not specifically named in the newspaper articles. If we think we have a correct name but are not certain, we put a question mark after it.

There are undoubtedly errors in this volume, both in the event notices themselves and in our transcriptions, including our understanding of maiden names and the names of parents. No transcription work of this size could be made error free. We have attempted to transcribe all articles in these volumes exactly as written in the newspaper, errors and all. However, a very few obvious typographical errors were corrected, and we inserted some comments into the articles, in brackets ([comment]). The serious researcher will want to see a copy of the original at the library.

The reader will find many instances of "errors" in grammar in these notices. We have tried to accurately duplicate the text in the original notices, making corrections only where there was clearly a case of incorrect typesetting. Writing styles changed noticeably during the years of these transcriptions. In some cases parts of the original text were unreadable. We used question marks in the transcription boxes where we had to interpret a word or phrase from a barely legible microfilm page.

The reader will find many variations in the spelling of surnames throughout these transcriptions. These should not necessarily be considered errors. Almost everyone who researches their family back into the nineteenth century will find spelling variations in the official records. Be creative about the spelling of surnames whenever you search for ancestors!

A common error is in the reporting of the dates of events. Sometimes it was weeks before the event was reported to the paper, and the exact date may have been lost or misinterpreted. Information in newspapers frequently got there through more than one person, and transmission errors were introduced along the way. Thus, the date in the newspaper and that in the official record may differ.

We undoubtedly introduced some errors of our own in the process of transcribing this large number of newspaper articles, and in interpreting the spelling of names, for which we apologize. Once again, we recommend that, after finding the article in these volumes, the reader will make a copy from the original in the local history room at the Alcona County Library.

Birth

Each entry in the Birth Notices section contains the following information: The name of the child in bold at the top of the entry, a box with the complete transcription of the article from the newspaper, an italicized citation of the newspaper and issue date of the notice, and the birth father and mother.

During the era of Volume 1, and for some time after, it was common usage to only give the father's name in a birth announcement (for example: "Joe Belair—a girl—happy man!"). Some notices did not even give the sex of the child ("F. O. Gullifer is the father of a brand new baby, and of course congratulations are in order. So here goes!"). The local correspondents who contributed these notices improved in their accuracy and completeness over time, but never got to the point of providing all of the vital information for all births.

The authors have used a number of sources to try to determine the names of the children, as well as the full names of both parents. For mothers who were previously married, we have included maiden names in brackets. We again apologize for any errors in interpretation of those sources. In the case of a stillborn child, or one who died within a few days of birth, the birth notice may also be a death notice. Please note that the names of parents in this section are not indexed, only that of the child.

Marriage

Entries in the Marriage Notices section contain the following: The full names of the two parties in the marriage, a box with the complete text of the relevant notice, and an italicized citation of the newspaper and issue date of the notice.

Marriage notices varied in length from a single sentence (see George Allen and Mary Lemon), to several paragraphs and two or three articles (George Theron Withington and Frances Bayley). Occasionally, the only article will be one stating that a marriage license has been issued, with no following marriage notice (John Rickle and Mary [Dewar] Mosseau). We make no claims that a marriage actually did or did not take place.

Divorce

Divorce Notices entries contain the following: The full names of the two parties in the divorce case, a box containing the full text of the notice, and an italicized citation of the newspaper and issue date of the notice.

The authors were surprised at the number of divorces in the early volumes. For the women in these entries, we again tried to determine their maiden names. Where this was not possible, we used "Mrs." Many of the articles are related to court proceedings.

Bigamy

Entries in the Bigamy Notices section contain the following: The full names of the parties involved in the Bigamy case, a box containing the full text of the notice, and an italicized citation of the newspaper and issue date of the notice.

Yes, there were some bigamy articles in the *Alcona County Review*, and they make interesting reading. As with the divorces, we tried to determine the names of all parties, including the wives' maiden names.

Death

The Death Notices section entries contain the following: The name of the deceased, a box containing the full text of the notice, an italicized citation of the newspaper and issue date of the notice, and an entry for the cemetery in which the deceased was buried. If no state, province, or country is shown, the cemetery is in Michigan. At times likely burial places were identified but could not be confirmed, and are marked "Probable."

As with the other categories, death notices varied considerably in length. Some were as short as a single article with a single sentence (Francis Bennaway). Others include multiple articles with many pages of text (William James Anderson). If an individual was seriously ill and died of that illness, or if there was a court case that extended over time, we included all relevant notices we could find. For some deaths, the probate process took years to complete. We included all of those notices, even if they went beyond the stated range of dates for the volume.

Males are indexed by their surnames. Women are indexed by both their married and maiden (where found) names. Maiden names in the index are in italics.

There were quite a few accidental deaths reported in the *Review*, including gruesome logging, railroad, and farming accidents. Some of the articles would probably be "R" rated today for violence. Also of note were the large number of infants and young children who died of diseases we no longer have to deal with, such as diphtheria, smallpox, and scarlet fever. In cases where several members of one family perished from the same cause, accident or illness, we often grouped them in the Death Notices section.

We have attempted to determine the location of burial for all of the deaths reported. Indexes to most of the local cemeteries (including our own for Mount Joy) were used in this effort. We give significant credit to Janet Higgins for her assistance in this phase of the project.

Sources

As stated above, the authors used a variety of sources to add information to the notices included in these volumes:

The most important sources for names for this volume were the Alcona County Birth Records (ACBR), Alcona County Marriage Records (ACMR), Alcona County Death Records (ACDR), and the U.S. Federal Census (Census). These records are available from a number of sources. The ACBR, ACMR, and ACDR sets are kept at the Alcona County Clerk's Office in Harrisville. The information on these records was also submitted to the State of Michigan Department of Public Health, and was microfilmed by the Latter Day Saints. The microfilms can be viewed at Family History Centers around the world. Of course, we also used notices from the Alcona County Review!

For privacy reasons the ACBR data set, which is a very valuable source of information on names of parents and children, has a 100 year restriction on release and therefore could not be accessed beyond 1915.

The U.S. Federal Census is taken every 10 years for purposes of Congressional redistricting. This census is of great help in putting family groups together and correlating names and ages of family members. Unfortunately for our Volume 1, the 1890 census was destroyed in a fire before it could be microfilmed, and was thus not available to us. Another problem with the census is that it is not released for 72 years. Thus, the latest census available is the one for 1940. That was a great handicap for our Volumes 6 and 7. We hand transcribed the U.S. Federal Census from microfilm for Alcona County in the early 1990s at the National Archives and Records Administration main location in Washington, D.C. For census records outside Alcona County, our primary source was the web site ancestry.com, a subscription site that has very good search capabilities. State of Michigan censuses were taken every 10 years on the "4s" but all have been lost for Alcona County (as well as several other counties in the state).

An additional source of death records is available at www.seekingmichigan.org. This searchable web site contains images of the original death certificates sent to the State of Michigan in Lansing, starting in 1897. The LDS web site www.familysearch.org has several decades of transcriptions of official Michigan death record submissions.

For burial information, the authors used the various cemetery transcriptions (including several by Kay Morley) available in the Alcona Library, searched the death record images at www.seekingmichigan.org, and checked the web sites www.findagrave.com, and www.familysearch.org. We also had the valuable assistance of Janet Higgins who looked at tombstones in the cemeteries in Alcona County.

Number of Events of Each Type per Volume

Volume	Date Range	Birth	Marriage	Divorce	Bigamy	Death
1	1877-1899	792	762	48	7	1,520
2	1900-1909	619	553	39	2	1,029
3	1910-1919	807	573	51	1	1,284
4	1920-1929	718	527	41	0	1,283
5	1930-1939	789	615	17	0	1,341
6	1940-1944	576	391	16	0	731
7	1945-1949	652	448	7	0	695
Total	All: 16,930	4,952	3,870	219	10	7,879

Acknowledgements

We would like to thank Cheryl Peterson of *The Alcona County Review* for making this work possible, Carol Luck for help in obtaining the microfilms and for providing access to the original newspapers, Kay Morley for her invaluable cemetery transcriptions, and Janet Higgins for her thorough review of cemeteries for the death records and all of her other support for this project. We also thank our spouses for putting up with us and giving us the time to complete it.

Introduction to Volume 1

This is the first volume of a series of transcriptions of life-event notices of interest to the people of Alcona County, Michigan, and the Lake Huron Shore.

Non-Native settlement of this part of the state began in the 1840s with the arrival of fishermen who used selected locations on the shore as seasonal fishing camps. Fishing was the main industry in the county into the 1860s, but was soon to be overwhelmed by lumbering, which reached its peak in the 1880s. By the turn of the century, farming of the timbered-over land and the services needed to support agriculture had become the primary employment of the citizens of Alcona County.

The period of Volume 1, 1877-1899, saw the first roads through Alcona County from Bay City to Alpena. The first railroads in the county were built to bring the timber from the lumber woods to saw mills on the shore, primarily in Black River and Harrisville. Passenger service by rail through the county seat of Harrisville was not begun until after the turn of the century. Travel to and from the county before this was almost exclusively by boat, both sail and steam.

While we expect most readers to use these volumes in tracing their own family members, a little "reading around" could be entertaining. In Volume 1, many entries were just plain interesting to read (see for example the birth of Carl Winter's children; all of the bigamy entries; deaths of William James Anderson and Ralph Pratt). Newspaper editors/publishers had great leeway in the late nineteenth century, and the local paper could be, as in Alcona County, strongly partisan. Note that Volume 7 (March 30, 1883 through April 11, 1884) of *The Review* is missing in its entirety, as are a few scattered pages from other issues of the paper.

This work has taken more than two decades to complete, including the early work on the federal census and county vital records. We sincerely hope that those who use these volumes will deem the effort worthwhile!

Bob and Don Ferrett (alconavitals@gmail.com)

Birth Notices

from the

Alcona County Review

Adams, Chester
MIKADO.
Born to Mr. and Mrs. Will Adams, a son.

Alcona County Review, April 15, 1897
Father: William H. Adams
Mother: Sarah A. McMillan

Alcorn, Charles
ALCONA ATOMS.

Mr. Alex Yuill became the father of a bouncing baby boy on Monday, the 1st day of February. Mr. Alcorn, of Alcona village, also became the father of a big boy on Friday last.

Alcona County Review, February 12, 1886
Father: Harry Alcorn
Mother: Elizabeth Mowcomber

Alcorn, John
ALCONA ATOMS.
A Shower of Babies in Alcona.
Mrs. Harry Alcorn presented her chappie with a baby boy, April 29th. All of the above are reported standard weight.

Alcona County Review, May 6, 1887
Father: Harry Alcorn
Mother: Elizabeth Mowcomber

Allen, {Girl}
Curtis Items.
Curtis, Jan. 20, 1896.--Curtis is increasing in population. Mrs. George McCollum has a bouncing 8 pound baby girl and Mr. and Mrs. Allen rejoice over a 10 pound baby girl; that shows we are not losing ground.

Alcona County Review, January 23, 1896
Father: Thomas Theodore Allen
Mother: Rosamund M. Dunn

Allen, Russell
Somewhat Personal.

Lyman H. Dunn has reached the proud period of a man's life when children rise up to call him grandfather. This one is a boy, born last Saturday at Au Sable to Mrs. T. T. Allen, nee Rose Dunn.

Alcona County Review, June 4, 1891
Father: Thomas Theodore Allen
Mother: Rosamund M. Dunn

Allen, Ruth E.
PERSONAL MENTION.
A son [daughter] was born to Mr. and Mrs. T. T. Allen at Au Sable on April 13.

Alcona County Review, April 16, 1896
Father: Thomas Theodore Allen
Mother: Rosamund M. Dunn

Alstrom, John Russell
CALEDONIA.
Spruce, Mar. 21, '99
The young son at the home of C. Alstrom will date his birth from March 14th last.

Alcona County Review, March 23, 1899
Father: Charles Alstrom
Mother: Catherine McDonald

Anderson, Julia
From Alcona.
Alcona, July 26th, 1878.
Mrs. Anderson, living near Hubbard Lake, presented her lieged lord with twin girls, and it is reported that they are as pretty as a picture. I cannot inform you how many were imported into Pearceville, all that I know of is two.

Alcona County Review, August 2, 1878
Father: John Kanute Anderson
Mother: Arvilla Ann Wood

Anderson, Junia
From Alcona.
Alcona, July 26th, 1878.
Mrs. Anderson, living near Hubbard Lake, presented her lieged lord with twin girls, and it is reported that they are as pretty as a picture. I cannot inform you how many were imported into Pearceville, all that I know of is two.

Alcona County Review, August 2, 1878
Father: John Kanute Anderson
Mother: Arvilla Ann Wood

Anderson, Walter
Along the Shore.

Born to Mrs. J. K. Anderson last Friday two boys, twins. This makes three children that Mrs. Anderson has presented her husband within a year. Gov. Jerome should make Mr. Anderson a present in behalf of the State.—*Alpena Pioneer.*

Alcona County Review, October 21, 1881
Father: John Knute Anderson
Mother: Arvilla Ann Wood

Anderson, William
Along the Shore.

Born to Mrs. J. K. Anderson last Friday two boys, twins. This makes three children that Mrs. Anderson has presented her husband within a year. Gov. Jerome should make Mr. Anderson a present in behalf of the State.—*Alpena Pioneer.*

Alcona County Review, October 21, 1881
Father: John Knute Anderson
Mother: Arvilla Ann Wood

Apsey, Edena
West Harrisville.

West Harrisville, Aug. 16.—Robt. Apsey was presented with a new daughter last week.

Alcona County Review, August 16, 1894
Father: Robert Apsey
Mother: Ida May House

Apsey, Glenn I.
Around the County.
West Harrisville Items.
Robert Apsey, who recently moved into our village, is father of a boy, who more recently arrived.

Alcona County Review, April 30, 1891
Father: Robert Apsey
Mother: Ida May House

Apsey, Milford McKinley
WEST HARRISVILLE.
Aug. 1, '96.

Born, to Mr. and Mrs. Robt. Apsey, a son.

Alcona County Review, August 13, 1896
Father: Robert Apsey
Mother: Ida May House

Atchison, Nellie M.
COUNTY JOTTINGS.
Andy, the shoemaker, is as "happy as a big sunflower, that nods and bends in the breezes." It's a girl, and weighs--well the scales have "gin out."

Alcona County Review, June 7, 1878
Father: Andrew Atchison
Mother: Mary E. Hunt

Atchison, William A.
County News and Gossip.

Andrew Atchison is exceedingly happy. It's another boy.

Alcona County Review, April 1, 1881
Father: Andrew Atchison
Mother: Mary E. Hunt

Atherton, Ashel
Curran Crumbs.
May 25, 1896.
Born to Mr. and Mrs. Samuel Atherton, a boy, May 5th.

Alcona County Review, May 28, 1896
Father: Samuel Atherton
Mother: Nellie Prudence Hensey

Atherton, Delbert
June 15, 1896.
Born, to Mr. and Mrs. Frank Atherton, a son.

Alcona County Review, June 18, 1896
Father: Frank Atherton
Mother: Minerva Inez Mooney

Bailey, Callie
PERSONAL MENTION.
Born to Rev. and Mrs. W. J. Bailey, a daughter, on Saturday, Aug. 11, 1894.

Alcona County Review, August 16, 1894
Father: William J. Bailey
Mother: Catherine Euphemia McDonald

Bailey, Effie Catherine
THE CRADLE.
Born—To Rev. and Mrs. W. J. Bailey, Saturday, January 30, a daughter.

Alcona County Review, February 4, 1892
Father: William J. Bailey
Mother: Catherine Euphemia McDonald

Bailey, Fred
MIKADO.
Herb Bailey has had a big smile on his face since last Thursday. Another big boy has arrived at his home.

Alcona County Review, November 23, 1899
Father: Herbert Bailey
Mother: Jane Parks

Baird, Clarence A.
HAWSE TOWNSHIP.
Mrs. Baird presented Mr. Baird with a fine big boy June 25. Both doing well.

Alcona County Review, July 6, 1899
Father: James Baird
Mother: Mary P. King

Baird, Henrietta
WEST HARRISVILLE.

Another happy man: Mr. Baird is very proud of his new daughter.

Alcona County Review, February 4, 1897
Father: James Baird
Mother: Mary P. King

Balch, Flora
THE CRADLE.
Born.--To Mr. and Mrs. Geo. Balch, Jr., Monday, January 25, a daughter.

Alcona County Review, February 4, 1892
Father: George W. Balch, Jr.
Mother: Carrie Bell Mudgett

Balch, George
LOCAL JOTTINGS

Geo. Balch, Jr., assumed a new responsibility Thursday morning. The responsibility is in the shape of a girl [boy], of usual weight, and George is glad of it.

Alcona County Review, March 16, 1888
Father: George W. Balch, Jr.
Mother: Carrie Bell Mudgett

Baldwin, Vernon B.
Curran Crumbs.
June 29, '96.
Born to Mrs. Anna Baldwin, a son.

Alcona County Review, July 2, 1896
Father: Edwin Baldwin
Mother: Anna E. Wilbur

Barber, Belle
KILLMASTER ECHOES.

Killmaster, June 7.--E. R. Barber is the happy father of a bouncing boy [girl].

Alcona County Review, June 15, 1888
Father: Eustache R. Barber
Mother: Margaret Wark

Barber, Daniel David
Little Strangers.
E. R. Barber of Henry Station reports another 11 lb. boy addition to his family on Sunday, May 6th.

Alcona County Review, May 17, 1894
Father: Eustache R. Barber
Mother: Margaret Wark

Barber, Hazen L.
PERSONAL POINTS.

Nicholas Barber is going around with a smile on his face: a ten pound boy is the cause of it.

Alcona County Review, March 31, 1898
Father: Nicholas N. Barber
Mother: Jessie M. Buyers

Barber, James E.
PERSONAL POINTS.

Mrs. Jas. Barber presented her husband with a bouncing baby boy Tuesday, May 2d.—Grand Marais Leader.

Alcona County Review, May 18, 1899
Father: James Barber
Mother: Cora May Hilliard

Barber, John B.
SOMEWHAT PERSONAL.

E. R. Barbour of Killmaster announces the birth of a son and heir Saturday morning weighing 14 lbs. Of Mr. Barbour's eight children only one weighed as low as 11 lbs. His second born weighed 15 lbs. and the others averaged 12 to 13 lbs. It is a family of heavy weights.

Alcona County Review, September 15, 1892
Father: Eustache R. Barber
Mother: Margaret Wark

Barber, Lyle Ross
PERSONAL MENTION.

Mr. and Mrs. N. Barber rejoice over the arrival of a nine-pound boy on Nov. 15.

Alcona County Review, December 5, 1895
Father: Nicholas N. Barber
Mother: Jessie M. Buyers

Barber, Margaret M.
MUD LAKE JC.
On May 11th there arrived at the home of E. R. Barber a visitor. They hope her stay may be a long one.

Alcona County Review, June 11, 1896
Father: Eustache R. Barber
Mother: Margaret Wark

Barber, Mary E.
EVENTS OF ONE WEEK
An 8-lb. girl recently arrived to gladden the hearts of Nich Barber and wife.

Alcona County Review, April 19, 1894
Father: Nicholas N. Barber
Mother: Jessie M. Buyers

Barnum, Delilah
Greenbush.

Greenbush, March 12.--Cigars on P. D. Barnum—daughter last Thursday.

Alcona County Review, March 15, 1894
Father: Phanuel Dick Barnum
Mother: Sarah Ellen Morgan

Baror, Maud

COUNTY JOTTINGS.

The family of Joseph Baror are happy. It's a nine pound girl.

Alcona County Review, June 14, 1878
Father: Joseph Baror
Mother: Anna Maria Aird

Basher, Frank

BLACK RIVER RIPPLES.

Chas. Basher—a boy—12 pounds.

Alcona County Review, August 14, 1885
Father: Charles Basher
Mother: Barbara Rhinehart

Batten, Amy Mae

Curtis Tid Bits.

Curtis, March 19.--A little stranger put in an appearance in the form of a housekeeper in the home of John Batten some time since.

Alcona County Review, March 22, 1894
Father: John W. Batten
Mother: Johanna H. Alexander

Batten, Grace Beulah

CURTIS NEWS.

Born, Saturday, Sept. 9, to Mr. and Mrs. John Batton, a daughter.

Alcona County Review, September 21, 1899
Father: John W. Batten
Mother: Johanna H. Alexander

Batten, Ida

CURTIS CRUMBS.

Curtis, Jan. 30.—Born, Jan. 17, to Mr. and Mrs. John Batten, a daughter.

Alcona County Review, February 3, 1888
Father: John W. Batten
Mother: Johanna H. Alexander

Batten, John M.

Curtis Items.

May 17, 1896.
Born to Mr. and Mrs. J. W. Batten a fine boy a short time ago. Also a boy to Mr. and Mrs. Wm. Wallace.

Alcona County Review, May 21, 1896
Father: John W. Batten
Mother: Johanna H. Alexander

Beard, Harold F.

County News and Gossip.

F. E. Beard, of Alcona, received a fine Christmas present in the shape of a big baby boy, presented by his wife.

Alcona County Review, December 27, 1878
Father: Frank E. Beard

Mother: Minnie A. Hewitt

Beard, James H.

COUNTY NEWS JOTTINGS.

Mr. F. E. Beard, of Alcona, is the happy father of a bouncing boy, the weight of which we did not get. The cherub was born in Bristol, Indiana last week, and therefore we are at a loss to determine whether we shall call him a Hoosier or Wolverine. "He looks just like his father, for all the world."

Alcona County Review, September 14, 1877
Father: Frank E. Beard
Mother: Minnie A. Hewitt

Beaton, Gertrude A.

Haynes Happenings.

Mrs. Beaton presented Henry with a baby girl on Decoration Day. Mother and daughter are reported as doing well.

Alcona County Review, June 10, 1897
Father: Henry Beaton
Mother: Sarah Anne Fettes

Beaton, Jessie Marie

SLEEPY HOLLOW.

Oct. 17th, 1899.
Born to Mr. and Mrs. Henry Beaton a daughter on Oct. 12.

Alcona County Review, October 19, 1899
Father: Henry Beaton
Mother: Sarah Anne Fettes

Beaton, John Murray

Haynes Happenings.

Haynes, Dec. 18.--Henry Beaton is the daddy of a big bouncing baby boy since Dec. 11.

Alcona County Review, December 20, 1894
Father: Henry Beaton
Mother: Sarah Anne Fettes

Beaumont, Charles Aruth

PERSONAL POINTS.

The many friends of Rev. Arthur Beaumont and wife will be interested in this little item of news:
"Born, to Rev. Arthur Beaumont and wife, at Henrietta, Mich., Sunday, Oct. 16th, a 10-pound son. Both doing well."

Alcona County Review, October 20, 1898
Father: Arthur Beaumont
Mother: Nellie Western

Beede, Charles H.

THE CRADLE.

January 21, to Mrs. F. A. Beede, a son.

Alcona County Review, January 29, 1891
Father: Fred Alger Beede
Mother: Caroline M. Storms

Beede, Fred Alger

HOME NEWS JOTTINGS.

Fred Beede wears the title of papa now with becoming dignity. His bouncing boy will be a voter just twenty-one years from to-day.

Alcona County Review, March 23, 1883
Father: Fred Alger Beede
Mother: Caroline M. Storms

Beede, Glenn Allison

LOCAL JOTTINGS.

Fred Beede is the father of two boys now, the second one putting in his claim for a share of the paternal blessings last Saturday.

Alcona County Review, November 28, 1884
Father: Fred Alger Beede
Mother: Caroline M. Storms

Beede, Mornelva

PERSONAL MENTION.

A daughter was born to Mrs. F. A. Beede on Saturday the 11th inst.

Alcona County Review, August 16, 1894
Father: Fred Alger Beede
Mother: Caroline M. Storms

Beede, Ray L.

LOCAL JOTTINGS.

Thursday, Feb. 4, Mrs. Fred Beede presented her husband with a bouncing boy.

Alcona County Review, February 12, 1886
Father: Fred Alger Beede
Mother: Caroline M. Storms

Beever, Esther Etta

PERSONAL.

Twin daughters were born to Geo. Beever and wife on Monday.

Alcona County Review, November 25, 1897
Father: George B. Beever
Mother: Hannah Melissa Cummings

Beever, Harold H.

PERSONAL.

Wm. Beever, Jr., is happy. It's a nine pound boy.

Alcona County Review, July 10, 1885
Father: William R. Beever, Jr.
Mother: Nellie

Beever, Raymond

PERSONAL MENTION.

Born to Mr. and Mrs. George Beever, a son, April 18.

Alcona County Review, April 23, 1896
Father: George B. Beever
Mother: Hannah Melissa Cummings

Beever, Robert Russell

LOCAL PICK UPS.

Born to Mr. and Mrs. Geo. Beever Monday evening, a boy.

Alcona County Review, August 10, 1899
Father: George B. Beever
Mother: Hannah Melissa Cummings

Beever, Ruth

PERSONAL.

Twin daughters were born to Geo. Beever and wife on Monday.

Alcona County Review, November 25, 1897
Father: George B. Beever
Mother: Hannah Melissa Cummings

Belair, {Girl}

LOCAL JOTTINGS.

Joe Belair—a girl—happy man.

Alcona County Review, August 14, 1885
Father: Joseph Belair
Mother: Emma LaFrance

Bell, {Boy}

PERSONAL MENTION.

Mr. and Mrs. Mitchell Bell are the parents of a 10 pound boy, since Monday, 7 inst.

Alcona County Review, September 10, 1896
Father: Mitchell Bell
Mother:

Bell, Martin J.

WEST HARRISVILLE GOSSIP.

Jas. Bell's countenance is a grand wreath of smiles over the arrival of a bouncing baby boy, who has come to stay, Saturday evening.

Alcona County Review, January 26, 1899
Father: James Bell
Mother: Fannie J. McRae

Bell, Martin J.

CURTISVILLE.

Nov. 28, '99.

Born to Mr. and Mrs. Bell on Saturday, a son. We are sorry to state that the infant lived only a few hours when it was laid to rest at West Curtis cemetery Sunday at 3 p.m. Mrs. Bell has the sympathy of a large circle of friends.

Alcona County Review, November 30, 1899
Father: Joseph Bell
Mother: Josephine LaFleur

Billings, Lucille

PERSONAL POINTS.

Born Tuesday, Sept. 10, to Mr. and Mrs. S. O. Billings, a daughter. Mother and child are doing nicely.— Tucker Co. (West Va.) Democrat.

Mrs. Billings was formerly Miss Anna Pearson of Harrisville.

Alcona County Review, October 6, 1898
Father: Samuel Olen Billings
Mother: Anna Louisa Pearson

Bissell, {Boy}

REVIEWINGS.

First a daughter, then a son, and the world is well begun. It's a nine pound boy, and Mr. and Mrs. J. T. Bissell are happy.

Alcona County Review, March 21, 1879
Father: Jerome T. Bissell
Mother: Mary E.

Bissonette, Anna B.

Curtis Items.

Feb. 3, 1896.

Born Jan. 27, to Mr. and Mrs. Jos. Buisnett, a girl.

Alcona County Review, February 6, 1896
Father: Joseph Anthony Bissonette
Mother: Emma Marie Beadle

Blakeney, {Boy}

PERSONAL POINTS.

A son was born to Mr. and Mrs. Earl Blakely last Thursday. A report that the child weighed 15 pounds has reached town but it is not verified.

Alcona County Review, May 5, 1898
Father: Earl D. Blakeney
Mother: Charlotte Emma Beever

Boardman, Eunice

REVIEWINGS.

Ah, ha!—here it is!—They were not twins, but they were born the same night and in the same house. One was a 10 pound boy to Mr. and Mrs. Chas. Twite, and the other was a 9 pound girl to Mr. and Mrs. John Boardman. There's a match for you, sure!

Alcona County Review, March 12, 1880
Father: John Boardman
Mother: Alvira

Boice, {Boy}

Haynes.

Mr. Joseph Hastings has a broad smile on his face—it is a boy. Ditto Mr. Boice.

Alcona County Review, March 31, 1892
Father: ? Boice
Mother:

Bond, {Boy }

LOCAL JOTTINGS.

Thomas Bond was highly complimented Tuesday night. His wife presented him with twins, son and daughter. Happy? "Well, I should say he was."

Alcona County Review, November 7, 1884
Father: Thomas Bond
Mother: Margaret J. Beals

Bond, {Girl}

LOCAL JOTTINGS.

Thomas Bond was highly complimented Tuesday night. His wife presented him with twins, son and daughter. Happy? "Well, I should say he was."

Alcona County Review, November 7, 1884
Father: Thomas Bond
Mother: Margaret J. Beals

Bond, {Girl}

HOME NEWS JOTTINGS.

Thomas Bond is happy, and the cause of his joy is the addition to his family of a pair of twin girls. They came last Monday, and weigh over twelve pounds.

Alcona County Review, February 23, 1883
Father: Thomas Bond
Mother: Margaret J. Beals

Bond, {Girl}

HOME NEWS JOTTINGS.

Thomas Bond is happy, and the cause of his joy is the addition to his family of a pair of twin girls. They came last Monday, and weigh over twelve pounds.

Alcona County Review, February 23, 1883
Father: Thomas Bond
Mother: Margaret J. Beals

Bond, Justus

LOCAL JOTTINGS.

To Mrs. Thos. Bond,—a son.

Alcona County Review, November 4, 1887
Father: Thomas Bond
Mother: Margaret J. Beals

Bonnard, Victor

MIKADO.

A baby boy arrived at the home of Mr. and Mrs. Joe Bonnards last week.

Alcona County Review, October 6, 1898
Father: Joseph Bonnard
Mother: Jane Ross

Bouford, {Girl}

Black River Sparks.

Born to Mr. and Mrs. Telesphore Bouford, a girl.

Alcona County Review, September 26, 1895
Father: Telesphore Bouford
Mother:

Brahaney, Florence

COUNTY REVIEWINGS.

Born, on Monday last, to Mr. and Mrs. James Brahaney, a girl.

Alcona County Review, July 30, 1880
Father: James Brahaney
Mother: Annie

Brennan, Josephine M.
LOCAL JOTTINGS.

Mrs. Andrew Brennan gave birth to a bouncing girl baby last Saturday. Mrs. B. has been a great sufferer from bronchial affections, having been confined to her room since last fall. She is now gaining slowly, and is hoped will entirely recover from her bronchial troubles.

Alcona County Review, March 12, 1886
Father: Andrew Brennan
Mother: Phoebe Bertrand

Bridgeman, {Girl}
LOCAL JOTTINGS.

Born, Feb. 5th, 1889, to Mr. and Mrs. Henry Bridgeman, of Duluth, Minn., a daughter.

Alcona County Review, February 22, 1889
Father: Henry Bridgeman
Mother: Charlotte D. Nevin

Bridgeman, Marion R.
LOCAL PICK UPS.
Born to Mr. and Mrs. H. Bridgeman, of Duluth, Minn., on June 28th, a daughter.

Alcona County Review, July 13, 1899
Father: Henry Bridgeman
Mother: Charlotte D. Nevin

Briggs, Bernard
PERSONAL POINTS.

Born to Mr. and Mrs. Frank H. Briggs, a son, at Ione, California, April 5th.

Alcona County Review, April 28, 1898
Father: Frank H. Briggs
Mother: Annie Dean

Briggs, Clara
Local News.
Word comes from Starkey, Oregon, that Mr. and Mrs. Frank H. Briggs of that place, formerly of Harrisville, are the proud parents of a handsome daughter, since Sept. 14th.

Alcona County Review, October 5, 1899
Father: Frank H. Briggs
Mother: Annie Dean

Briggs, Elam Owen
PERSONAL.

Born at Hilgard, Oregon, to Mr. and Mrs. J. C. Briggs, Jan. 7th, a son.

Alcona County Review, January 27, 1898
Father: James C. Briggs
Mother: Jennie M. Larson

Briggs, Kay John
PERSONAL POINTS.

A son was born to Mrs. Ernest Briggs at the residence of Mrs. Robt. Ludington Saturday last.

Alcona County Review, February 24, 1898
Father: Ernest A. Briggs
Mother: Alice M. [Fraser] McNally

Brooks, Florence
The Local News.

West Harrisville contributes another to the next census. A daughter was born to Mr. and Mrs. D. W. Brooks on March 22d.

Alcona County Review, March 28, 1890
Father: Daniel W. Brooks
Mother: Eliza Ann Brownlee

Brown, Erbert George
LOCAL JOTTINGS.

Born to Mr. and Mrs. James Brown, a son, weight 10 ½ pounds.

Alcona County Review, September 19, 1884
Father: James Brown
Mother: Elizabeth Henry

Brown, Ethel
HOME NEWS JOTTINGS.

James Brown of South Harrisville, since Wednesday of last week has worn one of the most smiling countenances you ever saw. It's a fine-looking daughter and weighs— well, the folks have been too much overcome with joy to yet read the figures on the "scales."

Alcona County Review, September 8, 1882
Father: James Brown
Mother: Elizabeth Henry

Brown, Elizabeth
Country Happenings.
Mr. and Mrs. Jas. Brown have welcomed a new comer to reign in their household, in the shape of another baby girl.

Alcona County Review, December 14, 1893
Father: James Brown
Mother: Elizabeth Henry

Brownlee, {Boy}
WEST HARRISVILLE.
To Mr. and Mrs. J. Brownlee, on March 15th, a son.

Alcona County Review, March 31, 1898
Father: Joshua Brownlee
Mother: Effie Jane Phillips

Brownlee, Sarah E.
The Local News.

Joshua Brownlee of West Harrisville feels proud of a little stranger of the female sex that recently came to brighten his fireside.

Alcona County Review, October 3, 1890
Father: Joshua Brownlee
Mother: Effie Jane Phillips

Bruce, William Wallace
PURELY PERSONAL.

Daniel D. Bruce and wife, of Mikado, are happy over the arrival of a son.

Alcona County Review, March 29, 1889
Father: Daniel D. Bruce
Mother: Mary Ann McGillis

Bryan, Clare
KILLMASTER RIPPLES.
Sept. 21, 1897.
Geo. Bryan is the new daddy of a 12 lb. boy.

Alcona County Review, September 23, 1897
Father: George Bryan
Mother: Mary M. Buyers

Buchanan, Anna Belle
LOCAL JOTTINGS.

Mrs. B. F. Buchanan presented her husband with a fine new baby girl Sunday night. This now gives Mr. B. a family of four daughters.

Alcona County Review, August 28, 1885
Father: Benjamin F. Buchanan
Mother: Flora

Buchanan, Earl
PERSONAL POINTS.

Born to Mr. and Mrs. Wm. Buchanan, Monday, March 21, a son.

Alcona County Review, March 24, 1898
Father: William Buchanan
Mother: Jennie Beever

Buchanan, Florence
PURELY PERSONAL.
Born—July 29th, to Mrs. B. F. Buchanan, a daughter.

Alcona County Review, August 5, 1887
Father: Benjamin F. Buchanan
Mother: Flora

Buchanan, Florence
Of Local Interest.
Born to Mr. and Mrs. Wm. Buchanan, Monday Dec. 25, a daughter.

Alcona County Review, December 28, 1899
Father: William Buchanan
Mother: Jennie Beever

Buchanan, Marguerite
PERSONAL MENTION.

"B. F. Buchanan and wife. At home March 8th, 1894. Marguerite—weight 9 lbs. Sixth member. Rising Sun, Ind." Thus reads a card received this week. Congratulations.

Alcona County Review, March 15, 1894
Father: Benjamin F. Buchanan
Mother: Flora

Buchanan, Mitchell
LOCAL JOTTINGS.

Born, to Mr. and Mrs. Wm. Buchanan, a son.

Alcona County Review, March 1, 1889
Father: William Buchanan
Mother: Jennie Beever

Burt, {Boy}
Local Sayings and Doings.

There's fresh joy at the home of John Burt, Jr., a son having come to greet its father and mother. We didn't get the weight.

Alcona County Review, April 14, 1882
Father: John Burt
Mother: Isabel M. McIntyre

Byce, {Boy}

Born, Jan. 7, 1890 to Mr. and Mrs. Daniel Byce another boy, which makes Daniel smile and in conversation with him Thursday he says he is the father of 10 boys, 8 now living.

Alcona County Review, January 10, 1890
Father: Daniel Byce
Mother: Sarah A. Fitch

Byce, Grace
West Harrisville.
October 1, 1895.
Walter Byce is the happy father of a nine-pound girl. I hope he will get here in time to treat.

Alcona County Review, October 3, 1895
Father: Walter Byce
Mother: Alice Lemon

Campbell, Eugene
LOCAL JOTTINGS.

Born, March 9th, to Mr. and Mrs. S. E. Campbell, a son.

Alcona County Review, March 15, 1889
Father: Samuel E. Campbell
Mother: Jennie E. Reynolds

Campbell, John Seal
ALCONA ATOMS.
Alcona, March 12.—Mrs. Archy Campbell presented her liege lord and master with a baby boy on Saturday.

Alcona County Review, March 16, 1888

Father: Archibald Campbell
Mother: Frances Elizabeth Armstrong

Campbell, Rachel Catherine
Haynes Happenings.

Received too late for Publication last week.

Haynes, Sept. 13th, 1894.--Tally a brand new daughter to Archey Campbell. Also one for Fred Teeple.

Alcona County Review, September 20, 1894
Father: Archibald Campbell
Mother: Frances Elizabeth Armstrong

Campbell, Sarah J.
ALCONA ATOMS.

And now Archy Campbell sings, "I am the daddy of a bouncing baby girl, with cheeks so cherry red." It arrived in Alcona last Saturday.

Alcona County Review, June 25, 1886
Father: Archibald Campbell
Mother: Frances Elizabeth Armstrong

Campbell, Sarah L.
ALCONA ATOMS.

Alcona, Feb. 28.—Duncan Campbell was the happy recipient last week of a young daughter.

Alcona County Review, March 2, 1888
Father: Duncan Campbell
Mother: Agnes Fettes

Card, Esther
Haynes Happenings.

Geo. Ritchie received a present of another son on the 21st, and it is reported that Fred J. Card is similarly happy, sex unknown.

Alcona County Review, November 1, 1894
Father: Frederick J. Card, Sr.
Mother: Eliza Miller

Card, Frederick, Jr.
Alcona Atoms.

Blow ye the trumpet and sound the dinner horn, for Fred J. Carde is father of a brand new sawyer.

Alcona County Review, May 26, 1882
Father: Frederick J. Card, Sr.
Mother: Eliza Miller

Cardy, Clarence

Mr. and Mrs. Louis Cardy, Jr., are the proud parents of a bouncing 10 pound baby boy, born on the 22d of last month.

Alcona County Review, September 3, 1891
Father: Louis J. Cardy, Jr.
Mother: Francis Ida F. Little

Cardy, Russel L.
PERSONAL MENTION.

A 12 pound son and heir arrived Tuesday morning at the residence of L. Cardy, Jr., to gladden the hearts of the parents.

Alcona County Review, February 1, 1894
Father: Louis J. Cardy, Jr.
Mother: Francis Ida F. Lytle

Carle, Myrtle May
COUNTY REVIEWINGS.

W. F. Carle and A. Noyes have each been made the happy father of a girl baby this week.

Alcona County Review, September 17, 1880
Father: William F. Carle
Mother: Sadie Code

Carr, {Boy}
ALCONA ATOMS.

Joseph Hasty is a daddy; it's a boy. Phillip Carr's little flock also numbers one more boy.

Alcona County Review, August 6, 1886
Father: Phillip Carr
Mother: Catherine

Carson, Joseph

Born, to Mrs. Carson, on Sunday, a boy.

Alcona County Review, September 13, 1889
Father: Matthew Carson
Mother: Jane Dobson

Chambers, Charles
EVENTS OF ONE WEEK.

Born, a son to Mrs. Will Chambers and a daughter to Mrs. A. Clark.

Alcona County Review, March 30, 1893
Father: William N. Chambers
Mother: Nellie Dora Angell

Chambers, Eva
Alcona County Leads.
There is rejoicing in the household of Wm. Chambers over the birth of a daughter.

Alcona County Review, September 29, 1898
Father: William N. Chambers
Mother: Nellie Dora Angell

Chambers, {Girl}
Your Folks and Our Folks.

A little stranger of the female sex arrived at the home of Mr. and Mrs. Will Chambers Thursday last.

Alcona County Review, May 7, 1891
Father: William N. Chambers
Mother: Nellie Dora Angell

Chapelle, Grace A.
THE CRADLE.

Born to Mrs. E. W. Chapelle,
Tuesday, January 15, a daughter.

Alcona County Review, January 17, 1890
Father: Edward W. Chapelle
Mother: Ida May Ralston

Chapelle, Zoe R.

PERSONAL.

A daughter was born to Mr. and
Mrs. E. W. Chapelle Monday noon.

Alcona County Review, December 30, 1897
Father: Edward W. Chapelle
Mother: Ida May Ralston

Chiritree, Eugene Russell

PERSONAL POINTS.

Mr. and Mrs. Chiritree gave
welcome to a little stranger of the
masculine gender yesterday.

Alcona County Review, December 8, 1898
Father: Calvin Chiritree
Mother: Isabella Sinton

Churchill, Alice

BLACK RIVER ITEMS.

We are glad to announce that Mr.
and Mrs. Peter Churchill are happy
again—a little girl. We didn't learn
the weight.

Alcona County Review, April 23, 1880
Father: Peter Churchill
Mother: Sarah Olmstead

Churchill, Frank

COUNTY JOTTINGS.

Mrs. James Churchill presented
her husband with a ten pound boy on
Sunday last.

Alcona County Review, September 20, 1878
Father: James S. Churchill
Mother: Mary Olmstead

Churchill, James

Black River Items.

James Churchill is the happy man
this time—a young son.

Alcona County Review, May 7, 1880
Father: James S. Churchill
Mother: Mary Olmstead

Churchill, Paul

Black River Sparks.

Born, Jan. 25, to Mr. and Mrs.
Arthur Churchill, a son.

Alcona County Review, January 30, 1896
Father: Arthur Churchill
Mother: Elizabeth

Clark, Chester B.

Haynes Happenings.

Wm. Clark is the father of a young
butcher boy for the past two weeks.

Alcona County Review, February 4, 1897
Father: William Clark
Mother: Florence Belle Jack

Clark, {Girl}

LOCAL JOTTINGS.

Increase of one in population of
Harrisville. It is Albert Clark this
time who is destined to bask in the
sunlight of a baby girl's warm smiles.

Alcona County Review, February 8, 1889
Father: Albert J. Clark
Mother: Sarah

Clark, Ida May

ALCONA ATOMS.

On the 3d there were several
venerable looking old ladies
congregated at the residence of Mr.
Clark, and in a short time he heard a
peculiar squall and one of the old
ladies stuck her head out of the room,
and he asked what is it? Answer, a
girl. "H—l, thunder, and lightning, I
wanted a boy!" Five girls and only
two boys.

Alcona County Review, March 12, 1886
Father: Charles Hope Clark
Mother: Elizabeth Miller

Clark, Samuel

SOMEWHAT PERSONAL.

Born to Mr. and Mrs. John Clark,
of the Mud Lake Branch, a son, Sept.
10th, inst.

Alcona County Review, September 15, 1892
Father: John G. Clark
Mother: Margaret Mary McKinnon

Clark, Sarah E.

EVENTS OF ONE WEEK.

Born, a son to Mrs. Will Chambers
and a daughter to Mrs. A. Clark.

Alcona County Review, March 30, 1893
Father: Albert J. Clark
Mother: Sarah

Clark, Thelma A.

Local News.

Al Clark has informed our
reporter, confidentially, that he is the
father of a 10 pound new girl since
Sunday morning.

Alcona County Review, September 14, 1899
Father: Albert J. Clark
Mother: Sarah

Cohen, {Boy}

Reviewings.

David Cohen is happy. It's a ten-
pound boy.

Alcona County Review, March 5, 1880
Father: David Cohen
Mother:

Collins, Robert McMullin

The Local News.

Patrick Quinlin appeared in
Justice Beede's court last week to
answer to a charge of bastardy,
preferred by Johanna Collins. The
examination was adjourned until
May 31, as the people were not
prepared with their witnesses. W. E.
Depew was present to represent
Quinlin. [Note: Born March
2, 1892.]

Alcona County Review, May 12, 1892

The Local News.

Patrick Quinlan was arraigned
Tuesday before Justice Beede, on the
charge of bastardy previously
noticed, and without examination
was bound over to the circuit court
for trial in the sum of $200 bail,
which was furnished with D.
LaBoueff as surety. The girl in the
case is Mary Ann McMullin, step
daughter of Thos. Collins.

Alcona County Review, May 12, 1892

For Court and Jury to Decide.

The following is a complete list of
cases to be tried at the next session of
court:

People vs. Patrick Quinlin,
Bastardy.

Alcona County Review, September 29, 1892
Father: Patrick Quinlan?
Mother: Mary Ann McMullin (Collins)

Colwell, Edith Gardiner

COUNTY NEWS JOTTINGS.

Another Man Made Happy.—One
of the most sublime thoughts of life is
that all the glories of this world do
not come to one particular person.
For instance, to illustrate: Born—to
Mr. George W. Colwell, of
Harrisville, Mich., on the 21st inst., at
Angelica, N. Y., a daughter; weight
10 ¼ pounds.

"Eureka!" George in ecstacy cries,
My head is all of a whirl!
I've waited so long—time heavily
flies—
But at last I've a ten pound girl!"

Alcona County Review, August 24, 1877
Father: George W. Colwell
Mother: Mary Jane Gardiner

Colwell, Ethel P.

COUNTY REVIEWINGS.

Mr. Geo. W. Colwell is the happy
one this time—a girl—this morning.

Alcona County Review, August 27, 1880
Father: George W. Colwell
Mother: Mary Jane Gardiner

Colwell, Grace L.

Local Sayings and Doings.

L. A. Colwell is the father of a bouncing baby girl. She tips the beam at ten pounds.

Alcona County Review, August 25, 1882
Father: Llewellyn A. Colwell
Mother: Josephine E. French

Colwell, Margaret Louise
County News and Gossip.

Lew A. Colwell is the happy father of another nice little daughter, presented to him last Friday—weight 9 pounds. May the little one become the joy of the household.

Alcona County Review, February 21, 1879
Father: Llewellyn A. Colwell
Mother: Josephine E. French

Colwell, Roscoe Stanley
Purely Personal.

Born, to Mrs. H. F. Colwell, Friday, May 16, a son.

Alcona County Review, May 23, 1890
Father: Henry F. Colwell
Mother: Jennie Burt

Colwell, Walter S.
COUNTY JOTTINGS.

Geo. W. Colwell is happy. It's a boy. Yesterday morning the date. Mother and son doing well. That's nice, for

First a daughter, then a son,
And the world is well begun.

Alcona County Review, September 20, 1878
Father: George W. Colwell
Mother: Mary Jane Gardiner

Colwell, William Wallace
LOCAL JOTTINGS.

The close of last week brought happiness to our townsman Geo. W. Colwell. His wife presented him with a handsome new boy.

Alcona County Review, September 4, 1885
Father: George W. Colwell
Mother: Mary Jane Gardiner

Conklin, Alton

Born Feb. 3, to Mr. and Mrs. Chas. Conklin, a son.

Alcona County Review, February 4, 1909
Father: Charles Conklin
Mother: Minnie A. LaChapelle

Conklin, Austin
The Local News.

Born to Mr. and Mrs. Chas. Conklin, a son. Thursday, March 3rd, inst.

Alcona County Review, March 10, 1892
Father: Charles Conklin

Mother: Minnie A. LaChapelle

Conklin, Harold

Born to Mr. and Mrs. Wm. Conklin, July 1st, a son. All hands, including the father, are doing well.

Alcona County Review, July 6, 1899
Father: William Frank Conklin
Mother: Jennie Anderson

Conklin, Laura Mae

A daughter was born to Mr. and Mrs. Chas. Conklin this morning.

Alcona County Review, March 31, 1898
Father: Charles Conklin
Mother: Minnie A. LaChapelle

Conklin, Lois
PERSONAL MENTION.

Born to Mr. and Mrs. Chas. Conklin, a daughter Dec. 20.

Alcona County Review, December 26, 1895
Father: Charles Conklin
Mother: Minnie A. LaChapelle

Conklin, Stuart
PERSONAL MENTION.

Born to Mr. and Mrs. Chas. Conklin, a son, Sunday, February 25.

Alcona County Review, March 1, 1894
Father: Charles Conklin
Mother: Minnie A. LaChapelle

Connors, {Boy}
KILLMASTER.
Feb. 26, 1896.
A son was born to Mr. and Mrs. Tom Connors last Friday.

Alcona County Review, February 27, 1896
Father: Thomas Connors
Mother: Ellen

Cook, Mary
ALCONA ATOMS.
A Shower of Babies in Alcona.
Mrs. John Cook made up her mind to be in the fashion and so presented John with a baby girl.
All of the above are reported standard weight.

Alcona County Review, May 6, 1887
Father: John Cook
Mother: Janet Wilson

Coon, Florence
LOCAL PICK UPS.
Born to Mr. and Mrs. Silas Coon Tuesday, a son.

Alcona County Review, January 19, 1899
Father: Silas Coon
Mother: Emma

Coon, Nellie M.
PERSONAL.

Born to Mr. and Mrs. Richard Coon, on Wednesday of last week, a girl.

Alcona County Review, November 18, 1897
Father: Richard Coon
Mother: Mary J.

Corbett, Ila G.
LOCAL PICK UPS.
Born to Mrs. Roland H. Corbet, May 7th, a baby girl.

Alcona County Review, May 11, 1899
Father: Roland H. Corbett
Mother: Minnie Foster

Corcoran, Lorena
LOCAL JOTTINGS

A baby girl was born to Mr. and Mrs. P. Corcoran, June 26.

Alcona County Review, July 6, 1888
Father: Peter K. Corcoran
Mother: Helen O'Keefe

Corcoran, Paul
Somewhat Personal.
A very small boy has made his appearance in the family of Mr. and Mrs. P. Corcoran and will be treated with due courtesy and consideration for an indefinite length of time.

Alcona County Review, May 28, 1891
Father: Peter K. Corcoran
Mother: Helen O'Keefe

Cowley, Lillian Celia
REVIEWINGS.

It's another girl baby. Mark it down to B. P. Cowley.

Alcona County Review, October 24, 1879
Father: Bernard P. Cowley
Mother: Helen C. Gates

Coyle, {Girl}
GREENBUSH GETTINGS.

J. F. Coyle appeared to be the happiest man in Greenbush on Xmas morning. What do you suppose Mr. Editor was the reason? Why in addition to the gifts he received on Xmas Eve., his wife, quite early Xmas morning, presented him with a fine daughter weighing 12 pounds avoir. This youthful individual is the only one we heard of that "kicked" on Christmas. Mr. C. was generous enough to "set up" the cigars for his friends in honor of the event.

Alcona County Review, January 1, 1886
Father: James F. Coyle
Mother: Abigail

Crane, {Girl}
Curtis Items.

Mr. and Mrs. Isaac Crane rejoice over a bright handsome daughter born to them a short time ago.

Alcona County Review, July 25, 1895
Father: Isaac Crane
Mother:

Crawford, {Boy}

About Black River.

On Saturday morning, to Mr. and Mrs. Jno. Crawford, a son.

Alcona County Review, October 31, 1895
Father: John Crawford
Mother:

Cronin, {Girl}

Notes and New Along the Shore

THE TAWASES.

A little daughter was recently born to Mr. and Mrs. Wm. Cronin.

Alcona County Review, December 26, 1884
Father: William Cronin
Mother:

Crougher, {Boy}

WEST HARRISVILLE.

W. Crougher is the happy father of a bouncing boy.

Alcona County Review, July 7, 1898
Father: W. Crougher
Mother:

Curriveau, David

LOCAL JOTTINGS

The family of Ralph Carribeau was increased last week by the birth of a son.

Alcona County Review, June 15, 1888
Father: Ralph Curriveau
Mother: Virginia Ducharme

Curriveau, Max Joseph

The Local News.

The census was increased last week by one, a very young person at the home of Ralph Carvo.

Alcona County Review, March 7, 1890
Father: Ralph Curriveau
Mother: Virginia Ducharme

Cuyler, Hazen Shirley

Mr. and Mrs. George A. Cuyler of Sturgeon Point are rejoicing over the birth of a son and heir. The little fellow made his appearance last Tuesday.

Alcona County Review, September 1, 1898
Father: George Alonzo Cuyler
Mother: Anna Rose Shirley

Deacon, Clyde

GLENNIE.

Born on the 21 inst. to Mr. and Mrs. Phillip Deacon, a son.

Alcona County Review, October 27, 1898

Father: Phillip Deacon
Mother: Maggie Vaughn

Decarie, Marie

Black River Sparks.

Born Sept. 2d, to Mr. and Mrs. O. E. Decarie, a girl.

Alcona County Review, September 3, 1896
Father: Oliver Edward Decarie
Mother: Anna Blanche Charlefour

Dege, William

About Black River.

To Mr. and Mrs. E. Diegie, Monday, a nine-pound boy.

Alcona County Review, October 24, 1895
Father: Ernest Dege
Mother: Anna Neubert

Dellar, Hattie

KILLMASTER.

Mr. and Mrs. Jim Dellar are jubilant and all on account of the arrival of a young daughter at their home.

Alcona County Review, June 29, 1899
Father: James Dellar
Mother: Emma J. Gordon

Dewar, Benjamin

THE LOCAL NEWS.

Born to Mr. and Mrs. Archie Dewar a son, usual weight.

Alcona County Review, January 8, 1891
Father: Archie Dewar
Mother: Sarah Thompson

Dewar, Roderick

LOCAL JOTTINGS.

Duncan Dewar, of W. Harrisville, is hilarious over the birth of a son and heir.

Alcona County Review, June 28, 1889
Father: Duncan Dewar
Mother: Catherine Florence McNeil

Dewey, Gladys

LOCAL PICK UPS.

Born Thursday, Aug. 24, to Mr. and Mrs. Louis Dewey, a daughter.

Alcona County Review, August 31, 1899
Father: Louis B. Dewey
Mother: Anna M. Schram

Dewey, Lynn Dana

EVENTS OF ONE WEEK.

Born—To Mr. and Mrs. John Dewey—Thursday, Sept. 3, —a son.

Alcona County Review, September 10, 1896
Father: John S. Dewey
Mother: Cora L. Tower

Dewey, Monica E.

PERSONAL MENTION.

We omitted notice last week of the birth of a daughter to Mrs. Jno. Dewey.

Alcona County Review, November 2, 1893
Father: John S. Dewey
Mother: Cora L. Tower

Dixon, {Boy}

Black River Sparks.

Born, 16th inst., a boy to Mr. and Mrs. James Dixon.

Alcona County Review, May 21, 1896
Father: James Dixon
Mother:

Dobson, Harry R.

Haynes.

Haynes, Feb. 15th, 1892.--Mrs. Supr. Dobson presented Robert with a brand new baby boy on Saturday morning, the 13th, inst.

Alcona County Review, February 18, 1892
Father: Robert Dobson
Mother: Emma A. Bertha Morton

Dobson, Pearl

ALCONA ATOMS.
A Shower of Babies in Alcona.

Mrs. Robert Dobson has presented her liege lord with a girl.

All of the above are reported standard weight.

Alcona County Review, May 6, 1887
Father: Robert Dobson
Mother: Emma A. Bertha Morton

Dougherty, Anna

REVIEWINGS.

They now call our harness-maker "pa Dougherty." It's a girl.

Alcona County Review, April 25, 1879
Father: Morris Dougherty
Mother: Mary

Douglas, {Boy}

Mites of Humanity.

An employe in Loud's planing mill by the name of E. Douglas has two mites of humanity at his home near the mill, in the shape of twins who were born to him and Mrs. Douglas two weeks since. They are a boy and a girl. The boy weighs two and the girl one and one half pounds. One can hardly conceive until they have seen, a human being weighing but one and a half pounds. A silver dollar placed over the face of the little girl would cover up nearly all of its head. A dessert coffee cup would almost fall down upon its shoulders. A tea cup would fall upon the shoulders and have room to spare. The little ones lie nearly all the time sleeping in their crib. Neither Mr. nor Mrs. Douglas are 21 years of age, so we are told, and besides these twins they have one boy.—Monitor.

Alcona County Review, August 27, 1891
Father: E. Douglas
Mother:

Douglas, Ethel E.
Mites of Humanity.
An employe in Loud's planing mill by the name of E. Douglas has two mites of humanity at his home near the mill, in the shape of twins who were born to him and Mrs. Douglas two weeks since. They are a boy and a girl. The boy weighs two and the girl one and one half pounds. One can hardly conceive until they have seen, a human being weighing but one and a half pounds. A silver dollar placed over the face of the little girl would cover up nearly all of its head. A dessert coffee cup would almost fall down upon its shoulders. A tea cup would fall upon the shoulders and have room to spare. The little ones lie nearly all the time sleeping in their crib. Neither Mr. nor Mrs. Douglas are 21 years of age, so we are told, and besides these twins they have one boy.—Monitor.

Alcona County Review, August 27, 1891
Father: E. Douglas
Mother:

Douglas, Margaret E.
Greenbush Gettings.

Mr. John Douglass wears a sunny smile this week. His wife presented him with a little girl on Tuesday, Oct. 26.

Alcona County Review, October 29, 1886
Father: John Douglas
Mother: Lucy R.

Downer, Aurelia F.
R. W. Downer, of Springport, has another boarder,--it's a 10 lb. girl-- twenty-first grandchild of Mr. and Mrs. I. Wilson.

Alcona County Review, November 25, 1887
Father: Romanzo William Downer
Mother: Ruthann Frances Wilson

Downer, {Girl}
REVIEWINGS.

Allen Downer now carries off the prize—a 11 ½ pound baby-girl.

Alcona County Review, April 11, 1879
Father: Allen Downer
Mother:

Downer, Olive I.
REVIEWINGS.

R. W. Downer is happy; it's a nine pound girl. Can't touch R. W. with a ten-foot pole.

Alcona County Review, March 7, 1879
Father: Romanzo William Downer
Mother: Ruthann Frances Wilson

Downie, Herbert Dewey
HAYNES HAPPENINGS.
Mrs. Ed. Downie has presented Edward with another promising young thresher, making the fourth son in succession.

Alcona County Review, April 21, 1898

PERSONAL POINTS.

Edw. Downie, the well known Haynes citizen, has named the latest male addition to his family "Dewey" in honor of the hero of Manila.

Alcona County Review, June 23, 1898
Father: Edward Downie
Mother: Frances Jane Slater

Downie, James R.
Haynes.
Mr. Ed. Downie is the father of another baby boy, presented to him last week by Mrs. Downie, and Wm. Johnston is the father of a bouncing baby girl presented to him by Mrs. Johnston.

Alcona County Review, November 17, 1892
Father: Edward Downie
Mother: Frances Jane Slater

Dreyer, Charity
AMONG OUR EXCHANGES.

Mrs. Abe Dreyer of Bay City gave birth to triplets on Sunday. They are all girls and have been named Faith, Hope and Charity.

Alcona County Review, May 11, 1893
Father: Abe Dreyer
Mother:

Dreyer, Faith
AMONG OUR EXCHANGES.

Mrs. Abe Dreyer of Bay City gave birth to triplets on Sunday. They are all girls and have been named Faith, Hope and Charity.

Alcona County Review, May 11, 1893
Father: Abe Dreyer
Mother:

Dreyer, Hope
AMONG OUR EXCHANGES.

Mrs. Abe Dreyer of Bay City gave birth to triplets on Sunday. They are all girls and have been named Faith, Hope and Charity.

Alcona County Review, May 11, 1893
Father: Abe Dreyer

Mother:

Dunham, {Girl}
West Harrisville.
Sept. 18, 1895.
Rev. F. P. Dunham is the happy father of a pretty baby girl.

Alcona County Review, September 19, 1895
Father: F. P. Dunham
Mother:

Durkee, {Girl}
LOCAL LACONICS.

Geo. Durkey is the happiest man in Greenbush. It is a girl, and arrived at his residence on Monday last.

Alcona County Review, May 8, 1885
Father: George W. Durkee
Mother: Jessie A. Perkins

Dyer, Clara
Local News.
Mr. and Mrs. Michael Dyer received a New Years gift last Saturday in the shape of a bouncing baby girl—their eleventh child.

Alcona County Review, January 5, 1899
Father: Michael Dyer
Mother: Mary LaChapelle

Dyer, Honor
PERSONAL MENTION.

A daughter was born to Mrs. M. Dwyer Monday, Oct. 5th, making the tenth child born to them.

Alcona County Review, October 8, 1896
Father: Michael Dyer
Mother: Mary LaChapelle

Earle, {Girl}
South Harrisville.

Mr. and Mrs. Geo. Earle gladly welcomed the arrival of a little daughter Feb. 4th, making a total of three boys and one girl. Mr. Earle is working in the woods near South Rogers.

Alcona County Review, February 14, 1895
Father: George Earle
Mother: Tillie

Edgar, Annabell
Somewhat Personal.
The census around shingle mill No. 1 was increased last Saturday morning by the arrival of two little strangers, one, a boy, at Jno. Nichols, the other—sex not named—at John Edgar's.

Alcona County Review, April 28, 1892

One birth only at the shingle mill last week, viz: to Mrs. Edgar. Our informant was mistaken.

Alcona County Review, May 5, 1892
Father: John D. Edgar

Mother: Isabella Barber

Edwards, Charles H.

REVIEWINGS.

Mr. and Mrs. Wm. Edwards are the happy parents of a nice large boy-baby. Their Harrisville friends extend congratulations.

Alcona County Review, April 2, 1880
Father: William Edwards
Mother: Augusta Lincoln

Edwards, Freeman W.

The Cradle.

Born—To Mrs. Wm. Edwards, a son.

Alcona County Review, January 31, 1890
Father: William Edwards
Mother: Augusta Lincoln

Edwards, Hazel Fern

Local News.

Born to Mr. and Mrs. Wm. Edwards, Monday, Sept. 18, a daughter.

Alcona County Review, September 21, 1899
Father: William Edwards
Mother: Augusta Lincoln

Edwards, James F.

Local Sayings and Doings.

And now comes the news to the Review that Wm. Edwards is once again "too happy for anything." It's a fine boy this time.

Alcona County Review, January 27, 1882
Father: William Edwards
Mother: Augusta Lincoln

Effrick, Ernest

PERSONAL MENTION.

The home of P. J. Effric was blessed by the birth of another son on Saturday, the 20th inst.

Alcona County Review, May 25, 1893
Father: Peter James Effrick
Mother: Emma E. Beever

Effrick, Milo G.

REVIEWINGS.

To Mrs. Peter Effric and Mrs. Joseph Speck—a son each. O, happy fathers!

Alcona County Review, January 23, 1880
Father: Peter James Effrick
Mother: Emma E. Beever

Elmer, Josephine

Local Sayings and Doings.

Gus. Elmer is happy. It's a six pound daughter.

Alcona County Review, March 17, 1882
Father: Rufus Augustus Elmer

Mother: Orilla McClure

Elmer, Nora

In Haynes.

Frank Elmer is the father of a fine daughter.

Alcona County Review, October 18, 1889
Father: Frank J. Elmer
Mother: Christina Illman

Elmer, Ralph

PERSONAL.

A son was born to Gus Elmer and wife yesterday.

Alcona County Review, October 28, 1897
Father: Rufus Augustus Elmer
Mother: Orilla McClure

Emerson, Arthur B.

COUNTY NEWS JOTTINGS.

And it is George Emerson's turn to chuckle;—by jove it's another boy, and a nine pounder, at that! Brethren, sing "suthin."

Alcona County Review, November 16, 1877
Father: George Emerson
Mother: Emma Beaver

Emerson, Clyde

PERSONAL MENTION.

Born to Mr. and Mrs. Fred Emerson Saturday, Dec. 15, a son.

Alcona County Review, December 20, 1894
Father: Fred Emerson
Mother: Minnie Showers

Emerson, Ina

Gustin Grist.

Gustin, Sept. 10, 1895.
Mr. and Mrs. Will Emerson are the happy parents of a pair of twin sisters.

Alcona County Review, September 12, 1895
Father: Willis Emerson
Mother: Margaret Adams

Emerson, John

REVIEWINGS.

Uriah Emerson is happy; it's a bouncing boy-baby. We almost forgot to mention it.

Alcona County Review, December 26, 1879
Father: Uriah J. Emerson
Mother: Lavina Evingham

Emerson, Murriel

Local News.

To Mr. and Mrs. Jas. Emerson, Feb. 10, a daughter.

Alcona County Review, February 16, 1899
Father: James E. Emerson
Mother: Mary S. Hudson

Emerson, Nina

Gustin Grist.

Gustin, Sept. 10, 1895.

Mr. and Mrs. Will Emerson are the happy parents of a pair of twin sisters.

Alcona County Review, September 12, 1895
Father: Willis Emerson
Mother: Margaret Adams

Emerson, Thomas

The Local News.

Born, to Mrs. Elias Emerson Monday, June 16, a boy.

Alcona County Review, June 27, 1890
Father: Elias Emerson
Mother: Charlotte Dewey

Emerson, Velma

PERSONAL POINTS.

A daughter to Mr. and Mrs. Curtis Emerson yesterday.

Alcona County Review, May 19, 1898
Father: Curtis Emerson
Mother: Melvina LaBoeuff

Emerson, Waldo

PERSONAL MENTION.

Mr. and Mrs. Elias Emerson are the parents of a child born recently at Rose City, Mich.

Alcona County Review, January 10, 1895
Father: Elias Emerson
Mother: Charlotte Dewey

Emmel, {Girl}

The Local News.

Oscar Emmel, formerly of Harrisville, has just added a girl, a very young one, to his family at Au Sable.

Alcona County Review, April 25, 1890
Father: Oscar Emmel
Mother: Orilla Rebelle

Evans, Mary E.

Local Sayings and Doings.

Joseph Evans is too happy for anything. It's a brand new 12 pound girl.

Alcona County Review, August 11, 1882
Father: Joseph Evans
Mother: Ellen

Evingham, {Boy}

Local Sayings and Doings.

Born—March 30, 1882, to Mr. and Mrs. Wm. H. Evingham, a son; weight, 8 pounds. Happiness reigns supreme.

Alcona County Review, April 7, 1882
Father: William Henry Evingham
Mother: Carrie Adeline Griswold

Fair, {Boy}

LOCAL JOTTINGS.

The family of J. E. Fair, a former citizen, has been blessed recently by the birth of a son.

Alcona County Review, May 26, 1898
Father: James E. Fair
Mother: Sarah C.

Fair, Mabel

LOCAL JOTTINGS.

County treasurer, J. E. Fair, has been presented by his wife with a very valuable holiday present--a fine new daughter. Weight, 16 ounces to the pound.

Alcona County Review, December 19, 1884
Father: James E. Fair
Mother: Agnes D.

Ferguson, Donald

LOCAL JOTTINGS

Born, Feb. 20 to Mr. and Mrs. Geo. G. Ferguson, a son.

Alcona County Review, February 24, 1888
Father: George G. Ferguson
Mother: Mary Nedeau

Ferris, Albert

LOCAL JOTTINGS.

Alcona county also has a freak of nature if a report can be believed, which states that a Mrs. Ferris, who lives a few miles back of Harrisville, recently gave birth to a child which had two well developed teeth.

Alcona County Review, March 2, 1888
Father: Theodore Allen Ferris
Mother: Emma E. Wixon

Ferris, Frank A.

West Harrisville.

Mrs. T. A. Fettes presented her husband with a son and heir last Friday morning. Mother and child are doing well.

Alcona County Review, February 2, 1893
Father: Theodore Allen Ferris
Mother: Emma E. Wixon

Ferris, Percy

West Harrisville, Feb. 27.—Born, to Mrs. T. A. Ferris, Feb. 24, a son. T. A. is doing well. Also to Mr. and Mrs. D. A. Thompson, a daughter, Feb. 26.

Alcona County Review, February 28, 1890
Father: Theodore Allen Ferris
Mother: Emma E. Wixon

Fettes, Charles Murray

HAYNES HAPPENINGS.

Mrs. Wm. Fettis presented Wm. with a son on St. Valentine's day.

Alcona County Review, February 23, 1899
Father: William Fettes
Mother: Elizabeth Clark

Fisher, Bertie

LOCAL JOTTINGS.

Joseph Fisher and wife take pleasure in entertaining a bright-eyed little boy, which arrived at their home on Friday last. He weighed eleven pounds.

Alcona County Review, February 26, 1886
Father: Joseph Fisher, Jr.
Mother: Adaline A. Lewis

Fisher, Eva Pearl

The Review of last week failed to chronicle the advent of a brand new daughter at the home of D. B. Mudgett, and one also at the home of Joseph Fisher, Jr.

Alcona County Review, May 9, 1884
Father: Joseph Fisher, Jr.
Mother: Adaline A. Lewis

Fisher, Guy

Local Sayings and Doings.

Joseph Fisher is once again made as happy as a big sun-flower that nods and bends in the breezes. It's a fine ten pound boy.

Alcona County Review, June 23, 1882
Father: Joseph Fisher, Jr.
Mother: Adaline A. Lewis

Fisher, Mary A.

Personalities.

And now you can't "touch Joseph Fisher, Jr., with a ten-foot pole." A handsome young Miss, fifteen hours old, and weighing 9 pounds, is at his house, and being well pleased with the surroundings, proposes to make it her permanent residence.

'Tis sweet to be remembered
Even by friends across the waters,
But sweeter still to have your wife
Present you with a daughter.
Isn't that so, Joseph?

Alcona County Review, October 4, 1878

Grandpa Lewis—a-hem!

Alcona County Review, October 4, 1878
Father: Joseph Fisher, Jr.
Mother: Adaline A. Lewis

Fisher, Sara Maria

COUNTY REVIEWINGS.

In the announcement of births last week, the Review reporter inadvertently omitted to say that Mr. and Mrs. Joseph Fisher, Jr., had just become the happy recipients of a nice large girl-baby. The census man will please tally two for Joseph.

Alcona County Review, July 30, 1880
Father: Joseph Fisher, Jr.
Mother: Adaline A. Lewis

Fisher, Sherman

LOCAL JOTTINGS

Saturday, Dec. 31st,—to Mrs. Jos. Fisher, Jr., a son.

Alcona County Review, January 6, 1888
Father: Joseph Fisher, Jr.
Mother: Adaline A. Lewis

Fitzpatrick, Viola

West Harrisville.

West Harrisville, Sept. 11, '95. J. Fitzpatrick is very happy. A baby girl came last Sunday eve.

Alcona County Review, September 12, 1895
Father: John Fitzpatrick
Mother: Margaret

Flanagan, Bertha M.

COUNTY REVIEWINGS.

Born, last evening, to Mr. and Mrs. Alex. Flanagan, of Alcona, a son [daughter].

Alcona County Review, May 28, 1880
Father: Sylvester Alex Flanagan
Mother: Mary J.

Fleck, {Boy}

LOCAL JOTTINGS.

Could (not) touch Chas. Fleck now with a ten foot pole nor a fish-net flag staff. Oh, of course it's a boy.

Alcona County Review, January 23, 1885
Father: Charles John Fleck
Mother: Lillian M. Aird

Fleck, {Boy}

Somewhat Personal.

Mrs. Chas. Fleck of Tawas City, gave birth to a son last week at the home of her mother, Mrs. A. Baror.

Alcona County Review, March 31, 1892
Father: Charles John Fleck
Mother: Lillian M. Aird

Fleck, {Girl}

PURELY PERSONAL.

Chas. Fleck steps about two feet high since last week, and wears a smile that would have done honor to the visage of a Chesterfield. It's a girl.

Alcona County Review, June 1, 1888
Father: Charles John Fleck
Mother: Lillian M. Aird

Fleming, Charles

Alcona Atoms.

Mr. Thos. Fleming is the daddy of another boy. Dr. McCormick was the accoucheur. Mother and child are doing well.

Alcona County Review, December 10, 1886

Father: Thomas A. Fleming
Mother: Annie Campbell

Fleming, Hattie S.

Haynes.

Mrs. Fleming presented Thomas with a daughter on Saturday morning, the 13, inst.

Alcona County Review, February 18, 1892
Father: Thomas A. Fleming
Mother: Annie Campbell

Fleming, William

Haynes Happenings.

Haynes, April 10.--Look at Isaiah 9-6 and you will see what happened to Mr. and Mrs. Jas. Fleming on the 8th. 1st line of verse.

Alcona County Review, April 12, 1894
Father: James Fleming
Mother: Catherine McKillop

Fleury, Hattie S.

LOCAL JOTTINGS.

Two more souls made happy, viz., Oliver Lemon and Morgan Flora, whose respective wives has presented each with a daughter. Thus the world moves.

Alcona County Review, January 15, 1886
Father: Morgan Fleury
Mother: Sarah Pyne

Fonger, {Girl}

Alice Fonger, the demented woman, was brought back from Traverse City last week and last night she gave birth to a healthy, fully matured female child. This seems to clear the poor farm of any blame in the matter as the woman did not come there until July 7th, 1892.

Alcona County Review, April 6, 1893
Father:
Mother: Alice Fonger

Forcleau, {Boy}

Black River Sparks.

BIRTHS.

Mr. and Mrs. P. Forcleau, a boy.

Alcona County Review, May 14, 1896
Father: P. Forcleau
Mother:

Ford, Mildred Mary

Black River Sparks.

Born to Mr. and Mrs. Fourd, a girl.

Alcona County Review, September 26, 1895
Father: Fred S. Ford
Mother: Mary

Forsythe, Myrtle

PERSONAL MENTION.

A 10-pound baby girl was born on the 6th, inst., to Mrs. Jas. Forsythe at Killmaster.

Alcona County Review, April 12, 1894
Father: James Forsythe
Mother: Florence Denison

Fortier, {Boy}

HAYNES HAPPENINGS.
July 18.

Mr. and Mrs. A. J. Fortier had the misfortune to lose a baby boy, stillborn. Interment took place Sunday afternoon.

Alcona County Review, July 21, 1898
Father: A. J. Fortier
Mother: Louisa [Bonville] Allen

Fortier, {Girl}

Black River Sparks.

Born to Mr. and Mrs. A. J. Fortier July 3d, a girl. Mother and babe doing well. Father will recover.

Alcona County Review, July 9, 1896
Father: A. J. Fortier
Mother: Louisa [Bonville] Allen

Foster, Oveld

Local Sparks.

Born—To Mr. and Mrs. C. Horton, a daughter; to Mr. and Mrs. James Foster, a son.

Alcona County Review, August 29, 1895
Father: James Foster
Mother: Minnie Martin

Fowler, Lyle

KILLMASTER.

Chas. Fowler is the happy possessor of a new baby boy.

Alcona County Review, March 9, 1899
Father: Charles Fowler
Mother: Emma Rose

Franklin, Edna

PERSONAL.

Born to Charles O. Franklin and wife, a daughter.

Alcona County Review, January 13, 1898
Father: Charles O. Franklin
Mother: Hannah C. Spencer

Franklin, Leonard

WEST HARRISVILLE.

B. Franklin is the happy father of a baby boy, who came last Wednesday to stay.

Alcona County Review, December 9, 1897
Father: Robert Franklin
Mother: Fannie Fitzpatrick

Fraser, Clementine

The Local News

Dan Fraser, of Haynes, and his good wife are happy over the arrival of a daughter on the 13th inst.

Alcona County Review, December 20, 1889
Father: Donald Fraser
Mother: Ellen D. Ritchie

Fraser, Esther

ALCONA ATOMS.

Mrs. Fraser presented Donald with a boy [girl], last week.

Alcona County Review, October 8, 1886
Father: Donald Fraser
Mother: Ellen D. Ritchie

Fraser, John

GREENBUSH GETTINGS.

"Hello, Andrew! What makes your usually benighted countenance cast such a halo of brightness around you, this morning?" "Didn't you hear the news?" "No." "Well, my wife presented me with a young blacksmith on Sunday, July 11—weights 11 lbs. I'm going to have him help me in the shop. What do you think of that?"

Alcona County Review, July 23, 1886
Father: Andrew Fraser
Mother: Elizabeth Chisolm

Fraser, Lawrence W.

Haynes Happenings.

Born to Mr. and Mrs. Donald Fraser, a son, on the 20th.

Alcona County Review, May 24, 1894
Father: Donald Fraser
Mother: Ellen D. Ritchie

Fraser, Maud

LOCAL JOTTINGS.

To all his friends John Fraser now has to "set up" two cigars each. A pair of twins—two daughters—that's what's the matter.

Alcona County Review, November 6, 1885
Father: John A. Fraser
Mother: Jennie [Bridgeman] McNally

Fraser, Myrtle

LOCAL JOTTINGS.

To all his friends John Fraser now has to "set up" two cigars each. A pair of twins—two daughters—that's what's the matter.

Alcona County Review, November 6, 1885
Father: John A. Fraser
Mother: Jennie [Bridgeman] McNally

Frederick, Harrison S.

Purely Personal.

We understand that L. Frederick and family are entertaining a little stranger at their home, whom they will endeavor to bring up in the way he should go.

Alcona County Review, November 1, 1889
Father: Lorenzo Frederick
Mother: Hannah Sutherland

Frederick, Herman

Lorenzo Frederick, the efficient Superintendent of Schools of Harrisville township, and who teaches the young idea to shoot out in the Dean district, has found it necessary to have another assistant. Therefore his wife presented him with a handsome new daughter [son], a few days ago, weighing sixteen ounces to the pound. The population of our township is rapidly increasing. Next.

Alcona County Review, January 15, 1886
Father: Lorenzo Frederick
Mother: Hannah Sutherland

Frederick, Howard

LOCAL JOTTINGS.

L. Frederick and his good wife rejoice over the addition to their flock this week of a bouncing baby boy.

Alcona County Review, October 28, 1887
Father: Lorenzo Frederick
Mother: Hannah Sutherland

Frederick, Myrtle E.

HOME REVIEWINGS.

Mr. Frederick, school teacher in the Fisher district, is happy over the advent of a new son [daughter].

Alcona County Review, April 22, 1881
Father: Lorenzo Frederick
Mother: Hannah Sutherland

Freer, {Girl}

LOCAL JOTTINGS.

Last Sunday George Freer became the happy father of a 3 1-2 pound daughter. At last accounts the child was breathing naturally, doing well, etc., and George had become fully reconciled to an attitude of thankfulness for "small favors."

Alcona County Review, December 25, 1885
Father: George G. Freer
Mother: Effie E. Weir

Freer, Jewel

PERSONAL.

Supr. and Mrs. Wm. Freer of Mitchell are the parents of another daughter since Saturday.

Alcona County Review, November 11, 1897
Father: William Sherman Freer
Mother: Linna Elizabeth Sovey

Freer, Joseph

PERSONAL MENTION.

Mrs. Will Freer presented her husband with a bouncing boy on Christmas eve—the daintiest and most precious gift yet reported.

Alcona County Review, December 29, 1892
Father: William Sherman Freer
Mother: Linna Elizabeth Sovey

Freer, Katie

PERSONAL.

John Freer came home for the 4th and was greeted by a 12-lb daughter, born Friday, the 2d.

Alcona County Review, July 8, 1897
Father: John S. Freer
Mother: Catherine Hill

Freer, Marion

PERSONAL MENTION.

Born to Mrs. John Freer, a daughter, Tuesday, August 13.

Alcona County Review, August 15, 1895
Father: John S. Freer
Mother: Catherine Hill

Freer, Orrin

Haynes Happenings.
Feb. 1, 1897.

George Freer is the daddy of a bouncing baby boy, came Jan. 2d.

Alcona County Review, February 4, 1897
Father: George N. Freer
Mother: Ida Lombard

Freer, Voil

Mitchell Rumblings.

Born, to Mr. and Mrs. John Freer, a son, Jan. 12th.

Alcona County Review, January 21, 1892
Father: John S. Freer
Mother: Catherine Hill

Fuller, Claude

County News and Gossip.

A. J. Fuller was very suddenly called home to the Sable, a few nights ago. It's a boy, even ten pounds. We've quit smoking!

Alcona County Review, January 10, 1879
Father: Andrew J. Fuller
Mother: Orilla

Fullerton, Robert John

Henry Fullerton of Curran welcomed a son and heir to the family circle recently.

Alcona County Review, October 11, 1894
Father: Henry J. Fullerton
Mother: Mary LaForge

Gage, {Boy}

WEST HARRISVILLE.

Frank Gage is happy. It is a boy.

Alcona County Review, January 10, 1890
Father: Frank Gage
Mother:

Gardiner, {Boy}

Somewhat Personal.

Harry Gardiner, brother of Mrs. Geo. W. Colwell and who has made frequent visits to Harrisville, is the proud father of a son and heir.

Alcona County Review, December 17, 1891
Father: Harry Gardiner
Mother:

Gardner, {Boy}

Black River Sparks.

Born to Mr. and Mrs. J. Gardner, a son.

Alcona County Review, March 26, 1896
Father: J. Gardiner
Mother:

Genge, Roy

BORN.

To Mr. and Mrs. Geo. Gange, W. Harrisville, a son March 5th.

Alcona County Review, March 21, 1890
Father: George Genge
Mother: Effadell Williams

Genge, William Lee

West Harrisville.

West Harrisville, Jan. 22.--John Genge is happy: A son, born last Tuesday.

Alcona County Review, January 24, 1895
Father: John Genge
Mother: Della M. Thornton

Gillam, Bruce Rupert

The Local News

Any shortcomings in this issue will be overlooked we feel sure. It's a boy, and the first. All parties, including the father, doing well.

Alcona County Review, April 28, 1892

Somewhat Personal.

Born to Mr. and Mrs. Geo. E. Gillam, Saturday, April 23, a son.

Alcona County Review, April 28, 1892
Father: George E. Gillam
Mother: Rena B. Tillotson

Gillam, Earl

PERSONAL MENTION.

Born to Mr. and Mrs. Geo. E. Gillam, an 8-lb. son, Sunday, March 4th.

Alcona County Review, March 8, 1894

EVENTS OF ONE WEEK.

Editor Gillam of the Harrisville Review gets out a mighty good paper for the size of the town, and he didn't let up a bit this week just because there was a new baby in the family, born last Sunday.—Oscoda Press.

Oh! don't; you make us blush.

Alcona County Review, March 15, 1894
Father: George E. Gillam
Mother: Rena B. Tillotson

Gillam, {Girl}
PERSONAL MENTION.

Born to Mrs. Geo. E. Gillam, Saturday, Nov. 2, a daughter.

Alcona County Review, November 7, 1895
Father: George E. Gillam
Mother: Rena B. Tillotson

Gillard, Reuben Clare
Caledonia.

Born to Mr. and Mrs. H. Gillard, a son.

Alcona County Review, December 22, 1892
Father: Henry Gillard
Mother: Catherine McKinnon

Girvin, Samuel
COUNTY JOTTINGS.

Samuel Girvin is now on his tip-toe of delight. It's a boy and weighs 11 3/4 pounds. How is that for a fisherman's luck.

Alcona County Review, March 1, 1878
Father: Samuel Girvin
Mother: Rachel Carpenter

Goheen, Ray

Mrs. E. Goheen presented her husband with a 10-lb. boy Tuesday.

Alcona County Review, September 13, 1889
Father: Ezra Goheen
Mother: Isabelle Joan Springstead

Goheen, Ward J.
West Harrisville.
October 23, 1895.

Congratulations are being tendered Mr. and Mrs. Goheen upon the arrival of a ten pound boy in the family circle.

Alcona County Review, October 24, 1895
Father: Ezra Goheen
Mother: Isabelle Joan Springstead

Good, William Darius
Gustin Grist.

Gustin, April 9.
Joseph Good is happy again—a boy this time.

Alcona County Review, April 11, 1895
Father: Josephus E. Good
Mother: Ida E. Stringer

Gould, Mary E.
Our Neighbors.

Haynes, Jan. 13, 1890:—Mrs. Gould presented Nathan with a daughter on Monday of last week.

Alcona County Review, January 17, 1890
Father: Nathan E. Gould
Mother: Jenette Husted

Gow, Harold R.
PERSONAL MENTION.

Sandy Gow is the happy father of another son born Monday August 3d. Mrs. Gow and child are getting along well.

Alcona County Review, August 13, 1896
Father: Alexander L. Gow
Mother: Elsie S. Baldwin

Gow, Logan
PERSONAL MENTION.

"Sandy" Gow and wife are the parents of a very young Gow, who made his appearance on the 9th inst.

Alcona County Review, August 10, 1893
Father: Alexander L. Gow
Mother: Elsie S. Baldwin

Gram {Girl}
COUNTY JOTTINGS.

John Gram, of the Sable, was in town on Wednesday, and illuminated our office with the light of his smiling countenance. Beats all what a peculiar aspect a man's countenance will assume, after he has become a "darling papa." But, such is life.

Alcona County Review, March 29, 1878
Father: John C. Gram
Mother: Annie Hutchinson

Gray, Rachel
The Cradle.

Born—To Mrs. Wm. Gray, a daughter.

Alcona County Review, January 31, 1890
Father: William Gray
Mother: Martha Fisher

Green, Birdie M.
LOCAL JOTTINGS.

A girl baby at Thos. Green's Monday night. Weight 9 1-2 pounds.

Alcona County Review, February 12, 1886
Father: Thomas M. Green
Mother: Alice M. Beacraft

Green, Ernest Valentine
Purely Personal.

Of all the valentines received or sent last week the one that came to the address of Mr. and Mrs. Thos.

Green came the nearest to giving perfect satisfaction and happiness. It is a boy and "looks just like his father."

Alcona County Review, February 21, 1890
Father: Thomas M. Green
Mother: Alice M. Beacraft

Green, Fred L.
PURELY PERSONAL.

Tom Green, ye butcher man, has worn a broad smile of contentment and happiness ever since an early hour Sunday morning. It's a boy this time.

Alcona County Review, May 20, 1887
Father: Thomas M. Green
Mother: Alice M. Beacraft

Green, Percy
THE CRADLE.

Mr. and Mrs. Ed Green of Black River are proud of a little stranger who has come to them within the week. It is a boy.

Alcona County Review, January 17, 1890
Father: Edward Green
Mother: Jewell Freer

Green, William
PURELY PERSONAL.

Thos. Green and wife feel justly proud over the advent of a son last week, their second born.

Alcona County Review, November 2, 1888
Father: Thomas M. Green
Mother: Alice M. Beacraft

Greenfield, {Girl}
Black River Sparks.

Born to Mr. and Mrs. Greenfield, a daughter.

Alcona County Review, June 18, 1896
Father: F. William Greenfield
Mother: Mary Ann Wilson

Greenfield, Margaret May
Haynes Happenings.

May 5, '96.
John Greenfield is the father of a baby girl.

Alcona County Review, May 7, 1896
Father: John Greenfield
Mother: Helen Wilson

Gullifer, {Child}
COUNTY REVIEWINGS.

F. O. Gullifer is the father of a brand new baby, and of course congratulations are in order. So here goes!

Alcona County Review, September 3, 1880
Father: Freeman O. Gullifer
Mother: Henrietta H. Hill

Gunther, Mary

> **SPENCER DISTRICT.**
>
> Mrs. B. Guenther has a baby girl.

Alcona County Review, December 8, 1898
Father: Benjamin Gunther
Mother: Sarah M.

Gurd, {Girl}

> **COUNTY REVIEWINGS.**
>
> --------
>
> A girl-baby was born to Mrs. Thos. Gurd, a guest of the McLellan House, last Friday. Mr. Gurd arrived on the Pearl yesterday from below.

Alcona County Review, October 1, 1880
Father: Thomas Gurd
Mother: Dora?

Hailey, Lottie

> **FISHER'S**
>
> Born to Mr. and Mrs. Geo. Hailey, a daughter Oct. 6th.

Alcona County Review, October 14, 1897
Father: George W. Hailey
Mother: Christina McDonald

Hale, {Boy}

> **PERSONAL.**
>
> --------
>
> A 11 lb. son was born to Mr. and Mrs. Will Hale at Killmaster Thursday, the 8th.

Alcona County Review, July 15, 1897
Father: William D. Hale
Mother: Esther Walker

Hale, {Boy}

> **LOCAL PICK UPS.**
>
> Wm. Hale wears a very broad smile these day, all on account of the arrival of a son at his home Tuesday, the 18th inst.——Grand Marais Leader.

Alcona County Review, July 27, 1899
Father: William D. Hale
Mother: Esther Walker

Hale, Claude

> **LOCAL JOTTINGS.**
>
> --------
>
> And unto Matthew Hale, on Monday last, a son was born. However, Mat. says the price of meat will remain the same.

Alcona County Review, October 22, 1886
Father: Matthew Hale
Mother: Jennie Gilbert

Hale, Myrtle May

> **HOME NEWS JOTTINGS.**
>
> --------
>
> Sherman Hale has recently received an addition to his family. It's a girl.

Alcona County Review, March 2, 1883
Father: Sherman Hale
Mother: Mary Farrington

Hall, Lagrand

> **COUNTY REVIEWINGS.**
>
> --------
>
> Another man made happy, and this is how it happened. Last Friday night, at 12 a.m., while the M. E. church bell was ringing in the Happy New Years morn, a ten-pound boy was born to Mrs. H. A. Hall of Harrisville. This was Mr. Hall's New Year's present.

Alcona County Review, January 7, 1881
Father: Hiram A. Hall
Mother: Lydia

Harris, Raymond

> **Black River Sparks.**
> **BIRTHS.**
>
> Mr. and Mrs. L. O. Harris are training a prospective Supervisor for the first ward. It is a nine pound boy, and was born last Monday morning, just in time for the special session of the Board that convened that day. His governor pronounces him a stalwart on the [unreadable] question.--Cadillac News.
>
> Harrisville, the namesake of the boy's father, sends greeting.

Alcona County Review, February 27, 1880
Father: Levi O. Harris
Mother: Georgine

Hartigan, Matthew

> **Black River Sparks.**
>
> --------
>
> **BIRTHS**
>
> Mr. and Mrs. M. Hartigan, a boy.

Alcona County Review, May 14, 1896
Father: Matthew Hartigan
Mother: Mary Nubert

Hastings, Anna Jane

> **Haynes Happenings.**
>
> --------
>
> Haynes, Dec. 26.--Reported that Wm. Hastings is the father of a boy [girl] born on the 22d.

Alcona County Review, December 27, 1894
Father: William John Hastings
Mother: Jane Ann Elizabeth Willoughby

Hastings, {Boy}

> **Haynes Happenings.**
>
> --------
>
> February 20, 1894.
> Robert Hastings received a valentine in the shape of a bouncing baby boy on the 14th. He is as happy as a boy with a new pair of boots.

Alcona County Review, February 22, 1894
Father: Robert F. Hastings
Mother: Sarah Jane Ritchie

Hastings, Evelina

> **SLEEPY HOLLOW.**

> Sept. 26, '99.
> Born to Mr. and Mrs. Joseph Hastings on the 19th inst. twin baby girls. Unfortunately one of them only lived eight hours and was interred in the cemetery Thursday.

Alcona County Review, September 28, 1899
Father: Joseph Alexander Hastings
Mother: Catherine Jane Elmes

Hastings, Joseph Ellsworth

> **Haynes.**
>
> Haynes, March 29.--Mr. Joseph Hastings has a broad smile on his face—it is a boy. Ditto Mr. Boice.

Alcona County Review, March 31, 1892
Father: Joseph Alexander Hastings
Mother: Catherine Jane Elmes

Hastings, Lavina S.

> **HAYNES HAPPENINGS.**
>
> Mrs. Wm. Hastings presented Wm. with a daughter last week.

Alcona County Review, February 23, 1899
Father: William John Hastings
Mother: Jane Ann Elizabeth Willoughby

Hastings, Mary

> Haynes, Dec. 2, 1891.—Robert Hasty is a happy father, so report says.

Alcona County Review, December 10, 1891
Father: Robert F. Hastings
Mother: Sarah Jane Ritchie

Hastings, Robert E.

> **Haynes Happenings.**
>
> --------
>
> Feb. 6th, 1894.
> Joseph Hasty is the father of a bouncing baby boy. Congratulations.

Alcona County Review, February 8, 1894
Father: Joseph Alexander Hastings
Mother: Catherine Jane Elmes

Hastings, Shirley Laselles

> **Haynes Happenings.**
>
> March 22, '97.
> Born—To Mr. and Mrs. W. J. Hastings, a son on the 16th. To Mr. and Mrs. Wm. Pyne, a son on Monday the 15th.

Alcona County Review, March 25, 1897
Father: William John Hastings
Mother: Jane Ann Elizabeth Willoughby

Hastings, Stella Belle

> **SLEEPY HOLLOW.**
>
> Sept. 26, '99.
> Born to Mr. and Mrs. Joseph Hastings on the 19th inst. twin baby girls. Unfortunately one of them only lived eight hours and was interred in the cemetery Thursday.

Alcona County Review, September 28, 1899
Father: Joseph Alexander Hastings
Mother: Catherine Jane Elmes

Hastings, Warren Erwin

ALCONA ATOMS.

Joseph Hasty is a daddy; it's a boy. Phillip Carr's little flock also numbers one more boy.

Alcona County Review, August 6, 1886
Father: Joseph Alexander Hastings
Mother: Catherine Jane Elmes

Hawkins, Harry B.

CURRAN EVENTS.

Born to Mr. and Mrs. S. Hawkins a son Feb. 19.

Alcona County Review, February 23, 1899
Father: Steven Hawkins
Mother: Harriet LaForge

Hawkins, Jennie

Curran, Jan. 8.—Mr. and Mrs. George McCormick are happy over the arrival of a baby boy on Dec. 19. Also Mr. and Mrs. Steve Hawkins a fine girl on January 3d.

Alcona County Review, January 10, 1895
Father: Steven Hawkins
Mother: Harriet LaForge

Hawse, Floyd J.

Mud Lake Jots.

Mr. and Mrs. Charles Hawse have a nice baby boy about a month old. As his arrival has not been spoken of and he "came to stay" it must be mentioned.

Alcona County Review, April 18, 1895
Father: Charles Hawse
Mother: Jane

Hayes, George Albert

Curtis.

Mrs. Harp Hase presented her husband with a beautiful son a short time ago.

Alcona County Review, December 29, 1892
Father: Joseph Hartwell Hayes
Mother: Fanny Vaughn

Hebener, Daniel Dewey

KILLMASTER.

Our worthy night watchman, Benjamin Hebener, grew six inches Monday morning, when he found that he was the papa of a seven pound boy.

Alcona County Review, September 15, 1898
Father: Benjamin Hebener
Mother: Phyllis Smith

Heilig, James Nolan

CURTISVILLE.

Mr. and Mrs. Heileg are the proud parents of a young son since Saturday, Oct. 7th.

Alcona County Review, October 12, 1899
Father: Peter Francis Heilig
Mother: Eva Goodfellow

Henderson, May E.

PURELY PERSONAL.

Capt. Henderson, of the L. S. S., had a welcome New Year's gift from his wife in the shape of a "blessed" baby girl, their first born.

Alcona County Review, January 13, 1888
Father: James E. Henderson
Mother: Minnie M. Lytle

Henderson, Norman J.

Born to Mrs. Capt. Henderson, a boy on the 6th.

Alcona County Review, January 7, 1897
Father: James E. Henderson
Mother: Minnie G. Kibbe

Heron, {Girl}

Black River News.

Born to Mr. and Mrs. John Heron a daughter.

Alcona County Review, August 8, 1895
Father: John W. Heron
Mother: Lulu H. Bailey

Heron, Mary Blanchard

Somewhat Personal.

Cards have been received here announcing the birth at Montesano, Wash., on Oct. 20, of a daughter— Mary Blanchard—to Mr. and Mrs. John Heron, popular young people of Greenbush up to two years ago.

Alcona County Review, November 5, 1891
Father: JohnW. Heron
Mother: Lulu H. Bailey

Herron, {Boy}

Additional Reviewings.

Andy Herron, who now lives at South Harrisville, is the happiest married man that trods the plains of this mundane sphere. A handsome seven-pound boy was placed in his arms Wednesday morning. Mother and child doing well.

Alcona County Review, May 13, 1881
Father: Andrew Herron
Mother: Rebecca E.

Heumann, {Boy}

Somewhat Personal.

Mr. and Mrs. F. G. Heumann welcomed a little stranger of the male sex to their household a few days ago. It is but a few weeks ago that they buried their eldest child.

Alcona County Review, January 7, 1892
Father: Fred G. Heumann
Mother:

Heumann, Clara

LOCAL JOTTINGS.

Fred Heumann, the Au Sable tailor, was in town Thursday. Fred is feeling happy over the arrival of a 10-lb. girl at this house last Sunday, and "set up" the cigars in honor of the event.

Alcona County Review, June 4, 1886
Father: Fred G. Heumann
Mother:

Higgins, Florence A.

BORN.

To Mr. and Mrs. L. H. Higgins, at Minneapolis, Minn. a daughter, March 13th.

Alcona County Review, March 28, 1890
Father: Leonard H. Higgins
Mother: Ina J.

Hill, Floyd R.

Gustin Grist.

July 1, 1896.
Milton Hill and wife are rejoicing over a bouncing boy.

Alcona County Review, July 2, 1896
Father: Milton Hill
Mother: Bertha E.

Hill, Fred

Black River Sparks.

Born to Mr. and Mrs. Sam Hill, a 12 lb. boy.

Alcona County Review, June 18, 1896
Father: Samuel Hill
Mother: Sarah S. Miller

Hill, Milton Adrian

SOMEWHAT PERSONAL.

Mr. and Mrs. Milton Hill of Killmaster are the proud parents of a very young son, who made his appearance at their home last week.

Alcona County Review, July 21, 1892
Father: Milton Hill
Mother: Bertha E.

Hill, Samuel

Haynes Happenings.

Haynes, Nov. 20.--Mrs. Hill presented Sam with a son on Friday, the 16th, making the fifth son in succession. No daughters.

Alcona County Review, November 23, 1888
Father: Samuel Hill
Mother: Sarah S. Miller

Hogue, Josephine

LOCAL JOTTINGS.

Can a man be happy when he has reached an age above forty years? Some of them can, on "special occasions." For instance, there is Wilder Hogue who is just now the happiest man on earth. He's the father of a fine boy, or girl, we didn't learn which—enough to make any thusly favored mortal cast a "broad grin."

Alcona County Review, April 10, 1885
Father: Wilder B. Hogue
Mother: Ida M. Elmer

Holmes, Alice M.

Haynes.

Births.—Mrs. Sam Johnson, a boy; Mrs. Wm. Ritchie, a girl; Mrs. John LaFrance, a girl; Mrs. Edwin Holmes, a girl.

Alcona County Review, July 27, 1893
Father: Edwin Holmes
Mother: Mary Jane Wilson

Holmes, Herbert F.

Somewhat Personal.

E. Holmes and wife are harboring another little stranger of the masculine persuasion since last week.

Alcona County Review, September 10, 1891
Father: Edwin Holmes
Mother: Mary Jane Wilson

Hooper, Guy S.

COUNTY NEWS JOTTINGS.

It laughs (!) lovingly, chirps beautifully, and weighs exactly nine pounds. Is a boy, and was born yesterday morning. L. W. Hooper is its paternal ancestor.

Alcona County Review, September 14, 1877
Father: Lewis William Hooper
Mother: Clara C. Wilson

Hornby, Alice M.

Dean District, Jan. 11, 1893.—A new arrival reported at the residence of Chas. Hornby.

Alcona County Review, January 12, 1893
Father: Charles W. Hornby
Mother: Elizabeth Maud DeForest

Hornby, Minnie

A Long String From Springport.

Springport, Jan. 15, 1895.
Born, Dec. 16th, 1894, a son to Mr. and Mrs. Joseph Specht. The evening previous a daughter to Mr. and Mrs. Chas. Hornby.

Alcona County Review, January 17, 1895
Father: Charles W. Hornby
Mother: Elizabeth Maud DeForest

Horton, {Girl}

Local Sparks.

Born—To Mr. and Mrs. C. Horton, a daughter; to Mr. and Mrs. James Foster, a son.

Alcona County Review, August 29, 1895
Father: C. Horton
Mother:

Houghton, {Girl}

BLACK RIVER.

Will Houghton says he is convinced that he has the biggest and finest baby, age considered, in town. It is prize girl, 10 weeks old and weighs 16 pounds.

Alcona County Review, October 13, 1898
Father: Charles William Houghton
Mother: Abigail McLaurin

Houghton, Edwin

GREENBUSH.

Born to Mrs. Geo. Houston, a son, last Tuesday.

Alcona County Review, July 1, 1897
Father: George Houghton
Mother:

Howitson, Albert

LOCAL JOTTINGS.

Samuel Howitson, Jr., of Greenbush, is the happy father of twin boys,—came about two weeks ago and bid fair to stay a long time.

Alcona County Review, December 9, 1887
Father: Samuel Howitson, Jr.
Mother: Sarah Gilbreath

Howitson, Alfred

LOCAL JOTTINGS.

Samuel Howitson, Jr., of Greenbush, is the happy father of twin boys,—came about two weeks ago and bid fair to stay a long time.

Alcona County Review, December 9, 1887
Father: Samuel Howitson, Jr.
Mother: Sarah Gilbreath

Hull, James Robert

County News and Gossip.

The happiest man in Alcona county—Is it one of the newly elected township officers? No; not by any manner of means. It is Mr. Robert Hull, whose good lady presented him with a fine bouncing boy, and Robert is just glorious over the advent of the interesting little stranger. Well, long may he be spared to fulfill the every wish of his now happy father.

Alcona County Review, April 8, 1881
Father: Robert Hull
Mother: Ellen

Hyke, Arthur Wellington

Haynes.

George Hyke is the happy father of a bouncing baby boy.

Alcona County Review, April 13, 1893
Father: George A. Hyke
Mother: Celia Ann McVeigh

Hyke, George Warren

Mud Lake Jots.

April 29.
Mr. and Mrs. George Hyke have three little sons; the latest came to stay last Wednesday, Apr. 24. Mother and child both doing finely. Mr. H. expects to have lots of help in his farming soon.

Alcona County Review, May 2, 1895
Father: George A. Hyke
Mother: Celia Ann McVeigh

Jackson, Chester E.

GREENBUSH GETTINGS.

Born—On Sunday, Dec. 27, 1885, to the wife of Seth Jackson, a son. This makes the second 12 pounder in Greenbush inside of 3 days. Seth, they say, is so happy he can hardly sleep.

Alcona County Review, January 8, 1886
Father: Seth Jackson
Mother: Mary Isabella Griswold

Jameson, Earl C.

The Local News.

Mr. and Mrs. C. E. Jameson have added another little stranger to their family this winter; a fact that speaks well for the climate of Washington. It is a boy.

Alcona County Review, April 4, 1890
Father: Clifton E. Jameson
Mother: Sarah E. Taft

Jameson, Eula V.

LOCAL JOTTINGS.

C. E. Jameson ought to be happy, and no doubt is exceedingly so. His wife presented him with a handsome daughter the latter part of last week.

Alcona County Review, January 15, 1886
Father: Clifton E. Jameson
Mother: Sarah E. Taft

Jameson, Harriet Roma

PURELY PERSONAL.

Mrs. C. E. Jameson, Aug. 12,—a girl.

Alcona County Review, August 19, 1887
Father: Clifton E. Jameson
Mother: Sarah E. Taft

Jantz, Howard

PERSONAL MENTION.

Born, to Mrs. Nich. Jantz, a son. The lady has been seriously ill since confinement.

Alcona County Review, May 14, 1896
Father: Nicholas Jantz
Mother: Pauline

Jantz, May

The Local News.

Nicholas Jantz has been celebrating the arrival of a new 10 ½ pound girl, born Sunday.

Alcona County Review, June 4, 1891
Father: Nicholas Jantz
Mother: Pauline

Jantz, Nichols

LOCAL PICK UPS.

Born, Friday June 23, to Mr. and Mrs. N. Jantz, a son.

Alcona County Review, June 29, 1899
Father: Nicholas Jantz
Mother: Pauline

Jantz, Pearl

PERSONAL MENTION.

Nich Jantz and wife are rejoicing over the birth of another daughter, Thursday, the 8th, inst.

Alcona County Review, June 15, 1893
Father: Nicholas Jantz
Mother: Pauline

Jenkins, {Boy}

GREENBUSH GETTINGS.

The population of Greenbush is increasing, in one way at least for, on 22nd inst. the wife of Wm. Jenkins presented him with a son of 10 lbs. weight. Billy followed Mr. Coyle's example and set up the cigars.

Alcona County Review, January 29, 1886

LOCAL JOTTINGS.

New settlers have arrived in Alcona County recently, as follows: Jan. 21, a boy each at the homes of Wm. Jenkins, Greenbush, and Geo. W. Stecker, Harrisville.

Alcona County Review, January 29, 1886
Father: William Jenkins
Mother: Martha J. Young

Johnson, Annie

Gustin Grist.

April 30.
Our blacksmith, Mr. Johnson, now has more than horses to shoe, he has a nine pound girl.

Alcona County Review, May 2, 1895
Father: Albert Johnson
Mother: Kate

Johnson, {Boy}

Haynes.

Births.—Mrs. Sam Johnson, a boy; Mrs. Wm. Ritchie, a girl; Mrs. John LaFrance, a girl; Mrs. Edwin Holmes, a girl.

Alcona County Review, July 27, 1893
Father: Samuel Johnson
Mother: Mary

Johnson, {Boy}

Haynes Happenings.

Jan. 14, 1896.
To Mr. and Mrs. Samuel Johnston, a son, born Jan. 4.

Alcona County Review, January 16, 1896
Father: Samuel Johnson
Mother:

Johnson, John

HAYNES HAPPENINGS.

Mrs. John Johnson presented an 8 pound boy to John last week. She is at her mother's in Alpena.

Alcona County Review, September 15, 1898
Father: John Johnson
Mother: Eleanor Roberts

Johnson, Newton E.

MIKADO.

C. A. Johnson, general merchant, is of the opinion that he was the receiver of the most valuable Christmas present in Mikado. It's a boy, ——10 pounds, and arrived on Christmas Eve.

Alcona County Review, January 6, 1898
Father: Canute A. Johnson
Mother: Mary J. [McFarland] McGillivary.

Johnson, Reginald?

Killmaster.

Born to Mr. and Mrs. Johnson, a boy Tuesday, Mar. 30.

Alcona County Review, April 8, 1897
Father: Albert Johnson
Mother: Hattie

Johnston, Annie

Haynes.

Mrs. Thomas Johnston gave birth to a daughter on Monday the 12th.

Alcona County Review, September 22, 1892
Father: Thomas J. Johnson
Mother: Eliza J.

Johnston, Arthur

HAYNES.

To Mr. and Mrs. Wm. R. Johnston—have not learned whether it is a boy or girl.

Alcona County Review, July 20, 1899

HAYNES.

July 25, '99.
It was a 10 lbs. boy which came to Mr. and Mrs. Wm. R. Johnston last week, and Wm. says it is gold standard weight—no 16 to 1 about it.

Alcona County Review, July 27, 1899
Father: William R. Johnston
Mother: Sarah Melinda Shaw

Johnston, Arvilla

Haynes.

Mrs. Wm. Johnson presented Will with a daughter last week.

Alcona County Review, March 30, 1893
Father: William A. Johnston

Mother: Ellen Lavina Hicks

Johnston, {Boy}

PERSONAL.

Mrs. Wm. R. Johnson of Haynes presented Wm. with a big baby boy Feb. 5.

Alcona County Review, February 11, 1897
Father: William R. Johnston
Mother: Sarah Melinda Shaw

Johnston, Cora

HAYNES HAPPENINGS.

Mrs. Wm. Johnston presented her husband with a 12 lbs. girl last week.

Alcona County Review, December 22, 1898
Father: William R. Johnston
Mother: Ellen Lavina Hicks

Johnston, {Girl}

Haynes.

John Johnston is the father of a bouncing baby girl, which arrived on Friday a. m., the 19th.

Alcona County Review, May 25, 1893
Father: John Johnston
Mother:

Johnston, Jennings Bryan

Haynes Happenings.

March 18, '96.
Born to Mr. and Mrs. Wm. Johnson, a son, on 11th.

Alcona County Review, March 19, 1896
Father: William R. Johnston
Mother: Sarah Melinda Shaw

Johnston, Margaret

ALCONA ATOMS.

Alcona, April 21.—Thos. Johnston is the daddy of a bouncing baby girl. If it had been a boy, he would have been the seventh son and a natural born doctor.

Alcona County Review, April 22, 1887
Father: Thomas J. Johnston
Mother: Eliza J.

Johnston, Minnie

Haynes.

Mr. Ed. Downie is the father of another baby boy, presented to him last week by Mrs. Downie, and Wm. Johnston is the father of a bouncing baby girl presented to him by Mrs. Johnston.

Alcona County Review, November 17, 1892
Father: William R. Johnston
Mother: Sarah Melinda Shaw

Johnston, Robert

Haynes Happenings.

Born to Mr. and Mrs. Wm. J. Johnson, a son on the 2d.

Alcona County Review, June 14, 1894

Father: William R. Johnston
Mother: Sarah Melinda Shaw

Johnston, Susie Jane

Haynes, May 28, 1895.--Give credit to Wm. R. Johnston for a new girl regulation weight.

Alcona County Review, May 30, 1895
Father: William R. Johnston
Mother: Ellen Lavina Hicks

Johnston, Teressa

ALCONA ATOMS.

Wm. Johnston is daddy to another bouncing baby girl.

Alcona County Review, January 28, 1887
Father: William R. Johnston
Mother: Ellen Lavina Hicks

Jordan, Erlin

GREENBUSH.

Born to Mr. and Mrs. Carl Jordan, a boy.

Alcona County Review, October 20, 1898
Father: Carl Jordan
Mother: Jennie Walton

Joseph, Clara A.

HAYNES HAPPENINGS.

Mrs. Joseph presented her husband with a daughter, and Joseph is happy.

Alcona County Review, December, 1888
Father: Alex Joseph
Mother: Magdalena S. Beck

Joughin, {Boy}

PERSONAL MENTION.

A son was born to Mr. and Mrs. H. A. Joughin, Thursday, August 13.

Alcona County Review, August 20, 1896
Father: Herbert A. Joughin
Mother: Lois E. Patterson

Kahn, Iver

Local News.

Born, at Bay City, to Mr. and Mrs. S. B. Kahn Thursday, Oct. 19, a son.

Alcona County Review, October 19, 1899
Father: Samuel B. Kahn
Mother: Nellie Sandorf

Kajawa, {Boy}

Black River Sparks.

Born Saturday, March 21st, to Mr. and Mrs. Simon Kajawa, twins, both boys, since deceased.

Alcona County Review, March 26, 1896
Father: Simon Kajawa
Mother:

Kajawa, {Boy}

Black River Sparks.

Born Saturday, March 21st, to Mr. and Mrs. Simon Kajawa, twins, both boys, since deceased.

Alcona County Review, March 26, 1896
Father: Simon Kajawa
Mother:

Keating, John

LOCAL JOTTINGS.

John Kating is now the happiest man in the county. It's a son, and was placed in the arms of its elated father June 2nd.

Alcona County Review, June 6, 1884
Father: John Keating
Mother:

Kell, {Boy}

LOCAL JOTTINGS.

Will Kell wears a smile of unusually large dimensions. It's a son and was born March 9th.

Alcona County Review, March 15, 1889
Father: William J. Kell
Mother: Clio Young

Kell, Finley

A little stranger of the male sex put in an appearance last week at the home of Wm. Kell.

Alcona County Review, April 5, 1894
Father: William J. Kell
Mother: Clio Young

Kelley, {Boy}

HOME REVIEWINGS.

We see by the Alpena Argus that W. H. Kelley, our former townsman, is the father of a brand new boy, born on Sunday last. The Argus says it is the second colored child every born in that city. Kelley could afford to send down a box of cigars to his Harrisville friends in honor of that event.

Alcona County Review, July 15, 1881
Father: W. H. Kelley
Mother: Winniford

Kelley, Jessie May

West Harrisville.

Benj. Kelly has a big smile and a little daughter.

Alcona County Review, April 7, 1892
Father: Benjamin E. Kelley
Mother: Sarah M.

Kennedy, Grace B.

Somewhat Personal.

Mr. and Mrs. John Kennedy of Skamokawa, Wash., are receiving congratulations on the birth of another daughter.

Alcona County Review, December 17, 1891
Father: John C. Kennedy
Mother: Ida Belle Wilson

Kennedy, Hazel B.

PURELY PERSONAL.

Mr. and Mrs. John Kennedy, of Fort Bragg, California, have been made happy by the recent birth of a daughter.

Alcona County Review, July 12, 1889
Father: John C. Kennedy
Mother: Ida Belle Wilson

Kennedy, Mary

LOCAL JOTTINGS.

A. W. Kennedy and his good wife, of Mikado, were made happy last week by the advent of a baby girl.

Alcona County Review, April 8, 1887
Father: Angus W. Kennedy
Mother: Christina

Keough, {Boy}

LOCAL JOTTINGS

Patrick Keough rejoices over the recent addition to his family of a son.

Alcona County Review, August 10, 1888
Father: Patrick Keough
Mother: Eliza Cole

Keough, Frank

SPENCER DISTRICT.

Mrs. John Keough has a young son.

Alcona County Review, November 17, 1898
Father: John Keough
Mother: Jane Ellen Walker

Kernohan, Grace Josephine

Additional Home Jottings.

J. P. Kernohan and wife, of Grand Island, Neb., formerly of Harrisville, are rejoicing over the advent of a daughter, born August 26. Grace Josephine is the name. A son and daughter now compose their family.

Alcona County Review, September 9, 1882
Father: J. P. Kernohan
Mother: Ella Packer

Kernohan, Jay Waldo

LOCAL JOTTINGS.

J. P. Kernohan, of Grand Island, Neb., formerly of Harrisville, received an elaborate present from his wife, New Year's Day, in the shape of a handsome new son. The youngster sends us his card with compliments of the season. We hope he may live long and prosper. Jay Waldo is his name.

Alcona County Review, January 15, 1885
Father: J. P. Kernohan
Mother: Ella Packer

Kerwin, {Boy}

COUNTY JOTTINGS.

A little stranger (boy, we believe) has come to make joyful the hearts of Mr. and Mrs. Kerwin, as well as little Stella.

Alcona County Review, April 12, 1878
Father: ? Kerwin
Mother:

Killmaster, Benjamin

PERSONAL MENTION.

Another judge, a small one of customary weight, received a warm welcome at the home of Hon. C. H. Killmaster on June 7th.

Alcona County Review, June 15, 1893
Father: Charles H. Killmaster
Mother: Nellie Duncan

Killmaster, Elspeth Storey

Mr. and Mrs. J. H. Killmaster, are the parents of a daughter since Apr. 4.

Alcona County Review, April 14, 1898
Father: John Henry Killmaster
Mother: Helen May Barlow

Killmaster, {Girl}

LOCAL JOTTINGS

All is sunshine now in the household of Mr. and Mrs. Chas. H. Killmaster. A daughter, their first born, brought gladness and joy to their hearts last Thursday morning.

Alcona County Review, June 15, 1888
Father: Charles H. Killmaster
Mother: Nellie Duncan

Killmaster, Henry

Gustin Grist.

Gustin, March 5th, 1895. Attorney Killmaster is shouting with joy. He expected a girl but it is a 12-pound boy.

Alcona County Review, March 7, 1895
Father: John Henry Killmaster
Mother: Helen May Barlow

Killmaster, Henry James

Somewhat Personal.

Born—To Mr. and Mrs. John H. Killmaster, Dec. 13, a son.

Alcona County Review, December 17, 1891
Father: John Henry Killmaster
Mother: Helen May Barlow

Kimball, {Boy}

ALCONA ATOMS.

Mrs. Geo. Kimball gave birth to twins (a boy and girl) on the 6th of Feb. Unfortunately the girl did not live, and was buried on Sunday, the 7th. Mother and boy are doing well.

Alcona County Review, February 19, 1886
Father: George Kimball
Mother: Eliza

Kimball, {Girl}

ALCONA ATOMS.

Mrs. Geo. Kimball gave birth to twins (a boy and girl) on the 6th of Feb. Unfortunately the girl did not live, and was buried on Sunday, the 7th. Mother and boy are doing well.

Alcona County Review, February 19, 1886
Father: George Kimball
Mother: Eliza

King, {Girl}

BLACK RIVER BRIEFLETS.

On the 7th inst. the wife of Harry King presented Harry with a young queen.

Alcona County Review, February 12, 1886
Father: Harry H. King
Mother: Rosa McKinley

King, John A.

MUD LAKE.

There is a new comer at Mr. and Mrs. Joseph King's. It is a nine pound boy.

Alcona County Review, July 13, 1899
Father: Joseph King
Mother: Emma E. Joseph

Korf, Mary E.

KILLMASTER RIPPLES.

Mrs. J. Korf has a young daughter, Feb. 8.

Alcona County Review, February 18, 1897
Father: John Korf
Mother: Della Belle

LaBoueff, Elita Leila

PERSONAL POINTS.

D. La Boueff has received news of the birth of a daughter. This happy event took place at St. Thomas, Ont., where his wife has been for several weeks.

Alcona County Review, February 10, 1898
Father: David LaBoueff
Mother: Elizabeth Branaghan

LaBoueff, {Girl}

PERSONAL MENTION.

The arrival of a daughter Sunday morning brought joy to the hearts of Davy and Mrs. LaBoueff, but Dave had rather spoken for a stage driver.

Alcona County Review, September 3, 1896
Father: David LaBoueff
Mother: Elizabeth Branaghan

LaChapelle, Belle

LOCAL JOTTINGS.

It's Alford LaChappell's turn to be happy this time. Another daughter.

Alcona County Review, April 17, 1885
Father: Alfred LaChapelle
Mother: Sarah Kennedy

LaChapelle, Edith

HOME NEWS JOTTINGS.

Alf. LaChapelle's home was invaded last Wednesday by a bouncing baby girl who "tips the beam" at a little over nine pounds.

Alcona County Review, January 5, 1883
Father: Alfred LaChapelle
Mother: Sarah Kennedy

LaChapelle, John

LOCAL JOTTINGS.

Republicans gain of one! A 10 lb. boy for Alf Chapelle.

Alcona County Review, September 21, 1888
Father: Alfred LaChapelle
Mother: Sarah Kennedy

LaChapelle, William L.

Local News.

We omitted to mention last week that a young conductor arrived at the home of Will La Chapelle at Alpena. He arrived on the 1st inst.

Alcona County Review, September 14, 1899
Father: William LaChapelle
Mother: Mary Elizabeth McIntosh

LaChapelle, William W.

REVIEWINGS.

Another boy for Alford LaChapelle.

Alcona County Review, April 11, 1879
Father: Alfred LaChapelle
Mother: Sarah Kennedy

LaCross, {Boy}

BLACK RIVER IN PRINT.

Born to Mr. and Mrs. Clay Lacross, a son, since deceased.

Alcona County Review, January 16, 1896
Father: Clayton LaCross
Mother: Julia

LaFrance, Alexander

Haynes Happenings.

Mrs. John La France presented her husband with a baby boy last week, which rounds out a baker's dozen of children for them.

Alcona County Review, October 24, 1895
Father: John LaFrance
Mother: Jane Bond

LaFrance, {Boy}

Haynes Happenings.

Feb. 6th, 1894.
Joseph La France is happy. It is a boy. Mother and child are well.

Alcona County Review, February 8, 1894
Father: Joseph LaFrance
Mother: Catharine Langton

LaFrance, {Girl}
HAYNES HAPPENINGS.

Haynes, May 22--Mrs. Joseph LaFrance presented her husband with a daughter, and Joseph is happy.

Alcona County Review, June 1, 1888
Father: Joseph LaFrance
Mother: Catharine Langton

LaFrance, Henry Joseph
'ROUND ABOUT.

Haynes, Nov. 24.--Mrs. LaFrance presented Joseph with a son on the 20th.

Alcona County Review, November 26, 1891
Father: Joseph LaFrance
Mother: Catharine Langton

LaFrance, Ida
Haynes.
Births.—Mrs. Sam Johnson, a boy; Mrs. Wm. Ritchie, a girl; Mrs. John LaFrance, a girl; Mrs. Edwin Holmes, a girl.

Alcona County Review, July 27, 1893
Father: John LaFrance
Mother: Jane Bond

LaFrance, John
Alcona Atoms.
John LaFrance is happy again. It is a boy.

Alcona County Review, March 10, 1882
Father: John LaFrance
Mother: Jane Bond

LaFrance, Sarah J.
ALCONA ATOMS.

Mrs. Jane LaFrance presented her liege lord and master with a daughter, lately.

Alcona County Review, October 1, 1886
Father: John LaFrance
Mother: Jane Bond

LaFrance, William Henry
Haynes Items.
Mrs. Jane LaFrance presented John with a daughter [son] on Thursday last.

Alcona County Review, May 7, 1891
Father: John LaFrance
Mother: Jane Bond

Laister, {Boy}
Purely Personal.

Born.—To Mrs. Jack Laister, a son.

Alcona County Review, November 22, 1889
Father: Jack Laister
Mother:

LaLonde, Joseph A.
HOME NEWS JOTTINGS.

Born.—On the 20th inst., to Mr. and Mrs. LaLonde, a son.

Alcona County Review, March 23, 1883
Father: Joseph A. LaLonde
Mother: Alice

Landon, Blanche Irene
WEST HARRISVILLE.

Dec. 29, 1896.
A baby girl came to the home of A. Landon on Christmas eve.

Alcona County Review, December 31, 1896
Father: Alexander Landon
Mother: Martha Genge

Landon, {Girl}
LOCAL JOTTINGS.

Tally one each for Dave Micho and Gill Landon. Both girls.

Alcona County Review, April 5, 1889
Father: Gilbert Landon
Mother: Anna Genge

Landon, Mary
West Harrisville.
West Harrisville, Mar. 23.—Mrs. Alex Landon presented her husband with a bouncing baby girl Thursday last week.

Alcona County Review, March 24, 1892
Father: Alexander Landon
Mother: Martha Genge

Lappan, {Boy}
Local Sayings and Doings.

Adolph Lapain is just now too happy for anything. His wife presented him with a fine healthy boy Wednesday night, and that's the reason. The census man can now put Lapain down for five girls and one boy. This is about how it affected him:

"Eureka!" 'Dolph triumphantly yelled,

"Ahoy! Ahoy!! AHOY!!!

Now what do you guess is the matter with me?—

Why, I'm the dad of a fine-looking boy!"

Alcona County Review, November 18, 1881
Father: Adolphus Lappan
Mother: Mary L.

Lappan, {Boy}

LOCAL JOTTINGS.

Somebody forgot to tell the Review that Adolph Lappan has recently been made happy again, over the advent of a new daughter.

Alcona County Review, October 30, 1885

LOCAL JOTTINGS.

Last week the Review said Adolph Lappan's new boy was a girl. We "take it all back," this week, after having received "official returns." Last week's erroneous announcement almost broke Adolph's heart.

Alcona County Review, November 6, 1885
Father: Adolphus Lappan
Mother: Mary L.

Lappan, Emma
REVIEWINGS.

Ah, la! Zat wazzer fine new daughter, and Dolph La Paine was happy!

Alcona County Review, February 27, 1880
Father: Adolphus Lappan
Mother: Mary L.

Larrett, {Girl}
Black River Sparks.

Born to Mr. and Mrs. John Larrett, on Friday a.m., a daughter. John is a happy man.

Alcona County Review, August 22, 1895
Father: John W. Larrett
Mother: Melinda E. Ferguson

Lathrop, Katie L.
REVIEWINGS.

Mrs. E. Lathrop--a nice new daughter.

Alcona County Review, December 12, 1879
Father: Eugene Lathrop
Mother: Sarah Maria

Lawrence, Clyde V.
Curtis Items.
Curtis, Jan. 27, '96.--Born to Mr. and Mrs. Wm. Lawerence, Jan. 22, a 9 pound boy. Mother and child doing finely.

Alcona County Review, January 30, 1896
Father: Wellington Lawrence
Mother: Rosanna LaFleur

Lawrence, Wellington
Curtis Tid Bits.

Curtis, March 19.--Wm. Lawrence and wife are very happy over a ten pound boy which arrived at their home last Sabbath.

Alcona County Review, March 22, 1894
Father: Wellington Lawrence
Mother: Rosanna LaFleur

Lawson, {Girl}

From Alcona.

Alcona, July 11th, 1877.
Born—at Alcona on the 10th inst., to Mr. and Mrs. Chas. J. Lawson, a daughter.

Alcona County Review, July 13, 1877
Father: Charles J. Lawson
Mother: Christiana

LeClair, Josephine

Black River Sparks.

BIRTHS.

Mr. and Mrs. Wm. LeClair, a boy [girl].

Alcona County Review, May 14, 1896
Father: William LeClair
Mother: Angeline Gauthier

Lecuyer, Howard

WEST HARRISVILLE.

Mr. and Mrs. P. Lecuyer are rejoicing over the coming of a young son.

Alcona County Review, March 31, 1898
Father: Peter Lecuyer
Mother: Emma J. Gallagher

Lecuyer, Irvine

WEST HARRISVILLE.

West Harrisville, June 10.--P. Lecuyer is building an addition to his store, also on his house. For Pete is the father of a bouncing boy.

Alcona County Review, June 11, 1896
Father: Peter Lecuyer
Mother: Emma J. Gallagher

Leith, Minnie E.

LOCAL JOTTINGS.

Rev. T. B. Leith was highly elated Tuesday. His wife presented him a handsome new daughter. Mother and child doing well.

Alcona County Review, November 6, 1885
Father: T. B. Leith
Mother: Louisa A.

Lemon, Jane

LOCAL JOTTINGS.

Two more souls made happy, viz., Oliver Lemon and Morgan Flora, whose respective wives has presented each with a daughter. Thus the world moves.

Alcona County Review, January 15, 1886
Father: Oliver Lemon
Mother: Eleanor Bond

Lepard, {Boy}

CALEDONIA.

Born to Mr. and Mrs. Ed Leopard, June 15, a son. All doing well.

Alcona County Review, June 15, 1896
Father: Edward Lepard
Mother: Mary E. O'Connor

Lewis, {Boy}

PERSONAL MENTION.

A letter to an Oscoda citizen from Mt. Clemens announces the arrival of a baby boy at the home of Rev. E. A. Lewis, formerly of this place.—Press.

Alcona County Review, September 17, 1896
Father: W. E. A. Lewis
Mother: Marion Barmby

Lewis, Claud B.

LOCAL JOTTINGS

Word comes from Tawas City that Mr. and Mrs. Grant Lewis, nee Lou Hall, rejoice over the birth of a son and heir.

Alcona County Review, January 6, 1888
Father: Grant Lewis
Mother: Lulu E. Hall

Lewis, Hattie M.

Born, to Mrs. Grant Lewis at East Tawas last Saturday, a daughter.

Alcona County Review, October 27, 1892
Father: Grant Lewis
Mother: Lulu E. Hall

Lincoln, Fred

EVENTS OF ONE WEEK.

Born to Mrs. Joe Lincoln, a son.

Alcona County Review, June 1, 1893
Father: Joseph Lincoln
Mother: Rose Anna Aird

Loney, {Girl}

Haynes.

Mrs. Abram Loney gave birth to a daughter on Monday, the 5th.

Alcona County Review, February 15, 1894
Father: Abram Loney
Mother: Elizabeth Marshall

Loney, Mabel

ALCONA ATOMS.

Mrs. Loney presented Abram with a daughter, last week.

Alcona County Review, September 3, 1886
Father: Abram Loney
Mother: Elizabeth Marshall

Long, Henry A.

Haynes Happenings.

Haynes, April 10.--Look at Isaiah 9-6 and you will see what happened to Mr. and Mrs. Jas. Fleming on the 8th. 1st line of verse. Also, a daughter

to Rev. Mrs. Long about the same time.

Alcona County Review, April 12, 1894

Haynes Happenings.

The child born to Rev. Long and wife was a boy, not a girl. My mistake and your treat.

Alcona County Review, April 19, 1894
Father: Henry A. Long
Mother: Caroline

Lott, Edith

REVIEWINGS.

Lott's baby!—That's what they call that new-born cherub at Black River.

Alcona County Review, April 11, 1879
Father: Robert L. Lott
Mother: Stella B. Fralic

Lott, Walter

Things Ain't as They Used to Be.

In the Lott family (R. L. Lott, prop'r) at Black River there used to be only two persons, but the latest telegraphic intelligence confirms the fact that they had an accident up there the other day, and now the family embraces three--nice boy. Our poetry machine has unfortunately "gin out," or we would grind out a couple of stanzas to dispel the melancholy feelings of the poor disconsolate father. However, congratulations and ten-cent cigars are in order, just the same.

Alcona County Review, February 22, 1878
Father: Robert L. Lott
Mother: Stella B. Fralic

Ludington, Hanley K.

PERSONAL MENTION.

Mrs. C. P. Ludington presented her husband with a bouncing boy Sunday.

Alcona County Review, October 17, 1895
Father: Kirk P. Ludington
Mother: Theresa Grace Renis

Lumbard, {Girl}

'ROUND ABOUT.

Haynes, Nov. 24.—Mrs. Lumbard presented her husband with a daughter last week.

Alcona County Review, November 26, 1891
Father: William Lumbard
Mother: Celia Cakman

Lumbard, {Girl}

Haynes Happenings.

Haynes, Jan. 22, 1895.--Wm. Lumbard tallies again—it is a daughter.

Alcona County Review, January 24, 1895
Father: William Lumbard
Mother: Celia Cakman

Lyman, Francis W.

THE CRADLE.

January 22, to Mrs. Don Lyman, a daughter.

Alcona County Review, January 29, 1891
Father: Don Lyman
Mother: Mary A. Sinclair

Lyman, Lena B.

LOCAL JOTTINGS.

Born, March 18, to Mr. and Mrs. Don Lyman, a daughter.

Alcona County Review, March 22, 1889
Father: Don Lyman
Mother: Mary A. Sinclair

Lyman, Maude

Local Sayings and Doings.

Somehow it utterly escaped our columns last week, but its true nevertheless that Don Lyman is the happy father of a fine new daughter.

Alcona County Review, April 21, 1882
Father: Don Lyman
Mother: Mary A. Sinclair

Lyman, St. Clair

COUNTY REVIEWINGS.

Don Lyman, of Black River, became the happy father of a boy-baby on Tuesday last.

Alcona County Review, August 20, 1880
Father: Don Lyman
Mother: Mary A. Sinclair

Lynch, Charles B.

Haynes Happenings.

Haynes, May 23.—Born to Mr. and Mrs. Lynch, a son, on the 20th.

Alcona County Review, May 24, 1894
Father: Stephen Lynch
Mother: Agnes B. Hood

Lynch, Robert

BLACK RIVER BRIEFLETS.

Mr. Steve Linch is the father of a ten lb. boy. There came a little stranger into the township some time ago, whose father has skipped out for a more congenial clime.

Alcona County Review, April 30, 1886
Father: Stephen Lynch
Mother: Agnes B. Hood

Madden, Earl C.

LOCAL JOTTINGS

Frank Madden is the happy father of a son and heir.

Alcona County Review, January 6, 1888
Father: Frank Madden
Mother: Mary Baker

Marble, Ralph N.

REVIEWINGS.

Hold on here!—stop the press! Register of Deeds R. N. Marble full of business—a curious deed just recorded (short form)—title good—description unlimited—consideration, a boy—weighs nine pounds, more or less—hoop-a-lah!

Alcona County Review, March 7, 1879
Father: Ralph N. Marble
Mother: Belle L.

Marshall, Frank

WEST HARRISVILLE.

Born, to Mrs. John Marshal, a son.

Alcona County Review, July 2, 1896
Father: John Marshall
Mother: Hannah Jane Brown

Marshall, Julia Elizabeth

West Harrisville.

John Marshall grins all over his face these days. It is a girl baby which arrived Tuesday that is the cause.

Alcona County Review, March 15, 1894
Father: John Marshall
Mother: Hannah Jane Brown

Martin, Charles C.

PERSONAL POINTS.

Born to Mr. and Mrs. Walter Martin, Monday March 27 inst., a son.

Alcona County Review, March 30, 1899
Father: Walter B. Martin
Mother: Mary Elizabeth Buchanan

Martin, Hurburt

SOMEWHAT PERSONAL.

Among many other items that escaped notice last week was the arrival of a 12-lb. girl at the home of Jas. Martin on the morning of August 25.

Alcona County Review, September 8, 1892
Father: James Martin
Mother: Margaret

Martin, Grace Belle

Purely Personal.

Born to Mrs. Jas. Martin, June 10,—a girl.

Alcona County Review, June 20, 1890
Father: James Martin
Mother: C. Mahala Milligan

Mather, Henry O.

COUNTY REVIEWINGS.

Here's a bit o' news for Harrisvillians: Mr. and Mrs. Albert Mather, of Alpena, who were formerly residents of Harrisville, have just been made parents of a bouncing boy. They will please accept Harrisville congratulations.

Alcona County Review, July 16, 1880
Father: Albert H. Mather
Mother: Sarah E. Jones

Maynard, Charlie A.

REVIEWINGS.

E. Maynard says there are ten pounds more of trick-maker at his house, now, than has heretofore been discovered. Not a *cry*-sis, either.

Alcona County Review, October 3, 1879
Father: Edward Maynard
Mother: Louise

McArthur, {Boy}

BLACK RIVER IN PRINT.

Born to Mr. and Mrs. C. Raney, a daughter; to Mr. and Mrs. Jno. McArthur, a son.

Alcona County Review, January 16, 1896
Father: John G. McArthur
Mother: Agnes Lamp

McArthur, Duncan Robert

ALCONA ATOMS.

Mr. Duncan J. McArthur is the father of a 14 lb. boy.

Alcona County Review, June 4, 1886
Father: Duncan John McArthur
Mother: Harriet Hastings

McArthur, George J.

GREENBUSH GETTINGS.

John McArthur was made happy by being presented with a young son on Saturday, July 31.

Alcona County Review, August 6, 1886
Father: John McArthur
Mother: Christie B.

McClain, {Girl}

BLACK RIVER BRIEFLETS.

On the 4th inst. the wife of Wm. McClain presented William with an eleven pound and a quarter girl baby.

Alcona County Review, February 12, 1886
Father: William McClain
Mother:

McClatchey, Charles

REVIEWINGS.

Would you believe it?——Abe McClatchy is the father of a bouncing babe.

Alcona County Review, August 29, 1879
Father: Abram McClatchey
Mother: Elizabeth Rivard

McClatchey, {Child}

The Last Sad Rites.

The remains of the late Mrs. Abram McClatchey were laid at rest last Friday morning in the cemetery west of town. The services were held at the M. E. Church. The pastor, Rev. W. Will preached a very impressive sermon, taking as his text Job 10:20-22, prefacing his remarks with the statement that whatever he might say was not intended to apply in any way to the dead but was intended as counsel for the living. The remains were encased in a beautiful casket, and lying on the mother's breast was the babe for which she sacrificed her life. The two hives of lady Maccabees attended in a body, accompanying the remains on foot from the residence to the church; from there they were conveyed by carriages to the cemetery where the Maccabee burial service was performed. There was a very large turnout of citizens.

Alcona County Review, August 12, 1897
Father: Abram McClatchy
Mother: Elizabeth Rivard

McClatchey, Earl E.

PERSONAL POINTS.

A son was born to Mr. and Mrs. M. McClatchey last evening.

Alcona County Review, June 9, 1898
Father: Moses McClatchey
Mother: Mary

McClatchey, Nellie

Local Sayings and Doings.

Abe McClatchey is twice happy. The father of a fine baby girl for sure.

Alcona County Review, January 20, 1882
Father: Abram McClatchey
Mother: Elizabeth Rivard

McClatchey, Rena

THE CRADLE.

Born——To Mrs. A. McClatchey, a daughter.

Alcona County Review, January 17, 1890
Father: Abram McClatchey
Mother: Elizabeth Rivard

McLeod, Benjamin Harrison Morton Maltz

NEIGHBORHOOD NOTES.

A small Alpena boy, born shortly after the recent election, will have to struggle through life with the ponderous name of Benjamin Harrison Morton Maltz McCloud. Poor lad.

Alcona County Review, January 25, 1889
Father: Alexander McLeod
Mother: Esther A.

McCollum, Georgena

Curtis Items.

Curtis, Jan. 20, '96.--Curtis is increasing in population: Mrs. George McCollum has a bouncing 8 pound baby girl and Mr. and Mrs. Allen rejoice over a 10 pound baby girl; that shows we are not losing ground.

Alcona County Review, January 23, 1896
Father: George McCollum
Mother: Ida

McConnell, Guy

West Harrisville.

West Harrisville, July 18, '94.-- Varnum McConley is the happy papa of a boy since Wednesday of last week.

Alcona County Review, July 19, 1894
Father: Varnum McConnell
Mother: Alice H. Genge

McConnell, Harwood

West Harrisville.

Dec. 4, 1895.
Born to Mr. and Mrs. V. McConnel, a son, Dec. 3.

Alcona County Review, December 5, 1895
Father: Varnum McConnell
Mother: Alice H. Genge

McCormick, {Boy}

The Local News

Born to Mr. and Mrs. Dr. McCormick of Black River, a son, Wednesday, August 10, 1892.

Alcona County Review, August 18, 1892
Father: Francis P. McCormick
Mother: Sarah McLean

McCormick, Earl

Curran, Jan. 8.——Mr. and Mrs. George McCormick are happy over the arrival of a baby boy on Dec. 19. Also Mr. and Mrs. Steve Hawkins a fine girl on January 3d.

Alcona County Review, January 10, 1895
Father: George C. McCormick
Mother: Alma M. Fullerton

McCoy, Clarence

Black River Sparks.

BIRTHS.

Mr. and Mrs. Jno. McCoy, a boy.

Alcona County Review, May 14, 1896
Father: John McCoy
Mother: Louisa Illman

McDonald, {Boy}

PURELY PERSONAL.

Ronald R. McDonald, of Mud Lake, pronounces himself the happiest man in Alcona county at present. Cause, birth of a son and heir, Sunday, Jan. 27th.

Alcona County Review, February 8 1889
Father: Ronald R. McDonald
Mother: Mary McQuaig

McDonald, {Boy}

LOCAL JOTTINGS.

"Jake" Y. McDonald is the father of a bouncing boy, 'tis said. Just think of that!

Alcona County Review, February 6, 1885
Father: Jake Y. McDonald
Mother:

McDonald, George L.

PERSONAL.

Sherman Hale enters just complaint against this paper for neglecting to mention the birth of a grand-daughter [grandson] at his residence June 9th. His daughter, Mrs. McDonald, has been at home since March.

Alcona County Review, June 24, 1897
Father: Dan E. McDonald
Mother: Jessie Eunice Hale

McDonald, {Girl}

LOCAL JOTTINGS.

Malcolm McDonald was never so extremely happy before. It's a nice baby girl.

Alcona County Review, February 6, 1885
Father: Malcolm McDonald
Mother:

McDonald, {Girl}

HAYNES HAPPENINGS.

Haynes, May 29——Geo. H. Lee is the grandfather of a Miss McDonald who lately came to Black River.

Alcona County Review, June 1, 1888
Father: John McDonald
Mother: Luella Lee

McDonald, Mary Loraine

EVENTS OF ONE WEEK.

A daughter was born last Friday to Mrs. D. E. McDonald, formerly Miss Jessie Hale.

Alcona County Review, April 19, 1894
Father: Dan E. McDonald
Mother: Jessie Eunice Hale

McDonald, Randall

> ### Your Folks and Our Folks.
> Born—to Mrs. R. R. McDonald, a son, Friday, April 23d. at Alpena.

Alcona County Review, April 30, 1891
Father: Ronald R. McDonald
Mother: Mary McQuaig

McDougall, {Boy}

> ### Somewhat Personal.
> --------
> Ernest McDougall, a former typo on the Review but better known as a publisher of the Oscoda Saturday Night is emulating G. Cleveland's example and will walk the floor o' nights. It's a boy.

Alcona County Review, October 15, 1891
Father: Ernest McDougall
Mother:

McDougal, William

> ### Gustin Grist.
> Gustin, Feb. 25, '96.
> Born to Mrs. Wm. McDogal, a son.

Alcona County Review, February 27, 1896
Father: William McDougal
Mother: Margaret McArthur

McGee, {Girl}

> ### ALCONA.
> Rev. and Mrs. McGee are happy. It is a daughter, born Dec. 2nd.

Alcona County Review, December 13, 1878
Father: ? McGee
Mother:

McGillis, Catherine M.

> ### GREENBUSH GETTINGS.
> --------
> Mrs. Duncan McGillis presented her husband with a daughter August 12th.

Alcona County Review, August 27, 1886
Father: Duncan McGillis
Mother: Sarah Jeneau?

McGillis, Mary

> ### Springport and Vicinity.
> --------
> Congratulations are due Wm. and Mrs. McGillis upon the arrival of an eleven and a half pound daughter July 16.

Alcona County Review, July 26, 1894
Father: William McGillis
Mother: Jane McDonald

McGregor, {Child}

> ### CALEDONIA.
> --------
> Mr. and Mrs. Gregor McGregor mourn the loss of their four days old baby.

Alcona County Review, May 14, 1896
Father: Gregor McGregor
Mother: Mary Martin

McGregor, John C.

> ### CALEDONIA.
> --------
> A young son has arrived to brighten the home of Mr. and Mrs. Gregor McGregor.

Alcona County Review, October 28, 1897
Father: Gregor McGregor
Mother: Mary Martin

McGuire, Ellen

> ### PERSONAL.
> --------
> Born, to John McGuire, of Alcona, a daughter.

Alcona County Review, June 26, 1885
Father: John McGuire
Mother: Isabel

McIntosh, {Girl}

> ### LOCAL JOTTINGS.
> --------
> John McIntosh received a telegram from his brother Jesse this morning, which contained the following delightful words: "Your niece sends her compliments!"--John is now extremely happy.

Alcona County Review, October 24, 1884
Father: Jesse McIntosh
Mother:

McIntyre, Arthur

> ### EVENTS OF ONE WEEK.
> --------
> Congratulations to Mr. and Mrs. John McIntyre on that 10-lb. boy born Tuesday morning.

Alcona County Review, April 19, 1894
Father: John H. McIntyre
Mother: Robena Nevins

McKinnon, {Boy}

> ### CALEDONIA.
> A young son has arrived to brighten the home of Mr. and Mrs. John McKinnon.

Alcona County Review, January 19, 1899
Father: John McKinnon
Mother: Catherine McLeod

McKinnon, Mary

> ### KILLMASTER.
> Born to Mr. and Mrs. McKinnon, on Monday morning, a 12 lb. girl.

Alcona County Review, September 29, 1898
Father: John D. McKinnon
Mother: Annie Dewar

McLachlan, {Boy}

> ### PERSONAL MENTION.
> --------
> Mr. and Mrs. J. A. McLachlan were presented with a fine pair of boys Tuesday evening. All doing well.

Alcona County Review, February 23, 1893
Father: John A. McLachlan
Mother: Mary A. McDonald

McLachlan, {Boy}

> ### PERSONAL MENTION.
> --------
> Mr. and Mrs. J. A. McLachlan were presented with a fine pair of boys Tuesday evening. All doing well.

Alcona County Review, February 23, 1893
Father: John A. McLachlan
Mother: Mary A. McDonald

McLain, {Boy}

> From the Skamokawa (Wash.) Eagle.
> Elias Cornell has a letter from Mr. Dan McLain dated April 23d. One paragraph will be interesting to that gentleman's Skamokawa friends, it reads as follows. "Well, Elias, I have something new to offer for the good of the order. It is a bouncing baby boy. He came on the 19th (April). Mother and baby doing fine." Dan also thinks the boy is a gold bug, judging from the color of his hair, which is red.

Alcona County Review, May 20, 1897
Father: Dan McLain
Mother:

McLaughlin, {Boy}

> ### PRITCHARD'S CAMP.
> There are children enough here to start a school; Wm. Johnson has three girls, Mike Quigly four boys, and Mr. McLaughlin had an addition to his family lately in the shape of a bouncing baby boy.

Alcona County Review, May 17, 1889
Father: ? McLaughlin
Mother:

McLelland, Alexander

> ### Haynes Happenings.
> --------
> Haynes, Feb. 5.--Dougall McLellan is the happy father of a big baby boy born on the 1st of February.

Alcona County Review, February 7, 1895
Father: Dougal McLelland
Mother: Mary Ellen Forbes

McLelland, {Girl}

> ### COUNTY REVIEWINGS.
> --------
> Jas. McClelland, the shoe maker, is the happy father of a bouncing baby girl.

Alcona County Review, July 23, 1880
Father: James McLelland
Mother: Sarah Hobbs

McLelland, Lizzie May

PERSONAL MENTION.

Aleck McNeil and Dougald McLelland, both of Haynes, are each happy as a clam in high tide over the birth of daughters on Saturday last.

Alcona County Review, May 11, 1893
Father: Dougal McClelland
Mother: Mary Ellen Forbes

McLeod, Lyman D.
HOME REVIEWINGS.

Born, Thursday morning, to Mr. and Mrs. John McLeod, a son.

Alcona County Review, August 5, 1881
Father: John McLeod
Mother: Catherine Graham

McLeod, Velma
Local News.
Born to Mr. and Mrs. Robt. McLeod of Greenbush—a daughter.

Alcona County Review, September 14, 1899
Father: Robert McLeod
Mother: Jane

McMaster, Catherine H.
Gustin Grist.
Duncan's face has a pleasant curl: this time it is a nine-pound girl.

Alcona County Review, March 7, 1895
Father: Duncan McMaster
Mother: Sarah Watson

McNally, Alice
LOCAL LACONICS.

S. J. McNally rejoices over a ten-pound daughter, who arrived at his residence on Wednesday last.

Alcona County Review, May 1, 1885
Father: Simon J. McNally
Mother: Margaret

McNally, George
LOCAL JOTTINGS

Geo. W. McNally and wife welcomed a little stranger to their home last Sunday—a boy.

Alcona County Review, July 20, 1888
Father: George Wesley McNally
Mother: Mary Sapphira Goodel

McNally, {Girl}
PURELY PERSONAL.

Mr. and Mrs. S. J. McNally mourn the death of an infant daughter, born Monday, Oct. 1st.

Alcona County Review, October 5, 1888
Father: Simon J. McNally
Mother: Margaret

McNally, Maurine
Local Sayings and Doings.

A bright-eyed little daughter has come to greet the home of Mr. and Mrs. S. J. McNally, of Alcona.

Alcona County Review, March 24, 1882
Father: Simon J. McNally
Mother: Margaret

McNeal, Maggie
West Harrisville, March 7.--If a true report there is a young daughter at John McNeals.

Alcona County Review, March 7, 1895
Father: John McNeal
Mother: Flora McLellan

McNeil, Annie Laura
Haynes Happenings.
March 18, '96.
Born to Mr. and Mrs. Donald McNeil, Jr., a daughter on the 10th.

Alcona County Review, March 19, 1896
Father: Donald McNeil
Mother: Ella Mae Milligan

McNeil, Blanche
Haynes Happenings.
Since my last communication our population has been increased by four young ladies, who are in favor of protection: One at the home of A. McNeil, one at Alex Yuill's, one at Ellison Milligan's, and one came to the home of Geo. S. Ritchie Sunday morning. They are all reported to be able to take their rations regularly from the commissary department.

Alcona County Review, November 19, 1896
Father: Alexander McNeil
Mother: Rebecca Johnson

McNeil, Gracie
PERSONAL MENTION.

Aleck McNeil and Dougald McLelland, both of Haynes, are each happy as a clam in high tide over the birth of daughters on Saturday last.

Alcona County Review, May 11, 1893
Father: Alexander McNeil
Mother: Rebecca Johnson

McNeil, Mae
HAYNES HAPPENINGS.
Born to Mr. and Mrs. Alex McNeil on the 19th, a son [daughter].

Alcona County Review, March 23, 1899
Father: Alexander McNeil
Mother: Rebecca Johnson

McNeil, Margery
ALCONA ATOMS.

Mrs. McNeil presented John with a brand new daughter lately. Mrs. Thorner presented her husband with a daughter on the "17th of Ireland," and it is reported that Addison

Silverthorn, of the life-saving crew, was recently made happy in a similar manner.

Alcona County Review, March 26, 1886
Father: John McNeil
Mother: Flora McLellan

McNeil, Olive Rebecca
HAYNES.
Haynes, Aug. 17, 1891.--Mrs. McNeil presented Alex with a daughter on Thursday last.

Alcona County Review, August 20, 1891
Father: Alexander McNeil
Mother: Rebecca Johnson

McNeil, Roy A.
Haynes Happenings.

Alex McNeil is the happy father of a bouncing baby boy since Dec. 2d.

Alcona County Review, December 13, 1894
Father: Alexander McNeil
Mother: Rebecca Johnson

McNeil, Wallace Lloyd
HAYNES HAPPENINGS.
A 9-lb. baby boy came last week to rejoice the hearts of Mr. and Mrs. Dan McNeil.

Alcona County Review, March 17, 1898
Father: Donald McNeil
Mother: Ella Mae Milligan

McPherson, Jean E.
PERSONAL POINTS.
Born to Mr. and Mrs. Wm. McPherson (Kittie Kimbal) at Grand Marais, a daughter.

Alcona County Review, April 7, 1898
Father: William Fraser McPherson
Mother: Kittie Maude Kimball

McRae, {Child}
Mrs. Duncan McRae, Jr.
It is our sad duty today to record the untimely death of Mrs. Duncan McRae, Jr., formerly Edith Miller, which occurred at 5 o'clock last night, at her late home in Greenbush from childbirth. The child survived the mother's death but a short time. The funeral services will probably beheld Saturday from the Harrisville M. E. church.

Alcona County Review, April 30, 1896
Father: Duncan McRae
Mother: Edith Madeline Miller

McRae, {Girl}
LOCAL JOTTINGS.

The population of Greenbush was increased, one day last week, by the advent of a bouncing 12-pound girl in the family of Duncan McRae.

Alcona County Review, February 25, 1887
Father: Duncan McRae

Mother: Isabella McGucken

McTamany, {Boy}

LOCAL JOTTINGS.

A son was born to Geo. McTamany, of Greenbush, Nov. 1st.

Alcona County Review, November 5, 1886
Father: George McTamany
Mother: Catherine

McVeigh, {Boy}

HAYNES HAPPENINGS.
August 2, 1898.
Bruce McVeigh is the daddy of a boy born July 28th.

Alcona County Review, August 4, 1898
Father: Bruce McVeigh
Mother: Ida Ritchie

Medor, Consuella

Local News.
Mr. Editor: Born to Mr. and Mrs. Peter Medor Feb. 20, a bouncing baby girl. Peter says he intends to have the worth of the high school tax he has been paying. Everybody doing well.

Peter Medor.

Alcona County Review, February 23, 1899
Father: Peter Medor
Mother: Josephine Tibeau

Medor, Frances

PERSONAL.

Peter Medor is the happiest man in town—a big baby girl put in its appearance at his house yesterday. All well.

Alcona County Review, April 22, 1897
Father: Peter Medor
Mother: Josephine Tibeau

Medor, Isadore

PERSONAL MENTION.
Peter Medor and wife are highly elated over the advent of another young blacksmith into the family circle on Thursday, Jan. 30th, ult.

Alcona County Review, February 6, 1896
Father: Peter Medor
Mother: Josephine Tibeau

Medor, Melvina

PERSONAL MENTION.

Peter Medor and wife added one to Harrisville's population bright and early on the morning of July 5th. A bouncing boy. All doing well, including the happy father.

Alcona County Review, July 12, 1894

EVENTS OF ONE WEEK.

The paragraph in our last issue, about a new son and heir born to

Peter Medor, was all right excepting that the boy is a girl. "He fine girl," says Mr. Medor.

Alcona County Review, July 19, 1894
Father: Peter Medor
Mother: Josephine Tibeau

Medor, Peter

LOCAL JOTTINGS.

A little stranger came to the house of Peter Medor Sunday night. The little fellow will be well taken care of until he gets old enough to pump the bellows in the blacksmith shop. After that he will probably begin to hoe his own row.

Alcona County Review, January 25, 1889
Father: Peter Medor
Mother: Josephine Tibeau

Medor, Selina C.

The Local News

A 14-lb. baby girl has made things very interesting since last Thursday, in the household of P. Medor, our worthy blacksmith.

Alcona County Review, May 26, 1892
Father: Peter Medor
Mother: Josephine Tibeau

Merritt, William T.

CURTISVILLE.
Too late for last week.
Born to Mr. and Mrs. J. Merritt a son.

Alcona County Review, November 23, 1899
Father: John V. Merritt
Mother: Sarah

Michelson, Sidney

LOCAL PICK UPS.

Born to Mr. and Mrs. J. Michelson, Wednesday, April 6, a son.

Alcona County Review, April 7, 1898
Father: James Michelson
Mother: Jennie Sandorf

Micho, Earle E.

WEST HARRISVILLE.

Born, to Mrs. Florence Micho, a big bouncing boy.

Alcona County Review, March 26, 1891
Father: Florence George Edgar Micho
Mother: Frances

Micho, Eva F.

LOCAL JOTTINGS.

Tally one each for Dave Micho and Gill Landon. Both girls.

Alcona County Review, April 5, 1889
Father: Florence George Edgar Micho
Mother: Frances

Micho, Philip Calvin

West Harrisville.
October 23, 1895.
D. Micho is wearing a broad smile. Cause—a big baby boy.

Alcona County Review, October 24, 1895
Father: David Micho
Mother: Mary Rivard

Middleton, Effie

CURTIS ITEMS.
Sept. 23, 1895.
Born to Mrs. Robert Middleton, a daughter.

Alcona County Review, September 26, 1895
Father: Robert Middleton
Mother: Viola Rice

Miller, {Child}

ALCONA ATOMS
Mrs. Thomas Miller gave birth to a still-born babe on the 18th. Dr. McCormick requested the assistance of Dr. Mitchell, as it was a very serious case, but their assistance was secured too late, and Mrs. Miller died on Monday evening.

Alcona County Review, January 28, 1887
Father: Thomas Miller
Mother: Margaret Graham

Miller, Frances Lillian

PURELY PERSONAL.

Mrs. Wm. Miller, Alcona, presented her husband with a charming little daughter, Wednesday.

Alcona County Review, May 18, 1888
Father: William Miller
Mother: Margaret Quinlan

Miller, Grace

HAYNES.
Charlie Miller has tallied the advent of a daughter on the head of the bed and is as happy as a big sunflower. It arrived on the 11th.

Alcona County Review, August 19, 1897
Father: Charles J. Miller
Mother: Cora Wilson

Miller, Harry H.

The Local News

Born to Mrs. Kane Miller, a son, Oct. 23, inst.

Alcona County Review, October 27, 1892
Father: Kane Miller
Mother: Minnie B. Hall

Miller, Henrietta

Haynes Happenings.
August 20, 1895.
John Miller is happy over the birth of a daughter born this morning. It weighs 11 ½ pounds.

Alcona County Review, August 22, 1895
Father: John F. Miller
Mother: Lydia A. Hudson

Miller, Henry Michael

Haynes.

Wm. Miller is happy: He is the father of another big boy.

Alcona County Review, April 20, 1893
Father: William Miller
Mother: Margaret Quinlan

Miller, Irena

HAYNES HAPPENINGS.

Haynes, May 14th.—Joseph Miller is a daddy. It is a girl.

Alcona County Review, May 18, 1888
Father: Joseph Miller
Mother: Martha Hastings

Miller, Joseph R.

Haynes Happenings.
Feb. 1, 1897.
Joseph Miller is as happy as a clam at high tide over the advent of an eleven pound boy which came Jan. 27.

Alcona County Review, February 4, 1897
Father: Joseph Miller
Mother: Martha Hastings

Miller, Josephine Q.

SLEEPY HOLLOW.
Oct. 10th, 1899.
Born to Mr. and Mrs. Wm. Miller, a daughter last week.

Alcona County Review, October 19, 1899
Father: William Miller
Mother: Margaret Quinlan

Miller, Myrtle M.

SOMEWHAT PERSONAL.

Our Haynes correspondent writes that a female addition to the family of Thos. Miller was announced Sunday evening last. All parties concerned are doing well.

Alcona County Review, June 30, 1892
Father: Thomas Miller
Mother: Rebecca Thorner

Miller, Russell Kane

PERSONAL MENTION.

Born, to Mr. and Mrs. Kane Miller, Monday, Sept. 9th, a son.

Alcona County Review, September 12, 1895
Father: Kane Miller
Mother: Minnie B. Hall

Miller, Vean Wellington

Haynes Happenings.

May 14, 1895.

Wm. Miller is as happy as a clam at high tide: it's a boy since Friday.

Alcona County Review, May 16, 1895
Father: William Miller
Mother: Margaret Quinlan

Miller, Wilson James

West Harrisville.
West Harrisville, Jan. 1896.--Chas. Miller is the father of a young son. Charley says he has the finest boy along the shore.

Alcona County Review, January 23, 1896
Father: Charles J. Miller
Mother: Cora Wilson

Milligan, Cora Belle

Haynes Happenings.
Since my last communication our population has been increased by four young ladies, who are in favor of protection: One at the home of A. McNeil, one at Alex Yuill's, one at Ellison Milligan's, and one came to the home of Geo. S. Ritchie Sunday morning. They are all reported to be able to take their rations regularly from the commissary department.

Alcona County Review, November 19, 1896
Father: Ellison Milligan
Mother: Mary London

Milligan, Jessie

Busy Times In Haynes.

Haynes, Jan. 9th, 1894. Elison Milligan is happy. He is a father for the eleventh time.

Alcona County Review, January 11, 1894
Father: Ellison Milligan
Mother: Mary London

Milligan, Leslie

Haynes Happenings.

Mrs. W. S. Milligan presented Will with a daughter as a Christmas present.

Alcona County Review, December 31, 1896
Father: William S. Milligan
Mother: Elizabeth J. London

Milligan, Margaret

Haynes.
Mrs. Milligan presented Ellison with a daughter last week. It is regulation weight.

Alcona County Review, November 12, 1891
Father: Ellison Milligan
Mother: Mary London

Milligan, Myrtle M.

HAYNES HAPPENINGS.

Mrs. Milligan presented William with a bouncing baby girl last week.

Alcona County Review, February 12, 1891
Father: William S. Milligan

Mother: Elizabeth J. London

Milligan, Ray

Haynes.
Haynes, Dec. 13, 1892.--Wm. Milligan is the father of a daughter. Mother and child reported as doing well.

Alcona County Review, December 15, 1892

Haynes, Dec. 20.
Mr. Editor, In my communication of the 13th I got the babies of Mrs. Milligan and Mrs. Slater vice-versa.

Alcona County Review, December 22, 1892
Father: William S. Milligan
Mother: Elizabeth J. London

Milligan, Sidney

HAYNES.
Mrs. Milligan presented Elison with a fine baby boy last week by the old reliable process.

Alcona County Review, September 6, 1889
Father: Ellison Milligan
Mother: Mary London

Mitchell, {Girl}

PERSONAL MENTION.

Born to Mrs. D. W. Mitchell, Tuesday, Nov. 5, a daughter.

Alcona County Review, November 7, 1895
Father: David William Mitchell
Mother: Carrie L. Colwell

Mitchell, Helen

PERSONAL MENTION.

Born to Mrs. D. W. Mitchell, Monday, June 5, a daughter.

Alcona County Review, June 8, 1893
Father: David William Mitchell
Mother: Carrie L. Colwell

Mitchell, Louise

The Local News.

Born, to Mrs. D. W. Mitchell, a daughter, Wednesday, April 22.

Alcona County Review, April 23, 1891
Father: David William Mitchell
Mother: Carrie L. Colwell

Monroe, {Boy}

Local Sayings and Doings.

Geo. Monroe is happy. Its another fine boy.

Alcona County Review, April 14, 1882
Father: George N. Monroe
Mother: Mary F. Van Buskirk

Monroe, Herbert A.

GREENBUSH GETTINGS.

We now have more foremen than mills in Greenbush. On June 24th the dark countenance of D. A.

Monroe was unusually brightly illuminated, and when questioned as to the cause he promptly replied, "I have another son—weighs 9 lbs."

Alcona County Review, July 9, 1886
Father: David A. Monroe
Mother: Mary C. Spencer

Monroe, Wilbur V.

Mr. and Mrs. George Munroe, of South Harrisville, are made happy once again. It's a nice boy-baby this time.

Alcona County Review, April 2, 1880
Father: George N. Monroe
Mother: Mary F. Van Buskirk

Moore, {Boy}

LOCAL JOTTINGS.

March 26th to Mrs. Jas. Moore, a boy.

Alcona County Review, April 1, 1887
Father: James Moore
Mother: Deborah?

Moore, Fanny

PURELY PERSONAL.

It's H. P. Moore's turn to buy the cigars and look pleasant. A girl.

Alcona County Review, September 30, 1887
Father: Henry P. Moore
Mother: Susan S.

Morrill, {Girl}

KILLMASTER.

Mrs. Levi Morrill is the happy possessor of a young daughter.

Alcona County Review, August 25, 1898
Father: Levi Morrill
Mother: Alice Electra Huntoon

Morrill, Mildred

KILLMASTER.

Mr. and Mrs. Jesse Morrill are proud of a new daughter, born Sunday morning.

Alcona County Review, September 22, 1898
Father: Jesse A. Morrill
Mother: Ellen M. Hulbert

Morris, Alice

LOCAL JOTTINGS

A brand new daughter arrived in the home of John Morris, Tuesday.

Alcona County Review, February 24, 1888
Father: John Morris
Mother: Isabella Lang

Morris, Charles G.

COUNTY REVIEWINGS.

Mr. James Morris was presented with an 11-lb. boy yesterday morning.

Alcona County Review, June 11, 1880
Father: James W. Morris
Mother: Mary A. Thompson

Morris, Ernest H.

LOCAL JOTTINGS.

Born—to Mr. and Mrs. James W. Morris a boy; weight, ten pounds.

Alcona County Review, September 5, 1884
Father: James W. Morris
Mother: Mary A. Thompson

Morris, Susan E.

HOME NEWS JOTTINGS.

Last Sunday being the birthday anniversary of James W. Morris, to make him extremely happy, his wife presented him with a daughter weighing nine pounds. It isn't every married man that can afford such a birthday present. Not much.

Alcona County Review, September 1, 1882
Father: James W. Morris
Mother: Mary A. Thompson

Morris, Warren

PURELY PERSONAL.

Born—to Mrs. Jas. Morris, Thursday morning, a son.

Alcona County Review, June 1, 1888
Father: James W. Morris
Mother: Mary A. Thompson

Morrison, Emma Blanch

TOWN LINE.

December 14, '96.
Born to Mr. and Mrs. James Morrison, a girl.

Alcona County Review, December 17, 1896
Father: James Morrison
Mother: Mary Ellen

Morton, {Boy}

Haynes, Dec. 20.
Lyman Morton is the happy father of a young son, born on the 15th.

Alcona County Review, December 22, 1892
Father: Lyman Morton
Mother: Sarah Clark

Mudgett, {Boy}

ADDITIONAL LOCAL.

We have wondered why D. B. Mudgett has been "dressed up" so much of late. The mystery is now solved. It's a brand new boy-baby.

Alcona County Review, April 28, 1882
Father: David B. Mudgett
Mother: Olive Burt

Mudgett, Edith May

HOME REVIEWINGS.

Mr. and Mrs. D. B. Mudgett are happy again. A new daughter.

Alcona County Review, April 22, 1881
Father: David B. Mudgett
Mother: Olive Burt

Mudgett, Florence

The Review of last week failed to chronicle the advent of a brand new daughter at the home of D. B. Mudgett, and one also at the home of Joseph Fisher, Jr.

Alcona County Review, May 9, 1884
Father: David B. Mudgett
Mother: Olive Burt

Mulholland,{Boy}

Our Neighbors.

Mrs. D. Mulholland of Haynes presented David with a son and heir on the 12th inst.

Alcona County Review, December 20, 1889
Father: David Mulholland
Mother: Eliza McNeil

Mulholland, John H.

ALCONA ATOMS.

Dr. McCormick and Mrs. Mulholland had a hunt through the straw on the 27th, and found an eight pound boy. They insisted that old Dave was the father. The doctor knows his business and don't you forget it. He was as cool as a cucumber and gave good satisfaction. The mother is doing well.

Alcona County Review, March 5, 1886
Father: David Mulholland
Mother: Eliza McNeil

Neil, Glenmore

PERSONAL.

Born to Mr. and Mrs. Archie Neil, Friday Oct. 22, a son.

Alcona County Review, October 28, 1897
Father: Archibald Neil
Mother: Cordelia Ann Loomis

Neil, Guy Ellison

PERSONAL MENTION.

Born, to Mr. and Mrs. Archie Neil, a son, weight 11 lbs.

Alcona County Review, September 19, 1895
Father: Archibald Neil
Mother: Cordelia Ann Loomis

Neil, Percy

LOCAL PICK UPS.

Dr. Mitchell reports the birth of a son to Mr. and Mrs. Nich Neil, on Saturday, 10th inst.

Alcona County Review, September 15, 1898
Father: Nicholas Neil
Mother: Keziah McLaurin

Neil, Sarah?

Nicholas Neal's young wife surprised her husband wonderfully yesterday morning when she presented him with a pair of twins, boy and girl.

Alcona County Review, May 2, 1884
Father: Nicholas Neil
Mother: Alice Irene Fick

Neil, Wallace Leonard

Nicholas Neal's young wife surprised her husband wonderfully yesterday morning when she presented him with a pair of twins, boy and girl.

Alcona County Review, May 2, 1884
Father: Nicholas Neil
Mother: Alice Irene Fick

Nestle, Grace

LOCAL JOTTINGS.

Wm. Nestle and wife rejoice over the recent addition to their household of a fine baby.

Alcona County Review, June 3, 1887
Father: William Nestle
Mother: Ida E. Tower

Nevin, Spray

The bright smile that has illuminated the countenance of David Nevin, Jr., of late is explained: A 10 lb. girl recently arrived upon the scene at his house and will dwell there indefinitely.

Alcona County Review, December 7, 1893
Father: David Alexander Nevin, Jr.
Mother: Lillie Margaret Gilpin

Newcomb, {Girl}

HOME REVIEWINGS.

J. B. Newcomb is the happy father of a 8 ¼ pound daughter, born Wednesday morning. She will go by the name of the "Miller's Daughter," we presume.

Alcona County Review, July 29, 1881
Father: James W. Newcomb
Mother: Maria

Newcomb, {Girl}

COUNTY REVIEWINGS.

Another bran new baby came to town Tuesday. J. W. Newcomb is the happy father of an 11-pound daughter.

Alcona County Review, September 10, 1880
Father: James W. Newcomb
Mother: Maria

Newell, John

PURELY PERSONAL.
Henry Newell rejoices over an increase in his family since Monday. It is a girl [boy] and weighs 10 lbs., or thereabouts.

Alcona County Review, September 23, 1887
Father: Henry Newell

Mother: Hattie

Nolan, James

KILLMASTER ECHOES.
Killmaster, Aug. 8.—A new boy made his appearance at the home of James Noland, last week.

Alcona County Review, August 10, 1888
Father: James Nolan
Mother:

Noyes, Caroline

COUNTY NEWS JOTTINGS.
Dan N. thinks it's all right to have a *little noise* in the family occasionally. This time it's a girl and weighs—well—confound it all, there's too much *wait* for Harrisville young uns, anyhow.

Alcona County Review, October 19, 1877
Father: Daniel H. Noyes
Mother: Sarah McLeod

Noyes, {Girl}

COUNTY REVIEWINGS.

W. F. Carle and A. Noyes have each been made the happy father of a girl baby this week.

Alcona County Review, September 17, 1880
Father: Abram Noyes
Mother: Clara Henning

O'Dell, Deborah

Reviewings.

To Mrs. Thomas O'Dell--a new daughter.

Alcona County Review, March 26, 1880
Father: Thomas H. O'Dell
Mother: Nancy M. Emerson

O'Dell, Miles

COUNTY NEWS JOTTINGS.
Thomas O'Dell is happy. It's a fine boy. We didn't get the weight.

Alcona County Review, August 24, 1877
Father: Thomas H. O'Dell
Mother: Nancy M. Emerson

O'Hearn, {Girl}

West Harrisville.

West Harrisville, Aug. 31.--Jas. O'Hearn rejoices over the fact that he is father to a bran new girl of 10 ½ pounds avoirdupois. Parentage began last Sunday.

Alcona County Review, August 30, 1894
Father: James O'Hearn
Mother:

Oliver, Eugene

CALEDONIA.
A young son arrived at the home of Mr. and Mrs. Oliver last Thursday morning.

Alcona County Review, November 3, 1898

Father: Eugene Oliver
Mother: Jennie Johnson

Oliver, Lawrence E.

Born to Mr. and Mrs. Harvey Oliver (Matie Taft) at Hoquiam, Wash., Saturday, June 24, a son. "All doing nicely," writes Mrs. Oliver.

Alcona County Review, July 6, 1899
Father: Harvey L. Oliver
Mother: Matie E. Taft

O'Neal, {Boy}

Aug. 27, a nine pound boy was presented to Mr. and Mrs. Jos. O'Neal of Tonawanda, New York. Quite a surprise, as their youngest child is 13 years of age.

Alcona County Review, September 12, 1895
Father: Joseph O'Neal
Mother: Anna Flora

Otto, Clara M.

HAYNES HAPPENINGS.
Fritz Otto is the father of a bouncing baby girl.

Alcona County Review, January 26, 1899
Father: Isadore Frederick Otto
Mother: Sarah Letitia Sanderson

Palmer, Claude

PERSONAL POINTS.

Word comes that a son was born to Mrs. Linna Reed Palmer at Cheyenne, Wyoming, the 11th inst., and mother and child were well.

Alcona County Review, July 21, 1898
Father: Walter S. Palmer
Mother: Linna Reed

Parks, {Girl}

West Harrisville, Nov. 19, '91. Mrs. Jos. Parks presented her husband with a girl last week.

Alcona County Review, November 19, 1891
Father: Joseph Parks
Mother: Mary Mudgett

Partridge, Ina

Somewhat Personal.

We learn that Phillip O. Partridge and wife, of Mikado, are ministering to the wants and comfort of a daughter, born Feb. 21.

Alcona County Review, March 3, 1892
Father: Phillip O. Partridge
Mother: Mary F. Lee

Partridge, Pearl

Mikado Murmurs.

Mikado, June 18.--Born to Mr. and Mrs. P. O. Partridge, a 10-pound girl.

Alcona County Review, June 21, 1894
Father: Phillip O. Partridge
Mother: Mary F. Lee

Patterson, {Boy}

LOCAL JOTTINGS.

A little son arrived at Ralph Patterson's, Sept. 17.

Alcona County Review, September 24, 1886
Father: Ralph Patterson
Mother: Melvina Griswold

Peacock, {Girl}

HOME NEWS JOTTINGS.

C. H. Peacock reports a bouncing baby girl as a recent addition to his happy home.

Alcona County Review, January 26, 1883
Father: C. H. Peacock
Mother:

Pearson, Armand

PURELY PERSONAL.

Mr. and Mrs. Jno. J. Pearson, Sturgeon Pointe, rejoice over the advent of a son and heir to their household.

Alcona County Review, May 25, 1888
Father: John J. Pearson
Mother: Luella V. Edgar

Pearson, Mabelle L.

Purely Personal.

Mrs. Jno. Pearson presented her husband with a daughter last week, their second born.

Alcona County Review, January 24, 1890
Father: John J. Pearson
Mother: Luella Edgar

Pelkie, {Boy}

Curtis.

Jack Pelkie and wife were blest by a fine son a week ago, but sad news came to the father the other day that the child was dead. He was working for J. W. Ferguson and being near Bryant he telephoned for a coffin, which came that night. On his return home he found the child living and it is living yet. This is quite a miracle.

Alcona County Review, March 30, 1893
Father: Jack Pelkie
Mother:

Peterson, {Boy}

PERSONAL MENTION.

The arrival on Friday night, March 15th inst., of a son and heir at the residence of Jack Peterson of Lakeside, has wreathed that gentleman's face in a 7x9 smile, for he just wanted another boy.

Alcona County Review, March 21, 1895
Father: Jack Peterson
Mother:

Philp, {Boy}

COUNTY REVIEWINGS.

The telegraph wires in this section ought to be kept in pretty good order now. Another line repairer has been placed on this route. He is boarding at the residence of Wm. Philp, and weighs just 11 pounds.

Alcona County Review, October 29, 1880
Father: William J. Philp
Mother: Susan McGillis

Pierson, {Girl}

The Tawases.

Born--to Mr. and Mrs. Daniel Pierson, of this village on the 25th ult., twins--boy and girl.

Alcona County Review, March 10, 1885
Father: Daniel Pierson
Mother: Sarah

Pierson, Wayne

LOCAL JOTTINGS.

Born, to Mrs. R. P. Pierson, a son.

Alcona County Review, May 27, 1887
Father: Robert F. Pierson
Mother: Alta Sheldon

Pierson, William

The Tawases.

Born--to Mr. and Mrs. Daniel Pierson, of this village on the 25th ult., twins--boy and girl.

Alcona County Review, March 10, 1885
Father: Daniel Pierson
Mother: Sarah

Pizer, Mildred

Somewhat Personal.

Born to Mr. and Mrs. Jacob Pizer, Tuesday, April 26, a daughter.

Alcona County Review, April 28, 1892
Father: Jacob Pizer
Mother:

Porter, Alma

LOCAL JOTTINGS.

Wells Porter is too happy for anything. It's a fine little daughter. Mother and child doing well.

Alcona County Review, June 27, 1884
Father: Wells Porter
Mother: Emanette A. Emerson

Potts, Gladys

West Harrisville.

E. Potts is wearing a broad smile over the arrival of a baby daughter.

Alcona County Review, September 9, 1897
Father: Emerson Potts
Mother: Anna Seaton

Potts, Grace I.

West Harrisville.

West Harrisville, April 3.--Mr. E. Potts is happy—another girl.

Alcona County Review, April 4, 1895
Father: Emerson Potts
Mother: Anna Seaton

Pratt, Harriet A.

LOCAL JOTTINGS.

As we met him on several occasions the fore part of the week, we noticed that our young friend George Pratt wore a rather peculiar smile of joy and satisfaction upon his face, but never for once did we "catch on" to the secret till Wednesday forenoon. He is the happy father of a bright seven-pound daughter.

Alcona County Review, December 5, 1884
Father: George B. Pratt
Mother: Hannah McClatchey

Pritchard, Jennie

LOCAL JOTTINGS.

Mr. Pritchard, of Black River, is made happy by the presence of a baby daughter in his home.

Alcona County Review, February 13, 1885
Father: James Robert Pritchard
Mother: Bridget B. Hood

Proctor, {Boy}

Black River Speaks.

Born to Mrs. W. Proctor, a boy.

Alcona County Review, August 27, 1896
Father: William F. Proctor
Mother: Elizabeth Hall

Putman, Mary

ALCONA BREEZES.

Mr. and Mrs. Putman are rejoicing over the arrival of a baby girl.

Alcona County Review, April 21, 1898
Father: Charles E. Putman
Mother: Celestine LaLonde

Pyne, Horatio Albert

PERSONAL MENTION.

Born, to Mr. and Mrs. Geo. Pyne, a son, Aug. 30.

Alcona County Review, September 5, 1895
Father: George Pyne
Mother: Margaret McIntyre

Pyne, Victoria B.

Haynes Happenings.

March 22, '97.

Born—To Mr. and Mrs. W. J. Hastings, a son on the 16th. To Mr. and Mrs. Wm. Pyne, a son on Monday the 15th.

Alcona County Review, March 25, 1897

Haynes Happenings.

Mrs. Wm. Pyne's baby turned out to be a girl.

Alcona County Review, April 1, 1897
Father: William C. Pyne
Mother: Harriet Laviolette

Quigley, Francis Patrick

Born, to Mr. and Mrs. M. Quigley, Tuesday of last week, a boy.

Alcona County Review, May 24, 1894

From a special correspondent:
Michael Quigly is sporting a pleasant face at present. Cause, a 12 lb. boy.

Alcona County Review, May 24, 1894
Father: Michael Quigley
Mother: Margaret Morrison

Ranney, {Girl}

BLACK RIVER IN PRINT

Born to Mr. and Mrs. C. Raney, a daughter; to Mr. and Mrs. Jno. McArthur, a son.

Alcona County Review, January 16, 1896
Father: C. Ranney
Mother:

Ranney, {Girl}

PERSONAL MENTION.

Supr. A. W. Ranney of Black River was called home from his duties on the Board, Tuesday, to rejoice over an important family event--A bouncing baby girl.

Alcona County Review, June 25, 1896
Father: Arthur W. Ranney
Mother: Lucy C. Cross

Reynolds, {Boy}

PERSONAL MENTION.

A son was born to Mr. and Mrs. Fred Reynolds Monday morning, but the little innocent's life was destined to be short and it passed away in the evening to the great sorrow of the young parents.

Alcona County Review, April 30, 1896
Father: Frederick C. Reynolds
Mother: Laura A. Sisson

Reynolds, {Girl}

Of Local Interest.

Mr. and Mrs. Fred Reynolds of Cleveland are the parents of a baby girl since Nov. 27.

Alcona County Review, December 7, 1899
Father: Frederick C. Reynolds
Mother: Laura A. Sisson

Reynolds, Paul F.

PERSONAL.

The birth of a lusty 10 lb. son and heir to Mr. and Mrs. Fred Reynolds, on the 7th inst., escaped mention in the last Review.

Alcona County Review, June 17, 1897
Father: Frederick C. Reynolds
Mother: Laura A. Sisson

Rice, Earl Blaine

LOCAL PICK UPS.

The Review received a friendly letter from Prof. E. R. Rice this week. Among other things he says "we have one of the finest boys if not the finest that may be found; he came Aug. 7 and everybody's well."

Alcona County Review, August 24, 1899
Father: Earl R. Rice
Mother: Josephine Mills

Rice, Frank Clarence

COUNTY JOTTINGS.

And now our illuminative fellow townsman, W. E. Rice, comes to the front with a new boy baby. This little joker kicks the beam at eight pounds, and takes his rations with commendable ability. In fact he seems to enjoy life first rate, and is the joy and pride of his father's heart. Tally three for Rice.

Alcona County Review, December 6, 1878
Father: William E. Rice
Mother: Mary

Richardson, Carl

West Harrisville.

T. Richardson is rejoicing over the arrival of a big baby boy at his house.

Alcona County Review, August 19, 1897
Father: Thomas Richardson
Mother: Adeline Jameson

Rifenbark, {Boy}

Tuscola County.

From your old friends George and Malinda Rifenbark. Our family has been obliged to call the doctor for all hands have been sick since we reached our new home. That is what never happened in our family while we lived 10 years in Alcona Co.

Archie's wife is not expected to live, though she made her husband a neat Fourth present of a big boy to remember her by should she be taken away. And Min, the old lady, was fetched home from Archie's sick--so you see I can't say much for this place as being healthy. As for crops they look good allowing for the wet weather. Our good wishes to all; good bye.

Family of Geo. and Archie Rifenbark.

Alcona County Review, July 20, 1899
Father: Archie Rifenbark
Mother: Emma Hackett

Ritchie, Bertrum W.

Haynes Tid Bits.

Mrs. William Ritchie has returned from Canada where she had been for some time past with relatives and friends and presented William with a bran new daughter [son].

Alcona County Review, April 2, 1891
Father: William Ritchie
Mother: Maria J. Lawrence

Ritchie, Edna S.

Haynes.

Births.—Mrs. Sam Johnson, a boy; Mrs. Wm. Ritchie, a girl; Mrs. John LaFrance, a girl; Mrs. Edwin Holmes, a girl.

Alcona County Review, July 27, 1893
Father: William Ritchie
Mother: Maria J. Lawrence

Ritchie, Georgie

HAYNES.

Haynes, Sept. 25—To Mr. and Mrs. George Ritchie, a daughter on Thursday, Sept. 18.

Alcona County Review, September 28, 1888
Father: George Samuel Ritchie
Mother: Anne Jane Hastings

Ritchie, Jennie P.

Haynes Happenings.

Since my last communication our population has been increased by four young ladies, who are in favor of protection: One at the home of A. McNeil, one at Alex Yuill's, one at Ellison Milligan's, and one came to the home of Geo. S. Ritchie Sunday morning. They are all reported to be able to take their rations regularly from the commissary department.

Alcona County Review, November 19, 1896
Father: George Samuel Ritchie
Mother: Anne Jane Hastings

Ritchie, Johnson

Haynes Happenings.

Geo. Ritchie received a present of another son on the 21st, and it is reported that Fred J. Card is similarly happy, sex unknown.

Alcona County Review, November 1, 1894
Father: George Samuel Ritchie
Mother: Anne Jane Hastings

Ritchie, Mae Lawrence

HAYNES HAPPENINGS.

Wm. Ritchie is the father of an eleven pound girl, born on the 19th. The mother was in a precarious condition on Saturday four doctors being in attendance. The latest report is that she is recovering.

Alcona County Review, May 31, 1889
Father: William Ritchie
Mother: Maria J. Lawrence

Ritchie, Robert G.

Haynes.

Mrs. Ritchie is also a record smasher. She presented George with a young daughter [son] lately that will knock the spots off any other baby in the county for size.

Alcona County Review, September 22, 1892
Father: George Samuel Ritchie
Mother: Anne Jane Hastings

Ritchie, Robert James

Late From Alcona.

On the 12th of March, Mrs. J. Ritchie, a boy of 12 pounds. How is that for Alcona?

Alcona County Review, March 19, 1880
Father: Joseph C. Ritchie
Mother: Ellen Lamb

Ritchie, Russell E. H.

ALCONA ATOMS.
A Shower of Babies in Alcona.

Mrs. Geo. Ritchie concluded to present George with a baby boy on the 29th day of April.

All of the above are reported standard weight.

Alcona County Review, May 6, 1887
Father: George Samuel Ritchie
Mother: Anne Jane Hastings

Roe, Inez M.

ALCONA BREEZES.

Born to Mr. and Mrs. Samuel Roe Aug. 29th, a fine baby girl.

Alcona County Review, September 15, 1898
Father: A. Samuel Roe
Mother: Marion E. Sayers

Rosenthal, {Girl}

AU SABLE AND OSCODA.

Sam Rosenthal has become the father of a nine-pound girl.

Alcona County Review, January 30, 1885
Father: Sam Rosenthal
Mother:

Ross, Leon Reeves

LOCAL JOTTINGS.

Mrs. Jno. Ross, of Mikado, presented Mr. Ross with a 9 ½ lb. boy on the 6th inst.

Alcona County Review, December 21, 1888
Father: John W. Ross
Mother: Rose Adams

Rouse, Edna B.

Greenbush Personal and Impersonal.

Born to Mr. and Mrs. Wellington Rouse, Jan. 22, a daughter.

Alcona County Review, February 10, 1898
Father: Wellington Rouse
Mother: Jessie Wallace

Rouse, Flora

GREENBUSH GETTINGS.

On Wednesday morning Feb. 3d the wife of Mr. Wellington Rouse

presented him with a daughter— both doing well.

Alcona County Review, February 5, 1886
Father: Wellington Rouse
Mother: Jessie Wallace

Ruston, Clare

CALEDONIA.
April 2, '98.

Andrew Ruston is the proud father of a bouncing baby girl.

Alcona County Review, April 7, 1898
Father: Andrew Ruston
Mother: Mary

Sampson, Lydia LeBurney

Curtis Items.
Nov. 30, 1896.

Mrs. Sampson gave a present of a young daughter to George. He is proud of the girl. It will soon call him papa.

Alcona County Review, December 3, 1896
Father: George Sampson
Mother: LaBurnia Regier

Sanborn, James Noble

PERSONAL.

W. H. Sanborn and wife of Greenbush have reason to feel proud over the birth of a 10-lb. son last Friday.

Alcona County Review, September 2, 1897
Father: Wilson Henry Sanborn
Mother: Sophronia Young

Scriver, William

ALCONA BREEZES.

Born to Mr. and Mrs. Geo. Scriver, a boy.

Alcona County Review, November 10, 1898
Father: George Scriver
Mother: Laura M. Hartman

Severance, Alice

LOCAL PICK UPS.

Born to Mr. and Mrs. L. Severance of Walled Lake, Mich., Thursday Aug. 24, a son.

Alcona County Review, August 31, 1899
Father: Lemuel Severance
Mother: Laura May LaChapelle

Shaw, {Boy}

Haynes Happenings.
October 8, 1895.

Mrs. May Shaw, nee Martin, is the mother of a son. Her husband died recently in Bay City. She is residing with her parents in Haynes.

Alcona County Review, October 10, 1895

Haynes Happenings.

In my last items I said Mrs. May Shaw nee Morton (erroneously printed Martin) is the mother of a son.

Alcona County Review, October 24, 1895

Father: ? Shaw
Mother: May Morton

Sheehan, Edith

Somewhat Personal.

A young lady of tender years is reported to have arrived yesterday at the home of Prof. W. B. Sheehan, where she will reside permanently.

Alcona County Review, March 17, 1892
Father: Walter B. Sheehan
Mother: Melissa

Sheehan, {Girl}

PERSONAL MENTION.

Born to Mr. and Mrs. W. B. Sheehan, Friday, Oct. 12, a daughter.

Alcona County Review, October 18, 1894
Father: Walter B. Sheehan
Mother: Melissa

Showers, Irene

PERSONAL.

Mr. and Mrs. Spencer Showers of Alpena, well known here where they once lived, are the parents of a very young daughter. This child comes as the first after a married life of 14 years and reports come that "Spen" is still celebrating. Mother and daughter are doing well.

Alcona County Review, February 18, 1897
Father: Spencer Showers
Mother: Eliza

Shwitzer, Leonard

LOCAL JOTTINGS.

Harry Shwitzer is the happy parent of a brand new son.

Alcona County Review, April 3, 1885
Father: Harry Shwitzer
Mother: Sarah Rosenthal

Shwitzer, Samuel

Local Sayings and Doings.

Harry Shwitzer was made exceedingly happy last Saturday morning. It's a fine boy. Congratulations are in order.

Alcona County Review, March 24, 1882
Father: Harry Shwitzer
Mother: Sarah Rosenthal

Sicord, Roland

GLENNIE.

Mrs. P. Sicord presented to her husband a fine baby boy for a Christmas present. Mother and child are both doing well.

Alcona County Review, January 5, 1899
Father: Procule Sicord
Mother: Agnes B. Chevrier

Silversides, {Boy}

The Local News.

Born, to Mrs. Wm. Silversides, a boy, Sunday, April 5.

Alcona County Review, April 9, 1891
Father: George William Silversides
Mother: Clara [Henning] Noyes

Silversides, Clara
LOCAL JOTTINGS.

Born, to Mrs. Wm. Silversides, Thursday, Sept. 12, a daughter.

Alcona County Review, September 20, 1889
Father: George William Silversides
Mother: Clara [Henning] Noyes

Silverthorn, Ernest Clifford
Dr. Ludlum reports the arrival of a new son at A. Silverthorn's home.

Alcona County Review, February 28, 1895
Father: Addison I. Silverthorn
Mother: Grace A. Aird

Silverthorn, Howard Charles
SOMEWHAT PERSONAL.

A. Silverthorn celebrates the arrival of an 11-lb boy at his house last Sunday.

Alcona County Review, September 29, 1892
Father: Addison I. Silverthorn
Mother: Grace A. Aird

Silverthorn, Mary J.
Gustin Grist.
Mack Silverthorn is the father of a girl.

Alcona County Review, April 23, 1896
Father: Alfred McFarlane Silverthorn
Mother: Jennette Good

Silverthorn, Ray
ALCONA ATOMS.

Mrs. McNeil presented John with a brand new daughter lately. Mrs. Thorner presented her husband with a daughter on the "17th of Ireland," and it is reported that Addison Silverthorn, of the life-saving crew, was recently made happy in a similar manner.

Alcona County Review, March 26, 1886
Father: Addison I. Silverthorn
Mother: Grace A. Aird

Silverthorn, Wilber
HOME REVIEWINGS.

Addison Silverthorn is supposed to be the happiest man that now perambulates the walks of this mundane sphere. It's a brand new boy, with good fighting weight.

Alcona County Review, August 12, 1881
Father: Addison I. Silverthorn
Mother: Grace A. Aird

Simons, Allen
Curtis, Nov. 22 (Special).--A bouncing boy has arrived at the home of Will Simons. Will is looking quite fatherly now.

Alcona County Review, November 30, 1893
Father: William Simons
Mother: Belle Alderton

Simons, George C.
Local Sayings and Doings.

This is the way she did it. Mrs. Charles Simmons, wishing to let her husband know that the 16th was her birthday, presented him with a fine, ten-pound baby boy, and Charlie is—well, just happy.

Alcona County Review, May 9, 1882
Father: Charles Simmons
Mother: Catherine McDonald

Simons, Lois
Curtis Crumbs.

James Simons is once more made happy by the arrival of a 12 pound girl.

Alcona County Review, February 22, 1894
Father: James Simons
Mother: Francis Stahl

Simons, Richard
Curtis Items.
Feb. 17, 1896.
Born to Mr. and Mrs. Truman Simons, a son.

Alcona County Review, February 20, 1896
Father: Truman Simons
Mother: Mary A.

Sinclair, {Boy}
EVENTS OF ONE WEEK.

Born to Mr. and Mrs. Chas. Sinclair Monday, March 22, a 10-lb. boy.

Alcona County Review, March 25, 1897
Father: Charles Sinclair
Mother: Mary McNabb

Sinton, {Girl}
COUNTY REVIEWINGS.

Another new daughter has come to greet and make happy the home of Mr. and Mrs. Geo. Sinton.

Alcona County Review, July 9, 1880
Father: George Sinton
Mother: Mary A. McDonald

Sinton, Ida M.
COUNTY NEWS JOTTINGS.
Our young friend Geo. Sinton is the happy father of another girl, born last week. George is 'sweet' on girls.

Alcona County Review, October 19, 1877
Father: George Sinton
Mother: Mary A. McDonald

Skuse, Charles
Dr. Tiffany reports the birth of twins, a boy and a girl at the home of Mr. and Mrs. Wm. H. Skuse on Tuesday of this week. Mother and children are doing nicely.

Alcona County Review, December 1, 1898
Father: William H. Skuse
Mother: Sarah M. J. Twite

Skuse, Eliza
PERSONAL.

Mr. and Mrs. Wm. Skuse rejoice over the birth of an 11-pound girl on the 23rd. inst.

Alcona County Review, January 28, 1897
Father: William H. Skuse
Mother: Sarah M. J. Twite

Skuse, Esther
PERSONAL MENTION.

Born to Mr. and Mrs. Will Skuse, a 12-pound girl on Oct. 1.

Alcona County Review, October 10, 1895
Father: William H. Skuse
Mother: Sarah M. J. Twite

Skuse, Fanny
Dr. Tiffany reports the birth of twins, a boy and a girl at the home of Mr. and Mrs. Wm. H. Skuse on Tuesday of this week. Mother and children are doing nicely.

Alcona County Review, December 1, 1898
Father: William H. Skuse
Mother: Sarah M. J. Twite

Slater, Everett
Haynes Happenings.
Walter Slater is the father of another baby boy since Jan. 22d.

Alcona County Review, February 4, 1897
Father: Walter Slater
Mother: Minnie [DeKett] Cade

Slater, Glenn
West Harrisville.
Mrs. Albert Slater made Al a present of a 9 pound boy for his New Years. This is Al's first present of the kind; shake.

Alcona County Review, January 7, 1892
Father: Albert Slater
Mother: Laura

Slater, Sadie
Haynes.
Mrs. Slater presented Walter with a young plowman on the 9th.

Alcona County Review, December 15, 1892

EVENTS OF ONE WEEK.
Haynes, Dec. 20.

Mr. Editor, In my communication of the 13th I got the babies of Mrs. Milligan and Mrs. Slater vice-versa.

Alcona County Review, December 22, 1892
Father: Walter Slater
Mother: Minnie [DeKett] Cade

Sly {Girl}
HAWSE ITEMS.
July 7, 1897.
Mr. and Mrs. Edwin Sly are the happy parents of a baby girl.

Alcona County Review, July 8, 1897
Father: Edwin Sly
Mother:

Smiley, {Girl}
LOCAL JOTTINGS.

A little girl is being entertained at J. S. Smiley's. She arrived on the 25th ult., and weighed ten pounds.

Alcona County Review, April 2, 1886
Father: John S. Smiley
Mother:

Smiley, {Girl}
PURELY PERSONAL.

Jno. Smiley smiles now as if he had something to smile for. He has. Girl; Tuesday morning.

Alcona County Review, June 1, 1888
Father: John S. Smiley
Mother:

Smith, {Boy}
Black River Sparks.

Born on Monday, May 25, to Mr. and Mrs. C. C. Smith, a boy.

Alcona County Review, May 28, 1896
Father: Christopher? C. Smith
Mother: Margaret?

Smith, Clark Harold
LOCAL JOTTINGS.

Lawyer Smith thinks he has the finest boy in the village; arrived first of the week; usual weight. Cigars expected.

Alcona County Review, November 11, 1887
Father: Osmund H. Smith
Mother: Clara N. Palmer

Smith, Gladys Gertrude
Killmaster.
Killmaster, Augus 28.--Mrs. Jas. Smith presented her husband with a fine baby girl a few days ago. Mother and child doing well.

Alcona County Review, August 30, 1894
Father: James Smith
Mother: Ida Bond

Smith, Helen Flora
PERSONAL MENTION.

Pros. Atty. Smith and wife are receiving congratulations over the birth of a bouncing baby girl last evening.

Alcona County Review, August 8, 1895
Father: Osmund H. Smith
Mother: Clara N. Palmer

Smith, Howard
PERSONAL.

Born to Mrs. W. R. Smith of Black River, a bouncing boy, March 11th.

Alcona County Review, March 11, 1897
Father: William R. Smith
Mother: Kate Reynolds

Smith, Maude J.
WEST HARRISVILLE.
Born, June 17th, to Mr. and Mrs. Frank Smith, a daughter. Mrs. Smith is quite low at this writing.

Alcona County Review, June 21, 1889
Father: Franklin E. Smith
Mother: Emma M. Clearwater

Smith, Percy
West Harrisville, Nov. 19, '91. Mrs. Frank Smith made a present to Frank of a boy of 9 pounds last Sunday.

Alcona County Review, November 19, 1891
Father: Franklin E. Smith
Mother: Emma M. Clearwater

Snowden, William
LOCAL JOTTINGS.

Mrs. Wm. Snoden, of Black River, presented her husband with a son on the 18th inst.

Alcona County Review, February 26, 1886
Father: William E. Snowden
Mother: Martha Churchill

Somers, Clifford
HAYNES HAPPENINGS.
Mr. and Mrs. Frank Somers of Haynes welcomed the arrival of a son Tuesday night.

Alcona County Review, January 19, 1899
Father: Frank Somers
Mother: Lillian Card

Sousie, {Boy}
Black River Sparks.

Born, Jan. 27, to Mr. and Mrs. Geo. Sousie, a boy.

Alcona County Review, January 30, 1896
Father: George Sousie
Mother: Mary Twite

Southgate, {Boy}
Local Sayings and Doings.

A certain son of Mr. and Mrs. Robert Southgate will be a man in 21 years from last Monday.

Alcona County Review, August 25, 1882
Father: Robert Southgate
Mother: Marietta Beever

Southgate, Jennie H.
LOCAL JOTTINGS.

The family of Robert Southgate have recently been made happy by the advent of a new daughter. Weight 12 pounds.

Alcona County Review, June 19, 1885
Father: Robert Southgate
Mother: Marietta Beever

Southgate, Nellie M.
Reviewings.

A girl baby was born in this village some three months ago, but our reporter was invited out to a buttermilk festival about that time and forgot to report the item to headquarters. Had not the editor discovered the "blessed little creature" in her mother's arms the other day, he would have remained in ignorance relative to her existence even longer than till now. We've discharged that neglectful reporter, and hired him over again.

Alcona County Review, July 18, 1879
Father: Robert Southgate
Mother: Marietta Beever

Southgate, Vidie L.
HOME REVIEWINGS.
How often is it the case in life that one's joy is soon turned into sorrow. Saturday morning last a beautiful ten-pound daughter was born to Mr. and Mrs. Robert Southgate, which remained to gladden their hearts only till Sunday evening when the spirit of the little one returned back to God who gave it. The lovely flower was too tender for the climes of this cold and uneven world and the Good Father has thus transplanted it in His garden of celestial clime and beauty where its bloom shall assume the brightness of eternal glory. "The Lord giveth and the Lord taketh away. Blessed be the name of the Lord."

Alcona County Review, July 1, 1881
Father: Robert Southgate
Mother: Marietta Beever

Sovey, Clair O.
PERSONAL MENTION.
A son was born to Mr. and Mrs. John Sovey Saturday, May 9th inst.

Alcona County Review, May 14, 1896
Father: John F. Sovey
Mother: Phoebe E. St. Clair

Sovey, Herbert
PERSONAL POINTS.

To Mr. and Mrs. John Sovey, a boy, Tuesday, 13th inst.

Alcona County Review, September 15, 1898
Father: John F. Sovey
Mother: Phoebe E. St. Clair

Sparr, Joseph
Shore Items.

Says the *Au Sable News*: Capt. Jones of the propeller St. Joseph appeared with great success in a new *role*, Saturday. Mrs. Philip Sparr of Au Sable was delivered of a child on Saginaw Bay on his steamer, and it is said Jones, the gallant fellow, was equal to the emergency and rendered every assistance in his power. On landing at Sable dock he sought out Mr. Sparr, who was expecting his wife home, and stipulated that the son just born to him should be called "Joseph," to which the happy but rather excited man at once acceded. Young Joseph and his mother are doing well.

Alcona County Review, May 2, 1879
Father: Phillip Sparr
Mother: Tracy

Specht, Joseph H.
REVIEWINGS.

To Mrs. Peter Effric and Mrs. Joseph Speck—a son each. O, happy fathers!

Alcona County Review, January 23, 1880
Father: Joseph Specht
Mother: Mary Henry

Specht, Raymond
A Long String From Springport.

Springport, Jan. 15, 1895.
Born, Dec. 16th, 1894, a son to Mr. and Mrs. Joseph Specht. The evening previous a daughter to Mr. and Mrs. Chas. Hornby.

Alcona County Review, January 17, 1895
Father: Joseph Specht
Mother: Mary Henry

Spencer, Ella
LOCAL PICK UPS.
Born, to Mrs. Nellie Southgate-Spencer, a daughter, Tuesday evening.

Alcona County Review, January 12, 1899
Father: Ernest E. Spencer
Mother: Nellie M. Southgate

Stecker, {Boy}

LOCAL JOTTINGS.

New settlers have arrived in Alcona County recently, as follows: Jan. 21, a boy each at the homes of Wm. Jenkins, Greenbush, and Geo. W. Stecker, Harrisville.

Alcona County Review, January 29, 1886
Father: George W. Stecker
Mother:

Steele, {Boy}
PERSONAL MENTION.

Mrs. C. B. Steele, wife of a former pastor of the Harrisville M. E. church, presented her husband with a son Sunday last.

Alcona County Review, June 1, 1893
Father: Charles B. Steele
Mother: Lillie

Steele, Lois E.
LOCAL JOTTINGS.

The hearts of the Rev. and Mrs. C. B. Steele were made happy last week Friday by the birth of a daughter, their first born.

Alcona County Review, March 18, 1887
Father: Charles B. Steele
Mother: Lillie

Sterritt, {Boy}
LOCAL JOTTINGS.

The new under-sheriff of Alcona county arrived less than a week ago. He is stopping in the family of sheriff Chas. Sterritt on the hill. He isn't very large yet (9 or 10 lbs.), but he has good grit and a strong pair of lungs, and will "git thar" in the season.

Alcona County Review, January 23, 1885
Father: Charles H. Sterritt
Mother: Nellie J. McIntyre

Stevens, Clara
LOCAL JOTTINGS.

It is said to be a lovely little boy-baby [girl], and papa Frank Stevens is just too happy for anything. Next.

Alcona County Review, July 18, 1884
Father: Frank E. Stevens
Mother: Susannah H. Taft

Stewart, {Boy}
Gustin Grist.
Gustin, May 11, '96.
Born to Mr. and Mrs. John Stewart, a bouncing boy on May 10. Mrs. Stewart is getting along nicely.

Alcona County Review, May 14, 1896
Father: John Stewart

Mother: Annie McDonald

Stewart, Earl
ALCONA ATOMS.

Mrs. Stewart gave birth to twins last spring, and both are alive and well. She also gave birth to twins in Canada, and they are both living.

Alcona County Review, February 19, 1886
Father: Joseph Stewart
Mother: Margaret

Stewart, Ethel
ALCONA ATOMS.

Mrs. Stewart gave birth to twins last spring, and both are alive and well. She also gave birth to twins in Canada, and they are both living.

Alcona County Review, February 19, 1886
Father: Joseph Stewart
Mother: Margaret

Stinchcombe, Gervin Lucean
Another fine son arrived at the home of Henry Stinchcombe on the 24th inst. All doing well, including the father.

Alcona County Review, June 27, 1895
Father: Henry J. Stinchcombe
Mother: Maggie J. Nevin

Stinchcombe, Guy
Little Strangers.
An 11 lb. boy arrived on Monday to bless the home of Henry Stinchcombe and wife.

Alcona County Review, May 17, 1894
Father: Henry J. Stinchcombe
Mother: Maggie J. Nevin

Stinchcombe, Margaret
Mr. and Mrs. Henry Stinchcombe are rejoicing over the birth of a handsome daughter Saturday morning last.

Alcona County Review, November 24, 1892
Father: Henry J. Stinchcombe
Mother: Maggie J. Nevin

Storms, Ben E.
LOCAL JOTTINGS.

It is now David Eugene Storms' turn to bask in the sunshine of congratulatory smiles. Last Sunday he became the happy father of a bright, ten pound boy. Mother and child doing well.

Alcona County Review, October 3, 1884
Father: David Eugene Storms
Mother: Marian O. Colwell

Storms, {Boy}
HOME REVIEWINGS.

Geo. Storms is the happy papa of a new boy-baby.

Alcona County Review, October 28, 1881
Father: George A. Storms
Mother: Evaline Beever

Storms, Bryan

PERSONAL MENTION.

Twins, a boy and a girl, were born to Mr. and Mrs. Geo. Storms, Friday, Sept. 18.

Alcona County Review, September 24, 1896
Father: George A. Storms
Mother: Evaline Beever

Storms, Edith M.

REVIEWINGS.

Mr. and Mrs. George Storms rejoice. It's a 10 pound girl.

Alcona County Review, May 2, 1879
Father: George A. Storms
Mother: Evaline Beever

Storms, Kate

PERSONAL AND SOCIAL.

Born, last Friday, to Mr. and Mrs. Geo. Storms, a daughter. Happiness reigns supreme.

Alcona County Review, August 21, 1885
Father: George A. Storms
Mother: Evaline Beever

Storms, Pansy

PERSONAL MENTION.

Twins, a boy and a girl, were born to Mr. and Mrs. Geo. Storms, Friday, Sept. 18.

Alcona County Review, September 24, 1896
Father: George A. Storms
Mother: Evaline Beever

Storms, Sanford

The Local News.

Geo. Storms is happy again. Another boy.

Alcona County Review, January 3, 1890
Father: George A. Storms
Mother: Evaline Beever

Storms, Vivienne

BLACK RIVER.

Aug. 9, '99.
Mr. and Mrs. Chas. Storms are the happy parents of a baby girl since Saturday.

Alcona County Review, August 10, 1899
Father: Charles A. Storms
Mother: Mary A. McGregor

Storms, Wilbert

Somewhat Personal.

Born to Mr. and Mrs. Geo. Storms, a son, Sunday, April 10.

Alcona County Review, April 14, 1892
Father: George A. Storms
Mother: Evaline Beever

Stringer, Angus E.

SPENCER DISTRICT.

Mrs. Stringer has a baby girl.

Alcona County Review, January 19, 1899
Father: Everett Stringer
Mother: Sarah Jane Emerick

Stringer, Clara (Hattie)

GREENBUSH GETTINGS.

Mr. James Stringer is the happy father of a young daughter, presented Nov. 19.

Alcona County Review, November 26, 1886
Father: James Stringer
Mother: Elizabeth

Strong, {Boy}

KILLMASTER RIPPLES.

Born to Mr. and Mrs. Allen Strong, a son Sunday evening, May 2nd.

Alcona County Review, May 6, 1897
Father: Allen Strong
Mother: Sarah E. [Lamb] Hetherington

Sweet, George H.

PERSONAL POINTS.

Born to Mr. and Mrs. Henry Sweet, at Sturgeon Point, June 24, a son.

Alcona County Review, July 7, 1898
Father: Henry Sweet
Mother: Ella M.

Swindlehurst, William John

EVENTS OF ONE WEEK.

A 12-lb. son was born to Mrs. Wm. Swindlehurst Monday morning.

Alcona County Review, March 12, 1896
Father: William Swindlehurst
Mother: Johanna Hendrie

Tacia, Mable

ALCONA ATOMS.

On March the 1st, Mrs. Lacey presented Joseph with a boy, and now he sings "rock the cradle pet, rock the cradle pet." Many's the man who would give his right hand to have a nice child like that.

Alcona County Review, March 12, 1886

ALCONA ATOMS.

Mrs. Tacey gave birth to a boy, not Mrs. Lacey, as stated in last week's paper.

Alcona County Review, March 19, 1886
Father: Joseph Tacia
Mother: Nancy Kilburn

Talmadge, {Boy}

COUNTY REVIEWINGS.

A young son arrived at the Methodist parsonage to-day.
[Note: The Methodist minister at the time was Charles H. Talmadge.]

Alcona County Review, September 24, 1880
Father: Charles H. Talmadge
Mother: Ella L. Freeman

Tanner, Earl K.

PERSONAL.

Mr. and Mrs. Harry Tanner (nee Miss Blanche Kimball) are rejoicing over the arrival of a bouncing baby boy.—Grand Marais Herald.

Alcona County Review, May 13, 1897
Father: Harry F. Tanner
Mother: Blanche F. Kimball

Teeple, Chester

Haynes Happenings.

March 10, 1896.
Mrs. Teeple presented Fred with a baby boy on the 6th and therefore could not attend the funeral of her dear sister.

Alcona County Review, March 12, 1896
Father: Frederick Oliver Teeple
Mother: Eliza J. [Hastings] Holden

Teeple, Clifford

ALCONA ATOMS.

Mrs. Teeples gave birth to a five pound boy on Washington's birthday the 22d.

Alcona County Review, March 5, 1886
Father: Frederick Oliver Teeple
Mother: Eliza J. [Hastings] Holden

Teeple, Cora E.

Haynes Items.

Mrs. Teeple presented Frederick with a daughter, regulation weight on Friday last.

Alcona County Review, May 7, 1891
Father: Frederick Oliver Teeple
Mother: Eliza J. [Hastings] Holden

Teeple, Earl Frederick

PURELY PERSONAL.

Fred. O. Teeple, of Haynes, rejoices over the birth in his household Mar. 22 of a son.

Alcona County Review, March 29, 1889
Father: Frederick Oliver Teeple
Mother: Eliza J. [Hastings] Holden

Teeple, George W.

Haynes, August 15, 1892.—Mr. Teeple is the happy father of another bouncing baby boy.

Alcona County Review, August 18, 1892
Father: Frederick Oliver Teeple
Mother: Eliza J. [Hastings] Holden

Teeple, Wilson

Haynes Happenings.

Received too late for Publication last week.

Haynes, Sept. 13th, 1894.--Tally a brand new daughter to Archey Campbell. Also one for Fred Teeple.

Alcona County Review, September 20, 1894
Father: Frederick Oliver Teeple
Mother: Eliza J. [Hastings] Holden

Thibideau, Arthur?

PURELY PERSONAL.

Levi Tibbido came down from camp to greet a new member of his family—a boy, his second, born Sunday evening.

Alcona County Review, August 16, 1889
Father: Levi Thibideau
Mother:

Thompson, Myrtle May

West Harrisville, Feb. 27.—Born, to Mrs. T. A. Ferris, Feb. 24, a son. T. A. is doing well. Also to Mr. and Mrs. D. A. Thompson, a daughter, Feb. 26.

Alcona County Review, February 28, 1890
Father: Daniel A. Thompson
Mother: Emma

Thorner, Grace

Haynes Happenings.

Haynes, July 24.--Wm. Thorner has tallied once more. Another girl last week.

Alcona County Review, July 26, 1894
Father: William Thorner
Mother: Martha Newell

Thorner, Sarah J.

ALCONA ATOMS.

Mrs. McNeil presented John with a brand new daughter lately. Mrs. Thorner presented her husband with a daughter on the "17th of Ireland," and it is reported that Addison Silverthorn, of the life-saving crew, was recently made happy in a similar manner.

Alcona County Review, March 26, 1886
Father: William Thorner
Mother: Martha Newell

Thornton, George A.

PERSONAL POINTS.

Born to Mr. and Mrs. Lyman Thornton, on Monday, a son.

Alcona County Review, May 26, 1898
Father: Lyman L. Thornton

Mother: Carrie Ethel Noyes

Thornton, Grace B.

MUD LAKE.
You ought to see the smile that Lime Thornton wears—it's all over that big 10 pound girl born last Monday.

Alcona County Review, August 3, 1899
Father: Lyman L. Thornton
Mother: Carrie Ethel Noyes

Tovey, Edward James

Born to Mrs. Michael Tovey, Nov. 18, a son.

Alcona County Review, November 24, 1892
Father: Michael Tovey
Mother: Ann Margaret Kehoe

Tovey, Mary

Somewhat Personal.
A little babe made its appearance last week at the residence of Michael [James] Tovey.

Alcona County Review, April 28, 1892
Father: James Tovey
Mother: Mary Agnes Shirley

Tovey, William

Born to Mrs. Jas. Tovey, a son.

Alcona County Review, November 19, 1896
Father: James Tovey
Mother: Mary Agnes Shirley

Trask, Charles S.

WEST HARRISVILLE.
Happy man. Another son at the home of Peter Trask.

Alcona County Review, May 6, 1897
Father: Peter Trask
Mother: Susanna K. Standlake

Twite, Arthur

Black River Sparks.
Born to Mr. and Mrs. H. Twite, Sept. 16th, a 12 lb. boy.

Alcona County Review, September 19, 1895
Father: Henry J. Twite
Mother: Mary Lamp

Twite, Nathaniel

REVIEWINGS.

Ah, ha!—here it is!—They were not twins, but they were born the same night and in the same house. One was a 10 pound boy to Mr. and Mrs. Chas. Twite, and the other was a 9 pound girl to Mr. and Mrs. John Boardman. There's a match for you, sure!

Alcona County Review, March 12, 1880
Father: Charles Twite
Mother: Margaret Higginson

Valentine, Marion K.

LOCALS.
Dr. and Mrs. D. W. Valentine, formerly A. Belle Colwell, of

Englewood, N. J., are rejoicing over the arrival of a little daughter.

Alcona County Review, August 26, 1897
Father: Daniel Webster Valentine
Mother: Ada Belle Colwell

Valentine, Margaret

PERSONAL POINTS.
Born to Mr. and Mrs. D. W. Valentine of Englewood, N. J., adaughter.

Alcona County Review, February 16, 1899
Father: Daniel Webster Valentine
Mother: Ada Belle Colwell

Van Alstine, David

COUNTY REVIEWINGS.

Wm. H. Vanalstine has been made happy. A ten pound boy is the cause.

Alcona County Review, April 30, 1880
Father: William H. VanAlstine
Mother: Martha Johnson

Van Alstine, Earl Russell

Haynes.
Mrs. Wm. Van Alstine is the mother of a 14 pound boy. It came Saturday last.

Alcona County Review, March 30, 1893
Father: William H. VanAlstine
Mother: Martha Johnson

Van Alstine, {Girl}

By due process of law we give Mrs. VanAlstine credit for a 11-pound girl and charge the same to the account of Wm. H. VanAlstine.
Haynes.

Alcona County Review, August 23, 1889
Father: William H. VanAlstine
Mother: Martha Johnson

Van Alstine, William H.

Alcona Atoms.

Sunday evening the 7th, Wm. H. Vanalstine was made happy. It is a 12 lbs. boy.

Alcona County Review, May 12, 1882
Father: William H. VanAlstine
Mother: Martha Johnson

Van Wagoner, Lewis P.

West Harrisville.
May 28, 1895.
Lew Van Wagner is the happy father of a bouncing baby boy.

Alcona County Review, May 30, 1895
Father: George Lewis Van Wagoner
Mother: Anne May Burkhart

Vaughn, Clara

LOCAL JOTTINGS.

Born, June 22, to Mr. and Mrs. Wm. Vaughn, W. Harrisville, a daughter.

Alcona County Review, June 28, 1889
Father: William Vaughan
Mother: Mary Bickel

Vaughn, Dorothy

HAYNES HAPPENINGS.
There arrived a 9 ½ lb. girl at the home of Wm. Vaughn Oct. 6.

Alcona County Review, October 13, 1898
Father: William Vaughn
Mother: Mary Bickel

Walker, {Boy}

County News and Gossip.

In our last issue we forgot to mention that John Walker was the happiest man under the canopy of Heaven. He's the father of a nine pound boy.

Alcona County Review, March 18, 1881
Father: John Walker
Mother: Adaline O'Dell

Walker, Herman

HAYNES.
Born to Mr. and Mrs. James Walker, a son, May 12, 1899.

Alcona County Review, May 18, 1899
Father: James G. Walker
Mother: Rillah Milligan

Walker, Rena Blanch

PERSONAL MENTION.

Born, to Mrs. Robt. Walker, Thursday, Jan. 4th, a daughter.

Alcona County Review, January 11, 1894
Father: Robert Walker
Mother: Mary Broadley

Wallace, Levi George

Curtis Items.
May 17, 1896.
Born to Mr. and Mrs. J. W. Batten a fine boy a short time ago. Also a boy to Mr. and Mrs. Wm. Wallace.

Alcona County Review, May 21, 1896
Father: William Wallace
Mother: Martha Nemitz

Ward, {Boy}

PERSONAL MENTION.

Born to Mrs. Geo. Ward, Jr., a son, Saturday, Nov. 11.

Alcona County Review, November 16, 1893
Father: George Ward, Jr.
Mother: Jennie Sinclair

Ward, Stewart T.

LOCAL PICK UPS.

Congratulations to John Ward and wife on the birth of a 10-lb. son and heir Tuesday afternoon.

Alcona County Review, October 14, 1897
Father: William John Ward
Mother: Rebecca Ferguson

Waters, Arley

People We Hear About.

Mr. and Mrs. J. Waters welcomed a little stranger of the feminine gender to their family circle Sunday evening.

Alcona County Review, July 11, 1890
Father: Jefferson L. Waters
Mother: Jessie Conklin

Webb, {Boy}

HAYNES HAPPENINGS.

Haynes, Nov. 9th, 1897.
Mr. and Mrs. Webb recently buried a child, aged 2 months, which died of whooping cough.

Alcona County Review, November 18, 1897
Father: Henry Webb
Mother: Elizabeth Fishleigh

Weinberg, Lillian

LOCAL PICK UPS.
Mr. and Mrs. A. S. Weinberg are happy over the birth of another daughter on Thursday, the 12th inst. Mother and daughter are doing nicely.

Alcona County Review, January 12, 1899
Father: Abraham S. Weinberg
Mother: Rosetta S. Sandorf

Weir, {Girl}

BLACK RIVER BRIEFLETS.

On Friday, Jan. 22d, the wife of Rev. Geo. S. Weir presented him with a bouncing daughter. All parties concerned are doing well.

Alcona County Review, January 29, 1886
Father: George S. Weir
Mother:

Weir, Lillian Belle

Notes and News Along the Shore

AU SABLE AND OSCODA.
Hiram Weir's Christmas present was a brand new daughter.

Alcona County Review, January 2, 1885
Father: Hiram Weir
Mother:

Welch, {Girl}

Local Sayings and Doings.

William Welch was made exceedingly happy last week over the birth of a fine girl.

Alcona County Review, January 27, 1882
Father: William Welch
Mother:

Wells, {Girl}

Black River Sparks.

BIRTHS.
Mr. and Mrs. J. C. Wells, a girl.

Alcona County Review, May 14, 1896
Father: J. C. Wells
Mother:

Welsh, {Girl}

BLACK RIVER SPARKS
--------.

Born to Mr. and Mrs. C. S. Welsh, a girl.

Alcona County Review, September 3, 1896
Father: C. S. Welsh
Mother:

Wheeler, Flossie Jane

BORN.
To Mr. and Mrs. Peter Wheeler, at W. Harrisville, a daughter, Mar. 5.

Alcona County Review, March 21, 1890
Father: Peter J. Wheeler
Mother: Nancy Fonger

White, {Boy}

KILLMASTER.
Killmaster, June, 1896.--Born, to Mrs. White, a son on Sunday. Mother and child are doing well.

Alcona County Review, June 11, 1896
Father: ? White
Mother:

White, {Boy}

PERSONAL POINTS.

Born to Mr. and Mrs. D. D. White of Parshallville, Mich., a son. Mrs. White was formerly Miss Ida Taylor of this place.

Alcona County Review, October 13, 1898
Father: D. D. White
Mother: Ida Taylor

White, {Child}

JOTTINGS ALONG THE SHORE.

Robert White, of East Tawas—the "biggest" lawyer on the shore—has just become a father. Next!

Alcona County Review, April 22, 1881
Father: Robert White
Mother: Mary A. Holbrook

Wiedbrauk, Lena

Curran Crumbs.

The excitement over at Wiedbrauk's since Jan. 26th is on account of his new daughter. "It's a girl!"

Alcona County Review, February 7, 1895
Father: William Henry Wiedbrauk
Mother: Eliza Jane Fullerton

Willard, Irma Julia

The Local News.

Mr. and Mrs. J. C. Willard welcomed a stranger of the tender sex at their Greenbush home a few days ago.

Alcona County Review, August 15, 1890

A Grist From Greenbush.

The old adage (Patience and perseverance will accomplish wonders.) was never better illustrated than in the case of the 9 lb. stranger who made her advent in Greenbush some four weeks or so ago. Well, five years of sticktoitaveness deserves its reward and we congratulate the happy parents.

Alcona County Review, August 29, 1890
Father: Joseph G. Willard
Mother: Polly Treadway

Williams, Ira David

Curran Crumbs.
July 15, 1895.
Born to Mr. and Mrs. Albert Williams, a son.

Alcona County Review, July 18, 1895
Father: Albert R. Williams
Mother: Phebe Rifenbark

Williams, Mattie

Greenbush Gettings.

Last Saturday the countenance of Asa Williams was all aglow over the presentation of a darling little girl. Papa Williams--ahem!

Alcona County Review, September 17, 1886

LOCAL JOTTINGS.

A little girl, who will be able to say "papa" in about twelve months, arrived at the residence of Asa Williams, of Greenbush, last Saturday, the 11th inst.

Alcona County Review, September 17, 1886
Father: Asa Williams
Mother: Mary Murphy

Wilson, {Boy}

We have a letter received from Seymour Wilson, now residing in Tacoma, in which he writes that Mrs. Wilson presented him with a nine-pound baby boy last Sunday morning and the little mother and baby were doing nicely. Skamokawa Friends send congratulations.

Alcona County Review, May 20, 1897
Father: Seymour Wilson
Mother: Emma Wagner

Winter, Earle
Winter, Frances
Winter, Henry

WINTER IN THE LAP OF SUMMER.
----
26 ½ Lbs. of Infant
Born to an Au Sable Woman.

Monday morning at 3 o'clock a boy weighing 7 ½ pounds was presented to Carl Winter of the Third ward. Carl's face blossomed all over with smiles as he saw a young Winter resting in the lap of summer. His joy was beyond expression, excepting Carl's face, which was all expression. The single blessedness of his joy was not of long life, as but a very short time elapsed before an 8 ½ pound girl was added to the list. Carl's joy was a little bit tangled just then. He considered one company, but two something the semblance of a crowd. He had about accommodated his mind to the old adage that "two is company" and had resolved to make the best kind of father to both of them. A boy and a girl was not to be sneezed at after six years of married life. Things about the Winter household had scarcely had time to gather themselves together, when a third little one, a boy weighing 10 ½ pounds, was ruthlessly thrust into Carl's lap. It is said that Carl did not collapse, but this is hardly conceivable under the circumstances. Two boys and one girl, weighing 26 ½ pounds, is quite a load for one man to meekly submit to. "Three is a crowd." Some people have a wonderful ability of adapting themselves to circumstances, and by 9 o'clock when Carl went down town, he had fully recovered his usual equilibrium and was anxiously awaiting for a fourth, which never came.

The little ones are all perfectly favored. One has a fine head of hair and the other two are quite well supplied. They are all bright and promise to live to good old age.

Hundreds have visited the home of Mr. and Mrs. Winter this week to inspect the three little ones, and all express themselves pleased with the charming sight.

Three children at one birth is of very rare occurrence and Au Sable will go down to history through the medium of the State press as being up to date in at least one thing.

Alcona County Review, July 5, 1894

EVENTS OF ONE WEEK.

Carle Winter's triplets, whose births were fully noted in the Review, were christened last week, the Rev. Osborn officiating. The ceremony took place at his home and something like 200 friends and admirers of the family and triplets were present, according to the Press. Addresses were delivered by the pastor and the mayor of the city and a baby carriage made to order for three occupants was presented as a gift from friends.

Alcona County Review, August 9, 1894
Father: Carl Winter
Mother: Cynthia Hall

Withington, Theron

BLACK RIVER.
A very pleasing expression was noticed on the countenance of George Withington Saturday. Later we learned the arrival of a young operator that morning. Mother and babe are doing well.

Alcona County Review, January 13, 1898
Father: George Theron Withington
Mother: Frances Bayley

Woo, Rosa Maud

West Harrisville.

W. Woo is the happy father of a 3 lb. girl.

Alcona County Review, May 14, 1896
Father: Willie C. Woo
Mother: Maud C. LePage

Yuill, Ethel

ALCONA ATOMS.
A Shower of Babies in Alcona.
Mrs. Alex Yuill presented her dear hubby with a baby girl, April 28.
All of the above are reported standard weight.

Alcona County Review, May 6, 1887
Father: Alexander Yuill
Mother: Frances McNeil

Yuill, Jennie R.

The Local News.

Born, on Friday last to Mrs. Alex Yuill, of Haynes township, a daughter.

Alcona County Review, February 19, 1891
Father: Alexander Yuill
Mother: Frances McNeil

Yuill, Joseph

Haynes.
Alex Yuill is the father of another boy. Mother and child are doing well.

Alcona County Review, June 1, 1893
Father: Alexander Yuill

Mother: Frances McNeil

Yuill, Leota Ruth

Haynes Happenings.

Since my last communication our population has been increased by four young ladies, who are in favor of protection: One at the home of A. McNeil, one at Alex Yuill's, one at Ellison Milligan's, and one came to the home of Geo. S. Ritchie Sunday morning. They are all reported to be able to take their rations regularly from the commissary department.

Alcona County Review, November 19, 1896
Father: Alexander Yuill
Mother: Frances McNeil

Yuill, Viola

Haynes Happenings.

Received too late for Publication last week.

Haynes, Sept. 13th, 1894.--Alex. Yuill is the father of a baby girl, born on the 12th.

Alcona County Review, September 20, 1894
Father: Alexander Yuill
Mother: Frances McNeil

Yuill, William

ALCONA ATOMS.

Mr. Alex Yuill became the father of a bouncing baby boy on Monday, the 1st day of February. Mr. Alcorn, of Alcona village, also became the father of a big boy on Friday last.

Alcona County Review, February 12, 1886
Father: Alexander Yuill
Mother: Frances McNeil

?, {Child}

COUNTY NEWS JOTTINGS.

The man living in the cottage across the street is happy. It's a boy--or girl.

Alcona County Review, February 8, 1878
Father:
Mother:

?, {Child}

Born on the Alpena.

The steamer City of Alpena had an experience last Sunday which seldom occurs on lake or river steamers. It was nothing less that the birth of a child Sunday morning shortly before the boat reached Oscoda. The parents of the child were from St. Ignace. The interesting event was not expected at the time, so that preparations for the young visitor, a fine boy, had not been made. The lady passengers on the steamer, however, among whom was Mrs.

Judge Simpson, of Au Sable, at once went to work and soon had all necessary clothing made for their guest. A collection was also taken up and $15 raised as a present to the child. The officers of the Alpena are highly delighted with the whole affair, as such an event is supposed to bring great good luck to the boat on which it occurs.—Saturday Night.

Alcona County Review, June 21, 1889
Father:
Mother:

?, {Child}

PERSONAL MENTION.

All last week we endeavored in vain to ascertain the inducement of that expansive smile worn by our genial stage driver. Now we learn that Ed. is rejoicing over the birth of another boy on the 22d last.

Alcona County Review, August 3, 1893
Father: Ed
Mother:

?, {Child}

EVENTS OF ONE WEEK.

A child was born in this village last Friday whose advent into this vale of sin and sorrow has been a matter of anxiety to more than one person besides the girl mother. Fortunately for all concerned the child died on Monday.

Alcona County Review, June 20, 1895
Father:
Mother:

Marriage Notices

from the

Alcona County Review

Adams, William H.
McMullen, Sarah A.

MIKADO.

Wm. Adams and Miss McMullen took the evening train to Ausable Friday where they were married and spent the 4th. Much joy and a happy future, Wm.

Alcona County Review, July 9, 1896

Agans, E. F.
Tool, Eugenie

CURRAN CRUMBS.

Curran, Mar. 23, 1896..--Miss Eugenie Tool and E. F. Agaus are to be married at the home of the bride's parents Tuesday, March 24, at 7 a.m.

Alcona County Review, March 26, 1896

Curran Crumbs.

Curran, March 28, 1896.
TOOL—AGANS.

Miss Eugine Tool of Curran and Mr. E. Agans of McKinley, were united in the holy bonds of matrimony, the Rev. Wolly officiating.

The wedding was solemnized last Tuesday morning at the home of the bride's parents. The most intimate friends of the bride and groom were present. The bride was arrayed in a handsome costume of blue velvet. Miss Eunice Tool, who acted as maid of honor, was arrayed in blue velvet also. Mr. C. H. Rix, groomsman, and Mr. Agans were clad in black.

After the ceremony an elaborate dinner was served. The guests present were:

Mr. and Mrs. Park and Mrs. Walker, Mr. and Mrs. Gabriel, C. H. Rix and Mrs. Rix, Mr. and Mrs. W. Freer, Messrs. H. J. St. Clair and J. Agans, Mrs. Pratt of Texas.

Mr. and Mrs. Agans departed on their wedding tour Wednesday last.

They will be at home in McKinley to their friends after April 10th.

Alcona County Review, April 2, 1896

Alcorn, Edward
Smith, Arvilla Evangelina

Local News.

Ed Alcorn was married last week to a Tawas young lady. They are visiting his parents here.

Alcona County Review, September 14, 1899

Allen, Frank J.
Bruneau, Sadie E.

At the Altar.

Allen-Bruneau.—At the M. E. parsonage, July 7, 1895, by the Rev. W. J. Bailey, Mr. Frank J. Allen of Harrisville to Miss Sadie E. Bruneau of Alpena.

Alcona County Review, July 11, 1895

Allen, George
Bonville, Louisa

LOCAL JOTTINGS.

Married.—On Xmas Eve, by the Rev. T. B. Leith, at the residence of the bride, George Allen to Louisa Bonville, all of Alcona.

Alcona County Review, January 8, 1886

Allen, George
Lemon, Mary

LOCAL JOTTINGS.

Justice Beede tied the knot that made Geo. Allen and Mary Lemon one last Saturday.

Alcona County Review, July 8, 1887

Allen, Theodore
Dunn, Rose A.

People We Hear About.

Theodore Allan, an Au Sable lumber inspector, was united in marriage last Sunday to Miss Rose

Dunn of this township. The ceremony was performed by the Rev. L. Hazard at the home of the bride's parents. The bride is a well known and popular young lady, having resided here from early childhood. The Review offers congratulations and best wishes.

Alcona County Review, October 10, 1890

People We Hear About.

Fred Reynolds drove up home last Sunday. He was accompanied by Theodore Allan and Clarence Parker, the former of whom carried away a Harrisville young lady with him when he left.

Alcona County Review, October 10, 1890

Allison, L.
Selves, Dora [Baldwin]

LOCAL PICK UPS.

Mrs. Frank Selves, formerly of Harrisville, was married at Carson City Thursday, to Mr. L. Allison of East Tawas.

Mrs. Selves was here the first of the week superintending the removal of her household goods to Tawas.

Alcona County Review, July 20, 1899

Alstrom, Charles
McDonald, Katherine

CALEDONIA.
McDonald—Alstrum

On Wednesday last at 2 o'clock occurred the marriage of Miss Kate McDonald to Mr. Charles Alstrum. The nuptial knot was tied by the Rev. Thomas Middlemiss of Alpena, in the presence of about 60 relatives and friends at the home of the bride's mother.

The house was beautifully decorated in green. The fragrant trailing arbutus and other cut flowers constituted the floral decoration.

The bride was tastefully dressed in green and tan and was attended by her sister, Miss Flora McDonald, while Mr. Bernard Alstrum was best man. After congratulations all retired to the dining room where a delightful supper was served; after supper the bride and groom amid a shower of rice and followed by many of their young friends, drove to their new home which is only a short distance from the bride's former home. No wedding party was held as the bride's brother is very sick in Chicago and also the groom has a sister in that city quite ill. The young people went to house-keeping at once in their fine new home.

Both bride and groom are very popular young people, and their many friends wish them every happiness in their wedded life. They were the receivers of many handsome and valuable presents.

Alcona County Review, May 5, 1898

Local History of One Year

Chronology of the Principal Events of the Year 1898.

April 27. Marriage Chas. Alstrome and Kate McDonald. Social event of Caledonia.

Alcona County Review, January 5, 1899

Alstrom, Gustav
Sedergren, Annie

Marriage Licenses.

April 13.—Gustave Alstrom, Black River, and Annie Sedergrin, Caledonia. [Note: Married 4/12/1897 in Caledonia Township.]

Alcona County Review, April 15, 1897

Amesbury, Austin
Hastings, Minnie

The Local News.

Austin Amesbury and Miss Minnie Hastings were united in marriage Sunday, April 6th, by the Rev. P. C. Goldie at the home of the bride's parents in Haynes township.

Alcona County Review, April 11, 1890

Anderson, Donald E.
Procunier, Beatrice

Anderson—Procunier.

A quiet wedding occurred Sunday afternoon at the residence of Mr. and Mrs. J. W. Anderson, when Donald

E. Anderson and Miss Beatrice Procunier were united in marriage. The ceremony was performed in the presence of only a few intimate friends and relatives, Rev. W. W. Will officiating.

Mr. Anderson is the youngest son of Thos. C. Anderson and the bride is a daughter of Peter Procunier. Both are highly respected young people and have the best wishes of a host of friends. The Review extends congratulations.

Alcona County Review, May 11, 1899

Anderson, J. William
McClatchey, Nancy

ANDERSON—McCLATCHEY.

Married last evening, June 20th, at the residence of the bride's parents, Mr. and Mrs. Robt. McClatchey, Mr. J. Wm. Anderson, to Miss Nancy McClatchey, the Rev. W. J. Bailey officiating.

This happy event has been long anticipated and its consummation gives little less pleasure to their many friends than to the bride and groom themselves. Both are too well known to require any introduction to the people of this county. Mr. Anderson has been employed in the store at South Harrisville by J. Van Buskirk for four years past, and his sterling Christian character and bright and cheerful disposition have won him the esteem of all with whom he has had business or social relations. The bride is "to the manor born" and Harrisville is her birthplace. She is an active worker in Sunday-School and the C. E. Society, in which work her husband is also deeply interested. It is a happy union of hearts and hands and we bespeak for them a pleasant voyage together down the stream of life. Like sensible young people they have already commenced housekeeping and will be at home after July 5, in their cozy little home at Springport.

Alcona County Review, June 21, 1894

Anderson, Joseph
Specht, Mary A.

A license was issued yesterday from the county clerk's office authorizing the marriage of Jos. Anderson to Miss Mary Specht, which will be solemnized tomorrow at Au Sable. The young people are popular residents of Harrisville township, the bride having been born

here. They will make their home in Au Sable this summer whither the best wishes of their many friends will follow them.

Alcona County Review, February 22, 1894

PERSONAL MENTION.

Jos. Anderson and Miss Mary Specht were married at the M. E. parsonage in Au Sable last Thursday evening by the Rev. F. L. Osborne.

Alcona County Review, March 1, 1894

Anderson, Walter
Ritter, May

LOCAL PICK UPS.

Married, Thursday evening, Aug. 24, at the Methodist parsonage, Mr. Walter Anderson of Harrisville, and Miss May Ritter of Greenbush. Rev. W. Will performed the ceremony.

Alcona County Review, August 31, 1899

LOCAL PICK UPS.

Mr. Walter Anderson, notice of whose marriage was made last week, is the latest Alcona business man to join the ranks of the Benedicts. He conducts a grocery business in the southwestern part of the township and was so successful that he was contemplating a trip to the state of Washington by way of recreation, when arrested by Cupid's darts, in consequence of which the trip was indefinitely postponed. He wants the people to know that he is doing what he can to help the county along--and respectfully solicits a continuance of patronage.

Alcona County Review, September 7, 1899

Anderson, William
Ferguson, Eliza Jane

Married.

In Harrisville, at the home of the bride's parents, April 28th, 1884, by Rev. J. H. McIntosh, William Anderson and Miss Eliza J. Ferguson, all of Harrisville, Mich.

Alcona County Review, May 2, 1884

Anthony, William
Cutting, Annie

Local Sayings and Doings.

Married—at the M. E. parsonage in Harrisville, April 6, by Rev. J. H. McIntosh, William Anthony of Black River and Miss Annie Cutting of Greenbush. Here's to their good luck!.

Alcona County Review, April 14, 1882

Argyle, William C.
Pringle, Catherine M.

SOMEWHAT PERSONAL.

Argyle—Pringle, married, at the home of Mr. Thomas Argyle, Gustin, by the Rev. D. H. Campbell, June 28th, 1892, Mr. William C. Argyle of Gustin, and Miss Catherine M. Pringle of Sault St. Marie.

Alcona County Review, June 30, 1892

HISTORY OF ONE YEAR.

Chronological History of the Past Year, 1892.

MARRIAGES.

June 28. Wm. C. Argyle to Catherine M. Pringle, at Killmaster.

Alcona County Review, January 5, 1893

Armstrong, James
Read, Ina

PERSONAL MENTION.

Jas. Armstrong and Miss Ina Read were united in marriage Sunday by the Rev. W. J. Bailey. The bride is an adopted daughter of Mr. and Mrs. Geo. Ward, Sr.

Alcona County Review, July 7, 1893

Atchison, William
Keating, Mrs. Jane [Nestle]

Married, December 27th, at the Baptist parsonage, by Rev. W. P. Tompkins, Mr. Wm. Atchison and Mrs. Jane Keating, all of Harrisville.

Alcona County Review, December 30, 1897

Atherton, Samuel
Hensey, Nellie Prudence

EVENTS OF ONE WEEK.

The marriage of Miss Nelly Hensey to Sam Atherton at the home of the bride's father, Philo Hensey, was quite an event in Mitchell township. It occurred Sunday, and an elaborate dinner was served to 63 guests. Elder Merritt performed the ceremony.

Alcona County Review, June 6, 1895

Aubin, Philip
Causley, Elizabeth Jane

BLACK RIVER BRIEFLETS.

Married—At Black River, Jan. 10, 1886, by justice Leach, Philip Aubin to Miss Elizabeth Jane Causley.

Alcona County Review, January 15, 1886

Babcock, Arthur R.
Woods, Rilla

Somewhat Personal.

Handsome wedding invitations were issued this week Tuesday for the marriage of Mr. Arthur R. Babcock of Ludington, Mich., to Miss Rilla Woods, daughter of Mr. and Mrs. Chas. Woods, at their residence Wednesday, June 3, 1891, at 8:30 p.m.—West Branch Herald-Times.

The above bridegroom taught school at Dean's two or three years ago. Since leaving here he has been gravitating between West Branch and several other Michigan towns as a job printer and compositor.

Alcona County Review, June 4, 1891

Backus, Austin D.
Anthony, Ella A.

The Local News.

Reported that a double wedding is likely to occur soon at Killmaster in which Will Noyes of Mud Lake will lead a Miss Backus to the altar and a brother of the latter will wed another popular young lady of Killmaster.

Alcona County Review, June 16, 1892

SOMEWHAT PERSONAL.

A Double Wedding.

Backus—Anthony, in Killmaster, by the Rev. D. H. Campbell, June 22d at the residence of the bride's parents, Mr. Austin D. Backus and Miss Ella A. Anthony, both of Killmaster.

Alcona County Review, June 30, 1892

HISTORY OF ONE YEAR.

Chronological History of the Past Year, 1892.

MARRIAGES.

June 22. Austin D. Backus to Ella A. Anthony at Killmaster.

Alcona County Review, January 5, 1893

Bailey, Herbert
Parks, Jennie

Somewhat Personal.

Herb Bailey led Miss Jennie Parks to the altar last Thursday, thereby entitling him to the congratulations of a wide circle of friends.

Alcona County Review, October 22, 1891

Balch, George W., Jr.
Mudgett, Carrie Bell

LOCAL JOTTINGS.

Miss Carrie Mudgett and George Balch, Jr., were quietly married before Justice Beede last Wednesday evening.

Alcona County Review, March 18, 1887

Barber, Eustache
Scott, Rachel

LOCAL JOTTINGS.

Eustache Barber and Miss Rachel Scott were married in Alpena last week. The groom is well known in this county.

Alcona County Review, July 12, 1889

Barber, James
?, Cora May

PERSONAL.

The employees of the Colwell shingle mill presented their fellow workman James Barbour, with an elegant piano lamp Tuesday, on the event of his marriage. It is needless to say "the shingle mill boys" have Jim's most hearty thanks.--Grand Marais Herald.

Alcona County Review, January 20, 1898

Barber, Nicholas N.
Buyers, Jessie M.

Married, Saturday, Aug. 1, Nicholas Barber and Miss Jessie Buyers, both of Alcona county. Ceremony performed by Rev. L. Hazard.

Alcona County Review, August 6, 1891

Barley, Archie
Miller, Anna

BLACK RIVER.

Black River, June 26.--Archie Baily went to Tawas last week on business. We don't know the name of the bride.

Alcona County Review, June 29, 1888

Barley, Archie
Bellmore, Victoria

Black River Sparks.

Reported that Archie Barley, a railroad "con," was united in marriage Tuesday at Harrisville to

Miss Victoria Bellmore. If true, allow us to congratulate.

Alcona County Review, September 26, 1895

Barnes, J. M.
Jouhgin, Jennie

Purely Personal.

The marriage of J. M. Barnes and Miss Jennie Joughin is announced. The latter is a niece of Pros. Atty. Smith and has many friends in this village, also at Au Sable where she has occupied a position for several years as a teacher in the public schools. Mr. and Mrs. Barnes will make their home at Sherwood, Mich. The Review extends congratulations and best wishes.

Alcona County Review, May 2, 1890

Baror, Henry
Betts, Bessie

LOCAL PICK UPS.

Friends of Henry Baror, a Harrisville boy popular with his associates, will be deeply interested in the announcement that comes from Hillsdale, Mich., of his marriage on Dec. 20th inst. to Miss Bessie Betts of that city. The Review sends congratulations.

Alcona County Review, December 29, 1898

Basher, Charles
Rhinehart, Barbara

REVIEWINGS.

Married.—In Harrisville, Mich., March 30th, 1880, by C. P. Reynolds, Esq., at his residence, Mr. Chas. Basher and Miss Barbara Rhinehart, all of Black River, Mich.

Alcona County Review, April 2, 1880

Beaton, Daniel
Lough, Hattie

ALPENA.

Daniel Beaton and Miss Hattie Lough were united in marriage Aug. 5th.

Alcona County Review, August 21, 1885

Beaton, Henry
Fettes, Sarah Anne

OTHER HAYNES NEWS.

Henry Beaton and Miss Sarah Fettis were united in marriage by the Rev. E. F. Smith, at the residence of the bride's father, on the 10th. I wish them joy on the happy event.

Alcona County Review, January 18, 1894

MARRIED.

Beaton—Fettes. At the residence of the bride's parents in Haynes, Jan. 10, 1894, Mr. Henry Beaton and Miss Sarah A. Fettis by Rev. E. F. Smith.

We judge by passing events that the hard times are teaching the young people that it is more economical to live together. As one Benedict said, his livery and confectionary bills were less.

The wedding of our young friends in Haynes was an occasion of much merriment, participated in by three generations, which about filled the house.

The bride and groom received numerous presents and congratulation, which, together with land and youth and love, will go far in enabling them to make a home for themselves. There was a tinge of sadness and an occasional tear would break through all efforts to conceal it, both on the part of the parents as they gave away their last daughter, and on the part of the bride as she realized that she must leave the dear associations of the old home, father, mother and brothers, and begin a new home.

May prosperity and joy attend them in their new venture in life, is the wish of their numerous friends.

Alcona County Review, January 18, 1894

Becker, Frederick Austin
Robinson, Esther S.

PERSONAL.

Married.—At the residence of the bridegroom's parents, Mr. and Mrs. Heath of Killmaster, on Thursday eve., Feb. 18th, '97, F. A. Becker and Miss Esther Robinson, both of Killmaster. Rev. F. S. Ford officiated. Only relatives and intimate friends were invited, and the evening was very pleasantly spent. After supper some very entertaining music was rendered and about midnight the friends retired, wishing the happy young couple a long prosperous life.

Mr. and Mrs. Becker are well known and very popular young people, and their many friends will wish them a peaceful voyage on the sea of life.

Alcona County Review, February 25, 1897

Beede, Fred Alger
Storms, Caroline M.

Local Sayings and Doings.

Married—In Harrisville, Sunday evening, June 25, 1882, by Rev. J. H. McIntosh, Mr. Fred A. Beede and Miss Carrie M. Storms, all of Harrisville, Mich.

The above named couple are well known to the people of this place, because of their long residence among us, and we may say their friends and well wishers are legion. The Review unites with all in wishing them a happy and prosperous future, hoping that their life may eventually be crowned by all those rich blessings which only Heaven hath the power to confer.

Alcona County Review, June 30, 1882

Beegle, Charles
?, {Bride}

ALL ALONG THE SHORE.

Oscoda and Au Sable Notes.

From the Democrat.

The sweetheart of Charles Beegle, of Big Creek township, Oscoda Co., arrived there June 28, direct from Germany. She traveled alone and was twenty-nine days on the way, and came all this distance to be married to Charley. And they were married. Constancy thou art indeed a jewel.

Alcona County Review, July 8, 1887

Beever, George B.
Cummings, Hannah Melissa

SOMEWHAT PERSONAL.

Geo. Beever, son of Robt. Beever, was married Saturday last to Miss Melissa Cummings at the residence of the bride's parents, the Rev. W. J. Bailey officiating.

Alcona County Review, August 18, 1892

HISTORY OF ONE YEAR.

Chronological History of the Past Year, 1892.

MARRIAGES.

August 12. Geo. Beever to Melissa Cummings, both of Harrisville.

Alcona County Review, January 5, 1893

Bell, James
McRae, Fannie J.

The Tie That Binds.

The marriage of Mr. James Bell of West Harrisville to Miss Fannie McRae of Greenbush, occurs today at the home of the bride's parents in Greenbush.

The bridegroom is the well known merchant. The bride is well known to a majority of Review readers and is a young lady possessed of many charms of person and manners. The review joins their many friends in wishing them all due happiness. They will be at home at West Harrisville after May 1st.

Alcona County Review, April 23, 1896

West Harrisville.

The people of this village extend congratulations to Mr. and Mrs. Bell and wish them every success in life.

Alcona County Review, April 30, 1896

Two Hearts That Beat as One.

On Thursday evening, April 23rd, at the home of the bride's father, Mr. Duncan McRae of Greenbush, Mr. James Bell of West Harrisville, and Miss Fannie McRae, of Greenbush, were united in marriage.

The house was very tastefully and profusely decorated with beautiful flowers. Mr. Bell was supported by James Blackstock, his business partner; Miss Ida McRae was maid of honor, the pastor, Rev. F. S. Ford, officiating.

After the service the bride and groom led the way to the dining room where the happy company were confronted with all the good things in and out of season and a very pleasant evening was spent.

Mr. and Mrs. Bell commence married life under favorable circumstances. Mr. Bell is a prosperous business man and his bride is an estimable young lady and both have a host of friends who will wish them a peaceful and pleasant voyage through life.

On Friday morning the happy couple left Greenbush for their new home at West Harrisville amid a shower of rice and old shoes—while the band played.

Our beautiful Fannie was married today.
Beautiful Fannie with soft brown hair,
Whose shadows fall o'er a face as fair
As the snowy blooms of the early May.
We have kissed her lips and sent her away
With many a blessing and many a prayer,

The pet of our home who was married to-day.

Alcona County Review, April 30, 1896

Bell, Manley A.
LaFleur, Harriett T.

CURTISVILLE.

Too late for last week.

Mr. Manly Bell and Miss Hattie La Fleur were quietly married at the bride's home on Sunday, Nov. 12. Mr. and Mrs. Bell have the best wishes of a large circle of friends.

Alcona County Review, November 23, 1899

Bennett, J. .F.
Bissell, Evelyn

Somewhat Personal.

A quiet wedding took place at the residence of the parents of the bride on Clark street Thursday evening, at which J. F. Bennett was united in marriage to Miss Evalin Bissell by Rev. J. R. Beach.—*Saginaw Herald*, April 23rd.

The bride was but recently a resident of Springport, where she resided with her parents.

Alcona County Review, April 28, 1892

Bernard, Joseph
Ross, Jane

The Local News.

The county clerk has issued a marriage license to Jos. Bernard of Haynes and Jane Ross of Au Sable, also one to Christ Regier and Evadne L. Deacon, both of Curtis township.

Alcona County Review, May 9, 1890

Our Neighbors.

Jos. Bernard of West Harrisville has enlisted in the noble army of Benedicts by taking unto himself an Au Sable lady for a wife.

Alcona County Review, May 9, 1890

Bessinger, George
Emmel, Mabel

Mabel Emmel, a former resident of this place was married to Geo. Bessinger Monday at Ausable.

Alcona County Review, September 22, 1898

Best, Arthur
?, {Bride}

Purely Personal.

Arthur Best was in town this week preparatory to a visit to Canada. Best committed the offence of getting

married last fall to a nice young lady across the line and keeping the matter a dead secret from all his friends until it accidentally came to the surface as all things will, in accordance with the old truism "Murder will out." This trip to Canada it is understood is for the purpose of bringing Mrs. Best to Michigan. Mr. and Mrs. Best have the best wishes of the bridegroom's many friends in Harrisville and the woods.

Alcona County Review, May 2, 1890

Bickell, W. R.
Norton, Mrs. Eva

LOCAL JOTTINGS.

Married—At Alcona M. E. Parsonage, by Rev. R. H. Balmer, on the evening of the 5th inst., W. R. Bickell and Mrs. Eva Norton, all of Alcona.

Alcona County Review, December 12, 1884

Bickle, George J.
Mason, Ellen

EVENTS OF ONE WEEK.

Married at the M. E. parsonage, Aug. 20, 1895, by the Rev. W. J. Bailey, Mr. George J. Bickle to Miss Ellen Mason, both of Harrisville, Mich.

Alcona County Review, August 22, 1895

Billings, Samuel Olen
Pearson, Anna Louisa

WEDDING BELLS.

From the Parsons, W. Va. Democrat.

One of the prettiest weddings that has taken place in Tucker county for a decade was celebrated at the residence of Mr. R. P. Pearson on last Tuesday, July 10, at 1:30 p.m.

The contracting parties were Mr. Samuel Olen Billings, Commissioner of the Circuit Court, and Miss Anna Louisa Pearson, both of this place.

Mr. Billings is one of our foremost business men: besides being Commissioner of the Court he is engaged in the real estate and insurance business and has before him a bright career. The bride is one of the charming and accomplished daughters of Mr. and Mrs. R. P. Pearson.

The parlor where the ceremony took place was beautifully decorated with flowers and evergreens, and as the wedding march was being played

Mr. Pearson entered with his charming daughter leaning upon his arm and gave her away. The officiating minister, Rev. C. E. Glenn, stood beneath a beautiful and artistic arch of evergreens with a horse shoe encircled by a handsome wreath of rhododendrons in the center.

After the congratulations common on such occasions, the party retired to the dining room where refreshments were served, consisting of ice-cream, cake and all fruits and delicacies of the season.

At 2:45 p. m. the carriage arrived at the door and the happy couple and their attendants, amid a shower of rice and slippers that have seen better days, were driven to the depot, where the two that is now one, took their departure on the east bound train to spend their honeymoon. At the depot they were treated to a second shower of rice until the train bore them away.

Alcona County Review, July 19, 1894

PERSONAL MENTION.

In another column the Review reprints an extract from the Tucker County (W. Va.) Democrat describing the recent marriage of Miss Anna Pearson, until quite recently a resident of this village. Cards have been received by many personal friends of the bride announcing the event, and this account of the ceremony will be read with special interest by them as well as by the many friends and acquaintances of the bride and her family.

Alcona County Review, July 19, 1894

Biron, Joseph
Maynard, Mary L.
BIRON--MAYNARD.
Miss Mary L. Maynard and Mr. Joseph Biron were quietly united in marriage in the city of Manchester, N. H., July 3, 1898. The bride is the eldest daughter of Mr. and Mrs. Edmund Maynard. Mr. and Mrs. Biron will make their home in Lawrence.

Alcona County Review, August 4, 1898

Birtch, Dresden E.
Baker, Mrs. J. C.
People We Hear About.

The Rev. Dresden Birtch was married a few days ago to Mrs. J. C. Baker at Bay City. The bridegroom is well known in this county.

Alcona County Review, October 10, 1890

Blackwell, Bert
Dalton, Pursie
Gustin Grist.

Gustin, Feb. 5.—Henry S. Dalton arrived home the 2d to be present at the wedding of his daughter, Pursie, which takes place this evening.

Alcona County Review, February 7, 1895

Gustin Grist.

A very fine evening was spent at H. S. Dalton's after the wedding on Tuesday evening.

Alcona County Review, February 14, 1895

Gustin Grist.

H. S. Dalton has gone back to Detroit, where he is engaged in the salt business. His new son-in-law, Bert Blackwell, has gone to Petrolia, Ont.

Alcona County Review, February 14, 1895

Gustin Grist.

Some of the Killmaster boys, as an act of courtesy, went out to serenade the newly married couple who came from Petrolia, Ont., to spend their honeymoon with the bride's parents at this place. The boys received a treat—I do not mean he came out and bought the cigars, for he did not, but the good mother-in-law came out and favored them with a temperance lecture which did not seem to satisfy the boys, so they came back the second time. Then the groom appeared and offered to fire the boys all in the snow bank and told them they had not been brought up in the woods. A mean trick, Bert.

Some of the bride's friends who did not have the pleasure of seeing her wish to congratulate her through this paper by wishing her much joy and many happy days. "Shorty" also wishes them many happy days.

("The Joker" sends a lengthy account of this same affair, but on account of its length and limited space, we are obliged to omit it. Thanks for it just the same.)
Feb. 12, 1895.

Alcona County Review, February 14, 1895

Blakeney, Earl D.
Beever, Charlotte Emma

Earl D. Blakney procured a marriage license from the county clerk Saturday, and bright and early Monday morning, accompanied by Miss Emma Beever, repaired to the M. E. parsonage in Harrisville where the twain were made one. The couple left on the stage for Au Sable the same morning. Geo. W. Beever, father of the bride, was somewhat incensed at the marriage for the girl had only reached her 16th birthday the morning of the marriage, although in the affidavit the age was given as 17 at her last birthday. As the couple are safely and securely married it is likely that the course of true love will not be interrupted.

Alcona County Review, July 7, 1892

HISTORY OF ONE YEAR.

Chronological History of the Past Year, 1892.

MARRIAGES.
July 4. Earl Blakney to Emma Beever.

Alcona County Review, January 5, 1893

Blanchard, Arthur H.
Campbell, Ina May
COUNTY REVIEWINGS.

We learn that Miss May Campbell, of Greenbush, and Mr. A. H. Blanchard, of Oscoda, were married at the latter place on the 12th inst.

Alcona County Review, July 16, 1880

Boddy, Edward E.
Blake, Charlotte Ann
LOCAL JOTTINGS.

Edward E. Boddy and Charlotte A. Blake are the names of two young people of Curtis township attached to a marriage license issued from the clerk's office Monday.

Alcona County Review, September 20, 1889

Bolster, William
Duggan, Maria
REVIEWINGS.

Married: At the Exchange Hotel, in Harrisville, June 26th, by Rev. D. VanDyke, Capt. William Bolster of Detroit, and Miss Maria Duggan of Harrisville.

The happy couple left for Detroit on Monday morning's boat, where the Capt. will take command of a passenger steamer, running from Detroit to the Islands. We wish them a long life of happiness and prosperity.

Alcona County Review, July 4, 1879

Bolton, Robert
Dove, Cynthia Ellen

ALONG THE SHORE.

General News-Gleanings From the Several Counties.

ALPENA.

Recent marriages hereabouts: May 26, Angus McDonald and Miss Margaret J. Hall. May 30, Robert Keen and Miss Eliza Ann Wilson. June 3, Robert Bolton and Miss Cynthia Ellen Dove.

Alcona County Review, June 11, 1880

Bond, Joshua
Carr, Violet

South Harrisville.

Joshua Bond was united in marriage to Miss Violet Carr at Tawas about three weeks ago.
South Harrisville, Apr. 10th.

Alcona County Review, April 11, 1895

Bonner, Thomas P.
Campbell, Minnie H.

LOCAL JOTTINGS.

Married—At the Church of the Sacred Heart, Oscoda, on Monday, August 4, by Rev. C. J. Roche, Thos. P. Bonner and Minnie H. Campbell, both of Oscoda.

The newly married couple were given a wedding dinner by Mrs. Arthur Blanchard, sister of the bride, at which there were several invited guests. The bride was the recipient of many beautiful presents. Both bride and groom are well known in Oscoda and Au Sable where each has numerous friends, with whom Saturday Night joins in wishing for the happy pair a joyous future.— Au Sable Saturday Night.

The bride is a daughter of Colin Campbell of Greenbush, but has been living with her sister in Oscoda for some time past. "Tom," as he is familiarly known, also has many friends among the young people of

this county who will join those of his native town in well wishes.

Alcona County Review, August 15, 1884

Bowser, Frederick N.
Dixon, Maude

Marriage licenses have been issued this week to Bartholomue McNally and Adelia Twite of Black River and Ferdinand Bowser and Maud Dixon of Curtis.

Alcona County Review, May 2, 1895

Curtis Items.

May 6, 1895.
Miss Maud Dickinson and Fred Bowser are to be married Tuesday, the 7th. A fine looking couple. Hope they will enjoy life as loving at the last of their days as they do at present.

Alcona County Review, May 9, 1895

Orange Blossoms.

Married at the Baptist church at Curtis, at the close of the evening service May 7th, by Rev. A. Waterbury assisted by their pastor elect, Rev. G. W. Fayette, Mr. Frederick N. Bowser and Miss Maud Dixon, both of Curtis, Mich.

Many friends of the parties were at the marriage feast at the home of the groom, in the afternoon: and nearly a church full of people gave their congratulations at the close of the ceremony in the evening.

The best wishes of all who know them accompany the bridal pair entering thus upon the voyage of life.

Alcona County Review, May 9, 1895

Boyer, John
Jarvis, Hattie

HOME REVIEWINGS.

Married, at the Catholic church in Harrisville, Monday, Aug. 1st, by Rev. C. J. Roche, Mr. John Boyer and Miss Hattie Jarvis (sister of Mrs. Jno. Oven) all of Harrisville.

Alcona County Review, August 5, 1881

HOME REVIEWINGS.

John Oven, fireman and assistant engineer in Colwell's mill, with family, and also John Boyer and wife, will take their departure for Bay City the fore part of next week to reside.

Alcona County Review, August 5, 1881

Bridgeman, Henry

Nevin, Charlotte D.

PURELY PERSONAL.

Henry Bridgeman, of Duluth, Minn., and Miss Charlotte Nevins, of this place, were united in marriage Monday evening. They left for their future home at Duluth this week.

Alcona County Review, September 23, 1887

MARRIED.

In Harrisville, Sept. 19th, at the residence of the bride's father, by the Rev. F. N. Barlow, Mr. Henry Bridgeman, of Duluth, Minn., and Miss Charlotte D. Nevins, of Harrisville.

Alcona County Review, September 23, 1887

LOCAL JOTTINGS.

Henry Bridgeman, who recently carried away one of Alcona county's fair daughters, sends this office the collateral for a year's subscription for the Review. His address is 1536 West Michigan st., Duluth, Minn.

Alcona County Review, November 11, 1887

Briggs, Ernest A.
McNally, Alice M. [Frasier]

At the Altar.

Briggs-Frasier—Mr. Ernest Briggs, son of Chas. C. Briggs, and Miss Alice McNally (Frasier) were quietly married Sunday evening by the Rev. W. W. Will at the home of the bride. They are among the most popular of the young people of Harrisville and a pleasant matrimonial journey should be theirs.

Alcona County Review, November 21, 1895

PERSONAL MENTION.

Mr. and Mrs. Ernest Briggs are comfortably housed in the residence of Chas. Briggs, Sr., who is living with his son this winter.

Alcona County Review, November 28, 1895

Briggs, Frank H.
Dean, Annie

Briggs—Dean.

Married at Oakland, Cal., Sept. 9, 1896, by the pastor of the Free Methodist church of Almeda, Mr. Frank H. Briggs and Miss Annie Dean, both of Almeda.

After the ceremony the bridal couple returned to Almeda, where the groom had a home prepared for its new occupant.

On Friday the 11th they took their departure for Ukiah, Cal., for a visit with the bride's mother and other relatives. They will be at home to their friends at Almeda, Cal., after Oct. 15th, '96.

The groom is a son of C. C. Briggs of Harrisville.

Alcona County Review, October 8, 1896

Briggs, J. C.
Prell, Blanch

Married, at the residence of the officiating clergyman in Alicel, Oregon, May 5, 1895, Mr. J. C. Briggs, of Starkey, and Miss Blanch Prell, of Island City; Rev. Reasoner officiating.

Alcona County Review, May 16, 1895

Bright, C.J.
Larson, Jennie M.

PERSONAL MENTION.

Married at Wasco, Oregon, June 14, 1896, by the Rev. Edward Baker, C. J. Bright and Jennie M. Larson. Miss Larson formerly resided at Harrisville.

Alcona County Review, July 2, 1896

Broadwood, Alexander
McMaster, Adaline

ECHOS FROM GREENBUSH.
Greenbush, Dec. 30.—By the Rev. J. Robbins, at the residence of Edward McMaster, Mr. Alexander Broadwood and Miss Adaline McMaster were united in the holy bonds of matrimony, on Sunday, Dec. 19. All the above of Gustin Center.

Alcona County Review, December 31, 1886

Brooks, John W.
Wolf, Mary

The Local News

Jno. Brooks and Mary Wolf were married last week at Black River.

Alcona County Review, March 24, 1892

Broun, Oscar
Fisher, Satie

LOCAL PICK UPS.
Cards have been received here announcing the marriage of Miss Satie Fisher, second daughter of Joseph Fisher, to Mr. Oscar Broun. The ceremony occurred yesterday at the M. E. church, St. Maries, Idaho.

Alcona County Review, June 8, 1899

Brower, Nicholas
Jordan, Ella

Somewhat Personal.

Miss Ella Jordan, a former Black River teacher, was married two weeks since to Nicholas Brower of Black River.

Alcona County Review, October 29, 1891

Brownlee, Robert
Atkins, Susan

PURELY PERSONAL.
Robert Brownlee, of West Harrisville, was married July 30 to Miss Susan Adkins, of Oscoda, by the Rev. J. B. Lambley.

Alcona County Review, August 12, 1887

LOCAL JOTTINGS.
The course of true love did not run as smooth as it might between Robert J. Brownlee and Sarah Atkins, and the twain have separated after a honeymoon lasting less than three weeks. Sarah is a giddy girl and skipped from her lord and the latter says that he is glad she did.

Alcona County Review, August 19, 1887

Bruce, Daniel D.
McGillis, Mary Ann

PURELY PERSONAL.

Daniel D. Bruce, Mikado, was in very happy frame of mind when he was in town Monday. Reason, going to get married.

Alcona County Review, June 8, 1888

MIKADO MATTERS.

Mikado, June 5.--The events of the season were the weddings of Christian Heinold, of Mikado to Miss Rodha, of Handy last Thursday, and D. D. Bruce and a Miss McGillis on Tuesday, June 5. The latter departed on the south bound train.

Alcona County Review, June 8, 1888

LOCAL JOTTINGS.

Daniel D. Bruce, of Mikado, and Mary Ann McGillis, Gustin, are the names that appear as principals in marriage license No 21. The Review extends best wishes for a long and happy married life.

Alcona County Review, June 8, 1888

Bryan, Peter W.
Cowan, Etta

MARRIED.
In Harrisville, Sept. 2d, 1887, by the Rev. F. N. Barlow, Mr. Peter W. Bryan and Miss Etta Cowan, both of Gustin Center.

Alcona County Review, September 16, 1887

Bryne, George W.
Buyers, Mary

MARRIED.
In Harrisville, July 2d, by Rev. F. N. Barlow, Geo. Bryne, of Gustin, to Miss Mary Buyers, of Harrisville.

Alcona County Review, July 6, 1888

Buchanan, William
Beever, Jennie

MARRIED.
At the residence of the bride's parents in this township, Saturday evening, June 30, by the Rev. C. B. Steele, William Buchanan and Miss Jennie Beever, both of Harrisville.

Alcona County Review, July 6, 1888

Buck, William A.
Lotz, Minnie

LOCAL JOTTINGS.

Wm. A. Buck, aged 22, and Minnie Lotz, aged 16, both of Mud Lake, have taken out a license to wed.

Alcona County Review, April 26, 1889

Budd, Warren A.
Clark, Martha

The county clerk issued a marriage license Nov. 23d to Warren A. Budd, aged 28, of Haynes and Martha Clark, aged 31, of Tawas. Yesterday Angus W. Smith, aged 25, of Grindstone City, was licensed to marry Florence Cowan, aged 17, of Gustin.

Alcona County Review, December 1, 1892

Budreaux, William
Bonan, Carrie

Somewhat Personal.
Fr. Mahar made a parochial call Monday on old Mr. Tovey, who is quite feeble at the advanced age of 97. While here the Father united two couples of young people from the French settlement in marriage.

Alcona County Review, March 3, 1892

Bunard, William
Hart, Julia

The Local News.

Wm. Bunard, aged 19, and Julia Hart, aged 18, were married Monday morning in the Catholic church by the Rev. Fr. Reusseman. They are residents of Harrisville township.

Alcona County Review, August 13, 1891

Burcham, James F.
Hyke, Elizabeth

EVENTS OF ONE WEEK.

James F. Burcham of Sherman and Elizabeth Hyke of West Harrisville were married at Tawas on Wednesday, Nov. 28, by Justice Murphy.

Alcona County Review, December 6, 1894

Burge, Edward
Somers, Anne Cordelia

Burge-Somers.—At the Methodist parsonage, Aug. 28, by the Rev. Wm. Bailey, Mr. Edw. Burge to Miss Annie Somers both of Hawse.

Alcona County Review, August 29, 1895

Burkhart, John
Hart, Selina

EVENTS OF ONE WEEK.

John Berkhart will wed Miss Salina Hart next Tuesday and a wedding dance at the bride's home will be given in the evening, to which they extend an invitation to all their friends.

Alcona County Review, October 24, 1895

West Harrisville.
Oct. 30, 1895.
A few of our people attended the wedding dance of John Burkhart and Miss Salina Hart.

Alcona County Review, October 31, 1895

Quite a crowd went out to the wedding at Hart's Tuesday evening and according to all reports they had a ga-lorious time.

Alcona County Review, October 31, 1895

Burkhart, William
Balch, Mrs. Elizabeth

LOCAL PICK UPS.
Wm. Burkhart and Mrs. Lizzie Balch were married March 23 by Rev. W. W. Will. The ceremony occurred at the residence of Mr. John Burkhart.

Alcona County Review, March 30, 1899

Burnham, Newton A.
Tweedley, Mary [Miller]

EVENTS OF ONE WEEK.

The following from the Buffalo Express of the 17th inst. explains the fate of a young man well known to many Review readers, as a brother-in-law of Prof. Sheehan.

A quiet wedding was celebrated at the home of the bride's mother, No. 21 Lawrence Place, on Thursday evening, when Mary Miller Tweedley was married to Newton A. Burnham. The ceremony was performed by the Rev. W. C. Wilbor. The bride wore cream silk and carried white roses. She was attended by her sister, Isabella M., while Norman L., brother of the groom, acted as best man. The newly-wedded couple will be at home at No. 347 Normal Avenue after April 1st.

Alcona County Review, March 28, 1895

Burnham, Smith
Caster, Ella E.

PERSONAL MENTION.

Ella E. Caster, daughter of Presiding Elder Caster, was recently married to Prof. Smith Burnham of Albion College.

Alcona County Review, September 14, 1893

Burt, George
Genge, Mary H.

MARRIED.
At the M. E. parsonage in Oscoda, 30th ult., by Rev. R. Woodhams, George Burt and Miss Mary H. Genge, both of Harrisville.

The Review extends congratulations to George and Mary, and wishes them a long life of unalloyed happiness and prosperity.

Alcona County Review, January 13, 1882

Burt, Jerome
McIntyre, Dora Emma

LOCAL JOTTINGS.

Married: On the 15th inst., by the Rev. T. B. Leith, at the residence of the bride's mother, Jerome Burt and Miss Dora Emma McIntyre, all of Harrisville. May heaven's richest blessing grow the union of Jerome and Dora, is the Review's best wish, which could not be more fully expressed were we to devote a column of "sweet words" to the subject.

Alcona County Review, February 20, 1885

Burt, John
McIntyre, Isabel M.

COUNTY JOTTINGS.
At the residence of the bride's mother, Mrs. Mary J. McIntyre, Nov. 13th, by Rev. N. N. Clark, Mr. John Burt and Miss Isabel M. McIntyre, all of Harrisville.

Alcona County Review, November 15, 1878

Burt, John H.
Hamilton, Flora [McRae]

MARRIAGE LICENSES.
The following marriage licenses have been issued by County Clerk Rutson:

Nov. 10, John H. Burt, Alcona, 64 [and] Flora Hamilton, Harrisville, 65.

Alcona County Review, November 18, 1887

Buxton, Benjamin Warder
Gullifer, Mildred

Married at Lansing.
From Republican, March 1st.
At 1 o'clock, this afternoon, a very small party witnessed a charming home wedding at the residence of Mr. and Mrs. Fred J. Hopkins, 710 Washington ave. north, when Miss Mildred Gullifer a daughter of Mr. and Mrs. F. O. Gullifer of Detroit and niece of Mrs. Hopkins, was united in marriage to Mr. Benjamin Warder Buxton, according to the ring service of the Congregational church, Rev. Clarence F. Swift officiating. The bride was attired in a handsome tailored gown of brown whipcord. Following the service an elaborate luncheon was served at which the decorations were pin carnations and smilax. Among the guests was Thomas Gullifer of Detroit, a brother of the bride. The groom is a very promising young business man of Detroit, being secretary of the firm of Moran, Fitzsimmons & Co., wholesale grocers, and the bride, formerly a resident of Lansing, is popularly known here. Mr. and Mrs. Buxton went to Detroit this afternoon, and after March 10 will be at home at 107 East High street.

Alcona County Review, March 10, 1898

Buyers, John F.
Kearly, Margaret J.

LOCAL JOTTINGS.

Married: On the 26th inst., at the M. E. Parsonage, by the Rev. T. B. Leith, John F. Buyers and Margaret J. Kearly.

Alcona County Review, October 2, 1885

Byce, Charles M.
Hart, Mary

LOCAL PICK UPS.

Mr. Charles Byce and Miss Mary Hart were united in marriage last evening by Justice Hale. The Review extends congratulations and best wishes.

Alcona County Review, April 13, 1899

Byce, Clarence
Simons, Lottie

Clarence Byce of Goodar, Mich., was licensed last week to marry Lottie Simons of Curtis.

Alcona County Review, April 14, 1892

Byce, Frederick S.
Thornton, Olla Alberta

Byce—Thornton. At the home of the bridegroom's parents, Mr. Daniel Byce, Feb. 6, 1894, by the Rev. W. J. Bailey, Mr. Frederick Byce to Miss Ollie Thornton, both of Harrisville, Mich.

Alcona County Review, February 8, 1894

Byce, Walter
Lemon, Alice

EVENTS OF ONE WEEK.

Walter Byce and Miss Alice Lemon, young people well and favorably known in this county, were married at Alpena this week.

Alcona County Review, July 7, 1893

EVENTS OF ONE WEEK.

The announcement in last week's issue of this paper of the marriage of Mr. Walter Byce and Miss Alice Lemon, was a little premature: They were not made one until Friday last, when the knot was securely tied by Rev. W. J. Bailey at the parsonage.

Alcona County Review, July 13, 1893

Campbell, Charles
Moore, May

BLACK RIVER.

Miss May Moore, daughter of Jas. Moore and one of Black River's popular young ladies, was united in the holy bonds of wedlock with Mr. Chas. Campbell, principal of the Tawas public schools, at East Tawas Monday evening of this week.

Alcona County Review, September 24, 1896

Campbell, Charles D.
Covelle, Jennie [Bloodgood]

LOCAL PICK UPS.

Chas. Campbell of Black River and Miss Jennie Bloodgood of Harrisville were married Tuesday at Harrisville. Rev. W. W. Will performed the ceremony.

Alcona County Review, February 23, 1899

Campbell, Duncan
Fettes, Agnes

MARRIED.

Campbell-Fettes.—In Harrisville, Feb. 2d, 1887, by Rev. F. N. Barlow, Duncan Campbell and Miss Agnes Fettes, both of Alcona.

Alcona County Review, February 4, 1887

Campbell, Fred E.
Byce, Ida

LOCAL PICK UPS.

We are informed that Mr. Fred Campbell and Miss Ida Byce two of Harrisville's popular young people were united in marriage at the home of the bride's parents last evening. May they live long and prosper is the Review's worst wish for them.

Alcona County Review, April 20, 1899

Campbell, McDonald N.
Hood, Margaret A.

County Reviewings.

Married.— At the residence of the bride's father, Alcona, June 21st, 1877, by Rev. N. N. Clark, McDonald N. Campbell and Margaret A. Hood, both of this county.

Alcona County Review, June 22, 1877

Campbell, Samuel E.
Reynolds, Jennie E.

PURELY PERSONAL.

Dr. S. E. Campbell went to Bay City Thursday where he was to be married on the evening of that day to Miss Jennie E. Reynolds.

Alcona County Review, January 13, 1888

Wedding Bells.

Brief mention was made last week of the marriage of Dr. S. E. Campbell, of this place, to Miss Jennie E. Reynolds, of Bay City, at that place, Thursday evening, Jan. 12th. The Tribune contains the following in regard to the event:

At the residence of Mr. and Mrs. F. H. Reynolds, Fremont avenue, Thursday evening, were assembled some 30 or 40 guests, the occasion being the marriage of their daughter Jennie to Dr. S. E. Campbell. The ceremony was performed in a very

impressive manner by Rev. E. Chesney, after which the company sat down to a bounteous repast, to which full justice was done. Upon reassembling in the parlors the guests, by request, affixed their autographs to a beautiful wedding souvenir or album, which will doubtless be highly prized by the happy couple. The presents, consisting of silverware, glassware, crockery, plush and bronze, books and pictures, were beautiful and useful, but too numerous and varied to admit of individual mention. The bride was one of the most popular and esteemed young ladies in this part of the city, and she will be greatly missed, especially in the church and Sunday school, where she has been a most active and zealous worker. In this our loss will be Harrisville's gain, as that village is to be their future home, the doctor having there an extensive and lucrative practice. The best wishes of their numerous friends are heartily extended.

Alcona County Review, January 20, 1888

PURELY PERSONAL.

Dr. S. E. Campbell and bride returned Monday evening from Bay City.

Alcona County Review, January 20, 1888

It is undoubtedly in entire accord with the custom of this section to subject a newly married couple to all the horrors of discordant sounds usually produced at a charivari party, the object, of course, being to thus compel the happy bridegroom to purchase quietness by "setting 'em up" to the boys. But the circumstances hardly justify the length to which the charivari of Monday night was carried, and much indignation is expressed on all sides at the wanton manner in which some reckless individual discharged firearms.

Alcona County Review, January 20, 1888

PURELY PERSONAL.

Dr. S. E. Campbell goes to Bay City Friday morning to accompany his wife back to Harrisville. They will go to housekeeping upon their return, having leased the residence of F. Kennedy.

Alcona County Review, June 1, 1888

Cardy, Louis J., Jr.

Lytle, Francis Ida

Purely Personal.

Louis Cardy, Jr., member of the Sturgeon Pointe life saving crew and son of the light house keeper at the same place, was married to Miss Ida Lytle of Sand Beach last Saturday evening. The happy event was celebrated at Sturgeon Pointe at the residence of Captain Henderson whose wife is a sister of the bride. The bridegroom is one of Alcona county's most highly respected young men. The bride has made many friends here during her frequent visits to Sturgeon Pointe. The Review extends congratulations.

Alcona County Review, December 20, 1889

Carle, William F.
Code, Sadie

REVIEWINGS.

Married: At Alcona, Sunday, July 6, by Rev. D. VanDyke, Mr. Willie F. Carle and Miss Satie Code, all of Harrisville.

We most heartily congratulate this young happy couple upon the new relations in life which they have assumed, and hope they may live long, always be happy, and enjoy never failing prosperity. May God speed them in the right.

Alcona County Review, July 11, 1879

Carle, William F.
McGillis, Sarah

Married.

Carl—McGillis Tuesday, Jan. 31, 1893, at the Alcona House in the village of Harrisville, Mr. Will F. Carle of Joliet, Ill., to Miss Sarah McGillis of Alcona County.

The groom is a son of Mrs. E. Carle, proprietor of the Alcona House, and was a resident for many years of this county, having been engaged in the hotel and merchantile business in Alcona village in its palmy days, coming to Harrisville at the opening of the Alcona House. Since leaving Harrisville he has been railroading and is at present located in Illinois. The bride is well and favorably known as a resident of Harrisville and Mikado townships and enjoys the friendship and esteem of a wide circle of acquaintances.

The ceremony was performed at 4 o'clock p.m. by Justice Beede in the presence of fifteen invited guests and

an hour later they sat down to discuss an elaborate menu, served in Mrs. Carle's most approved style. This was followed by music and an enjoyable evening was passed, oysters being served at 9 o'clock, making a pleasing variation. The bride and groom were the recipients of many valuable gifts. They will remain in Harrisville until Saturday, when they will take their departure for Joliet, Ill., where they will make their home for the present.

The following were present by invitation: Mr. and Mrs. W. C. Lee of Mikado, Mrs. J. Taft, Mr. and Mrs. E. W. Chapelle, Mr. and Mrs. Chas. Conklin, the Misses Matie and Lyda Taft, and Messrs. Chas. Mayo, F. A. Beede, L. W. Taft, Fred Reynolds, H. A. Joughin, Walter Chapelle.

Alcona County Review, February 2, 1893

Carlson, Charles
Anderson, Jennie

The Local News.

Peter Carlson, aged 21, was licensed last week to marry Mary John, aged 31. The same day Chas. Carlson, aged 26, was licensed to marry Jennie Anderson, aged 30. All parties are residents of Caledonia.

Alcona County Review, September 24, 1891

Carlson, Peter
Jehn, Mary

The Local News.

Peter Carlson, aged 21, was licensed last week to marry Mary Jehn, aged 31. The same day Chas. Carlson, aged 26, was licensed to marry Jennie Anderson, aged 30. All parties are residents of Caledonia.

Alcona County Review, September 24, 1891

Carpenter, O. N.
Scott, Mrs. George

TAWAS CITY.

O. N. Carpenter and Mrs. Geo. Scott, of East Tawas, were married last week.

Alcona County Review, January 9, 1885

Carson, Amond
Lyman, Emma [Eilbert]

LOCAL JOTTINGS.

"Kit Carson" and Mrs. Emma Lyman, of this place, are said to have been married at Black River, Wednesday.

Alcona County Review, March 6, 1885

LOCAL JOTTINGS.

The Review is informed that "the boys" who imbibe saloon atmosphere more or less in the lower part of town, "did up" Kit Carson very disgracefully one day this week. Getting him "stone drunk" at one of the saloons, as we are told, they put him into a sleigh, formed a line with pall bearers, etc., and proceeded to give unconscious Kit the benefits of a mock funeral, by escorting him to the home of his new wife.

Alcona County Review, March 13, 1885

Cavanagh, Charles
Brahaney, Maud

PERSONAL MENTION.

Chas. Cavanagh and bride nee Maud Brahany, both former residents of Black River, were enjoying a few days of their honeymoon in Harrisville the past week, the guests of Jas. McClelland and family. They will reside at Flint, Mich.

Alcona County Review, October 1, 1896

Chambers, William N.
Angell, Nellie

People We Hear About.

A marriage license was issued last week to Will Chambers and Miss Nellie Angell. The marriage was solemnized a couple of days later at the home of the bride's parents in Au Sable. The bridegroom is an Alcona county boy, having resided here since early childhood, and is a young man of excellent habits. The bride is a school teacher. Mr. and Mrs. C. will go to housekeeping soon and will make their home in Harrisville. We extend congratulations and best wishes.

Alcona County Review, August 22, 1890

People We Hear About.

Will Chambers returned Monday evening. His bride is teaching and will be in Harrisville in a couple of weeks when they will go to house-keeping at once.

Alcona County Review, August 22, 1890

People We Hear About.

Mrs. Jas. Nevin accompanied her son Will to Au Sable last week and was present at his marriage Sunday.

Alcona County Review, August 22, 1890

People We Hear About.

Will Chambers Sundayed in Au Sable. He has leased the Ellis cottage on South Lake street and will go to housekeeping there on the arrival of Mrs. Chambers.

Alcona County Review, August 29, 1890

People We Hear About.

Mrs. Will Chambers, bride of our young townsman, arrived in the village last week and they are now keeping house in one of the Ellis cottages on South Lake street.

Alcona County Review, September 12, 1890

Chambers, William N.
Perry, Nellie Dora
PERSONAL.

Will Chambers caused a small sized sensation by returning from Bay City Monday night accompanied by Mrs. Chambers, nee Nellie Perry. They were married New Years eve at the home of the bride's parents in Bay City. Mr. Chambers made it all satisfactory to the Review staff and congratulations are hereby extended.

Alcona County Review, January 6, 1898

Chapelle, Edward W.
Ralston, Ida May
Ring Those Chiming Bells.
A social event that has been among the probabilities for a number of months past transpired at Au Sable Monday and Edward W. Chapelle and Miss Ida M. Ralston, two of our best known young people, were united in the holy bonds of matrimony. Miss Ralston did not accompany her parents to Astoria, Oregon, but since their departure she has been visiting relatives at East Saginaw and Au Sable. The newly wedded couple will return to Harrisville in a few days where they will reside this winter, when they expect to swell the tide that has been setting in for a couple of years past towards the boundless West. They have the best wishes of the Review.

Alcona County Review, September 21, 1888

MARRIED.
Chapelle-Ralston-Sept. 17, 1888, at Au Sable, by the Rev. R. L. Williams, Edward W. Chapelle, of Harrisville, and Miss Ida May Ralston, of Au Sable.

Alcona County Review, September 21, 1888

PURELY PERSONAL.

Edward W. Chapelle and bride, nee Miss Ida M. Ralston, came up to Harrisville Sunday evening by boat, and they are now keeping house at the home of the former's parents in this village.

Alcona County Review, September 28, 1888

Chase, Martin J.
Carr, Mary Jane
Somewhat Personal.

Martin Chase, engineer of the flour mill, was married last week to Mary Carr of Alpena.

Alcona County Review, March 10, 1892

Chiritree, Calvin
Sinton, Isabella
PERSONAL POINTS.

Calvin Chiritree and Miss Belle Sinton, two of our best known young people, were quietly married last Friday evening.

Alcona County Review, June 16, 1898

Churchill, James S.
Olmstead, Mary
COUNTY NEWS JOTTINGS.
Our young friend Jas. S. Churchill, who was recently married to one of Au Sable's fair daughters, has built himself a comfortable dwelling at his work near Alger & Co's camp, and himself and wife have gone to housekeeping. We hope they may experience much joy and prosperity in their new home.

Alcona County Review, December 14, 1877

Clark, John G.
McKinnon, Margaret
MARRIED.
Clark—McKinnon.—In Harrisville, July 3d, by Rev. P. C. Goldie, John Clark, of Haynes, and Miss Margaret McKinnon, of Caledonia.

Alcona County Review, July 5, 1889

Clark, Samuel J.
Beebe, Emma
HAWSE TOWNSHIP.
The ice is broken. Another bachelor made happy. Thanksgiving Day celebrated by the father of Hawse. He has broken the ranks of the Bachelor Club by taking to himself a wife of beauty and merit. He was married in Alpena on Thanksgiving Day, that sacred day—a sacred deed—to one Emma Beebe, a sister of James Beebe.

Alcona County Review, December 1, 1898

HAWSE TOWNSHIP.
Mrs. Clark, mother of Supervisor Clark, is well pleased with her new daughter, and well she might be, for she is getting along in years and it relieves her greatly, for the young guest is so very kind to the old lady. Mrs. Clark has always been a mother to all her neighbors in time of need and it is the wish of all that her last days, be they many or few, may be made happy.

Alcona County Review, December 15, 1898

Clark, William
Bray, Ella
Somewhat Personal.

Wm. Clark of Crystal Falls, upper peninsula, a former Harrisville boy, was recently married to Miss Ella Bray of Ishpeming.

Alcona County Review, January 14, 1892

Clark, William
Jack, Florence Belle
Haynes Happenings.
Haynes, Mar. 3rd, 1896.-- Reported that Wm. Clark and Bella Jack were united in the holy bonds of wedlock yesterday. I wish them success and may their journey through life be as prosperous and happy as the poet sang
Two souls with but a single thought,
Two hearts that beat as one.

Alcona County Review, March 5, 1896

EVENTS OF ONE WEEK.

Married. At the Methodist parsonage on Monday evening, William Clarke and Florence B. Jack.

Alcona County Review, March 5, 1896

Cleveland, Frank G.
Scarlett, Alice
EVENTS OF ONE WEEK.

Frank G. Cleveland of Lewiston came down to Au Sable in search of a housekeeper. He struck a bargain with Alice Scarlett, but changed his mind before night and concluded to marry her. She was willing and the twain were made one in due form. They had never met before.

Alcona County Review, January 19, 1893

Code, William
Devlin, Martha

Wedding Bells—The following from the Sunday Times of Bay City describes a social event that took place in Bay City last week. The bride is a niece of R. L. Lott of this village and during her frequent visits to Harrisville has made many friends. The bridegroom is also well known here, having at one time been a resident.

Code—Devlin.

The marriage of Miss Martha Devlin of this city and William Code, of Mesa, Arizona, was a happy event that gave great pleasure mixed with the pain of parting, to a large circle of acquaintances. Miss Devlin has taught a number of years in the city schools and for several years also has been the organist of the Madison avenue M. E. church Sunday school, and has acquired innumerable warm friends. Mr. Code was formerly a resident of Saginaw, a graduate of the Michigan University and is the civil engineer of the Bowen, Ferry & Chandler Canal company, Arizona. The wedding took place at the residence of the bride's parents, 1412 Sheridan street, Thursday evening, Rev. M. C. Hawks officiating. The guests numbered about 50, including friends from Detroit, Saginaw, Harrisville and Arizona. The bride was pronounced more than lovely in white china silk and lace, the only ornament a diamond pin a gift of the groom. He looked all a bride could crave, in conventional black. The presents were many and valuable. The couple departed after the wedding supper for Detroit, from where they go this week to Chicago and thence to their home in Arizona.

Alcona County Review, September 21, 1893

Colwell, George L.
Habersham, Emma [Keene]

EVENTS OF ONE WEEK.

The Skamokawa Eagle of Jan. 10th, inst., is at hand and contains the following paragraph, which will be read with interest by readers of the Review, to whom Mr. Colwell is well known as a pioneer citizen of Alcona county:

Married--At the residence of Mrs. A. K. Strobel, Portland, Or., Jan. 3, 1895, Mr. George L. Colwell, of Ilwaco, Wash., and Mrs. Emma Keene Habersham, of Portland.

The marriage of Mr. Colwell, so long a resident of Skamokawa, comes as a surprise to his old friends, and while a little tardy, their congratulations are none the less sincere and hearty.

Alcona County Review, January 17, 1895

Conklin, Charles
LaChapelle, Minnie A.

MORE LOCAL.

An event that has been long expected by friends of the principals to the transaction, was the marriage of Chas. Conklin and Miss Minnie Chapelle, two of our well and favorably known young people. Therefore the announcement of their marriage Tuesday morning at the home of the bride's parents in Harrisville township will cause no surprise. Mr. and Mrs. Conklin left by rail for a short visit at Bay City and Flint. The Review offers best wishes and congratulations.

Alcona County Review, May 16, 1890

Conklin, William Frank
Anderson, Jennie

At the Baptist Church.

A quiet wedding took place last evening at the Baptist Chapel, Mr. William F. Conklin and Miss Jennie Anderson being the happy couple.

They marched from the vestibule to the altar to the strains of a wedding march and Rev. W. P. Tompkins performed the ceremony under a canopy of stars and stripes.

Mr. and Mrs. Conklin have a host of friends who wish them a happy and prosperous life.

Alcona County Review, June 30, 1898

Connelley, Ret
Johnson, Laura

Somewhat Personal.

Miss Laura Johnson, a former teacher in the Fisher district, was married July 29 at Warren O., to Ret Connelley.

Alcona County Review, August 20, 1891

Connors, James J.
Atherton, Lottie

Mitchell Crumbs.

Oct. 5, 1896.

Miss Lottie Atherton of Mitchell and James Conors of Fairview, were united in the holy bonds of matrimony at the residence of Kimble McCollum, Sept. 21st. We wish the young couple much joy and happy dreams.

Alcona County Review, October 8, 1896

Conrad, Albert
Dunham, Lizzie

PERSONAL POINTS.

At Ossineke on June 8th occurred the marriage of Miss Lizzie Dunham to Mr. Albert Conrad of Vernon, Mich., Rev. O. W. Willets of Alpena officiating. A large number of guests were present and the bride and groom were the recipients of many useful and valuable presents. Mr. and Mrs. Conrad are now in this city where they will visit for a few days before going to their pleasant home in Vernon.—Pioneer.

The bride is well known in this county where she formerly resided.

Alcona County Review, June 16, 1898

Cook, Lawrence
Hugill, Frances

HAYNES.

July 25, '99.

I congratulate Mr. and Mrs. Geo. Hastings and Mr. and Mrs. Lawrence Cook on the happy event of their unions.

You will have a weary race to run,
The end you cannot see;
Look over on the sunny side
And always cheerful be.

Alcona County Review, July 27, 1899

Corbin, Fred
Hamilton, Henrietta

PERSONAL POINTS.

Mr. Fred Corbin and Miss Henney Hamilton, both of Harrisville township, were united in marriage last Thursday. Congratulations.

Alcona County Review, September 7, 1899

Cotte, Fred
Paquet, Caroline

Along the Shore.

General News-Gleanings From the Several Counties.

Au Sable and Oscoda.

Recent marriages: Fred Cotte and Caroline Paquet, June 28; Andrew Rennell and Mary M. Norman, and John Omen and Mary Emma

Minord, June 22d; Stephen Murphy and Mary Williams, June 20th.

Alcona County Review, July 2, 1880

Covie, Porter
Byce, Alvie

Covie—Byce.

Mr. Porter Covie and Miss Alvie Byce both of Harrisville were married at the Methodist parsonage on Monday evening, by Rev. W. Will.

Mr. and Mrs. Covie have the best wishes of a large number of friends, including the Review.

Alcona County Review, July 6, 1899

Cowley, John H.
McClelland, Lillian

COWLEY-McCLELLAND.

Married, June 15th inst., at Sacred Heart church, Au Sable, John H. Cowley and Lillian McClelland, both of Harrisville. Miss Marie Cowley acted as bridesmaid and Mr. F. G. Cowley as groomsman. The bride and bridesmaid were attired in travelling costumes, the bride and groom wearing lillies-of-the-valley, the bride's favorite flower.

The church was beautifully and artistically decorated with flowers by Prof. Gauthier, the altar being almost a solid mass of flowers to a height of twelve feet. The altar rail was covered with beautiful flowers, large branches of begonia arching over them as they knelt. A grand wedding march was played as the bridal party entered, and soft, sweet music continued throughout the impressive services which lasted for about three-quarters of an hour. Prof. Gauthier presided at the organ throughout the ceremony and played Lohengrin's Wedding March as the bridal party left the church. An elegant repast was served at 1:30 at the Sherman House, the party including Fr. Mahar and Prof. Gauthier. Mr. and Mrs. Cowley left by steamer Atlantic for a trip down the St. Lawrence and other points of interest. The contracting parties have been residents of Harrisville from childhood and both enjoy a wide circle of acquaintance in the community. The groom as a rising young business man and the bride as a successful public instructor, have won places in the community that entitle them to the best wishes of all for a bon voyage through life.

Alcona County Review, June 16, 1892

SOMEWHAT PERSONAL.

Mr. and Mrs. Jno. H. Cowley have returned from their wedding trip.

Alcona County Review, June 30, 1892

HISTORY OF ONE YEAR.

Chronological History of the Past Year, 1892.

MARRIAGES.

June 15. Jno. H. Cowley, Lillian McClelland of Harrisville, at Sacred Heart church, Au Sable.

Alcona County Review, January 5, 1893

Cram, George W.
Frederick, Margaret L.

EVENTS OF ONE WEEK.

Rev. Geo. Cram and Miss Maggie Frederick are to be married at 5 o'clock p.m. Jan. 1, at the Baptist church in this village.

Alcona County Review, December 26, 1895

Mid-winter Wedding Bells.

The interior of the Calvary Baptist church was never more beautifully decorated than on the evening of Jan. 1, 1896. The occasion was the marriage of Miss Margaret L. Frederick, eldest daughter of Mr. and Mrs. L. Frederick, and a young lady of rare personal attractions, to Rev. Geo. W. Cram, a former pastor of this place.

Long before the appointed hour the church was filled by the invited guests. At 5:30 o'clock the sweet strains of the Lohengrin wedding march pealed from the organ, played by Miss Beatrice Wilson.

The wedding party entered and passed slowly up the aisle, preceded by the ushers, Messrs. A. N. Springer and L. A. Colwell. First came the groom and his best man, Mr. Chas. Mayo, followed by the bridesmaid, Miss Allie M. Colwell, carrying a lovely boquet of pink carnations. The ring was borne in a small silver basket by little Miss Pearl Woods. Last came the bride, leaning upon her father's arm, and looking lovely in a cream-colored dress, trimmed with satin and lace, her long tulle veil fastened on her head with white hyacinths and carrying in her hand a shower boquet of American Beauty roses tied with cream satin ribbon.

The groom met the bride at the altar, where, under a white canopy

and beneath a pendant floral horse shoe, Rev. C. E. Conley of Detroit pronounced the beautiful and impressive marriage ceremony, after which the bridal party marched down the aisle headed by the newly married couple. The parents of the bride gave a reception to the bridal party at Maple Lodge, which was kindly placed at their disposal by its genial mistress, whither they all repaired. Congratulations followed, then an elaborate supper was spread: after which the remainder of the evening was spent by the merry party in music and conversation until a late hour when the farewells were spoken and sincere wishes expressed for the happiness and prosperity of Rev. and Mrs. Cram, who left the next morning for their future home in Port Huron.

The presents were unusually numerous and valuable, owing to the extensive acquaintance and popularity of the contracting parties. Great credit is due the young people of the church for the artistic arrangement of the decorations.

Alcona County Review, January 2, 1896

Crannell, George Edward
Hill, Helen Genevieve

BLACK RIVER.

Oct. 4, '99.

Invitations are out announcing the marriage of Geo. E. Cranelle to Miss H. Genevieve Hill at the residence of A. W. Ranney at high noon, next Monday.

Alcona County Review, October 5, 1899

BLACK RIVER.

Black River records one more swell social event. Miss Helen G. Hill, a popular and talented young lady of this city, was married at high noon on Monday to Geo. E. Cranell, owner and proprietor of the Black River Drug Store.

The ceremony, at which several guests were present, was performed by Rev. A. C. Austin at the residence of A. W. Ranney, Miss Sue Hill acting as bridesmaid and Mr. L. G. Ranney as groomsman. Mr. and Mrs. Cranell accompanied their mother, Mrs. F. J. Hill, and Sue as far as Bay City.

Alcona County Review, October 12, 1899

Craven, George F.
Morton, Lizana

MARRIAGE LICENSES.

The county clerk has issued the following marriage licenses during the month of September:
Geo. F. Craven, Haynes.
Lizana Morton, Harrisville.

Alcona County Review, September 26, 1890

Craven, James P.
Atchison, Maggie

PESONAL MENTION.

Jas. Craven and Maggie Atchison were united in marriage Saturday evening at the parsonage by the Rev. W. J. Bailey.

Alcona County Review, October 4, 1894

Craven, William J.
Elmes, Sarah

HAYNES HAPPENINGS.

Haynes, Nov. 9th, 1897.
Times are improving in Haynes. Quite a number of young men are erecting houses preparatory to splicing to better halves. Among them are Will Fettes and Will Craven. Miss Hattie McArthur is to be married on Wednesday next (Nov. 17) to a young man who resides at Black River. Your scribe wishes them joy and happiness during the journey of life. Miss McArthur is a model young lady and the daughter of Donald McArthur. Her mother died while she was an infant. She was reared by Mrs. Hastings, her grandmother.

Alcona County Review, November 18, 1897

Crenshaw, Albert B.
Wilson, Allie

Our Neighbors.

A Tawas city young lady Miss Allie Wilson has caused a sensation by eloping with A. B. Crenshaw, a resident of Cleveland, Ohio.

Alcona County Review, November 1, 1889

Crinian, Thomas
McFarlan, Margaret

Married:—In East Tawas, November 13, 1879, Mr. Thomas Crinian, of Oscoda, and Miss Margaret McFarlan, of Au Sable. This wedding was an entire surprise to even the friends of the parties. In plain terms, it was an elopement. The well-laid plans and faithful execution of them, the attending circumstances, the hour of starting-- all cast around this union the hue and tinge of delicious romance. For our part we trust they may never encounter rougher weather on the matrimonial sea than they have already triumphed over, and their further course be marked only by gentle winds and smooth sailing. God bless them.—*Au Sable News.*

Alcona County Review, November 28, 1879

Cummings, Lester L.
Martin, Emma A.

Lester Cummings will be down from Grand Marais this week and rumor has it that he comes for the purpose of taking away one of Alcona's fairest young ladies.

Alcona County Review, October 21, 1897

Cummings—Martin.

A very pretty home wedding was solemnized last Saturday night when Mr. Lester L. Cummings and Miss Emma A. Martin were joined in wedlock at the residence of the bride's parents, Rev. W. W. Will officiating.

A large company of guests witnessed the ceremony and immediately afterward all were seated to a magnificent wedding supper.

The ceremony was performed in the cozy parlor, which was tastefully decorated with plants and flowers. The bride looked charming in a pale blue gown of Lansdown, garnitured with cream lace and ribbon, as did the bridesmaid, Miss Matie McIntyre who was dressed in a pink gown of the same material, trimmed with cream chiffon. Mr. James Martin actcd as groomsman.

The bride is the only daughter of Mr. and Mrs. Chas. Martin, old and respected citizens of this township, and has a wide circle of relatives and friends, who hold her in high esteem.

The groom is a young man with a promising future before him. He is also well and favorably known here where he spent most of his life until a few years ago when he went to the booming town of Grand Marais and identified himself with the interests of that community, and where he has built a home for himself and bride.

The presents were pretty and appropriate. The happy couple left Tuesday afternoon for their future home, whether the best wishes of their host of friends here will follow them.

Alcona County Review, October 28, 1897

PERSONAL.

Mr. and Mrs. Cummings are now nicely located in their new and comfortable residence, in the Gamble & Millen addition. Mr. Cummings has been a resident of this city for the past two years and is a favorite of the community both in business and socially. Miss Martin is one of Harrisville's most highly esteemed young ladies, and it is with a hearty welcome we greet her to our midst.-- Grand Marais Herald.

Alcona County Review, November 11, 1897

Curran, Philip
Cutting, Mary

LOCAL JOTTINGS.

Married—By C. P. Reynolds, Esq., at his residence in Harrisville, on the 29th ult., Philip Curan and Mary Cutting, all of West Greenbush.

Alcona County Review, April 2, 1886

Currie, John
?, Christina

LOCAL JOTTINGS.

John Currie returned from Canada last week Wednesday, bringing with him a bonnie bride.

Alcona County Review, November 19, 1886

Currie, William D.
Crandall, Mae

PERSONAL POINTS.

Will Curry, a former Harrisville boy, was married recently to a Tawas young lady. They reside at Au Sable.

Alcona County Review, August 25, 1898

PERSONAL POINTS.

Mrs. Chas. Peacock and sister, Miss Sarah Curry, went back to Oscoda last week to attend the wedding of their brother, Wm. Curry. They have returned to Harrisville to complete their visit. Mrs. Peacock's home is in London, Ont.

Alcona County Review, August 25, 1898

Curtis, Peter
Boulieu, Clarissa

Jottings Along the Shore.

Married, May 31st, by Rev. C. J. Roche Peter Curtis, of Au Sable, and Miss Clarissa Boulieu, of Oscoda.

Alcona County Review, June 10, 1881

Curtis, Richard E.
Goodfellow, Mary

Somewhat Personal.

Richard E. Curtis and Miss Mary Goodfellow, two of Curtis township's most promising young people, were in the village last Friday and while here secured the necessary papers and were made man and wife. Congratulations being in order we beg leave to extend them to Mr. and Mrs. Curtis.

Alcona County Review, May 28, 1891

Cuyler, George Alonzo
Shirley, Anna Rose

Geo. A. Cuyler and Ed. Green drove down Tuesday evening from the River. The former carried home with him a license to wed Annie R. Shirley of Black River. Mr. C. is well and favorably known here having pulled an oar the past season in the Sturgeon Pointe life boat. The young lady in the case is highly spoken of by those who know her and we bespeak for them a happy voyage on the troublous seas of matrimony.

Alcona County Review, December 31, 1891

Davelay, Alexander Louis
Herron, Jennie Electra

LOCAL JOTTINGS.

Married.
On the 5th inst., at the residence of the bride's father, by Rev. R. H. Balmer, Alex L. Davelay and Miss Jennie E. Herron, all of Black River.

The Review wishes this young couple a happy, useful life.

Alcona County Review, October 17, 1884

Dayton, James O.
Smith, Lizzie

Jottings Along the Shore.
Married.—At the M. E. Church, East Tawas, Jan'y 1st, 1880, by Rev. J. B. Atchinson, James O. Dayton, of Alcona, and Miss Lizzie Smith, of East Tawas.—*Tawas Gazette.*

Alcona County Review, January 9, 1880

Deacon, Delormy
Vaughn, Margaret

The Local News.

Married.—At the home of the bride in Curtis, Sept. 7, by Rev. R. L. Mulholland, Mr. Delormy Deacon and Mrs. Maggie Vaughn, both of

Curtis, in the presence of a large circle of friends.

Alcona County Review, September 17, 1891

Crumbs from Curtis.
Curtis, Sept. 14, 1891.—Mr. Delormy Deacon, Jr., and Miss Margaret Vaughn were married Sept. 7th, at the bride's residence, by Rev. R. N. Mulholland of Au Sable. They are going to live in Mr. Claudius Hood's house.

Alcona County Review, September 17, 1891

DeCarie, Oliver Edward
Charlefour, Anna Blanche

BLACK RIVER IN PRINT.
Cards are out announcing the wedding of O. E. DeCarie to Miss Anna Blanche Charlefour on January 22d.

O. E. DeCarie spent a few days in Alpena on business of "importance."

Alcona County Review, January 16, 1896

Black River Sparks.

Owing to the late hour of the DeCarie—Charlefour wedding O. O. Jr. will get his skates on and have a full account by next week.

Alcona County Review, January 23, 1896

Black River Sparks.

A very pretty church wedding was solemnized here Wednesday, Jan. 22, at St. Gabriel's which united Mr. Oliver Decarie and Arma Blanch Charlefour, both of this place.

The ceremony took place at 9 a.m.

The Rev. Fr. Poulin performing the beautiful marriage service of the Catholic church. The beautiful church was filled with friends of the bride and groom, including a number from Alpena, Au Sable, and Harrisville. Promptly on the hour the wedding party wended their way down the aisle while Prof. Gauthier played the sweet strains of Mendlesohn's Wedding March. Mr. John Elie of Alpena acted as best man and Miss Clinia Charlefour of Oscoda, cousin of the bride, as bridesmaid.

The church was beautifully decorated with flowers and ferns. The royal mass was sung by Messrs. Eugene Croteau and Leo Bertrand of Alpena assisted by Prof. Gauthier.

O'Salutaris was sung by Mrs. Sauve of East Tawas with splendid effect and the Ave Maria by Messrs.

Croteau and Bertrand was delightfully rendered.

After the ceremony the happy couple and their friends adjourned to the newly purchased home of Mr. Decarie where they partook of a wedding dinner. They were the recipients of a number of beautiful and costly gifts.

Mr. and Mrs. Decarie left on the evening train for a visit with friends in Alpena and will be at home Feb. 1. The Review and O. O. Jr. extend their congratulations.

Alcona County Review, January 30, 1896

DeCoste, William
Deacon, Ethel

A Variety of Interesting Paragraphs from Curtis.

Jan. 22, '94.
Decause—Deacon. Were married at the residence of the bride's parents in Curtis December 31st, 1893, Mr. William Decaus and Miss Ethel Deacon, by the Rev. I. B. Nun. They gave a very pleasant party; their house was crowded with friends and neighbors and a fine supper was served at midnight. All enjoyed themselves. We wish them as neighbors a happy and peaceful life.

Alcona County Review, January 25, 1894

Dege, Ernest
Neubert, Anna

People We Hear About.
MARRIAGE LICENSES.

The county clerk has issued the following marriage licenses during the month of September:

Ernest Dege, aged 23, Black River. Anna Newbert, aged 19, Haynes.

Alcona County Review, September 26, 1890

DeKett, George
Hohenstein, Alida

Married.
In Harrisville, at the M. E. parsonage, April 26th, 1884, by Rev. J. H. McIntosh, Geo. Deket and Miss Alida Hohenstein, all of Alcona, Mich.

Alcona County Review, May 2, 1884

Derby, Arthur W.
Stafford, Alice

Among Our Exchanges.

From the Alpena Echo:

Mr. Arthur Derby and Miss Stafford, of Black River, came up on the train last night and were married in this city this morning.

Alcona County Review, May 26, 1892

SOMEWHAT PERSONAL.

Arthur Derby and Alice Stafford, both of Black River, were married July 14 at the Central hotel, Oscoda, by the Rev. R. N. Mulholland.

Alcona County Review, July 21, 1892

Derby, Edwin
Kehoe, Kittie

LOCAL JOTTINGS.

A party bent on matrimony passed through Harrisville last Sunday on their way to Au Sable where the nuptial knot was to be tied. It has to be a colder day than Sunday to prevent Cupid from playing his pranks. Edwin Derby was the bridegroom, and Miss Kittie Kehoe the blushing bride.

Alcona County Review, March 4, 1887

DeRosia, Louis, Sr.
Filkins, Roena C. [Ingraham]

Louis De Rosie, age 61, has wooed and won the heart of Roena C. Filkins, aged 61, and the county clerk has issued a marriage license permitting the union of hearts and homes and fortunes. The young couple will reside in Caledonia.

Alcona County Review, October 27, 1892

Devault, Mr.
Van Meter, Mrs. H. K.

LOCAL PICK UPS.

Friends of Mrs. H. K. Van Meter have received notice of her marriage on the 20th ult., at La Rose, Ind., to Mr. Devault, a wealthy citizen of La Rose.

Alcona County Review, July 13, 1899

Dewar, Daniel
McLellan, Isabella

Local Sayings and Doings.

Married: November 12, 1881, at M. E. Parsonage, Harrisville, by Rev. J. H. McIntosh, Daniel Dewar and Miss Isabella McLellan, all of Harrisville.

Alcona County Review, November 18, 1881

Dewey, John S.
Tower, Cora L.

SOMEWHAT PERSONAL.

Jno. Dewey and Miss Cora Tower were united in marriage by the Rev. W. J. Bailey last Thursday evening at the home of the bride's mother.

Alcona County Review, May 26, 1892

Schram, Anna

Dewey—Scram.

Mr. Lewis Dewey of Harrisville and Miss Anna Scram of West Harrisville were united in wedlock at the Methodist parsonage last evening by the Rev. W. W. Will.

The groom is well and popularly known here, where he has lived most of his life.

The bride is a daughter of David Scram and is one of West Harrisville's most estimable young ladies. The Review joins with the large circle of friends in extending congratulations and best wishes.

Alcona County Review, November 3, 1898

Dickerson, John
Durkee, Charlotte L.

GREENBUSH GETTINGS.

Two more souls made happy! On Saturday, April 17th, at the residence of Geo. Goff, of South Harrisville, Mr. John Dixon of Black River and Miss Charlotte Durkee were united in marriage by Rev. J. Robbins.

Alcona County Review, April 23, 1886

Dickinson, James A.
Twite, Kittie

LOCAL JOTTINGS.

Married, in Harrisville, Feb. 3d, 1889, by the Rev. P. C. Goldie, Miss Kittie Twite and Jas. A. Dickinson.

Alcona County Review, February 22, 1889

Dobson, Robert
Morton, Emma A.

LOCAL JOTTINGS.

Married: At the residence of the bride's father, on the 13th inst., by the Rev. R. H. Balmer, Robert Dobson and Bertha Morton, all of Alcona.

Alcona County Review, February 20, 1885

Dodge, Benjamin
McLelland, Elizabeth

LOCAL JOTTINGS.

A very pleasant social event took place in Harrisville, Monday evening July 6th, 1885, at the residence of our townsman Mr. James McLelland, it being the marriage of his niece, Miss Lizzie McLelland to Benjamin Dodge, all of Harrisville. The ceremony was performed in a very impressive manner by Rev. G. R. Bisby, Pastor of the First Baptist Church. Although none but immediate relatives were present, their numerous friends all unite in wishing them happiness and prosperity.

Alcona County Review, July 10, 1885

Dodge, Frank
Langdon, Priscilla

PERSONAL MENTION.

Frank Dodge has been heard from. He has committed matrimony in England.

Alcona County Review, March 2, 1893

The following paragraph clipped from an English journal, concerning the marriage of Frank Dodge Jan. 8th, at Chiselborough, Somersetshire, Eng., will interest many readers of this paper:

A marriage took place on Wednesday between Mr. Frank Dodge, son of Mr. Mark Dodge, and Miss Pricilla Langdon, second daughter of the late Mr. John Langdon. Great interest was taken to the event by the villagers, and the bells pealed forth merrily. The bride wore a stylish dress of light fawn material, with trimmings of dark brown velvet; she also wore a wreath and veil and carried a lovely boquet of flowers. The bridesmaids were Miss Thirza Langdon (sister of the bride) who wore a dress of dark helitrope with banners to match, and Miss Susie Dodge (sister of the bridegroom), who wore a fawn dress with hat to match. The bride was given away by Mr. Warry, of Merriott. Mr. A. Holland acted as best man. The Rev. Preb Newell officiated. The party were well showered with rice on leaving the church. The presents were numerous.

Alcona County Review, March 16, 1893

Douglas, William Lester
Thornton, Ada

MARRIAGE LICENSES.

April 21, Wm. L. Douglas, 32, Alpena, and Ada Thornton, 26, Harrisville.

Alcona County Review, April 25, 1890

The Local News.

Miss Ada Thornton was united in marriage Monday evening at her father's residence in Harrisville township to Wm. L. Douglas of Alpena. The Rev. L. Hazard officiated.

Alcona County Review, April 25, 1890

Downer, Frederick W.
Coyle, Mattie

SOMEWHAT PERSONAL.

Married, Sept. 12, at the Methodist E. parsonage, Harrisville, by the Rev. Wm. J. Bailey, Mr. Frederick W. Downer of Harrisville to Miss Mattie Coyle of Greenbush, Mich.

Alcona County Review, September 15, 1892

HISTORY OF ONE YEAR.

Chronological History of the Past Year, 1892.

MARRIAGES.

Sept. 12. Frederick Downer to Mattie Coyle of Greenbush.

Alcona County Review, January 5, 1893

Downer, Isaac Jefferson
Monroe, Mary Frances

PERSONAL MENTION.

Isaac Downer and Miss Matie Monroe were united in marriage Monday by Rev. W. J. Bailey, at the home of the bride's parents in Greenbush township. The Review extends congratulations.

Alcona County Review, November 1, 1894

A Long String From Springport.

Springport, Jan. 15, 1895. Mr. and Mrs. Isaac Downer started housekeeping at Greenbush this week. They have been living with Mr. D.'s parents.

Alcona County Review, January 17, 1895

Downie, Edward
Slater, Frances Jane

LOCAL JOTTINGS.

Married.—April 21st, at the residence of the bride's father in Alcona, by Rev. T. B. Leith, Edward Downie and Francis J. Slater, all of Alcona.

Alcona County Review, April 23, 1886

Drennon, William W.

Nelson, May

Reviewings.

Married: November 13, 1879, at the Presbyterian Parsonage in Harrisville, by Rev. D. VanDyke, Mr. William W. Drennon and Miss May Nelson, both of Oscoda.

Alcona County Review, November 14, 1879

Duff, Ralph M.
Wilson, Hattie

PERSONAL.

Miss Hattie Wilson, who resided in Skamokawa some five years ago, was married in Tacoma, Sunday, May 30th, to Mr. Ralph M. Duff, son of a prominent contractor in that city.—Skamokawa (Wash.) Eagle.

The bride formerly resided in Harrisville and is a sister of Mrs. Wm. Ludington.

Alcona County Review, June 17, 1897

Duggan, Daniel
Hill, Mrs. Mary A. [Moss]

REVIEWINGS.

Married: At the residence of the Bride, Tuesday evening, June 3rd, by the Rev. D. VanDyke, Mr. Daniel Duggan and Mrs. Mary A. Hill, all of Harrisville.

The editor extends congratulations to the new couple, and wishes them a happy, prosperous future.

Alcona County Review, June 6, 1879

Duggan, John
Richmond, Mrs. Margaretta

REVIEWINGS.

We learn that Mr. John Duggan, of the Huron House, and Mrs. Richmond, of this place, were married last Sunday. The editor extends congratulations, and hopes they may enjoy long life, happiness and prosperity.

Alcona County Review, September 26, 1879

Duggan, Thomas
Mickley, Susan

COUNTY REVIEWINGS.

Married.—At the residence of Mr. Michael Kerwin, Au Sable, May 5th, by Rev. A. McKinnon, Mr. Thomas Duggan and Miss Susan Mickley, both of Harrisville.

Alcona County Review, May 14, 1880

Dunbar, John
Lee, Charlotte

WEST HARRISVILLE.

Married at the M. E. parsonage, on May 11, John Dunbar and Lottie Lee, both of Haynes, Rev. F. S. Ford, officiating.

Alcona County Review, May 19, 1898

Duncan, Robert
Edmundson, Margaret Ann [Morgan]

GREENBUSH GETTINGS.

Married. On Sunday afternoon, by Rev. J. Bain of Harrisville, at the residence of A. W. Frazer, Mrs. Edmunson, sister of Mrs. G. Rouse, to Mr. Robert Duncan. Both parties are of age at least. We heartily congratulate Robert and wish the couple all happiness and prosperity. Mr. Bain must have experienced some difficulty in tying the knot or the bee must have been quite enough to satisfy him for that afternoon, for he did not deem it necessary to have service as usual in the church.

Alcona County Review, December 11, 1885

LOCAL JOTTINGS.

Married, at Greenbush on Sunday, Dec. 6, 1885, by Rev. J. Bain, of Harrisville, at residence of Mr. Frazer, Robert Duncan and Mrs. Margaret Ann Edminson, all of Greenbush.

Alcona County Review, December 11, 1885

Durkee, George W.
Perkins, Jessie A.

LOCAL JOTTINGS.

Married, June 19, 1884, at the M. E. parsonage in Harrisville, by Rev. J. H. McIntosh, Geo. W. Durkee and Miss Jessie A. Perkins, all of Greenbush.

Alcona County Review, June 20, 1884

Dyer, W. R.
Heuston, Martha

LOCAL JOTTINGS.

State Representative W. R. Dyer has put his head into Hymen's noose. He was married July 10 to Miss Martha Heuston of Thompsonville, Conn., at that place. Mr. Dyer has a handsome face and a good bank account.

Alcona County Review, July 26, 1889

Eager, {Male}
?, {Bride}

LOCAL JOTTINGS.

Prof. Eager, on his recent trip below, it is said went after his family. Well, that statement is true in one sense, and in another it isn't. The Prof. was *not* a married man when he left here on said trip, and therefore had no family, that any body knew of, but on his arrival at Saranac, Ionia county, he was married to one of the fair daughters of that burg. He informs the Review that the happy event took place on the 5th inst. Mrs. Eager will not arrive in Harrisville until the opening of spring.

Alcona County Review, March 20, 1885

Earl, George E.
Ferguson, Margaret Matilda

MARRIED.

Earl—Ferguson.—March 28th, at the residence of the bride's father, Jas. Ferguson of Harrisville township, by the Rev. P. C. Goldie, Geo. E. Earl and Miss Matilda Ferguson, both of Harrisville township.

Alcona County Review, March 30, 1888

Edgar, George
Micho, Frances [LaChapelle]

ADDITIONAL LOCAL.

It is rumored that a wedding will occur this week in which the contracting parties will be Mr. Geo. Edgar and Mrs. F. Micho.

Alcona County Review, August 31, 1899

LOCAL PICK UPS.

Geo. Edgar and Mrs. Frances Micho were united in marriage by Rev. Fr. Poulin last Friday evening.

Alcona County Review, September 7, 1899

Edgar, George
Neal, Lizzie

COUNTY REVIEWINGS.

George Edgar and Miss Lizzie Neal of this place were united in the bonds of wedlock at Au Sable, on the 7th inst. May they always enjoy each other's company even as they do now, and thus experience a happy life.

Alcona County Review, August 13, 1880

Edgar, John D.
Barber, Isabella

Married—In Harrisville March 22, 1883, by the Rev. J. H. McIntosh, John D. Edgar, and Miss Isabella Barber, all of Harrisville, Mich.

Alcona County Review, March 23, 1883

Edgar, William
Morrell, Mary

Wm. Edgar and Mary Morelle were married last week.

Alcona County Review, October 11, 1894

Edwards, William
Lincoln, Augusta

County News and Gossip.

Married:—On New Year's evening, 1879, by Rev. N. N. Clark, at the residence of Sherman Hale, Esq., Harrisville, Mich., Mr. William Edwards and Miss Augusta Lincoln, all of Harrisville.

An unusually pleasant time was had on the occasion of the wedding above announced, which is long to be remembered. The bride and groom were the recipients of some nice presents in the shape of silver and glass. The editor was kindly remembered with a handsome supply of the wedding cake, for which thanks are returned. We wish the new couple a "Happy New Year," together with a long life of prosperity and pleasure.

Alcona County Review, January 3, 1879

Effrick, Albert F.
Sinclair, Anna M.

PERSONAL.

Bert Effric and Miss Anna Sinclair, two well and favorably known young people of Harrisville township, were quietly married last evening at the M. E. parsonage by Rev. Will, in the presence of a few friends.

Alcona County Review, July 8, 1897

Ellis, Charles
?, {Bride}

People We Hear About.

Chas. Ellis has been in the village this week. Charlie recently slipped his head into the matrimonial noose by marrying an Alpena young lady.

Alcona County Review, July 11, 1890

Ellis, Chauncey
Hasty, Sarah

Somewhat Personal.

Chauncey Ellis and Sarah Hasty yielded to the tender influence of cupid's Fourth of July love tipped darts and Sunday evening their hearts, hands and fortunes were united forever by the tie that binds. This was a somewhat Hasty match but the bride's Chauncey's are the best that could be expected under the circumstances, and no doubt both will live long and be very happy.

Alcona County Review, July 9, 1891

Elmer, Frank J.
Illman, Justina

Married.

Elmer—Illman.—At the residence of Wm. Houge, Harrisville, by the Rev. W. R. Waters, December 21st, Frank J. Elmer and Miss Yestina Illman, both of Alcona.

Alcona County Review, December 28, 1888

Elmer, Milo
Glover, Amanda

Elmer—Glover.

Married at Killmaster Thursday, May 11, by Rev. Geo. Nixon, Mr. Milo Elmer of Harrisville and Miss Amanda Glover of Killmaster. The ceremony was performed at the home of the bride's parents in the presence of a small party of friends.

Alcona County Review, May 18, 1899

Emerson, Curtis
LaBoueff, Melvina (Lena)

PERSONAL.

Curtis Emerson and Miss Lena La Boueff, two well-known young people of this place, were quietly married Saturday evening by Fr. Poulin at his residence. The Review wishes them all manner of happiness.

Alcona County Review, September 23, 1897

Emerson, Fred
Showers, Minnie

Somewhat Personal.

Fred Emerson provided himself with one of those beautifully engraved licenses on sale only at the county clerk's office, and yesterday took his departure for Alpena. It is the old story over again. The young lady in the case is, or was, Miss Minnie Showers, well and favorably known here where she has resided for a number of years.

Alcona County Review, November 12, 1891

Somewhat Personal.

Fred Emerson and bride, nee Miss Minnie Showers, returned from Alpena last week.

Alcona County Review, November 19, 1891

Emerson, James E.
Hudson, Mary Sophia

Married.

On Wednesday evening, Oct. 6, by Rev. W. P. Tompkins, at the Baptist parsonage, Mr. James E. Emerson and Miss Mary S. Hudson.

Alcona County Review, October 7, 1897

Emmel, Oscar
Nestle, Fannie

COUNTY JOTTINGS.

Married.—At the residence of L. H. Dunn, South Harrisville, Sept. 29th, 1878, by Rev. N. N. Clark, Mr. Oscar Emmel, of Harrisville and Miss Fannie Nestle, of Wales, St. Clair county.

Alcona County Review, October 4, 1878

Emmel, Oscar
Rebelle, Aurelia

LOCAL JOTTINGS

Oscar Emmel, aged 34, and Aurelia Rebelle, aged 26, both of Harrisville, are the signatures that grace a marriage certificate issued by the county clerk Feb. 4th.

Alcona County Review, February 10, 1888

Emmorey, David C.
Conklin, Mrs. Emma

LOCAL JOTTINGS.

Married: On the 27th inst., at the residence of the bride, by Rev. T. B. Leith, David C. Emmorey and Mrs. Emma Conklin, all of Harrisville. The Review extends congratulations to the happy pair, and trusts that their union may be fraught with joy and usefulness until death do them part.

Alcona County Review, January 30, 1885

Evans, Joseph
Sloan, Mrs. Ellen

Additional Local.

Joseph Evans went east about a week ago to see his brother as he said, but returned home a few days ago accompanied by his bride. He married Mrs. Ellen Sloan, formerly of Harrisville. Here's to their good health, hoping that they may enjoy a long life of happiness and prosperity. So mote it be.

Alcona County Review, November 4, 1881

Evringham, Philip H.
Emerson, Orilla T.

REVIEWINGS.

Married: March 6, 1879, at the residence of the bride's father, Nathan P. M. Emerson, esq., by Rev. N. N. Clark, Mr. Philip H. Evringham and Miss Orilla T. Emerson, all of Alcona County, Mich.

Two more hearts now beat as one. May the happy couple strive to keep off the thorns of life, and thus their earthly bliss will be complete, and they shall receive plenteous prosperity.

Alcona County Review, March 7, 1879

Evringham, William Henry
Griswold, Carrie Adeline

COUNTY REVIEWINGS.

Married, at the residence of the bride's father, Nov. 2d, by the Rev. Calvin Gibbs, Mr. William H. Everingham and Miss Carrie A. Griswold, both of Harrisville.

Alcona County Review, November 19, 1880

Ewar, Duncan
McNeil, Catherine

LOCAL JOTTINGS.

Duncan Ewar and Catherine McNeil journeyed to the hub on Tuesday from Alcona, and were made one by the Rev. C. B. Steele, at the M. E. parsonage.

Alcona County Review, December 31, 1886

Fassett, James
Carr, Mary

EVENTS OF ONE WEEK.

Licenses were issued on the 8th inst. permitting the marriage of James Fassett to Mary Carr, and Nelson Palmer to Mina Mooney.

Alcona County Review, April 11, 1895

Ferguson, John
McArthur, Mary [Argyle]

Gustin Grist.

Sept. 2, 1896.

After 11 years courtship John Ferguson and Mary McArthur concluded to wed, and on Friday last the pair drove to Harrisville and had the knot tied.

Alcona County Review, September 3, 1896

John Ferguson and Mrs. Mary McArthur of Gustin were married by Rev. W. W. Will at the parsonage on last Friday evening.

Alcona County Review, September 3, 1896

Fettes, William
Clark, Elizabeth

HAYNES HAPPENINGS.

Haynes, Nov. 9th, 1897.

Times are improving in Haynes. Quite a number of young men are erecting houses preparatory to splicing to better halves. Among them are Will Fettes and Will Craven. Miss Hattie McArthur is to be married on Wednesday next (Nov. 17) to a young man who resides at Black River. Your scribe wishes them joy and happiness during the journey of life. Miss McArthur is a model young lady and the daughter of Donald McArthur. Her mother died while she was an infant. She was reared by Mrs. Hastings, her grandmother.

Alcona County Review, November 18, 1897

Wedding Bells.

On June 1st, at the parsonage West Harrisville, Mr. William Fettis, son of Mr. and Mrs. J. M. Fettis of Haynes, was married to Betsy Eliza Clark of Haynes. Both are popular among their acquaintances and commence life with the good wishes of many friends. Rev. F. S. Ford officiating.

Alcona County Review, June 9, 1898

Finch, William H.
McLaurin, Letitia B.

Finch-McLauren.

Mr. William H. Finch and Miss Letitia B. McLaurin were united in marriage by Rev. W. W. Will at the Methodist parsonage on Tuesday evening, July 4th.

The groom is a popular member of the life-saving crew and is well known in Harrisville and vicinity. The bride is the daughter of Mr. and Mrs. Robt. McLaurin of Haynes and has lived in Harrisville a number of years. They have a wide circle of friends and acquaintances who will join the Review in wishing them a long and happy life.

Alcona County Review, July 6, 1899

Fish, Thomas A.
Meaney, Catherine

'ROUND ABOUT.

Thos. A. Fish of Mud Lake, a well known and popular citizen of the pine districts, was licensed last week to wed Miss Catherine Meaney of Black River. A long and happy life to you, Tom.

Alcona County Review, June 4, 1891

Fisher, Hogue
?, {Bride}

PURELY PERSONAL.

Hogue Fisher, a former Alcona county boy, is married. This event happened a number of weeks ago but as the distance is so great it probably is'nt too late to send congratulations to Cour d'Alene.

Alcona County Review, October 4, 1889

Fisher, John W.
McMurray, Cora L. [Bailey]

Cards have been received in the village this week announcing the marriage of John Fisher, formerly of Harrisville township, to a Cedar Springs (Mich.) young lady.

Alcona County Review, January 31, 1895

Fisher, Joseph, Jr.
Lewis, Adelaide A.

COUNTY NEWS JOTTINGS.

Married: Sept. 26, 1877, at the residence of the bride's father, Guy C. Lewis, Esq., by Rev. N. N. Clark, Mr. Joseph Fisher Jr. and Miss Addie A. Lewis, all of Harrisville. The well wishes of a host of intimate friends go with the happy couple. Mr. Fisher is a young man of good habits, steady, industrious, and enterprising, and his bride bears equally as good a reputation as himself. The printers acknowledge the receipt of a generous supply of the wedding cake, and extend hearty congratulations to bride and groom.

Alcona County Review, September 26, 1877

Fiske, Louis R.
Tillotson, Lewella J.

MARRIED.

At the residence of Geo. Rutson, Harrisville, Sunday evening, May 28, 1882, by Rev. F. W. Weatherwax, Mr. Louis R. Fiske, of Black River, and Miss Lewella J. Tillotson, of Harrisville.

The above young couple are well known to Harrisville people. The groom is the son of the eminent Michigan educator and clergyman, Rev. Dr. Fiske, Pres't of Albion college, and is at present superintendent of the store and mercantile business of Alger, Smith & Co., at Black River, this county. The bride has been a teacher in the Harrisville schools for the past year, and as such has won many golden opinions from pupils and parents who will regret to lose her from the schoolroom. She is also an accomplished musician and fine singer, standing very high as such in the estimation of our people. Tuesday evening a formal reception was given the happy couple at Agricultural hall, participated in by the *elite* of Harrisville, Black River and other points in the county, the occasion being one of the most pleasant and enjoyable order.

The Review takes this opportunity to congratulate Mr. and Mrs. Fiske, hoping that their pathway in life may be strewn with the richest blessings which heaven and earth can give, and that exceeding great prosperity may attend all their laudable undertakings.

Alcona County Review, June 2, 1882

Flawes, William
Titus, Ada Laura

PURELY PERSONAL.

Wm. Flawes, the handsome Black River shoemaker, was recently married to Miss Laura Titus of the same village.

Alcona County Review, November 23, 1888

Fleck, Joseph
McFadyen, Mary

The Local News.

Jos. Fleck, of Tawas City, and Miss Mary McFadyen, of Harrisville were united in marriage Thursday, March 27, by the Rev. L. Hazard at the residence of Mrs. A. Baror. The following Sunday Mr. Hazard officiated at the marriage of Albert McDonald, of Black River, and Ella Stafford, of South Harrisville, at the home of the latter's parents.

Alcona County Review, April 4, 1890

Forsythe, George Henry
Wilson, Hattie

Marriage Licenses.

April 10.—To Geo. H. Forsythe, Harrisville, and Hattie Wilson, Gustin.

Alcona County Review, April 15, 1897

PERSONAL.

Mr. Geo. Forsythe of Harrisville and Miss Hattie Wilson of Gustin were married last Thursday afternoon at the M. E. parsonage by Rev. W. W. Will.

Alcona County Review, April 22, 1897

Fortier, A. J.
Allen, Louisa [Bonville]

MARRIED.

Fortier—Allen.

Married at Duluth, Minn., July 23, Mr. A. J. Fortier to Mrs. Louisa Allen, at the residence of the bride's sister. Mr. Fortier was formerly with Alger, Smith & Co. at Black River, after with Sinclair & Co. of Alpena and at present with Panton & Weston of Duluth. The bride is well known here, being a former resident of Alcona.

Alcona County Review, August 3, 1893

Foster, James
Martin, Minnie

Jas. Foster, son of Robt. Foster, and Miss Minnie Martin were united in marriage Tuesday morning at the Catholic church by the Rev. Fr. Reussemann. Miss Annie Shirley stood up with the bride and Dan Hayden was best man. The bride is a daughter of Jas. Martin, the well known Harrisville citizen, who resides just north of town. A dance in the evening at the home of the bride's parents was given to the friends of the happy couple, in honor of the occasion. Many Black River friends were present.

Alcona County Review, August 29, 1890

Foster, Robert N.
Pyne, Ellen J.

Robert N. Foster of Black River, and Miss Ellen J. Pyne of Haynes were married Tuesday evening at the Nevins House. Rev. W. Will performed the ceremony. Mr. and Mrs. Foster will leave for Washington state next week, where Mr. Foster expects to engage in the lumber business.

Alcona County Review, October 27, 1898

Fowler, Charles
Rose, Emmer

LOCAL PICK UPS.

Chas. Fowler of Killmaster and Miss Emmer Rose of West Harrisville were united in marriage last evening by the Rev. Tompkins.

Alcona County Review, August 18, 1898

Franklin, Charles O.
Spencer, Hannah C.

Married at the home of the bride's parents in Gustin on Wednesday, Dec. 16 at 2 p.m., by Rev. W. P. Tompkins, Mr. Chas. O. Franklin, West Harrisville, and Miss Hannah Spencer.

Alcona County Review, December 17, 1896

Fraser, Donald
Ritchie, Ellen D.

LOCAL JOTTINGS.

Married: On Christmas Eve, Dec. 24th, at the Alcona House in Harrisville, by Rev. J. Bain, Donald Frazer and Miss Ellen Ritchie, all of Alcona.

Alcona County Review, January 1, 1886

Fraser, John A.
McNally, Jennie [Bridgeman]

REVIEWINGS.

Married: Aug. 31st, at the residence of Joseph Tayler, by Rev. N. N. Clark, Mr. John A. Fraser, and Mrs. Jennie McNally, all of Harrisville. The editor extends happy congratulations.

Alcona County Review, September 5, 1879

Freer, Andrew J.
Sovey, Mabel

Mr. Andrew J. Freer and Miss Mabel Sovey were quietly married on last Thursday evening at the residence of Mr. and Mrs. Kane Miller in Harrisville. Rev. W. P. Tompkins performed the ceremony.

Alcona County Review, July 14, 1898

Freer, George G.
Weir, Effie E.

Married.

In Harrisville, July 4, 1882, at the residence of the groom's father, by Rev. J. H. McIntosh, George G. Freer and Miss Effie E. Weir, all of Harrisville.

The editor of the Review rises to extend hearty congratulations to all the above named new couples, hoping that they may pick up pearls of happiness all along their respective pathways through life, and part in the terrestrial world only to meet in the never ending blissful celestial.

Alcona County Review, July 7, 1882

Freer, John S.
Hill, Catherine

Purely Personal.

It was very quietly done. So quietly in fact that but a favored few knew anything about it, but done it is, and Mr. and Mrs. Jno. S. Freer, nee Miss Kittie Hill are ready to receive the congratulations of their friends. The ceremony was performed Saturday evening at the residence of Mrs. Hotchkiss, sister of the bridegroom, by the Rev. P. C. Goldie. The Review wishes them a long and happy married life.

Alcona County Review, November 22, 1889

Freer, William Sherman
Sovey, Linna Elizabeth

Purely Personal.

Will Freer came home from the woods Sunday morning and rather surprised himself and his acquaintances by getting married before night. The bride was Miss Linna Sovey, daughter of Mr. and Mrs. Jos. Sovey. The young couple started out Sunday morning for a drive and in the course of a couple of hours had "seen the minister," the pastor of the M. E. church and were made man and wife. The bride attended school at Harrisville last Friday as usual. The Review wishes them nothing but happiness and prosperity.

Alcona County Review, February 28, 1890

Friedlander, Charles Millen
Dunlop, Ethel Amelia

Easter Wedding Bells.
From Alpena Pioneer.

The marriage of Mr. Charles Millen Friedlander of Black River, Mich., and Miss Ethel Amelia Dunlop of this city took place at the residence of the bride's parents, Washington Avenue, on Tuesday afternoon, the 5th inst. The beautiful marriage ceremony of the Episcopal church was performed in a most solemn manner by the Rev. Warren Hasting, in the presence of friends and a number of invited guests from the city and outside.

The bride was attended by her sister, Miss Viola Dunlop, and both looked charming in their becoming gowns of white silk organdy and heliotrope respectively, each carrying a large bouquet of roses. The groom was supported by his cousin Mr. John Baily of Black River. The rooms were very tastefully decorated and draped with evergreens and smilax. The curtains were drawn and the house artificially lighted a great profusion of pink, white and American Beauty roses, carnations and other flowers making a delightful effect.

An elaborate luncheon was served after which the 4:45 train carried the happy couple off amidst showers of rice and the best wishes of their hosts of friends. Mr. and Mrs. Friedlander will go east on their wedding tour visiting Detroit, New York and Washington.

Alcona County Review, April 14, 1898

Fullerton, Henry J.
LaForge, Mary

Around the County.
Mitchell Mites.

Mary La Forge and Henry Fullerton were united in marriage last week. We wish them a full measure of happiness.

Alcona County Review, April 30, 1891

Fulsher, Joseph
Good, Emma

LOCAL JOTTINGS.

Joseph Fulsher, of Au Sable, has a better half who as a maiden was Good. If the good will only leaven the other half Joseph's chances for a front pew in Kingdom come will be good. Miss Emma Good, of Greenbush, was married to the aforesaid Fulsher at Au Sable, April 15, by the Rev. W. R. Waters.

Alcona County Review, April 26, 1889

Gardiner, Harry
?, {Bride}

Your Folks and Our Folks.

Harry Gardiner, a brother of Mrs. Geo. W. Colwell, and well known here was recently united in marriage to a Buffalo young lady.

Alcona County Review, November 28, 1890

Gardner, Llewellyn
Tuttle, Helen

LOCAL JOTTINGS.

At the residence of the bride's parents in East Tawas, on Christmas Day, Llewellyn Gardner and Miss Helen Tuttle, only daughter of Judge and Mrs. J. B. Tuttle, were united in the bonds of wedlock. The groom is now a resident of Detroit, but was raised in the Review editor's native town, Lowell. The Review sends congratulations.

Alcona County Review, January 8, 1886

Genge, John
Thornton, Della M.

Yoked Together.

At the Hawkins House, Au Sable, Dec. 25th, by Rev. F. Bradley, John Genge and Della Thornton, both of Harrisville.

At the same time and place, by the same, Roland P. McDonald and Ida Thornton, both of Harrisville.

Alcona County Review, December 29, 1882

Gerlatt, R. B.
Reefer, Ada

WORLDLY WISDOM.

Detroit News: "R. B. Gerlatt, of Bay City, as been married to Miss Ada Reefer, of Kansas City. The lady is a Jewess, and Mr. Gerlatt was compelled to adopt that faith in order to secure his wife. Accordingly he sought a rabbi, who put him upon 18 months probation, and decided to take him into the faith without the performance of the ceremonial rites. This was done after an endorsement of his decision had been made by many of the American rabbis. The event is almost unprecedented in the history of the Jewish church. Gerlatt is a nephew of the late Geo. W. McCrary, secretary of war in President Hayes' cabinet."

Alcona County Review, September 5, 1890

Gillam, George E.
Tillotson, Rena B.

PURELY PERSONAL.

Geo. E. Gillam, accompanied his sister, Miss Mabel, to Detroit last Saturday. The former was to go East from Detroit to Oneida, N. Y., where he was to wed on Wednesday of this week Miss Rena Tillotson, a young lady well and favorably known in this village. Mr. and Mrs. Gillam will be at home to their friends after July 10.

Alcona County Review, June 14, 1889

WEDDING BELLS.

Gillam-Tillotson.—The following from papers published at Oneida, Syracuse and Utica, N. Y., is descriptive of the wedding of Geo. E. Gillam and Miss Rena Tillotson, of Oneida. The ceremony, which was privately celebrated at 9 o'clock a. m. Wednesday, June 12th, at the home of the bride's parents on Park Ave., in the presence of Mr. and Mrs. W. I. Tillotson, father and mother of the bride, Misses Carrie and Daisy Tillotson, Mr. and Mrs. L. R. Fiske, Jr., of Marine City, Mich., Mrs. R. L. Lott and daughter, Edith, of Harrisville, and Mrs. H. M. Shaw, of Oneida. The floral decorations were beautiful and were furnished by florist Burt of Syracuse. After an elegant wedding breakfast which was provided by caterer Smith, of Oneida, the newly married couple were driven to the depot of the N. Y. Central where they took a train for the East. They visited briefly the chief points of interest in Albany, on the Hudson, and in N. Y. City.

Notwithstanding that the ceremony was strictly private the bride was the recipient of many beautiful presents. Mr. and Mrs. Gillam will be at home to their friends at their future home in Harrisville after July 10.

Alcona County Review, June 21, 1889

ADDITIONAL LOCAL.

Geo. E. Gillam and bride are expected home this week.

Alcona County Review, June 28, 1889

Glode, James
Forsythe, Rachael Ann

PERSONAL MENTION.

James Glode, a handsome young man from Marquette, and a marine engineer by occupation, is to be united in marriage this evening at Killmaster to one of Alcona county's fair daughters, viz., Miss Annie Forsythe of Harrisville township. The marriage ceremony will be performed by the Rev. W. J. Bailey at the hotel in Killmaster in the presence of a few invited guests. Mr. and Mrs. Glode will remain at Killmaster until the opening of navigation, when they expect to go north. The Review extends congratulations and best wishes.

Gustin Grist.

Gustin, Feb. 5.--A fine evening was spent at the hotel after the wedding of Mr. Glode and Miss Forsythe.

Alcona County Review, February 7, 1895

Wedding at Killmaster.

Mr. James Glode, of Marquette, and Miss Rachael Ann Forsythe, of Harrisville, were united in marriage last Thursday evening at 4 o'clock p. m., by the Rev. Wm. J. Bailey in Harrisville.

Many friends and well-wishers were present to witness the happy union. I am told the bride and groom looked a little bashful about that time, but that is natural on such occasions—but they pulled through all right without fainting. The weather was rather cold that day and the thermometer stood at the freezing point with the couple. Those present thought it might turn warmer before morning. Next after this stage of proceedings was over, followed a very pleasant evening party at which every one present seemed to have a good time and enjoyed themselves until the clock began to strike the little ones next morning, Feb. 1. At this time the party began to disperse for the several places of abode, leaving behind them wishes of much joy to the newly married couple.

> *May virtue guide thy footsteps*
> *Where're on earth you roam,*
> *And when your earthly journey's o'er,*
> *May Heaven be thy home.*

Alcona County Review, February 7, 1895

Glover, William John
Bryne, Elizabeth

Greenbush Gettings.

The following item was handed us for publication a month ago, but its appearance at this late date is due to a treacherous memory:

Married.—By Rev. Jesse Robins, at the residence of the bridegroom's father, in Gustin Center, Oct. 6, Wm. J. Glover and Elizabeth Bryne, all of the above place.

Alcona County Review, November 12, 1886

Goff, George
?, {Bride}

LOCAL LACONICS.

Geo. Goff returned from York State, on Friday last, and surprised his friends by bringing a newly-wedded wife with him. The Review extends congratulations.

Alcona County Review, May 8, 1885

Goheen, Ezra
Springstead, Isabelle Joan

LOCAL JOTTINGS.

MARRIED.

At the residence of Mr. Geo. Goff, in Springport, on Tuesday, May 4th, by Rev. Jesse Robins, Mr. E. Goheen, formerly of Port Hope, Ontario, and Miss Belle Springstead, formerly of Bosanquet, Ontario.

Both of the above contracting parties are well and favorably known in Greenbush and vicinity, where they have resided for some time, Mr. Goheen having been principal of the Greenbush school for the past two years. The happy couple went to Bay City on the steamer Metropolis, Wednesday morning. The Review joins in the many good wishes for their future prosperity and happiness, and hopes the new relation assumed by Mr. Goheen will not prevent him from acting as our Greenbush correspondent in the future, as he has so acceptably done in the past.

Alcona County Review, May 7, 1886

GREENBUSH GETTINGS.

The happy couple who went to Bay City on Wednesday morning, May 5, had a pleasant trip. After reviewing the city, they left for Sterling on Friday afternoon, and were met at the depot by Mr. and Mrs. Ling, pastor of the M. E. church, in that place, and late pastor in Greenbush, and were at once claimed as their guests. The few days spent in that place gave great pleasure to all. Acquaintances was formed with some of the leading citizens of that town, and each evening was made pleasant by the presence of the above. We were pleased with the appearance of Sterling and surrounding country, which is an excellent agricultural district. Sterling is a town of 600 inhabitants, contains four stores, a good school, and a fine church, in which we had the pleasure of again hearing a

sermon from the Rev. Mr. Ling. On Monday afternoon we took the train for West Greenbush and were met there by Mr. Code and driven to his residence, where a very pleasant and agreeable surprise awaited in the form of

A RECEPTION PARTY.

We found a goodly number of friends assembled, and after having a season of enjoyment, all were introduced to a table loaded with everything that would tempt the appetite, and the beautiful bunches of flowers rendered fragrant the rooms of the house. After satisfying the demands of the appetite, another season of merriment was indulged in after which the party went to their homes. Myself and Mrs. E. G. feel very grateful for the kindness shown to us from every side.

Alcona County Review, May 14, 1886

Good, Josephus E.
Stringer, Ida E.

Licensed to Wed.

The following marriage licenses were issued this month and escaped notice at the time.

Josephus E. Good, of Harrisville, and Ida E. Stringer, of Gustin.

Alcona County Review, February 26, 1891

Goodfellow, Robert
Fraser, Jennie [Bridgeman]

Joined in Wedlock.

Robt. Goodfellow, one of the substantial and prosperous citizens of Curtis township, was united in marriage to Mrs. John Fraser of Harrisville last week, the Rev. Will officiating. They will make their home in Curtis.

Alcona County Review, July 1, 1897

Goodsell, C. William
Johnson, Annie

PERSONAL MENTION.

Married.—At the parsonage, Ossineke, Mich., Dec. 24, 1892, by the Rev. E. F. Warner, Mr. C. W. Goodsell of Alcona township, and Miss Annie Johnson of Haynes township.

Alcona County Review, December 29, 1892

HISTORY OF ONE YEAR.

Chronological History of the Past Year, 1892.

MARRIAGES.

Dec. 24. At Ossineke, C. W. Goodsell and Annie Johnson of Alcona county.

Alcona County Review, January 5, 1893

Goodwin, Harvey
Mooney, Mary

Curran Crumbs.

April 6, 1896.
Miss Mary Mooney and Harvey Goodwin were united in the holy bonds of matrimony, Long John officiating. The wedding was solemnized last Tuesday night, Mar. 31, between the hours of 12 and 1 at the home of Long John at Myo, Oscoda county. The most intimate friends of the bride and groom were present. After the ceremony an elaborate supper was served at the Hotel de Log at Myo. Mr. and Mrs. Goodwin departed on their wedding tour Wednesday last and will be at home in Curran after April 1st.

Alcona County Review, April 9, 1896

Gorbutt, T. H.
McClymont, Minnie

PERSONAL MENTION.

Cards have been received announcing the marriage of Miss Minnie McClymont, a former teacher in the Harrisville schools, to T. H. Gorbutt, at Three Rivers, Mich., Oct. 14th.

Alcona County Review, October 8, 1896

Gougiou, John
Eastman, Emma

LOCAL JOTTINGS.

Sheriff Sterritt returned last week from Seney, Mich., having in custody Jno. Gougon, who is charged by Emma Eastman, of Black River, with being the father of her child. The prisoner has a hearing this week before Justice Snowden, of Black River.

Alcona County Review, November 25, 1887

Marriage Licenses.

John Gougion, aged 28, to Emma Eastman, aged 18, both of Black River.

Alcona County Review, December 2, 1887

LOCAL JOTTINGS.

Jno. Gougiou and Emma Eastman settled their disagreement in a very sensible manner by agreeing to get married, and the ceremony was performed at Black River the first of the week.

Alcona County Review, December 2, 1887

Gow, Alexander L.
Baldwin, Elsie S.

People We Hear About.
MARRIAGE LICENSES.

The county clerk has issued the following marriage licenses during the month of September:

Alexander L. Gow, aged 26, Harrisville.

Elsie Baldwin, aged 19, Mitchell.

Alcona County Review, September 26, 1890

People We Hear About.

Mr. and Mrs. A. L. Gow, nee Miss Elsie Baldwin, but recently married, are passing their honeymoon at the St. Lawrence House in this village.

Alcona County Review, October 3, 1890

Gray, Albert
Pyne, Ella

LOCAL JOTTINGS.

Married, in Haynes, April 22, by the Rev. F. N. Barlow, Albert Gray to Miss Ella Pyne, all of Haynes.

Alcona County Review, April 26, 1889

Gray, William
Fisher, Martha

Married.—At the residence of the bride's parents, in this township, Oct. 15, by Rev. C. B. Steele, Mr. Wm. Gray and Miss Mattie Fisher, all of Harrisville.

Alcona County Review, October 15, 1886

Green, Edward M.
Donahue, Lizzie

Marriage Licenses.

Edward Green, aged 24, to Lizzie Donahue, aged 22, both of Harrisville.

Alcona County Review, December 2, 1887

LOCAL JOTTINGS.

Edward Green and Lizzie Donahue, two of our most estimable young people, were united in marriage last Saturday at Au Sable by the Rev. Fr. Winter. We wish them a full cup of joy and happiness.

Alcona County Review, December 2, 1887

Green, Edward M.
Parrow, Julia [Freer]

EVENTS OF ONE WEEK.

The marriage of Mr. Ed Green of Black River to Mrs. Julia Parrow took place on Christmas Day at the residence of the bride's parents, Mr. and Mrs. A. J. Freer, the Rev. Will officiating. Only a few immediate friends were invited.

Alcona County Review, December 26, 1895

Green, John
?, {Bride}

LOCAL JOTTINGS.

When John Green returned from Port Huron last Friday, the Review was not apprised that he had become a married man during his absence from Harrisville, and that his bride had accompanied him on his return to this place. But 'tis true, and the Review wishes the happy couple all manner of prosperity and bliss.

Alcona County Review, March 20, 1885

Green, Will
Blumberg, Nettie

Your Folks and Our Folks.

Will Green, of Au Sable, well-known along the shore as manager of the old stage line, was married to Miss Nettie Blumberg, of the same place, on the 16th ult.

Alcona County Review, July 2, 1886

Griswold, Francis Hosmer
Moshier, Hanna Salome

Additional Reviewings.

Married: Sunday evening, Aug. 28th, at the M. E. Parsonage, by Rev. C. Gibbs, Mr. F. Hosmer Griswold and Miss Salama Mosher, all of Harrisville. The Review extends congratulations to the happy couple and hopes they may never regret the union.

Alcona County Review, September 2, 1881

Groves, John M.
Mason, Victoria

COUNTY REVIEWINGS.

Married: At the M. E. Parsonage in Harrisville, Jan. 6, 1881, by Rev. Calvin Gibbs, of said place, Mr. John M. Groves and Miss Victoria Mason, both of Oscoda.

Alcona County Review, January 7, 1881

Gustin, H. K.
Avery, Ruth Huntington

Gustin—Avery.

The wedding of Representative H. K. Gustin and Miss Ruth Huntington Avery, took place yesterday at 3:30 o'clock p.m. The ceremony was performed by Rev. Warren Hastings at the residence of Mr. and Mrs. E. O. Avery, parents of the bride, at Alpena. The newly-married couple left on the southbound steamer Alpena the same evening for their wedding trip. The Review extends congratulations.

Alcona County Review, June 15, 1899

KILLMASTER.

George B. Killmaster, American consul at Port Rowan, Ont. made our village a brief, but interesting call from Sunday until Tuesday. He left for Alpena to attend the wedding of his cousin, H. K. Gustin.

Alcona County Review, June 15, 1899

Hackett, Percy
Graham, Lucy

The Local News.

Percy Hackett, the popular railroad conductor, has entered Hymen's noose by wedding Miss Lucy Graham of Tawas. They will reside in Alpena.

Alcona County Review, October 3, 1890

Haggett, William H.
McNeil, Annie

MARRIED.

Sept. 3, at the Methodist E. parsonage, Harrisville, by the Rev. Wm. J. Bailey, Mr. William H. Haggett of Black River, to Miss Annie McNeil of Au Sable, Mich.

Alcona County Review, September 8, 1892

HISTORY OF ONE YEAR.

Chronological History of the Past Year, 1892.

MARRIAGES.

Sept. 3. Wm. H. Haggett of Black River to Miss Annie McNeil of Au Sable.

Alcona County Review, January 5, 1893

Hale, William D.
Walker, Esther

PERSONAL MENTION.

Mr. Wm. Hale and Miss Birdie Walker were united in marriage yesterday at the residence of the bride's parents, Mr. and Mrs. Robt. Walker, the Rev. C. H. Holden of Alpena officiating. The young couple sensibly concluded to begin housekeeping at once and they had furnished the Carl Lund house ready for immediate occupancy. As a slight testimonial the boys around town put up a shake purse and bought a handsome lounge, which was set up in the house as a surprise. The Review extends congratulations and best wishes.

Alcona County Review, May 7, 1896

Haley, George W.
McDonald, Christine

Local Sayings and Doings.

Married—Sunday, May 7, by Justice LaChapelle at his residence, George W. Haley to Miss Christie McDonald.

Alcona County Review, May 12, 1882

Hall, William
Pyne, Meda

BLACK RIVER.
Nov. 22, '99.

A very pretty wedding took place at the home of Mr. and Mrs. Harry Hall, on Wednesday Nov. 15 at four o'clock in the afternoon, when their son, Will, was united in marriage with Miss Meda Pyne, a highly respected young lady of this place, Rev. Austin officiated. Miss Margaret McClellan of Alpena acted as bridesmaid and Freeman Hill as best man. The happy couple were the recipients of many very pretty and useful gifts. A party was given in the I. O. O. F. Hall in the evening at which a large crowd had a very enjoyable.

Alcona County Review, November 23, 1899

Hamilton, Alexander B.
Thornton, Mary Esther

MARRIED.

Sept. 5, at the Methodist E. parsonage, Harrisville, by the Rev. Wm. J. Bailey, Mr. Alexander B. Hamilton to Miss Mary Esther Thornton, both of Harrisville, Mich.

Alcona County Review, September 8, 1892

HISTORY OF ONE YEAR.

Chronological History of the Past Year, 1892.

MARRIAGES.

Sept. 5. Alexander B. Hamilton to Miss Mary Thornton, both of Harrisville.

Alcona County Review, January 5, 1893

Hamilton, George
Evans, Lizzie

PURELY PERSONAL.

Geo. Hamilton quietly folded his tent and like the Arab stole away during the mild winter weather of the past season. George went to Cheapside, Ont., where he was united in marriage to one of the fair ladies of that place, Miss Lizzie Evans by name. The Review extends congratulations and best wishes. They will reside in Cheapside for the present.

Alcona County Review, April 26, 1889

Purely Personal.

Geo. Hamilton returned from Cheapside, Ont., last week. His sojourn in Cheapside was not wholly in vain for George brought back with him his bride of a few months. He will remain here this winter.

Alcona County Review, October 11, 1889

Hamilton, James
Haley, Rebecca

Marriages.—In the last issue of the Au Sable News we find noted the following marriages of residents of Alcona county:

At the same time and place, by the Rev. R. Woodhams, James Hamilton and Rebecca Haley, both of Harrisville.

The Review extends congratulations to the newly wedded couples, and hopes their cup of bliss and prosperity may ever be overflowing. Walk uprightly, step lightly, and keep off the thorns, young friends. So shall unalloyed happiness follow you all.

Alcona County Review, March 25, 1881

Handy, T. P.
Dease, Ollie

NEIGHBORHOOD NOTES.

T. P. Handy, paymaster on the Detroit, Bay City & Alpena R. R., was married last week to Miss Ollie Dease, of East Tawas.

Alcona County Review, February 8, 1889

Harrington, {Groom}
?, {Bride}

Neighborhood Notes.

Mr. Harrington, the Alpena gentleman who recently accepted the position of cashier of the state treasury is soon to accept the heart and hand of a lovely Pontiac young lady.

Alcona County Review, September 6, 1889

Harris, Ben
Lostutter, Florence

Somewhat Personal.

Miss Florence Lostutter of Rising Sun, Ind., who visited family of B. F. Buchanan a few years ago and formed pleasant acquaintances here, was married last week to Mr. Ben Harris, a popular and well established young man of the same place. They contemplate a trip here and elsewhere in near future. She is a niece of Mrs. B.

Alcona County Review, November 12, 1891

Hartigan, Matthew
Nubert, Mary

It has been announced that Mr. M. Hartigan and Miss M. Nubert will soon join hands in wedlock.

Alcona County Review, November 21, 1895

Wedding Bells a Ringing.

Matthew Hartigan, a well-known Harrisville boy, took the all important step in a man's life this week, when he joined hands and fortunes with Miss May Nubert, of Black River. The ceremony was performed at St. Raphael's church, Black River, Tuesday, in the presence of a few friends. They will make their home for the present at Black River. The Review extends best wishes.

Alcona County Review, November 28, 1895

Hastings, George
Fleming, Annabel

HAYNES.
July 25, '99.

I congratulate Mr. and Mrs. Geo. Hastings and Mr. and Mrs. Lawrence Cook on the happy event of their unions.

You will have a weary race to run,
The end you cannot see;
Look over on the sunny side
And always cheerful be.

Alcona County Review, July 27, 1899

Hastings, Joseph Alexander
Elmes, Catherine Jane

LOCAL JOTTINGS.

Married: Oct. 20, 1885, at the residence of Widow Hastings, by the Rev. T. Leith, Joseph Alexander Hastings to Catherine Jane Elms, both of Alcona.

Alcona County Review, October 23, 1885

Hastings, Robert Thomas
Ritchie, Sarah Jane

The Local News.

Robt. F. Hastings and Sarah J. Ritchie, are the names attached to the last marriage license issued from the County Clerk's office. Both reside in Haynes.

Alcona County Review, December 12, 1890

Hastings, William John
Willoughby, Jane Ann
Elizabeth

Hastings—Willoughby.

On the evening of Dec. 25, 1893, at the residence of the bridegroom's brother-in-law at Black River, by Rev. E. F. Smith, Mr. Wm. J. Hastings and Miss Jane A. E. Willoughby.

Although it had been storming the greater part of the day, it ceased in time for the parties interested to assemble at Mr. Ellis', where two individuals who had been going alone agreed from this time on to walk together the journey of life.

Mr. and Mrs. Hastings are worthy young people and will doubtless be useful citizens in their town, where they are respected and have the best wishes of all who know them.

Christmas is indeed a day most fitting on which to begin life together, if those united have, or at the beginning of their married life will, receive into their hearts and home the Savior, whose advent to earth we celebrate this day. Then on each returning anniversary will the marriage bells and Christmas bells ring out in harmony to the world, of love in the home "and on earth peace, good will to men."

Merry Christmas and many, and may the New Years as they come and go add to your happiness, is the wish of your friends.

Alcona County Review, December 28, 1893

Busy Times In Haynes.

I congratulate Mr. and Mrs. Wm. Hastings and may their shadows never grow less.

Alcona County Review, January 11, 1894

Hawkins, Stephen
LaForge, Harriet

EVENTS OF ONE WEEK.

A license to marry was issued last week to Stephen Hawkins and Miss Hattie La Forge, the latter a daughter of Jas. La Forge. Both are residents of Mitchell township. The nuptials were to have been celebrated last evening at the home of the bride's parents.

Alcona County Review, March 1, 1894

Curran Items.

Married, at the residence of the bride's parents, Feb. 28, Mr. Stephen Hawkins to Miss Hattie La Forge, by Rev. Ferington of Fair View.

A large party of friends and neighbors was present, there being 35 who partook of the wedding dinner. May they have a long and prosperous life is the wish of
One Who Was There.

Alcona County Review, March 8, 1894

Hay, P.
Noyle, C.

Black River Sparks.

Cards are out announcing the wedding of Captain P. Hay to Miss C. Noyle at Mooretown, Ont. Capt. Hay is well known here and will command the tug Wescott the coming season, succeeding Capt. Howes who has resigned.

Alcona County Review, February 13, 1896

Black River Sparks.

Captain P. Hay has returned with his bride and will make his home with us. A cordial welcome is extended to Mrs. Hay.

Alcona County Review, February 27, 1896

Hayden, Daniel
Collins, Joanna

Hayden—Collins.

The marriage of Daniel Hayden and Miss Joanna Collins, two well known young people of this township, was solemnized Monday morning at the Catholic church by Fr. Ruessman. The groom is a steady

and industrious young man and his bride is a popular young lady who graduated from the Harrisville high school last spring with high honors. The Review proffers congratulations and wishes them a long and happy life.

Alcona County Review, October 1, 1891

Hayes, John Hartwell
Vaughn, Fannie

The following have been licensed to wed by the county clerk: Fred St. Peter and Flora Dewar, both of Gustin; Hartwell Hayes and Fannie Vaughn, both of Curtis.

Alcona County Review, June 27, 1890

Curtis Trifles.

Heartwell Hayes and Fannie Vaughn, both of Curtis township, were married by Justice Barker June 24.

Alcona County Review, July 4, 1890

Healy, Welcome
Snooks, Mrs. Mary

GLENNIE.

Welcome Healy, son of J. H. Healy, post master of Glennie, was married Oct. 19 to Mrs. Mary Snooks at the home of the bride's parents in Rose City. He has the well wishes of all his friends. They are now visiting with his parents. They intend to make their home in the future at Rose City, where he has a farm.

Alcona County Review, October 27, 1898

Heinold, Christian
Rudy, Marie

MIKADO MATTERS.

Mikado, June 5.--The events of the season were the weddings of Christian Heinold, of Mikado to Miss Rodha, of Handy last Thursday, and D. D. Bruce and a Miss McGillis on Tuesday, June 5. The latter departed on the south bound train.

Alcona County Review, June 8, 1888

LOCAL JOTTINGS.

Christian Heinold, of Greenbush, aged 47, and Marie Rudy, of Mikado, took out license No 18, and Justice C. P. Reynolds tied the nuptial knot for them in due legal form last week Thursday.

Alcona County Review, June 8, 1888

Henderson, {Groom}
?, {Bride}

The Local News.

Clerk Henderson, of the steamer City of Mackinac, is to be married in January to a Cheboygan young lady. The Democrat says that Cheboygan girls are going off like hot cakes.

Alcona County Review, November 29, 1889

Purely Personal.

Clerk Henderson of the City of Mackinaw has married a Cheboygan young lady.

Alcona County Review, January 31, 1890

Henderson, James E.
May, Minnie G. [Kibbee]

ADDITIONAL LOCAL.

A very interesting and happy event will take place this evening at the residence of H. C. Kibbee in this village, being nothing less than the marriage of their daughter, Minnie, to Capt. Jas. E. Henderson, of Sturgeon Pointe. Both the bride and groom are held in the highest esteem in this community and the match is an excellent one. The Review joins their hosts of friends in wishing them every joy and happiness that comes from such a union.

Alcona County Review, July 6, 1893

Married.: Henderson—May. At the residence of the bride's parents in Harrisville, July 6th, by the Rev. W. J. Bailey, Mr. James E. Henderson, of Sturgeon Point, to Mrs. Minnie G. May, of Harrisville.

Alcona County Review, July 13, 1893

Heron, Charles
Sousie, Clara

The Local News.

A happy event was the marriage last Thursday at Au Sable of Mr. Chas. Heron and Miss Clara Sousie, both of Black River. Mr. and Mrs. Heron returned to their home at once and the next evening entertained their friends in a royal manner in Malta Hall, with free dancing and refreshments. The Review extends congratulations and best wishes.

Alcona County Review, September 3, 1891

Heron, John W.
Bailey, Lulu H.

WEDDING BELLS.
Married—John W. Heron of Centralia, Wash., to Miss Lulu H. Bailey of Skamokawa, Wash., on

Sunday, Aug. 31, by Rev. Mr. Short, Rector of Grace Church, Astoria, Oregon.

The Gazette extends its hearty congratulations to the young couple and trusts that all the happiness and prosperity that is possible in this world may be theirs. Miss Bailey is a most estimable lady and made a host of warm friends while teaching here. Mr. Heron is a very exemplary young man, with marked business abilities, and is worthy of her in every respect. The happy couple left for Centralia Tuesday morning where they will make their future home.— Chathlamet Gazette.

Congratulations are in order here also, where both parties to this happy event enjoy the warm friendship of a wide circle of acquaintants.

Alcona County Review, September 19, 1890

Hewett, John
Nancy Atchison

HOME REVIEWINGS.

Married: On Sunday evening, Sep. 13, at the residence of Andy Atchison, by Geo. W. LaChapelle, Justice of the Peace, Mr. John Hewett and Miss Nancy Atchison, all of Harrisville. May the union be one of life-long happiness and prosperity, is the Review's best wish.

Alcona County Review, September 23, 1881

Hickey, John
Henderson, Mrs. Libbie

Local Sayings and Doings.

Married—At the Presbyterian parsonage of this place, Sunday evening, March 5, 1882, by Rev. W. Weatherwax, Mr. John Hickey, of Oscoda, and Mrs. Libbie Henderson, of Harrisville. The Review extends congratulations, and wishes the new couple an overflowing cup of bliss, all the way through life.

Alcona County Review, March 10, 1882

Hill, Benjamin
Anthony, Laura

GUSTIN.
Gustin loses one more of its fair young ladies. Miss Laura Anthony of Gustin and Mr. Benjamin Hill of Black River were united in marriage at Black River July 12th. Congratulations are extended by this community.

Alcona County Review, July 13, 1899

BLACK RIVER.
The swell event of the year was the marriage in their future home Wednesday, July 12th, of Miss Laura Anthony, daughter of Mr. Geo. Anthony of Killmaster, to Mr. Ben Hill. Rev. C. C. Austin performed the ceremony. Mr. Joe Whitsett was best man, Miss Belle Hill was maid of Honor and Miss Thema Anthony was bridesmaid. Everything was on an elaborate scale, from the rich dresses of the ladies, to the dinner. Many attended the party given in Odd Fellows hall in honor of Mr. and Mrs. Hill.

Alcona County Review, July 20, 1899

Hill, Fitz James
Hull, Lesbia H.

LOCAL JOTTINGS.

Married—In Brooklyn, N. Y., July 21st, 1885, by Rev. Arthur Mitchell, Fitz James Hill, of Black River, Mich., and Miss Lesbia H. Hull, of Brooklyn, N. Y.

The Review unites with the people of Black River and other acquaintances of Mr. Hill in this county in their offer of congratulations to the happy pair. Mr. Hill is book-keeper for Alger, Smith & Co., at B. R., and also treasurer of Alcona township. He is a very exemplary young man and has won a legion of friends during his residence within this county. May himself and bride enjoy a very profitable matrimonial sail down the dream of time, is the Review's wish.

Alcona County Review, July 31, 1885

BLACK RIVER RIPPLES.
F. J. Hill, on his return from a trip East, gave some of his friends quite a surprise, by bringing home with him a wife. He married an accomplished lady from Brooklyn.

Alcona County Review, August 14, 1885

Hill, Greeley
Taylor, Jennie

PERSONAL MENTION.
Miss Jennie Taylor, sister of Mrs. A. McLearn, left yesterday noon for Chicago, where Miss Taylor and Greeley Hill, formerly of this place, will be united in marriage. From Chicago Mr. and Mrs. Hill will go to Alexander, Wis., where they will make their home.—Press.

Alcona County Review, November 8.1894

Hogan, James J.
Morrison, Bena

MARRIED.

In Harrisville, Jan. 7, 1882, at the M. E. parsonage, by Rev. J. H. McIntosh, James J. Hogan, of Black River, and Miss Bena Morrison, of Oscoda.

Alcona County Review, January 13, 1882

Hogue, Wilder B.
Elmer, Ida M.

LOCAL JOTTINGS.

Married, at the home of the bride's parents in Harrisville township, June 4th, 1884, by the Rev. J. H. McIntosh, Wilder Hogue and Miss Ida M. Elmer, all of Harrisville.

At last two more hearts beat as one, while time rolls on and Cupid still lives to throw his love tipped darts at others. The happy couple have the best wishes of the Review for a prosperous, happy life.

Alcona County Review, June 6, 1884

Holmes, Ellsworth G.
?, Forest

HAYNES.

E. G. Holmes, teacher of District No. 4, has arrived with his bride and will fix up a residence before the school year commences. I wish them much happiness.

Alcona County Review, August 19, 1897

Holmes, Frank C.
Spratt, Lizzie

Along the Shore.

Frank C. Holmes and Miss Lizzie Spratt, of Alpena, were united in marriage Thursday evening of last week.

Alcona County Review, October 7, 1881

Hompstead, George
Burkhart, Elizabeth Jane

PERSONAL.

George Hompstead Jr. and Elizabeth Jane Burkhart have been licensed to wed.

Alcona County Review, April 1, 1897

EVENTS OF ONE WEEK.

George Hompstead of Haynes and Miss Elizabeth Burkhart of West Harrisville, were united in marriage at West Harrisville on Thursday, April 8, Rev. F. S. Ford officiating.

Alcona County Review, April 15, 1897

Hompstead, George
Erb, Catherine [Dewar]

PERSONAL POINTS.

Mr. George Hompstead and Mrs. Catherine Erb were united in marriage by Rev. W. Will on Tuesday evening. The ceremony was performed at the residence of Mr. Daniel Dewar, brother to the bride.

Alcona County Review, December 15, 1898

Hompstead, Samuel
O'Niel, Lile

LOCAL JOTTINGS.

The marriage of Samuel Hempstead, of Grayling, Mich., to Miss Lile O'Niel, of Tawas city, late of Harrisville, took place at Tawas city Thursday, March 14.

Alcona County Review, March 15, 1889

PURELY PERSONAL.

Mrs. Tinkey and son, Kane, and Mrs. Geo. Balch, Jr., attended the wedding Thursday of Miss Lile O'Niel to Sam'l Hempsted at Tawas city.

Alcona County Review, March 15, 1889

Hopkins, Fred
Hill, Belle

Cupid Scores Another Victory.

Miss Bell Hill, well known here as a former leading belle of Alcona county, was married Sept. 20 at Detroit to Fred Hopkins, one of the leading young men of the Capital city. The Lansing Journal in speaking of the happy event says:

Fred J. Hopkins, the popular teller of the City National bank, and Miss Belle Hill were married this afternoon at the home of the bride's sister, Mrs. F. O. Gullifer, in Detroit, in the presence of a few of the most intimate friends. The bride was arrayed in a beautiful costume of brocaded pink silk and wore corsage and hand boquets of cream tea roses. Mr. and Mrs. Hopkins will reside in Lansing, and will hereafter be at home at 321 Walnut street north.

Alcona County Review, October 5, 1888

Hopkins, Harvy
Cole, Mrs. Sarah

Your Folks and Our Folks.

Married.—At the Alcona House, in this village, on Sunday, Aug. 8th, by F. A. Beede, Esq., Harvy Hopkins and Sarah Cole, all of this township.

Alcona County Review, August 13, 1886

Hopper, Thomas J.
Dwyer, Kathrine

WEST HARRISVILLE.

Dec. 8, 1896.

A very pretty wedding was solemnized at the residence of I. Rose, Wednesday, Dec. 3d, inst. The contracting parties were Mr. Thos. J. Hopper of Tawas City, and Miss Kathrine Dwyer, of this city.

The bride was attended by her cousin, Miss Bryde Rose, and the groom was attended by his friend, W. J. McMullan, of this village.

After the ceremony, which took place at 3 o'clock p.m., and which was performed by Rev. Fr. Poulin, supper was served for the intimate friends and relatives. The happy couple left for Alpena amid a shower of old shoes and rice.

The bride has many friends in this city who join in wishing her every happiness.

Alcona County Review, December 10, 1896

Hornby, Charles W.
DeForest, Elizabeth Maud

The Local News.

Particulars are not at hand but news comes that Chas. Hornby and Miss Lizzie De Forrest were united in marriage on Christmas day at the home of the bride's parents southwest of this village.

Alcona County Review, December 27, 1889

The Local News.

The marriage of Chas. W. Hornby and Miss Elizabeth DeForest, which was to have taken place Christmas day, did not occur until the 27th of December when it was solemnized by the Rev. P. C. Goldie. The delay was on account of bad weather.

Alcona County Review, January 3, 1890

Houghton, Charles William
McLaurin, Abigail

Houghton—McLaurin.

At the parsonage, March 15th, 1895, by the Rev. W. J. Bailey, Mr. Charles William Houghton to Miss Abigail McLaurin, both of Harrisville, Mich.

Alcona County Review, March 21, 1895

Howard, George F.
Apsey, Flavia

Your Folks and Our Folks.

Geo. F. Howard, the jovial station agent and operator at West Harrisville, has joined the army of Benedicts. His bride was Miss Flavia Apsey, also a resident of West Harrisville.

Alcona County Review, November 14, 1890

Howe, William
Geer, Nettie

LOCAL JOTTINGS.

Wm. Howe, or "Billy," as he is more generally called, is handy man about the Nevins House, and the owner of a dulcet voice that would rival in sweetness that of the famous Nightengale, or, mayhap, the Sweet Singer of Michigan, My Michigan. The refrains that Billy sings to the delight of the frequenters of the above hostelry, are sources of pride and happiness to himself, no doubt, but thrice as happy, yea, three times thrice as happy, is Billy since he took to himself a wife from among the fair young ladies of the Provinces. This happy event took place a short time ago at Oriel, Canada. If it is not yet too late the Review begs leave to congratulate the happy bridegroom and his bride. The bride was Miss Nettie Geer.

Alcona County Review, February 8, 1889

Howitson, William S.
Kramer, Minnie May

Married, June 8, 1898, at the residence of the brides' parents, Mr. W. S. Howitson of Greenbush and Miss Minnie May Kramer of Gustin, W. P. Tompkins officiating.

Alcona County Review, June 16, 1898

Hubert, Fred
Thibeau, Minnie

LOCAL JOTTINGS.

We neglected to mention last week the marriage of Fred Hubert and Miss Minnie Tebo by Esq. Reynolds.

Alcona County Review, August 5, 1887

Huffman, Joseph
Baker, Minnie

Local Sayings and Doings.

Married—At the Presbyterian parsonage in Harrisville, June 13, 1882, by Rev. F. W. Weatherwax, Joseph Huffman, of Black River, Mich., and Miss Minnie Baker, of Norfolk, Ont.

Alcona County Review, June 16, 1882

Hugill, Henry
Wheeler, Mary M.

Married.—At the M. E. parsonage, Oct. 6, by Rev. C. B. Steele, Henry Hugill and Mary M. Wheeler, both of Harrisville.

Alcona County Review, October 22, 1886

Hull, George
Buchanan, Ida Ella

LOCAL JOTTINGS.

Married: On the 10th inst., at the residence of John Buchanan, by the Rev. T. B. Leith, George Hull and Ida Ella Buchanan, all of Harrisville. Here's hoping that the young couple may have a prosperous, happy voyage through life, and the *hull* of their bark ne'er be wrecked on the reef of disunion.

Alcona County Review, January 15, 1885

Hulme, James
Brown, Annie [Huffman]

PERSONAL MENTION.

For 14 years Jas. Hulme and Mrs. Annie Brown have lived together as man and wife, but the marriage tie was not made in strict conformance with the law of the land, a fact that was never divulged to Mrs. Hulme until a few years since. Before that she lived on in blissful ignorance that she was not lawfully wedded. On Tuesday Mr. Hulme procured a regular marriage license and the error of 14 years ago will thus be rectified.

The Hulmes live at Handy station.

Alcona County Review, May 31, 1894

CORRESPONDENCE.

Curran P. O., June 5.—Jas. Hulme and wife of Handy Station were happily married Monday afternoon by Justice McClatchey. Regular readers of the Review will readily see the peculiarity of this seemingly anomalous statement.

Alcona County Review, June 7, 1894

Huot, Joseph
Ducharme, Vina

LOCAL PICK UPS.

On Monday evening at St. Anne's church, Joseph Huot was married to Miss Vina Ducharme, Rev. C. H. DeQuoy officiating. Both are well known in the city and have many friends who wish them an abundance of happiness.--Alpena Echo.

Alcona County Review, June 8, 1899

Hyke, George A.
McVeigh, Celia Ann

Haynes.

Mr. George Hyke and Miss Annie McVeigh were united in marriage at Tawas last week. Both of Haynes township.

Alcona County Review, May 5, 1892

HISTORY OF ONE YEAR.

Chronological History of the Past Year, 1892.

MARRIAGES.

April 2. Geo. Hyke, Annie McVeigh of Haynes at Tawas.

Alcona County Review, January 5, 1893

Irwin, George Wilfred
Beech, Bessie May

PERSONAL POINTS.

A quiet wedding occurred at the home of Mr. and Mrs. Fred Kirkendall on Saturday evening last, when Mr. Geo. W. Irwin of Forestville, and Miss Bessie Beech of Greenbush were united in marriage by the Rev. W. W. Will.

Mr. and Mrs. Irwin left for Forestville Monday.

Alcona County Review, March 31, 1898

Jack, George
Walker, Jennie [Malotte]

COUNTY JOTTINGS.

Married: April 9th, at the Carle House, Alcona, by Rev. N. N. Clark, Mr. George Jack and Mrs. Jennie Walker, all of Alcona.

Alcona County Review, April 12, 1878

Jack, James
Milligan, Rilla

Haynes Happenings.

October 8, 1895.
Reported that James Jack and Rilla Milligan were married. We wish them all kinds of prosperity in their matrimonial venture.

Alcona County Review, October 10, 1895

James, Ephraim
Lyon, Mrs. Sarah Ann
HOME REVIEWINGS.

We see by the Alpena Argus that on the 30th ult., in that city, Mr. Ephraim James of Alpena and Mrs. Sarah Ann Lyon of Harrisville were united in the holy bonds of matrimony by Rev. Wm. Donnelly. Of course, this explains conclusively why Mrs. Lyons likes Alpena better. The Review with hosts of Harrisville people extend congratulations to the happy, new-made couple.

Alcona County Review, September 9, 1881

Jenkins, William
Young, Martha J.
COUNTY JOTTINGS.
A double wedding occurred at the residence of J. B. Young, in Greenbush, Monday, his two eldest daughters being married at that time. Wm. Jenkins and Wm. J. Kell are the young gentlemen who carried off the prizes. May happiness and prosperity crown the lives of these newly married couples.

Alcona County Review, July 5, 1878

Johnson, Canute A.
McGillivary, Mary J.
[McFarland]
Wedding Bells A Ringing.
Johnson—McGillivary
Canute A. Johnson, the popular Mikado merchant, was married last evening at the residence of John McMaster to Mrs. Mary J. McGillivary of Au Sable, the Rev. Collins of Au Sable officiating. Mr. and Mrs. Johnson have gone to Saginaw and Ludington on a short bridal tour and at the conclusion of their visit with friends in those places, they will return and begin housekeeping at Mikado.

Alcona County Review, November 28, 1895

Johnson, Oscar
Nelson, Dora
SPRUCE.
Oscar Johnson, one of Caledonia's returned soldiers, and Miss Dora nelson of Alpena were married last week. Best wishes to the young couple.

Alcona County Review, July 20, 1899

Johnson, Samuel
Keegan, May Emmalene

SOMEWHAT PERSONAL.

Married at the residence of Mr. Samuel Johnson in Haynes, on June 30, 1892, by J. L. Shaw, Esq.: Mr. Samuel Johnson of Haynes twp. and Miss May E. Keegan of Mikado, all of Alcona county, Mich.

Alcona County Review, July 7, 1892

HISTORY OF ONE YEAR.

Chronological History of the Past Year, 1892.

MARRIAGES.
June 30. Samuel Johnson to Mary Keegan.

Alcona County Review, January 5, 1893

Johnson, William R.
Shaw, Sarah Melinda
Married, Johnson-Shaw.—At the home of the bride's parents in Haynes township, May 12, Wm. R. Johnson and Sarah M. Shaw, the Rev. P. C. Goldie officiating.

Alcona County Review, May 24, 1889

LOCAL JOTTINGS.

Wm. R. Johnson and Sarah Shaw both of Haynes were recently married.

Alcona County Review, May 24, 1889

Johnston, Edward
Hicks, Mary Ann
COUNTY REVIEWINGS.

Married.—At Harrisville, April 20, 1880, by Rev. D. Van Dyke, Edward Johnston and Mary Ann Hicks, both of Alcona. May they enjoy a long and happy wedded life.

Alcona County Review, April 23, 1880

Johnston, John
Morton, Elizabeth
Haynes Items.
Haynes, July 27—Mr. Lyman Morton and Miss Sarah Clark, and Mr. John Johnston and Miss Elizabeth Morton were united in matrimony by the Baptist minister of Harrisville, on Saturday afternoon at the residence of Mr. Mark Morton. There was a large concourse of relatives and friends present at the ceremony and the presents were numerous and appropriate to the occasion.

Alcona County Review, July 30, 1891

Somewhat Personal.
A double wedding took place last Saturday morning at the residence of Mark Morton in Haynes township at which his son, Lyman, was united in the holy bonds of matrimony to Miss Sarah Clark, and his daughter, Elizabeth, to John Johnston. The happy ceremony was performed by the Rev. G. W. Cram of Harrisville.

Alcona County Review, July 30, 1891

Johnston, William
Ritchie, Susan
COUNTY REVIEWINGS.

Married—At the Presbyterian parsonage, by Rev. D. Van Dyke, May 2d, Mr. William Johnston and Miss Susan Ritchie.

Alcona County Review, May 7, 1880

Jones, Edward
Martin, Annie
LOCAL JOTTINGS.

Married: At the M. E. Parsonage, August 20th, 1885, Rev. T. B. Leith, Edward Jones and Annie Martin, all of Harrisville.

Alcona County Review, August 28, 1885

Jones, George
Emerson, Gertie
EVENTS OF ONE WEEK.

By the Northwestern Review we note that Miss Gertie Emerson, a daughter of Mr. and Mrs. Nathan Emerson of Harrisville, was married at the residence of Chas. Ellis to Geo. Jones of Alpena on Christmas, the Rev. F. N. Barlow officiating. The bride's parents were present and over one hundred guests partook of the wedding feast. Mr. Jones owns a farm in Long Rapids township, where they will make their home.

Alcona County Review, January 4, 1894

Jones, Joseph D.
Kelley, Mary Ann
LOCAL JOTTINGS

J. D. Jones, aged 25, and Mary Ann Kelley, aged 19, both of Killmaster, took out a marriage license this week.

Alcona County Review, April 13, 1888

Jones, Richard
?, Kate
BLACK RIVER ITEMS.

Black River, Oct. 24.--Dick Jones has taken unto himself a partner to share his joys and sorrows. May prosperity and happiness brighten their way along life's stormy path.

Alcona County Review, October 28, 1887

Jordan, Martin
Murray, Emma
BLACK RIVER.

A modest wedding occurred here last Saturday when Mr. Martin Jordan and Miss Emma Murray, two of our popular young people, were made one. Rev. Fr. Poulin performed the ceremony. A wide circle of friends wish the young people a successful voyage over life's troublous sea.

Alcona County Review, October 13, 1898

Joughin, Herbert A.
Patterson, Lois E.
EVENTS OF ONE WEEK.

Cards are out announcing the marriage of Herbert A. Joughin to Lois E. Patterson at Pittsford, Mich., Monday, Aug. 26, inst. This explains Mr. Joughin's quiet and mysterious departure from Harrisville a few days ago, and so far as known few were in the secret. The Review extends heartiest congratulations and wishes the happy couple all the pleasure and happiness of married life and none of its sorrow. They will make Harrisville their home and will be at home after Oct. 10th.

Alcona County Review, August 29, 1895

PERSONAL MENTION.

H. A. Joughin and bride arrived home on the Sunday boat and will enjoy the hospitality of O. H. Smith until they begin housekeeping.

Alcona County Review, September 5, 1895

Kahn, Samuel B.
Sandorf, Nellie
Married at Bay City.

At 5 o'clock p.m. on Tuesday Samuel B. Kahn, the energetic and popular young merchant, was united in marriage to Miss Nellie Sondarf at Washington Hall, Bay City. The bride has visited in Harrisville and is an attractive young lady both in manner and person. The bridegroom has been a resident of Harrisville for the past two years and by his uniform courtesy and gentlemanly bearing has won the respect and friendship of

a large circle who will wish him unqualified joy in his new relation in life.

Alcona County Review, December 30, 1897

PERSONAL.

Samuel B. Kahn and bride arrived home yesterday and are receiving congratulations today.

Alcona County Review, January 6, 1898

Karhan, James
Bruce, Annie
HOME REVIEWINGS.

Married.—At Harrisville, Mich., Oct. 26, 1881, by Rev. J. H. McIntosh, James Karhan of Harrisville and Miss Annie Bruce of Greenbush.

Alcona County Review, November 11, 1881

Keen, Robert
Wilson, Eliza Ann
ALONG THE SHORE.

General News-Gleanings From the Several Counties.

ALPENA.

Recent marriages hereabouts: May 26, Angus McDonald and Miss Margaret J. Hall. May 30, Robert Keen and Miss Eliza Ann Wilson. June 3, Robert Bolton and Miss Cynthia Ellen Dove.

Alcona County Review, June 11, 1880

Kell, William J.
Young, Clio
COUNTY JOTTINGS.

A double wedding occurred at the residence of J. B. Young, in Greenbush, Monday, his two eldest daughters being married at that time. Wm. Jenkins and Wm. J. Kell are the young gentlemen who carried off the prizes. May happiness and prosperity crown the lives of these newly married couples.

Alcona County Review, July 5, 1878

Kelley, Charles
Morris, Cora
HOME NEWS JOTTINGS.

At the residence of the bride's parents, in Alpena, Sunday last, Mr. Charles Kelley, of Pack, Woods & Co.'s store, Au Sable, and Miss Cora Morris (daughter of Web. Morris, late foreman of our Au Sable paper),

were united in marriage. The Review extends congratulations to the happy pair, and hopes for their highest matrimonial joy and prosperity through all the future years of their life.

Alcona County Review, December 1, 1882

Kelley, Hiram
Leach, Libbie
MARRIED.

Kelly--Leach--At Baptist parsonage in Harrisville, June 23d, 1887, Hiram Kelley, of St. Ignace, and Libbie Leach, of Pickford, Mich.

Alcona County Review, July 8, 1887

Kelley, John
McGillis, Mary
MARRIED.

A double marriage occurred Tuesday morning at the Catholic church, the Rev. Fr. Mahar officiating. The contracting parties were John McGillis and Mary McDonald and John Kelley and Mary McGillis. All the young people are residents of this county, all having resided in Greenbush or adjoining townships for many years.

Alcona County Review, January 11, 1894

Kennedy, John C.
Wilson, Ida Belle

The Review is credibly informed that a quiet wedding will take place some day next week. The bride is one of Harrisville's most estimable young ladies; the prospective bridegroom has been a leader in all the social events of this village. The Review begs leave to extend congratulations and well wishes.

Alcona County Review, June 1, 1888

LOCAL JOTTINGS

The prospective marriage mentioned in the Review last week took place Monday evening at the home of the bride's parents in this village. The contracting parties were John Kennedy and Miss Belle Wilson. The wedding was private, the ceremony being performed by the Rev. P. C. Goldie. The happy couple left the same evening by the steamer City of Mackinac for Bad Axe, the former home of the bride. After visiting friends there for a few days they will join the rest of the Harrisville party and will continue their journey to Skamokawa, Washington Ter., at which place Mr.

Kennedy has been employed by Colwell & Montgomery for a number of months past.

Alcona County Review, June 8, 1888

Kenville, John
Eneuf, Mary

People We Hear About.
MARRIAGE LICENSES.

The county clerk has issued the following marriage licenses during the month of September:

Jno. Kenville, aged 24, Black River.

Mary Eneuf, aged 23, Black River.

Alcona County Review, September 26, 1890

Kersten, Adelbert
Wilson, Sarah F.

Married.

At the residence of the bride's father, October 26, 1882, by Rev. J. H. McIntosh, Anthony Kersten of Otsego Lake, and Miss Sarah F. Wilson of South Harrisville, Mich.

Alcona County Review, October 27, 1882

HOME NEWS JOTTINGS.

A communication relative to the occasion of the late marriage of Sarah F. Wilson, has been received, but too late for insertion this week.

Alcona County Review, November 3, 1882

Wedding Celebration.

Some time ago we received a communication from one of the guests at the wedding of Miss Sarah F. Wilson, youngest daughter of Isaac Wilson of South Harrisville, and Adelbert Kirsten of Otsego Lake, Mich., but owing to the pressure of other matters, we were obliged to put off its appearance until now, when we can give but a synopsis of the well written article. The communication gives the following:

"The evening was one of the pleasantest of the season and about thirty-five guests were in attendance, some of them from a distance, but the most of the company was immediate neighbors. The ceremony was performed in a beautiful and impressive manner by Rev. J. H. McIntosh. The supper was a real wedding feast. The 'bride's cake' was a mammoth one and as good as it was large, each of the ladies especially appropriating a piece as a kind of 'extra.' The presents were many, beautiful and some of them costly. Among these were two elegant lamps, a heavy gold ring, silver ware, etc., some of which came from the groom's friends, a beautifully bound family Bible and hymnal neatly lettered on the lids, being the gift of the bride's mother, and last but not least, a piano from the bride's father.

Altogether the occasion was a very enjoyable one, and a fitting tribute of the esteem and love in which both the young bride and the fortunate young man are held by all who know them. The good wishes of hosts of friends follow them to their new home in Otsego.

Alcona County Review, November 10, 1882

Kerwin, Michael
McKay, Tillie

COUNTY NEWS JOTTINGS.

And now our young friend, Michael Kerwin, of Harrisville, has fallen overboard into the matrimonial sea. He was married on Wednesday to Miss Tillie McKay, of AuSable. A few hours after marriage, the happy couple started off on a trip to the southern part of the State. May prosperity and happiness crown their life, and their shadows never grow less.

Alcona County Review, September 7, 1877

Ketchepaw, John
Hawkins, Adella Williams

LOCAL JOTTINGS.

Married—By the Rev. T. B. Leith, at the M. E. parsonage, on the 15th inst., John Ketchepaw and Adella Williams, all of Alcona.

Alcona County Review, February 19, 1886

Kibbee, Albert Howard
Peterson, Sarah Myrtle

PERSONAL MENTION.

The marriage of Sergt. Albert Kibbee and Miss Myrtle Peterson is an interesting social event that will take place in Harrisville before October.

Alcona County Review, September 10, 1896

PERSONAL MENTION.

The marriage of Miss S. Myrtle, youngest daughter of Mr. and Mrs. J. Peterson, formerly of Detroit, to Mr. A. H. Kibbee, of that place, takes place in the Methodist church Tuesday, Sept. 29, at noon.

Alcona County Review, September 17, 1896

Albert H. Kibbee and his best man, Mr. Fessenden, are up from Detroit for the nuptial ceremony, which occurs next Tuesday at the M. E. church.

Alcona County Review, September 24, 1896

Kibee—Peterson.

Albert H. Kibbee and Myrtle S. Peterson, were united in the holy bonds of matrimony at the Methodist church at Tuesday 2 o'clock p.m., Rev. Will officiating.

The ceremony was performed under an arch of evergreens and in the presence of a small company of invited guests. At the opening strains of Lohengrin's wedding march the bridegroom and his best man, Mr. Fessenden, of Detroit, both neatly clad in conventional suits of black, entered from the rear and took their places at the right of the altar. The bride entered at the front of the church and passed down the aisle to altar upon the arm of her father. She was attended by her cousin, Miss May Sisson, and two little maids of honor, Pearl and Dolly Henderson, bearing boquets of asters. The bride was beautifully attired in a cream satin dress en train and her figure was completely enveloped in a tulle veil.

The bridal party left the church at the conclusion of the ceremony for Lakeside, where a sumptuous wedding dinner was spread in their honor.

Mr. and Mrs. Kibbee took their departure on the afternoon train for Detroit, which city will be their home. Warm congratulations follow them. Mr. Kibbee is a Harrisville boy and a young man of high character and bright prospects.

Alcona County Review, October 1, 1896

PERSONAL MENTION.

Ed. Myers attended the wedding of his old friend and comrade, Albert H. Kibbee.

Alcona County Review, October 1, 1896

PERSONAL MENTION.

Miss Ida Peterson came up from Detroit for the Kibbee-Peterson nuptials.

Alcona County Review, October 1, 1896

Killmaster, Charles H.

Duncan, Nellie

LOCAL JOTTINGS.

Many of their acquaintances in this place will no doubt be pleased to hear that Chas. H. Killmaster and Miss Nellie Duncan, of Oscoda, were united in marriage, Wednesday. The Review extends congratulations.

Alcona County Review, August 29, 1884

Killmaster, John Henry
Barlow, Helen May

Purely Personal.

Reported that Jno. H. Killmaster was married in Bay City a few days ago to Miss Nellie M. Barlow of Au Sable.

Alcona County Review, July 4, 1890

Kimball, Fred M.
Harshaw, Mary E.

ALL ALONG THE SHORE.

Alpena Drift.

From the Pioneer.

Mr. Fred M. Kimball, Senator Harshaw's partner in the hardware business, and Mary E. Harshaw, the Senator's oldest daughter, were united in marriage at the residence of the bride's father on Wednesday evening of last week. The young couple are well known and highly respected.

Alcona County Review, June 10, 1887

King, Harry H.
McKinley, Rosa

LOCAL LACONICS.

Harry King and Rosa McKinley, both of Black River, were married at Alcona by the Rev. Balmer, on Thursday of last week. May they "live long and die happy."

Alcona County Review, May 22, 1885

King, Joseph
Joseph, Emma

King—Joseph.

A quiet wedding took place at St. Anne's church last Tuesday morning when Mr. Joseph King and Miss Emma Joseph were united in the holy bands of wedlock, by Rev. Fr. Poulin, at 8 o'clock.

The bridesmaid was Miss Agnes Tovey and best man was Mr. Albert Joseph, brother of the bride. After the wedding they drove to Mr. M. Tovey's, where they partook of a wedding breakfast. After this they drove to their home at Mud Lake, accompanied by Mrs. M. Tovey, and son Richard and daughter Agnes.

In the evening there was a dance at the home of the bride's parents, Mr. and Mrs. Aleck Joseph.

Mr. and Mrs. King received congratulations and showers of rice and many presents.

Alcona County Review, October 6, 1898

Kirkendall, Wesley
Monroe, Myrtle

PERSONAL MENTION.

Married.

At the residence of the bride's father, D. A. Monroe, Greenbush, Jan. 14th, 1895, by the Rev. W. J. Bailey: Mr. Wesley Kirkendall to Myrtle Monroe, both of Greenbush.

Alcona County Review, January 17, 1895

Knight, Adelbert
Doughty, Clara

MARRIAGE LICENSES.

The following marriage licenses were issued from the county clerk's office within the past week:

July 29.—Albert Knight, Alpena; Miss Clara Doughty, Harrisville.

Alcona County Review, August 3, 1893

Koch, W. E. C.
Heumann, Minnie

ALL ALONG THE SHORE.

Oscoda and Au Sable Notes.

From the Saturday Night.

Miss Minnie Heumann, of Bay City, a sister of Messrs. Fred and George Heumann, of Oscoda, was recently married at Denver, Col., to Mr. W. E. C. Koch, of Aspen, Col.

Alcona County Review, August 5, 1887

Kohlman, Louis W.
Mulhatten, Maggie A.

CURRAN.

A very pretty wedding was solemnized at the residence of Mr. Mulhatten last Wednesday evening. The occasion was the marriage of Mr. Mulhatten's daughter, Miss Maggie, to Mr. Louis Kohlman, of Mud Lake.

The bride was attired in a becoming suit of white. Miss Agnes La Forge acted as maid of honor and Mr. Edward La Forge as groomsman. After the ceremony the guests retired to Mr. H. F. Fullerton's where a reception was given.

Owing to the illness of her father, Mrs. Kohlman will remain in Mitchell for an indefinite period.

Their many friends wish them a pleasant voyage through life.

Toot Freer drove to Harrisville on Tuesday and back Wednesday so as to attend the wedding. His sister, Miss Martha, accompanied him back to Curran. She also went out to attend the wedding. This is the quickest trip Casey has made this year.

Frank Noyes drove to Curran Wednesday to attend the Kohlman-Mulhatten wedding. Miss Mae Freer and Miss Eunice Toole were numbered among the invited guests.

Alcona County Review, May 19, 1898

Kruger, William
Harrison, Maud

EVENTS OF ONE WEEK.

William Kruger and Miss Maud Harrison, both of Gustin, were united in marriage at the Methodist parsonage last Thursday evening.

Alcona County Review, December 10, 1896

LaBoueff, David
Branaghan, Lizzie

LABOUFF—BRANNAGAN.

The marriage of David LaBoueff to Miss Lizzie Brannagan was consummated yesterday afternoon at Au Sable, whither the wedding party drove from Harrisville. The event has been long expected and is looked upon as a happy union. The bridegroom is too well known as one of Harrisville's prosperous business men, to require any introduction to the readers of this paper. He is a self made man, as the term is used, and by diligence and good management has acquired a comfortable property, including one of the best residences in the village, viz. the Gram house, in which they have already begun housekeeping. The bride is of a modest, retiring disposition, and those who enjoy her acquaintance speak in high terms of her many virtues. The Review extends congratulations and best wishes for a long and happy married life.

Alcona County Review, December 28, 1893

EVENTS OF ONE WEEK.

A horse on La Boueff. He got half way to Harrisville one day last week only to find that he had left the mail at the station. Absent minded. Recently married. Excusable. Will get over it.

Alcona County Review, January 11, 1894

EVENTS OF ONE WEEK.

The Ladies of Alcona Hive No. 285, L.O.T.M., desire to thank the Ladies of Dalton Hive, No. 143, L.O.T.M., for the very pleasant entertainment given them on the occasion of their visit of Tuesday evening, Jan. 30th, and the excellent refreshments served to them.

Also especial thanks are due Mr. La Boueff for the very enjoyable sleigh-ride so kindly tendered them as a wedding treat on the event of his marriage.

Margaret Laverty, M. at A.

Alcona County Review, February 1, 1894

LaChapelle, Louis
?, {Bride}

LOCAL PICK UPS.
Louis La Chapelle, oldest son of Alfred La Chapelle, was married last week to an Alpena young lady.

Alcona County Review, August 10, 1899

LaChapelle, Peter
McLaughlan, {Bride}

COUNTY REVIEWINGS.

It will, no doubt, interest our readers to know that Peter La Chapelle, formerly of this place, has recently been married to Miss McLaughlan of Spencer Creek.

Alcona County Review, April 30, 1880

La Chapelle, William Francis
McIntosh, Mary Elizabeth

LaChapelle—McIntosh.
The marriage of Will LaChapelle, one of Harrisville's most popular and exemplary young men, and son of Geo. W. LaChapelle, to Miss Mary Elizabeth McIntosh occurred at 8 o'clock Tuesday morning at St. Bernard's church in the city of Alpena, the Rev. Fr. Flannery officiating. Michael Kennedy a friend of the bridegroom acted as best man and Miss Minnie McDougall was bridesmaid.

Mr. and Mrs. Geo. W. LaChapelle, Misses Addie and Hattie, and Winfield were present at the happy ceremony.

A wedding reception was held at The Exchange in the evening. Mr. and Mrs. LaChapelle will make their home in Alpena and will reside on Lockwood street. Warmest congratulations of Harrisville friends of the bridegroom will be extended to the happy pair.

They were the recipients of many wedding gifts, the railroad boys showing the esteem in which they held their associate by a gift of a costly silver service. Some 70 couples were present at the reception and the evening was made jolly and memorable by dancing.

Alcona County Review, November 17, 1898

PERSONAL POINTS.

Misses Hattie and Addie LaChapelle have arrived home from Alpena where they went to attend Will's wedding. Miss Hattie is located in Bay City and it is her first visit home in some time.

Alcona County Review, December 1, 1898

Lacy, Van Albert
Tillotson, Daisy Elizabeth

PERSONAL MENTION.

The marriage of Miss Daisy Elizabeth Tillotson to Dr. Van Albert Lacy of Buffalo is announced to take place Aug. 20, at the home of the bride, 18 Park Ave., Oneida, New York. Miss Tillotson is a sister of Mrs. Geo. E. Gillam and has made frequent visits to Harrisville and she has many acquaintances here.

Alcona County Review, August 8, 1895

PERSONAL MENTION.

Dr. Van A. Lacy and bride, formerly Miss D. Elizabeth Tillotson, of Oneida, N. Y., are guests at the residence of Geo. E. Gillam, Mrs. Lacy and Mrs. Gillam being sisters.

Alcona County Review, August 29, 1895

Lafferty, Alexander
Rouse, Susan

GREENBUSH.
Dec. 5, '99.

Married on Nov. 25, at Tawas by Elder Grant of the Latter Day Saints, Mr. Alex Lafferty to Miss Susie Rouse, both of this place.

Alcona County Review, December 7, 1899

LaFleur, Joseph
Simons, Cora

CURTISVILLE.
Joe La Fleur and Miss Cora Simons were married at the home of the bride's parents last Monday at 10:30. Several guests were present to witness the ceremony, which was performed by Rev. Nunn of Hale.

Alcona County Review, December 21, 1899

LaFrance, Joseph
Langton, Catherine

ALCONA ATOMS.

Jos. LaFrance has provided himself with a bran new wife and has moved out to his place. He will occupy the house of John McNeil until he can erect one for himself on his adjoining farm.

Alcona County Review, May 27, 1887

Lagace, Felix
Caszes, Mary

County Reviewings.

Mr. Felix Lagace and Miss Mary Caszes, both of this place, were married by Father C. J. Roche at the Catholic church, Monday evening of last week.

Alcona County Review, June 4, 1880

LaLiberty, Joseph
Parreau, Mena

La Liberty—Parreau.
At the Methodist Episcopal parsonage, Harrisville, Aug. 28, 1893, by the Rev. Wm. J. Bailey, Mr. Joseph La Liberty to Miss Mena Parreau, both of Haynes, Mich.

Alcona County Review, August 31, 1893

Landon, Alexander
Genge, Martha

MARRIED.
In Harrisville, October 16, 1882, by Rev. J. H. McIntosh, Alexander Landon and Miss Martha Genge, all of Harrisville.

Alcona County Review, October 27, 1882

Lang, John
Haynes, Georgie

Wedding Bells a Ringing.

Married at the Episcopal rectory at Marshall, Mich., by the Rev. Sidney Beckinth, on Monday, Nov. 18, Miss Georgie Haynes, of Albion, and Mr. John Lang, of Harrisville.

Alcona County Review, November 28, 1895

Larrett, John W.

Manning, Melinda E. [Ferguson]

Larrett—Manning.

Married, at the home of the bride's parents, Mr. and Mrs. Jas. Ferguson, Nov. 6th, 1894, by the Rev. Wm. J. Bailey, Mr. John W. Larrett of Black River to Mrs. Melinda E. Manning of Harrisville.

Alcona County Review, November 8, 1894

Larson, Erik
Janson, Matilda

Yoked Together.

At the Methodist parsonage in Alpena, Dec. 21st, by Rev. L. H. Riddick, Erik Larson and Matilda Janson, both of Alcona.

Alcona County Review, December 29, 1882

Lasare, Gilbert
Tibot, Mathilda

ALONG THE SHORE.

Gilbert Lasare and Mathilda Tibot of Oscoda, were united in matrimony Jan. 11th.

Alcona County Review, January 21, 1881

Latraill, Joseph
Fecto, Mary

PURELY PERSONAL.

A double wedding took place Tuesday morning in the Catholic church, the Rev. Fr. Winter officiating. The parties were Joseph Latraill, of Au Sable, and Miss Mary Fecto, of Alcona, and Daniel McDonald, superintendent of the poor farm, and Miss Mary McDonald, daughter of Supervisor McDonald of Greenbush.

Alcona County Review, March 8, 1889

Lavier, Melvin
McGregor, Jane E. J.

MARRIED.
Lavier—McGregor.

At the parsonage, Harrisville, August 21, by the Rev. Wm. J. Bailey, Mr. Melvin Lavier to Miss Jane E. J. McGregor, both of Millen, Mich.

Alcona County Review, August 24, 1893

Laviolette, Adolph D.
Burkhart, Celina [Hart]

Laviolette—Burkhart.
Adolph Du Laviolette, one of our successful farmers, and Mrs. Celina Burkhart, daughter of Mr. and Mrs.

Peter Hart, were united in marriage today at St. Anne's church, by Rev. Fr. Poulin.

Alcona County Review, July 6, 1899

Lawrence, David, Jr.
Meddaugh, Emma

The Local News.

David Laurence, aged 21, and Emma Meddaugh, aged 19, both of Alcona, were licensed to wed by the county clerk July 3.

Alcona County Review, July 11, 1890

Leavitt, William
Smith, Satie

Leavitt—Smith.
Mr. William Leavitt of Black River and Miss Satie Smith of Roe Lake were united in marriage Tuesday at the Methodist parsonage, by Rev. W. W. Will. They were accompanied by Mr. J. J. Richards and Miss Ida Leavitt.

The newly married couple we understand will make their home at Black River, where they have a wide acquaintance and hosts of friends. Congratulations.

Alcona County Review, June 15, 1899

LeClair, William
Gauthier, Angeline

Black River Sparks.
Married at St. Gabriel's church, on Feb. 17, Mr. Wm. Le Clair to Miss Angeline Gokey, both of Black River. The wedding breakfast was served at the residence of Peter Rose, after which the bride and groom left for a visit with Alpena friends.

Alcona County Review, February 27, 1896

Lecuyer, Peter
Gallagher, Emma J.

Miss Emma Gallagher and Peter Lecuyer were married Wednesday in Au Sable. All friends extend congratulations.

Alcona County Review, November 16, 1893

West Harrisville, Nov. 15.--Peter Lecuyer has taken to himself a new wife and gone to housekeeping. Congratulations are the order of the day.

Alcona County Review, November 16, 1893

Lecuyer, Peter
Hunt, Mary Luella

LOCAL JOTTINGS.

Married--On the evening of July 4th at the Parsonage in Alcona, by Rev. R. H. Balmer, W. E. Snowdon to Martha Churchill. Also at the same time and place Peter Lecuier to M. Luella Hunt. All parties of Alcona.

Alcona County Review, July 17, 1885

Lee, Grant A.
McLain, Maud

Mikado Mites.
Mikado, Jan. 22, 1896.—Mr. Lee of Ontonagon and Miss McClair of Chicago arrived on the train last evening and were joined in the holy bonds of wedlock, at the residence of Mr. Partridge, where they will remain for a short visit. Mr. Lee is a brother of Mrs. Partridge and W. J. Lee.

Alcona County Review, January 23, 1896

Lee, John William
Leland, Emma

A correspondent sends us an account of a double wedding which occurred last week at the residence of John Lockhart, of Oscoda. The contracting parties were A. H. Meston and Miss Janet Lockhart, and Wm. Lee and Miss Emma Leeland, all of Oscoda and Au Sable. Rev. Conway, the Baptist minister officiated. A large number of guests were present and the lists of gifts to each couple were numerous. Among the guests were Mr. and Mrs. J. W. Ferguson of Curtis township. Our space and limited time prevents the publication of the long list of presents.

Alcona County Review, February 22, 1894

Lee, Thomas
Fraser, Ella

LOCAL PICK UPS.
Miss Ella Fraser, daughter of Andrew Fraser of Greenbush, was married this week to Mr. Thos. Lee of Au Sable. The ceremony was performed at Tawas.

Alcona County Review, August 3, 1899

Lee, William C.
McGillis, Mary

LOCAL JOTTINGS.

We hear that Miss Mary, daughter of Jas. McGillis, of this township, was married to a young gentleman at East Tawas about two weeks ago. Our eye escaped the notion of the marriage, which is said to have appeared in the Tawas Gazette, and therefore we haven't yet learned the groom's name. However, we wish Mary and her husband a very pleasant sail upon the matrimonial sea, hoping the union may prove a mutual blessing.

Alcona County Review, November 27, 1885

Lepard, Edward
O'Connor, Mary E.

SOMEWHAT PERSONAL.

Edward Lepard and J. Monaghan of Black River were in the city yesterday, the former to secure a license to lead Miss Mary E. O'Connor to the altar. The wedding occurs Friday evening.

Alcona County Review, June 16, 1892

Levette, Alexander
Gillett, Frances [Tompkins]

Somewhat Personal.

Alex Levett and Frances Ginett of Black River were licensed to wed last week.

Alcona County Review, July 2, 1891

One Wife Better Than Two.

Less than two short weeks ago Alex Levett procured a license and led to the alter Frances Gillett, both parties hailing from Black River. Now it transpires that there is a Mrs. Levette No. 1, who has not lived with her husband for some time, although they were not separated by any legal process. No. 1 lived in Detroit but she was not long in finding out that Aleck had bestowed his affections upon another lassie; last week she appeared upon the scene and thereby hangs a tale of woe. Levett was arrested for unlawful cohabitation with a second wife, arraigned before Squire Beede, waived examination and was bound over the circuit court for trial in the sum of $300 bail which was furnished by Chas. Conklin and D. C. Emmorey.

Alcona County Review, July 9, 1891

Lewis, Grant
Hall, Lulu E.

LOCAL JOTTINGS.

Grant Lewis and Miss Lulu Hall surprised their acquaintances, last Sunday, by the announcement that they had been married by the Rev. F.

N. Barlow that afternoon. Cigars received.

Alcona County Review, July 15, 1887

MARRIED.

Lewis—Hall.—In Harrisville, July 10th, 1887, by the Rev. F. N. Barlow, Mr. Grant Lewis and Miss Lou Hall, all of Harrisville.

Alcona County Review, July 15, 1887

Lewis, W. E. A.
Barmby, Marion

CHURCH AND SOCIETY.

Rev. W. E. A. Lewis is to be married Oct. 15 at Bay City to Miss Marion Barmby.

Alcona County Review, October 3, 1895

Liberty, Benjamin
Fecto, Amanda

MARRIAGE LICENSES.

The following marriage licenses have been issued by County Clerk Rutson:

Nov. 11, Benj. Liberty, Alcona, 26 [and] Amanda Fecto, Alcona, 18.

Alcona County Review, November 18, 1887

Lincoln, Joseph
Aird, Rosa Anna

LOCAL JOTTINGS.

Married, In Harrisville, July 20, 1884, by the Rev. J. H. McIntosh, Joseph Lincoln and Miss Rosa Anna Aird, all of Harrisville. The Review extends congratulations.

Alcona County Review, July 25, 1884

Lindsay, William
Somers, Selena A.

Dr. Wm. Lindsay, of Georgia, Vermont, secured a license Tuesday to marry Miss Selena A. Somers, daughter of Robert Somers of Haynes. The marriage ceremony was performed yesterday at the residence of the bride's parents by the Rev. Wm. J. Bailey of Harrisville. Dr. and Mrs. Lindsay will reside in Vermont.

We regret to lose Miss Somers as she is a lady of sterling virtue and true modesty; who has made many friends, by whom she will be greatly missed, but we wish the newly named pair every success in their new home in Vermont.

Alcona County Review, August 1, 1895

Lipscomb, A. L.
Pearson, Minnie

PERSONAL MENTION.

Miss Minnie Pearson, until a short time ago a resident of Harrisville, was married at Parsons, W. Va., on Oct. 30, to Mr. A. L. Lipscomb, editor of the Tucker County Democrat.

Alcona County Review, November 7, 1895

Little, Richard C.
McDonald, Flora

Little—McDonald.

A pretty home wedding occurred Tuesday, May 9, at the home of Mrs. Margaret McDonald of Caledonia, when Flora, eldest daughter of Mrs. McDonald, and Richard C. Little of Duluth, Minn. were united in marriage.

The ceremony was performed in the presence of only a few intimate friends and relatives, Rev. Austin of Black River officiating.

The young couple were attended by Miss Belle Melville of Alpena and Roderick McDonald, brother of the bride.

The rooms were handsomely decorated with plants and flowers, the wedding taking place under a spider web composed of red and pink carnations and evergreens. The bride was prettily gowned in military blue trimmed with white silk and wore cream roses.

After the ceremony was over the guests participated in a wedding feast and had a highly enjoyable time.

Guests were present from Alpena, Ossineke, Harrisville and Black River.

The bride and groom were the recipients of many costly and useful gifts from their friends. The Lady Maccabees of Alpena, to which the bride belonged, presented a handsome oxidized silver carving set.

Amid a shower of rice the wedding party took their departure on the evening train for their new home in Duluth where they will be at home to their friends after June 14.

Alcona County Review, May 18, 1899

Littlefield, Edgar E.
Boardman, Nattie

YOUR FOLKS AND OUR FOLKS.

Miss Nattie Boardman, a former popular young lady of Harrisville, was recently married to Edgar E.

Littlefield, of Minneapolis, at the home of her parents.
Alcona County Review, February 26, 1891

Livingstone, George
Lavin, May

Somewhat Personal.

Married, last evening in this village by Justice Beede, Geo. Livingstone of Camp 8 to Miss May Lavan.
Alcona County Review, November 5, 1891

The Local News.

The Review erred in reporting Livingstone-Lavin marriage last week. The facts will be found in our West Harrisville correspondence.
Alcona County Review, November 12, 1891

West Harrisville.
West Harrisville, Nov. 4, 1891.-- Geo. Livingstone and Miss May Lavin were married last Wednesday evening in this village. Rev. Munday, of Alpena, came and tied the knot. The couple drove to camp 8 the same night where they intend to reside.
Alcona County Review, November 12, 1891

Logan, C. C.
Fulton, Minnie

PERSONAL MENTION.
Word comes from Flint that Minnie Fulton, niece of Wm. C. Gray, was recently married to C. C. Logan of that city, which they have made their home.
Alcona County Review, May 21, 1896

Longstreet, William R.
?, Adelaide

PERSONAL MENTION.

W. R. Longstreet and bride, of Saginaw, passed a few days with Mr. Longstreet's parents at the parsonage the past week.
Alcona County Review, May 21, 1896

Lostutter, Robinson
Hogue, Mattie B.

PERSONAL POINTS.
Mr. Robinson Lostutter, formerly of Rising Sun and Miss Mattie B. Hogue were united in marriage in Indianapolis Tuesday, Aug. 29. Friends here extend congratulations.—Rising Sun Local.
Alcona County Review, September 7, 1899

Lott, Robert L.

Fralic, Stella B.

County Reviewings.
Married—At Bay City, on the 11th inst., at the residence of Rev. Mr. Vinning, Mr. Robert L. Lott and Miss Stella B. Fralic, all of Black River.
Immediately after the nuptials Mr. and Mrs. Lott took the train for Detroit, where a portion of their honeymoon was enjoyed among friends. They are a young couple much esteemed by the people of this county, and the well-wishes of all are heartily extended. May their pathway through life be long and pleasant and may supreme joy and unalloyed happiness ever be theirs to enjoy.
Alcona County Review, May 18, 1877

Alcona.
May 18th, 1877.
Editor Alcona County Review.
Married, at Bay City, Mich., on Friday evening, May 11th, 1877, Mr. Robert Lott of Black River, and Miss Stella Fralic, of the same place.
Alcona County Review, May 18, 1877

County Reviewings.

The Alcona County Review announces the marriage of Miss Stella Fralic to Mr. Robert L. Lott. How on earth a woman who has ever read the Bible can consent to become Lott's wife, with the historic precedents all in favor of her being turned into a pillar of salt, is beyond our conception. Will the Review explain? Flint Globe.
Well, Mr. Globe, as you seem to be in a peck of trouble over the matter, we'll try and help you out. In the first place it is well to consider that circumstances always govern cases. Previous to her marriage, we understand Miss Stella faithfully promised herself that she would never look back toward the doomed city, and as she has never been known to go back on her word, even in her most trying circumstance of life, you may depend upon it that she is safe from that "pillar of salt," and will flee with Lott to the "mountains of refuge," with nary a turn to the right or to the left.
Alcona County Review, June 8, 1877

Loud, Edward F.
Ammack, Annabel

Jottings Along the Shore.

The marriage of Mr. E. F. Loud and Miss Annabel Ammack, of Oscoda, is announced to take place at the M. E. Church in that place on the 27th inst.
Alcona County Review, January 9, 1880

Loud, George A.
Glennie, Elizabeth

LOCAL JOTTINGS.

Oscoda was graced with a brilliant wedding on Tuesday, the contracting parties being Mr. Geo. A. Loud, of the H. M. Loud & Sons Lumber Co., of Oscoda, and Miss Lizzie Glenny, an accomplished and leading member of Oscoda and Au Sable society. The ceremony was performed by the Revs. Williams and C. B. Steele. About sixty couples of leading society people, relatives and friends of the bride and groom were present, among them Mr. and Mrs. L. A. Colwell, of Harrisville. Mr. and Mrs. Loud departed Wednesday per special train for Detroit. Their wedding tour will extend through several Eastern states.
Alcona County Review, December 8, 1888

NEIGHBORHOOD NOTES.

The swell social event of the season was the reception tendered to Geo. A. Loud, of Oscoda, and bride on their return last week from their wedding tour.
Alcona County Review, January 4, 1889

Loyer, George G.
Hart, Edith

Killmaster Scrapings.
Killmaster, Feb. 18.--The marriage ceremony of Mr. G. Lalouy to Miss Hart was solemnized Tuesday, Rev. Poulin officiating. They gave a reception at Mikado. A number of people from Killmaster attended.
Alcona County Review, February 20, 1896

Roy Ripples.
Feb. 18th, '96.
In this season of Valentines, golden hearts and Cupid's darts, this vicinity has caught the infection and in consequence Mr. George Loyer of Mikado township leads Miss Edith Hart of Harrisville township to Hymen's alter. There will be a dance this evening in Maccabee Hall in honor of the event. The friends of both parties congratulate them and wish them a long and happy life. It is

said their residence will be with the bridegroom's parents for some time.

Alcona County Review, February 27, 1896

Lubenew, Adolph
Benway, Eunice Ann [Vary]

LOCAL JOTTINGS.

Married—At Black River, March 22d, by R. S. Leach, Esq., Adolph Lubenew and Mrs. Eunice A. Benway, all of Black River.

Alcona County Review, March 26, 1886

BLACK RIVER BRIEFLETS.

The usual quiet of our village was interrupted Monday night by the noise of tin-pans, horns, fire-arms and human voices. The "boys" were celebrating the marriage of Mr. A. Lubenew to Mrs. Benway, widow of the Indian doctor who died here last year.

Alcona County Review, March 26, 1886

BLACK RIVER BRIEFLETS.

Mr. A. Lubenew moved away on Monday with his bride. They went to Alpena.

Alcona County Review, April 30, 1886

Ludean, William
Neil, Laura

Oscoda County News.

During the day Mr. Wm. Ludean was married to Miss Laura Neil, both of Rose, by Justice O. K.VanTine.

Alcona County Review, June 22, 1881

Ludington, Kirk P.
Renis, Theresa Grace

LOCAL JOTTINGS.

Married.—In Alcona township, on the 20th inst., by Rev. James Bain, Kirk Ludington, of Alcona, and Grace Renes, of Detroit.

Alcona County Review, April 23, 1886

Ludlum, H. O.
Henry, Bertha

PERSONAL MENTION.

H. O. Ludlum, brother of Dr. Ludlum and who was here most of last year, was recently married to a Bay City young lady, Miss Bertha Henry by name.

Alcona County Review, February 14, 1895

Lyman, Don
Sinclair, Mary A.

REVIEWINGS.

Married:—On the 17th inst., at the residence of Dr. J. Lyman in Harrisville, by Rev. D. VanDyke, Mr. Don Lyman and Miss Mary Sinclair, all of Harrisville.

The editor extends congratulations to the new couple, and hopes theirs may be a long life, complete with bliss and prosperity, and minus flying rolling pins, potato-mashers, and other semi death-producing instruments. They should continually strive to walk in the garbs of truth, virtue, morality and religion, and thus keep off the thorns.

Alcona County Review, November 21, 1879

Greenbush Items.

Don Lyman and _____ _____ , well yes, they're married.

Alcona County Review, November 21, 1879

Lyman, George A.
Balch, Elizabeth

Lyman—Balch.

Married, at the Methodist parsonage Dec. 25th, 1893, by the Rev. W. J. Bailey, Mr. George A. Lyman of Mud Lake, Mich., to Miss Lizzie Balch of Harrisville, Mich.

Alcona County Review, December 28, 1893

Lyman, Frank J.
Hawse, Ella

Married, at the M. E. parsonage, March 12th, 1894, by the Rev. W. J. Bailey, Mr. Frank J. Lyman to Miss Ella Hawse, both of Millen township.

Alcona County Review, March 22, 1894

Affairs at Mud Lake.

Well, I promised to tell you all about the wedding: It took place in Harrisville, but the dance did not take place; too many of the dancing people were sick.

Alcona County Review, March 22, 1894

Lynch, Stephen
Craven, Delia

COUNTY JOTTINGS.

Married: On the 9th inst., by Rev. N. N. Clark, at the residence of Hosmer Griswold, Mr. Stephen Lynch and Miss Delia Craven, all of Harrisville.

Alcona County Review, April 12, 1878

Lynch, Stephen
Hood, Agnes B.

LOCAL JOTTINGS.

Married: On the 10th inst., at the M. E. Parsonage, by the Rev. T. B. Leith, Stephen Lynch to Agnes B. Hood, both of Alcona. Here's hoping that the individual whoever attempts to *hood*wink them into temporary or permanent unhappiness, may be *lynch*ed on the spot.

Alcona County Review, January 15, 1885

Macomb, John
Buerbee, {Bride}

Local News.

John Macomb of Alpena and Miss Buerbee of Mikado, were married by Rev. Fr. Poulin last week.

Alcona County Review, November 3, 1898

Madden, Frank D.
Baker, Retty May

PERSONAL PICKUPS.

Married.—At the M. E. parsonage, Saturday evening, July 3d, by Rev. T. B. Leith, Mr. Frank D. Madden and Miss May Baker, all of Harrisville.

Alcona County Review, July 9, 1886

Madden, Lewis A.
Roberts, Kate Agnes

PURELY PERSONAL.

Cards are out announcing the marriage at the home of the bride's parents in Knoxville, Tenn., of Miss Kate Agnes Roberts to Louis A. Madden. The bride is a daughter of Mr. and Mrs. R. Z. Roberts, former residents of Harrisville.

Alcona County Review, May 25, 1888

GAY WEDDING BELLS AT KNOXVILLE.

The following from the Knoxville (Tenn.) Daily Journal, June 7, inst., is an account of the marriage in that city of a young lady well known in this and surrounding towns as a former resident of Harrisville and daughter of R. Z. Roberts formerly Prosecuting Attorney of Alcona county:

The most brilliant of the many weddings that have already graced the roseate month of June in Knoxville was that of Mr. Lewis B. Madden, of New York, and Miss Katie Roberts at St. John's church last night. The church was crowded with friends and admirers of the bride, who has filled an enviable position in society for quite a time, and of the groom also.

All the society people were there in full dress and the scene was one of unequaled splendor. The floral decoration were rich and tastefully arranged in clusters and wreathes about the altar and chancel. The bridal party stood beneath a massive arch of evergreen and flowers as the ceremony was being performed by Rev. S. Ringgold, rector of St. John's.

The bridesmaids were Miss Mary Cowan and Miss Ada Meek. Mr. J. M. McRae was best man, and the other attendants were George S. Andes and J. H. Cowan.

Shortly after nine o'clock the bridal party and the bride leaning upon her father's arm walked slowly down the aisle as the groom and his best man approached from the vestry. They met under the arch of roses and the venerable rector performed the full ceremony from the ritual of the Episcopal church.

After the ceremony the bridal party was driven at once to the palatial home of the bride's parents, Mr. and Mrs. R. Z. Roberts, on "The Circle," West Knoxville, where a splendid reception was held.

There was almost a crush of society notables and it was one of the most magnificent affairs of the kind ever given in Knoxville.

The young bride is beautiful, highly educated and fully accomplished in all that goes to make life a pleasure. She will be greatly missed from a circle of loving friends and her place in Knoxville society will be a void.

The groom is peculiarly fortunate in his choice of a wife and she is fortunate in the choice of a husband. Mr. and Mrs. Madden left on the 2 a.m. train for New York.

The Knoxville Daily Tribune commenting on the same event says of the happy couple:

The groom is a young man of his city where he is a leader in the business world and of the highest social standing. The bride is the daughter of our well known citizen, Mr. R. Z Roberts, and has friends without number. She is one of the most popular young ladies of the city, esteemed and loved for her beauty of character as well as person.

Alcona County Review, June 15, 1888

Magahay, David Charles

Anger, Ellonera

A Wedding and a Donation.

A correspondent sends us the following, under date of March 23d.

At the residence of the bride's uncle, Mr. Samuel Anger of West Harrisville, March 20th, 1886, by the Rev. J. Robins, Mr. David Charles Magahay, formerly of Victoria, Canada, and Miss E. Anger, of St. Clair county, Mich. They have the well wishes of their many friends. May grace and peace adorn their married life.

Alcona County Review, March 26, 1886

Manlove, Stephen P.
Kaupman, Maggie

Was She From Our Town?
The following dispatch was in Monday's Free Press. The Review knows of no family in Harrisville by the name of Kaupman.

LaPort, Ind., Nov. 6.--Stephen P. Manlove, a wealthy farmer of Starke county, was married yesterday to Miss Maggie Kaupman, who gave her home as Harrisville, Mich. Manlove gave his age at 74, while the Wolverine bride is but 24. The nuptials were the sequel of an advertisement for a wife and the conditions under which Miss Kaupman assumed marital duties were the deeding of a fine farm and the bequeathing to her of the wealth of Manlove, which is estimated to be up in the thousands. Manlove is a highly respected citizen and has buried three wives.

Alcona County Review, November 10, 1898

Mann, Samuel K.
Cook, {Bride}

Samuel K. Mann, who is well known through this section of the country was married last week at Blood's Station, N. Y., to a Miss Cook. Samuel is an exemplary young man and will make his wife a good husband. His many friends here will only be too glad to hear in the future that "Sam" and his bride are meeting with much prosperity and happiness, and that all their troubles are but *little ones.*

Alcona County Review, March 18, 1881

Manning, Edward B.
Laviolette, Josephine

Haynes Happenings.

Edw. B. Maynard gave a dance in honor of his recent wedding. Hope he will live long and prosper.

Alcona County Review, June 13, 1895

Manson, John
Bradshaw, Donna

PERSONAL MENTION.
Mr. and Mrs. John Manson of Grand Rapids enjoyed a few days of their honeymoon in Harrisville and were guests at the residence of R. L. Lott. The bride was Miss Donna Bradshaw, for many years a resident of Harrisville, and she has received the warm congratulations of many friends this week. They took their departure Tuesday for their home in the Valley City.

Alcona County Review, April 30, 1896

Marble, Ralph N.
?, Belle H.

Hymeneal.
Our young friend, new townsman and attorney, Ralph N. Marble, arrived from Lansing on the St. Paul, Sunday night, but was not under the circumstances in which he has previously been accustomed to inhabit this mundane sphere. Beg pardon, but 'tis a fact: he navigates no longer under the mottoed banner of "single blessedness." He went down to Lansing, sang "Meet me at the gate, sweet darling Belle;" the fair young lady acquiesced and now the "two hearts beat as one." 'Tis well, and may the new couple live a long, happy and prosperous life. Ladies, you will find the new bride at the McLennan House.

Alcona County Review, June 14, 1878

COUNTY JOTTINGS.

The upright to John Morris' house is being re-fitted for the use of R. N. Marble and wife, who are soon to go to housekeeping on their own book.

Alcona County Review, June 28, 1878

Marchefski, Ignatius
Budnik, {Bride}

There was a wedding up in Posen, Presque Isle county last week. The bridal couple—Ignatius Marchefski and Miss Budnik—started with friends in wagons drawn by oxen and horses. A young duffer who sat near the groom wanted to have a little celebration and whipped out a revolver to make a noise. The thing went off too soon and the bullet entered the tender hide of Ignatius. The procession kept on just the same and the couple were married. Then they began looking for the bullet. Ignatius found a lump in his sock and pulling off his boot the ball fell out. There was much joy thereat. A piece of courtplaster was pasted over the wound in his body, the wedding dance went on and they all had a splendid time.

Alcona County Review, June 20, 1890

Martin, Walter B.
Buchanan, Mary Elizabeth

PERSONAL MENTION.

Mr. Walter B. Martin and Miss Mary Buchanan were united in marriage Thursday evening last by the Rev. W. W. Will at the parsonage. Both are well-known young people of the township and congratulations are in order.

Alcona County Review, October 24, 1895

Mather, Albert H.
Jones, Sarah

REVIEWINGS.

Married: Thursday evening, July 3d. at the residence of John Millen, Jr., in Harrisville, by Rev. D. VanDyke, Mr. Albert H. Mather and Miss Sarah Jones, all of Harrisville.

We extend congratulations to the new couple, and wish them a long life of usefulness, complete with joy and bliss.

Alcona County Review, July 4, 1879

Mather, Increase
Freer, Ann M.

Married.

In Harrisville, July 4, 1882, at the residence of the bride's father, by Rev. J. H. McIntosh, Increase Mather and Miss Ann M. Freer, both of Harrisville.

The editor of the Review rises to extend hearty congratulations to all the above named new couples, hoping that they may pick up pearls of happiness all along their respective pathways through life, and part in the terrestrial world only to meet in the never ending blissful celestial.

Alcona County Review, July 7, 1882

May, Ralph
Kibbe, Minnie

LOCAL JOTTINGS.

Marriage license No. 41 bears the names of Ralph May and Miss Minnie Kibbe, two well known young people.

Alcona County Review, April 5, 1889

McArthur, John G.
Lamp, Agnes

Black River.
McArthur—Lamp.

Married, at the bride's residence on Wednesday, Oct. 26, Mr. John McArthur to Miss Agnes Lamp. The services were conducted by the Rev. J. A. Gone. The wedding was private and only a few friends were present, the groom's brother and Miss Kittie Foster assisting. The presents were numerous. Mr. and Mrs. McArthur left on the morning train for Mud Lake where they begin housekeeping.

Alcona County Review, November 3, 1892

HISTORY OF ONE YEAR.

Chronological History of the Past Year, 1892.

MARRIAGES.

Oct. 26. Jno McArthur to Agnes Lamp at Black River.

Alcona County Review, January 5, 1893

McCambridge, Michael
McTamminy, Mary

REVIEWINGS.

Married: At Au Sable, on the 10th inst., by Rev. C. J. Roche, Michael McCambridge and Miss Mary McTamminy, all of Greenbush.

Well, that makes another good match. Michael and Mary are pretty good sort of young folks. We hope they may trot together in double harness to perfection the rest of their natural lives, and never meet with any of those obstacles which make life unpleasant.

Alcona County Review, February 20, 1880

McCary, John
Moore, Satie

MARRIED.

McCary-Moore.—In Harrisville, August 15th, 1888, John McCary, of Alcona, and Miss Satie Moore, of Harrisville.

Alcona County Review, August 17, 1888

McClatchey, Abram
Rivard, Elizabeth

Married: January 12th, 1879, at the M. E. Parsonage, Harrisville, Mich., by Rev. N. N. Clark, Mr. Abram McClatchey and Miss Elizabeth Revard, all of Harrisville.

The above announcements come to hand for publication at a rather late date, but then we can congratulate the elated parties just the same. May their future anticipations, joy, prosperity, etc., be fully realized, and life pass on admirably.

Alcona County Review, January 31, 1879

McClatchey, Abram
Sisson, Charlotte E.
[Peterson]

Wedding Bells.

Married, at the bride's residence at Lakeside, Tuesday evening, Mr. Abram McClatchey to Mrs. C. E. Sisson. The ceremony was performed by Rev. W. W. Will in the presence of a few friends and members of the two families. After the ceremony the bridal party were driven to the Union Dock where they boarded the Thompson steamer for Detroit, from whence they go on to Niagara Falls and Buffalo.

A very large number of their friends were at the dock to see them off and bride and groom were showered with rice and received warm congratulations.

The union is a happy one from every point of view, and the Review extends its heartiest congratulations and best wishes.

Alcona County Review, August 4, 1898

PERSONAL POINTS.

Mr. and Mrs. Abram McClatchey have returned from their bridal tour and are at home in Mr. McClatchey's residence.

Alcona County Review, August 25, 1898

Local History of One Year

Chronology of the Principal Events of the Year 1898.

August 2. Marriage of Abram McClatchey--Mrs. C. E. Sisson.

Alcona County Review, January 5, 1899

McClatchey, Bert
Tompkins, Minnie

Purely Personal.

Bert McClatchey of Bay City a former resident of Harrisville, was married a few days ago to Miss Minnie Tompkins of the above city.

Alcona County Review, December 20, 1889

McClellan, Dougal
Forbes, Mary Ellen

Haynes.

Haynes, March 23.—Mr. Dugall McClellen starts for Ontario Wednesday with the intention of capturing one of the fair daughters of the Dominion for his better half. We wish him success.

Alcona County Review, March 24, 1892

Somewhat Personal.

Dougall McClellan, of Haynes, arrived home from Ontario last Saturday, bringing a bran new bride with him.

Alcona County Review, April 28, 1892

McConnell, Varnum
Genge, Alice H.

EVENTS OF ONE WEEK.

Varnum McConnell and Miss Alice Genge, both of West Harrisville, the latter a daughter of Geo. Genge, were married last evening at the home of the bride's parents. The Review extends congratulations.

Alcona County Review, September 28, 1893

Mr. Varnum McConnell and Miss Alice Genge, both of West Harrisville, were united in marriage by Rev. S. Brundy, at the home of the bride's parents, Mr. and Mrs. G. Genge, Sept. 27th, 1893. They are both very highly respected by those who know them and the bride was the happy recipient of many valuable presents. They have gone to Canada to spend a month with his people, after which they intend to return and settle down here at West Harrisville.

Alcona County Review, October 5, 1893

McCormick, Francis P.
McLean, Sarah

Purely Personal.

A pleasant event that has been long expected in society circles was the marriage of Dr. F. P. McCormick of Black River and Miss Sarah McLean of East Saginaw. It was consummated a few days ago at the home of the bride's parents in the latter city. The party of the first part

is too well known to need any further introduction to our readers; the bride is an accomplished young lady, vivacious and brilliant and we have no doubt will make a most welcome addition to Black River society. The Review begs leave to extend congratulations to both and best wishes for their happiness and prosperity.

Alcona County Review, December 6, 1889

McCormick, George C.
Fullerton, Alma M.

Somewhat Personal.

Geo. McCormick and Alma M. Fullerton, two of Mitchell township's young people, have been licensed to wed by the county clerk.

Alcona County Review, April 7, 1892

McCoy, John
Illman, Louisa

PERSONAL MENTION.

Jno. McCoy of Black River and Louisa Ellman of Alcona have been licensed to wed.

Alcona County Review, January 5, 1893

BLACK RIVER'S BUDGET.

Black River, Jan. 9, 1893.
McCoy—Ellman. The marriage of Mr. John McCoy to Miss Ellman took place at the latter's residence on the 5th inst. Mr. and Mrs. McCoy will retain their residence at Black River. Here's joy to you.

Alcona County Review, January 12, 1893

McDermaid, Daniel
Sousie, Sarah

Daniel McDermid and Miss Sarah Sousie were united in marriage Sept. 15, by Justice F. A. Beede. Both reside at Black River and are well known and popular young people.

Alcona County Review, September 22, 1892

HISTORY OF ONE YEAR.

Chronological History of the Past Year, 1892.

MARRIAGES.
Sept. 15. Daniel McDermaid and Sarah Sousie, both of Black River.

Alcona County Review, January 5, 1893

McDonald, Albert
Gibson, Josephia

Greenbush Jottings.
Married: At the Presbyterian parsonage, in Harrisville, Nov. 8th, 1879, by Rev. D. VanDyke, Mr. Albert McDonald and Miss Josephia Gibson, both of Greenbush.

Alcona County Review, November 14, 1879

McDonald, Albert
Stafford, Ella

The Local News.

Jos. Fleck, of Tawas City, and Miss Mary McFadyen, of Harrisville were united in marriage Thursday, March 27, by the Rev. L. Hazard at the residence of Mrs. A. Baror. The following Sunday Mr. Hazard officiated at the marriage of Albert McDonald, of Black River, and Ella Stafford, of South Harrisville, at the home of the latter's parents.

Alcona County Review, April 4, 1890

McDonald, Angus
Hall, Margaret J.

ALONG THE SHORE.

General News-Gleanings From the Several Counties.--------
Alpena.

Recent marriages hereabouts: May 26, Angus McDonald and Miss Margaret J. Hall. May 30, Robert Keen and Miss Eliza Ann Wilson. June 3, Robert Bolton and Miss Cynthia Ellen Dove.

Alcona County Review, June 11, 1880

McDonald, Archibald
McDonald, Catherine

COUNTY REVIEWINGS.

Married, at the Catholic Church in Harrisville, Monday morning, September 6th, by Rev. C. H. Roche of Au Sable, Miss Catherine McDonald and Archibald McDonald, both of Harrisville.

Alcona County Review, September 10, 1880

McDonald, Archibald
O'Connor, Frances

MARRIAGE LICENSES.

April 18, Archie McDonald, aged 25, and Miss Frankie O'Connor, aged 19, Greenbush. [Note: Married on 4/21/1890 in Greenbush Township.]

Alcona County Review, April 25, 1890

McDonald, Archie

Kennedy, Isabel

COUNTY JOTTINGS.

At the Catholic Church, in this village, Nov. 11, by Rev. Father Roche, Mr. Archie McDonald and Miss Isabel Kennedy, all of Harrisville.

Alcona County Review, November 25, 1878

McDonald, Arthur D.
Coyle, Maud

Miss Maud Coyle, daughter of the well known Greenbush citizen, was united in marriage Tuesday evening at her late home to Arthur McDonald of Au Sable. Mr. and Mrs. McDonald have gone to Bay City where the bridegroom's parents reside.

Alcona County Review, July 4, 1890

Social Event at Greenbush.

Married, July 1st, at the residence of the bride's parents, Miss Maud Coyle to Mr. Arthur McDonald, of Au Sable. A large circle of friends being present at a little after nine o'clock the bride and groom made their appearance supported by Miss Alice McCoy and Mr. John Madison, of Au Sable. The ceremony was performed by the Rev. Mr. McAllay after which the guests adjourned to the dining room where tables were spread with a bountiful supply of the good things of the land. After supper the guests repaired to the Town Hall, where they tripped the light fantastic until the "wee sma' hours." The occasion was enjoyed by all the participants. We wish the happy couple a happy journey down the stream of life.

Alcona County Review, July 11, 1890

A Grist From Greenbush.

Arthur D. McDonald and wife, of Au Sable, are visiting the bride's parents.

Alcona County Review, August 29, 1890

McDonald, Dan E.
Hale, Jessie Eunice

PERSONAL MENTION.

Dan E. McDonald, a highly respected citizen of the township of Caledonia, secured a license last Friday to wed Miss Jessie E. Hale, an esteemed young lady and eldest daughter of our fellow townsman, Sherman Hale. The twain drove to Au Sable and united in marriage that evening. The Review extends best wishes.

Alcona County Review, March 8, 1894

McDonald, Daniel
McDonald, Mary

PURELY PERSONAL.

A double wedding took place Tuesday morning in the Catholic church, the Rev. Fr. Winter officiating. The parties were Joseph Latraill, of Au Sable, and Miss Mary Fecto, of Alcona, and Daniel McDonald, superintendent of the poor farm, and Miss Mary McDonald, daughter of Supervisor McDonald of Greenbush.

Alcona County Review, March 8, 1889

McDonald, Donald
Hecox, Iva Maud

Somewhat Personal.

Donald McDonald of Caledonia, aged 20 years, was licensed on the 20th inst. to marry Iva Maud Hecox, of the same age, daughter of D. A. Hecox the well known Black River citizen.

Alcona County Review, November 26, 1891

McDonald, Hugh H.
Scott, Henrietta

LOCAL JOTTINGS.

Married. At Harrisville, on the 26th inst., at the residence of Mrs. E. Carle, by the Rev. M. Lowry, Mr. Hugh McDonald of Black River and Miss Henrietta Scott of Alcona.

Alcona County Review, May 30, 1884

McDonald, John
McAdams, Elizabeth

LOCAL JOTTINGS.

Married—In Harrisville, July 15, 1884, by B. F. Buchanan, Esq., John McDonald and Miss Elizabeth McAdams, of Kintail, Canada.

Alcona County Review, July 25, 1884

McDonald, John J.
Dewer, Christina

LOCAL JOTTINGS.

Married: At the M. E. Parsonage, August 18th, 1885, by Rev. T. B. Leith, John J. McDonald and Christina Dewer, all of Harrisville.

Alcona County Review, August 28, 1885

McDonald, Ranald R.
McQuaig, Mary

LOCAL JOTTINGS

R. R. McDonald, well known here, and Miss Mary McQuaig were married at Au Sable Monday by the Rev. Fr. Winters.

Alcona County Review, April 27, 1888

McDonald, Roland P.
Thornton, Ida

Yoked Together.

At the Hawkins Home, Au Sable, Dec. 25th, by Rev. F. Bradley, John Genge and Della Thornton, both of Harrisville.

At the same time and place, by the same, Roland P. McDonald and Ida Thornton, both of Harrisville.

Alcona County Review, December 29, 1882

McDougal, Chesley
Procunier, Carrie

LOCAL PICK UPS.

Chesley McDougall and Carrie Procunier of Gustin were married on Monday afternoon at the home of the bride, Rev. W. Will officiating.

Alcona County Review, February 23, 1899

McDougal, J. E.
Stephens, Cora

Our Neighbors.

J. E. McDougall, publisher of the Oscoda Saturday Night, was married last week Tuesday at St. Johns, Mich., to Miss Cora Stephens, a niece of postmaster R. B. Emmons of Oscoda. The first named has many friends in this village who will wish Mr. and Mrs. McDougall all the blessings and few of the troubles commonly supposed to be incidental to married life.

Alcona County Review, November 22, 1889

McDougal, William
McArthur, Margaret

PERSONAL MENTION.

McDougall-McArthur. At the Nevin Hotel, Harrisville, July 14th, by the Rev. W. J. Bailey, Mr. William McDougall of Millen township was united in marriage with Miss Maggie McArthur of Gustin.

Alcona County Review, July 20, 1893

McDougall, Neil
?, Nellie M.

West Harrisville.

Miss Sara McDougall leaves Wednesday for her home at Siloam to be present at the marriage of her brother. Her sister, Mrs. Gaylord Freeman accompanies her.

Alcona County Review, April 16, 1896

West Harrisville.

April 21, 1896.
Mr. and Mrs. Freeman have returned from Reno, where they went for the purpose of attending the wedding of Mrs. Freeman's brother.

Alcona County Review, April 23, 1896

McElroy, John
Freer, Julia

LOCAL JOTTINGS.

Jno. McElroy, of East Tawas and Miss Julia Freer, of this place, were made one at the former place a few days since.

Alcona County Review, January 14, 1887

McFadyen, Murdoch
?, {Bride}

"Send my paper to Great Falls, Mont. until further notice," writes Murdoch McFadyen. The Review has just learned that Murdoch was married Nov. 26 to an estimable lady of the silver state.

Alcona County Review, December 20, 1894

McGillis, John, Jr.
McDonald, Mary

MARRIED.

A double marriage occurred Tuesday morning at the Catholic church, the Rev. Fr. Mahar officiating. The contracting parties were John McGillis and Mary McDonald and John Kelley and Mary McGillis. All the young people are residents of this county, all having resided in Greenbush or adjoining townships for many years.

Alcona County Review, January 11, 1894

Greenbush.

Feb. 5, 1894.
John McGillis, Jr., and wife have started housekeeping. Success to John.

Alcona County Review, February 8, 1894

McGregor, Gregor
Martin, Mary

At the Altar.

McGregor-Martin.—At the M. E. parsonage, July 3, 1895, by the Rev. W. J. Bailey, Mr. Gregor McGregor

to Miss Mary Martin, both of Caledonia, Mich.

Alcona County Review, July 11, 1895

McIntosh, Jesse
Diem, Rose B.

HOME REVIEWINGS.

Well, well, well! Jesse McIntosh went to Detroit last week to buy goods and returned home Thursday morning accompanied by his bride, completely astonishing the natives hereabouts. The marriage took place at Port Austin on Wednesday, the bride's name being Miss Rose B. Diem. The Review extends congratulations to the happy couple, and hopes that a prosperous and blissful future may be in store for them.

Alcona County Review, October 14, 1881

McIntyre, Donald
Morrison, Kate

Additional Reviewings.

Married, at the St. Lawrence House in Harrisville, Tuesday evening, May 10, by A. J. Grout, Esq., Donald McIntyre and Kate Morrison, both of Au Sable.

Alcona County Review, May 13, 1881

McIntyre, John H.
Nevin, Robena

MCINTYRE—NEVIN.

Tuesday evening Mr. John H. McIntyre and Miss Robena Nevin were united in marriage at the home of the bride's parents by Rev. W. J. Bailey. Mr. and Mrs. McIntyre will be home after the 25th inst. The young people are life-long residents of Harrisville township and consequently have a wide range of friends and acquaintances who will congratulate them on this happy event.

Alcona County Review, June 22, 1893

McKinnon, Hector
Gircke, Dora

MARRIED.

McKinnon—Gerky.—In Harrisville, July 3d, by the same [Rev. P. C. Goldie], Hector McKinnon and Miss Dora Gerky, both of Caledonia.

Alcona County Review, July 5, 1889

McLain, Alexander
Taft, Mrs. Harriet

COUNTY REVIEWINGS.

Married, at the M. E. Parsonage, by Rev. Talmadge, Sept. 23, Alexander McLain and Mrs. Harriet Taft.

Alcona County Review, October 8, 1880

McLaughlin, John
Boudreau, Selena [Richway]

HAWSE TOWNSHIP.

Mr. John McLaughlan was married on Wednesday, Feb. 8, to one Mrs. Boudray, a lady of beauty and wealth and by all appearances one to make the lonesome home of so honest and well respected a citizen happy and pleasant. John wears a smile now when he comes in to find dinner on the table and no potatoes to be peeled no pork to fry—All in readiness now.

Alcona County Review, February 9, 1899

McLellan, Alexander
McCullough, Mary Jane

LOCAL JOTTINGS.

Married—March 11th, at the Methodist Episcopal parsonage, by the Rev. T. B. Leith, Alexander McLellan and Mary Jane McCullough, all of Black River.

Alcona County Review, March 19, 1886

McLennan, Daniel D.
Twite, Emma S.

HOME REVIEWINGS.

Daniel D. McLennan, of Black River, and Miss Emma S. Twite of Harrisville, were married at Alpena, by Rev. N. L. Little, on the 19th inst. They arrived home last Sunday morn.

Alcona County Review, September 30, 1881

McLennan, James
Holden, Carrie J.

LOCAL JOTTINGS.

Our citizens no doubt will be surprised to learn that James McLennan, of Duluth, Minn., (formerly of this place), and Miss Carrie J. Holden, of Harrisville, were, on May 27, 1884, united in marriage by Rev. John Wilson, pastor of Jefferson Avenue M. E. church, at East Saginaw. We understand that the happy couple will reside at Duluth. Well, here's hoping that they may ever be useful as well as ornamental in the world, and enjoy a prosperous, happy life.

Alcona County Review, May 30, 1884

McLennon, Donald
Wilson, Jane

Social and Tea Party.

Married, April 21st, at M. E. Parsonage, Harrisville, by Rev. C. Gibbs, Mr. Donald McClennon and Miss Jane Wilson of Black River.

Alcona County Review, April 22, 1881

McLeod, John
McCauley, Mary

AMONG OUR EXCHANGES.

A license has been issued at Detroit for the marriage of John McLeod of this city and Mary McCauley of Detroit.

Alcona County Review, July 14, 1892

McLochlin, John
McDonald, Mary Ann

Purely Personal.

Father Winters had a pleasant duty to perform at the Catholic church Monday morning. It was the union in the holy bonds of matrimony of Jno. McLochlan, son of postmaster McLochlan, of Handy station, and Mary Ann McDonald, daughter of Duncan McDonald, of the same place. Chas. McDonald of Au Sable and Mary A. McDonald of Greenbush stood up with the happy young couple.

Alcona County Review, October 18, 1889

Purely Personal.

Chas. McDonald of Au Sable dropped into the Review office Monday while in town attending the McLochlin-McDonald wedding.

Alcona County Review, October 18, 1889

McMaster, Duncan
Watson, Sarah Ann

The Local News.

Married, Dec. 9th, at the McFarlane House, Au Sable, by the Rev. R. L. Williams, Mr. Duncan McMaster and Miss Sarah Watson, both of Harrisville.

Alcona County Review, December 17, 1891

McMaster, Hugh H.
Watson, Maggie

People We Hear About.

Hugh H. McMaster, present keeper of the Poor Farm, was married July 15, at Au Sable to Miss Maggie Watson. The Review extends congratulations.

Alcona County Review, July 25, 1890

One Year's History.

Record of Local Happenings for the Year 1890.

JULY.

15 H. H. McMaster, Supt. of Poor Farm, married to Miss Maggie Watson.

Alcona County Review, January 1, 1891

McMillan, William
?, {Bride}

LINCOLN.

Grand Marais reports say that Wm. McMillan, formerly of this place, is to be married in the near future. Congratulations; also wish him success in his "soon to be adventure."

Alcona County Review, August 31, 1899

McNally, Bartholomew
Twite, Adelia

Marriage licenses have been issued this week to Bartholomue McNally and Adelia Twite of Black River and Ferdinand Bowser and Maud Dixon of Curtis.

Later—The former couple were married at the parsonage yesterday by Rev. Bailey.

Alcona County Review, May 2, 1895

McNally, George Wesley
Goodell, Mrs. Mary Sapphira

LOCAL JOTTINGS.

The marriage of Geo. W. McNally and Mrs. Goodell, widow of the late Alfred Goodell, was solemnized by the Rev. C. B. Steele Tuesday evening. A charivari party vexed the night air later on with the din of loud sounding saws of uncertain age, and other hideous noises. It didn't last long, however, for George has been there before, knows how it is himself, and quieted the clamor by emptying his pocketbook into the hand of the captain of the serenaders.

Alcona County Review, August 5, 1887

McNeil, Alexander

Johnson, Rebecca

HAYNES HAPPENINGS.

Married.—McNeil-Johnson.—At the home of the bride's parents in Haynes township, by the Rev. C. B. Steele, Alexander McNeil and Rebecca Johnson.

Alcona County Review, August 31, 1888

PURELY PERSONAL.

The wedding of Aleck McNeil last week to Miss Rebecca Johnson at Haynes was a happy affair. A large number of friends of the happy couple were present including the Misses Dean of Harrisville. The presents were numerous and appropriate.

Alcona County Review, September 7, 1888

McNeil, Donald
Milligan, Ella Mae

PERSONAL MENTION.

Married at the M. E. parsonage, Apr. 24th, by Rev. Wm. J. Bailey, Mr. Donald McNeil to Miss Ella Milligan, both of Haynes.

Alcona County Review, May 2, 1895

McPhee, Archie
Kramer, {Bride}

PERSONAL MENTION.

Archie McPhee, the well-known camp foreman, and Col. Reynolds, both popular and who enjoy a wide acquaintance in Alcona county, committed matrimony last week in the city of Alpena by wedding two sisters named Kramer, who are estimable ladies. The particulars of the affair are not at hand, but the Review joins with the many friends of the two gentlemen in extending congratulations and best wishes.

Alcona County Review, March 30, 1893

McPherson, William Fraser
Kimble, Kittie Maude

PERSONAL.

Invitations have been received here to the wedding of Miss Kittie Maude Kimble to Mr. William Fraser Macpherson, at Grand Marais, Mich., at eleven o'clock on the morning of Wednesday, January 20, 1897. Miss Kimble has many friends here who will wish her happiness and prosperity on the matrimonial sea.

Alcona County Review, January 14, 1897

Wedding Bells at Grand Marais.

From the Herald.

The wedding of Miss Kittie Maud Kimball to Mr. William McPherson was solemnized Wednesday, shortly after 11 o'clock in the forenoon at the home of the bride's parents on Campbell street, Rev. Mr. McGillivery performing the impressive ceremonies. A large number of friends and relatives of both the contracting parties were present. Miss Flora McLaughlan acted as bridesmaid and the groom was supported by Mr. Frederick Brace; the waitingmaids were the Misses Bertha Lencoe, Jennie Glover, Carrie Staats, Mattie Tait, Minnie Moriarty and Minnie Davidson; the ushers were Misses Rose Chisholm and Cassie Crinnian. The bride was beautifully dressed in a handsome cream silk dress trimmed with gorgeous lace and carried a large boquet of carnations and the groom wore a black suit. The wedding ceremony and everything connected with the pleasant union was a happy event and one long to be remembered by the contracting parties and their numerous friends.

The wedding presents were numerous and some very costly, which showed the high esteem in which the bride and groom were held. The happy young couple left on the noon train on their wedding tour to be gone three weeks, during that time they will visit the groom's parents at Montreal, returning via Chicago.

Alcona County Review, January 28, 1897

McRae, Duncan, Jr.
Miller, Edith Madaline

Somewhat Personal.

The nuptials of Miss Edith Miller, of Greenbush, and Mr. Duncan McRae, of Alpena, were celebrated Saturday evening at the home of the bride's parents, the Rev. Campbell of Greenbush officiating. Both young people have many friends and acquaintants in this vicinity who will wish them abundant joy and happiness. Mr. and Mrs. McRae will make their home in Alpena.

McRae—Miller, married at the residence of the bride's parents, Greenbush, Mich., April 23rd, by Rev. D. H. Campbell, Mr. Duncan McRae and Miss Edith Madaline Miller, both of Greenbush.

Alcona County Review, April 28, 1892

HISTORY OF ONE YEAR.

Chronological History of the Past Year, 1892.

MARRIAGES.

April 23. Duncan McRae and Edith Miller at Greenbush.

Alcona County Review, January 5, 1893

McVeigh, Thomas B.
Ritchie, Ida L.

PERSONAL MENTION.

Married, at the residence of Thos. McVeigh Feb. 22, 1896, Thomas B. McVeigh and Miss Ida L. Ritchie by Rev. I. L. Shaw. All of the township of Haynes.

Alcona County Review, March 5, 1896

Meddaugh, John
Lavine, Lena

BLACK RIVER RIPPLES.

John Meddaugh and Lena Lavine, both of Black River, were married at Alcona by Rev. R. H. Balmer, Wednesday, Aug. 6th.

That relic of barbarism the "chivaree," was indulged in by some of the more illiterate men and boys a few nights since. The victims, as usual, a new married couple.

Alcona County Review, August 14, 1885

Micho, David
Rivard, Mary

LOCAL JOTTINGS.

Married.—In the Catholic church in this village, on Monday, June 14, by Rev. Father Winters, Mr. David Micho and Miss Mary Rivard, all of Harrisville. In the evening a party was given the friends of the happy pair at the residence of the bride's father, Lewis Rivard. The Review wishes the couple a long and happy life.

Alcona County Review, June 18, 1886

Middleton, Frank
Marsh, Etta Jane

Curtis Items.

I am informed that Frank Middleton and Miss Etta March are married. The latter was teacher in district No. 1 last fall. All wish them a long and happy life.

Alcona County Review, July 25, 1895

Middleton, Robert
Rice, Viola

EVENTS OF ONE WEEK.

Robert Middleton and Viola Rice, aged 23 and 16, both residents of Curtis township, were licensed to wed last week.

Alcona County Review, January 3, 1895

Millen, John
Fiske, Luella J. [Tillotson]

PERSONAL POINTS.

The marriage of Mrs. Luella J. Fiske to Mr. John Millen of Black River, will occur at Detroit the last week in June. The wedding will be private.

Alcona County Review, June 15, 1899

Millen—Fiske.

The wedding of Mr. John Millen, of Black River, and Mrs. Luella J. Fiske occurred last evening at eight o'clock at the residence of Mr. and Mrs. J. Q. Ramsey, 245 Merrick avenue, Detroit.

Mr. and Mrs. Millen will take a wedding trip up the St. Lawrence river.

Alcona County Review, June 29, 1899

PERSONAL POINTS.

Several Alcona County citizens were present at the Millen-Fiske nuptials at Detroit last week, viz: Mr. and Mrs. John Whyte and Major C. H. Safford of Black River; Mr. and Mrs. Geo. E. Gillam, Mrs. Stella B. Lott and Miss Edith Lott of Harrisville.

Alcona County Review, July 6, 1899

Millen, John Alfred, Jr.
Yokom, Olive Mary

Another Black River Wedding

John Millen, Jr., and Miss Olive Yokom were united in marriage Tuesday at the home of the bride's parents, Mr. and Mrs. I. C. Yokom. It is reported as a very pretty home wedding. The bridegroom is a nephew of Supt. Millen and has been in the employ of the company for three years past in the capacity of scaler. The bride is one of Black River's popular and handsome young ladies. The marriage ceremony was performed by Rev. J. C. Cram of the Black River Presbyterian church.

Alcona County Review, June 24, 1897

PERSONAL.

Capt. and Mrs. Henderson were up to the Millen-Yokom wedding Tuesday.

Alcona County Review, June 24, 1897

PERSONAL.

Mr. and Mrs. John Millen Jr. wen north on their wedding trip.

Alcona County Review, July 1, 1897

Millen, Walter
McLeod, Bessie
PURELY PERSONAL.

Walter Millen, son of Thos. Millen, was recently married at St. Ignace to Miss Bessie McLeod of Seney.

Alcona County Review, March 29, 1889

Miller, Charles J.
Wilson, Cora
MARRIED.
Miller—Wilson. At the M. E. parsonage, Harrisville, Oct. 4th, 1894 by the Rev. Wm. J. Bailey, Mr. Charles J. Miller of Gustin, Mich., to Miss Cora Wilson of Gustin, Mich.

Alcona County Review, October 11, 1894

West Harrisville.

Chas. Miller, who recently launched a matrimonial ship, has taken refuge in D. W. Brook's house from the storms of winter.

Alcona County Review, November 15, 1894

Miller, Eli
Cumming, Mary
HOME NEWS JOTTINGS.

Married—In Harrisville, January 8, 1883, at the residence of Hiram Hall, by the Rev. J. H. McIntosh, Eli Miller and Miss Mary Cumming, all of Au Sable.

Alcona County Review, January 19, 1883

Miller, John F.
Hudson, Lydia A.
LICENSED TO WED.
Jno. F. Miller, Alcona, aged 24, and Lydia A. Hudson, Alcona, aged 24 years.

Alcona County Review, January 6, 1888

Miller, Joseph
Hastings, Martha
ALCONA ATOMS.
Alcona, July 18.--Joseph Miller and Miss Martha Hasty were united in marriage last week. Joseph has the best wishes of a host of admiring friends in this vicinity.

Alcona County Review, July 22, 1887

Miller, Kane
Hall, Minnie B.
Your Folks and Our Folks.

Married—At the residence of the bride's mother, in Harrisville, Oct. 3d, by Rev. F. N. Barlow, Mr. Kane Miller and Miss Minnie Hall, all of Harrisville.

The Review joins with numerous friends in congratulations and wishes for a happy future.

Alcona County Review, October 8, 1886

Miller, Thomas
Thorner, Rebecca
LOCAL JOTTINGS.

The county clerk has issued marriage licenses to Seymour H. Spencer, aged 37, and Louisa S. Ricker, aged 27, both of Harrisville, and to Thos. Miller, aged 31, and Rebecca Thorner, aged 16, both of Alcona.

Alcona County Review, December 6, 1887

MARRIED.
In Harrisville, Dec. 6th, 1887, by the Rev. F. N. Barlow, Thomas Miller and Miss Rebecca Thorne, both of Alcona.

Alcona County Review, December 23, 1887

Milligan, William S.
London, Elizabeth J.
The Local News.

Wm. S. Milligan and Miss Lizzie I. London, both of Haynes township, were united in marriage on Christmas by the Rev. P. C. Goldie.

Alcona County Review, January 3, 1890

Mills, Matthew
Jordan, Maggie
Married.
Matthew Mills of Black River and Maggie Jordan of Alpena have been married under an Alpena county license.

Alcona County Review, November 15, 1894

Monroe, David A.
Spencer, Mary E.
REVIEWINGS.

Married: On the 15th inst., at the residence of the bride's parents, by Rev. D. Van Dyke, David Monroe and Miss Mary E. Spencer, all of Harrisville.

We extend congratulations to the new couple, and wish them a life's journey of unalloyed happiness.

Alcona County Review, February 20, 1880

Monroe, William R.
Taylor, Olive
PERSONAL POINTS.

Wm. R. Monroe and Miss Olive Taylor, both of Mikado, were married last evening at the Baptist parsonage by Rev. W. P. Tompkins.

Alcona County Review, August 18, 1898

Moore, William S.
Bayne, Christina
COUNTY REVIEWINGS.

Married.—At Au Sable, April 13, by Rev. R. Woodhams, Mr. William S. Moore and Miss Christina Bayne, both of Black River.

Alcona County Review, April 30, 1880

Morissey, William
Smith, Anna Belle
Local News.
Miss Belle Smith, daughter of Mr. and Mrs. Jas. Smith, was married Tuesday at Grand Marais to Mr. Wm. Morissey.

Alcona County Review, November 9, 1899

Smith-Morissey Wedding.
The marriage of Miss Anna Belle Smith to Mr. William Morissey took place at Holy Rosary church Tuesday morning, Nov. 7, 1899, the Rev. Fr. Mockler officiating.

The ceremony was performed in the presence of a large number of the friends of the contracting parties.

Miss Mary Conway was bridesmaid and Mr. Louis Williams best man.

A reception was tendered the newly wedded couple at the Carpenter House. In the evening dancing was indulged in and a very enjoyable time was had.

Mr. and Mrs. Morissey began housekeeping at once in pleasant rooms in the house of Mr. and Mrs. Peter Petitpren.

They are both highly respected by their many Grand Marais friends who join in wishing them a long and prosperous married life.—Grand Marais Leader.

Mr. and Mrs. Morissey were the recipients of many and costly presents. Congratulations and best wishes are extended to them by Harrisville friends.

Alcona County Review, November 16, 1899

Morrill, Thomas Alvin
Burton, Mary Jane

Thos. A. Morril of Killmaster and Mary J. Burton of Greenbush were married yesterday by Rev. Geo. Nixon. Congratulations.

Alcona County Review, January 26, 1899

Morris, John
Lang, Mrs. Isabella

HOME NEWS JOTTINGS.

Married--at the residence of the bride's sister in Harrisville, on Wednesday March 7, 1883, John Morris and Mrs. Isabella Lang, all of Harrisville.

Alcona County Review, March 23, 1883

Morrow, J. L.
Thornton, Carrie

PERSONAL.

Lieut. J. L. Morrow of Alpena and Miss Carrie Thornton, daughter of Silas Thornton of Harrisville township, were united in marriage Wednesday, the 15th inst., at the bride's home. They will make their home in Alpena.

Alcona County Review, September 23, 1897

Morton, Lyman
Clark, Sarah

Haynes Items.

Haynes, July 27—Mr. Lyman Morton and Miss Sarah Clark, and Mr. John Johnston and Miss Elizabeth Morton were united in matrimony by the Baptist minister of Harrisville, on Saturday afternoon at the residence of Mr. Mark Morton. There was a large concourse of relatives and friends present at the ceremony and the presents were numerous and appropriate to the occasion.

Alcona County Review, July 30, 1891

Somewhat Personal.

A double wedding took place last Saturday morning at the residence of Mark Morton in Haynes township at which his son, Lyman, was united in the holy bonds of matrimony to Miss Sarah Clark, and his daughter, Elizabeth, to John Johnston. The happy ceremony was performed by the Rev. G. W. Cram of Harrisville.

Alcona County Review, July 30, 1891

Morton, Thomas H.
Fick, Lizana J.

Married.—At the residence of the bridegroom's father, in Alcona, Oct. 21st, 1886, by Rev. Charles B. Steele, Thomas H. Morton, of Alcona, and Lizana J. Fick, of Harrisville.

Alcona County Review, October 29, 1886

Mothersell, Jesse
Woods, {Bride}

Our Neighbors.

The prospective bride ran away with another fellow while waiting for the justice to marry the couple was the experience of the Woods family, who live five miles north of Atlanta, Monday. J. L. Woods has a daughter, about 16 years old. She became engaged to a young fellow by the name of George Covey. He obtained a marriage license at Hillman Saturday and they were to be married Monday. But while waiting for the justice, Jesse Mothersell, who had a previous claim upon the girl got wind of the affair and with a mutual friend went over to the place and while Mothersell waited out side the friend went in and coaxed the girl out doors and with a little persuasion got her to fly with Mothersell. They returned to Atlanta and in the evening drove to Hillman where a license was procured and they were happily married. Covey, the forsaken, is disconsolate.

Alcona County Review, December 27, 1889

Mowat, William
Haviland, Elnore

ALONG THE SHORE.

AU SABLE AND OSCODA.

Married at the residence of the bride's parents by Rev. R. Woodhams, on the 4th inst., Mr. William Mowat and Miss Elnore Haviland, all of Au Sable, Mich.

Alcona County Review, February 10, 1882

Muncey, Frank S.

McClelland, Margaret

PERSONAL MENTION.

The marriage of Margaret McClelland of Harrisville to Mr. Frank Muncey of Au Sable, which took place on July 5th at the residence of Rev. P. C. Goldie near Tawas City, was quite a surprise to the bride's friends, who were not let into the secret until after the knot had been safely tied. However, they will not be backward in extending congratulations for the bride has a large circle of friends in this county, where she has been reared and has taught successfully several terms in the public schools.

Alcona County Review, July 18, 1895

Munday, John
Mason, Flora [Richardson]

Somewhat Personal.

The Rev. John Munday, Episcopal clergyman at Alpena, and Mrs. Flora Richardson Mason were married with great pomp and ceremony by Bishop Davies last week. They have gone to Europe for a wedding trip of several months.

Alcona County Review, May 5, 1892

Munson, John
McDougall, Jessie

From Alabaster.

On Saturday, April 9, John Munson, of Alabaster, and Jessie McDougall, of Whetstone Point, were joined in the holy bonds of matrimony by Justice Cavanaugh, of Point Lookout. The happy couple then came to Alabaster, where they will reside.

Alcona County Review, April 21, 1882

Murch, Chauncey M.
Martin, Joanna M.

Black River Sparks.

Cards are out announcing the wedding of Miss B. Martin to C. H. Murch, all of Black River, which will take place at Harrisville, May 14. Congratulations.

Alcona County Review, May 14, 1896

Black River Sparks.

Martin—Murch.

One of those extremely pleasant events which occur to the average mortal once in a lifetime took place on Thursday morning, May 14th last at Harrisville and caused not a little ripple of excitement among the younger maidens and bashful swain. It is almost unnecessary to state then that the event was a marriage, the contracting parties being C. M. Murch and Miss Joanna M. Martin (second daughter of Mr. and Mrs. Jas. Martin) all of Black River. The bride was a picture of loveliness, being attired in cream silk. She was attended by Miss Anna Collins, while the groom was supported by Frank Martin, brother of the bride.

The bridal party, attended by a large number of friends, repaired to the residence of the bride's parents. The bride was the recipient of many handsome and valuable presents.

Mr. and Mrs. Murch will take up their residence in Black River. The Review and O. O. Jr., together with the many friends of the couple, wish them all happiness.

Alcona County Review, May 21, 1896

Murphy, Stephen
Williams, Mary

Along the Shore.

General News-Gleanings From the Several Counties.

Au Sable and Oscoda.

Recent marriages: Fred Cotte and Caroline Paquet, June 28; Andrew Rennell and Mary M. Norman, and John Omen and Mary Emma Minord, June 22d; Stephen Murphy and Mary Williams, June 20th.

Alcona County Review, July 2, 1880

Mutch, William
Mitchell, Jennie

MARRIED.

Mutch—Mitchell. At the home of the bride's parents, Harrisville, Mich., December 2, 1892, by the Rev. Wm. J. Bailey: Mr. William Mutch to Miss Jennie Mitchell.

Alcona County Review, December 8, 1892

HISTORY OF ONE YEAR.

Chronological History of the Past Year, 1892.

MARRIAGES.

Dec. 2. William Mutch to Jennie Mitchell, at Harrisville.

Alcona County Review, January 5, 1893

Myers, George Edward
Kruger, Minnie

Married.

Myers—Kruger. Saturday, Oct. 24th, by Rev. Wm. J. Bailey, at the home of the bride at West Harrisville, Mr. Geo. E. Myers to Miss Minnie Kruger.

Alcona County Review, November 12, 1891

Neil, Archibald
Loomis, Cordelia Ann

SOMEWHAT PERSONAL.

Married, Mr. Archie Neal of Harrisville, and Miss Delia Loomis of Au Sable, Sept. 21st. At the residence of Nicholas Neal, by the Rev. S. Boundy.

Alcona County Review, September 22, 1892

HISTORY OF ONE YEAR.

Chronological History of the Past Year, 1892.

MARRIAGES.

Sept. 21. Archie Neil of Harrisville and Delia Loomis of Au Sable.

Alcona County Review, January 5, 1893

Neil, Archibald
McDonald, Kate

Somewhat Personal.

A happy event was the marriage last Saturday evening of Archie Neil to Miss Kate McDonald, both of whom are known throughout the township as industrious and upright young people. The knot was tied by the Rev. L. Hazard. The Review extends congratulations.

Alcona County Review, May 28, 1891

Neil, Nicholas
Fick, Alice Irene

Yoked Together.

At the Bonner House, Au Sable, Dec. 26th, by the same [Rev. F. Bradley], Nicholas Neal and Alice Irene Fick, both of Harrisville.

Alcona County Review, December 29, 1882

HOME NEWS JOTTINGS.

On Tuesday Harrisville turned out the youngest bride in the shore country. Only a few months past fifteen summers.

Alcona County Review, December 29, 1882

Neil, Nicholas

McLaurin, Keziah

PERSONAL MENTION.

Nicholas Neil was united in marriage last night to Miss Cassie McLaurin, the Rev. W. W. Will officiating. The Review wishes them happiness and prosperity.

Alcona County Review, June 11, 1896

Nestle, Lafayette
Lee, Carrie May

Licensed to Wed.

The following marriage licenses were issued this month and escaped notice at the time.

Lafayette Nestell, of Wales Center, Mich., and Carrie May Lee, of Haynes township.

Alcona County Review, February 26, 1891

Nestle, William
Tower, Ida E.

Local Sayings and Doings.

Married—On Sunday evening, March 26, 1882, by Rev. F. W. Weatherwax, William Nestle and Miss Ida Tower, all of Harrisville. The Review extends congratulations to the happy couple, and wishes them a long life of unalloyed happiness, peace and prosperity.

Alcona County Review, March 31, 1882

Nevin, Andrew
Morrell, Annie

LOCAL JOTTINGS.

Married.—On Sept. 23d, 1885, at the M. E. Parsonage, Harrisville, by Rev. T. B. Leith, Andrew Nevins to Annie Morrell, both of Harrisville.

Alcona County Review, September 25, 1885

Nevin, Andrew W.
Donahue, Katie

LICENSED TO WED.

Andrew W. Nevin, aged 28, and Katie Donahue, aged 18, both of Harrisville.

Alcona County Review, January 6, 1888

LOCAL JOTTINGS

Andrew Nevins and Miss Katie Donahue surprised their friends by getting married Monday, although the event was not unexpected. They left Tuesday for Bay City, from which place they will go to Seney.

Alcona County Review, January 6, 1888

Nevin, David Alexander, Jr.
Gilpin, Lillian Margaret

David Nevin, Jr. and Miss Lillian Gilpin, both well known and highly esteemed young citizens of Harrisville township, were united in marriage last evening at the home of the bride's parents, the Rev. W. J. Bailey officiating. The wedding was a quiet home affair none but the immediate relatives and friends being present. Mr. and Mrs. Nevin will be at home after Dec. 5th. The Review wishes them bon voyage on life's journey.

Alcona County Review, December 1, 1892

MARRIED.

Nevin—Gilpin. At the home of the bride, Harrisville, Mich., Nov. 30, 1892, by the Rev. Wm. J. Bailey: Mr. David Nevin to Miss Lillian M. Gilpin, both of Harrisville.

Alcona County Review, December 8, 1892

HISTORY OF ONE YEAR.

Chronological History of the Past Year, 1892.

MARRIAGES.

Nov. 30. David Nevin, Jr., to Lillian Gilpin of Harrisville.

Alcona County Review, January 5, 1893

Nevin, Lincoln
Ottinger, Katie S.

PERSONAL MENTION.

The marriage of Lincoln Nevin, a Harrisville boy, is announced to take place June 10th at Duluth. The bride is Katie S. Ottinger of Duluth.

Alcona County Review, June 4, 1896

Newcomb, Charlie
Silverthorn, Lida

COUNTY REVIEWINGS.

We have been informed by Willie Carle of East Saginaw, that Miss Lida Silverthorn, of this place, and Charlie Newcomb, of Bay City, were recently married at the latter place; also that Walter Newcomb of said place has taken to himself one of the fair daughters of Bay City. If true, we extend congratulations, and hope all may enjoy a long, prosperous and happy life.

Alcona County Review, December 3, 1880

Newell, John
Hugill, Mary Ellen

MARRIAGE LICENSES.

April 19, John Newell, 21, and Mary E. Hugell, 16, Harrisville.
[Note: Married on 4/26/1890 in Greenbush Township.]

Alcona County Review, April 25, 1890

Nichol, John
Barber, Annie C.

County News and Gossip.

Married: At the residence of Matthew O'Neal, Tuesday evening, Feb. 22nd, by Rev. D. VanDyke, Mr. Jno. Nichol and Miss Annie C. Barber, all of Harrisville.

Alcona County Review, February 25, 1881

Nicholson, Donald
Spencer, Minnie L.

SOMEWHAT PERSONAL.

Donald Nicholson of Au Sable and Minnie L. Spencer of Harrisville township were duly licensed to marry July 1. The latter is a daughter of Seymour Spencer.

Alcona County Review, July 7, 1892

Nolan, Richard
Fraser, Jessie

The Tie That Binds.

Mr. Richard Nolan of Alpena and Miss Jessie Fraser of Greenbush, were married by Rev. W. W. Will on Wednesday, April 15, at 2 o'clock at the home of the bride.

They left on the evening train for Alpena where they will reside.

Alcona County Review, April 23, 1896

Nolan, Thomas
Forsyth, Sarah

LOCAL LACONICS.

A double wedding took place at Alcona House, Wednesday afternoon, May 7, the interested parties being Warren Roberts, of Black River, and Miss Eliza Deforest, of this village, and Thos. Nolan and Sarah Forsyth, both of this place. Rev. Mr. Lowry performed the ceremony, after which an elegant repast was partaken of. The presents were elegant and numerous. Mr. and Mrs. Roberts left for their home at Black River on Thursday morning.

Alcona County Review, May 8, 1885

Noonday, Lyman

Nad-nig-na-by, Julia

Somewhat Personal.

Mr. Lyman Noonday, of Saginaw, and Miss Julia Nad-nig-na-by, of Mikado, were married last week by an Au Sable parson. The parties are both Indians.

Alcona County Review, September 3, 1891

North, Alfred
Bruce, Jessie

Alfred North and Miss Jessie Bruce the latter a sister of that worthy citizen D. D. Bruce of Mikado were married this week.

Alcona County Review, November 9, 1888

North, Alfred
Hortwick, Eliza

They Were Legally Married.

It having been reported about that Alfred and Eliza North, of this township, were never legally married; and to show the fallacy and utter untruthfulness of any and all such reports, Mrs. North has handed the editor of the Review the certificate of their marriage which we copy. It reads as follows:

State of Michigan.
County of Cheboygan.
Township of Duncan.

I do hereby certify that on the first day of January, A. D. 1862, at the house of W. E. Jennings in said county above written, and that Alfred North and Eliza Hortwick, of the town above written, to me personally came and proved by W. E. Jennings, the aforesaid, to be the person described in this certificate, were by me joined together, with their mutual consent, in the bonds of wedlock; and I did first ascertain that the said parties were of sufficient age to consent to the same, which marriage took place in the presence of W. E. Jennings and wife of the aforesaid.

I do hereby certify to the above certificate this first day of January, A. D. 1862.

F. M. Sammons,
Justice of the Peace.

Alcona County Review, March 27, 1885

Norton, Clarence S.
Kelly, Katherine

Dr. Clarence S. Norton and Miss Katherine Kelly of Killmaster were married Nov. 1st inst., at Au Sable. They are at home at Killmaster since

Nov. 7. The Review extends congratulations and best wishes.

Alcona County Review, November 10, 1892

HISTORY OF ONE YEAR.

Chronological History of the Past Year, 1892.

MARRIAGES.

Nov. 1. Dr. Clarence S. Norton to Katherine Kelly.

Alcona County Review, January 5, 1893

Noyes, Abram
Henning, Clara

HARRISVILLE.

Married—June 27th, 1877, at the M. E. Church Parsonage, Harrisville, Mich., by Rev. N. N. Clark, Mr. Abram Noyes and Miss Clara Henning, all of Harrisville.

A reception party was given the bride and groom at the Good Templars Hall, Wednesday evening, which was a very pleasant and sociable affair. About one hundred invited guests were present to congratulate the new couple and participate in the other festivities of the occasion. Delicious refreshments were served in abundance, which was a decidedly prominent feature of the entertainment provided. The many friends of Mr. and Mrs. Noyes will wish them a long and pleasant journey through life. May they in their new relation in life receive a full measure of joy and happiness.

Alcona County Review, June 29, 1877

Noyes, William E.
Backus, Clara A.

The Local News.

Reported that a double wedding is likely to occur soon at Killmaster in which Will Noyes of Mud Lake will lead a Miss Backus to the altar and a brother of the latter will wed another popular young lady of Killmaster.

Alcona County Review, June 16, 1892

SOMEWHAT PERSONAL.

A Double Wedding.

Noyes—Backus, in Killmaster, by the Rev. D. H. Campbell, June 22d, Mr. Wm. E. Noyes of Mud Lake and Miss Clara A. Backus of Killmaster.

Alcona County Review, June 30, 1892

HISTORY OF ONE YEAR.

Chronological History of the Past Year, 1892.

MARRIAGES.

June 22. Wm. E. Noyes to Clara A. Backus, at Killmaster.

Alcona County Review, January 5, 1893

O'Brien, J. V.
King, Nellie

LOCAL JOTTINGS.

J. V. O'Brien and Miss Nellie King, daughter of postmaster King, were married Wednesday morning of last week.

Alcona County Review, January 23, 1885

O'Brien, Patrick
Shirley, Martha

PERSONAL MENTION.

Pat O'Brien and Miss Martha Shirley were united in marriage by the Rev. Fr. Mahar at Au Sable Tuesday, the 24th, inst. They will reside at Sturgeon Pointe where Mr. O'Brien is one of the boys of the life-saving crew. Mrs. O'Brien is a sister of Mrs. Geo. Cuyler. We extend congratulations.

Alcona County Review, April 26, 1894

Oglesby, {Groom}
Sutherland, Laura K.

PURELY PERSONAL.

Miss Laura K. Sutherland, who has been a teacher in the Au Sable school for several years past, has sent in her resignation to take effect at the close of the present school term, a couple of weeks from now. Miss Sutherland will be united in marriage shortly afterwards to the Rev. Oglesby, a Canadian clergyman. A host of friends offer congratulations.—Saturday Night. Miss Sutherland, who is a sister of Mrs. P. C. Goldie, has numerous admiring acquaintances in Harrisville who will also extend hearty congratulations.

Alcona County Review, March 22, 1889

Oliver, Harvey L.
Taft, Matie E.

Married at Grand Marais.

At 10:30 o'clock yesterday morning the marriage of Mr. Harvey L. Oliver and Miss Matie Taft was solemnized at Grand Marais, Mich. Mr. and Mrs. Oliver left on the afternoon train for ———, Wash., Mr. Oliver's home, where they will reside.

The bride is one of the most popular young ladies of Harrisville, where she has lived nearly all her life. She has taught in the public schools of the village and county and has endeared herself to a host of friends whose best wishes will follow her to her new home in the far distant state of Washington. The groom is not known here, but he is to be congratulated upon becoming

"The happy bridegroom of so fair a bride."

Alcona County Review, April 14, 1898

The Oliver-Taft Wedding.

The Herald of Grand Marais has the following report of the marriage of Miss Matie Taft to Harvey L. Oliver, which took place at 10 a.m. Wednesday, 13th inst., at the home of the bride's brother, L. W. Taft.

"The ceremony was strictly private only relatives of the bride being present. Presiding Elder Fraser officiated assisted by Rev. W. J. Datson. After the ceremony the party partook of a sumptuous repast. At 1 o'clock the happy young couple left amid showers of congratulations and good wishes, for McMinnville, Oregon, where they go to take up their future abode."

The groom has been a resident of Grand Marais for three years, most of that time being employed at the Colwell mill as drag sawyer.

Both bride and groom were active in church and society circles and had hosts of friends whose good wishes follow them.

Alcona County Review, April 21, 1898

Local History of One Year

Chronology of the Principal Events of the Year 1898.

April 13. Marriage Matie Taft to Harvey L. Oliver at Grand Marais.

Alcona County Review, January 5, 1899

Oliver, James
Budworth, Mrs. Sarah Ann

HOME REVIEWINGS.

Married, at Harrisville, May 12, 1881, by Rev. C. Gibbs, James Oliver of Alpena, to Mrs. Sarah Budworth, of Harrisville. The couple left for the bridegroom's home at Alpena on the steamer Flora yesterday afternoon. The congratulations of the bride's numerous friends in Harrisville are extended to the couple.

Alcona County Review, May 13, 1881

Oliver, Louis W.
McNally, Jennie

Somewhat Personal.

Louis W. Oliver of Ossineke and Miss Jennie McNally of Black River were united in marriage this week.— Alpena Pioneer.

Alcona County Review, March 17, 1892

Oliver, Norman J.
Ferris, Nellie S.

CALEDONIA.

Invitations have been received in Caledonia for the wedding of Mr. Norman J. Oliver and Miss Nellie Ferris of Black River. Mr. Oliver has many warm friends in Caledonia who wish him and his fair bride happiness and prosperity over life's tempestuous sea.

Alcona County Review, October 28, 1897

PERSONAL.

The marriage of Norman J. Oliver to Nellie S. Ferris was performed at Black River Wednesday of last week in the presence of a large company of their friends. They are among the most popular citizens of the town and both have many warm friends throughout the county who will wish them all manner of happiness. Mr. Oliver has a two weeks furlough from his duties as station agent.

Alcona County Review, November 4, 1897

LOCAL PICK UPS.

Hosa Funk of Tawas is acting as relief agent at Black River during the absence of Mr. Oliver on his wedding trip.

Alcona County Review, November 4, 1897

Olsen, Henry
Nelson, Anna Christina

ALONG THE SHORE.
Henry Olsen and Anna Christina Nelson were married at Oscoda on the 8th inst.

Alcona County Review, January 21, 1881

Omen, John
Minord, Mary Emma

Along the Shore.

General News-Gleanings From the Several Counties.

Au Sable and Oscoda.
Recent marriages: Fred Cotte and Caroline Paquet, June 28; Andrew Rennell and Mary M. Norman, and John Omen and Mary Emma Minord, June 22d; Stephen Murphy and Mary Williams, June 20th.

Alcona County Review, July 2, 1880

O'Neal, James
?, {Bride}

Somewhat Personal.

Jas. O'Neal returned from Tawas Saturday night where he has been working for some time. He was accompanied by Mrs. O'Neal, to whom he was married the previous Wednesday.

Alcona County Review, December 10, 1891

O'Neal, William
Deucharme, Mary

Wedding Bells.
The Catholic church at this place was crowded Monday morning with friends and relatives who came to witness the marriage ceremony of William O'Neal and Miss Mary Deucharme. The church had been very tastily decorated with flowers for the occasion, and the floral offerings were numerous and appropriate. The bride and bridegroom were assisted by Miss Carrie Deucharme, of Au Sable, sister of the bride, and W. B. Fitzmaurice, of Alpena, brother-in-law of the bridegroom. The nuptial knot was tied by the Rev. Father Winter. After the impressive marriage ceremony was completed the bridal party was driven to the home of the bridegroom, where they did ample justice to a bountiful repast.

Mr. O'Neal and wife have settled down on the former's place near Harrisville.

Alcona County Review, July 15, 1887

Osborn, James K.
Killmaster, Isabell

PURELY PERSONAL.

Miss Isabell Killmaster, sister of Chas. and Geo. Killmaster, was recently married at Brantford, Ont., to Jas. K. Osborn.

Alcona County Review, September 28, 1888

O'Toole, Felix
?, {Bride}

Along the Shore.

General News-Gleanings From the Several Counties.

Au Sable and Oscoda.
Mr. Felix O'Toole, formerly of Au Sable, now of Albany, Oregon, who for the past 75 years has enjoyed single blessedness, will shortly be married to a young miss of 14 years, of the latter place.

Alcona County Review, July 30, 1880

Ottley, Robert
McDonald, Elizabeth

Somewhat Personal.

Miss Annie Gothro who accompanied Mr. and Mrs. Robt. Ottley upon a visit to the Pointe and the Fair, returned to her home at Au Sable on Saturday. Mr. and Mrs. Ottley returned home last Monday and will be "at home" to their friends after Nov. 1st. Congratulations. Mrs. O. is a sister of Mrs. Finch and a niece of Mrs. D. C. Emmory.

Alcona County Review, October 22, 1891

Otto, Isadore Frederick
Sanderson, Letitia Sarah

Mr. Isadore F. Otto of Haynes and Letitia Sanderson of Avoca, Mich., were married by the Rev. Will Wednesday afternoon at the Methodist parsonage.

Alcona County Review, December 23, 1897

Owen, John H.
McKay, Pearl

Local News.
John Owen, son of S. H. Owen of Harrisville township, and Miss Pearl McKay of Greenbush, were united in marriage at the parsonage by Rev. W. P. Tompkins Saturday afternoon.

Alcona County Review, November 3, 1898

Local News.
The young friends of John H. Owen and wife took them by surprise Hallowe'en. Sixteen gathered at his

home. A good time and many wishes and all went home happy.

Alcona County Review, November 3, 1898

Owen, Samuel H.
Spencer, Rhoda J.

County News and Gossip.

Married.—At the M. E. Church, Christmas Eve, 1878, by Rev. N. N. Clark, Mr. Samuel H. Owen and Miss Rhoda J. Spencer, all of Harrisville.

Alcona County Review, December 27, 1878

Palmer, Nelson
Mooney, Mina

EVENTS OF ONE WEEK.

Licenses were issued on the 8th inst. permitting the marriage of James Fassett to Mary Carr, and Nelson Palmer to Mina Mooney.

Alcona County Review, April 11, 1895

Curran Crumbs.

This week has run smoothly until tonight, 9th of April, we hear of a surprise party of six meeting at James LaForge's headed by Nelson Palmer and Miss Mina Moony. A marriage license being placed into the hand of Justice LaForge which meant business, the nuptial knot was tied according to the law of the state. Tables were spread with the best in the land; after doing justice a pleasant evening was spent. A beautiful night for a wedding tour. Henry Fullerton drove up with the little oxen, three seats were filled and away they drove. We wish Mr. and Mrs. Palmer much joy and a long life together.

Alcona County Review, April 18, 1895

Palmer, Walter S.
Reed, Linna

PERSONAL MENTION.

The wedding of Miss Linna Reed to Walter S. Palmer is announced to take place Monday, Nov. 25th, at 8 o'clock (whether morning or evening is not stated) at the M. E. church.

Alcona County Review, November 14, 1896

At the Altar.

Palmer-Reed—The marriage of Mr. Walter S. Palmer of Chicago and Miss Linna Reed of Harrisville will be solemnized Monday evening next at 8 o'clock at the M. E. church. Mr.

and Mrs. Palmer will make their home in Chicago.

Alcona County Review, November 21, 1895

Wedding Bells a Ringing.

Palmer—Reed.

The leading society event of the season in Harrisville took place at the M. E. church Monday evening, when Mr. Walter S. Palmer, U. S. weather observer at Chicago, led to Hymen's altar Miss Linna Reed, eldest daughter of our esteemed fellow citizen, Supervisor Abram Reed.

The church was prettily decorated for the occasion with evergreens, autumn leaves and flowers. A large number of invited guests came early to witness the ceremony, which removes from Harrisville society a social favorite and a lady possessed of many graces of person and manners.

Miss Alie M. Colwell presided at the organ and preluded the wedding march proper by a careful selection of music. At 8 o'clock the bridal party arrived at the church. The groom and his best man, Mr. Walter L. Chapelle, entered by the right aisle and preceded by the ushers, Messrs. Fred C. Reynolds and Arthur W. Emerson, took their places at the right of the altar. The bride, charmingly attired in a crushed rose gown of Lansdowne, entered by the left aisle and was escorted to the altar on the arm of her venerable father. She was attended by her sister, Miss Martha Reed.

The beautiful marriage service was very impressively rendered by the pastor of the church, Rev. W. W. Will. At the conclusion of the service the wedding party left the church by the right aisle and were at once driven to the residence of the bride's parents, where a wedding supper was served and congratulations were showered upon Mr. and Mrs. Palmer.

The bride is a lifelong resident of Harrisville, while the groom is not a stranger to the majority of our people and has created a most favorable impression during frequent visits. Mrs. Palmer has been an active worker in church and social affairs for years and she will be greatly missed by a large circle of friends, who will wish her joy and happiness, however, in her new home.

Mr. and Mrs. Palmer took the train Tuesday morning enroute for

Jackson and their new home at Chicago.

List of Presents.

Angora goat rug, Mr. and Mrs. Gynn.
Embroidered center-piece, Mrs. Gynn.
Cracker jar, Miss A. Bell Colwell.
Bonbon spoon, Mr. and Mrs. L. M. Reed.
Framed picture of apple blossoms, Mr. and Mrs. L. A. Colwell.
Clock in Dresden china case, Mrs. Elliott.
Hand-painted thermometer, B. F. Buchanan and family.
Emb. linen handkerchief, Mrs. E. Chapelle.
Orange knife and spoon, Lewis Dewey.
½ doz. nut picks and portfolio, Mr. and Mrs. Van Buskirk.
Traveling case, Mrs. Geo. Monroe.
Match safe, Inez Monroe.
Vase with flowers, Mr. and Mrs. J. W. Anderson.
Orange knife and spoon, Mr. and Mrs. S. Hale.
"Evangeline" illustrated, W. L. Chapelle.
Linen towel, Mr. and Mrs. R. McClatchey.
Knitted lace, Mrs. Helen Reynolds.
Doyley, Mr. and Mrs. Peterson and Ella.
Celery dish, Mrs. Sisson.
Silver butter knife, Mr. and Mrs. F. A. Beede.
Table cloth and napkins, Mr. and Mrs. A. Reed.
Silver syrup pitcher and tray, Mattie Reed.
Flowers, Carrie Moore.
Sugar Spoon, Arthur Emerson.
Cut glass salt and pepper shakers, Chas. Mayo.
China bread tray, O. H. Smith family.
Set silver knives and forks, Mr. and Mrs. Evans.
Photo basket, Mr. and Mrs. F. Reynolds.
Pair after dinner coffee cups and saucers, Edith Lott.
Dozen china berry dishes, Mr. and Mrs. H. F. Colwell.
Pair napkin rings, Mr. and Mrs. Anson Beebe.

Alcona County Review, November 28, 1895

Parks, Joseph
Mudgett, Mary

LOCAL JOTTINGS.

Married.

On Thursday, the 9th inst., by Justice C. P. Reynolds at his office, Joseph Parks, of Lapeer, Mich., and Miss Mary Mudgett, of Harrisville.

May happiness and good luck ever attend them.

Alcona County Review, October 17, 1884

Parrow, Henry
Freer, Julia

LOCAL JOTTINGS.

Henry Parrow and Julia Freer were married Wednesday at the residence of Mrs. Weir, of W. Harrisville, the Rev. W. R. Waters officiating.

Alcona County Review, October 5, 1888

Partridge, Philip O.
Lee, Mary F.

Licensed to Wed.

The following marriage licenses were issued this month and escaped notice at the time.

P. O. Partridge and Mary F. Lee, both residents of Mikado.

Alcona County Review, February 26, 1891

Paterson, Ralph
Griswold, Melvina

HOME REVIEWINGS.

We see by the Au Sable News that Mr. Ralph Paterson and Miss Melvina Griswold, of Harrisville, were married in that village on the 17th inst., by Rev. R. Woodhams.

Alcona County Review, August 26, 1881

Patterson, George
McDonald, Dora

Note and News Along the Shore

TAWAS CITY.

George Patterson and Dora McDonald were married Dec. 24th, by Justice Dixon.

Alcona County Review, January 2, 1885

Peck, Miner
Stockton, Minnie Jane

Orange Blossoms.

At ten o'clock in the morning of Dec. 25, 1899, Miss Minnie Stockton, daughter of Mr. and Mrs. L. M. Stockton, of Gustin, and Mr. Mino Peck of Curtis, were married in the presence of a company of friends at the home of the bride's parents. Rev. G. Sanderson of Lincoln performed the ceremony. The groom and bride received many useful and expensive

presents, among which was a handsome organ and a sewing machine. Their many friends extend congratulations.

Alcona County Review, January 11, 1900

Pepper, Solomon
Monette, Marian May

EVENTS OF ONE WEEK.

Solomon Pepper, aged 27, and May Monette, aged 20, both of Black River, were licensed to wed a few days ago. Also John Rickle, aged 33, and Mary Mosseau, aged 35, both of Gustin.

Alcona County Review, November 7, 1895

Perry, Byron
McGillis, Elizabeth

Married.—In Harrisville, Dec. 8, 1886, by Rev. F. N. Barlow, Mr. Byron Perry and Miss Elizabeth McGillis, all of Harrisville.

Alcona County Review, December 10, 1886

Phelps, Myron
Wedge, Elizabeth [Quigley]

EVENTS OF ONE WEEK.

Reported that Hick's hustling salesman, Phelps, has taken unto himself a better half in the person of Mrs. Wedge.

Alcona County Review, December 19, 1895

Phillips, Frank A.
Curly, Susie May

CURTIS.

It is reported that Frank Phillips and wife are on their way home from an extended wedding trip. May long life and happiness be their lot.

[Note: married on 9/7/1897]

Alcona County Review, October 7, 1897

Phillips, George E.
Wood, Emma R.

AU SABLE AND OSCODA.

Geo. E. Phillips and Miss Emma R. Wood were married on the 4th inst.

Alcona County Review, February 13, 1885

Philp, William
McGillis, Susan

REVIEWINGS.

Well yes, they're married! It happened on Tuesday evening—Rev. D. VanDyke officiating—and Mr. Wm. Philp and Miss Susie McGillis

are the victims. Ah, what a change in life! Now somebody has a brother in law, some one else a sister in law— and aunts and uncles follow next.

"'Twas never thus in childhood's hour!" May the new couple live long to enjoy unalloyed happiness and prosperity, which cometh only to those who keep inviolate the nuptial vows.

Alcona County Review, January 16, 1880

REVIEWINGS.

Mr. and Mrs. Wm. Philip, newly married, have gone to housekeeping on their own hook in a portion of the residence occupied by J. W. Newcomb and family.

Alcona County Review, January 23, 1880

Pierson, John
Edgar, Lewella

Married.—In Harrisville, Nov. 24, 1886, by F. Beede, Esq., Mr. John Pierson and Miss Lewella Edgar, both of Harrisville.

Alcona County Review, December 10, 1886

Pizer, Julius
Friedman, Annie

SOMEWHAT PERSONAL.

Cards have been received announcing the marriage at Denver, Col., Sunday evening, August 14, of Mr. Julius Pizer of Harrisville to Miss Annie Friedman of Denver.

Alcona County Review, August 11, 1892

SOMEWHAT PERSONAL.

Julius Pizer and bride arrived on the Atlantic Sunday eve, and are stopping at the Nevins House.

Judging by the handsome presents received by the happy couple it would appear that the wedding ceremony must have been an elaborate affair. The bride is a daughter of a wealthy Denver merchant. The bride and groom have been acquainted from childhood. During Mr. Pizer's residence in Harrisville, covering a period of about four years, he has conducted himself as a gentle man and an upright business man. He enjoys the respect of the community, who will wish him and his bride abundant happiness. The Review extends a welcome back to Harrisville.

Following are some of the presents received by Mr. and Mrs. Pizer:

check for $1,500 from bride's parents, $500 from bride's brother, $100 from I. Harris of Kearney, Neb., $100 from E. Harris of Detroit, $100 from S. H. Cominskey of Denver, $100 from M. A. Nathan of Marshaltown, Ia., and many other valuable presents. After their marriage they took a trip to the mountains, Colorado Springs, Pike's Peak, Manitou and many other points of interest.

Alcona County Review, September 1, 1892

HISTORY OF ONE YEAR.

Chronological History of the Past Year, 1892.

MARRIAGES.

August 14. Julius Pizer of Harrisville to Anna Friedman at Denver, Col.

Alcona County Review, January 5, 1893

Potter, Arthur
Stone, Adella

PERSONAL MENTION.

Arthur Potter of Alpena, the gentleman who has occupied the pulpit of the Baptist church in this village on two occasions the past summer was married last week at Hamilton, N. Y. to Miss Adella Stone.

Alcona County Review, September 13, 1894

Potter, Emerson
Seaton, Anna

Local Sayings and Doings.

Married—At the Presbyterian parsonage, Monday, March 6, 1882, by Rev. F. W. Weatherwax, Mr. Emerson Potter and Miss Anna Seaton, all of Alcona, Mich.

Alcona County Review, March 10, 1882

Poultny, James C.
Forbes, Jennie

MARRIED.

POULTNY—FORBES.—At Black River, Jan. 20, 1887, by the Rev. Geo. E. Weir, James C. Poultny and Jennie Forbes, both of West Bay City.

Alcona County Review, January 28, 1887

Preston, Henry
Barret, Mary

Last Tuesday evening Cupid cut up one of his pranks with a young lady of this city. Miss Mary Barret was living with Capt. Henry Vosburg and his wife but was engaged to be married to Henry Preston, of Bay City, and expected the nuptial knot to be tied next fall. Henry came to see Mary last Tuesday, and Captain Vosburg and his wife, being jolly people, challenged them to be married. We suppose that Cupid commenced immediately to practice his arts of archery, for the challenge was accepted, the Justice was called, Mr. and Mrs. Vosburg acted as groomsman and bridesmaid while the nuptial tie was made solid. The occasion, though impromptu, was very pleasant.—*Alpena Pioneer.*

Alcona County Review, August 5, 1881

Pritchard, James Roberts
Hood, Jetta B.

MARRIED.

In Harrisville, Mich., Dec. 25, 1881, at residence of C. P. Reynolds, by Rev. J. H. McIntosh, James Roberts Pritchard and Miss Jetta B. Hood, both of Black River.

Alcona County Review, December 30, 1881

Proctor, William F.
Hall, Elizabeth

PERSONAL MENTION.

Proctor—Hall.—In Black River at the residence of the bride's parents, William F. Proctor and Miss Lizzie Hall, both of Black River, were married Oct. 9, 1893, by the Rev. E. F. Smith.

Alcona County Review, October 12, 1893

Procunier, Anthony
Good, Mrs. Mary J.

MARRIED.

At the M. E. church parsonage in Harrisville, October 14, 1882, by Rev. J. H. McIntosh, Anthony Procunier and Mrs. Mary J. Good, all of Harrisville, Mich.

Alcona County Review, October 27, 1882

Procunier, Dessmus
Lynham, Harriet E.

Married.

Procunier—Lynham. Sunday, Oct. 25th, at the Methodist parsonage, Harrisville, by the Rev. Wm. J. Bailey, Mr. Dessmus Procunier of Harrisville, to Miss Harriet E. Lynham of Mikado.

Alcona County Review, November 12, 1891

Provencher, Napolean

Maynard, Josephine

Provencher—Maynard.

Miss Josephine Maynard and Mr. Napolean Provencher were united in marriage in the city of Manchester, N. H. June 25, 1898. The bride is a daughter of Mr. and Mrs. Edmund Maynard, who for many years resided in Harrisville township.

The bride was attired in navy blue trimmed with white chiffon. Immediately after the ceremony a wedding breakfast was served, after which the party left for Boston for a short honeymoon. On their return Mr. and Mrs. Provencher will make their home in Manchester.

Alcona County Review, July 7, 1898

Pyne, George
McIntyre, Margaret

OUR NEIGHBORS.

Married at the M. E. parsonage, Au Sable, April 28, by Rev. F. L. Osborne, Mr. Geo. Pyne of Harrisville and Miss Maggie McIntyre of Oscoda.--*Press.*

Alcona County Review, May 9, 1895

Pyne, William C.
LaViolette, Harriet

PERSONAL MENTION.

Wm. C. Pyne of Haynes and Miss Hattie Laviolette of Harrisville were married by Rev. W. W. Will Saturday evening at the parsonage.

Alcona County Review, March 26, 1896

Quesnell, Hermidas
DeForrest, Maggie

LOCAL JOTTINGS.

Hermidas Quesnell, of Au Sable, recently of Harrisville, and Miss Maggie DeForrest, were united in marriage, Tuesday, Dec. 13, at the residence of L. A. Colwell, by Rev. W. R. Waters. A pleasant company witnessed the ceremony, and several valuable and useful presents were presented to the bride by Mr. and Mrs. L. A. Colwell; also from several friends in Harrisville and vicinity. They departed at once for Au Sable, at which place Mr. Quesnell is engaged in business. The worthy couple have the best wishes of their Harrisville friends for a long and happy life.

Alcona County Review, December 21, 1888

Quinlan, Thomas J.
Bloomingdale, Harriet

PERSONAL.

Mr. Thos. Quinlan and Miss Hattie Bloomingdale were united in wedlock this week by Rev. Fr. Poulin.

Alcona County Review, April 29, 1897

Raciat, Joseph
Talbot, Lea

EVENTS OF ONE WEEK.

Joseph Raciat and Miss Lea Talbot, both of Black River, were married at Harrisville Monday by Fr. Poulin.

Alcona County Review, August 20, 1896

Ranney, Arthur W.
Cross, Lucy

Black River.

Cards are out giving notice of the marriage of Mr. Arthur Ranney to Miss Cross of Rochester, N. Y., on the 16th inst. Mr. Ranney left yesterday for his former home.

Alcona County Review, June 9, 1892

HISTORY OF ONE YEAR.

Chronological History of the Past Year, 1892.

MARRIAGES.

June 16. Arthur W. Ranney to Miss Cross, at Rochester, N. Y.

Alcona County Review, January 5, 1893

Read, Nelson H.
Webster, Clara J.

COUNTY NEWS JOTTINGS.

Married: At the residence of Albert H. Leland, Black River, Alcona County, Mich., Nov. 6th, 1877, by Rev. N. N. Clark of Harrisville, Mr. Nelson H. Read, of Buffalo, N. Y., and Miss Clara J. Webster, of Eden Center, N. Y. This is said to be the first wedding in Black River village. The gifts presented to Mrs. Read by her numerous friends, were many and useful. Mr. and Mrs. Leland will long be remembered by the forty-five guests who were so hospitably entertained by them.

Alcona County Review, November 16, 1877

Reed, Matt
Stewart, Charlotta

LOCAL JOTTINGS.

Matt Reed of the life saving station, went up to Alpena, Monday.

Don't know why it was that Matt took a bath in Lake Huron that morning with all his good clothes on unless there was something in the rumor that said he didn't intend to come back alone.

Alcona County Review, July 15, 1887

PURELY PERSONAL.

Matt Reed, of Sturgeon Pointe, had "business" in Au Sable last Sunday, and he attended to it so well that next time there will be very little come up under the head of "unfinished business."

Alcona County Review, September 2, 1887

PURELY PERSONAL.

Word comes from Alpena that Matt Reed, a popular member of the Sturgeon Pointe L. S. crew, has joined the grand army of Benedicts. Matt's enamoratta was formerly Miss Charlotta Stewart, one of Alpena's fairest young ladies.

Alcona County Review, January 13, 1888

PURELY PERSONAL.

Matt Reed, of Sturgeon Pointe L. S. S. was married since the closing of navigation to one of Alpena's fairest young ladies. The most blissful period of married life according to the most reliable reports has been embittered in his case by a severe attack of inflammatory rheumatism which has confined him to the house nearly all winter.

Alcona County Review, April 13, 1888

Regier, Christ
Deacon, Evadne Leburney

First Marriage License.

The first and only license issued thus far by Co. Clerk Rutson under the provisions of the new marriage license law was issued Oct 11th to Christ Regur, of Curtis. The bride is Miss Evadne Leburney Deacon, daughter of ex-supervisor Deacon, of Curtis. In accordance with our promise made some time since to send the Review one year free to the first couple married under the new law, we now place the happy bride-groom's name upon our mailing list, trusting that in perusing its columns he and his bride will discover something that will lend a flavor to their enjoyment of the honeymoon. Here's luck, Christ.

Alcona County Review, November 4, 1887

The Local News.

The county clerk has issued a marriage license to Jos. Bernard of Haynes and Jane Ross of Au Sable, also one to Christ Regier and Evadne L. Deacon, both of Curtis township.

Alcona County Review, May 9, 1890

Rennell, Andrew
Norman, Mary M.

Along the Shore.

General News-Gleanings From the Several Counties.

Au Sable and Oscoda.

Recent marriages: Fred Cotte and Caroline Paquet, June 28; Andrew Rennell and Mary M. Norman, and John Omen and Mary Emma Minord, June 22d; Stephen Murphy and Mary Williams, June 20th.

Alcona County Review, July 2, 1880

Reynolds, {Groom}
Kramer, {Bride}

PERSONAL MENTION.

Archie McPhee, the well-known camp foreman, and Col. Reynolds, both popular and who enjoy a wide acquaintance in Alcona county, committed matrimony last week in the city of Alpena by wedding two sisters, named Kramer, who are estimable ladies. The particulars of the affair are not at hand, but the Review joins with the many friends of the two gentlemen in extending congratulations and best wishes.

Alcona County Review, March 30, 1893

Reynolds, Frederick C.
Sisson, Laura A.

PERSONAL MENTION.

The wedding of Mr. Fred Reynolds and Miss Laura Sisson, two of Harrisville's popular young people, is announced to take place at the M. E. church on the evening of June 27.

Alcona County Review, June 13, 1895

PERSONAL MENTION.

The marriage ceremony of Mr. Fred Reynolds to Miss Laura Sisson takes place this evening at the M. E. church. The seats of the church are all reserved for invited guests. A reception at the residence of the bride's mother at Lakeside will follow the ceremony.

Alcona County Review, June 27, 1895

PERSONAL MENTION.

Miss Ida Peterson arrived from Detroit last week and remains for the Reynolds-Sisson nuptials this evening.

Alcona County Review, June 27, 1895

Miss Maud Reynolds of Black River is in town for the wedding this evening.

Alcona County Review, June 27, 1895

WEDDING BELLS.

Reynolds-Sisson.—The marriage of Mr. Fred C. Reynolds to Miss Laura A. Sisson was solemnized at the M. E. church Thursday evening, June 27th, in the presence of a house full of invited guests, every seat having been reserved. A large number not knowing this came to the church and expressed great disappointment when they learned that all the seats had been reserved. The groom was assisted by Messrs. W. L. Chapelle and H. A. Joughlin, all being dressed in conventional black. The bride, looking very charming in a cream silk dress and white bridal veil, came in on the arm of her grandfather, Mr. J. Peterson. The maids of honor were the bride's sister, Miss May Sisson, and her aunt, Miss Myrtle Peterson. They were also dressed in white silk and the bride and maids carried bouquets of natural flowers. The ushers were Messrs. A. N. Springer and Geo. E. Gillam. The wedding ceremony was performed by the pastor of the church, Rev. W. J. Bailcy, and took place under an arch of evergreens. The church had been tastefully decorated for the occasion with potted plants, evergreens, ribbon, etc. and looked very attractive. On the rear wall and facing the bridal couple a large horseshoe of evergreen enclosing the motto "Bonum fortuna."

Following the ceremony a reception was given at Lakeside from 9 to 10 p. m. and a number of guests repaired thither to congratulate Mr. and Mrs. Reynolds. The newly married couple had their arrangements made to begin housekeeping and after the reception they were driven to their new home on South Lake street, where they are now at home to their many friends.

The groom, as all know, is a Harrisville boy by birth and he is in every way worthy of the hand and heart of his lovely bride. The bride came from North Platte, Neb., two years ago, but during her short residence she has endeared herself to a large circle of friends. Since coming to Harrisville she has united with the M. E. church and as an officer the member of the C. E. Society and worked faithfully and zealously.

The presents were many and nice. Here is a complete list.
Class of '95, silver cake basket.
W. L. Chapelle and H. A. Joughin, china and silver berry dish.
Mr. and Mrs. L. A. Colwell, silver berry spoon.
Mr. and Mrs. O. H. Smith and Jessie, set china cups and saucers.
Geo. Rutson, silver pickle dish.
Chas. Mayo, pair bronze vases.
Mr. and Mrs. Jas. Morris, sugar sifter and china cake plate.
Mr. and Mrs. G. W. Chapelle and family, china salad dish.
Rev. and Mrs. W. J. Bailey, cocoa pot.
Miss Ida Peterson, Detroit, set Carlsbad china berry dishes.
Walter S. Colwell, Harrisville, souvenir spoon.
Mrs. D. E. Storms, Jean Ingelow's poems.
Mr. and Mrs. B. P. Cowley, set silver knives & forks.
Mr. and Mrs. Beede, silver berry spoon.
Miss Allie Colwell, china rose jar and handsome bouquet.
Mr. and Mrs. Smith and family, Black River, set dishes.
"Phidias." Miss Anna Duggan.
Thos. F. McClatchey, gold pen.
Mrs. Helen Reynolds, large Bible.
Mrs. Elliot, Chinese embroidered silk handk'chf.
Miss Stella Witter, Greeley, silver buttoner, moss agate handle.
Miss Anna Gusslee, North Platte, Neb., ottoman cover and head rest.
Mr. Thos. Pugh, Au Sable, silver goblet.
Miss Cora Hoover, North Bend, Neb., pair silver napkin rings.
Mrs. K. A. Stimson, Greeley, Col., "Scenes Among the Rockies."
Mr. and Mrs. S. Hale, silver butter knife, sugar spoon.
Mr. and Mrs. G. C. Lewis, Allie Fisher, silver card receiver.
Mr. and Mrs. Geo. Ward, Jr., glass water set.
Miss M. McClelland, hand embroidered doily.

Mr. and Mrs. M. McClatchey, wool duster.
Mrs. John Cowley, set crocheted table mats.
Mrs. Geo. H. Sisson, check for fifty dollars.
Mrs. J. B. Peterson and family, bed linen.
Mr. and Mrs. Dwyer, North Platte, table cloth.
Miss. F. Thaler, Palmyra, Neb., hand-painted pin-cushion.
Mr. and Mrs. D. La Boueff, china lamp.
Miss Allie Frasher, pair doilies.
Mr. and Mrs. A. Saylor, nickle comb, brush, tray.
Mr. and Mrs. Robt. McClatchey, pair towels.
Mr. and Mrs. H. F. Colwell, set ice-cream dishes, china sugar bowl and cream pitcher.
Dr. and Mrs. Mitchell, handsome picture.
May Sisson, veil case.
Mr. and Mrs. J. B. Peterson, Sr., bed linen.
Mr. and Mrs. J. B. Peterson, Jr., rocking chair.
Mrs. Mary Hoover, Iliff, Colo., head-rest.
Miss Maude Hoover, tidy.
M. Minainyer, table lamp.
Mrs. C. H. Bennett, Brady, Neb., souvenir spoon.
Jessie E. Vroman, Vroman, Neb., embroidered doily.
Mr. and Mrs. A. N. Springer, Mr. and Mrs. G. E. Gillam, hanging lamp.
Thos. Green, roast and roaster.
Miss Jennie Ware, Hershey, Neb., fancy pepper and salt indo.
Capt. and Mrs. Henderson, half-dozen napkins.
Misses Ella and Myrtle Peterson, fancy wall pocket.
Mrs. Van Meter, 3 cans fruit.

Alcona County Review, July 4, 1895

Reynolds, Thomas W.
Lowdy, Katie

LOCAL JOTTINGS.

Married—On the 14th inst. at the M. E. parsonage, by Rev. T. B. Leith, Thos. W. Reynolds and Katie Lowdy all of Sand Beach.

Alcona County Review, November 21, 1884

Rice, Earle R.
Mills, Josephine

PERSONAL.

Mr. Earle R. Rice, principal of the Harrisville schools, and Miss Josephine Mills, one of the department teachers, were married last week and are now receiving the congratulations of their many friends here.

Alcona County Review, September 2, 1897

Richards, Lewis H.
Briggs, Anna

WEDDING BELLS.
Richards—Briggs.

From Evening Telegram, Adrian.

Of all the numerous gods of myth the world hears very little to-day except of that one who is smallest of them all and yet whose silent power moves the world. Cupid is yet with us and the 75 guests who gathered on State street on Tuesday evening were of one opinion, that Cupid had done a good job and joined two hearts of like disposition.

The bride, Miss Anna Briggs, has lived in our city long enough to gain for herself a wide circle of friends and exerted a helpful influence wherever she was found. As bookkeeper for Moreland Brothers & Crane, she filled her position excellently and gave the best satisfaction. Her place there has been filled by her sister, Miss Ella Briggs.

The groom, Mr. Lewis H. Richards, is better known at the college than in the city. Mr. Richards spent several years in our institution and graduated in the class of '95 of which he was president. He was always a favorite with the boys. After graduation, he worked for some time as bookkeeper for the Wilcox Hardware Co., and last fall accepted a position as principal of the high school at Harrisville, Mich., in which work he is still engaged.

About seventy-five guests assembled at the home of the bride last evening and at 7:30 the ceremony was performed by Rev. Dr. Shaffer, of the city. The wedding march was played by Mr. Richard E. Fox and was one of his own compositions, entitled "The Smilox March."

Perhaps a prettier, daintier nook cannot be found in our city than a little apartment of the Briggs home, which heretofore has been very fittingly termed "the angel's bower." It was here that the ceremony was performed last evening. The

apartment is a little addition to the sitting room and is about nine feet square. It was beautifully lined with white, trimmed with smilax. From the ceiling were draped large pink and blue ribbons. Upon the floor a large white rug, upon which the bride and groom stood.

The bridesmaid was the bride's sister, Miss Ella Briggs, who was dressed in white and carried a beautiful bouquet of pink carnations. The best man was the groom's nephew, Mr. Roy Montjoy, a student at the college. The bride was dressed in pink silk with white organdie over, and was the personification of sweetness and beauty. The groom wore a neat black suit.

After the ceremony and the profusion of kisses and wishes, the guests passed through an archway to the next room, where the gifts were displayed. They were plentiful and valuable.

Refreshments were served by several of the prettiest young ladies who were dressed in white. The dining room table was also beautifully decorated with smilax and ribbons. Everywhere was pink and white, and the decorations were neat and pretty.

Mr. and Mrs. Richards arrived in Harrisville Saturday evening, where the first intimation anyone had of this happy event was when the Professor began to introduce his charming bride. Mr. Richards is already well and favorably known in our village and Mrs. Richards will be welcome among us.

Alcona County Review, January 7, 1897

Richardson, John S. R.
McKinnon, Jessie A.

Richardson—McKinnon.
(communicated)

At the home of the bride's parents in Caledonia, Mich., Nov. 29, 1893, by Rev. E. F. Smith, Mr. John S. R. Richardson and Miss Jessie A. McKinnon.

The occasion was full of interest and joy, participated in by a housefull of friends and neighbors. After the two had promised to be one, and had received numerous congratulations that the ordeal was safely passed, the guests sat down with the handsome bride and smiling bridegroom to a table loaded with those things that tickle the palate and please the eye.

Among them towered a huge pyramid cake crowned with orange blossoms, while California fruit, nuts and sweetmeats interlarded the substantials.

Mr. and Mrs. Richardson are young people of high moral and religious character, and will doubtless be a great help in Christian work wherever they make their home.

They have the best wishes of all who know them and may the blessing of the Lord, which only can bring true happiness and peace, go with them through the journey of life.

Alcona County Review, December 7, 1893

Rickle, John
Mosseau, Mary [Dewar]

EVENTS OF ONE WEEK.

Solomon Pepper, aged 27, and May Monette, aged 20, both of Black River, were licensed to wed a few days ago. Also John Rickle, aged 33, and Mary Mosseau, aged 35, both of Gustin.

Alcona County Review, November 7, 1895

Ritchie, George Samuel
Hastings, Anne Jane

MARRIED.

Ritchie—Hastings.—At the residence of the bride's mother, in Watford, Ont., July 9, by Rev. J. Wilson, B. A., Geo. S. Ritchie, of Alcona, Mich., and Miss Annie J. Hastings, of Watford.

The Watford *Advocate* of the 23d inst., contains the following account of the wedding:

The orange buds whose interesting unfolding we modestly alluded to last week, blossomed fragrantly and sweetly on Monday, when Mr. Geo. S. Ritchie, of Alcona, Mich., and Miss Annie Hastings, of this place, were made man and wife. At five o'clock the ceremony was performed by Rev. Jasper Wilson, B. A., in presence of a large circle of relatives and intimate friends. The contracting pair were gracefully supported by Mr. W. J. Hastings, of Tilsonburg, brother of the bride, and Miss Ritchie, sister of the groom. The wedding robe was an exceedingly pretty one of green and garnet changeable silk; while the presents were particularly handsome, and included among other articles: Two silver cruets, one in colored glass; silver fruit dish, two silver syrup pitchers, silver tea set, four silver pickle casters, silver honey server, wine set, toilet bottles, butter cooler, cut glass perfume bottles, silver knives and forks, silver card receiver, China set, gold card receiver, set vases, butter cooler, set tea spoons, etc. On the evening train, amidst a heavy discharge of rice, Mr. and Mrs. Ritchie left on a little tour to Detroit, and thence went to their Michigan home.

Alcona County Review, July 30, 1886

Rivet, John
Hulme, Ida

Roy.

The little birds are whispering to each other that Miss Ida Hulme and John Rivett are to be united in marriage.

Alcona County Review, April 27, 1893

'Round About the County.
Another One From Roy.
Miss Ida Hulme and John Rivett were married Monday, April 24th, in Au Sable by the Baptist minister.

Alcona County Review, April 27, 1893

Rivet, Leon
Noel, Florence

PERSONAL MENTION.
A double French wedding occurred in town Tuesday. The gaily bedecked brides and their bridegrooms stopped at the Huron house for an hour or so, and their hilarity was so manifest that it could be heard for blocks.

Alcona County Review, August 6, 1896

Roberts, Warren
Deforest, Eliza

LOCAL LACONICS.

A double wedding took place at Alcona House, Wednesday afternoon, May 7, the interested parties being Warren Roberts, of Black River, and Miss Eliza Deforest, of this village, and Thos. Nolan and Sarah Forsyth, both of this place. Rev. Mr. Lowry performed the ceremony, after which an elegant repast was partaken of. The presents were elegant and numerous. Mr. and Mrs. Roberts left for their home at Black River on Thursday morning.

Alcona County Review, May 8, 1885

Robidoux, Francoise

Liberty, Virginia

MARRIAGE LICENSES.
The following marriage licenses have been issued by County Clerk Rutson:
Nov. 11, Francis Robidoux, Au Sable, 21 [and] Virginia Liberty, Alcona, 18.

Alcona County Review, November 18, 1887

Rochon, Victor
Harvey, Mary J.

LOCAL JOTTINGS.

Married.—at Alpena, Aug. 20, by Rev. Wm. Donnelly, Victor Rochon and Mary J. Harvey, all of Black River.

Alcona County Review, September 11, 1885

Roe, A. Samuel
Sayers, Marion E.

PERSONAL MENTION.
A. S. Roe of Alpena and Miss May E. Sayers of Alcona township were married at Alpena on Wednesday, Dec. 14.

Alcona County Review, December 22, 1892

Ross, David W.
Lombard, Flora

EVENTS OF ONE WEEK.

David W. Ross of Black River and Flora Lombard of Alcona were united in wedlock yesterday at the home of the bride's parents by Rev. Will.

Alcona County Review, August 13, 1896

Ross, George
Richway, Mary Agnes

EVENTS OF ONE WEEK.

George Ross, aged 24, and May Richway, aged 16, both of Haynes, were licensed to wed Saturday last. The bride being under 18 years of age consent of her father to the marriage had be filed.

Alcona County Review, October 17, 1895

Ross, John W.
Adams, Rose

LOCAL JOTTINGS.

Jno. Ross and Miss Rose Adams were united in marriage at Killmaster last Tuesday by the Rev. Mr. Johnson.

Alcona County Review, December 30, 1887

Rutherford, Grant

Beckman, Agnes

NEIGHBORHOOD NOTES.
Grant Rutherford, member of the firm of Depew & Rutherford, was united in marriage last week to Miss Agnes Beekman, one of Alpena's nicest young ladies.

Alcona County Review, September 6, 1889

Rutson, George B.
Joughin, R. Anna

PERSONAL.

County Clerk Rutson took his departure for southern Michigan Monday. It is no secret that Mr. Rutson goes away to be married to a very estimable young lady, viz: Miss Anna Joughin, niece of Pros. Atty. Smith. The lady is no stranger in Harrisville, having lived with her uncle's family for a long time. She is much admired for many estimable qualities and our county clerk is to be congratulated on securing the heart and hand of so charming a woman.

Alcona County Review, June 24, 1897

PERSONAL.

Co. Clerk Rutson and bride, formerly Miss Anna Joughin, arrived home on last evening's train.

Alcona County Review, July 8, 1897

Sampson, George
Regier, Laburnia [Deacon]

Married.
Sampson—Regier.
At the St. Lawrence House Harrisville, June 4, by the Rev. Wm. J. Bailey, Mrs. Laburnia Regier to Mr. George Sampson, both of Curtis.

Alcona County Review, June 6, 1895

Sanborn, William H.
Dafoe, Eleanor

Jottings Along the Shore.
W. H. Sanborn of Ossineke, and Miss Eleanor Dafoe of Alpena, were united in matrimony on the evening of the 5th inst.

Alcona County Review, February 13, 1880

Sanborn, Wilson Henry
Young, Sophronia

EVENTS OF ONE WEEK.

Rev. W. J. Bailey repaired to Greenbush last evening to solemnize the marriage of Mr. Wilson H. Sandburn, the popular school teacher, to Miss Fronia Young,

daughter of Jno. B. Young. Congratulations.

Alcona County Review, September 20, 1894

Sandorf, Albert
?, Esther C.

Albert Sandorf was married on Wednesday to a Bay City young lady.

Alcona County Review, December 31, 1896

PERSONAL.

F. C. Reynolds, has been in charge at Sandorf Kahn & Co.'s store part of this week, during the absence of the proprietors at Bay City to attend the marriage of Mr. Albert Sandorf to [line stops here]

Alcona County Review, December 31, 1896

Sayer, Robert
Napper, Margaret

The Local News

Robt. Sayer, aged 21, of Alcona, has taken out a license to marry Maggie Napper, aged 20, of Alpena.

Alcona County Review, October 20, 1892

Schall, Frank E.
Durfee, Nettie M.

SCHALL—DURFEE.

On Tuesday Frank E. Schall, the gentlemanly and popular principal of the Harrisville school for two years past left for a brief trip to Southern Michigan where he is to join heart and fortune with those of a young lady who, report says is an estimable and accomplished woman. Today is the day set for the celebration of the nuptials, at Plymouth, Mich., the home of the bride's parents. The wedding is to be private and only a few of the immediate relatives of the bride and groom are expected to be present. Mr. and Mrs. Schall will arrive in Harrisville Saturday evening and will be at their home to their friends on and after the Saturday following. The bride is wholly unknown to the people of this community, but no doubt she will meet with a hearty welcome from the many friends and admirers of the bridegroom, who has won the respect of this community by his courteous bearing and upright character.

Alcona County Review, April 2, 1891

Schleicher, Henry
Somers, Minnie

The following marriage license was issued from St. Clair county and reported in the last issue of the Marine City Reporter: Henry Schleicher of Marine City, Minnie Summers of West Harrisville.

Alcona County Review, May 7, 1896

METHODIST EPISCOPAL CHURCH.

Married at the home of the bride's parents at Mud Lake Junction on May 6th, Henry Schleicher of Marine City and Minnie Somers of West Harrisville. Both these young people are well known in church circles and their many friends will wish them well. The happy couple left for their new home in Marine City on Saturday evening. Rev. F. S. Ford officiated.

Alcona County Review, May 14, 1896

Schreiber, Edward J.
Cowley, Marie Catherine

PERSONAL MENTION.

Mr. and Mrs. B. P. Cowley announce the engagement of their daughter, Marie C. Cowley, to E. J. Schreiber, of Detroit. The marriage will take place in January, 1895.

Alcona County Review, November 1, 1894

CHURCH AND SOCIETY.

Invitations have been issued by Mr. and Mrs. B. P. Cowley for the marriage of their charming and accomplished daughter, Miss Marie, to Edward J. Schreiber, of Detroit, which will be consummated at the chapel of St. Anne's in this village next Tuesday morning at 10 o'clock a.m. The bride is a native of this village and her circle of friends is as wide as her acquaintance and she therefore requires no introduction. Mr. Schreiber is the commercial salesman of the well-known house of Edson, Moore & Co., of Detroit, and during his frequent visits to Harrisville of late years has made many acquaintances and friends, who must concede that he is well worthy the prize he has won.

Alcona County Review, January 3, 1895

WITH POMP AND CEREMONY.

Celebration of the Nuptials of Miss Marie Cowley and Edw. J. Schreiber.

The marriage of Marie Catherine Cowley, daughter of Mr. and Mrs. B. P. Cowley of Harrisville, and Mr.

Edward J. Schreiber, of Detroit, was duly solemnized Tuesday morning in the chapel of St. Anne, in the presence of a large congregation of invited guests and citizens. It was the first ultra fashionable wedding that has taken place in Harrisville in many years, and this fact, taken in connection with the general esteem in which the bride is held, was incentive sufficient to fill the little chapel to its utmost capacity long before the hour set for the consummation of the nuptials.

At 10 o'clock the organ pealed forth the notes of the wedding march and the bridal procession entered the portal of the church and proceeded slowly up the aisle to the altar, where the bridegroom, modestly attired in a conventional suit of black, awaited them.

The bride entered on the arm of her father, who gave her away. They were preceded by the ushers, F. G. Cowley, brother of the bride, and Mr. John White, of Indianapolis. Following them were S. G. M. Gates of Bay City, and Miss Lillian Cowley, maid of honor and the five little bridesmaids. Mr. John Walsh of Detroit was best man. The bride wore cream silk with a diamond star at the throat, a gift of the bridegroom, her figure being enveloped in a veil of tulle. She carried a prayer book and a boquet of yellow roses. The bridesmaids were Ethel Springer, Ethel Colwell and Susie Hotchkiss, of Harrisville, Blanche Heron of Black River, and Annie Schrieber of Monroe, two of whom were daintily dressed in Nile green with pink carnations, and three dressed in white with white carnations.

The marriage ceremony of the Catholic church was rendered deeply impressive by the celebration after the marriage of solemn high mass by Fr. Schreiber of Detroit, brother of the bridegroom, Fr. Whalen of Midland, and Fr. Doucette. The marriage ceremony was performed by Fr. Schreiber.

After mass Fr. Whalen delivered an eloquent general address upon the sacredness of the married relation, the Savior's attitude towards it and the duties of the couple assuming such a relation, concluding with some excellent advice directed to the newly married couple.

The church was especially decorated for the occasion and about the chancel and altar was massed a profusion of potted plants which added variety and color to the interior.

A wedding breakfast was served at St. Bernard's at 1 o'clock. Covers were laid for 20, including the bridesmaids. The refreshments were elaborate and were served in the height of style.

Mr. and Mrs. Schreiber remained at St. Bernard's until Wednesday morning when they took their departure for their future home at Bay City, which awaited them ready furnished. They were accompanied as far as destination by the out-of-town guests.

Each of the bridesmaids was presented by Mr. Schreiber with a pin set with pearls in remembrance of the occasion.

Music was furnished by the young ladies' choir of Au Sable under the direction of Prof. Gauthier.

Alcona County Review, January 10, 1895

PERSONAL MENTION.

Dr. and Mrs. McCormick of Black River attended the Schreiber-Cowley wedding Tuesday morning and were entertained at the residence of Geo. E. Gillam.

Alcona County Review, January 10, 1895

PERSONAL MENTION.

Miss Theresa Schreiber, of Detroit, attended her brother's wedding Tuesday and was entertained at St. Bernard's.

Alcona County Review, January 10, 1895

PERSONAL MENTION.

Mrs. F. J. Hill and Miss Susie Hill were among the invited guests at the Schreiber-Cowley wedding. They were entertained by Geo. W. Colwell.

Alcona County Review, January 10, 1895

PERSONAL MENTION.

Mr. and Mrs. John Heron and little daughter came down from the River Monday morning and remained over to attend the Schreiber-Cowley nuptials.

Alcona County Review, January 10, 1895

PERSONAL MENTION.

Misses Minnie McDonald, Kate Dunn, Lizzie Johnson, Katie Johnson, Loretta Fitzpatrick, Victoria Fitzpatrick, Katie McDonald, and Thos. Garner, members of the Au Sable Catholic choir, drove up Tuesday morning to be in attendance at the wedding ceremony.

Alcona County Review, January 10, 1895

Schunck, J. D.
Rix, Linnie
HOME NEWS JOTTINGS.
Dr. J. D. Schunck and Miss Linnie Rix, of Oscoda, were married last Sunday.

Alcona County Review, December 15, 1882

Scriver, Joseph
?, {Bride}
EVENTS OF ONE WEEK.

A license to marry was issued last Thursday to Joseph Scriver and wife of Haynes Township. In explanation of the rather unusual procedure Joseph wishes to make the following statement: "I have been told that certain persons are making statements to the effect that we were not married. I was married three years ago in Shiawassee County; the justice who married us got into trouble about that time and left the county without giving us our marriage certificate. That is why we have no certificate to show. Now, in order to stop people's tongues; and as it is cheaper to get re-married than to get proofs and secure a certificate, we concluded to get married again; and that is all there is of it."

Alcona County Review, April 8, 1897

Secord, Joseph
Anderson, Nellie
GREENBUSH GETTINGS.

Married—By Rev. J. Robins, Sunday, Nov. 21, at the residence of the bride's father, Joseph Secord and Nellie Anderson, all of Harrisville township.

Alcona County Review, November 26, 1886

Sedergreen, Oscar
Nelson, Annie C.
MARRIED.
Sedergreen—Nelson. At the house of the bridegroom's parents in Caledonia, Jan. 6th, 1894, by Rev. E.

F. Smith, Mr. Oscar Sedergreen and Miss Annie C. Nelson, both of Caledonia, Mich.

Alcona County Review, January 11, 1894

Seguin, Tellespore
Bassett, Delia
LOCAL JOTTINGS.

Married: At Black River, June 21st, 1885, by Justice R. S. Leach, Tellesphore Seguin and Miss Delia Bassett, all of said village.

Alcona County Review, July 3, 1885

Selves, Frank
Baldwin, Dora
LOCAL JOTTINGS.

Frank Selves of Au Sable and Miss Dora Baldwin of Gustin township were united in marriage Wednesday evening at the Alcona House by the Rev. P. C. Goldie.

Alcona County Review, October 4, 1889

Severance, Lemuel
LaChapelle, Laura May
PERSONAL POINTS.

Mr. L. Severance of Walled Lake, Oakland county, and Miss May LaChapelle, daughter of Mr. and Mrs. Frank LaChapelle, were united in marriage at 2 o'clock yesterday afternoon at the family residence, the Rev. W. W. Will officiating. Only a few friends were present. Mr. and Mrs. Severance left on the evening train for their future home at Walled Lake. Mr. Severance, the fortunate bridegroom, will be remembered as a former teacher of the Fisher school, a young man of high character and purpose.

Alcona County Review, June 16, 1898

Seyan, Ameda
Manette, Lia
Somewhat Personal.
Fr. Mahar made a parochial call Monday on old Mr. Tovey, who is quite feeble at the advanced age of 97. While here the Father united two couples of young people from the French settlement in marriage.

Alcona County Review, March 3, 1892

Shaw, Jesse
Oulton, Lizzie
LOCAL JOTTINGS.

Married: At the residence of Mr. Chas. Sterritt in Harrisville, Mich., October 3, 1885, by Rev. T. B. Leith, Jesse Shaw, of Black River, and Lizzie Oulton, of Prince Edward Island. Mr. Shaw is a young man well known in this county, having been in the employ of Alger, Smith & Co. for several years past. His numerous friends in the county will unite with the Review in wishing Jesse and his bride a long, useful and happy matrimonial life. May they step on nary a thorn.

Alcona County Review, October 9, 1885

Shepard, William B.
Hike, Elizabeth

Paragraphs of Local Interest.

Wm. B. Shepard, aged 41, secured a license on Monday to marry Elizabeth Hike, aged 42. Both are residents of Millen township.

Alcona County Review, January 18, 1894

Shorter, Horace
Boyce, Carrie

LOCAL JOTTINGS.

Married—At Black River, November 30, 1884, by R. S. Leach, Justice of the Peace, Horace Shorter of Black River and Miss Carrie Boice of Alcona.

Alcona County Review, December 5, 1884

Shorter, John
Hedroig, Friederika D.

LOCAL JOTTINGS.

Married—At Black River, on the 9th instant, by the Rev. R. H. Palmer, John Shorter to Friederika D. Hedroig, both of Black River, Mich.

Alcona County Review, November 14, 1884

Showers, Spencer
?, Eliza

LOCAL LACONICS.

Spencer Showers left on the steamer Arundell yesterday morning for Detroit via. Bay City. Spencer will be absent from our village about ten days and when he returns Mrs. S. will accompany him. The wedding will take place at Bellview, near Detroit, on Tuesday next. The Review extends congratulations, if it is not too soon.

Alcona County Review, May 15, 1885

LOCAL LACONICS.

Spencer Showers and bride are expected on the steamer Mackinac on Sunday evening.

Alcona County Review, May 22, 1885

Shwitzer, Harry
Rosenthal, Sarah

COUNTY REVIEWINGS.

Hebrew custom, if not law, requires the man and woman proposing to unite their fortunes in marriage to sign a marriage contract, which specifies the date the wedding is to take place, the wife's dowry and the proposed husband's gift to his bride; also, the portion the bride will bring to her husband, if any. Such an engagement was concluded Thursday evening between Harry Schweitzer of Harrisville, and Miss Sarah Rosenthal of East Tawas. Further than that the marriage will be celebrated in April, particulars can not be made public.—Au Sable News.

So our Harry is to be married at last. Well, well; good for Harry. "Suthin" more anon.

Alcona County Review, February 11, 1881

HOME REVIEWINGS.

We learn from splendid authority that Harry Shwitzer will convert the upper portion of his store building into a dwelling suitable for himself and that little wife which he is soon to bring to Harrisville.

Alcona County Review, April 22, 1881

HOME REVIEWINGS.

Our young friend and fellow townsman, Harry Shwitzer, and Miss Sarah Rosenthal, of East Tawas, are to be married, Sunday next, at the home of the bride's parents.

Alcona County Review, May 27, 1881

HOME REVIEWINGS.

At the residence of the bride's parents, at East Tawas, last Sunday afternoon, by Rabbi Landow, of the Jewish Reform Church of Bay City, Mr. Harry Shwitzer, of Harrisville, and Miss Sarah Rosenthal were united in marriage. The ceremony was witnessed by many friends and relatives from all along the Shore. The presents which were comprised largely of silver were numerous and costly. The happy couple left on

Monday's boat for a short visit at Detroit and Chicago, after which they will return to Harrisville for future residence. The Review wishes Harry and his bride a long and pleasant life, complete with unalloyed happiness.

Alcona County Review, June 3, 1881

HOME REVIEWINGS.

Philip Shwitzer has been "head boss," "fancy clerk" and "check boy," in his brother Harry's store during the latter's "honeymoon."

Alcona County Review, June 10, 1881

HOME REVIEWINGS.

Harry Shwitzer and bride have arrived at their home in Harrisville.

Alcona County Review, June 10, 1881

HOME REVIEWINGS.

Mr. and Mrs. Harry Shwitzer have settled down to housekeeping in their new home.

Alcona County Review, June 17, 1881

Shwitzer, Julius
?, Rachel

Note and News Along the Shore

AU SABLE AND OSCODA.

Julius Shwitzer, late of this place was married in New York last Sunday.

Alcona County Review, January 2, 1885

Sicord, Joseph A.
Charlefour, Celina

Black River Sparks.

A very quiet wedding occurred at Harrisville on Sunday, April 12, the contracting parties being Joseph Sicord and Miss Celina Charlefour, both of Black River. The wedding was solemnized by Rev. Fr. Poulin.

The happy couple returned to Black River where they received the congratulations of their many friends. On Monday eve a wedding party was held at the IOOF Hall in which a large crowd participated.

Alcona County Review, April 16, 1896

Silversides, George W.
Noyes, Clara [Henning]

MARRIED.

In Harrisville, July 3d, by the same [Rev. F. N. Barlow], George W. Silversides to Mrs. Clara Noyes, both of Harrisville.

Silverthorn, Addison J.
Aird, Grace A.

Married.

Sept. 1st, 1878, at the residence of the bride's mother, in Harrisville, Mich., by Rev. N. N. Clark, Mr. Addison J. Silverthorn, of Alcona, and Miss Grace A. Aird, of Harrisville.

The many friends of the happy couple will wish them a long and pleasant journey together through life.

Alcona County Review, September 6, 1878

Silverthorn, Alfred McFarlane
Good, Jennette

Married.
Silverthorn—Good.

At the M. E. parsonage Nov. 11, 1894, by the Rev. Wm. J. Bailey, Mr. Alfred McFarlane Silverthorn of Harrisville to Miss Jennette Good of Gustin, Mich.

Alcona County Review, November 15, 1894

Silverthorn, Perley
Kiah, Helen W.

LOCAL JOTTINGS.

Married--On the 16th inst., by Rev. T. B. Leith, at the residence of the bride, Pearley Silverthorn of Alcona, to Helen W. Kiah of Harrisville.

Alcona County Review, December 18, 1885

Simmons, James
Sthall, Frances

REVIEWINGS.

Married: On the 11th inst., by George Hamilton, Esq., at the residence of Mr. Aaron Byce in Harrisville, brother-in-law of the bridegroom, Mr. James Simmons and Miss Frances Sthall, all of Au Sable.

Alcona County Review, May 23, 1879

Simms, Andrew
Mills, Mary B. [Allen]

Married at Gustin, on June 15, by Rev. Geo. Nixon, Mr. Andrew Sims to Mrs. Poole Mills, both of Mikado. The ceremony was performed at the residence of Stephen Price.

Alcona County Review, June 22, 1899

Simons, Charles
McDonald, Catherine

Marriages.—In the last issue of the Au Sable News we find noted the following marriages of residents of Alcona county:

At the Benner House, on Thursday, March 17, by Rev. R. Woodhams, Charlie Simons and Catherine McDonald, both of Harrisville.

The Review extends congratulations to the newly wedded couples, and hopes their cup of bliss and prosperity may ever be overflowing. Walk uprightly, step lightly, and keep off the thorns, young friends. So shall unalloyed happiness follow you all.

Alcona County Review, March 25, 1881

Simons, William
Alderton, Belle

A SPECIAL FROM CURTIS.

Married.—William Simons of Curtis, to Miss Belle Alderton of Goodertown, at the home of the bridegroom by Rev. I. B. Nunn.

Alcona County Review, February 16, 1893

Simpson, William
Marsh, Ella M.

Lake Shore Gossip.

Mr. Wm. Simpson, of Au Sable, prosecuting attorney of Iosco county, and Miss Ella M. Marsh, of Saginaw, were married at the residence of the bride's parents, on the 28th ult. The *News* gives them a good "send off" on the matrimonial sea.

Alcona County Review, August 10, 1877

Sissons, Frank
McDonald, Lizzie

Marriages.—In the last issue of the Au Sable News we find noted the following marriages of residents of Alcona county:

At the Methodist parsonage, Mar. 16th, by Rev. R. Woodhams, Frank Sissons and Lizzie McDonald, both of Greenbush, Michigan.

The Review extends congratulations to the newly wedded couples, and hopes their cup of bliss and prosperity may ever be overflowing. Walk uprightly, step lightly, and keep off the thorns, young friends. So shall unalloyed happiness follow you all.

Alcona County Review, March 25, 1881

Skuse, Thomas

McDonald, Annie

COUNTY REVIEWINGS.

Married, at Au Sable by Rev. C. J. Roche, Sunday, Sept. 26th, Mr. Thos. Skuse and Miss Annie McDonald, both of Harrisville.

Alcona County Review, October 1, 1880

Skuse, William H.
Twite, Sarah M. J.

MARRIAGE LICENSES.

The following marriage licenses were issued from the county clerk's office within the past week:

July 26.—William H. Skuse, Miss Sarah M. J. Twite, both of Harrisville township.

Alcona County Review, August 3, 1893

MARRIED.
Skuse—Twite.

At the residence of the bride, Harrisville, July 30, by the Rev. Wm. J. Bailey, Mr. William H. Skuse to Miss Sarah M. J. Twite, both of Harrisville.

Alcona County Review, August 3, 1893

Slaght, Richard
Becker, Sarah E.

MARRIED.

In Harrisville, June 10th, by the Rev. F. N. Barlow, Richard Slaght, of Harrisville, to Miss Sarah Becker, of Gustin.

Alcona County Review, June 22, 1888

Slater, Arthur
Lemon, Annie

PERSONAL.

There was a wedding in this village Saturday at the residence of Mary Bond, whereby Arthur Slater and Annie Lemon were made man and wife. Rev. Will performed the ceremony.

Alcona County Review, November 25, 1897

Slater, Walter
Cade, Minnie [DeKett]

SOMEWHAT PERSONAL.

Married at the parsonage, Harrisville, Aug. 14, 1892, by the Rev. W. J. Bailey, Mr. Walter Slater to Mrs. Minnie Cade, both of Haynes township.

Alcona County Review, August 25, 1892

HISTORY OF ONE YEAR.

Chronological History of the Past Year, 1892.

MARRIAGES.

August 14. Walter Slater to Mrs. Minnie Cade of Haynes.

Alcona County Review, January 5, 1893

Sloan, Alexander
Thompson, Elizabeth

LOCAL JOTTINGS.

Married—At the residence of Daniel Dewey, Harrisville, on March 10, 1886, by Rev. J. Bain, Alexander Sloan to Miss Elizabeth Thompson.

Alcona County Review, March 12, 1886

Sloan, Samuel
Elmes, Susanna

Haynes Happenings.

Mr. Samuel Slone and Miss Susanna Elms were united in marriage yesterday. Wish them a long and prosperous journey in their matrimonial venture.

Alcona County Review, June 13, 1895

Small, J. W.
Smith, Ella

PERSONAL POINTS.

Mr. and Mrs. Wm. Hilliard of the Point are in Alpena in attendance at the marriage of Mr. Hilliard's sister, Ella, to Dr. J. W. Small, which occurs at the family residence this evening.

Alcona County Review, July 14, 1898

Smith, Angus W.
Cowan, Florence

The county clerk issued a marriage license Nov. 23d to Warren A. Budd, aged 28, of Haynes and Martha Clark, aged 31, of Tawas. Yesterday Angus W. Smith, aged 25, of Grindstone City, was licensed to marry Florence Cowan, aged 17, of Gustin.

Alcona County Review, December 1, 1892

MARRIED.

Smith—Cowan. At the M. E. parsonage, Harrisville, Nov. 30, 1892 by the Rev. Wm. J. Bailey: Mr. Angus W. Smith to Miss Florence Cowan, both of Gustin, Mich.

Alcona County Review, December 8, 1892

HISTORY OF ONE YEAR.

Chronological History of the Past Year, 1892.

MARRIAGES.

Nov. 30. Angus W. Smith to Florence Cowan, both of Gustin.

Alcona County Review, January 5, 1893

Smith, Fred H.
Anchutz, May B.

PERSONAL MENTION.

Miss Helen Reynolds of Black River has been visiting East Tawas friends and was present at the marriage of Fred H. Smith of Seney to May B. Anchutz.

Alcona County Review, February 22, 1894

Smith, Joseph
Cooper, Edna

Wedding Bells.

After a long courtship, Mr. Joseph Smith won the love and affections of the beautiful and accomplished daughter of Hiram Cooper of Curtis. They drove to Harrisville, June 1st and were united in matrimony by Rev. W. W. Will. They stopped over night at the residence of Aaron Byce, the groom's uncle. Returning home the next evening the groom's parents gave a reception for them at which 60 guests were present. A sumptuous supper was served at a late hour: the company was highly entertained and dispersed, wishing the newly married couple a pleasant voyage on the sea of life. Presents were numerous and some quite costly.

Alcona County Review, June 11, 1896

Smith, Jude A.
Clearwater, Rachel A.

Married.

In Harrisville, July 22, 1882, by Rev. J. H. McIntosh, Jude A. Smith and Miss Rachel A. Clearwater, all of Black River, Mich.

Alcona County Review, July 28, 1882

Smithers, John H.
Wilson, Etta

HOME REVIEWINGS.

Married.—At the same place [Harrisville], Oct. 13, 1881, by the same [Rev. J. H. McIntosh], John H. Smithers and Miss Etta Wilson, all of Harrisville.

Alcona County Review, November 11, 1881

Smithers, William
McGillis, Kate

MARRIED.

In Harrisville, Mich., Dec. 28, 1881, at M. E. Parsonage, by Rev. J. H. McIntosh, William Smithers and Miss Kate McGillis, all of Harrisville.

Alcona County Review, December 30, 1881

Snowdon, William E.
Churchill, Martha

LOCAL JOTTINGS.

Married--On the evening of July 4th at the Parsonage in Alcona, by Rev. R. H. Balmer, W. E. Snowdon to Martha Churchill. Also at the same time and place Peter Lecuier to M. Luella Hunt. All parties of Alcona.

Alcona County Review, July 17, 1885

Socient, Napoleon
Thibault, Mary

EVENTS OF ONE WEEK.

Mr. Napoleon Socient of Au Sable and Miss Mary Thibault of Harrisville were married at Black River on Monday the 10th, inst., by the Rev. Fr. Dousette of Au Sable.

Alcona County Review, July 13, 1893

Somers, Frank
Card, Lillian

HAYNES HAPPENINGS.

April 18.--Frank Somers has rented Mrs. Loney's farm and intends to migrate to the state of matrimony.

Alcona County Review, April 21, 1898

PERSONAL POINTS.

A marriage license has been issued to Mr. Frank Somers, son of Robert Somers of Haynes, and Miss Lillian Card, daughter of Mrs. Fred Card, of the same town. The marriage is to be solemnized today at the M. E. parsonage by Rev. Will. They will make their home on the old Jos. Yuill farm in Haynes. The Review joins the many friends of the young couple in well-wishes for their success and happiness.

Alcona County Review, October 13, 1898

Soura, Edward
Nevins, Annie

LOCAL JOTTINGS.

Married.--On the 17th inst. at the M. E. parsonage by Rev. T. B. Leith, Edward Soura to Annie Nevins, both of Harrisville.

Alcona County Review, December 30, 1887

Sousie, George
Twite, Mary

LOCAL JOTTINGS.

Geo. Sousie and Miss Mary Twite were united in marriage last Saturday. The Review extends congratulations and well wishes.

Alcona County Review, December 30, 1887

Sousie, Silas
Hartion, Mary Ellen

LOCAL JOTTINGS.

Married—At Catholic church, on Sunday, Aug. 9, 1885, by Rev. P. C. A. Winters, Silas Sousie and Miss Mary Hartion, all of Harrisville.

Alcona County Review, August 14, 1885

Sovey, John F.
St. Clair, Phoebe E.

Curran Crumbs.

At the residence of Mr. William Freer, on Thursday eve., between the hours of 7 and 8 o'clock, Mr. John Sovey and Miss Phoebe St. Clair were united in marriage. Justice of the Peace W. H. Wiedbrauk officiated.

A supper was partaken of a short time later. Few were present except those directly interested. We did not hear anything about old shoes and showers of rice, but Curranites do wish the young couple all happiness and that their journey across the matrimonial sea may be unimpaired by storms.

Feb. 25, 1895.

Alcona County Review, February 28, 1895

Spain, Elmer R.
Johnson, Margaret

A Pleasant Event.

On Saturday afternoon at 3 o'clock one of those pleasant affairs occurred that bring pleasure to all interested, when Elmer R. Spain of Flanders, was married to Miss Margaret Johnson of Harrisville, Mich.

It was a quiet home wedding, and took place at the home of Mr. and Mrs. Fred Emerson, 126 McKinley avenue, this city. The ceremony was performed by Rev. D. B. Davidson, pastor of the Baptist church.

The young couple left for their home at Flanders Saturday evening. The Argus joins in congratulations.--Alpena Argus.

Alcona County Review, April 30, 1908

Spencer, Ernest E.
Southgate, Nellie M.

PERSONAL.

A happy event was the marriage last evening at the residence of the bride's parents, of Miss Nellie Southgate, daughter of Mr. and Mrs. Robt. Southgate, to Mr. Ernest Spencer, son of Seymour Spencer. The ceremony was performed by the Rev. W. W. Will in the presence of the family and near relatives.

The contracting parties are two of the most estimable young people of the township. The groom has shown good judgment by providing a home for his bride and they will pass their honeymoon under their own roof.

The Review wishes them a long life and prosperity.

Alcona County Review, November 25, 1897

Spencer, Frank H.
Nevin, Charlotte M.

MARRIED.

Also by the same [Rev. F. N. Barlow], Sept. 11th, in Harrisville township, Mr. Frank H. Spencer and Miss Charlotte M. Nevins both of Harrisville township.

Alcona County Review, September 16, 1887

LOCAL JOTTINGS.

Frank Spencer and Miss Lottie Nevins were united in marriage by the Rev. F. N. Barlow last week.

Alcona County Review, September 16, 1887

Spencer, John A.
McGregor, Catherine E.

LOCAL PICK UPS.

Mr. John Spencer of Harrisville and Miss Catherine McGregor of Mud Lake were united in wedlock on Wednesday April 5. They are housekeeping at the old Spencer homestead, where they will be pleased to receive their friends.

Alcona County Review, April 20, 1899

Spencer, Lincoln Edward
Nevin, Mary Jane

LOCAL JOTTINGS.

Lincoln Spencer and Mary Jane Nevins were united in marriage last week. The Review extends congratulations.

Alcona County Review, June 14, 1889

Spencer, Seymour H.

Ricker, Louisa S.

LOCAL JOTTINGS.

The county clerk has issued marriage licenses to Seymour H. Spencer, aged 37, and Louisa S. Ricker, aged 27, both of Harrisville, and to Thos. Miller, aged 31, and Rebecca Thorner, aged 16, both of Alcona.

Alcona County Review, December 16, 1887

MARRIED.

In Harrisville, Dec. 15th, by the Rev. F. N. Barlow, Seymour H. Spencer and Miss Louisa L. Ricker, both of Harrisville.

Alcona County Review, December 23, 1887

St. Laurent, George Victor
Budreau, Christina

Black River.

St. Laurent—Budeaw. Married, at the residence of F. C. Grealeau, Mr. St. Laurent to Miss Budeaw, both of Black River. The happy couple were recipients of many congratulations and good wishes.

Alcona County Review, February 23, 1893

St. Peter, Fred
Dewar, Flora

The following have been licensed to wed by the county clerk: Fred St. Peter and Flora Dewar, both of Gustin; Hurtwell Hayes and Fannie Vaughn, both of Curtis.

Alcona County Review, June 27, 1890

Steere, Edwin M.
Monroe, Edith R.

A Pretty Home Wedding.

Harbor Beach Times.

On Tuesday evening of last week at the home of Mr. and Mrs. Geo. N. Monroe in the presence of the relatives and a few friends of the family, was solemnized the marriage of their daughter, Edith R., to Edwin M. Steere, the popular young mail clerk of this division of the F. & P. M. The spacious home of the bride was handsomely decorated for the occasion with flowers and potted plants. Promptly at the hour of 10:00 the contracting parties, accompanied by the parents of the bride entered the parlor to the strains of the wedding March played by Miss Laura Reynolds and the ceremony, which united the lives and fortunes of two of our popular young people, was performed by Rev. F. L. Leonard, of the M. E. church, of this place. At the conclusion of the ceremony and the congratulations of the happy couple all were invited to the dining room to partake of the wedding supper.

After supper an hour was spent in social enjoyment. As each guest bade the happy couple good-night and took their departure for their respective homes it was with the firm conviction that it had been one of the prettiest home weddings that it had ever been their good fortune to attend, as well as an occasion greatly enjoyed and long to be remembered.

Mr. and Mrs. Steere will be at home to their friends after Dec. 25. May good fortune ever attend them through the voyage of life. The happy couple will live with the bride's parents this winter.

The bride is a grand daughter of Mr. and Mrs. Jos. Van Buskirk and has many friends in Harrisville.

Alcona County Review, December 21, 1899

Stevens, Arbor C.
Snell, Francis M.

LOCAL JOTTINGS.

Arbor Stevens and Francis M. Snell, two strangers, were securely bound together as man and wife by Justice Beede last week.

Alcona County Review, September 21, 1888

Stevens, George T.
McCrae, Agnes Catherine

LOCAL JOTTINGS.

George T. Stevens and Miss Aggie McCrae, both of Greenbush, were married in Oscoda on the 9th inst., by the Rev. F. Bradley.—(Saturday Night.)

Alcona County Review, April 18, 1884

Stewart, Duncan
Ralston, Hattie

PERSONAL MENTION.

Cards have been received announcing the marriage on April 5th, at Astoria, Oregon, of Miss Hattie Ralston to Duncan Stewart. The bride formerly lived in Harrisville with her parents and is a sister of Mrs. E. W. Chapelle.

Alcona County Review, April 20, 1893

Stinchcomb, Henry J.
Nevin, Maggie J.

STINCHCOMB—NEVIN.

A happy event was the marriage last evening at the residence of the bride's parents, of Mr. Henry Stinchcombe to Miss Maggie Nevin, daughter of Mr. and Mrs. David Nevin. Both of these young people are well known and respected citizens of Harrisville township, the bride having been born here and the bridegroom having resided here the past five years. The marriage ceremony was performed by the Rev. L. Hazard. Mr. and Mrs. Stinchcombe will go to housekeeping at once in their own house which their foresight has already furnished and equipped with most of the essentials of a well appointed house. Their wide circle of friends will join with us in wishing them God speed on life's journey, with as many of its blessings and as few trials and tribulations as possible.

Alcona County Review, August 13, 1891

Stockman, Harry W.
Atchison, Emma Gwendolyn

The Tie That Binds.

Harry W. Stockman, scaler, of Au Sable, secured a license at the clerk's office on Monday to wed Miss Emma G. Atchison, one of Harrisville's fair young ladies. The ceremony was performed the same evening at the home of the bride's sister in Oscoda, Rev. F. L. Osborn officiating.

Alcona County Review, April 23, 1896

Storms, Charles A.
McGregor, Mary A.

Cards are out announcing the marriage of Mr. Chas. A. Storms to Miss Mary McGregor, eldest daughter of Mr. and Mrs. P. C. McGregor of Black River, to occur at the home of the bride's parents on Wednesday evening, Dec. 30th, inst.

Alcona County Review, December 24, 1896

WEDDING BELLS.

Storms—McGregor.

Mr. Chas. A. Storms and Miss Mary McGregor, both of this place, were united in marriage, Wednesday last, Rev. Middlemiss of Alpena officiating. A reception was given at the bride's home from 8 until 10 in the evening, after which invited guests to the number of about 80 adjourned to Malta hall, where they tripped the light fantastic until a late

hour. The presents were very numerous and costly, which showed the appreciation of their many friends.

Black River, Jan. 4, '97.

Alcona County Review, January 7, 1897

Storms, David Eugene
Colwell, Mae O.

HOME NEWS JOTTINGS.

Will Storms left town last Sunday to attend the marriage ceremony of his brother, Eugene.

Alcona County Review, January 19, 1883

HOME NEWS JOTTINGS.

Cards have been issued announcing the marriage of our townsman, D. E. Storms, to Miss Mae O. Colwell, of Portville, N. Y., Wednesday, the 17th inst., being the day set for the happy occasion. Miss Colwell is well known to most of the Review readers, having been for a long time a resident in our village, and a teacher in our school. Besides the educational interests, she was connected with the social and musical entertainments in such a manner as won her many friends, and caused her to be greatly missed after her return to Portville. Mr. Storms has held several county offices, his term as sheriff having just expired, and with his good nature combined with the faithful discharge of his official duties, it is not necessary to add that the people of the whole county join with the Review in expressions of good wishes and congratulations. We hope they may conclude to make Harrisville their future home.

Alcona County Review, January 19, 1883

HOME NEWS JOTTINGS.

D. E. Storms and bride, nee Miss Mae Colwell, arrived from Portville, N. Y., last Sunday afternoon. They stopped for a couple of days at Au Sable with Mr. and Mrs. J. C. Gram. Their many friends and the Review gladly welcome them back to Harrisville, and hope they will find it to their advantage to reside here.

Alcona County Review, February 2, 1883

Storms, George A.
Beever, Evaline

COUNTY JOTTINGS.

Married.—Sunday evening, July 21st, 1878, at the residence of the bride's father, in Harrisville township, by Rev. N. N. Clark, Mr. Geo. A. Storms and Miss Evaline Beever, all of Harrisville.

May joy, prosperity and happiness crown the lives of the new couple, and make their pathway smooth.

Alcona County Review, July 26, 1878

Strong, Albert F.
Silverthorn, Jennie

The following concerns a former Harrisville young lady, a daughter of Perley Silverthorn:

Miss Jennie Silverthorn and Albert F. Strong were united in marriage last evening at the home of the bride's sister in Detroit. The bride was for six years employed in the office of the James Stewart company, and for the past two years she had been in the employ of the Saginaw Manufacturing company. The groom was also formerly employed in Saginaw, but he is now in business in Detroit, where they will make their future home. They were well remembered by Saginaw friends with several useful and beautiful gifts.--Saginaw Herald.

Alcona County Review, September 29, 1898

Strong, Allen
Hetherington, Sarah E. [Lamb]

WEDDING BELLS.

Strong—Hetherington. Married at the Methodist parsonage, July 17, 1894, by the Rev. Wm. J. Bailey, Mr. Allen Strong of Gustin, Mich. to Mrs. Sarah Hetherington of Harrisville, Mich.

Alcona County Review, July 19, 1894

Stuart, Angus
Leslie, Jessie

PERSONAL MENTION.

Angus Stuart of Caledonia surprised his neighbors last Saturday by bringing home a bride to his bachelor quarters. The bride, Jessie Leslie by name, was a bonnie Canadian lass who came over only last week. On pretence of engaging a cook, Mr. Stuart went to Alpena, where they met and were married.

Alcona County Review, October 18, 1894

Swindlehurst, William
Hendrie, Johanna

PURELY PERSONAL.

Married, June 2d, at the Manse, Harrisville, by the Rev. P. C. Goldie, Joanna Hendrie and William Swindlehurst, both of Alcona county.

Alcona County Review, July 13, 1888

Taft, Lester W.
Staats, Carrie M.

Taft—Staats.

Invitations have been received to a wedding which is to take place at Grand Marais next Tuesday, Oct. 12, in which Lester W. Taft, a Harrisville boy, and Miss Carrie M. Staats will unite their destinies for better or for worse. That it may be for the better will be the earnest wish of the many friends of Mr. Taft, who have known him from childhood as one of the most exemplary and promising young men in this community. The bride elect is very highly spoken of for excellent qualities of mind and person. She went to Grand Marais from East Tawas a few years ago.

Alcona County Review, October 7, 1897

PERSONAL.

Lester Taft and bride—Miss Carrie Staats—who were married Tuesday at Grand Marais, are to take a two week's trip to East Tawas, the bride's former home and to Harrisville. Let's many friends are thus to have an opportunity to personally extend congratulations to him and also to become acquainted with his better half.

Alcona County Review, October 14, 1897

The Taft-Staats Wedding.
Grand Marais Leader.

On Tuesday afternoon at one o'clock, at the M. E. church, Miss Carrie M. Staats was joined in holy wedlock to Mr. Lester W. Taft, both of this place, Rev. James Ivey, of Newberry, officiating.

Immediately after the ceremony Mr. and Mrs. Taft took the train for a wedding trip to East Tawas and Harrisville, where they will visit friends and relatives for a couple of weeks, returning here about the 25th inst.

The happy couple are among the most popular young people of Grand Marais and their wedding was witnessed by a large concourse of friends, the larger portion of whom accompanied them to the train, where they were showered with rice and the best wishes of all.

Mr. and Mrs. Taft were the recipients of a large number of useful and valuable presents, including a handsome sideboard from the employees of the Colwell shingle mill.

The bride is the daughter of Mr. J. R. Staats, one of Grand Marais' most honored citizens and has been here for the past three years. Mr. Taft came here from Harrisville some two or three years ago, and is noted as one of our most honored and upright citizens. Both are known and loved by all Grand Marais for their true worth.

Upon the departure of the train many of the mills and vessels in the harbor blew their whistles as a parting salute, bidding them Godspeed on their journey through life.

Upon their return home a reception will be tendered them by the Grand Marais Club, a notice of which appears in another column.

Alcona County Review, October 21, 1897

Lester Taft and bride arrived from Tawas Monday night, and will make a short visit at his mother's before returning to their future home at Grand Marais.

Alcona County Review, October 21, 1897

Tanner, Harry F.
Kimball, Blanche F.

PERSONAL MENTION.

The marriage of Miss Blanche Kimball and Mr. Harry Tanner, both of Grand Marais, was solemnized in that town Wednesday, April 8. Miss Kimball is a young lady very well and favorably known in this place, where she formerly resided. Mr. Tanner is a nephew of John Millen, and a young man of fine prospects. The newly married couple will take a trip to Alabama to visit the groom's relatives and upon their return will make their home at Grand Marais. Many congratulations are extended to both Mr. and Mrs. Tanner.

Alcona County Review, April 16, 1896

Black River Sparks.

John Millen and niece, Miss F. Bayley, attended the Tanner—Kimball wedding at Grand Marais.

Alcona County Review, April 16, 1896

Tate, Robert
?, {Bride}

CALEDONIA.

Robt. Tate, one of our Caledonia boys, surprised himself and his acquaintances by getting married June 22d. The bride's maiden name is unknown to the writer. We hope that Robert may prosper.

Alcona County Review, July 1, 1897

Taylor, {Groom}
Middleton, {Bride}

Curtis, Dec. 23, 1889.--Miss Middleton of Curtis was married on the 22nd to Mr. Taylor from across the Bay.

Alcona County Review, December 27, 1889

Teeple, Frederick Oliver
Holden, Eliza [Hastings]

LOCAL LACONICS.

Fred Teeple and Mrs. Eliza Holden, both of Alcona, were married at the residence of the bride's father, in the 20th inst., by the Rev. R. H. Balmer, of Alcona.

Alcona County Review, May 29, 1885

Terry, C. W.
White, Grace

AMONG OUR EXCHANGES.

Editor C. W. Terry of the East Tawas Epitomist, was married last week to Miss Grace White, a most estimable young lady of Tawas.

Alcona County Review, July 20, 1893

Terry, John
Kerr, Mrs. Jennie

Married: January 11th, 1879, at the residence of John McRae, Harrisville, Mich., by Rev. N. N. Clark, Mr. John Terry and Mrs. Jennie Kerr, all of Harrisville.

The above announcements come to hand for publication at a rather late date, but then we can congratulate the elated parties just the same. May their future anticipations, joy, prosperity, etc., be fully realized, and life pass on admirably.

Alcona County Review, January 31, 1879

Thibault, Charles
Cyr, Mable

EVENTS OF ONE WEEK.

Chas. Thibault, formerly of Harrisville, was married Friday evening of last week at Oscoda to Miss Mable Cyr.

Alcona County Review, December 17, 1896

Thibideau, Albert
Meddaugh, Hannah

The Local News.

Married, July 19, by Justice La Chapelle, Albert Tibbido, of Alpena, and Hanna Meddaugh, of Alcona.

Alcona County Review, July 25, 1890

Thompson, Alfred
Good, Hattie

Alfred Thompson of Alpena procured a license today to marry Hattie Good of Gustin.

Alcona County Review, February 7, 1895

Black River News.
Married, Feb. 9th, at the house of Daniel Thompson, by Justice Flaws, Alfred Thompson and Hattie Good.

Alcona County Review, February 21, 1895

Gustin Grist.

Alfred Thompson and wife, formerly Miss Good, took train today for Black River.

Alcona County Review, March 14, 1895

Thompson, Broughton
Thornton, Emma

Curtis, Oct. 26.—Mr. Braten Thompson of Curtis, and Miss Emma Thornton of Oscoda were joined in marriage Oct. 21, by Mr. W. T. Blake, Justice of the Peace, at the home of the bride's aunt Mrs. Middleton. Both of the age of 22 yrs.

Alcona County Review, October 29, 1891

Thompson, Henry
Diamond, Kate [Lapier]

COUNTY JOTTINGS.
Married. On Saturday evening, Aug. 17th, by Rev. A. McKinnon, Henry Thompson, of Au Sable, and Mrs. Kate Diamond, of Harrisville. The ceremony was performed at the residence of Mrs. Warren Evans.— *Au Sable News.*

The editor of the Review extends congratulations to the new couple, and wishes them a bright and happy future.

Alcona County Review, August 30, 1878

Thorner, Joseph
Milligan, Mahala

The Local News.

Jos. Thorner and Mahala Milligan, both of Haynes, have joined their fortunes for life.

Alcona County Review, January 8, 1891

Thornton, James T.

Hamilton, Hattie

Married.

In Harrisville, at the residence of the bride's father, July 1, 1882, by the Rev. J. H. McIntosh, James T. Thornton and Miss Hattie Hamilton, all of Harrisville.

The editor of the Review rises to extend hearty congratulations to all the above named new couples, hoping that they may pick up pearls of happiness all along their respective pathways through life, and part in the terrestrial world only to meet in the never ending blissful celestial.

Alcona County Review, July 7, 1882

Thornton, Lyman L.
Noyes, Carrie Ethel

Married.

At West Harrisville Nov. 4th, '96, Miss Carrie E. Noyes, of Mud Lake, and Mr. Lyman L. Thornton, of Sanilac, Rev. F. S. Ford officiating.

Alcona County Review, November 12, 1896

Tiffany, George L.
Fox, Maud A.

PERSONAL MENTION.

It is now Dr. and Mrs. Tiffany. At a quiet home wedding on Tuesday evening, Geo. L. Tiffany, M. D., and Miss Maud A. Fox were united in marriage by Rev. W. Will. No cards.

The bridegroom is a recent comer to Harrisville, but the air of refinement and education he carries have favorably impressed those with whom he has had business or social relations and they can congratulate him on his conquest of the heart of so fair a bride. The Review wishes both a full measure of happiness.

Alcona County Review, September 3, 1896

Tillotson, Sherwood D.
Loomis, Hattie G.

S. D. Tillotson, of the Union office, was united in marriage Sunday last, to Miss Hattie G. Loomis, of Joliet, Ill. The ceremony took place at the residence of the bride's sister, in Joliet. The newly married have been traveling in the west visiting relatives and friends during the past week, and intend reaching their Ovid home next week. We trust this union may prove in every way as well "made up" as have other Unions which Sherwood has had occasion to put to press.--Ovid Union. Mr. Tillotson was formerly a resident of Alcona county. He is a brother of Mrs. L. R. Fisk of Black River. The Review wishes Sherwood and his bride all manner of happiness and prosperity.

Alcona County Review, September 22, 1882

Tipler, Frank E.
Carr, Katie

The Local News.

Frank E. Tipler, aged 28, and Miss Katie Carr, aged 23, were licensed to wed by the county clerk last week.

Alcona County Review, July 16, 1891

Towner, William E.
Johnson, Fannie

Forty Years Married.

On June 28, 1909, Mr. and Mrs. W. E. Towner, well known residents of Centralia, celebrated the fortieth anniversary of their wedding at their home in Salzer Valley, four miles east of Centralia. All the children and grandchildren were present for a family reunion. Many relatives and friends were invited, making about a hundred guests in all.

Dinner was served in the orchard on long tables spread under a bower of fir boughs and were decorated with flowers. A beautiful wedding cake occupied the center of the table, and was cut by the bride of forty years. Ice cream and cake were served for dessert.

In the afternoon the company was entertained with a few selections of music and singing by a number of guests.

Many beautiful gifts were presented to the host and hostess as wedding gifts from the relatives and friends.

Plans had been made for a family picture to be taken, but owing to the uncertain weather it was postponed and will be taken later.

The day passed very successfully and all reported a good time. Good wishes were poured upon the happy family by all.

Mr. and Mrs. Wm. E. Towner were married June 28, 1869, in Harrisville, Mich., where they spent the first years of their married life. In 1880 they moved to South Dakota, and in 1891 to Centralia, Wash., where they have since resided.

There are twelve children in the family, eight of whom are married and residing in Centralia and

vicinity. There are twenty-three grandchildren.

Centralia, (Wash.) News Examiner.

The "bride" was Miss Fannie Johnson, sister of W. R. Johnson, Mrs. C. W. Goodsell and Mrs. Alex MacNeil of Haynes.

Alcona County Review, July 15, 1909

Tremain, E. A.
Duncan, Jennie M.

ALONG THE SHORE.

The marriage of E. A. Tremain and Miss Jennie M. Duncan, of Au Sable, on the 15th inst. was a brilliant affair.

Alcona County Review, July 15, 1909

Turner, Robert
Reynolds, Helen

Local Sparks.

Cards are out announcing the marriage of Miss Helen, eldest daughter of Mr. and Mrs. W. R. Smith, to Robert Turner, on Sept. 10.

Alcona County Review, August 29, 1895

PERSONAL MENTION.

Mrs. H. E. Reynolds has gone to Black River to be present at the marriage of her grand daughter which occurs next Tuesday. After the wedding Mrs. Reynolds will go to Alpena to visit the family of her son, Colwell.

Alcona County Review, September 5, 1895

Mrs. H. E. Reynolds is here to attend the wedding of her grand daughter.

Alcona County Review, September 12, 1895

Black River Sparks.

Married—Mr. Robt. Turner to Miss Helen Reynolds.

Swell Social Event. A Happy Union of Two Popular Young People.

It was a pretty home wedding which took place at the residence of the bride's parents, Tuesday morning, Sept. 10th, when Miss Helen Reynolds and Mr. Robert Turner were joined in holy bonds of wedlock. The ceremony was performed in a spacious parlor which was beautifully decorated with flowers for the occasion. Promptly at 8 o'clock the family and relatives

entered the parlor, when the strains of the Lohengrin Bridal March, played by Major Safford, announced the coming of the bridal party down the main staircase and through the parlor to an alcove draped with lace and flowers.

The bride was attended by her sister, Miss Maud Reynolds, and the groom by Mr. Joseph Whitsett. The ceremony was performed by Rev. W. J. Bailey of Harrisville in his usual impressive way. After the ceremony a reception was held and an elegant wedding breakfast served, after which they took their departure on the morning train amid many good wishes and showers of rice and old shoes. They will visit relatives in the eastern cities and expect to be gone about three weeks. They were the recipients of many beautiful and costly gifts. The following guests were present.

Harrisville: Mr. and Mrs. L. A. Colwell, Mr. and Mrs. Fred Reynolds, Mrs. H. Reynolds, Mrs. Elliott, Chas. Mayo, Misses Allie, Grace and Louise Colwell.

Alpena: Mrs. E. H. Barlow, Miss Kate Jordan, E. O. Johnston, D. T. Cutting, editor Alpena Echo.

Misses Kittie and Blanche Kimball of Grand Marais; Miss Matie Smith, of Milwaukee.

Black River: Dr. and Mrs. McCormick, Mr. and Mrs. Ed. Lemere, Mr. and Mrs. James Pritchard, Mr. and Mrs. F. J. Hill, Mr. and Mrs. John White, Mr. and Mrs. P. C. McGregor, Mr. and Mrs. A. J. Fortier, Mr. and Mrs. John Wells, Mr. and Mrs. Sam Hill, Mrs. Dysinger, Mrs. J. D. Walker, Mrs. Jas. Johnston. The Misses Allie Lemere, Frances Bayley, Myrtle Dysinger, Susetha and Genevieve Hill, Annie Johnston, Mary McGregor, May Moore, Irene Pritchard, M. A. Hill, Messrs. Jno. Millen, Major Safford, John Bayley, Geo. Withington, O. E. Decarie, Charles Storms, Clarke Yokom, Jno. McGregor.

Alcona County Review, September 12, 1895

Black River Sparks.

By an oversight on the part of your correspondent the names of Mr. Peter Churchill and daughter, Alice, were omitted from the list of guests at the late Turner-Reynolds wedding.

Alcona County Review, September 19, 1895

Twite, Henry J.
Lamp, Mary

Purely Personal.

Mr. Henry Twite of Harrisville and Miss Mary Lamp of Black River were united in marriage by the Rev. L. Hazard Saturday.

Alcona County Review, January 3, 1890

Twite, William J.
Dickinson, Annie R.

HOME NEWS JOTTINGS.

Married: At the M. E. parsonage in the village of Harrisville, on November 23, 1882, by Rev. J. H. McIntosh, William J. Twite of Harrisville and Miss Annie R. Dickinson of Black River, Mich.

Alcona County Review, November 24, 1882

Tye, George
Drake, Janie

LOCAL JOTTINGS.
George Tye of Gustin took out a license Saturday to wed Miss Janie Drake whose home has been in Oscoda county.

Alcona County Review, September 20, 1889

Uptegrove, {Groom}
McArthur, Hattie

HAYNES HAPPENINGS.

Haynes, Nov. 9th, 1897.
Times are improving in Haynes. Quite a number of young men are erecting houses preparatory to splicing to better halves. Among them are Will Fettes and Will Craven. Miss Hattie McArthur is to be married on Wednesday next (Nov. 17) to a young man who resides at Black River. Your scribe wishes them joy and happiness during the journey of life. Miss McArthur is a model young lady and the daughter of Donald McArthur. Her mother died while she was an infant. She was reared by Mrs. Robert Hastings, her grandmother.

Alcona County Review, November 18, 1897

Valentine, Daniel Webster
Colwell, Ada Belle

Invitations are out for the marriage of Miss Ada Belle Colwell to Dr. Daniel W. Valentine for Wednesday, October 28th inst., at the Presbyterian church, Harrisville. They will be at home at 15 Dean St., Englewood, New Jersey.

Alcona County Review, October 15, 1896

PERSONAL MENTION.

Dr. Daniel Valentine of Englewood, New Jersey, and his best man, Mr. Harry Maybee of New York, arrived Monday and formed a few pleasant acquaintants in the village.

Alcona County Review, October 29, 1896

WEDDING BELLS.
The marriage of Ada Belle Colwell, youngest daughter of Benj. S. Colwell of Portville, N. Y., to Dr. Daniel W. Valentine of Englewood, N. J., was solemnized last evening at 7 o'clock at the Presbyterian church, Rev. Warren Hasting, rector of Trinity church of Alpena, officiating.

The church was elaborately trimmed with ground pine, plants and cut flowers, white and green being the predominating colors. Suspended above the arch was an immense butter fly bow, the streamers from which extended gracefully from arch to arch the entire length of the church. Huge bunches of white carnations and smilax adorned the pews reserved for the family.

While awaiting the arrival of the bridal party Arthur Wilson beautifully rendered that sweet song, "O Promise Me." Presiding at the organ was Mrs. E. J. Schreiber, of Bay City and as the first strains of the wedding march pealed from the organ, the vestry door at the rear opened and the groom, his best man and the officiating rector took their places at the altar. At once all eyes were turned towards the vestibule, the ushers stepped in place and the bridal party proceeded slowly up the broad aisle, carpeted with white for the occasion. Following the four ushers came the little ribbon bearers, masters Willie Colwell and Ben Storms, nephews of the bride. The bridesmaid entered alone followed by the maid of honor carrying the bride's boquet of yellow roses. The bride, leaning on the arm of her father, completed the bridal party. The marriage ceremony was according to the beautiful and impressive ceremony of the Episcopal Church, rendered doubly impressive by the low strains of music through the entire ceremony

and the dignified bearing of the officiating clergyman.

Following the service a delightful reception was given at the home of Mr. and Mrs. Geo. W. Colwell, only the bridal party, relatives and immediate friends attended.

The bridal gown was of rich ivory satin, dutchess, en train; corsage adorned with dutchess lace and pearl trimmings, while a diamond sunburst, a gift of the groom, held the tulle veil in place.

The maid of honor, Miss Grace Ludington, looked charming in white serge and satin. The bridesmaid, cousin of the bride, Miss Almira Colwell, was gowned very becomingly in white silk and chiffon, with diamond ornaments.

Mr. Harry Maybee, of New York, acted as best man. The ushers were Messrs. D. McGregor, Geo. E. Gillam, Chas. Mayo and Arthur Wilson, with boutonnieres of white chrysanthemums.

Never was witnessed such a charming wedding in Harrisville. The bride a great and general favorite endeared to all requires no description.

She will be especially missed in the educational circles. She was an ideal teacher and won the hearts of scholars and friends alike by her bright sunny disposition and winning ways. Never has anyone lived among us who will leave so great a void in the home and social life. The groom is a gentleman of pleasing address who stands high in his chosen profession, and is to be congratulated upon winning so talented a bride. The wedding gifts were numerous and consisted largely of silver, cut glass, Hariland china, linen, checks, and gold.

The happy couple left this morning for Englewood, N. J., where their future home is in readiness for immediate occupancy.

Alcona County Review, October 29, 1896

PERSONAL MENTION.

F. J. Hill and wife attended the Valentine—Colwell wedding Wednesday.

Alcona County Review, October 29, 1896

PERSONAL MENTION.

Mrs. E. J. Schrieber of Bay City came up for the Valentine-Colwell nuptials.

Alcona County Review, October 29, 1896

Van Alstine, Culver
Deacon, Edith

Culver Van Alstine of Alcona and Edith Deacon of Curtis were married at the Alcona House on Monday evening, Rev. W. W. Will officiating.

Alcona County Review, May 18, 1899

Van Buskirk, Stewart
Dunn, Ruth Agnes

PERSONAL MENTION.

The marriage of Mr. Stewart Van Buskirk to Miss Ruth Dunn will occur on Sunday, June 30th, at the residence of the bride's parents.

Alcona County Review, June 20, 1895

Van Buskirk-Dunn.—Married at the residence of the bride's parents, Harrisville, Mich., Sunday, June 30, 1895, Mr. Stewart Van Buskirk to Miss Ruth A. Dunn, the Rev. W. J. Bailey officiating.

This happy event was consummated at 5 o'clock Sunday afternoon in the presence of but a few invited guests besides the immediate relatives. Mr. John Macgregor was best man and the bride was sustained by her particular friend, Miss Effie Graham of Tawas city. At the conclusion of the marriage ceremony the guests were invited to discuss an elaborate menu, but they did not omit bestowing their warmest congratulations upon Mr. and Mrs. Van Buskirk.

The groom is one of Harrisville's rising young business men. Although born in Genessee county he has lived in Alcona county practically all his life and as a boy and man has made many warm friends, who will unite with the Review in wishing him health, wealth and happiness in this new relation in life. His bride was also raised in the county and is too well known to require an introduction. She is a general favorite and her bright and sunny disposition makes friends for her wherever she goes. She is a graduate of the Harrisville public schools, coming out with the class of '90. Since then she has taught several terms of school with signal success, both in Alcona county and at Tawas, where she has been for the past year.

Mr. and Mrs. Van Buskirk, we are pleased to state, will make their home in Harrisville, and will be at home to their friends after July 20th.

Alcona County Review, July 4, 1895

Van Horn, Scott
Marcellus, Clara

VANHORN—MARCELLUS.

Married at the Baptist church, West Harrisville, Wednesday evening, December 18th, inst., Scott Vanhorn to Clara Marcellus, the Rev. C. H. Holden of Alpena officiating.

The bride is one of the fairest and most charming young ladies in Alcona county, of sweet and lovable disposition and a great favorite.

The groom has been the pastor for many years of the church in which the marriage ceremony was performed and has likewise filled the pulpit of the Harrisville church for several months. He is therefore well known to a large number of our citizens who can congratulate him upon securing so charming a bride.

Alcona County Review, December 19, 1895

A Happy Event.

One of the most noteworthy events in the history of the quiet little city of West Harrisville was the wedding of the Rev. Scott Vanhorn, the popular young pastor of the Harrisville and West Harrisville Baptist churches, to Miss Clara Marcellus, a charming young lady of culture and refinement and a devout christian, which was celebrated on the evening of Dec. 18, 1895, in the Baptist church. The house, which was beautifully and tastefully decorated, was crowded to its utmost capacity with interested friends, among whom was the school consisting of about seventy-five children, pupils of the bride. Miss Beatrice Wilson presided at the organ and rendered with much skill and excellence Mendelson's wedding march.

The bride in white silk, the groom in full dress, were accompanied by six attendants led by a little maid, a sister of the bride, bearing the wedding ring upon a silver tray. Marching to the platform, which was beautifully draped, the party formed a semi-circle facing the audience when the officiating clergyman, Rev. C. H. Holden, of Alpena, stepped on the platform and in an earnest and impressive manner pronounced the marriage ceremony.

The evening passed most pleasantly in greetings, congratulations, feasting, etc., in the spacious and cheerful home of the bride's parents, Mr. and Mrs. A. Marcellus. From first to last the evening was most happy and unique. The happy couple received many beautiful presents among which are the following:

Rug and Japanese tray from school.
Silver sugar shell, Miss Laty Haven.
Parlor lamp, James Blackstock.
Silver cream pitcher, Edna Anderson, Saginaw.
Silver and china cracker bowl, James Bell.
Tea set, Mr. and Mrs. Donahue.
Teapot, Miss Kate Dyer.
Water set, Mr. and Mrs. Rose.
Silver jewel casket, Miss Lucy Beggam, of Saginaw.
Pickle crstor, Mr. and Mrs. Guy Lewis.
Clock, Chas. Mayo.
Linen tablecloth, D. McGregor.
Toilet bottle, Mr. and Mrs. John Marshal.
Individual pepper and salt shakers, Mr. and Mrs. A. Hamilton.
Carving set, T. E. Reynolds, Bay City.
China cake dish, Miss Alice Cowell.
Silver sugar shell and butter knife, Mrs. M. Bolster.
Cream spoon, Beatrice and Harry Wilson.
Berry spoon, J. E. McGregor, Black River.
Table doily, Miss Frances Bayley, Black River.
Silver photo frames, Wallace Chapelle.
½ doz. silver teaspoons, Mrs. L. A. Colwell and Mrs. Elliott.
Glass cream pitcher, Allie Barker.
Glass tea set, Mr. and Mrs. J. Miller.
Carving set, ½ doz. silver fruit knives, ½ doz. silver nut picks, gold sugar shell, from Mr. and Mrs. Leon Smith of Detroit.
Silver and glass berry dish, Mr. and Mrs. M. Nolan.
½ doz. silver nut picks, R. Cummings and J. Emerson.
Butter chips, Miss Emmer Rote.
Fancy plate, Mr. and Mrs. Grant Lewis.
Picture, Miss Minnie Chevrier, Oscoda.
Silver sugar shell and Butter knife, Mr. and Mrs. Owens.
Picture drawe, Misses Fannie and Belle McRae.

Handkerchief box and gloves box, Miss Clara Holst of Saginaw.

Linen tablecloth, Wm. Waterbury, Tawas.

2 silver napkin rings, Mr. Whitney, Alpena.

China fruit dish and fruit plates, Jno. Macgregor.

Slumber robe, Mr. and Mrs. T. A. Ferris.

2 Doileys, Miss Nell Ferris.

Silver butter knife, Henry Baror.

Breakfast castor, N. Oliver.

Silver individual salts and spoons, Mr. and Mrs. Livingstone, Louisiana.

1 doz. linen napkins, Mr. and Mrs. L. Frederick.

1 silver berry spoon, from a friend.

Alcona County Review, December 26, 1895

Van Wagoner, George Lewis
Berkhart, Annie May

Married.
Van Wagner—Berkhart.

At the M. E. parsonage, Dec. 17th, by the Rev. Wm. J. Bailey, Mr. Geo. Lewis Van Wagner to Miss Annie May Berkhart, both of Harrisville.

Alcona County Review, December 20, 1894

An ancient custom was awakened at the residence of John Berkhart, Jr., last Monday night to do honor to "Lue" Van Wagner and his bride. It has become a custom to have a "quiet wedding" in this county, but the boys say "Lue's" was the reverse. Many invitations were extended and accepted and many self-invitations were also accepted. Everything that would create a noise, from a shot gun to a cow bell, was used. Good feeling ruled the hour. Everybody was in the height of delight and everything went off lovely, specially the guns.

Alcona County Review, December 20, 1894

Van Wagoner, John
Beever, Rose

Local News.

Mr. John Van Wagner, son of J. A. Van Wagner, and Miss Rose Beever, daughter of Geo. W. Beever, were united in marriage Tuesday evening by Rev. W. W. Will.

Alcona County Review, November 2, 1899

Van Wagoner, John
Miller, Jennie

Your Folks and Our Folks.

Marriage license No. 107 bears the names of Jno. Van Wagner and Miss

Jennie Miller, both of Greenbush. Both young people are well and favorably known in this vicinity, the latter having made her home for many years with her parents in Harrisville. The marriage ceremony was celebrated Sunday at the home of the bride's parents in Greenbush, the Rev. L. Hazard officiating. They commence keeping house at once on the bridegroom's farm in Greenbush township. May long life, joy and happiness attend them.

Alcona County Review, April 30, 1891

Vaughn, Prescott R.
Louderbaugh, Ida M.

The Local News.

Prescott R. Vaughn aged 29, and Ida M. Louderbaugh aged 17, have been licensed to wed. Both parties are credited to Mitchell township.

Alcona County Review, January 15, 1891

Vennard, Robert
McArthur, Catherine Jane

PERSONAL MENTION.

Thursday afternoon, July 2d, Rev. W. Will united in marriage Robert Venard and Miss Catherine J. McArthur, all of Haynes.

Alcona County Review, July 9, 1896

Vollett, Charles R.
Brownlee, Roxena

Wedding Bells.

Married, at the residence of the bride's parents, Mr. and Mrs. Brownlee of West Harrisville June 1, their daughter Roxena to Mr. Charles R. Vollett of Oscoda. Only relatives were present. Rev. F. S. Ford officiating.

Alcona County Review, June 9, 1898

Wagner, D. H.
Sinton, Mary Jane

The Local News.

Miss Mary Jane Sinton, daughter of our fellow townsman, Geo. Sinton, was married on the 13th inst. to D. H. Wagner, an Au Sable barber.

Alcona County Review, December 26, 1890

Waldron, Fred Augustus
Whitham, Dianthe Lodenra

Wedding Bells at Hintonburg.

At the residence of Mr. Francis Whitham, 10th avenue, last evening the wedding of his daughter Dianthe

Lodenra, to Mr. Fred Augustus Waldron, of the E. B. Eody Co., was celebrated. The bride was prettily attired in a traveling suit of fawn cloth. She was assisted by Miss Edie Dowler. Mr. James Whitham performed the duties of groomsman. The ceremony was performed by Rev. Robert Eady, of Bethany Presbyterian church. After the ceremony about sixty guests sat down to a sumptuous repast. The happy couple left on the 10:35 C. P. R. express for Harrisville. On their return they will take up their residence in Hull.

The following is a list of the presents: Rocking chair and table, members of Bethany Presbyterian church; rocking chair, Mrs. G. Dowler; easy chair, Messrs. H. and J. Dowler; silver fruit dish, Miss B. Dowler; silver bread plate, Mr. and Mrs. Freeman; berry set, Mrs. J. Dowler; berry spoon, Miss Edie Dowler; berry spoon, Mrs. J. Lewis; butter knife and sugar spoon, R. Dowler; toilet set, Mr., Mrs. and Miss Henry; lamp, Mr. W. and Miss H. Purdy; toilet set, Mrs. W. Gillespie; toilet set, Mrs. Adam Thompson; butter knife and pickle fork, Mr. and Mrs. W. Dowler; egg cruit, Mrs. W. Armstrong; silver butter dish, Mrs. E. Lewis; cheese dish, Miss MacFarlane; set of three pictures, Mr. E. Lewis; clock, Mr. Ludington; salt and pepper cruet, Mrs. Dunning; cheese knife, Mrs. R. Dowler; sugar spoon, Mr. R. Dowler; jardinière, Mrs. T. Gillespie; wall mirror, Mr. Crown; comforter, Mrs. McConnell; drape, Miss Ada McConnell; set smoothing irons, Mrs. H. Albright.—Ottawa Citizen.

Alcona County Review, October 5, 1899

PERSONAL POINTS.

Mr. Fred Waldron and bride of Ottawa, Ont., arrived Saturday morning for a two week's visit with his mother, Mrs. E. Waldron and family.

Alcona County Review, October 5, 1899

Walker, Frank
Rutherford, Lottie

Along the Shore.

Alpena.

On Wednesday of last week, Mr. Frank Walker and Miss Lottie Rutherford, both of this village, were united in marriage at the residence of the bride's uncle, J. J. Whitters, Oscoda, in the presence of a limited few of their friends.

Alcona County Review, March 3, 1882

Walker, John
O'Dell, Adaline

COUNTY REVIEWINGS.

Married.—At Au Sable, April 18, 1880, Miss Addie O'Dell and Mr. John Walker, both of Harrisville. The Review extends congratulations to the happy pair.

Alcona County Review, April 23, 1880

Wallace, Robert
Hodges, Ella

Local Sayings and Doings.

The Review has just learned of the marriage of Robert Wallace and Miss Ella Hodges, (formerly of Harrisville) which occurred about two weeks since. The happy couple are now living in Detroit, and the Review unites with their many Harrisville friends in wishing them a life of continued happiness and prosperity.

Alcona County Review, November 18, 1881

Wallace, William
Nemitz, Martha

Curtis Items.

May 6, 1895.
W. Wallace took a trip to Sanilac and brought a brand new wife home. They are a fine looking couple and brought a good lot of stock with them. They have rented E. Dickinson's farm. We wish them good success and prosperity through life.

Alcona County Review, May 9, 1895

Ward, Alfred Burton
Kirkendall, Elizabeth May

Christmas Wedding Bells.

Married at the home of the bride's parents, Mr. and Mrs. Kirkendall of Greenbush, on Christmas Day, Miss Libbie Kirkendall to Mr. Alfred B. Ward.

Capt. Ward is owner of a schooner and is very popular among the lake sailors, being a young man of very congenial spirit. His young wife is one of Greenbush's most popular young ladies and is everywhere a favorite. Rev. F. S. Ford, pastor of Greenbush, officiated.

Their many friends will wish them a long, happy and prosperous life.

Alcona County Review, December 30, 1897

Ward, Charles
Underhill, Dorthie

HOME NEWS JOTTINGS.

Married—In Harrisville, November 27, 1882, by Rev. J. H. McIntosh, Chas. Ward and Miss Dorthie Underhill, all of Harrisville, Mich.

Alcona County Review, December 15, 1882

Ward, George
Sinclair Jennie

REVIEWINGS.

Rev. D. VanDyke sends us from Plainwell this week the following marriage notice: Married at the Presbyterian Parsonage in Harrisville, June 23, 1881, by Rev. D. Van Dyke, Mr. George Ward and Miss Jennie Sinclair. We suppose congratulations to the happy couple are in order even at this late date, so the Review hopes for the eternal sweetness of the lives of the united couple.

Alcona County Review, July 22, 1881

Ward, William John
Ferguson, Rebecca

EVENTS OF ONE WEEK.

On Thursday evening, Oct. 29, Wm. J. Ward and Miss Rebecca Ferguson were united in marriage by Rev. W. Will. The wedding occurred at the home of the bride's parents, in the presence of a score or more of relations and friends. After the ceremony the company sat down to a most elegant supper. The young couple have hosts of friends that wish them many happy and prosperous years.

Alcona County Review, November 5, 1896

Slightly Mixed.

The marriage notice of John Ward and Miss Rebecca Ferguson became mixed last week with some lines written to commemorate the death of a son of Jas. McKinnon of Caledonia. The result was not just in line with such a happy event as a marriage, but we trust the incident has not in anyways affected the happiness of Mr. and Mrs. Ward and that their future may be one of unalloyed happiness.

Alcona County Review, November 12, 1896

Watrous, Edgar H.
Smith, Mary E.

Jottings Along the Shore.

Dr. E. H. Watrous, dentist, and Miss Mary E. Smith, teacher in the city schools, all of Alpena, were married, the 30th ult.

Alcona County Review, January 9, 1880

Watson, Wellington
Switzer, Lucy

BLACK RIVER.

Sept. 20, '99.
Wednesday afternoon of last week twenty five friends and relatives witnessed the marriage of Miss Lucy Switser, a popular young lady of this place, to Wellington Watson, a prosperous and well-to-do farmer of Sanilac Co. Rev. A. C. Austin united the happy couple; Mr. Levi Gardner acted as best man and Miss Gardner as bridesmaid. Mr. and Mrs. Watson left on the evening train amid showers of rice for their future home near Croswell. The best wishes of the entire community go with them.

Alcona County Review, September 21, 1899

Watters, Jeff L.
Conklin, Jessie

Two Souls Made Happy.

Jeff Watters went below last Saturday morning on a business trip. He brought up at Flint, where an "attraction" has been located that has caused his attention for some considerable time past. Saturday he made a direct line Flintward to capture the prize, and we believe succeeded admirably in the attempt. That is to say, on Sunday evening, at the residence of Mrs. Thomas Foster, in the city of Flint, Jeff (or Mr. J. L. Watters) and Miss Jessie Conklin, all of Harrisville, were united in marriage, an event which numerous of our young people were satisfied would soon happen. The Review rises up to extend hearty congratulations to the newly wedded pair, wishing them a happy and prosperous life.

O, set the bells a ringing
And fire off the guns.
Blow your trumpets inside out
And bang the biggest drums.
And if any one should ask you
The cause of all the fun,
Tell them Jeff and Jessie's married,
And the great transaction's done.

Alcona County Review, October 23, 1885

LOCAL JOTTINGS.

Mr. and Mrs. Jeff Watters arrived in Harrisville last Saturday night, and have since been receiving the hearty congratulations of their numerous friends here.

Alcona County Review, October 30, 1885

Weadock, Thomas J.
Curtis, Nancy E.

PERSONAL MENTION.

Congressman Weadock of this district was united in marriage on Jan. 1, to Miss Nannie Curtis. The bride has been housekeeper for Mr. Weadock since the death of his first wife, which occurred about three years ago. She is well and favorably known in Harrisville and a few years ago was frequently here, where her services as dressmaker were in great demand.

Alcona County Review, January 10, 1895

Weldon, James M.
Downing, Mrs. Rose Etta

Married.

In Harrisville, Mich., on the 15th inst. By Rev. N. N. Clark, Mr. James M. Weldon and Mrs. Rose Etta Downing, all of Harrisville.

The editor was kindly remembered by the bride and groom with a good supply of wedding viands, for which thanks are returned. May the felicity of the happy couple be complete and their walk together through life be long and unclouded.

Alcona County Review, October 18, 1878

Weston, Arthur H.
Lockhart, Janet

A correspondent sends us an account of a double wedding which occurred last week at the residence of John Lockhart, of Oscoda. The contracting parties were A. H. Meston and Miss Janet Lockhart, and Wm. Lee and Miss Emma Leeland, all of Oscoda and Au Sable. Rev. Conway, the Baptist minister officiated. A large number of guests were present and the lists of gifts to each couple were numerous. Among the guests were Mr. and Mrs. J. W. Ferguson of Curtis township. Our space and limited time prevents the publication of the long list of presents.

Alcona County Review, February 22, 1894

White, Caleb

Wertman, Mrs. Hannah E.
[Doughty]

MARRIAGE LICENSES.

The following marriage licenses were issued from the county clerk's office within the past week:

July 29.—Caleb White, Mrs. Hanna E. Wertman, both of Gustin.

Alcona County Review, August 3, 1893

White, James
Hall, Hattie

CALEDONIA.

Hattie Hall of Caledonia was married June 22 to Jas. White of Maple Ridge, by Rev. Thos. Middlemus of Alpena.

Alcona County Review, July 1, 1897

White, Robert
Holbrook, Mary A.

Jottings Along the Shore.

Miss Mary Holbrook is to be married at Miltion, Mich., on the 6th inst. to Robert White, Esq., of Tawas, Mich.--Alpena Reporter. Can it be possible that Bob would do such a thing.

Alcona County Review, January 9, 1880

White, W. A.
Sawyer, Allie

ALONG THE SHORE.

Married—Saturday, Aug. 8, W. A. White of Chicago, and Miss Allie Sawyer of East Tawas.

Alcona County Review, August 21, 1885

White, Wells D.
Taylor, Ida

PERSONAL MENTION.

Miss Ida Taylor has resigned her position in the Tawas City schools and has gone to Bay City, where it is reported there is to be a wedding soon. The young lady is well known and a favorite in Harrisville.

Alcona County Review, March 12, 1896

Taylor—White.

The marriage of Miss Ida Taylor, late a teacher in the Tawas City schools, took place at Bay City on March 9th, inst.

The ceremony was performed at the residence of J. W. Tolmie, 800 18th street, the Rev. C. B. Steele officiating.

The fortunate bridegroom is Wells D. White, of Parshallville, Mich., also a school teacher.

It was a pretty home wedding and took place at 7:30 p.m. After lunch the bridal pair left at 9:30 for their home and Parshallville. Their departure was accompanied by the usual shower of rice, old shoes, and bon mots.

Alcona County Review, March 26, 1896

Whitsett, Joseph M.
Anthony, Ruthema

BLACK RIVER.

Aug. 9, '99.

People here are much interested in a knot that is being tied at Killmaster today, where Rev. A. C. Austin will unite in holy matrimony Mr. Joe Whitsett, a popular business man of this place, and Miss Ruthema Anthony of Killmaster. Mr. Whitsett, his mother, Mrs. J. D. Walker of Millersburg, his sisters Mrs. J. F. Pepper of Millersburg, and Mrs. C. W. Ranney of Alpena, accompanied him to Killmaster this morning. Mr. and Mrs. Whitsett will arrive this evening and if the proposed reception is carried out the happy couple will be in China town for a time.

Alcona County Review, August 10, 1899

GUSTIN.

Gustin loses one more of its fair young ladies. Joseph Whitsett of Black River and Miss Ruthema Anthony of Gustin, were united in marriage at her home in Gustin Monday, Aug. 9th. Miss Anthony is one of our most popular young ladies and the best wishes of this community are extended to the happy pair.

Alcona County Review, August 10, 1899

Whittaker, Frank R.
Cummings, Ella

EVENTS OF ONE WEEK.

Cards have been received by friends of the bride announcing the marriage at Detroit on Wednesday evening of this week, of Miss Ella Cummings to Frank R. Whittaker.

Alcona County Review, June 7, 1894

Whittemore, Henry R.
Lindner, Lucille

PURELY PERSONAL.

Henry R. Whittemore, clerk of the propeller Arundell, and royal good fellow to boot, was married last week to Miss Lucile Lindner, at the bride's home in Lexington, Ky.

Alcona County Review, March 8, 1889

Whitter, James
Fowler, Nettie

KILLMASTER JOTS.

"Two hearts that beat as one; two minds with but a single thought" is the result of the visit made by the Rev. Mr. Robins at the residence of P. H. Ives, where James Whitter and Miss Nettie Fowler were united in the holy bonds of matrimony—all of our village. The steady stream of congratulations that is pouring in upon the happy couple from all sides indicates that they have a warm place in the hearts of all their acquaintances. So here goes our bran new slipper after them.

Alcona County Review, January 8, 1887

Wiley, Fred C.
Southern, Jennie L.

EVENTS OF ONE WEEK.

Dr. Wiley and bride arrived from Sarnia last Friday. The Doctor has wisely provided a house for his bride and everything was ready for them to begin housekeeping.

Alcona County Review, December 3, 1896

Willard, Joseph C.
Treadway, Polly

LOCAL LACONICS.

We are informed that Joseph C. Willard, of Greenbush, who was recently joined in wedlock's bands to Miss Polly Treadway, niece of Mrs. H. H. Kibler, will commence housekeeping the present week in the house purchased by him of Jas. F. Coyle.

Alcona County Review, June 5, 1885

Willett, Wilfred
Lessard, Julia

The Local News

Wilfred Willett and Julia Lessard, both of Haynes, were married at Au Sable last week by Fr. Langlois.

Alcona County Review, August 4, 1892

Williams, Asa
Murphy, Mary

LOCAL JOTTINGS.

Married: On Sunday, Sept. 20th, 1885, by Rev. J. Bain at his residence, Mr. Asa Williams and Miss Mary Murphy.

Alcona County Review, October 2, 1885

Williams, William W.
Baror, Maud Lula

Bits of News.

Miss Maude Baror and Mr. William W. Williams were quietly married Thursday evening at the residence of the bride's mother, Mrs. A. Baror, on Lake St.

Alcona County Review, December 7, 1899

Wilson, Arthur H.
Ash, Mrs. Edith E.

LOCAL PICK UPS.

Last Wednesday afternoon, at the Episcopal church in East Tawas, occurred the marriage of Mrs. Edith E. Ash, of that city, and Arthur H. Wilson, of Detroit, Rev. Wye officiating. The bride is the daughter of Mr. and Mrs. E. G. Ash and has a large circle of friends in the Tawases who join in wishing her a long and happy wedded life. The happy couple left on the afternoon train for Oscoda, where they took the boat for Detroit.—Tawas Herald.

Mr. Wilson at one time had charge of the St. Andrew's Episcopal Mission of Harrisville.

Alcona County Review, August 10, 1899

Wilson, John
Anderson, Nettie J.

JOTTINGS ALONG THE SHORE.

Mr. John Wilson and Miss Nettie J. Anderson, of Au Sable, were married April 14th.

Alcona County Review, April 22, 1881

Wilson, Seymour
Wagner, Emma

Married at Skamokawa, Wash., Sunday, May 10th, Mr. Seymour Wilson to Miss Emma Wagner. The bridegroom was a former resident of Harrisville and is a brother of Mrs. Wm. Ludington.

Alcona County Review, May 21, 1896

Winchester, William
Brabant, Jennie S.

The Shore dentist, Dr. Winchester, was married to Miss J. S. Brabant of Alpena, the first of the present month.

Alcona County Review, November 26, 1880

Winkleman, Louis
Yalomstein, Fanny

PERSONAL.

Louis Winkleman will be married Aug. 31, inst. to Miss Fanny Yalomstein of Detroit.

Alcona County Review, August 12, 1897

Winkleman, M. P.
?, {Bride}

Somewhat Personal.

M. P. Winkleman, a former Harrisville merchant, was married last week at Detroit. His home at present is Manistique.

Alcona County Review, July 23, 1891

Winkleman, Sam
Rosenthal, Fanny

PERSONAL.

Sam Winkleman will be married on the 7th of Sept., to Miss Fanny Rosenthal of Petoskey. Sam will go into business at Manistee soon after getting married. The boys are at St. Ignace.

Alcona County Review, August 12, 1897

Sam Winkleman's Brilliant Wedding.

Mrs. Will Fitzmaurice, who is at Bay View, sends the Review a copy of the Daily Resorter, published at Petoskey, containing a report of the wedding of Samuel Winkelman of Manistee and Miss Phenie Rosenthal of Petoskey. The paper reports the affair as a "brilliant social event," and say: "One of the most brilliant events in Petoskey's history was the marriage of Miss Phenie Rosenthal, who was wedded to Mr. Samuel Winkleman, of Manistee, at the home of the bride's father, Mr. Samuel Rosenthal, Tuesday evening, Sept. 7th. The bride was one of Petoskey's popular young ladies and the prominent position occupied by Mr. and Mrs. Rosenthal added interest to the occasion.

The spacious residence and ground were most tastefully decorated. Carpets covered the ground from the veranda to the large pavilion, which had been erected on the west lawn. Electric lights had been placed at intervals on the porch and in adjoining trees, brilliantly illuminating the scene and producing a very pretty effect.

At 6:00 o'clock the bridal cortege entered, under direction of Mr. Louis Winkleman, master of ceremonies.

The Rev. Dr. Rappenport, of Chicago, performed the marriage ceremony.

Alcona County Review, September 16, 1897

Wiseman, Alex
Urquhart, Ida

At the Altar.

Wiseman, Urquhart.—At the M. E. parsonage, July 8, 1895, by the Rev. W. J. Bailey, Mr. Alex Wiseman to Miss Ida Urquhart, both of Alpena, Mich.

Alcona County Review, July 11, 1895

West Harrisville.

July 9, 1895.

Mr. Aleck Wiseman and Miss Urquhart of Alpena arrived in town Monday afternoon. A. McMillan drove them to Harrisville where they were united in matrimony and returned to Alpena Tuesday.

Alcona County Review, July 11, 1895

Withey, Joseph S.
Stafford, Mrs. Eleanor M.

Married.

In Harrisville, July 23, 1882, by Rev. J. H. McIntosh, Joseph S. Withey and Mrs. Elleanor Stafford, all of Harrisville, Mich.

Alcona County Review, July 28, 1882

Withington, George Theron
Bayley, Frances

PERSONAL.

Cards are out announcing the marriage of Mr. Geo. T. Withington and Miss Frances Bayley, both of Black River, to occur on Wednesday, June 16th next, at Grace Mission, Black River, Mich.

Alcona County Review, June 3, 1897

Withington—Bayly.

The Withington—Bayly nuptials, which united in the holy bonds of matrimony two of Black River's most popular young people, was probably the swellest affair of the kind that has ever taken place in that town, where the swell set take special pride in doing all things in the social line in the top of the prevailing mode.

The bride, Miss Frances Bayly, is a favorite niece of John Millen, and his

princely generosity was unbounded in providing for the arrangements.

The ceremony took place at high noon at Grace Mission in the presence of about 50 invited guests, including several from Alpena and Harrisville.

The bride was attired in white satin en train, with bridal veil. She was attended by Miss Nellie Ferris of Black River. George Withington, the bridegroom, wore the conventional black. John E. McGregor of Black River was best man. The ceremony was performed by the Rev. Warren Hastings of Alpena, after which the party repaired to Gray Gables where a sumptuous banquet was served and congratulations were showered upon the happy couple. The presents were numerous and costly, including a check for $500 from Mr. Millen.

Mr. and Mrs. Withington took their departure on the evening train for the south. They will return in about ten days and make their home at Black River. They were attended to the train by a large number of their friends who showered them with rice and good wishes.

Alcona County Review, June 17, 1897

PERSONAL.

Mr. and Mrs. Geo. W. Colwell, Mrs. D. E. Storms and John Macgregor attended the Withington-Bayly nuptials at Grace Mission, Black River, Tuesday.

Alcona County Review, June 17, 1897

PERSONAL.

Mr. and Mrs. Geo. T. Withington have returned to Black River from their wedding trip.

Alcona County Review, July 1, 1897

Witter, Charles W.
Jacob, Bertha

SOMEWHAT PERSONAL.

Chas. W. Witter and Miss Bertha Jacob were married at Au Sable June 27. The first named is a former resident.

Alcona County Review, July 21, 1892

Woo, Willie C.
LePage, Maud C.

AU SABLE AND OSCODA.

Willie Woo, the Chinese laundrymen, and Miss Maud LePage, were recently married by Rev. Goldie.

Wood, Arthur D.
Goupell, Sophia

PERSONAL POINTS.

Cards have been received here announcing the marriage of Arthur D. Wood, editor of the Grand Marais Herald, to Sophia Goupell; The Review extends congratulations.

Alcona County Review, October 19, 1899

Wood, John
McKenzie, Margaret

LOCAL JOTTINGS.

John Wood and Margaret McKenzie are names that appear upon marriage license No. 40, issued from the county clerk's office March 23d.

Alcona County Review, March 29, 1889

Yearn, Louis F.
Rice, Minnie

LOCAL JOTTINGS.

The Rev. and Mrs. F. N. Barlow left per train for Detroit Tuesday morning where the former will officiate by request at the marriage of Miss Minnie Rice, a young lady well known in Harrisville.

Alcona County Review, November 25, 1887

MARRIED.

Yearn—Rice.—At the home of the bride's parents, Capt. and Mrs. W. E. Rice, No. 129 Eighteenth st., Detroit, Nov. 23d, 1887, by the Rev. F. N. Barlow, of Harrisville, Louis F. Yearn, of St. Clair, and Miss Minnie Rice, of Detroit.

The wedding was intended to be private with the exception of a few of the most intimate friends of the parties, yet the bridal pair were the recipients of many rich and valuable presents from their numerous friends present and abroad, and after partaking of a bountiful repast the young couple left for their future home in St. Clair, where they commence life together under the most pleasant auspices.

The bride is well and favorably known in Harrisville and her many friends here and elsewhere, will be delighted to learn that her choice of a husband has fallen upon one who is every way worthy of her. He is engaged in mercantile pursuits, and his employer, Mr. Hubel, of St. Clair, in whose family he has lived for several years, speaks of his character, ability and habits in the most flattering terms and showed his appreciation of his services by magnificent presents.

The best wishes of their large circle of friends and acquaintances will follow them.

Alcona County Review, December 2, 1887

Yockey, Fred H.
Boddy, Rachael

LOCAL JOTTINGS.

Married: On the 27th inst., at the Nevins' House, by the Rev. T. B. Leith, Fred H. Yockey and Rachael Boddy, both of Oscoda.

Alcona County Review, October 2, 1885

Young, Ernest
Kirkendall, Myrtle [Monroe]

PERSONAL.

Mr. Ernest Young and Miss Myrtle Kirkendall, two popular young people of Greenbush, were united in marriage yesterday afternoon at the residence of W. H. Sanborn by Matthew Hale, Esq. This was the latter's first wedding.

Alcona County Review, December 22, 1898

Young, William
LaFlambois, Louisa

Young—LaFlambois.

Last Thursday evening at the Baptist chapel there occurred a ceremony which gave to the Benedicts one of Harrisville's popular young men, when Mr. Wm. Young and Miss Louisa La Flambois were united in marriage.

The groom is a native born citizen of Harrisville and has a host of

friends who will join with the Review in wishing the young couple life-long happiness in their married life. The bride's home is in Alpena, where she enjoys the friendship and esteem of a wide circle.

Mr. and Mrs. Young are at home with the groom's parents, Mr. and Mrs. Geo. W. Young.

Alcona County Review, October 13, 1898

Zorn, A. William
Ashley, Anna

PERSONAL MENTION.

A copy of the Cheboygan Tribune of June 7th has been received at this office with the following paragraph marked:

A. William Zorn, assistant post master, and Miss Anna Ashley were married Tuesday morning by Rev. K. J. Whalen, of St. Mary's church, and immediately settled down to housekeeping in a cozy home, 122 Huron street, furnished ready for the occasion by Mr. Zorn prior to the marriage. The happy couple have hosts of friends in our city who will join with the Tribune in wishing them a long, happy and prosperous life.

Alcona County Review, June 14, 1894

?, {Groom}
?, {Bride}

Black River.
General News.

Mrs. A. W. Ranney will spend ten days visiting friends at Howell, Mich., attending her cousin's wedding. Miss Ranney, sister of A. W. of Rochester, N. Y., will accompany Mrs. Ranney.

Alcona County Review, September 15, 1892

?, {Groom}
Clayton, {Bride}

HAYNES.

Miss Redhouse has a ten days vacation from her school to act as bridesmaid at the marriage of her friend, Miss Clayton.

Alcona County Review, May 25, 1899

?, {Groom}
Collins, Lulu

CALEDONIA.

Miss Mary Ford has gone to Alpena to attend the wedding of her friend, Miss Lulu Collins, which takes place Tuesday evening, Oct. 4th.

Alcona County Review, October 6, 1898

?, {Groom}
Madden, Edna

People We Hear About.

Reports from Skamokawa, Wash., are to the effect that Miss Edna Madden, formerly of Harrisville, is married. Further particulars not learned.

Alcona County Review, September 5, 1890

?, {Groom}
Morgan, Millie

A Greenbush Grist.

Miss Millie Morgan, formerly of Greenbush, was married to a gentleman in Detroit on Thursday last.

Alcona County Review, October 18, 1894

Divorce Notices

from the

Alcona County Review

Allan, George
Allan, Mary [Lemon]

STATE OF MICHIGAN--Judicial circuit in Chancery. Suit pending in circuit court for the county of Alcona in Chancery, at Harrisville on the 25th day of February, 1897.

Mary Allen, Complainant,

vs.

George Allen, Defendant.

In this cause it appearing from affidavit now on file that George Allen, defendant has been a resident of the state of Michigan for the past eight years, until on or about November 10, 1896, and that on or about November 10, 1896, said defendant left his residence in this state and has not since returned and it's not learned from diligent search and inquiry whether said George Allen is in this state or out of it, and that if he is in this state he is secreted or concealed so that his whereabouts cannot be ascertained, and that process for his appearance has been duly issued but could not be served by reason of his absence from his place of residence and his whereabouts are unknown.

On motion of Fred A. Beede, Complainant's solicitor, it is ordered that George Allen, the Defendant, cause his appearance to be entered herein within five months from the date of this order, and in case of his appearance that he cause an answer to the complainant's bill of complaint, to be filed and a copy thereof to be served on complainant's solicitor within twenty days after service on him of a copy of said bill and notice of this order, and in default thereof said bill be taken as confessed by said defendant; and it is further ordered that within twenty days the said complainant cause a notice of this order to published in the Alcona County Review, a

newspaper printed and published and circulated in said county, and that said publication be continued therein at least once in each week for six [6] weeks in succession or that she [complainant] cause a copy of this order to be personally served on said defendant at least twenty [20] days before the time above prescribed for his appearance.

William H. Simpson,

Circuit Judge.

Fred A. Beede,

Complainant's Solicitor.

George Rutson, Register.

Alcona County Review, March 11, 1897

Circuit Court.

Court convened at 10 o'clock Tuesday morning, Judge Simpson on the bench.

The calendar for the term comprised the following cases:

Elizabeth Lyman vs. Geo. Lyman, Mary Allan vs. Geo. Allan, Fred M. Bowser vs. Maud B. Bowser, Julia Welch vs. Wm. Welch, divorces.

Alcona County Review, February 17, 1898

Circuit Court Round-Up.

Mary Allan vs. Geo. Allan. Decree of absolute divorce.

Alcona County Review, February 24, 1898

Anderson, Walter
Anderson, Mrs. Sylinda

CHANCERY NOTICE.

Sylinda Anderson, Complainant,

vs.

Walter Anderson, Defendant.

STATE OF MICHIGAN:--In the Circuit Court for the County of Alcona, in Chancery.

Upon due proof by affidavit that Walter Anderson, defendant in the above entitled cause pending in this court, resides out of the said State of Michigan and in the State of Washington and on motion of Mortimer D. Snow, solicitor for the

Complainant, it is ordered that said Defendant do appear and answer the Bill of complaint filed in said cause within four months from the date of this order, else the said bill of complaint shall be taken as confessed: And further, that this order be published within twenty days from this date in the Harrisville Review, a newspaper printed in the said County of Alcona, and be published therein once in each week for six weeks in succession; such publication, however, shall not be deemed necessary in case a copy of this order be served on the said Defendant, personally, at least twenty days before the time herein prescribed for his appearance.

Dated this 27th day of August, A. D. 1891,

WILLIAM H. SIMPSON, Circuit Judge.

Mortimer D. Snow, Solicitor for Complain't.

Alcona County Review, September 10, 1891

For Court and Jury to Decide.

Sylinda Anderson vs. Walter Anderson, divorce.

Alcona County Review, December 31, 1891

Somewhat Personal.

The divorce case of Mrs. Walter Anderson vs. Walter Anderson is in progress as we go to press. At its conclusion court will adjourn.

Alcona County Review, January 7, 1892

Bond, Josh
Bond, {Female}

Josh Bond was granted a divorce from his unfaithful wife last week. The woman has for a long time been and still is living with another man in Sanilac county.

Alcona County Review, December 27, 1894

Bond, William, Jr.

Bond, Mrs. Eliza

Order of Publication.

The Circuit Court for the County of Alcona--in Chancery.

William Bond, Junior,

vs.

Eliza Bond.

Suit pending in the circuit court for the county of Alcona, in chancery, at the village of Harrisville in said county, on the 14th day of September, 1885.

It satisfactorily appearing by affidavit on file, that the defendant Eliza Bond, has departed from her last known place of residence and her residence cannot be ascertained, on motion of W. E. Depew complainant's solicitor it is ordered that the said defendant Eliza Bond cause her appearance to be entered herein within five months from the date of this order and in case of her appearance that she cause her answer to complainants bill of complaint to be filed and a copy thereof to be served on said complainants solicitor within twenty days after service on her of a copy of said bill and notice of this order and that in default thereof said bill be taken as confessed by said defendant.

O. H. Smith, Circuit Court Commissioner for the County of Alcona, Mich.

W. E. Depew, Solicitor for Complainant.

Alcona County Review, September 18, 1885

Circuit Court Matters.

William Bond, Jr. vs. Eliza Bond, Divorce, Decree granted.

Alcona County Review, February 5, 1886

Bowser, Fred M.
Bowser, Maud B. [Dixon]

Curtis Items.

Sept. 9, 1895.

I have been informed that Freddy Bowser and wife have parted, having been married about four months. It is a sad affair; they should have weighed each other well in the balance before taking this step and lived in peace the remainder of their lives.

Alcona County Review, September 12, 1895

Notice is hereby given that my wife, Maud Bowser, has left my bed and board, Sept. 7, without cause. I hereby notify and forbid any and all persons from harboring or trusting her on my account.

Fred Bowser.

Curtis, Sept. 9, 1895.

Alcona County Review, September 12, 1895

Circuit Court.

Court convened at 10 o'clock Tuesday morning, Judge Simpson on the bench.

The calendar for the term comprised the following cases:

Elizabeth Lyman vs. Geo. Lyman, Mary Allan vs. Geo. Allan, Fred M. Bowser vs. Maud B. Bowser, Julia Welch vs. Wm. Welch, divorces.

Alcona County Review, February 17, 1898

Circuit Court Round-Up.

Fred M. Bowser vs. Maud R. Bowser. Testimony was taken in divorce proceedings but case was not completed.

Alcona County Review, February 24, 1898

Brabant, Richard
Brabant, Mrs. Elizabeth

The Local News.

Richard Brabant asks the circuit court of Alcona county to grant him a divorce from his wife Ella, on the grounds of desertion, cruelty and infidelity. They were married October 6, 1881, at Alpena and have no children.

Alcona County Review, August 20, 1891

To Be Tried Next Week.
CHANCERY.

Richard Brabant vs. Elizabeth Brabant, divorce.

Alcona County Review, November 12, 1891

Budworth, Thomas
Budworth, Mrs. Sarah Ann

Reviewings.

"Thomas Cope" has finally got up on his ear again it would seem. A recent issue of the Detroit Evening News contains the following, which shows that some body else is getting mad too: "Sarah Ann Budworth has instituted proceedings for divorce against Thomas Budworth. The parties were married in England. Budworth has deserted his wife and gone back, and from Liverpool he writes to her that if she does not send him his tools and clothes, and $100 cash, he will return and send her to h-- with a revolver before she has a chance to say her prayers. She dislikes the prospect.

Alcona County Review, August 1, 1879

State of Michigan, in the circuit court for the county of Alcona. In chancery,

Sarah Ann Budworth, complainant,

vs.

Thomas Budworth, defendant.

Upon due proof by affidavit that Thomas Budworth, defendant in the above entitled cause pending in this court, could not be served with process by reason of his absence from or concealment within the state, said process having been issued and returned not found. And on motion of W. A. Weeks, solicitor for complainant, it is ordered that the said defendant do appear and answer the bill of complaint filed in the said cause, within three months from the date of this order, else the said bill of complaint shall be taken as confessed, and further that this order be published within twenty days from this date in the Alcona County Review, a newspaper printed in said county of Alcona, and be published therein once in each week for six weeks in succession; such publication however shall not be necessary in case a copy of this order be served on the said defendant personally, at least twenty days before the time herein prescribed for his appearance.

Dated this Ninth day of November, A. D. 1880.

J. B. Tuttle.

Circuit Judge.

Alcona County Review, November 12, 1880

HOME REVIEWINGS.

The May term of circuit court for Alcona county was short. The court was opened Tuesday morning at 9:30 with Judge Tuttle on the bench, and the only business that came up before the court was the divorce case of Sarah Budworth vs. Thomas Budworth, in which a decree of divorce was granted to Mrs. B. The session lasted only about half an hour.

Alcona County Review, May 6, 1881

Carle, Frederick
Carle, Elizabeth [Clark]

LOCAL JOTTINGS.

Judge Tuttle granted a divorce to Elizabeth Carle from her husband,

Frederick Carle, at the recent term of the circuit court.

Alcona County Review, December 17, 1886

Carson, Amon
Carson, Emma [Eilbert]

CIRCUIT COURT MATTERS.

Court opened Tuesday, Judge Tuttle presiding. Most of the cases were put over to the next term, and but little business was transacted, no jury having been summoned. The following cases were disposed of as noted:

Emma Carson vs. Amond Carson, Divorce. Decree granted.

Alcona County Review, June 4, 1886

Chambers, William
Chambers, Nellie M. [Angell]

Court of Chancery.

THE CASES.

William Chambers vs. Nellie M. Chambers. Plaintiff granted a decree of divorce.

Alcona County Review, October 28, 1897

Crannell, George Edward
Crannell, Ida [Woods]

Oct. 28.

In the Circuit Court for the County of Alcona, in Chancery.

George Edward Crannell, Complainant vs. Ida Woods or Crannell, defendant.

Suit pending in the circuit court for the county of Alcona, in Chancery, at the village of Harrisville, on the 22d day of October, A.D. 1897.

It satisfactorily appearing to this court by affidavit on file that the defendant, Ida Woods or Ida Crannell, is not a resident of this state, but resides in the state of New York. On motion of L. G. Dafoe, complainant's solicitor, it is ordered that the said defendant, Ida Woods or Ida Crannell, cause her appearance to be entered herein within 4 months of the date of this order, and in case of her appearance, that she cause her answer to the complainant's bill of complaint to be filed, and a copy thereof to be served on the complainant's solicitor within twenty days after service on her of a copy of said bill and notice of this order; and that in default thereof said bill be taken as confessed by said non-resident defendant.

And it is further ordered that within twenty days after the date hereof the said complainant cause a notice of this order to be published in the Alcona County Review, a newspaper printed, published and circulated in said county, and that said publication be continued therein at least once in each week for six weeks in succession, or that he cause a copy of this order to be personally served on said non-resident defendant at least twenty days before the above time prescribed for her appearance.

William H. Simpson,
Circuit Judge.
L. G. Dafoe,
Complainant's Solicitor.

Alcona County Review, November 4, 1897

Circuit Court.

Decree of divorce was granted Geo. Crannell from Ida Crannell.

Alcona County Review, February 17, 1898

Davison, William
Davison, Mrs.

Mrs. Wm. Davison, the divorced wife of Wm. Davison, both of whom are well known former residents of Harrisville, died at Bay City last Sunday.

Alcona County Review, March 9, 1888

Deacon, Washington H.
Deacon, Mrs. Mary E.

STATE OF MICHIGAN: In the Circuit Court for the County of Alcona, in Chancery.

Mary E. Deacon, Complainant, vs. Washington H. Deacon, Defendant.

It satisfactorily appearing to the Court from the affidavit of Mary E. Deacon on file herein that the above named defendant, Washington H. Deacon, does not reside in the State of Michigan,

It is hereby ordered that the said Washington H. Deacon cause his appearance to be entered in this cause in four months from the date hereof, and that this order be published, as the statute requires, in the Alcona County Review.

Harrisville, March 8th, 1894.
WILLIAM H. SIMPSON,
Circuit Judge.
Charles R. Henry, Solicitor for Complainant.

Alcona County Review, May 3, 1894

In the Court Room.

Mary Deacon was granted a divorce from Washington Deacon yesterday.

Alcona County Review, October 18, 1894

Deklyne, William P.
Deklyne, Mrs. Ella

Ella DeKlyne of West Bay City has begun proceedings to secure a divorce from her husband, Wm. P. DeKlyne, alleging extreme cruelty. The DeKlynes were residents of Harrisville about six years ago. They were married in 1878 and have several children.

Alcona County Review, February 28, 1895

EVENTS OF ONE WEEK.

Ella Deklyne was granted a divorce from Wm. P. Deklyne a few days ago in the Bay county circuit court on the ground of cruelty. Mrs. Deklyne was given the custody of their youngest child but nothing was said as to the disposition of the oldest children.

Alcona County Review, August 22, 1895

DeRosier, Louis
DeRosier, Mrs. Mary

Court of Chancery.
THE CASES.

Louis De Rosier vs. Mary De Rosier. Decree of divorce granted.

Alcona County Review, October 28, 1897

di Cenda, Emil R.
di Cenda, Mrs. Emma

HOME REVIEWINGS.

On Tuesday, decrees of divorce were granted by the Circuit Court, Emma di Cenda from Emil R. di Cenda, on ground of failure to support; also to Sarah A. Lyon from McCormick Lyon, for extreme cruelty and failure to support. Taft & Smith were the attorneys for the applicant.—*Pontiac Gazette*, June 10, 1881.

Sarah A. Lyon, above referred to, is now a resident of Harrisville, this county.—Ed. Review.

Alcona County Review, June 24, 1881

Dingwell, William
Dingwell, Mrs. Mary

Mary Dingwell was granted a divorce from William Dingwell on the ground of desertion and non-support.

Alcona County Review, November 19, 1896

Fitz, William

Fitz, Mrs. Lena

The Calendar for May.

Chancery, 1st Class.
Lena Fitz vs. Wm. Fitz, divorce.

Alcona County Review, May 10, 1894

Fitzmaurice, William B.
Fitzmaurice, Tillie [O'Neal]

CIRCUIT COURT.

A divorce was granted to Mrs. W. B. Fitzmaurice from her husband on the grounds of habitual drunkenness and non-support.

Alcona County Review, October 25, 1894

Fraser, Donald
Fraser, Ellen [Ritchie]

Took the Children.
Donald Fraser Abducts His Two Children From Haynes.

Donald Fraser, a former resident of Haynes township, returned to Munising a few days ago, concluding his first visit to Haynes in about five years. He was accompanied by his two daughters, Esther, aged 12, and Clementine, aged 8. Fraser and his wife have been separated several years and the latter now has a divorce suit pending.

On the day of the abduction Mrs. Fraser and Fred Landon, who has a lease of the Fraser farm, were in Harrisville. Mr. Fraser saw them in town and hiring a rig at La Boueff's he drove to Haynes and securing the two children brought them to Harrisville, and after buying them shoes and other articles he left with them for the upper peninsula.

Mrs. Fraser is much exercised over the abduction of her children. Her husband has done nothing for their support for several years. The neighbors give Mrs. Fraser credit for having given them excellent care.

Alcona County Review, September 22, 1898

Adjourned Term of Circuit Court.
CHANCERY.
Ellen Fraser vs. Donald Fraser, Divorce.

Alcona County Review, December 15, 1898

Pretty Tame Term of Court

Ellen Fraser of Haynes was granted a divorce from Donald Fraser, on the ground of desertion and non-support. No answer was made to her bill.

Alcona County Review, December 22, 1898

Gardiner, William C.
Gardiner, Mrs. Christina

Circuit Court.
The May term of Circuit Court for Alcona county was commenced at the Court House in Harrisville Wednesday morning, and up to the time of going to press Friday noon the following cases have been disposed of. Judge Tuttle presiding:

William C. Gardiner vs. Christina Gardiner, divorce; decree granted.

Alcona County Review, May 5, 1882

Gullifer, Freeman O.
Gullifer, Harriett [Hill]

The family troubles of Freeman O. Gullifer, now of Detroit, have reached the courts and the newspapers. A divorce suit is pending. On Sept. 17, 1895, an injunction was issued restraining him from visiting his house, 81 Park Place, and interfering with his wife's boarders. The injunction has been infringed by Mr. Gullifer and now he is summoned to show cause why he should not be fined for contempt.

Alcona County Review, July 30, 1896

Hawse, Frank
Hawse, Mrs. Agnes Catherine

Mrs. Hawse Takes a Hand.
Another phase of the much complicated Hawse family troubles is a replevin suit instituted by Mrs. Hawse to recover possession of household goods which she claims are her property. The goods were in the possession of her husband but when the officer went to look for them the goods were scattered, some of them being found out on the plains in the possession of a woman named Mrs. Robinson. Monday was return day of the suit but Mrs. Hawse was not ready for trial and an adjournment was taken for one week. O. H. Smith is attorney for Frank Hawse. Mrs. Hawse was without counsel, but it is presumed that L. G. Dafoe will handle the case.

Alcona County Review, June 24, 1897

Witness Wouldn't Testify.
The complaint made by Frank Hawse against Hiram McKenna and Mrs. Frank Hawse for adultery was dismissed by Pros. Attorney Smith, because of the unwillingness of important witnesses--children of Hawse--to testify on the stand to what they had subscribed to in private. The hearing was held Friday before Squire Southgate, L. G. Dafoe of Alpena appearing for the defendants.

Those having some knowledge of the facts say that if the case came to trial and all the facts were drawn out it would open up a very unsavory tale of moral depravity.

Alcona County Review, June 24, 1897

PERSONAL.

Denies the Statement.
Attorney L. G. Dafoe, counsel for the defendants in the Hawse adultery case, enters an emphatic denial of the published statement that the Hawse children refused to testify on the stand what they had subscribed to in private. He says one witness was on the stand when the case was nolle prossed and that she stated under oath that the statements alleged to have been made by her were suggestions of her father and not her own. Mr. Dafoe says he stated to the court before the dismissal of the case that his clients courted the fullest investigation and were ready to stand trial.

Alcona County Review, July 1, 1897

All Suits Off Except Divorce.
The Hawse family troubles which have kept three justices pretty busy for a few days with suits and counter suits, criminations and re-criminations, reached a partial settlement on Tuesday, when the principals and their attorneys, O. H. Smith for Hawse and L. G. Dafoe for Mrs. Hawse, agreed upon a division of the property the possession of which has been in dispute. The title of all the property has been vested in Mrs. Hawse, but it was finally agreed to divide and quit each other and call all suits off. Hawse takes 24 sheep, a yoke of steers, mare, cart and harness, blacksmith tools, sleighs, a farm bell which is an heirloom. The value of the stuff is about $200. Mrs. Hawse retains their farm in Tuscola county, and the rest of the sheep and truck located in Hawse township. Chas. Mayo, coroner, will act as official go-between and will see that Hawse gets his share as above agreed. A divorce suit instituted by

Mrs. Hawse is not included in those discontinued.

Alcona County Review, July 1, 1897

PERSONAL.

Hon. L. G. Dafoe of Alpena gave up several days of his time this week to the Hawse cases as attorney for Mrs. Hawse.

Alcona County Review, July 1, 1897

The following paragraph was written for our last issue, but failed to get in:

Alfred Williams, husband of the woman, whose fair name was alleged to have been slandered by Mrs. Burcham, is a brother of Mrs. Hawse. He denies that the slander case was an outgrowth of the Hawse family troubles, and says further that Mrs. Burcham was not a principal witness on any of those cases, although if the adultery case against Mrs. Hawse and McKenna had come to trial she would have been a witness for the people.

Alcona County Review, July 15, 1897

PERSONAL.

Hawse is Suspicious.

Frank Hawse came in Monday and offered the information that his wife took her departure on a boat last Thursday for the south, and that Hiram McKenna took the same boat at Oscoda. The couple were accused of adultery recently by Hawse and were arrested, but the complaint was dismissed.

Alcona County Review, July 15, 1897

Hawses at it Again.

McKenna Arrested for Assault. Mrs. Hawse Gets a Horse on Hubby.

Frank Hawes has had Hiram McKenna arrested on a charge of assault and battery upon his oldest daughter. From the story told by the girl there are some features of the case preceding the alleged assault that are more serious even than the assault and battery, the girl charging him with indecent exposure, but the circumstances were such that it could not be reached under the statute.

The examination of McKenna is set for today before Squire Hale. L. G. Dafoe will defend him.

A few days ago Hawse drove into town with the horse and cart which had been turned over to him as a part of the terms of the settlement with Mrs. Hawse. The latter happened in town the same day. The two met in the rear of the court house and a war of words ensued. A crowd was soon attracted. The dispute became so noisy that Under Sheriff Balch was summoned to abate the nuisance.

Hawse then went into the court house leaving his wife behind and his horse and cart hitched in the county's $2,500 shed. Mrs. Hawse thereupon took possession of the outfit and drove for home as fast as the horse could go. Hawse was outwitted and had no horse to follow his fleeing wife; but he invoked the aid of the law and started a suit in replevin. Mrs. Hawse manifested no disposition to hold the horse and cart, and as soon as service was made upon her she gave up the fight and the outfit.

Mrs. Burcham sued Mrs. Hawse for $7.12 alleged to be due her for wages. The case was tried yesterday before Squire Hale. O. H. Smith was plaintiff's attorney; L. G. Dafoe for defendant. The case took up nearly an entire day and was not given to the jury until a late hour last night. The jury aimed apparently to split the difference between the litigants and gave plaintiff a verdict for $3.62.

Alcona County Review, July 22, 1897

Court of Chancery.

THE CASES.

Agnes Catherine Hawse vs. Frank Hawse. Decree of divorce granted.

Alcona County Review, October 28, 1897

Again in Limelight

Hiram McKinney of Hawes Township Fame Again in Court.

Review readers will remember the scandalous doings in Hawes township several years ago when the domestic troubles of Frank Hawes and family occupied the attention of the courts and also of the so-called "White Caps" of that locality. It will be remembered that Mrs. Hawes secured a divorce from her husband and later married Hiram McKinney, the man who had been involved to

some extent in the troubles above mentioned.

A sequel to that disgraceful affair is mentioned in the following clipping taken from the Alpena Evening News:

"The examination of Hiram McKinney, who is charged with criminal assault on the person of his 12-year-old step daughter. Ethel Hawes, on the night of Oct. 28, was taken up before Justice Malcomson this morning and a 2:30 o'clock this afternoon the complaining witness, Mrs. Alice Harrigan, was still on the stand. A physician's testimony was taken at the opening of the afternoon session."

McKinney was bound over and will have to stand trial in the circuit court. Bail was fixed at $1,000 and the defendant was remanded to the county jail in default of bail. The father of the girl, Frank Hawes, has appeared on the scene and it is said will interest himself in the prosecution of McKinney.

Alcona County Review, November 23, 1905

Hiram McKenna, charged with attempted assault on the person of his step-daughter, Ethel Hawes, was tried in Alpena county last week and found not guilty.

Alcona County Review, December 14, 1905

Hazen, Charles
Hazen, Mrs. Mary

Circuit Court.

The May term of Circuit Court for Alcona county was commenced at the Court House in Harrisville Wednesday morning, and up to the time of going to press Friday noon the following cases have been disposed of. Judge Tuttle presiding:

Mary Hazen vs. Charles Hazen, divorce; decree granted.

Alcona County Review, May 5, 1882

Heumann, Fred G.
Heumann, Mrs. Fred G.

LOCAL PARAGRAPHS.

From The Press, Oscoda.

Mrs. F. G. Heumann has recently been granted a divorce from her husband. The divorce was obtained at Alpena, where Mrs. Heumann has been living for some time back with her parents, and carries with it a considerable sum for alimony, also an allowance for the maintenance of the children. Mrs. Heumann is said to have made an engagement to travel with a theatre company as pianist.

Alcona County Review, November 22, 1894

From the Monitor.

The domestic troubles of Fred Heumann are at an end perchance. They have been many and were ended by Mrs. Heumann getting a divorce in the Alpena Circuit Court with alimony and support of children. The question which would suggest itself is, why did not Mr. Heumann secure the divorce which he was a thousand times entitled to if all reports concerning the actions of this wife are true.

Alcona County Review, November 29, 1894

Houghton, Ansel
Houghton, Mrs. Elizabeth

THE FEBRUARY CALENDAR.

The list of cases already noticed for trial at the next general term of Court are as follows:
Chancery—First Class.
Elizabeth Houghton vs. Ansel Houghton: divorce.

Alcona County Review, January 29, 1891

THE LAST COURT NEWS.

The long session of the February term of court was concluded Friday evening last and Judge, lawyers, jurymen and witnesses deserted the village the following day.

A decree was granted in the divorce case of Elizabeth Houghton vs. Ansel Houghton.

Alcona County Review, February 26, 1891

Keating, Michael J.
Keating, Jane [Nestle]

The Local News.

Jane Keating asks for a divorce from Michael Keating on the ground of desertion and non-support. They were married June 21, 1888, but have not lived together since June 5, 1889.

Alcona County Review, August 20, 1891

Latham, Edward
Latham, Mrs. Mary

Circuit Court.

The September term of Circuit Court for Alcona county opened and closed Tuesday, Judge Tuttle presiding. The following cases were disposed of:

Chancery—First Class.

Mary Latham vs. Edward Latham, divorce. Decree granted.

Alcona County Review, October 2, 1885

Lott, Robert L.
Lott, Mrs. Stella B.

CIRCUIT COURT.

Chancery--First Class.

Stella B. Lott vs. Robert L. Lott, divorce. M. J. Connine for plf. Continued.

Alcona County Review, November 19, 1896

Lyman, George A.
Lyman, Elizabeth [Balch]

Notice.—My wife, Mrs. Lizzie Lyman, having left my bed and board without just cause or provocation, I will not pay any bills that she does contract, nor will I pay any hotel bills that she runs.

George A. Lyman.

Mud Lake, Mich., Feb. 4, 1894.

Alcona County Review, February 8, 1894

EVENTS OF ONE WEEK.

Geo. Lyman gives notice that his wife of a month has left his bed and board and that he will not be responsible for any debts of her contracting.

Alcona County Review, February 8, 1894

Circuit Court.

Court convened at 10 o'clock Tuesday morning, Judge Simpson on the bench.

The calendar for the term comprised the following cases: Elizabeth Lyman vs. Geo. Lyman, Mary Allan vs. Geo. Allan, Fred M. Bowser vs. Maud B. Bowser, Julia Welch vs. Wm. Welch, divorces.

Alcona County Review, February 17, 1898

Circuit Court Round-Up.

Elizabeth Lyman vs. Geo. Lyman. Decree for absolute divorce granted.

Alcona County Review, February 24, 1898

Lyon, McCormick
Lyon, Mrs. Sarah A.

HOME REVIEWINGS.

On Tuesday, decrees of divorce were granted by the Circuit Court, Emma di Cenda from Emil R. di Cenda, on ground of failure to support; also to Sarah A. Lyon from McCormick Lyon, for extreme cruelty and failure to support. Taft & Smith were the attorneys for the

applicant.—*Pontiac Gazette*, June 10, 1881.

Sarah A. Lyon, above referred to, is now a resident of Harrisville, this county.—Ed. Review.

Alcona County Review, June 24, 1881

Martin, Frank
Martin, Mrs. Lillian

Short Session.

Lillian Martin was granted a decree of divorce from Frank Martin of Black River.

Alcona County Review, March 2, 1899

McDonald, Albert
McDonald, Josephia [Gibson]

LOCAL JOTTINGS.

An assault and battery case in which Mrs. Albert McDonald and Mrs. O'Conner were respectively complainant and defendant was tried before Justice Reynolds Friday. A jury of six good men were divided in their opinions and the result in consequence was a disagreement of the jury. The parties reside in 28-8. The complainant is at present endeavoring to secure a divorce from her husband in the circuit court, and the assault grew out of an alleged attempt of Mrs. McDonald to steal one of her children, which had been placed under the care of Mrs. O'Conner.

Alcona County Review, June 8, 1888

February Calendar.—The circuit court docket for the February term of the circuit court contains the following cases: 4th class—14. Albert McDonald vs. Josephia McDonald, divorce.

Alcona County Review, February 8, 1889

THE COURT RECORD.

Albert McDonald vs. Josephine McDonald divorce. Decree granted applicant.

Alcona County Review, November 1, 1889

McDonald, Dougal
McDonald, Mrs. Mary

Order of Publication.

The Circuit Court for the County of Alcona--in chancery.

Mary McDonald, Complainant,
vs.
Dougal McDonald, Defendant
Suit pending in the Circuit Court for the county of Alcona in Chancery,

on the 2nd day of September A. D. 1885.

It satisfactorily appearing in the court by affidavit on file, that the defendant Dougal McDonald is not a resident of this state but resides in the state of New York, on motion of W. E. Depew, complainant's solicitor, it is ordered that the said defendant Dougal McDonald cause his appearance to be entered herein within four months from the date of this order, and in case of his appearance, that he cause his answer to the complainant's bill of complaint to be filed, and a copy thereof to be served on said complainant's solicitor within twenty days after service on him of a copy, of said bill and notice of this order and that in default thereof said bill be taken as confessed, by the said non resident defendant.

And it is further ordered that within twenty days after the date hereof the said complainent cause a notice of this order to be published in the Alcona County Review, a newspaper printed, published, and circulated in said county, and that said publication be continued therein at least once in each week for six weeks in succession, or that a copy of this order be personally served on said non resident defendant at least twenty days before the above time prescribed for his appearance.

J. B. Tuttle, Circuit Judge.

W. E. Depew, Complainant's Solicitor.

Alcona County Review, October 9, 1885

McLean, Alexander
McLean, Harriett S. Taft [Witter]

The Circuit Court for the County of Alcona, in Chancery:

Harriet S. McLean
vs.
Alexander McLean

Suit pending in the Circuit Court for the County of Alcona, in Chancery, on the sixth day of January, 1892.

It satisfactorily appearing to this Court by affidavit on file that the Defendant, Alexander McLean, is not a resident of this State, but resides in the State of New Hampshire, on motion of Depew & Rutherford, Complainant's solicitors, it is ordered that the said defendant Alexander McLean, cause his

appearance to be entered herein within four months from the date of this order, and in case of his appearance that he cause his answer to the complainant's bill of complaint to be filed and a copy thereof to be served on said complainant's solicitors, within twenty days after service on him of a copy of said bill and notices of this order, and in default thereof said bill be taken as confessed by the said non resident defendant.

And it is further ordered that within twenty days after the date hereof the said complainant cause a notice of this order to be published in the Alcona County Review, a newspaper printed, published and circulated in said County, and that such publication be continued for six weeks in succession, or that she cause a copy of this order to be personally served on said no- resident defendant, at least twenty days before the above time prescribed for his appearance.

WILLIAM H. SIMPSON, Circuit Judge.

Depew & Rutherford, Complainant's Solicitors.

Alcona County Review, May 7, 1880

Millen, John Alfred
Millen, Olive Mary [Yokom]

Adjourned Term of Circuit Court.

CHANCERY.
Olive Millen vs. John A. Millen, Divorce.

Alcona County Review, December 15, 1898

Pretty Tame Term of Court

A divorce was granted by default to Olive Mary Millen from John Alfred Millen. Mrs. Millen charged her husband with extreme cruelty and if half that was related is true her brief association with him must have been very unhappy.

Her husband did not appear to contest the proceedings or answer the wife's charges and an absolute divorce was granted by default. Millen had retained I. S. Canfield but the latter did not appear for his client.

Alcona County Review, December 22, 1898

Morrison, Hugh R.
Morrison, Mrs. Etta P.

The Circuit Court for the County of Alcona, in chancery; Ettie P. Morrison vs. Hugh R. Morrison.

Suit pending in the Circuit Court for the County of Alcona, in Chancery, at Harrisville on the 29th day of September, A. D. 1890.

It satisfactorily appearing to this Court by affidavit on file, that the defendant, Hugh R. Morrison, is not a resident of this state, but resides in the State of Wisconsin, on Motion of Depew & Rutherford, complainant's solicitors, it is ordered that the said defendant, Hugh R. Morrison cause his appearance to be entered herein, within four months from the date of this order, and in case of his appearance that he cause his answer to the complainant's bill of complaint to be filed, and a copy thereof to be served on said complainant's solicitors, within twenty days service on him of a copy of said Bill, and Notice of this Order; and that in default thereof, said Bill be taken as confessed by said non-resident defendant.

And it is further ordered, that within twenty days after the date hereof, the said complainant cause a Notice of this Order to be published in the Alcona County Review, a newspaper published, printed and circulating in said County, and that such publication be continued therein at least once in each week, for six weeks in succession, or that she cause a copy of this Order to be personally served on said non-resident defendant at least twenty days before the above time prescribed for his appearance.

WILLIAM H. SIMPSON, Circuit Judge.

Depew & Rutherford, Solicitors for Complainant.

Alcona County Review, October 31, 1890

THE FEBRUARY CALENDAR.
The list of cases already noticed for trial at the next general term of court are as follows:

Chancery—First Class.
Etta P. Morrison vs. Hugh R. Morrison: divorce.

Alcona County Review, January 29, 1891

IN THE COURT ROOM.
Minor Court News.
A decree was granted in the divorce case of Etta P. Morrison against H. R. Morrison.

Alcona County Review, February 19, 1891

Nevin, James
Nevin, Mary Lambert
[Chambers]

Circuit Court Cullings.

Mrs. Mary Nevin filed an application for divorce from Jas. Nevin, alleging cruel treatment and infidelity.

Alcona County Review, May 24, 1894

The taking of testimony in the divorce suit of Mary Nevin vs. James Nevin was begun and Mart Young and Lizzie Balch were placed on record for such knowledge as they possessed. The case was continued at this point until the next regular term of court, which convenes January 15.

Alcona County Review, December 27, 1894

Proceedings at Court.

Chancery Cases.

Mary Nevin vs. James Nevin. Bill for divorce.

Alcona County Review, January 17, 1895

EVENTS OF ONE WEEK.

Some additional testimony in the divorce case of Mary Nevin vs. James Nevin was taken last week, but the case was not completed and goes over until the May term. The testimony as far as completed has not been as sensational as the public was led to expect, but it nevertheless discloses a rather unhappy state of affairs.

Alcona County Review, January 24, 1895

Mrs. Nevin was granted a divorce at the recent term of court.

Alcona County Review, November 14, 1895

Before Judge and Jury.

The docket for the February term of court comprises…a hearing for alimony--Mary Nevin vs. Jas. Nevin, comprise the matters in chancery.

Alcona County Review, February 13, 1896

THE CIRCUIT COURT.

Briefs.

Mary Nevin was given full possession of all the property of Jas. Nevin as the result of the hearing for alimony. The court gave her the hotel, hotel barn, and all the appurtenances to which dfdt. might have had any right or title.

Alcona County Review, February 27, 1896

EVENTS OF ONE WEEK.

The decree in the Nevin divorce proceedings was placed on record yesterday, and Mrs. Nevin now has full and legal possession of the hotel, barn and all the appurtenances.

Alcona County Review, March 26, 1896

Richter, James
Richter, Mrs. Claudia

The Circuit Court for the County of Alcona, in Chancery:

Claudia Richter, Complainant, vs. James Richter, Defendant.

Suit pending in the Circuit Court for the County of Alcona, in Chancery, on the 20th day of November, A. D. 1894, wherein said Complainant prays for divorce from the bonds of matrimony.

It satisfactorily appearing to me by affidavit on file that the defendant is not a resident of this state, but resides in the city of Portland in the State of Oregon, on motion of R. J. Kelley, Complainant's solicitor, it is ordered that the said defendant, James Richter, cause his appearance to be entered herein within four months from the date of this order, and in case of his appearance that he cause his answer to the complainant's bill of complaint to be filed, and a copy thereof to be served on said complainant's solicitor within twenty days after service on him of a copy of said bill and notice of this order and that in default thereof said bill will be taken as confessed by said non-resident defendant.

And it is further ordered that within twenty days after the date hereof, the said complainant cause a notice of this order to be published in the Alcona County Review, a newspaper printed, published and circulated in said county, and that such publication be continued therein at least once in each week for six weeks in succession, or that she cause a copy of this order to be personally served on said non-defendant at least twenty days before the above time prescribed for his appearance.

O. H. Smith,
Circuit Court Commissioner for Alcona County.
R. J. Kelley, Complainant's Solicitor.

Alcona County Review, December 6, 1894

CIRCUIT COURT.

Mrs. Claudia Richter was granted a decree of divorce from her husband, James Richter, and was given the custody of three small children.

Alcona County Review, May 23, 1895

Seligman, Jacob
Seligman, May E. [Buckland]

MICHIGAN, MY MICHIGAN.

Saginaw: Little Jake Seligman is defendant in a divorce suit. The case has been given a bad turn for Jake by his arrest on a charge of unlawful parentage, the complainant being a young girl named Trombley. Jake says he has already settled the case several times and that it is a case of blackmail.

Alcona County Review, February 2, 1893

Sloan, Malcolm A.
Sloan, Mrs. Esther Jane

Circuit Court.

The May term of the Circuit Court for this county, Hon. Judge Tuttle presiding, opened on Monday morning last and closed Wednesday night. The following cases were disposed of:

Esther Jane Sloan vs. Malcolm A. Sloan--divorce--decree of divorce granted to complainant.

Alcona County Review, May 7, 1880

Smith, Alva J.
Smith, Isabelle E. [Barlow]

THE FEBRUARY CALENDAR.

The list of cases already noticed for trial at the next general term of Court are as follows:

Chancery—First Class.

Bella Smith vs. Alva Smith: divorce.

Alcona County Review, January 29, 1891

IN THE COURT ROOM.

The divorce case of Belle Smith vs. A. J. Smith occupied the evening session and will be concluded this evening.

Alcona County Review, February 12, 1891

IN THE COURT ROOM.

The Smith Divorce Case.

The taking of testimony in the Smith divorce case which occupied the evening sessions of court up to and including Monday evening was racy, sensational and unfit for publication. Miss Belle Barlow aged 16 was married in 1869 to Alva J. Smith, her senior by 13 years. Up to eight years ago the course of true love ran as smoothly as in most families, when dissensions arose that separated husband and wife until the yoke of matrimony became intolerable to both. A fine homestead, 65 acres of which are cleared, located in Mikado township is the result of their joint labors and seven children came in the course of time. Mrs. Smith in her bill alleges extreme cruelty, neglect and non support. Smith filed a cross bill containing a general denial of all these and put in a few of his own. Each charges the other with infidelity. Mrs. Smith commenced an action early in the winter against her husband for non-support; this was settled out of court but was soon followed by the filing of the above bill for divorce. Smith enjoys the reputation among his neighbors and acquaintances of a sober, hardworking and industrious man. Mrs. Smith asks in her bill for a division of the property and the custody of their children. Smith asks that he be given the custody of the four children under 14 years of age. The proofs are all in and the arguments will be made before Judge Simpson at Au Sable at some future date.

Alcona County Review, February 19, 1891

Divorced for Life.
Judge Simpson granted a decree of divorce this week to Belle Smith of Mikado from her husband, Alva J. Smith. The matter has been hanging fire since the February term of court, pending a settlement of the question of alimony. By the terms of the decree Mrs. Smith retains possession of the five minor children until they reach the age of 14. The homestead is reserved to her use for the maintainance of herself and children until further orders of the court. The defendant is restrained from entering upon the premises or in any way disturbing the complainant in the peaceful possession of the farm.

Alcona County Review, May 14, 1891

Court Pickings.
A. J. Smith asked that the decree of divorce granted his former wife,

Belle Smith (now Mrs. A. S. Vincent) of Mikado, be modified. Under the decree Mrs. Smith was given possession of the farm until the youngest son was 14 years old, or until further order of the court. The son is 21 now and Smith wants possession of the farm. The case was heard Monday.

Alcona County Review, October 5, 1911

In the case of Bell Smith (Vincent) vs. Alva J. Smith for a readjustment of alimony, Mrs. Smith (now Vincent) was given six months in which to buy Smith's interest in the property, consisting of a farm in Mikado township, for $500. In case she does not buy Alvah has six months in which to buy Mrs. Smith's interest at $750. In case neither takes advantage of the privilege to buy, the land shall be sold and the proceeds evenly divided.

Alcona County Review, February 8, 1912

Swindlehurst, William
Swindlehurst, Joanna
[Hendrie]

Circuit Court Matters.

William Swinehurst vs. Joanna Swinehurst. Divorce. Decree granted.

Alcona County Review, February 5, 1886

Tibbets, George
Tibbets, Mrs. Adella

Adella Tibbets was granted a divorce from George Tibbets.

Alcona County Review, October 5, 1893

Tinkey, Abram
Tinkey, Mrs. Catherine

Order for publication.
State of Michigan--In the Circuit Court for the County of Alcona--In Chancery.
Catherine Tinkey
vs.   Action pending for divorce
Abraham Tinkey.
Upon due proof by affidavit that Abraham Tinkey defendant in the above entitled cause pending in this court resides out of the said State of Michigan and in Colorado, and on motion of R. Z. Roberts, Solicitor for Complainant, it is ordered that the said defendant do appear and answer the bill of complaint, filed in the said cause within three months from the date of this order, else the said bill of complaint shall be taken as confessed; and further that this order be published, within twenty days

from this date, in the Alcona County Review, a newspaper printed in the said county of Alcona, and be published therein once in each week for six weeks in succession; such publication however shall not be necessary in case a copy of this order be served on the said defendant, personally, at least twenty days before the time herein prescribed for his appearance.
Dated this 22nd day of June A. D. 1881.
J. B. Tuttle, Circuit Judge.

Alcona County Review, July 22, 1881

Circuit Court.
The October term of circuit court for this county, Hon. J. B. Tuttle presiding, opened Tuesday morning, and closed Wednesday afternoon. The cases noticed for trial were few, and consequently a "lengthy" session was not had. The following were disposed of:
Catherine Tinkey vs. Abram Tinkey, divorce. Decree granted.
Catherine Tinkey vs. Abram Tinkey, foreclosure. Judgment for plaintiff.

Alcona County Review, October 28, 1881

Welch, William
Welch, Julia [Paul]

Oct 7-Nov18
State of Michigan. The Circuit court for the county of Alcona. In Chancery.
Julia Welch, complainant,
vs.
John Welch, defendant.
State of Michigan, 23d Judicial Court, in Chancery: Suit pending in the Circuit Court for the County of Alcona, in Chancery, at the village of Harrisville, on the 28th day of Sept., 1897.
It satisfactorily appearing to this Court by affidavit on file, that William Welch, said defendant, is a resident of this state, but is concealed within the same for the purpose of avoiding the service process: on motion of O. H. Smith, complainant's solicitor, it is ordered that the said defendant, William Welch, cause his appearance to be entered herein, within three months from the date of this order, and in case of his appearance, that he cause his answer to the complainant's bill of complaint to be filed and a copy thereof to be served on said complainant's solicitor, within twenty days after a

copy of said bill of complaint and notice of this order, and that in default thereof said bill be taken as confessed by said defendant.

And it is further ordered that within twenty days after the date hereof, the said complainant cause a notice of this order to be published in the Alcona County Review, a newspaper printed and published and circulating in said county and continued therein at least once in each week for six weeks in succession, or that he cause a copy of this order to be personally served on said defendant at least twenty days before the time prescribed for his appearance.

Fred A. Beede,

Circuit Court Commissioner, Alcona County.

O. H. Smith, Complainant's Solicitor.

Alcona County Review, October 7, 1897

Circuit Court.

Court convened at 10 o'clock Tuesday morning, Judge Simpson on the bench.

The calendar for the term comprised the following cases:

Elizabeth Lyman vs. Geo. Lyman, Mary Allan vs. Geo. Allan, Fred M. Bowser vs. Maud B. Bowser, Julia Welch vs. Wm. Welch, divorces.

Alcona County Review, February 17, 1898

Circuit Court Round-Up.

Julia Welch vs. Wm. Welch. Decree for absolute divorce.

Alcona County Review, February 24, 1898

Widman, Christopher
Widman, Mrs. Anna

Circuit Court Matters.

The Circuit Court for the County of Alcona--in Chancery.

Anna Widman, Complainant,

vs.

Christopher Widman, Defendant.

It satisfactorily appearing by affidavit on file, that the defendant Christopher Widman, is not a resident of this state but resides in Alleganey City in the State of Pennsylvania, on motion of W. E. Depew complainant's solicitor it is ordered that the said defendant Christopher Widman cause his appearance to be entered herein within four months from the date of this order and in case of his

appearance that he cause his answer to complainants bill of complaint to be filed and a copy thereof to be served on said complainants solicitor within twenty days after service on him of a copy of said bill and notice of this order and that in default thereof said bill be taken as confessed by said defendant.]

O. H. Smith, Circuit Court Commissioner for the County of Alcona, Mich.

W. E. Depew, Solicitor for Complainant.

Alcona County Review, September 18, 1885

Order of Publication.

Anna Widman vs. Christopher Widman. Divorce. Decree granted.

Alcona County Review, February 5, 1886

Williams, Albert R.
Williams, Mrs. Adell

Circuit Court Matters.

Adell Williams vs. Albert R. Williams. Divorce. Decree granted.

Alcona County Review, February 5, 1886

Bigamy Notices

from the

Alcona County Review

Brown, C. J.
Brown, Mrs.

Our Neighbors.

C. J. Brown a former Au Sable restaurateur has involved himself in complications by having one more wife than the law allows.

Alcona County Review, November 1, 1889

Corbett, Rolland J.
Rice, Jessie
Foster, Minnie
Young, Mrs.

R. J. Corbett Is a Bigamist

A Former Harrisville Girl is Wife No. 2 and Will Prosecute for Bigamy.

San Francisco, Cal., Jan. 24.— Three women call Rolland J. Corbett husband and one at least proposes to see what virtue there is in law to punish bigamists. Mrs. Corbett No. 2, who was formerly Miss Minnie Forster, the daughter of a rich lumberman of Harrisville, Mich., is now a resident of this city. They eloped and were married on June 10 of last year.

Two months later, the young wife says, she learned that she was not the only woman who had married Corbett. In fact, according to her story, he admitted when she discovered his deception and accused him, that he had a wife in Detroit from whom he had never been divorced; that he had when 17 years old eloped with Miss Jessie Rice, of Detroit, she being then 30 years old. He begged wife No. 2 not to leave him and induced her to come to San Francisco with him. She consented and they came here.

Soon after they came to California Corbett eloped with a Mrs. Young.

Mrs. Corbett thereupon wired her relatives in Michigan and they sent her money by telegraph. She says she will go to Detroit and hunt up wife No. 1 and together they will take steps to prosecute Corbett for bigamy.

The foregoing dispatch concerns a former Harrisville girl, Minnie Foster, daughter of Robert Foster— the name "Forster" in the dispatch evidently being a misprint. Mr. Foster says he sent his daughter money a week ago for her return east and expects that she is now on her way home.

Alcona County Review, January 26, 1899

Corbett is Not Captured Yet

The Bigamist is Still at Large, But Officers Are Hot on His Trail.

R. J. Corbett, the bigamist, is still at large, though officers are after him and if the prayers of the women he has wronged are answered his freedom will be of short duration.

Corbett, the Detroit papers state, has quite a history. He was educated originally for the priesthood, but his evil propensities early led him to abandon that calling. At one time he was quite prominent in Detroit politics. Published letters to his first wife and also to Robt. Foster of Harrisville, show the man to be about as deep dyed and slick a villain as ever perpetrated his nefarious practices out of prison.

Mrs. Corbett arrived home Tuesday evening and is staying with her sister, Mrs. Geo. Twite. A great deal of sympathy is expressed for her and it will give satisfaction to this community when it is known that Corbett is where he belongs—behind bars.

Alcona County Review, February 2, 1899

LOCAL PICK UPS.

Born to Mrs. Roland H. Corbet, May 7th, a baby girl.

Alcona County Review, May 11, 1899

Crenshaw, Albert B.
Wilson, Allie Grace

Our Neighbors.

A Tawas city young lady Miss Allie Wilson has caused a sensation by eloping with A. B. Crenshaw, a resident of Cleveland, Ohio.

Alcona County Review, November 1, 1889

A. B. Crenshaw, the man who created a great sensation last year by marrying a Tawas City young lady while he already had a wife, died in the Detroit House of Correction last Saturday of consumption. He was serving a term of one year in that institution for bigamy. His term would have expired Feb. 4, 1891.

Alcona County Review, December 4, 1890

Among Our Exchanges.

Allie Grace Wilson Crenshaw Sabine the young Tawas woman who has figured extensively of late as a matrimonial sensationalist attempted suicide at the National hotel in Au Sable a few days ago, by taking morphine. A doctor restored her to a normal state of health in a very short time. Her latest husband, Wells Sabine, an Au Sable saloon keeper has left her, hence her grief.

Alcona County Review, January 29, 1891

Levette, Alexander
Gillett, Frances [Tompkins]

One Wife Better Than Two.

Less than two short weeks ago Alex Levett procured a license and led to the alter Frances Gillett, both parties hailing from Black River. Now it transpires that there is a Mrs. Levette No. 1, who has not lived with her husband for some time, although they were not separated by any legal process. No. 1 lived in Detroit but she was not long in finding out that Aleck had bestowed his affections upon another lassie; last week she appeared upon the scene and thereby hangs a tale of woe. Levett was arrested for unlawful cohabitation with a second wife, arraigned before Squire Beede, waived examination and was bound over the circuit court for trial in the sum of $300 bail which was furnished by Chas. Conklin and D. C. Emmorey.

Alcona County Review, July 9, 1891

The Local News.

Alex Levette, the gay Black River Lothario whose indignant spouse No. 1 began legal proceedings against him for having more wives that the law allows, is reported to have taken leg bail for parts unknown. His bondsmen are D. C. Emmory and Chas. Conklin, who are secured by notes.

Alcona County Review, July 30, 1891

Will Not Go Away Again Soon.
Alex Levett, the Black River gentleman who was married in June and was arrested early in July on a charge of having more wives than the law usually allows, is with us again. He returned to Black River very unexpectedly last week after a few weeks' sojourn in the Queen's domain. He was placed under arrest by order of his bondsmen and on Monday Deputy Sheriff McGregor brought him to Harrisville where he is now resting as quietly as could be expected behind the bars in the county jail. The old bondsmen felt a little shaky and refused to go his bail again and it is now improbable that he will regain his liberty again before the next term of court.

Alcona County Review, August 20, 1891

To be Tried Next Week.
Criminal Cases.
People vs. Edwin Day, larceny; People vs. David La France, larceny; People vs. Jas. Conklin, assault; People vs. Alexander Levette, unlawful cohabitation.

Alcona County Review, November 12, 1891

CIRCUIT COURT.

A jury was secured last evening in the case of the People vs. Levette, the too much married man. Both his wives are present and both are prepossessing, and both seem imbued with a desire for revenge. Levette's troubles came to a focus June 20th last when he married Francis Gillet at Black River, Mrs. L. No. 1 having previously forsaken him and taken up her residence in Detroit. The latter soon heard of this invasion of her domestic sphere and the result was Levette's arrest on a charge of bigamy which was subsequently altered to the charge of unlawful cohabitation. The trial is still in progress as we go to press.

Alcona County Review, November 19, 1891

CIRCUIT COURT.

The trial of Alex. Levette which was in progress last Thursday as we went to press, was given to the jury that evening after the able counsel had poured whole oceans of eloquence into the attentive ears of the twelve good men. The jury took one hour and twenty minutes to deliberate over the prisoner's fate, finally returning with a verdict of guilty as charged. The defense made a strong fight to debar Mrs. Levette No. 1 from testifying against her husband but Judge Simpson allowed it to go in under an exception. The jury decided Levette's fate on the fourth ballot, the first, which was taken immediately after retiring, standing 5 for conviction and 7 for acquittal. This order was reversed on the next ballot, standing 11 to 1 for conviction on the third and clear for conviction on the next.

Alcona County Review, November 26, 1891

THE LOCAL NEWS.

Alex Levette is alone in his misery at the jail. Some sympathy is felt for the man and it needn't surprise the public if it results in his release on suspended sentence before a great while. The argument is used that no good can come from his further punishment, his confinement in the jail here for three months being punishment enough in the estimation of his friends.

Alcona County Review, December 3, 1891

The Local News.

Alex Levette has been released on bail with Geo. Rutson and Chas. Mayo as sureties in the sum of $300 for his appearance at the next term of court. His attorneys will be prepared to take his case to the Supreme Court in case Judge Simpson does not suspend sentence.

Alcona County Review, December 10, 1891

Levette Is Freed On Suspended Sentence.
At the opening of the court this week Judge Simpson has his attention called to a couple of petitions, one numerously signed from Black River and another from Harrisville praying the suspension of sentence, for the reasons subjoined, on Alex Levette who was convicted at the last term of court of unlawful cohabitation. The court favorably entertained the petitions and suspended sentence accordingly.

1. We think the conviction was on technical grounds.

2. That he unwittingly committed the offence and that on account of his long imprisonment waiting for trial he had been sufficiently punished.

3. That he is not a man of criminal practices but an industrious and steady man.

4. That his family require his parental care and the results of his labor for their support.

Alcona County Review, January 1, 1892

HISTORY OF ONE YEAR.
Chronological History of the Past Year, 1892.
January 5. Circuit court. Sentence suspended on Alex Levette.

Alcona County Review, January 5, 1893

Repkey, Frederick
Repkey, Mrs.
NEIGHBORHOOD NOTES.

Frederick Repkey, of Au Sable, is a too much married man for Michigan, and the cold, clammy hand of the law has therefore taken him into custody.

Alcona County Review, March 15, 1889

Snyder, {Male}
Body, {Female}
Arrested for Bigamy.
Sheriff Dawson of Sanilac county arrived in Alcona county last week and made the arrest of a man named Snyder and a woman named Body, who were living near Mater's farm in the vicinity of West Harrisville. The couple, accompanied by the woman's 10-year-old boy, arrived at Harrisville last fall on the Pilgrim

and at once settled in the neighborhood where they were found. They had eloped from near Marlette, where one had left a wife and family and the other a husband. Those who saw Snyder wondered how any woman could be led astray by him, for his personal attractions were principally conspicuous by their absence.

Alcona County Review, January 31, 1895

Vaughn, Wallace
Vaughn, Mrs. Mary J.

The Au Sable Times publishes a report to the effect that Wallace Vaughn, the Curtis lumberman and farmer, has left the country. The Times gives him a hard reputation, crediting him with five wives, three of whom were living at one time.

Alcona County Review, September 5, 1890

Death Notices

from the

Alcona County Review

Adams, Annie

LOCAL JOTTINGS.

Miss Annie Adams, oldest daughter of Frederick Adams, one of the new farmers of Greenbush township, died last Monday from consumption. She had been sick a long time. She was aged 22 years. Funeral services of the deceased were held at Greenbush on Wednesday, Rev. McIntosh of this village officiating.

Alcona County Review, April 18, 1884
Cemetery: Probably Springport, Alcona Co.

Aird, Mrs. Amanda A.

County Reviewings.

Mrs. H. J. Aird, living about a mile north of Harrisville, died on the morning of April 30th. Consumption was the cause of her death.

Alcona County Review, May 4, 1877
Cemetery: Springport, Alcona Co.

Aird, Hercules J.

REVIEWINGS.

The sad intelligence of the death of H. J. Aird, our townsman, which occurred at Harper Hospital in Detroit, on Tuesday, has been received. "Pete," as he was familiarly known, had long been a resident of our county, and went to Detroit for treatment only a few days since. He was a member of the Royal Templar organization of this place, and by his death his only heir, a boy of 7 years, is entitled to $2,000. The remains of the deceased are expected to arrive here to-day, for interment to-morrow, at 10:30 A. M., funeral services will be held from the M. E. church. The Royal Templars will turn out as an order.

Alcona County Review, January 2, 1880

HONORS TO DEAD HEROES.

A magnificent demonstration of the patriotic spirit of the citizens of Alcona county was the observance on Monday of the time honored custom of decorating the graves and commemorating the deeds of valor of the nation's dead heroes.

The roster of soldiers who are buried here is as follows: Harrisville, (West), A. Marcellus, John Pelton, W. W. Douglass: Catholic, Louis Rivard, Geo. Bernizer: South Harrisville, R. Richmond, Chas. Miller, H. J. Aird, A. Noyes, Jas. Johnson.

Alcona County Review, June 2, 1898
Cemetery: Springport, Alcona Co.

Alcorn, Arthur

May Have Died From a Dog's Bite.

A two years' old child of Stephen Alcorn died last week and the family entertain the opinion that the child died from the effects of a bite from the house dog, which they claim had been poisoned. Dr. Mitchell attended the case. He states that there were symptoms of blood-poisoning and there was the merest scratch on the child's leg which might have been caused by the dog's tooth. The child died after two days of suffering. The funeral was held Sunday afternoon with services at the Baptist church.

Alcona County Review, May 25, 1893

Died From Her Injuries.

The daughter of Harry Alcorn, who was so frightfully burned on June 16th, was relieved by death from her sufferings Sunday afternoon. She suffered untold agony, which was partially relieved by the free use of opiates.

The child was buried Monday afternoon. This is the second death in the same family within a month. Both were accidental, the other, a child of two years, having died from the

effects of blood poisoning caused by the bite of a dog.

Alcona County Review, June 29, 1893
Cemetery:

Alcorn, Elizabeth

DEADLY KEROSENE.
A Girl's Clothing Catches Fire with Serious Results.

Last Friday morning the neighborhood on North Lake street was disturbed by the most piercing screams coming from the direction of the house occupied by Harry Alcorn and family. In a few moments one of the children came rushing from the building and it was seen that her clothing was on fire. As she ran across the street the flames from her burning garments completely enveloped her. Ferd Burnham and others who were near at hand rendered such assistance as they could in extinguishing the flames and they tore the remnants of the burning clothing from the child. She was very seriously burned, especially about the legs and the abdomen and it was thought also that she inhaled some of the flames; but if inflammation does not set in she will recover.

The girl, who is about 13 years of age, was lighting a fire with kerosene which she was pouring from a glass can. The can was broken and a quantity of the oil spilled upon the floor and in some way became ignited. She attempted to extinguish it by throwing water on it but the only effect was to scatter the oil and fire about and some of it splashed upon her clothing with the above fearful results.

Alcona County Review, June 22, 1893

Died From Her Injuries.

The daughter of Harry Alcorn, who was so frightfully burned on June 16th, was relieved by death from her sufferings Sunday afternoon. She suffered untold agony, which was partially relieved by the free use of opiates.

The child was buried Monday afternoon. This is the second death in the same family within a month. Both were accidental, the other, a child of two years, having died from the effects of blood poisoning caused by the bite of a dog.

Alcona County Review, June 29, 1893
Cemetery:

Alger, Allan Sheldon

The Local News.
General R. A. Alger lost his youngest son, Allan, last week Monday. He was 8 years of age.

Alcona County Review, February 19, 1891
Cemetery: Elmwood, Crawford Co.

Alger, {Child}

Affliction in General Alger's Family.
General and Mrs. R. A. Alger's baby died in this village Monday morning.--Another child, a daughter, seven years of age, is seriously ill of congestion of the brain, with probable cerebral hemorage. Dr. Brown, of Detroit, the family's physician, arrived from Detroit in this village Monday night, and Tuesday morning the General and wife, with the little sick daughter, and the doctor returned to Detroit per the tug City of Alpena, accompanied by the remains of the deceased baby which go to Detroit for interment. The balance of the family returned to Detroit Wednesday night. The kind sympathy of our community is extended to the General and family in their sore affliction.

Alcona County Review, August 16, 1878
Cemetery:

Allen, {Child}

LOCAL JOTTINGS.

A young child of Geo. Allen of Haynes was buried in the Harrisville cemetery last Friday.

Alcona County Review, June 14, 1889
Cemetery:

Allen, George S.

LOCAL JOTTINGS

George Allen, a young man well known in Alcona county, died very suddenly last Sunday morning at his home in Alcona township. Relatives in Boston were notified and the burial delayed until their arrival.

Deceased was married but, we are informed, had no children.

Alcona County Review, February 17, 1888

CARD OF THANKS.
To the friends and neighbors who so kindly assisted me in my late great affliction in the death of my husband, I extend to each and all of them my sincere thanks for their kindness in the hour of my greatest sorrow.
                              Louisa Allen.
Alcona, Feb. 13, 1888.

Alcona County Review, February 17, 1888

ALCONA ATOMS.
Alcona, Feb. 15.--George Allen's uncle and aunt came from Buffalo, N. Y., to attend his funeral. His sister and brother-in-law could not attend as they had lost a child themselves and the sister was also sick at the time.

Alcona County Review, February 17, 1888
Cemetery: Probably Mt. Joy, Alcona Co.

Allen, J. E.

COUNTY JOTTINGS.
At Oscoda, Monday afternoon, a young man named J. E. Allen was drowned while attempting to swim from a raft to a tug.

Alcona County Review, July 5, 1878
Cemetery:

Allen, Thomas Theodore

PERSONAL POINTS.

Thomas Theodore, the 13 months' old son of Mr. and Mrs. T. T. Allen of Au Sable, died last Thursday morning of congestion of the brain. The remains were interred in the family lot at the South Harrisville cemetery on Saturday.

The parents and grandparents are deeply grieved over the loss of their precious little one, who was the joy and light and hope of the household.

Alcona County Review, December 22, 1898
Cemetery: Springport, Alcona Co.

Allen, William

HERE AND THERE.
Wm. Allen was killed by rolling logs at Whittemore Monday.

Alcona County Review, February 11, 1892
Cemetery:

Anderson, Charles J.

DROWNED HIMSELF!

CHAS. ANDERSON, TEMPORARILY INSANE, JUMPS INTO HUBBARD LAKE.

He was a Prosperous Farmer But Went Crazy on Religion.

Chas. Anderson, aged 51, one of the leading citizens of Caledonia, committed suicide on Wednesday, the 6th inst., by jumping into Hubbard Lake at 1 o'clock in the morning of that day.

About midnight, Tuesday, he arose from his bed and put on a pair of overalls and started outdoors. His son-in-law was awakened and following, asked where he was going. He answered that he was going to look about the premises and see if everything was all right. No more attention was paid to him until the next morning, when his non-appearance aroused the anxiety of the household, and a search was instituted.

In their search they met two fishermen returning from Hubbard Lake, who were followed by a dog owned by the deceased. They stated they had picked the dog up from the water where they discovered him swimming. After an hour's search the body of Mr. Anderson was discovered floating on the waters of Hubbard Lake.

From tracks in the road leading down to the lake there appeared footprints about five feet apart, showing that the deceased must have made for the lake, a mile distant from his home, on the run, followed by his faithful dog. His hat was found under his arm, also a rope.

Mr. Anderson had of late attended religious services very frequently and became deranged over the subject.

His unnatural condition had been noticeable for two or three years, but friends thought the derangement but temporary.

He would take a bible and commence preaching to an imaginary audience and would remain for hours in his barn in prayer, and all through the day would be mumbling and talking on religious subjects.

Anderson was in Harrisville a short time ago and it was remarked then that he acted a little queer.

Alcona County Review, May 14, 1896

CALEDONIA.

Another Account of Anderson's Death.
The many friends of Chas. Anderson of Hubbard lake were

shocked to hear of his death last Tuesday. He had been in poor health for some time, but nothing serious was thought of it. He got up about 12 o'clock Monday night and dressed and remarked to his wife that he was just going to the barn, but suspecting something, she got up and followed and found he was gone. She woke the family and they searched till morning but were unable to find him. Two men who were fishing on the lake found Anderson's dog on the beach, but thought nothing more of it till the next forenoon when they heard he was missing. After a short search at the lake the body was recovered.

Anderson was an old pioneer, having lived here a number of years. He was a kind neighbor, a loving husband and a conscientious Christian. The funeral was held Friday afternoon and was conducted by Rev. Wang of Alpena and followed by a large number of sorrowing friends and relatives.

Alcona County Review, May 14, 1896

Nov. 11--Dec. 9.
STATE OF MICHIGAN,
County of Alcona.

Notice is hereby given, that by an order of the Probate Court for the County of Alcona, made on the 9th day of November, A.D. 1897, six months from that date were allowed for creditors to present their claims against the estate of Chas. J. Anderson, late of said County, deceased, and that all creditors of said deceased are required to present their claims to said Probate Court, at the Probate office, in the Village of Harrisville, for examination and allowance, on or before the 9th day of May next, and that such claims will be heard before said Court, on the 9th day of January and on the 9th day of May next, at ten o'clock in the forenoon of each of those days.

Dated Nov. 9th, A.D. 1897.
W. H. GILPIN, Judge of Probate.

Alcona County Review, November 18, 1897
Cemetery:

Anderson, Frank Lincoln
THE GRIM REAPER.

The three months-old child of Mr. and Mrs. Wm. H. Anderson died Tuesday morning. The burial occurred yesterday at the south cemetery.

Alcona County Review, January 20, 1898

Cemetery: Springport, Alcona Co.

Anderson, George
EVENTS OF ONE WEEK.

A little son of Wm. H. Anderson, aged 7 years, died Sunday of diphtheria. Others of the children were taken with the disease, but they are recovering.

Alcona County Review, June 29, 1893

EVENTS OF ONE WEEK.

W. H. Anderson, who lost two children from diphtheria, last week burned his house and the greater part of its contents, as the only way to destroy the germs of the terrible disease.

Alcona County Review, July 13, 1893

EVENTS OF ONE WEEK.

Union funeral services were held last Sunday in the Dean school house for the children of the families of Wm. H. Anderson, Jos. Specht and Jas. Ferguson, who died the past summer from diphtheria. The services were largely attended and the Rev. S. Boundy preached a very feeling and impressive sermon, taking as his text St. Matt. xxiv., 44.

Alcona County Review, September 7, 1893

South Harrisville, Oct. 18.
A few improvements of late are noticeable at the S. Harrisville cemetery.

Wm. H. Anderson has a fine monument placed at the head of his children's graves, also Wm. Silversides to the memory of his wife and Mrs. Fowler of Killmaster in memory of her husband.

Each of the three former have their plots raised and graveled. All show forth the love still cherished for those they have committed to their Creator.

Alcona County Review, October 19, 1893
Cemetery: Springport, Alcona Co.

Anderson, Mrs. Laura
Gustin Grist.
Oct. 13, 1896.

Walter Anderson extends sincere thanks to the people in the Fisher district, also the Wilson district, for their kindness in his late bereavement by the death of his wife.

Alcona County Review, October 15, 1896
Cemetery: Springport, Alcona Co.

Anderson, Lottie C. E.
LOCAL JOTTINGS.

A ten-months-old babe of Mr. and Mrs. Lew Anderson of this township was buried on Monday.

Alcona County Review, August 15, 1884
Cemetery: Springport, Alcona Co.

Anderson, Lulu M.
DIPHTHERIA'S HARVEST.
The Dreadful Disease Adds to the Long List of Dead.

Another death from diphtheria occurred in the family of Wm. H. Anderson last week, making the second death from the same disease.

Alcona County Review, July 7, 1893

W. H. Anderson, who lost two children from diphtheria, last week burned his house and the greater part of its contents, as the only way to destroy the germs of the terrible disease.

Alcona County Review, July 13, 1893

EVENTS OF ONE WEEK.

Union funeral services were held last Sunday in the Dean school house for the children of the families of Wm. H. Anderson, Jos. Specht and Jas. Ferguson, who died the past summer from diphtheria. The services were largely attended and the Rev. S. Boundy preached a very feeling and impressive sermon, taking as his text St. Matt. xxiv. 44.

Alcona County Review, September 7, 1893

South Harrisville, Oct. 18.
A few improvements of late are noticeable at the S. Harrisville cemetery.

Wm. H. Anderson has a fine monument placed at the head of his children's graves, also Wm. Silversides to the memory of his wife and Mrs. Fowler of Killmaster in memory of her husband.

Each of the three former have their plots raised and graveled. All show forth the love still cherished for those they have committed to their Creator.

Alcona County Review, October 19, 1893
Cemetery: Springport, Alcona Co.

Anderson, {Male}
Had a Fortune Left Him.

Jas. Anderson, who has for many years past occupied a prominent position in the history of Alcona county as a lumberman and farmer, and who has been entrusted at various times with town and county offices by his fellow citizens, recently received the sad news of his father's sudden demise at his Canadian home on the St. Lawrence River. Mr. Anderson was unable to attend the funeral, but on Wednesday of this week he left for his old home to look after the settlement of his father's estate, which amounts to something like $30,000. Mr. Anderson is the only direct heir, but two farms and some village property valued at $8,000 are left by the provisions of the deceased's will to the children of a dead brother. Mr. Anderson had one other brother who has not been heard from in twenty-five years, and it is presumed that he is dead. Mr. Anderson expects to get in the neighborhood of $20,000, which amount is in cash and interest bearing securities.

Alcona County Review, August 10, 1888

When James Anderson's father died a couple of years ago he left an estate valued at $30,000. The only heirs to this property were the above and a brother whose whereabouts had been a mystery for many years. It was not known whether he was alive or not. By the provisions of the will the estate was to be divided between the two sons, but in case the other brother did not claim his share after a certain length of time James was to get the whole of it. Nothing has been heard of this brother until last week when he surprised Jim by dropping into Harrisville very unexpectedly. Further particulars have not been learned.

Alcona County Review, February 21, 1890
Cemetery:

Anderson, Pearl

Gustin Grist.
Dec. 18, 1895.
Walter Anderson is having considerable sickness in his family.

Alcona County Review, December 19, 1895

Gustin Grist.
Walter Anderson lost a small child Sunday night from paralysis. Funeral yesterday.

Alcona County Review, December 26, 1895
Cemetery:

Anderson, Peter

MIKADO.
Mr. Anderson leaves a wife and eight children to mourn their loss. He had a brother in Oscoda. The family have the sympathy of the community.

Weep not for a father deceased,
Your loss is his infinite gain.

His soul is from prison released
And freed from its bodily chain.

With songs may you follow his flight
And mount with his spirit above.
Escaped to the mansions of light
And lodged in the Eden of love.

Your father the haven hath gained,
Outflying the tempest and wind.
His rest he hath sooner obtained
And left his dear ones behind

Still tossed on a sea of distress.
Hard toiling to make the blest shore,
(Where all is assurance and peace
And sorrow and sin are no more.)

Alcona County Review, July 21, 1898

Local History of One Year

Chronology of the Principal Events of the Year 1898.

July 16. Peter Anderson, aged 54, died at Mikado.

Alcona County Review, January 5, 1899
Cemetery: Probably Pinecrest, Iosco Co.

Anderson, William James

Awful Tragedy!

On the Main Street of Our Village.

W. James Anderson Shot and Instantly Killed.

Tuesday Afternoon While Sitting in His Buggy.

Shooting Done by Mrs. Robert Dobson of Haynes.

Never before has this community been shocked and horrified as it was Tuesday by the shooting and instant death of W. James Anderson.

The shooting occurred about 3 o'clock and was done by Mrs. Robt. Dobson of Haynes township. Mrs. Dobson had accompanied her husband to Harrisville Tuesday morning ostensibly for the purpose of attending the State farmers institute, which was in progress at the Court House. She attended the morning session of the Institute and also went in the afternoon for a short time. At about 3 o'clock she left the court room alone and went directly down the main street, on the north walk. As she was about opposite the Alcona

House, Mr. Anderson came around Cowley's corner in his buggy and drove up to the Huron House horse block, where he stopped for his wife and daughter who were to ride home with him. Mrs. Dobson came on down the street, crossed over and approaching her victim from behind fired four shots at short range at his back. Death was instantaneous. One shot passed through his heart and one just below, a third lodged in the left arm, and the fourth cut through the clothing between the arm and body. The horse turned around and ran down road. Mr. Anderson fell out in the street. He was immediately picked up and placed upon the horse block: efforts were made to revive him but they were of no avail, he evidently having been dead before falling from the buggy.

A number of persons were witnesses of the crime and within a few minutes time a crowd had gathered on the spot. The news soon reached the court house and the institute immediately adjourned.

After the shooting Mrs. Dobson stepped to the south walk and started up street in the direction of McClelland's shoe shop. Sheriff Edwards, who was in Sandorf, Kahn & Co.'s store at the time of the shooting, came out just at this time. Mrs. Anderson heard the shots and came running out of the hotel and was horrified to see her husband lying dead in the street. She realized what had happened and cried out in a wild, incoherent way to Mrs. Dobson as the latter, with the revolver still in her hand, walked up the street. She turned and said, "You watch out," and kept on her way. Others say she flourished the revolver and cried, "Yes, I have shot him and I will shoot you too!" The sheriff crossed over and overtook the woman but a short distance from the scene of the murder. She willingly gave up the revolver, remarking that she had no further use for the weapon. She was immediately taken to the jail.

At six o'clock Coroner Mayo and Ex-Coroner Beede impaneled a jury and took the evidence of C. C. Smith of Black River. Mr. Smith had passed Anderson just before the shooting commenced. He turned at the first shot and saw the woman still firing. Mrs. Dobson was present at the inquest but showed little or no emotion. After the taking of Mr. Smith's testimony the inquest adjourned until Wednesday afternoon at the Anderson residence, where the body was removed. The jury returned a verdict in accordance with the facts in the case. Drs. Ludlum and Wiley probed the wounds and found them to have taken effect as above stated.

Bert Chapelle was crossing the road just in front of the horse just as the shots were fired; Arthur Emerson was also a witness of the whole affair from the windows of the Review office, Nathan Gould was driving by; others were also on the street at the time or immediately after. The whole affair happened so suddenly and unexpectedly that there was no time for interference by anyone.

During an interview with the writer on the evening of the murder Mrs. Dobson was tearful and a trifle nervous, but she expressed no regret for her awful act, nor did she seem to comprehend the heinousness of the crime or its consequences.

She said:

"My motive for shooting Anderson was because he has brought a horrid disgrace upon me and my family. He followed me to Bay City last August, where I went for medical treatment. He made use of an opportunity to drug me; he drugged me several times; while I was in this condition he offered me indignities and insults and caused me to disgrace and dishonor myself and family. Upon my return home I found that scandalous stories were being circulated by the Andersons about me. I and my husband both wrote Anderson and asked him to deny the stories through the paper, to do something, anything to help rid me of the disgrace he had brought upon me. He refused to do anything and only sneered at us. He sneered at me to my husband on the street, I could not stand the shame. I was snubbed on every hand, no one would notice me and I thought I would rather die than stand that sort of thing any longer. This feeling grew on me as the drugs worked out of my system and I resolved that he must either explain away some of the stories, or I would shoot him. This is the first time I have seen Anderson since my return from Bay City."

"Did you come down to-day with that intention."

"Not altogether. I hardly knew what I was going to do but I saw him there and I did it."

"Did any one else know of your intentions in this matter?"

"No, I said nothing to anyone."

"Did you threaten any other members of the Anderson family?"

"No. I had no grudge against them, though they have slandered me greatly."

"You say Mr. Anderson drugged you."

"He did. He gave me water that I know now was drugged; he gave me candy also that looked as if it had been dipped in water and sprinkled with powder of some kind. One time he told me not to take too many at a time. He said he would give anything to influence me against my husband, and while I was under the influence of the drug, I was completely in his power. I had no control over myself."

"Have you any of the drugged candy now?"

"No, I have not."

Mrs. Dobson has always been a highly respected and esteemed lady in her neighborhood. Those who know her best say she is of a retiring and modest disposition, which makes this unfortunate affair all the more to be lamented.

Alcona County Review, January 7, 1897

Mrs. Dobson was arraigned this morning before Justice Beede, charged with murder in the first degree. The examination was adjourned until Wednesday, next at 10 a.m.

A revolver and a box of cartridges were found on Mr. Anderson's person after the shooting. Whether there is any significance in this fact or not is not known.

Alcona County Review, January 7, 1897

W. James Anderson was born at Athens, Leeds county, Ont. in the year 1849. He came to Michigan in 1870, and he was employed at different points along the Huron shore until he came to Alcona county some twenty years ago. He was married to Charlotte Ward May 13, 1876. He leaves a widow and two children who have the sympathy of the community in their affliction.

John Anderson, nephew of the murdered man, came from Athens to attend the funeral.

The funeral services will be held at the Anderson home tomorrow (Friday) morning at 10 o'clock.

Alcona County Review, January 7, 1897

The Examination.

Mrs. Dobson Bound Over to the Circuit Court.

The examination of Mrs. Robert Dobson for the murder of W. James Anderson took place at the court house yesterday. The taking of testimony consumed part of the morning and nearly all the afternoon.

Mrs. Dobson was brought into court and sat with bowed head through all the proceedings, and occasionally bringing her handkerchief to her eyes. She apparently paid little attention to the testimony.

The first witness sworn was Nathan Gould:

"I reside in the Township of Haynes, Alcona County and have been acquainted with Mrs. Dobson 12 or 13 years. I saw her on the morning of January 5 in the Register of Deeds' office, Harrisville, and afterwards on the street between Green's meat market and the Huron House.

"Go on and state what you saw her do."

"I was in my wagon going east, saw Mrs. Dobson coming west, to my right and between me and the sidewalk. She walked up behind Mr. Anderson to within seven feet: he was sitting in his buggy in front of Huron House. Mrs. Dobson threw open her coat, drew a revolver from her pocket and discharged at Anderson's back. Am positive she fired 3 shots perhaps 4. Mr. Anderson was facing west. After second shot horse turned north, Anderson was then quartering to Mrs. Dobson; horse started to run and Anderson fell out in street. I was not close to him after the shooting, saw him at a distance; was driving down street."

The cross-examination was conducted by W. E. Depew:

"It was about one o'clock when I saw Mrs. Dobson in Register's office, did not know that the women's section of the Farmers Institute was held there that morning. Mr. and Mrs. Dobson and others were there. I passed time of day with Mrs. Dobson, She and her husband were whispering together, did not notice her talking with anyone else. They left before I did. Next saw Mrs. Dobson on the street near Huron House. Know nothing of her action between the time I saw her at Register office and when I saw her just before the shooting. I was standing up in my wagon driving along street when I saw Mrs. Dobson; I had just come out of Huron House barn yard, my team was headed west when I hitched up in yard, had crossed the walk and was in the road west of the front of LaBoue's jewelry store and even with Anderson's buggy. She walked about 10 feet after I first saw her before she shot. I noticed nothing peculiar about her conduct only her eyes were fixed intently upon Anderson. She was walking possibly a little faster than an ordinary walking gait. Anderson's horse ran to the east, I saw him fall out: when I looked back Mrs. Dobson was standing near where Anderson fell out on the street and was waving her right arm; could not see the body at that time; a crowd was gathering from all directions. I saw nothing more of her that day."

Bert Chapelle was the next witness called:

"I reside in Harrisville, have been here continuously during this month. On January 5 I was at Huron House. I saw the shooting on that day. I was crossing the street from the Huron House barn to the hotel. I had just helped Mr. Gould hitch up his team and had closed the barn doors; he was behind me when the shooting occurred. I saw Mr. Anderson sitting in his buggy by the horse-block. I saw Mrs. Dobson first about in the center of the road and about twenty feet east of Anderson coming towards him. I at this time was crossing the north walk and going towards Huron House. She walked up and stopped behind Mr. Anderson possibly 2 or 3 feet from him. She raised a revolver and fired four shots, aiming at Anderson. Horse took fright at shots, turned around to north and Anderson was thrown out on north side of road. After the shots I saw Mrs. Dobson in road near Anderson's body. I help pick Mr. Anderson up;

he was alive, lived long enough to be carried to horse-block. I went into hotel and came out again, he gasped twice after that. I saw the wounds: one was through the left shoulder blade, the other about 3 inches below on same side. I saw no other wounds."

Cross examination:

"I am 18 years old. Was employed at the Huron House at time of this shooting. I saw Mr. and Mrs. Dobson going up street toward court house in the morning. Saw nothing more of her until the shooting. I hitched up Gould's team, turned and went into barn; think Gould left yard before I did. I was coming from barn to house when first saw Mrs. Dobson in afternoon; she was in center of street and about 20 feet east of Anderson. She went straight for Anderson's buggy from the point where I first saw her to within 2 or 3 feet and fired. She walked at ordinary pace; when about six feet from him she raised the revolver and walked right up close to him. She was still walking leisurely when she drew the revolver and did not quicken her pace. I saw her face; she looked at me when I was crossing the north walk and the rest of the time at Anderson. I did not hear her say anything; she shot four times very rapidly. I helped pick him up. After the shooting I saw Mrs. Dobson in center of road; she walked up street on south walk; she said. "That man has caused me trouble enough," I think she also told Mrs. Anderson to "Be careful," or something to that effect. The shooting occurred about 3 o'clock p.m."

But two other witnesses were called, Thos. Duggan and Dr. Wiley. Mr. Duggan saw the shooting from the front of the Review office. Dr. Wiley helped pick Anderson up; said he lived from 1 to 2 minutes after that. The doctor had also made an examination of the body; one of the bullets passed through the apex of the heart and was sufficient alone to cause death.

The defense offered no testimony. Mrs. Dobson was bound over without bail, (the statute in such cased not providing for bail) to appear for trial at the next term of the circuit court, Feb. 16.

Mrs. Dobson broke down completely as she was leaving the

court room and sobbed and cried "Oh, my children, my poor children."

Alcona County Review, January 14, 1897

IS SHE INSANE?

Mrs. Dobson Once Had a Brain Disease.

From the Detroit Journal.

Standish, Mich., Jan. 9.--Special.-- Mrs. Robert Dobson, who shot and killed James Anderson, of Harrisville, is well known in this place, being the wife of Robert Dobson, whose parents have resided on a farm near here for years, and whose father died about a year ago. Dobson has two brothers, "Jim" and "Joe" who are prominent young men of the county. Mrs. Dobson has been ill for some time with an affliction of the head, and many think here she was insane at the time the crime was committed.

Alcona County Review, January 14, 1897

A Large Funeral.

The funeral services of the late W. J. Anderson were held at the Presbyterian church last Friday morning.

The shocking death of Mr. Anderson had aroused the sympathy of the friends, neighbors and acquaintances of the family in every section of the county where the news had spread, and a vast concourse of people came to pay their last respects to the dead and to thus express their sympathy for the bereaved family. Fully a quarter of the people were obliged to remain outside the church.

The funeral sermon was delivered by the Rev. Tompkins, who took his text from Eccl. 14:7; "In the day of prosperity be joyful, but in the day of adversity consider." The reverend gentleman's remarks were earnest and impressive and were well fitted for the solemn occasion.

The remains were interred in the west cemetery.

Alcona County Review, January 14, 1897

Card of Thanks.

We desire to publicly thank our friends and neighbors who willingly aided us in so many ways during our recent bereavement: and who by their sympathy and consoling words, have helped us in a great measure to submissively bow to the will of an all wise God in taking from us our beloved husband and father.

Mrs. W. Jas. Anderson and Family.

Alcona County Review, January 14, 1897

The Circuit Court.

The Calendar Pretty Well Cleaned Up. Dobson Murder Trial Now In Progress.

The most important case of the February term of court, which convened at the court house at 10 o'clock Tuesday morning, is without question the Dobson murder trial. The interest in this trial is great and the court room has been packed to the doors since the case was called.

The freshness of the details of this tragedy in the public mind makes it superfluous to reprint them at this time, and we herewith give a bare statement of the facts connected with the shooting:

On the afternoon of January 5th last, as W. Jas. Anderson was sitting in his buggy on the main street of this village, he was shot three times from behind by Mrs. Dobson. Death resulted almost instantly.

The above facts are indisputable as proven by the testimony given at the examination by witnesses who saw the shooting. In view of this the curiosity of the public is excited and there is much speculation as to what the nature of the defense will be. Prosecuting attorney Smith is assisted by C. R. Henry, and the defense will be conducted by W. E. Depew and Judge Kelly. With these giants arrayed against each other a legal battle of rare interest may be looked for, and it is needless to say that every inch of the ground will be bitterly contested.

The general impression prevails that the defense will endeavor to convince the jury that at the time of the shooting Mrs. Dobson was temporarily insane; that for some time past the defendant has been afflicted with a trouble of the head; and that this trouble together with worrying over the stories circulating regarding herself and Anderson, had served to unbalance defendant's mind--and she was therefore not responsible for her act.

The above is regarded generally as the only avenue of escape for the accused and many are of the opinion that a strong defense can be raised on these grounds. The Bay City physician who treated Mrs. Dobson has been summoned by the defense to appear in court.

Mrs. Dobson was arraigned Tuesday morning, and upon her refusal to plead, a plea of not guilty was entered. The impanelling of a jury was begun but the regular panel was soon exhausted and a special panel of 75 jurors was ordered summoned. Pending the return of the summons further consideration of the case was postponed.

The other business of the court was disposed of by 10:30 Wednesday and a recess taken till one o'clock, when the impanelling of the jury was recommenced. The examining of jurors consumed all of the afternoon and up to 10 o'clock this morning, when a recess was taken to await the arrival of officers with more jurors. It is not improbable that a jury can not be obtained in this county and a change of venue may be taken.

Alcona County Review, February 18, 1897

To the Jury!

Mrs. Dobson's Fate Is Now In Their Hands.

Diversity of Opinion as to the Result of Their Deliberations.

The Dobson murder case will be given to the jury to day, and within a short time Bertha Dobson will know her fate.

Whether or not a verdict of guilty is returned the fact remains that the sympathies of by far the majority of this community are with the defendant. While they do not attempt to excuse her awful act of taking a human life, still the evidence shows that the provocations were great and it seems as if the hand of Providence can be traced throughout all this miserable affair.

From the evidence offered at the trial there was not one thing brought out that went to show that Mrs. Dobson was not as pure and chaste as any other woman from her childhood up to the time of the Bay City affair.

The Trial.

Mrs. Dobson was arraigned last week Tuesday at the opening of court. W. E. Depew and R. J. Kelley, attorneys for the defendant were present and Prosecuting attorney Smith and C. R. Henry appeared for the People.

The regular panel, a special panel of 75 and nearly the whole of a second special of 75 were exhausted before the attorneys were satisfied that they had twelve men who were qualified to sit in judgment upon the case. It was three o'clock Saturday afternoon when the jury was finally completed as follows, viz: Hector McKinnon, William Wilson, Joseph H. Grantham, Richard Case, Thomas Burton, Fred Denler, Stephen Hawkins, Peter Carleson, Joseph Herr, Hiram McKenna, Peter Anderson. Before the jury were sworn the defense challenged the array, presenting their reasons, but was over ruled by the court.

The taking of testimony was at once begun. One witness, C. C. Smith of Black River, was examined, when court adjourned to Tuesday of the present week, Monday being a legal holiday.

Mr. Smith was an eye witness of the shooting; he helped pick Mr. Anderson up afterwards and he testified to that effect.

Tuesday morning there was nothing to delay and the trial was begun in earnest.

The mother and two children of Mrs. Dobson were present in court and occupied a seat within the bar. It was the first meeting of the mother and her children since the former's arrest and many eyes dimmed as they witnessed the scene. Mrs. Dobson, who had retained a degree of composure up to this time, broke down completely and sat with her head bowed during the remainder of the day.

A large amount of evidence was submitted to prove that Mrs. Dobson did the shooting.

Bert Chapelle was called and gave his testimony in a straight forward way. He had seen Mrs. Dobson cross the street, walk up behind Anderson and fire a revolver. This story was corroborated in the main by a number of witnesses whose testimony varied only so much as might be natural considering that they viewed the tragedy from different parts of the street.

Sheriff Edward produced the revolver with which the shooting was done, just as it was when handed to him by defendant on the day of the shooting. It was a 32-caliber, self-action pattern, and 4 empty shells were found in the chambers. Defendant had told the sheriff that she had borrowed the revolver to shoot a dog.

D. McGregor testified to selling Mrs. Dobson about ten days before the shooting a revolver like the one exhibited in court. She stated at the time that she wanted to kill a dog. She inquired the price and said she did not have the money to spare that day. Got some cartridges also and wanted to know if she killed the dog and returned the revolver in two or three weeks would he take it back and only charge her for the cartridges.

Mrs. Kate Fleming of Haynes testified that she visited Mrs. Dobson a week or two before Christmas, and they had talked over the scandal regarding Mrs. Dobson and Anderson. That Mrs. Dobson told her at that time that Anderson had followed her to Bay City and had drugged and disgraced her. Said she had not seen Anderson since her return, from Bay City, but as sure as she did she would shoot him. Witness said; "I told her I would not shoot him, but if I was not guilty, I would put him where the gods would not bite him."

At 5 o'clock the prosecution rested their case.

The plan of the defense was outlined by Mr. Depew. He stated they would prove that at the time of the shooting Mrs. Dobson was suffering from emotional insanity. That misled and deceived by the hypocricy of Anderson, she had trusted him implicitly and had thus permitted herself to be placed in a position, while at Bay City for medical treatment, which made it possible for deceased Anderson by the use of drugs to accomplish her downfall and disgrace her forever. That after her return from Bay City she found herself the subject of scandalous stories, that she was practically ostracized and threatened with expulsion from lodges of which she was a member, that Anderson refused to retract, deny, or help her in any way to clear from shame. And that after brooding for weeks upon her troubles she came to Harrisville, with her husband to attend the

Farmers Institute. She attended the women's section of the institute, where she met former acquaintances who refused to recognize her, and unfortunately listened to a very touching discourse upon the subject of "Mothers and Daughters." It seemed as if every word of the lecture was directed at her. With her mind wrought up to a high pitch she left the court room and walked she knew not where, but while in this condition of mind she saw Anderson, the man who had caused all her trouble and shame. The impulse seized her, she had a borrowed revolver in her pocket which she was returning to D. McGregor, and driven on by an uncontrollable impulse she walked up to Anderson and shot him. That they would also prove that Mrs. Dobson's ancestors had been afflicted with insanity.

Matthew Hale testified that he was a juryman at the inquest over Anderson's body. That among other things a 38 caliber revolver and a box of cartridges of same caliber, was taken from one of deceased's pockets.

Mrs. Morton, defendant's mother, testified that Mrs. Dobson is 31 years old, and is the 4th child of a family of 13 children. Witness said, "My grand mother was insane and was kept confined in a room for 8 or 10 years prior to her death, at the age of 70. My father's brother was insane at times and my own brother was insane shortly before he died. As a child Bertha was very nervous and delicate. She could not stand through her classes at school without fainting, for same reason she had to lie down to have her hair combed. She was of a very retiring disposition and at times very melancholy. She has been married 12 years. After her return from Bay City I noticed that she seemed downhearted, and that her eyes were red: she had a wild look at times.

Dr. Fred. D. Heisordt, eye and ear specialist of Bay City, testified that he had treated Mrs. Dobson for eye trouble, that on the occasion of her first visit to his office, in August last he had noticed a peculiar wild expression on her face and had thought at the time she might be deranged mentally. Taking into consideration the evidence he had heard and what he of his own personal knowledge knew, his

opinion is that Mrs. Dobson was insane at the time of the shooting. Emotional insanity may be premeditated, but usually is not.

Dr. Mitchell evidence was to the effect that he had treated Mrs. Dobson for the trouble with her eye and head and had advised her to consult a specialist. Also that Mrs. Dobson was ill and that he was called to attend her in October, and that Mrs. Dobson was delirious for several hours at that time.

Mrs. Dobson was sworn in her own behalf and occupied the witness stand for three hours. She was remarkably composed while on the stand and gave her testimony in a firm voice. In substance it was as follows:

"I became acquainted with the Andersons last May and through our associations in the Eastern Star and L. O. L. lodges we became quite intimate and visited back and forth. During the summer I was troubled considerably with my eye and head and was advised by Drs. Mitchell and Wiley to consult a specialist. I accordingly made arrangements to go to Bay City for this purpose sometime in August. The night before I left for Bay City my husband and I stayed at Andersons, and Mr. and Mrs. Anderson accompanied us to the boat the next morning. Up to this time I had always regarded Mr. Anderson as a Christian and a gentleman for I had no reason to think otherwise. I had often heard him speak in religious meetings and say grace at the table. He had exhorted me and had asked his wife to speak to me on the subject of religion. I went to Bay City. About a week after that Miss Helen Beever called at the house where I was staying in West Bay City and I went with her to have some dental work done. After that at her suggestion we went down to the boat that came from Harrisville, as she thought there might be someone from home. At the dock we saw Anderson; he spoke to use and walked up street with us. He said he was down for the Democrat convention. The next day I had an engagement to go to a picnic in the afternoon. I went to the doctor's office first to be treated; Anderson came there too. We went out on the street and he detained me so I missed the car for the picnic. He said he had some special news from home for me and asked me to go into the public sitting room of a hotel while he told me. We went in and sat down and talked. He brought me a glass of water; I thought it tasted queer but he said it was poor water. The water must have been drugged for I soon became unconscious. When I came to my senses it was night and I was in Anderson's room I did not know what to do. I arose and sat on a chair until daylight when I went to my sister's where I was staying. Anderson left for home a day or two after this and on the dock I asked him not to let this get out and to protect my name from scandal. My husband came down later he having heard some scandals about me. We went home a few days later."

Here the witness' testimony touching upon her treatment by the neighbors and former friends after her return and up to the day of the tragedy was practically the same as stated in the plan of the defense outlined by Mr. Depew.

Mrs. Dobson also stated that from the time of leaving the north walk by La Boueff's jewelry store until the next morning when she heard the grating of a key in her cell door, her mind was a blank and she has no remembrance of anything that transpired during that time.

Cross-examination--"I was never alone with Anderson in a huckleberry patch; I never followed him to the barn or to a pig pen. I borrowed the revolver from Mr. McGregor to shoot a dog which Anderson had given us. I did not shoot the dog and brought the revolver with me that day to return it. My husband did not know I had the revolver. I do not remember of telling Mr. Chapelle about my trip, nor of seeing him at all on the night of the shooting. (A letter was produced which Mrs. Dobson read and disclaimed any knowledge of it. The letter was not offered in evidence.) Mr. Dobson and myself started home at noon on the day of the institute but changed our minds and came back for the afternoon. The scandal never caused any trouble between myself and husband. After taking the water that was drugged it was about 15 minutes before I felt effect of it and later I became unconscious."

William Conklin testified that he let Anderson have a 38 caliber revolver on the day of the shooting, but did not know for what purpose he borrowed it.

Miss Helen Beever testimony corroborated that part of Mrs. Dobson testimony relating to herself (Miss B.).

Here the defense rested and W. L. Chapelle was called to the stand on behalf of the People. He testified to having interviewed Mrs. Dobson on the night of the tragedy in the capacity of a reporter. He stated that he had met Mrs. Dobson once before this time and that she recalled the circumstance. Witness also stated that he had quite a lengthy conversation with her in regard to her motive for shooting Anderson and the causes leading up to it.

Mrs. Wm. Edwards also stated that she had had a talk with Mrs. Dobson in cell the same evening of tragedy about her connection with the Star lodge and her reasons for shooting Anderson.

Mrs. Anderson testified that at camp-meeting last summer Mrs. Dobson and Anderson were together most of the time; that she saw them walking around the edge of the woods. In meeting they sat together and Jim held his hat before their faces while they whispered; Mr. and Mrs. Anderson and Mr. and Mrs. Dobson drove to au Sable last summer to a meeting of the Orangemen; Mrs. Dobson and Mr. Anderson were together a good deal and coming home Mrs. Dobson leaned her head against Jim's back; That the night before Mrs. Dobson went to Bay City she suggested that her husband go home and look after the farm while she stayed all night at Anderson's; but Mrs. Anderson insisted on Dobson staying too. She saw Mrs. Dobson follow Jim to the barn one morning: another time she followed Jim to pig-pen behind the barn.

Jennie Anderson corroborated in part her mother's testimony.

Dr. Godfrey of Alpena was subpoenaed to testify in behalf of the People but his evidence was not admitted.

Dr. J. E. Emerson, of Detroit, a specialist on nervous diseases, was next sworn. He was at one time

assistant at the Kalamazoo insane asylum. His testimony was brief but weighty. His answers to hypothetical questions covering Mrs. Dobson's case were considered very damaging evidence against the defense. Dr. F. P. McCormick of Black River also gave testimony along this line.

At the close of Wednesday evening's session both sides rested.

Thursday morning the arguments of council were begun. Mr. Henry opened the argument for the People and spoke eloquently for an hour and thirty minutes. He was followed by Mr. Depew who spoke for two hours in behalf of the defendant. Judge Kelley consumed nearly two hours in the delivery of a masterly plea; he was followed by Prosecuting Atty. Smith and Mr. Henry again spoke for a short time, closing the arguments at 6 o'clock.

On this day Mrs. Dobson's four children were present in court. She was very much affected on seeing her little girls, and clasped the youngest to her bosom and sobbed brokenly during the whole day. As she was leaving the court house for supper she again broke down crying, "Oh, My God, help me." After supper she was carried into the court room on a couch, but owing to her condition Judge Simpson adjourned court until this (Friday) morning at 9 o'clock.

Mrs. Dobson was able to be at court this morning. Judge Simpson at once began his charge to the jury. He stated to them that if they found defendant guilty, they could bring in either of three verdicts, viz: murder in the first degree, murder in the second degree or manslaughter. It took 40 minutes to deliver the charge, which was considered by the attorneys on both sides to be a very fair one. The jury retired at 10 o'clock.

Alcona County Review, February 25, 1897

PERSONAL.

The Dobson trial has been the all absorbing event this week. Never before in this county has the interest in any case been so great. Every day the court room has been packed almost to suffocation by the crowds of people who were anxious to hear every detail of the case, the ladies being but less numerous in attendance than the men. Many brought their meals with them to the court room in order to reserve their seats. Judge Simpson was good natured and courteous and his platform was crowded by the ladies at every session.

Alcona County Review, February 25, 1897

Not Guilty!

SO SAID THE JURY IN THE DOBSON MURDER TRIAL.

After Deliberating for 8 Hours Upon the various Phases of the Case.

"Not guilty!" Such was the conclusion reached by the twelve men who sat in judgment upon the Dobson murder trial last week. The decision was reached at 6 o'clock Friday night, the jury having been out eight hours.

The first ballot showed six for acquittal and six for conviction as charged; the second ballot stood 7 to 5 in favor of acquittal and the third stood 9 for acquittal and the other three held that she was partially insane and wanted to bring in a verdict of manslaughter. The jury here came out for instructions from the Court, and were informed that if they found the accused insane, then their verdict must be not guilty; an insane person cannot be guilty of any crime. The jury again retired and in a short time returned with a verdict of not guilty.

Before the jury was allowed to announce their verdict, Judge Simpson cautioned the crowd of spectators against making any disturbance or demonstration of any kind. The crowd, however, was not less demonstrative than the accused herself, who sat perfectly motionless while the verdict was announced and the jury discharged. She was supported from the court room by two attendants and left the jail with her husband the same evening.

Thus endeth the most celebrated criminal case ever entered upon the court annals of Alcona county. While many have expressed surprise at the result of the trial, yet we believe that the majority of the community, especially those who heard the evidence, are satisfied with the verdict.

The prosecution presented a very strong case and when the jury retired there were but few of the spectators who did not look for a conviction or at least a disagreement. It was a great victory for Messrs. Depew and Kelley.

Alcona County Review, March 4, 1897

STATE OF MICHIGAN, County of Alcona.

At a session of the Probate Court for said County, held at the Probate office, in the Village of Harrisville, on the eighteenth day of January in the year one thousand eight hundred and ninety-seven.

Present, W. H. Gilpin, Judge of Probate.

In the matter of the estate of William James Anderson, deceased.

On reading and filing the petition duly verified of Jennie Anderson, asking that a certain instrument now on file in this court, purporting to be the last will and testament of said deceased, may be admitted to probate, and that Carl M. Lund and Bernard P. Cowley be appointed executors of said last will and testament.

Thereupon it is ordered, that Saturday, the 27th day of March next, at ten o'clock in the forenoon, be assigned for the hearing of said petition, and that the heirs at law of said deceased and all other persons interested in said estate, are required to appear at a session of the Probate Court, then to be holden at the Probate office, in the Village of Harrisville and show cause, if any there be, why the prayer of the petitioner should not be granted.

And it is further ordered that the petitioner give notice to the heirs at law and persons interested in said estate, of the pendency of said petition, and the hearing thereof, by causing a copy of this order to be published in the Alcona County Review, a newspaper printed and circulating in said county three successive weeks previous to said day of hearing.

W. H. Gilpin,
Judge of Probate.

Alcona County Review, March 4, 1897

State of Michigan, County of Alcona.

Notice is hereby given, that by an order of the Probate Court for the County of Alcona made on the 30th day of January A.D. 1899, six months from that date were allowed for

creditors to present their claims against the estate of William James Anderson, late of said County, deceased, and that all creditors of said deceased are required to present their claims to said Probate Court, at the Probate office, in the Village of Harrisville, for examination and allowance, on or before the 7th day of August next and that such claims will be heard before said Court, on Monday, the 10th day of April and on Monday the seventh day of August next, at ten o'clock in the forenoon of each of those days.

Dated January 31st, A.D. 1899.

W. H. Gilpin,
Judge of Probate.

Alcona County Review, February 9, 1899
Cemetery: West Lawn, Alcona Co.

Anger, {Male}

Your Folks and Our Folks.

S. B. Anger returned last week from Sanilac county where he had been called by the sudden illness and death of his youngest brother.

Alcona County Review, February 26, 1891
Cemetery:

Anger, William C.

West Harrisville.

West Harrisville, Nov. 5th,— William Anger of Mayville, Tuscola county, died suddenly while on his way to visit his brother, S. B. Anger. Mr. Anger started up here to hunt and expected to meet his brother at the depot. The latter was there but Mr. Anger did not see him so he started to walk down the track to his brother's. When he reached the crossing he dropped dead. The jury's verdict was that he died from natural causes beyond the skill of the jury to determine.

Alcona County Review, November 7, 1895

We wish to return our heartfelt thanks to our neighbors and friends for their assistance in our bereavement, the loss of our dear brother.

Mr. and Mrs. S. B. Anger.

Alcona County Review, November 14, 1895

EVENTS OF ONE WEEK.

The remains of the late W. C. Anger, an account of whose sudden death was reported in the last issue of the Review by the West Harrisville correspondent, were removed to his late home at Mayville from whence they were taken to Lakeport in St.

Clair county for burial. His brother S. B. Anger accompanied the remains. Deceased was 66 years of age. He was a member of the M. E. church and a Maccabee in which order he carried insurance to the amount of $1,000.

Alcona County Review, November 14, 1895
Cemetery: Lakeport, St. Clair Co.

Anjajakilski, Valentine

ALONG THE SHORE.

ALPENA.

Yesterday some Polanders were at work felling trees for Mr. Blakely about two miles out of town, just beyond J. A. Case's farm, when one felled a tree which struck the other on the top of his head, crushing his brains out and killing him instantly. The dead man's name was Valentine Anjajakilski. The body was brought to town, and the inquest was held today.

Alcona County Review, January 20, 1882
Cemetery:

Argyle, Emelia Charlotte [White]

SOMEWHAT PERSONAL.

Mrs. Thos. Argyle of near Gustin is dead, having expired yesterday after a short illness of four hours.

Alcona County Review, September 1, 1892
Cemetery:

Arldt, George

Jottings Along the Shore.

George Arldt, whose skull was fractured by Carl Knuphf on the 17 instant, died in the jail at Rogers City at ten o'clock Wednesday morning.

Alcona County Review, May 21, 1880
Cemetery:

Arnold, Mrs. Joseph

LOCAL JOTTINGS.

During a heavy thunder storm at Au Sable last Saturday, a bolt of the electric fluid struck the house of Jos. Arnold, on Smith st., instantly killing Mrs. Arnold. Lightning also struck several other houses in the neighborhood, but beyond slight shocks to the inmates, no one else was injured.

Alcona County Review, July 8, 1887
Cemetery:

Atchen, Maggie

Haynes Happenings.

The remains of a young lady who died at West Harrisville from consumption, were interred in our cemetery on Friday last.

Alcona County Review, June 3, 1897

Haynes Happenings.

The remains of Miss Maggie Atchen were brought from West Harrisville and laid to rest in Mount Joy Cemetery.

Alcona County Review, June 3, 1897
Cemetery: Mt. Joy, Alcona Co.

Atchison, Johnny

COUNTY REVIEWINGS.

Johnny Atchison, a little son of James Atchison, of Oscoda, was drowned in the Au Sable river on Wednesday. Andrew Atchison of this place left on the mail boat yesterday morning to attend his nephew's funeral.

Alcona County Review, August 13, 1880
Cemetery: Pinecrest, Iosco Co.

Atchison, Rebecca [Anderson]

Mrs. Atchison, a daughter of Wm. Anderson, died Monday morning at her home west of this village.

Alcona County Review, April 11, 1890
Cemetery: Springport, Alcona Co.

Aubin, John A.

The remains of a boy named Aubin were brought here Sunday from the River for interment in the Catholic cemetery. The lad met a violent death on the log rollway.

Alcona County Review, March 10, 1898

Black River, March 8, 1898.
We wish to thank our many friends through the columns of your paper for their kindness during our sore bereavement.

Mr. and Mrs. Philip Aubin.

Alcona County Review, March 10, 1898
Cemetery: Probably St. Anne's, Alcona Co.

Avery, E. O.

Personal and Local.

E. O. Avery, the well known Alpena citizen, died Sunday at Detroit.

Alcona County Review, October 12, 1899
Cemetery: Woodmere, Wayne Co.

Axtell, Mrs. Paulina A.

SUICIDE AT HOWELL.

A Former Resident of Harrisville Hangs Herself to a Door Hinge in a Fit of Temporary Insanity.

Howell, Mich., April 12.——Special. Mrs. George Axtell committed suicide today at 12:30 o'clock by hanging herself to a doorhinge in her room at George Clark's residence. Brooding over poor health and financial losses led to temporary insanity. The family always held a high social position. Mr. Axtell has been foreman in the Livingston Republican office for the last four years. The dead woman leaves two children, Jessie, a music teacher in Honolulu, and Ford, a student at Ann Arbor.

_____

Mrs. Axtell was the wife of George W. Axtell, Geo. E. Gillam's predecessor as publisher of the Review. Mr. Axtell and wife resided here eleven months in 1886 and will doubtless be well remembered by many of our citizens.

Alcona County Review, April 15, 1897
Cemetery: Lakeview, Livingston Co.

Backus, Ella May [Anthony]

A Sudden Death.

Mrs. Austin Backus died very suddenly at her home in the township of Gustin Sunday morning, after a brief illness of but a few hours. The lady attended the dance at Agricultural Hall in the village of Harrisville on Thursday evening last. She had but recently recovered from an attack of la grippe. The following day she was taken ill but no serious consequences were anticipated until Sunday morning when it became apparent to her husband that she was very ill. A neighbor was called in and a physician was summoned but she had expired before the latter's arrival. Deceased was the eldest daughter of Mr. and Mrs. Geo. A. Anthony and was not yet 20 years of age. She was united in marriage to Austin Backus in 1892. A little daughter, a child of 7 months, survives. Her sudden death is a sad blow to her parents, her husband and her many friends, as she was held in general esteem.

The remains were brought to the South Harrisville cemetery Tuesday where they were placed at rest in the family lot.

Alcona County Review, March 1, 1894

Affairs at Mud Lake.

Mr. and Mrs. Backus were suddenly called to their home in Killmaster by the death of their daughter-in-law, Mrs. Austin Backus.

Alcona County Review, March 1, 1894
Cemetery: Springport, Alcona Co.

Backus, James Russell

JAMES R. BACKUS

Died of consumption, at his late home in Killmaster on Wednesday, July 28th, aged 49 years. Deceased was born at Malahide, Ontario, in 1849. A widow and two children, Mrs. Austin Backus and Mrs. Wm. Noyes survive to mourn their loss. Interment will take place Friday morning.

Alcona County Review, July 29, 1897
Cemetery: Springport, Alcona Co.

Bailey, William

Oscoda County Mail Items.

A brother of Mr. Clark Bailey of this county died a few days ago in Clare county from the effects of a falling limb. He had a homestead claim near here.

Alcona County Review, April 14, 1882
Cemetery: Maple Grove, Clare Co.

Bailey, Sarah

MIKADO.

Sadie, youngest child of Mr. and Mrs. Bailey, died Friday morning last. They were up town in the evening and the child seemed in usual health; she was taken sick about midnight and lived but a few hours. The funeral took place Saturday afternoon.

Sympathy of many friends is extended in their sad bereavement.

Alcona County Review, July 9, 1896
Cemetery:

Baker, Freddie

ALONG THE SHORE.

ALPENA.

Last Monday little Freddie Baker, aged four years, son of Mrs. Mary Baker, was pulling a little child around on his little sled. When last seen alive he was on the ice walking backwards and pulling the little child. Shortly afterwards the attention of those near by was attracted by the crying of the child. It was close to a water hole where horses are watered, and Freddie was missing. Search was made for the body, but it was not found until the next day.

Alcona County Review, January 20, 1882
Cemetery: Evergreen, Alpena Co.

Baker, Thomas

Thos. Baker, the Mikado citizen who was adjudged insane a few days ago and was sent home pending an opening at the asylum, has been relieved by death from further suffering.

Alcona County Review, September 15, 1898

Local History of One Year

Chronology of the Principal Events of the Year 1898.

September 9. Thos. Baker died at Mikado. Had been judged insane.

Alcona County Review, January 5, 1899
Cemetery:

Balch, Carrie Bell [Mudgett]

LOCAL PICK UPS.

News was received here Monday of the sudden death of Mrs. Geo. Balch in a Detroit hospital.

Alcona County Review, August 4, 1898

Mr. and Mrs. Geo. Wilson have adopted the five year old daughter of Mr. Geo. Balch. The little girl is a very handsome child, and with Mr. and Mrs. Wilson will have a most pleasant home.—Grand Marais Herald.

Alcona County Review, March 23, 1899
Cemetery:

Balch, George

LOCAL JOTTINGS.

The infant daughter [son] of Mr. and Mrs. Geo. Balch, Jr., died Sunday morning.

Alcona County Review, March 30, 1888

Card of Thanks.
We extend our heartfelt thanks to those friends who assisted us during our recent bereavement.
　　　　Mr. and Mrs. Geo. Balch, Jr.

Alcona County Review, March 30, 1888
Cemetery:

Baldwin, Freddie

CURRAN EVENTS.
　　　　　　　Oct. 9. '99.
Another one of Mr. Baldwin's children is dangerously ill.

Alcona County Review, October 12, 1899

CURRAN EVENTS.
　　　　　　　Oct. 16. '99.
After fourteen days of intense suffering little Freddie Baldwin passed away at the age of six years. He was buried Friday in the family plot at their own home.

Alcona County Review, October 19, 1899

Cemetery:

Bamfield, Mrs. Adaline

CURTIS.

Died, March 9th, 1898, Mrs. William Bamfield age 55 years. Mrs. Bamfield has long resided in this place and many will miss her, for her kindness and hospitality were known to all.

Alcona County Review, April 7, 1898

Local History of One Year

Chronology of the Principal Events of the Year 1898.

March 9. Death of Mrs. Wm. Bamfield aged 55, of Curtis.

Alcona County Review, January 5, 1899
Cemetery: Curtisville, Alcona Co.

Barber, Peter

PERSONAL MENTION.

Peter Barber, aged about 20 years, son of Jas. Barber, died yesterday at the residence of his parents after a lingering illness from consumption.

Alcona County Review, May 24, 1894

By request we publish the following concerning the late Peter Barber, beloved son of Mr. and Mrs. James Barber, who died May 23. His illness covered a period of 2 years and 6 months. At the time of his death he was 24 years of age. Prior to his death he expressed a desire that Rev. E. F. Smith of Black River should preach his funeral sermon and that he should be assisted by Rev. W. J. Bailey of Harrisville. He also selected the pall bearers. Early on the morning of his death he called his mother to take the lamp from his room and rollup the curtain that he might see the dawn of another day and the rising of the sun. He admonished his sorrowing parents and sisters and brothers who stood weeping about the bedside, to live Christian lives that he might meet them in Heaven. He bade them all good bye and at 12 o'clock noon, Wednesday, May 23, his spirit left its earthly tabernacle.

Eustache Barber and Mr. and Mrs. J. Nichol of Alpena were among the relatives who attended the funeral services on May 25.

From the depths of our sorrowing hearts we return thanks to our many friends whose services and sympathies during the last illness and death of our dear son were so acceptable.

                    Mr. and Mrs. Jas. Barber.

Alcona County Review, June 14, 1894
Cemetery: Springport, Alcona Co.

Barber, William R.

LOOKS LIKE A FAKE

Edward Barber in Washington Jail, "Confesses" to Murdering His Brother in Alcona Co.

The sheriff of Alpena county last Friday received a telegram from the sheriff of Everett, Wash., stating that Edward Barber was in jail there and had confessed that he had murdered his brother near Black River 15 years ago while the two were going to camp, and threw the body into the lake.

Nothing is known at Alpena or at Harrisville of such a murder and it is generally believed by the officials that the story is not true. There are several families of Barbers both at Alpena and in Alcona county, but none of them know Edward Barber.

Since the foregoing was written, a second telegram has been received in which the confessor states that his father's name is David Barber and that the brother killed was William R. Barber. This throws a little light on the subject. David Barber, a respected Haynes township farmer, has a son named Eustache somewhere in the West, who left here about six years ago. This son joined the navy and served for several years, being discharged at Seattle, since which time the parents have heard little of him. The brother, Wm. R. Barber, whom the man in the west confesses to "murdering," is a respected school teacher of this county. There seems to be no doubt but that the man who made the "confession" is the Eustache here mentioned. What his object is in making such a statement no one knows. It is possible that the young man has got into difficulty with the Washington authorities and has made this "confession" in the belief that he would get a free ride back to Michigan. if such was his intention, he undoubtedly forgot to reckon on the telegraph, or he would not have sent out a story of this kind to bring such unpleasant notoriety to himself and to his relatives.

Alcona County Review, April 26, 1906

Deputy Sheriff Noyes of Alpena, was down Tuesday trying to trace out the "Barber murder mystery." He went home satisfied that there was nothing in the story.

Alcona County Review, April 26. 1906

IS THIS THE BARBER?

Sheriff Peterson has received a letter from the chief of police at Everett, Wash., relative to Edward Barber, who confessed that he murdered his brother near here 15 years ago and threw the body into the lake. The authorities there believe the man's statement.

A few years ago a man by the name of Edward Barber, having no relatives living in this county, made his home in Alpena. He said he served in the American navy during the Cuban war. He always wore a discarded army uniform with brass buttons, a fatigue cap and sported several cheap badges which he displayed with great pride. He was regarded here as slightly demented.

The Everett chief enclosed newspaper clippings and other material in the letter to Sheriff Peterson.—Alpena Echo.

Alcona County Review, May 3. 1906
Cemetery:

Barclay, Mrs. Eliza

LOCAL JOTTINGS.

The remains of Mrs. Eliza Barclay who died at the residence of her son-in-law, Mr. R. Z. Roberts of the Southern Car Works, in West End, Saturday night, have been expressed to Sinnemahoning, Penn., her former home, for interment. Deceased died at the age of 63, of heart disease.—Knoxville, Tenn., *Tribune.*

Mrs. Barclay, the deceased, was well known to many of the people of this place. During the residence of R. Z. Roberts and family here she was often a visitor in Harrisville, spending several months at a time, especially during the summer season. She was a very active Christian lady, and did much while here to further religious interests. She was a good conversationalist, and her society was always pleasant to have at socials and other gatherings of the people. She has hosts of friends in Harrisville whose eyes will not be dry and whose hearts will not fail to well up with sorrow on reading this notice of her death.

Alcona County Review, December 5, 1884
Cemetery: Wyside, Cameron Co., PA

Barkley, Mrs. E. A.

PERSONAL MENTION.

The Drayton (N. D.) Echo of Feb. 10 contains a notice of the death of Mrs. J. K. Fairchild's mother, Mrs. E. A. Barkley, at Grand Rapids, Mich. The lady was known to citizens of Harrisville, where she visited frequently when Mr. Fairchild published the Review.

Alcona County Review, February 23, 1893
Cemetery: Probably Fairplains, Kent Co.

Barley, Mrs. Anna

Mrs. Archie Barley of Black River was buried at Alcona Monday. She died from cancer from which she had suffered for a year or more. She was about 25 years of age and leaves two children besides her husband.

Alcona County Review, April 6, 1893

PERSONAL MENTION.

Mrs. M. Bolster returned Tuesday from Black River where she had been for five weeks previous nursing Mrs. Barley who died last week.

Alcona County Review, April 6, 1893

Haynes, Jan. 23, 1894.
Peter Churchill has caused to be erected a very artistic monument in remembrance of his wife, in our cemetery. Archie Barley has also erected a beautiful monument as a memorial to his wife. Both came from Port Huron.

Alcona County Review, January 25, 1894
Cemetery: Mt. Joy, Alcona Co.

Barlow, Edwin

COUNTY JOTTINGS.

There was no service in the Baptist church last Saturday, the pastor, Rev. F. N. Barlow, having been called to Williamston by the death of a brother.

Alcona County Review, October 29, 1886
Cemetery: Summit, Ingham Co.

Barlow, Mrs. Elizabeth J.

Your Folks and Our Folks.

The Alpena paper report that Mrs. F. N. Barlow suffered a stroke of paralysis Saturday morning and is in a critical condition.

Alcona County Review, April 2, 1891

Passed to Eternal Rest.

Mrs. F. N. Barlow, whose serious illness was briefly noted in these columns last week, passed away at her late home in the city of Alpena last Saturday evening after a brief illness of one week. She was conscious to the last but was unable to speak to those gathered around her bedside. The deceased was a much esteemed woman and during a residence of two years in Harrisville, while her husband was first pastor of the Baptist church, she endeared herself to a large circle of friends who will hear with sorrow that the summons of death came so suddenly upon her. At the time the deceased was stricken Mr. Barlow was prostrated by an attack of la grippe from which he has not yet recovered. He will have the sympathy of this community in his deep affliction.

Alcona County Review, April 9, 1891

Resolution of Respect and Condolence.

At a meeting of the 1st Baptist church of Harrisville held April 10, 1891, the following preamble and resolutions were unanimously adopted by the church. Whereas, the hand of death has removed [the wife of] our former pastor, and so long and intimately associated with us in all church work, therefore

Resolved, that we as a church unite with her many friends, here in this vicinity and elsewhere, in expressing to her bereaved husband and family our tenderest sympathy and heart felt sorrow, in this, their great affliction in the loss of one whose life has been spent in good works, and who so closely identified with all that tended to further her Master's cause on earth.

Resolved, that while we bow in submission to the will of God in removing our sister from the church Militant to the church Triumphant, We feel assured that He who has said "I will never leave thee nor forsake thee" will sustain and strengthen our brother in this trying ordeal.

Resolved, that a copy of these resolutions be sent to our dear brother Barlow, also a copy be sent to the Alcona County Review for publication.

By order, and behalf of the church

Mrs. M. L. Elliott, Ch. Clk.

Alcona County Review, April 16, 1891
Cemetery:

Barrett, Robert

EVENTS OF ONE WEEK.

Robt. Barrett, aged 85 and deaf, was run over by the cars and killed at Alpena last Saturday.

Alcona County Review, August 2, 1894
Cemetery:

Bartley, Alexander

Mrs. Baror has just been apprised of the death of her favorite brother and his wife within three days of each other at St. Clair. Alexander Bartley was his name. He had been an inmate of the Pontiac Asylum for a number of years, but prior to his insanity, which was caused by paralysis, he was a prominent citizen of St. Clair county, having been sheriff of the county at one time. Mrs. Bartley had been an invalid for many years.

Alcona County Review, November 10, 1892
Cemetery: Hillside, St. Clair Co.

Bartley, Mrs. Rose L.

Mrs. Baror has just been apprised of the death of her favorite brother and his wife within three days of each other at St. Clair. Alexander Bartley was his name. He had been an inmate of the Pontiac Asylum for a number of years, but prior to his insanity, which was caused by paralysis, he was a prominent citizen of St. Clair county, having been sheriff of the county at one time. Mrs. Bartley had been an invalid for many years.

Alcona County Review, November 10, 1892
Cemetery: Hillside, St. Clair Co.

Batton, Frederick A.

Curtis

Sickness has attended nearly every house and in some death followed. Death entered the home of J. W. Batton and took their second oldest boy, aged seven years and six months. He had a relapse from scarlet fever, complicated by kidney complaint. They took him to Au Sable for about ten days' treatment when they thought him some better. The fond mother brought him home but he got worse and Dr. Weir was called twice but it proved of no avail. For two weeks he suffered more than human tongue could tell and then passed away. He was buried in the cemetery on Sunday, the 5th. Nearly everyone

that had not sickness attended the funeral. It was sad to see the little angel laid in its mother earth, but God giveth and God taketh away; blessed by the name of the Lord. J. W. Ferguson took charge of the funeral and Rev. Elder Nunn preached the funeral sermon, which was remarked as the best ever preached in this place.

Alcona County Review, March 30, 1893
Cemetery: Glennie, Alcona Co.

Baucus, Frank

Local News.

Frank Baucus is very ill.

Alcona County Review, June 15, 1899

GREENBUSH.

Frank Baucus, son of David Baucus, died Monday at the home of his parents in Greenbush, from consumption. The interment occurred yesterday.

Deceased was a member of the Maccabee fraternity and also of the Union Life Guards, carrying $1000 in each order.

Alcona County Review, October 19, 1899

Mikado Tent K. O. T. M.

The action of the Mikado Tent K. O. T. M. in connection with the case of the late Frank Baucus, a member of the ten, is worthy of special mention and is one of those instances that argue so strongly in favor of beneficiary organizations.

Early in the period of Mr. Baucus' sickness the Tent assumed the payment of his assessments, nurses were provided and no effort was spared to make the last days of their brother Sir Knight as comfortable as possible.

While this may all be within the bounds of duty and brotherhood prescribed by the rules of the order, still one cannot but notice these things and get their opinion of the various orders from just such incidents. As before stated the action of Mikado Tent in this case is especially commendable.

Fifty dollars were paid the deceased, from the disability fund during his illness, and after his death the balance of the $1,000 insurance was paid promptly.

Alcona County Review, December 7, 1899

Resolutions of Condolence

Whereas, under mortality's law, Comrade Frank Baucus was taken from our midst on October the 17th, 1899, therefore it is

Resolved that Hancock Post 29, Union Life Guards, tender to the father, sister and brothers of Comrade Baucus their heartfelt sympathy in the loss sustained. Further it is

Resolved, to bear in mind that Comrade Baucus was ever a Guardsman who attended not only strictly to his own interests as a beneficiary, but also to the interest of others of our fraternity, by frequence of attendance at Post meetings, being always a ready worker and willing help. Further, it is

Resolved, that a copy of these resolutions be sent to the father, sister, and brothers of Comrade Baucus, also that a copy be printed in the Alcona County Review and in the Guardsman and enscribed in full upon the records of Hancock Post 29 Union Life Guards, an entire page being allowed for such inscription. Further it is

Resolved, that the charter of Hancock Post 29, Union Life Guards be draped in mourning for sixty days. Fraternally yours,
　E. Van Horn
　J. F. Coyle　Committee
　J. L. Waters.

Alcona County Review, December 7, 1899
Cemetery: Springport, Alcona Co.

Baxter, Stephen

Local Sayings and Doings.

Stephen Baxter, a former resident and township treasurer of Alcona, died at Detroit, recently. He was one of the pioneer farmers of that township, and had been in failing health for some years past. He went to Detroit to be treated, but it seems medical skill could not help him.

Alcona County Review, December 16, 1881
Cemetery:

Beach, John

Up and Down the Shore.
A terrible and fatal accident occurred at the iron mill of the O. S. & L. Co. about half past eight this morning, resulting in the death of John Beach, who for eleven years had been a valued employee of the company. Mr. Beach was running one of the big circulars and in attempting to remove some bark from in front of the saw with a stick, the stick slipped and he fell, his shoulder and head striking the saw. His shoulder was badly lacerated, and his head split open nearly to the

ears. He was immediately conveyed to his home where in spite of his terrible injuries he continued to breathe nearly an hour. Mr. Beach leaves a wife who is the daughter of Joseph Kirkendall, and two children, a boy of six and a girl nearly two years of age. He was a steady, industrious man, universally respected by his fellow workmen and all who knew him. By strict economy he had bought a little home, and was beginning to get his surroundings in comfortable shape when he was snatched into eternity. His wife is nearly heartbroken and has the sympathy of the whole community in her terrible bereavement.—Au Sable News, Sept. 3.

Alcona County Review, September 9, 1881

NOTICE OF SALE OF REAL ESTATE.
STATE OF MICHIGAN,
County of Alcona.
In the matter of the estate of Henry J. Beach and Bessie May Beach, infants.

Notice is hereby given that in pursuance of an order granted to the undersigned, David Kirkendall, guardian of the estate of said Henry J. Beach and Bessie May Beach, infants, by the Honorable George S. Ritchie, Judge of Probate for the county of Alcona, on the 23rd day of July, A. D. 1892, there will be sold at public vendue, to the highest bidder, at the east front door of the court house in the village of Harrisville, in the County of Alcona, in said State, on Saturday, the 17th day of September, A. D. 1892, at 11 o'clock in the forenoon of that day (subject to all incumbrances existing at date of sale), the following described real estate, to-wit: All that certain piece of land situate in said county and described as follows: The South-west quarter of the North-west quarter of section eighteen (18), in town twenty-five (25) North of range nine East.
　DAVID KIRKENDALL, Guardian.

Alcona County Review, August 11, 1892
Cemetery: Pinecrest, Iosco Co.

Beach, Rhoda J.

STATE OF MICHIGAN,
County of Alcona.
At a session of the Probate Court for said County, held at the Probate office, in the village of Harrisville, on the 17th day of Oct., in the year one

thousand eight hundred and ninety-one.

Present, Hon. Geo. S. Ritchie, Judge of Probate.

In the matter of the estate of Rhoda J. Beach.

On reading and filing the petition, duly verified, of David Kirkendall praying that administration of said Estate be granted to him or some other suitable person.

Thereupon it is ordered, that Saturday, the 14th day of November next, at ten o'clock in the forenoon, be assigned for the hearing of said petition, and that the heirs at law of said deceased, and all other persons interested in said estate, are required to appear at a session of said Court, then to be holden in the Probate office, in the Village of Harrisville and show cause, if any there be, why the prayer of the petitioner should not be granted: And it is further ordered, that said petitioner give notice to the persons interested in said estate, of the pendency of said petition, and the hearing thereof, by causing a copy of this order to be published in the Alcona County Review, a newspaper printed and circulated in said county, four successive weeks previous to said day of hearing.
　Geo. S. Ritchie, Judge.

Alcona County Review, October 22, 1891

The Local News.

Judge Ritchie held a short session of his court Tuesday p. m. to dispose of the petition of D. Kirkendall for administration of the estate of Rhoda J. Beach, deceased.

Alcona County Review, November 19, 1891
Cemetery:

Beadle, Joseph

Jos. Beadle is No More.
Jos. Beadle, an historic character of Iosco county, who kept a "half way" house for many years up the Au Sable river, died last week at the home of his daughter, Mrs. Jos. Bisonette of Curtis township. He was 79 years of age.

Alcona County Review, July 1, 1897
Cemetery: Glennie, Alcona Co.

Beadore, Frank

LOCAL JOTTINGS.

Frank Beadore, of Oscoda, died Tuesday morning from the effect of over-work. He had a job of moving lumber for the Gratwick, Smith & Fryer Lumber Co. He had always been a very hard worker and went into this job in his usual way, working with all his might, which resulted in his death. Beadore was quite well off—being worth between $3,000 and $4,000. He owned a good farm in Canada, the American House, and one or two other buildings in Oscoda. He was about 34 years of age. He left a wife, but no children.

Alcona County Review, July 31, 1885
Cemetery:

Beam, Thomas
Curtis Items.
Nov. 30, 1896.
A young man named Thos. Beem went to the raising of Bill Lawrence's shanty Nov. 10th. A log fell off the building; he tried to hold it when he was warned it was going. No one seems to know just how it happened, but they think the log fell on another and in trying to get out of the way he fell and one log jammed him against another. Three ribs were broken loose from the backbone and one of the ribs punctured the lung, so the doctor said. He died on the 12th and was buried on the 14th. Deceased was a member of the Harvest Home Baptist church. The sermon was preached by a McKinley minister. His father told me that the same night Tom was hurt Lawrence came and borrowed his gun and never went to see him afterwards nor even to the funeral.

It is a warning to the living, though we are in health and vigor we know not how soon we may be cut down as he was. He was the only son and was about 26 years of age.

Alcona County Review, December 3, 1896
Cemetery:

Beams, Benjamin
NEIBHBORHOOD NOTES.

Body of a boy named Benjamin Beams was found in the Au Sable river last week. Boy had been missed for a month past.

Alcona County Review, May 24, 1889
Cemetery:

Beard, Fred
COUNTY REVIEWINGS.

Last Monday while Fred Beard was helping unload a stick of timber at Alcona, the car upon which it was

placed tipped up, causing the log to roll off and fall upon him. One leg was broken and it is feared that he is injured internally. He went down on the Marine City, Monday evening, to Port Huron, where his friends are living.

Alcona County Review, May 7, 1880

COUNTY REVIEWINGS.

Fred Beard, who was injured at Alcona on the 3d of May, died at the home of his parents in Port Huron, on Monday, May 10. He suffered the most excruciating pain while consciousness remained, and death was really a relief from his tortures. Deceased was but twenty years of age, and an enterprising young business man. His death is deeply regretted by his large circle of friends.

Alcona County Review, May 21, 1880
Cemetery:

Beard, Ida
HOME REVIEWINGS.

Died—At Alcona, Saturday morning, July 16th, Ida, infant daughter of Mr. and Mrs. Frank E. Beard; aged 7 months and 13 days. In this case, as with many others in this life death came suddenly and was not expected by the grief-stricken parents, and is another exhibition of the truthfulness of the Divine statement that "In an hour when ye think not the Son of man cometh." The remains of the little one were taken to Port Huron on steamer Flora, Saturday afternoon and interred in the cemetery of that city.

Alcona County Review, July 22, 1881

HOME REVIEWINGS.
F. E. Beard and wife passed up to their home at Alcona on the steamer Flora yesterday morning. They had been to Port Huron to bury their little daughter.

Alcona County Review, July 22, 1881
Cemetery: Probably Lakeside, St. Clair Co.

Beard, James
Alcona Atoms.
F. E. Beard returned home the latter part of last week from the bedside of his father, Jas. Beard, of Port Huron, who is very ill and is expected will hardly recover.

Alcona County Review, January 13, 1882

Local Sayings and Doings.

F. E. Beard and wife passed down in their own conveyance Tuesday, en

route to Port Huron, to see Mr. Beard's father, who is not expected to live long.

Alcona County Review, January 20, 1882

Alcona Atoms.

Mr. F. E. Beard received a dispatch announcing that his father was very sick. He and his wife started for Port Huron immediately.

Alcona County Review, April 28, 1882

JAMES BEARD.

Death of this Popular Citizen and Pioneer of Port Huron—A Sketch of his Life.
James Beard, one of the pioneers of Port Huron, a popular citizen, active, liberal and successful in business, and an honest, upright and generous man, died at his residence on Military street at 10 minutes after 8 o'clock this morning. Mr. Beard has suffered greatly from kidney diseases during the past two or three years, and last summer his friends did not think it possible for him to last through the winter. His strong constitution and will sustained him, however, but for several weeks past he has been too weak to speak above a whisper, and his death has been considered a matter of but a few hours or days.

Mr. Beard was born in Green, Chenango Co., N. Y., May 22, 1815, and was therefore nearly 68 years old at the time of his death. His childhood was spent at and near the place of his birth until October, 1833. Being then in the nineteenth year of his age he removed to Michigan, locating in St. Clair county. His brother David came with him. They landed at Port Huron early in the morning and neither of the boys having money enough left to board them in town until they could get a chance to their father's mill in Clyde, they started out on foot and walked to Wadham's mills, where they got breakfast and then walked the remainder of the way. Arriving at the mills they went to work for their father driving oxen at $12 a month. David Beard soon after returned to New York.

Here Mr. Beard's brother John was at work when he arrived, and they both continued to work for their father at $12 per month for some time, saving all to enable them to buy a yoke of oxen for themselves, so they could take a job of logging. They afterwards succeeded in obtaining a job of Mr. Cameron, now living in Sarnia. In 1842 James and John bought their father out of the saw mill and operated it summers together. In the winters James drove the oxen and John did the cutting. They lived in a small log house on Mill creek, not large enough to be divided into rooms, so that at night they had to hang up a blanket for a partition between the rooms. Mrs. John Beard, who is now living at Ruby, did the cooking.

In the mill James and John worked together at this time, one doing the sawing and the other rafting the timber. They had to raft their lumber to Detroit then as vessels were scarce and freights high.

Their father was very strict with them, making them meet all payments on the property when due; but they managed to get through with it.

In 1845 Mr. Beard removed to Detroit, and started a lumber yard near where the old water works dock is. In the spring of 1846 he started a fire company, and was made its foreman. The number of the engine was 7, and he held the position as long as he continued to live in Detroit.

In 1853 he returned to Port Huron. In 1856 James and John Beard bought the Whitman mill and continued to run it until 1859, when the firm of J. & J. Beard was dissolved and E. R. Haynes was taken in as a partner. The mill stood in front of the present family residence here.

In 1863, he, with John Johnston, F. H. Vanderburg and E. R. Haynes started lumbering at Alcona, Mich., the firm being Johnston, Haynes & Co. In 1872 Messrs. Vanderburg and Johnston sold out, and Haynes and Beard continued under the old firm name.

In 1875 Mr. Haynes sold out to Mrs. James Beard and Frank E. Beard bought a fourth interest in the business of his father, the new firm being James Beard & Co.

Mr. Beard was one of the first stockholders of the Port Huron Savings Bank, the Times Company, the Port Huron City Railway and the Port Huron and Northwestern

railway. He was elected alderman of the second ward at the first election of the city of Port Huron, and once since has served in the same office.

In 1863 he was appointed assistant U. S. assessor, which office he held until it was consolidated with that of collector, excepting during one year of Johnson's administration. When the offices were consolidated he was appointed deputy collector, and held the office until 1878. he was frequently offered the office of collector of the district, but declined.

Of the family of Ai Beard, James Beard's father, but one remains alive--Mrs. Louis Brockway, who for several months has been a member of her brother's family. David Beard, John Beard, Ai Beard, a half brother and Mrs. Kingsley of Clyde, have all died within the past three years.

Mr. Beard leaves four children, Frank, Ida, (Mrs. W. C. Anderson) Ella and Alexander. Mrs. A. Beard, who survives her husband, was his third wife.

In Mr. Beard's death Port Huron loses a citizen whom everybody respected and loved. Generous almost to a fault, liberal in all public enterprises, genial in manners kind and considerate under all circumstances, he was one of natures true noblemen.

To the memory of such a man praise is superfluous; his good deeds and noble qualities are a lasting monument before the eyes of all who knew him.

The funeral services were held at 2 o'clock, Tuesday, May 2d.--*Port Huron Times.*

Alcona County Review, May 12, 1882
Cemetery:

Beard, James

L. A. Colwell received a telegram yesterday from Frank Beard of Port Huron stating that his son, James, had been drowned.

Yesterday's dailies bring particulars of the sad accident. The young man who was but 16, was one of a party who had just started on a pleasure excursion to Huronia beach on the steam yacht Vulcan. James started forward by walking on the rail and holding by the stanchion, when he slipped and fell into the river. He was a good swimmer and could have easily reached the shore but followed the boat. Chairs and life preservers

were thrown out to him but he did not reach them and before the yacht could get back to him he sank from sheer exhaustion.

Alcona County Review, July 30, 1896
Cemetery: Lakeside, St. Clair Co.

Beaumont, Charles Aruth

PERSONAL POINTS.

Rev. and Mrs. Arthur Beaumont have had the sad misfortune to lose their baby boy. The sympathy of many friends here will go out to them.

Alcona County Review, November 3, 1898
Cemetery: Mt. Evergreen, Jackson Co.

Becker, George Henry

KILLMASTER.

Died at his home in Gustin after an illness of only nine days, George, the only son of Solomon and Lucy Becker. He leaves an aged father and mother and three sisters. Mrs. Wm. Dellar, Mrs. James Morrison, Mrs. Lou Anderson, and a large circle of friends to mourn his loss. The family has the sympathy of the entire community.

Alcona County Review, December 14, 1899

KILLMASTER.

Lou Anderson, Will Deller and James Morrison are home from camp to attend the funeral of George Becker.

Alcona County Review, December 14, 1899
Cemetery: Springport, Alcona Co.

Beebe, Mrs. Hannah

West Harrisville.

The funeral of the late Mrs. Beebe was held at the Baptist church this morning, Rev. VanHorn officiating.

Alcona County Review, April 18, 1895

Haynes Happenings.

Wm. Pyne has our sympathy in the loss of his wife; also Mr. Beebe in his affliction.

Alcona County Review, April 25, 1895
Cemetery:

Beebe, James

EVENTS OF ONE WEEK.

The six year old son of Jas. Beebe of Haynes township died this week of inflammation of the lungs.

Alcona County Review, March 16, 1893
Cemetery:

Beever, Esther

PERSONAL POINTS.

George Beever and wife are mourning the death of their remaining twin child which occurred yesterday. The funeral occurs today.

Alcona County Review, October 6, 1898
Cemetery: Springport, Alcona Co.

Beever, Ruth

One of Geo. Beever's twin baby girls died Wednesday morning, aged 9 months. The interment takes place this afternoon.

Alcona County Review, September 1, 1898
Cemetery: Springport, Alcona Co.

Bejin, Joseph Stanley

LOCAL PICK UPS.

Died, June 22, at his home, 428 Anthon street, Detroit, Joseph Stanley, beloved son of Joseph Bejin and Hattie Leonard, aged 2 months and 16 days.—Tribune.

Mr. and Mrs. Bejin have relatives in this county.

Alcona County Review, June 30, 1898
Cemetery: Mt. Elliot, Wayne Co.

Bell, Jacob J.

KILLED BY A SCANTLING.

An Accident Which Happened at Beard's Mill, Alcona.

A very painful accident happened at James Beard & Co's mill, at Alcona, last Friday afternoon. Jacob J. Bell, a middle-aged man, employed on the edger in the mill, was struck in the right side between the ribs and hip, by a 2x4 scantling which, with considerable velocity, accidentally gigged back from the saws, bursting a blood vessel. He lived until Saturday morning when death relieved him of his sufferings. The deceased was a native of Canada, and had been in this county but a short time. He was a cousin of Joseph Taylor, of Alcona. He leaves a wife and three children.

Alcona County Review, July 19, 1878
Cemetery:

Bell, Jane Sarah [Curtis]

Curtis.

Mrs. Jennie Bell, after an illness of a few hours, passed peacefully from this earth to try the realities of another world. The deceased was thirty-four years of age, and the daughter of Mr. and Mrs. E. D. Curtis. She leaves a husband and seven children to mourn their loss.

It was a terrible blow to the community, as she was loved by all who knew her. She died on Saturday

morning. The funeral was held in the Baptist church Monday afternoon at half past two.

Alcona County Review, November 10, 1892

HISTORY OF ONE YEAR.

Chronological History of the Past Year, 1892.

THE DEATH RECORD.

Oct. 29. Mrs. Jennie Bell, Curtis.

Alcona County Review, January 5, 1893
Cemetery: Curtisville, Alcona Co.

Bell, Martin J.

CURTISVILLE.

Born to Mr. and Mrs. Bell on Saturday, a son. We are sorry to state that the infant lived only a few hours when it was laid to rest at West Curtis cemetery Sunday at 3 p.m. Mrs. Bell has the sympathy of a large circle of friends.

Alcona County Review, November 30, 1899
Cemetery: Curtisville, Alcona Co.

Benaire, William

Bound To Keep Up Her Record.

Margaret Harvey, the reputed wife of the notorious sinner, who was recently sentenced from the Iosco circuit court to states prison for the murder of Jos. Kennedy is in a fair way to soon reach the end of her rope. Last week she shot and killed a young man named Wm. Benaire, while the latter was passing a notorious resort at Otsego Lake, of which she was an inmate. This woman goes by the happy sobriquet of "The Shooter," having earned this distinguished appellation by a bloody record of crimes and misdemeanors. She has shot four men in this state but has succeeded in escaping conviction through lack of evidence. She has been jailed at Gaylord.

Alcona County Review, July 1, 1887

She Got Off With Three Years.

"Shooter" Harvey, the woman who was mentioned in this paper recently as having shot and killed a young man at Otsego Lake, had her trial before Judge Emerick soon after the commission of the crime, and was convicted and sentenced to the Detroit House of Correction for three years.

Alcona County Review, July 8, 1887
Cemetery:

Bennaway, Francis

LOCAL JOTTINGS.

Dr. Benway, the Indian physician, died at Black River last evening.

Alcona County Review, March 20, 1885
Cemetery: Mt. Joy, Alcona Co.

Bennett, {Male}

The trial of Atherton and McCallum at Mio last week for the murder of an Indian named Bennett resulted in their acquittal although the dead man's widow testified positively that she saw them do the deed. W. E. Depew defended the prisoners and his electrical eloquence must have taken due effect upon the jury.

Alcona County Review, November 2, 1893
Cemetery:

Benway, Silas [aka Causley]

Victim of the Iron Horse.

Silas Benway was buried at Black River last Sunday. He was a young man but 22 years of age, of handsome physique and powerful frame. He met with a frightful accident the Wednesday previous while engaged in the discharge of his duties as conductor of a Potts logging train. In attempting to board the engine by swinging onto the "cow catcher" he slipped and fell under the wheels of the moving train. One leg was completely severed below the thigh. He was taken at once to the Yockey House in Au Sable, but medical skill could not save him and he expired the next day. His mother, who has resided at Black River, was called to his bedside and after his death took the remains to Black River for interment.

Alcona County Review, July 4, 1890

One Year's History.

Record of Local Happenings for the Year 1890.

MAY.

27 Silas Benway, aged 22, killed Wednesday on Pott's railroad, and buried at Black River.

Alcona County Review, January 1, 1891
Cemetery: Mt. Joy, Alcona Co.

Bernhizer, George H.

PERSONAL MENTION.

Geo. Bernizer is reported very low with dropsy, resulting from asthma, at his home in Mikado township. He has been confined to his bed for several weeks.

Alcona County Review, April 4, 1895

Geo. H. Bernizer died at his late home in Mikado township early Monday morning, April 8th, 1895.

Deceased was 62 years of age and had been a resident of Alcona county for upwards of twenty years. He had been a sufferer from asthma for a long time and during the winter dropsy set in, resulting in his death as above stated. He leaves a wife, but no children.

Alcona County Review, April 11, 1895

EVENTS OF ONE WEEK.

Geo. Bernizer was awarded an increase of pension last week by the department. The increase comes a little late for Mr. Bernizer, for he has been dead these two months, but it will be quite acceptable to his widow.

Alcona County Review, July 4, 1895

HONORS TO DEAD HEROES.

A magnificent demonstration of the patriotic spirit of the citizens of Alcona county was the observance on Monday of the time honored custom of decorating the graves and commemorating the deeds of valor of the nation's dead heroes.

The roster of soldiers who are buried here is as follows: Harrisville, (West), A. Marcellus, John Pelton, W. W. Douglass: Catholic, Louis Rivard, Geo. Bernizer: South Harrisville, R. Richmond, Chas. Miller, H. J. Aird, A. Noyes, Jas. Johnson.

Alcona County Review, June 2, 1898
Cemetery: St. Anne's, Alcona Co.

Berry, William H.
BLACK RIVER BRIEFLETS.

We regret to state that Mr. Wm. Berry is seriously ill.

Alcona County Review, April 9, 1886

BLACK RIVER BRIEFLETS.

We regret to chronicle the death of Mr. Wm. Berry, which occurred Sunday afternoon. He had been in a low state of health for sometime from a complication of chronic diseases. During a visit to Harrisville he contracted a severe cold, which brought on alarming symptoms. His demise adds another to the list of deceased veterans of the civil war. One by one they pass away, and soon there will be no one left to tell the story of the sufferings of that stirring time. He leaves a wife and two sons

to mourn his loss, who have the sympathy of the whole village, in their sad bereavement.

Alcona County Review, April 23, 1886
Cemetery: Mt. Joy, Alcona Co.

Bertrand, Frank
PERSONAL MENTION.

Frank Bertrand, who was employed in the Colwell saw mill some ten years ago, and who is a relative of Andrew Brennan, died a few days ago near Port Huron of consumption. He was a married man.

Alcona County Review, November 28, 1895
Cemetery:

Betz, Frank J.
LOCAL PICK UPS.

Frank Betz, a respected citizen of Au Sable, died last week from the effects of la grippe. Deceased was commander of Papineau Tent, K. O. T. M.

Alcona County Review, April 27, 1899
Cemetery: Pinecrest, Iosco Co.

Betz, George
REVIEWINGS.

George Betz, an Au Sable man, was shot at Port Sanilac by Albert Kinney, of Oscoda, on Nov. 9th. The men had been picking up a raft of logs for the Loud Co. On the night in question they were drinking when a quarrel resulted and Kinney deliberately shot his companion. Betz died the next day.

Alcona County Review, November 21, 1895

Al Kinney, who shot and killed George Betz in a Port Sanilac saloon last fall has been convicted of murder in the second degree and sentenced to 17 years imprisonment at Jackson. Both Kinney and Betz were residents of Au Sable and were in the employ of the Loud Co. They were engaged at Port Sanilac in picking up a raft. Kinney was under the influence of liquor but his general reputation was good.

Alcona County Review, February 6, 1896

The damage suit of Mrs. Betz against the bondsmen of the saloon keeper in whose saloon her son, George Betz, was killed a year or so ago, has been on trial in Sanilac county for the past two or three days. C. R. Henry and Judge Kelley are conducting the case for Mrs. Betz.-- Oscoda Press.

Alcona County Review, June 10, 1897
Cemetery: Pinecrest, Iosco Co.

Biddle, Joseph W.
A TERRIBLE ACCIDENT.

Seven Men Buried Alive Beneath a Mass of Brick.

THE FRIGHTFUL OCCURRENCE AT AU SABLE.

On Monday afternoon the citizens of AuSable and Oscoda were suddenly thrown into a state of excitement and terror, by the announcement of a horrible accident which had occurred at Gram's mill burner, by which five persons lost their lives, seven in all being victims to the terrible calamity. The particulars of the sad occurrence we glean from the Saturday Night extra of Wednesday, as follows:

"There were seven men at work in the burner at Gram's mill. They were Joseph W. Biddle, Thomas Mitchell, George Fulton, John Hardwick, William Miner, George Santerneau, George Gordon. The men were engaged in taking down the brick wall of one of the refuse burners of Gram's mill. A scaffolding had been built inside the burner, and upon the scaffolding the men worked and upon it the brick was also laid as they were taken from the wall. The men began taking the wall down from the top. They had been working in the burner about a week and had the walls about half down. The brick from the part of the wall already taken down were of course lying on the platforms of the scaffolding above the heads of the workmen. While the men were engaged at work, continuing the tearing down of the wall—with about 20,000 brick, or from 40 to 50 ton's weight, above them, the scaffolding gave way, and in an instant the seven men were buried beneath this immense amount of brick and the lumber and timber of which the scaffolding was made. The alarm was given by Michael Gerrard, who was working but a few feet from the burner. Before an hour had passed there were from 1000 to 1500 men collected at the scene of the accident. The task of uncovering the men was begun as soon as possible after the accident occurred, but under the circumstances it was a very slow job. The bricks, and lumber composing the scaffolding, had all to be thrown out through two small openings—two feet by two and one half—and of course only a small number of them could work at a time. The scaffolding fell about half past four o'clock. At half past seven the first body was reached and taken out. It proved to be that of Joseph Biddle. A short time after young Gordon was taken out alive and seemingly not fatally injured, though at this writing his recovery is doubtful. A few minutes later Fulton and Santerneau were taken out, the former alive and the latter dead. Then the bodies of Mitchell, Miner, and Hardwick were taken out in the order named, it being about nine o'clock, or four and one-half hours after the accident, when the last body was removed. When the scaffolding fell some of the scantlings happened to wedge in such a position that they kept the principal weight of the brick off from Gordon, and he was able to converse at intervals with the men who were removing the brick. The men could also hear groans from one of the other imprisoned victims—probably Fulton, he was the only other one taken out alive. Five of the victims—Biddle, Fulton, Miner, Santerneau and Hardwick—were married men with families. Mr. Hardwick, familiarly called "Happy Jack," leaves a wife and six children, the oldest a daughter of seventeen. Mr. Biddle leaves a wife and two children, Mr. Miner the same. Mr. Fulton has a wife and three children, and Mr. Santerneau leaves a wife and baby.

Later.—Fulton died Wednesday evening.

Alcona County Review, April 17, 1885

LOCAL JOTTINGS.

Register of Deeds Jamison and Gene Taft spent Monday night at Au Sable, and brought to town early Tuesday morning the news of the killing of the 5 men at Au Sable.

Alcona County Review, April 17, 1885
Cemetery: Pinecrest, Iosco Co.

Bigelow, James Harvey
LOCAL JOTTINGS.

Harvey Bigelow of Hudson, a noticeable character on the village streets every Saturday for many years past, died recently. He was well to do, but preferred the life of a recluse and the companionship of his dogs, pigs,

and chickens. He always had a warm nest for these, and their society seemed the highest happiness of his life. 'Tis said his chickens roosted every night for years on the footboard of his bed and his highest delight was to be awakened by their crows and cackle.

Alcona County Review, February 20, 1885
Cemetery: Maple Grove, Lenawee Co.

Biggam, Thomas

Thos. Biggam, a county charge, died at the county poor farm Wednesday night of pneumonia. He had no known relatives.

Alcona County Review, May 2, 1890
Cemetery:

Birch, Ransom

His Name Was Ransom Birch.
From the Alpena Echo.

Yesterday the remains of an aged man were found at Mud Lake Junction and taken to West Harrisville for burial. Owen Fox, learning of the fact, left on the noon train, thinking perhaps the remains were those of his brother who disappeared from here a week ago.

Alcona County Review, December 8, 1892

A brother of Ransom Birch, who died two weeks ago at Noyes' Hotel, Mud Lake, came up from Port Huron as soon as he was apprised of his relative's death. The remains had been already buried and were not disturbed. The dead man was a member of the Forresters and had a policy for $2,000 insurance therein.

Alcona County Review, December 15, 1892

HISTORY OF ONE YEAR.

Chronological History of the Past Year, 1892.

THE DEATH RECORD.
Dec. 3. Ransom Birch, Mud Lake.

Alcona County Review, January 5, 1893
Cemetery: Probably Twin Lakes, Alcona Co.

Bissell, {Boy}
REVIEWINGS.

Mr. and Mrs. J. T. Bissell buried their two months' old baby, Tuesday.

Alcona County Review, May 23, 1879
Cemetery:

Bissell, {Male}
KILLMASTER ECHOES.

D. D. Bissell went to Bay City Tuesday to attend the funeral of his father.

Alcona County Review, June 1, 1888
Cemetery: Elm Lawn, Bay Co.

Bissell, Jerome T.
PESONAL MENTION.

Frank Springer returned this week from a trip to Saginaw.

Mr. Springer was called to Saginaw to attend the funeral of his brother-in-law, Jerome T. Bissell, a former resident of Harrisville. Mr. Bissell had been a confirmed invalid for a number of years and had been an inmate of the Soldier's Home at Grand Rapids on different occasions and at the time of his death was an inmate of the Soldiers' Home at Dayton.

The circumstances of his death were rather painful to his family who resided in Saginaw. During his last illness he was unconscious from first to last, and as he had said nothing concerning his private affairs his attendants knew nothing of his family. He died Friday, April 7, and was buried in the cemetery in Dayton. Hearing nothing from or concerning him the family telegraphed and wrote to Dayton, only to learn that the husband and father was dead and buried. The remains were disinterred after they had been buried a week and were shipped to Saginaw where they were again buried on the 16th inst., the G. A. R. Post of which he was a member taking charge of the ceremonies.

Alcona County Review, April 20, 1893
Cemetery: Forest Lawn, Saginaw Co.

Bissell, Maria [Gustin]
The Local News

A middle aged lady named Bissel died at Killmaster last week. The remains were conveyed to Bay City for interment.

Alcona County Review, May 26, 1892

ORDER FOR PUBLICATION
Appointment of Administrator
State of Michigan,

The Probate Court for the County of Alcona.

At a session of said court, held at the Probate Office in the City of Harrisville, in said County, on the 18th of August, 1913.

Present: Hon. Geo. W. Burt, Judge of Probate.

In the matter of the estate of Martha Bissell, Deceased.

Douglas D. Bissell, son of said deceased, having filed in said court a petition praying that the administration of said estate be granted to Alice C. Gustin, or some other suitable person.

It is ordered, that the 13th day of Sept., A. D. 1913, at two o'clock in the afternoon, at said probate office, be and is hereby appointed for hearing said petition;

It is further ordered, that public notice thereof be given by publication of a copy of this order, for three successive weeks previous to said day of hearing, in the Alcona County Review, a newspaper printed and circulated in said county.

GEO. W. BURT,
Judge of Probate.

Alcona County Review, August 21, 1913
Cemetery: Probably Elm Lawn, Bay Co.

Bissonette, Margaret [Jacobson]

CURTIS.

Died, October 21, at her home in this place, Mrs. Bisnet. The funeral services were held in the school house Saturday, Oct. 23. She leaves many children and grand children to mourn her loss.

Alcona County Review, November 4, 1897
Cemetery: Glennie, Alcona Co.

Bittner, Herbert Paul

PERSONAL MENTION.

Paul Bittner, aged 14, was killed at Rogers City last week by the accidental discharge of a gun. Mrs. Mary Gould, wife of a farmer living near Hillman, was mistaken for a bear by a fool hunter and was shot and instantly killed about the same time.

Alcona County Review, October 26, 1893
Cemetery: Rogers Township, Presque Isle Co.

Blackburn, Hannah [Barton]

HOME REVIEWINGS.

Mrs. G. N. Blackburn of Alpena died on Friday morning last. She had been an invalid for many years past, and especially during the past six months had been a great sufferer.

Alcona County Review, July 15, 1881
Cemetery: Evergreen, Alpena Co.

Blair, Jane

LOCAL JOTTINGS.

Miss Jane Blair died at the home of John Gray on Wednesday, aged 75 years. The funeral will be held at the Presbyterian church, at 2:30 o'clock this (Friday) afternoon.

Alcona County Review, April 23, 1886
Cemetery: West Lawn, Alcona Co.

Blakely, Abram Randolph

A. R. Blakely, a prominent Alpena citizen, was accidentally shot and killed in his own home Monday while cleaning his rifle, preparatory to going for a day's hunt.

Alcona County Review, November 17, 1898

The late A. R. Blakely of Alpena carried $45,000 life insurance. One policy in the N. Y. Life for $3,000 was taken out only two weeks before his tragic death, but this reliable company was first to pay.

Alcona County Review, December 15, 1898
Cemetery: Evergreen, Alpena Co.

Blanchard, Hannah [Hicks]

GREENBUSH ITEMS.

Mrs. Geo. O. Bailey arrived home from Tawas on Friday evening, at which place she has been for two weeks past, having been called there to minister unto her mother, Mrs. Hannah Blanchard, with tender and loving hands during her last sickness and death, which occurred on Saturday, March 12th, at the age of 74 years. The Iosco Gazette says that Mrs. Blanchard lived and died beloved and respected by a large host of friends and her funeral, that took place at the residence of her daughter, Mrs. C. W. Howard, was attended by a large number of neighbors and friends.

Alcona County Review, March 27, 1887
Cemetery: Greenwood, Iosco Co.

Blanchard, Norman

GREENBUSH GETTINGS.

Mr. Bailey and family attended the funeral of Mr. Blanchard, Mrs. Bailey's father, on Tuesday of last week, in Tawas. Mr. Bailey, daughter and youngest son returned next day. Mrs. Bailey returned Monday night last. Wm. and Thos. Bailey are attending school in Tawas.

Alcona County Review, January 8, 1886
Cemetery: Greenwood, Iosco Co.

Plunkett, Catherine

COUNTY NEWS.

There has been another death this week from diphtheria. Miss Kittie Blanket, sister of Mrs. R. Reed (recently from Deckerville), who had been ill less than a week, died Wednesday evening. She was a bright girl and aged about 13 years. Her sudden decease leaves another vacant chair and lonely household. Be ye also therefore ready "for in an hour when ye think not the Son of Man cometh." Burial takes place to-day at 2:30 p.m.

Alcona County Review, February 11, 1881
Cemetery:

Bloomingdale, Catherine [Mitchell]

Another Pioneer Gone.

Once more the Review is called upon to chronicle the death of another of the well-known lady pioneers of this county. This time it is Mrs. Kate Bloomingdale, wife of Stephen Bloomingdale and sister of William Mitchell and Mrs. Andrew J. Freer, of this place, who is summoned to the spirit land by the messenger of death, she having died Monday night, after a long and painful illness.

The deceased was born at Alton, Ill., and in early life moved to Detroit. In 1853 she removed to Alcona county, and was joined in marriage to Willis Roe in 1856, by whom she had three children (two sons and one daughter) Sylvanus and Lansing Roe still being alive, the daughter dead. She was married to Stephen Bloomingdale, her present husband, in 1866, by whom she had three children (one son and two daughters) Rillie, Hattie and Coatie, all still alive. She has lived in this county continuously for about 31 years, and was therefore one of our early pioneers. She died at the age of 47 years.

The deceased was a person who was known by almost everybody in this vicinity, and her friends were exceedingly numerous. She was a kind and affectionate wife and mother.

Funeral services were held from the Presbyterian Church in this village Thursday afternoon, Rev. M. Lowry officiating. The church was filled with citizens who had gathered to pay respects to the memory of the departed.

Alcona County Review, December 12, 1884

LOCAL JOTTINGS.

Stephen Bloomingdale, on behalf of himself and family, desires to return thanks to friends and neighbors for their kindness and assistance during the late sickness and death of his wife.

Alcona County Review, December 12, 1884
Cemetery: Springport, Alcona Co.

Bloomingdale, Courtney

DEATH'S SAD DOINGS.

Court Bloomingdale was brought down from Rogers City on the steamer Flora one week ago last Sunday by his brother. He had been working on the Ocqueoc, near Rogers City and had been taken seriously ill with what was termed bloody piles by his physician. This turned into cholera morbus. His brother brought him to Harrisville with the intention of bringing him to his home near Alcona, but after he was taken to the St. Lawrence House he was too ill to be removed. His brother has been in constant attendance. He grew gradually worse until Tuesday morning when death relieved his sufferings. The funeral services were held Wednesday morning in the Presbyterian church the remains being interred at South Harrisville. The deceased is well known at Alcona where he formerly resided.

Alcona County Review, August 30, 1889

NEIGHBORHOOD NOTES.

To my friends and citizens of Harrisville who so kindly assisted and rendered so much kindness to my son during his late sickness, I extend to each and all of them my sincere thanks.

Stephen Bloomingdale.

Alcona County Review, September 6, 1889
Cemetery: Springport, Alcona Co.

Bloomingdale, Stephen

The Local News.

Stephen Bloomingdale died Sunday morning at his late home after a brief illness of four days from inflammation. He was aged about 55 years and had been a resident of Alcona county for the last quarter of a century, being identified during a great portion of that time with the fishery interests at Alcona. He leaves two daughters. The remains were interred Monday afternoon in the cemetery at South Harrisville.

Alcona County Review, July 30, 1891

Cemetery: Springport, Alcona Co.

Blush, Harriet

A Long String From Springport.

Springport, Jan. 15, 1895.
Mrs. Geo. Blush has been quite seriously ill the past few weeks. She is unable to eat any food and those in attendance fear she is fast fading away.

Alcona County Review, January 17, 1895

South Harrisville.

S. Harrisville, Jan. 21.--Miss Miller of Lansing, niece of Mrs. Blush, arrived last week to attend her in her sickness.

The days of Mrs. Blush are undoubtedly numbered. The doctors have given her up. All that can be done now is to make her remaining days as comfortable as possible.

Alcona County Review, January 24, 1895

CROSSED THE DARK RIVER.

Mrs. Geo. H. Blush departed this life Sunday, February 3rd, 1895, at her late residence south of the village of Harrisville, after a long illness from cancer of the stomach. Thus death removes another from the rapidly thinning ranks of the pioneer citizens of Alcona county. She was a good and kind neighbor and died in the faith of a Christian.

Deceased was a native of Green county, N. Y., where she was born Dec. 28, 1819. In her younger days she was a school teacher. Oct. 10, 1860, she was married to Geo. H. Blush, so that their married life covered a third of a century. They became residents of Alcona county the same year as their marriage and have resided here continuously ever since, and were consequently witnesses to and participants in all the many changes that have taken place in that time.

The funeral services were conducted at her late residence by the Rev. W. J. Bailey Tuesday afternoon and the remains were borne thence for interment in the South Harrisville cemetery.

Alcona County Review, February 7, 1895

South Harrisville.

Mrs. Abram Reed, the faithful attendant upon the late Mrs. Blush, for the three weeks prior to her death, rightfully merits the esteem of friends and neighbors in the community for her faithfulness. Who other than she would have left home and fireside and devote night and day to the care of a friend. It illustrates her Christian spirit in Christ's words, "Greater love hath no man than this, that he lay down his life for his friends."

South Harrisville, Feb. 11, 1895.

Alcona County Review, February 14, 1895

While still fresh in our minds of the good neighbors that surround us, who so kindly assisted in the care of my beloved wife and friend in her long spell of sickness and her death, especially to Mrs. Abram Reed, who devoted so much of her time for her relief and comfort: I cannot pay them, but would say from the bottom of our hearts, thanks and may Heaven bless you.

Geo. H. Blush
Miss Adelle Miller.

Alcona County Review, February 21, 1895
Cemetery: Springport, Alcona Co.

Bock, Anna [Schultz]
Bock, John, Jr.
Bock, John, Sr.
Bock, Josephine
Bock, Catherine
Bock, William

BURNED TO A CRISP.

An Entire Family of Six Destroyed in the Ruins of Their Home.

The village of Omer, Arenac county, was the scene of an awful calamity on the morning of Wednesday, Feb. 6 inst. It was nothing less than the destruction by fire of the dwelling house of John Bock, and all the inmates, comprising father, mother, two sons and two daughters were burned in it.

The fire broke out about 5 o'clock in the morning. Neighbors hastened to the scene with pails of water, but they were too late to be of any assistance except to remove the charred and blackened remains of the former inhabitants.

It is supposed that the weather being intensely cold they had started a fire and then retired again and when awakened by the heat or smoke they were too much overcome to make their escape.

Bock and his wife, the latter having her baby in her arms, were found in the main living room. They looked as though they had made a great effort to escape, but had been overcome by the smoke or flames, and perished miserably. Their arms and limbs were burned to stubs.

The other children were found in other parts of the ruins, the bodies burned beyond semblance of human form

Bock was a hard-working, steady man, about 35 years of age. He had lived at Omer about six or seven years and the family had many friends.

Alcona County Review, February 14, 1895
Cemetery: Probably Evergreen, Arenac Co.

Bock, Sylvester C.

COUNTY JOTTINGS.

S. C. Bock, of Falmouth, Missaukee county, formerly a resident of this place, died of heart disease about 10 days ago.

Alcona County Review, November 22, 1878
Cemetery:

Bollet, {Male}

KILLED.

Last Wednesday morning a man by the name of Bollet was killed at Mason's camp, which is located about 8 miles west of Harrisville. He was helping to load logs on a car when a log from the top rolled down upon him, killing him instantly. His body was brought in from the camp yesterday forenoon and placed at the St. Lawrence House, and in the afternoon it was taken to Alpena, where he has a brother living.

Alcona County Review, January 22, 1886
Cemetery:

Bonaher, George

LOCAL JOTTINGS.

An employee of Alger, Smith & Co., at Black River, was killed at Moore's camp this afternoon by a falling tree. Name not learned.

Alcona County Review, March 6, 1885
Cemetery:

Bond, Elijah H.

COUNTY REVIEWINGS.

Died, in Harrisville, October 9th, Elijah Bond, aged 16.

Alcona County Review, October 15, 1880
Cemetery: West Lawn, Alcona Co.

Bond, Mary [Banks]

Mrs. Wm. Bond, aged 74, died Monday afternoon of acute dysentery after a brief illness of three days. The old lady attended the funeral of Asa

Emerson Friday afternoon and went to the Crusader's meeting in the evening at the town hall. She was taken sick that night. Dr. Wiley was called, also Dr. Mitchell later on but they could do nothing for her. Deceased had lived in Alcona county a great many years and was the mother of a numerous family. She was rough and rugged both in character and physical endurance. She has been known to shoulder a 25 lb. sack of flour in town and carry it nearly three miles to her home.

The funeral services were held over until this morning on receipt of a telegram from her son, Josh, that he would get home last night. The burial took place in the West cemetery.

Alcona County Review, August 6, 1896

STATE OF MICHIGAN, County of Alcona.

Springport, Jan. 15, 1895.
At a session of the Probate Court for said County, held at the probate office, in the village of Harrisville, on the 25th day of January in the year one thousand eight hundred and ninety-seven.

Present, W. H. Gilpin, Judge of Probate.

In the matter of the estate of William Bond and Mary Bond, husband and wife.

On reading and filing the petition, duly verified, of Jayne La France, praying that Fred A. Beede of Harrisville or some other suitable person, be appointed administrator of the estate of the aforesaid William Bond and Mary Bond, husband and wife.

Thereupon it is ordered, that Monday, the 29th day of March next, at ten o'clock in the forenoon, be assigned for the hearing of said petition, and that the heirs at law of said deceased and all others interested in said estate, are required to appear at a session of said Court, then to be holden at the Probate office, in the Village of Harrisville and show cause, if any there be, why the prayer of the petitioner should not be granted: And it is further ordered, that the petitioner give notice to the heirs at law and persons interested in said estate, of the pendency of said petition, and the hearing thereof by causing a copy of this order to be published in the Alcona County Review, a newspaper

printed and circulated in said county, three successive weeks previous to said day of hearing.

W. H. Gilpin,
Judge of Probate.

Alcona County Review, March 4, 1897

STATE OF MICHIGAN, County of Alcona.

At a session of the Probate Court for said county, held at the Probate office, in the

village of Harrisville, on the 11th day of July in the year one thousand eight hundred and ninety-eight.

Present, Hon. Wm. H. Gilpin, Probate Judge.

In the matter of the estate of Mary Bond, deceased.

On reading and filing the petition, duly verified, of Miss Mary Bond, praying that the estate of said Mary Bond deceased may be administered and that administration of said estate be granted to David LaBoueff, or some other suitable person.

Thereupon it is ordered, that the eighth day of August, next, at 10 o'clock in the forenoon, be assigned for the hearing of said petition, and that the heirs at law of said deceased, and all other persons interested in said estate, are required to appear at a session of said court, then to be holden at the Probate office, in the village of Harrisville, and show cause, if any there be, why the prayer of the petitioner should not be granted: and it is further ordered that said petitioner give notice the persons interested in said estate, of the pendency of said petition, and the hearing thereof, by causing a copy of this order to be published in the "Alcona County Review" a newspaper printed and circulated in said county, three successive weeks previous to said day of hearing.

Wm. H. Gilpin,
Judge of Probate.

Alcona County Review, July 14, 1898

Notice is hereby given, that by an order of the Probate Court for the County of Alcona, made on the 8th day of August A.D. 1898, six months from that date were allowed for creditors to present their claims against the estate of Mary Bond deceased late of said County, deceased, and that all creditors of said deceased are required to present their claims to said Probate Court, at the Probate office, in the Village of

Harrisville, for examination and allowance, on or before the 8th day of February next and that such claims will be heard before said Court, on Monday, the 10th day of October and on Wednesday the 8th day of February next, at ten o'clock in the forenoon of each of those days.

Dated August 8th, A.D. 1898.

Wm. H. Gilpin,
Judge of Probate.

Alcona County Review, August 11, 1898

STATE OF MICHIGAN, County of Alcona.

At a session of the Probate Court for said County, held at the Probate office, in the Village of Harrisville on the 20th day of March in the year one thousand eight hundred and ninety-nine.

Present, Hon. W. H. Gilpin, Judge of Probate.

In the matter of the estate of Mary Bond Sr. deceased.

On reading and filing the petition duly verified of David La Boueff, administrator of said estate praying that license and authority be granted to him to sell the real estate of said estate at private sale to pay the indebtedness existing against same, which said lands are described as follows, to-wit: Lot nineteen (19) of Cowley & Roberts addition to the village of Harrisville, in said county and state.

Thereupon it is ordered that Monday, the 17th day of April next, at ten o'clock in the forenoon, be assigned for the hearing of said petition, and that the next of kin and heirs at law of said deceased and all other persons interested in said estate, are required to appear at a session of the Probate Court, then to be holden at the Probate office, in the Village of Harrisville and show cause, if any there be, why the prayer of the petitioner should not be granted. And it is further ordered that the petitioner give notice to the next of kin, heirs at law and persons interested in said estate, of the pendency of said petition, and the hearing thereof, by causing a copy of this order to be published in the Alcona County Review, a newspaper printed and circulated in said county three successive weeks previous to said day of hearing.

Wm. H. Gilpin,
Judge of Probate.

Alcona County Review, March 23, 1899

STATE OF MICHIGAN, County of Alcona.

Probate Court for said County.

At a session of the Probate Court for said County, held at the Probate office in said county on Wednesday the fourteenth day of August in the year of our Lord one thousand eight hundred and ninety nine.

Present, Hon. W. H. Gilpin, Judge of Probate.

In the matter of the estate of Mary Bond, deceased. David La Boueff, administrator of said estate, comes into Court and represents that he is now prepared to render his account as such administrator.

Thereupon it is ordered, that Monday, the 4th day of September next, at ten o'clock in the forenoon, be assigned for the examining and allowing of such account and that the heirs at law of said deceased and all other persons interested in said estate are required to appear at a session of said Court, then to be holden at the Probate Office in the village of Harrisville in said County, and show cause, if any there be, why the said account should not be allowed. And it is further ordered, that said David La Boueff give notice to the persons interested in said estate, of the pendency of said account and the hearing thereof, by causing a copy of this order to be published in the "Alcona County Review" a newspaper printed and circulated in said county, two successive weeks previous to said day of hearing.

Wm. H. Gilpin,
Judge of Probate.

Alcona County Review, August 24, 1899

LOCAL PICK UPS.

The final settlement of the estates of William and Mary Bond Sr. was effected at the probate court Tuesday. About $150 of the estates remained after all indebtedness was paid, which amount was divided between the six heirs. Geo. H. Lee of Haynes appeared as attorney for the heirs and ably represented their interests before the court.

Alcona County Review, September 7, 1899
Cemetery: West Lawn, Alcona Co.

Bond, William, Sr.

An Aged Man Suddenly Expires.

Wm. Bond, aged 80 years, dropped dead Tuesday afternoon as he was about to enter the doorway of his own house. They had been digging potatoes all day and the old gentleman had a bag on his shoulder. He was subject to sinking spells and at first it was supposed to be one of these spells, but with one gasp life became extinct. Coroner Beede was summoned, but after viewing the body and investigating all the circumstances he decided not to hold an inquest. The funeral took place this morning, the interment at the west cemetery. The funeral service consisted simply of a prayer at the house by Rev. Will. Sermon was reserved for next Sunday, when it will be delivered at the usual hour in the morning.

Alcona County Review, October 3, 1895

STATE OF MICHIGAN, County of Alcona.

Springport, Jan. 15, 1895.

At a session of the Probate Court for said County, held at the probate office, in the village of Harrisville, on the 25th day of January in the year one thousand eight hundred and ninety-seven.

Present, W. H. Gilpin, Judge of Probate.

In the matter of the estate of William Bond and Mary Bond, husband and wife.

On reading and filing the petition, duly verified, of Jayne La France, praying that Fred A. Beede of Harrisville or some other suitable person, be appointed administrator of the estate of the aforesaid William Bond and Mary Bond, husband and wife.

Thereupon it is ordered, that Monday, the 29th day of March next, at ten o'clock in the forenoon, be assigned for the hearing of said petition, and that the heirs at law of said deceased and all others interested in said estate, are required to appear at a session of said Court, then to be holden at the Probate office, in the Village of Harrisville and show cause, if any there be, why the prayer of the petitioner should not be granted: And it is further ordered, that the petitioner give notice to the heirs at law and persons interested in said estate, of the pendency of said petition, and the hearing thereof by causing a copy of this order to be published in the Alcona County Review, a newspaper printed and circulated in said county, three successive weeks previous to said day of hearing.

W. H. Gilpin,

Judge of Probate.

Alcona County Review, March 4, 1897

Order of Hearing.

14 July 98.

STATE OF MICHIGAN, County of Alcona.

At a session of the Probate Court for said County, held at the Probate office, in the

Village of Harrisville on the eleventh day of July in the year one thousand eight hundred and ninety-eight.

Present, Hon. W. H. Gilpin, Judge of Probate.

In the matter of the estate of William Bond, deceased.

On reading and filing the petition duly verified of Miss Mary Bond, praying that the estate of said Wm. Bond deceased, may be administered and that administration of said estate may be granted to David LaBoueff or some other suitable person.

Thereupon it is ordered, that the eighth day of August next, at ten o'clock in the forenoon, be assigned for the hearing of said petition, and that the heirs at law of said deceased and all other persons interested in said estate, are required to appear at a session of the Probate Court, then to be holden at the Probate office, in the Village of Harrisville and show cause, if any there be, why the prayer of the petitioner should not be granted.

And it is further ordered that the petitioner give notice the persons interested in said estate of the pendency of said petition, and the hearing thereof, by causing a copy of this order to be published in the Alcona County Review, a newspaper printed and circulating in said county three successive weeks previous to said day of hearing.

W. H. Gilpin,
Judge of Probate.

Alcona County Review, July 14, 1898

Notice is hereby given, that by an order of the Probate Court for the County of Alcona, made on the 8th day of August A.D. 1898, six months from that date were allowed for creditors to present their claims against the estate of William Bond deceased late of said County, deceased, and that all creditors of said deceased are required to present their claims to said Probate Court, at the Probate office, in the Village of Harrisville, for examination and allowance, on or before the 8th day of February next, and that such claims will be heard before said Court, on Monday the 10th day of October and Wednesday the 8th day of February next, at ten o'clock in the forenoon of each of those days.

Dated Aug. 8th, A.D. 1898.

Wm. H. Gilpin,
Judge of Probate.

Alcona County Review, August 11, 1898

State of Michigan, County of Alcona.

At a session of the Probate Court for said County, held at the probate office in the village of Harrisville on the 27th day of March, in the year 1899. Present, Hon. Wm. H. Gilpin, Judge of Probate.

In the matter of the estate of Wm. Bond, deceased.

On reading and filing the petition, duly verified, of David La Boueff, administrator of said estate, praying for license and authority to sell to pay the indebtedness and expenses of administration, the following described lands belonging to said estate, all that piece or parcel of land situate and being in the township of Harrisville, Alcona county and state of Michigan and describes as follows to-wit: The S W ¼ of the N W ¼ of section fifteen (15) in township twenty-six (26) north range nine (9) east; and also that he be authorized and empowered to sell the personal property as scheduled in said petition at public or private sale as he may find to be most beneficial for said estate for the purpose of paying the indebtedness aforesaid or so far as it will go toward paying same.

Thereupon it is ordered that Monday, the 24th day of April next, at ten o'clock in the forenoon be assigned for the hearing of said petition, and that the next of kin and heirs at law of said deceased and all other persons interested in said estate, are required to appear at a session of said court then to be holden in the probate office in the village of Harrisville and show cause, if any there be why the prayer of the petitioner should not be granted. And it is further ordered that said petitioner give notice to the next of kin and other persons interested in said estate of the pendency of said petition, and the hearing thereof, by causing a copy of this order to be published in the Alcona County Review, a newspaper printed and circulated in said county, 3 successive weeks previous to said day of hearing.

Wm. H. Gilpin,
Judge of Probate.

Alcona County Review, March 23, 1899

STATE OF MICHIGAN,
County of Alcona.

In the matter of the estate of Wm. Bond, deceased.

Notice is hereby given, that in pursuance of an order granted to the undersigned administrator of the estate of said Wm. Bond, by the Hon. Judge of Probate for the county of Alcona, on the 24th day of April A.D. 1899, there will be sold at public vendue, to the highest bidder at the court house in the village of Harrisville in the county of Alcona, in said state, on the 10th day of June, A.D. 1899, at 10 o'clock in the forenoon of that day, (subject to all incumbrances by mortgage or otherwise existing at the time of the death of said deceased, or at the time of said sale) the following described real estate, to-wit: The Northwest quarter of the Northwest quarter of section fifteen (15) in Township twenty-six (26) north range nine (9) east.

David LaBoueff, Administrator.

Alcona County Review, April 27, 1899

The above sale is adjourned for want of bidders, to July 10, 1899, at 2 o'clock p.m. at same place.

D. La Boueff, Administrator.

Alcona County Review, July 6, 1899

STATE OF MICHIGAN, County of Alcona.

Probate Court for said County.

At a session of the probate court for said County held at the probate office in said county on Monday, the 14th day of August in the year one thousand eight hundred and ninety-nine.

Present, Hon. Wm. H. Gilpin, Judge of Probate.

In the matter of the estate of William Bond, Sr. deceased. David La Boueff administrator of said estate, comes into court and represents that he is now prepared to render his account as such administrator.

Thereupon it is ordered, that Monday, the 4th day of September next at ten o'clock in the forenoon, be assigned for the examining and allowing of such account and that the heirs at law of said deceased and all other persons interested in said estate are required to appear at a session of the said court then to be holden in the probate office in the village of Harrisville in said county and show cause if any there be why the account should not be allowed. And it is further ordered, That said David La Boueff give notice to the persons interested in said estate, of the pendency of said account by causing a copy of this order to be published in the Alcona County Review, a newspaper printed and circulated in said county two successive weeks previous to said day of hearing.

W. H. Gilpin,
Judge of Probate.

Alcona County Review, August 17, 1899

LOCAL PICK UPS.
The final settlement of the estates of William and Mary Bond Sr. was effected at the probate court Tuesday. About $150 of the estates remained after all indebtedness was paid, which amount was divided between the six heirs. Geo. H. Lee of Haynes appeared as attorney for the heirs and ably represented their interests before the court.

Alcona County Review, September 7, 1899
Cemetery: West Lawn, Alcona Co.

Bonneville, Mrs. Joseph
A young married woman, Mrs. Jos. La Bonneville by name, died in the French settlement in Haynes township in confinement. She was but 19 years of age.

Alcona County Review, March 9, 1893
Cemetery:

Boothroyd, William H.
EVENTS OF ONE WEEK.

W. H. Boothroyd, the well-known book agent, who has canvassed the Huron shore towns for many years, meeting with great success by his quiet, courteous bearing, dropped dead in a Masonic hall in Detroit Tuesday evening of last week. He was a 32d degree Mason. One of his last works was the compilation of a Masonic directory, comprising the portraits and biographical sketches of several members of a great majority of the lodges of the state. He was 58 years of age.

Alcona County Review, January 25, 1893
Cemetery: Probably Woodmere, Wayne Co.

Boquest, Frank

The body of Frank Bovkist, a Swede about 30 years of age, was found floating in the river at Oscoda, last week Thursday. Accidentally drowned while intoxicated, was the verdict of the coroner's jury.

Alcona County Review, September 3, 1886
Cemetery:

Bothwell, James
SOMEWHAT PERSONAL.
Murdoch McLean and wife attended the funeral of a friend and veteran at Au Sable on Sunday. The deceased was Jas. Bothwell, aged about 60 years. His wife died last spring. He was a member of John Earl Post G. A. R., the members of which attended the funeral.

Alcona County Review, August 18, 1892
Cemetery:Sacred Heart, Iosco Co.

Boutyette, Charles
Chas. Boutyette Killed.
Charlie Boutyette, son of Henry Boutyette, formerly landlord of the National Hotel at Au Sable and of the Golling at Alpena, was shot and instantly killed last week at a lumber camp near Lake Charles, La.

Charles was foreman of the camp and the trouble which resulted in his death arose out of his refusal to give work to a couple of men. The men returned the next day after being refused work and created trouble among the men. One of them carried a gun. Boutyette was trying to quiet the trouble when he was shot dead. The shooting took place in view of Mrs. Boutyette, who warned her husband of danger. One of the men was captured, but the one who did the shooting escaped.

Alcona County Review, November 23, 1899

Of Local Interest.
The murderers of Charley Boutyette, formerly of Au Sable have been convicted at Lake Charles, La. Boutyette was murdered in November, 1899, by two men whose hatred he had engendered while acting as foreman for a lumber company at Lake Charles.

Alcona County Review, October 11, 1900
Cemetery: Orange Grove, Calcasieu Parish, LA

Brahaney, Florence
DIED.
Saturday morning, Jan. 7, 1882, Florence, daughter of James and Annie Brahaney; aged 1 year, 5 months and 11 days.

Another light from our household is gone.

Another voice we loved is stilled.
Another place is vacant at our hearth.
Which never can be filled

Deep sorrow now pervades each heart,
And grief our bosom swells;
Another loved one from our midst departs,
In that new home to dwell.

Nipped in the opening bloom of youth,
With scarce a moment's warning given;
Summon'd early from this earth,
To grace with smiles the courts of heaven.

Rest, little Florence in thy happiness rest!
Mingling with angels, we know thou'rt blest;
Far from the trials that tempt us to stray,
God in His mercy has called thee away.

Alcona County Review, January 13, 1882

Local Sayings and Doings
Mr. and Mrs. James Brahany desire the Review to return thanks to W. E. Rice and wife, and many other friends and neighbors for the sympathy and acts of kindness tendered during the sickness, death, and burial of their little daughter.

Alcona County Review, January 13, 1882
Cemetery:Pinecrest, Iosco Co.

Brannigan, Ed
PURELY PERSONAL.

Edward Brannigan was called to St. Thomas, Ont., last week by a telegram announcing the sudden demise of his father.

Alcona County Review, August 3, 1888
Cemetery:

Brannigan, Mrs. Jane
The serious illness of Mrs. Brannigan has brought some of her children here from distant points. Edward and Alfred have arrived from the Soo, Mrs. G. F. Thoncroft from Ontario, Thomas and Mrs. David La Boueff were already here. There are ten children altogether. Two of the remaining five reside in Ontario and are unable to come, the others are on the Pacific coast. Mrs. Brannigan has long been a sufferer from a tumor. This has been further complicated by inflammation of the lungs. She is in a very critical condition and little hope is entertained of her recovery.

Alcona County Review, April 16, 1896

OBSERVATIONS.

Mrs. Jane Brannigan, whose serious illness was noted last week, passed away Thursday night, April 16th.

Deceased was a native of Ireland and was 76 years of age. The funeral services were held Sunday afternoon at the M. E. church, the Rev. Will officiating. The interment took place at South Harrisville.

Alcona County Review, April 23, 1896

We, the children of the late Mrs. Jane Brannigan, feel deeply indebted and grateful to those kind citizens of Harrisville who administered in any way to the comfort of our dear mother during her long illness. The debt of obligation is larger than we can ever hope to pay: we can only thank one and all.

Her Children.

Alcona County Review, April 23, 1896

PERSONAL MENTION.

Edward and Alfred Brannigan returned to the Soo Monday.

Alcona County Review, April 23, 1896
Cemetery: Springport, Alcona Co.

Bratt, Jacob

Jacob Bratt.

Death claimed this citizen at 11 A.M. Sunday. Mr. Bratt was taken sick three days before with inflammation of the lungs. The funeral services were held Thursday morning at 10 o'clock at the Dean school house, the Rev. Will officiating. Mr. Bratt was a native of Canada and had been a resident of Alcona County about 10 years, and was engaged in farming. He is well spoken of by his neighbors; he is survived by his wife, having no children of their own.

Alcona County Review, December 10, 1896

Card of Thanks.

Recognizing the Omnipotent hand in the death of my dearly beloved husband, I cannot do otherwise than submit to the will of him who doeth all things well.

During the saddest hours of my late bereavement kind friends have surrounded me with open hearts and hands, especially C. C. Briggs and family. My heart overflows with gratitude towards all for the sympathy and kind acts bestowed upon me, and though I feel the burden of loneliness very great, I trust it will be the means of drawing myself and friends nearer our God.

Mrs. Jacob Bratt.

Alcona County Review, December 24, 1896

SPRINGPORT AND VICINITY.

Mrs. Bratt has removed from the North house on C. C. Briggs' farm to her old home again.

Since her husband's death friends have been very charitable towards her. Four teams were on hand to move her back home, and a few days before six young men cut, split and piled 13 cords of wood for her.

Alcona County Review, February 4, 1897

I return thanks to Mr. Effrick and family, to Mr. Sinclair and family, also Mr. Duncan McGillis and family for assisting me, and also many other kind friends for putting in my crops and also for their kindness and sympathy. I also desire to express my sincere thanks to my many friends who were so kind in giving me their sympathy and assistance in my recent bereavement.

Ann Jane Braat.

Alcona County Review, June 24, 1897
Cemetery:

Braun, John

CUT HIS HEAD OFF.

Shocking Railroad Accident in the Village of Pinconning.

Pinconning, July 13.—John Braun, a respected citizen of this village, met a shocking death yesterday.

He was walking across the Michigan Central track near the depot. He had just been engaged in conversation with Louis Landsberg about matters in reference to the Pinconning tent, K.O.T.M., of which he was record keeper. Just as they finished talking Braun started to go across the track. The Gladwin train was backing up to the station; it was coming noiselessly, and as Braun did not see it he failed to get warning of its approach and was struck by the coach on the shoulder, knocked down and the wheels of the truck passed over his head, severing the head from the body. Death was instantaneous.

Braun was a married man and the father of three children. Deceased carried an insurance of $2,000 in the Maccabees.

Alcona County Review, July 18, 1895
Cemetery: Pinconning Township, Bay Co.

Brault, John

PERSONAL.

We regret to announce that Jno. Brault is again seriously ill. He is

attended by Dr. Tiffany, who ascribes his illness to heart trouble.

Alcona County Review, March 4, 1897

Death of John Brault.

Last night at 6:15 o'clock the slender thread by which John Brault had clung to this life for days past, parted and the sufferer passed to the silent majority.

Deceased had been sick for two months or more and for two weeks his physicians have had little or no hope of his recovery. Years of hard work was the primary cause of death. He was working at Cowley's camp the early winter and came home about Christmas sick with a cold; later he went back to camp but was again taken sick. His health went from bad to worse until the time of his death, heart failure being the immediate cause.

Deceased was born at Harrisville and was an only child. He was 28 years old and well liked by his companions. He was a hard worker. His favorite work was dock wholloping and it was often said of him that he was as good as any other two men at that kind of labor. This fact was known and appreciated by the master of every vessel that calls here, and John was a favorite with them. But it was undoubtedly the hard work which caused his early death. He was the only support of his widowed mother, who has the sincere sympathy of this entire community. There are no relatives of the family living here.

The funeral services will be conducted by Rev. Fr. Poulan tomorrow at 9 o'clock.

Alcona County Review, March 11, 1897

EVENTS OF ONE WEEK.

John Brault, whose death was mentioned in last week's issue, was buried from the Catholic church in this place last Friday, and all that is earthly of him now rests in the Catholic cemetery beside his father, who died about ten months since. His memory will live long in the hearts of all who knew him, for Johnie was a most faithful and devoted son and a good citizen, and it can be truly said he had no enemies in the world. He was born Nov. 20th, 1896, and had spent his life here with the exception of a few years when he was quite young, when he removed with his parents to the Mining districts of Lake Superior, where he acquired a great love for the study of geology, and he collected many fine specimens. His doubly bereaved mother has the sympathy of all the community.

Alcona County Review, March 18, 1897
Cemetery: St. Anne's, Alcona Co.

Brault, Prosper
PROPER BREAULT.

This old and respected citizen of Harrisville passed from earth about 3 o'clock in the afternoon of Friday, May 29th, ult., after a long illness from pulmonary troubles which had kept him confined to the house and his bed for many months. The funeral services were held Monday morning, according to the rites of the Roman Catholic church of which deceased was a devout and consistent member.

Alcona County Review, June 4, 1896

Card of Thanks.

From the bottom of our hearts we return thanks to the friends and neighbors who so kindly and thoughtfully aided and comforted us by their kind acts and words of sympathy during the long illness and death of our beloved husband and parent.

We trust a kind providence will spare them a like affliction.

Mrs. Prosper Breault.
John Breault.

Alcona County Review, June 4, 1896
Cemetery: St. Anne's, Alcona Co.

Brenner, Patrick
NEIBHBORHOOD NOTES.

Patrick Brenner a woodsman died at the Yockey House, in Au Sable. Remains were buried at the expense of Iosco county as the whereabouts of his relatives was unknown and he left no property so far as known.

Alcona County Review, May 24, 1889
Cemetery:

Bridgeman, Robert Sr.
OBITUARY.

Died—In Greenbush, Monday, December 4, 1882, Robert Bridgeman, aged 68 years.

Robert Bridgeman was born at Cambridgeshire, Eng., and came to this count[r]y in 1837, being then 23 years of age. After living a few years in New York he went to Ontario, Canada, where he lived a number of years, during which time he was married, when he removed with his

family to Ohio. He had nine children born to him, two of whom have died, while five daughters—Mrs. R. B. Ludington of Greenbush, Mrs. Thomas Davis and Mrs. J. C. Taylor of Harrisville, Mrs. Wm. Henson of Alcona, and Mrs. John A. Frazer of Black River, —and two sons— Frank of this place and Henry of Duluth, Minn. are still living. Since the death of his wife, seven years ago, he has resided in Alcona county, living with his different children, and at the time of his death was at the home of his daughter at Greenbush. During his stay in this vicinity he made a number of friends who remain to mourn his loss.

The funeral services were held last Wednesday forenoon at his recent home, Rev. Mr. Riggs officiating. He was buried at Alcona where are also a number of his relatives.

Alcona County Review, December 8, 1882
Cemetery: Mt. Joy, Alcona Co.

Briggs, Albert G.
OBITUARY.

Albert G. Briggs died Dec. 5th, from dilatation of the stomach, associated with chronic inflammation of the stomach and bowels, the result of the typhoid fever, which he had at Harper Hospital, Detroit. He had tried different doctors and most every remedy he could hear of, but to no purpose. Some of them would help him but for a short time only. He literally starved to death, for he was unable to eat one single thing long before he died or to drink anything but a little clear water. (The deceased realizing that death was near at hand wrote the foregoing himself with a view to its publication after his death. The date was left blank of course by him.—Ed. Review) The deceased was twenty years and three months of age. He was born and always resided on the farm with his parents, and was a young man of exemplary habits and left many friends. He was buried Sunday last from the M. E. church, his remains being interred in the cemetery at South Harrisville.

Alcona County Review, December 12, 1890

Card of Thanks.

C. C. Briggs and family wish to thank their kind friends for their assistance during the late sickness and death of their son and brother.

Alcona County Review, December 12, 1890

One Year's History.

Record of Local Happenings for the Year 1890.

DECEMBER.
5 Death of Albert Briggs.

Alcona County Review, January 1, 1891
Cemetery: Springport, Alcona Co.

Briggs, Grace M.

We are called upon to chronicle the sad death of Miss Grace M. Briggs, which occurred at an early hour this morning, from heart failure. The young lady resided with Mrs. Hurlbert, by whom she was employed as trimmer. When Mrs. Hurlbert went to awaken her this morning, she was found unconscious, and Drs. Darling and Thatcher were immediately summoned, but death had claimed her.

The home of the deceased was at Battle Creek where her parents reside. She came here last spring to take charge of the trimming department in Mrs. Hurlbert's Store and returned again this fall. The young lady was about 23 years of age. (—Tawas Herald).

Miss Briggs was in Harrisville a few weeks ago with a line of millinery, and the friends she made while here deeply regret the sudden call of death.

Alcona County Review, November 14, 1895
Cemetery: Oak Hill, Calhoun Co.

Briggs, Lilian Edith
REVIEWINGS.

Died, March 27th, 10 o'clock p.m., Lilian Edith, infant daughter of Charles C. and Frances A. Briggs, aged seven months and eleven days. He shall carry the lambs in His bosom.

Alcona County Review, April 2, 1880
Cemetery: Springport, Alcona Co.

Briggs, Roy John
LOCAL PICK UPS.

The infant son of Mr. and Mrs. E. A. Briggs died Tuesday morning from inflammation of the bowels. The funeral occurred yesterday morning.

Alcona County Review, April 7, 1898
Cemetery: Springport, Alcona Co.

Broadwell, Hilliard S.
LOCAL PICK UPS.

Harry Broadwell, formerly a keeper of the Sturgeon Point L. S. S., and later a citizen of this village, died last week at Wayne, Mich. Deceased was an uncle of Mrs. Fred Emerson, who was present at the funeral.

Alcona County Review, April 20, 1899
Cemetery: Newburg, Wayne Co.

Brophy, Timothy

REVIEWINGS.

Our aged townsman, Mr. Brophy, lies very sick at his home. It is not expected that he can live but a short time. Father Roche, the priest, of Au Sable, visited him yesterday, pronounced the extreme unction, and administered to him the last rites of the Catholic church.

Alcona County Review, March 7, 1879

REVIEWINGS.

Aged Mr. Brophy is still dangerously ill.

Alcona County Review, March 28, 1879

REVIEWINGS.

Timothy Brophy, Esq., who has been a resident of this village for quite a few years past, died Monday evening, after a lingering illness of quite a few months. He had been a sufferer of rheumatism many years, which affected his spine and made him a life-long cripple in the back. He died at the mature age of 75 years, and leaves a wife and three children to mourn his decease.

Alcona County Review, May 30, 1879
Cemetery: St. Anne's, Alcona Co.

Brouthaker, Charles

Small-Pox in Alcona Township.

One Man Has Died—Seven Other Victims to the Terrible Disease.

The surprising announcement, in this vicinity, last Saturday evening, that the small-pox was raging near Hubbard Lake, in the northwestern portion of the county, threw people into a lively state of excitement. No one in this vicinity had been made aware of the fact, or dreamed of the existence of the contagion in the county, until it had been announced that one man had died with the disease. The people in that portion of the county have been accustomed to do their trading, and other business not necessarily connected with this county, at Ossineke in Alpena county, that, on account of roads and distance, being a more accessible point for them, and perhaps that is

how the Alpena people had cognizance of the location of the disease prior to our own people. We are indebted to the *Alpena Argus* for the following information explaining how the small-pox was brought into the county:

"It appears that one Frank Fifer came from Wisconsin a few weeks since, coming through this city, via Mackinaw, and proceeded to his half brother, Chas. Brouthaker, Hubbard Lake, in Alcona county. Fifer was broke out, and soon after his arrival, his brother, who was boarding with the family of Frank O'Dell, came down with the disease, and died on Friday last. Six children in O'Dell's family are also down with the malady, two of whom are now recovering, the other four being bad cases."

Of the condition in which the patients were first found by a physician, the *Argus* further says;

"Dr. Shelton, of this city, was called to see the patients last Sunday, and found them in a suffering condition. In the house, which is a small log cabin, he found the body of the man who died on Friday, he being so bad that it was impossible for any one to remain near him long enough to remove the body for burial, and thus it remains in the house unburied. In the house in another room is a young man very sick with the same disease, who could not be removed safely. Out of doors the doctor found two children, also very bad, and these he removed to the barn, where they were made as comfortable as the circumstances would admit. Fifer and two of the children, all of whom were afflicted but lightly, are now recovering. Mrs. O'Dell was absent from home, and was on Monday of last week confined; but last Sunday she walked three miles to the Cushman shanty, where she will remain and cook the necessaries of life for the afflicted, and send them across the lake."

In connection with the above, it would perhaps be well for us to state that the Supervisor of Alcona township, Mr. Adam Scarlett, was first informed of the matter Sunday night, and very early Monday morning he convened the Board of Health and took action in regard thereto. The Board immediately

dispatched Mr. David Mulholland to the afflicted spot to note the condition of the patients, provide for their wants and comfort as far as possible, and then report progress. Mr. M. removed the patients to a lumber camp near by, and arranged things as comfortable for them as the surrounding circumstances would allow. He then, finding it impossible to bury the body of Brouthaker, set fire to the building and burned up it and its contents. The services of Dr. Shelton, of Alpena, were secured to care for the afflicted ones continually, until they may recover. He will remain with them day and night.

LATER.

The lumber camp to which the small-pox victims were removed, caught fire yesterday and was burned to the ground. Dr. Shelton succeeded in getting the patients out all right, and there being no other house or shanty near by to which they could be removed, they were taken to a cedar swamp, where he built a shelter over them out of bark, and arranged things as best he could with the limited conveniences at hand. O'Dell and Potts, who left the house and went into the woods to escape the small-pox at the time Brouthaker was about to die, came back to headquarters Wednesday all broken out with the disease—Mrs. O'Dell and babe have been exposed and we learn the baby has come down with the malady. We further learn that another family, living near by O'Dell's, have been exposed to the disease, and are not allowed to go outside the yard surrounding their dwelling. The township authorities are using every precaution to keep the contagion from spreading further, and will look after the best comfort and care of the patients, possible.

Alcona County Review, June 1, 1877
Cemetery:

Brown, George W.

Our Neighbors.

Geo. W. Brown, register of deeds for Arenac county was found dead in bed with a bullet through his heart. It was purely accidental.

Alcona County Review, January 17, 1890
Cemetery: Arenac Township, Arenac Co.

Brown, John

The Local News.

John Brown, aged 21 years, was killed at Potts May 10th. He fell under a moving log train. Both legs and one arm were crushed. Amputation was resorted to, but the young man died in a couple of hours. The remains were taken to the home of his parents in Huron county.

Alcona County Review, May 23, 1890

Great Town, that Detroit.

Potts had another shooting last Sunday morning, and a man called by the classic name of "Billy Dutch" was the victim. He was badly wounded, but as is usual in this reckless town, no arrests were made. The next day a man was killed under a logging car and all the mill men went out on a strike. Great town, that Potts.— Detroit Evening News.

Let's see: Detroit never has any shooting affairs, murders, fatal railroad accidents, nor strikes! Oh no! It is only in the wild woods of the north that such things happen.— Saturday Night.

Alcona County Review, May 30, 1890
Cemetery:

Brown, Joseph
LOCAL JOTTINGS.

Joseph Brown, employed at David Nevins' camp, Mud Lake, who was brought to Harrisville last week for medical treatment, having contracted a severe cold which settled on his lungs, died at the Nevins House at 12 o'clock Tuesday night. Mr. Brown was about 55 years old, and had been employed in lumbering on this shore for a number of years. He had no relatives in this country, coming originally from New Brunswick where his people now reside. The body was interred in the Harrisville cemetery.

Alcona County Review, February 25, 1887
Cemetery: Springport, Alcona Co.

Brown, Joshua
LOCAL JOTTINGS

Joshua Brown, an old and respected resident of Black River, died last week of consumption, aged 55 years. The remains were buried Sunday.

Alcona County Review, June 22, 1888
Cemetery:

Brown, Phillip G.
From the Saturday Night.

Phillip G. Brown was accidentally killed at Cartwright's camp last Saturday. A tree fell and struck an axe he had over his shoulder, driving the blade into his neck and nearly severing his head. Brown was an old soldier and was about 58 years of age. His funeral took place Tuesday.

Alcona County Review, November 17, 1892
Cemetery:

Brown, Warren
LOCAL JOTTINGS.

Warren Brown, a single man aged 27, was killed last Saturday morning on Fletcher, Pack & Co's railroad near Hubbard Lake. A log rolled off the train and struck him.

Alcona County Review, April 19, 1889
Cemetery:

Brown, William
THE GREAT STORM.

Probable Loss of the Propeller Oconto--A Terrible Experience.

One of the greatest storms that has prevailed upon the lakes for the past half century, came forth in its wild fury from the northeast last Friday evening, about 5 o'clock, and raged fiercely all night. The air was filled with snow and sleet, and the wind blew at the rate of about 50 miles an hour. The steamer Oconto left Oscoda about an hour before the fierceness of the storm had commenced for Harrisville and Alpena heavily laden with merchandise, horses, etc., for shore people, with also a goodly number of passengers. No clue was had of the steamer from the time she left Oscoda until Monday, and it was feared she had gone down into the lake with all on board, an old sailor said it could not have been possible for her to have "weathered the storm." But Tuesday a dispatch was received from Caseville, on the opposite shore of the Bay, announcing that the steamer was ashore on the east side of Charity Island, about 17 miles from Caseville, that passengers and crew were all safe ashore on the Island.

There was one person in Harrisville who was more than specially anxious about the fate of the Oconto. It was D. C. Emery, whose sister, Margaret Emery of Muskegon, was aboard the same on her return to Harrisville, in answer to a telegram

sent to her by her brother from here. One can imagine his feelings and the lengthiness with which the hours appeared to him, as he waited for some news concerning the unfortunate craft and the status of his aged and beloved sister, during Saturday, Sunday and Monday.

From the Bay City Tribune of Wednesday we glean the following:

Four victims of the propeller Oconto disaster reached Bay City last evening, having come by the way of the Pontiac, Oxford, & Port Austin railroad to Clifford and thence to this city over the Port Huron & Northwestern railway. They were J. R. Vanslyke, clerk, James Ross, second mate, both of Detroit, Walter Bostwick, Wheelsman, of Forestville, and N. C. Potts, passenger, of Forestville. They in company with Thomas Cracker, lookout, John Cavanaugh, wheelsman, and Frank Teiper, second engineer all of Detroit, left the Oconto Monday, the three latter going through to their homes in Detroit yesterday. Ascertaining that some of the victims were in Bay City, the Tribune reporter called upon Mr. Vanslyke and Mr. Ross at the Lefever house and held an interview with them regarding the mishap, which is herewith presented, substantially as told by the writer. The Oconto left Oscoda Friday afternoon at 3 o'clock for Alpena. The passenger list numbered twenty-two, nineteen men, two ladies and a child. The boat was in command of Capt. Gregory W. McGregor, a master whose name is familiar to many people of Bay City, Detroit and citizens of the shore towns, and a crew of twenty-four men, all numbering forty-seven person. After a run of about fifteen minutes from Oscoda the wind freshened from the northeast and rapidly increased in velocity, bringing with it a blinding snow storm, and a furious sea that lifted the boat high in the air as each wave struck it. The fury of the storm was so great that it was seen she could not proceed toward Alpena, her destination, so she was brought about and headed for Tawas light, it being intended to seek shelter in Tawas bay. Darkness set in and the light at Tawas was invisible. The gale increased and the snow fell in sheets. The lake became a living sea of foam, and spray fell over the propeller in torrents, and the snow uniting with it, froze solid to every point it touched. The decks, cabin and all upper works were one coating of ice. The bearings were lost and the Oconto was at the mercy of the waves. Everyone on board prepared to meet the death of drowning, and each wore a life preserver that their bodies might wash ashore and thus be returned to their friends. The two larger life boats were swept from the upper deck, the davits being broken short off at the deck. The third and smallest boat was stove in and rendered useless. The sheets of water that rolled over the sides broke in the windows and partially filled the staterooms. So certain did it appear that they must go down that each was furnished with a list of the passengers and crew, so that should any reach shore safely, they could report the number and the names of those drowned.

Wm. Brown, a colored cook whose home was in Cincinnati, was frightened to death and breathed his last in the forecastle shortly before 12 o'clock Friday night.

At 10 minutes past 12 o'clock a light was observed ahead of the propeller. It was only seen occasionally, but often enough so that the course of the steamer could be changed with the assistance of the surf to the south, southeast in order to clear the land ahead. At 20 minutes past twelve, a monster wave picked the Oconto up and in receding left her hard aground on a sandy bottom in six feet of water. The propeller drew twelve feet of water and the reader can imagine the sea that was running to carry her ashore in that depth. As each wave struck her she rose and settled in the sand and soon became fast, while the sea washed over and about her. The hurricane slowly died away and the weather began to grow colder, but the passengers and crew did not suffer, having plenty of fuel and keeping the apartments well warmed. When daylight dawned and the snow ceased falling, it was seen that the land near was big Charity Island in Saginaw bay. They had gone ashore about three quarters of a mile from the island, heading southeast, or nearly in the direction of the Little Charity. The sea was too heavy then to go ashore. The remaining lifeboat was

repaired and at the first opportunity was launched, manned and put out for the island, which was reached with great difficulty. Charles McDonald, keeper of the light, his wife and children, gave them a cordial welcome, and it was decided to bring all the persons from the Oconto, which was done by using a skiff obtained from the island. Some of the passengers and crew were given quarters in the light house and others in fish shanties, so that all were comfortable. They have plenty to eat, provisions having been brought from the stranded steamer.

On Sunday the remains of the colored man were brought ashore and given a burial.

Monday morning it was decided to summon assistance, and the seven persons above named volunteered to try and go ashore to Caseville, 11 miles distant. They took the light house sail boat, and made the trip safely, reaching Caseville early in the evening.

Alcona County Review, December 11, 1885
Cemetery:

Brownlee, {Boy}
WEST HARRISVILLE.
The infant child of Mr. and Mrs. J. Brownlee was buried in the West Harrisville cemetery last Saturday, and they have the sympathy of all their friends in their trouble.

Alcona County Review, April 7, 1898
Cemetery: Probably Twin Lakes, Alcona Co.

Brownlee, Robert John
WEST HARRISVILLE.

The remains of John Brownlee, the young man who was killed on the railroad, were conveyed to the Harrisville cemetery Tuesday.

Alcona County Review, January 10, 1890

RIGHTEOUS INDIGNATION.
Editor Review:——The deed did at the cemetery near Harrisville last Sunday or Monday calls forth condemnation without precedence. The parents of John Brownlee, with a lady friend, fashioned flowers into beautiful forms and decorated the grave of the late William Brownlee last Saturday. On Monday his father returned to the grave and found every flower stolen. The feelings of the parents, friends and other relatives can be better imagined than expressed. Is there no law to prohibit

this sacrilegious practice? I would advise shot guns to be brought into requisition and used with telling results, unless the graves are exempt from being robbed.

Yours truly,
Geo. F. Howard.
West Harrisville, Sept. 16, 1890.

Alcona County Review, September 26, 1890

One Year's History.

Record of Local Happenings for the Year 1890.

JANUARY.
January 4. Jno. Brownlee killed by cars.

Alcona County Review, January 1, 1891
Cemetery: Twin Lakes, Alcona Co.

Bruce, Duncan James
Mikado Mites.
Mikado, Jan. 22, 1896.--Mr. Bruce, one of the oldest residents of this village, died this morning. His exact age is not known but his relatives say that he was about 105 years of age. He has been in feeble health for several years and was confined to his bed since fall.

Alcona County Review, January 23, 1896

Card of Thanks.
Mikado, Feb. 4, '96.
We wish to thank our neighbors and many friends for their kindness and aid in our late trouble and death of a kind husband and loving father.
Mrs. Duncan Bruce and Family.

Alcona County Review, February 6, 1896
Cemetery: Springport, Alcona Co.

Bryant, Clyde Wellington
EVENTS OF ONE WEEK.

A three-year-old child of George Bryant of West Harrisville came down with diphtheria last Thursday. Dr. Ludlum was called but pronounced the case as hopeless and the child died on Monday.

Alcona County Review, August 24, 1893

ANOTHER DIPHTHERIA VICTIM.

A Variety of Interesting Happenings at West Harrisville.

Harrisville, Aug. 22.--Geo. Bryan's boy, 4 years old, died of diphtheria last Monday afternoon.

Alcona County Review, August 24, 1893

West Harrisville.

Diphtheria is reported as being in the house of Geo. Bryan. Mrs. Byers, grandmother of the little boy that was buried last week, has it but she is getting well again.

Alcona County Review, August 31, 1893
Cemetery:

Bryant, Edith

Died: At Alcona, February 25th, Edith, infant daughter of George and Mary Bryant; aged 9 months.

The Savior says, "Suffer little children to come to me, and forbid them not, for of such is the kingdom of heaven." While it may be hard to part with those we love, it is gratifying to feel that they are safe in another world, and it is our privilege to meet them again, by and by, if we will.

Alcona County Review, February 25, 1881

County News and Gossip.

The funeral services of Mr. and Mrs. Geo. Bryant's child were held at Alcona last Sunday afternoon, Rev. D. Van Dyke officiating.

Alcona County Review, March 4, 1881

County News and Gossip.

Mr. and Mrs. George Bryant, of Alcona, wish the Review to return thanks to the citizens of Alcona for their kind, neighborly assistance during the recent illness and death of their little daughter Edith. Such sympathy and kindness will not soon be forgotten by the bereaved parents.

Alcona County Review, March 11, 1881
Cemetery: Mt. Joy, Alcona Co.

Buchanan, Elizabeth [Winslow]

PERSONAL MENTION.

Mrs. Walter Martin has received the sad news of the death of her mother in New Brunswick.

Alcona County Review, January 30, 1896
Cemetery: St. Peter's Presb, York Co., NB

Buchanan, {Male}

Local Sayings and Doings.

B. F. Buchanan was made sad the fore part of last week by the receipt of a telegram announcing the death of a brother. His death was of very sudden, unexpected order.

Alcona County Review, April 14, 1882
Cemetery:

Buchanan, {Male}

Miss Mary Buchanan has received the sad news of the death of a brother

in New Brunswick. The young man was in charge of a crew of men on the drive. He went out early one morning alone to dislodge some logs; the first log he loosened started others and several rolled over him, killing him almost instantly.

Alcona County Review, May 16, 1895
Cemetery:

Buhlman, Francis

Our Neighbors.

The Karter brothers were convicted at West Branch of manslaughter. This is the result of a drunken brawl last April in which Frank Buhlman was killed.

Alcona County Review, November 22, 1889

Our Neighbors.

It cost Ogemaw county about an even $1,000 to convict the two Karter brothers of the crime of murder and now a paper is being circulated for signatures asking Judge Simpson's clemency. This maudlin sympathy for convicted criminals is disgusting in the extreme. The heinousness of the crime is forgotten.

Alcona County Review, November 29, 1889
Cemetery: St. Francis, Ogemaw Co.

Burcer, Jerry

KILLED INSTANTLY.

Jerry Burcer the Victim of a Frightful Accident.

At 10 o'clock Friday morning another frightful accident took place on Pack's railroad near Hubbard Lake. Jerry Burcer was the victim of this sad affair. Mr. Burcer left Tuesday for the woods to work at Pack's camps on the railroad. Friday morning he went to his work as usual and was engaged in top loading on a log car. While rolling a large log up on the car one of the chains broke, which started the car and threw Burcer on the track ahead of it. He did not have time to recover himself before the car was upon him, running over his neck and nearly severing the head from the body. Before the load could be started back from the body, the whole load had to be removed, and then by the aid of a few more men the car was pushed back and the remains of Burcer taken from the track. The deceased leaves a wife to mourn his loss, as well as plenty of friends. His home was in Alpena.

Alcona County Review, January 28, 1892

HISTORY OF ONE YEAR.

Chronological History of the Past Year, 1892.

January.

22. Jerry Burcer instantly killed by a log train near Hubbard Lake.

Alcona County Review, January 5, 1893
Cemetery:

Burkhart, John, Jr.

Young Man Died.

John Burkhart Jr. died at his father's residence Sunday morning of consumption after a year's illness. The funeral occurred Tuesday afternoon. Service was held at the M. E. church by the pastor. The young man was 25 years of age.

Mr. Burkhart Sr. expresses his gratitude to friends for their kindness in his recent troubles and thanks them for it.

Alcona County Review, November 24, 1898

We are indebted to our neighbors and friends and the Home Missionary Society of the Methodist church more than mere words can tell for many acts of kindness rendered during our recent troubles and bereavements. We thank all and ask God's blessing upon you.

Mr. and Mrs. John Burkhart.
George Hompstead.

Alcona County Review, November 24, 1898

State of Michigan, The Probate Court for the County of Alcona:

At a session of said court, held at the probate office in the city of Harrisville, in said county, on the 29th day of August, A. D. 1910.

Present: Hon. Geo. W. Burt, Judge of Probate.

In the matter of the estate of Edmond Burkhart, a minor: Peter Hart, guardian of said minor, having filed in said court a petition, praying for license to sell the interest of said estate in certain real estate therein described.

It is ordered, That the 24th day of September A. D. 1910, at 2 o'clock in the afternoon, at said probate office, be and is hereby appointed for hearing said petition, and that all persons interested in said estate appear before said court, at said time and place, to show cause why a license to sell the interest of said estate in said real estate should not be granted;

It is further ordered, That public notice thereof be given by publication of a copy of this order, for three successive weeks previous to said day of hearing in the Alcona County Review, a newspaper printed and circulated in said county.

GEO. W. BURT, Judge of Probate.

Alcona County Review, September 1, 1910
Cemetery: Probably West Lawn, Alcona Co.

Burnham, Fred H.

BLACK RIVER.

Gen. Supt. John Millen, upon his last visit here, called upon Mrs. Fred H. Burnham, whose husband committed suicide, recently, and presented her with $50.—Gd. Marais Ex.

Alcona County Review, December 1, 1898
Cemetery:

Burt, Anna [Ginn]

Died Suddenly.

The following obituary notice from the Oscoda Press is of interest to Harrisville people who remember the subject of the sketch as Anna Ginn when she lived here in her girlhood and attended the public schools:

———

Mrs. Anna Burt, wife of Frank Burt, died at her home in Au Sable at 3:15 o'clock Sunday morning, the immediate cause of death being convulsions.

Mrs. Burt was a daughter of Mrs. Thos. Wilson of Au Sable. She was born in Grant township, this county, in January, 1868. Her husband and two children survive her, Earle, 9 years, and Henrietta, 3 years of age.

Mrs. Burt's death was very unexpected. She had attended to her household duties up to Thursday afternoon, when she was taken ill with malarial fever and congestion of the lungs. Her illness was not at first thought to be serious and she appeared Saturday to be improving. Sometime after midnight she was taken with convulsions and at 3:15 Sunday morning she died. A number of relatives and friends, including her husband and her mother, were present at her death bed.

The funeral was held Tuesday afternoon from the Presbyterian church and was a large one.

Alcona County Review, April 28, 1898
Cemetery: Pinecrest, Iosco Co.

Burt, Mrs. Elizabeth

COUNTY REVIEWINGS.

———

Again we are called upon to record the death of the wife of one of our township's foremost farmers. This time Mrs. John Burt is called to the realities of terrestial life. Mrs. Burt was feeling usually well Wednesday morning, but shortly after dinner she was taken with a convulsion and died. It is thought that heart disease was the cause of her death. She was a few days past 57 years of age, a most amiable christian wife and mother, and her sudden departure cannot fail to leave an aching void in the hearts of the husband, children and large circle of friends left behind. The funeral services of the deceased will be held from the M. E. church at 2 o'clock p.m. today.

Alcona County Review, January 28, 1881
Cemetery: Springport, Alcona Co.

Burt, Minnie

REVIEWINGS.

———

Died: at the residence of D. B Mudgett, in Greenbush, on Sunday, February 29th, of typhoid pneumonia, Minnie, youngest daughter of John H. and Elizabeth Burt, of Harrisville, Mich., aged 17 years.

Minnie was a sister of Mrs. D. B. Mudgett, and had come down from the farm home in Harrisville to Greenbush to pay her sister a visit. She was taken sick on Sunday, the 22d inst., and remained unconscious the greater part of the time until her death. She was born at Addison, Stuben Co., N. Y. in 1862, where she remained the greater part of her life, until two years ago, when she removed to this county with her parents, where she has since resided. During her residence in this county she had gained a large circle of intimate friends, and of her it may be said:

"None knew her but to love her;
None named her but to praise."

The bereaved parents, brothers and sisters have the most heartfelt sympathy of our citizens, in the great loss which they have sustained by the death of the loved one.

Alcona County Review, March 5, 1880

REVIEWINGS.

———

There was a large attendance at the funeral obsequies of Miss Burt, at Greenbush, Monday afternoon last.

Alcona County Review, March 5, 1880

REVIEWINGS.

———

The bereaved parents and other near relatives of the deceased Minnie Burt, desire to express their sincere thanks through the columns of the Review, to the people of Harrisville and Greenbush, for the kindness and sympathy manifested in their large attendance upon the occasion of the funeral obsequie of the deceased, and also for assistance rendered during her recent sickness.

Alcona County Review, March 5, 1880
Cemetery: Springport, Alcona Co.

Burt, Sarah [Brown]

LOCAL PICK UPS.

———

The mother of Mrs. Geo. Gill of Killmaster is reported dead.

Alcona County Review, August 18, 1898

OBITUARY.

Mrs. Sara Burt was born in Canada, February 3, 1821, died at Killmaster August 17, 1898. The remains were brought to South Harrisville cemetery for interment on Saturday. The funeral and burial services were conducted by Rev. F. S. Ford.

Deceased came to Michigan in 1857 and settled in St. Clair county, and has resided at Killmaster for several years. She was the mother of fourteen children nine of whom survive her. Two sons were killed and one died from disease in the war of the rebellion.

Alcona County Review, August 25, 1898

KILLMASTER.

We wish to extend our heartfelt thanks to the many kind friends and neighbors who so kindly assisted us during the illness and death of our beloved mother, especially to those who contributed so many nice flowers; also to those who sang.

Mr. and Mrs. Gill.
Abe Robinson.
Justin Robinson.

Alcona County Review, August 25, 1898

Local History of One Year

———

Chronology of the Principal Events of the Year 1898.

———

August 17. Mrs. Sara Burt, aged 77, died at Killmaster.

Alcona County Review, January 5, 1899
Cemetery: Springport, Alcona Co.

Burton, Antonio
LOCAL JOTTINGS.

A three years old son of Thomas Burton, of Greenbush, died this week.

Alcona County Review, November 4, 1887
Cemetery: Probably Springport, Alcona Co.

Bushaw, Mrs. Joseph
PERSONAL POINTS.

Mrs. Jos. Bushaw died at Mud Lake yesterday morning of pulmonary consumption. The remains will be brought to Harrisville tomorrow for interment in the Catholic cemetery.

Alcona County Review, March 17, 1898
Cemetery: St. Anne's, Alcona Co.

Byce, Dan

The family of Daniel Byce have been plunged in the deepest sorrow by the death of their son, Dan, aged 17 years. The young man had la grippe, from which he had not fully recovered when he returned to his work last week. A relapse followed and his decline was rapid until this morning when he passed away.

Alcona County Review, May 4, 1893
Cemetery: West Lawn, Alcona Co.

Byce, Grace E.
LOCAL JOTTINGS.

Mr. and Mrs. Frank Byce, living west of the village, buried their six-year-old daughter last Saturday. Sorrow and loneliness now fills the home, in the absence of the dear one. Only those parents who have lost a son or daughter can understand fully the depths of grief which such a separation brings to the heart.

Alcona County Review, August 28, 1885
Cemetery: Probably West Lawn, Alcona Co.

Byce, Grace Stella
LOCAL JOTTINGS.

During the past two weeks, cholera-infantum has been having a terrible rage in this community, no less than a dozen small children and babes having died from the same. This naturally leaves many houses of mourning in our community, and to those of us who are as yet free from the scourge in our own homes, should come forth hearty sympathy and fitting words for the bereaved. Friday

last, the scourge took away a little, human flower each from the homes of William Nestle and James Stringer. Tuesday the family of Chas. Larson were bereft of their babe, and Wednesday evening Frank Stevens and wife were called to part with their first-born. Gilbert Landon, one of the Messrs. Byces, and the Ducharms have also each lost a babe, and there are several others in the community apparently nearly at death's door, at the time we go to press. Thus many of the homes in our community are being darkened. May the Lord remove the dark cloud speedily, and give consolation to the sorrowing parents.

Alcona County Review, August 29, 1884
Cemetery: West Lawn, Alcona Co.

Byce, Nettie
LOCAL JOTTINGS.

Miss Nettie Byse, daughter of Aaron Byse, aged 14 years, died Tuesday at her father's residence near Harrisville, of congestion of the brain.

Alcona County Review, February 4, 1887
Cemetery: West Lawn, Alcona Co.

Cade, Robert N.
Death on the Rail.

Robert Cade is the latest victim of the logging railroad. He was killed on Monday while engaged in the discharge of his duties as conductor on the Mud Lake branch. A fellow employee noticed something dragging under the wheels and soon discovered to his horror that it was poor Cade who had evidently slipped on a log and went down under the deadly wheels. The train was stopped at once and the mangled remains of the unfortunate man were gathered up. They were tenderly cared for and taken to Black River and then to Alcona for interment. His death must have been almost instantaneous. He leaves a wife and two children. Cade was popular among the woods boys and was considered one of the best conductors on the branch.

Alcona County Review, March 26, 1891
WEST HARRISVILLE.

This community was shocked to hear of the death of Robert Cade, a conductor on the D. B. C. & A. R. R. He slipped off his car and was dragged a quarter of a mile before he

was missed. His wife is reported at the point of death.

Alcona County Review, March 26, 1891
Haynes Tidbits.

Robert Cade was buried on Sunday, the 29 inst. There was a very large concourse of relatives and friends who followed the remains to the burial ground overlooking the village of Alcona and the broad waters of magnificent Lake Huron. Mr. Cade was respected by all who knew him. May his remains rest in peace. The genial and ever accommodating David LaBoueff brought [the body] from Black River in his elegant hearse.

Alcona County Review, April 2, 1891
The Local News.

Robert Cade, the D. B. C. & A. conductor, was not buried until Sunday last to give his fellow employees an opportunity to attend the last sad rites.

Alcona County Review, April 2, 1891
Haynes Items.

Haynes, July 27.--Mrs. Robt. Cade has caused to be erected a monument to the memory of her late husband. The design is the same as the one erected to the memory of W. J. Proctor; it has engine and tender No. 20 and D. B. C. & A. R. R. engraved on it. There is one fault that I find, and that is this, in place of "died" on such a day, I would have inserted killed. There are a good many who have been killed who are buried in our cemetery, who are marked simply as having died; it would show that they had not died a natural death and would be more impressive to the public. The fence of the graveyard is in a very bad condition and the hogs of the neighborhood are running at large in it and rooting and destroying the graves. The Board of Health should take some action in the matter or the graveyard will soon be in a worse condition than the township highway assessment roll, which I think is not yet made out and no labor performed by the overseers of highways so far this season.

Alcona County Review, July 30, 1891
Cemetery: Mt. Joy, Alcona Co.

Cadieux, Procule
ALONG THE SHORE.

AU SABLE AND OSCODA.

It becomes the painful duty of the News to chronicle a fatal accident which happened to Procule Cadieux Saturday afternoon last, at John Dudgeon's camp in Alcona county. Mr. Cadieux was engaged in felling a tree and by some manner accidentally slipped and fell under the "butt" of the same just in time to have it fall upon him. He was killed instantly, his body being horribly mangled. Mr. C. was a Frenchman and formerly from the country below Quebec. He resided in Au Sable with his family during last summer and fall, but had been at Dudgeon during the past two months. He leaves a wife and three children to mourn his sudden and horrible death. We learn that the remains of the deceased accompanied by his family, were started yesterday for Canada where they will be interred at his former place of residence.

Alcona County Review, February 10, 1882
Cemetery:

Cady, Dave

How Dave Cady Was Killed.

The following particulars concerning the death of David Cady, a former well known citizen of Alcona county are taken from the Skamokawa (Wash.) Eagle of August 20, and are republished for the benefit of those of the Review's readers who may not have been aware of the manner of his death:

Last Friday evening about 5 o'clock David Cady was killed at McIntire & Hepburn's logging camp. Mr. Cady was cutting the tops off a fallen tree, and when the log fell off he jumped onto the top end, this threw him and he fell under the log and was dragged down the steep ravine a distance of twenty feet or more. The poor fellow was terribly crushed, but lived an hour, during which time he recognized his friends who surrounded him.

Deceased was nearly 45. He was a native of Pennsylvania and was unmarried. he was buried under Macabee auspices.

Alcona County Review, September 24, 1896
Cemetery: Fern Hill, Wahkiakum Co, WA

Cady, Sarah [Jacobs]

LOCAL JOTTINGS.

Mrs. Cady, of Springport, died suddenly Wednesday evening. The supposed cause of her death was heart disease. Mrs. Cady was about 70 years of age.

Alcona County Review, August 5, 1887

Card of Thanks.

I desire in behalf of myself and my sisters to publicly thank the many friends who so kindly rendered assistance in our recent bereavement. David Cady.

Alcona County Review, August 12, 1887
Cemetery: Springport, Alcona Co.

Cameron, Daniel

Around the County.

Within the past few days two of the county charges at the poor farm have crossed the dark river. One, Jerry Reeves by name, about 70 years of age, died suddenly, the other, Daniel Cameron, was about 65 and had been failing for a number of months past from consumption and his death was not unexpected. Neither had any friends in this country. There are four charges still at the farm.

Alcona County Review, June 11, 1891
Cemetery:

Cameron, John

LOCAL JOTTINGS.

Jno. Cameron, a resident of Limerick died at that place Saturday.

Alcona County Review, May 27, 1887
Cemetery: St. Anne's, Alcona Co.

Cameron, Mrs. Martha A.

A Whole Family Sacrificed.

East Tawas, Mich., March 14.— Mrs. Cameron, wife of the late Henry A. Cameron, a pioneer, died at 3 o'clock this morning of consumption. Her son Willie died about a year ago; afterwards his father, and now his mother. A daughter, Lily, is very low. All were victims of consumption.

Alcona County Review, March 19, 1886
Cemetery: Greenwood, Iosco Co.

Cameron, Roderick

Rhoderick Cameron, aged 30, residing with his parents near Mikado, died Saturday last. The funeral occurred Monday from the Mikado Catholic church, Rev. Fr. Poulin officiating. The young man's death was the result of injuries received while working in the woods several years ago.

Alcona County Review, October 7, 1897
Cemetery: St. Raphael, Alcona Co.

Campbell, Colin

Death of Colin Campbell.

A telegram received here Wednesday announced that Colin Campbell died Tuesday night in Au Sable, at the home of his son-in-law, John Ward. The cause of his death we learn was inflammation of the lungs. He was aged 55 years.

Colin Campbell was one of the pioneers of this county. He had been a resident here for twenty years or more, his business being lumbering and land looking. He resided at Greenbush, and passed much of his service in the employ of E. Mors & Co., and other lum-bermen who have operated in that vicinity. As a township official elected by the votes of his fellow citizens, he on various occasions served Greenbush in the capacity of Supervisor, Justice of the Peace, and Highway Commissioner. He had wide acquaintance among the people on the shore, especially in the counties of Alcona and Iosco, and his friend-ship was very extensive with the same. He was not without faults, and yet he was a man who had brought large benefit to our county in his day. He was of a kind, jovial and generous disposition, and very neighborly. He leaves a wife and large family of children, most of whom are grown up to womanhood.

Alcona County Review, November 6, 1885

LOCAL JOTTINGS.

The old pioneers of Alcona county are leaving us one by one. Colin Campbell is no more.

Alcona County Review, November 6, 1885

PROBATE ORDER.

STATE OF MICHIGAN, County of Alcona.

At a session of the Probate Court for said county, held at the Probate Office in the village of Harrisville, on the 9th day of June, in the year one thousand eight hundred and eighty-eight. Present, Allen Nevins, Judge of Probate. In the matter of the

ESTATE OF COLIN CAMPBELL,

Late of said county, deceased. On reading and filing the petition, duly verified, of Christy Campbell praying that an administrator be appointed for said estate.

Thereupon it is ordered that Saturday, the Thirtieth Day of June, 1888, next, at 11 o'clock in the forenoon, be assigned for the hearing of said petition, and that the heirs at law of said deceased, and all other persons interested in said estate, are required to appear at a session of said court then to be holden at the Probate office, in the village of Harrisville, and show cause if any there be, why the prayer of the petitioner should not be granted. And it is further ordered that said petitioner give notice to the heirs at law, and other persons interested in said estate, of the pendency of said petition, and the hearing thereof, by causing a copy of this order to be published in the Alcona County Review, a newspaper printed and circulated in said county, three successive weeks previous to said day of hearing.

ALLEN NEVINS, Judge of Probate.

Henry & Cornville, Attorneys for Petitioner.

Alcona County Review, June 15, 1888
Cemetery: Sacred Heart, Iosco Co.

Campbell, Daniel Angus

A seven year old child of Colin Campbell, of Greenbush, died from diptheria, Thursday afternoon, and was buried the following afternoon.

Alcona County Review, December 13, 1878
Cemetery:

Campbell, George G.

Two More Victims.

Two Pewabic Wreckers Lose Their Lives in the Diving Bell.

Geo. G. Campbell and Peter Olson lost their lives Saturday while at work on the wreck of the Pewabic, which lies in deep water off Thunder Bay.

The men went down in the diving bell. Campbell, who was the superintendent of the expedition, telephoned up to the steamer Root for hooks. Communication was then suddenly suspended and an effort to hoist the bell disclosed that it had fouled in the wreck and could not be moved. A heavy sea came on and it was several hours before the bell was finally hoisted and towed into smooth water. A window in the bell was found broken and both men were found dead, of course.

These make a total of four lives lost in the effort to secure the treasure of the Pewabic. Wm. Hike of Buffalo died from exposure in 1865 and Oliver Pelkey became entangled in the wreckage in 1891.

Alcona County Review, June 23, 1898
Cemetery: Forest Home, Milwaukee Co., WI

Campbell, Sarah J.

WEST HARRISVILLE.

Archie Campbell's baby girl died last Thursday after a short illness, aged 20 months. The burial occurred at Harrisville cemetery, Saturday, June 8, 1889.

Alcona County Review, June 21, 1889

WEST HARRISVILLE.

On account of Rev. Mr. Goldie's sickness the funeral sermon of Archie Campbell's little baby, which was to have been preached Wednesday night was postponed indefinitely as Mr. Campbell had to make a business trip to the southern part of the state.

Alcona County Review, June 21, 1889
Cemetery: Probably West Lawn, Alcona Co.

Campbell, Thomas W.

LOCAL PICK UPS.

Thos. Emerson writes of a sad accident that occurred at Rose City July 1st in the mill in which he was working. The sawyer, a man named Campbell, fell on the circular saw and was sawed open from his left shoulder down to his stomach. Mr. Emerson helped removed him from the saw. The unfortunate man left $4,000 insurance to his wife and child.

Alcona County Review, July 6, 1899
Cemetery: Rose Township, Ogemaw Co.

Canada, John

REVIEWINGS.

A young man named John Canada, who had been sick for some weeks past, died at the "Old Boarding House" in this village last Saturday. He had been a hard drinker, we are informed, and it is thought that his system became so poisoned with alcohol that it finally killed him. He was buried Sunday afternoon in the Catholic cemetery.

Alcona County Review, October 24, 1879
Cemetery: St. Anne's, Alcona Co.

Carle, Frederick

OBITUARY.

Died at the Alcona House in the village of Harrisville, Sunday, July 8, 1894, Frederick Carle, aged 67 years, 5 months and 1 day.

Frederick Carle was born on the border land between Germany and France, February 7, 1827. He was brought to this country while yet an infant and until 1866 he was a resident of Detroit, from whence he came north and settled in Alcona county. He was a carpenter and mill wright by trade. He constructed the Beard saw mill at Alcona and was foreman for Beard for 9 years thereafter. He was a thorough mechanic and while in Detroit his services were in great demand. The wood work on the interior of St. Paul's church in that city was finished by him or under his supervision, as was also that of many others of Detroit's buildings of earlier days. His death was caused by dropsy, from which he has been a patient sufferer for a long time, the malady having manifested especially dangerous symptoms about three weeks ago, when it became apparent to himself as well as others that his life was rapidly nearing its end. He was confined to his bed but little and was up and around his room the night before his death. He was prepared for death. He died about 6 o'clock Sunday morning. His sister, Mrs. Zerga of Detroit, and brother, John Carle of Alpena, were with him for two weeks prior to his death.

He was brought up in the Catholic faith and the funeral services were held Tuesday morning from that church.

Alcona County Review, July 12, 1894
Cemetery: St. Anne's, Alcona Co.

Carlson, John

EVENTS OF ONE WEEK.

John Carlson, an Oscoda groceryman, was found dead on the 9th inst. and a coroner's jury found him guilty of committing suicide. No cause assigned.

Alcona County Review, December 15, 1892
Cemetery: Pinecrest, Iosco Co.

Carpenter, Seth L.

Hon. Seth L. Carpenter, city attorney, of Alpena, died Sunday night of paralysis. Mr. Carpenter was a pioneer of the Shore Country, and the very first Mayor of Alpena city had. He served also one term in the Michigan legislature (lower house) from this district. He was a gentleman well known in this county. But for the use of strong drink to excess, he might have reached a very high pinnacle of fame in the legal and political world. He was an able lawyer and very capable man. Strong drink was his great enemy.

Alcona County Review, October 23, 1885
Cemetery: Evergreen, Alpena Co.

Carpenter, Edward
Carpenter, Willard H.

Victims of the Gale.

Willard Carpenter and Boat Crew Meet Death in Lake Superior.

A Free Press special says that a disaster has just come to light at Deer Park, Lake Superior, which indicates that eight lives were lost in a recent gale that swept the lakes. A drifting fish boat was picked up Sunday by the crew of the Muskalonge lifesaving station. The craft was found to be a fishing boat that had left Whitefish Point October 6 for Au Train, one hundred miles west. On board there were at least eight persons, including W. H. Carpenter his wife and child and crew of five men. A report that Carpenter had two children on board was not verified. No one was found on the wrecked boat and there is no reason to believe that anyone escaped.

The Carpenters who were victims of this disaster are known to many people in this county. Carpenter was a grandson of Gilbert VanBuren and a decade or more ago he was a resident of this village and occupied the house in which Dr. Mitchell lives at the present time. He was engaged in fishing along this shore.

A subsequent dispatch states that the body of Carpenter has been washed ashore. Willard Carpenter's brother Edward was one of the ill-fated crew. Carpenter's wife, who was an Alpena girl, was not on the boat but is at Au Train with her two children. They are left destitute, as all Carpenter's money and fishing equipment were on the boat. This was to have been the last trip of the season.

Geo. Emerson, Jr., who returned to Harrisville two weeks ago was in the employ of Carpenter on the lost boat during the past summer.

Alcona County Review, October 12, 1893

Were They Murdered?

The remains of Willard and Edward Carpenter have been brought to Alpena for burial. It transpires now that when the men started out on the voyage which proved to be their last, they had between $500 and $600 in currency on their persons. Not one cent was found on their bodies and there are suspicions that they were foully dealt with. A watch belonging to one of them was found in the possession of another man and he has been arrested on suspicion.

Alcona County Review, October 19, 1893

Haynes, Nov. 15th, 1893.
Editor Review:——Mr. Gilbert Van Buren wishes me to state that Willard Carpenter came ashore and that there was no foul play, as everything was all right on his person. His wife stayed till the body was found. Mr. Van Buren went up and ascertained all the facts of the case. They were caught in the storm and their boat was upset.

Alcona County Review, November 23, 1893
Cemetery:Evergreen, Alpena Co.

Carr, Mrs. Catherine

Haynes Items.

Philip Carr who moved to Buffalo after the spring election has had bad luck since he left the shore, his wife and family were taken down with the grip and his wife died in less than three weeks after arriving in Buffalo. He has the sympathy of a good many of the residents of Haynes and your correspondent in his affliction.

Alcona County Review, May 7, 1891
Cemetery:

Carr, Emory

LOCAL JOTTINGS.

Three brothers, Waldo, Eugene, and Emory Carr, were killed last week by the explosion of the boiler in their shingle mill situated a few miles from Alpena. The men, whose ages were 35, 33, and 31 years, respectively, had lived in Alpena a number of years, where they were well known and highly respected. They were the three eldest of a family of five brothers, and had only recently purchased the property where they met such a sad fate.

Alcona County Review, March 18, 1887

The shingle mill opposite Middle Island seems to have an unfortunate time of it. Last winter, it will be remembered, the boiler exploded, killing three Carr brothers, proprietors of the mill. The other day a part of the mill was destroyed by fire.

Alcona County Review, August 5, 1887
Cemetery: Evergreen, Alpena Co.

Carr, Eugene

LOCAL JOTTINGS.

Three brothers, Waldo, Eugene, and Emory Carr, were killed last week by the explosion of the boiler in their shingle mill situated a few miles from Alpena. The men, whose ages were 35, 33, and 31 years, respectively, had lived in Alpena a number of years, where they were well known and highly respected. They were the three eldest of a family of five brothers, and had only recently purchased the property where they met such a sad fate.

Alcona County Review, March 18, 1887

The shingle mill opposite Middle Island seems to have an unfortunate time of it. Last winter, it will be remembered, the boiler exploded, killing three Carr brothers, proprietors of the mill. The other day a part of the mill was destroyed by fire.

Alcona County Review, August 5, 1887
Cemetery: Evergreen, Alpena Co.

Carr, Waldo

LOCAL JOTTINGS.

Three brothers, Waldo, Eugene, and Emory Carr, were killed last week by the explosion of the boiler in their shingle mill situated a few miles from Alpena. The men, whose ages were 35, 33, and 31 years, respectively, had lived in Alpena a number of years, where they were well known and highly respected. They were the three eldest of a family of five brothers, and had only recently purchased the property where they met such a sad fate.

Alcona County Review, March 18, 1887

The shingle mill opposite Middle Island seems to have an unfortunate time of it. Last winter, it will be remembered, the boiler exploded, killing three Carr brothers, proprietors of the mill. The other day a part of the mill was destroyed by fire.

Alcona County Review, August 5, 1887
Cemetery: Evergreen, Alpena Co.

Carr, Walter

FOUL MURDER.

Walter Carr Murdered by His Partner, Charles Wightman.

THE MURDERER IN JAIL.

Fatal Termination of a Quarrel Over a Woman.

In a lonely log cabin fifteen miles to the west and north of Harrisville occurred a frightful tragedy last Thursday night, which breaks the record for immunity from serious crime that this county has enjoyed for many years. The tragedy occurred at Hanshaw's old lumbering camps, which were the scene of active lumbering operations two years ago, but which passed into the hands of Walter Carr, the camp blacksmith, at the conclusion of the lumbering. Carr set out to clear a home in the wilderness and made a livelihood by farming and lumbering. Last winter he had a contract for putting in a quantity of cedar for John Millen, and in this enterprise he was assisted by Chas. Wightman. The two men worked in partnership and Wightman lived with Carr, who had a wife and a family of four children. Carr's wife is a woman of 50 or thereabouts, not particularly prepossessing, but having a reputation for virtue that has become somewhat tarnished by her past conduct. An intimacy sprung up between Wightman and his partner's wife, and as Carr became aware of the unfaithfulness of his spouse and the treachery of his partner, matters became more and more strained between them as time passed on. Last Thursday Carr was working at Mud Lake Jc. for Chas. Foley. Wightman and Mrs. Carr came down there in the afternoon to do some trading. Late in the afternoon the trio started home up the railroad, but they had not gone far before the two men renewed their dispute and soon came to blows, Wightman getting considerably the worst of it. Wightman and the woman continued on their way home but Carr returned to the Junction, and Mr. Foley endeavored to dissuade him from going home that night as he feared that there might be more trouble. Carr persisted, however, and accompanied by his son-in-law, David La France, left for home by a short cut through the woods.

Wightman and Mrs. Carr arrived first. The former was sitting on a bench outside the house as Carr came up, and with a sullen glance he said, "This is a pretty face you've given me, aint it?" referring to his injuries. "It is no more than you deserved," answered Carr, and he passed into the house. Wightman went to the barn and secured a Winchester rifle of 40-60 caliber and returned to the house. The testimony on this point varies a little but not materially.

The only witness who saw the whole affair was David La France, who was present to the end. His testimony at the examination was briefly as follows:

"I came home with Mr. Carr. Wightman was sitting on a bench outside the house. Carr and Wightman bade each other 'good evening,' Carr passed into the house, Wightman followed and said, 'Are you mad at me, Walter?' 'No, Charlie, I am not,' was Carr's reply. 'This is a pretty face you put on me,' said Wightman. 'You deserved it, Charlie, or you wouldn't have got it.' was Carr's rejoinder. Wightman then went outdoors and Mrs. Carr came in. In a moment more Wightman was heard to say, 'Come out here, Walt Carr, you ―― ―― you can't do me now.'" Mrs. Carr left the house at this. Carr arose to go out, but the witness who was standing near the door, observed that Wightman had a Winchester in his hand, the lever of which he reversed once, and said to Carr, "Don't go out Mr. Carr, he's going to shoot you." "Two can play at that game," said Carr, and he stepped into the bedroom and took down another gun and reversing the lever started for the door. The two angry men met on the threshold. The steel barrels of their rifles resounded as they struck together in an attempt to divert each other's aim. Wightman fired. Carr snapped his gun without exploding it and dropped to his knees. Wightman fired again and Carr snapped his gun a second time with the same effect as before and fell forward on his face a dead man. Carr had several wounds: the fingers of his left hand had been struck by the first fire, which must also have struck the sight on his gun detaching it. A rough flesh wound in the neck was evidently caused by the broken sight. The principal wound, which was the fatal

one, entered Carr's right breast and passing through his body came out about two inches to the left of the navel. It was an ugly wound and death was instantaneous.

Mrs. Carr, La France and the children gathered around to witness Wightman's bloody work. "I've a notion to blow his brains out," Wightman said, leveling his gun as if to fire again, but the others entreated him not to do so and he desisted. After the shooting all started up the road with the intention of notifying the authorities, but after going a short distance Wightman said he was too weak to go any farther, and all excepting La France returned home. Carr's body was not disturbed. His rifle laid beside him. Officers arrived about 11 o'clock that night, but owing to the heavy rain fall they were compelled to remain the night. The prisoner was brought to Harrisville and placed in confinement Friday morning.

An inquest and an examination of the prisoner was conducted by Justices Shaw and Campbell, but these proceedings were held to be irregular by the authorities here and Coroner Beede, D. W. Mitchell and Pros. Atty. Snow repaired to the scene of the shooting Friday, where they viewed the remains and the surroundings. A jury returned that Carr came to his death from a bullet wound caused by a bullet fired from a Winchester rifle in the hands of Chas. Wightman, with malicious and felonious intent.

The examination was conducted Monday before Justice Beede at the court house. The prisoner, a man of good appearance—barring his right eye, which was heavily draped in mourning—was brought into court. He had no counsel but paid close attention to the proceedings, casting a furtive glance at Mrs. Carr as she gave her testimony.

Dr. Mitchell, the first witness, testified as to the nature of the wounds.

Mrs. Carr was next on the stand. It was undoubtedly the murderer's intention to set up a plea of self defence, but Mrs. Carr was threatened with prosecution for complicity in the crime, and as the price of immunity she promised the prosecuting attorney that she would make a clean breast of the whole affair. Her testimony proves that Carr's murder was the result of a diabolical plot, and that Mrs. Carr is not entirely free from guilt. While on their way home Wightman said, "He'll be sorry for this. I'll shoot him." She testified that when she and Wightman arrived home the latter went into the room where two Winchester guns were always kept. She heard the click of the gun as Wightman unloaded it, the shells falling on the floor. Wightman picked these up and put them in his pocket. He came out with Carr's gun. He said, "I'll go up the hill and I'll shoot him up there." Mrs. Carr said, "No, he won't come from that way." In answer to a question she said she believed from Wightman's actions and remarks that he intended to shoot Carr, but in the next breath, when asked why she did not tell her husband when he came home, she said she did not give it a second thought and did not think Wightman would do it. Mrs. Carr went to milk and Carr arrived during her absence. She returned to the house as soon as she had finished milking, just in time to hear Wightman challenge Carr to come out. She left the house again with her children because she expected a fuss and did not want to see it. After the shooting and the arrival of the officers, the gun Carr had was found to contain four loaded cartridges and one empty one. Mrs. Carr admitted on the stand that she believed that they were replaced in the gun after the tragedy by Wightman. After the tragedy all of them started to go to the settlement to notify the authorities, but after going a short distance all but La France returned, and on their way home Wightman said he had a notion to load Carr's gun. Mrs. Carr supposed he did but she did not see him do it.

At this juncture the prisoner was permitted to cross examine the witness and he asked the following questions:

"Are you positive which gun I drew those cartridges from?"

Ans.—"No, sir, I am not."

"Did you see me pick that gun up after we came back?"

Ans.—"No, sir, I did not."

"Did you see me put any shells in it?"

Ans.—"No, sir, I did not."

The prisoner was not put on the stand Monday but an adjournment was taken until yesterday afternoon. He was asked if he desired to say anything or make any statement, but he answered in the negative. He has no attorney. He expected to retain O. H. Smith, but the latter did not care to handle it. The People rested their case and the prisoner having nothing to say was bound over for trial to the circuit court without bail. He at first expressed a willingness to have the trial take place at the ensuing term of court, but now pleads his inability to secure a certain witness by that time. He does not divulge who this witness is.

BEHIND THE BARS.

The Review scribe paid the murderer a visit in his cell. He is a man of 35 years of age, rather pleasing in appearance and address and of more than average intelligence. He is unmarried and says he is a native of Watkins, Schuyler county, N. Y. He has not heard from his relatives in many years. He was closely questioned in regard to the various features of the case. He says that Carr and himself quarreled at times but he did not know that Carr was jealous and that he was never accused by him of intimacy with his partner's wife. The fight on the railroad track he says was unprovoked; as they were walking along Carr suddenly said, "I have a notion to cut the heart out of you," and in a moment more Carr knocked him down and kicked him. He denies removing the cartridges from Carr's gun, but says he took them from the gun he used himself and then put in fresh ones. He entered a general denial to all the criminating testimony offered by Mrs. Carr upon the stand.

He evidently does not realize the enormity of his crime, and appears confident that he can establish his innocence, or rather that he was not the aggressor, although he would not divulge his reasons for expecting to clear himself. He and Carr were general partners, owning the farm and crops together and generally working together.

The general reputation of the Carr family, especially the female part of it, is not good. Many of the depredations that have been committed in that section during recent years have been charged to them.

MRS. CARR IN LIMBO.

Suspecting that Mrs. Carr might not be on hand when she was most wanted a warrant was issued for her. Yesterday morning Sheriff McDonald started for the Carr house and arrived at West Harrisville just in time. She was at the station and was prepared to take the train south, she said for Au Sable. She was brought to Harrisville and is now in jail pending the furnishing of $500 bonds for her appearance at circuit court.

Alcona County Review, September 29, 1892

For Court and Jury to Decide.

The following is a complete list of cases to be tried at the next session of court:

People vs. Chas. Wightman, Murder.

Alcona County Review, September 29, 1892

DONE BY THE COURT.

Chas. Weightman, the murderer of Walter Carr (or Kerr) was arraigned and a plea of not guilty entered by direction of the court, the prisoner refusing to plead. The defense not being ready to proceed the case was continued. C. R. Henry has been retained by Pros. Atty. Snow to assist him in the prosecution.

Alcona County Review, October 6, 1892

SOMEWHAT PERSONAL.

The Rev. N. C. Kerr of Watrousville, Tuscola county, Mich., was present at the opening of court this week. He is a brother of the man who was murdered two weeks ago.

Alcona County Review, October 6, 1892

The crops of Kerr & Wightman have been taken care of by John Millen, to whom they were indebted for $60. If anything remains after deducting this amount it will be used to defray the expenses of defending Murderer Wightman. W. E. Depew will assist in his defence.

Alcona County Review, October 27, 1892

The next term of court in Alcona county is expected to be considerable of a term. There will be the case of the People vs. Wightman for murder and there is a possibility that the two damage suits of McNally and Cowley & Lott vs. Geo. L. Colwell may be taken up again. There will also be the usual number of other suits.

Alcona County Review, November 24, 1892

FOR COURT AND JURY.

Cases Awaiting Trial at the Next Term of Court.

The following is a list of cases noticed for trial at the ensuing term of court which convenes at Harrisville Tuesday, Jan. 3, next. There are seven criminal cases, the largest number at one term for many years.

Criminal.

The People vs. Charles Weightman, murder.

Alcona County Review, December 29, 1892

MATTERS IN COURT.

Several Important Cases Go Over to the Next Session.

The star case of the present session of court, which convened at Harrisville Tuesday morning, is unquestionably the Weightman murder trial. The freshness of the details of this atrocious crime in the public mind and the absolute certainty beyond peradventure that Weightman is the man who killed Walter Carr, have served to excite the curiosity of the public and make them wonder what the methods and what the nature of the defense will be. With W. E. Depew as attorney for the defendant and Hon. C. R. Henry associated with M. D. Snow in the prosecution, everyone has looked forward to this as a legal battle of rare interest. The defense will endeavor to satisfy the jury unquestionably that it was a case of justifiable homicide, to a certain extent. They will endeavor to prove that Weightman had been subject to constant abuse by Carr and that this was aggravated on the day of the murder, when the two men had a fight on the railroad track near Mud Lake Jc. The defense will claim that Carr was generally the aggressor. To many it seems that any other verdict than that of guilty of murder is out of the question. Weightman killed Carr unquestionably. He does not deny it. Mrs. Carr, wife of the murdered man, admitted last fall to Pros. Attorney Snow that before Carr's return Weightman loaded a rifle and carried the same outside the house; also that he emptied the cartridges from another rifle which was the weapon that Carr seized and held in his hand

when the tragedy occurred. John LaFrance's testimony at the examination is also very damaging to Weightman.

Weightman was arraigned Tuesday and the impaneling of a jury was begun, but the regular panel was soon exhausted and the court ordered the sheriff to summon a special panel of 100 talesmen. Pending the return of the summons further consideration of the case was postponed. The prosecution asked leave of the court to endorse the names of four new witnesses on the information. The defense objected and asked for continuance of the case until next term. The motion for a continuance was afterward withdrawn and the case was resumed this morning and the attempt to secure a jury is now being made.

At the opening of court, as Pros. Attorney Smith had advised with the defendants in most of the criminal cases, the court appointed Ex-Pros. M. D. Snow to act as prosecutor in the cases against Weightman for murder, Karpel, hawker and peddler, and the LaLiberty larceny case.

Alcona County Review, January 5, 1893

PERSONAL MENTION.

W. E. Depew arrived in the city Friday last to fortify himself with facts, figures and law in several cases in which he appears as attorney, including among others the Wightman murder case, in which he appears for the defendant.

Alcona County Review, January 5, 1893

HISTORY OF ONE YEAR.

Chronological History of the Past Year, 1892.

September.

22. Walter Carr murdered by his partner, Chas. Wightman, near Mud Lake Jc. Weightman arrested and bound over for trial.

Alcona County Review, January 5, 1893

Gone Up for Life

The Murderer of Walter Carr at the Bar of Justice.

A FAIR AND IMPARTIAL TRIAL

Clearly Establishes the Guilt of Charles Weightman.

HE IS NOW BEHIND PRISON BARS.

The Weightman murder trial is ended. It ended without a shadow of doubt as it should have done. A jury of his peers, sitting in solemn judgment on his case has passed a verdict that convicts Chas. Weightman of the fearful crime of taking a fellow creature's life with malice aforethought, and as a penalty for this crime he has been sentenced to the penitentiary for life at hard labor.

THE CRIME &C.

The crime for which Charles Weightman stands convicted, was committed on Sept. 22, 1892. The scene of the tragedy was a lonely log house which had once been part of a set of log camps located about 5 miles by an indirect route, west from Mud Lake Jc. and in the township of Haynes. The nearest neighbors lived three miles away through the woods. In this house lived Weightman with Walter Carr and the latter's family, consisting of his wife and their children. Carr and Weightman had been co-partners for a year prior to this. They had purchased a quarter section of land of Alger, Smith & Co. and had made a small clearing on it and had planted crops of corn, potatoes, bagas and buckwheat. The also took cedar jobs and cut hemlock bark and did such other work as came to hand, sharing equally in the profits and dividing the expense of maintaining the establishment. At the time the crime was committed they were engaged in building a barn at Mud Lake Jc. for Chas. Foley. From testimony that was taken at the examination before Justice Beede, which was excluded at this trial, it appears that an intimacy had sprung up between Weightman and his partner's wife or at least Carr suspected that such was the case and many jangles were the result. The Carr house bore rather a hard reputation among the neighbors and it was suspected that it was a rendezvous for a class of petty malefactors, who sallied forth on lawless errands, secure in their retreat from public espionage.

On the morning of September 22nd Carr went to the Junction as usual. Weightman remained at home until about 10 o'clock, when he and Mrs. Carr started for the Junction to get needed provisions. Carr and Weightman had a drink together there in Foley's saloon but neither drank to excess or became intoxicated. After the arrival of the freight all started home up the railroad track. When they had gone about 60 rods the two men had an altercation. The woman's testimony as to details of this encounter is the same as Weightman's. Not a word had been spoken between the two men since they left the station. There had been no words and no dispute. Dropping a cradle he carried in his hand Carr suddenly stepped up to Weightman and catching him by the shoulder turned him around and with an oath, exclaimed "I've a notion to cut the heart out of you!" dealt him a blow in the temple which felled him to the ground. Pouncing on his prostrate form Carr turned Weightman's face up to him and dealt him three more blows. Weightman took his licking like a little man, offering no resistance either by word or act to Carr's treatment. This bit of romance was further embellished by a statement that he arose and reaching out his hand offered it to Carr at the same time saying to him, "What have you got against me, Walter?" Then Walter knocked him down again and kicked him. Weightman then arose and without more ado started for home with Mrs. Carr, Carr himself returning to Mud Lake Jc.

Leaving the Junction, Carr started home by a short cut accompanied by his son-in-law, David La France. Friends endeavored to dissuade him from going home that night as more trouble was feared. Arriving home they found Weightman sitting in front of the house. They exchanged greetings, Carr passed into the house followed by La France; Weightman came in after them.

"Are you mad at me, Walter," he said, speaking to Carr.

"No, Charlie, I am not," was the reply.

"This is a pretty face you have put on me, ain't it?" he rejoined, referring to his injuries.

"You deserved it, Charlie, or you wouldn't have got it," was the reply.

Weightman turned then and went out of the house. In a few minutes La France, who was standing by the door inside, put his head out and saw him approaching the house with the rifle in his hand. Weightman exclaimed, "Come out here, Walt Carr, you --- of a ----, you can't do me now," at the same time reversing the lever of his gun to throw a cartridge in position for firing. Carr started to go out but La France urged him not to do so for he had a gun and intended to shoot him. "Two can play at that game, " said Carr, and he stepped into the adjoining room and taking down the rifle from which the cartridges had been extracted started for the door.

The two men met on the threshold. Their rifles clashed as they strove to divert each other's aim. Weightman fired, the shot knocking the sight off Carr's gun, which grazed his knuckles and his throat, and lodged in his right shoulder. Carr's gun snapped and Weightman fired again. This was the fatal shot, penetrating his right breast and passing through the body, striking the heart in its passage, producing instant death. The first shot brought Carr to his knees; after the last one he fell over on his face a dead man.

Mrs. Carr had taken the children as soon as her husband came home and went with them off to the barn. At the examination she gave as reason for this that she feared trouble and did not want to see it.

As the body of the murdered man lay prostrate before them, and the smoking Winchester was still in the murderer's hand, he said, "I've a notion to blow his brains out," but the wife and La France implored him not to do so saying that he had done enough.

After the tragedy the murderer, accompanied by all the witnesses to it, started for the settlement, the murderer expecting to give himself up, but after going a mile all but La France and the oldest girl returned to the house, the latter going on to notify the authorities of the tragedy.

The officers returned at 11 o'clock. The murderer submitted quietly to arrest and after a quasi examination before Justice Shaw was brought to Harrisville and lodged in jail the following morning, where he has been since confined.

THE TRIAL.

The murderer was arraigned Tuesday at the opening of court. W. E. Depew, who had been appointed to defend him, was present and Ex-Pros. Atty. Snow and Hon. C. R. Henry appeared for the People.

The regular panel and nearly the whole of a special panel of 100 jurors was exhausted before 12 men satisfactory to both sides could be found to try the case. It was not until late Thursday afternoon that the jury was completed as follows: Anthony Procunier, Peter Carlson, Geo. Layor, Wm. Balance, jno. S. Fullerton, Rosell Lee, Donald McIvor, Josiah D. Coon, Jacob Kramer, Lauchlin C. McIvor, Louis DeRosia, Jr., Albert Ducharme.

The taking of testimony was begun at the evening session. Mrs. Carr, wife of the murdered man, was put on the stand. She had been forcibly detained as a prisoner in the county jail since the murder to secure her presence at this trial.

After the impanelling of a jury had begun, an attempt was made to secure a change of venue, but Judge Simpson put an emphatic veto on it and declared that the case would have to be tried in Alcona county and at that time if every man it the county had to be subpoenaed.

We shall not attempt to give Mrs. Carr's testimony, or in fact any of it in detail. Space is too limited. She was on the stand until 9 o'clock Thursday evening, at which time one of the jurors became so sleepy that an adjournment was taken until Friday morning, when she was put on the stand again.

Her testimony showed an evident purpose to shield Weightman as far as lay in her power at every possible point. She told a story at the trial that bore little resemblance to her testimony at the examination. At that time Pros. Atty. Snow had threatened her with prosecution for complicity in the crime and she promised to make a clean breast of the crime, which she did, as the price of her immunity from prosecution.

But her long confinement in jail had given her time to reflect and as the cell she occupied and the one occupied by her paramour were within whispering distance, it was the theory of the prosecution that they had had ample time and opportunity to make their stories harmonize so as to give Weightman every appearance of having acted wholly in self defense.

No testimony taken at the examination was admitted in evidence on this trial. At the examination this witness stated that on their way home Weightman said Carr would be sorry for what he had done for he would shoot him, but last week Mrs. Carr testified that Carr said on the day of the murder that he would have Weightman's life before night.

La France succeeded Mrs. Carr on the stand. He was a remarkably good witness and his testimony did not vary an iota in any important particular from that given at the examination. He was standing within two feet of the men when the tragedy occurred. His testimony was straightforward and he was as immovable as the rocks of Gibraltar. He recited Weightman's challenge to Carr to come out, how Weightman fired first, and poured a second and fatal shot into the body of Carr, who had fallen to the ground.

It was La France's testimony that convicted the murderer unquestionably.

Considerable other testimony of less importance was introduced. Weightman was put on the stand in his own defense. He denied ever having had any trouble with his partner. He related a pretty romance which was the main hope of the defence in clearing the murderer. He stated that blackbirds were destroying the buckwheat and that on the night of the murder and the night previous he had taken his rifle to scare them away. After scaring the blackbirds away he was carrying the rifle back to the house to put it up in its customary place. He had no thought of using it with murderous intent until he saw a rifle thrust out of the house in his face with Carr at the trigger end of it. He claimed that Carr's rifle struck his and discharged his rifle and he claimed to have fired but one shot. His story was the only evidence put in by the defense.

Arguments were commenced Friday evening, M. D. Snow opening the case for the People. He was followed by W. E. Depew for the defense, who made the best of a bad case, bringing everything to bear

upon the jury to secure an acquittal on the ground of justifiable homicide, or at least a disagreement.

C. R. Henry closed the People's case in a masterly manner Saturday morning. He completely riddled the defense. He destroyed the force of the blackbird story by stating that blackbirds, or any birds, in fact, never feed at the time of day mentioned by the prisoner, and further that they never feed on buckwheat. He demonstrated the untruth of Weightman's claim that his rifle was discharged by Carr's rifle barrel striking his hand by showing that Carr's rifle barrel was shorter than Weightman's. Furthermore the sight of Carr's gun was shot off and this could not have been done had Carr's rifle barrel reached as far as the trigger hand of the murderer.

Judge Simpson's charge was lengthy and gave the prisoner every show.

The jury went out at 11:30 a.m. They at once took a ballot which stood 10 for conviction and 2 for acquittal. Twenty minutes were taken up in discussing the testimony and another ballot was taken which showed a clear ballot for conviction as charged. The result was not announced until the reconvening of court at 1 o'clock.

Judge Simpson at once pronounced sentence upon the prisoner, which is to Jackson for life at hard labor.

The general opinion is that it is a just verdict, although but few believed that the jury would agree to anything greater than second degree.

Weightman was taken to Jackson Monday morning by Sheriff Lund.

Alcona County Review, January 12, 1893

EVENTS OF ONE WEEK.

Weightman, the murderer, was rather taciturn and uncommunicative on his trip to Jackson. He maintained his innocence to the last, however.

Alcona County Review, January 19, 1893

EVENTS OF ONE WEEK.

It is a singular fact that three adjoining shore counties, Iosco, Alcona and Alpena, have each contributed a life convict to Jackson prison within the past month: Iosco county sent Benson; Alpena county sent Grossman and Alcona county

sends Wightman. A pretty trio of murderers.

Alcona County Review, January 19, 1893

PERSONAL MENTION.

The Review has received a letter from the Hon. C. R. Henry congratulating it upon the full and complete report of the Weightman murder trial published by this paper.

Alcona County Review, January 19, 1893

TO PARDON WEIGHTMAN

He Now Serving a Life Sentence in Jackson State Prison.

Sent Up From Alcona County for the Killing of Walter Carr.

B. O. Cady of Grass Lake, Mich., has been in the village several days this week in the interest of Charles Wightman, now serving a life sentence in Jackson state prison for the murder of Walter Carr in Sept. 1892.

Mr. Cady was formerly a keeper in the prison and while acting in that capacity he became intimately acquainted with Wightman. Becoming interested in the man, he made himself acquainted with the circumstances surrounding Wightman's conviction. After a thorough investigation of the case he is satisfied that Wightman was too severely dealt with. While he does not attempt to free Wightman from guilt in the killing of Carr, he believes that the character of the evidence was not such as to warrant the finding of a verdict of a greater degree than manslaughter, and also that the character and reputation of the main witness, David La France, was such that had it been shown up by the defense no jury could have sent a man to prison upon his testimony.

Wightman was tried and convicted before Judge W. H. Simpson during the January term of court in this county in 1893. He was taken to prison Jan. 9, 1893. At that time he was 35 years of age and of more than ordinary intelligence. those who remember the man think the associations and influences which surrounded him at the time of the tragedy had more to do with the crime than any natural viciousness on the part of the prisoner. His conduct since his incarceration has been above reproach and it is this fact that has interested the prison officials in his case. Wightman is now head cook of the prison and a member of the prison band.

[The remainder of the article is taken verbatim from the January 12, 1893 article.]

Alcona County Review, November 26, 1903

News Items.

One of the cases that came before the Pardon Board in session at Lansing last week was that of Charles Weightman, who, it will be remembered, was sent from here 12 years ago to life imprisonment at Jackson for the murder of Walter Carr at Mud Lake Junct. The pardon was refused.

Alcona County Review, November 24, 1904

Chas. Wightman Pardoned.

Postmaster Lund yesterday received word from Charles Wightman, convicted of the murder of Walter Carr in Alcona county in January, 1894, and sentenced to life imprisonment, that his sentence has been cut to 25 years and that he is now out on parole.

Alcona County Review, September 6, 1906

Chas. Wightman, sent up for life from Alcona county for shooting Walter Carr, and later paroled, is under arrest at Marshall, charged with intoxication.

Alcona County Review, June 6, 1907
Cemetery:

Carroll, Jane [Janes]

Family Poisoned.

Dr. Wiley was summoned to Springport to attend the Carrol family. It is a case of poisoning and Gus and Mrs. Carrol are in a serious condition. No particulars as we go to press.

Later——Mrs. Carrol is dead.

Alcona County Review, July 28, 1898

Was It Poison.

Cause of Mrs. Carrol's Sudden Death a Mystery.

The serious sickness of the Carrol family at Springport and the death of Mrs. Carrol, were briefly noted in the Review of last week. Mrs. Carrol's death and the violent illness of her son, Gus, and also of her husband, bore every evidence of having been

caused by poison. Wild rumors were afloat that they were the victims of a malicious plot of another son who had left home a few days previously after a serious disagreement with the rest of the family. As this son had not been home since the quarrel there seemed to be little or no foundation for such a suspicion and this theory was dismissed. Another theory and the most likely one is that the sickness of the family and the death of Mrs. Carrol were occasioned by eating canned beef from a tin can that had been opened and the contents left standing in it for several hours. The milder sickness of the old gentleman is attributed to the fact that he ate his portion of the beef seasoned with vinegar, which may have neutralized the poison from the tin.

Gus Carrol, the son, was very ill and it was stated could not recover. His symptoms were alarming and by Monday had developed into a serious case of typhoid fever.

No inquest and no post mortem were held on the body of Mrs. Carrol and the cause of death is open to speculation.

Dr. Wiley, the attending physician, reports a most unsanitary condition of affairs around the Carrol home. He says it was indescribably filthy, and while he is inclined to the opinion that there were undoubted evidences of poisoning he still believes that the filthy surroundings must have seriously impaired the health of the family. The well water in constant use was in an abominable condition.

The worst of the filth has been removed and the health authorities will see that the conditions are improved.

Alcona County Review, August 4, 1898

Local History of One Year

Chronology of the Principal Events of the Year 1898.

July 28. Carrol family poisoned from canned beef. Mrs. Carrol died, Gus Carrol never fully recovered.

Alcona County Review, January 5, 1899

August Carroll's Hard Luck.

Gus Carroll, the subject of this sketch, and his mother were poisoned at Harrisville in 1898, from eating canned meat. The mother died as

above stated. There was considerable gossip about the affair at the time, and there are those who even now think that it should have been more thoroughly investigated. The step father suffered slightly from the effects of eating the meat.

Alcona County Review, October 11, 1900

The NEWS

A. B. Crow of Alpena and his local agent, S. S. Dorr, placed a beautiful monument in the Carroll lot in the Catholic cemetery Monday. They also placed one in Ernest Baake's lot in the South cemetery.

Alcona County Review, May 29, 1902
Cemetery: St. Anne's, Alcona Co.

Carson, Amon

The Local News.

The Detroit Free Press contained a Toledo dispatch last week to the effect that the body of a man had been found on the Bay Shore railroad who was identified as A. Carson of Michigan. He was an old soldier. It is believed that this is Amon, otherwise known as Kit Carson, a familiar character in this county for many years past.

Alcona County Review, November 8, 1889
Cemetery:

Carson, Matthew

Matthew Carson Receives a Sudden Call to Join the Silent Majority.

Matthew Carson, of Haynes township, died very suddenly Saturday evening. He had been cutting cedar that day and was seemingly in his usual good health. He retired to his bed shortly after supper, having made no complaint of feeling otherwise than perfectly well. About 9 o'clock he spoke to his wife, saying that he felt very sick at his stomach, and asked for some salt and water. He was unable to swallow the mixture, and, pushing it aside, remarked, "I guess I'm done for." At 10 o'clock he was dead. Evidence adduced at the inquest on Monday makes internal rupture, produced by over lifting, appear as the probable cause of death.

Mr. Carson was about 45 years of age, and had been a resident of this county many years. He leaves a wife and five children.

Alcona County Review, December 21, 1888
Cemetery:

Carter, Tom

"Long Tom" Carter, a familiar figure for many years in every hamlet, camp and stopping place along the Huron shore, has been gathered to his ancestors. He died two weeks ago at Plainfield's on the south side of the Au Sable river in Curtis township, this county, of pneumonia caused by exposure. His was a checkered career and the end was characteristic of that part of his life which he has spent in this section, being one protracted spree. Liquor was the bane of his life, the cause of his downfall and his death. Carter was an unreconstructed rebel having fought against the Union and he often boasted of the part he took in that memorable struggle. Carter was a beautiful penman and gained a livelihood in his latter days in that way. A wealthy brother residing at Windsor, Illinois, when notified of his death, wired to Au Sable that the remains should be buried there at the public expense as he would bear no expenses.

Alcona County Review, May 2, 1890
Cemetery:

Cassidy, Peter

Probably Found a Watery Grave.

Three weeks or more ago the trader C. R. Truax in charge of Captain Peter Cassidy and a boy named Gonyou, whose home is in Alpena, left Sand Beach bound for Oscoda with a cargo of apples and potatoes. When she left Sand Beach a stiff gale was blowing off land and the boat was undoubtedly driven out of her course. As no tidings have yet been received of either boat or crew they must have perished on Saginaw Bay. A passing boat reports seeing a lot of floating apples off Southampton, Ont. Cassidy's home was in Oscoda where he has a wife and five children. He had $1000 insurance in the Foresters which his family will get when proofs of his death are forthcoming.

Alcona County Review, November 26, 1891

$50 reward is offered by the widow of Peter Cassiday, captain of the scow C. R. Truax, who is sup-posed to have been lost with his boat on Saginaw bay about October 31st last, for any information leading to the recovery of his body or con-cerning his whereabouts if he is alive.

Alcona County Review, January 7, 1892

AMONG OUR EXCHANGES.

After waiting three years the Forresters have paid Mrs. Peter Cassidy of Au Sable $1,000 insurance carried by her late husband, who is supposed to have perished on Saginaw bay while crossing it in a gale three years ago last fall. Cassidy's body was never found and a story is current that he has been seen in the upper peninsula since his supposed death.

Alcona County Review, May 10, 1894
Cemetery:

Caton, Herbert Frank

Drowned in Rainy Lake.——On July 4th Frank Caton and a number of companions went for a swim in Rainy Lake, Alpena county. Caton was unable to swim and venturing beyond his depth he saw his danger and called lustily for help, but before his companions could reach him he sank to rise no more. Caton was a son of Mrs. Sarah Mills who resides near West Harrisville, and the remains were brought there for burial. The funeral services were held Sunday.

Alcona County Review, July 11, 1895

West Harrisville.

July 9, 1895.
Herbert Caton, second son of Mrs. S. L. Miller of Mud Lake Jc., was drowned July 4, while bathing in Rainy Lake north of Alpena. The deceased was a young man aged 20 years, 9 months and 15 days and had been a resident of this place for a few years. He was well liked by all who knew him and will be much missed by all his associates. The funeral services were held in the Baptist church and were largely attended. Rev. Long conducted the services assisted by Revs. Dunham and Van Horn. The people of this community extend their heartfelt sympathy to the bereaved family.

Alcona County Review, July 11, 1895

Card of Thanks.——I wish to thank the many kind friends that showed us such great kindness, sympathy and help in our bereavement. How kind and thoughtful everyone was. I feel that words are inadequate to express my feelings towards them. May God bless and reward them in my prayers.
Sarah L. Mills.
West Harrisville, July 8, 1895.

Alcona County Review, July 11, 1895
Cemetery: Probably Twin Lakes, Alcona Co.

Chambers, Charles

Mr. and Mrs. Wm. Chambers have suffered the loss of their infant child, making three babes they have lost. The child died Thursday the 16th. inst., and was buried Saturday afternoon. The bereaved parents have the sympathy of the community.

Alcona County Review, November 23, 1893
Cemetery:

Chambers, {Child}

The Local News.

Mr. and Mrs. Will Chambers mourn the loss of their only child which died last week of cholera infantum. They wish to express their deep and heartfelt thanks to the many kind friends who rendered valued assistance during the trying moments of the babe's death and burial.

Alcona County Review, September 3, 1891
Cemetery:

Chambers, {Male}

Took His Own Life.

Last Sunday a man named Chambers committed suicide at Mud Lake by shooting himself with a rifle. The ball entered his forehead and the top of his head was blown off. He was living with his family in Ward's old camps. He was about 35 years of age and had a wife and child and a mother-in-law. A family row in which the latter figured immediately preceded the rash act. Justice Snowden of Black River held an inquest.

Alcona County Review, October 31, 1890
Cemetery:

Chapman, Bidwell

Local Sayings and Doings.

Bidwell Chapman, Esq., well known to our citizens as a former lumberman in this county, died at Nashville, Tenn., the fore part of last week, whither he had gone in search of health.

Alcona County Review, November 25, 1881
Cemetery: Elm Lawn, Bay Co.

Chapman, John

COUNTY REVIEWINGS.

John Chapman was accidentally shot at Ossineke on Thursday of last week. Chapman and J. D. Spratt had been looking over some timber, and arrived at their tent in evening when it was found necessary to go to a creek half a mile away after water. When a short distance from the tent, Spratt's gun was discharged in some unaccountable way, the ball lodging in his companion. A doctor was immediately obtained and the ball extracted, but Chapman died Saturday night.

Alcona County Review, October 1, 1880
Cemetery: Holy Cross, Alpena Co.

Charlebois, John

FATAL ACCIDENT.

A Young Man Run Over by the Cars at Black River and Killed.

Again it becomes our painful duty to record another terrible accident happening in this county, by which a young man named John Charlebois suffered instantaneous death. The accident occurred Monday afternoon. Young Charlebois was, we believe, employed as a brakeman on R. A. Alger & Co's timber railway at Black River. The train was moving at rapid rate back toward the skidways. Charlebois was riding upon a bale of hay which by some means was caused to roll off the car, taking the young man with it, and throwing him in such a manner across the track as that several cars loaded with grain passed over his head and body, mutilating the same in a most horrible manner. The train was immediately stopped and the torn and bleeding form picked up, but all life was found to be extinct.

A coffin was immediately dispatched for to this place, and on Tuesday the remains were brought down on the tug Ballentine and interred in the Catholic cemetery, south of the village, the fellow employees of the deceased turning out almost *en masse* to pay him the last tribute of respect.

Deceased was a native of Coteau de Luc Ontario. Was 21 years of age, and unmarried. Has a brother, married, also in the employ of R. A. Alger & Co. at the River.

The sad affair has cast a gloom over the entire community.

Alcona County Review, August 22, 1879
Cemetery: St. Anne's, Alcona Co.

Charlefour, Bertha M.

From the Lakeside Monitor:
A case occurred in Au Sable this week where one child lay dead of diphtheria, a second very ill, while the mother was confined to bed with a child a few days old. The family was destitute, the father being compelled to quit his work to care for the others.

Alcona County Review, February 9, 1893
Cemetery:

Charlefour, Matheldia

Black River Sparks.

Died on Thursday, Feb. 20th, of consumption, Miss Matheldia Charlefour, aged 19 years.

The remains were taken to Au Sable on Saturday for interment. The family have the sympathy of the entire community.

Alcona County Review, February 27, 1896
Cemetery:

Charlevoix, Sifroi

A Hunter Killed.

Oscoda, Nov. 19.—Shortly after noon yesterday, while Sifroi and Octave Charlevoix were hunting about four miles north of Oscoda, they raised a flock of partridges. Octave took a shotgun, handing his rifle to his brother, and started to one side to shoot some of them. While his back was turned the rifle was discharged, and as he turned around he saw his brother fall. A bullet had entered the lower part of his abdomen, coming out near his shoulder and killing him instantly. His clothing caught fire and the body was badly burned. It was brought to town and an inquest is being held. Deceased was about 40 years of age and leaves a wife and 10 children in poor circumstances.

Alcona County Review, November 22, 1889
Cemetery:

Chevrier, Joseph A. C.

J. A. C. Chevrier Dies Suddenly.

The death of J. A. C. Chevrier, the well known Oscoda business and society man, occurred rather suddenly Wednesday afternoon, Nov. 6th, from heart failure.

"Mr. Chevrier," says the Press, "had been troubled with asthma for some years and about six weeks previous to his death was taken with an attack of bronchitis from which he had not entirely recovered when he was called to McKinley on business. On this trip he took cold and for a few days was confined to his bed. Wednesday, however, he was up and around the house. About 4 p.m. he complained of feeling faint. His wife assisted him in removing his overcoat when he fell on the bed unconscious and expired in a few minutes.

Mr. Chevrier was a native of France and was born in 1841. He came to this country in '62 and next year enlisted on the Union side. He was a prominent Odd Fellow and an active republican and was well known in Alcona. He was buried Sunday with Grand Army honors.

Alcona County Review, November 14, 1895

EVENTS OF ONE WEEK.

Mrs. Chevrier and son Edw. of Oscoda were in town Tuesday on business connected with the estate of the late Jos. Chevrier.

Alcona County Review, April 16, 1896

STATE OF MICHIGAN.

In the circuit court for the County of Alcona--in chancery.

John B. Thompson, Complainant,
vs.

Joseph A. C. Cheverier, Iosco County Savings Bank, Claire V. Cheverier, administratrix of the estate of said Joseph A. C. Cheverier, deceased, Agnes B. Cheverier, Joseph Edward C. Cheverier, Josephine Philomena F. Cheverier, Amos Edgar R. Cheverier and George Rutson, guardian, Defendants.

In pursuance of a decretal order of the court of chancery of said Alcona county made in the above cause in said court on the 26th day of February, A.D. 1897, will be sold under the direction of the subscriber, at public auction, at the front door of the court house in the village of Harrisville, Alcona county, Michigan--that being the place for holding the circuit court for the said Alcona county--on the 3rd day of May, A.D. 1897, at one o'clock p.m., all those certain pieces or parcels of land situate in the township of Curtis, Alcona county, Michigan, and described as follows, to-wit: The east half of southeast quarter of section thirteen (13) and the northeast quarter of the northeast quarter of section twenty-four (24) all in township twenty-five (25) north range five (5) east.

Dated March 17th, A.D. 1897.
Fred A. Beede,
Circuit Court Commissioner.
O. H. Smith, Solicitor for Plaintiff.

Alcona County Review, March 18, 1897
Cemetery: Pinecrest, Iosco Co.

Chiritree, Eugene Russell
LOCAL PICK UPS.
The infant child of Mr. and Mrs. Calvin Chiritree died last Saturday morning. The funeral took place Sunday from the Catholic church.

Alcona County Review, February 23, 1899
Cemetery: St. Anne's, Alcona Co.

Chisolm, Eunice D. [Carpenter]
COUNTY NEWS JOTTINGS.
Just as we go to press we are informed of the death of Amy L., wife of Roderick Chisolm, of this township. No particulars learned, yet.

Alcona County Review, February 15, 1878
Cemetery:

Churchill, Florence
HAYNES.
Haynes, July 14.--Mr. and Mrs. Arthur Churchill buried a child, aged 16 months, on Monday, the 13th, in the cemetery west of Alcona village.

Alcona County Review, July 16, 1891
Cemetery: Mt. Joy, Alcona Co.

Churchill, James
COUNTY REVIEWINGS.

We regret to learn that the infant child of James Churchill died at Black River Wednesday morning. It is only about six weeks since the death of Mr. Churchill's wife, and this double affliction certainly calls forth the most heartfelt sympathy of all friends. The little one was taken to Au Sable, yesterday, for burial.

Alcona County Review, June 25, 1880
Cemetery: Pinecrest, Iosco Co.

Churchill, Mary [Olmstead]
Black River Items.
Died--at Black River, May 13, at 5 a.m., Mrs. Mollie Churchill, wife of J. S. Churchill.

Many are left to mourn the loss of a dear friend and a kind and gentle woman. She was loved and respected by all who knew her. Two small children are left to mourn the loss of a fond and faithful mother. The remains will be buried at Au Sable on Saturday.

Alcona County Review, May 14, 1880
Cemetery: Pinecrest, Iosco Co.

Churchill, Mrs. Sarah J.
OBITUARY.
Mrs. Sarah Churchill, wife of Peter Churchill of Black River, died at her home last week Thursday.

The deceased was an estimable lady and was highly respected by the community in which she lived. Her untimely death, which resulted from lung trouble, is deeply regretted by those who knew her, and the people of Black River deeply sympathize with the bereaved family. Mrs. Churchill was 37 years of age and leaves a husband and a family of six small children to mourn their loss. The remains were buried Sunday in Alcona cemetery, whither they were followed by a large concourse of sympathizing friends and relatives.

Alcona County Review, July 20, 1893

Resolutions of Condolence.
To the memory of Sarah Churchill, wife of P. G. Peter Churchill.

Hall of Black River Lodge No. 385 I.O.O.F.

Whereas, It has been necessary for the kind Creator to remove from our midst Sarah Churchill, wife of our brother, P. G. Churchill:

Resolved, That we tender our heartfelt sympathy to our brother and his children in their bereavement, who have lost a kind and loving wife and mother.

Resolved, That a copy of these resolutions be presented to our brother, and have them published in the Alcona County Review.

Wm. F. Bens,
Jas. Scott,   Com'tee.
J. G. McArthur.
Black River, July 15, 1893.

Alcona County Review, July 20, 1893

Haynes, Jan. 23, 1894.
Peter Churchill has caused to be erected a very artistic monument in remembrance of his wife, in our cemetery. Archie Barley has also erected a beautiful monument as a memorial to his wife. Both came from Port Huron.

Alcona County Review, January 25, 1894
Cemetery: Mt. Joy, Alcona Co.

Cicero, Paulette
COUNTY JOTTINGS.
Paulette Cicero, well-known to nearly every person on the shore, died at Alpena last Sunday.

Alcona County Review, September 20, 1878
Cemetery: Holy Cross, Alpena Co.

Clark, {Girl}
LOCAL JOTTINGS.

Albert Clark buried an infant daughter last week.

Alcona County Review, April 12, 1889
Cemetery:

Clark, Mabel
A Beast's Work.
Oscoda and Au Sable were thrown into a high state of excitement and indignation, last week, over the fiendish work of Dr. D. H Weir, proprietor of the Lake Shore Hospital, in Oscoda. The terrible facts, which came to light from the victim's own lips, are most appalling. Miss Mable Clark, an orphan girl about 21 years old, while lying helplessly sick in the hospital was brutally and repeatedly assaulted by Weir. Some lady friends, learning of Miss Ward's [Clark's] illness, called at the hospital to see her, when the girl related to them the terrible truth. The ladies at once had her removed to the home of a friend where the girl died in great agony on Thursday of last week. Before a warrant could be issued Weir fled, but the beast's capture will doubtless soon be accomplished, as large rewards are offered and the people are thoroughly aroused in a determination to see that he receives his just deserts. According to his biography as published in the Au Sable papers, this Weir has been guilty of crimes heretofore for which he ought to have been hanged two or three times.

Alcona County Review, November 12, 1886
Cemetery:

Clark, Margaret (Maggie)
Haynes Happenings.

Mrs. Lyman Morton has been under Dr. Mitchell's care for several days; her case was critical but now she is reported as improving.

Alcona County Review, August 8, 1895

Haynes Happenings.
October 8, 1895.
Miss Margaret Clork is not improving. Her sister, Mrs. Lyman Morton, is very poorly. Consumption is thought to be the cause.

Consumption is the most fatal and frequent disease in our township.

Alcona County Review, October 10, 1895

Haynes Happenings.
In my last items I said Mrs. May Shaw nee Morton (erroneously printed Martin) is the mother of a son; and Miss Margaret Clark (not Clork) is not improving: she is now confined to her bed with that dread disease consumption.

Alcona County Review, October 24, 1895

A SAD COINCIDENCE.

Two sisters Die on Succeeding Days and Are Buried in One Grave

----

Haynes, November 12, 1895. Mrs. Lyman Morton, nee Sarah Clark, passed away quietly on the morning of the 7th at the home of her parents. Her sickness commenced about three months ago, when she gave premature birth to a child, after which she fell into a decline or quick consumption. She was aged 21 years.

Her sister, Miss Maggie Clark, took her departure on the evening of the 8th, at 9 o'clock p.m., aged 19 years, after a lingering illness of three years from that dread disease, consumption.

The mortal remains of both sisters were conveyed to the Presbyterian church about noon Sunday, when the Rev. H. A. Long preached a very effective funeral sermon. The remains were then borne to the cemetery, followed by a large concourse of relatives and sympathizing friends. Both were interred in one grave side by side.

Memory will their vigils keep,
Gathered 'round their narrow coffins,
Stand a mourning funeral train;
While for them redeemed too early,
Tears are falling down like rain.
Hopes are crushed and hearts are bleeding,
Drear the fireside now and lone;
They, the best loved and dearest,
Far away to Heaven hath flown.
Long, long will we miss thee, Sarah,
Long watch for Maggie keep;
And through many nights of sorrow,
Memory will thy vigils keep.

The bereft parents and husband of the departed have the sympathy of the whole community in their great sorrow in the loss of their beloved ones.

Quite a number of the deceased's friends and relatives from Black River and West Harrisville were present at the funeral.

Alcona County Review, November 14, 1895
Cemetery: Mt. Joy, Alcona Co.

Clark, Mary [Leggett]

Local Sayings and Doings.

Mrs. E. Carle, who went to Sarnia, Ont., two weeks ago, summoned by the sickness of her parents, returned on the steamer Flora. She arrived in Sarnia but a few days prior to the death of her mother, and from her we learn that the death of her father may come at any moment.

Alcona County Review, March 31, 1882
Cemetery: Lakeview, Lambton Co, ONT

Clayton, Elizabeth [Brown]

AT REST.

Mrs. Chas. Clayton, wife of our esteemed fellow citizen, passed away Friday morning last after a long and painful illness. For thirteen months she has been confined to her bed, but she bore her suffering with patience and Christian fortitude, never a murmer or complaint passing her lips. Her death was due to chronic bronchitis and liver complaint. The funeral services were held Sunday afternoon at the family residence, which was in accordance with a request of the deceased that she be buried from her home. Rev. W. P. Tompkins officiated.

Mrs. Clayton was 46 years of age. She was born at Guelph, Ont. A husband and three children, the youngest aged 13, survive her.

Mr. Clayton desires the Review to express his heartfelt thanks to the neighbors who have been so constant and helpful in the hour of his great need.

Alcona County Review, September 15, 1898

GREENBUSH.

Sept. 12, 1898.
Many from here attended the funeral service of Mrs. Clayton Sunday afternoon.

Alcona County Review, September 15, 1898

Local History of One Year

Chronology of the Principal Events of the Year 1898.

August 8. Death of Mrs. Chas. Clayton aged 46.

Alcona County Review, January 5, 1899
Cemetery: Probably Springport, Alcona Co.

Cloutier, Annie

A child was buried from the French settlement on Sunday and another, an 18 months' old boy, died yesterday. The latter belonged to a family named Oulette. Neither died from diphtheria, so far as known.

Alcona County Review, February 2, 1893
Cemetery:

Codera, Alexander

EVENTS OF ONE WEEK.

A Maccabee cannot make out an insurance policy in favor of a mere friend or acquaintance, and expect that friend or acquaintance to draw any money. Alexander Codera, of Saginaw, tried it. The beneficiary he named was J. H. Hambeau. When Codera died Hambeau tried to get the money on the plea that he was a dependent, but the supreme body of the Maccabees ruled against him, and now Judge McNight has done the same. The judge says that the Maccabee contract is plain, and after it has been passed upon by the great camp no action can be taken by the courts.

Alcona County Review, February 8, 1894
Cemetery:

Cole, Joseph

NEIGHBORHOOD NOTES.

Two citizens of Oscoda and Au Sable died last week of delirium tremens. Their names were Henry Erb and Joe Cole.

Alcona County Review, September 6, 1889
Cemetery:

Collins, Hugh

DIPHTHERIA'S HARVEST.

The Dreadful Disease Adds to the Long List of Dead.

A 13-year-old son of Thos. Collins died last Friday of diphtheria and was buried the same night.

Alcona County Review, July 7, 1893
Cemetery:

Collins, Mrs. Isabell

COUNTY JOTTINGS.

Mrs. Thomas Collins is lying very ill at the residence of Isaac Wilson. She is not expected to live from one moment to the next.

Alcona County Review, August 16, 1878

COUNTY JOTTINGS.

The wife of Thomas Collins died at the residence of Isaac Wilson, Saturday afternoon last, from the effects of a cancer. She had been a great sufferer for several years. Funeral services were held from the M. E. Church, Sunday afternoon.

Alcona County Review, August 23, 1878
Cemetery:

Collins, Isabell

EVENTS OF ONE WEEK.

Another death, a girl of 12 years, occurred from diphtheria in the family of Thomas Collins on Sunday last. The remains were buried in the Catholic cemetery.

Considerable indignation was excited by the manner in which this child was buried. Hugh Kearley and Alec Stewart brought the body to the cemetery Sunday Night. Next morning it was discovered that the men (?) had only thrown a few spadefulls of earth in the grave and that the box was partly uncovered. Clerk McClatchey was notified and he at once sent a man to properly bury the remains.

Alcona County Review, July 20, 1893

Alec Stewart and Hugh Kearley, the young men we reported as being the persons who buried the Collins child two weeks since, wish to say that the report was a mistake. They prepared the grave but had nothing to do with the burying of the child.

Alcona County Review, August 3, 1893
Cemetery: St. Anne's, Alcona Co.

Colwell, Edith G.

DIED.

In Harrisville, Sunday, Aug. 23d, 1885, Edith G., eldest daughter of Geo. W. and Mary G. Colwell; aged 8 years and 2 days.

Little Edith died very suddenly and unexpectedly. She had complained of not feeling well at various times for a week past, and Saturday morning became confined to her bed, complaining of a terrible headache in the earlier part of the next day. In the early part of Sunday afternoon her parents thought her very sick, but did not realize that such illness was unto death. About four o'clock she became unconscious and ceased to breath, and then for the first did her attendants realize that the terrible ordeal had come. Her spirit took its flight to the celestial abode of the purified ones. And now, because the precious soul of the dear one is not with them longer, but abideth with the spirits of the just made perfect in the paradise above, no doubt the hearts of the parents and brother and sisters are made sorrowful and grevious, and loneliness overshadows them. But amid all this, if they are trustful in God, there shall come to them that sweet consolation that "It is well with the child." The flower was too tender for earth, and the precious Father has only removed it that he might transplant it in his own beautiful garden in heaven. May the afflicted ones be able to say: "Thy will, O Lord, be done!"

> *"Safe in the arms of Jesus,*
> *Safe on his gentle breast,*
> *There by his love o'er shaded,*
> *Sweetly my soul shall rest."*

Alcona County Review, August 28, 1885

Edith Colwell's Obsequies.

The obsequies of Edith G., eldest daughter of Mr. and Mrs. Geo. W. Colwell, of this place, took place from the Presbyterian Church Wednesday forenoon, a few minutes past 10 o'clock. The attendance of sympathizing friends who had gathered to tender their tributes of respect to the memory of the departed one was very large. The services were conducted by Rev. J. Bain, pastor of the church, in an impressive manner, according to the Presbyterian custom. The address, though not lengthy, was full of many good points worthy of the most thoughtful consideration of all people. A beautiful red cedar casket, encased in elegant white felt, with gorgeous trimmings in white figured satin, satin fringe and tassels contained the remains, the whole resting upon two beautiful pedestals of like covering and trimmings. The floral tribute at the church was very large and elaborate. Among the pieces most conspicuous in the group were large-sized designs representing a cross, an anchor, a lyre, and a pillow, the latter bearing across its face, in small, beautifully arranged flowers the name "Edith." Taken altogether, it was the most beautiful and elaborate floral offering we have ever seen in this place upon any occasion. Excellent music was furnished by the choir, Mrs. L. R. Fiske, of Black River, presiding at the organ. The remains were conveyed from the church to the beautiful site selected for their interment on the summit of the large hill, at the South Harrisville cemetery. The site is very commanding, over-looking Lake Huron and all the country round about. Here, upon this altitude of ground, rising above Lake Huron probably over two hundred feet, the closing tribute of honor and respect was paid to all that remained on earth of little Edith Colwell, and the casket containing its precious remains were fittingly entombed.

Alcona County Review, August 28, 1885

LOCAL JOTTINGS.

Benj. S. Colwell, of Portville, and Mrs. Gardiner, of Angelica, N. Y., arrived in town Tuesday night to attend the obsequies of their granddaughter, Edith Colwell.

Alcona County Review, August 28, 1885

LOCAL JOTTINGS.

J. C. Gram and wife came up from AuSable Tuesday night to attend the funeral of Geo. W. Colwell's oldest daughter, Edith.

Alcona County Review, August 28, 1885

LOCAL JOTTINGS.

Out of honor for the memory of Edith G. Colwell, and the services attendant upon the burial of the remains of the deceased, G. L. Colwell's mill did not run on Wednesday.

Alcona County Review, August 28, 1885

Card of Thanks.

We hereby extend our most heartfelt thanks to the host of friends, both one and all, who so kindly assisted us in our late sad bereavement. May you be spared the necesity of such assistance as long as possible, but sooner or later it certainly will come, then may you be as spontaneously helped, is the sincere wish of
Mr. and Mrs. Geo. W. Colwell.

Alcona County Review, August 28, 1885
Cemetery: Springport, Alcona Co.

Colwell, Margaret A.[Weldon]

PERSONAL MENTION.

Geo. L. Colwell received a telegram Friday that his wife was again very ill and on Saturday he started back to the state of Washington.

Alcona County Review, June 22, 1893

PERSONAL MENTION.

L. A. Colwell has gone west again. His mother's health is very bad and there is more than a possibility that this highly esteemed lady will not survive an operation, which we understand is to be performed for the removal of a cancer.

Alcona County Review, June 29, 1893

OBITUARY.

Mrs. George L. Colwell passed quietly away to the life beyond at five o'clock Friday morning, Sept. 15th, 1893, at the Sanitarium at East Oakland, Cal., where she was under treatment for malignant cancer.

Besides her husband, her son, L. A. Colwell, and her daughter, Mrs. John C. Gram, survive her. What disposition will be made of the remains is not known here.

Later—Later information conveys the intelligence that the interment was to take place at Skamokawa, Wash.

Margaret Weldon was born in Steuben county, New York, March 19th, 1825, where she resided until her marriage with George L. Colwell in 1847. In the spring of 1862 they removed to Titusville, Penn., and in the fall of 1866 they came to Harrisville, Mich., which was then little more than a wilderness, since which time until their removal to Washington a few years ago, she has been closely identified with the interests of this town.

At that time there was no Protestant church building and the organization (Methodist) was in a feeble condition. She at once united with the church and from that time her best efforts were put forth for the advancement of the cause she had espoused and those who knew her best knew the efficient manner in which she overcame all difficulties. She was the first president of the first Ladies' Aid Society held in Harrisville, and many were the garments made under her direction.

In her the needy ever found a friend and those in want were never turned unheeded from her door.

After living to see several church societies started here, upon her removal west she partially lived over her first experience, as there was no church in Skamokawa, and though advanced in years her zeal for the cause of Christ was unabated. It was mainly due to her untiring efforts that a new church was completed and dedicated early in August of this year. Like Moses who was denied an entrance to the "promised land," so she was never permitted to hear a sermon within its walls, but the Savior she had loved so long and served so faithfully decreed otherwise. Death held for her no terrors, and when the summons came it found her "Waiting and watching," glad and happy to lay aside the pain racked body and to enter into the rest which remains for the people of God. The sorrow is not for her, but for those who are left and have yet to cross the dark stream.

Alcona County Review, September 21, 1893

EVENTS OF ONE WEEK.

For the excellent obituary notice of the late Mrs. Geo. L. Colwell the Review is under obligations to Mrs. L. A. Colwell.

Alcona County Review, September 21, 1893

STATE OF MICHIGAN, County of Alcona.

At a session of the Probate Court for said County, held at the Probate office in the Village of Harrisville, on the Thirty-first day of March, in the year one thousand eight hundred and ninety-four.

Present, C. H. Killmaster, Judge of Probate.

In the matter of the estate of Margaret A. Colwell.

On reading and filing the petition, duly verified, of Llewllyn A. Colwell, praying that a day may be fixed for hearing a petition for the appointment of an administrator on the above named estate: Thereupon it is ordered that Saturday, the Twenty-Eighth day of April next, at ten o'clock in the forenoon, be assigned for the hearing of said petition, and that the lawful heirs at law of said deceased, and all others interested in said estate, are required to appear at a session of said Court, then to be holden in the Probate office, in the Village of Harrisville, and show cause, if any there be, why the prayer of the petitioner should not be granted: And it is further ordered, that said petitioners give notice to the persons interested in said estate, of the pendency of said petition, and the hearing thereof by causing a copy of this order to be published in the Alcona County Review, a newspaper printed and circulated in said county, three successive weeks previous to said day of hearing.

C. H. Killmaster,
Judge of Probate.

Alcona County Review, April 12, 1894

LOCAL PICK UPS.

Mr. D. McGregor has caused to be erected at McGregor Park a fine granite stone, in memory of the late Margaret A. Colwell.

Alcona County Review, August 31, 1899
Cemetery: Greenwood Hills, Multnomah Co., OR

Colwell, Rosalie E. [Hooper]

HOME NEWS JOTTINGS.

H. F. Colwell left Tuesday for Scottsville, N. Y., to visit his wife, who is quite ill at that place.

Alcona County Review, February 9, 1883

Obituary.

Died—At Scottsville, N. Y., February 9, 1883, Rosalie E., wife of Henry F. Colwell, of Harrisville, aged 35 years.

Mrs. Colwell, then Rosalie E. Hooper, was born at Scottsville, N. Y., January 18, 1848. At the age of 20 she was united in marriage to Mr. Colwell, and with her husband has been a resident of this village a little over two years. For a year past she had been more or less indisposed, being a victim of the dread disease, consumption, and thinking to gain strength, left just before the close of navigation last fall for a visit among friends outside.

She first visited an old school mate at Cleveland, and went from there to Scottsville, visiting with her sister. During the past few weeks she had been visiting with Mrs. Robinson, an old acquaintance, at their hotel, and where she was taken seriously ill. Mr. Colwell was telegraphed for, and started Tuesday, the 6th inst., arriving at her bedside the following Friday, but a few hours before she died. The funeral took place last Monday, and she was buried near the place where she was born. B. S. Colwell, of Portville, N. Y., a brother of H. F. Colwell, with his wife, and Geo. W. Colwell of this place, were among the friends who attended the funeral. Although not a member of any church society, Mrs. Colwell was a regular attendant, when health would allow, of the Presbyterian church in this place and of the Methodist church at her old home.

Mr. Colwell returned this morning to his duties in Harrisville. The Review joins with his many friends in expressions of heartfelt sympathy in his sad bereavement.

Alcona County Review, February 16, 1883
Cemetery: Oatka, Monroe Co.

Colwell, Sally [Orr]

Local Sayings and Doings.

A telegram was received Monday from Portville, N. Y., announcing the death of the mother of Geo. L. and

Henry F. Colwell, of this place, a lady over 80 years. She had been a great sufferer for years, and death could not but be to her a great relief. She had been a member of the M. E. Church for about 60 years. Mr. and Mrs. G. L. Colwell attended the funeral.

Alcona County Review, June 30, 1882
Cemetery: Chestnut Hill, Cattaraugus Co., NY

Compo, John

From Alcona.

Alcona, Oct. 14th, 1878.
Mr. John Compo, who was lost off a tug twenty miles from Bay City, has not been found as yet. He leaves a wife and two small children.

Alcona County Review, October 18, 1878

ALCONA.

Alcona, November 25, 1878.
Messrs. Joseph and Frank Compo started, last week, to Canada after the remains of their brother John who was drowned in Saginaw Bay. The body was washed ashore on the Canadian side of the Lake.

Alcona County Review, November 29, 1878

The body of a man drifted ashore at Kincardine on Saturday, the 2nd inst. In a pocket was found a letter addressed to "John Compo, Alpena, Mich.," and signed "Your brother, Frank Compo." The following description is given of the body: Stoutish built, light complexion, 5 feet 8 inches in height, almost 30 years of age, had on a pair of chequered brown overalls, with grey pants underneath, grey undershirt and check cotton shirt; when taken out of the water there was on the left foot a boot, with the upper part cut off. The body came ashore face downward, and it is supposed from the bruised condition of the breast that the unfortunate man had been hanging to some spar for a long time until weakness compelled him to loosen his hold.

Alcona County Review, December 13, 1878
Cemetery:

Comstock, Joseph Baker

Alpena is in mourning over the death of Jos. B. Comstock, cashier of the Alpena Banking Co., and prominent as a business man and member of society. His death was due to softening of the brain and came suddenly.

Alcona County Review, August 23, 1894
Cemetery: Evergreen, Alpena Co.

Conklin, William Frank

Wm. Conklin, an Extensive Lumberman at Greenbush, Shoots Himself.

With half our edition off, we stop the press to chronicle the fact that Wm. Conklin, of Greenbush, shot himself through the head with a pistol, at 5. p.m. today. He expired instantly. Had been drinking considerably for several days past we learn. Will give full particulars next week.

Alcona County Review, July 6, 1877

THE GREENBUSH TRAGEDY.

No Cause yet Shown Why the Suicidal Act was Accomplished.

We expected to be able this week to give full particulars concerning the causes which led Wm. Conklin, Esq., the Greenbush lumberman, to commit the rash act of self destruction, on Friday afternoon last. But, as yet, the matter remains a mystery, no evidence having been produced to show that the tragical act was premeditated and deliberately performed while the mind was in a sane condition, or otherwise. We can not learn that Mr. Conklin was insolvent in any degree that would likely prey upon and cause great stress and probable temporary abberation of the mind; neither are we assured that domestic affairs were of such nature as to hold out an inducement to him to commit the act. In fact, all clear evidence which we have gained is decidedly unfavorable especially to the latter of these two causes. All statements corroborate the fact that of late years the home of Mr. Conklin has been pleasant and agreeable, and that up to the time of his death there was no dissention or unfriendly feeling existing between himself and wife. If Mr. C. was heavily involved in any way pecuniarily, it is unknown by his wife or other persons in this county. It is generally believed, to the contrary, that his financial standing was of the first order, and he was abundantly able to pay all his debts without injury or discommodure to his business. But we probably shall know more about his matter when the estate of Mr. C. comes to be administered.

The inquest held over the body of the deceased, brought out no

evidence other than that common with the intelligence of the people. The verdict of the jury was: "That William Conklin came to his death at Greenbush, on the sixth day of July, 1877, by a pistol shot fired by himself, while laboring under temporary insanity."

William Conklin was a large-hearted, generous man, highly respected by all who knew him. He had faults, to be sure (what man has not), but his good qualities overcame his faults, in most cases, and made him very popular with the world. As a business man he took rank among the first of the Shore, and we may truthfully say he was successful in amassing considerable of a fortune, honestly. He was supervisor of Greenbush township, this county, at the time of his death, which office he has held—with the exception of about six months—since the organization of the county, in 1869. He was apparently always jovial and in good humor, and invariably met his friends, which were legion, with a warm salutation. He was a member, in good standing, of the Masonic fraternity, at AuSable, and also of the Knights of Pythias at Detroit. He leaves a wife and three children to mourn his untimely departure, all of whom have the tender sympathy of a large circle of near friends.

The funeral services of the deceased were held in the Methodist church in Harrisville last Sunday afternoon, under the auspices of the Masonic order, of Au Sable. The attendance upon the occasion was very large, more persons being present than the church could accommodate with seats. The sermon was preached by Rev. N. N. Clark, from the appropriate text, found in Chronicles:
"And Saul took a sword and fell upon it."

Alcona County Review, July 13, 1877

Greenbush, Mich., July 9, 1877.
Mr. Editor:—At the inquest held over the body of my husband, it was stated by Edward Chapelle, that he had heard Mr. Conklin complain of *domestic* trouble, leaving the jury to believe that these complaints were of a recent date. I wish to inform the public, as I consider it but justice to my departed husband, myself and children, that these complaints must have been some time ago, which was

at the commencement and in consequence of the business partnership between my husband and Mr. Chappelle, and that there has been no trouble between us since that partnership terminated. I leave the public to judge from the results upon my husband both morally and pecuniarily, whether my repugnance to the partnership, and consequent association, was groundless or not.

Mrs. Emma Conklin.

Alcona County Review, July 13, 1877

The Conklin Estate.

The time appointed by the Commissioners for the reception of claims against the Conklin, deceased, expired some two weeks ago. The total claims received against the estate were about $29,000, $14,000 of which were rejected by the Commissioners. We learn that $10,000 of the rejected claims comprise the bonds which were given by Mr. Conklin as one of the sureties for Edward Chapelle, late County Treasurer. The county has appealed to the Circuit Court for judgment, we believe.

Alcona County Review, June 7, 1878

Circuit Court.

Stephen B. Grummond vs. Estate of Wm. Conklin, for indebtedness-- judgment of $2,535.30.

Alcona County Review, May 16, 1879

Messrs. Geo. Rutson, D. B. Mudgett and G. W. LaChapelle attended the suit in the Saginaw Circuit, as witnesses and defendant, last week--Suit vs. D. B. Mudgett as administrator in Conklin estate, relative to the Chapelle horse.--We believe the suit terminated against the estate, and the horse, now in possession of W. H. Davison, of this place, we suppose belongs to plaintiff at Saginaw. It's a considerably mixed up matter.

Alcona County Review, June 13, 1879

Circuit Court.

The May term of the Circuit Court for this county, Hon. Judge Tuttle presiding, opened on Monday morning last and closed Wednesday night. The following cases were disposed of:

Gilbert Traverse vs. Estate of Wm. Conklin, deceased--appeal from commissioner on claims--tried by court; not decided.

Alcona County Review, May 7, 1880

HOME REVIEWINGS.

In the suit of Alcona county against the estate of Wm. Conklin, deceased, to recover from said estate on account of Mr. Conklin, who was one of the bondsmen for Edward Chapelle, late defaulting county treasurer, Judge Tuttle has recently rendered his decision in favor of the county in the sum of about $8,000.

Alcona County Review, May 27, 1881
Cemetery: Springport, Alcona Co.

Connor, William
NEIGHBORHOOD NOTES.

The body of Wm. Connor, drowned a month ago at Sand Beach has been recovered at Port Hope.

Alcona County Review, August 30, 1889
Cemetery:

Corcoran, {Girl}
LOCAL JOTTINGS.

A five weeks' old daughter of P. Corcoran died last week and was buried on Monday.

Alcona County Review, April 15, 1887
Cemetery: Probably St. Anne's, Alcona Co.

Corcoran, Lorena
DEATH'S SAD DOINGS.

Another of the little ones was called Tuesday morning. It was Lorena, the infant daughter of Mr. and Mrs. P. Corcoran aged 14 months and one day. She was ill but a few hours previous to death.

Alcona County Review, August 30, 1889
Cemetery: St. Anne's, Alcona Co.

Corcoran, Sarah [Kennedy]
LOCAL JOTTINGS.

The venerable Mrs. Corcoran, mother of Mr. Peter Corcoran, of this place, died early this morning from gangrene. She had been a terrible sufferer from this dread disease during the past twelve months, and so intense had been her pain during the past few weeks that it almost wholly deranged her mind. She was upwards of 70 years of age. We shall try to secure data for a more extended obituary notice of the deceased next week.

Alcona County Review, February 6, 1885

Obituary.

There is quite a history connected with the late Mrs. Sarah Corcoran

that would doubtless make interesting reading could we produce it, but we are unable to do so, and must therefore be contented with a few facts, concerning her life, in the make up of this obituary.

The deceased, whose maiden name was Sarah Kennedy, was born in the county of Tipperary, Ireland, in about the year 1808. At the age of 24 years she emigrated to Canada, and a short time afterward was united in marriage to Thomas Corcoran. After the death of her husband she removed to Michigan, in 1872, residing at Saginaw and Bay City until 1879, when she removed to this county with her son Peter, living in Harrisville most of the time since her death. The deceased was the mother of six children, five sons and one daughter. Three of the sons are dead, two of whom are buried in Canada beside their father, and one in Bay City. Her only daughter, Catherin, is married and lives in Bay City, and her two surviving sons, Peter and Matthew, reside in Harrisville.

In April last the deceased was taken with a severe pain in the large tow of her left foot, and about a month later the flesh broke back of the nail of said toe and gangrene set in. The work of amputating the toe next followed, but it seems to have been too late to accomplish any permanent good, as the sufferer gradually grew worse and finally died, having reached the advanced age of 72 years. The venerable lady had been a firm believer in the Catholic faith from her youth up, and died as she had thus lived.

Alcona County Review, February 20, 1885

LOCAL JOTTINGS.

Quite a word error occurred in the obituary of Mrs. Corcoran, last week's Review. The word TILL should have appeared in place of "since" where it read, "where she had resided 'since' her death."

Alcona County Review, February 27, 1885
Cemetery: St. Anne's, Alcona Co.

Coroskey, {Male}
EVENTS OF ONE WEEK.

Dr. J. W. Hauxhurst, of West Bay City, representing the State Board of Health, was in town Tuesday, having been sent to this and adjacent counties to look after the threatened diphtheria epidemic. He first went to Killmaster and then came to Harrisville, in which towns he found that the disease had been eradicated. Tuesday evening the Doctor went to Alpena, where a few cases had been reported and Wednesday he went to camp 8, this county, which seems to be the locality from which all the diphtheria cases in this and Iosco counties sprung. What was done or what will be done at that place will be reported next week.

From camp 8 Dr. Hauxhurst will go to Oscoda. Some weeks ago a man by the name of Coroskey was taken ill at camp 8 and went to Oscoda for treatment. He died there with what one of the local physicians termed tonsillitis and the remains were sent across the bay to Huron county. The doctor says that thirteen cases of diphtheria developed from exposure to the remains of this man, and that he will inquire into the matter while in Oscoda.

Health Officer Mitchell informs us that there is not a case of diphtheria now in Harrisville township and so far as he knows, outside of camp 8 there are but two cases in the county, they being in the family of Dunc. McDonald in Mikado township, where it will be remembered one of the boys carried the disease from camp 8.

Later.—We learn this morning that one of the children of Wm. Hilliard at Sturgeon Pointe is very low with diphtheria. The child has been ailing since last Saturday, but the cause was not known until last night, when a doctor was sent for. It is known that a number of persons have been exposed to this case since Saturday.

Alcona County Review, July 27, 1893
Cemetery:

Court, Thomas

DEATH IN THE WOODS.

Thomas Court Found Dead Near Mud Lake.

Was He Foully Dealt With?

Sunday evening James Callahan, engineer on the Loud branch of the railroad, brought the startling intelligence to Harrisville that two men had been found that morning on the railroad, one of whom, Thomas Court, by name, was dead, and the

other, George Dow, nearly so, both frozen. Prosecuting attorney Depew, accompanied by Justice Beede and Constable Noyes, started for the scene the same evening. A jury was impaneled the next morning, the testimony disclosing the following facts: Court and Dow, who were employed at Loud's camp No. 8, started on the afternoon of Saturday for Mud Lake, a distance of about six miles, arriving at the Nevins House about 8 o'clock in the evening. They stayed there until 10 p.m., when they started out with the avowed intention of returning to camp. The testimony of Dow, which is the only testimony bearing upon the movements of the two from this time, goes to show that they took the wagon road until they reached Nevins' camp, where they struck the Loud branch of the railroad, up which they walked towards the camp. The night was bitter cold, in fact, the coldest of the season. Court stumbled into a ditch, getting his feet and legs wet. After walking a short distance farther Court complained of the cold. Dow urged his companion forward, but after walking for a half or three quarters of a mile, Court insisted that he couldn't go any farther. Dow made an effort to rouse him, but in vain, and leaving his companion lying on the ground, he started in the direction of Nevins' for assistance; but he claims that he was unable to find the place, and it was discovered next day that his steps led him to within eighty rods of camp 8, and at the point at which he turned around his hat was afterwards discovered. Dow seems to have wandered around aimlessly after this, finally lying down when near the railroad track, overcome by the intense cold. The body of Court was discovered at an early hour Sunday morning by Chas. Rutel, who was on his way to camp. The body was lying face upwards, the head and feet being partially submerged in the waters of a narrow creek or ditch, the ice having apparently been broken by the falling of Court upon it. He was not drowned, however. Near here, on the banks of the creek, which is very narrow and barely wide enough to hold Court's body, were evidences of scuffling, the snow being tramped down for a considerable distance around, probably done by Dow in his

efforts to revive Court. Court's hands were drawn up around his head and face as if to shield himself. Rutel, after satisfying himself that life was extinct, hastened on to Camp 8 to notify them of his ghastly discovery. Proceeding about a mile he was horrified to see the body of another man, partly concealed under a projecting root. A movement of the body showed that life was not extinct. The camp was at once aroused by Rutel's story and a party hastened to recover the bodies of the two men. Court was found frozen stiff, having apparently been dead several hours. Dow was very badly chilled but the warmth of the camp at once revived him, and he soon regained his wonted vigor.

Before leaving Mud Lake the men had one or two drinks, taking a couple of quart bottles with them, but when they left there they seemed not to have been intoxicated, and Court is spoken of by his companions as one who was never the worse for liquor. One of the bottles was found half filled, which together with the remaining one was found in Dow's possession. Dow, it is reported has since left camp 8.

Justice Beede's jury returned a verdict in accordance with the facts as presented to them, viz.: that Court was frozen to death.

The dead man had been employed at this camp for some time, having previously worked as a fireman on the Loud branch. He was an Englishman by birth, and had no known relatives in this country. He was unmarried, and was about 32 years of age. The remains were taken to Au Sable for burial.

Later.—It is reported that Dow has left Camp 8, since the holding of the inquest.

Alcona County Review, January 7, 1887
Cemetery:

Cowan, Sarah [Anderson]

Mrs. Sarah Cowan, aged 39 died June 1st after a lingering illness. The funeral services will be held today, (Friday) at 1:30 P. M.

Alcona County Review, June 3, 1887
Cemetery: Springport, Alcona Co.

Cowley, Richard

COUNTY JOTTINGS.

County treasurer, B. P. Cowley, received by dispatch, Monday, the sad intelligence of his brother Richard, who was instantly killed that day, on the Syracuse, Geneva & Corning Railroad. The deceased was a conductor on said road. No particulars were given as to how he met his death.

Alcona County Review, October 18, 1878
Cemetery:

Coyle, John
COUNTY REVIEWINGS.

Died.—At Greenbush, April 26, 1880, of diphtheria, Johnny, only son of Mr. and Mrs. James Coyle, aged 4 years.

Alcona County Review, April 30, 1880
Cemetery: Springport, Alcona Co.

Cravan, Albert
EVENTS OF ONE WEEK.

Albert Cravan, an employee of Alger, Smith & Co., fell between the wheels of a moving train in the vicinity of Lake May and received injuries which caused death in 20 minutes.

Alcona County Review, July 4, 1895
Cemetery:

Craven, Barbary
PERSONAL MENTION.

The two-year-old child of Mr. and Mrs. Geo. Craven was buried Monday morning in the South Harrisville cemetery. Death resulted from inflammation of the lungs.

The death of this, the last of their little ones, is indeed a sad blow to the parents, who are now left childless. They have the sympathy of the community.

Alcona County Review, June 25, 1896

We desire to thus publicly thank our friends and neighbors who helped us in any way during the sickness, death and burial of our little one.

Mr. and Mrs. Geo. Craven.

Alcona County Review, June 25, 1896
Cemetery: Springport, Alcona Co.

Craven, Belle
REVIEWINGS.

Died, on Thursday last, Belle, daughter of Mr. and Mrs. William Craven, of Harrisville township; aged 17 years past. The deceased was first taken with the measles last summer, which being superceded by sickness

of a more acute form, finally resulted in her death. The bereaved family have the sympathy of a large circle of friends.

Alcona County Review, October 10, 1879
Cemetery:

Craven, {Boy}
Local Sayings and Doings.

The Review learns of the death of William Craven's four year old son, (a cripple) which occurred last evening. The little fellow had never seen but few well days.

Alcona County Review, January 6, 1882
Cemetery:

Craven, {Child}
Mr. and Mrs. Geo. Craven buried a year old child Sunday.

Alcona County Review, October 8, 1891
Cemetery:

Craven, Mrs. Isabel
The funeral services of the mother of Wm. Craven, living at Backusville, who died last Friday, were held from the M. E. Church in this village Sunday afternoon. The deceased was aged about 35 years [65 years]. She was a Baptist in Christian doctrine, and died as she had lived, a Christian.

Alcona County Review, March 18, 1881
Cemetery:

Craven, James
Local Sayings and Doings.

The Review learns of the death of the venerable James Craven (father of Mrs. James Pyne) which occurred at Black River yesterday. Mr. Craven as an old resident of the county and aged 86 years.

Alcona County Review, August 4, 1882
Cemetery:

Crawford, Charles
People We Hear About.

Chas. Crawford was killed on the Potts railroad last week, adding another victim to the already long list.

Alcona County Review, October 3, 1890
Cemetery:

Crawford, Ella
The body of Ella Crawford, a 13 months old child that died in Black River on Saturday, was brought here this morning and buried in the Catholic cemetery.—Alpena Echo.

Alcona County Review, January 19, 1899

Cemetery:

Crawford, Frank
AMONG OUR EXCHANGES.

Frank Crawford, a Presque Isle county pioneer, died last week from the effects of opium poisoning. His wife is accused of administering the poison.

Alcona County Review, April 26, 1894

AMONG OUR EXCHANGES.

Mrs. Frank Crawford, of Crawford's Quarry, who had been on the rack for the past few weeks, charged with the killing of her husband, has been discharged. The court decided that the testimony was insufficient to bind Mrs. Crawford over and ordered her discharge. The verdict was such a verdict as the people who knew the parties had expected and completely exonerated Mrs. Crawford.

Alcona County Review, May 10, 1894
Cemetery:

Crawford, John
ALONG THE SHORE.

THE TAWASES.
On Friday last a young man named John Crawford, employed at one of the Thompson camps on the Au Sable, was instantly killed by being caught in a log rollway which carried him down an embankment into the river among scores of logs. His body was not recovered for some time, but when found was brought to this village and encased by undertaker Quackenbush, and on Sunday the body was sent to relatives in Canada his former home. He was about 25 years of age and not married. Crawford is said to have been an honest and industrious workman, and had labored for Mr. Thompson during the last two years.—*Gazette*.

Alcona County Review, March 3, 1882
Cemetery:

Crawford, Leonard C.
Along the Shore.

Leonard C. Crawford, one of the oldest settlers of Presque Isle county, and after whom the port of Crawford Quarry was named, died at his residence on Friday night.

Alcona County Review, November 4, 1881
Cemetery:

Crawford, Thomas

Shore Pickings.

Thomas Crawford, formerly of Crawford's Quarry, died lately at Leadville, Colorado.

Alcona County Review, September 5, 1879
Cemetery:

Creighton, John

Purely Personal.

John Creighton, a well-to-do business man of Alpena, has been missing for several weeks and his friends are much alarmed. The last seen of him was at midnight on Dock street, and fears are entertained that he has fallen into the river.

Alcona County Review, April 25, 1890

The body of John Creighton was found floating in Alpena river last week. He was a prominent business man who suddenly disappeared on the night of April 7. It is supposed that he walked into the river through the open draw bridge in the dark.

Alcona County Review, May 23, 1890
Cemetery: Evergreen, Alpena Co.

Crenshaw, Albert B.

A. B. Crenshaw, the man who created a great sensation last year by marrying a Tawas City young lady while he already had a wife, died in the Detroit House of Correction last Saturday of consumption. He was serving a term of one year in that institution for bigamy. His term would have expired Feb. 4, 1891.

Alcona County Review, December 4, 1890
Cemetery:

Crinnian, Thomas

From the Saturday Night.
When Thos. Crinnian went to Greenbush on Wednesday to inform his wife of the disastrous fire which had left them homeless, he found one of his children, a bright little boy of three years of age, at the point of death. The child died Thursday night of membranous croup. Mrs. Crinnian had gone to Greenbush with her four children a few days previous to get away from the diphtheria prevailing in Au Sable.

Alcona County Review, December 1, 1892
Cemetery:Probably Pinecrest, Iosco Co.

Crockard, Alex

LOCAL JOTTINGS.

Lakeside Monitor: Alex Crochard, who has been employed as bookkeeper at A. Cartwright's camp

on Sage creek for a number of years, met his death on Wednesday by being caught in a jam of logs near the banking grounds. He was alone at the time, about 9 a.m., and was not missed until noon, when a search for him was instituted and he was found crushed to death, his injuries being terrible. The deceased was taken to his home at or near Port Austin yesterday.

Alcona County Review, January 22, 1886
Cemetery: Port Austin Township, Huron Co.

Cross, Philip

A Double Tragedy at Alpena.

A fearful double tragedy occurred at Alpena last week Thursday, resulting in the death of Philip Cross and Jno. O'Hara in the former's saloon. The two men were discovered about 5 o'clock in the afternoon. O'Hara being shot through the body, Cross having received a deadly blow on the head from an axe. Both men have since died. The affair at latest accounts is shrouded in mystery, but the circumstances indicate that a third party did the fearful deed. O'Hara, one of the victims, was once a respected citizen of Harrisville, having in early days worked as a teamster. He then went into the saloon business and has drifted from bad to worse until at the time of his death he was accounted a hard citizen. Cross did not bear the most savory reputation either.

Alcona County Review, November 4, 1887

LOCAL JOTTINGS.

It is now believed at Alpena that O'Hara and Cross must have had some trouble in the latter's saloon, whereupon O'Hara struck Cross with a hatchet, and seeing he had hurt him more severely than he had calculated, he seized a revolver and shot himself.

Alcona County Review, November 11, 1887
Cemetery: Holy Cross, Alpena Co.

Crossett, Benjamin

EVENTS OF ONE WEEK.

Benjamin Crosset, an old and highly respected resident of Harrisville township, passed away at his late home Monday morning after a lingering illness from Brights disease and dropsy. Deceased was of a quiet, gentlemanly disposition and general regret is expressed that he has been called away at the comparatively early age of 58. The funeral services were held Tuesday

afternoon. The interment took place in the cemetery west of Harrisville whither they were followed by an unusually large number of people, some 40 teams following the hearse. Rev. W. J. Bailey preached the funeral sermon and paid fitting tribute to the virtues of the deceased.

Alcona County Review, August 8, 1895

STATE OF MICHIGAN, County of Alcona.

At a session of the Probate Court for said County, held at the Probate office, in the Village of Harrisville, on the 14th day of September in the year one thousand eight hundred and ninety-five.

Present, C. H. Killmaster, Judge of Probate.

In the matter of the estate of Benjamin Crossett:

On reading and filing the petition, duly verified, of Mercy Crossett, praying that a certain instrument now on file in this Court, purporting to be the last will and testament of said deceased, may be admitted to probate, and that she be appointed executrix of said estate and will.............................There upon it is ordered, that Saturday, the 12th day of October next, at ten o'clock in the forenoon, be assigned for the hearing of said petition, and that the heirs at law of said deceased, and all others interested in said estate, are required to appear at a session of said Court, then to be holden in the Probate office, in the Village of Harrisville and show cause, if any there be, why the prayer of the petitioner should not be granted: And it is further ordered, that said petitioner give notice to the persons interested in said estate, of the pendency of said petition, and the hearing thereof by causing a copy of this order to be published in the Alcona County Review, a newspaper printed and circulated in said county, three successive weeks previous to said day of hearing.

C. H. Killmaster,
Judge of Probate.

Alcona County Review, September 19, 1895

The Benj. Crossett estate had a hearing in probate court Monday, but the executorship matter was not settled.

Alcona County Review, October 17, 1895

Anyone having accounts against the estate of the late Benj. Crossett should file same with me at once as the estate will be closed up this month.

B. P. Cowley, Administrator.

Alcona County Review, December 12, 1895
Cemetery: West Lawn, Alcona Co.

Culling, William F.

AMONG OUR EXCHANGES.

From the Alpena Pioneer.

Mr. W. F. Culling, Alpena's first settler and oldest inhabitant, died at the county house on Tuesday at the advanced age of 93 years. "Uncle Billy," as he was familiarly known, was the first white man to come to this section, reaching here in 1835. He was a hunter, fisherman and trapper, and traveled along the shore in a sail boat, knowing every foot of the coast between Mackinac and Saginaw Bay.

Alcona County Review, July 28, 1892
Cemetery:

Cunning, Mrs. Catherina

The Local News.

Tuesday afternoon the remains of Mrs. Edward Cunning, wife of a Mitchell township citizen, were brought to Harrisville and interred in the Catholic cemetery. The Rev. Fr. Reussemann conducted the funeral services.

Alcona County Review, April 23, 1891
Cemetery: St. Anne's, Alcona Co.

Cunning, {Child}

Around the County.
Mitchell Mites.

The infant child of Edward Cunning was buried last Saturday. Mr. C. has the sympathy of his neighbors in his recent bereavements.

Alcona County Review, April 30, 1891
Cemetery: St. Anne's, Alcona Co.

Cunningham, Josephine [Steffes]

PERSONAL MENTION.

Mrs. Wm. Cunningham is seriously ill from pneumonia.

Alcona County Review, May 11, 1893

OBITUARY.

Cunningham--Josephine Cunningham, wife of Jos. Cunningham, at Harrisville, Friday, May 12, 1893.

Mrs. Josephine Cunningham, wife of Jos. Cunningham, who was reported last week as seriously ill, was released by death from her sufferings Friday morning, May 12th.

Deceased was a member of the Catholic church. She was 30 years of age and was the mother of eight children, five of whom survive her. The funeral services were held Sunday afternoon at the church, from which a large concourse followed the remains to their last resting place. Deceased was a charter member of the Harrisville Hive L. O. T. M., and a large delegation of Lady Maccabees from West Harrisville joined their Harrisville sisters and the two lodges marched in a body to the grave. A beautiful floral cross bearing the letters "L. O. T. M." was a gift of the Harrisville Lady Maccabees, and was conspicuous among the other floral contributions.

The certificates of membership for the lady Maccabees were received on Thursday, the day before Mrs. Cunningham's death, so that her heirs will receive $1,000 from that source.

Alcona County Review, May 18, 1893

For myself and family I desire to offer a public expression of our deep gratitude to all whose kindness, sympathy and delicate attention have been a source of comfort during the last sickness, death and burial of my beloved wife.

Jos. Cunningham.

Alcona County Review, May 25, 1893

EVENTS OF ONE WEEK.

Proofs of death of the late Mrs. Cunningham have already been filed and an early settlement of the insurance on her life is looked for. Deceased had never paid an assessment except the one required in advance.

Alcona County Review, May 25, 1893

EVENTS OF ONE WEEK.

Jos. Cunningham received a check for $1,000 in Tuesday's mail, being the amount of insurance on the life of his deceased wife. Mrs. Cunningham died May 12th. Proof of death was mailed May 22d and the amount of insurance was received in just a week. The prompt settlement of the insurance is a credit to the order of Lady Maccabees and will tend to inspire greater confidence in the local membership.

Alcona County Review, June 1, 1893
Cemetery:

Cunningham, Mary

LOCAL JOTTINGS.

Little Mary Cunningham aged 14, was crowded off a bridge into the Au Sable river by a cow last week and drowned.

Alcona County Review, September 21, 1888
Cemetery:

Cunningham, Mr.

EVENTS OF ONE WEEK.

Jos. Cunningham and family have gone to Carleton, Monroe county, to reside.

We since learn that Mr. Cunningham had been called to Carleton since the recent death of his wife by the death of his father. He arrived too late, however, to attend the funeral. The old gentleman died suddenly at the advanced age of 93. He was born in Ireland but came to America at an early age and helped to build the first railroad constructed in this country, viz: the Albany and Schennectady R. R. He came to Michigan when it was yet a territory and settled in Monroe county, where he resided continuously until his death. His wife, aged 82, and six children survive him. His son Jos., who has lived in Harrisville nearly three years, inherits a furniture and undertaking business left to him by will and goes to Carleton for the purpose of taking charge of it.

Alcona County Review, June 29, 1893
Cemetery:

Curley, {Boy}

A SPECIAL FROM CURTIS.

Mr. and Mrs. Curley, recently of Bay City, now of this place, lost their little boy. The death was caused by whooping cough.

Alcona County Review, February 16, 1893
Cemetery: Probably Curtisville, Alcona Co.

Curriveau, David

A second child of Ralph Carvo died of diphtheria and was buried on Friday. The premises have been closely quarantined since the death of the first patient and so far there is no evidence that the disease has any further hold on the rest of the community.

A third child of Mr. Carvo's has had the disease but is reported convalescent.

The Board of Supervisors allowed Ralph Carvo the sum of $30 for clothing and personal property which had to be destroyed by the authorities to prevent the spread of the diphtheria, which had a foothold in his house, and from which he lost two children.

Alcona County Review, April 21, 1892
Cemetery:

Curriveau, Ralph, Jr.
Somewhat Personal.

A case of diphtheria at Ralph Carvo's.

Later—The patient, a boy of twelve years, died this morning.

Alcona County Review, March 31, 1892

The Board of Supervisors allowed Ralph Carvo the sum of $30 for clothing and personal property which had to be destroyed by the authorities to prevent the spread of the diphtheria, which had a foothold in his house, and from which he lost two children.

Alcona County Review, April 21, 1892

HISTORY OF ONE YEAR.

Chronological History of the Past Year, 1892.

THE DEATH RECORD.

April. Ralph Carvo, Harrisville, of diphtheria.

Alcona County Review, January 5, 1893
Cemetery:

Curry, Mrs. Alex
LOCAL JOTTINGS.

Word comes of the recent death at Windsor, Ont., of the young wife of Alex Curry. Mr. Curry is well known in this community, having formerly clerked here for several firms.

Alcona County Review, February 4, 1887
Cemetery:

Cutting, John
PURELY PERSONNAL.

Jno. Cutting, son of Chas. Cutting, of Mikado, returned recently from an absence of several years in Dakota and the west. He is considerably broken in health and is at present at Ann Arbor under care of the University physicians.

Alcona County Review, September 9, 1887

LOCAL JOTTINGS.

Chas. Cutting, of Mikado, was called to Ann Arbor last Saturday morning by telegram announcing that the malady with which his son John is afflicted had assumed a serious aspect, and desiring his immediate presence.

Alcona County Review, September 16, 1887

Death of Jno. Cutting.

Jno. Cutting, eldest son of Chas. Cutting, of Mikado, who was mentioned in the last issue of this paper as having recently returned from the West considerably broken in health, died at Ann Arbor last Sunday of inflammation of the lungs. The remains were brought back to this county by the deceased's father and interred Tuesday in the Catholic cemetery of this place.

Alcona County Review, September 16, 1887

Card of Thanks.

I take this means of thanking the many friends who rendered assistance during our recent bereavement in the death of my son, Jno. Cutting.

Chas. Cutting.

Alcona County Review, September 16, 1887
Cemetery: Probably St. Anne's, Alcona Co.

Cuyler, Elmer James
Expression of Sympathy.

Whereas, Death having entered the home of our sister, Lady Cuyler, and taken her little boy, Elmer James: Therefore, we, the officers and Ladies of Eveland Hive No. 159, extend to her our heartfelt sympathy.

Helen McGregor,
Sarah Hill,
Christena E. Creighead,
Committee.

Black River, Oct. 21.

Alcona County Review, October 26, 1893

Thomas Cuyler has erected a very neat monument in memory of his infant son, Elmer J., in our cemetery.

Alcona County Review, December 6, 1894
Cemetery: Mt. Joy, Alcona Co.

Dafoe, Phillip

Card of Thanks—To friends and relatives who have been so very kind to the bereaved Mrs. Phillip Dafoe and family during the sickness and death of her husband Phillip Dafoe, who died Aug. 16, at 8 o'clock a.m., '99. At Glennie, Alcona Co., Mich.

Mrs. Phillip Dafoe.

Alcona County Review, August 31, 1899

STATE OF MICHIGAN, THE PROBATE COURT FOR THE COUNTY OF ALCONA.

At a session of said Court, held at the Probate Office in the City of Harrisville in said County, on the 8th day of January, A. D. 1908.

Present: Hon. Geo. W. Burt, Judge of Probate.

In the matter of the estate of Mable, Floyd, Philip and Effie Dafoe, minors.

Mrs. Sarah Cooper, guardian of said estate, having filed in said court a petition, praying for license to sell at private sale the interest of said estate in certain real estate therein described.

It is ordered, That the 7th day of February, A. D. 1908, at ten o'clock in the forenoon, at said probate office, be and is hereby appointed for hearing said petition, and that all persons interested in said estate appear before said court, at said time and place, to show cause why a license to sell the interest of said estate in said real estate should not be granted.

It is further ordered, That public notice thereof be given by publication of a copy of this order, for three successive weeks previous to said day of hearing, in the Alcona County Review, a newspaper printed and circulated in said county.

GEO. W. BURT,
Judge of Probate.

Alcona County Review, January 16, 1908
Cemetery: Glennie, Alcona Co.

Daily, John
OUR NEIGHBORS.

The last day of December an old soldier by the name of John Daily started for the train to go to Cartwright's camp. He was too late for the train and either started on foot for the camp or to return to town. This was the last seen of him until his body was found in the river behind a boom stick near the boom bridge Thursday morning. Daily was 52 years of age and was about to receive a pension. He has a wife in Bay City with whom he has not lived for several years. His body was taken to Chevrier's undertaking rooms and an inquest was held which resulted in a verdict of accidental drowning. The body was buried yesterday, John Earle Post taking charge of the matter.--Monitor.

Alcona County Review, April 18, 1895
Cemetery:

Davis, James

MUD LAKE.

It is reported here that James Davis of McKinley was drowned in Au Sable river last Friday. He was a colored man and a fine fellow—am very sorry to hear of his death.

Alcona County Review, July 13, 1899

CURRAN EVENTS.

Sept. 25, '99.

The body of Jimmy Davis of McKinley, who fell off from a scow and was drowned in Au Sable river last July, was found last week by some of the Yockey crew while taking dead heads out of the river. Jimmy was a colored boy and he was very amiable and much respected by those who knew him.

This is the second time the Au Sable river was ever known to give up its dead.

Alcona County Review, September 28, 1899
Cemetery:

Davis, Mrs. George

EVENTS OF ONE WEEK.

Dr. Mitchell reports a case of diphtheria at Mud Lake in the La Vier settlement. The victim is Mrs. Geo. Davis.

Alcona County Review, December 15, 1892

PERSONAL MENTION.

Mrs. Geo. Davis, the Mud Lake woman reported last week as suffering from diphtheria, is dead. The case was a sad one, as the young woman had been confined but a short time before her death. Hers was the fourth death in the same family in five weeks. Her mother, who has been living at or near Cartwright's camp, lost two children while there and still another one after she came to Mud Lake to attend her daughter. No physician was called but it seems likely from the reports that all the children must have died of diphtheria and that it was thus brought to the Mud Lake settlement. The premises were not quarantined but a public funeral was held and neighbors passed in and out of the house with impunity.

Alcona County Review, December 22, 1892

HISTORY OF ONE YEAR.

Chronological History of the Past Year, 1892.

December.

15. Diphtheria reported at Mud Lake. Mrs. Geo. Davis died.

Alcona County Review, January 5, 1893

HISTORY OF ONE YEAR.

Chronological History of the Past Year, 1892.

THE DEATH RECORD.

Dec. 15. Mrs. Geo. Davis, Mud Lake.

Alcona County Review, January 5, 1893
Cemetery:

Davis, Lewis. P.

Presiding Elder Davis Dead.

Rev. L. P. Davis, who will be remembered as Presiding Elder of the Bay City district a decade ago, died Monday at Bay View after an illness of but one day's duration. He had gone to Bay View but a few days before to superintend the worship meetings of the Bay View association of which he was trustee.

Dr. Davis was born in 1835, 10 miles from Romeo.

At the time of his death he was presiding elder of the Adrian district and resided in Detroit.

He is survived by his wife, a daughter and a son.

Alcona County Review, July 15, 1897
Cemetery: Woodmere, Wayne Co.

Davison, Crozier

CROZIER DAVISON DEAD.

Another Old Citizen Goes Over to the Majority.

Detroit Tribune, Tuesday, Jan. 8:—

Sunday evening James N. Dean was calling at Crozier Davison's house, 424 Woodward avenue. During the evening Mr. Davison cheerfully said: "I'm going home tonight Nod. My ship sails at two o'clock sharp." Just before the stroke of two he tried to sit up. A violent fit of coughing seized him, and within four or five minutes he was dead. It is a curious coincidence that his wife, who died last July, passed away at 2 A. M. He had ever since expressed a wish that he might die at the same hour.

Mr. Davison was born in England, but came to this state early in life. After a short time spent at Royal Oak he went "up the lakes" as a fisherman. At the age of 27 he was

one of the most noted fishers on the lakes. The large catches of fish were shipped direct to Detroit dealers. In 1861 he left the water and went into the lumber business, in which he proved very successful, locating pine lands and selling at large profits to big lumber firms. He was interested with Gen. Alger in a number of important land transactions. In 1870 he was obliged to give up most of his active work, and came to Detroit where he has since lived. He was often transacting business down town when hardly able to get about. For the past two months he had been confined to his room, and though very feeble, he was cheerful and contented to the very end.

Mr. Davison was a Mason, and a member of St. John's Episcopal church. The funeral will be held from his residence at 2 o'clock Wednesday afternoon. He leaves a son, William, who is a farmer in Dakota and two daughters, Hattie and Carrie.

(The above sketch of the life and death of one of Detroit's wealthy citizens recounts briefly the eventful career of a man whose name in this section is a synonym for business shrewdness and success. It was along this shore that he cast his nets into the inland seas and made the lifts that proved the foundation of the princely fortune he leaves behind him. Like most of his fellows he was a plain blunt and rough mannered man, but underneath this rough veneering there beat a kindly heart. He early drifted into land and timber speculations and prospered as he seems to have done in all his undertakings. He had many thousands of dollars invested in Alcona county mortgages. The firm of C. Davison & Son for years conducted a merchandise business in the stand now occupied by Cowley & Lott.)

Alcona County Review, January 11, 1889

ADDITIONAL LOCALS.

An inventory of the estate of the late Crozier Davison comprises $41,383.14 in notes and bonds, $80,654.50 in Wayne county real estate and about the same valuation of real estate outside Wayne county. The Detroit home is appraised at $42,000.

Alcona County Review, April 12, 1889

DAVISON'S LAST WILL.

The will of the late Crozier Davison was filed in the probate court of Wayne county last Saturday. To his wife, who has died since the drawing of the will, he bequethed a life interest in their Detroit home, and the household effects. In addition she was to have had $6,000 a year while both or either of her two daughters remained single and stayed at home. The two daughters are each to receive $2,000 a year while they remain at home. If either one marries and leaves home the other is to get $1,500 a year. Wm. H. Davison, the only son, is to receive $600 a year until the youngest daughter attains the age of 25. At that time he is to receive $10,000, and the remainder of the estate is to be equally divided between the two daughters. Should the son contest, or endeavor to have the will interpreted, he is to forfeit everything. The estate is worth half a million dollars.

Alcona County Review, January 18, 1889

The Crozier Davison estate has commenced foreclosure proceedings against Jas. M. Johnson of Mikado.

Alcona County Review, November 22, 1889

STATE OF MICHIGAN, COUNTY OF ALCONA, S. S.—At a session of the Circuit Court for the County of Alcona, in Chancery, convened and held at the Circuit Court room, in the Village of Harrisville, on the thirty-first day of October, in the year one thousand eight hundred and eighty-nine. Present, Hon. William H. Simpson, Circuit Judge. In re the estate of Crozier Davison, deceased. Upon reading and filing the petition of James H. Dean and William H. Davison, executors of the last will and testament of said deceased, praying that the following lands: N. e. $\frac{1}{4}$, s. w. $\frac{1}{4}$ section 25, town 27, north of range 9 east; n. 1/8, n. w. $\frac{1}{4}$ section 25, town 27, north of range 9 east; n. e. $\frac{1}{4}$ n. w. $\frac{1}{4}$ section 11, town 27, north of range 9 east; n. w. $\frac{1}{4}$ n. e. $\frac{1}{4}$ section 10, town 27, north of range 9 east; s. e. $\frac{1}{4}$ n. w. $\frac{1}{4}$ section 25, town 27, north of range 9 east; lot 31 of Cowley & Robert's addition to the Village of Harrisville, lot 33 of Cowley & Robert's addition to the Village of Harrisville, lot 35 of Cowley & Robert's addition to the Village of Harrisville, s. e. $\frac{1}{4}$ n. w. $\frac{1}{4}$ section 25, town 27, north of range 9 east, except a parcel of land commencing at the

south-east corner of the s. e. $\frac{1}{4}$ of n. w. $\frac{1}{4}$ section 25, thence northerly along the east line of said s. e. $\frac{1}{4}$, n. w. $\frac{1}{4}$ sec, 25, 80 rods to the north line of s. e. $\frac{1}{4}$ n. w. $\frac{1}{4}$ thence westerly along said north line 16 rods, thence southeasterly in a straight line to the place of beginning; also n. w. $\frac{1}{4}$ of n. e. $\frac{1}{4}$, section 3, town 27 n. range 9 east; n. e. $\frac{1}{4}$ of s. e. $\frac{1}{4}$ section 5, town 26 n. range 9 east; east $\frac{1}{2}$ of n. e. $\frac{1}{4}$, sec, 33, town 26, n. range 9 east, in this county, devised to them in trust without power of sale, may be sold and the proceeds thereof invested in accordance with the provisions of Act No. 233 of the session laws of 1887, on the ground that said lands are wholly unproductive and exposed to waste. On motion of Wisner, Speed & Henry, of Detroit, Mich., solicitors for said petitioners, it is ordered that all persons interested in said property do appear before this court on Monday, the Sixteenth day of December, 1889, at 10 o'clock in the forenoon, and then and there show cause, if any exists, why the prayer of said petition should not be granted.
WILLIAM H. SIMPSON,
Circuit Judge.

Alcona County Review, August 24, 1893

State of Michigan: In the Circuit Court for the County of Alcona: In Chancery.
James N. Dean and William H. Davison, Executors of the last will and testament of Crozier Davison, deceased.
Complainants,
vs.
David E. Storms and William M. Storms.
Defendants.
In pursuance of a decretal order of the Court of Chancery made in the above cause will be sold under the direction of the subscriber, at public auction at the front door of the court house in the village of Harrisville, (that being the place of holding the Circuit Court for said County of Alcona) on Monday, the 20th day of April A.D. 1896, at 10 o'clock a.m., all that certain piece or parcel of land situate and being in the Township of Harrisville, Alcona county and State of Michigan, and described as follows, to-wit: The North East quarter of the North East quarter of Section Eleven (11) in Township Twenty-six (26) North of Range Nine (9) East, containing forty acres more

or less according to Government survey thereof.
Dated March 4th, A.D. 1896.
CARL M. LUND,
Special Commissioner.
O. H. Smith,
Solicitor for Complainant.

Alcona County Review, March 5, 1896
Cemetery: Woodmere, Wayne Co.

Davison, Mrs. William

Mrs. Wm. Davison, the divorced wife of Wm. Davison, both of whom are well known former residents of Harrisville, died at Bay City last Sunday.

Alcona County Review, March 9, 1888
Cemetery:

Deacon, Mrs. Archibald

Curtis Tid Bits.

Curtis, March 19.--March 16th, at four o'clock a. m., Mrs. Archibald Deacon passed from earth after a lingering sickness of sixteen years duration. She died very peacefully. She leaves a husband and two daughters, and brothers and sisters and many warm friends to mourn her absence, for she will be missed. She was a mother to the motherless and a mother to those in sickness. She was respected by all who knew her. The funeral took place on Sunday at 2 o'clock p. m. Rev. H. S. Merritt preached the funeral sermon, his text being from Job, 14th chapter and 14th verse: "If a man die, shall he live again?" It was a grand text and many great thoughts were dropped from the sermon. The funeral was a very large one and was conducted by J. H. Healy. Our great hope is that she lives again.

Alcona County Review, March 22, 1894
Cemetery: Probably Glennie, Alcona Co.

Deacon, William H.

Curtis Items.
Sept. 23, 1895.
Laid to Rest.—William H. Deacon who has been sick for some time and was thought to be better at last week's writing, died at the home of his son-in-law, Eli M. Barker, at 1:20 p.m. Saturday.
Deceased was born in Ireland in 1809. When seven years of age his parents moved to Canada, where he was reared. He was married and raised a large family, eleven in all, ten boys and one girl, but while in the midst of prosperity his beloved wife died. He moved to the States in 1858.

When the war broke out he enlisted in the service of the Union. Though a competent soldier he was never called into action as he belonged to the Home Guards. His parents belonged to the English church in which he was reared. When about thirty years of age he was converted and joined the Baptist church, to which belief he has clung since, being a member of the Curtis Harvest Home church.

The funeral sermon was preached at the school house by Elder Fayette of Rose City, present pastor of the Baptist church of this place.

A large procession followed the remains to the cemetery at Vaughn Lake.

Alcona County Review, September 26, 1895
Cemetery: Glennie, Alcona Co.

Dean, Birdie

The Local News.

Haynes.

Miss Birdie Dean was compelled by sickness to resign her contract with school district No. 1, which is regretted by the scholars as they were becoming very much attached to her and they all wish for her quick recovery.

Alcona County Review, October 1, 1891

BIRDIE DEAN.

After a lingering illness of nearly a year's duration Miss Birdie Dean gained that haven of rest whither all are drifting, at 6 o'clock p.m. Sunday last. The end had been long anticipated by friends and the patient sufferer looked forward with a cheerfulness and Christian fortitude that well became the closing scenes of a pure and gentle life on earth. The remains were placed beside those of her sister and father, who have only preceded her by a short period of time. The funeral services were held Tuesday morning in the Methodist church, the Rev. W. J. Bailey officiating. A very large concourse of people followed the remains to their last resting place in the cemetery at south Harrisville.

The deceased was born Sept. 22, 1870. She was a member of the Harrisville Baptist church and was ever known as a devout and exemplary Christian character. The first serious symptoms of consumption manifested themselves in June, 1891, and since that time she

has gradually drawn nearer and nearer to the border of that undiscovered land where sorrow and pain and anguish are unknown.

Alcona County Review, May 26, 1892

HISTORY OF ONE YEAR.

Chronological History of the Past Year, 1892.

THE DEATH RECORD.
May 22. Birdie Dean, Harrisville.

Alcona County Review, January 5, 1893
Cemetery: Springport, Alcona Co.

Dean, David

LOCAL JOTTINGS.

David Dean, 64 years of age, and a public charge, died at the county poor farm Tuesday morning. He was buried Wednesday in the potter's field at Springport.

Alcona County Review, November 16, 1888
Cemetery: Springport, Alcona Co.

Dean, Thomas

Passed to His Eternal Rest.

Thomas Dean entered the valley of the shadow of death at an early hour Wednesday morning, after an illness of but a few weeks. His death has been expected momentarily for ten days past and was due to that dread malady consumption.

Dr. Weir of Oscoda, his last medical attendant, informed him a number of days prior to his death that he should make his peace with God and man without delay. Accordingly the Rev. W. J. Bailey and Attorney Snow were summoned to his bedside last Saturday to assist him in settling his earthly affairs. That accomplished he seemed prepared and willing to go and his decline was rapid until his final dissolution.

The deceased was aged about 50 years and has long been recognized as one of the substantial and successful farmers of the county, with the history of which he has been closely identified for nearly a quarter of a century. At the time of his death he held the office of Supervisor of Harrisville township, it being his third term. He was chairman of the Board. For three years past he held the office of President of the Agricultural Society. As a public man and a private citizen he was noted for the inflexible determination of his

will. Nothing could move him when once he had taken a stand. He was a determined advocate of economy in public affairs and practiced what he preached by cutting his own salary in two the first year he was elected. In his business dealings it was said of him that his word was as good as his bond. The fine farm property he leaves is a monument to a long life of self denial, frugality and careful systematic husbandry.

The death of Mr. Dean is attended by peculiarly sad circumstances: One year ago he buried his eldest daughter, who also died of pulmonary consumption. His oldest surviving daughter is lying at this time on a bed of pain and sickness caused by the same dread malady, and there is no hope of her recovery. The surviving members of this afflicted family have the sympathy of this community in this the hour of their great bereavement. Mrs. Dean and two daughters survive him. The funeral services will be held Friday morning at 10 o'clock. A short service will be held at his late residence and then the remains will be born to the Methodist church and from thence to their last resting place.

Alcona County Review, March 31, 1892

The Local News

The remains of the late Thomas Dean were interred last Friday in the South Harrisville cemetery, whither they were followed by a large number of friends who came from many miles around. The services were held at the Methodist church, the Rev. W. J. Bailey officiating.

Alcona County Review, April 7, 1892

Resolutions of Respect.

Mr. Thos. E. Dean, of Harrisville, died March 30th, 1892, aged 52 years. The deceased was a member of Fisher association P. of I. 3,366 which adopted the following resolutions of respect:

Whereas Death has for the first time entered our association and taken from our midst our beloved brother Thomas E. Dean, therefore be it

Resolved, That while we bow in submission to Him whose ways are full of wisdom, we feel that in the death of our brother our association has lost a worthy and beloved member and his family a devoted husband and father,

Resolved, That we offer the bereaved family our sincere sympathy in their sorrow,

Resolved, That as a token of respect of our deceased brother the charter of this association be draped in mourning for thirty days and a copy of these resolutions be placed in the minutes of this association and a copy be sent to the bereaved family. Also copies be sent to the Alcona County Review and to the Patron's Guide for publication.

 C. C. Briggs,
 Sidney Dorr,
 George Earle,
 Committee.

Alcona County Review, April 14, 1892

We sincerely thank our many kind friends for their kindness and consideration during our late bereavement. That any who are called upon to suffer likewise may meet with equal kindness is our earnest wish.

 Mrs. Thos. Dean and Family.

Alcona County Review, April 14, 1892

HISTORY OF ONE YEAR.

Chronological History of the Past Year, 1892.

THE DEATH RECORD.
March 30. Supervisor Thomas Dean, Harrisville.

Alcona County Review, January 5, 1893

EVENTS OF ONE WEEK.
The death of Supervisor John Roy McDonald removes the chairman of the Board of Supervisors of Alcona county by death for the second time within a year. The other death was that of Supervisor Thos. Dean.

Alcona County Review, January 19, 1893
Cemetery: Springport, Alcona Co.

Dease, Charles Johnson Watts
A BAY CITY MYSTERY.

CHARLES DEASE OF EAST TAWAS, FOUND DEAD.

Killed by the Cars.
Charles Dease, a member of the East Tawas lumber firm of Dease & Graham, went to Bay City Friday of last week to purchase a carload of horses for the woods and camp supplies. It was expected by his friends that he would return home the same night, and he was seen

shortly before 11 p.m. waiting for the train at the Bay City depot. Saturday morning the mutilated remains of a man, which were identified as those of Mr. Dease, were found near the depot. The body was frozen and both legs were cut off. Suspicions of foul play were rife but the discovery of a roll of bills on his person amounting to $250 expelled this theory, and it is now believed he must have fallen from the outgoing train.

The deceased was a prominent citizen of the Huron shore, was a successful lumberman and had amassed a comfortable fortune. He leaves a wife and two daughters, one of whom was married only a few days ago to Paymaster T. P. Handy, of the Detroit, Bay City & Alpena railroad.

Alcona County Review, February 8, 1889

NEIGHBORHOOD NOTES.

The friends of Charles Dease are nearly convinced that he was murdered. He was known to have had a much larger amount of money on his person than was found. Suspicion has fastened upon a Bay City individual whose actions since the murder have been so peculiar as to lead to placing him under police surveillance.

Alcona County Review, February 22, 1889
Cemetery: Greenwood, Iosco Co.

Dege, Ernest J.
A year-old child of Mr. and Mrs. Dege, of Black River, died Monday and was buried Tuesday in the Catholic cemetery at this place. The funeral services were conducted by the Rev. Fr. Winters of Au Sable.

Alcona County Review, August 6, 1891
Cemetery: Probably St. Anne's, Alcona Co.

DeKlyne, Leonard E.
SOMEWHAT PERSONAL.

Mr. and Mrs. W. P. DeKlyne have the sympathy of all in their great sorrow over the loss of their infant son, who died about noon Friday from cholera infantum. The funeral took place Saturday afternoon from the family residence, the services being conducted by Rev. Buckley of St. James church. The floral tributes from many kind friends were beautiful and numerous.

Alcona County Review, September 29, 1892
Cemetery: Pine Hill, Cheboygan Co.

DeKlyne, William
LOCAL JOTTINGS.

A late copy of the New York Tribune received at this office announces the death of William DeKlyne, father of W. P. DeKlyne of this village, which occurred at Plainfield, N. J., on Sunday morning last. He was aged 74 years.

Alcona County Review, March 6, 1885
Cemetery: Hillsdale, Union Co., NY

Delahanty, Pat
LOCAL JOTTINGS.

Killed.—Pat Delehanty, working at Dease & Pratt's lumber camp near East Tawas, was struck by a falling tree a few days since and so badly injured that he died soon afterward. He is the third man killed this winter near the same spot.

Alcona County Review, February 19, 1886
Cemetery:

Deland, Mrs.
COUNTY REVIEWINGS.

Mrs. Deland, of Harrisville, on a visit to her sister in this city, died very suddenly at the residence on Twenty-first street, Sunday, of heart disease. The remains will be taken to Harrisville for interment.—*Bay City Tribune.*

Alcona County Review, November 19, 1880
Cemetery:

Delano, Hiram H.
GREENBUSH.
Hiram Delano, father of Mrs. John Code, and an old and respected citizen died here Saturday evening as the result of a fall less than a week before his death.

On Monday 9th inst., Mr. Delano was working about the yard when he slipped on the ice and fell striking heavily upon his face. At the time the hurt was not thought dangerous but later in the week it developed into congestion of the brain from which he died.

The deceased was born near Rochester, N. Y. April 12, 1820. While a young man he came to Mich. and for the past twenty two years he has lived in Alcona county, thirteen of which has been spent in Greenbush.

The funeral service was held from the house Tuesday afternoon and the large attendance shows the esteem which was held for our departed friend.

Alcona County Review, January 19, 1899

Gone From our Home.

The funeral of the late Hiram H. Delano was held from the residence of his daughter, Mrs. J. S. Code at Greenbush last Tuesday afternoon, January 17th inst.

The remains were followed to the cemetery by a large concourse of friends and relatives which told of the love and esteem in which the deceased was held by the people of the community in which he had resided so long. Mr. Delano was born in York state in the year of 1820 and came to Mich. when but a young man. Twenty-two years ago he settled in Alcona Co., thirteen of which he has spent in the little village of Greenbush, where he has been a much loved and respected citizen. His death is a sad shock to all who knew him. Mr. Delano was of a kind and loving disposition and was never at rest unless he was doing something for those whom he loved. In the death of Mr. Delano, his wife and family not only lose a faithful husband and loving father but the community loses a good citizen.

A wife and one daughter and son, Mr. and Mrs. J. S. Code, survive him.

Alcona County Review, January 26, 1899

Card Of Thanks.—Words cannot express the heartfelt thanks of the wife and family of the late Hiram Delano to the neighbors and friends who so kindly assisted us during the sickness and death of a loving husband and father. Especial thanks are tendered to the Harrisville choir for the music.

Mrs. H. Delano.
Mr. and Mrs. J. S. Code.

Alcona County Review, January 26, 1899
Cemetery: Springport, Alcona Co.

DeLavolette, Alexander

LOCAL JOTTINGS.

A. D. DeLavolette, of this township, received the sad tidings Saturday of the drowning on May 1 of his father, Alexander DeLavolette, at Two Rivers, Ont. The drowned man was 61 years old.

Alcona County Review, July 5, 1889
Cemetery:

Dellar, James

Jas. Dellar, 16 years old, died of acute peritonitis or inflammation of the bowels on Monday and was buried yesterday in the South Harrisville cemetery. Services were held at the Dean school house by the Rev. W. P. Tompkins.

Alcona County Review, November 11,1897
Cemetery: Springport, Alcona Co.

Delorme, Joseph

County News and Gossip.

Last Tuesday, at Au Sable, we learn two young men, while skating, accidentally ran into an air-hole and went down under the ice and were drowned. We did not get their names.

Alcona County Review, February 21,1879
Cemetery:

Demarro, Willie

ALONG THE SHORE.

Au Sable and Oscoda.

Willie Demarro, a 14-year-old boy employed at the O. S. & L. Co.'s mill had his head so badly cut with a saw, last Saturday that he died.

Alcona County Review, September 4, 1885
Cemetery:

Demott, Charlotte M [Bailey].

Curtis Items.
Nov. 30, 1896.

Death came to the home of John Demont and took his beloved wife from him. She passed away Nov. 21 and was buried Nov. 24th. There was a very large funeral. She was laid away in a beautiful coffin and shroud surrounded by wreaths and roses. She left a husband and five small children, 4 boys and a girl, to mourn the loss of a dear wife and mother. The funeral sermon was preached by a minister from McKinley. Procule Secord conducted the funeral procession very nicely. The pall bearers were Messrs. Lott Simons, Jos. Smith, Allan Paul, Joseph Herr, Frank Middelton, Robt. Deacon. Mr. Demont's mother and brother were present. I was informed deceased's age was 39 years. Young in life the flower was laid away to rest in the cold earth.

Alcona County Review, Dec. 3, 1896
Cemetery: Glennie, Alcona Co.

Dennis, Mrs. Alex

KILLMASTER.

Killmaster, Jan. 16.—A sad event took place on Sunday evening, Jan. 13th. Mrs. A. Dennis, one of the first settlers of Killmaster, died from an illness of three months standing. She leaves three children, two girls and one boy. Funeral took place Wednesday.

Alcona County Review, January 18, 1889

LOCAL JOTTINGS.

Mrs. Alex. Dennis died at her home in Killmaster Monday morning, aged 44 years. She leaves a husband and five children.

Alcona County Review, January 18, 1889
Cemetery:

Dennis, Lorena M. [Brown]

PERSONAL MENTION.

Mrs. W. W. Dennis, a sister of the late Mrs. Geo. Rutson, and who has frequently visited in Harrisville, died Sunday at her late home in Ovid. Mrs. R. L. Lott of this village went to Ovid Monday in response to a telegram.

Alcona County Review, May 28, 1896

PERSONAL MENTION.

Mrs. W. I. Tillotson of Oneida, N. Y., is expected to arrive this week from Ovid, where she was called by the death of her sister, Mrs. W. W. Dennis. She will make an extended visit with her daughter, Mrs. Geo. E. Gillam.

Alcona County Review, May 28, 1896
Cemetery: Maple Grove, Clinton Co

Depew, William E.

William E. Depew.

This Well-Known Lawyer Died Yesterday at the Alcona House.

The death of William E. Depew at the Alcona House yesterday morning was a shock to the community, as but few knew that he was so seriously ill.

He came down Wednesday of last week to conduct the defendant's case in the suit of La France versus Campbell. He had been indisposed for several days prior to coming here, but he became so much worse that he was forced to relinquish the case and was taken to the Alcona House. Dr. Mitchell was called and diagnosed the case as an acute bilious attack. The patient became worse and Dr. Mitchell advised sending for the family physician, but Mr. Depew and others did not favor it. Mrs. Depew was summoned and arrived Monday and remained until the end. Tuesday he seemed a little better but in the night he had several bad spells. Dr. Mitchell remained in the house all night and every means was used to rally the patient. He had an acute attack at 7:30 in the morning and all efforts to restore him were unavailing.

The death of Mr. Depew removes one of the greatest and most powerful advocates of the bar of northern Michigan. He was a man of brilliant parts and of great power and persuasive force as a public speaker and a law advocate. He was very successful in the practice of law and had a lucrative business, though he accumulated little or no property. He was prosecuting attorney of Alpena county by appointment at the time of his death and was in line to succeed Judge Kelley on the bench.

He was born at Chelsea, Mich., in November, 1848, and spent his boyhood on a farm. He entered the Ann Arbor University and graduated with the law class of 1875 and practiced law at Chelsea until 1882, when he came to Harrisville. He was elected prosecuting attorney that year and served until his removal to Alpena in 1887.

He was a member of the subordinate lodge of Odd Fellows and was made a member of Harrisville lodge March 18, 1885. He withdrew Feb. 20, 1889, and joined at Alpena. Mr. Sinaberger, representing the Alpena lodge, came down yesterday and accompanied Mrs. Depew to Chelsea. He brought a fine floral emblem for the lodge.

Deceased was also a member of the Harrisville Masonic Lodge and local members looked after the arrangements for the disposition of the remains, which were encased in a suitable casket and shipped this morning to Chelsea, Mich., the birthplace of Mr. Depew.

J. Van Buskirk accompanied Mrs. Depew to Chelsea as representative of the lodge, to relieve her of any annoyance so far as arrangements are concerned.

He was a stalwart Republican and an active campaigner.

While Mr. Depew left no property, he left a nice line of insurance, which is placed at $14,000, of which $4,000 was in the Maccabees and Union Life Guards.

Telegrams of sympathy poured in upon Mrs. Depew, among others one from the Alpena bar offering any assistance in their power.

Alcona County Review, September 22, 1898

Memorial to W. E. Depew.

The following resolutions were adopted at Monday's session of court as a slight memorial to the late Wm. E. Depew on motion of F. A. Beede.

On the 21st day of September, 1898, Wm. E. Depew, a member of this bar for many years, died at the age of 50 years. It has been deemed fitting and proper that the court and bar take formal notice of his death; and for that purpose the following memorial is offered as bearing testimony to his personal worth and his standing and ability as a lawyer.

Mr. Depew was 50 years of age and had been practicing law 22 years; he had lived and practiced at Ann Arbor, Harrisville and Alpena.

As a man Mr. Depew was ever honorable and upright; as a friend he was companionable and true; as a lawyer he attained high standing both for integrity and ability, and ranked as one of the leading lawyers of northern Michigan. His presence and his voice will indeed be missed at this court, where his eloquence was so well known, and where he was so universally admired.

As a testimonial to his memory the court is moved to accept this memorial, to have the same spread at length upon its records and a copy forwarded to his wife.

Signed in behalf of all members practicing at this court.

Alcona County Review, December 22, 1898

Any legal business that was in the hands of W. E. Depew, deceased, if placed with me will receive my best attention.

Fred A. Beede,
Attorney at Law.
Harrisville, Mich.

Alcona County Review, September 22,1898

LOCAL PICK UPS.

Judge Kelley has appointed James Collins to fill the vacancy in the office of prosecuting attorney for Alpena county occasioned by the death of the late William E. Depew.

Alcona County Review, October 6,1898

LOCAL PICK UPS.

The Union Life Guards have paid $1,175 to Mrs. W. E. Depew being the amount of insurance on her late husband's life.

Alcona County Review, December 29,1898

Local History of One Year

Chronology of the Principal Events of the Year 1898.

September 21. Death of Wm. E. Depew occurred at Alcona House.

Alcona County Review, January 5, 1899
Cemetery : Vermont, Washtenaw Co.

Derby, Leonard Edwin

Card of Thanks.

We desire to express our heartfelt thanks to our many friends who so kindly assisted us in our bereavement in the loss of our infant son.

Mr. and Mrs. A. Derby.
Black River, Mich., July 12.

Alcona County Review, July 15, 1897
Cemetery:Springport, Alcona Co.

Derochie, William

Black River Sparks.

William Derochie of Bay City, who has been visiting his step father, Jos. Reno, was taken ill and died from consumption from which he has been suffering for some time. His death occurred on the 7th of April, his 30th birthday. The remains were interred in the R. C. cemetery at Harrisville.

Alcona County Review, April 16, 1896
Cemetery: St. Anne's, Alcona Co.

DeRosia, Lewis

Haynes Happenings.

Jan. 8, 1896.
Lewis De Rosier, a boy of 16 years and a resident of Caledonia, slipped off a log while hunting rabbits and discharged the contents of his gun into his abdomen. He only survived a short time after being taken to his home. His remains were interred in the Catholic cemetery at Alpena.

Alcona County Review, January 9, 1896
Cemetery:Probably Holy Cross, Alpena Co.

DeRosia, Roena C. [Gilbert]

STATE OF MICHIGAN, County of Alcona.

At a session of the Probate Court for said County, held at the Probate office, in the Village of Harrisville, on the 21st day of December in the year one thousand eight hundred and ninety-five.

Present, C. H. Killmaster, Judge of Probate.

In the matter of the estate of Roena C. Derosie.

On reading and filing the petition, duly verified, of Don A. Heacox, praying that he be appointed administrator of the estate of the above named deceased.....................

Thereupon it is ordered, that Saturday, the 12th day of January next, at two o'clock in the afternoon, be assigned for the hearing of said petition, and that the heirs at law of said deceased, and all others interested in said estate, are required to appear at a session of said Court, then to be holden in the Probate office, in the Village of Harrisville and show cause, if any there be, why the prayer of the petitioner should not be granted: And it is further ordered, that said petitioner give notice to the persons interested in said estate, of the pendency of said petition, and the hearing thereof by causing a copy of this order to be published in the Alcona County Review, a newspaper printed and circulated in said county, three successive weeks previous to said day of hearing.

C. H. Killmaster,
Judge of Probate.

Alcona County Review, December 26, 1895
Cemetery:

Detrick, Thomas
LOCAL PICK UPS.
Thomas Detrick, an old and respected resident of Tawas was instantly killed last Friday while removing machinery from a mill. He was 47 years old and a mill wright; and leaves a wife and five children.

Alcona County Review, July 20, 1899
Cemetery: Greenwood, Iosco Co.

Dewar, John
LOCAL JOTTINGS.

John Dewar, a brakeman, loses a foot as a result of an accident at Black River last week.

Alcona County Review, August 9, 1889
LOCAL JOTTINGS.

John Dewar, the man who was injured at Black River a couple of weeks ago, was taken to Alpena where his foot was amputated three times in an attempt to save his life but without avail.

Alcona County Review, August 16, 1889
Cemetery: Evergreen, Alpena Co.

Dewar, Mrs.
Card of Thanks.
We extend our heart felt thanks to our kind friends and neighbors who shared our sorrow and assisted us in

our late bereavement in burying our dear mother. I hope they will accept of our sincere thanks for their unspeakable kindness.

Archie Dewar.

Alcona County Review, May 2, 1890
Cemetery:

Dewar, Mrs. Sarah
WEST HARRISVILLE.
Mrs. Archie Dewar, formerly of Harrisville township, departed this life at her late home near Standish, Thursday, Oct. 15, after a lingering illness from consumption. The funeral occurred Saturday. Mr. and Mrs. A. J. McMillan of this village and Dan Dewar attended the funeral. Deceased was 37 years of age. She was possessed of many excellent traits of character. Her husband and five children are left to mourn their deep loss.

Alcona County Review, October 22, 1896
Cemetery:

Dewey, Monica E.
PERSONAL MENTION.

Died, May 20th, Monica E., aged 7 months, infant daughter of Mr. and Mrs. John Dewey.

Alcona County Review, May 24, 1894
Cemetery: Springport, Alcona Co.

Dewitt, Charles
LOCAL JOTTINGS.

Charles Dewitt, aged 86 years, died at Gustin Tuesday. He had been a resident of the county but a short period.

Alcona County Review, August 7, 1885
Cemetery:

DeWitt, Julian F.
Probate Notice.
State of Michigan, County of Alcona.

At a session of the Probate Court for said county, held at the Probate Office in the village of Harrisville, on the sixth day of May, in the year one thousand eight hundred and eighty-four, present B. P. Cowley, Judge of Probate. In the matter of the estate of Julian F. DeWitt, deceased.

A copy of the will of said deceased, and the probate thereof in the State of New York, duly authenticated, having been produced in said Probate Court by William G. De Witt, executor in said will named, by William H. Simpson his attorney,

and petition being made that proceedings thereon according to the statute in such case made and provided may be had:

Thereupon it is ordered, that Monday the second day of June next, at ten o'clock in the forenoon, be assigned for the hearing of said petition, and that the heirs at law of said deceased, and all other persons interested in said estate, are required to appear at a session of said court, then to be holden in the Probate Office in the village of Harrisville, and show cause, if any there be, why the prayer of the petitioner should not be granted.

And it is further ordered, that said petitioner give notice to the persons interested in said estate, of the pendency of said petition, and the hearing thereof, by causing a copy of this order to be published in the Alcona County Review, a newspaper printed and circulated in said county three successive weeks previous to said day of hearing.

B. P. Cowley,
Judge of Probate.

Alcona County Review, May 9, 1884
Cemetery:

Deyermond, Henry
PERSONAL MENTION.
Henry Deyarmond, a prominent Mio citizen, is dead.

Alcona County Review, May 21, 1896
Cemetery: Probably Kittle, Oscoda Co.

Dickenson, Hiram Alexander
Local News.
Private Hiram A. Dickenson of the 34th Mich., who died at Traverse City Tuesday of fever, was a former resident of Curtis township, this county.

Alcona County Review, September 22, 1898

GLENNIE.
L. O. L. No. 408 have resolved to drape their charter for 60 days, in memory of Alex Dickinson, who died at Traverse City Sept. 20, and also to have a funeral sermon preached by Rev. Nunn on Oct. 16. Alex was a member in good standing at the time of his demise and his untimely death is greatly mourned.

Alcona County Review, October 13, 1898

GLENNIE.
The funeral service held at the school house in Dist. No. 1 by the L. O. L. was in memory of Alex

Dickinson. Rev. I. B. Nunn preached a Grand sermon.

Alcona County Review, October 20, 1898

Local History of One Year

Chronology of the Principal Events of the Year 1898.

September 20. Death of Alex Dickenson at Traverse City. A private in 33rd. Mich. Former resident of Curtis.

Alcona County Review, January 5, 1899
Cemetery: Oakwood, Grand Traverse Co.

Dickinson, Mrs.

BLACK RIVER BRIEFLETS.

We regret to record the death of Mrs. Dickinson, mother of Mrs. Walter JoKoin. The sad event occurred on Friday last. She has been suffering for some time from asthma, but inflammation of the lungs was the cause of death. The funeral sermon was preached in the M. E. Church on Sunday, by Rev. G. S. Weir, from Mathew 24:44.

Alcona County Review, January 22, 1886
Cemetery: Probably Springport, Alcona Co.

Dietz, Cornelius

EVENTS OF ONE WEEK.

Cornelius Dietz an old and respected citizen of Au Sable died last week of peritonitis at the age of 67.

Alcona County Review, August 29, 1895
Cemetery: Pinecrest, Iosco Co.

Dietz, William

Among Our Exchanges.

Wm. Dietz, a Presque Isle county farmer, aged 23, had some trouble with his mother and also with his sweetheart, and ended the matter by shooting himself twice with his rifle, once in the abdomen and once in the breast. His determination to die showed stoicism worthy of a better cause: after shooting himself in the abdomen he reloaded his rifle and put a ball into his breast. That not being sufficient to finish the job he begged the bystanders to give him his knife that he might complete the act of self destruction. They refused of course and he lingered in agony for several hours.

Alcona County Review, June 9, 1892
Cemetery: Belknap Township, Presque Isle Co.

Dimmick, Joseph

An Old Pioneer Gone.

Joseph Demmick, the well-known merchant of East Tawas, died very suddenly at that place last week Wednesday. He had been in feeble health for some time past. On the above day after eating a hearty supper, he started for the barn to attend to his customary duties of milking. Not returning as soon as he should have done, his wife and daughter started to look for him when they discovered his dead body lying by the pathway where he had apparently fallen while returning to the house from the barn. The deceased was born Oct. 29, 1816, in Plymouth, Chenango Co., N. Y., and was consequently in his 71st year.

Alcona County Review, July 1, 1887
Cemetery: Greenwood, Isoco Co.

Dobson, Robert

Haynes Happenings.

Robert Dobson has returned home from Standish where he was called last week to be present at the death of his father.

Alcona County Review, April 25, 1895

Laid to Rest.

The following is taken from a lengthy obituary sketch published in the Arenac Independent of Apr. 19. The subject was father of Robt. Dobson of Haynes who was present at the funeral.

Robert Dobson died at his home in Johnsfield April 12, after an illness of a few weeks. Mr. Dobson was born in Ireland in 1827, was 68 years of age. He emigrated to Ontario, Canada, in 1846, and was married Jan. 14, 1852, his wife surviving him. They have 12 children, eleven of whom are still living. His wife, six sons and five daughters are left to mourn the loss of a true husband and kind father. Thirty-five years ago he and his wife joined the M. E. church of which he was ever since a member.

Mr. Dobson was a very quiet man, a good neighbor and honored by all who knew him. His funeral took place on Sunday and was conducted by the Orangemen.

Alcona County Review, May 9, 1895
Cemetery: Woodmere, Arenac Co.

Dolson, John

LOCAL JOTTINGS.

John Dolson, aged 22 years, son of Wm. Dolson, a Mikado farmer died at the home of his parents last

Thursday. The remains were buried Saturday afternoon in the Oscoda cemetery.

Alcona County Review, October 4, 1889
Cemetery:

Donnelly, William

ALPENA DRIFT.

The Rev. Wm. Donnelly died on the 22d inst., aged 79 years. He left a wife and six children, of whom Col. R. M. Donnelly, Miss M. J. Donnelly, and Mrs. C. M. McKim live in Alpena.

Alcona County Review, December 31, 1886
Cemetery: Evergreen, Alpena Co.

Donohoe, Tommie

ALONG THE SHORE.

There were two drownings at Oscoda last week—Geo. Woods, aged 17 years, in Van Ettan Lake, and a seven-year-old boy in Potts bayous.

Alcona County Review, June 19, 1885
Cemetery:

Dorr, Jennette [Harris]

GUSTIN.

Oct. 31, '99.

Mrs. L. R. Dorr took train for Detroit to receive medical treatment last week.

Alcona County Review, November 2, 1899

Local News.

Friends of Mrs. L. R. Dorr will regret to learn that it has become necessary for her to go again to Detroit for further treatment of the cancer which she had removed by Detroit specialists early in the summer. She will remain away two weeks, when it is hoped she will be far on the road to recovery.

Alcona County Review, November 2, 1899

GUSTIN.

Nov. 21, '99.

Mrs. L. R. Dorr has returned from Detroit where she has had three cancers removed. She is somewhat better at this writing.

Alcona County Review, November 2, 1899

Mrs. L. R. Dorr.

This Pioneer Settler Died Peacefully at Her Home, Dec. 2.

Another pioneer has dropped from the rapidly thinning ranks of the earlier settlers of Alcona county.

This time it is Janette, wife of our respected townsman, L. R. Dorr, who on Saturday passed peacefully, as one in slumber, to the other side of the river.

Deceased died from the effects of operations performed for the removal of cancers. Some months ago she was treated by a Detroit physician and a cancer removed. She returned home and for a time seemed to improve, but about three weeks ago she returned to Detroit for further treatment and three more cancers were removed. From the effects of these operations she never recovered. She suffered considerably, but at the last sank into a peaceful sleep, from which she did not awaken on this earth.

Deceased came to Harrisville township in 1865 when Alcona county was, with the exception of a few scattering hamlets along the lake shore, an unbroken wilderness. She, with her husband, was among the earliest settlers and they took up the land which is now the Dorr homestead, the same year they came. She was loved and respected by all who knew her and the sorrowing husband and family have the sympathy of the community. A faithful wife, a loving mother and a good neighbor has gone to her reward.

Janett Harris was born July 3rd, 1840, in Huron county, Ohio. At the age of ten years she moved with her parents to Saginaw county, west of where the city of Saginaw now stands. At this time there were very few settlers along the Saginaw river, excepting Indians, and during a period of her childhood her playmates were mostly Indian children. In 1856 she was married to John Earl of Saginaw and in the following year she with her husband came to Au Sable where they resided until 1862, when Mr. Earl joined the 23rd regiment of volunteers as first Lieut. of Co. E. He died the same year at Frankfort, Ky. Of this union there were two children, viz: George Earl of Longmont, Col., and Mrs. Celia Sparks, of Seattle, Wash.

John Earl Post G. A. R. of Harrisville takes its name from Lt. Earl.

Janet Earl was married in 1864 to Laurence R. Dorr at Au Sable and in 1865 they came to Alcona county and settled on the farm where the family now reside.

Deceased was the mother of five children: Sidney, John, Dan, Laurence and Fred and one adopted child, Flossie, aged 10 years.

The funeral services were held at the Methodist church. The interment took place at South Harrisville cemetery, whither the remains were followed by a large number of friends and neighbors.

Mr. and Mrs. Harris, brother of the deceased, and Mrs. Holloway, a niece, and her husband, of Tawas City, were present at the funeral.

Alcona County Review, December 7, 1899

CURRAN EVENTS.
We regret to learn of the death of Mrs. Dorr of Harrisville. We extend our sympathy to Mr. Dorr and family.

Alcona County Review, December 14, 1899

Card of Thanks.
To those kind friends and neighbors who assisted us during our bereavement in the death of our beloved wife and mother, we desire to extend our sincere thanks. May they be spared a like affliction is our prayer.

L. R. Dorr and family.

Alcona County Review, December 14, 1899
Cemetery: Springport, Alcona Co.

Douglass, William Wallace
West Harrisville.
Mr. Wallace Douglass, an old veteran of the late war, died at the residence of his son William, last Wednesday.

Alcona County Review, April 7, 1892

HISTORY OF ONE YEAR.

Chronological History of the Past Year, 1892.

THE DEATH RECORD.
March 30. Walter Douglas, West Harrisville.

Alcona County Review, January 5, 1893

HONORS TO DEAD HEROES.

A magnificent demonstration of the patriotic spirit of the citizens of Alcona county was the observance on Monday of the time honored custom of decorating the graves and commemorating the deeds of valor of the nation's dead heroes.

The roster of soldiers who are buried here is as follows: Harrisville, (West), A. Marcellus, John Pelton, W. W. Douglass: Catholic, Louis Rivard,

Geo. Bernizer: South Harrisville, R. Richmond, Chas. Miller, H. J. Aird, A. Noyes, Jas. Johnson.

Alcona County Review, June 2, 1898
Cemetery: West Lawn, Alcona Co.

Downer, Albert C.
A Fatal Kick.
Bert Downer, the 20 year old son of Mr. and Mrs. R. W. Downer died at the residence of his parents in Greenbush Tuesday, Jan. 19.

Death resulted from injuries received by a kick from a horse. The young man was engaged in skidding logs below Greenbush about three weeks ago, when one of the horses kicked him in the abdomen. He has been under treatment of Dr. Wiley and also of Dr. Wier of Oscoda, but their united efforts were unavailing to save his life. The most serious injury resulting from the kick and the one which caused death was what is known to physicians as intussusception or telescoping of the large bowel.

Deceased was 20 years of age, and was a bright and promising young man. In his death the parents lost one who would have proved a comfort and a main stay in their declining years. He was born and reared in Alcona County and was well liked by those who knew him. The funeral will be held from Greenbush school house at 10 a.m. tomorrow.

Deceased had been a member of the Mikado Tent of Maccabees but had dropped out of the order a short time before his death.

Alcona County Review, January 21, 1897

SPRINGPORT AND VICINITY.

A. Kirsten and little son, Guy, came over from McKinley Wednesday of last week to attend the funeral of his nephew, Bert Downer. He returned Friday, leaving Guy to visit with his grandparents, Mr. and Mrs. I. Wilson.

Alcona County Review, January 28, 1897

Card of Thanks.
To the friends who were so kind and helpful to us during the sickness, death and burial of our beloved son, Bert, we extend our heartfelt thanks. We especially desire to thank those who contributed the beautiful flowers.

Mr. and Mrs. R. W. Downer.

Alcona County Review, January 28, 1897
Cemetery: Springport, Alcona Co.

Downie, Mrs. Catherine

Haynes Happenings.

Mrs. Catheran Downie, aged 65 years Dec. 9th, 1895, died in Detroit Feb. 12th of paralysis. She survived her husband 13 years. Her remains were brought to the home of her son, Ed. Downie, in this township, Friday evening, accompanied by four of her daughters and her son, William. The remains were interred Sunday afternoon. The Rev. McBride preached the funeral sermon to a large congregation of relatives and friends. She leaves seven daughters and three sons to mourn their loss. Two daughters live in Detroit, two in Chicago, two in Rochester N. Y., and one in Hamilton, Ont. Her son William is on the police force in Detroit. Her son Richard lives in Saginaw and drives delivery. Edward resides in Haynes, has a good farm, steam thresher and portable saw mill. The floral offerings were numerous; one from the ladies of the Womans Meeting, one from a Mrs. Edgar of Detroit and others. She was a member of the Methodist church and the Women's Relief Association of Detroit.

Alcona County Review, February 20, 1896
Cemetery: Mt. Joy, Alcona Co.

Drefka, Max

Max Drafka of Tawas City, a young man of 22 years, was shot and mortally wounded last week by Julius Fisher of Bay City. The affair occurred near Tawas at a dance given by Fisher's brother-in-law, Chris. Gedeke. Fisher claims he shot in self defense.

Alcona County Review, August 30, 1894

OUR NEIGHBORS.

Julius Fischer, the Bay City policeman who killed Max Drifke at a dance near Tawas last August, was acquitted of the charge of murder in the Iosco county circuit court last week. This is Fischer's second trial; he has been in the Iosco county jail since his arrest.

Alcona County Review, May 23, 1895
Cemetery: Emanuel Lutheran, Iosco Co.

Druer, {Child}

Your Folks and Our Folks.

A 16-month's old child of Daniel Druer of this township died Wednesday evening of cholera

morbus. Funeral at the Baptist church to-day (Friday) at 1 p.m.

Alcona County Review, September 10, 1886
Cemetery:

Dube, Michael

PERSONAL MENTION.

Michael Dube, a ne'er do well, but a man who had the advantage in early life of a good education, was burned to death in his house in Oscoda last week.

Alcona County Review, October 26, 1893
Cemetery:

Duby, Tom

Hunter Savidge Capsized.

The schooner Hunter Savidge, owned by John Mullerwise of Alpena capsized in a sudden squall off Point Aux Barques Sunday afternoon. Mrs. Mullerwise and 6-year old son, the Captain's wife and son and the mate of the boat were lost.

Alcona County Review, August 24, 1899

The schooner Hunter Savidge, which capsized off Point Aux Barques August 19th, has not been found and it is thought the vessel has gone to the bottom, taking with it the bodies of Mrs. Mullerweiss and daughter, of Alpena and Mrs. Capt. Sharpstein.

Alcona County Review, August 31, 1899
Cemetery:

Ducharme, {Child}

LOCAL JOTTINGS.

During the past two weeks, cholera-infantum has been having a terrible rage in this community, no less than a dozen small children and babes having died from the same. This naturally leaves many houses of mourning in our community, and to those of us who are as yet free from the scourge in our own homes, should come forth hearty sympathy and fitting words for the bereaved. Friday last, the scourge took away a little, human flower each from the homes of William Nestle and James Stringer. Tuesday the family of Chas. Larson were bereft of their babe, and Wednesday evening Frank Stevens and wife were called to part with their first-born. Gilbert Landon, one of the Messrs. Byces, and the Ducharms have also each lost a babe, and there are several others in the community apparently nearly at death's door, at the time we go to press. Thus many of the homes in our community are being darkened. May

the Lord remove the dark cloud speedily, and give consolation to the sorrowing parents.

Alcona County Review, August 29, 1884
Cemetery: Probably St. Anne's, Alcona Co.

Duchemin, Floy G.

GREENBUSH GETINGS.

The majority of the children of this village are suffering from a severe cough. The Drs. are unable to decide whether it is "whooping cough" or "chin cough."

Drs. Manzer and Mitchell have been called to see Mrs. McTamney's youngest child, and one or both of the above has been called to attend Mrs. Duchermin's infant child.

Alcona County Review, December 11, 1885

GREENBUSH GETINGS.

With sorrow we record the deaths of those infants referred to last week as being so ill.

Alcona County Review, December 18, 1885

GREENBUSH GETINGS.

Died—On Wednesday evening of last week the infant daughter of Mrs. Duchimen, aged 3 months. On Tuesday morning of this week, Mrs. McTamney's youngest child, aged 7 months.

Alcona County Review, December 18, 1885
Cemetery: Springport, Alcona Co.

Duchemin, William

A Greenbush Boy Meets Death in Wisconsin.

The following is sent to us for publication from Hurley, Wis., under date of Dec. 21, by Mr. S. H. McNally:

Killed at the Iron Belt Mining Co.'s Mine, at the town of Iron Belch, William Duchemin, (pronounced Dishinin) son of Joseph Duchemin, who was a well known resident of Greenbush village, Alcona county.

The deceased was born at Greenbush Oct. 6th, 1874. After his coming to this state he was a clerk for some time in one of the prominent hardware stores, which occupation he abandoned and then pursued the position of an engineer and pump man in this mine. He showed himself a very active boy and filled a man's position to the letter. He died on Sunday, the 13th day of December, 1891. His body was found in the pit, which was only a test pit, at a depth of 120 feet. His remains were buried in the M. E. church cemetery with much respect shown by the community, who deeply sympathize with the parents and family of this young man, who are heart broken by their loss. Just how the accident happened will never be known as he was alone; he may have fallen into the pit a distance of 20 feet, may be more. His skull and neck were broken. The body lay in water a depth of 3 feet when found.

Alcona County Review, December 31, 1891
Cemetery: Probably Springport, Alcona Co.

Dudgeon, Mrs. Margaret

ALONG THE SHORE.
Au Sable and Oscoda.

Last Friday afternoon Mrs. Margaret Dudgeon, mother of Joseph Dudgeon, died. She had reached the advanced age of 104 years, May last.

Alcona County Review, September 4, 1885
Cemetery: Probably Pinecrest, Iosco Co.

Duffey, {Male}

REVIEWINGS.

From Messrs. Jas. Fleming and David Mulholland, of Alcona, who where in the village on Wednesday, we learn that an aged farmer of Alcona Township, named Duffey, died very suddenly early Wednesday morning. We were unable to gain particulars relative to his death.

Alcona County Review, March 26, 1880
Cemetery:

Duggan, John

One Year's History.

Record of Local Happenings for the Year 1890.

NOVEMBER.

November 14. Death of John Duggan, aged 85 years.

Alcona County Review, January 1, 1891
Cemetery: Probably West Lawn, Alcona Co.

Dunbar, John, Sr.

LOCAL JOTTINGS.

The funeral services of John Dunbar were held in the M. E. church at Alcona last Sunday afternoon, Rev. J. Bain, of Harrisville, preaching the sermon. Mr. Dunbar died some two weeks ago, leaving a wife and several small children. He was aged 37 years, and the cause of his death was inflammation of the lungs, brought on by exposure and excessive labor in the woods during

the winter. The text for the sermon was John 11:25. "Jesus said unto her, I am the resurrection and the life."

Alcona County Review, April 30, 1886
Cemetery: Probably Mt. Joy, Alcona Co.

Duncan, James Stuart

Capt. Duncan is Dead.

Capt. James S. Duncan, the venerable Au Sable citizen, drove his cow to pasture Sunday, the 19th inst. An hour or two later he was found dead in a sitting posture leaning back against a shed. Capt. Duncan was a native of Scotland and was 62 years of age.

Alcona County Review, September 30, 1897
Cemetery: Pinecrest, Iosco Co.

Duncan, Robert

PERSONAL MENTION.

C. M. Lund and wife, Chas. Conklin and wife, E. W. Chapelle and wife, W. Jas. Anderson, and Wm. Edwards attended the funeral of Robt. Duncan at Au Sable today.

Alcona County Review, March 28, 1895
Cemetery: Pinecrest, Iosco Co.

Dunham, {Child}

PERSONAL MENTION.

Rev. F. P. Dunham lost a 5 week's old child last week from cholera infantum.

Alcona County Review, September 20, 1894
Cemetery: Probably Twin Lakes, Alcona Co.

Dunham, {Child}

WEST HARRISVILLE.

March 30.
Rev. Dunham of Ossineke brought the remains of his infant child here for burial. He was formerly pastor here and the many friends sympathize with the afflicted family.

Alcona County Review, April 1, 1897
Cemetery: Probably Twin Lakes, Alcona Co.

Dunn, Dan

The Local News

"You killed my brother, and I've killed you" was the remark made by Jim Harcourt when he shot Dan Dunn of Seney. Dunn used to be a resident of East Tawas, where he bore an unsavory reputation which events show did not improve with the lapse of time.

Alcona County Review, August 6, 1891

'ROUND ABOUT.

The trial of Jas. Harcourt for the murder of Dan Dunn in Jno. Nevins' saloon at Seney is in progress at Sault Ste. Marie, and is exciting a great deal of interest. Self defense is the card worked by Harcourt.

Alcona County Review, September 24, 1891

'ROUND ABOUT.

James Harcourt was found guilty of manslaughter at Sault Ste. Marie for the killing of Dan Dunn at Seney and motion for a new trial will be made.

Alcona County Review, October 1, 1891

OUR NEIGHBORS.

James Harcourt who killed Dan Dunn at Seney in 1891, and who was convicted of manslaughter and received a sentence of ten years in Marquette prison on that account, has been pardoned by Gov. Ritch. It will be remembered that the killing of Dunn was looked upon more in the light of an act for the public good than a crime and many thought that Harcourt should have received a pension rather than a conviction.

Alcona County Review, May 16, 1895
Cemetery: Probably Lakeview, Marquette Co.

Dunn, Mary A.

PERSONAL MENTION.
L. H. Dunn recently received the sad intelligence of the death of his only surviving sister, Miss Mary A. Dunn, in the town of Florida, N. Y. This leaves Mr. Dunn the only survivor of a family of nine children.

Alcona County Review, April 2, 1896
Cemetery:

Dunton, Alton C.

Lost in the Storm.

A Curtis Township Man Supposed to Have Perished

The Rose City News states in its last issue that A. C. Dunton, a homesteader of Alcona county, had been missing for ten days and it was assumed that he perished in the big storm of Jan. 31st.

On that day he went to South Branch P. O. in Ogemaw county to post a letter and do some trading. He was afoot and the storm broke upon him after he left South Branch on the return trip. He was last seen by a neighbor named Wells, who lives on the Au Sable river a mile and a half from Dunton's cabin. At 4 p.m. Jan. 31st Wells was hailed by Dunton who said he had some mail for him. The river lay between them and Dunton deposited the mail at the root of a tree and went on, declining an invitation to stay all night.

Next afternoon Wells was again hailed from the opposite bank of the Au Sable, this time by Dunton's boy, who said he feared his father had been frozen to death in the storm as he had not returned home.

Wells at once set out to look up the missing man. He found his bag of groceries hanging on a broken Norway and tracks leading into a thicket and a place where he had whittled some shavings, also unlighted matches. The tracks led on out of the swamp in the opposite direction but darkness coming on the trail could not be followed. Further search was made on succeeding days, but no trace was found of Dunton, and he was given up for lost.

Dunton came up from Battle Creek last year as did Wells also. They were to have been followed this spring by other settlers from Battle Creek, but Dunton's death, which is believed to be certain, may check the tide of immigration that was setting in to Curtis.

Alcona County Review, February 17, 1898

His Body Found.

The Curtis Township Settler who Lost His Way in the Big Storm of January.

The body of the Curtis township homesteader who was lost in the big storm of January 31st, has been found.

The man's name was A. C. Dunton. It will be remembered that he was returned from South Branch with some groceries when the storm arose. Not arriving home a search was made and the bag of groceries was found hanging on a tree and near by was found matches and shavings, showing that he had made an attempt to build a fire. The falling snow had covered the tracks beyond this point rendering further search futile.

Dunton and a young son went to Curtis from Battle Creek about a year ago and located on a homestead near

the county line. The son was at home alone when the storm came up and next morning he gave the alarm that he feared his father had perished in the storm. Although diligent search was made for several days, the body was not found.

Some suspicion was attached to another homesteader named Wells, who came from Battle Creek with Dunton and who knew of the latter's trip to South Branch on that day and that Dunton also expected some money through the mail, and he was under suspicion until the finding of the body last Thursday.

The story of the finding of the body is told as follows by the Tawas Gazette:

"In Battle Creek, the man had a wife and two small children, and a host of friends; and on Wednesday two gentlemen came from that city to search for the missing man, after the snow had disappeared. Thursday they went to the spot where the unfortunate was last seen, and the search began, and at 3:30 p.m. they were rewarded by finding the body where, apparently, the man had wandered a short distance from the trail, had lost his way, become exhausted, and had lain down and died. The body had not been disturbed, and in the pockets were found all of the money and the articles belonging to the deceased, and there was not one thing to bear evidence of foul play.

The deceased was a member of the Maccabees, and one of the gentlemen who came this week to search was a representative of that order. The names of these two gentlemen referred to are Abbey and Wright; and after finding the body they came to this city and purchased a casket from undertaker King, and after encasing the body, and getting the necessary permit, the remains were shipped to Battle Creek for interment."

Alcona County Review, March 24, 1898

Local History of One Year

Chronology of the Principal Events of the Year 1898.

February 1. A. C. Dunton a Curtis homesteader, lost in snow storm. Body found in March.

Alcona County Review, January 5, 1899
Cemetery: Oak Hill, Calhoun Co.

Dupont, {Girl}

HOME REVIEWINGS.

Died—At Alcona, Wednesday morning, July 20th, infant daughter of Mr. and Mrs. Benj. E. Dupont; aged 2 months, 15 days. This was the only daughter of Mr. and Mrs. Dupont. The sad affliction came upon them suddenly and unexpectedly, the little one having been sick only a few days. Funeral services took place yesterday, the remains of the deceased being interred in the cemetery at Harrisville.

Alcona County Review, July 22, 1881
Cemetery: West Lawn, Alcona Co.

Durfee, Mary Wightman

The Local News.

Mrs. F. E. Schall received the shocking intelligence by telegraph last Friday morning, that her mother was dead. She left the same morning accompanied by her husband for her mother's late home at Plymouth, Mich. Her mother's death was caused by heart disease and half an hour prior to her death she was apparently in her usual state of good health.

Alcona County Review, June 4, 1891

Somewhat Personal.

Prof. F. E. Schall returned on the Atlantic Sunday evening. Mrs. Schall will not return to Harrisville.

Alcona County Review, June 4, 1891
Cemetery: Newburgh, Wayne Co.

Durkee, Gilbert James

COUNTY REVIEWINGS.

Another very sad accident occurred in this county last Saturday, by which one James Durgie lost his life. He was employed at Perkins' camp, back of Greenbush and was instantly killed by a falling tree.

Alcona County Review, December 3, 1880
Cemetery:

Durkee, {Child}

LOCAL JOTTINGS.

Wm. Durkee lost an infant child last Sunday.

Alcona County Review, April 1, 1887
Cemetery:

Dyer, Mrs. Hattie N.

HOME REVIEWINGS.

Mrs. F. H. Dyer of Alpena, who has been a great sufferer for several years past, while temporarily insane, shot herself through the left breast with a revolver, Monday morning, from the effects of which she died Wednesday morning.

Alcona County Review, May 27, 1881
Cemetery: Evergreen, Alpena Co.

Edgar, Andrew K.

Local Sayings and Doings.

The venerable Squire Edgar, living a mile north of the village is very ill and not expected to live. While piling wood about two weeks since he very suddenly lost the use of his legs and fell to the ground, almost helpless. He succeeded, however, in crawling into his house on hands and knees and has been confined to his bed since, with no apparent improvement in his condition, so we learn.

Alcona County Review, November 25, 1881

Local Sayings and Doings.

Squire Edgar is still very ill at his home.

Alcona County Review, December 9, 1881

Another Pioneer Gone.

Andrew K. Edgar, Esq., one of the pioneer farmers of Harrisville township, is no more, his death having occurred at his residence one mile north of this village, Sunday morning last, after an illness of seven weeks. Mr. Edgar was born in the State of Vermont in March 1802, and consequently at the time of his death was past 79 years of age. After spending the greater part of his young manhood in his native State, he subsequently removed to Detroit, Mich., but in what year we have not been informed. Here he met with Margaret Warrington, whose hand in marriage he courted and finally won in 1855, and who now survives his death with a family of three sons and four daughters. Eighteen years ago last May the deceased with his family removed to this county, and located a farm just above the village of Harrisville, where he remained to the day of his death. He always bore a prominent part in township and county matters, and was elected Justice of the Peace for several terms. In his death Harrisville township loses one of her oldest citizens and public benefactors.

Funeral services of the deceased were held from the M. E. church Monday afternoon. The attendance of friends and neighbors was unusually large.

Alcona County Review, December 30, 1881
Cemetery: Springport, Alcona Co.

Edgar, {Boy}

The three-year-old son, and only child of Mr. and Mrs. Wm. Edgar died Sunday. The burial took place Monday afternoon. The services were conducted by the Rev. C. B. Steele.

Mr. and Mrs. Edgar are grateful to friends who have assisted them in their trouble.

Alcona County Review, July 22, 1897
Cemetery:

Edgar, Eliza [Neil]

PERSONAL POINTS.

Mrs. Geo. Edgar is reported to be very ill at her home north of the village.

Alcona County Review, November 3, 1898

PERSONAL POINTS.

Mrs. Edgar died last evening. She was a devout Christian and a faithful member of the Baptist church. She was a faithful wife, a loving mother and a good neighbor and her demise is a cause for sorrow to a large number of friends. Deceased was a sister of Archie and Nicholas Neil and Mrs. Jas. Barber. She is survived by her husband and four children.

Alcona County Review, November 3, 1898

Card of Thanks--We desire to extend our heartfelt thanks to our friends and neighbors who rendered so many kindnesses and such timely help during the long illness and death of our beloved wife and mother. Only when deep sorrow comes upon us can we appreciate such acts of kindness and from the bottom of our hearts again we thank you.

Geo. Edgar and Family.

Alcona County Review, November 17, 1898

Local History of One Year

Chronology of the Principal Events of the Year 1898.

November
1. Death of Mrs. Geo. Edgar.

Alcona County Review, January 5, 1899
Cemetery: Springport, Alcona Co.

Edgar, George

Sick at Jackson.

On Saturday Geo. Edgar received a dispatch from a Jackson physician stating that his son, George, was ill with typhoid fever in a hospital in that city.

The young man left home about six weeks ago in the employ of Perrine's circus. He became sick down in Southern Michigan somewhere and the manager of the show started him for home in charge of another young man. When they arrived at Jackson George's companion deserted him at the Eagle hotel and he was soon taken to the hospital. At last accounts he was doing nicely.

Alcona County Review, September 14, 1899

Local News.

Supt. Effrick yesterday received a telegram from Jackson notifying him of the death at a hospital in that city of Geo. Edgar, the young man who was reported sick at Jackson two weeks ago with typhoid fever. The deceased, it will be remembered, was on his way home from the employ of Perrine's circus, when he was abandoned at Jackson by the man who was bringing him home. He was about 17 years old and was the oldest child of George Edgar. The interment will take place at Jackson.

Alcona County Review, September 28, 1899
Cemetery: Mount Evergreen, Jackson Co.

Edgar, Loyle

EVENTS OF ONE WEEK.

A three-year-old child of Geo. Edgar died yesterday morning of inflammation of the lungs.

Alcona County Review, February 11, 1897

Loyle Edgar infant son of Mr. and Mrs. Geo. Edgar died Wednesday morning, Feb. 10th, age 2 years eight months. The funeral service was conducted by Rev. Tompkins at the Baptist church.

A Bud the gardener gave us.
A pure and holy child.
He gave it to our keeping to cherish undefiled,
And just as it was opening
To the glory of the day,
Down came the heavenly gardener
And took our bud away.

Alcona County Review, February 18, 1897

Card of Thanks.

I wish to express our sincere thanks for the many kindnesses rendered us by our kind friends and neighbors during the illness, and death of our child.

Mr. and Mrs. Geo. Edgar.

Alcona County Review, February 18, 1897
Cemetery:

Edgar, Margaret [Warrington]

Once more death has visited this community and laid his icy finger upon one of its citizens. This time the summons was for Mrs. Margaret Edgar. She had been ailing for some time with la grippe and the infirmities of age, which culminated in her death Friday afternoon of last week. Deceased was surrounded by her children at her last moments and passed away very peacefully.

Marguerite Warrington was born in Ireland July 23, 1832. She came to Detroit in 1852 and three years later was married to Andrew K. Edgar. In May, 1863 she came to Harrisville with her husband, whom she survived by 15 years. There are five children, all of whom survive their parents.

The funeral services were held Monday at the Episcopal church, Rev. A. H. Wilson officiating.

Alcona County Review, March 4, 1897

PERSONAL.

Mrs. James Graham of Detroit was in attendance at the funeral of her sister, Mrs. M. Edgar.

Alcona County Review, March 4, 1897

Card of Thanks.

We desire to express our heartfelt gratitude to the kind neighbors who helped us in any way during the illness and death of our beloved mother; and who their kind and cheering words helped to cheer and comfort her during the last hours.

Mrs. Edgar's Children.

Alcona County Review, March 4, 1897

Order of Hearing.
Feb. 10, 98.
STATE OF MICHIGAN, County of Alcona.

At a session of the Probate Court for said County, held at the Probate office, in the Village of Harrisville on the tenth day of February in the year one thousand eight hundred and ninety-eight.

Present, Hon. W. H. Gilpin, Judge of Probate.

In the matter of the estate of Margarette Edgar, deceased.

On reading and filing the petition duly verified of Luella Pearson praying among other things that administration of said estate may be granted to William Finch, of Haynes township, Alcona county, Mich., or some other suitable person.

Thereupon it is ordered, that Monday, the 7th day of March next, at ten o'clock in the forenoon, be assigned for the hearing of said petition, and that the heirs at law of said deceased and all other persons interested in said estate, are required to appear at a session of the Probate Court, then to be holden at the Probate office, in the Village of Harrisville and show cause, if any there be, why the prayer of the petitioner should not be granted.

And it is further ordered that the petitioner give notice to the heirs at law and all persons interested in said estate, of the pendency of said petition, and the hearing thereof, by causing a copy of this order to be published in the Alcona County Review, a newspaper printed and circulating in said county three successive weeks previous to said day of hearing.

W. H. Gilpin,
Judge of Probate.

Alcona County Review, February 10, 1898

State of Michigan, County of Alcona.

Notice is hereby given, that by an order of the Probate Court for the County of Alcona, made on the 11th day of April A.D. 1898, six months from that date were allowed for creditors to present their claims against the estate of Margrete Edgar deceased late of said County, deceased, and that all creditors of said deceased are required to present their claims to said Probate Court, at the Probate office, in the Village of Harrisville, for examination and allowance, on or before the 11th day of October next, and that such claims will be heard before said Court, on Monday, the 20th day of June and on Tuesday, the 11th day of October next, at ten o'clock in the forenoon of each of those days.

Dated April 11th, A.D. 1898.

W. H. Gilpin,
Judge of Probate.

Alcona County Review, April 14, 1898
Cemetery: Springport, Alcona Co.

Edwards, Anne [Thompson]

HOME REVIEWINGS.

Wm. Edwards, of this place, received a telegram, Wednesday, announcing the death of his mother at her home in Sand Beach.

Alcona County Review, September 30, 1881
Cemetery: Probably Rock Falls, Huron Co.

Edwards, Bertie.

Sad Case of Drowning.

While little Bertie Edwards, in company with his little sister and brothers, was fishing Monday morning at the lower pond, he lost his balance and fell in where the water was deepest. The children were alone at the time and the others ran at once for assistance, but when the little fellow was taken out he must have been in the water 20 to 30 minutes and all efforts to resuscitate him were unavailing. He was 7 years of age and his shocking death was a cruel blow to the bereaved parents. The remains were buried Tuesday, the funeral services being conducted at the Baptist church by the Rev. Boundy.

Alcona County Review, May 18, 1893

Our kind, sympathetic neighbors will please accept our heartfelt thanks for their sympathy and kindness in our recent affliction.

Wm. Edwards and Family.

Alcona County Review, May 18, 1893
Cemetery: Probably West Lawn, Alcona Co.

Edwards, Wilbert L.

LOCAL JOTTINGS.

One of the twin babies of Mr. and Mrs. Wm. Edwards died yesterday, and funeral will be held to-day.

Alcona County Review, September 12, 1884
Cemetery: West Lawn, Alcona Co.

Effrick, Christina [Kramer]

PERSONAL MENTION.

P. J. Effric was called to Fonthill, Ont., yesterday by a telegram announcing the death of his mother.

Alcona County Review, January 18, 1894
Cemetery: Prob. Hillside, Niagara Region, ONT

Ellico, Harry Russell

LOCAL JOTTINGS.

The fore part of last week, the year-old child of Mr. and Mrs. Ellico, at Gustin Center, this county, was fatally scalded. The mother had taken a boiler of hot water off the stove and placed it on the walk at the back door of the house. The child was walking near the boiler, and accidentally stepping off the walk, it caught hold of the said boiler to save itself tipping the same off the walk, and spilling the contents thereof upon itself. The child was terribly scalded all over the lower part of its body, hips and legs. The little sufferor died about 24 hours thereafter.

Alcona County Review, November 13, 1885
Cemetery: Springport, Alcona Co.

Elliott, William N.

COUNTY NEWS.

A telegram came to L. A. Colwell yesterday, announcing the death of Dr. M. N. Elliott, of White Pigeon, husband of Mrs. L. A.'s sister. Mr. Colwell left last night to attend the funeral.

Alcona County Review, February 4, 1881

County News and Gossip.

It is rumored that Mrs. Dr. W. N. Elliott, of White Pigeon, whose husband recently became deceased, will make her home in Harrisville the coming year, with her sister, Mrs. L. Colwell.

Alcona County Review, February 25, 1881

HOME REVIEWINGS.

Mrs. Elliott of White Pigeon, Mich., has arrived in Harrisville to remain with her sister Mrs. L. A. Colwell. It will be remembered that the husband of Mrs. E., Dr. M. N. Elliott, died the past winter.

Alcona County Review, June 3, 1881
Cemetery: White Pigeon Township, St. Joseph Co.

Ellis, Charles B.

Chas. B. Ellis, a private of Co. B, 33d Mich. Vol., died of fever on the hospital ship Seguranca. The remains weighted with 300 pounds of scrap iron, were buried at sea with soldier's honors. He enlisted at Alpena. John McGregor of Black River and Cyrus Dunham of Ossineke, a son of Rev. F. P. Dunham, were aboard the Seguranca and were convalescent from fever.

Alcona County Review, August 18, 1898
Cemetery: At sea

Ellis, Sarah J. [Hastings]

Black River News.

Correspondence Alpena Echo.
Mrs. Chancey Ellis left here some time ago for her health. Reports have come that the doctors have given her up with no hopes of recovery, which is sad news to her many friends in this town.

Alcona County Review, August 1, 1895

Haynes, Nov. 4th, 1895.——Mrs. R. Hastings returned home last Wednesday from Ontario accompanied by her son-in-law, Mr. Ellis, and wife. She has been in Canada attending to her sick daughter who has recovered sufficiently to come here.

Alcona County Review, November 7, 1895

Haynes Happenings.
Haynes, Jan. 28, '96.--Mrs. Chancey Ellis is in very poor health.

Alcona County Review, January 30, 1896

Haynes Happenings.
March 10, 1896.
Obituary.
Died March 5th, 1896, beloved wife of Chauncey Ellis, aged 22 years, of dropsy. Three small children are left to mourn their great loss. The funeral services were held at the home of her mother, Mrs. Robt. Hastings. The Rev. McBride officiated. There was a large attendance of relatives and friends of the family to follow the mortal remains to the cemetery.

Let fall the sympathetic tear
With those who weep,
That one whom tender hearts hold dear
Lies in her last long sleep

Mr. Armstrong and wife and Geo. Hastings arrived Saturday evening from the camps of Alger, Smith & Co., not knowing their beloved sister was dead.

Mrs. Teeple presented Fred with a baby boy on the 6th and therefore could not attend the funeral of her dear sister.

Alcona County Review, March 12, 1896
Cemetery: Mt. Joy, Alcona Co.

Emerson, Asa

CALLED IN THE NIGHT.

Asa Emerson Now Sleeps the Sleep of the Just.
This old and upright citizen, passed peacefully away about 2 o'clock yesterday morning without a moment's warning that the unbidden guest was in wait beside the "half-closed door" of a peaceful and honorable existence. His aged wife was awakened by his gasping for breath, but before she could secure a light and get to his side the thread of life had broken.

Mr. Emerson was in town the day before and was in usual good health.

The funeral services will be held tomorrow afternoon at the Methodist church. The Odd Fellows, of which order he was a faithful member, will be in charge to discharge their last obligations to a departed brother.

Deceased was aged 65. He was a man of simple habits and trustful disposition. His strict honor and integrity, his earnest endeavor to do right by all, won for him universal respect. He was not great, as the world judges men, but the world was better for his having lived. Peace to the ashes of "Honest Asa Emerson."

Alcona County Review, July 30, 1896

All members of Harrisville Encampment No. 104, of Harrisville Lodge No. 218, IOOF, and of Huron Rebecca Lodge No. 256, are requested to be at the hall at 13:20 tomorrow to attend the funeral of our late worthy Brother, Asa Emerson.
M. Hale, C. P.
C. M. Lund, N. G.
Mary E. Young, N. G.
Sister lodges are requested to join.

Alcona County Review, July 30, 1896

PERSONAL MENTION.

Thos. Emerson of Rose City came to Harrisville to attend the funeral of his brother, Asa.

Alcona County Review, August 6, 1896

PERSONAL MENTION.

Mr. and Mrs. Jas. E. Smith of West Bay City were called to Harrisville last week by the death of Mrs. Smith's brother, the late Asa Emerson.

Alcona County Review, August 6, 1896

PERSONAL MENTION.

I thank the Odd Fellows particularly for their kindness and assistance in my late bereavement, but I would not forget the numerous other friends for their welcome assistance in my hour of greatest need.
Mrs. Lucinda Emerson.

Alcona County Review, August 6, 1896

The remains of the late Asa Emerson were interred at Springport Friday afternoon after the burial service of the Independent Order of Odd Fellows. The solemn occasion was made the subject for a very impressive sermon over the remains by the pastor of the M. E. church who discoursed at length upon the uncertainty of life and the necessity for some preparation for the transition from mortality to immortality. The remains were not exposed to view.

Alcona County Review, August 6, 1896

Whereas, Death has entered our Lodges and removed from our midst our beloved Brother, Asa Emerson, and

Whereas, We the undersigned members of Harrisville Lodge No. 218 I. O. O. F., Harrisville Encampment No. 104, and Huron Rebekah Lodge 256, while we bow in humble submission to the will of the Deity, whom we recognize as the light and guide of our united Orders, it is

Resolved, That we sincerely regret the decease of said Brother and that we open our hearts in sympathy to the bereaved widow in this her deep sorrow, And be it also

Resolved, That we drape our charters in mourning for a period of thirty days, that these resolutions be spread upon the records of our several orders, and that they also be printed in the Alcona County Review.

Encampment Com. C. M. Lund, D. H. Noyes, S. Kahn.

Sub. Lodge Com.——M. Hale, H. P. Moore, Kane Miller.

Rebekah Com.——Mary Young, Matie Taft, Kate Wier.

Alcona County Review, August 13, 1896
Cemetery: Springport, Alcona Co.

Emerson, Nancy Estella

COUNTY JOTTINGS.

That dreaded disease, diptheria, is raging quite extensively among the children in the southern portion of Alcona township. One of Supervisor A. T. Scarlett's little sons died with the disease Sunday night, and children in the families of Ephriam Waldron, John Hayden and Uriah Emerson are now down with the same. Let all necessary precautions be taken to prevent the further spreading of the disease.

Alcona County Review, October 25, 1878

COUNTY JOTTINGS.

Estella, only daughter of Mr. and Mrs. Uriah Emerson, died of typhoid fever, yesterday morning, aged 11 years and 6 months. She had just recovered from a severe attack of the diptheria when the fever set in and accomplished her death. Her decease is a sad blow to the parents, being the only daughter in the family. Their grief will be hard to overcome. Verily,

"the Lord giveth and the Lord taketh away." Even our choicest flowers be spareth not. The remains of the deceased will be buried today. Funeral services at the M. E. Church next Sunday at 10:30 a.m.

Alcona County Review, November 1, 1878
Cemetery: Springport, Alcona Co.

Emerson, Goldie

LOCAL JOTTINGS.

An infant child of Elias Emerson died last week and was buried Saturday afternoon.

Alcona County Review, June 17, 1887

LOCAL JOTTINGS.

The mill shut down last Saturday afternoon to give some of the employees an opportunity to attend the funeral of Elias Emerson's child.

Alcona County Review, June 17, 1887
Cemetery: Springport, Alcona Co.

Emerson, Jared

Death of Jared Emerson.

Jared Emerson, for twenty years past a resident of Alcona county, died at his late residence in this place, at 8 o'clock Wednesday evening. He was well and favorably known in this community and leaves numerous progeny and a large circle of friends to mourn their loss. He had been troubled with a distressing disease of the kidneys for several years past, and this, complicated with old age, was the immediate cause of his death. The deceased was 81 years of age, and was born in Petersburg, Rensellaer county, N. Y., April 15, 1806, coming to Michigan in middle age, where he has resided ever since. He was buried yesterday afternoon, at Springport. The Rev. F. N. Barlow will preach the funeral sermon Sunday morning in the Methodist church.

Alcona County Review, December 24, 1886

LOCAL JOTTINGS.

There were no services at the Baptist chapel, Sunday morning, but the two congregations assembled in the M. E. church to listen to the funeral address on the late Jared Emerson, which, at the request of the relatives of the deceased, was preached by the Rev. F. N. Barlow in that church. The reverend gentleman drew a graphic description of the biblical heaven, and concluded a fervent address with a touching tribute to the memory of the

deceased. The surviving relatives of the deceased were present.

Alcona County Review, December 31, 1886

Card of Thanks.

We, the undersigned, desire to return our heartfelt thanks to our many friends and neighbors who so kindly assisted during the last illness of our father, Jared Emerson.

The Children of Jared Emerson.

Alcona County Review, December 31, 1886

PROBATE ORDER.

At a session of the Probate Court for said county, held at the Probate Office in the village of Harrisville, on the 31st day of March, in the year one thousand eight hundred and eighty-seven. Present, Hon. Allen Nevins, Judge of Probate. In the matter of the **ESTATE OF JARED EMERSON, DECEASED.**

On reading and filing the petition, duly verified, of George Emerson praying that administration of said estate be granted to William E. Depew or some other suitable person.

Thereupon it is ordered, that Saturday, the Twenty-Third Day of April next, at 10 o'clock in the forenoon, be assigned for the hearing of said petition, and that the heirs-at-law of said deceased, and all other persons interested in said estate, are required to appear at a session of said court, then to be holden in the Probate Office, in the Village of Harrisville, and show cause, if any there be, why the prayer of the petitioner should not be granted; And it is further ordered, that said petitioner give notice to the persons interested in said estate, of the pendency of said petition, and the hearing thereof, by causing a copy of this order to be published in the Alcona County Review, a newspaper printed and circulated in said county, three successive weeks previous to said day of hearing.

Allen Nevins, Judge of Probate.

Alcona County Review, April 1, 1887

PROBATE ORDER.

State of Michigan, County of Alcona.

Notice is hereby given that by order of the Probate Court for the county of Alcona, made on the 23d day of April, 1887, six months from that date were allowed for creditors to present their claims against the estate of Jared Emerson, late of said county, deceased, and that all creditors of said deceased are required to present their claims to said Probate Court, at the Probate office in the village of Harrisville, for examination and allowance on or before the 24th Day of October, 1887, next, and that such claims will be heard before said Court, on Monday, the 25th day of August, 1887, and on Monday, the 24th day of October, 1887, next, at 10 o'clock in the forenoon of each of those days.

Dated April 23d, 1887.

Allen Nevins, Judge of Probate.

Alcona County Review, July 8, 1887

PROBATE ORDER.

STATE OF MICHIGAN, County of Alcona.

At a session of the Probate Court for the County of Alcona held at the Probate office in the village of Harrisville, on the tenth day of July, in the year one thousand eight hundred and eighty-eight. Present, Hon. Allen Nevin, Judge of Probate. In the matter of the

ESTATE OF JARED EMERSON, DECEASED.

On reading and filing the petition, duly verified of Simon J. McNally, administrator of the estate of Jared Emerson, deceased, praying that he may be empowered and licensed to sell the real estate of said deceased, situated in the township of Harrisville, County of Alcona, State of Michigan, known and described as follows: The north half of lot seventeen, south half of lot nineteen, entire lot eighteen, a strip of land four rods wide off the east end of the north half of lot four, the east end of lot three, and the east end of the south half of lot two, all in block thirteen of the recorded plat of the village of Harrisville. Also the south-east quarter of the north-west quarter of section twenty-six, lot one of section twenty-six, except so much of said last parcel as was conveyed by said Jared Emerson, for an addition, to South Harrisville Cemetery, all of said land in township twenty-six north of range nine east.

Thereupon it is ordered that Monday, the Sixth Day of August next, at 10 o'clock in the forenoon, be assigned for the hearing of said petition, and that the heirs at law of said deceased, and all other persons interested in said estate, are required to appear at a session of said court, then to be holden in the Probate office, in the village of Harrisville, and show cause, if any there be, why the prayer of the petitioner should not be granted. And it is further ordered, that said petitioner give notice to the heirs at law and persons interested in said estate, of the pendency of said petition, and the hearing thereof, by causing a copy of this order to be published in the Alcona County Review, a newspaper printed and circulating in said county of Alcona, three successive weeks, previous to said day of hearing.

ALLEN NEVIN, Judge of Probate.

Alcona County Review, July 13, 1888

Notice of Sale of Real Estate.

(First Publication Aug. 10, 1888, No. 19.)

STATE OF MICHIGAN, County of Alcona.

In the matter of the ESTATE OF JARED EMERSON, deceased. Notice is hereby given, that in pursuance of an order granted to the undersigned, administrator of the estate of said Jared Emerson, by the Hon. Judge of Probate for Alcona county, on the 6th day of August, A. D. 1888, there will be sold at public vendue to the highest bidder, at the front door of the Court House, in the village of Harrisville, in the County of Alcona, in said State, on Saturday, the Twenty-second Day of September, A. D. 1888, at eleven o'clock in the forenoon of that day (subject to all encumbrances by mortgage or otherwise existing at the time of the death of said deceased, or the time of the said sale, and also subject to the right of dower and the homestead rights of the widow of said deceased therein), the following described real estate, to wit: Situate in the township of Harrisville, County of Alcona, and State of Michigan, described as follows: The north half of lot seventeen, south half of lot nineteen, entire lot eighteen, a strip of land four rods wide off the east end of the north half of lot four, the east end of lot three, and the east end of the south half of lot two, all in block thirteen of the recorded plat of the village of Harrisville; also the south-east quarter of the north-west quarter of section twenty-six, lot one of section twenty-six, except so much of said last parcel as was conveyed by said Jared Emerson, for an addition, to South Harrisville Cemetery. All of said land in township twenty-six north of range nine east.

SIMON J. McNALLY,

Administrator of the Estate of Jared Emerson, Deceased.

The above sale is hereby adjourned until the 18th day of December, A. D. 1888, at 2 o'clock in the afternoon.

Dated September 22d, 1888.

SIMON J. McNALLY,

Administrator.

Alcona County Review, September 28, 1888

STATE OF MICHIGAN,

County of Alcona.

At a session of the Probate Court for said County, held at the Probate office, in the village of Harrisville, on the 30th day of Dec., in the year one thousand eight hundred and ninety-one.

Present, Hon. Geo. S. Ritchie, Judge of Probate.

In the matter of the Estate of Jared Emerson.

On reading and filing the petition, duly verified, of H. P. Moore praying that F. A. Beede or some other suitable person be appointed administrator of said Estate.

Thereupon it is ordered, that Saturday, the 30th day of January, next, at ten o'clock in the forenoon, be assigned for the hearing of said petition, and that the heirs at law of said deceased, and all other persons interested in said estate, are required to appear at a session of said Court, then to be holden in the Probate office, in the Village of Harrisville and show cause, if any there be, why the prayer of the petitioner should not be granted: And it is further ordered, that said petitioner give notice to the persons interested in said estate, of the pendency of said petition, and the hearing thereof, by causing a copy of this order to be published in the Alcona County Review, a newspaper printed and circulated in said county three successive weeks previous to said day of hearing.

Geo. S. Ritchie, Judge.

Alcona County Review, December 31, 1891

The Local News.

Another turn has been taken in the estate of the late Jared Emerson, by which Geo. Emerson petitions the probate court for the removal of Simon J. McNally, who was duly appointed administrator of said estate a number of years ago, but who is now a non-resident of the state.

Alcona County Review, March 31, 1892

STATE OF MICHIGAN,
County of Alcona.

Probate Court for said County.

In the Matter of the Estate of Jared Emerson Citation.

To Simon J. McNally, Greetings:

Whereas, George Emerson has filed a verified petition with this Court, on the 30th day of January, 1892, alleging that said Simon J. McNally was and had been for some time Administrator of the above Estate, and that he ought to be removed as such administrator for the following reason, viz: That said Simon J. McNally is now, and has been for six months immediately preceding this date, a non-resident of the State of Michigan and a resident of the State of Wisconsin, and that he is now incompetent to discharge the duties of the office.

In the Name of the people of the State of Michigan:

You are Therefore hereby Cited and Required personally to be and appear at the said Probate Court, at the Probate Office in the Village of Harrisville on the 23rd day of April, at Two O'clock in the afternoon of that day, and then and there (or show cause, of any, why) you should not be removed from the office of Administrator of the aforesaid Estate and your former letters of administration be revoked. And the sheriff, or any deputy, coroner or constable, of said county, is hereby authorized to serve and make due return hereof. This citation is to be served Twenty days before the return day hereof.

Witness, The Honorable George S. Ritchie, Judge of the Probate Court, for the county of Alcona, this 30th day of January, in the year of our Lord, one thousand eight hundred and ninety-two.

GEORGE S. RITCHIE, Judge of Probate.

STATE OF MICHIGAN,
County of Alcona

I hereby Certify and Return, That after diligent search I have not been able to find the within named Simon J. McNally within my bailiwick, nor in said State.

Dated at Harrisville March 29th, 1892.

JOHN Y. McDONALD, Sheriff of said County.

Alcona County Review, March 31, 1892

The Local News.

Judge Ritchie held a session of court Saturday and moved the Emerson estate matter one peg nearer a final settlement.

Alcona County Review, May 19, 1892

STATE OF MICHIGAN,
COUNTY OF ALCONA.

At a session of the Probate Court for said County, held at the Probate office, in the village of Harrisville, on the 14th day of May, in the year one thousand eight hundred and ninety-two.

Present, Hon. Geo. S. Ritchie, Judge of Probate.

In the Matter of the Estate of Jared Emerson, deceased:

On reading and filing the petition, duly verified, of O. H. Smith, administrator of said estate, praying that he be granted a license to sell the real estate of said Jared Emerson, deceased, for the purpose of paying the debts of said deceased and expenses of administration, which real estate is described as follows, to-wit: All the real estate situate in the Township of Harrisville, County of Alcona and State of Michigan and described as follows, to-wit: The north half of lot seventeen (17) south half of lot nineteen (19), the entire lot eighteen (18), all the east end of lot three (3) being four rods wide east and west and width of said lot north and south; all of the east end of the south half of lot two (2), being four rods wide east and west and width of said half lot north and south; all the east end of the north half of lot four (4), being four rods wide east and west and width of said half lot north and south, all in block thirteen of the recorded plat of the Village of Harrisville. Also the southeast quarter of the northwest quarter of Section Twenty-Six (26), lot one (1) of Section Twenty-Six (26), except so much of said last parcel as was conveyed by said Jared Emerson for an addition to the South Harrisville cemetery; all of said land in Township Twenty-Six (26) North of Range Nine east.

Thereupon it is ordered, that Saturday, the 18th day of June, next, at ten o'clock in the forenoon, be assigned for the hearing of said

petition, and that the heirs at law of said deceased, and all other persons interested in said estate, are required to appear at a session of said Court, then to be holden in the Probate office, in the Village of Harrisville and show cause, if any there be, why the prayer of the petitioner should not be granted:

And it is further ordered, that said petitioner give notice to the persons interested in said estate, of the pendency of said petition, and the hearing thereof, by causing a copy of this order to be published in the Alcona County Review, a newspaper printed and circulated in said county four successive weeks previous to said day of hearing.

Geo. S. Ritchie,
Judge of Probate.

Alcona County Review, May 19, 1892

STATE OF MICHIGAN,
COUNTY OF ALCONA.

In the Matter of the Estate of Jared Emerson, deceased:

Notice is hereby given, that in pursuance of an order granted to the undersigned, of O. H. Smith, Administrator of the estate of said Jared Emerson, by the Hon. Judge of Probate for the County of Alcona, on the 18th day of June A. D. 1892, there will be sold at public venue, to the highest bidder, at the front door of the Court House in the Village of Harrisville, said county (that being the place of holding circuit court in the County of Alcona), in said State, on Saturday the 20th day of August A. D. 1892, at one o'clock in the afternoon of that day (subject to all incumbrances by mortgage or otherwise existing at the time of the death of said deceased, or at the time of said sale, and also subject to the dower and homestead rights of the widow of said deceased therein) the following described real estate, to-wit: The north half of lot seventeen (17) south half of lot nineteen (19), the entire lot eighteen (18), all the east end of lot three (3) being four rods wide east and west and width of said lot north and south; all of the east end of the south half of lot two (2), being four rods wide east and west and width of said half lot north and south; all the east end of the north half of lot four (4), being four rods wide east and west and width of said half lot north and south, all in block thirteen of the recorded plat of the Village of Harrisville. Also the southeast quarter of the northwest quarter of Section Twenty-Six (26), lot one (1) of Section Twenty-Six (26), except so much of said last parcel as was conveyed by said Jared Emerson for an addition to the South Harrisville cemetery; all of said land in Township of Harrisville, County of Alcona and State of Michigan, being Township Twenty-Six (26) North of Range Nine (9) east.

O. H. Smith, Administrator.

Alcona County Review, July 7, 1892
Cemetery: Springport, Alcona Co.

Emerson, Lorena [Effingham]

PERSONAL.

Mrs. Uriah Emerson is near unto death's door and but slight hopes are entertained for her recovery. The lady has been sick nearly all winter, and unless a change for the better occurs soon, her friends fear she cannot recover.

Alcona County Review, April 22, 1897

PERSONAL.

Mrs. Uriah Emerson departed this life on Tuesday of this week, after a long and tedious illness covering a period of several months.

Lovenia Effingham was born in Alleghany county, N. Y., January 27, 1849, and was therefore aged 48 years and 4 months. She was the mother of six children, four of whom and her husband survive to mourn her demise.

The funeral takes place from the Baptist chapel at 2 o'clock this afternoon.

Alcona County Review, April 29, 1897

Card of Thanks.

To the friends and neighbors who assisted us by their many acts of kindness and Christian sympathy, during the great affliction which has befallen us in the illness and death of our dear companion and mother, we extend our heartfelt thanks and trust our heavenly father will reward them. And especially do we desire to thank the Baptist Young People's Union for the lovely flowers which they placed upon the casket.

Uriah Emerson and Family.

Alcona County Review, May 6, 1897
Cemetery: Probably Springport, Alcona Co.

Emerson, Nancy [O'Dell]

LOCAL JOTTINGS.

Mrs. Jared Emerson is confined to her bed most of the time with rheumatism. She is 76 years old.

Alcona County Review, July 23, 1886

Your Folks and Our Folks.

Mr. Enos Emerson, of Alleganey county, N. Y., arrived in Harrisville last week Thursday evening, being called here by the dangerous illness of his mother, Mrs. Jared Emerson.

Alcona County Review, August 6, 1886

LOCAL JOTTINGS.

Mrs. Jared Emerson died at 10 A.M. Thursday. Time and place for holding funeral not decided upon before Review went to press.

Alcona County Review, August 13, 1886

Your Folks and Our Folks.

Died.—In this village, on the 12th inst., Mrs. Jared Emerson, aged 78 years.

The deceased was born in Petersburg, Rensselaer county, N. Y., in April, 1808; was married in Sept., 1826, and came to Michigan with her family 19 years ago, settling in Harrisville, where they have since resided. The funeral service was held in the M. E. church, at 2 o'clock p. m. on Friday, Revs. Barlow and Leith both taking part in the service. The remains were interred in the Springport cemetery. It will be sixty years next Sept. since Mr. and Mrs. Emerson were married—a longer period of married life being rarely known.

Alcona County Review, August 20, 1886

Your Folks and Our Folks.

Enos Emerson, of Bolivar, N. Y., who was called here during the fatal illness of his mother, returned home last Sunday.

Alcona County Review, August 20, 1886

LOCAL JOTTINGS.

The "dry spell" was broken by a fine rain storm last Friday afternoon. For a time it was very dark. The funeral services of Mrs. Jared Emerson were being held in the M. E. church, and when the storm came up, about three o'clock, it was so dark the church lamps were lighted.

Alcona County Review, August 20, 1886

Card of Thanks.—We hereby extend our most heartfelt thanks to

the host of friends, one and all, who so kindly assisted us in our late sad bereavement in the sickness and burial of our dear mother. That you may be spared the necessity of such assistance as long as possible is the sincere wish of

Mr. and Mrs. Geo. Emerson.

Alcona County Review, August 20, 1886
Cemetery: Springport, Alcona Co.

Emerson, Nina

EVENTS OF ONE WEEK.

Mr. and Mrs. Willis Emerson, of Mikado, mourn the death of one of their year-old twins. The little one died from inflammation of the lungs, resulting from whooping cough.

Alcona County Review, November 26, 1896
Cemetery: Prob. Mikado Township, Alcona Co.

Emery, Hiram A.

NOTICE OF SALE OF REAL ESTATE.

State of Michigan, County of Bay.

In the matter of the estate of Ella Emery and Diana Emery, minors.

Notice is hereby given, that in pursuance and by virtue of an order granted to the undersigned as guardian of the estate of said minors, by the Judge of Probate in and for Bay County, Michigan, on the 21st day of February, A.D. 1898, there will be sold at public vendue to the highest bidder at the front door of the Alcona County court house in the village of Harrisville in said county, on the 17th day of August, A.D. 1898, at 9 o'clock a.m. of said day, all the right, title and interest of said minors in and to the following described lands and premises situated in said Alcona County and State of Michigan, to-wit: The S W ¼ of N W ¼, N W ¼ of S W ¼, S ½ of S E ¼ Sec. 30; S ½ of S W ¼ of Sec. 29; N E ¼, E ½ of N W ¼, E ½ of S W ¼, S ½ of S E ¼ of Sec. 31: N W ¼; S W ¼; W ½ of S E ¼ of Sec. 32, all in Town 25 north, range 5 east. All subject to the right of dower therein of Eunice Emery, widow of Hiram A. Emery, late of Bay County, deceased.

Henry S. Lewis,
Guardian.

Dated June 30, 1898.

Alcona County Review, June 30, 1898

Henry S. Lewis of Bay City, guardian of two minor children of the late H. A. Emery, was here yesterday morning and conducted a sale of county realty belonging to the Emery estate. He then went across to McKinley on his wheel on a similar mission in Oscoda county. The estate comprises a large amount of real estate in northern Michigan.

Alcona County Review, August 18, 1898
Cemetery:

Emmel, {Child}

LOCAL JOTTINGS.

The infant child of Oscar Emmel died October 2d, after a few hours illness.

Alcona County Review, October 16, 1885
Cemetery: Probably Springport, Alcona Co.

Emmel, Fanny [Nestle]

PERSONAL DRIFT.

Mrs. Oscar Emel, who has been very sick for two months past, is reported as being no better.

Alcona County Review, July 16, 1886

LOCAL JOTTINGS.

The wife of Oscar Emmel, of this place, died Wednesday afternoon after a lingering illness. Mrs. Emmel was 27 years of age, and leaves three small children to mourn their loss.

Alcona County Review, February 4, 1887

LOCAL JOTTINGS.

The funeral services of Mrs. Oscar Emmel were held last Sunday morning in the M. E. church, the Rev. C. B. Steele officiating.

Alcona County Review, February 11, 1887

LOCAL JOTTINGS.

A paper was circulated last week and a considerable sum of money raised for the benefit of Oscar Emmel. Mr. Emmel is a worthy man, whom the long sickness and death of his wife has left in rather straightened circumstances.

Alcona County Review, February 11, 1887
Cemetery: Springport, Alcona Co.

Emmorey, David C.

WITHOUT WARNING.

D. C. Emmorey Receives a Sudden Call.

The community received another shock last Friday when the news spread rapidly that D. C. Emmorey, another respected citizen, had received a sudden call from his Maker to appear and render an account of his stewardship. Mr.

Emmorey had come down town Friday morning in his usual health, and after attending to the morning mail, drove a pig to the Fair Grounds for exhibition. The animal was a little fractious and the exertion of driving it must have caused his death. He was taken suddenly ill. Mrs. Emmorey and daughter, Mrs. Waters, were sitting in their buggy near by and Mr. Emmorey jumped in and was driven rapidly to his store. He got out there but just as he was passing through the door he sank to his knees and with one gasp he fell backwards and his soul took its flight.

Deceased had not been in good health for a couple of years, not since he was thrown out in a runaway accident which must have injured him internally, and his sudden demise was not, therefore, so surprising to those who realized the delicate condition of his health.

Mr. Emmorey had been a resident of Harrisville about eight years. He was born in 1820 and but little is known of his life previous to his coming here. In 1885 he was married to Mrs. Wm. Conklin, who survives him. In the same year he joined the Harrisville M. E. church of which he has ever since been a devout and faithful member. He was universally well liked and by honesty, fair and easy dealing had built up an excellent business in agricultural implements, buggies, wagons, stoves and tinware.

The funeral services were held Sunday morning at the M. E. church and the remains were interred at South Harrisville, whither they were followed by an unusually large number of citizens.

It is a singular coincidence that on last Thursday a brother of Mr. Emmorey died at Grand Rapids, Mich. No particulars are at hand.

Alcona County Review, October 13, 1892

The Local News.

Judge Ritchie held a session of court Monday and listened to a petition of Emma Emmory praying for the appointment of Chas. Conklin as administrator of the estate of the late D. C. Emmory.

Alcona County Review, October 20, 1892

STATE OF MICHIGAN, County of Alcona.

At a session of the Probate Court for said County, held at the Probate office, in the village of Harrisville, on

the 17th day of October, in the year one thousand eight hundred and ninety-two.

Present, Hon. Geo. S. Ritchie, Judge of Probate.

In the matter of the Estate of David C. Emmory, deceased:

On reading and filing the petition, duly verified, of Emma Emmory, praying that administration of said estate may be granted to Charles Conklin or some other suitable person.

Thereupon it is ordered, that Saturday, the 12th day of November, next, at ten o'clock in the forenoon, be assigned for the hearing of said petition, and that the sole heirs at law of said deceased, and all other persons interested in said estate, are required to appear at a session of said Court, then to be holden in the Probate office, in the Village of Harrisville and show cause, if any there be, why the prayer of the petitioner should not be granted: And it is further ordered, that said petitioner give notice to the persons interested in said estate, of the pendency of said petition, and the hearing thereof, by causing a copy of this order to be published in the Alcona County Review, a newspaper printed and circulated in said county, 3 successive weeks previous to said day of hearing.

Geo. S. Ritchie,
Judge of Probate.

Alcona County Review, October 20, 1892

STATE OF MICHIGAN, County of Alcona.

Notice is hereby given that by an order of the Probate Court for the County of Alcona, made on the twelfth day of November, A. D. 1892: six months from that date were allowed for creditors to present their claims against the estate of David C. Emmory, late of said county deceased, and that all creditors of said deceased are required to present their claims to said Probate Curt at the Probate office, in the Village of Harrisville, for examination and allowance, on or before the Twelfth Day of May, 1893 next, and that such claims will be heard before the Court on Monday, the Thirteenth Day of February, 1893, and on Friday, the Twelfth Day of May, A. D. 1893, next, at 2 o'clock in the afternoon of each of those days.

Dated at Harrisville, Mich., this 12th day of November, A. D. 1892.

GEORGE S. RITCHIE,
Judge of Probate.

Alcona County Review, October 20, 1892

EVENTS OF ONE WEEK.

Wants a Share of the Estate.

A brother of the late D. C. Emmory, residing at Kingsville, Ont., was in the village last week. His mission here was to endeavor to establish a claim upon his brother's estate through a former wife of the deceased, whom he claims is still living. Chas. Conklin, administrator of the estate, visited Kingsville in the fall and offered the claimant a sum of money in satisfaction of any claims he might have upon the estate but the offer was rejected. The administrator says that the business of the deceased was left in such shape that assets, consisting largely of book accounts, will be barely sufficient to meet the liabilities.

Alcona County Review, January 5, 1893

MATTERS IN COURT.

Several Important Cases Go Over to the Next Session.

Owing to the death of D. C. Emmory, the main witness, a nolle pros. was entered in the case of the People vs. M. Karpel, charged with hawking and peddling in Harrisville.

Alcona County Review, January 5, 1893

HISTORY OF ONE YEAR.

Chronological History of the Past Year, 1892.

October.

7. Sudden death of D. C. Emmory of Harrisville.

Alcona County Review, January 5, 1893

HISTORY OF ONE YEAR.

Chronological History of the Past Year, 1892.

THE DEATH RECORD.

Oct. 6. D. C. Emmory, Harrisville.

Alcona County Review, January 5, 1893

EVENTS OF ONE WEEK.

"Closed to take Stock" is the language of a notice posted on the front door of the tinshop. Since D. C. Emmorey's death the business has been conducted by Chas. and Will Conklin with the latter in charge. The first named has not been satisfied with the way the business was run and he decided to lock the doors and close out the stock unless a better solution of the present difficulties offers.

Alcona County Review, October 5, 1893

Probate Order.

--Aug. 19 '97.

STATE OF MICHIGAN, County of Alcona.

At a session of the Probate Court for said County, held at the Probate office, in the Village of Harrisville, on the 16th day of August, in the year one thousand eight hundred and ninety-seven.

Present, Hon. W. H. Gilpin, Judge of Probate.

In the matter of the estate of David C. Emmorey, deceased.

On reading and filing the petition duly verified of Charles Conklin, Administrator, praying among other things that he be granted a license to sell at private sale, for the purpose of paying indebtedness outstanding and unpaid against said estate, the following real estate, viz: All that part or parcel of land situate in the village of Harrisville, Alcona county and State of Michigan, described as follows, to-wit: Lots 2 and 7 and the east thirteen feet of lots 3 & 6, excepting 50 feet off the north end of lot 6, all in block fifteen in the village of Harrisville, in said county.

Thereupon it is ordered, that Monday, the 20th day of September next, at ten o'clock in the forenoon, be assigned for the hearing of said petition and that the heirs at law of said deceased, and all other persons interested in said estate, are required to appear at a session of said Court, then to be holden at the Probate office in the village of Harrisville, and show cause, if any there be, why the prayer of the petitioner should not be granted; and it is further ordered that said petitioner give notice to the heirs at law and all persons interested in said estate of the pendency of said petition, and the hearing thereof, by causing a copy of this order to be published in the Alcona County Review, a newspaper printed and circulated in said county, three successive weeks previous to said day of hearing.

W. H. Gilpin,
Judge of Probate.

Alcona County Review, August 19, 1897
Cemetery: Springport, Alcona Co.

Emmorey, Emma [Reeves]
Conklin, Emma [Reeves]

Mrs. D. C. Emmery who has been seriously ill for a long time shows little or no signs of improvement.

Alcona County Review, November 26, 1896

Mrs. Emmorey is very low and her friends express no hope of her recovery.

Alcona County Review, December 10, 1896

MRS. D. C. EMOREY.

This estimable lady passed quietly and peacefully from this life at 2 o'clock Monday afternoon after a long and tedious illness from a complication of diseases. The deceased had been a great sufferer during her illness and death was looked upon by herself and her friends as a welcome relief. At the last moments the sufferer seemed to find rest and she passed away so peacefully that it was some moments before the watchers realized that the end had come.

Emma Reeves was born in England on Nov. 8, 1844. She came to America with her parents at a very early age and settled at St. Williams, Ont. In 1861 she married William Conklin of New York state and four years later moved from St. Williams to Saginaw with her husband. The following year they came to Alcona county and settled at Greenbush, where Mr. Conklin engaged extensively in the lumber business. Mr. Conklin died July 6, 1877, and the next year his widow came to Harrisville and has since resided continuously in this village. On Jan. 27, 1885, Mrs. Conklin was married to David C. Emorey who died Oct. 7, 1892. Deceased was the youngest of a family of ten children and was 52 years, two months and 13 days of age when death claimed her. She is survived by three children., Charles and William Conklin of Harrisville and Mrs. J. L. Waters of Greenbush; also by two brothers, Amram Reeves of Chettowac, B. C.; Viol Reeves of St. Williams, Ont.; and two sisters, Mrs. Julia Price of St. Williams and Mrs. Elizabeth Adams of Mikado.

The funeral services were conducted Wednesday morning by Rev. W. Will and in accordance with the wishes of the deceased, were held at the family residence. A large number of friends and relatives attended, though many remained away owing to a mistaken impression that the service was to be private. The remains were laid to rest in the family lot at South Harrisville.

Alcona County Review, February 4, 1897
Cemetery: Springport, Alcona Co.

Erb, Henry

NEIGHBORHOOD NOTES.

Two citizens of Oscoda and Au Sable died last week of delirium tremens. Their names were Henry Erb and Joe Cole.

Alcona County Review, September 6, 1889
Cemetery: Pinecrest, Iosco Co.

Erb, Johnny

The remains of Johnny Erb of Au Sable were brought here Saturday for interment in the West Harrisville cemetery. He died of diabetes, aged 9 years, 1 month, 13 days. He was the nephew of Dan Dewar.

Alcona County Review, August 23, 1894
Cemetery: Probably Twin Lakes, Alcona Co.

Erskine, James

PERSONAL MENTION.

James Erskine, of Rogers City, who died the other day, was at one time one of the heaviest lumbermen in northern Michigan. Most of his wealth, however, was spent in impracticable schemes, one of which was the digging of an immense ditch 12 miles long to float logs. This was before railroad logging was dreamed of.

Alcona County Review, January 10, 1895
Cemetery: Rogers Township, Presque Isle Co.

Esmond, Lorinda [Knight]

LOCAL JOTTINGS.

The Bay City Tribune says that Mrs. Clark Esmond, wife of sheriff of Iosco county, died Wednesday morning from a dose of laudanum, supposed to have been taken with suicidal intent.

Alcona County Review, September 5, 1884
Cemetery: Esmond-Evergreen, Iosco Co.

Evans, Joseph

Some of the Worst Grip Cases.

Joseph Evans is seriously if not dangerously ill. He had the grip, which has brought on a complication of other diseases; and his friends feel much concerned about his condition.

Alcona County Review, February 9, 1899

Local News.

Jos. Evans' condition is still very serious.

Alcona County Review, February 16, 1899

PERSONAL POINTS.

Geo. Evans arrived home last Friday, called hither by the serious illness of his father. He left camp near Lewiston, Montmorency county, Thursday morning and walked the entire distance (about 100 miles) except for a chance ride of a few miles. He "hoofed it" all night Thursday when the mercury was down to 24 below zero.

Alcona County Review, February 16, 1899

JOSEPH EVANS DEAD.

Joseph Evans died at his home in Harrisville last Friday night. Deceased was first taken with the grip about four weeks ago, but neglected to care for himself until he was compelled to take to his bed about three weeks since. A complication of diseases set in and his condition was serious from the first and for a week past his friends had grave doubts as to his recovery.

Joseph Evans was a native of Canada. He went from Canada to western New York and in 1869 he came to Alcona County to work for a brother who was engaged in lumbering in this section. He followed lumbering for two winters, and cleared up a farm about four miles from Harrisville. In the fall of 1876 he was elected sheriff of this county and served one term. In 1882 he was again elected to that office and served one term, since which time he has not taken an active part in politics. He was 52 years of age.

Beside a wife deceased leaves four children, viz: George and Charles and Mary Evans of Harrisville and Mrs. Spicer of Canton, Mich. Four brothers and a sister also survive, viz: Warren Evans and Jas. Evans of Bay City, Edw. Evans of Tonawanda, N. Y., Mrs. Wingrove of Tawas, and another brother of Amy, Mich.

The funeral was held from the M. E. church Tuesday afternoon, Rev. W. Will officiating.

Deceased carried a $2,000 policy in the Knights of Honor.

Alcona County Review, February 23, 1899

PERSONAL POINTS

Jas. Evans of Bay City and Mrs. Wingrove and daughter of Tawas, attended the funeral of Joseph Evans, Tuesday.

Alcona County Review, February 23, 1899

We desire to express our heartfelt thanks to the kind neighbors and friends who so willingly aided us by their help and sympathy during our sad bereavement, the death of our beloved husband and father.

Mrs. Jos. Evans and family.

Alcona County Review, February 23, 1899

LOCAL PICK UPS.

A check for $2,000, the amount of insurance held by the late Joseph Evans, in the Knights of Honor, has been received this week. The delay in payment of the insurance was occasioned by the absence of some of the family whose signatures to certain papers were necessary. The money is divided $500 to Mrs. Evans, $500 each to George, Charles and Mary.

Alcona County Review, June 1, 1899
Cemetery: Springport, Alcona Co.

Evarts, David

REVIEWINGS.

David Evarts, a young man in the employ of D. B. Mudgett at Greenbush, died last Saturday of congestion of the brain. He had no relatives in this country, and therefore was buried by companions and friends. Great credit is due the citizens of Greenbush for the en masse manner in which they turned out to honor the departed dead, by giving him a very honorary burial. Mr. Evarts was a young man much respected in Greenbush.

Alcona County Review, September 5, 1879
Cemetery: Probably Springport, Alcona Co.

Everingham, Aurelia T. [Emerson]

Died, in Harrisville, Monday, March 8, Aurelia T., wife of Philip Everingham, and daughter of Nathan and Hellen Emerson; aged 22 years, 10 months and 8 days. The deceased was born at Scio, Alleghaney Co., N. Y., and was married a year ago the sixth of the present month. She had been ailing for a number of months prior to her death, but as to the exact cause of her death we are not advised. We are informed that she passed away with a firm belief and trust in Him who gave His life to save the souls of mankind; and if so, she is no doubt safe on the other shore. The grief stricken husband and other relatives have the sympathy of our citizens.

Alcona County Review, March 12, 1880

REVIEWINGS.

The parents and other relatives of the deceased Aurelia T. Everingham, desire the Review to return thanks to friends and neighbors of Harrisville for kindness and sympathy expressed in their late affliction.

Alcona County Review, March 12, 1880
Cemetery:

Evingham, Mrs. Sarah

County News and Gossip.
Just as we go to press we learn the sad news of the death of Mrs. _____ Evingham. Funeral services will be held at the M. E. Church, Saturday afternoon at 2 o'clock.

Alcona County Review, January 3, 1879
Cemetery: Springport, Alcona Co.

Evingham, Sarah [Crow]

PERSONAL.

Mrs. Effingham, aged 75, mother of Mrs. Harris Bonney, died Monday of this week. The funeral was held at the M. E. church, Rev. Will conducting the service. The remains were interred at South Harrisville.

Alcona County Review, February 25, 1897
Cemetery: Springport, Alcona Co.

Fadden, Sarah S. [Craven]

EVENTS OF ONE WEEK.
Mr. and Mrs. Wm. Craven received a telegram last week, announcing the sad news of the death of their eldest daughter, Mrs. N. F. Fadden, at Ironwood, Mich. The deceased leaves a husband and three children and many friends to mourn their loss.

Alcona County Review, May 11, 1893
Cemetery: Probably Riverside, Gogebic Co.

Fairchild, Clarence

Drowned in the Red River.

News of the sad death by drowning of Clarence Fairchild was received in the village last week by friends of the family. Deceased was the bright young son of J. K. Fairchild, founder and for many years publisher of the Review. The young man was skating on the Red river at Drayton, Nor. Da. when he broke through and was drowned. He was but 22 years of age. He had recently graduated from the University of North Dakota and at the time of his death was publishing the Drayton Echo, which was also founded by his father. He had a bright future before him and his untimely death must be a sad blow to his parents.

————————

The accident occurred Tuesday, Nov. 22. The following account of it is given in the Cavalier, North Dakota, Chronicle, of which J. K. Fairchild is publisher.

He repaired to the Red river to enjoy a skate upon the treacherous ice. The river had been frozen immediately in front of the main street for nearly a week but a short distance to the north quite a large space of open water still remained. It is thought that Clarence had no knowledge of this, and in the darkness, encumbered with a heavy overcoat, he skated directly into the opening. His cry for help was heard by William Ehrky who gave the alarm but 'ere assistance arrived a noble promising life had gone out. His glove was found immediately adjoining the open space through which he had skated to his death and the tracks of his skates indicated that he proceeded nearly direct from the starting point on the bank to the open space, showing clearly that he was unaware of its existence.

On his way to the ice he met Geo. Countryman who tried to dissuade him from the trip remarking that he did not consider the ice safe, but Clarence with a merry laugh and with that buoyancy of spirits which ever characterized him through life, hurried on determined to have a little recreation after many hours patient toil in the editorial room.

Owing to the darkness it was impossible to recover the body Tuesday night though every effort was made and it was not until about Wednesday noon that their search was rewarded.

He was still clad in his heavy overcoat and it was noticed that several of the buttons had been torn off evidently in his struggles to remove it, and one skate was also missing. He was a powerful young man and one of the foremost athletes in the state and it was clear that he made a desperate though futile attempt to save himself.

Alcona County Review, December 1, 1898

Local History of One Year

Chronology of the Principal Events of the Year 1898.

November 22. Clarence Fairchild, son of founder of Review, drowned at Drayton, N. D.

Alcona County Review, January 5, 1899
Cemetery: Drayton, Pembina Co., ND

Fairchild, {Female}

The Local News.

News has reached here of the death of the mother of J. K. Fairchild, formerly a publisher of this paper. The deceased was known to many of our old residents.

Alcona County Review, February 11, 1892
Cemetery:

Fairchild, George

ALONG THE SHORE.

ALPENA.

Last week Charles Fairchild, of Hubbard Lake had the misfortune to lose two children from the effects of diphtheria.

Alcona County Review, March 3, 1882
Cemetery: Probably Evergreen, Alpena Co.

Fairchild, Henry

ALPENA.
Last week Charles Fairchild, of Hubbard Lake had the misfortune to lose two children from the effects of diphtheria.

Alcona County Review, March 3, 1882
Cemetery: Probably Evergreen, Alpena Co.

Fairchild, Nina May

DIED:
Thursday evening, December 12, 1878, Nina May, only daughter of Joseph K. and Fannie M. Fairchild; aged 4 years, 11 months, and 8 days.

Mamie, as we called her, was much beloved in our household, and we cannot but feel that in her death, we have lost one of the greatest of earthly treasures. She loved the Sabbath School very much and most always for each Sabbath's attendance, had committed to memory some short passage of Scripture to repeat to her teacher. She took great delight in talking with papa and mama about the Savior and heaven, and never retired for the night without uttering her little prayer—"Now I lay me down to sleep"—to which she always added: "God bless papa and mama, and make me a good little girl." But our little darling Mamie is no more on earth; her spirit has returned to God who gave it and to that heaven of which she loved to talk and sing. We shall miss her voice and merry laughter and prattlings on earth, but there comes to us the sweet consolation that we shall meet her again by and by, if we live on earth the life that it is our privilege to do. While our grief may seem to us almost unbearable, yet we feel to-day in our hearts, "Thy will, O Lord, be done!"

The manner of Mamie's death was very sudden. She was apparently as well and lively as ever up to about 4 ½ o'clock p.m. Thursday, when she complained of dizziness, and shortly afterward was taken with spasms, of which she died in about 1 ½ hours. She had eaten an apple just before being taken with dizziness. She was buried Friday afternoon.

Alcona County Review, December 13, 1878

COUNTY NEWS AND GOSSIP.

The editor and wife will ever remember with grateful hearts the sympathy and kindness extended to them during the brief sickness and death of their little daughter. We trust we shall not fail to reciprocate whenever any of our neighbors or friends are thus afflicted.

Alcona County Review, December 13, 1878

To Our Readers.

Apology to our readers for the thin local appearance of this week's Review is unnecessary. The fact that death has entered our family circle within the past few days and taken away a loved one we believe will be accepted by our readers as sufficient apology. Without any assistance in our office, it could not justly be expected that we would issue any paper at all this week, under the circumstances, but not wishing to miss the publication entirely, we have done the best we could and issue, Saturday evening.

Alcona County Review, December 13, 1878

County News and Gossip.

Many thanks are due to our brethren of the State press for the kind words of sympathy extended to us in the loss of our darling little daughter. May God bless you, brethren!

Alcona County Review, January 10, 1879

Cemetery: Springport, Alcona Co.

Fairchild, Timothy

Death in a Well.

On Tuesday afternoon last one of those sad accidents which shock the entire community occurred at Hubbard Lake, Ossineke township. The particulars of the accident, as related to us by a neighbor of the deceased are as follows: Mr. Timothy Fairchild, assisted by two of his neighbors, had been engaged during the day digging a well, and at 6 p.m. had reached a depth of thirty feet, and had the well about completed. Mr. Fairchild was at the bottom of the well and the two men were hauling the dirt up and as the last bucket-full was being pulled up Mr. Fairchild asked the parties above to hurry up, but before they had time to reply the earth began to cave in very rapidly, and before any assistance could be rendered the unfortunate man was buried beneath twelve feet of earth. The men at once set to work to rescue him, assisted by the neighbors who soon learned of the accident, but the nature of the soil necessitated the building of curbing and when our informant left at six o'clock the following morning the body had not been recovered. Mr. Fairchild took up the farm on which he met with his untimely death, about one year ago. He had just completed and moved into a new house and was in a fair way of enjoying the fruits of his labor. He was about 45 years of age and a man of exemplary character. Mr. Fairchild leaves a wife, but no children. His mother, who resides in St. Clair county, has been telegraphed for.— *Alpena Pioneer.*

Alcona County Review, October 28, 1881
Cemetery: Evergreen, Alpena Co.

Farrington, Mrs. Mary

Purely Personal.

Mrs. Guy C. Lewis and Mrs. Sherman Hale were called to Big Rapids this week by the dangerous illness of their mother who resides near that city.

Alcona County Review, February 7, 1890

Purely Personal.

Mrs. Guy C. Lewis and Mrs. Sherman Hale returned Tuesday evening from Big Rapids. Their mother, to whose bedside they were

called, died last week and was buried Sunday. Both ladies were ill on their return home although not seriously it is hoped.

Alcona County Review, February 14, 1890
Cemetery:

Feaban, George

Capt. Sawyer Drowned.

It is our sad misfortune to chronicle the death of Capt. Joseph Sawyer, by drowning, which occurred near Rogers City Wednesday morning. Capt. Sawyer, in company with the captain of the life saving station at Forty Mile Point, and one of the station crew, while going from the point to Rogers in a small sail boat, were capsized by the gale, and the two captains drowned. Capt. Sawyer was Supt. of the U. S. life-saving service for the 10th district, and quite well known in this vicinity from his numerous visits here. His residence was in Detroit, and he was off on a tour of inspection at the time of his death.

Alcona County Review, October 22, 1880

County Reviewings.

According to the Presque Isle Advance the body of Capt. Feaben, who was drowned in company with Capt. Sawyer some time ago, was found seven miles above Rogers City. No trace of Capt. Sawyer's body yet, though a vigilant search has been maintained.

Alcona County Review, November 26, 1880
Cemetery:

Fecteau, Marie Eliza [Guimond]

Mrs. Fecto, a very aged lady living in Alcona township, was buried from the Catholic church in this village on Monday.

Alcona County Review, November 13, 1885
Cemetery: Probably St. Anne's, Alcona Co.

Fenilon, Daniel

Spontaneous Combustion.

On Saturday afternoon last, at three o'clock, Daniel Fenilon was sent from W. P. & V. Whitney's drive on the Au Gres river to help raise a dam ten miles above. The man at the dam waited for help until early Sunday morning, but no one appearing, he started down to ascertain the cause. A mile and a half below the dam he found Fenilon lying on his hands and face dead. There were no marks of violence on the body, but it was as black as a coal.

Fenilon had been a heavy drinker, but during the two or three days that he had been at camp he had remained sober. It looks like a case of spontaneous combustion—that is to say, where the tissues of the body had become so saturated with alcohol that they burst into flame, and the victim expires in great agony. A case of spontaneous combustion is graphically described in the celebrated novel, "Jacob Faithful." Fenilon resided at Tawas.—Bay City Tribune.

Alcona County Review, July 5, 1878
Cemetery:

Ferguson, Arthur G.
LOCAL LACONICS.

A five-year-old son of James Ferguson, a farmer living about four miles west of this village, died on Wednesday last.

Alcona County Review, May 1, 1885
Cemetery: Springport, Alcona Co.

Ferguson, Donald
LOCAL JOTTINGS.

An infant child of Geo. G. Ferguson was buried Sunday.

Alcona County Review, December 8, 1888
Cemetery: West Lawn, Alcona Co.

Ferguson, Henry Melvin
EVENTS OF ONE WEEK.

Jas. Ferguson lost two sons from diphtheria, one on Saturday and the other Sunday, ages seven and ten years.

Alcona County Review, July 13, 1893

EVENTS OF ONE WEEK.

Union funeral services were held last Sunday in the Dean school house for the children of the families of Wm. H. Anderson, Jos. Specht and Jas. Ferguson, who died the past summer from diphtheria. The services were largely attended and the Rev. S. Boundy preached a very feeling and impressive sermon, taking as his text St. Matt. xxiv. 44.

Alcona County Review, September 7, 1893

South Harrisville, Oct. 18.
A few improvements of late are noticeable at the S. Harrisville cemetery.

Mr. Ferguson has erected a fine monument erected to the memory of his four children.

Alcona County Review, October 16, 1893
Cemetery: Springport, Alcona Co.

Ferguson, Wallace C.
EVENTS OF ONE WEEK.

Jas. Ferguson lost two sons from diphtheria, one on Saturday and the other Sunday, ages seven and ten years.

Alcona County Review, July 13, 1893

EVENTS OF ONE WEEK.
Union funeral services were held last Sunday in the Dean school house for the children of the families of Wm. H. Anderson, Jos. Specht and Jas. Ferguson, who died the past summer from diphtheria. The services were largely attended and the Rev. S. Boundy preached a very feeling and impressive sermon, taking as his text St. Matt. xxiv. 44.

Alcona County Review, September 7, 1893

South Harrisville, Oct. 18.
A few improvements of late are noticeable at the S. Harrisville cemetery.

Mr. Ferguson has erected a fine monument erected to the memory of his four children.

Alcona County Review, October 16, 1893
Cemetery: Springport, Alcona Co.

Ferris, W. B.
REVIEWINGS.

Just before going to press we learn that W. B. Ferris was found dead in his bed at Black River, this morning. He was manager of the shingle mill and store at that place, and was around yesterday attending to business as usual. Cause of his death unknown. He leaves a wife and child.

Alcona County Review, November 14, 1879
Cemetery:

Fick, Francis
LOCAL JOTTINGS.

Walter Fick, a minor, of Port Huron, and a second cousin of Francis Fick, who died at Killmaster on the 8th of June last, fell heir by devise to 80 acres of land owned by the deceased, and his representatives re endeavoring to perfect his title thereto through the medium of the Probate court.

Alcona County Review, September 23, 1887

PROBATE ORDER.
STATE OF MICHIGAN, County of Alcona.

At a session of the Probate Court for said County held at the Probate

office in the village of Harrisville, on Tuesday, the tenth day of January, in the year one thousand eight hundred and eighty-eight. Present, Hon. Allen Nevin, Judge of Probate. In the matter of the

ESTATE OF FRANCIS FICK, DECEASED.

On reading and filing the petition, duly verified, of Carlton Fick, praying that a certain instrument now on file in this court, purporting to be the last will and testament of said deceased, may be admitted to probate, and that said Carlton Fick may be appointed executor of said estate. Thereupon it is ordered that Saturday, the Fourth Day of February, 1888 next, at ten o'clock in the forenoon, be assigned for the hearing of said petition, and that the heirs at law of said deceased, and all other persons interested in said estate, are required to appear at a session of said court, then to be holden at the Probate office, in the village of Harrisville, and show cause, if any there be, why the prayer of the petitioner should not be granted. And it is further ordered, that said petitioner give notice to the persons interested in said estate, of the pendency of said petition, and the hearing thereof, by causing a copy of this order to be published in the Alcona County Review, a newspaper printed and circulated in said county, three successive weeks previous to said day of hearing.

ALLEN NEVIN, Judge of Probate.

Alcona County Review, January 13, 1888

PROBATE ORDER.
STATE OF MICHIGAN, County of Alcona.

Notice is hereby given, that by an order of the Probate Court for the County of Alcona, made on the 4th day of February, A. D. 1888, six months from that date were allowed for creditors to present their claims against the

ESTATE OF FRANCIS FICK,
late of said County, deceased, and that all creditors of said deceased are required to present their claims to said Probate Court, at the Probate office, in the village of Harrisville, for examination and allowance, on or before the fourth day of August 1888, next and that such claims will be heard before said Court on Friday, the fourth day of May 1888, and on Saturday the 4th day of August, 1888

next, at ten o'clock in the forenoon of each of those days.

Dated February, 4th, A. D. 1888.

ALLEN NEVIN, Judge of Probate.

Alcona County Review, February 24, 1888

Order of Publication.

STATE OF MICHIGAN, County of Alcona.

At a session of the Probate Court for said county, held at the Probate office, in the village of Harrisville, on the Tenth day of November, in the year one thousand eight hundred and eighty-eight. Present, Allen Nevin, Esq., Judge of Probate. In the matter of the

ESTATE OF FRANCIS FICK,

deceased. On reading and filing the petition, duly verified, of Carlton Fick, administrator of the estate of said Francis Fick, deceased, praying that he may be empowered and licensed to sell the real estate of said deceased, situate in township of Gustin, county of Alcona, and state of Michigan, known and described as follows, viz: The east half of the north-west quarter of section twenty-three, town twenty-six north, range eight east, containing eighty acres, for the purpose of paying the debts due against said estate, and the expenses of administration of said estate. Thereupon it is ordered, that Monday, the Tenth Day of December next, at ten o'clock in the forenoon, be assigned for the hearing of said petition, and that the widow and heirs at law of said deceased, and all other persons interested in said estate, are required to appear at a session of said Court, then to be holden in the Probate office, in the village of Harrisville, and show cause, if any there be, why the prayer of the petitioner should not be granted: And it is further ordered, that said petitioner give notice to the heirs at law and all persons interested in said estate, of the pendency of said petition, and the hearing thereof, by causing a copy of this order to be published in the Alcona County Review, a newspaper printed and circulated in said county, for three successive weeks previous to said day of hearing.

ALLEN NEVIN, Judge of Probate.

Alcona County Review, November 16, 1888

Notice of Sale of Real Estate.

STATE OF MICHIGAN, County of Alcona.

In the matter of the ESTATE OF FRANCIS FICK, deceased. Notice is hereby given, that in pursuance of an order granted to the undersigned, Executor of the estate of said Francis Fick, deceased, by the Honorable Judge of Probate for the county of Alcona, on the tenth day of December, A. D. 1888, there will be sold at public venue, to the highest bidder, at the front door of the Court House, in the village of Harrisville, in the county of Alcona, in said state, on Wednesday, the Third Day of April, A. D. 1889, at Two o'clock in the forenoon of that day (subject to all encumbrances by mortgage or otherwise existing at the time of the death of said deceased, or at the time of the said sale, and also subject to the right of dower and the homestead rights of the widow of said deceased therein), the following described real estate, to wit: All that certain lot and parcel of land situate in Alcona County, in the State of Michigan, known and distinguished as the east half of the north-west quarter, section twenty-three (23) town twenty-six north range eight east.

CARLTON FICK, Executor.

Dated January 16th, 1889.

Alcona County Review, February 22, 1889

LOCAL JOTTINGS.

The estate of Francis Fick was closed up Saturday by Judge Ritchie. The forty acres of land which constituted the principle part of the estate was bid in at the sale by B. P. Cowley.

Alcona County Review, May 31, 1889
Cemetery:

Finch, Annie L. [Ferris]

Death of Mrs. Wm. Finch.

It is our sad duty this week to record the death of Mrs. Wm. Finch of Sturgeon Point.

The death of this lady occurred Tuesday under particularly sad circumstances. She had not been in good health for some time and it became necessary for her to undergo a surgical operation. Monday morning her husband drove her out to the train and she departed for Detroit to enter a hospital. Tuesday about 3 o'clock a telegram was received by Mr. Finch stating that his wife had died at the hospital before the operation was attempted.

This is a sad blow to Mr. Finch and the relatives of the deceased, and they

have the sympathies of a large number of friends.

The funeral services will be held tomorrow at 1:30 p.m. from the Episcopal Church.

Alcona County Review, January 13, 1898

LOCAL PICK UPS.

The funeral of the late Mrs. Wm. Finch was held from the Episcopal church last Friday afternoon, Rev. A. Beaumont officiating. A large congregation of relatives and sympathizing friends filled the church. The floral offerings were very beautiful, principal of which were an anchor of yellow roses, white carnations and ferns, and a large wreath of pink roses from the L. S. S. crew; and a beautiful gift of hot house flowers from the Ladies Guild.

At the cemetery the grave had been lined with white and at the close of the burial ceremony a screen of evergreens was lowered, the final covering taking place after the departure of the mourners.

Alcona County Review, January 20, 1898

I wish to express my heartfelt gratitude to those kind friends who rendered me such timely assistance during the hour of my deep sorrow, in the loss of my beloved wife. May God spare them a like affliction is my sincere wish.

William Finch.

Alcona County Review, January 20, 1898

Local History of One Year

Chronology of the Principal Events of the Year 1898.

January 11. Death Mrs. Wm. Finch at Detroit.

Alcona County Review, January 5, 1899
Cemetery: Springport, Alcona Co.

Finch, Bertie

LOCAL LACONICS.

Bertie, a ten-year-old daughter of Mr. and Mrs. Alvin Finch, formerly of this village, died of diphtheria on Saturday evening last, at Pott's railroad.

Alcona County Review, May 29, 1885
Cemetery: East Berlin, St. Clair Co.

Finger, Herman T.

Still another case of diphtheria has been reported from Mud Lake, this time in the family of Wm. Finger.

Alcona County Review, January 12, 1893

MORE DIPHTHERIA.

Destitution and Disease Rampant in the La Vier Settlement.

On Sunday Health Officer Beede paid another visit to the diphtheria stricken settlement at Mud Lake. Matters there were even worse than on the occasion of his last visit, if that were possible. In the family of Wm. Finger he found five cases of the disease, two girls in a fair way to recover, one boy, Herman, apparently in the last stages of dissolution and two other cases, one a boy and one a girl, the termination of which was uncertain. Previous to going to the settlement he had been informed that the family were in destitute circumstances, owing to long illness and the continuance of the quarantine under which they were placed. To relieve their distress he took along supplies of pork, beef and beans, besides gingham, cotton and factory cloth. Dr. Parr had had charge of the cases but Mr. Beede ordered Dr. Mitchell to visit the settlement also. Sickness was reported in another family, McAdam by name, but he was not able to say whether this was diphtheria or not.

Alcona County Review, January 19, 1893

Progress of the Diphtheria Cases.

Another child, a son of William Finger, died in the Mud Lake settlement Friday last of diphtheria. Health officer Beede received notice Monday that new cases had developed in the family of Louis Beach in the same locality.

Alcona County Review, February 2, 1893
Cemetery:

Finger, Julia V. S.

MORE DIPHTHERIA.
Destitution and Disease Rampant in the La Vier Settlement.

On Sunday Health Officer Beede paid another visit to the diphtheria stricken settlement at Mud Lake. Matters there were even worse than on the occasion of his last visit, if that were possible. In the family of Wm. Finger he found five cases of the disease, two girls in a fair way to recover, one boy, Herman, apparently in the last stages of dissolution and two other cases, one a boy and one a girl, the termination of which was uncertain. Previous to going to the settlement he had been informed that the family were in destitute circumstances, owing to long illness

and the continuance of the quarantine under which they were placed. To relieve their distress he took along supplies of pork, beef and beans, besides gingham, cotton and factory cloth. Dr. Parr had had charge of the cases but Mr. Beede ordered Dr. Mitchell to visit the settlement also. Sickness was reported in another family, McAdam by name, but he was not able to say whether this was diphtheria or not.

Alcona County Review, January 19, 1893

DEATH'S HARVEST.

An 11-year-old daughter of Wm. Finger died at Mud Lake this week. The child had the diphtheria from which she was in a fair way to recover when she caught a severe cold which resulted fatally.

Alcona County Review, March 2, 1893
Cemetery:

Fisher, Guy

EVENTS OF ONE WEEK.

G. C. Lewis received word last night that Jos. Fisher, Jr.'s oldest child, Guy, was dying at St. Marie's, Idaho.

Alcona County Review, December 15, 1892

PERSONAL MENTION.

Little Guy, the 10 year old son of Mr. and Mrs. Jos. Fisher, Jr., of St. Marie's P. O., Idaho, and grandson of Mr. and Mrs. Guy Lewis of this place, died on the 8th inst. The malady from which he suffered was spinal meningitis.

Alcona County Review, December 22, 1892
Cemetery:Woodlawn, Benewah Co., ID

Fisher, Joseph, Sr.

PERSONAL MENTION.

Joseph Fisher, Sr., is dead. The old gentleman passed away at St. Maries, Idaho, Wednesday, Sept. 4, of malignant inflammation of the urinary organs. Deceased was about 70 years of age. He was one of the pioneer settlers of Alcona county, cleared up one of the best farms in the county, which is now owned by Jas. Anderson, raised a large family, sold out his farm for a song a few years ago and followed his boys west. He was a good citizen although somewhat eccentric, and in the early days he participated in the public events which constitute the county's history. He was one of those who in

1859 petitioned the county of Alpena, to which Alcona was then attached, for the organization of a separate township and the township of Harrisville, comprising nearly the whole of the present county of Alcona, was organized in answer to the petition.

Alcona County Review, September 19, 1895

Wm. Beever, neighbor and life-long friend of the late Jos. Fisher, Sr., adds the following from their joint experience to what has been printed regarding the early life of deceased: They came to Michigan and Harrisville from N. Y. State in the year 1857 and found an antiquated saw mill with an old "muly" saw at this place and a mere handful of people. "The present site of Harrisville," says Mr. Beever, "was the worst cedar swamp I ever saw." In 1858 he and Jos. Fisher located their homesteads and they were laughed at for what was considered at that early day the insane folly of attempting to raise any farm products in this northern latitude. They were the first to break ground in Alcona county for farming purposes. Their wise choice has been fully justified and both lived to enjoy the fruits of their early application to pioneer farming. The forest was so dense and unbroken in that early day that Mrs. Fisher carried a lantern in broad daylight when coming to the settlement. This to frighten away the wild beasts. Wm. Beever and Jos. Fisher had the honor of hauling the first two sticks for the Methodist Episcopal church of Harrisville. They made the first move also for a schoolhouse in their neighborhood, resulting in the construction of the Fisher school house.

Alcona County Review, September 26, 1895
Cemetery: Woodlawn, Benewah Co., ID

Fisher, Sherman

LOCAL JOTTINGS

J. Fisher Jr., and wife, mourn the loss of their three months old son, Sherman. The little fellow died Sunday morning after a long illness from inflammation of the lungs.

Alcona County Review, March 30, 1888

Card of Thanks.

To those friends who assisted us in our late bereavement we extend our heartfelt thanks and especially to those who contributed flowers.

Mr. and Mrs. Jos. Fisher, Jr.

Alcona County Review, March 30, 1888
Cemetery:

Fitzpatrick, Michael

The Local News

The remains of a middle aged man named Michael Fitzpatrick were buried Saturday in the West Harrisville cemetery. He had lived here for some time. His death occurred at Mud Lake.

Alcona County Review, May 12, 1892

HISTORY OF ONE YEAR.

Chronological History of the Past Year, 1892.

THE DEATH RECORD.

May 6. Michael Fitzpatrick, at Mud Lake.

Alcona County Review, January 5, 1893
Cemetery: Twin Lakes, Alcona Co.

Fitzpatrick, Mrs. Mary A.

LOCAL PICK UPS.

The death of Mrs. Fitzpatrick, sister of Mrs. Edw. Saylor, is reported as having taken place yesterday at Oscoda, where she was stopping with relatives.

Alcona County Review, October 14, 1897
Cemetery: Sacred Heart, Iosco Co.

Flanders, Mont

The Local News.

A man named Mont Flanders was killed Tuesday on the Mud Lake railroad. A long stick of timber rolled over him crushing his head. His remains were taken to his late home in Alpena.

Alcona County Review, July 18, 1890

One Year's History.

Record of Local Happenings for the Year 1890.

JULY.

15 Mont Flanders killed at Mud Lake.

Alcona County Review, January 1, 1891
Cemetery:

Flaws, Jessie Lulu

Black River.

Mr. Flaws' two children are quite ill. No further particulars in now.

Alcona County Review, May 26, 1892

SOMEWHAT PERSONAL.

Wm. Flaws of Black River buried a child nine months old in the cemetery west of Harrisville, on Tuesday.

Alcona County Review, June 16, 1892

Card of Thanks.——Our deep and heartfelt thanks are due to our many kind and sympathetic friends and neighbors. Their many acts of kindness during the sickness and death of our little daughter, Jessie Lulu, will ever live in our grateful remembrance. May they be spared a similar affliction is our earnest wish.

Mr. and Mrs. Wm. Flaws.
Black River, Mich., June 15.

Alcona County Review, June 16, 1892
Cemetery: West Lawn, Alcona Co.

Fleck, Charles Addison

Died, April 11.——The infant son of Mr. and Mrs. Charles Fleck, of East Tawas.

Alcona County Review, April 14, 1892
Cemetery: Greenwood, Iosco Co.

Fleming, Abram

Alcona Atoms.

Alcona, July 12, 1882.
Editor Review:——We have just received the news that Abram Fleming has been severely hurt out at Mudgett's camp, by a limb falling from a tree. He was senseless when the man left for the Dr. and he thought he would not recover. James Fleming, his son, started to see his father as soon as he received the sad news.

Alcona County Review, July 14, 1882

Alcona Atoms.

Alcona, July 13.
Abram Fleming died yesterday at 10 o'clock a.m., aged 67 years and 11 months, respected by all in the township who knew him.

Alcona County Review, July 14, 1882

Fatal Accident.

A very sad accident happened Tuesday at D. B. Mudgett's camp back of Alcona. Abram Fleming, an aged gentleman, of about 67 years, and one of the old residents of Alcona township, who was employed at the camp, was struck on the head and one shoulder by a heavy, falling limb from a tree and so badly injured that he died the following day.

Of Mr. Fleming's life and general history, the Review knows but very

little, more than that he had the reputation of being a fine old gentleman and hard worker. He leaves two sons, James and Thomas Fleming, also farmer residents of Alcona.

Alcona County Review, July 14, 1882
Cemetery: Mt. Joy, Alcona Co.

Fleming, Maggie Belle

Haynes Happenings.

October 8, 1895.
Miss Maggie Fleming died in Harper Hospital, Detroit, on Friday, the 4th day of October, after an operation performed for the removal of an abscess from her lung. The disease was of long standing, but it was thought she would recover after an operation performed in Alpena. They did not reach the seat of the disease, however. The doctors at Harper Hospital said she could not live long as she was and there might be a chance for her after an operation. She lived only a few minutes after the operation and complained of pain in her back and asked for her sister, when the spirit took its flight. She would be 16 years of age on the 20th of November next. Her remains were brought home Saturday. The Rev. Mr. Long preached the funeral sermon on Sunday in the Presbyterian church. The remains were followed to the cemetery by a large concourse of relatives and friends of the bereft and stricken parents. She was the flower of the family and beloved by her schoolmates and acquaintances.

Gently, how gently, departed her breath,
No anguish or grief pervaded her breast;
Sweetly, how sweetly, she slumbers in death,
Wearing the smile of the pure and the blest.

Rev. Long's discourse was from the text, "She is not Dead, but Sleeping." There were more wet eyes and sympathy manifested in the congregation than I have seen in Haynes since I have been in the township.

Mrs. Joseph Ash of Alpena accompanied Mr. Fleming to Detroit with his daughter and Mr. Ash and Donald McKillop and Mrs. Belle Woliver of Alpena attended the funeral.

Alcona County Review, October 10, 1895
Cemetery: Mt. Joy, Alcona Co.

Fleming, Willie

Alcona Atoms.

Jas. Fleming buried an infant son, aged 4 months and 2 days, last Sunday.

Alcona County Review, March 10, 1882
Cemetery: Mt. Joy, Alcona Co.

Flint, Moses

LOCAL JOTTINGS.

Killed.—We learn from our exchanges that Moses Flint, of East Tawas, was killed by a falling tree last Friday, while at work on the Au Gres river.

Alcona County Review, February 12, 1886
Cemetery:

Foley, Anna [Hooley]

LOCAL PICK UPS.

Mrs. Chas. Foley, well known in Alcona county, died last week at Pinconning, where she had resided principally since the death of her husband a few years ago. The remains were buried at Alpena beside those of her husband. She was aged 35 years.

Alcona County Review, August 4, 1898
Cemetery: Holy Cross, Alpena Co.

Foley, Charles

Chas. Foley Has Passed Away.

From the Alpena Echo.

Charley Foley, a new-comer in the city but a man well known here died at his home at 5:30 this morning. For some years he kept an hotel at Mud Lake Junction and was well known along the line of the railroad. Last spring he gave up the place and came up to Alpena and has been engaged in business here since. He was sick but a few days and on Saturday last celebrated his 37 birthday. Heart trouble is given as the cause.

Charlie Foley was well known in Alcona county where for many years he has been a resident. His untimely death revives memories of the bright, sociable, courteous, and companionable Charlie Foley of less than ten years ago, then a general favorite, a young man of bright prospects, whom to know was to esteem. In an evil hour he engaged in the liquor business at Mud Lake Jc. We will not dwell upon the painful details of the succeeding years, with which all are familiar. He tried the gold cure, but it was not permanent, unfortunately.

Mr. Foley left a wife but no family.

Alcona County Review, September 13, 1894

West Harrisville.

West Harrisville, Sept. 14, 1894.-- Quite a large number of our people went to Alpena last Saturday night and attended the funeral of Chas. Foley there Sunday.

Alcona County Review, September 13, 1894

PERSONAL MENTION.

Mrs. Chas. Foley has received $1,000 from the Liquor Dealers Association for insurance held on the life of her late husband.

Alcona County Review, October 18, 1894
Cemetery:Holy Cross, Alpena Co.

Foley, Michael

The Local News.

Michael Foley, father of Chas. Foley, was killed at Tawas City last week by being thrown from his express wagon.

Alcona County Review, October 3, 1890

The Local News.

The Michael Foley killed at Tawas City was not the father of Chas. Foley of Mud Lake Jc.

Alcona County Review, October 10, 1890
Cemetery:

Fonger, {Girl}

Alice Fonger, a single woman of unsound mind, was sent to the asylum at Traverse City a few months ago. The sad fact has been learned that she is pregnant. The authorities at the asylum refuse to allow her to remain there and it has been found necessary to have her returned to this county in charge of an attendant. Judge Killmaster endeavored to find a suitable place for her at Traverse City, but it was found impossible to do so.

Alcona County Review, March 23, 1893

PERSONAL MENTION.

The Fonger woman is to be taken back to the Traverse City Asylum. Her child has died.

Alcona County Review, April 20, 1893
Cemetery:

Forrest, James E.

Death of James E. Forrest.

James E. Forrest, one of Au Sable's best known and leading business men died last week Thursday of typhoid pneumonia. In Mr. Forrest's death Au Sable suffers a severe loss. He was a public spirited and very successful business man, to whom Au Sable is largely indebted

for her prosperity. He was a Royal Arch Mason and was buried Sunday with Masonic honors. The funeral was one of the most imposing and impressive that has ever taken place on the shore. Special train ran from Alpena carrying Masonic brethren and other friends from that city and other points along the line.

Mr. Forrest was born in Blackburn, Lancashire, England, Oct. 25, 1845. Came to the United States in 1861 and to Au Sable in '62, where he engaged in the fishing business, in which he was successful. He has held repeatedly the offices of supervisor, treasurer and postmaster. He was engaged principally in the banking business. He leaves an estate valued at $75,000. A wife and son survive him.

Alcona County Review, March 22, 1889

PURELY PERSONAL.

Chas. Sterritt, Chas. Conklin, C. M. Lund and Jas. Nevins, representing Alcona Lodge, F. & A. M., attended the funeral of Jas. E. Forrest at Au Sable last Sunday.

Alcona County Review, March 22, 1889

Postmaster McMahon, of Au Sable, In the Toils.

Frank McMahon, the retiring democrat postmaster of Au Sable, is in a limbo. He was arrested last week by Detective Pat O'Neil of Detroit, and U. S. Marshal LaRoux, charged with stealing a registered package containing $2,000 from the Au Sable postoffice. The missing package was sent by the Detroit National Bank to J. E. Forrest, banker of Au Sable, and should have arrived there March 12, two days prior to Mr. Forrest's death. Inspector O'Neil claims to have a sure case against McMahon. McMahon is held in the Bay City jail until the examination in default of $3,000 bail.

Alcona County Review, June 14, 1889
Cemetery: Au Sable Township, Iosco Co.

Forrest, William Edwin

ALONG THE SHORE.

Au Sable and Oscoda.

The infant son of James E. Forrest died on Wednesday, July 28.

Alcona County Review, August 6, 1880
Cemetery: Au Sable Township, Iosco Co.

Forsythe, Henry

Henry Forsythe was quite seriously injured on the 5th inst. by an infuriated bull. The animal knocked him to the ground and gored him in a frightful manner, breaking several ribs and otherwise injuring him. He is recovering slowly.

Alcona County Review, November 17, 1892

HISTORY OF ONE YEAR.

Chronological History of the Past Year, 1892.

November.

5. Henry Forsythe gored by an infuriated bull.

Alcona County Review, January 5, 1893

PERSONAL MENTION.

Henry Forsythe is slowly regaining his strength and has been in town several times lately, although he is still unable to use his limbs but little. His disability dates from Nov. 5, 1892, when he was nearly killed by a vicious bull.

Alcona County Review, August 24, 1893

EVENTS OF ONE WEEK.

Henry Forsythe has been very low this week with heart trouble.

Alcona County Review, January 23, 1896

The death of Henry Forsythe, which has been expected daily for several weeks, occurred Wednesday. The old gentleman's illness dates back to injuries received from a vicious bull three years ago. he was confined to his bed much of the time until last year, when he was able to get to town occasionally. He never recovered fully. Early in the winter he began to fail and his death became only a matter of time. The interment took place this morning.

Alcona County Review, February 20, 1896

HENRY FORSYTHE.

Passed to his rest Tuesday, Feb. 18, at 8:42 p.m. after about six weeks confinement to his bed, suffering almost incessant pain from heart trouble, supposed to have been caused from injuries received about three years ago from an infuriated animal owned by himself and kept on the farm.

Deceased was a native of Ireland. He was born Tuesday, May 12th, 1836, at 2 o'clock a.m., and was therefore aged 59 years, 9 months, 6 days and 6 hours. He moved to Ontario and in the fall of 1872 came

to Alcona county, and has remained here until when God in his infinite wisdom, who doeth all things well, came with his last and welcome message to summon the sufferer from his earthly tabernacle of cares and troubles to that better land where trouble and care are unknown. Then as his death bell was tolling he kindly summoned all his children present to his bedside and kissed them good bye.

His mission on earth being finished,
He no longer cared to stay;
And then, without a struggle,
His spirit passed away.

The deceased leaves a family of seven children, consisting of four boys and three girls to mourn their loss.

The funeral services were held from deceased's late residence Thursday, Feb. 20th, the Rev. Ford officiating.

The family feel deeply indebted to the neighbors for their kindness, and particularly to Mr. and Mrs. L. R. Dorr, who were untiring in their efforts to relieve the sufferings of the departed.

Alcona County Review, February 27, 1896

Henry Forsythe was born Tuesday, May 12th, 1830, at 3 o'clock a.m. and was therefore 66 years old the 12th of May, 1896. The family that is left gives many kind thanks to all their kind friends and neighbors which have all acted like a brother or sister to their loving father and theirselves which is left to mourn the loss of a kind father.

George Henry Forsythe.

Alcona County Review, March 5, 1896

STATE OF MICHIGAN, County of Alcona.

At a session of the Probate Court for said County, held at the Probate office, in the Village of Harrisville, on Monday the second day of March in the year one thousand eight hundred and ninety-six.

Present, C. H. Killmaster, Judge of Probate.

In the matter of the estate of Henry Forsythe.

On reading and filing the petition duly verified of George Forsythe, praying that a certain instrument now on file in this Court, purporting to be the last will and testament of said deceased, may be admitted to probate.

Thereupon it is ordered, that Saturday, the 21st day of March next, at ten o'clock in the forenoon, be assigned for the hearing of said petition, and that the heirs at law of said deceased and all others interested in said estate, are required to appear at a session of the Probate Court, then to be holden at the Probate office, in the Village of Harrisville and show cause, if any there be, why the prayer of the petitioner should not be granted.

And it is further ordered that the petitioner give notice to the heirs at law and persons interested in the estate, of the pendency of said petition, and the hearing thereof, by causing a copy of this order to be published in the Alcona County Review, a newspaper printed and circulating in said county three successive weeks previous to said day of hearing.

C. H. KILLMASTER,
Judge of Probate.

Alcona County Review, March 5, 1896

Order for Probate of Will.
Aug 12--Sept 2, 97.
STATE OF MICHIGAN, County of Alcona.

At a session of the Probate Court for said County, held at the Probate office, in the Village of Harrisville, on the ninth day of August in the year one thousand eight hundred and ninety-seven.

Present, Hon. W. H. Gilpin, Judge of Probate.

In the matter of the estate of Henry Forsythe, deceased.

On reading and filing the petition duly verified of George Henry Forsythe, praying that a certain instrument now on file in this court, purporting to be the last will and testament of said deceased, may be admitted to probate and that L. R. Dorr be appointed executor of said last will and testament.

Thereupon it is ordered, that Tuesday, the 7th day of September next, at ten o'clock in the forenoon, be assigned for the hearing of said petition, and that the heirs at law of said deceased and all other persons interested in said estate, are required to appear at a session of the Probate Court, then to be holden at the Probate office, in the Village of Harrisville and show cause, if any there be, why the prayer of the petitioner should not be granted.

And it is further ordered that the petitioner give notice to the heirs at law and all persons interested in said estate, of the pendency of said petition, and the hearing thereof, by causing a copy of this order to be published in the Alcona County Review, a newspaper printed and circulating in said county three successive weeks previous to said day of hearing.

W. H. Gilpin,
Judge of Probate.

Alcona County Review, August 12, 1897

Forsythe Estate Somewhat Mixed.

The late Henry Forsythe executed a will leaving his farm to his son, George. The latter applied to the probate court for the appointment of L. R. Dorr as executor of the will. On investigation it was found that Henry Forsythe had deeded his farm a number of years before to his wife, since deceased, and the title to the property had never been changed. Mr. Dorr refused to act as executor. Matters have remained in this situation for a year, and now the court has reopened the matter by issuing another order for the probate of the will and also for the appointment of an administrator of the estate of Lavina Forsythe, on the petition of George Forsythe who asks for the appointment of L. R. Dorr as executor in one case and administrator in the other.

Alcona County Review, August 12, 1897

State of Michigan, County of Alcona. Probate Court for said County.

Estate of Henry Forsythe, deceased.

The undersigned having been appointed by the Judge of Probate of said County, Commissioners on Claims in the matter of said Estate of Henry Forsythe, and six months from the 23rd day of February, A.D. 1898, having been allowed by said Judge of Probate to all persons holding claims against said estate, in which to present their claims to us for examination and adjustment.

Notice is hereby given, that we will meet on Saturday, the 30th day of April, A.D. 1898, and on Friday, the 23d day of September, A.D. 1898, at 10 o'clock a.m. of each day, at Register of Deeds' office in the Village of Harrisville in said County, to receive and examine such claims:

Dated, February 28, A.D. 1898.
John MacGregor,
E. W. Chapelle, Commissioners.

Alcona County Review, March 3, 1898

STATE OF MICHIGAN, County of Alcona.

At a session of the Probate Court for said county, held at the probate office, in the village of Harrisville, on the 13th day of March in the year one thousand eight hundred and ninety-nine.

Present, Hon. W. H. Gilpin, Judge of Probate.

In the matter of the estate of Henry Forsythe deceased.

On reading and filing the petition, duly verified, of L. R. Dorr, executor, praying that license be granted license to sell the west half of the east half of the southwest quarter of section twenty-eight (28) in township twenty-six (26) north of range nine (9) east, for the payment of indebtedness existing and now due against said estate. Also on reading and filing the petition of said L. R. Dorr praying that the personal property of said estate be sold to pay said indebtedness and that license be given him to sell same.

Thereupon it is ordered, that Monday the 10th day of April next, at ten o'clock in the forenoon, be assigned for the hearing of said petition, and that the next of kin and all others interested in said estate, are required to appear at a session of said Court, then to be holden at the Probate office, in the Village of Harrisville and show cause, if any there be, why the prayer of the petitioner should not be granted: And it is further ordered, that said petitioner give notice to the persons interested in said estate, of the pendency of said petition, and the hearing thereof by causing a copy of this order to be published in the Alcona County Review, a newspaper printed and circulated in said county, three successive weeks previous to said day of hearing.

W. H. Gilpin,
Judge of Probate.

Alcona County Review, March 16, 1899

Probate Court.

Lawrence R. Dorr, administrator has applied to the court for license to sell the real and personal property of the estate of Lovina and Henry Forsyth, deceased, to pay off indebtedness against said estate.

Alcona County Review, March 16, 1899

State of Michigan, County of Alcona.

In the matter of the estate of Henry Forsythe deceased.

Notice is hereby given, that in pursuance of an order granted to the undersigned, executor of the estate of said Henry Forsythe, by the Hon. Judge of Probate for the County of Alcona, on the 22d day of May A.D. 1899, there will be sold at public vendue, to the highest bidder, at the farm described below, in the county of Alcona, in said state, on Monday, the tenth day of July A.D. 1899, at ten o'clock in the forenoon of that day (subject to all encumbrances by mortgage or otherwise existing at the time of the death of said deceased, or at the time of sale, the following described real estate, to-wit: The west half of the east half of the south west quarter of section twenty-eight [28] in town twenty-six [26] north of range nine [9] east.

L. R. Dorr, Executor.

Alcona County Review, May 25, 1899

State of Michigan, County of Alcona.

Probate Court for said County.

At a session of the Probate Court for said county, held at the Probate office, in said county, on Monday the 17th day of July, in the year one thousand eight hundred ninety-nine.

Present, Hon. Wm. H. Gilpin, Probate Judge.

In the matter of the estate of Henry Forsythe deceased.

L. R. Dorr, administrator of said estate comes into court and represents that he is now prepared to render his account as such administrator.

Thereupon it is ordered that Monday the 7th day of August next, at 10 o'clock in the forenoon, be assigned for the examining and allowing of such account and that the heirs at law of said deceased and all other persons interested in said estate, are required to appear at a session of said court, then to be holden at the Probate office, in the village of Harrisville, and show cause, if any there be, why the said account should not be allowed: and it is further ordered that said L. R. Dorr give notice to the persons interested in said estate, of the pendency of said account, and the hearing thereof, by causing a copy of this order to be published in the "Alcona County Review" a newspaper printed and circulated in said county, two successive weeks previous to said day of hearing.

Wm. H. Gilpin,
Judge of Probate.

Alcona County Review, July 20, 1899

STATE of Michigan, County of Alcona.

Probate Court for said County.

At a session of the Probate Court for said county, held at the Probate office, in said county on Monday the 24th day of July, in the year one thousand eight hundred and ninety-nine.

Present, Hon. Wm. H. Gilpin, Probate Judge.

In the matter of the estate of Henry Forsythe deceased.

L. R. Dorr, executor of said estate comes into court and represents that he is now prepared to render his account as such executor.

Thereupon it is ordered that Monday the *** day of August next, at 10 o'clock in the forenoon, be assigned for the examining and allowing of such account and that the heirs at law of said deceased and all other persons interested in said estate, are required to appear at a session said court, then to be holden at the Probate office, in the village of Harrisville, in said county and show cause, if any there be, why the said account should not be allowed: and it is further ordered that said L. R. Dorr give notice to the persons interested in said estate, of the pendency of said account, and the hearing thereof, by causing a copy of this order to be published in the "Alcona County Review" a newspaper printed and circulated in said county, three successive weeks previous to said day of hearing.

Wm. H. Gilpin,
Judge of Probate.

Alcona County Review, July 27, 1899
Cemetery: Springport, Alcona Co.

Forsythe, John T.

Death of John T. Forsythe.

A telegram received Monday morning announced the death of John T. Forsythe, second son of Henry Forsythe, at Ann Arbor, where he had been taken last week by his father for medical treatment. The deceased had only just passed his majority, having been born Feb. 15, 1866, in the county of Gray, Ont., Canada. He gave promise at an early age of a long and healthful life, as nature had endowed him with a powerful constitution that it seemed could withstand the onslaught of any disease. He stood 6 feet and 2 inches in his stockings and weighed, before his sickness, 190 pounds. He was stricken with rheumatism in April of last year, and since that time he has been a constant sufferer, being wholly confined to the house for the past three months. He received the best medical treatment in this section, but with apparently little benefit, and his parents decided to take him to Ann Arbor. But it was too late, blood poisoning had developed, and the skill of the celebrated physicians of the University could not save him. The physicians at Ann Arbor discovered the dangerous symptoms of blood poisoning and advised that he be taken home. It was while he was being carried to the boat in Detroit, we are informed, that the deceased expired.

The remains were brought back on the steamer City of Alpena, Tuesday. The funeral services were held Wednesday at the Dean school house, the remains being interred in the South Harrisville cemetery.

Alcona County Review, June 3, 1887
Cemetery: Springport, Alcona Co.

Forsythe, Lavina [Ferguson]

PURELY PERSONAL.

Mrs. Henry Forsythe is a sufferer from cancer in the stomach. The insidious disease has assumed a serious aspect, and the sufferer has been confined to her bed for some weeks past.

Alcona County Review, September 2, 1887

OBITUARY.

FORSYTHE.——At her late residence, Dec. 1st, 1887, Lavina, wife of Henry Forsythe, aged 46 years 2 months and 19 days. Deceased was born in Watertown, Conn. The funeral services were held Saturday at the Baptist church, the Rev. F. N. Barlow officiating.

————

Some one has gone from this strange world of ours,
No more to gather its thorns with its flowers;
No more to linger where sunbeams must fade.
Where on all beauty death's fingers are laid;
Weary with mingling life's bitter and sweet,
Weary with parting and never to meet.
Some one has gone to the bright golden shore;
Ring the bell softly, there's crape on the door!
Ring the bell softly, there's crape on the door!

Some one is resting from sorrow and sin,
Happy where earth's conflicts enter not in.
Joyous as birds when the morning is bright,
When the sweet sunbeams have brought us their light.
Weary with sowing and never to reap,
Weary with labor, and welcoming sleep.
Some one's departed to heaven's bright shore;
Ring the bell softly, there's crape on the door!
Ring the bell softly, there's crape on the door!

Angels were anxiously longing to meet
One who walks with them in heaven's bright street;
Loved ones have whispered that some one is blest,—
Free from earth's trials and taking sweet rest.
Yes! there is one more in angelic bliss,—
One less to cherish and one less to kiss;
One more departed to heaven's bright shore;
Ring the bell softly, there's crape on the door!
Ring the bell softly, there's crape on the door!

Alcona County Review, December 9, 1887

Card of Thanks.

I wish to thank the many friends and neighbors who rendered such kindly assistance during the last illness and death of my wife. My especial thanks are due Mrs. L. A. Colwell and Mrs. A. Noyes for floral tributes. Henry Forsythe.

Alcona County Review, December 9, 1887

LOCAL JOTTINGS.

A paper was circulated this week for the relief of Henry Forsythe, one of our old and most respected farmers. Mr. Forsythe has been carrying a heavy load of troubles during the past two years. The expenses attending the death and burial of a son then of his wife, followed later by the loss of two work horses has seriously crippled him financially.

Alcona County Review, May 31, 1889

Order of Hearing.
First Publication August 12, '97.

STATE OF MICHIGAN, County of Alcona.

At a session of the Probate Court for said county, held at the probate office, in the village of Harrisville, on the 9th day of August in the year one thousand eight hundred and ninety-seven.

Present, Hon. W. H. Gilpin, Judge of Probate.

In the matter of the estate of Lavina Forsythe, deceased.

On reading and filing the petition, duly verified of George Henry Forsythe praying that L. R. Dorr of Harrisville or some other suitable person, be appointed administrator of the said estate.

Thereupon it is ordered, that Tuesday, the 7th day of September next, at ten o'clock in the forenoon, be assigned for the hearing of said petition, and that the heirs at law of said deceased and all others interested in said estate, are required to appear at a session of said Court, then to be holden at the Probate office, in the Village of Harrisville and show cause, if any there be, why the prayer of the petitioner should not be granted: And it is further ordered, that said petitioner give notice to the heirs at law and all persons interested in said estate, of the pendency of said petition, and the hearing thereof by causing a copy of this order to be published in the Alcona County Review, a newspaper printed and circulated in said county, three successive weeks previous to said day of hearing.

W. H. Gilpin,
Judge of Probate.

Alcona County Review, August 12, 1897

State of Michigan, County of Alcona. Probate Court for said County.

Estate of Lavina Forsythe, deceased.

The undersigned having been appointed by the Judge of Probate of said County, Commissioners on claims in the matter of said estate of Lavina Forsythe, and six months from the 23rd day of February, A.D. 1898, having been allowed by said Judge of Probate to all persons holding claims against said estate, in which to present their claims to us for examination and adjustment. Notice is hereby given, that we will meet on Saturday the 30th day of April, A.D.

1898, and on Friday, the 23d day of September, A.D. 1898, at 10 o'clock A.M. of each day, at the Register of Deeds' office in the Village of Harrisville in said County, to receive and examine such claims:

Dated, February 28, A.D. 1898.
John MacGregor,
E. W. Chapelle,
Commissioners.

Alcona County Review, March 3, 1898

STATE of Michigan, County of Alcona.

At a session of the Probate Court for said county, held at the Probate office, in the village of Harrisville, on the 13th day of March in the year one thousand eight hundred and ninety-nine.

Present, Hon. Wm. H. Gilpin, Probate Judge.

In the matter of the estate of Lovina Forsythe deceased.

On reading and filing the petition, duly verified of L. R. Dorr, administrator, praying that he be granted license to sell the east half of the east half of the southwest quarter of section twenty-eight (28) in township twenty-six north, range nine (9) east, for the payment of indebtedness existing and due against said estate.

Thereupon it is ordered that Monday the 10th day of April next, at 10 o'clock in the forenoon, be assigned for the hearing of said petition, and that the next of kin and all other persons interested in said estate, are required to appear at a session of said court, then to be holden at the Probate office, in the village of Harrisville and show cause, if any there be, why the prayer of the petitioner should not be granted: and it is further ordered that said petitioner give notice to the persons interested in said estate, of the pendency of said petition, and the hearing thereof, by causing a copy of this order to be published in the "Alcona County Review" a newspaper printed and circulated in said county, three successive weeks previous to said day of hearing.

Wm. H. Gilpin,
Judge of Probate.

Alcona County Review, March 16, 1899

Probate Court.

Lawrence R. Dorr, administrator has applied to the court for license to sell the real and personal property of

the estate of Lovina and Henry Forsyth, deceased, to pay off indebtedness against said estate.

Alcona County Review, March 16, 1899
Cemetery: Springport, Alcona Co.

Fortier, {Boy}

HAYNES HAPPENINGS.

July 18.
Mr. and Mrs. A. J. Fortier had the misfortune to lose a baby boy, stillborn. Interment took place Sunday afternoon.

Alcona County Review, July 21, 1898
Cemetery: Mt. Joy, Alcona Co.

Fortier, {Child}

Haynes Happenings.

Mr. and Mrs. A. J. Fortier buried an infant a few hours old in our cemetery. I sympathize with them in their sorrow.

Alcona County Review, June 13, 1895
Cemetery: Mt. Joy, Alcona Co.

Fortier, Louisa [Bonville]

Bits of News.

The remains of Mrs. A. J. Fortier, of Oscoda, were interred at Mount Joy cemetery, Haynes, yesterday. Deceased was a daughter of Mr. and Mrs. A. Bonnville.

Alcona County Review, December 7, 1899

HAYNES.

Dec. 12, `99.
Mrs. Louisa Fortier, daughter of Mr. and Mrs. Amos Bondville, Sr., died at Au Sable Dec. 4th, `99, of abcess of the throat and tonsils, aged 32 years, 5 months and 10 days. She leaves two children, a girl aged 3 years and an infant boy 4 days old, a sorrowing husband and father and mother. Mrs. Bondville was at the bedside of her daughter when she died. The remains were brought up to Black River and interred Wednesday, 6th, in Haynes Tp. cemetery. The Rev. Mr. Austin preached the funeral sermon.

Alcona County Review, December 14, 1899

Our sincere thanks are due to people of Black River for unremitting kindness and sympathy and assistance during our recent great bereavement. May the Giver of all good reward you and give you friends in time of need.

A. J. Fortier
Mr. and Mrs. Bondville
and family

Alcona County Review, December 14, 1899
Cemetery: Mt. Joy, Alcona Co.

Foster, Ella B.

Black River Sparks.

Died at Chicago, May 29, 1896, Miss Ella Foster, second daughter of Robert Foster of Harrisville, aged 25 years.

The remains arrived by the evening train Monday and were taken to the residence of her brother, James Foster. Miss Foster was an estimable young lady and well known in Black River, where she had many warm friends. The funeral took place at Harrisville on Tuesday. The remains were followed by a large crowd of friends and relatives. The pall bearers were Wm. Hill, A. Heron, Joe Whitsett, P. Collins, M. Titus, I. Hohenstein.

Alcona County Review, June 4, 1896

PERSONAL MENTION.

The remains of Ella B. Foster, aged 24, a daughter of Robert Foster, were brought here for burial from Chicago this week. The young woman died from a cancer of the stomach. She had been working in the city of Chicago prior to her last illness.

Alcona County Review, June 4, 1896

Card of Thanks.

We desire to thank the people of Black River, and others, who aided us in any way during the illness, death and burial of our beloved sister and daughter, Ella B. Foster.

Robt. Foster and Family.

Alcona County Review, June 4, 1896

In Memory of Ella Foster, Deceased.

In memory of a daughter dear,
A sister kind and true.
These lines are dedicated
In fondest love to you.

Thou hast left us dearest Ella,
Thy spirit is at rest.
Thou hast gone to join thy mother
Up in heaven with the blest.

Though absent thou art not forgotten;
Thy image will ever be near,
In the warmest spot in our hearts
Will thy memory be ever dear.

We trust that we may meet thee
When God in his infinite love
Shall call to us to enter
Into his beautiful home above.

--M. A. F.

Alcona County Review, July 23, 1896
Cemetery: Probably Springport, Alcona Co.

Foster, {Boy}

LOCAL PICK UPS.

The remains of the infant child of Mr. and Mrs. Robt. Foster, Jr., were buried at Harrisville cemetery last Friday.

Alcona County Review, January 19, 1899
Cemetery: Springport, Alcona Co.

Foster, Mrs. Mary Ann

COUNTY REVIEWINGS.

Mrs. Robert Foster died at her home above Harrisville on Thursday night. She leaves a husband and seven children to mourn her loss.

Alcona County Review, December 10, 1880
Cemetery: Springport, Alcona Co.

Foster, Oveld

Black River Sparks.

Died on Wednesday, May 20, Oveld, the infant son of Mr. and Mrs. James Foster, aged nine months. The funeral will take place Thursday, May 21 from St. Gabriel's church. Burial at the Harrisville R. C. cemetery. "Suffer the little children to come unto me, for of such is the kingdom of heaven."

Alcona County Review, May 21, 1896

Black River Sparks.

To our friends and neighbors who so kindly aided and comforted us in the hour of our recent sad trouble, the death of our little son, we return our sincere thanks.

Mr. and Mrs. Jas. Foster.
Black River, May 21, 1896.

Alcona County Review, May 28, 1896
Cemetery: St. Anne's, Alcona Co.

Fowler, George

LOCAL JOTTINGS

The body of a man supposed to be that of Geo. Fowler, second engineer of the barge Cowle, who disappeared at Alpena last October, was found floating in the river at that place last week Tuesday.

Alcona County Review, July 6, 1888
Cemetery:

Fowler, Kate

KILLMASTER HAPPENINGS.

Killmaster, April 27.--We are pleased to record that Miss Kittie Fowler, who has been very sick for a long time, is slowly improving. Hopes

are now entertained of her final recovery.

Alcona County Review, April 29, 1887

KILLMASTER FLASHES.

Killmaster, May 26.--It is with feelings of deep sorrow that we announce the death of our young friend, Miss Kitty Fowler. She passed away a little before noon on Tuesday, the 24th inst. at the home of C. Dedrich. Miss Fowler was highly respected by all, and leaves a large circle of mourning friends. Her parents and family have the sympathy of the entire community.

Alcona County Review, May 27, 1887
Cemetery: Springport, Alcona Co.

Fowler, William

EVENTS OF ONE WEEK.

Wm. Fowler, a resident of Gustin township, died Tuesday afternoon after a lingering illness from pulmonary consumption. He leaves a family whose present needs are provided for by a policy for $1,000 in the Maccabees, deceased being a member of the Killmaster Tent. The funeral will be held to-day.

Alcona County Review, June 8, 1893

Resolved, That the wife has lost a kind and loving husband and this Tent laments the loss of a brother who was ever ready to proffer the hand of aid and the voice of sympathy to the needy and distressed of the fraternity, and

Resolved, That we, the members of Mineral Water Tent, No. 403 K.O.T.M, extend to the bereaved widow and sorrowing relatives our heartfelt sympathy in their irreparable loss and that the same be spread upon the records of this Tent, and be it further

Resolved, That our charter be draped in mourning for the period of 90 days, that a copy of these resolutions be sent to the widow and also that they be published in the Alcona County Review and Michigan Maccabee.

H. S. Dalton,
J. H. Killmaster,   Com.
D. Procunier.

Alcona County Review, June 15, 1893

PERSONAL MENTION.

Mrs. Wm. Fowler of Killmaster has received a K.O.T.M. check for $1,000, as the amount of insurance carried by her husband, who died June 5.

Alcona County Review, July 27, 1893

South Harrisville, Oct. 18.

A few improvements of late are noticeable at the S. Harrisville cemetery.

Wm. H. Anderson has a fine monument placed at the head of his children's graves, also Wm. Silversides to the memory of his wife and Mrs. Fowler of Killmaster in memory of her husband.

Each of the three former have their plots raised and graveled. All show forth the love still cherished for those they have committed to their Creator.

Alcona County Review, October 19, 1893
Cemetery: Springport, Alcona Co.

Fox, Bub

Local Sayings and Doings.

Bub Fox, the idiot, who has been a county charge for numerous years past, died at the poor farm last Friday morning, and was buried beside his mother in the village cemetery on Saturday.

Alcona County Review, November 18, 1881
Cemetery: West Lawn, Alcona Co.

Fox, Mrs. Sarah A.

Mrs. Fox, the blind woman who has been a county charge at the poor farm for several years past, died last Friday, and was buried in the cemetery west of this place last Sunday. She was the mother of "Bub" Fox, the "idiot," and quite an aged lady.

Alcona County Review, February 25, 1881

C.P.R. IN REPLY TO G.H.B.
[From a longer article by C. P. Reynolds complaining of the treatment of the poor by George H. Blush, who managed the poor farm.]

How did he [George H. Blush] bury old Aunt Fox, the oldest of the pioneers of Alcona county? While many old neighbors were waiting to pay a last tribute to her memory, and wondering at the delay of the procession, where was GHB? One solitary team, a box and a blanket— only that and nothing more. Not a prayer, nor a christian act of any kind to her memory—buried like a dog. GHB despises God's poor. Oh Shame! "Where is thy blush?"

Alcona County Review, August 5, 1881

C.P.R.'s REPLY TO G.H.B.

[Another discussion of Sarah Fox's burial and the funeral provided by neighbors, from a longer article.]

He is very tender about that burlesque funeral of Aunt Fox. He says he did the best he could under the circumstances. The minister says that G. H. B. told him that "there were no relatives nor friends, and that he could dispense with such services." He evidently thought himself the Boss of that funeral, as well as of the graveyard, and could run it to suit himself—and he did.

Compare that funeral with the one provided by the neighbors of Mr. Fox, and note the differences between the cold, calculated neglect and the warm heartedness of the people of this county, where kindly sympathy did the work and G. H. B. drew the pay. C. P. R. has frequently, more frequently than any other man in the county, met the women and with them did the best offices to humanity. The ladies never failed; with rich or poor they make no distinctions. To them be all the honor for the decency of Aunt Fox's funeral, but to G. H. B. nothing but its extreme cheapness. It only lacked his praying and singing to make it too sweet for earth and too holy for Heaven. Besides, it was so cheap that the county could well afford two such funerals in one day.

Alcona County Review, August 5, 1881
Cemetery: West Lawn, Alcona Co.

Frank, {Boy}

LOCAL JOTTINGS.

A six-months old babe of Mr. and Mrs. Frank, living on the old LaChapelle place below town, died last Sunday.

Alcona County Review, June 20, 1884
Cemetery:

Franklin, Adella M.

LOCAL JOTTINGS.

Miss Della Franklin, of Springport, is dead after a lingering illness.

Alcona County Review, September 28, 1888

OBITUARY.
Miss Della Franklin, who died at Springport after a lingering illness of ten months, was born at Clio, Mich., Dec. 17th, 1867, and was nearly 21 years old at the time of her death. Her sufferings, which were intense most of the time from the beginning of her sickness, were borne with fortitude and patience remarkable in one so young. She realized that she was passing away and had made her peace with God. She was an affectionate daughter, and in her loving and thoughtful care for her parents when in health, leaves an example worthy of imitation by her many youthful friends. The home is lonely now, and never will be quite the same to them again, yet they sorrow not without hope, but know if they love the same Saviour they will meet their loved one where parting will come no more.

Rest for the toiling hand,
Rest for the anxious brow.
Rest for the weary, waysore feet,
Rest from all labor now.

Rest for the fevered brain,
Rest for the throbbing eye;
Through those parched lips of thine
No more shall pass a moan or sigh.

Ye dweller of the dust,
Awake, come forth and sing;
Sharp has your frost of winter been,
Big bright shall be your spring.

'Twas sown in weakness here,
'Twill there be raised in power;
That which was sown an earthly seed
Shall rise a heavenly flower.
W. D. and A. Franklin,
Springport, Oct. 10, 1888.

Alcona County Review, October 12, 1888

We wish to thank our many kind friends and neighbors for their kindness and sympathy during the long illness of our dear daughter and in our bereavement.
W. D. and A. Franklin.

Alcona County Review, October 12, 1888
Cemetery: Springport, Alcona Co.

Fraser, John A.

KILLED ON THE MUD LAKE BRANCH.

Jno. A. Fraser, an Old Lumberman, Meets His Death Under the Wheels While on his way to work at Camp 8.

Jno. A. Fraser, an old and well known lumberman in this section, and employed as a teamster in Loud's camp No. 8, had been visiting his family in this place for a few days and had started about dusk Monday evening to return to camp. At W.

Harrisville he boarded night train No. 10, which soon started on its usual night run up the Mud Lake Branch for a load of logs. It was within forty rods of the place where he wanted to get off, and when the train was running about five miles an hour, that Fraser started forward over the flat cars in company with the brakeman. The night was dark and stormy and Fraser having no lantern made a misstep and fell between two of the flats. Eight cars passed over him, mangling both legs in a painful manner. The train was stopped at once and Fraser's mangled form lifted tenderly on board. The train was backed down to W. Harrisville where the injured man was made as comfortable as possible at the Duggan House. Drs. Mitchell and Campbell, of Harrisville, were sent for at once, but on their arrival they could do nothing for him. He retained consciousness to the last, expiring at 4 o'clock Tuesday morning. No inquest was held, it not being deemed necessary.

The deceased was about 45 years of age and leaves a wife and six children. He had been lumbering on this shore for the past twenty years, and has occupied several positions of importance. The funeral services were held Wednesday afternoon at 2 o'clock under the auspices of Harrisville Lodge No. 218, I. O. O. F. The Rev. F. N. Barlow delivered the funeral sermon.

Alcona County Review, September 16, 1887

Resolutions of Condolence.

Whereas, It has seemed good to the Almighty disposer of events to remove from our midst our late worthy and esteemed Brother, John A. Frazer, and,

Whereas, The intimate relations long held by the deceased with the members of this order render it proper that we should place upon record our appreciation of his services as an Odd Fellow and his merits as a man, therefore,

Resolved, That we deplore the loss of John A. Frazer with deep feelings of regret, softened only by the confident hope that his spirit is with those who have fought the good fight here and are now enjoying perfect happiness in a better world,

Resolved, That we tender to his afflicted family our sincere condolence, and our earnest sympathy in their affliction through the loss of one who was a kind husband and father, a good citizen, a devoted Odd Fellow, and an upright man.

Resolved, That the members of this Lodge will attend our deceased Brother to the grave in a body; that the hall of meeting be hung with the emblems of mourning until after the funeral ceremony shall have been performed, and that the lodge room be draped with black for thirty days,

Resolved, That a copy of the foregoing resolutions, signed by the Nobel Grand and certified by the Secretary under seal of this lodge, be transmitted to the family of the deceased Brother. Also that a copy be furnished the editor of the village paper for publication, and that the foregoing be spread upon the records of the lodge.

Fraternally submitted,
F. A. Beede.

Alcona County Review, September 23, 1887

ORDER OF HEARING.

State of Michigan, County of Alcona.

At a session of the Probate Court for said county, held at the Probate Office in the village of Harrisville, on the 26th day of September, in the year one thousand eight hundred and eighty-seven. Present, Allen Nevins, Judge of Probate. In the matter of the

ESTATE OF JOHN FRASER, DECEASED.

On reading and filing the petition, duly verified, of Jennie Fraser, praying that she or some other suitable person be appointed administratrix of the estate of said John Fraser, deceased. Thereupon it is ordered that Saturday, the 22d Day of October, 1887, next, at ten o'clock in the forenoon, be assigned for the hearing of said petition, and that the heirs at law of said deceased, and all other persons interested in said estate, are required to appear at a session of said court then to be holden at the Probate office, in the village of Harrisville, and show cause if any there be, why the prayer of the petitioner should not be granted. And it is further ordered that said petitioner give notice to the heirs at law, and other persons interested in said estate, of the pendency of said petition, and the hearing thereof, by causing a copy of this order to be published in the Alcona County Review, a newspaper printed and circulated in said county, three successive weeks previous to said day of hearing.

Allen Nevins, Judge of Probate.

Alcona County Review, September 30, 1887
Cemetery: Springport, Alcona Co.

PROBATE ORDER.

STATE OF MICHIGAN, County of Alcona.

Notice is hereby given that by an order of the Probate Court for the County of Alcona, made on the 22d day of October, A. D. 1887, six months from that date were allowed for creditors to present their claims against the

ESTATE OF JOHN FRASER.

late of said county, deceased, and that all creditors of said deceased are required to present their claims to said Probate Court, at the Probate office, in the village of Harrisville, for examination and allowance, on or before the 23d Day of April, 1888 next, and that such claims will be heard before said court on Monday, the 23d day of January, 1888, and on Monday, the 23d day of April, 1888, at ten o'clock in the forenoon of each of those days.

Dated October 22d, 1887.

ALLEN NEVINS, Judge of Probate.

Alcona County Review, January 6, 1888
Cemetery: Springport, Alcona Co.

Fraser, William

A Sudden Call.

From the Saturday Night.

Last Saturday a man by the name of Wm. Fraser came down on the train from Black River and stopped at the Central Hotel. He told Landlord Cherrytree that he was not well and had come down to consult a doctor. He sat around the hotel for some time and finally said as he was not well he would go to his room. No more attention was paid him until one of the men around the hotel went to his room to see how he was getting along. He seemed to be in a bad condition so a doctor was sent for and he was given something to quiet him. On going to his room Monday morning it was found that he died in the night. Mr. Cherrytree at once notified the authorities and telegraphed Black River to see if he had any friends. No one coming to claim the remains he was buried Tuesday. Fraser was a man about fifty years of age and had been a hard drinker all his life. He had been working for Alger, Smith & Co. for some time. It is said that he had a large amount of money coming to him from the Co. Dr. Weir, who attended him, said he died of malarial fever. A brother in Detroit was notified of his death but he failed to put in an appearance or express any wish as to the disposal of the remains.

Alcona County Review, September 29, 1892
Cemetery:

Frasier, {Male}

Haynes.

Haynes, March 23.—Mr. Donald Frasier has been called away from home to accompany the remains of a beloved brother to Ontario, where they will be interred.

Alcona County Review, March 24, 1892
Cemetery:

Frasier, Mary [McDonald]

LOCAL JOTTINGS.

Mrs. Angus Frasier, of Greenbush, died last night at 12 o'clock, of consumption, aged about 35 years. She leaves husband and one child.

Alcona County Review, April 24, 1885
Cemetery:

Frederick, Barton

Murdered in Arkansas.

A message came by wire last night to Lorenzo Frederick that his brother Bart had been murdered the day before at Kingsland, Arkansas, but giving no particulars.

The murdered man was well known here where he resided 15 years ago. He was a member of the Sturgeon Point Life Saving Station crew at one time. He visited his brother two years ago. He is well spoken of as a man of kindly, genial disposition.

Alcona County Review, December 30, 1897

Unknown.

Murderer of Bart Frederick Not Yet Captured.

Mr. Editor:--I desire to pay for the information of the public that my beloved brother was murdered by some person unknown. A reward of $1200 is offered for the arrest of the party who did the cowardly act. All communications regarding the case should be addressed to Dr. William Buarhive, Kingsland, Ark.

In sorrow,

L. Frederick.

Alcona County Review, January 13, 1898

Bart Frederick's Murder

Story of the Atrocious Crime Related by an Arkansas Physician.

Negroes Did the Deed. Robbery was their Motive.

Mr. L. Frederick has received the following letter from Arkansas in explanation of the details of the recent atrocious murder of his brother:

Kingsland, Ark. Jan. 1, 1898.

My Dear Brother:—Your letter of 10th came this morning also one of 12th; in reply beg to say that Bart was shot 1 ½ miles south of town. He was going from town tank to station tank where he resided. It was on Tuesday afternoon between 3 and 4 o'clock, and to add to the horror of the affair the perpetrators of the deed had only about 25 minutes to do their work, as the south bound passenger train was due here at 4 o'clock and the pile driver train was at work at noon and had to come here for switch track, so you see it had to leave work about 3:30 so as to be sure and be on time. The murder was well planned and quickly executed. He was on his car, was stopped on the point of a high grade and evidently shot from behind at very close range as powder was embedded in the flesh about the neck and ear. The bullet entered just below the left ear ranging upward at an angle of about 3 degrees, passing through the base of the brain and lodging on the inside, fracturing the jaw bone on the right side just at the angle. He was shot with a 38 pistol. I took the bullet out and gave it to the detective who was present. Death was instantaneous, i. e. there was no sign of struggling, and even if there was struggling he was conscious of no pain. He fell backwards on his car and a great pool of blood poured out on the rail. He was then dragged down the dump into a clump of pine bushes, robbed and left a prey to the wild beasts of the field and the vultures of the air. His car was simply turned bottom upwards beside the track. The pile-driver people saw his car and said that they supposed he

was off filling a can of water or something like that.

About 9 o'clock Wednesday morning Mr. McKenna, section foreman, found his car and dinner bucket and on further investigation found his body. He came immediately to town and told us of it. I got on my horse and with the sheriff and a number of others went out and held an inquest, brought the body to town, extracted the bullet, dressed him, and on Thursday we gave him a decent Masonic burial. Our lodges turned out from Entered Apprentice to Royal Arch, and there were at least 500 people at the funeral. There were a large number of his A. A. (railroad) friends present.

Since writing you we have caught one of the murderers and will in a short time catch the others. The one we have has made a partial confession. They were negroes and there is a possibility of a white man being the instigator. The A. A. Co.'s detective and the sheriff of the county have used untiring efforts to catch the murderers. The robbers and murderers took his watch and in their hurry to get away they pulled the watch away and left the chain ring on the guard. We have the watch; it was pawned at Berden, 15 miles south of here.

Bart will live always in our memory because we loved him. Please accept the sympathy of a brother in these your dark days of sorrow. Bart often told us that he was the black sheep of the paternal fold, but Oh! my God, how we loved that big hearted brother, whose faults the world knows and whose deep seated, God-given love we share. May God, who gives and takes, console your wounded spirit. I loved Bart as a friend; you loved him for other and deeper causes. I give you my hand across the stretch of miles and could you feel its warm grasp you would know how I loved him. We are, perhaps, of different politics and different tribes, as it were, but, my brother, these things are too meager, too superfluous; below, deep down, is a fellow feeling that reaches the heart and goes out to you as if I had known you always. God bless you.

I have given the minute details of the crime. There are many things connected with the chase of criminals

I would like you to have, but time and space will not admit of it. If I can serve you in any capacity I will do it, barefooted and bareheaded if necessary. So never hesitate to communicate me.

Your sincere friend,
Dr. Wm. Buerhive.

Alcona County Review, January 27, 1898

PERSONAL POINTS.

Prof. L. Frederick was in Harrisville Saturday and stated to the Review that he expected to leave this week for Kingsland, Ark., where his brother Barton was recently murdered. The latter left some unsettled business matters and also carried some insurance which awaits the action of the heirs.

Alcona County Review, February 17, 1898

PERSONAL POINTS.

Prof. Lorenzo Frederick closed up a $2,000 life insurance policy in the Aetna Life Ins. Co. last week, which was placed on the life of his late brother Bart, whose atrocious murder a few weeks ago in Arkansas was duly chronicled in the Review at the time. The policy was an accident. The company was a little inclined to fight payment on the ground that Bart's death was not purely accidental, so to avoid litigation Prof. Frederick, the sole beneficiary, accepted a settlement at a figure of $400 less than the face of the policy.

Alcona County Review, May 12, 1898
Cemetery: Kingsland, Cleveland Co., AR

Frederick, {Child}
PERSONAL MENTION.

Mr. and Mrs. L. Frederick have the sympathy of the community in the loss of their baby, a child of about one year of age which died at an early hour Friday morning, June 1st, after a three weeks' illness.

Alcona County Review, June 7, 1894

Editor Review:—
Dear--Sir. Permit us through the columns of the Review to thank our neighbors and friends for their assistance and sympathy in our late bereavement.

Mr. and Mrs. L. Frederick.

Alcona County Review, June 14, 1894
Cemetery:

Frederick, Stanley
The Local News.

L. Frederick and wife mourn the loss of an infant child which died last week when but five months old.

Alcona County Review, August 27, 1891
Cemetery:

Freer, {Boy}
PERSONAL MENTION.

Mr. and Mrs. John Freer were called upon last week to part with their youngest child, a boy, aged six months. We are informed that the child was found dead in its bed in the morning. The funeral was held Saturday from the residence of A. J. Freer.

Alcona County Review, June 8, 1893

For himself and wife John Freer desires to express their thanks through these columns to their kind neighbors and friends of Mitchell and Harrisville, whose timely sympathy and aid were so welcome in their late bereavement.

Alcona County Review, June 8, 1893
Cemetery: Probably Springport, Alcona Co.

Freer, Voil
DEATH'S HARVEST.

Mr. and Mrs. John S. Freer were called upon last week to part with their little son, aged 11 months. The interment took place on Sunday at South Harrisville. The child died of the cold which is so prevalent among children this winter.

Alcona County Review, March 2, 1893
Cemetery: Springport, Alcona Co.

French, Almira C. [Chapelle]
OBITUARY.

On the afternoon of May 1st, 1890, at the residence of her son-in-law, L. A. Colwell, Mrs. Almira C. French, aged seventy-nine years. Although she had been in feeble health for some time, yet death came suddenly, but it found her ready and watching. She retained her faculties to a marvelous degree to the last moment, bidding each member of her family farewell, and expressing herself as desiring to "Depart and be with Christ."

The funeral services were conducted at her late residence by her former pastor, Rev. F. N. Barlow of Alpena, assisted by the Rev. P. C. Goldie of Harrisville.

Alcona County Review, May 9, 1890

We desire to extend our sincere thanks to the friends and neighbors who so kindly assisted us during an illness, death and burial of our dear mother.

Mr. and Mrs. L. A. Colwell.
Mrs. Elliott.

Alcona County Review, May 9, 1890

The Local News.

The Alpena Pioneer made a mistake in its last issue by stating that Mrs. Colwell had died at the home of her son in this village whereas it was Mrs. French, mother of Mrs. L. A. Colwell.

Alcona County Review, May 9, 1890

Purely Personal.

The Rev. F. N. Barlow and G. A. Shannon of Alpena were in Harrisville last Saturday to attend the funeral of Mrs. French.

Alcona County Review, May 9, 1890

One Year's History.

Record of Local Happenings for the Year 1890.

MAY.

1 Death of Mrs. Almira C. French.

Alcona County Review, January 1, 1891
Cemetery: Springport, Alcona Co.

Fry, William
LOST THEIR CHILD.

A Couple From Alcona County Have a Sorrowful Journey.

From Bay City Tribune, Jan. 7.
While coming from their home in Alcona county on Thursday, the 14 month's old child of a couple named Fry was taken seriously ill on the train. Arriving in this city the train officials ordered the child taken care of and it was taken by the parents to a hotel near the Michigan Central depot. The proprietor upon learning that the child was ill, would not permit it to be cared for in his house. Entreaties were in vain and the parents were obliged to seek other quarters. Being strangers they went to the depot and told their story to Superintendent Martin. The case was put in charge of the railroad physicians, Drs. Newkirk, who had the child removed to the McIntosh House. Mr. and Mrs. McIntosh not only found accommodations for the family, but gave the sick child every possible care. The child lived until yesterday morning when death came to its relief. The physicians pronounced it a case of membraneous croup.

Mr. McIntosh was seen by a Tribune reporter yesterday afternoon. He said: "The family left here this noon taking with them the dead child. They were bound for Sebawaing where Mr. Fry is to work in the mines. The child was brought here in a dying condition. It showed the need of nursing and we agreed to take it. My wife stayed up nearly all night with the baby and did everything she could to bring it through, but it was too far gone. I think it was cruel to turn the family out of a hotel because of a sick child. There were two other children in the family.

Alcona County Review, January 12, 1893
Cemetery:

Fullerton, Harvey

HEIR TO THOUSANDS.

Postmaster Fullerton Gets a Windfall by the Death of an Uncle.

John S. Fullerton, a leading citizen of the township of Mitchell and postmaster at Curran, was deeply pained recently to learn of the death of an uncle at West Troy, N. Y., Harvey Fullerton by name. The grief over the death of his aged relative was somewhat ameliorated however, by the later and more agreeable information that the deceased left an estate worth from $25,000 to $30,000 and that this will be divided equally between four heirs, viz: John S. Fullerton of Alcona county, Mich., John Houghtaling of Jonesville, Mich., E. Houghtaling of Springfield, Mo., and Rebecca Hulbert of West Troy, N. Y.

The necessary legal steps are being taken to settle the estate and Postmaster Fullerton will ere long come into possession of his share.

Alcona County Review, August 24, 1893
Cemetery:

Fullerton, Henry John

CURRAN.

Henry Fullerton, who has been on the sick list for a week or more, was obliged to call the doctor who pronounced his case spinal fever and heart disease. He is very low at present.

Alcona County Review, October 20, 1898

CURRAN EVENTS.

Death of a Respected Citizen.

We are sorry to state that Henry J. Fullerton passed away peacefully to try the realities of an untried world, after a short period of severe suffering, Nov. 1st, at 1:30 a.m.

Deceased was 28 years of age. Death was due to spinal fever and heart failure. He was buried in the family cemetery in Mitchell. Services were conducted by the Rev. R. T. Ferrington of Fair View.

Mr. Fullerton was a member of McKinley True Blues No. 320, of the Loyal Orange Institution. Our lodge loses from its ranks a faithful member, faithful in attendance and in his daily life a faithful and upright Orangeman. In his death we all feel a personal loss. In conformance with his expressed wish he was committed to the grave according to our ritual. We laid him in the sleep that comes to all and left him to his rest. We would say in behalf of the bereaved wife, that however severely we may feel our loss we know that it is infinitely less than yours. You miss the gentle presence and strong support of a worthy husband. Only those who have similarly trod the vale of sorrow can sound its depths. "No mystic chain, no mortal art, can bid our loved companion stay; the bands that clasp them to our heart, snap in death's frost and fall apart; like shadows fading with the day, they pass away." Such is the destiny of all. Too soon, alas, we also will be summoned to join him in the great beyond. There the tears of earth are dried, there the hidden things are clear, there the work of life is tried by a juster judge than here.

Grace Fullerton is some better at this writing.

Alcona County Review, November 10, 1898

Condolence.

The following letter of condolence has been sent to Mrs. Henry Fullerton.

Whereas, The Divine Master has seen fit to remove from the trials and sorrows of earth to the celestial realms above, your beloved husband, we desire to extend to you our sincere sympathy in this the time of your loneliness, when all seems dark and dreary. We would bow to this affliction and feel assured that God cannot err, and that He is too good to be unkind. We would bow in humble submission to Him and say, "Thy will

be done." We would offer our tribute of respect to the memory of the deceased, and feel we would not be carrying out the principles of our association were we not to extend to you and your family our heartfelt sympathy through your sore bereavement. From our intimate associations with him we can testify to his loyalty to the Orange institution. May God's richest blessings rest upon you and may your heart be comforted by the thought that you and he who has gone before may some day meet in that happy home where parting is no more. Signed in behalf of McKinley True Blue Lodge No. 320. L. O. L.

Jas. LaForge, W. M.
Stephen Hawkins, Rec. Sec.
Curran, Alcona Co., Michigan

Alcona County Review, November 10, 1898

Local History of One Year

Chronology of the Principal Events of the Year 1898.

November 1. Death of Henry J. Fullerton of Mitchell.

Alcona County Review, January 5, 1899
Cemetery: Fullerton Family, Alcona Co.

Fullerton, John Stephen

Received a Sudden Call.

John S. Fullerton, a pioneer citizen of the township of Mitchell, expired very suddenly Monday evening from heart disease. He had been suffering considerable of late from the disease and had laid off work for a day or two on account of it. He was conversing with those about him at the time, and without warning gave a gasp and the spark of life went out. He was about 57 years of age and leaves his wife and one son. Deceased recently fell heir to a quarter interest in a $30,000 estate, by the death of an uncle, but he had not yet come into possession of his fortune. He was postmaster at Curran.

Alcona County Review, November 9, 1893

Curran, Nov. 10.--The death of Postmaster Fullerton occurred last Sunday at 9 o'clock p.m. His friends think it heart disease. It came unexpectedly to all as he was well on Saturday and went to McKinley with Henry Wiedbrauk. The funeral took place at his residence at Curran. Rev. Merritt, of Curtis, preached a good sermon that ought to warn all that heard his voice that day.

Alcona County Review, November 16, 1893

PERSONAL MENTION.

Pretty Good, If True.

Proceedings for the appointment of L. R. Dorr as administrator of the estate of the late John S. Fullerton, commenced Saturday before Judge Killmaster. A quarter interest in a property worth $30,000, left by a deceased uncle of John S. Fullerton was supposed to be the only property, but it is now reported that a deposit of upwards of $80,000 has been discovered in a Pennsylvania bank and the Fullerton heirs, viz.: the widow and son, will come in for a proportionate share of that also.

Alcona County Review, November 23, 1893

STATE OF MICHIGAN, County of Alcona.

At a session of the Probate Court for said County, held at the Probate office, in the Village of Harrisville, on the Eighteenth day of November, in the year one thousand eight hundred and ninety-three.

Present, C. H. Killmaster, Judge of Probate.

In the matter of the Estate of John S. Fullerton:

On reading and filing the petition, duly verified, of Mrs. E. J. Fullerton, widow, and Henry J. Fullerton, son, praying that letters of administration be granted to L. R. Dorr, or some other suitable person: Thereupon it is ordered that Saturday, the Fourteenth day of December next, at ten o'clock in the forenoon, be assigned for the hearing of said petition, and that the lawful heirs at law of said deceased, and all others interested in said estate, are required to appear at a session of said Court, then to be holden in the Probate office, in the Village of Harrisville, and show cause, if any there be, why the prayer of the petitioner should not be granted: And it is further ordered, that said petitioners give notice to the persons interested in said estate, of the pendency of said petition, and the hearing thereof by causing a copy of this order to be published in the Alcona County Review, a newspaper printed and circulated in said county, three successive weeks previous to said day of hearing.

C. H. Killmaster,

Judge of Probate.

Alcona County Review, November 23, 1893

PERSONAL MENTION.

Curran, Nov. 27, 1893. Please allow me to correct a mistake that was made a few weeks ago:

John S. Fullerton was 59 years and ten months old and died Sunday the 5th of Nov. He leaves a wife and seven children, six daughters and one son, to mourn his loss—all of whom are married, except one.

Alcona County Review, November 30, 1893

PERSONAL MENTION.

The estate of the late John S. Fullerton, which at one time was reported would be worth between $20,000 and $30,000, it is now positively known will not exceed $3,000 after all debts are paid. L. R. Dorr, administrator, is getting the affairs of the estate in shape for the final settlement.

Alcona County Review, March 8, 1894

STATE OF MICHIGAN, County of Alcona.

At a session of the Probate Court for said County, held at the Probate office, in the Village of Harrisville on Saturday the 11th day of January in the year one thousand eight hundred and ninety-six.

Present, C. H. Killmaster, Judge of Probate.

In the matter of the estate of John S. Fullerton:

L. R. Dorr, the administrator of said estate, comes into Court and represents that he is now prepared to render of said estate a final account as such administrator.

Thereupon it is ordered, that Saturday the eighth day of February next, at ten o'clock in the forenoon, be assigned for reexamining and allowing such account, and that the heirs at law of said deceased, and all other persons interested in said estate, are required to appear at a session of said Court then to be holden at the Probate office in the village of Harrisville in said county, and show cause, if any there be, why the said account should not be allowed.

And it is further ordered that L. R. Dorr Adm'r, give notice to the persons interested in said estate, of the pendency of said account, and the hearing thereof, by causing a copy of this order to be published in the Alcona County Review, a newspaper

printed and circulating in said county three successive weeks previous to said day of hearing.

C. H. KILLMASTER, Judge of Probate.

Alcona County Review, January 16, 1896

CURRAN.

Mrs. John Fullerton has had a tombstone erected over her late husband's grave.

Alcona County Review, May 26, 1898
Cemetery: Fullerton Family, Alcona Co.

Fullerton, Robert John

GUSTIN.

Curran, Sept. 13, '97.

We are sorry to announce that the messenger of death has come and taken Robert, the eldest son of Henry and Minnie Fullerton, after a very brief illness. He was taken sick Thursday evening between the hours of six and seven with a convulsive fit, out of which he rallied and appeared to be in a fair way to recovery until one o'clock in the morning, when he was taken again. At 3:30 he passed peacefully away. Robert was two years and eleven months old, died on the morning of the 11th of Sept. The disease was so quick in its action that it rendered it impossible to reach medical aid. The funeral took place Saturday afternoon, Rev. R. T. Ferrington of Fariview officiating. Interment at the family cemetery in Mitchell.

Alcona County Review, September 16, 1897

GUSTIN.

We hereby tender our heartfelt thanks to one and all of our neighbors whose aid and sympathy were so acceptable in the sickness, death and burial of our beloved son, especially Mr. and Mrs. Samuel McCormick, also Mason Mooney.

Henry J. Fullerton.

Alcona County Review, September 16, 1897
Cemetery: Fullerton Family, Alcona Co.

Fulton, George

A TERRIBLE ACCIDENT.

Seven Men Buried Alive Beneath a Mass of Brick.

THE FRIGHTFUL OCCURRENCE AT AU SABLE.

On Monday afternoon the citizens of AuSable and Oscoda were suddenly thrown into a state of excitement and terror, by the announcement of a horrible accident which had occurred at Gram's mill burner, by which five persons lost their lives, seven in all being victims to the terrible calamity. The particulars of the sad occurrence we glean from the Saturday Night extra of Wednesday, as follows:

"There were seven men at work in the burner at Gram's mill. They were Joseph W. Biddle, Thomas Mitchell, George Fulton, John Hardwick, William Miner, George Santerneau, George Gordon. The men were engaged in taking down the brick wall of one of the refuse burners of Gram's mill. A scaffolding had been built inside the burner, and upon the scaffolding the men worked and upon it the brick was also laid as they were taken from the wall. The men began taking the wall down from the top. They had been working in the burner about a week and had the walls about half down. The brick from the part of the wall already taken down were of course lying on the platforms of the scaffolding above the heads of the workmen. While the men were engaged at work, continuing the tearing down of the wall—with about 20,000 brick, or from 40 to 50 ton's weight, above them, the scaffolding gave way, and in an instant the seven men were buried beneath this immense amount of brick and the lumber and timber of which the scaffolding was made. The alarm was given by Michael Gerrard, who was working but a few feet from the burner. Before an hour had passed there were from 1000 to 1500 men collected at the scene of the accident. The task of uncovering the men was begun as soon as possible after the accident occurred, but under the circumstances it was a very slow job. The bricks, and lumber composing the scaffolding, had all to be thrown out through two small openings—two feet by two and one half—and of course only a small number of them could work at a time. The scaffolding fell about half past four o'clock. At half past seven the first body was reached and taken out. It proved to be that of Joseph Biddle. A short time after young Gordon was taken out alive and seemingly not fatally injured, though at this writing his recovery is doubtful. A few minutes later Fulton and Santerneau were taken out, the former alive and

the latter dead. Then the bodies of Mitchell, Miner, and Hardwick were taken out in the order named, it being about nine o'clock, or four and one-half hours after the accident, when the last body was removed. When the scaffolding fell some of the scantlings happened to wedge in such a position that they kept the principal weight of the brick off from Gordon, and he was able to converse at intervals with the men who were removing the brick. The men could also hear groans from one of the other imprisoned victims—probably Fulton, he was the only other one taken out alive. Five of the victims—Biddle, Fulton, Miner, Santerneau and Hardwick—were married men with families. Mr. Hardwick, familiarly called "Happy Jack," leaves a wife and six children, the oldest a daughter of seventeen. Mr. Biddle leaves a wife and two children, Mr. Miner the same. Mr. Fulton has a wife and three children, and Mr. Santerneau leaves a wife and baby.

Later.—Fulton died Wednesday evening.

Alcona County Review, April 17, 1885

LOCAL JOTTINGS.

Register of Deeds Jamison and Gene Taft spent Monday night at Au Sable, and brought to town early Tuesday morning the news of the killing of the 5 men at Au Sable.

Alcona County Review, April 17, 1885
Cemetery: Au Sable Township, Iosco Co.

Gagne, Zorilla

Mr. and Mrs. Jos. Gagnie's daughter, aged one year, died yesterday morning at the home of her parents at Black River. The remains were brought (to) this city on the noon train to-day for interment in the Catholic cemetery.—Tuesday's Echo.

Alcona County Review, August 6, 1891
Cemetery: Holy Cross, Alpena Co.

Gallagher, Hattie

WEST HARRISVILLE.

July 21, 1896.

On the second of July the little daughter of Mr. and Mrs. James Gallagher was taken from their midst by the messenger of death and was interred in the cemetery west of Harrisville on Sunday, July 5th.

This was a sad blow to the family, as little Hattie was the child of their

old age, the idolized pet of the entire family. She was two years and six months old when called from earth to heaven.

> Oh weep no more for Hattie,
> From sorrowing now refrain;
> The cause of our affliction
> Brings her eternal gain.

The family have the sincere sympathy of the community and some few days after the remains were interred several of the neighbors gathered one day and cut Mr. Gallagher's hay and later others raked and hauled in the crop.

Alcona County Review, July 23, 1896
Cemetery: West Lawn, Alcona Co.

Gallagher, James William

West Harrisville, July 26.

William Gallagher, aged 23 years, died at his home last Friday after several weeks' illness with consumption. The heartfelt sympathy of all in this vicinity goes out to the parents and relatives in this their sad bereavement.

The remains were buried Saturday in the cemetery west of Harrisville.

Alcona County Review, July 28, 1892

HISTORY OF ONE YEAR.

Chronological History of the Past Year, 1892.

THE DEATH RECORD.

July 22. Wm. Gallagher, W. Harrisville.

Alcona County Review, January 5, 1893
Cemetery: West Lawn, Alcona Co.

Gannon, Mrs.

PERSONAL MENTION.

The remains of Mrs. Gannon, of Ewen, upper peninsula, were brought to Harrisville last week by her husband for interment. Deceased was a cousin of Mrs. P. Corcoran.

Alcona County Review, December 14, 1893
Cemetery:

Gardiner, Daniel D.

DEATH'S HARVEST.

Mrs. Geo. W. Colwell received the sad and startling intelligence Monday morning by telegraph that her father, D. D. Gardiner, of Angelica, N. Y., had passed to the other side the day before. Mrs. Colwell left Tuesday morning for Angelica.

The deceased was well known to many of our citizens, having been a frequent visitor here, his last visit having been only last summer. He had been treasurer of the county in which he lived for upwards of 39 years, and was held in the highest esteem by his fellow citizens, as his exceptionally long and unbroken public service will bear witness.

Alcona County Review, March 2, 1893

A Tribute to a Good Man.

The following tribute from Every Week, published at Angelica, N. Y., to the memory of the late D. D. Gardiner, father of Mrs. Geo. W. Colwell of Harrisville, so emphatically impresses the truth of the proverb, "a good name is better than great riches," that we reprint it for the benefit of our readers. They can not fail to profit by it whether they knew the subject of the sketch or not.

Died—In Angelica, February 26, 1893, Daniel D. Gardiner, aged 60 years.

It is with a feeling of personal loss that we record the death of our honored friend, Daniel D. Gardiner, who passed from his long labors to that longer rest of the Great Unknown on Sunday afternoon, Feb. 26, 1893.

Beyond the Vale no tender thoughts can reach him, but he knew of the esteem in which he was held, for his fellow citizens have placed implicit confidence in him, as they have testified by their constantly returning him to a most responsible post of duty, which has been most faithfully and efficiently performed.

Daniel D. Gardiner was born in Eaton, Madison County, N. Y., March 2, 1823. He came to Angelica when he was eleven years of age, and entered the merchantile business, where he remained until he was elected County Treasurer in 1854. In 1848 he was married to Miss Julia Porter, who with two children, Mrs. Colwell, who lives in Michigan, and Harry Gardiner, of Buffalo, survives him.

Mr. Gardiner was elected Treasurer of Allegany county in 1854, which office he has faithfully held for thirty-eight years and two months. His public record has been one of credit and honor to the county; it stands almost without parallel for uprightness and accuracy. He has honored his office, his constituents, his town and himself with an honor that will never die.

The Allegany County Republican adds the following tribute to the rectitude of his actions as a public servant in the following language.

During this long period of 38 years Treasurer Gardiner handled a very large total of public money— estimated at about $7,000,000.00.—and not one dollar, nor one dime, nor one penny of this very large sum of public money, in all these years, has been lost or stolen.

Formerly this officer was paid by allowing a certain per cent, upon all monies handled—not to exceed, however, $500 a year. But during the war period the Board of Supervisors (who have charge of the matter) changed the compensation to $1000 a year, which has since remained the salary. One less familiar with the duties of this office, and less methodical and studious in attention to business, would be compelled to employ an assistant, at least during the busiest part of the year.

It is a very important trust—the entire charge of the public monies of a county; and this is one reason why Treasurer Gardiner had been so long retained in this office. The people feeling that in all respects he served them as no other man could possibly excel, they settled down in the determination to continue him as their public servant in this office so long as his physical and mental powers remained.

He was subjected to perhaps the severest strain of his life six years ago. We refer to the absconding to Canada of Cashier Robinson and collapse of the Bank—an institution of which he was a Director and in which he had on deposit when the doors closed, about $15,000 of the public funds.

But conscious of his own integrity and possessing physical vigor beyond that of his companions who fell, he survived the storm. Abundant offers of money, from neighboring Bankers were made to him; but it so happened he was in no present need of the $15,000 of public funds on deposit in the broken Bank—which money was in time all recovered by him from the Receiver.

And when November of that most trying year came, he met with the Board of Supervisors in annual settlement, as for thirty years—and his books, as ever, balanced to a penny.

Alcona County Review, March 9, 1893

PERSONAL MENTION.

Geo. W. Colwell has gone to Angelica, N. Y., where his time will be taken up for a few days in discharging the duties of executor of the estate of his father-in-law, the late D. D. Gardiner, acting in that capacity jointly with Mrs. Gardiner. In addition to closing up his private estate they will have to effect a settlement with the county treasurer who succeeds Mr. Gardiner. Mr. Colwell's familiarity with the duties of that office and his expertness will make the task an easy one for him.

Alcona County Review, April 6, 1893
Cemetery: Until the Day Dawn, Allegany Co., NY

Gardner, Mrs. Annie

LIKE A ROMANCE.

A Distracted Mother's Long Search For Her Children.

AN INHUMAN FATHER

The Sudden Death of the Mother Ends a Pitiable Story of Wrong.

Last Friday morning Mrs. Annie Gardner did not respond as usual to the call for breakfast. In the silent watches of the night the final summons from her Maker had come, and the poor broken soul was released from its tenement of clay. A jury was impaneled by Justice Beede and an inquest was held on the remains. It was the jury's solemn opinion that the death of the deceased was a "visitation of God" through natural causes. So the book of her life was closed. Not a word about the long weary years of patient suffering. An examination of her effects disclosed how much the fond mother and heartbroken wife had dwelt with loving tenderness and vain regret on a past that would rival in sadness and tender pathos the simple devotion of Evangeline, which Longfellow has immortalized by weaving the story in the measured and stately verse of his beautiful poem. Her trunk was carefully packed as if its owner were about to go on a journey. There were all kinds of articles of feminine attire which had apparently not been used for years. Small articles of children's attire and little trinkets which delight the baby heart; all so carefully and tenderly packed away. She had no other effects. Everything showed that this poor woman's life was wrapped up in sad memories of the past.

For a number of years Mrs. Gardner found a home in Harrisville. She endeavored apparently to smooth the pathway of those with whom she came in contact, and to so live that when the final summons came she would hear her Maker say, "Well done good and faithful servant enter thou into the joy of thy Lord." She has found a home for a few years past in the family of Jas. Morris, all of whom speak in the highest terms of her character and daily life. Her story is a sad one. It reads like a chapter from a romance. She would have been 46 years of age in May, but the bowed form and whitened locks gave her the appearance of greater age. The following from the Ottawa Daily Citizen, a copy of which, dated March 3, 1883, was found in her trunk, tells the story of her life. The Greenbush and Limerick mentioned are in Alcona county, which gives the story a more than ordinary local interest.

————

Some nine years ago a man named William Gardner, at that time residing in the township of Clarence in the county of Russell, married a woman some years his senior. Gardner was a farmer, working for his father, who owned a large farm in the township named. His parents more especially his father, were much averse to his marriage, but notwithstanding, for some years he and his wife, a most estimable woman, lived very happily together.

Two children were born to them, a girl and a boy, and for a time all went well, the elder Gardner seeming to become reconciled to his daughter-in-law. The reconciliation however was but superficial, the old animosity lying underneath and only awaiting a favorable opportunity to burst out anew.

The Gardners (the younger) lived in a small cottage in the bush, at some distance from their nearest neighbors. William used to leave his home early in the morning for his father's farm and not return until late in the evening. In the summer of 1881, he began to absent himself at night also, sleeping at his father's house, where it is needless to say, every argument that could be addressed, was brought to bear upon him to excite a quarrel between him and his wife. The father succeeded only too well. On the night of the 16th of July, 1881, about ten o'clock in the evening, as Mrs. Wm. Gardner was sitting in her lonely cottage occupied in some housewifely cares, the children (the girl then aged six, the boy five), sleeping quietly in the adjoining room, a knock was heard at the door. On Mrs. Gardner opening it her husband entered, and without saying a word to her passed into the further room and awoke the children, ordering them to get up and put on their clothes. Half frantic, the mother threw herself before them, but in vain. The father still persisted in his inhuman purpose, and refused to answer her agonizing appeal. Suddenly a thought struck the mother. She rushed out and searched the back yard where, cowering behind a shed door, she found her father-in-law. She at once accused him of inciting her husband to take away her children, and the cowardly fellow had no reply to make. He followed her into the house and sat down without speaking. Meanwhile the younger man had got the children dressed, and the well matched pair, father and son, carried them off, leaving the poor mother fainting on the floor. In the morning the distracted woman ran to the house of the father-in-law, but found no trace of her recreant husband and children. From information gleaned in the neighborhood, however, she learned that he had probably taken them to some place in the neighbourhood of the Gatineau. She then came to Ottawa and sought advice from an eminent lawyer, who, however, could do but little to help her. Acting on his advice, she went to the Gatineau, and for days traveled over the entire district searching for news of the lost babes. At last she heard incidentally that the man was in Michigan, at the place of an uncle of his, and the children, presumably, were with him. After many difficulties the heroic woman reached Limerick, Michigan, the place where he was supposed to

be, and found that he had learned of her indefatigable pursuit, and had left for the Black Hills.

Nothing daunted, she set forth for the Hills, only to find that the object of her search had gone. Through a cousin of her husband's (a woman too) she was informed that he had gone further into the Hills, but, as she heard afterwards, this was a deliberate lie, told to put her off the track. By the merest accident she met a woman who kept a hotel at Greenbush Dock, who told her that the man with the children had started a few days previously for Bay City. This charitable woman told a pitiful story of the condition in which the wretched children were. They barely clothed, and both thin and weak from exposure and insufficient food. She said that the father did not appear to take the least interest in them, and had she not had compassion on their misery, they must have died on the voyage in the boat. Spurred to greater exertion, if possible, by this recital, the mother pushed on to Bay City, only to lose the thread, no further trace being found of husband and lost children. Heartbroken she returned to Clarance, having almost lost hope of ever again in this life seeing her beloved babes.

Last November a rumor reached her that her husband had been heard of working in Potsdam, N. Y. Faint as was the hope held out, it was enough to carry the deserted mother thither, and there a tale was told her sad enough to move the most strong heart.

It appears that in the month of September, 1881, Gardner went to the house of a farmer in Potsdam and asked for work. Work was plentiful then, and he was engaged. He represented himself as, or at least did not deny that he was, a single man. Nothing was said about his children until in November, 1882, he said he was going to leave Potsdam for a week or two. From Potsdam he went to Bay City, to obtain possession of his children, and bring them back to Potsdam with him. On the 26th November he returned, not alone. With him was his little girl, apparently in the last stage of consumption, and the corpse of his boy, who had died of diphtheria.

Leaving the little shell at the depot and carrying the emaciated form of the girl, he arrived at his master's house. Although amazed at learning that her labourer was a married man, his mistress' motherly heart warmed to the poor sickly child, and every care was taken of it. On hearing of the dead child at the depot she persuaded her husband to get a permit for its burial, and the child's body was laid, not in the cemetery, but in the corner of a field.

The heartless father told his employer he was a widower, but on close cross-examination, he admitted that his wife was alive, but that he had been forced to take away his children on account of her continual ill usage of them.

Twelve days after her arrival the little girl followed her brother. The doctor said the actual cause of her death was diphtheria, but that had she not had that disease she must have succumbed to the severe inflammation of the lungs from which she was suffering, and which was brought on by exposure and neglect. Her body was laid beside her brother's in the same unconsecrated ground.

All these particulars were told to the heart-stricken mother on her arrival at Potsdam by the kind-hearted woman who had befriended her child. She spoke in the highest terms of the sweet, loving disposition of the little girl, and sympathetic tears rolled down her cheeks as she told the sad, sad story of her death. Mrs. Gardner at once had the two coffins disinterred and laid in hallowed ground at Potsdam, and the little cemetery plot is tended carefully by the children of the farmer, whose name it is not necessary here to mention.

The villainous father left immediately after the death of his daughter and returned to Canada, and is supposed to have settled somewhere near Toronto.

Mrs. Gardner has recently been in the city, having only just returned from Potsdam, where she learned the particulars of the melancholy end of her unfortunate children.

The sympathy of the whole community will be extended to the noble, true-hearted long suffering woman, who braved so much for the sake of her helpless little ones. She has now returned to her bereaved home much shaken in health, and her only desire is to soon rejoin her murdered (for murdered they were) children.

Alcona County Review, April 12, 1889
Cemetery:

Garland, Edward
Horrible Death on the Rail.

Sunday morning as the night log train, engine No. 13, was on its way with a load to Black River, an object was noticed by engineer Shorter lying across the track at a point about midway between Nevins' hotel and the "Exchange." The whistle was blown, but the object did not stir. The heavily loaded train had such momentum that it was impossible to stop and the entire train consisting of an engine and eighteen cars passed over what proved to be the body of Edward Garland, a woodsman who was employed at Pyne & Boney's camp in Mud Lake country. The body was horribly mangled, the head being crushed beyond all semblance to that of a human being, the right leg being cut off below the knee and also the left arm at the elbow. The entire body was crushed and mangled in a frightful manner. The remains were gathered up and taken to the Nevins House and Justice Brahaney, of Black River, summoned to hold an inquest. The latter, upon his arrival and investigation of the facts, did not deem an inquest advisable. No blame attaches to the railroad company. Garland was undoubtedly stupefied from the effects of liquor and his tragical death can be attributed to nothing else than this. The remains were taken to Black River and from thence to Alcona where they were interred Sunday afternoon, the dead man having no friends here to claim his remains. Garland was about thirty years of age, unmarried, and hailed from Canada.

Alcona County Review, August 5, 1887
Cemetery: Mt. Joy, Alcona Co.

Gaulait, Theodore
'ROUND ABOUT.

Theodore Gouleit, an Oscoda veteran, was run over at Detroit by a street car. His leg had to be amputated but he did not survive the shock.

Alcona County Review, August 13, 1891
Cemetery:

Gauthier, Joseph
NEIGHBORHOOD NOTES.

Joseph Gauthier, a resident of Tawas City, was run into by the passenger train one day last week while attempting to cross the track. Resulted fatally to both man and his horse. Railroad company exonerated from blame.

Alcona County Review, January 11, 1889
Cemetery: Probably St. Joseph, Iosco Co.

Gaymer, Anna [Fisher]
PERSONAL POINTS.

Mrs. Gamer, mother of Mrs. Wm. D. Mitchell and known to the older inhabitants of Harrisville, died last Thursday at Cadillac, Mich. Mrs. Mitchell was unable to attend the funeral owing to the illness of her son, John.

Alcona County Review, February 16, 1899
Cemetery: Maple Hill, Wexford Co.

Genge, Eliza [Brady]
COUNTY JOTTINGS.

Just as we go to press we learn of the death of Mrs. Eliza Genge, wife of Nathaniel Genge, deceased. Funeral services will be held from the M. E. Church to-morrow (Saturday) afternoon.

Alcona County Review, October 18, 1878
Cemetery:

Genge, Herbert
LOCAL JOTTINGS.

Mr. and Mrs. John Genge lost their 15 months' old child yesterday morning.

Alcona County Review, January 23, 1885
Cemetery: Springport, Alcona Co.

Genge, Nathaniel
Probate Notice.
State of Michigan--County of Alcona--ss.

At a session of the Probate Court for said county, held at the Probate office in Harrisville on the 25th day of September, 1879. Present, R. Z. Roberts, Judge of Probate.

In the matter of the estate of Nathaniel Genge, deceased.

An instrument purporting to be the last will and testament of said deceased having been deposited in the said Court. Thereupon it is ordered, That Monday, the 20th day of October next, at ten o'clock in the forenoon, be assigned for the proving of said will, and that all persons concerned or interested in said estate, are required to appear at the Probate office to attend the session of the Probate Court then and there to be holden, to show cause, if any there be, why probate of said will should not be granted. And it is also ordered that notice of said hearing by given to persons interested in said estate, by the publication of a copy of this order in the Alcona County Review--a paper printed and circulating in said county of Alcona--three successive weeks previous to said day of hearing.

R. Z. Roberts, Judge of Probate.

Alcona County Review, September 23, 1879
Cemetery:

Genge, Mrs. Nettie Elizabeth

West Harrisville.

West Harrisville, Aug. 16.--Mrs. Nelson Genge died at the residence of her mother in this village last Monday evening.

Alcona County Review, August 16, 1894
Cemetery: Probably Twin Lakes, Alcona Co.

Genge, Roy

Diphtheria Claims More Victims.

Geo. Genge of West Harrisville lost a little son Saturday, also from the same malady [diphtheria].

Alcona County Review, June 15, 1893

We wish to thank our many friends of West Harrisville for their friendly aid in our hour of sorrow, the death of our little boy.

Mr. and Mrs. G. Genge
and Family.

Alcona County Review, June 15, 1893
Cemetery: Probably Twin Lakes, Alcona Co.

Gibbs, Montgomery

A Strange Story.

MINNIE CLARKE ALLEN CONFESSES TO A MURDER.

Belief That She is the Victim of an Hallucination.

James Glode, who lives at Killmaster when he is at home, but who is sailing the lakes at present, sends the Review a 4 ½ column article clipped from the Buffalo Enquirer of May 20th, which recites the story of the strange life of a woman who claims relationship to many prominent citizens of Alcona county.

Just at present the woman is an inmate of the Wisconsin state prison at Waupun, where she is serving a two years term for burglary, which expires Jan. 18, 1897. During her confinement in prison she professed conversion under the influence and counsel of the prison chaplain and to that official she unburdened her mind of an alleged guilty secret, which was nothing less than the murder of a former lover and betrayer, Montgomery Gibbs by name, a Buffalo man, for whose murder two persons are now serving life sentences in the State prison at Auburn, N. Y. Strange to say these two persons also made confession of their guilt prior to their conviction.

After her confession the Buffalo chief of police went to Waupun, but she gave him no satisfactory information and her connection with the crime was dismissed as an hallucination of the woman's brain.

Her story, however, as told to the reporter, is full of romantic interest, and as some of the incidents are related as having taken place in this county, a local interest is imparted to it, and the Review will briefly summarize for its readers, some of whom will remember the unfortunate woman when, full of the freshness and beauty of young womanhood, she lived in Harrisville for a brief period with her husband, Richard Allen, who was subsequently killed in the lumber woods.

Her maiden name was Clarke. She was born in 1866 near Owen Sound, Ont. Her family subsequently moved to Nottawassoga, where she clandestinely made the acquaintance of Montgomery Gibbs, a dashing young fellow, who won the susceptible girl's heart at first sight.

Subsequent to this meeting with Gibbs, who temporarily dropped out of sight, the girl's family arranged that she should marry a man much her senior in years, but a man of means. She had a lover, however, with whom she eloped to avoid the marriage with the man who was the choice of her parents, which union was very distasteful to her.

The scene now shifts to Harrisville and Alcona county, where the family came to reside in the early 80's. On May 22, 1885, a son was born to her at Harrisville who received the name

of Garfield. But the course of true love did not run smoothly. Differences arose between husband and wife and just at this inopportune stage the man Gibbs once more crossed the pathway of her life. He had ascertained her whereabouts and wrote to her from Buffalo urging her to go to Cleveland where he had secured a position for her. She went and there met Gibbs, whose influence over her from that time was supreme. He provided her with money and she traveled to San Francisco and other parts of the country.

Gibb's liaison with the woman was looked upon by him as a mere past-time. Her husband was dead, but Gibbs refused to marry her. Her love finally turned to hate and for a long time she meditated his murder, but no opportunity presented itself until in April, 1894, she went to Buffalo, met Gibbs, made an appointment with him and on Saturday evening April 28, 1894, she shot him dead with his own revolver which he handed to her at her request to see it. She was never suspected of any connection with the crime.

This is the substance of the confession. The authorities are not inclined to treat it seriously as they have secured the conviction on strong evidence and their own admission of two persons for the Gibbs murder, and they treat this confession as the vagary of a diseased mind.

Three brothers, a sister, and the mother of this unhappy woman now live in this county, not many miles from West Harrisville. They are among our most highly respected citizens. Their names are given in the Enquirer's long article, but the Review withholds them out of consideration for their feelings.

Alcona County Review, May 28, 1896
Cemetery: Forest Lawn, Erie Co., NY

Gillam, Bruce Rupert

The Local News

Died, Tuesday, May 24, Bruce Rupert Gillam, infant son of Mr. and Mrs. Geo. E. Gillam.

Alcona County Review, May 26, 1892
Cemetery: Springport, Alcona Co.

Gillam, Florence Luella

LOCAL PICK UPS.

Florence, the little daughter of Repr. and Mrs. Geo. E. Gillam has been seriously ill for two weeks from gastritis and nervous prostration.

Alcona County Review, May 25, 1899

LOCAL PICK UPS.

Florence Luella, daughter of Representative and Mrs. Geo. E. Gillam died in the city hospital at Lansing Thursday afternoon last week after two weeks of intense suffering from spinal meningitis. Her sickness was not considered serious at first either by the parents or the attending physician but as the fatal disease progressed her condition became so alarming that it was thought best to remove her to the city hospital where the little sufferer could have the benefit of the tenderest care from skilled nurses. She was not conscious during the last four days of her little life. The remains were interred Saturday at Lansing in Mt. Hope cemetery. Lansing friends and the associate members of Mr. Gillam were very kind. Their sympathies were genuine and their floral gifts were many and beautiful. Florence was three years six months and twenty three days old.

Alcona County Review, June 1, 1899

The following resolutions were adopted by the House of Representatives upon the death of Repr. Gillam's little daughter:

Whereas, The House has learned with profound regret of the death of Florence, the little daughter of our esteemed Speaker pro tem, Representative Gillam, therefore be it

Resolved, That this House tenders to our honored associate and his stricken family our deepest sympathy in this their dark hour of grief and commend them to the Giver of every good and perfect gift for consolation and health,

Resolved that a copy of these resolutions be spread upon the Journal and a copy thereof be presented to the family of our afflicted brother,

Resolved, That as a further mark of respect for our bereaved associate, the House do now adjourn,

Which was unanimously adopted.

Alcona County Review, June 1, 1899
Cemetery: Mt. Hope, Ingham Co.

Gillis, Donald

Murder at Onoway.

Dan Gillis of Cheboygan was murdered near Onoway last Saturday evening. The man was shot from ambush. The murderer has not yet been apprehended, though the officers think they know the man.

Alcona County Review, May 4, 1899
Cemetery: Forest Lawn, Cheboygan Co.

Gilpin, Norman

EVENTS OF ONE WEEK.

Norman Gilpin, the 12 year old son of Mr. and Mrs. W. H. Gilpin, died on the afternoon of Thursday, April 9th, inst., from diabetes from which the boy had been a constant sufferer for the past two years. The funeral services were held Sunday afternoon at the Fisher school house. Public sympathy and respect for the bereaved family manifesting itself in a very large attendance. Rev. W. W. Will conducted the service. The interment was made in the west cemetery.

Alcona County Review, April 16, 1896
Cemetery: West Lawn, Alcona Co.

Glendennie, John

An old man named John Glendennie, died Tuesday at Mikado, aged about 80 years. Funeral to-day.

Alcona County Review, December 1, 1892

HISTORY OF ONE YEAR.

Chronological History of the Past Year, 1892.

THE DEATH RECORD.

Nov. 29. John Glendennie, Mikado.

Alcona County Review, January 5, 1893
Cemetery:

Glennie, John W.

TERRIBLE STORM!

Wreck of the Chriss Grover. Jno. W. Glennie Killed While Trying to Rescue Her Crew.

The latter part of last week we experienced one of the most severe storms that has visited this shore in a number of years. Thursday afternoon the schooner Chriss Grover was first struck by the storm while off South Point, near Thunder Bay. She was driven helpless before the wind until 9 o'clock that night, when she was cast ashore about a mile below Au Sable. Friday morning three of her crew succeeded in coming ashore in the yawl, but went back on board again shortly afterward. At ten o'clock a.m. the wind increased in violence and the waves began to wash over the doomed vessel. The crew, having failed to come on shore while the opportunity presented, were now in great peril, their yawl having been washed away by the sea. The Grover was driven within 40 rods of the shore, in 5 or 6 feet of water. A crowd soon gathered on the beach and means were devised as to how the crew might be rescued. The telegraph wires were down, and no dispatches could be sent. At noon teams were sent to the Tawas life-saving station, twelve miles distant, after the life-boat and crew. It was then thought that the rescue might be effected by firing a line out to the vessel, and a small cannon (weighing about 100 pounds) belonging to Geo. Loud, was procured and heavily loaded. An iron bar, to which a rope was attached, was placed in the muzzle, and after several unsuccessful attempts the gun was fired by Mr. Glennie. A terrible explosion followed, and when the smoke had cleared away the fact was revealed that the gun had burst, and that Mr. Glennie, Geo. Loud, Jno. C. Gram and Frank Fortier were knocked down, and for the time supposed to be killed. Fortier was not hurt; Geo. Loud and Mr. Gram were but slightly injured. Mr. Glennie presented a horrible appearance. His right arm was terribly mutilated, and his right leg broken in half a dozen places. He was conveyed to the home of his sister, Mrs. Geo. H. Keating, and Drs. Bredin, Wier and Sutherland summoned, who pronounced amputation of the leg and arm absolutely necessary. But before the operation was commenced, in less than two hours after the accident, John W. Glennie had breathed his last. At the time of the accident both Mrs. Glennie and her daughter Lizzie were away from home—the former visiting the latter, a pupil in the state normal school. Dispatches were immediately carried to Standish and forwarded to them.

At 12 o'clock Friday night the boat and crew of the life-saving station arrived on the scene. The boat was launched and in less than half an hour the entire crew (six men and one woman) was landed safely on shore. The Grover is said to be a total wreck. She was built at Black River in June, 1878, by W. A. Jones, who then owned her, and in 1879 rated A2. Her insurance value in 1879 was $7,000, but as vessel property has greatly advanced, she could not probably be replaced for less than $10,000 or $12,000.

Mrs. Glennie and daughter arrived in Bay City at 5 o'clock Sunday morning. The tug Music was secured and shortly after noon they started for Au Sable. When off Pinconning they were met by the tug Balize, which had been sent to meet them at Bay City. They were transferred to the Balize, which started back to Au Sable.

A meeting of the citizens of Au Sable was held on Saturday, the 17th, for the purpose of passing resolutions and expressing the keen sorrow and loss of the community in the death of their most public spirited and highly esteemed citizen. The funeral of the deceased took place Tuesday afternoon. At the time of his death, Mr. Glennie was custom collector of that port, village treasurer and an extensive dealer in lumber and pine lands. He was one of the leading citizens of Au Sable and one of the most enterprising business men on the shore. His loss is keenly felt by the entire community in which he lived.

The schooner H. D. Root and barge Athenian, at Oscoda, were both scuttled by their captains to prevent their pounding to pieces on the bottom.

Alcona County Review, April 23, 1880

Along the Shore

General News-Gleanings From the Several Counties.

Mrs. Glennie has been appointed administratrix of the estate of her late husband, Jno. W. Glennie, at Au Sable.

Alcona County Review, June 4, 1880

JOTTINGS ALONG THE SHORE.

"To-day is the anniversary of the sad accident whereby Mr. J. W. Glennie lost his life in a noble effort to save others. The citizens of Au Sable will not soon forget April 16, 1880."--News.

Alcona County Review, April 22, 1881
Cemetery: Pinecrest, Iosco Co.

Glosienke, Alexander

LOCAL SAYINGS AND DOINGS.

Alexander Glosienke, steward of the barge H. W. Weeks, belonging to J. E. Potts' line, fell overboard at the mouth of the Au Sable river Sunday afternoon, and was drowned. No traces of the body have yet been discovered, although the river's mouth was thoroughly dragged, and it is thought the same has been carried out into the lake by the swift current. Sad affair.

Alcona County Review, May 19, 1882
Cemetery:

Goddard, Charles

LOCAL JOTTINGS.

Charles Goddard, a Mikado farmer, died at the home of his son in Au Sable last week Friday, aged 69 years. He was one of the pioneers of Oscoda. He leaves a wife and four children, two of whom are John and Abram Goddard, of Mikado.

Alcona County Review, March 8, 1889
Cemetery: Pinecrest, Iosco Co.

Godfrey, Alice S. [Bell]

LOCAL JOTTINGS.

The wife of Dr. V. F. Godfrey died at their home in Alpena last week Thursday after a short illness from inflammation of the bowels. She had been seriously ill before Dr. Godfrey made his last professional visit to Harrisville, but she was supposed to be out of danger at that time. The deceased was an estimable woman, and a devoted wife and mother. She left two sons.

Alcona County Review, August 24, 1888

LOCAL JOTTINGS.

Owing to the death and burial of his wife, Dr. Godfrey was unable to meet his engagements here this week, but hopes to be able to do so on the same day of next week.

Alcona County Review, August 24, 1888
Cemetery: Evergreen, Alpena Co.

Goldie, Georgeana M.

The Local News.

It is with regret that we note that death has entered the family of P. C. Goldie at Tawas and taken there from little Georgie, a bright, lovable child, after a brief illness of but 3 days from

diphtheria. Others of their children have been taken with the disease but they have had a happier termination.

Alcona County Review, November 3, 1892
Cemetery:

Golling, Agnes

Alpena Items.
Mr. Charles Golling has been greatly afflicted by the loss of two of his children within one week's time by the membranous croup. A little girl and a little boy swiftly took their departure leaving the household desolate from their mournful absence.

Alcona County Review, November 22, 1878
Cemetery: Evergreen, Alpena Co.

Golling, Jacob

Alpena Items.
Mr. Charles Golling has been greatly afflicted by the loss of two of his children within one week's time by the membranous croup. A little girl and a little boy swiftly took their departure leaving the household desolate from their mournful absence.

Alcona County Review, November 22, 1878
Cemetery: Evergreen, Alpena

Gonyea, {Male}

Probably Found a Watery Grave.
Three weeks or more ago the trader C. R. Truax in charge of Captain Peter Cassidy and a boy named Gonyou, whose home is in Alpena, left Sand Beach bound for Oscoda with a cargo of apples and potatoes. When she left Sand Beach a stiff gale was blowing off land and the boat was undoubtedly driven out of her course. As no tidings have yet been received of either boat or crew they must have perished on Saginaw Bay. A passing boat reports seeing a lot of floating apples off Southampton, Ont. Cassidy's home was in Oscoda where he has a wife and five children. He had $1000 insurance in the Foresters which his family will get when proofs of his death are forthcoming.

Alcona County Review, November 26, 1891
Cemetery:

Gonyea, Jerry Albertis

HAYNES HAPPENINGS.
Mr. and Mrs. Alex Gonue also lost a child about that date [the 4th], aged about 3 weeks, from la grippe. Interment in Harrisville.

Alcona County Review, February 9, 1899
Cemetery: Probably St. Anne's, Alcona Co.

Good, William Darius

Gustin Grist.

August 27, 1895.

A small child of Joseph Good died Sunday and was buried yesterday. The services were conducted by Rev. Van Horn. The child died with cholera infantum.

Alcona County Review, August 29, 1895
Cemetery: Springport, Alcona Co.

Goodell, Alfred

Death of Alfred Goodell.

Alfred Goodell died at his residence in this place Monday evening at the ripe old age of 85. He was born Nov. 7, 1802, at a little hamlet in Onondagua county, N. Y., where he lived with his parents until he was 20 years of age, when he started on a tour through the southern states. Going back to his native state after the lapse of several years, he married a Miss Griswold, at Watertown, in 1828. Four years after this event he came to Michigan, settling at a point near Memphis, where he followed his business, of millwright. He accumulated considerable property, bought land and was one of the leading men in that section. Indeed, Goodell station, nine miles from Memphis, bears his name. Here he lived until 1868, honored and respected by his neighbors. His first wife dying, he married Miss Mary Boynton, in the year 1867, and the following year came to Tawas and built a mill on the upper West Branch. This proved a disastrous investment, and through unfortunate business complications Mr. Goodell lost his property. His health gave out about the same time. In 1872 he moved to Tawas City where he lived until 1880 when he came to Harrisville. He died from old age. Nine months ago he lost his mind and since Christmas he has slept only five nights, his passion being to work to retrieve his broken fortunes. The deceased during his business career was noted for his sterling integrity and honesty and his word was considered as good as his bond. He had no children by his first wife, but his second wife and a son fifteen years of age survive him.

Alcona County Review, May 27, 1887
Cemetery: West Lawn, Alcona Co.

Goodfellow, Agnes [Clelland]

Curtis Items.

July 4, 1895.

Mrs. Goodfellow was buried June 23. It was a largely attended funeral. The Rev. Sharp of McKinley preached the funeral sermon. His text was, "But a Step from Life unto Death," a very good sermon. Deceased became a Christian at the age of thirteen and was a member of the Presbyterian church and so lived and died. She was beloved by all her neighbors and friends. She has left a husband, four sons and four daughters to mourn the loss of so good a wife and mother.

Alcona County Review, July 11, 1895

STATE OF Michigan
County of Alcona

At a session of the Probate Court for said County, held at the Probate office in the Village of Harrisville on the third day of June, in the year one thousand nine hundred and one.

Present W. H. Gilpin, Judge of Probate. In the matter of the estate of Agnes Goodfellow, deceased. On reading and filing the petition duly verified of Peter Heilig, praying among other things that an administrator may be appointed and that administration of said estate may be granted to Peter Heilig or to some other suitable person.

Thereupon it is ordered, that Monday, the 1st day of July next, at ten o'clock in the forenoon at said Probate office, be assigned for the hearing of said petition.

And it is further ordered, that the petitioner give notice to the heirs at law and all persons interested in said estate by causing a copy of this order to be published in the Alcona County Review, a newspaper printed and circulated in said county three successive weeks previous to said day of hearing.

W. H. GILPIN,
Judge of Probate.

Alcona County Review, June 6, 1901
Cemetery: Curtisville, Alcona Co.

Goodwin, Myrtle

'ROUND ABOUT.

Willie Kane, aged 13, threw stones at little Myrtle Goodwin, ages 3 years, which struck the child on the head causing hemorrhage of the brain, from which the child died the same day. This happened at Au Sable last week, and a jury has held young Kane responsible for the killing. The only witnesses of the affair were very young children.

Alcona County Review, August 13, 1891
Cemetery: Probably Dale, Gladwin Co.

Gordon, Charlotte [Simons]

Curtis Items.

Death entered the home of Swayze Gordon and took from his side his beloved wife, leaving three children, two boys and one girl. Her funeral sermon was preached in the Curtis First Baptist church by a Methodist minister from McKinley. He preached a splendid sermon. He told when she first started in the Lord's service at the age of 16 and ever since she has endeavored to do her Master's will. She never failed to teach her children in the way they should go to gain eternal life. She was loved by all who knew her. "Neighbors and friends," the minister said, "we would as leave be in that sister's place as not, if the Lord was to come down and put his arms around us and take us up as he did the prophet in flesh and blood." He had great faith in the departed one. We trust that she is in a heaven of rest. The funeral took place Thursday, Feb. 7th, and she was buried on this side of the river. Thos. Phillips conducted the funeral with great credit. The pall bearers were Messrs. Peter Helig, John Bowser, Robert Goodfellow, Joseph Bell, E. M. Barker and J. W. Ferguson. Many relatives and friends and neighbors followed the remains to their last resting place. Great sympathy for husband and family is expressed.

Curtis, Feb. 11, 1895.

Alcona County Review, February 14, 1895
Cemetery: Curtisville, Alcona Co.

Goshman, Lewis

LOCAL JOTTINGS.

Lewis Goshman, employed at Black River by Alger, Smith & Co., was hit upon the head by a falling limb of a tree last Monday, from the affects of which he died Wednesday, his skull being fractured. He leaves a wife and one child. His home was at Brockway Center, whither his remains were taken for interment.

Alcona County Review, January 30, 1885
Cemetery: Probably Lakeside, St. Clair Co.

Gould, Lulu Jane

Card of Thanks.—To citizens of Alcona township we return our sincere thanks for your kindness to us in our sad bereavement, and especially to Mrs. Mark Morton, and Mrs. Mary McDonald for preparing the deceased for burial; also to Mrs. Donald McNeil, Mrs. Geo. Ritchie and Miss Sarah Ritchie for floral tributes, and may God in his infinite goodness spare you and your loved ones many years from a similar bereavement.

Mrs. Nettie and Nate Gould.

Alcona County Review, November 5, 1886
Cemetery: Mt. Joy, Alcona Co.

Gould, Mrs. Mary

PERSONAL MENTION.

Paul Bittner, aged 14, was killed at Rogers City last week by the accidental discharge of a gun. Mrs. Mary Gould, wife of a farmer living near Hillman, was mistaken for a bear by a fool hunter and was shot and instantly killed about the same time.

Alcona County Review, October 26, 1893
Cemetery:

Gould, Rilla Ann

HAYNES HAPPENINGS.

Miss Rilla Gould, aged 17 years, 11 months and 25 days, daughter of Nathan Gould, died November 25th from meningitis. She was interred in Mount Joy Cemetery on Sunday. Rev. W. W. Will preached an impressive funeral sermon. The remains were followed to their last resting place by a large and sympathetic concourse of friends.

Alcona County Review, December 1, 1898

Local History of One Year

Chronology of the Principal Events of the Year 1898.

November 24. Death of Retta Gould, aged 17 at Haynes.

Alcona County Review, January 5, 1899
Cemetery: Mt. Joy, Alcona Co.

Graham, William C.

Wm. C. Graham, aged 61 years, died at his home 3 miles south of the village of Greenbush, Thursday night, Feb. 4, from inflammation of the bowels.

Deceased had been ailing all winter but was able to be about and worked in the woods the day previous to his death. He had no relatives in this country. He was a carpenter by

trade and built David Nevin Sr.'s new house last year.

The funeral was held Sunday at Greenbush, W. D. Graham of Tawas City, a nephew of the deceased, being the only relative present.

Alcona County Review, February 11, 1897

I wish to express my sincere thanks and appreciation of the many kindnesses extended to my lamented uncle, the late W. C. Graham, during his illness and death, and myself, a perfect stranger, during my stay here, by D. Baucus, W. B. Chase, Alex. McDonald, and any others to whom thanks is due.

W. D. Graham.

Alcona County Review, February 11, 1897
Cemetery:

Gram, {Girl}

COUNTY JOTTINGS.

The infant daughter of Mr. and Mrs. John C. Gram died at Au Sable Monday night.

Alcona County Review, April 12, 1878
Cemetery: Probably Pinecrest, Iosco Co.

Grantham, Joseph H.

Greenbush.

The infant child of Mr. and Mrs. W. Grantham died on Tuesday last and was buried in the Springport cemetery. On account of the absence of Brother Smith of the church of the Latter Day Saints, Rev. Dunham officiated.

Alcona County Review, February 1, 1894

Paragraphs of Local Interest.

Mr. and Mrs. Wm. Grantham, of Greenbush, buried their 5 months' old child last week.

Alcona County Review, February 1, 1894
Cemetery: Springport, Alcona Co.

Graves, Amandus

A. R. Graves of Marblehead, Ohio called at the Review office Wednesday; he is in quest of information concerning a brother who was lost off the schooner, Our Son, in the gales last Thursday at a point about twenty miles east of Sturgeon Pointe.

Alcona County Review, June 7, 1889

$25 Reward For Body!

Last Thursday my brother, Amandus Graves, was lost overboard from the schooner Our Son at a point about twenty miles east of Sturgeon Pointe. I will give Twenty-five dollars

for information leading to the recovery of his body. He weighed about 150-lbs., had sandy hair and reddish mustache. His Union card will probably be found in his watch pocket.

A. R. Graves.
Address Care of Hugh McDonald.
East Tawas Mich.

Alcona County Review, June 7, 1889

E. R. Graves, of Marblehead, Ohio, requests us to say that he is still at E. Tawas searching for the body of his brother who was lost from the schooner "Our Son."

Alcona County Review, June 14, 1889

PURELY PERSONAL.

E. R. Graves, of Marblehead, O., who is still searching for the body of his brother, Amandus Graves, recently lost overboard from the schooner Our Son, was in the village Monday.

Alcona County Review, July 5, 1889
Cemetery:

Gray, John

Victim of the Flowing Bowl.

A man named John Gray met with a fatal accident on the Mud Lake branch last week. He was lying on the track in an intoxicated condition when he was run over by a logging train. His leg was so badly crushed that amputation was necessary but he died at the completion of the operation, which was conducted by Dr. Parr assisted by two Alpena surgeons. Gray had been employed in the woods for a number of years.

Alcona County Review, September 17, 1891
Cemetery:

Gray, John

PASSING OF JOHN GRAY.

John Gray, an old and respected pioneer settler of Alcona county, died at his home three miles from Harrisville, last Saturday night.

Mr. Gray had been suffering from grip for several weeks, at times being in a critical state, but had so far recovered that he was able to be down town several days prior to his death. He suffered a relapse and the end came so suddenly that the announcement of his death was a surprise to all.

Mr. Gray has been a resident of the county for upward of thirty years, the greater part of which time he has lived on the farm where he died. He is survived by a wife and two children, Mrs. Alex McLennan of

Haynes, and Wm. Gray of St. Marie's, Idaho.

The funeral occurred Wednesday afternoon from the Methodist church, Rev. W. W. Will officiating. A large procession followed the remains to their last resting place at the west cemetery.

Deceased was 78 years of age.

Alcona County Review, February 23, 1899

PERSONAL POINTS.

Mrs. Kirker of Toledo and W. E. Rogers of Alpena, children of Mrs. Gray, attended the funeral of the late John Gray.

Alcona County Review, February 23, 1899

Card of Thanks.

Mrs. John Gray and her children wish to thank their neighbors and friends for the kindness they showed in their sad bereavement, the loss of their beloved husband and father.

Mrs. Jno. Gray and Children.

Alcona County Review, March 2, 1899

The NEWS

Mrs. John Gray's name has been restored to the pension list and she will now receive $12 per month, widow's pension. She formerly received a pension as the widow of Mr. Rogers, but upon her marriage to Mr. Gray the pension was discontinued. Mr. Gray has since died. Under a late ruling of the pension department in cases of this kind she was entitled to again receive her pension and by the help of Attorney Beede her name was restored to the pension list.

Alcona County Review, June 5, 1902

The NEWS

When a man dies and the widow marries again and the second husband dies, is she the widow of the first husband, or of the second one, or of both? That is the conundrum recently before the pension authorities. The widow of a federal soldier was drawing a pension as such widow. She married again and the pension stopped. Then the second husband died and the widow made application for reinstatement as the widow of the first husband, and the claim was allowed. Consequently, under that ruling, a widow can never be a widow of any but her first husband.--Mt. Pleasant Enterprise.

Alcona County Review, December 4, 1902

STATE OF MICHIGAN
County of Alcona

At a session of the Probate Court for said County, held at the Probate Office in the village of Harrisville, on the 16th day of March in the year one thousand nine hundred and three.

Present, W. H. Gilpin, Judge of Probate. In the matter of the estate of John Grey, deceased.

On reading and filing the petition, duly verified, of Alma Grey, praying among other things that an administrator may be appointed over the above named estate and that she may be appointed as said administratrix.

Thereupon it is ordered, that Monday, the 13th day of April next, at ten o'clock in the forenoon, at said Probate Office, be assigned for the hearing of said petition.

And it is further ordered, that notice be given to the heirs at law and all persons interested by causing a copy of this Order to be published in the Alcona County Review, a newspaper printed and circulated in said County, three successive weeks previous to said day of hearing.

W. H. Gilpin,
Judge of Probate.

Alcona County Review, March 19, 1903

STATE OF MICHIGAN
County of Alcona

Probate Court for said County.

The undersigned having been appointed by the Judge of Probate of said County, Commissioners on Claims in the matter of said estate of John Grey, and six months from the 15th day of April A. D. 1903, having been allowed by said Judge of Probate to all persons holding claims against said estate, in which to present their claims to us for examination and adjustment:

Notice is hereby given, that we will meet on Monday, the 15th day of June, A. D. 1903, and on Thursday, the 15th day of October, A. D. 1903, at ten o'clock A. M. of each day, at the Probate office in the Village of Harrisville in said County, to receive and examine such claims.

Dated, April 14, A. D. 1903.
Chas. A. Mayo,
Robt. Southgate. Commissioners.

Alcona County Review, April 30, 1903

The NEWS

Mrs. John Grey had a monument erected on her husband's grave Memorial day.

Alcona County Review, June 4, 1903

The NEWS

Attorneys Cobb and Dafoe of Alpena were here Monday, representing clients at a hearing before the commissioners of claims in the John Gray estate.

Alcona County Review, December 31, 1903

STATE OF MICHIGAN
County of Alcona

At a session of Probate Court for said county held at the Probate office, in the Village of Harrisville on the 16th day of March, in the year one thousand nine hundred and four.

Present, Wm. H. Gilpin, Judge of Probate. In the matter of the Estate of John Grey, deceased.

On reading and filing the petition, duly verified, of Alma Grey, widow of said deceased, praying for an order allowing her such portion of the personal property as she is entitled to as widow of said deceased under the statues of this state and such same of money for her support and maintainence as she is entitled to during the settlement of the estate.

Thereupon it is ordered, that Monday, the 11th day of April next, at one o'clock in the afternoon, be assigned for the hearing of said petition, and that the heirs at law of said deceased, and all persons interested in said estate, are required to appear at a session of said Court, there to be holden in the Probate office, in the Village of Harrisville, and show cause, if any there be, why the prayer of the petitioner should not be granted. And it is further ordered, that said petitioner give notice to the heirs-at-law and the administrator and persons interested in said estate, of the pendency of said petition, and the hearing thereof, by serving the administrator and each of the heirs-at-law interested in said estate personally at least 14 days before the term herein fixed for the hearing of said petition with a citation or notice of said hearing.

W. H. Gilpin,
Judge of Probate.

Alcona County Review, March 17, 1904
Cemetery: West Lawn, Alcona Co.

Gray, {Male}

PERSONAL.

Mrs. John Gray went to Bay City this morning in response to a telegram, stating that her son was dying there.

Alcona County Review, July 1, 1897

Mrs. John Gray returned from Bay City after burying her son. He died the 4th after an illness of two and a half years. He suffered a great deal from rheumatism. He died in a Christian faith. He leaves a wife and two little daughters, a mother, three brothers and a sister. We mourn for him here but we know he has gone to the better land where no sickness or sorrow ever comes.

Alcona County Review, July 22, 1897
Cemetery:

Gray, Mrs. Mary

Mrs. John Gray the Victim of Apoplexy.

Mrs. Gray, the estimable wife of our worthy farmer citizen, John Gray, of Harrisville township, was stricken down by an apoplectic stroke while visiting the family of Frank Smith, of West Harrisville, last Sunday evening, dying immediately. Mrs. Gray went to W. Harrisville Sunday afternoon, intending to remain with Mr. Smith's family over night and take the train Monday morning for Au Sable to visit a sick daughter. Mrs. Gray, who was a very large woman, appeared to be in excellent spirits and the best of health. At the conclusion of the evening meal she started to walk into the sitting room, chatting gaily with members of the family. Suddenly, and without a moment's warning, she fell to the floor, gasped once and was dead.

Mrs. Gray was about 50 years of age. She leaves a husband and two children, a son and daughter by a former marriage. Her remains were taken to Au Sable Tuesday for burial.

Alcona County Review, December 21, 1888

Card of Thanks.—To those kind friends, and especially those at West Harrisville, who rendered such willing and valued aid and sympathy at the death of my beloved wife, I return my heartfelt thanks.
John Gray.

Alcona County Review, December 28, 1888
Cemetery: Pinecrest, Isoco Co.

Green, Elizabeth [Donahue]

EVENTS OF ONE WEEK.

Mrs. Ed Green of Black River is very ill.

Alcona County Review, July 19, 1894

EVENTS OF ONE WEEK.
For the third time in a few weeks death has entered the home of Edw. Green at Black River and taken from it a member of the little circle. At 2

o'clock on Monday morning, Sept. 3d. the beloved wife and mother received the summons which comes to all mortals freeing her spirit from its earthly home and a long period of illness and suffering was ended forever. Deceased was a victim of that relentless disease, consumption, and though the best medical skill was invoked to check its ravages, it long ago became apparent that any effort to stay the hand of death would be futile.

Deceased was 28 years of age and was a daughter of Thos. O'Donahoe of Harrisville. She was married in 1887 and four children were the fruit of this union, but one of whom is now living. The remains were brought to Harrisville yesterday morning for interment in the Catholic cemetery. A large number of sympathizing friends and sorrowing relatives followed them to their last resting places.

Alcona County Review, September 6, 1894

A sense of the obligation which I am under to the many warm hearted friends and neighbors at Black River, whose kindness, sympathy and help have been so freely offered, and so acceptable in my hour of need, impels me to publicly express my heartfelt thanks to them and a wish that they may be spared a similar sorrow.
Edw. Green.

Alcona County Review, September 6, 1894
Cemetery: St. Anne's, Alcona Co.

Green, Harry

EVENTS OF ONE WEEK.

Mrs. Ed. Green of Black River is very ill.

Mr. Green also has a very sick child whose life is hanging on a very slender thread.

Later—The child died this morning.

Alcona County Review, July 19, 1894

EVENTS OF ONE WEEK.

The 3-year-old child of Ed Green, of Black River, which died on the 29th, was buried in the Catholic cemetery of Harrisville last Friday.

Alcona County Review, July 26, 1894
Cemetery: St. Anne's, Alcona Co.

Green, {Male}

NEIGHBORHOOD NOTES.

Will Green, an East Tawas painter, has struck it rich. Had a rich "dad" who died and left him $10,000.

Alcona County Review, November 23, 1888
Cemetery:

Green, Myra

LOCAL JOTTINGS.

Mr. and Mrs. Ed Green are mourning the loss of an infant son, their only child.

Alcona County Review, July 12, 1889
Cemetery: St. Anne's, Alcona Co.

Green, William

PERSONAL MENTION.

Mr. and Mrs. Ed Green of Black River mourn the loss of an infant child aged about two months, which died Monday night at the home of Thos. Donahoe. They have the sympathy of the entire community.

Alcona County Review, August 30, 1894
Cemetery: St. Anne's, Alcona Co.

Green, Willie

DEATH'S SAD DOINGS.

Mr. and Mrs. Thos. Green mourn the loss of their baby boy Willie. The child was only ten months old. Its death occurred Monday afternoon.

Alcona County Review, August 30, 1889

PURELY PERSONAL.

Mr. and Mrs. Ed Green of Black River attended the funeral of his brother's baby Tuesday.

Alcona County Review, August 30, 1889
Cemetery: Springport, Alcona Co.

Greenfield, {Boy}

Haynes Happenings.

Wm. Greenfield of Hawse township buried an infant child in our cemetery lately.

Alcona County Review, July 12, 1892
Cemetery: Mt. Joy, Alcona Co.

Greenman, Charles

Under a Saw

Fatal Accident to a Black River Young Man.

Chas. Greenman, a young man 20 years old, was brought into town at noon today from Thompson's shingle mill near Long Lake, terribly injured.

A flying bolt hit him about 9 o'clock this morning and sent him under the circular saw. It cut deep into his right leg, so that amputation above the knee was necessary. The operation was performed by Drs. McKnight and Miller at the Union house this afternoon. Greenman's left arm was also cut by the saw.

The home of the young man is at Black River. His sister is employed in a laundry here. Word has been sent to his mother and she is expected on the evening train.—Alpena Echo.

The young man died the same evening. He was a son of J. Greenman of Black River, and had been gone from home but one week when the accident occurred. The burial took place at Alpena.

Alcona County Review, May 25, 1899
Cemetery: Evergreen, Alpena Co.

Gregory, Ramsey

Ramsey Gregory, a young man well known and highly respected in Bay City, was shot and killed by an unknown man whom Ramsey caught stealing harness.

Alcona County Review, March 5, 1886
Cemetery: Elm Lawn, Bay Co.

Grice, Joseph

Another Railroad Fatality.

The remains of Wm. Mercier were hardly buried ere another fatality has been added to the long list of those which have occurred on the logging railroads of Alcona county. Tuesday night as Conductor Joseph Grice was making up his train at McPhee's camp to run into Black River, he was thrown under the wheels and fatally injured. The remains were badly mutilated and death was almost instantaneous. Deceased leaves a wife and one child.

Alcona County Review, September 1, 1892

HISTORY OF ONE YEAR.

Chronological History of the Past Year, 1892.

August.

28. Joseph Grice, a conductor, run over and killed on railroad.

Alcona County Review, January 5, 1893
Cemetery:

Griswold, Freddie

REVIEWINGS.

Mr. and Mrs. Hosmer Griswold lost a four months old child Monday. Verily "the Lord giveth and the Lord

taketh away. Blessed be the name of the Lord."

Alcona County Review, May 2, 1879
Cemetery: Springport, Alcona Co.

Griswold, Harvey C.

Gone.

Again the Review is called upon to announce the death of another of the pioneer residents of Harrisville. This time it is the venerable Mr. H. C. Griswold, who died on Tuesday at the advanced age of nearly 70 years, after a lingering illness of several weeks, principally caused by general dropsy. Mr. Griswold's native home was in New York State, and at one time he was in very prosperous circumstances and had accumulated a considerable property, but like many others he met with misfortune and lost all, and his latter years found him struggling against poverty and other adverse circumstances. He was a man of more than usual intelligence, strictly honest, and commanded the respect of a majority of our citizens. He leaves a wife and seven children, four of whom were dependent upon him for support. He was buried yesterday afternoon, Rev. J. H. McIntosh officiating.

Alcona County Review, October 7, 1881
Cemetery: Probably Springport, Alcona Co.

Griswold, Hattie

REVIEWINGS.

Died, on Monday last, Hattie, youngest daughter of Francis H. and Jennie Griswold; aged 3 years, 3 months and 27 days. Verily the little one is safe, for Jesus has called her to himself. He loveth our little ones, and assures us that "of such is the kingdom of heaven."

Alcona County Review, October 17, 1879
Cemetery: Springport, Alcona Co.

Griswold, Jennie [Craven]

REVIEWINGS.

Died, in Harrisville, Nov. 12th, Jennie, wife of F. Hosmer Griswold; aged 24 years, 11 months and 24 days. The deceased had been a sufferer from consumption for a long period, and had been confined to her bed most of the time since last June. She gradually wasted away, until death came to her relief, and gently bore her spirit away. The grief-stricken husband has the sympathy of the community.

Alcona County Review, November 14, 1879

Cemetery: Springport, Alcona Co.

Groom, Willie

DEATH'S SAD DOINGS.

Mr. and Mrs. Thos. Groom mourn the loss of their baby boy Willie. The child was only ten months old. Its death occurred Monday afternoon.

Alcona County Review, August 30, 1889
Cemetery:

Gullickson, Thora M.

Among Our Exchanges.

From the Pioneer,

A terrible accident occurred in the northern part of the county on Friday last. The Gullickson family were driving home from this city, when the team ran away. Miss Flora Gullickson was thrown out and instantly killed, her neck being broken. She was a very estimable young lady.

Alcona County Review, June 2, 1892
Cemetery: Leer Lutheran, Alpena Co.

Gullifer, Eliphas

COUNTY NEWS JOTTINGS.

Mr. Eliphas Gullifer, one of the most extensive lumbermen in the Saginaws and a highly respected and very prominent citizen of East Saginaw, died on the morning of the 28th ult. of paralysis. The deceased was an only brother of Mr. Thomas Gullifer of Harrisville, and was sixty-one years old. He was a native of the State of Maine, and has been engaged in the lumber business since fourteen years of age.

Alcona County Review, October 5, 1877
Cemetery: Brady Hill, Saginaw Co.

Gullifer, Sarah [Nason]

Mrs. Thos. Gullifer has become quite feeble this winter. She has reached the advanced age of 75.

Alcona County Review, April 21, 1892

SOMEWHAT PERSONAL.

F. O. Gullifer, of Detroit, is in the village, the serious illness of his mother calling him here.

Alcona County Review, June 2, 1892

SOMEWHAT PERSONAL.

Mr. and Mrs. H. A. Gullifer, of Cleveland, Ohio, were called to Harrisville last week by the serious illness of the latter's mother.

Alcona County Review, June 2, 1892

OBITUARY.

Mrs. Sarah Gullifer, nee Nason, was born in Athens, Maine, August 4, 1815, and had she lived until the 4th of next August would have been 77 years old. She came from good old revolutionary stock, her grandfather Garcelon having served seven years in the continental army during the war of revolution. Mrs. Gullifer was one of a family of 14 children, of which she was the last survivor. Her father, Abram Nason, dying young the older children were obliged to go out into the world and battle for themselves. In January, 1834, she was married to the late Thomas Gullifer, with whom she lived until death separated them January 8, 1887, a period of 53 years. Six children, all of whom lived to reach man's estate, and five of whom survive their parents, were born to them: Mrs. Leander Boardman and Mrs. Leonard Higgins, of Minneapolis, Mrs. Henry Fox of this place, Henry A. Gullifer, of Cleveland, Freeman O. Gullifer, of Detroit, all of whom, except Mrs. Higgins, were at their mother's bedside to cheer and comfort her last hours.

Mrs. Gullifer joined the Methodist Episcopal church at the age of 19 and for 58 years lived the life of an earnest, consistent christian. Her love for her church and her bible was second only to her love for her family. Coming to Harrisville in 1871, where she has since resided, except when visiting her children, the history of our village has been her history, its joys her joys, and its sorrows her sorrows.

Strengthened by the knowledge of a life work well done, assured that when she had crossed the dark river she would be greeted with "Well done good and faithful servant," confident that the husband of her youth would be waiting to greet her on the other side, she was ready and anxious to go. Her last hours were free from pain and the final dissolution came like a gentle sleep to a tired soul. A good wife, a good mother, a good neighbor, and a good christian. She has gone to her reward.

Alcona County Review, June 2, 1892

A Card.
The children of the late Mrs. Thomas Gullifer take this method of returning their most sincere thanks to the people of Harrisville, not only for their kindness to them and their mother during her last illness, but for the uniform kindness and courtesy which has ever been extended to them all by this community. For 21 years this village has been the home of our mother and the gathering place of her children and we have always felt that we were welcome among you. We thank you one and all and trust that you may always meet with as good friends as you have been to us.

Alcona County Review, June 2, 1892

HISTORY OF ONE YEAR.

Chronological History of the Past Year, 1892.

THE DEATH RECORD.
May 31. Mrs. Sarah Gullifer, Harrisville.

Alcona County Review, January 5, 1893
Cemetery: West Lawn, Alcona Co.

Gullifer, Thomas
LOCAL JOTTINGS.

Mr. Thomas Gullifer, who has been in ill health for some time from the infirmities of old age, lies in a very enfeebled condition at his home in this village, having been confined to his bed for the past four weeks, and it is recognized that he is gradually passing away. His son, F. O. Gullifer, of Lansing, is now with him.

Alcona County Review, November 26, 1886

LOCAL JOTTINGS.

The Hon. F. O. Gullifer of Lansing, was called this week to the bedside of his father, Thomas Gullifer, who lies very sick at his home in this place.

Alcona County Review, January 8, 1887

OBITUARY.
GULLIFER—At his home in Harrisville, January 8th, 1887, Thomas Gullifer, aged 73 years.

Thomas Gullifer was born in Brodley, Me., Dec. 28th, 1813, and was, therefore, at the time of his death 73 years and 10 days old. His father and mother were also natives of Maine. His father died when he was but nine years of age and his mother two years later, leaving the subject of this sketch and two younger brothers to depend on their own exertions. Finding he must shift for himself he secured a position as choreboy in a lumber camp. From that time until he was 65 years of age he followed the life of a lumberman, filling all positions from choreboy to owner. He was married to Miss Sarah Nason, also a native of the state of Maine, January 13th, 1835. His life partner survives him after over 50 years of married life. The deceased leaves five children: Mrs. L. Boardman, Mrs. H. H. Fox, and Henry Gullifer of this county; Mrs. L H. Higgins, of Minneapolis, Minn., and Freeman O. Gullifer, of Lansing. All of his children except Mrs. Higgins were with him during his last sickness.

In the fall of 1867 the deceased came to Michigan, and in 1870 he located with his family in this village, where they have since resided. His death resulted from old age and general decay. Although confined to his bed for nearly four months, during all that time he suffered very little pain, but gradually grew weaker as the sands of life slowly ebbed away, until when the final end came he appeared to gently fall asleep. During his residence here he made many friends, who admired him for his quiet unostentatious manner of living, and his faith and patience in adversity. As one of his neighbors said on the day of his funeral, "It is doubtful if he had an enemy in the world." An honest, industrious, upright man, his family has lost a good husband and father, and the community a good citizen.

Alcona County Review, January 14, 1887

Card of Thanks.
The family of the late Thomas Gullifer desire to express their sincere and heartfelt thanks to the many friends who so nobly stood by them during their recent affliction. May these friends always find help and assistance when needed.

Alcona County Review, January 14, 1887
Cemetery: West Lawn, Alcona Co.

Gurnsay, John
COUNTY NEWS.

On Friday of last week, John Gurnsay, a farmer of Alpena county, was struck by the butt of a falling tree, and so badly injured that he died Sunday morning.

Alcona County Review, February 11, 1881
Cemetery: Probably Evergreen, Alpena Co.

Gustin, Richard P.
PURELY PERSONAL.
R. P. Gustin Dead.—The news of the death of this well known business

man was received in this village Tuesday, and caused such remarks as the death of a man of his prominence naturally would, a man whose life and business interests have been closely identified with the history of the Huron shore. The deceased died Monday evening at his residence in Bay City after a brief illness. He was born in the county of Middlesex, Ont., in 1837. He moved to Bay City in 1866, engaging in the wholesale grocery business, first alone and then successively with Gustin & Co., Gustin & Merrill, and Gustin, Merrill & Co. He was senior member of the lumbering firm of Gustin & Killmaster, of Killmaster, which was succeeded last year by Jno. H. Killmaster & Co. It is reported here that the deceased sold his individual half interest in his Alcona county property only a few days prior to his death. He leaves a widow and six children. Mrs. Gustin was a daughter of the Hon. William Killmaster, of Norfolk county, Ont., to whom he was married in 1863.

Alcona County Review, March 1, 1889

LOCAL JOTTINGS.

It is said that the late R. P. Gustin had insurance to the amount of $43,000 on his life. One policy of $12,000 was unfortunately allowed to lapse only a few days prior to his last sickness.

Alcona County Review, March 8, 1889
Cemetery:

Gustin, Ruth Huntington [Avery]

Mrs. H. K. Gustin Dead.
Word was received here yesterday of the death of Mrs. H. K. Gustin, at her home in Alpena. Cause of death was appendicitis.

This sad news comes as a shock to Mr. Gustin's friends in this county. Deceased had been married but a few months and it is only three weeks since E. O. Avery, father of Mrs. Gustin, passed away at Detroit. Mr. Gustin has the sympathy of a large number of friends in this vicinity.

Alcona County Review, October 26, 1899
Cemetery: Woodmere, Wayne Co.

Hackett, Ralph

EVENTS OF ONE WEEK.
Capt. Ralph Hackett of Alger, Smith & Co.'s tug Torrent and a brother of Conductor Percy Hackett of the D. & M. railroad was killed last

Wednesday in the St. Clair Flats Ship Canal by getting foul of the tow line of the schooner Yukon which swept the decks of the Torrent. Hackett was struck by the line and instantly killed as was also David Kanary the watchman. Another man was swept in to the lake and drowned.

Alcona County Review, July 25, 1895
Cemetery: Woodmere, Wayne Co.

Hagen, William

AMONG OUR EXCHANGES.

Something like a race war is on in Presque Isle county. The accused murderers of Edward Molitor are Germans, and their trial has been postponed from time to time, and has now gone over to the June term. The murderer of William Hagen is John Idalski, a Pole. He has been promptly tried, convicted and sentenced. The Poles now say that all murderers must be treated alike in Presque Isle county; that the murderers of Molitor, even though they be well-to-do Germans, must be tried, convicted and sentenced, and that if they are not they will take the law into their own hands.

Alcona County Review, January 28, 1892
Cemetery: Rogers Township, Presque Isle Co.

Haining, Mrs. Addie

Somewhat Personal.

Died at West Bay City of Consumption, Mrs. Jas Haining, formerly of Harrisville. Died January 28. She leaves a husband and four children to mourn their loss.

Alcona County Review, February 25, 1892
Cemetery:

Halcrow, Andrew

County Reviewings.
Marine Disaster.— On Monday evening, the steam barge D. W. Rust, Captain Pringle, collided with the schooner F. B. Berriman, Captain Thomas, about ten miles off Sturgeon Point, near this place. The Berriman was loaded with forty-two thousand bushels of wheat, and sunk in less than fifteen minutes after the collision took place. Andrew Halcrow and Charles Myers were lost. One of the crew, whose name we did not learn, had his leg badly fractured. All but the two parties named were taken on the barge and saved. The Rust, loaded with coal, was considerable injured, and now lies at East Tawas in a sinking condition.

Alcona County Review, May 11, 1877
Cemetery:

Hale, Bessie E.

PERSONAL POINTS.

M. Hale and wife are much concerned for their daughter whose condition is serious.

Alcona County Review, May 5, 1898

LOCAL PICK UPS.

Bessie Hale, daughter of Mr. and Mrs. Matthew Hale, passed away last evening after a long wasting illness from consumption. She was a bright child, of gentle disposition and was a general favorite. The funeral will not be held until Sunday morning at 11 o'clock at the Methodist church.

Bessie was in her fourteenth year and her parents are heart-broken at the untimely death of a favorite child and only daughter.

Alcona County Review, June 9, 1898

PERSONAL POINTS.

A sister of Mrs. Matthew Hale, whose home is at Lansing, came up to attend the funeral of her niece.

Alcona County Review, June 16, 1898

PERSONAL POINTS.

The mortal remains of little Bessie Hale, whose death was noted in the last Review, were laid at rest in the South Harrisville cemetery Sunday morning after very affecting and impressive services at the Methodist church. The remains were preceded on the way to the church by six little girls dressed in white and on foot. They were members of Bessie's Sunday school class. The pall bearers were boys of about the same age as Bessie and were her school and playmates. Rev. W. W. Will preached a sermon of excellent points that was full of hope and consolation for the stricken parents. The remains were encased in a beautiful white casket which was covered with fragrant blossoms of the summer season.

The grave was draped with white cloth and the earth was concealed under banks of flowers.

Alcona County Review, June 16, 1898

Resolutions of Condolence.
Whereas, The divine Ruler of the Universe has, in his infinite wisdom, seen fit to remove by death Bessie, the beloved daughter of Brother and

Sister Matthew and Jennie Hale, therefore be it

Resolved, That we, the members of Huron Rebeckah Lodge No. 295, do hereby extend to said Brother and Sister Hale and family our sincere and heartfelt sympathy in their hour of sorrow, and be it further

Resolved, that these resolutions be spread upon the records of our Lodge, that a copy be sent to the bereaved family, and that they be published in the Alcona County Review.

Fred A. Beede,
Mrs. Young,   Com'tee.
Winnifred Moore.

Alcona County Review, June 30, 1898

Local History of One Year

Chronology of the Principal Events of the Year 1898.

June 8. Death of Bessie Hale aged 14.

Alcona County Review, January 5, 1899
Cemetery: Springport, Alcona Co.

Hale, Eunice [Burdick]

COUNTY REVIEWINGS.

Matthew Hale received a dispatch Monday night from Bridgeport, Con., announcing the death of his wife, and left on the boat Tuesday morning *en route* for that place. Mrs. Hale it will be remembered was taken to Connecticut from Harrisville the early part of the spring, with hopes that she might recover, but her health was only improved for the time, it seems, and her many friends in this village will regret to learn that she has now passed away into the sphere of immortality.

Alcona County Review, July 2, 1880
Cemetery: Spring Grove, Hartford Co, CT

Hall, Fredrick C.

REVIEWINGS.

Saturday morning last, Fred Hall, a resident of East Tawas, died in his chair while waiting for breakfast. Dropsy of the heart was the cause.

Alcona County Review, February 13, 1880
Cemetery: Greenwood, Iosco Co.

Hall, Mrs. H. E.

LOCAL JOTTINGS.

Mrs. Grant Lewis received a telegram Wednesday announcing the death of her mother, Mrs. H. E. Hall,

formerly of this place, which occurred at Rising Sun, Ind., on Christmas day.

Alcona County Review, December 28, 1888
Cemetery:

Hall, Harry

LOCAL JOTTINGS.

Private letters received by B. F. Buchanan state that Harry Hall, a young man who formerly resided in Harrisville died of typhoid fever in the new state of Washington a few weeks since. Mrs. Hall, his mother, was proprietress of the McLennan house. Mrs. Kane Miller of Harrisville and Mrs. Grant Lewis of Tawas, are sisters of the deceased.

Alcona County Review, September 27, 1889
Cemetery:

Hall, Mrs. Lydia

Weighed in the Balance.

Mrs. Hi. Hall, at one time a resident of Harrisville, died at Bay City about two weeks ago of pulmonary consumption.

Alcona County Review, January 11, 1894
Cemetery:

Hall, Thomas

Reported that many of the men who went to West Virginia with Lindsay & Grant are disgusted with the country and will soon return to Michigan. Thos. Hall, who went from Alpena with them, was instantly killed week before last by being caught between two rolling logs.

Alcona County Review, April 18, 1890
Cemetery:

Halverson, Olof

EVENTS OF ONE WEEK.

Olof Halverson, an Au Sable lad aged 16 years, broke through the ice off Fish Point while skating on Lake Huron and was drowned.

Alcona County Review, February 8, 1894
Cemetery: Pinecrest, Iosco Co.

Hamilton, Dell

Local Sayings and Doings.

Dell. Hamilton, a young man working at Pyne's camp back of Black River, died very suddenly last night.

Alcona County Review, March 17, 1882
Cemetery:

Hamilton, George, Sr.

KILLED BY A TREE.

Sudden Taking Away of George Hamilton, Sr.

At no time in the history of this county has there hovered over the people a greater cloud of mourning than that caused by the sudden death of our worthy pioneer townsman, George Hamilton, Sr., last Saturday afternoon. Mr. Hamilton, in company with one of his younger sons was in the woods a short distance from the house felling hemlock trees, to secure the bark from the same which he was selling to a Harrisville shipper. He had just finished sawing from the stump one of these trees and had stepped a few feet back from the same till it fell. In falling the top of this tree struck against an adjacent beech tree, bending over the top of the latter considerably, and from thence fell to the ground. The beech tree, in springing back quickly from its forced position, broke off at the top and came down upon Mr. Hamilton, striking him on the head and badly fracturing the skull. He was picked up in an insensible condition and conveyed to his house, when medical aid was summoned with all possible haste, but to no avail, as he lived only about one and a half hours after the accident. Thus in an unexpectedly sudden manner has passed away a noble Christian gentleman, and honored citizen, a public benefactor, and a beloved husband and father.

George Hamilton, Sr., was born near Glasgow, Scotland, in the year 1823, and at the age of eighteen years he sailed across the Atlantic to America and at once took up his residence in Canada, where he remained until about twenty years ago, when he removed with his family to this township taking up his residence in South Harrisville, and there working at the cooper's trade in company with the father of the La Chapelle boys. Here he worked for about five years, when he took up a piece of land under the government homestead act about four miles west of this village and there lived until the day of his death. About fifteen years ago he became converted, and took a strong, active stand for Christianity and temperance. For several years past he had often filled the sacred office of local preacher in the M. E.

church (of which he was a member), preaching in many of the school houses throughout the county, and aiding materially in the organization of Sunday schools. in all temperance movements he assumed a leading position, and never ceased trying to do what he could to make temperance a success in this community. In fact as a temperance man he was enthusiastic, having himself personally known the terrible destroying effects of intemperance in former years. He was a natural orator and a man of much ability, and could he but have had proper advantages and training in the earlier part of his life he would no doubt have assumed a high position among the most useful men of the present day and age. At the time of his death he was holding his second term as Supervisor of Harrisville township, and was chairman of the Board of Supervisors. During the fifteen years past he had also held other offices within the gift of the town and county, among which were Register of Deeds, President of the Agricultural Society, Justice of the Peace, School Inspector, etc. He was one of the most useful men and valued public servants the township and county ever had, and he departed this life with the highest esteem of all his fellow citizens. Well may the populace mourn when such a good, useful man dies, for indeed by his death all lose a friend.

Mr. Hamilton leaves a wife and 10 living children. In all 15 children were born to Mr. and Mrs. H., five of which are dead.

The funeral services of the deceased were held from the M. E. church in Harrisville at 11:30 Monday morning, Pastor J. H. McIntosh officiating in his usually impressive manner, and preaching from the text in 2d Timothy: "I have fought a good fight, I have finished my course, I have kept the faith." The attendance upon this funeral occasion is said to have been the largest ever had in the county upon a similar occasion. So great was the crowd of people in the church and consequent strain upon the floor that props had to be put under the joists to keep them from breaking through. Sixty teams were in the procession from the church to the cemetery.

To the wife and family of the deceased the Review unites sincerely with all citizens in extending heartfelt sympathy in this day of deep affliction, which has so suddenly come upon them, and commends them to the care of Him who "Doeth all things well."

Alcona County Review, July 14, 1882

RESOLUTIONS OF CONDOLENCE.

The following resolutions were adopted by the Board of Supervisors at a meeting held on the 10th day of July, 1882, Supervisors Kirkendall, McGuire and Thompson present:

Whereas, It has seemed good to the Almighty Disposer of all human events to remove from our midst our late worthy fellow member and Chairman of this Board, George Hamilton, and

Whereas, The intimate relations held by the deceased with the members of this Board, and with public affairs in general, render it proper that we should place upon record our appreciation of his services as a county officer, and his merits as a man; therefore

Resolved, That we deplore the loss of George Hamilton with deep feelings of regret, softened only by the confident hope that his spirit is with those who, having fought the good fight here, are enjoying perfect happiness in a better world.

Resolved, That we tender to his afflicted wife and children our sincere condolence, and our earnest and heartfelt sympathy in their affliction at the loss of one who was a good citizen, an efficient county officer and an upright and honorable man.

Resolved, That the members of this Board will attend our deceased brother to the grave in a body, to pay our last sad token of respect to him who has ceased to preside in the counsels of this Board.

Resolved, That a copy of the foregoing resolutions, certified by the Clerk of this Board, be transmitted to relatives of the deceased, and also published in the Alcona county Review.

David Kirkendall,
Chairman, pro tem.
Geo. Rutson, Clerk.

Alcona County Review, July 14, 1882

A Card.

Gratitude prompts me to return our heartfelt thanks to the many friends and neighbors who manifested such tender interest in us during our recent bereavement and sudden deep affliction. May God's richest blessing be their portion.

Mrs. G. Hamilton.
July 14, 1882.

Alcona County Review, July 14, 1882

Local Sayings and Doings.

The Town Board have appointed D. B. Mudgett Supervisor of Harrisville, vice Geo. Hamilton, deceased. The choice is a good one.

Alcona County Review, July 21, 1882

Resolutions.

The following resolutions were adopted by the Sunday school of district No. 2:

Whereas, According to the will of the Great Father it has seemed good in His sight to remove from us by death our Superintendent, George Hamilton, and

Whereas We, as a school, feel his loss most deeply, by being deprived of his wise counsel and untiring labor for our prosperity, we deem it prudent to offer the following:

Resolved, That while we bow in submission to the decree of God, yet we do deeply deplore the loss of our Superintendent, still believing that his death was but the entrance into that blissful rest that remaineth for the children of God.

Resolved, That while we mourn his death, we shall strive with more diligence to follow his example, pay more heed to his council and labor more faithfully for the welfare of our school.

Resolved, That we extend our heartfelt sympathy to his bereaved wife, who thus suddenly has been called upon to part with a loving companion, and to his orphaned children, who are henceforth deprived of the kind care and counsel of a kind father.

Resolved, That a copy of these resolutions be presented to the family of the deceased and also published in the Alcona County Review.

B. E. Bubar,
Peter Effric,
George Ward,
Committee.

Alcona County Review, July 28, 1882

Alex'r Hamilton, son of the late Geo. Hamilton, who died intestate in 1882, filed a petition to the court Tuesday praying for a distribution to heirs of the estate of his father, which consists at the present time of an 80 acre farm in section 8, town 26-9, and valued at $2,000. A former petition to the probate court to the probate court for the appointment of an administrator was denied last July. The petitioner sets forth that the farm has proved a source of contention among the heirs and that an equitable distribution is the only way out of the difficulty.

Alcona County Review, December 20, 1894

EVENTS OF ONE WEEK.

Geo. Hamilton, Sr., died some twelve years ago. His estate, consisting principally of an 80-acre farm, has never been legally settled. This week a petition was filed for the appointment of an administrator, which will be heard on July 2.

Alcona County Review, June 7, 1894

STATE OF MICHIGAN, County of Alcona.

At a session of the Probate Court for said County, held at the Probate office in the Village of Harrisville, on the Fourth day of June, in the year one thousand eight hundred and ninety-four.

Present, C. H. Killmaster, Judge of Probate.

In the Matter of the Estate of George Hamilton, Sr.:

On reading and filing the petition, duly verified, of Alexander Hamilton, praying that an administrator be appointed in the aforesaid estate:

Thereupon it is ordered that Monday, the Second day of July next, at ten o'clock in the forenoon, be assigned for the hearing of said petition, and that the heirs at law of said deceased, and all other persons interested in said estate, are required to appear at a session of said Court, then to be holden in the Probate office, in the Village of Harrisville, and show cause, if any there be, why the prayer of the petitioner should not be granted: And it is further ordered that said petitioners give notice to the persons interested in said estate, of the pendency of said petition, and the hearing thereof, by causing a copy of this order to be published in the Alcona County Review, a newspaper printed and circulated in said county, three successive weeks previous to said day of hearing.

C. H. Killmaster,
Judge of Probate.

Alcona County Review, June 7, 1894
Cemetery: Springport, Alcona Co.

Hammond, James
A Fatal Mistake.

Jas. Hammond Swallowed Carbolic Acid and Died in Fifteen Minutes.

Jas. Hammond, a laborer, who had been in the employ of J. Van Buskirk the past season, went home to his boarding place at Wm. Swindlehurst's about 4 o'clock last Friday morning from the village, where the day before he had attended the Fair and in the evening the dance. During the day he was drinking a little, a very unusual thing for him to do, and when he went home he took a bottle of whiskey with him. He went to bed on reaching home but before retiring he placed the bottle of liquor on a stand on which was also a bottle containing carbolic acid. The two bottles were of equal size and not dissimilar in form. He arose at 11 o'clock and took a drink from what he supposed was the bottle of liquor. In a moment more he said to Mrs. Swindlehurst:

"What was in that bottle."

"Carbolic acid," she replied.

"Oh, My God! I'm gone." he cried, and these were his last words.

He died in about 15 minutes from the time he swallowed the awful dose.

Dr. Ludlum, who was at Springport, was summoned but poor Hammond was dead before the physician reached the house.

Hammond came from Middleport, N. Y., last spring where he left a family consisting of a wife and six children. A disagreement over property matters had separated them. During his residence here he has been a quiet, industrious citizen and he was not addicted to the use of intoxicants, so far as known.

His relatives were wired and three brothers arrived here Sunday, coming up to Tawas on the freight and driving the rest of the way. They decided to bury him here and the interment took place Monday morning in the Catholic cemetery.

Coroner Beede held an inquest on the remains but no new facts bearing on the case were discovered and a verdict was rendered that deceased came to his death from poison accidentally administered by his own hand.

Alcona County Review, October 11, 1894
Cemetery: St. Anne's, Alcona Co.

Hankinson, Joseph T.
Social and Religious

The Rev. J. T. Hankinson, pastor of the Tawas circuit M. E. churches, died last week, aged 61 years.

Alcona County Review, March 2, 1893
Cemetery: Greenwood, Iosco Co.

Hannah, Jacob
Fatal Accident.

Wednesday afternoon, Jacob Hannah, an employee on E. M. Fowler's long timber banking ground, met with his death. He, with others, was engaged in unloading long timber from the cars, and by some means was struck a terrible blow upon the head with a cant hook, killing him almost instantly. He was a young man, but we did not learn whether he was married or not.

Alcona County Review, June 14, 1878
Cemetery:

Hardwick, John
A TERRIBLE ACCIDENT.

Seven Men Buried Alive Beneath a Mass of Brick.

THE FRIGHTFUL OCCURRENCE AT AU SABLE.

On Monday afternoon the citizens of AuSable and Oscoda were suddenly thrown into a state of excitement and terror, by the announcement of a horrible accident which had occurred at Gram's mill burner, by which five persons lost their lives, seven in all being victims to the terrible calamity. The particulars of the sad occurrence we glean from the Saturday Night extra of Wednesday, as follows:

"There were seven men at work in the burner at Gram's mill. They were Joseph W. Biddle, Thomas Mitchell, George Fulton, John Hardwick, William Miner, George Santerneau, George Gordon. The men were engaged in taking down the brick wall of one of the refuse burners of Gram's mill. A scaffolding had been built inside the burner, and upon the scaffolding the men worked and upon it the brick was also laid as they were taken from the wall. The men began taking the wall down from the top. They had been working in the burner about a week and had the walls about half down. The brick from the part of the wall already taken down were of course lying on the platforms of the scaffolding above the heads of the workmen. While the men were engaged at work, continuing the tearing down of the wall—with about 20,000 brick, or from 40 to 50 ton's weight, above them, the scaffolding gave way, and in an instant the seven men were buried beneath this immense amount of brick and the lumber and timber of which the scaffolding was made. The alarm was given by Michael Gerrard, who was working but a few feet from the burner. Before an hour had passed there were from 1000 to 1500 men collected at the scene of the accident. The task of uncovering the men was begun as soon as possible after the accident occurred, but under the circumstances it was a very slow job. The bricks, and lumber composing the scaffolding, had all to be thrown out through two small openings—two feet by two and one half—and of course only a small number of them could work at a time. The scaffolding fell about half past four o'clock. At half past seven the first body was reached and taken out. It proved to be that of Joseph Biddle. A short time after young Gordon was taken out alive and seemingly not fatally injured, though at this writing his recovery is doubtful. A few minutes later Fulton and Santerneau were taken out, the former alive and the latter dead. Then the bodies of Mitchell, Miner, and Hardwick were taken out in the order named, it being about nine o'clock, or four and one-half hours after the accident, when the last body was removed. When the scaffolding fell some of the scantlings happened to wedge in such a position that they kept the principal weight of the brick off from Gordon, and he was able to converse at intervals with the men who were removing the brick. The men could also hear groans from one of the other imprisoned victims—probably Fulton, he was the only other one taken out alive. Five of the victims—

Biddle, Fulton, Miner, Santerneau and Hardwick—were married men with families. Mr. Hardwick, familiarly called "Happy Jack," leaves a wife and six children, the oldest a daughter of seventeen. Mr. Biddle leaves a wife and two children, Mr. Miner the same. Mr. Fulton has a wife and three children, and Mr. Santerneau leaves a wife and baby.

Later.—Fulton died Wednesday evening.

Alcona County Review, April 17, 1885

LOCAL JOTTINGS.

Register of Deeds Jamison and Gene Taft spent Monday night at Au Sable, and brought to town early Tuesday morning the news of the killing of the 5 men at Au Sable.

Alcona County Review, April 17, 1885
Cemetery: Pinecrest, Iosco Co.

Hare, Nicholas

Curtis Items.

Nov. 30, 1896.

Mrs. J. W. Ferguson was called to the death-bed of her father, Nicholas Hare, of St. Clair county. She left Nov. 17th, but was too late to see him; he had gone home. He was a deacon of the Presbyterian church for many years. Besides his aged wife he left a family of 10 children, all men and women, 5 daughters and five sons. His age was nearly 80. He died happy and was willing to go to the better land. There was a very large funeral. The old must go as well as the young. 'Tis well for all ages to prepare for the better world, where sorrow is no more and the weary find rest.

Alcona County Review, December 3, 1896
Cemetery:

Harris, William

Alcona—Death Notice.

Alcona, Feb. 8th, 1879.

Editor Review:—William Harris died at the Carle House on Friday the 7th, at 1 o'clock P.M., of Pleurisy; aged 32 years; unmarried. This would have been his 16th year in the lumber woods. By his steady industry and good habits he has accumulated property to the amount of three thousand dollars. He was a resident of Newbury, Ont., and was in the employ of Martin Brennan, at Hubbard Lake. He was taken to Newbury by Willie F. Carle of Alcona.

Alpena and Canada papers please copy.

Alcona County Review, February 14, 1879
Cemetery:

Harrison, Calista M. [Huntley]

LOCAL JOTTINGS.

Mrs. Jas. Harrison, living west of Springport, died Wednesday morning, leaving a husband and five children.

Alcona County Review, August 13, 1886
Cemetery: Springport, Alcona Co.

Harrison, Georgia

Along the Shore.

The body of Miss Georgia Harrison, one of the unfortunate four drowned near Rogers City recently, has been recovered.

Alcona County Review, November 4, 1881
Cemetery:

Hart, Joseph Albert

LOCAL JOTTINGS.

A two-year-old child of Peter Hart, Harrisville, died on Friday last.

Alcona County Review, March 19, 1886
Cemetery: St. Anne's, Alcona Co.

Hartigan, Howard J.

EVENTS OF ONE WEEK.

The infant child of Mr. and Mrs. Matthew Hartigan of Black River was buried in the Catholic cemetery Friday, the 18th.

Alcona County Review, September 24, 1896

PERSONAL MENTION.

We wish to express our sincere thanks to the kind friends and neighbors who assisted in any way during the illness and death of our little son Howard.

Mr. and Mrs. M. Hartigan.

Alcona County Review, September 24, 1896
Cemetery: St. Anne's, Alcona Co.

Hartman, August

One Way to Die.

August Hartman, a well-to-do farmer residing near East Tawas, loaded a gun with a heavy charge of powder, filled the barrel with water, placed the muzzle in his mouth, fired the gun with a stick and blew himself into kingdom come. Domestic troubles.

Alcona County Review, May 28, 1896
Cemetery:

Hastings, Evelina

SLEEPY HOLLOW.

Sept. 26, '99.

Born to Mr. and Mrs. Joseph Hastings on the 19th inst. twin baby girls. Unfortunately one of them only lived eight hours and was interred in the cemetery Thursday.

Alcona County Review, September 28, 1899
Cemetery: Mt. Joy, Alcona Co.

Hastings, Lloyd

HAYNES HAPPENINGS.

A child of Robt. Hastings died from grip Tuesday. Aged 3 months.

Alcona County Review, February 9, 1899
Cemetery: Mt. Joy, Alcona Co.

Hastings, Robert

Another Pioneer Gone.

Robert Hastey who has lived in Alcona township, this county, for 15 years or more, departed this life last Friday evening; heart disease being the pronounced cause of his death. He had the week previous been over in Canada purchasing a lot of working horses, to be used in the lumber woods the coming winter, and returning home on Friday or Saturday of said week, he was taken ill. The Monday following he was able to be about the house again and remained up for several days. He was subsequently taken suddenly ill, and passed away within a few hours. He was over sixty years of age.

Robert Hastey came to this county and commenced carving out a home for himself in our forests, when neighbors were few and far between; but he lived to develop a good farm himself, and see the country all about thickly settled with others whose clearings and agricultural developments are the admiration of all who visit this county. Mr. Hastey devoted much of his time the past few years to jobbing in the lumber woods for Alger, Smith & Co., and his recent purchase of additional horses was for the enlargement of his operations in that line of work. He leaves a wife and seven or eight children. Most of the children are grown to manhood and womanhood.

Alcona County Review, September 25, 1885

Probate Order.

State of Michigan,
County of Alcona.

At a session of the Probate Court for the County of Alcona holden at the Probate office, in the village of Harrisville, on the twenty-second day of September, in the year one thousand and eight hundred and eighty-five.

Present, Allen Nevins, Judge of Probate.

In the matter of the estate of Robert Hastey, deceased.

On reading and filing the petition, duly verified, of Joseph Hastey, praying among other things for the probate of an instrument in writing heretofore filed in this court, purporting to be the last will and testament of Robert Hastey, deceased.

Thereupon it is ordered, that Monday, the nineteenth day of October, 1885 next, at ten o'clock in the forenoon, be assigned for the hearing of said petition, and that the heirs at law of said deceased, and all other persons interested in said estate, are required to appear at a session of said Court, then to be holden in the Probate office, in the village of Harrisville, and show cause, if any there be, why the prayer of the petitioner should not be granted. And it is further ordered, that said petitioner give notice to the persons interested in said estate, of the pendency of said petition, and hearing thereof, by causing a copy of this order to be published in the Alcona County Review, a newspaper printed and circulated in said county, three successive weeks previous to said day of hearing.

Allen Nevins,
Judge of Probate.

Alcona County Review, September 25, 1885

Commissioners' Notice.

State of Michigan,
County of Alcona.

Probate Court for said County.
Estate of Robert Hastey, deceased.

The undersigned having been appointed by the Judge of Probate of said County, Commissioners on claims in the matter of said estate, and six months from the seventh day of April, A. D. 1886, having been allowed by said Judge of Probate to all persons holding claims against said estate, in which to present their claims to us for examination and adjustment.

Notice is hereby given, that we will meet on Wednesday, the seventh day of July, A. D. 1886, and on Thursday, the seventh day of October, A. D. 1886, at ten o'clock A. M. of each day, at the office of George Rutson in the village of Harrisville, in said County, to receive and examine such claims.

Dated, April 7th, A. D. 1886.
George Rutson, Commissioners.
Simon McNalley.

Alcona County Review, April 30, 1886
Cemetery: Mt. Joy, Alcona Co.

Hawkins, Harriet [Williams]

EVENTS OF ONE WEEK.

The remains of Mrs. Chas. Hawkins of Mud Lake Jc. were brought to Harrisville for burial Tuesday.

Alcona County Review, September 9, 1897
Cemetery:

Hawkins, {Boy}

Mud Lake Jots.

Charles Hawkins buried an infant child about four weeks old. He bought Chas. Hawse's place, built a house and has lived here but a short time. They have the sympathy of our people.

Alcona County Review, July 4, 1895
Cemetery:

Hawkins, Luther

DEATH'S HARVEST.

A young man named Hawkins, whose parents reside at West Harrisville, died there Saturday of consumption after a lingering illness. He was about 19 years of age.

Alcona County Review, March 2, 1893

OBITUARY.

Luther Hawkins, eldest son of Mr. and Mrs. Charles Hawkins, of Haynes township, this county, departed this life Feb. 25, 1893.

Deceased was 17 years old the 9th day of last April. Three years ago this winter this dear boy took la grippe, from which he never recovered. It terminated in consumption of the lungs of which disease he died. Tongue cannot tell what this poor boy suffered, but it has all ceased now. His sufferings are over. We verily believe he was fully prepared to go to the land where suffering never comes. May God help those that remain to prepare to meet him in the happy land. Rev. H. A. Long.

Alcona County Review, March 2, 1893

West Harrisville.

The Review.--Luke Hawkins, who for the past year or two has been fading away by consumption, was released by death last Friday. He was 17 years of age.

Alcona County Review, March 2, 1893

Cemetery:

Hawse, Francis

WEST HARRISVILLE.

Francis Hawse, son of Mr. and Mrs. Frank Hawse, departed this life Sept. 14, 1892. He was born Oct. 18, 1886, and has been afflicted for the last four years. He has suffered much, but God has taken the dear little fellow to himself and ended his suffering. May God bless the dear parents in their affliction and sanctify it to their good.

Alcona County Review, September 22, 1892
Cemetery:

Hawse, {Girl}

Somewhat Personal.

Frank Hawse lost a daughter Tuesday morning which died from inflammation of the bowels. The child was aged between two and three years.

Alcona County Review, March 24, 1892
Cemetery:

Hayden, Annie [Donahue]

Card of Thanks.

We wish to thank our friends and neighbors for the kind assistance they rendered us during the sickness and death of our beloved wife and mother.

John Hayden and Family.

Alcona County Review, October 8, 1891
Cemetery: St. Anne's, Alcona Co.

Hayden, {Child}

A SAD ACCIDENT.
Infant Child Killed by Another Infant.

The infant child of Mr. and Mrs. Dan Hayden of Black River met its death in a very lamentable manner. It was but a few months old and the parents had just administered a quieting potion containing laudanum. The bottle containing the laudanum was set down within easy reach of a two-year-old child belonging to a neighboring family. The child picked up the bottle unbeknown to the adults in the room and gave it to the babe and before the family realized what had taken place the infant had swallowed a large part of the contents of the bottle. Every means was taken to counteract the effects of the poison but the child died at noon the next day. Interment took place at Harrisville on Sunday.

Alcona County Review, August 27, 1896

Black River Sparks.

We wish to thank our many friends and neighbors for their kindness and timely assistance during the illness and death of our beloved little one.

Mr. and Mrs. Dan Hayden.

Alcona County Review, August 27, 1896
Cemetery: Probably St. Anne's, Alcona Co.

Hayden, {Child}

LOCAL JOTTINGS.

Thomas Hayden lost a small child the fore part of the week.

Alcona County Review, October 10, 1884
Cemetery: Probably St. Anne's, Alcona Co.

Hayden, John

COUNTY JOTTINGS.

That dreaded disease, diptheria, is raging quite extensively among the children in the southern portion of Alcona township. One of Supervisor A. T. Scarlett's little sons died with the disease Sunday night, and children in the families of Ephriam Waldron, John Hayden and Uriah Emerson are now down with the same. Let all necessary precautions be taken to prevent the further spreading of the disease.

Alcona County Review, October 25, 1878

COUNTY JOTTINGS.

The twelve year old son of Joseph Hayden, living about one mile north of the village, died with the diptheria last Saturday night. Other members of the family are afflicted with the disease.

Alcona County Review, November 8, 1878
Cemetery: St. Anne's, Alcona Co.

Hayden, Mrs. Mary

Mrs. Thos. Hayden departed this life Wednesday morning at 6 o'clock after a very brief illness. She was subject to convulsions and death was due to an unusually severe attack which continued until death released her.

Deceased was an estimable wife and mother. She was a devout Catholic and the remains will be buried tomorrow morning under the rites of that church.

Alcona County Review, November 21, 1895
Cemetery: St. Anne's, Alcona Co.

Hayes, {Male}

This morning telegrams announced that a man named Hayes was shot and killed, in a drunken brawl, at Tawas yesterday. No particulars are given.

Alcona County Review, July 5, 1878
Cemetery:

Hayes, William

Curtis.

Sad to say, Mr. and Mrs. Harp Hase's only child took its departure on March 6th to the realms of the blessed. It was buried in the cold earth but Christ says, "Suffer little children to come unto me." The Rev. Nunn preached a grand sermon.

Alcona County Review, March 30, 1893
Cemetery: Glennie, Alcona Co.

Haynes, Elijah R.

Probate Order.

State of Michigan,
County of Alcona.

At a session of the Probate Court for said county, held at the Probate Office in the village of Harrisville on the 6th day of July, A. D. 1881.

Present B. P. Cowley, Judge of Probate. In the matter of the estate of Elijah R. Haynes, deceased.

James Beard, executor of said estate, comes into court and represents that he is now prepared to render his final account.

Thereupon it is ordered that Saturday, the Thirtieth day of July A. D. 1881, at ten o'clock in the forenoon, be assigned for examining and showing such account, and that the legatees named in the will of said estate, heirs at law of said deceased, and all other persons interested in said estate are required to appear at a session of said court then to be holden at the Probate office in the village of Harrisville in said county, and show cause, if any there be, why the said account should not be allowed. And it is further ordered that said James Beard give notice to persons interested in said estate of the pendency of said account, and the hearing thereof, by causing a copy of this order to be published in the Alcona County Review, a newspaper printed and circulated in said county, three successive weeks previous to said day of hearing.

B. P. Cowley.
Judge of Probate.

Alcona County Review, July 8, 1881

The Local News.

When E. R. Haines, a former Alcona lumberman died he left an estate consisting of $5,000 life insurance, the annual interest of which was bequeathed in trust to a boy named Augustus Fish, to whom he had taken a great liking. Geo. P.

Voorheis was appointed administrator. Fish has grown to man's estate and is not satisfied with the manner in which his affairs have been handled. Judge Ritchie is now entertaining a petition for the removal of Voorheis and the appointment of another administrator.

Alcona County Review, December 17, 1891

LOCAL PICK UPS.

Benj. Whipple, a young law student of Port Huron, was in town Tuesday looking over the records of the probate court in the matter of the estate of Elijah R. Haynes, deceased. Haynes was at one time a large property owner in Alcona township and the estate has never been settled up.

Alcona County Review, March 2, 1899

State of Michigan. In the probate court for the county of Alcona. At a session of the probate court for the county of Alcona, held at the office of the Judge of Probate, on the 12th day of April, 1899.

Present, Hon. W. H. Gilpin, Judge of Probate.

In the matter of the estate of Elijah R. Haynes deceased.

On reading and filing the petition, duly verified of Augustus D. Fish, Janette Brockway, Emma Lothian, Adele Smith, Elijah Tremain and Frederick D. Tremain, praying that George P. Voorheis, administrator de Bonis non of said estate, account for his doings as such administrator and that he be removed from such office.

...it is ordered, that Tuesday, the 16th day of May A.D. 1899 at ten o'clock in the forenoon, be assigned for the hearing of said petition, and that the administrator of said estate, George P. Voorheis and all persons interested in said estate, are required to appear at a session of said Court, then to be holden in the office of the Judge of Probate in the Village of Harrisville in said county and show cause, if any there be, why the prayer of the petitioners should not be granted: And it is further ordered, that said petitioners give notice to George P. Voorheis, administrator, etc., of said estate of the pendency of said petition, and the hearing thereof by causing a copy of this order together with a copy of the petition to be personally served on the said George P. Voorheis at least two weeks prior to said day of hearing and also that a copy of said order and notice be published in the Alcona County Review a newspaper printed and circulated in said county, three successive weeks previous to said day of hearing.

W. H. Gilpin, Judge of Probate.

Alcona County Review, April 13, 1899

STATE OF MICHIGAN, County of Alcona.

At a session of the Probate Court for said County, held at the Probate office, in the Village of Harrisville on the twenty-fourth day of July in the year one thousand eight hundred and ninety-nine.

Present, Hon. W. H. Gilpin, Judge of Probate.

In the matter of the estate of Elijah R. Haynes, deceased.

On reading and filing the petition duly verified of Augustus D. Fish, praying among other things that an administrator be appointed with the will annexed and that administration of said estate of said estate may be granted to Jacob Haynes or some other suitable person.

Thereupon it is ordered, that Monday, the 21st day of August next, at ten o'clock in the forenoon, be assigned for the hearing of said petition, and that the heirs at law of said deceased and all other persons interested in said estate, are required to appear at a session of the said Court, then to be holden in the Probate office, in the Village of Harrisville and show cause, if any there be, why the prayer of the petitioner should not be granted. And it is further ordered that the petitioner give notice to the heirs at law and persons interested in said estate of the pendency of said petition, and the hearing thereof, by causing a copy of this order to be published in the Alcona County Review, a newspaper printed and circulated in said county three successive weeks previous to said day of hearing.

W. H. Gilpin, Judge of Probate.

Alcona County Review, July 27, 1899

Of Local Interest.

The probate court was occupied Tuesday with matters pertaining to the Elijah R. Haynes estate. This estate has been in an unsettled condition ever since the death of Haynes in 1874. Recently steps have been taken by beneficiaries of the estate to have the administrator, Geo. P. Voorhees, removed and another administrator appointed.

The hearing was adjourned until next Monday.

The following persons were present at the court: Geo. P. Voorhees of Cleveland, administrator; Frank T. Wolcott, Frank Whipple Sr. and A. D. Fish of Port Huron, Mr. Boyce, son of one of Voorhees' bondsmen.

Alcona County Review, November 16, 1899

STATE of Michigan, County of Alcona.

Probate Court for said County.

At a session of the Probate Court for said County, held at the Probate office, in the Village of Harrisville on the twentieth day of November A.D. 1899.

Present, Hon. W. H. Gilpin, Judge of Probate.

In the matter of the estate of Elijah R. Haynes, deceased.

George F. Voorheis, administrator, de bonis non, of said estate comes into court and files his final account as such administrator.

Thereupon it is ordered that the 19th day of December next, at ten o'clock in the forenoon, be assigned for the examining and allowing of such account and that Augustus D. Fish, Elijah A. Tremain, Fred D. Tremain, Janette Brockway, Emma Lothian, and Adele Smith, legatees under the will of said deceased and all other persons interested in said estate, are required to appear at a session of said court, then to be holden at the Probate office, in the village of Harrisville, in said county, and show cause, if any there be, why the said account should not be allowed: and it is further ordered that said George P. Voorheis give notice to the persons interested in said estate, of the pendency of said account, and the hearing thereof, by causing a copy of this order to be published in the "Alcona County Review" a newspaper printed and circulated in said county, three successive weeks previous to said day of hearing.

Wm. H. Gilpin, Judge of Probate.

Alcona County Review, November 23, 1899

Of Local Interest.

Messrs. A. D. Fish, Frank Whipple and Judge Wolcott of Port Huron and W. P. Voorheis of Toledo were transacting business in the Probate Court Tuesday. Their business was in onnection with the Elijah R. Haynes estate.

Alcona County Review, December 21, 1899

STATE OF MICHIGAN
County of Alcona

Probate Court for said County:

At a session of the Probate Court for said county, held at the Probate office in said County on Monday, the 4th day of November in the year of our Lord one thousand nine hundred and one.

Present W. H. Gilpin, Judge of Probate. In the matter of the estate of Elijah R. Haynes, deceased, Jacob P. Haynes, administrator of said estate, comes into court and represents that he is now prepared to render his final account as such administrator.

Thereupon it is ordered, that Tuesday, the 3rd day of December next, at ten o'clock in the forenoon be assigned for the examining and allowing such account and that the heirs at law of said deceased, and all other persons interested in said estate are required to appear at a session of said court then to be holden at the Probate office in the Village of Harrisville in said County and show cause, if any there be, why the said account should not be allowed.

And it is further ordered, that said administrator give notice to the persons interested in said estate, of the pendency of said account and the hearing thereof, by causing a copy of this order to be published in the Alcona County Review, a newspaper printed and circulated in said county three successive weeks previous to said day of hearing.

W. H. Gilpin,
Judge of Probate.

Alcona County Review, November 28, 1901

Doings of the Week

The hearing of the final account of the administrator of the estate of Elijah R. Haynes was the business that occupied the Probate court Tuesday. Jacob P. Haynes, the administrator, and atty., H. W. Stevens of Port Huron were present. The account was accepted, but as one of the heirs of the estate has been missing for several years the administrator and his bondsmen will not be released until the missing heir

has been gone long enough to be legally dead, under the statute in such case made and provided.

Alcona County Review, December 5, 1901
Cemetery:

Hazen, James
PERSONAL MENTION.

Jim Hazen, a character well known in Alcona county, died last Friday at Chiritree's hotel in the village of Oscoda. Hazen bore a reputation for remarkable ability as a toper. It was no feat at all for him to hold a pint flask of whiskey to his lips and drink it to the last drop, and a gallon of the fiery liquid was his regular daily portion at one time. Like many another man of his class, he had a soft spot in his heart and he was not a stranger to generous impulses. His death was caused, the Press says, by a fibrous growth in the larynx. He was 55 years of age. He had a wife and son in Canada but they had lived apart for years. He had enough money to pay for his funeral expenses.

Alcona County Review, April 12, 1894

Some friends of the late Jas. Hazen were somewhat wrathy at the way in which the Review referred to his habit of drinking. No disrespect to Hazen's memory was intended by this paper in that article. The facts as stated were practically true in the main, but often times the truth is better left untold. The Review humbly apologizes to Mr. Hazen's many friends.

Alcona County Review, April 26, 1894
Cemetery:

Hebener, Daniel Dewey
KILLMASTER.

The infant child of Benjamin Heboner that was suffering from inflammation of the lungs, died Tuesday morning.

Alcona County Review, February 23, 1899
Cemetery: Springport, Alcona Co.

Henderson, James
OUR STATE.

A body found in the river near Mason's mill, Alpena, was identified as that of James Henderson, who came there from Goderich, Ont., last fall, and was seen in a saloon for the last time alive. The body bore marks of violence, and it is probable Henderson was murdered for his money, as he had considerable.

Alcona County Review, May 15, 1885
Cemetery:

Henderson, Minnie M. [Lytle]
Somewhat Personal.

Mrs. Capt. Henderson is lying quite dangerously ill at her home at Sturgeon Pointe from inflammation of the lungs, which originated with la grippe.

Alcona County Review, January 7, 1892
REQUIESEAT IN PACE.

It becomes our sad and painful duty this week to record the death of one who was in life a happy wife and devoted mother, a christian woman, who was beloved by all who enjoyed the pleasure of her acquaintance, viz: Mrs. Jas. E. Henderson, wife of the Captain of the Sturgeon Pointe Life Saving Crew, whose serious illness was briefly announced last week. The deceased sang at the Christmas Eve exercises at the Baptist church and attended the dance at Agricultural Hall the next evening, at which time she contracted a severe cold, or rather la grippe, which became worse and worse with the lapse of time until it finally developed in to that dreaded malady, pneumonia. The friends who attended her realized that she was very ill, but her bereaved husband, who was constantly at her bedside, had no intimation of the extremely dangerous nature of the invidious disease from which she suffered until a few minutes before she breathed her last, when he was aroused from slumber by the attendant and was called to the bedside. She died at 4 o'clock on Saturday, January 9th, inst.

The death of hardly anyone in this community could have shocked the public as did the news of the death of this estimable young woman. She was universally esteemed as well for her womanly graces as for the genial hospitality with which she welcomed the many who have visited Sturgeon Pointe each year since her husband has been in charge of the station. Her untimely death removes from the little circle at the Pointe one of its brightest and most winsome members, but saddest of all is the vacant place in the family circle at the station and the void in the desolate heart of the husband, who has the heartfelt sympathy of the entire community in this irreparable loss. A few of the many friends of the family sent to Bay City Saturday and procured two beautiful floral pieces which arrived by express the same evening and were sent to the Pointe Sunday as delicate testimonials of the esteem in which the living and the dead are universally held. One piece was a cross with foundation of cream carnations and a setting of cream hyacinths with a centre of marguerites and roses. The other piece consisted of palm leaves and roses. There were other floral tributes also. The deceased was about 25 years of age. Her parents reside at Sand Beach where she was married about six years ago. One child is the only fruit of their marriage.

The funeral services were held at the M. E. church and was attended by a large assembly of sympathizing friends and relatives. The funeral sermon was preached by Rev. F. J. Bailey and the remains were interred in the South Harrisville cemetery. Mr. Young, representing J. E. Denton, an Alpena undertaker, officiated.

Alcona County Review, January 14, 1892

Somewhat Personal.

W. R. Smith and wife, Clark Yokom and wife, Geo. and Thos. Coyle, Jas. Monahan and Boney Burt, all of Black River, were down Tuesday and attended the funeral of Mrs. J. E. Henderson.

Alcona County Review, January 14, 1892

Somewhat Personal.

Mr. Lytle, father of the late Mrs. Jas. E. Henderson, arrived in the village Sunday, having come to Tawas Saturday on the freight, from whence he drove to Harrisville.

Alcona County Review, January 14, 1892

The following extract will explain why Mr. Robillard, the Au Sable Baptist minister, did not fulfil his engagement to preach the funeral sermon of Mrs. J. E. Henderson:

Au Sable, Mich., Jan. 13, '92.
B. F. Buchanan.

Dear Sir:—I have just returned from my attempt to fill my engagement yesterday, (and God knows I was anxious to keep my word) but am here. Who carelessly directed me well nigh caused my perishing last night. I was gone all night and came in town at 1 p.m.

today. I took a span of horses purposely as not to be delayed or miss appointment.   Yours,
J. C. Rubillard.

Alcona County Review, January 14, 1892

Somewhat Personal.

Capt. Ferris, of the Point Aux. Barques L. S. S., who attended the funeral of Mrs. J. E. Henderson last week, returned home last Saturday morning. Mr. Ferris is a particular friend of Capt. Henderson's, the two having been fellow surfmen in the Sand Beach station for five years.

Alcona County Review, January 21, 1892

Card of Thanks.

I wish to extend thanks to all the friends who kindly assisted in my late bereavement and also for the selection of flowers from kind friends.
J. E. Henderson.

Alcona County Review, January 21, 1892

The Local News

A good price will be paid for copies of the Review bearing date of January 14th, 1892, or for the obituary of the late Mrs. Capt. Henderson published therein. If any friends having same will kindly forward them to this office it will be esteemed as a favor also.

Alcona County Review, February 18, 1892

HISTORY OF ONE YEAR.

Chronological History of the Past Year, 1892.

THE DEATH RECORD.

Jan. 9. Death of Mrs. Capt. Henderson.

Alcona County Review, January 5, 1893
Cemetery: Springport, Alcona Co.

Henderson, Samuel

HOME NEWS JOTTINGS.

Samuel Henderson, recently in the employ of Moore & Tanner, of Au Sable, committed suicide by shooting, Monday evening. Henderson's home is in Alcona. The funeral took place Wednesday.

Alcona County Review, September 1, 1882
Cemetery: Probably Mt. Joy, Alcona Co.

Hendricks, William

William Hendricks, aged 28, was struck in the head by a stick which flew from the edger in the Miner saw mill in Alpena. The stick penetrated entirely through his head, exiting the

jaw and lacerating the roof of his mouth in a terrible manner. Yet he lived for several hours.

Alcona County Review, May 28, 1896
Cemetery: Probably Evergreen, Alpena Co.

Hendrie, Annie [Miller]

DEATH'S SAD DOINGS

The wife of John Hendrie, one of the pioneer farmers of Alcona county, died at his late residence in Harrisville township Sunday at the age of 64 years 6 months and 11 days. The funeral which was held Tuesday morning from the Catholic church was largely attended by the residents of the county.

Annie Miller Hendrie was born in Lanlasgoshire, Scotland, in 1825, where about 1845 she married John Hendrie who survives her. In 1853 they came to what was then called the highlands of Au Sable, which is now included in this county, and four years later they moved onto the land which for thirty years has been their home. All around them then was a dense and unbroken forest of pines. The deceased was the mother of three children all of whom are married and survive her.

Alcona County Review, August 30, 1889

ADDITIONAL LOCAL.

John Hendrie thanks his friends and especially the ladies of Springport for their kindness during the recent illness and death of his wife.

Alcona County Review, August 30, 1889
Cemetery: Probably St. Anne's, Alcona Co.

Hendrie, John

Another Pioneer Gone.

As a faithful chronicler of passing events it becomes the duty of the Review to record the death of one more of the old pioneer citizens' of Alcona county:

John Hendrie, having passed the limit of years allotted to man as the period of his existence upon the earth, was gathered to his fathers Sunday morning, February 18th, at the ripe old age of 76 years. Mr. Hendrie was a native of Scotland. He has been a resident of Alcona county since the year 1855, when he and his wife came here and entered the employ of Crosier Davison, who was in that early day conducting the business of fishing off this coast on an extensive scale. Sometime afterwards Mr. Hendrie bought 40 acres of government land which was increased by a subsequent purchase of 120 acres. He built a cabin, made a garden, planted an orchard and struggled along earning money in the saw mill to carry him along while clearing his farm. In his pioneer days he was ably assisted by his wife, who shared his privations with true heroism, often carrying their supplies home on her back. Thus they made a home in the wilderness. In the year 1859 the deceased was one of 17 electors who petitioned the county of Alpena for a separate township organization. Among that number were Isaac Wilson, Geo. H. Blush, Perley Silverthorn, Chas. Briggs, Wm. Noyes, Jos. Fisher, Francis La Chapelle, Sr., L. O. and L. H. Harris, Henry Gibbons, Jas. Higginson, Wm. Hill and Wm. Cullings, many of whom still survive. Their prayer being granted afforded the first opportunity to the citizens of the then wilderness to cast a vote for public officers. It does not appear that the deceased ever held public office. His wife died about four years ago. He is survived by three daughters, viz: Mrs. Jos. Specht, Mrs. Jas. Brown and Mrs. Swindlehurst.

The funeral services were held Monday afternoon at the Methodist church.

Alcona County Review, February 22, 1894

Card of Thanks.

We, the undersigned, herewith desire to extend our sincere and heartfelt thanks to the many kind friends and neighbors who so liberally lent a helping hand during our recent bereavement; the illness, death and burial of our beloved father.

Mrs. Mary Specht,
Mrs. Lizzie Brown,
Mrs. Joanna Swindlehurst.

Alcona County Review, March 8, 1894
Cemetery:

Henry, John

Shore News.

This morning telegrams announced that a man named Hayes was shot and killed, in a drunken brawl, at Tawas yesterday. No particulars are given.

Alcona County Review, July 5, 1878
Cemetery: Greenwood, Isoco Co.

Henson, William

PERSONAL MENTION.

Wm. Henson was brought down from Ward's camp Tuesday by a comrade. Henson was and is a very sick man and is suffering from low fever which had sapped his vitality until his friends feared that recovery was impossible. His condition today is serious.

Later.——He died at 3 p.m.

Alcona County Review, August 29, 1895

EVENTS OF ONE WEEK.

The Review had part of its last edition printed when the forms were opened to announce the death of William Henson which occurred at 3 p.m. Thursday, August 29. Deceased was a native of Canada and was born at Dannville, Ont., April 22, 1849. He was therefore 46 years old at the time of his death. He came to Michigan in 1874. In February, 1877, he was united in marriage to Mrs. Elizabeth Bailey. Four children, two sons and two daughters, were the product of this union. Mr. Henson was made a Master Mason in December, 1874, in Alcona Lodge No. 292 and four years later he became a member of Harrisville Lodge No. 218 I.O.O.F. He had followed a lumberman's life for many years and was known among his fellows as a patient hard working man honorable in his dealings, moral in character and a good friend. He had been employed in Ward's camp 10 years and his chief looked upon him as one of his most reliable men and frequently left him in charge. His death was due in a measure to hard work. He was taken ill less than a week before his death and was brought home two days before his demise so that in his last moments, he was surrounded by his family. The funeral services were held Sunday morning at the Methodist church and were in charge of the Masonic and Odd Fellow fraternities who turned out 100 strong to discharge this last solemn obligation to their departed friend and brother. Rev. W. J. Bailey preached an excellent funeral sermon. The procession was a large one, the Masons and Odd Fellows leading the way on foot, marching to and from the South Harrisville cemetery where the interment took place. The services at the grave followed the

beautiful and impressive ritual of the Masons.

The flowers and pieces were fine.

Alcona County Review, September 5, 1895

Black River Sparks.

Little Sparks.

Several members of the I.O.O.F. of Black River attended the funeral of William Henson at Harrisville Sunday.

Alcona County Review, September 5, 1895

Resolutions of Respect and Condolence.

Whereas, It has pleased Almighty God in his infinite wisdom to remove from our midst our esteemed friend and brother, William Henson, a member of Alcona Lodge No. 292 F. & A. M. therefore be it

Resolved, that while submitting to the will of God who doeth all things well, we deplore the loss of our absent brother.

Resolved that the charter be draped for 30 days, that a copy of these resolutions be sent to the relatives of the deceased, entered upon the records of our lodge and published in the Alcona County Review.

Harrisville, Mich., Sept. 1, 1895.
C. M. Lund.
Geo. E. Gillam.   Com.
L. A. Colwell.

Alcona County Review, September 5, 1895

Resolutions of Respect and Condolence.

Resolved, that to his respected and bereaved family we extend our sincere sympathy and as a further token thereof, as engrossed copy of these resolutions be presented to them and

Resolved, that as a further token of our love and respect for our deceased brother, that these resolutions be spread upon the lodge records, a copy be sent to our local paper for publication, and that our lodge room be suitably draped in mourning for a period of 30 days. And it is further.

Resolved, that we join the Masonic Order in paying the funeral expenses.

Harrisville, Sept. 5, 1895.
Matthew Hale.
Carl M. Lund.   Com.
Lyman H. Dunn.

Alcona County Review, September 5, 1895

We sincerely thank our many friends for their help and sympathy in the hour of our deep affliction. May they all find friends equally kind in the hour of need.

Mrs. Henson and Family.

Alcona County Review, September 5, 1895
Cemetery: Springport, Alcona Co.

Heron, George Colburn

ALL ALONG THE SHORE.

Alpena Drift.

From the Argus.

Geo. C. Herron, a well known pioneer of this county, and a leading citizen of Wilson township, died at his residence on Tuesday of last week, aged 51 years. He was one of the first settlers of Wilson township and has held the office of township clerk many terms. He leaves many friends behind.

Alcona County Review, May 27, 1887
Cemetery: Wilson Township, Alpena Co.

Heron, Henry

Probate Order.

State of Michigan,
County of Alcona.

Notice is hereby given, that by an order of the Probate Court for the County of Alcona made on the seventh day of April A. D. 1886, six months from that date were allowed for creditors to present their claims against the estate of Henry H. Herring, late of said County, deceased, and that all creditors of said deceased are required to present their claims to said Probate Court, at the Probate office, in the village of Harrisville, for examination and allowance, on or before the seventh day of October 1886, next, and that such claims will be heard before said Court, on Wednesday, the seventh day of July, and on Thursday, the seventh day of October, next, at ten o'clock in the forenoon of each of those days.

Dated, April 7th, A. D. 1886.
Allen Nevins,
Judge of Probate.

Alcona County Review, May 27, 1887
Cemetery: Probably Springport, Alcona Co.

Heron, John Bailey

BLACK RIVER.

Mr. and Mrs. John Heron of Alpena came down Saturday morning with the remains of their little month old baby boy, who died Friday.

Alcona County Review, September 22, 1898

LOCAL PICK UPS.

Mr. and Mrs. Jno. Heron of Alpena, formerly of Black River,

mourn the loss of another little one. The remains were interred in the South Harrisville cemetery Saturday.

Alcona County Review, September 22, 1898
Cemetery: Springport, Alcona Co.

Heron, Priscilla Alden

The infant child of John Heron is quite ill.

Alcona County Review, September 12, 1895

PERSONAL MENTION.

John Heron came down from the River this morning to make arrangements for the burial of his infant child which died yesterday.

Alcona County Review, September 12, 1895

Black River Sparks.

The infant child of Mr. and Mrs. John Heron died here on Thursday morning, Sept. 12th. The funeral took place on Friday a.m. The services were conducted by the Rev. Earle of E. Tawas at the church here. Major Safford presided at the organ during the services. The interment was made at the South Harrisville cemetery.

A sad but pretty sight was presented as the little white casket was borne to the church by four little girls, assisted by four boys. The floral offerings were very beautiful.

Alcona County Review, September 19, 1895

Black River Sparks.

Mrs. Geo. O. Bailey returned from the Soo, whence she was summoned by telegram announcing the serious illness of her granddaughter, the infant child of Mr. and Mrs. John Heron.

Alcona County Review, September 19, 1895

We sincerely thank our friends for the many words of sympathy and acts of kindness tendered us during the sickness and death of our little one and particularly those who personally cared for Mrs. Heron and child.

Mr. and Mrs. Jno. Heron.

Alcona County Review, September 19, 1895
Cemetery: Springport, Alcona Co.

Hershey, John

Jottings Along the Shore.

John Hershey, a young man about 22 years of age, was drowned on Fletcher, Pack & Co.'s drive on Thunder Bay river Monday of last week.

Alcona County Review, May 27, 1881
Cemetery: Probably Evergreen, Alpena Co.

Heumann, Frank Faust

PERSONAL MENTION.

Fred G. Heumann, merchant tailor of Traverse City, formerly of Oscoda, was greeting old business acquaintances in town Tuesday. He had been called to Alpena by the death of his little son.

Alcona County Review, December 5, 1895
Cemetery: Evergreen, Alpena Co.

Heumann, Clara Louise

Somewhat Personal.

Mr. and Mrs. Fred Heumann of Oscoda buried their daughter Clara, aged five years, on Sunday. She had been ill a couple of weeks.

Alcona County Review, November 12, 1891
Cemetery: Pinecrest, Iosco Co.

Heumann, George

LOCAL JOTTINGS.

Dr. Geo. Heumann, a resident of Bay City since 1853, father of Ferdinand and Geo. Heumann, of Oscoda, died last Friday afternoon, aged 64 years.

Alcona County Review, September 10, 1886
Cemetery: Probably Green Ridge, Bay Co.

Hike, William

Two More Victims.
Two Pewabic Wreckers Lose Their Lives in the Diving Bell.

Geo. G. Campbell and Peter Olson lost their lives Saturday while at work on the wreck of the Pewabic, which lies in deep water off Thunder Bay.

The men went down in the diving bell. Campbell, who was the superintendent of the expedition, telephoned up to the steamer Root for hooks. Communication was then suddenly suspended and an effort to hoist the bell disclosed that it had fouled in the wreck and could not be moved. A heavy sea came on and it was several hours before the bell was finally hoisted and towed into smooth water. A window in the bell was found broken and both men were found dead, of course.

These make a total of four lives lost in the effort to secure the treasure of the Pewabic. Wm. Hike of Buffalo died from exposure in 1865 and Oliver Pelkey became entangled in the wreckage in 1891.

Alcona County Review, June 23, 1898
Cemetery:

Hiler, Joseph

EVENTS OF ONE WEEK.

Jos. Hiler was shot and instantly killed at Alpena Tuesday by Wellington Scrimshaw. Hiler and a woman were quarreling when Scrimshaw interfered with a shotgun and fatal results to Hiler.

Alcona County Review, September 21, 1893

Scrimshaw, the Alpena murderer, has received a sentence of 15 years at Jackson.

Alcona County Review, November 16, 1893
Cemetery:

Hill, Abram

The Local News

Mr. Milton Hill of Killmaster was summoned home on Monday to attend the funeral of his father, Abram Hill, of Goodrich, Genessee county, who died Sunday evening, May 22. Mr. Hill keeps the store and postoffice at Killmaster and is town treasurer. He is highly respected as a merchant, officer and citizen and has the sincere sympathy of the people in his bereavement and sorrow.

Alcona County Review, May 26, 1892
Cemetery: Goodrich, Genesee Co.

Hill, Ezra N.

PERSONAL MENTION.

F. J. Hill of Black River was called to Holley, N. Y., last week by the death of his father, Ezra N. Hill, which occurred Nov. 5th inst. Death was sudden and resulted from dropsy of the lungs.

From the Holly Standard, a copy of which has reached us, we observe that deceased was born upon the same farm where he died 72 years ago. He had been married twice and F. J. Hill was the eldest of his four children.

The Standard says of him:

In this vicinity, where Mr. Hill has lived practically all his life, no citizen was more highly esteemed. In business matters his integrity was spotless, socially he was one of the most genial and companionable of men, and the calls of religion and benevolence always found him ready with open heart, hand and purse.

Alcona County Review, November 15, 1894
Cemetery:

Hill, Milton Abram

PERSONAL.

It is with genuine regret that we are called upon this week to chronicle the death of Milton Hill of Gustin township. Mr. Hill died Monday morning last at his home of pneumonia.

During his five years of residence in Alcona county, the deceased made many friends in his own and neighboring towns. He was a man of sterling worth, honest and upright in his dealings with his fellows, and who commanded the respect of all who knew him. For two years he served in the capacity of treasurer, and had just concluded his third term as town clerk. Kind and generous, his untimely death is felt deeply by the community in which he lived.

Deceased was born in Genesee county, Mich., and had he lived one day longer would have been 37 years of age. Six years ago he married Bertha Graham. Five years ago he came to Alcona county and has since been doing a general merchantile business at Gustin and Killmaster. He leaves a wife, two sons, five brothers and two sisters to mourn their loss. His last words were addressed to his wife and were: "I am going to heaven with the angels, mother and father: meet me there with the children."

The funeral services were held at the M. E. church, Harrisville, yesterday afternoon, Rev. Ford officiating.

Alcona County Review, March 4, 1897

Card of Thanks.

To all the kind neighbors and friends who helped us during the last illness and death of our beloved husband and father, and who offered words of comfort in our deep sorrow, we desire to express our heartfelt thanks.

Mrs. Milton Hill and Family.
Gustin, Mich., Mar. 5, 1897.

Alcona County Review, March 11, 1897

PERSONAL POINTS.

Mrs. Bertha Hill of Killmaster was transacting some business before the probate court Monday relative to the estate of her late husband which is nearing a settlement.

Alcona County Review, February 10, 1898

At a session of said court, held at the Probate Office in the city of Harrisville, in said county, on the 13th day of November, A. D. 1911.

Present: Hon. Geo. W. Burt, Judge of Probate.

In the matter of the estate of Milton Abram Hill and Floyd Robert Hill, minors.

Bertha E. Hacker, guardian of said minors, having filed in said court a petition praying for license to sell the interest of said estate in certain real estate therein described.

It is ordered, That the 9th day of December, A. D. 1911, at two o'clock in the afternoon at said probate office, be and is hereby appointed for hearing said petition, and that all persons interested in said estate appear before said court, at said time and place, to show cause why a license to sell the interest of said estate in said real estate should not be granted.

It is further ordered, That public notice thereof be given by publication of a copy of this order, for three successive weeks previous to said day of hearing, in the Alcona County Review, a newspaper printed and circulated in said county.

GEO. W. BURT, Judge of Probate.

Alcona County Review, November 30, 1911
Cemetery: Springport, Alcona Co.

Hill, Mrs.

KILLMASTER RIPPLES.

Mr. Hill received a telegram Friday night, stating the sad news of his mother's death. She was a very estimable old lady.

Alcona County Review, February 18, 1897
Cemetery:

Hill, Will

LOCAL PICK UPS.

East Tawas has made its first sacrifice on account of the war in the death of Will Hill, a young man of 21 who enlisted with a Mississippi regiment and died of typhoid fever at Jacksonville, Fla. The remains were embalmed and brought north for burial.

Alcona County Review, August 25, 1898
Cemetery:

Hill, William

Haynes Happenings.

Haynes, Jan. 29th.--Wm. Hill Sr. is reported to be very ill; so low that he is speechless. He is residing at Black River, but was formerly a resident of Haynes and he was familiarly known as "Commodore" Hill in this neck o' woods.

Alcona County Review, January 31, 1895

The funeral services of the late Wm. Hill were held this forenoon, interment taking place at Alcona.

Alcona County Review, March 21, 1895

Black River News.

Black River, March 27.--William Hill, one of the oldest residents of Alcona county, died here Tuesday morning. His death was in no way a surprise to the community for he had a paralytic stroke some time ago and has been lying at death's door ever since.

Alcona County Review, March 21, 1895

Black River News.

Black River, March 27.--Mrs. Hopkins returned home to Lansing last week after paying her last respects to her father, Wm. Hill.

Alcona County Review, March 28, 1895

Haynes Happenings.

The remains of William Hill were interred in our cemetery on Thursday March 21st, whither they were brought from Black River and were followed by a large number of relatives and friends. The floral offerings were large and very beautiful.

Alcona County Review, March 28, 1895

The following facts in the life of the late Wm. Hill are taken from the biographical sketches in the History of the Huron Shore:

William Hill was born at Lockport, Niagara County, N. Y., 1823, and lived there to manhood. He was married at Lewiston, N. Y., to Lydia A. Horton, in 1857, who died at Alcona in 1877 and was buried in Alcona cemetery.

Mr. Hill came to Presque Isle May 1845, and to Alcona County the same year and worked for Goodwin Bros., at Thunder Bay Island, at $14 per month. He bought a gill net and commenced the business on his own hook. He afterward got more nets and the next year got a boat and increased his business. He came to the Cove in 1853 and had at one time five boats full rigged and did the largest fishing business on the shore. In the fall of 1855 Mr. Hill opened a store of supplies for fishermen, and Robert White acted as clerk. This store was also a hotel where men got food and lodging and did not pay

anything. In 1857 Mr. Hill bought out Morrison McKinly which included his fishing rigs and shanties, and then secured lots 2, 3, and 4 at the Cove, being in section 1 and section 11 in Alcona Township. Mr. Hill afterward owned land in Harrisville Township, where the principal part of the village now stands, which he sold to Harris Bros. In 1857 and '58 Mr. Hill was appointed deputy state land commissioner by James W. Sanborn, state land commissioner, and was, during that time, engaged in preventing and prosecuting trespassers on the public lands. Mr. Hill was elected highway commissioner of his township and held several successive terms of that office. He laid out and superintended the building of the Harrisville and Black River Turnpike Road of thirteen miles, the longest road of the kind in the county.

Alcona County Review, March 28, 1895

We thank the friends who so kindly contributed in any way to render easy the last moments of our late father, Wm. Hill. Also those ladies for the beautiful church decorations for the funeral.

HIS CHILDREN.

Alcona County Review, March 28, 1895
Cemetery: Mt. Joy, Alcona Co.

Hinckley, Mary

Overboard.

Friday night last, the steamer Metropolis had on board a young lady passenger named Miss Mary Hinckley, who was registered for Alpena. She occupied a stateroom with a Mrs. Griggs, and the last time she was seen was in her room shortly after the boat had left Oscoda. As her shawl and hat were found near one of the steamer's wheel-houses and her valise had been left in the state-room, it is evident that she either accidentally fell or jumped overboard and was drowned. She was not missed until the boat neared this port and as no person got off at Greenbush, she must have found a watery grave somewhere between Oscoda and Harrisville. She was a woman of unusual intelligence, 35 years of age, and resided in Arbela, Tuscola county. The clerk of the Metropolis after reaching Alpena telegraphed the intelligence of her death to relatives in various parts of the State. No attempt as yet has been

made to recover the body, but search will probably be instituted after the time shall have elapsed when the same would float on the surface of the water and probably come ashore. We understand that the young lady had attempted suicide several times before.

Alcona County Review, August 19, 1881

Miss Hinckley's Death.

We copy the following from a recent number of the Bay City Evening Press:

The readers of the Press will remember the mysterious fate of Miss Hinckley, who was evidently drowned, last week, in some manner from the steamer Metropolis, near Harrisville, while proceeding from this city to Alpena. Several of our exchanges have alluded to her death as a case of suicide; but her friends and relatives think that this idea does injustice to them and to the deceased. The Vassar Times in alluding to the case says:

"Miss Hinckley was at her sister's in Vassar for two days prior to her departure for Alpena, and seemed to be in excellent health and a happy frame of mind. As she bade her sister good bye she exacted a promise to join her in Alpena at a later date, and they would come home together: she also left messages for the friends at home, all indicating anticipation of a pleasant visit in Alpena and an early return home. Her parents and other relatives know of no reason why she should have sought death, and they firmly believe that her sad fate is solely attributable to accident.

Miss Hinckley was 35 years of age and a woman of marked intelligence and warm affections. Her life had been passed almost wholly at home, and her affection for father, mother, brothers and sisters was very strong. To her home was the one dear spot on earth, and within its sacred precincts she appeared to be content. She was never known to intentionally wound the feelings of friends, and had endeared herself to all within the range of her acquaintance by deeds worthy of her generous nature. Her heart went out in sympathy to all the afflicted, and she will be mourned by many who had no kinship.

Alcona County Review, August 26, 1881

HOME REVIEWINGS.

Capt. Robertson informs the Review that Miss Hinckley went overboard from the steamer Metropolis somewhere between South Harrisville and Harrisville, as she was last seen just as the boat was backing out from the former place.

Alcona County Review, August 26, 1881

Additional Reviewings.

The body of a woman, supposed to be Miss Mary Hinckley who was drowned between Harrisville and South Harrisville two weeks since, was found floating in Tawas Bay, Wednesday afternoon, by the captain of the Metropolis. The remains were in a terribly decomposed state and were only recognizable by the clothing which they had on.

Alcona County Review, August 26, 1881

The body of Miss Hinckley, which was found floating a short distance from Tawas, reached the city this morning about two o'clock on the shore boat and proceeded to Clio on the 7 o'clock F. and P. M. train, where it will be buried to-morrow. Mr. Miller, the brother-in-law of the deceased, says the body was decomposed past recognition, the features bearing no semblance to a human being. The body was in the water two weeks, and floated at least 30 miles, directly in the track of the shore boats, making it somewhat remarkable that it had not been discovered before. There is a theory advanced in regard to it, however, that possibly it might have fastened by the clothing to some vessel which passed over it, and been dragged the greater portion of the distance, but that would hardly seem probable.— *Bay City Press*, Aug. 27.

Alcona County Review, September 2, 1881
Cemetery: Pine Grove, Tuscola Co.

Hoard, Eugene Temple
REVIEWINGS.

Death has again entered the domestic circle of Bro. Hoard, of the Tawas *Gazette*, and snatched from the arms of father and mother a bright-eyed little boy, scarce a year old. 'Tis sad to part with those little ones we love, and the weight of grief presses heavily upon our hearts when the dear Savior calls for the infant souls, that he may take them up in His arms to bless them, and we consign their little, lifeless forms to

the narrow limits of the tomb. But the hope that they shall live again, and we shall be privileged to meet them in a glorious immortality of life! Ah, that comforteth us, and casts a glimmer of light upon our sorrowing countenances, while we go on hoping and striving for that "sweet by and by." Yes, our hopes are not buried in the grave.

Alcona County Review, September 19, 1879
Cemetery:

Hogan, Matt
FATAL ACCIDENT.

Conductor Matt Hogan Instantly Killed on the Mud Lake Railroad.

Special Correspondence of the Review.

We regret to chronicle the death of Conductor Matt Hogan which occurred on the Mud Lake branch of the D. B. C. & A. railroad on the morning of the 7th inst. at 6:44 A.M.

Engine No. 10, Cal McDonald, engineer, was employed in bringing the men of Brook's camp to their work, and in backing in on the Whitney branch the train struck a tree which had fallen across the track. The train was made up of two flat cars and a way car containing the men, two teams of horses, some hay and the necessary tools for working; the flat cars were ahead on the train—the way car between them and the engine.

The ill fated conductor was at his post of duty on the head flat, and the force of the concussion threw him ahead of his train on the track. The platform of the car on which he had been standing left its trucks and shot forward on the rails, crushing Hogan beneath it. Death must have been instantaneous as the body was terribly mangled. The engine crashed into the way car wounding several of the men but none fatally—one of the horses was killed.

A large wrecking crew was on hand in a short time, and the body of the unfortunate man was taken from beneath the car and sent to Black River and thence to his home in Lucan, Ont.

The dead conductor was a gentleman in every sense of the word—genial, whole-souled and obliging, and his untimely death is deeply regretted by a large circle of friends.

Alcona County Review, November 15, 1889
Cemetery:

Hohenstine, Truth W.
The Local News

A child of Mrs. Honestine was buried yesterday.

Alcona County Review, February 25, 1892
Cemetery:

Holcomb, {Male}
Killmaster.
April 22, 1896.
Charles Holcomb received a telegram Saturday saying his brother had been killed at Yale, Mich.

Alcona County Review, April 23, 1896
Cemetery: Probably McFadden, St. Clair Co.

Holcomb, Mary Jane [Oles]
Killmaster.
Sept. 12th, '99.
Mrs. Charles Holcomb of Yale, formerly of this place, died last Wednesday after a long illness. Mr. Holcomb and family have the sympathy of all in this place.

Alcona County Review, September 14, 1899

Resolutions of Condolence.
Sanborn Hive No. 79: Lady Mary Holcomb age 40 years.

Whereas, the angel of death has passed the sentinel and picket of our hive for the second time since its organization and has removed from our circle our beloved sister, Mary J. Holcomb

Resolved, as it has been the will of him who doeth all things well, who has seen fit to remove from her earthly home Lady Holcomb,

Resolved, that we as members of Sanborn Hive No. 79 L. O. T. M. extend to the bereaved husband and friends our heartfelt sympathy in this hour of affliction.

Resolved that we drape our charter for sixty days as a token of respect and a copy of these resolutions sent to the husband and son and entered upon the records of our Hive and published in the county paper.
Killmaster, Sept. 9, 1899.
Eliza Heath
Maude Graham Com'tee.
Lizzie Wood

Alcona County Review, September 14, 1899

KILLMASTER.
Nov. 1, '99.
On the 26th of October Chas. H. Holcomb received a check for $500, being the amount of insurance carried by his wife, a member of the Sanborn Hive No. 79.

Alcona County Review, November 2, 1899
Cemetery: McFadden, St. Clair Co.

Holden, Carrie

REVIEWINGS.

Brother Holden, of the Farwell *Register*, has lost his only daughter, a bright little seven-year-old. We can truly sympathize with him in this great affliction, having ourself been called upon to part with an only daughter of five summers just one year ago to-day. We know the depth of grief that causes the tears to well up in the eyes of the father thus deprived of so lovely a household flower, and if it were not for the sweet consolation that we may meet them again in more glorious surroundings than earth can afford, Oh, who can tell the weight of sorrow we should then bear. Dear Brother, let us strive to meet our little ones in that glorious immortality.

Alcona County Review, December 12, 1879
Cemetery: Surrey Township, Clare Co.

Holden, Lewis

County News and Gossip.

Wednesday forenoon Miss Carrie Holden received a telegram from Bay Co. that her brother there was dangerously ill. Miss Holden, accompanied by her brother Edward and Mrs. C. E. McLennan, left from Au Sable on yesterday morning's stage for Standish, where they would take the cars for Bay City. Mr. McLennan drove them down to the Sable Wednesday evening.

Alcona County Review, January 3, 1879

County News and Gossip.

Mrs. C. E. McLennan, Miss Carrie and Edward Holden, who, last week Wednesday, went down to Mason, Ingham county, to see a sick brother of Carrie and Ed's, arrived just in time to see him die, and follow his remains to the cemetery. They arrived home again on Wednesday of this week.

Alcona County Review, January 10, 1879
Cemetery: Maple Grove, Ingham Co.

Holmes, Beatrice M.

PERSONAL MENTION.

A small child of E. Holmes has suffered a stroke of paralysis, the result of a severe attack of diphtheria, from which it was recovering.

Just as we go to press we learn that another child of Mr. Holmes, a girl of 6 years, died this morning from a relapse of diphtheria.

Alcona County Review, July 20, 1893
Cemetery: Mt. Joy, Alcona Co.

Holmes, Eva L.

Diphtheria Claims More Victims.

The cruel hand of death has been laid heavily upon the family of Edwin Holmes and two of his children have been ruthlessly taken away, innocent victims to the dreadful disease diphtheria. The children had been ill but the nature of the disease was unknown and the parents supposed it was some simple summer complaint. When a physician was finally called the youngest child was found in the last stages of dissolution. The death of this child on Saturday was followed by the death of their 11 year old daughter, Eva, on Sunday.

Six other cases developed in the same family but all are reported as recovering. The disease was brought from camp by one of the boys.

Alcona County Review, June 15, 1893

Last Monday Dr. Mitchell thoroughly disinfected the house of Edwin Holmes and the family were released from quarantine. There has been no diphtheria in the family for a month and no fear need be felt by anyone who may come in contact with them.

Alcona County Review, August 10, 1893
Cemetery: Mt. Joy, Alcona Co.

Holmes, Herbert F.

Diphtheria Claims More Victims.

The cruel hand of death has been laid heavily upon the family of Edwin Holmes and two of his children have been ruthlessly taken away, innocent victims to the dreadful disease diphtheria. The children had been ill but the nature of the disease was unknown and the parents supposed it was some simple summer complaint. When a physician was finally called the youngest child was found in the last stages of dissolution. The death of this child on Saturday was followed by the death of their 11 year old daughter, Eva, on Sunday.

Six other cases developed in the same family but all are reported as recovering. The disease was brought from camp by one of the boys.

Alcona County Review, June 15, 1893

Last Monday Dr. Mitchell thoroughly disinfected the house of Edwin Holmes and the family were released from quarantine. There has been no diphtheria in the family for a month and no fear need be felt by anyone who may come in contact with them.

Alcona County Review, August 10, 1893
Cemetery: Mt. Joy, Alcona Co.

Hompstead, Elizabeth Jane [Burkhart]

Mrs. Geo. Olmstead, a daughter of John Burkhart, died Tuesday morning at the family residence from consumption. She was but 19 years of age and had been married about two years. John Burkhart Jr., a son, is also very ill with the same wasting disease, and the stricken family should have not only the sympathy but the substantial aid of all citizens. The funeral of Mrs. Olmstead occurred today.

Alcona County Review, November 10, 1898
Cemetery: Mt. Joy, Alcona Co.

Hompstead, Emma [Price]

Haynes Happenings.

March 16, 1897.

Mrs. George Hompsted died very suddenly at 2 o'clock a.m. Wednesday March 10th. She was at Miller's store on the 9th and appeared in good health. She leaves a husband and three sons, two of whom were working in the lumber woods. One has not arrived home yet. The funeral will be held tomorrow.

Alcona County Review, March 18, 1897

Haynes Happenings.

March 22, '97.

The remains of Mrs. George Hompsted were interred in the cemetery on the 17th. Her three sons were present to mourn with their father over his loss.

Alcona County Review, March 25, 1897
Cemetery: Mt. Joy, Alcona Co.

Hompstead, Mrs.

Haynes Happenings.

Mrs. Hempstead, mother-in-law of Peter Churchill, died last week and the remains were buried Friday in our cemetery. Consumption was the cause of death.

Alcona County Review, September 6, 1894
Cemetery: Mt. Joy, Alcona Co.

Hood, Charles

PURELY PERSONAL.

Killed at Black River.—Last Friday afternoon Chas. Hood, a well known young man employed by Alger, Smith & Co. as a teamster, was instantly killed on the rollway at Black River. He was fastening a chain to a deck when the rollway broke and a log came down striking him on the head with force sufficient to break his neck. He was 26 years of age and unmarried. He was well and favorably known throughout the county. His remains were buried in the Catholic cemetery at Harrisville, a large number of his friends following them to their final resting place.

Alcona County Review, July 19, 1889
Cemetery: St. Anne's, Alcona Co.

Hood, {Girl}

Mr. Claudius Hood's folks lost their baby last week. They went to town with it and it died the next day. It was about six months old.

Alcona County Review, January 10, 1890
Cemetery:

Hood, Robert

REVIEWINGS.

Robert Hood, living four miles west, was buried to-day. He was an aged man and considerably crippled. Had been a resident of this county for a number of years.

Alcona County Review, June 6, 1879
Cemetery: St. Anne's, Alcona Co.

Hooper, Lewis W.

Lewis W. Hooper, a former resident of Harrisville, is dead. He was a member of Webster Lodge No. 1099, Knights of Honor of Harrisville, and was insured in that order for $2,000.

Alcona County Review, February 7, 1890

OBITUARY.
A friend of the Review sent the following obituary notice too late for publication last week:

L. W. Hooper, who was for many years a resident of Harrisville, died at Greeley, Col., Jan. 31, of a complication of diseases of long standing, aged 45 years, 1 mo. and 17 days.

He was born in England, his parents emigrating to Canada when he was 12 years of age. When about 16 years of age he came to Michigan where he resided until about seven years ago when, having poor health, he removed to Colorado and while there he regained his health. It no

doubt prolonged his life. He was many years in the employ of J. Van Buskirk of S. Harrisville. He was a man of strict integrity and unblemished character, of more than ordinary business capacity, one to be missed in a community. He was a member of the Masonic order, the Knights of Honor and also of the I. O. O. F. He leaves a wife, one child and a large circle of friends to mourn their loss.

Alcona County Review, February 14, 1890

Lewis W. Hooper whose death at Greeley, Col., was reported Jan. 3rd was a member of Webster Lodge No. 1099, K. of H. A certificate for $2,000, the amount of insurance held by Mr. Hooper in the order, was received by the officers of the Lodge last week. It was payable to Mrs. Hooper and has been forwarded to her address.

Alcona County Review, May 2, 1890
Cemetery: Fairmount, Denver Co, CO

Hoover, Eli

LOCAL JOTTINGS

Eli Hoover, of West Bay City, is 78 years old and for 25 days he has not touched food because he maintains that the Lord is able to keep the faithful right along without the inconvenience of eating. Eli ought to be old enough to know that the Lord helps only those who help themselves.

Alcona County Review, July 20, 1888

LOCAL JOTTINGS

Eli Hoover, the West Bay City faster, stood it for forty-five days without tasting food and then—died.

Alcona County Review, August 10, 1888
Cemetery:

Hotchkiss, Charles

LOCAL JOTTINGS

Chas. Hotchkiss, of Killmaster, is very low with inflammation of the lungs. He cannot recover.

Alcona County Review, March 9, 1888

DEATHS.
Hotchkiss.—Charles Hotchkiss, mentioned last week as very low with inflammation of the lungs, at his home in Killmaster, died Friday and was buried Sunday. The funeral services were held at the Baptist church in this place, Rev. F. N. Barlow officiating.

Alcona County Review, March 16, 1888

Cemetery: Springport, Alcona Co.

Houghton, Eliza [Smith]

COUNTY REVIEWINGS.

Died, in Harrisville, Nov. 11, 1880, Mrs. Eliza Houghton, aged 73 years, 5 months and 24 days, wife of Mr. Jehial Houghton, and mother of Mr. Ansel Houghton and Mrs. M. S. Madden. Deceased has been a member of the Baptist Church for the past 40 years.

Alcona County Review, November 12, 1880
Cemetery: Springport, Alcona Co.

Houghton, Jehial

LOCAL JOTTINGS.

We understand that "Uncle" Houghton, father of Mrs. M. L. Madden, is quite ill at the home of the latter. He is past 80 years of age.

Alcona County Review, February 19, 1886

LOCAL JOTTINGS.

Jebiel Houghton died on the 22d inst. at the residence of his daughter, Mrs. M. Madden. Mr. Houghton was born January 24, 1806, in New Lisbon, Otsego county, N. Y., and was aged 80 years, 1 month and 29 days. The funeral services were held at the Methodist Episcopal church on Wednesday afternoon, Rev. T. B. Leith taking for his text: "For David after he had served his own generation by the will of God, fell on sleep and was laid unto his fathers." There was a large attendance.

Alcona County Review, March 26, 1886
Cemetery: Springport, Alcona Co.

Houston, Peter

LOCAL PARAGRAPHS.
Mrs. Jos. Evans received a telegram Saturday announcing the serious illness of her brother, Peter Houston by name, at the Central Hotel, Oscoda. Houston died at noon of the same day. On Sunday the remains were brought to Harrisville and interred Tuesday in the South Harrisville cemetery.

Houston was 36 years of age and his sister had not heard from him before in nine years until the telegram was received announcing his fatal illness. Mrs. John Morris is the other sister referred to by the Press.

The Oscoda Press contains the following concerning Houston's sickness and death:

Peter Houston died at the Central Hotel just before noon today. A week ago today he was brought down from Yockey's camp, where he had been working and where he was taken sick with inflammation of the lungs. Dr. Weir has attended him. A few minutes before his death Houston said that he had a brother in Cheboygan and two sisters in Harrisville, one of whom was Mrs. Jos. Evans. When asked by Mr. Coppinger earlier in the week if he had any relatives or friends who could be notified of his sickness, he evaded the question by saying that he would be all right in a few days. He evidently thought all the time that he was going to get well and did not wish to make his relatives any trouble. Not until he was dying did he tell of his brother and sisters, and they were immediately notified by telegram. Mr. Houston had been stopping at the Central Hotel off and on since August when he was out of work.

Alcona County Review, December 20, 1894

We thank our friends and neighbors for many kindnesses rendered after the death and at the burial of the late Peter Houston.
Mrs. Jos. Evans
Mrs. Jno. Morris.

Alcona County Review, December 20, 1894
Cemetery: Springport, Alcona Co.

Howard, {Child}

ALCONA ATOMS.

Mr. L. A. Howard's child died in Alpena, last week, where he had taken it for better skilled medical treatment.

Alcona County Review, August 13, 1886
Cemetery:

Howard, E. G.

West Harrisville.

The Review:--Geo. F. Howard and his brother, of Alpena, were called away Tuesday of this week, presumably to the death bed of their father in Muskegon, Mich.

Alcona County Review, September 8, 1892
Cemetery: Oakwood, Muskegon Co.

Howard, Flavia [Apsey]

OBITUARY.

We regret to announce the death of Mrs. George F. Howard, wife of our station agent, which occurred at 3 o'clock Sunday morning. She was ill only a few moments before her death, it being caused by a paroxysm of coughing which burst an internal abcess. She was loved by all as she was a woman of sterling worth and Christian principles.

Flavia Apsey was born in St. Clair county on the 15th of May, 1863, and moved shortly afterward to Sanilac county, where she lived all her life until moving here with her parents in March 1889. She was married to Mr. Howard Nov. 8, 1890, and was baptized and admitted to the Baptist church last September. She was an honorary member of the L. O. T. M. Hive of this place which was present with Mrs. Dalton, lady organizer. The funeral sermon was preached at the house by Rev G. W. Cram, who was called from Tawas to officiate.
West Harrisville, May 18, 1892.

Alcona County Review, May 19, 1892

Whereas, death has entered the home of our worthy Sir Knight and brother, Geo. Howard, and taken from him his beloved wife. Therefore be it.

Resolved, that we, the members of Dalton Hive No. 143, extend our deepest sympathy to the sorely bereaved husband and mourning friends, and point them for comfort to the all-wise God and we humbly submit to the will of Him who doeth all things for the best. And be it further

Resolved, that while we cannot but feel that in the midst of life we are in death, we will bow in submission to the Divine will and strive to lead sisterly lives, bearing in mind the good deeds of our dear sister.

Resolved, that we drape our charter in mourning for 30 days and that a copy of these resolutions be sent to the bereaved husband and friends and the same be published in the Alcona County Review and the Michigan Maccabee.
Mrs. Chas. Foley.
Mrs. A. Marcellus.
Mrs. I. Rose.

Alcona County Review, May 19, 1892

Whereas, Death has entered the home of our beloved Brother, Geo. F. Howard, and taken therefrom his beloved wife, and

Whereas, we, the members of this Court, while bowing in humble submission to the will of the Deity, whom we recognize as the light and joy of that family, be it

Resolved, That we open our hearts in sympathy to the Brother in the loss of his beloved wife, and that a copy of these resolutions be sent to our beloved Brother, also the Independent Forester and also to the Alcona County Review and placed on the records of our Court.
Geo. Wm. Beever,
T. E. Reynolds,
Jas. Thornton,
Committee.

Alcona County Review, May 26, 1892

HISTORY OF ONE YEAR.

Chronological History of the Past Year, 1892.

THE DEATH RECORD.

May 15. Mrs. Geo. F. Howard, West Harrisville.

Alcona County Review, January 5, 1893
Cemetery: West Lawn, Alcona Co.

Howard, George Francis

PEACE BE TO HIS ASHES.

The Review is pained to announce the fatal termination of the illness of Geo. F. Howard, station agent at West Harrisville. his death occurred Friday night after an illness of less than a week from pneumonia.

The funeral occurred Sunday afternoon, when the remains were brought to Harrisville through the fierce storm that was raging and placed beside those of his late wife.

Deceased was upwards of 45 years of age and possessed may sociable qualities that attracted friends and made him a favorite. He had excellent habits, was attentive to business and was rarely absent from his post of duty.

The Review feels a personal loss in his demise. He was one of those rare individuals who, actuated by no other motive than an inborn liking for the work, assumes the task of collecting the news of his neighborhood for the local paper, without hope or expectation of reward. He had been the regular correspondent of the Review from West Harrisville for several years and his contributions, which appeared under the signature of "H. O. Ward," were frequent and very acceptable. He was of a bright and cheerful disposition, and the "copy" he sent in was always free from personalities and captious criticism. His copy now goes to a higher power, where the proof reading will be more exact and the reward more adequate. Peace to his ashes.

The following from West Harrisville contains some facts relative to the life of the deceased and is a tribute to his excellent qualities:

Station Agent G. F. Howard, one of West Harrisville's most honored citizens, departed this life Friday evening, Jan. 11, 1895.

A feeling of sorrow, which has not been equaled in this place for many years, is caused by the sad and untimely death of Mr. Howard, who had gained the confidence of all who knew him.

The subject was born in New York City and had passed his forty-sixth birthday. He had been a resident of this state for twenty-nine years and during this time had been constantly engaged by the R. R. Co. He has been the station agent at this place since '89; was married to Flavie Epsey in '91, which happy union only lasted one year and a half when she was called away by death.

Mr. Howard united with the Baptist church soon after he located here and has done much toward the interests of the church and village.

Funeral services were conducted on Sunday at 1 o'clock p.m., the pastor of the church officiating. Two of his brothers, L. A. Howard of Detroit and "D." Howard of Alpena, arrived here not long before his death and remained until after the funeral. Notwithstanding the stormy day a large number of people attended the funeral services. The remains were interred in the Harrisville cemetery.

The writer can scarcely realize that he is gone. He leaves a host of friends to mourn his loss. When at the close of his eighth day's suffering the veil grew thin which separates time from eternity and he quietly passed away.
W. C. R.

Alcona County Review, January 17, 1895

PERSONAL MENTION.

The lamentable death of Station Agent Howard has resulted in the transfer of Gaylord Freeman from Mikado to West Harrisville. Agent Oliver of Ossineke, who temporarily supplied the post, has succeeded to Freeman's former position.

Alcona County Review, January 17, 1895

Whereas, It has pleased Almighty God in his infinite wisdom to remove from our midst our esteemed friend and brother, Sir Knight Geo. F. Howard, a member of Brook's Tent No. 577 K.O.T.M.

Therefore be it

Resolved, that while submitting to the will of God, who doeth all things well, we deplore the loss of our absent brother.

Resolved that our charter be draped for 60 days, that a copy of these resolutions be sent to the relatives of the deceased, entered upon the records of out Tent and published in the Alcona County Review and in the official organ of the order.

W. Harrisville, Jan. 15, 1895.
J. Marshall,
A. Landon,   Com.
E. Goheen,

Alcona County Review, January 17, 1895

Card of Thanks.

We wish to sincerely return thanks to the many friends who so kindly aided our brother and ourselves during his illness and death. We wish especially to thank Mr. Mack Apsey, and Ed. Miller for their untiring attention and kindness, and also other members of the Knights of the Maccabees for the brotherly offices.

When the angel of death comes, the kind help and sympathy of friends is most appreciated.

L. A. Howard, Detroit.
G. A. Howard, Alpena.

Alcona County Review, January 17, 1895

PERSONAL MENTION.

D. Howard of Alpena was at West Harrisville last week settling up the business affairs of his brother, the late Geo. F. Howard.

Alcona County Review, January 31, 1895

STATE OF MICHIGAN, County of Alcona.

At a session of the Probate Court for said County, held at the Probate office, in the Village of Harrisville, on the Third day of June in the year one thousand eight hundred and ninety-five.

Present, C. H. Killmaster, Judge of Probate.

In the matter of the estate of George F. Howard, deceased:

On reading and filing the petition, duly verified, of Lafayette A. Howard, praying that a certain instrument

now on file in this Court, purporting to be the last will and testament of said deceased, may be admitted to probate, and that administration of the said estate of George F. Howard, deceased be granted to the petitioner.

Thereupon it is ordered, that Monday, the first day of July next, at two o'clock in the afternoon, be assigned for the hearing of said petition, and that the heirs at law of said deceased, and all persons interested in said estate, are required to appear at a session of said Court then to be holden in the Probate office, in the Village of Harrisville, and show cause, if any there be, why the prayer of the petitioner should not be granted: And it is further ordered, that said petitioner give notice to the persons interested in said estate, of the pendency of said petition, and the hearing thereof, by causing a copy of this order to be published in the Alcona County Review, a newspaper printed and circulated in said county, three successive weeks previous to said day of hearing.

C. H. Killmaster,
Judge of Probate.

Alcona County Review, June 6, 1895
Cemetery: West Lawn, Alcona Co.

Howard, Henry

COUNTY REVIEWINGS.

The Alpena Argus says that Henry Howard, who was at work at the camp of Robert Black, on Hunt Creek, was killed by a falling tree, on Thursday afternoon last. The remains were brought to the city, and an inquest held by coroner Tims. The deceased was a native of Canada, and had no relatives in that vicinity.

Alcona County Review, December 3, 1880
Cemetery:

Hoyt, Frankie A. [Kennedy]

PERSONAL AND SOCIAL.

We hear that the wife of Frank Hoyt, formerly of Alcona, died at Mason, Mich., recently.

Alcona County Review, August 21, 1885
Cemetery: Maple Grove, Ingham Co.

Hubert, Sarah Delia

EVENTS OF ONE WEEK.

The remains of a 7-year-old daughter of Fred Hubert of Black River were buried in the Harrisville Catholic cemetery Tuesday. Death was caused by an abscess on the child's head.

Alcona County Review, August 2, 1894
Cemetery: St. Anne's, Alcona Co.

Hugill, Mrs. William

ADDITIONAL LOCAL.

The wife of Wm. Hugill, living in the Spencer neighborhood, died on Thursday night last after an illness of several weeks. She was 46 years of age.

Alcona County Review, April 28, 1882
Cemetery:

Hulbert, Montville

Our Neighbors.

Monte Hulbert, superintendent of the Au Sable & Northwestern railroad, died at Tawas last week of the fever.

Alcona County Review, October 25, 1889
Cemetery:

Hunt, A. Jackson

Jackson Hunt Found Dead.

Lying in a pool of blood the dead body of Jackson Hunt, who resided 1 mile north of this village, was found Monday morning about 9 o'clock by Leo Quigley, who was taking a cow to pasture at Hunts.

Seeing the door open he stepped inside and noticed Mr. Hunts body lying partly under the stove. Leo thought he was asleep and called to him; on getting no answer he went to where the body lay. Three hogs were in the house and horribly mutilated his head and he was scarred beyond recognition. Young Quigley tried to drive the hogs out, but instead they gave chase to him. He ran for assistance and an alarm was spread among the townspeople who immediately gathered to the spot. Coroner Hale happened to be in town also Dr. Norton and an inquest was held but the jury will not render their verdict until Saturday evening. He was buried Monday evening in the cemetery west of the village.

He had been in town Saturday and two parcels were found on the table unopened. He apparently has been dead since Saturday evening.

He has one daughter whose whereabouts is unknown, and two brothers one in Canada and one in Imlay City, Mich. Both well-to-do and highly esteemed in their neighborhood.

Jackson was 72 years old last 12th of July and was well known throughout the county. His brother is expected to arrive from Imlay City tonight and take charge of his affairs.

Alcona County Review, July 20, 1899

LINCOLN.

July 26, '99.

The jury in the inquest over the body of Jackson Hunt rendered their verdict Saturday evening as death from natural causes.

Alcona County Review, July 27, 1899

LOCAL PICK UPS.

Miss Melissa Hunt of Bridgeport, Canada, arrived in town this week to look after the property of the late Jackson Hunt of Hawse. She is staying at D. La Boueff's.

Alcona County Review, August 10, 1899

STATE OF MICHIGAN,
County of Alcona.
Probate Court for said county.
At a session of said court held at the Probate office in the village of Harrisville, on the 8th day of August, A.D. 1899.

Present the Hon. Wm. H. Gilpin, Judge of Probate.

In the matter of determining who are the lawful heirs of A. J. Hunt, deceased.

On reading and filing the petition duly verified of Melissa Hunt, praying that this court adjudicate and determine who were the lawful heirs, minor heirs or legal representatives of said A. J. Hunt, deceased, at the time of his death and their respective rights, in and to the real estate whereof said deceased died seized by virtue of land contract and also to determine who are now lawfully entitled to the same and the share or portion of each.

Thereupon it is ordered that the 1st day of September next at 10 o'clock in the forenoon be assigned for the hearing of said petition and that the heirs at law of said deceased, minor heirs or legal representatives of said deceased and all other persons interested in said estate are required to appear at a session of said court then to be holden at the probate office in the Village of Harrisville and show cause if any there be, why the prayer of the petitioner should not be granted. And it is further ordered that said petitioner give notice to the heirs at law, minor heirs or legal representatives of said deceased and

all other persons interested in said estate, of the pendency of said petition, and the hearing thereof, by causing a copy of this order to be published in the Alcona County Review, a newspaper published and circulating in said county, three successive weeks previous to said day of hearing.

W. H. Gilpin,
Judge of Probate.

Alcona County Review, August 10, 1899
Cemetery: West Lawn, Alcona Co.

Hunt, Annie M. [Hillman]

Jottings Along the Shore.

Mrs. Annie M., wife of Hugh Hunt, of Alpena, died on Wednesday of last week, after a painful and somewhat lengthy illness.

Alcona County Review, March 12, 1880
Cemetery: Evergreen, Alpena Co.

Hunt, James E.

LOCAL JOTTINGS.

A telegram was received by Mr. B. P. Cowley, Wednesday morning, announcing the death at his home in Toledo, Wednesday morning at 6 o'clock, of Jas. E. Hunt, an intimate friend of the family, and a former resident of Harrisville.

Alcona County Review, August 17, 1888

JAMES E. HUNT.

A Testimonial of Respect Placed on the Court Records.

Yesterday morning in Judge Pike's court room James E. Pilliod arose and in the presence of the Lucas county bar, read the following, which was ordered placed upon the court records by Judge Pike:

Testimonial.

James E. Hunt, a member of the bar of Lucas county, O., died on the 16th day of August, 1888, at this home in this city. By his death a life promising in all that went to make up a true lawyer, the earnest Christian and honorable man was cut off. Possessed of abilities of no common order, studious in application and zealous in the pursuit of knowledge in his chosen profession, polite and affable to all, he bade fair to occupy and ornament high and distinguished places at the bar and in the community. While, perhaps, not intimately known to the majority of the members of the bar, his death creates a void in the ranks of those who knew and appreciated his many grand qualities of head and heart.

May it please your honor to order this slight testimonial to the worth of our departed friend and brother to be entered on the records of this court.—Toledo Commercial.

Alcona County Review, October 19, 1888
Cemetery: Calvary, Lucas, OH

Hunt, John

LOCAL JOTTINGS.

John Hunt, of Rust township, Montmorency county, was shot dead by Herman Besser of the same place, on election day in a dispute over election matters.

Alcona County Review, November 16, 1888
Cemetery:

Hunter, John

EVENTS OF ONE WEEK.

Word has been received of the death of John Hunter at Minden City. Deceased was many years ago a resident of Harrisville, and he retained his membership in the Harrisville Lodge of Odd Fellows up to the time of his death. Suitable action has been taken by his brethren of the three links and the benefits he was entitled to have been forwarded to his widow.

Alcona County Review, January 18, 1894

RESOLUTIONS OF RESPECT.

Whereas, It has pleased the Supreme Ruler of the Universe and of the destinies of Mankind, to call from earth our late brother, John Hunter, of Minden City, Mich., therefore be it

Resolved, That we learn with deep regret of the demise of our brother, who has ever been faithful to his obligations as an Odd Fellow, and honorable and upright in his relations with his fellowmen, so far as we know.

Resolved, That we, the members of Harrisville Lodge, No. 218 I.O.O.F. extend our sincere sympathy to the bereaved widow and children of our deceased brother. Further, that these resolutions be published and a copy thereof be transmitted to them.

By Order of Com.

Alcona County Review, January 18, 1894
Cemetery: Minden, Sanilac Co.

Hunter, Mrs. W. J. [Silverthorn]

PERSONAL MENTION.

Addison Silverthorn left for Detroit Monday morning in response to a telegram announcing the death of his youngest sister, Mrs. W. J. Hunter, which occurred in that city Sunday. Deceased had been an invalid for a long period, but particulars of her death could not be secured. [Note: possibly Mabel Grace, born April 25, 1875.]

Alcona County Review, March 26, 1896
Cemetery:

Hunter, W. H.

THE BLIZZARD CLAIMS A VICTIM.

W. H. Hunter, a Piano Tuner, Frozen While Attempting to Walk from Mikado to Oscoda.

Last Thursday morning the engineer on the north bound freight train discovered the body of a man lying beside the track at a point about three miles north of Oscoda. He was taken aboard and although frozen stiff life was not extinct. He was transferred to the south bound passenger train and taken to Au Sable where he was placed in Wier's hospital. Restoratives were administered and all that medical skill could do was probably done to bring the victim back to consciousness and life but without avail, and he died Thursday night at 10 o'clock.

The inanimate form of the victim was recognized as that of W. H. Hunter, a youthful piano tuner, whose parents are mentioned as highly respected citizens of Alpena, formerly in affluent circumstances at London, Ont., but who were reduced to penury by business reverses, going to Alpena about a year since.

The young man had been doing considerable work in his line in Oscoda, Au Sable and Greenbush, and many residents of Harrisville will recollect him as the slight gentlemanly appearing young man who was in this place the first of last week soliciting work. He stopped at the Alcona House when in this village, and the landlady of that hotel speaks in high terms of his conduct while he enjoyed the hospitality of her house. He had stated Wednesday morning that he had an engagement to play at a ball to be given in Oscoda that evening, and said that he was going around by way of Greenbush to

catch the train for that place. He had no baggage excepting a small satchel in which he carried his tools, and a change of linen which was since found in his room at the Alcona House. He did not say that he would return to Harrisville, and Mrs. Carle is unwilling to believe from her guest's deportment while in her house that he harbored any intention of defrauding her of a board bill of $10 which he neglected to pay on his departure. Mrs. Carle states that he was lavish in his expenditure of money, and exhibited a roll of bills at the breakfast table one morning that seemed amply sufficient to place him far above want, yet he did not pay a livery bill of $1.50 at La Boueff's; and it was a dispute over another livery bill of $5.00 claimed by "Todd" Young, of Greenbush, that led indirectly to young Hunter's death. It was while engaged in a scuffle with Young that the freight train which Hunter wished to board pulled out from the station at Mikado. He paid Young $2, alleging that that was all the money he had. He stopped at VanWagner's hotel a few minutes, and then started to walk to Au Sable. He was urged to stay at Mikado, but he stated to those present that it was imperative for him to be in Au Sable that night. Hunter stopped at Frank McLaughlin's house, four miles from Mikado, for supper, and made himself agreeable by playing and singing. He was again urged to remain and the dangers of a ten mile tramp on such a terrible night as that of Wednesday were pointed out, but Hunter turned a deaf ear to this friendly advice and tramped on to his death. He was lightly clad for such a tramp on such a wild fierce night.

The remains were claimed by a sister who resides with her parents in Alpena. The coroner's verdict was that Hunter came to his death by freezing.

A story, which has not been substantiated, is to the effect that the driver of the sprinkler at Gordon's camp discovered Hunter early Thursday morning. He rubbed him with snow in a vain endeavor to resuscitate him, but left him lying there, returning to camp, where, strange to say, he said nothing of his discovery until the news of the finding of the body of young Hunter reached the camp from other sources.

Alcona County Review, January 6, 1888
Cemetery:

Hurd, William

REVIEWINGS.

William Hurd, a man of about 40 years, who has resided in this vicinity for a year past, working in Colwell's mill last summer, died at the residence of J. B. Guenette this morning. He had been ailing for a number of months past, at times suffering severely with the asthma, but the exact cause of his death we have not learned. He had no relatives here, but previous to his death stated that he had a brother and sister living at Quebec, Ont.

Alcona County Review, January 9, 1880
Cemetery:

Irons, Mrs. Mary

HOME NEWS JOTTINGS.

Died--In Alpena, October 24, 1882, Mrs. Mary Irons, aged 72 years.

Mrs. Irons was well known in and about this village, having passed some time as a resident here. Her death was partially if not wholly caused by paralysis.

Alcona County Review, November 24, 1882
Cemetery:

Jack, Charles

School Closed in Haynes.

Another Account of the Diphtheria Cases.

Haynes, Dec. 4.—An epidemic of Diphtheria has broken out in our township. Five of the children of Geo. Jack are down with it and one of Mrs. Donald Fraser's children, a girl about 12 years of age. Dr. Mitchell was called by Health officer Jas. Fleming for the Fraser child and he also visited Mr. Jack's children. He pronounced the disease diphtheria. Mr. Fleming has posted notices on these premises, and the school board of District No. 4 have closed the school in consequence of the outbreak of the dread disease.

Alcona County Review, December 6, 1894

Diphtheria in Haynes Township.

Diphtheria has made its appearance again in Alcona County, this time from the direction of Haynes township, where four cases exist in the family of George Jack;

one of these was very low on Monday. One case also reported in the family of Donald Fraser.

Dr. Mitchell is giving the cases his closest attention and it is the hope of the neighborhood that the disease will be confined in its present limits.

A few isolated cases of diphtheria are reported in Alpena and Presque Isle counties. In Detroit the disease is quite epidemic and the public schools have been closed to give the health officers a better chance to fight the disease.

Alcona County Review, December 6, 1894

Haynes Happenings.

George Jack's son Charles died Saturday evening of diphtheria and was buried Sunday morning. He was aged about 14 years. Mr. Jack and family have the sympathy of the inhabitants of Haynes in this their hour of great sorrow.

Alcona County Review, December 13, 1894

EVENTS OF ONE WEEK.

One of the diphtheria patients in the family of George Jack of Haynes township resulted fatally on Saturday. The victim was a boy of seventeen and the eldest child.

Alcona County Review, December 13, 1894

Alcona.

There has been some artistic and costly tombstones erected in Mount Joy cemetery this spring in memory of Mr. Bridgeman, a son and daughter of A. Yuill, Peter McGregor, Jas. E. Fleming and Geo. Jack erected one to the memory of his children Fred, Mary and Charles and F. O. Teeple to his son, Clifton. There are a number who take pride in keeping their lots in good order but the majority of the graves and lots are neglected, which don't speak well for the relatives. Sunken graves and toppling tombstones speak louder than words.

Alcona County Review, July 2, 1903
Cemetery: Mt. Joy, Alcona Co.

Jack, Mary

Haynes Happenings.

Haynes, Dec. 18.--Reported that Geo. Jack's family are recovering from diphtheria. It was Mary, not Bella, who was not expected to live.

Alcona County Review, December 20, 1894

EVENTS OF ONE WEEK.

A daughter of George Jack, of Haynes township, died last week after a long illness. The child was sadly afflicted from birth, but its death was due to other causes.

Alcona County Review, January 17, 1895

Haynes, Jan. 15th, 1895.—Mr. and Mrs. George Jack buried their daughter Mary on the 11th. She was aged about nine years.

Alcona County Review, January 17, 1895

ALCONA.

There has been some artistic and costly tombstones erected in Mount Joy cemetery this spring in memory of Mr. Bridgeman, a son and daughter of A. Yuill, Peter McGregor, Jas. E. Fleming and Geo. Jack erected one to the memory of his children Fred, Mary and Charles and F. O. Teeple to his son, Clifton. There are a number who take pride in keeping their lots in good order but the majority of the graves and lots are neglected, which don't speak well for the relatives. Sunken graves and toppling tombstones speak louder than words.

Alcona County Review, July 2, 1903
Cemetery: Mt. Joy, Alcona Co.

Jacques, Mrs. Margareth

Two Centenarians Dead.

Mrs. Jacque of Presque Isle died last week at the age of 103 years.

Alcona County Review, March 2, 1899
Cemetery: Belknap Township, Presque Isle Co.

Jacques, Pierre

THE SHORE COUNTRY.

The Rogers City Advance chronicles the death of Pierre Jaque at 90 years of age. He served in the Mexican war, and the rebellion, applied for a pension but died before it was granted.

Alcona County Review, November 27, 1885
Cemetery:

James, Sarah A. [Seyers]

OBITUARY.

Mrs. E. James, an old resident of Harrisville, died rather suddenly Wednesday morning. She had been confined to the house for a few days previous to her death with what was considered nothing worse than a bad cold. The deceased was about sixty years of age, and leaves a son and daughter by a former marriage. The former, named Hall, resides in

Oscoda. The latter is married and resides in California.

Alcona County Review, March 2, 1888

LOCAL JOTTINGS

The funeral services of the late Mrs. E. James will be held Friday afternoon.

Alcona County Review, March 2, 1888

OBITUARY.
On the morning of Feb. 29th, at 6 o'clock, Mrs. Sarah E. James, wife of Ephraim James, passed away to her eternal rest. Mrs. James had been confined to her home for a few days with a severe cold, but was not thought by her friends to be in a serious condition until a day or two before her death. She died peacefully in the triumph of the Christian. In the latter years of her life she connected herself with the Methodist Episcopal church, of which she was an exemplary member at the time of her death. The funeral services were held at her late residence Friday afternoon, March 2d, Rev. C. B. Steele officiating, assisted by Revs. Goldie and Barlow. Mrs. James was born in Providence, Rhode Island, June 10th, 1825. Her maiden name was Seyers. She leaves a husband, son and daughter.

Alcona County Review, March 9, 1888

PURELY PERSONAL.

H. A. Hall, of Oscoda, attended the funeral of his mother, the late Mrs. James, last week.

Alcona County Review, March 9, 1888

LOCAL JOTTINGS

H. A. Hall, of Oscoda, petitions the probate court to appoint an administrator of the estate of Sarah A. James, deceased, mother of the petitioner.

Alcona County Review, March 16, 1888

PROBATE ORDER.
STATE OF MICHIGAN, County of Alcona.

At a session of the Probate Court for the County of Alcona held at the Probate office in the village of Harrisville, on Saturday, the tenth day of March, in the year one thousand eight hundred and eighty-eight. Present, Hon. Allen Nevin, Judge of Probate. In the matter of the **ESTATE OF SARAH A. JAMES, DECEASED.**

On reading and filing the petition, duly verified, of Hiram A. Hall, praying for the appointment of an administrator for the estate of Sarah A. James, deceased.

Thereupon it is ordered that Saturday, the Fourteenth Day of April, at eleven o'clock in the forenoon, be assigned for the hearing of said petition, and that the heirs at law of said deceased, and all other persons interested in said estate, are required to appear at a session of said court, then to be holden at the Probate office, in the village of Harrisville, and show cause, if any there be, why the prayer of the petitioner should not be granted. And it is further ordered, that said petitioner give notice to the persons interested in said estate, of the pendency of said petition, and the hearing thereof, by causing a copy of this order to be published in the Alcona County Review, a newspaper printed and circulating in said county of Alcona, four successive weeks, and also by causing the same to be personally served at least ten days previous to said day of hearing upon Sarah E. Shoaf, 812 Polk Street, San Francisco, California, if they be found in said county.

ALLEN NEVIN, Judge of Probate.
Henry & Cornville, Att'ys for Petitioner.

Alcona County Review, March 16, 1888
Cemetery:

Jantz, {Child}

Events of One Week.

A four weeks' old child of Nich Jantz died last Thursday afternoon of convulsions.

Alcona County Review, March 7, 1895
Cemetery: Probably Evergreen, Alpena Co.

Jaquet, Paul

Man Killed at Oscoda.

Paul Jaquet, aged 29 years, was struck by a falling pile of lumber while working on the tram at Potts' mill in Oscoda, last Saturday, and knocked into the lake. It is supposed that in falling his head struck a timber, as his neck was broken.

Alcona County Review, August 27, 1886
Cemetery:

Jeffers, Emmor

Emmor Jeffers died Monday, Nov. 21, at the advanced age of 84 years. He was born in Stueben county, N.

Y., where he was married in 1829. He was the father of eight children, five of whom survive him, viz: Mrs. Asa and Mrs. Thos. Emerson of Harrisville township, Mrs. Sarah Storms of Red Cloud, Neb., Mrs. Elias Cornell of Skamokawa, Wash. and George Jeffers of Hornellsville, N. Y. He settled in Michigan in 1877. The remains were interred Tuesday in the West Harrisville cemetery beside those of the partner of his joys and sorrows.

Alcona County Review, November 24, 1892

Card of Thanks.
We wish to extend our sincere thanks to our neighbors and friends for their kindness shown in the death and burial of our dear father, Emor Jeffers.

Mr. and Mrs. Asa Emerson.

Alcona County Review, December 1, 1892

HISTORY OF ONE YEAR.

Chronological History of the Past Year, 1892.

THE DEATH RECORD.
Nov. 21. Emmor Jeffers, Harrisville.

Alcona County Review, January 5, 1893
Cemetery: West Lawn, Alcona Co.

Jeffries, Elizabeth [Butler]

The Local News
Mrs. E. Jeffries died Monday morning at an early hour at the home of her daughter, Mrs. Thos. Emerson, aged 70 years. The remains were buried yesterday afternoon in the West Harrisville cemetery. The husband of the deceased survives her, also her daughters, Mrs. Thos Emerson and Mrs. Asa Emerson of Harrisville, and Mrs. Elias Cornell of Skamokawa, Wash.

Alcona County Review, March 10, 1892

Mrs. E. Jefferies, who recently died, was 80 years old, had another daughter and a son not mentioned before, Mrs. Sarah Storms of Webster Co., Neb., and Mr. Geo. Jefferies of Hornellsville, Stuben Co., N. Y.

Alcona County Review, March 17, 1892

Card of Thanks.
Mr. and Mrs. Thos. Emerson extend their sincere thanks to their neighbors and friends for kindness shown in the death and burial of their mother, Mrs. Jeffries.

Mr. and Mrs. Thos. Emerson.

Alcona County Review, March 17, 1892

HISTORY OF ONE YEAR.

Chronological History of the Past Year, 1892.

THE DEATH RECORD.

March 6. Mrs. E. Jeffers, Harrisville.

Alcona County Review, January 5, 1893
Cemetery: West Lawn, Alcona Co.

Jeffries, May

Miss May Jeffries, a daughter of Geo. Jeffreys, of Hornellsville, N. Y., had the misfortune to run a splinter into her foot a few days ago. It was extracted and she felt little inconvenience or pain until Friday night when lockjaw set in from which she died the following Sunday. She was a niece of Mrs. Thos. Emerson.

Alcona County Review, September 10, 1891
Cemetery: Hillside, Steuben Co., NY

Jenkins, Martha J. [Young]

HELEN JENKINS.

Mrs. Helen Jenkins passed peacefully away Tuesday night after a long illness from consumption. She was surrounded by her family as her spirit released itself from the earthly tenement. This ends the life of a woman whose virtues were so conspicuous that she was held in universal esteem. Mrs. Jenkins was the daughter of the late John B. Young of Greenbush. She was left a widow several years ago, but by heroic efforts she sustained her family, though health was failing.

The funeral is held this afternoon at 1 o'clock from the Methodist church.

Alcona County Review, September 2, 1897
Cemetery: Springport, Alcona Co.

Jenkins, William

Somewhat Personal

The death of Wm. Jenkins, which occurred last Monday morning at an early hour, was not unexpected as for the past three years he has suffered greatly from a tumor which had assumed dangerous proportions. He began to fail about three weeks ago, since which time his decline has been rapid. The remains were buried yesterday at the South Harrisville cemetery. The deceased was born in New York March 31, 1848. He came to Harrisville in 1877 and was married the following year. His wife and four children survive him.

Alcona County Review, January 21, 1892

Somewhat Personal

D. H. Noyes and wife, of Mud Lake, attended the funeral of Wm. Jenkins.

Alcona County Review, January 21, 1892

Card of Thanks.

We sincerely thank the friends, and especially the members of the I. O. O. F., who so kindly aided in the late illness and death of our beloved husband and father.
Mrs. Wm. Jenkins and Family.

Alcona County Review, January 21, 1892

Friends of the family of the late Wm. Jenkins will give a benefit dance for them in Shwitzer's Hall Friday evening, March 11.

Alcona County Review, March 3, 1892

The Local News.

Bear in mind the dance at Shwitzers Hall tomorrow evening, for the benefit of the family of the late Wm. Jenkins.

Alcona County Review, March 10, 1892

The Local News.

The dance for the benefit of Mrs. Wm. Jenkins at Shwitzer's Hall last Friday evening was largely attended. Music was provided by Greely Hill, who played on this occasion at a great reduction over his usual rates. The proceeds of the dance were augmented by private contributions. The total amounted to the handsome sum of $82, which was presented to Mrs. Jenkins yesterday afternoon by Sam Anderson, who has been one of the leading spirits in this charitable enterprise.

Alcona County Review, March 17, 1892

HISTORY OF ONE YEAR.

Chronological History of the Past Year, 1892.

THE DEATH RECORD.

Jan. 18. Death of Wm. Jenkins.

Alcona County Review, January 5, 1893
Cemetery: Springport, Alcona Co.

Johnson, Elizabeth E. [Morton]

Haynes.

Mrs. John Johnson is reported to be very sick. Dr. Mitchell stayed with her all Sunday night.

Alcona County Review, June 1, 1893

Haynes.

Mrs. John Johnston died Sunday about noon, after a two months' sickness. She was buried on Tuesday. D. La Boueff of Harrisville had charge of the funeral.

Alcona County Review, August 3, 1893

CAN HAVE HIS OWN CHILD.

Possession of His Offspring Restored to John Johnson by Habeas Corpus.

A few weeks ago the wife of John Johnson of Haynes township died leaving a child some two or three months old. The dead woman was the daughter of Mrs. Emily Morton of the same township, who after her daughter's death claimed possession of the child on two peculiar and somewhat unusual grounds. In the first place she claimed that Johnson was indebted to her for board of himself and his deceased wife. In the second place she claimed that prior to her daughter's death the latter had given her the child. Johnson's efforts to gain peaceable possession of the child did not meet with success so he sought legal advice and retained O. H. Smith. Habeas corpus proceedings were begun last week and service was made on Mrs. Morton on Friday. The writ was returnable yesterday at Tawas but on Monday attorney Smith was informed that the case would not be contested but that peaceable possession of the child would be given to Mr. Johnson without further ado.

Alcona County Review, August 17, 1893

Haynes Happenings.

Mark Morton has erected a beautiful monument in memory of his three children and two grandchildren.

Alcona County Review, May 24, 1894
Cemetery: Mt. Joy, Alcona Co.

Johnson, James M.

Roy, Feb. 5th, 1896.
Jas. Johnson of Mikado died Monday night. His funeral will be held Thursday. His family, who are in quite destitute circumstances it is believed, have the sympathy of the entire community. Mr. Johnson has not been sick long I believe. He was a blacksmith by trade and was following that business when taken sick. He had been a resident of this

county many years and by his death Alcona county loses another of its old landmarks.

Alcona County Review, February 6, 1896

Mikado.

Mikado, Mich. Feb. 12, 1896--Mr. Johnston, whose death O. Crackie mentioned last week, was 63 years of age and leaves a wife and three children with whom we all sympathize. He has been working at his trade, blacksmithing, in one of Loud's camps on the Mud Lake branch where he was taken sick and lived but a few days after arriving home.

Alcona County Review, February 13, 1896

Resolutions by VanEttan Hive, Mikado.

Whereas, Our Heavenly Father has in His infinite wisdom permitted the angel of death to enter the home of our beloved sister, Alice E. Johnston, and touch with his icy finger the husband and father of that family.

Therefore be it Resolved, That while she submits to our all-wise Providence in her dispensation, we bow in humility to the will of Him who doeth all things well.

Resolved, That while she mourns in this bereavement, we deeply deplore her loss and tender our heart-felt sympathy to her family and assure of our watchful care in the future,

Resolved, That a copy of these resolutions be sent to the sorrowing family and published in the County paper.

Dated this tenth day of February, 1896.

Maggie Cummings,
Mrs. M. Johnston,
Mrs. B. Smith,
Committee

Alcona County Review, February 13, 1896

Mikado, Feb. 24, '96.
Editor Review:——We desire to thank friends and neighbors through the columns of your paper, for their kindness during the last illness and death of our beloved husband and father.

Mrs. J. M. Johnson and Family.

Alcona County Review, February 27, 1896

HONORS TO DEAD HEROES.

A magnificent demonstration of the patriotic spirit of the citizens of Alcona county was the observance on Monday of the time honored custom of decorating the graves and commemorating the deeds of valor of the nation's dead heroes.

The roster of soldiers who are buried here is as follows: Harrisville, (West), A. Marcellus, John Pelton, W. W. Douglass: Catholic, Louis Rivard, Geo. Bernizer: South Harrisville, R. Richmond, Chas. Miller, H. J. Aird, A. Noyes, Jas. Johnson.

Alcona County Review, June 2, 1898
Cemetery: Springport, Alcona Co.

Johnson, Minnie Elizabeth

Your Folks and Our Folks.

Died.—In this township, on the 31st ult., Minnie Elizabeth, infant daughter of Alex. and Katie Johnson, aged 21 months. The funeral was held in the M. E. church last Thursday.

Alcona County Review, September 10, 1886
Cemetery:

Johnson, Robert

Received a Sudden Call.

The startling news has reached here that another pioneer citizen has gone the way of all flesh. Robt. Johnston, one of the leading and most highly respected citizens of Haynes township, received the final summons which no mortal can defy, at 3 o'clock yesterday morning. The cause of his death is attributed to dropsy, from which he has been a sufferer for a year or more past. Alcona county has lost an excellent citizen. The funeral will take place tomorrow (Friday) at two o'clock p.m. from his late residence.

Alcona County Review, June 11, 1891

Around the County.

Haynes Items.

There was a very large attendance at the funeral of the late Robt. Johnson on Friday last. Mr. Hazard preached a very excellent sermon which was commented on favorably by a great many of his hearers.

Alcona County Review, June 18, 1891

The remains of the late Robt. Johnson were laid to rest in the Alcona cemetery last Friday afternoon, whither they were followed by a large concourse of sorrowing relatives and sympathizing friends and neighbors. So endeth the life of another good citizen. Peace be to his ashes.

Alcona County Review, June 18, 1891
Cemetery: Mt. Joy, Alcona Co.

Johnson, Robert, Jr.

Paul McNally of Arcata Cal., writes to his son S. J. McNally of this place enclosing a newspaper clipping describing the death in the woods near Arcata of Robt. Johnson, Jr. son of Robt. Johnson of Alcona. He was run over by a heavily loaded wagon causing his death after two days of suffering.

Alcona County Review, October 21, 1887
Cemetery:

Johnson, Wallace

Our Neighbors.

Potts, Oscoda county, must be a very unhealthy place. Dr. Wallace Johnson, a physician who located there, was stricken with malaria shortly after his arrival in the place and died. Dr. Minthorn who succeeded him has also fallen a victim of the same disease and is now lying very ill at his home in Oscoda.

Alcona County Review, November 22, 1889
Cemetery:

Johnston, Aleck

Word was received last week from Gladstone of the death of Aleck Johnston, a former resident of this county. Deceased was raised at Black River and lived in this vicinity all his life, until eight or nine years ago. He had numerous relatives in this county.

Alcona County Review, January 11, 1894
Cemetery:

Johnston, Garnet W.

LOCAL JOTTINGS.

Mr. and Mrs. Thomas Johnson of Alcona township bury a two year old babe to-day. The little one died very suddenly Wednesday evening.

Alcona County Review, September 5, 1884
Cemetery: Mt. Joy, Alcona Co.

Johnston, {Girl}

HAYNES.

Haynes, July 14,——Mr. and Mrs. Thomas Johnston buried a daughter aged 10 days on Friday last.

Alcona County Review, July 16, 1891
Cemetery: Mt. Joy, Alcona Co.

Johnston, James

Jas. Johnston, a lumberman, a little the worse for liquor, went to sleep on the railroad track near Alpena. He was run over by a log train, terribly mangled, one leg amputated, died from loss of blood and exposure.

Alcona County Review, August 9, 1894
Cemetery:

Johnston, Mrs. Jane

EVENTS OF ONE WEEK.

Mrs. N. J. Johnston of Black River died Saturday. A correspondent sends us a simple obituary notice but no particulars. Information from other sources states that the lady died very suddenly under somewhat distressing circumstances.

Alcona County Review, May 18, 1893

OBITUARY.

Johnston.—Mrs. Jane Johnston, wife of N. J. Johnston, died at her home in Black River, Mich., May 13, 1893. Aged 38 years.

Alcona County Review, May 18, 1893
Cemetery: Probably Mt. Joy, Alcona Co.

Johnston, Joseph

ADDITIONAL LOCAL.

Mr. Jos. Johnston and wife lost their baby boy on the morning of the 26th. He was three months old.

Alcona County Review, April 28, 1882
Cemetery:

Johnston, Thomas J.

Death of Thos. Johnston.

On Saturday last the remains of Thos. Johnston, a highly esteemed citizen of Haynes township, were laid to rest in the cemetery at Alcona. The deceased's illness dated from the previous Sunday and he expired Thursday night at 11 o'clock.

Deceased was about 45 years of age and leaves a wife and six children in fair circumstances. He was a member in good standing of the local lodge of the Black Knights of Malta, by which order he was buried. The funeral was one of the largest in point of attendance ever held in Haynes township. Rev. S. Boundy of Harrisville preached the funeral sermon.

From our regular correspondent:

Mr. Thomas Johnston was buried on Saturday, the 18th. The Knights of Malta took charge of the remains, assisted by the Baptist minister from Harrisville. There was a very large attendance of relatives and friends at the funeral. Several of the Knights of Malta from Harrisville and Black River were in attendance to pay their last tribute of respect to their departed brother. Relatives of the deceased came from Canada, a brother and a sister-in-law.

The deceased was taken with cramps on Monday evening and died Wednesday evening about 11 o'clock. He had been a resident of the township for the past 16 years and

had been a justice of the peace since the organization of Haynes township.

Alcona County Review, June 23, 1892

At a regular convocation of Haynes Commandery No. 63 Black Knights of Malta, held June 15, the following preamble and resolutions were adopted:

Whereas, It has pleased the great Architect of the Universe to remove from our midst our late companion, Thos. Johnson, and

Whereas, It is but just that a fitting recognition of his many virtues should be had: therefore be it

Resolved, That the charter of this Commandery be draped in mourning for sixty days.

Resolved, By Haynes Commandery No. 63 on registry of the Grand Commandery of Michigan B. K. of Malta, that while we bow with humble submission to the will of the Most High, we do not the less mourn for our companion who has been taken from us.

Resolved, That in the death of Thomas Johnson this Commandery laments the loss of a companion who was ever ready to proffer the hand of aid and the voice of sympathy to the needy and distressed of that fraternity, an active member of this Society, whose utmost endeavors were exerted for its welfare and prosperity; a friend and companion to all; a citizen whose upright and noble life was a standard of emulation to his fellows.

Resolved, That the heartfelt sympathy of this Commandery be extended to his family in their affliction,

Resolved, That these resolutions be spread upon the records of the Commandery, and a copy thereof be transmitted to the family of our deceased companion and to the county newspaper in Harrisville.

Alex Yuill,
G. S. Ritchie,   Committee.
Stephen Lynch.

June 25, 1892.

Alcona County Review, July 7, 1892

HISTORY OF ONE YEAR.

Chronological History of the Past Year, 1892.

THE DEATH RECORD.

June 15. Thos. Johnston, Haynes.

Alcona County Review, January 5, 1893

ORDER FOR PUBLICATION

State of Michigan, the Probate Court for the County of Alcona.

At a session of said Court, held at the Probate Office in the City of Harrisville, in said County, on the 26th day of March, A. D. 1919.

Present: Hon. Geo. W. Burt, Judge of Probate.

In the Matter of the Estate of Thomas Johnston, deceased.

Eliza Johnson, widow of said deceased, having filed in said court a petition praying that said court adjudicate and determine who were at the time of his death the legal heirs of said deceased and entitled to inherit the real estate of which deceased died seized.

It is ordered that the 19th day of April, A. D. 1919, at ten o'clock in the forenoon, at said probate office, be and is hereby appointed for hearing said petition.

It is further ordered that public notice thereof be given by publication of a copy of this order, for three successive weeks previous to said day of hearing, in the Alcona County Review, a newspaper printed and circulated in said county.

GEO. W. BURT, Probate. Judge.

Alcona County Review, March 27, 1919

ORDER FOR PUBLICATION

State of Michigan, The Probate Court for the County of Alcona. At a session of said court, held at the probate office in the City of Harrisville, in said County, on the 8th. day of October, A. D. 1926.

Present: Hon. Geo. W. Burt, Judge of Probate.

In the matter of the Estate of Thomas Johnson, deceased. John R. Johnson, son of said deceased, having filed in said court his petition praying that the administration of said estate be granted to himself or to some other suitable person, It is Ordered, That the 6th day of November, A. D. 1926, at ten o'clock in the forenoon, at said probate office, be and is hereby appointed for hearing said petition:

It is further Ordered, that public notice thereof be given by publication of a copy of this order, for three successive weeks previous to said day of hearing, in the Alcona County Review, a newspaper printed and circulated in said county.

GEO. W. BURT, Judge of Probate.

ORDER FOR PUBLICATION

State of Michigan. The Probate Court for the County of Alcona. At a session of said court, held at the Probate office, in the City of Harrisville, in said County, on the 18th day of April A. D. 1927. Present, Hon. Geo. W. Burt, Judge of Probate.

In the matter of the estate of Thomas Johnson, deceased. John R. Johnson, having filed in said court his final account as administrator of said estate, and his petition praying for the allowance thereof,

It is irdered, that the 14th day of May, A. D. 1927, at ten o'clock in the forenoon, at said Probate Office, be and is hereby appointed for examining and allowing said account;

It is further ordered, that public notice thereof be given by publication of a copy of this order for three successive weeks previous to said day of hearing, in the Alcona County Review, a newspaper printed and circulated in said county.

GEO. W. BURT, Judge of Probate.

Alcona County Review, April 21, 1927
Cemetery: Mt. Joy, Alcona Co.

Jones, Horace

LOCAL JOTTINGS.

Horace Jones, aged 2 years and 6 months, a son of Mrs. H. H. Jones, of Detroit, who is visiting her parents, Mr. and Mrs. Chas. Sexton, of this place, died last Saturday morning and was buried Sunday in the Harrisville cemetery.

Alcona County Review, August 12, 1887
Cemetery:

Jones, {Male}

Captain Jones is Dead.

The death of Captain Jones occurred at a hospital in Cleveland on Tuesday, Jan. 8. He was one of the best known of the lake captains who have sailed on this coast and was for many years in command of the old Atlantic, on which he opened navigation at this port for several consecutive seasons.

Alcona County Review, January 17, 1895
Cemetery: Prob. Woodland, Cuyahoga Co., OH

Jones, William E.

HOME REVIEWINGS.

W. E. Jones, one of the pioneer settlers of Long Rapids township, Alpena county, died at his residence Tuesday morning.

Alcona County Review, July 1, 1881
Cemetery:

Jordan, Mrs. Mary

ADDITIONAL LOCAL.

The remains of Mrs. Jordan, an elderly lady who resided at Black River, were buried this morning in the Catholic cemetery at South Harrisville.

Alcona County Review, September 28, 1893
Cemetery: St. Anne's, Alcona Co.

Joseph, {Girl}

West Harrisville.

A child of Alex. Joseph, and one of John Kelley, died in the last week, presumably of diphtheria.

Alcona County Review, January 5, 1893

Another case of diphtheria developed at Mud Lake and terminated fatally last week. The victim was a child of 5 years of age, a daughter of Albert Joseph. She was living with a family named Ranger.

Alcona County Review, January 5, 1893
Cemetery:

Joslyn, {Boy}

LOCAL JOTTINGS

An infant son of Ex-Sup. Geo. A. Joslyn, of Greenbush, died last week.

Alcona County Review, August 10, 1888
Cemetery: Springport, Alcona Co.

Joslyn, George A.

Greenbush Jottings.

Mr. and Mrs. Geo. A. Joslyn mourn the loss of a darling child, which died last week.

Alcona County Review, November 14, 1879
Cemetery: Springport, Alcona Co.

Joslyn, Ida M.

GREENBUSH.

Miss Ida Joslyn passed away at her late home last Thursday evening after an illness of two months from quick consumption. Deceased was 22 years of age. The interment took place Saturday, Elder Smith of the Latter Day Saints officiating.

Alcona County Review, July 8, 1897

WEST HARRISVILLE.

Mr. and Mrs. E. Goheen went to Greenbush Thursday evening of last week to see Ida Joslyn, but she was dead when they arrived. They attended the funeral on Saturday.

Alcona County Review, July 8, 1897

Card of Thanks.

We desire to extend our sincere thanks to the kind friends who so willingly and tenderly ministered to the wants and comforts of our

beloved Ida during her last illness and may the God who knoweth and seeth all bestow the merited reward.

Alice Joslyn.
In behalf of the family.
Greenbush, July 6th, 1897.

Alcona County Review, July 8, 1897
Cemetery: Probably Springport, Alcona Co.

Joslyn, Kezia [Springstead]

LOCAL JOTTINGS.

Death of Mrs. Geo. A. Joslyn.— Tuesday evening at 9 o'clock occurred the death of the estimable wife of Ex-Supervisor Geo. A. Joslyn at their home in the village of Greenbush. Mrs. Joslyn had been sick only a few days prior to her death, the immediate cause of which, as stated by the physician who attended her during the last hours of her sickness, was blood poisoning. The deceased was born in Hamilton, Ont., in 1853. She leaves a family of seven children, the youngest of which is but two weeks old. Mrs. Joslyn was a sister of Mrs. E. Goheen, and had other relatives at Lansing, Cheboygan and in Canada. The funeral services were to be held from her late home in Greenbush, Thursday afternoon at 2 o'clock.

Alcona County Review, August 23, 1889
Cemetery: Springport, Alcona Co.

Judd, John

Killed in the Woods.

Wednesday morning a woodsman employed in Graham's camp at Mud Lake was struck by a falling tree from the effects of which he died in three hours. He had been employed at the camp but a few days and no one knew his name or where his home was until after his death when a letter from his wife was discovered among his effects. After he was injured he was asked if a doctor should be sent for but he replied that he would be all right in a little while. He seemed to be getting along nicely until three hours later when he dropped dead. His name was John Judd. His remains were sent to his late home in Sanilac county.

Alcona County Review, January 24, 1890

One Year's History.

Record of Local Happenings for the Year 1890.

JANUARY.

January 22. John Judd fatally injured by a falling tree in Graham's camp.

Alcona County Review, January 1, 1891
Cemetery:

Kayga, Phelix E.

Towns Round Here.

Last November a 13 year old boy of Twining became lost in the woods and, though diligent search was made, he could not be found. Last week the body was found lying across a log with both hands and feet frozen in the ice. Part of the flesh from one arm and leg had been eaten by animals.

Alcona County Review, February 2, 1899
Cemetery:

Keegan, {Girl}

HOME REVIEWINGS.

A ten years old daughter of Jas. Keegan, of Mikado, was buried in the Catholic cemetery last Sunday.

Alcona County Review, March 15, 1889
Cemetery: Probably St. Raphael, Alcona Co.

Keen, Robert

DROWNED!

Robert Keen Lost off the Tug Eliza Williams.

From the Review Extra of Wednesday.

One of the saddest affairs of the season was the drowning of Robert Keen from the tug Eliza Williams, twelve miles off Harrisville, last Saturday afternoon. The tug is engaged in fishing off this place, and Mr. Keen was her engineer. Prior to the accident he had gone aft where there was a hand pump used to pump the water from the hold of the boat, employed on occasions when it was desired to apply full head of steam on the propelling wheel. All steam was applied and the boat was doing her best by way of speed and Mr. Keen was operating the above named pump by means of a rough pine stick improvised for a handle. Suddenly the handle broke and Mr. Keen went overboard, unseen save only by one of the crew, an unexperienced hand, who instead of giving the alarm ran to stop the engine. Before however the captain was made aware of what had happened and the boat brought around to where the drowning man was floundering, he being unable to swim had gone down for the third

and last time, and of course was then beyond recovery. The place where he went down was in about 35 fathoms of water, and the probabilities are that his body will never by recovered. Mr. Keen was an exemplary young man of about 27 years of age, and usually made it his home at Bay City, where reside his parents and some other relatives. He leaves in Harrisville a wife and five-months-old babe who were dependent upon him. His father, Wm. Keen, and a brother from Bay City have been in the village this week in hopes that they might make some successful effort to recover his body, but such effort seems impossible in view of the unknown place and depth of water where the same now lies. The terribly grief-stricken wife and other relatives of the drowned man have the sympathy of all our citizens.

Alcona County Review, September 16, 1881

HOME REVIEWINGS.

The fish tug Eliza Williams went out into the lake Sunday to look for the body of Robert Keen, who was drowned off here a week ago last Saturday. No trace of the body was discovered, however.

Alcona County Review, September 16, 1881
Cemetery:

Keightley, Wilson C.

A Sad Accident.

Drowning of Wilson Keightley Near the Greenbush Dock.

This community was shocked to hear that a man had been drowned at Greenbush Friday night and when it was learned that the unfortunate was Wilson Keightley, general regret was expressed by all who knew him. The dead man and Will Grantham went out after supper to set a gill net at a point 40 to 50 rods from shore and about 90 feet from the dock. Their boat was heavily loaded and there was considerable sea running but neither thought much of that. They finished their task but when they started back the boat had taken in a great deal of water; soon after she sank under them and both jumped into the lake. Each had an oar. Grantham was not a swimmer but Keightley was supposed to be at home in the water. The former

observed that his companion seemed to be in trouble and hallooed to him but received no answer. Grantham then struck out for shore which he reached with the assistance of an oar but not until he was greatly exhausted. When he looked around his late companion was not to be seen. The villagers were soon on the spot and measures were promptly resorted to to recover the body, which was finally secured by drawing a seine net; it had been in the water for a long time and life was extinct. There was only about 8 feet of water where he went down and but 15 to 20 feet from that point it was possible to wade. Why a good swimmer and a strong man should sink under such circumstances while his companion who was no swimmer escaped is explainable only by assigning it to cramps or heart paralysis from sudden immersion in the cold lake water.

Keightley had recently joined the order of the Maccabees and held insurance to the amount of $1000 which goes to his parents. The funeral was held Sunday afternoon and was very largely attended. Elder Smith of the Latter Day Saints preached the sermon. Coroner Beede held an inquest Saturday afternoon but no facts were ascertained to show that the death was anything but an accident.

Deceased was a man nearly 37 years of age. He was unmarried and was the mainstay of his aged parents who are bowed down with grief over the death of this beloved son. Deceased was a man of real worth and sterling principles and was esteemed by all who knew him. His untimely death is deeply deplored at Greenbush.

Alcona County Review, July 25, 1895

IN MEMORIAM.

Whereas, The Angel of Death has secured our password, evaded our pickets watchful eye, entered our Tent, and removed from our midst our beloved brother, Sir. Knight Wilson Keightly, who was drowned in Lake Huron at Greenbush, Mich., on the evening of July 19, 1895.

Whereas, This Tent has lost a worthy Sir Knight and faithful worker and his family a dutiful son and loving brother; therefore be it

Resolved, That we, the members of Mikado Tent No. 13, K.O.T.M., bow in humble submission to the Divine will and deeply regret the untimely and sudden death of Sir Knight Keightly which confronts us with the second demise that ever occurred in our Tent, be it, also.

Resolved, The we extend to the bereaved father and mother of the deceased our heartfelt sympathy and compassion; and may He who has promised to be a defender of the defenceless care tenderly for them in this sad hour of affliction. May the heavy stroke which has befallen them be softened by the consolations of Him who rules us all, as no man can minister to grief so deep and dark; yet the Great Commander of the Supreme Tent above can give solace and in his tender mercy they may find resignation and peace. Be it, also.

Resolved, That as a mark of respect to the departed Sir Knight the charter of this Tent be draped for a period of Sixty days; and be it further.

Resolved, That a copy of these resolutions be delivered to the mother and father of our deceased brother; that they be spread upon the record of our Tent; and that a copy be sent to the Alcona County Review for publication.

W. H. Sanborn,
J. F. Coyle,   Com.
D. N. McRae.

Alcona County Review, July 25, 1895

Card of Thanks.--Words cannot express the deep sense of gratitude we feel towards the friends and neighbors for many kind acts and for the grateful expressions of sympathy tendered to us during our recent sad affliction and irreparable loss. May their lives be blessed accordingly. We feel especially grateful to the Maccabees for the interest taken by them and for their assistance.

Mr. and Mrs. Chas. Keightley

Alcona County Review, July 25, 1895

The officers and members of Mikado Tent No. 13 wish to extend their thanks to the members of Alcona Tent who so kindly assisted them in the funeral ceremony of their late brother, Sir Knight Wilson Keightly.

J. P. McDonald, Record Keeper.

Alcona County Review, July 25, 1895

STATE OF Michigan,
County of Alcona.

At a session of the Probate Court for the County of Alcona, holden at the Probate office in the Village of Harrisville, on Monday, the 9th day of Nov., in the year one thousand nine hundred and three. Present Hon. W. H. Gilpin, Judge of Probate. in the matter of the Estate of Wilson Keightley, deceased.

On reading and filing the petition duly verified, of Charles Keightley.

Thereupon it is ordered, that Monday, the 7th day of December, A. D. 1903, at 10 o'clock in the forenoon, be assigned for the hearing of said petition. Heirs at law and all other persons interested in said estate are required to appear at a session of said court, then to be holden in the probate office, in the Village of Harrisville, and show cause if any there be why the prayer of the petitioner should not be granted.

And it is further ordered, that said petitioner give notice to the persons interested in the estate of the pendency of said petition and the hearing thereof, by causing a copy of this order to be published in the Alcona County Review, a newspaper printed and circulated in said County of Alcona, for three successive weeks previous to said day of hearing.

W. H. Gilpin,
Judge of Probate.

Alcona County Review, November 12, 1903
emetery: Springport, Alcona Co.

Kell, {Boy}

LOCAL JOTTINGS.

An infant son of Wm. Kell died last Friday.

Alcona County Review, March 29, 1889
Cemetery: St. Anne's, Alcona Co.

Kelley, Mrs. Cora

LOCAL JOTTINGS

Mrs. Chas. Kelley, late of Au Sable, was terribly and perhaps fatally burned recently at her home in Chesterfield, Mich. Her recovery is not thought possible.

Alcona County Review, May 11, 1888

LOCAL JOTTINGS

Mrs. Chas. Kelley, who was so terribly burned at her home in Chesterfield, died from the effects of her injuries after six weeks of suffering. She was 22 years of age and leaves two infant children.

Alcona County Review, May 18, 1888

Cemetery: Union, Macomb Co.

Kelley, Stephen J.

West Harrisville.

A child of Alex. Joseph, and one of John Kelley, died in the last week, presumably of diphtheria.

Alcona County Review, January 5, 1893

Health officer Beede paid a visit to the La Vier settlement Sunday. In his opinion the sanitary condition of this locality is in a deplorable state and he expresses surprise, not that diphtheria has caused several deaths, but that there have not been more. Another death occurred there Saturday, a child of two years named Kelley. The remains were brought to the cemetery west of Harrisville and interred there. The locality was placarded and health tracts upon the subject of diphtheria and its treatment were distributed and a warning given to the settlers to observe more rigid precautions to prevent the spread of the contagion.

Alcona County Review, January 5, 1893
Cemetery: West Lawn, Alcona Co.

Kelly, John F.

Jno. F. Kelly, for many years register of deeds for Alpena county and candidate for re-election, died a few days ago aged 80 years. His daughter had performed the duties of the office for the last few years.

Alcona County Review, October 27, 1892
Cemetery: Evergreen, Alpena Co.

Kennedy, Donald

GREENBUSH GETTINGS.

Died, on Saturday morning last, the son of Angus Kennedy, aged 3 years. This makes the third death in two weeks. The loss is greatly felt by the parents.

Alcona County Review, January 1, 1886
Cemetery: Springport, Alcona Co.

Keough, Ethel

PERSONAL MENTION.

The infant child of Mrs. Keough, nee Jennie Walker, died this week and was buried yesterday morning.

Alcona County Review, August 6, 1896

PERSONAL MENTION.

We thank our friends for their kindly interest, sympathy and assistance during the trying hours attending the sickness, death and burial of our little one.

Mr. and Mrs. John Keough.

Alcona County Review, August 13, 1896
Cemetery: West Lawn, Alcona Co.

Kernohan, Ella [Packer]

Death of a Former Resident.

Advice to the Review from Grand Island, Nebraska, report the death at that place on the 14th inst. of Mrs. Ella Packer Kernohan, who will probably be remembered by the older residents of Harrisville. Graduating from the Normal School at Ypsilanti, in 1874, she at once entered upon the duties of assistant principal in the public schools of Harrisville. August 19, 1875, she was married to Mr. Kernohan and remained in her station with him for two succeeding years. Poor health compelled her to retire from school life, and she removed with her family to Nebraska in 1878, and to Grand Island in 1880. The local press of that city speak of her as an earnest and consistent christian woman. She leaves her husband and three children to mourn their loss.

Alcona County Review, May 28, 1886
Cemetery: Grand Island, Hall County NE

Kibler, Henry H.

FATAL ACCIDENT.

Henry H. Kibler, of Greenbush, Killed in a Saw Mill.

It becomes the painful duty of the Review this week to record the horrible death of Henry H. Kibler of Greenbush, this county, which occurred in the lumber mill of T. F. Thompson & Co., Au Sable, Wednesday noon. The report of the accident, as we learn it, is as follows:

The mill had shut down for noon, and Mr. Kibler, filer in the mill, had proceeded to change the large circular saw. Two other employees of the mill were engaged below in putting some repairs upon machinery connected with the steam feed, and had forgotten, before commencing their work, to turn off the steam operating the feed. Without thought, the workmen misplaced a bolt holding the lever that lets steam into the long cylinder operating the carriage, when the carriage immediately shot forward with lightning speed. Mr. Kibler standing between the carriage and saw was crowded onto and over the latter, the same cutting into the lower part of his abdomen, virtually disemboweling him, and mangling his limbs in a horrible manner. It was only the work of an instant, but the screams of the unfortunate Kibler at once reminded the two men below of the horrible work that had been done through their carelessness. The unfortunate man, despite all medical skill used to save him, died in about four hours after the accident.

Henry H. Kibler first came to this county about five years ago, locating at Greenbush, where he had purchased a small farm adjoining the village. During the summer seasons prior to the present one, he filed in the mills of J. Van Buskirk at Greenbush and South Harrisville, and also tended his farm work, and his winters were devoted to getting out timber and cedar posts and ties. His former home was in Buffalo, N. Y., where he had lived for a large number of years. As a citizen he was well liked, and was very prominent in public matters about his home. Twice he was elected treasurer of Greenbush township, his last term expiring last April. He was a fine musician and had been a leader of cornet bands in Buffalo. He was a man of about 38 years of age, and leaves a wife and one child. The funeral services of the deceased were held at Greenbush this morning at 10:30 o'clock, Rev. F. Bradley of Oscoda officiating. Thus again we are forcibly reminded that "in the midst of life we are in death."

Alcona County Review, September 5, 1884

LOCAL JOTTINGS.

Mrs. H. H. Kibler, of Greenbush, received last week from the A. O. U. W. society a bank check for $2,000, being the amount of the policy due her on account of the death of her husband, who was killed in a saw mill at Au Sable last fall. Mr. Kibbler was a member of the Order at the latter place. Mrs. Kibbler desires the Review to say for her that she now hopes those Greenbush gossipers who have had so much to say about her not getting this money, will let their minds and unfeeling tongues be quietly put to rest.

Alcona County Review, January 23, 1885
Cemetery:Springport, Alcona Co.

Kieffer, May F.

Local Sayings and Doings.

Died—In the city of Buffalo, May 21, 1882, May F. Kiefer, daughter of Antona and Anna J. Kieffer, aged 22 years, 10 months and 26 days. The family and deceased were formerly residents of Alcona and Black River, Mich.

Alcona County Review, May 26, 1882
Cemetery:

Killmaster, Benjamin

The death of Benj. Killmaster is reported at Port Rowan, Ont., last week. Deceased was father of Chas. H. and Geo. B. Killmaster, both of whom were at his bedside during his last illness and death. He was a man of wealth and influence and a citizen highly esteemed in the community in which he lived and died.

Alcona County Review, November 8, 1894
Cemetery: Bayview, Norfolk County, ONT

Killmaster, Charles H.

Charles H. Killmaster.

C. M. Lund received a telegram Tuesday from Geo. B. Killmaster, Port Rowan, announcing the death of his brother, Charles H. Particulars have not been received.

Deceased was at one time a well known and popular citizen of this county. He was Supervisor of Gustin township and also Judge of Probate. About three years ago his mind became affected and it became necessary to place him in an asylum for treatment.

Alcona County Review, October 26, 1899

KILLMASTER.

Nov. 2, '99.

The late C. H. Killmaster carries an insurance of $2000 in the K. O. T. M. He is a member of Mineral Water Tent No. 403 at Killmaster.

Alcona County Review, November 2, 1899

The NEWS.

Geo. B. Killmaster left Saturday evening for Port Rowan, Ontario. He had been at Harrisville and Killmaster for the past two months settling up the affairs of the estate of his brother, C. H. Killmaster, deceased.

Alcona County Review, May 1, 1902

ORDER FOR PUBLICATION

State of Michigan. The Probate Court for the County of Alcona.

At a session of said court, held at the Probate office in the City of

Harrisville, in said county, on the 17th day of August, A. D. 1915.

Present: Hon. George W. Burt, Judge of Probate.

In the matter of the estate of Charles H. Killmaster, Deceased.

C. O. Duncan, one of the Administrators of said estate, having filed in said court his final account as Administrator of said estate, and his petition praying for the allowance thereof,

It is ordered that the 14th day of September, A. D. 1915, at ten o'clock in the forenoon, at said Probate Office, be and is hereby appointed for examining and allowing said account;

It is further ordered, that public notice thereof be given by publication of a copy of this order, for three successive weeks previous to said day of hearing, in the Alcona County Review, a newspaper printed and circulated in said county.

GEO. W. BURT,
Judge of Probate.

Alcona County Review, August 19, 1915
Cemetery: Bayview, Norfolk County, ONT

Kimball, Beecher M.

EVENTS OF ONE WEEK.

The death of Beacher Kimball, the ell-known electrician, occurred at his home in Au Sable Wednesday evening, Feb. 19th, from inflammation of the brain. Deceased made several trips to Harrisville last year to put the local telephone exchange in running order, and he created a favorable impression by reason of his bright and energetic manner. He was but 28 years of age, yet he was a successful electrician and was in a fair way to attain more than ordinary success in that line. He left a wife and two children.

Alcona County Review, February 27, 1896
Cemetery: Pinecrest, Iosco Co.

Kimball, Mrs. Catherine

LOCAL LACONICS.

Mrs. Kimball, wife of Wm. Kimball, employed at S. Milligan's shingle mill, died Tuesday morning after a short illness. She leaves five children, the youngest being only three months old. Mr. Kimball has the sympathy of all who know him in this severe affliction. The funeral took place on Wednesday afternoon.

Alcona County Review, May 8, 1885
Cemetery:

Kimball, {Girl}

ALCONA ATOMS.

Mrs. Geo. Kimball gave birth to twins (a boy and girl) on the 6th of Feb. Unfortunately the girl did not live, and was buried on Sunday, the 7th. Mother and boy are doing well.

Alcona County Review, February 19, 1886
Cemetery:

Kimball, Etta [Belknap]

Mrs. Herbert Kimball, a young married woman residing at Alpena, died very suddenly on Dec. 16, under circumstances that led to the suspicion that she had been poisoned. A month after she died the remains were exhumed and the vitals were sent to Ann Arbor for analysis. It now seems certain that she was poisoned, but no arrests have yet been made pending the arrival of a full report from Ann Arbor. The case is shrouded in much mystery.

Alcona County Review, February 23, 1893

The coroner's jury, sitting in solemn judgment on the remains of Mrs. Herbert Kimball of Alpena, found that she came to her death from arsenical poisoning administered by some person or persons unknown. Pros. Atty. Dafoe is proceeding very carefully and it is likely that some arrests will follow.

Alcona County Review, March 2, 1893
Cemetery: Evergreen, Alpena Co.

King, Henry Clay

Henry Clay King.

Oscoda has lost one if its oldest and most prominent citizens in the death of Henry Clay King, who passed away Thursday morning, Dec. 26, at the age of 66 years.

He was a native of the state of Massachusetts, but came to Michigan in 1852 and in 1873 removed to Oscoda, where he has since been closely identified with the business and social interests of that town. He was post-master for 15 years.

The funeral services were held Sunday afternoon and were under the auspices of the Knights of Pythias.

Alcona County Review, January 2, 1896
Cemetery:

King, Robert B.

NEIGHBORHOOD NOTES.

Robert B. King, the well known business man of Au Sable, died last Saturday morning, aged 64 years.

Alcona County Review, March 15, 1889
Cemetery:

Kirkendall, David H., Jr.

PERSONAL MENTION.

David Kirkendall, Jr., son of the pioneer citizen of that name of Greenbush township, died at the home of his parents, Monday, the 21st, of consumption. The remains were followed to their last resting place at South Harrisville, Wednesday afternoon by a large number of sympathizing friends and sorrowing relatives. Deceased was 26 years of age and unmarried.

Alcona County Review, March 23, 1893
Cemetery: Springport, Alcona Co.

Kirkendall, George E.

Geo. Kirkendall, aged 30 years, son of David Kirkendall of Greenbush died Monday from consumption. The funeral was held at Greenbush yesterday, Rev. Tompkins officiating.

Alcona County Review, May 13, 1897

Card of Thanks.

We desire to thank our many friends, especially the Knights of the Maccabees, who so kindly assisted us during the last illness and the death of our son. May He who is the rewarder of all, reward them for their kindnesses.

David Kirkendall and Family.
Greenbush, Mich., May 17, 1897.

Alcona County Review, May 20, 1897
Cemetery: Springport, Alcona Co.

Kirkendall, John

LOCAL JOTTINGS.

John Kirkendall, one of the oldest settlers of Oscoda, died on the 8th inst., aged 86 years.

Alcona County Review, September 17, 1886
Cemetery:

Kirkendall, Wesley

EVENTS OF ONE WEEK.

Wesley Kirkendall died a little after midnight last night at his home in Greenbush.

Deceased was strong and robust until a couple of weeks ago he contracted typhoid fever while working on the government piers at Grand Marais. He came home and has had the best of care, but the disease gained a victory over medical skill. He was 21 years of age. Deceased was married only last January to Miss Monroe, daughter of David Monroe, and the young wife is heart broken. Funeral will take place tomorrow at 10 a.m. from the Greenbush school house. Burial at South Harrisville.

Alcona County Review, October 24, 1895
Cemetery: Springport, Alcona Co.

Kissock, Mrs. William

REVIEWINGS.

A Mrs. Kissock, living back of Greenbush, was buried yesterday.

Alcona County Review, May 16, 1879
Cemetery:

Kline, Jacob

RESULT OF A SALOON ROW.

Ed Gauthro Behind the Bars for the Murder of Jacob Kline.

Another exciting event that happened at Au Sable last week was a saloon row in which Jacob Kline received a blow from Ed. Gauthro which resulted in Kline's death from hemorrhage.

Kline and Ed. Gauthro, the latter well known as an ugly and vicious fellow when drunk, met in Fred Welch's saloon early Sunday morning. They had some words, but no blows, and Kline started to go out the back door. He was followed by Gauthro, who struck him in the face when he reached the step. Kline fell from the step and in falling struck his head on a plank. Failing to get up he was dragged into the saloon, where he lay in an unconscious condition until Sunday evening, when Dr. Hovis and Dr. Cattanash were called. Kline was removed to his home near by, where examination revealed that a blood vessel had been ruptured and hemorrhage inside of the skull had resulted, causing a pressure upon the brain, resulting in congestion. Kline lingered in a comatose condition until Friday evening, when he passed away without having once regained consciousness. He leaves a wife and three small children, for whom provision is made by a $2,000 policy in the Maccabees. On Monday Gauthro was arraigned before Justice Cosgrove on a charge of murder. He waived examination and was bound over to the circuit court without bail.

Alcona County Review, August 13, 1891

THE LOCAL NEWS
Edward Gothro, who killed Jacob Kline in a fracas at Au Sable Aug. 2nd

last, while both men were under the influence of liquor, was acquitted of the charge of murder last week to the circuit court for Iosco county. While engaged in a dispute Gothro pushed or knocked Klein from the stoop at the back of the saloon and the latter in falling struck on the back of his head. He never regained consciousness but remained in a comatose state until three days later when he died. Gothro was at once arrested on a charge of murder and has languished in jail since in default of bail.

Alcona County Review, December 24, 1891
Cemetery:

Klock, Monroe

Among Our Exchanges.

Ex-Mayor Monroe Klock of Alpena died at Flint last Saturday morning, aged 48 years. He had been ill for some time.

Alcona County Review, May 19, 1892
Cemetery: Evergreen, Alpena Co.

Kloppenburg, Julius S.

Au Sable and Oscoda.

Major Julius S. Kloppenburg, a former lumberman and salt manufacturer of Tawas died at Chicago last week.

Alcona County Review, March 24, 1882
Cemetery:

Kruger, FredericaMinnie [Krantz]

Mrs. Kruger, an elderly lady of German nativity, residing in the western part of Harrisville township, died this morning of inflammation of the bowels after an illness of about four weeks.

Alcona County Review, February 8, 1894
Cemetery: West Lawn, Alcona Co.

Kujawa, {Boy}

Black River Sparks.
Born Saturday, March 21st, to Mr. and Mrs. Simon Kajawa, twins, both boys, since deceased.

Alcona County Review, March 26, 1896
Cemetery: Probably Holy Cross, Alpena Co.

Kujawa, {Boy}

Black River Sparks.
Born Saturday, March 21st, to Mr. and Mrs. Simon Kajawa, twins, both boys, since deceased.

Alcona County Review, March 26, 1896
Cemetery: Probably Holy Cross, Alpena Co.

LaBoueff, {Girl}

EVENTS OF ONE WEEK.

The infant daughter of Mr. and Mrs. David La Boueff died at 5 o'clock last evening from spasms. The funeral will be held at 10 o'clock tomorrow morning at the Catholic church.

Alcona County Review, April 15, 1897
Cemetery: Probably St. Anne's, Alcona Co.

LaBoueff, Louis

AN EPIDEMIC OF

TERRIBLE ACCIDENTS!

TWO MEN KILLED AND A LITTLE GIRL SEVERELY INJURED.

The Death of Antoine Laliberttey and Louis Laboueff.

Saturday evening last, Antoine Laliberttey, aged about 50 years, met his death at West Harrisville, being run over by a log train. The particulars are as follows: Saturday morning he took the train to Au Sable to get his daughter to come home and care for her mother, who was ill. She accompanied him home on the evening train. They got off the cars at West Harrisville, and were met by his son-in-law. The old man stopped to speak with some one, and the son-in-law and daughter started on up the track towards home, which they reached soon afterward. Sometime later Antoine followed, walking on the track, and when near Kimball's camp, was struck by a log train which was backing up the road, and killed, his body being horribly mangled by the wheels. During the night the sad intelligence of his death was conveyed to his family. The funeral service was held by Rev. Father Winter in the Harrisville Catholic church, on Monday afternoon. Sunday evening following occurred the

Sad Death of Louis Laboeuff,
who was killed by a run-away team under most distressing circumstances. Louis was a young man, being only 20 years of age. He came here recently from Canada to enter the employ of his brother, David Laboeuff, proprietor of the livery stable. He was quiet,

industrious, of good habits, and was steadily gaining friends. Sunday evening he took a load of men out to the camps, and returned safely, changed teams and started with another load. On his return he was met by Matt. Morrison, an employe of the stable who was also taking out a load of passengers, near the cemetery just west of the village, and was then all right. He was driving the stage-wagon, the front (or driver's) seat of which is provided with a foot-board having a low iron railing along the outer edge, and is located above and a trifle back from the whiffletrees. It is supposed that while driving down the Court House hill he fell forward from the seat while asleep, (or from some other cause), his body striking on and doubling over the evener and whiffletree, with his head and shoulders dragging on the ground directly behind the off horse, his body being held in that position by the evener pressing it against the foot-board. The horses ran down Main street to the McLennan House corner, and turned south past the livery barn down Lake street to the foot of the street, where they were soon afterward found standing, with Louis' dead body lying across the whiffletree in the position above described, the scalp torn off, the skull fractured, and the arms torn and bruised. Help was secured and the body taken out from the wagon. Pros. attorney Depew was notified, and arriving on the scene appointed S. J. McNally to act as coroner. The following jury was impaneled and viewed the remains: M. S. Madden, Dr. J. Currie, E. Barbour, Guy C. Lewis, A. Atchison and Jas. Nevins; and then adjourned to Monday afternoon. The body was washed and dressed and tenderly cared for, and friends vied with each other in expressions of sympathy and offers of assistance. Many handsome floral tributes were sent to Mr. Morrison's residence, where the remains lay, during Monday, and many viewed the remains. The funeral was held in the Catholic church Tuesday morning, and was largely attended.

INCIDENTS OF THE ACCIDENT.

Numerous theories as to how the accident occurred are advanced, and while all are probable, the late hour (nearly midnight) at which the accident occurred precludes the probability of the facts ever being known.

Louis' cap was picked up opposite Geo. Rutson's residence, and his rubber coat and under coat, bearing evidence of having been torn from his body by the wheel, were found in front of the Dr. Lyman residence.

Blood marked the course of the team, which took to the sidewalk near Wm. Reynolds' residence, on Lake street, and kept it for some distance. It is reported that two or more parties saw the team running and heard Louis cry "whoa!" but nothing definite is known as yet.

The coroner's jury met at G. C. Lewis' shop Monday afternoon as per adjournment; but owing to the non-appearance of an important witness the inquest was again adjourned until Thursday afternoon, and is still in progress was we go to press.

Alcona County Review, August 13, 1886

Verdict of the Coroner's Jury.

STATE OF MICHIGAN, County of Alcona.

An inquisition, taken at the shop of Guy C. Lewis, in the village of Harrisville, in said county, on the 12th day of August, 1886, in said county of Alcona, before Simon J. McNally, a coroner for said county, upon the body of Louis LaBoueff, deceased, whose body was viewed by said jurors on the 8th day of August, 1886, then and there lying dead, by the oaths of the jurors whose names are hereto subscribed, who being sworn to enquire in behalf of the people of this state when and in what manner and by what means the said Louis LaBoueff came to his death, upon their oaths do say, that said Louis LaBoueff, late of the Village of Harrisville, at the Township of Harrisville, in the County aforesaid, on the 8th day of August, in the year one thousand eight hundred and eighty six, (1886), came to his death by accidentally falling from a wagon he was driving and being kicked by one of the horses attached to said wagon.

The facts and circumstances connected with the death of said Louis LaBoueff, as we find them, are as follows, viz.; On said 8th day of August, 1886, said Louis LaBoueff, deceased, was in the employ of his brother, David LaBoueff, in a livery stable, in the village of Harrisville, in said county; and on said last named day, about fifteen (15) minutes after nine (9) o'clock in the evening, said David LaBoueff sent said Louis LaBoueff with a team attached to a covered spring wagon, to carry some passengers to West Harrisville, in said county; said Louis LaBoueff returned to the village of Harrisville, arriving there about thirty (30) minutes after eleven (11) o'clock, and when near the residence of George Rutson, in said village of Harrisville, said Louis LaBoueff accidentally fell from said wagon and was caught in the outside trace of the right-hand horse, or off horse, in which position he was carried to the south end of Lake street, in said village of Harrisville, where his body was found dead.

In Testimony Whereof, The said coroner and the jurors of this inquest have hereunto set their hands the twelfth (12th) day of August, 1886, at the place aforesaid
Dr. John Currie,
Samuel Anderson,
Eustache Barber,   Jurors.
Michael S. Madden,
James Nevins,
Guy C. Lewis,
SIMON J. McNALLY, Coroner.

Alcona County Review, August 20, 1886
Cemetery: St. Anne's, Alcona Co.

LaChapelle, Alice Sarah

EVENTS OF ONE WEEK.

Alice, the nine-year-old daughter of Mr. and Mrs. Frank La Chapelle, died Saturday of convulsions, to which the child was subject for several years past. The remains were placed? at rest Monday afternoon in the family lot in the South Harrisville cemetery, the Rev. W. J. Bailey officiating.

At the crystal river's brink,
Some sweet day bye and bye,
We shall find each broken link,
Some sweet day bye and bye;
There the star that fading here
Left our hearts and homes so drear,
We shall see more bright and dear
Some sweet day bye and bye.

Alcona County Review, November 1, 1894

PERSONAL MENTION.

At a meeting of Wyrum Hoyt Post G. A. R. held Thursday evening, Nov.

1st, 1894, the following resolution was unanimously adopted:

Resolved, That this Post do tender our heartfelt sympathy to Comrade Francis La Chapelle and family in their late loss and bereavement.

Harrisville, Mich., Nov. 1, 1894.
Howard C. Kibbee,
Post Commander.

Alcona County Review, November 15, 1894
Cemetery: Springport, Alcona Co.

LaChapelle, Charles J.

HOME REVIEWINGS.

Charles LaChapelle, aged about 19 years, son of Mrs. Catherine Micho, died at the residence of Isaac Rose in this township, Monday morning last. "Charley," as he was called, had been overtaken by the quick consumption, and his confinement to home and bed had only been about three weeks. He knew that he was going to die, and was prepared to meet the solemn change. Sunday morning early, as he was sitting up in his chair, or lying in the same, he called his mother to remove the curtain from an east window so that he might see the sun rise once more, saying that it would be the last time, as he should die before it rose again, and sure enough his prophesy was true, for the following morning at about three o'clock he passed away as in a calm sleep, there being not the slightest death struggle observable. The grief stricken mother, brothers and sisters of the deceased have the entire sympathy of the community in this their hour of affliction.

Alcona County Review, June 3, 1881
Cemetery: St. Anne's, Alcona Co.

LaChapelle, Francis

Very Sudden.

Frank La Chapelle Expires in a Chair After a Hard Day's Work.

Very suddenly came the death summons to Frank La Chapelle last Friday. He had been working hard nearly all day in the grain fields of his sick neighbor, Chas. Martin, and finished the day's work by cutting some grain of his own. While awaiting the coming of the men from the field for supper he sat out in the yard in a reclining easy chair to rest as was his wont. A member of the family prepared some lemonade for

him of which he drank freely. Shortly after this while the others were inside the house, they heard a choking sound and ran out to him but he died before they could reach his side.

A messenger was dispatched to Harrisville for a physician, hope being entertained that life still lingered, but long before his arrival the family realized that the final summons, to which all mortals must respond, had come.

The sudden death of Mr. La Chapelle was a shock to the community as all sudden deaths must be, but his intimate friends were not surprised, though pained at the suddenness of his demise, for it has been known to them for many months that he was suffering from heart disease of a very dangerous type. He knew his condition well and frequently alluded in a joking and cheery way to the probability of his sudden departure at any moment as if he had no fear of death and no hope of a long life.

The funeral services were conducted Sunday afternoon at the family residence with interment at Springport. There was a great concourse of people from far and wide, most of whom followed the remains to their last resting place.

Rev. Will preached the sermon.

The burial service conformed to the beautiful and touching ritual of the Grand Army of the Republic and was conducted by members of John Earle Post of Au Sable, of which deceased was a member. Wyrum Hoyt Post of Harrisville turned out in force and assisted at the grave and furnished the pall bearers. The casket was draped with the national flag, a most appropriate tribute to the deceased, for if there was any trait in his character that was more conspicuous and praiseworthy than any other it was his intense devotion to the flag and the government it represents, under which and for which he fought and marched from first to last of the great rebellion. Never a camp fire, a memorial observance or a reunion that he could attend but that found him present, and full of the fire of patriotic zeal. To such types of men as he the country is indebted in greater measure than is often realized until they are numbered among the dead. They

pass from among the living and their personality is soon forgotten, but the everlasting impress of their invincible spirits is left upon succeeding generations for ages. Though they never become great or famous as the world considers greatness and fame, they may have the individual weaknesses and the foibles of mankind in large degree, yet in the hearts and affections of a great unified people they have an enduring monument, for the tremendous sacrifices and the glorious deeds of this grand army of veterans never can be effaced or forgotten, as long as liberty continues to enlighten the world.

Deceased was about 54 years of age. He was a native of Canada but came to Alcona when a boy and was one of the early pioneers. He leaves a widow and a grown up family in comfortable circumstances.

Alcona County Review, August 4, 1898

PERSONAL POINTS.

Alfred La Chapelle and daughter, Miss Lillian, of Alpena, attended the funeral of Francis La Chapelle Sunday. Miss La Chapelle remained in Harrisville for the week.

Judge Simpson and Comrades Mead, Worth, Craft and Phillips of John Earl Post, Au Sable, came up Sunday on the Dietz steam launch, to officiate at the burial of their deceased comrade, Francis La Chapelle.

Alcona County Review, August 4, 1898

Haynes Happenings.

August 2, 1898.

I was surprised to learn of the death of Comrade Francis La Chapelle. I sympathize with the family in their loss. The old vets are dropping off one by one and it won't be long until we all have passed over the silent river to meet the comrades gone before.

Alcona County Review, August 4, 1898

PERSONAL POINTS.

Will La Chapelle was down from Valentine Lake Sunday to attend the funeral of his uncle.

Alcona County Review, August 4, 1898

PERSONAL POINTS.

Mrs. May Severance-La Chapelle was summoned from Walled Lake, Mich., by the death of her father.

Alcona County Review, August 4, 1898

A correction of the obituary notice of Francis La Chapelle published last week has been handed to the Review. Mr. La Chapelle was born at Ogdensburg, N. Y., in the year 1842 and was therefore a native born citizen of the United States, of which fact the deceased was especially proud.

Alcona County Review, August 11, 1898

Local History of One Year

Chronology of the Principal Events of the Year 1898.

July 29. Sudden death of Francis LaChapelle aged 56.

Alcona County Review, January 5, 1899

Memorial Day Remembered.

One by one the ranks of the veterans are thinning. The addition since last memorial Day of three graves to the list of those interred in local cemeteries was a present reminder of this fact. They were those of Patrick McGrath, Francis La Chapelle and Epriam Waldron.

Alcona County Review, June 1, 1899

Of Local Interest.

Pension attorney Baede reports the allowance of a pension for Mrs. F. La Chapelle and minor children. The amount of pension is $8 per month widow's pension and $2 per month for the minor children, with a crude pension from Sept. 3, 1898.

Alcona County Review, May 3, 1900

Of Local Interest.

A. B. Crow of Alpena has this week placed a monument at the grave of Francis La Chapelle at the South Harrisville cemetery.

Alcona County Review, May 31, 1900

Honored the Nation's Dead.

Despite the threatening weather of Tuesday night and early Wednesday morning, there never was a more perfect day for such an occasion than was yesterday, Memorial Day. When the rain ceased and the clouds lifted, Dame Nature came forth in her best bib and tucker, while Old Sol beamed cheerfully down.

People began to arrive in town quite early and by 10 o'clock the line of march was formed and the procession started for the Catholic and South Harrisville cemeteries. An

advance guard of fifty or more bicycles led the way, followed by the veterans, daughters of veterans, U. L. G., schools, citizens, the procession being about a half mile long.

At the cemeteries the graves of the dead heroes were decorated with flags and strewn with flowers and evergreens. At the grave of Daniel Noyes, the last of the veterans of this locality to respond to the final roll call, the veterans gave the impressive grave service of the G. A. R., and at the grave of Francis LaChapelle the Fisher school children sang a song.

Alcona County Review, May 31, 1900
Cemetery: Springport, Alcona Co.

LaChapelle, Matthew

Matthew Chapelle, aged about 40 years, died at the home of Isaac Rose at West Harrisville last Monday. Deceased had been subject to fits for years and of late the disease had grown on him to such an extent that he experienced three and four a day. His death was due to this cause.

The funeral services were conducted by the Rev. Fr. Poulin at St. Anne's church Tuesday morning.

Alcona County Review, April 22, 1897
Cemetery: St. Anne's, Alcona Co.

LaClair, Joseph

FATAL HOTEL FIRE.
The Miner House at Tawas Burned.
Two of its Inmates Incinerated in the Ruins.

Last week Thursday the Miner House in East Tawas was discovered to be on fire, but not until it had gained such headway that all efforts to check it were of no avail. Jos. Widdifield, the proprietor, and his family had barely time to escape. All the guests were aroused, it was thought, in time to make their escape but E. F. Roney, the barkeeper and a lumberman named Joseph La Clair were missed and an investigation of the ruins after the fire was over revealed the charred remains of the two men. A coroner's jury returned a verdict to the effect that the two men came to their death from suffocation by smoke. The hotel was a total loss with but little insurance.

Alcona County Review, December 13, 1889
Cemetery:

LaCross, {Boy}

Born to Mr. and Mrs. Clay Lacross, a son, since deceased.

Alcona County Review, January 16, 1896

Cemetery:

LaFleur, Armadas

Black River News.

May 1, 1895.
Armadas, the only child of Henry Lefour, died here Friday morning. He took sick Thursday noon. Dr. McCormick was sent for but said he could do nothing for him and did not answer the call. The remains were interred in the Harrisville cemetery Sunday.

Alcona County Review, May 2, 1895

EVENTS OF ONE WEEK.

A child from the French settlement back of Black River was buried in the Catholic cemetery Sunday morning.

Alcona County Review, May 2, 1895
Cemetery: St. Anne's, Alcona Co.

LaFrance, {Boy}

Haynes.

Daniel La France buried a five month's old boy last week.

Alcona County Review, March 23, 1893
Cemetery: Probably Mt. Joy, Alcona Co.

LaFrance, {Child}

A small child of Jno. La France of Haynes was buried in the Catholic cemetery this week.

Alcona County Review, April 23, 1896
Cemetery: St. Anne's, Alcona Co.

LaFrance, {Girl}

CORRESPONDENCE.

Haynes, Jan. 26th.—David La France buried a daughter about three months old last Monday week.

Alcona County Review, January 28, 1892
Cemetery: Probably Mt. Joy, Alcona Co.

LaFrance, {Girl}

PERSONAL MENTION.

Jos. LaFrance of Haynes township buried a young daughter last Saturday who had died from inflammation.

Alcona County Review, August 31, 1893
Cemetery: Mt. Joy, Alcona Co.

LaFrance, Mary

ALCONA.

Mr. John Lafrance buried a daughter, on Sunday 24th, aged about three years. Disease— whooping cough and worm fever.

Alcona County Review, November 29, 1878
Cemetery: Mt. Joy, Alcona Co.

LaFrance, William

HAYNES.

Sept. 5, '99.

Wm. La France, aged 8 years died Friday in Hawse twp. of dropsy and was interred in Haynes cemetery Sunday.

Alcona County Review, September 7, 1899

LOCAL PICK UPS.

The eight-year-old son of Mr. and Mrs. Jno. LaFrance of Ritchie, died last Friday and was buried Saturday at Mt. Joy cemetery. Chas. Mayo conducted the funeral.

Alcona County Review, September 7, 1899
Cemetery: Mt. Joy, Alcona Co.

LaGrange, B. S.

Hon. B. S. LaGrange.

The death of B. S. LaGrange occurred Sept. 24th ult., at his home in LaGrange, Col.

Deceased lived at Harrisville for a few years prior to 1870, when he was inspired by the New York Tribune emigration articles of that period to go west and grow up with the country. He was one of a number, including the late Wm. Noyes, who joined the Union Colony Association and assisted in laying the foundation of the now prosperous Colorado city of Greeley. "During the stormy days through which this community passed," says a newspaper article, "he was one of the few who stood firm, never allowing his confidence in the ultimate success of the colony to waver. For many years he served on its Board of Directors and at an early date became one of its canal superintendents. He was the guiding spirit and the master hand in conquering all the early difficulties of canal management. He devised and successfully carried through the legislature the first irrigation law which Colorado placed upon its statute books and more than all by his personal effort and tact succeeded in carrying its provisions into beneficial and peacable effect." He was a member of the board of directors of the Colorado Agricultural College for nineteen years. During the past twenty years he held many important appointive positions, his last public service being as world's fair commissioner. He was never a politician in the ordinary sense of the term and never ran for an elective office. He is survived by his wife, four children and five grand children.

Alcona County Review, October 10, 1895
Cemetery: Linn Grove, Weld County, CO

Lalibertty, Antoine

AN EPIDEMIC OF

TERRIBLE ACCIDENTS!

TWO MEN KILLED AND A LITTLE GIRL SEVERELY INJURED.

The Death of Antoine Laliberttey and Louis Laboueff.

Saturday evening last, Antoine Laliberttey, aged about 50 years, met his death at West Harrisville, being run over by a log train. The particulars are as follows: Saturday morning he took the train to Au Sable to get his daughter to come home and care for her mother, who was ill. She accompanied him home on the evening train. They got off the cars at West Harrisville, and were met by his son-in-law. The old man stopped to speak with some one, and the son-in-law and daughter started on up the track towards home, which they reached soon afterward. Sometime later Antoine followed, walking on the track, and when near Kimball's camp, was struck by a log train which was backing up the road, and killed, his body being horribly mangled by the wheels. During the night the sad intelligence of his death was conveyed to his family. The funeral service was held by Rev. Father Winter in the Harrisville Catholic church, on Monday afternoon.

Alcona County Review, August 13, 1886
Cemetery: Probably St. Anne's, Alcona Co.

LaLonde, Alex

LOCAL JOTTINGS.

A little child of David LaLonde, aged about six months, died Saturday morning. The funeral was held at the Catholic church, Sunday afternoon.

Alcona County Review, February 19, 1886
Cemetery: St. Anne's, Alcona Co.

Lambley, J. B.

THE GRAVE.

The Rev. J. B. Lambley, a bright young Baptist divine who filled the Oscoda pastorate a couple of years ago with great credit to himself, passed over to the silent majority a

few days ago at Manistique after a brief illness from typhoid fever.

Alcona County Review, January 17, 1890
Cemetery:

Lamont, George P.

OVERBOARD!

George P. Lamont Steps Off the Faxton and is Lost.

The steamer Faxton lost a passenger about five miles out of Tawas on her way up last Saturday night. His name was George P. Lamont, of Saginaw, and he was employed as advance agent for the Newell show.

When the boat was at Tawas Lamont was out on deck with other passengers and they all retired shortly after the boat pulled out. About half an hour later the young man came out of his room, walked to the rail and stepped off.

Lamont was in the habit of walking in his sleep and members of the show company think he walked overboard in his sleep.

A member of the Glass Blowers, who performed here this week, says he met Lamont in Tawas last week and thought at the time that he acted rather queer. He says he thinks it was a case of suicide.

Alcona County Review, June 25, 1896
Cemetery:

Lamp, Michael Henry

A Busy Life Has Ended

Engineer Lamp, Veteran Railroad Man of Black River, Has Crossed Over.

Michael Lamp, senior engineer of the D.& M., died at his home in Black River early Sunday morning, at the age of 51.

He was taken sick on the morning after New Year's with a complication of the grippe and pneumonia. It developed heart trouble and his busy life was ended at 2 on Sunday morning.

Engineer Lamp had handled the throttle in this vicinity since 1880, just 20 years. He was engaged on the D.& M. from the starting of the road. Previously he worked on Alger Smith and Co.'s timber line. He had also worked on roads in Southern Michigan.

He leaves a large family, which is well protected by extensive life insurance. Mrs. John McArthur, of Alpena, wife of a well known engineer, is his daughter.

The funeral was held today with interment at Alcona. An appropriate floral offering was ordered by the Alpena boys for the casket of their dead associate. Engineer Tom Kennedy represented them at the funeral.

Knowing and known to every one of the railroad employees, Engineer Lamp was universally esteemed and respected by them. That is a sufficient tribute to his manhood, for in the hard life around an engine the nobler characteristics are easily blunted, and his associates are sensitive to a man's faults. The comments of bereavement over "Mike's" death are the best eulogies that could be pronounced.—Alpena Echo.

Alcona County Review, January 12, 1899

BLACK RIVER.

For promptness in settling its obligations or death claims we know of no order or insurance company that will compare with the Maccabees. Another instance of their promptness along this line is noted in the case of Sir Michael Lamp, deceased. Proofs of death and other necessary papers were sent to headquarters on Monday of last week and on Saturday following the widow received a warrant for $2,000, the amount of her husband's policy.

Alcona County Review, February 2, 1899

HAYNES.

Mrs. M. Lamp has caused a splendid monument to be erected in our cemetery in memory of her husband.

Alcona County Review, July 20, 1899
Cemetery: Mt. Joy, Alcona Co.

Landon, Elizabeth

LOCAL JOTTINGS.

During the past two weeks, cholera-infantum has been having a terrible rage in this community, no less than a dozen small children and babes having died from the same.— This naturally leaves many houses of mourning in our community, and to those of us who are as yet free from the scourge in our own homes, should come forth hearty sympathy and fitting words for the bereaved. Friday last, the scourge took away a little, human flower each from the homes of William Nestle and James

Stringer. Tuesday the family of Chas. Larson were bereft of their babe, and Wednesday evening Frank Stevens and wife were called to part with their first-born. Gilbert Landon, one of the Messrs. Byces, and the Ducharms have also each lost a babe, and there are several others in the community apparently nearly at death's door, at the time we go to press. Thus many of the homes in our community are being darkened. May the Lord remove the dark cloud speedily, and give consolation to the sorrowing parents.

Alcona County Review, August 29, 1884
Cemetery:

Landon, Mary E.

LOCAL JOTTINGS.

A nine-year old daughter of Gil. Landon died Monday morning after a short illness.

Alcona County Review, June 22, 1888

LOCAL JOTTINGS.

A daughter of Gilbert Landon died June 17th of consumption, aged 9 years.

Alcona County Review, July 6, 1888
Cemetery: Twin Lakes, Alcona Co

Lane, Harriett [Hugill]

West Harrisville.
Oct. 30, 1895.
The funeral services of Mrs. Lain, who died on Saturday, took place in the church here Tuesday, Rev. Ford occupying the pulpit.

Alcona County Review, October 31, 1895
Cemetery: Twin Lakes, Alcona Co.

Langtree, John W.

FROM OUR EXCHANGES.
John W. Langtree, ex-sheriff of Iosco county died last week at East Tawas.

Alcona County Review, August 19, 1897
Cemetery: Brady Hill, Saginaw Co.

LaPage, Delima

STATE OF MICHIGAN, County of Alcona.

At a session of the Probate Court for said County, held at the Probate office, in the Village of Harrisville on the eleventh day of April in the year one thousand eight hundred and ninety-six.

Present, C. H. Killmaster, Judge of Probate.

In the matter of the estate of Delima La Page.

On reading and filing the petition duly verified of George La Page, praying among other things for the Probate of an instrument in writing filed in this court, purporting to be the last will and testament of Delima La Page, deceased, and that O. H. Smith may be appointed executor thereof.

Thereupon it is ordered, that Saturday, the ninth day of May next, at ten o'clock in the forenoon, be assigned for the hearing of said petition, and that the heirs at law of said deceased and all other persons interested in said estate, are required to appear at a session of the Probate Court, then to be holden at the Probate office, in the Village of Harrisville and show cause, if any there be, why the prayer of the petitioner should not be granted.

And it is further ordered that the petitioner give notice to the heirs at law and persons interested in the estate of the pendency of said petition, and the hearing thereof, by causing a copy of this order to be published in the Alcona County Review, a newspaper printed and circulating in said county three successive weeks previous to said day of hearing.

C. H. KILLMASTER,
Judge of Probate.

Alcona County Review, April 9, 1896
Cemetery:

Laperre, Louis

ACCIDENT AT BLACK RIVER.

An Employee of the Company Fatally Injured.

From Monday's Echo:
Friday night a man named Leparre, employed in Alger, Smith & Co's mill at Black River, met with an accident which cost him his life. Leparre was employed back of the saw and a heavy timber caught on the saw and flew back, striking him in the stomach and almost disemboweling him. Dr. McCormick attended him, but yesterday called Dr. Cameron, of this city, to assist. A special train was sent up and Dr. Cameron went to the injured man. He returned home last evening, but says Mr. Leperre cannot live.

Alcona County Review, June 2, 1892

Black River.

Louis Laperre was badly injured in the mill while sawing pickets. It seems that the young man had started a picket through the saw and it in some way caught on the saw and was returned with great force, striking Laperre near the pit of the stomach and inflicting a frightful wound. The picket punctured the intestine, which has made it necessary to perform some feats in medical surgical skill.

Alcona County Review, June 9, 1892

The Local News.

Dr. Seaman of Alpena is attending the man Lapere, who was injured at Black River last week, and under his care the patient is rapidly recovering. Writing to the Echo he states that he found Laperre very low with every indication of approaching death, but that at the date of writing—June 1—he had got the case under subjection; the patient was taking nourishment, sleeping well and comparatively free from pain.

Alcona County Review, June 9, 1892

Black River.

The young man Laperre, who was so frightfully injured in the mill some days since, is now in the care of Dr. Seaman of Alpena. The young man's case was given up by several physicians, who pronounced him incurable and that a few hours at the longest would terminate his earthly career.

It is two days since Dr. Seaman operated upon the case and the young man is steadily improving. Dr. Seaman is by the boy's bedside and keeps careful account of pulse and temperature and will operate again on Friday next and close up the wound in the large intestine by wire sutures. The Dr. expects his son from Germany to assist him in this last operation.

Alcona County Review, June 9, 1892

SOMEWHAT PERSONAL.

Leperre, the young man whose serious injury has been chronicled in these columns, died while Dr. Seaman was removing him to the train for the purpose of taking him to Detroit for treatment. The remains were brought to this place Sunday and interred in the Catholic cemetery.

Alcona County Review, June 16, 1892
Cemetery: St. Anne's, Alcona Co.

Lapham, James

Goes Up For Fifteen Years.

The case of the people vs. William L. Churchill for murder, on trial all last week at Hillman, Montmorency county. The case was given to the jury Friday night and Saturday morning a verdict of murder in the second degree was rendered. Judge Kelly at once sentenced Churchill to 15 years at Jackson. He takes his sentence easily and says he will be out in 11 years. He is 55 years of age. The crime of which Churchill is convicted is the killing of James Lapham on June 30 last. Churchill kept a hotel at Atlanta and he was accused of outraging a 15-year-old girl in his employ, which was probably untrue. There was talk of lynching him and he threatened to shoot any one who came near the house. Lapham walked past the house and Churchill riddled him with shot, the victim dying in 20 minutes. Churchill was defended by Sleator and Greening of Alpena and the case will probably not be appealed.

Alcona County Review, September 26, 1890
Cemetery:

Laraway, George

HORRIBLE DEATH.

George Laraway Killed at the Peninsular Car Works.

A fatal accident occurred at the Peninsular Car Works, corner of Adair and Wight streets, at 10:30 Wednesday night. George Laraway, a night foreman, turned a belt off from a pulley and while attaching it to its fastening his sleeve was caught in the pulley and he was jerked up and whirled around the shafting with great force. The accident was discovered by several of the employees, who came to Laraway's assistance, and when he was taken down it was found that his arm was broken and he had received a severe cut over one of his eyes. The fact was soon established that he was injured internally, and he was cared for until 11:50 o'clock, when he died. A reporter of the Free Press arrived at the works shortly afterward, and in conversation with a number of the employees, learned that Laraway's

death was caused by his own carelessness in getting too close to the pulley The remains were placed in the care of an undertaker. An inquest will be held to-day. Laraway lived at the corner of Larned and Russell streets, and leaves a wife. He was 35 years old.--*Detroit Free Press, Dec. 17.*

Many of the citizens of Harrisville and Black River, in this county, will remember Mr. Laraway, as, for over a year, he was in the employ of R. A. Alger & Co. as locomotive engineer on their railroads both at Harrisville and Black River. He left our county and accepted a position in the Peninsular Car Works at Detroit about a year ago. His sudden death must prove a sad blow to his wife, who has many sympathizing friends in this county.

Alcona County Review, December 24, 1880
Cemetery:

LaRocque, Albert

The Local News.

The remains of Albert La Rocque of Black River were buried Tuesday in the Catholic cemetery at this place. The deceased died from a paralytic stroke and was ill but two or three days. He was about 30 years of age and unmarried.

Alcona County Review, June 25, 1891
Cemetery: St. Anne's, Alcona Co.

Larson, {Child}

LOCAL JOTTINGS.

During the past two weeks, cholera-infantum has been having a terrible rage in this community, no less than a dozen small children and babes having died from the same. This naturally leaves many houses of mourning in our community, and to those of us who are as yet free from the scourge in our own homes, should come forth hearty sympathy and fitting words for the bereaved. Friday last, the scourge took away a little, human flower each from the homes of William Nestle and James Stringer. Tuesday the family of Chas. Larson were bereft of their babe, and Wednesday evening Frank Stevens and wife were called to part with their first-born. Gilbert Landon, one of the Messrs. Byces, and the Ducharms have also each lost a babe, and there are several others in the community apparently nearly at death's door, at the time we go to press. Thus many of the homes in our community are being darkened. May the Lord remove the dark cloud speedily, and give consolation to the sorrowing parents.

Alcona County Review, August 29, 1884
Cemetery: Probably Mt. Joy, Alcona Co.

Larson, {Girl}

COUNTY NEWS JOTTINGS.

Mr. and Mrs. Chas. Larson, of Alcona, lost an infant daughter, by death, Monday last.

Alcona County Review, February 8, 1878
Cemetery: Mt. Joy, Alcona Co.

Laverty, Margaret [McDonald]

SOMEWHAT PERSONAL.

Mrs. Lafferty, wife of Peter Lafferty, who resides to the southwest of Springport, died last Thursday and was buried Saturday in the Catholic cemetery. She was about 52 years of age and had been a confirmed invalid for many years. She leaves a family of grown up sons and daughters to mourn their loss.

Alcona County Review, September 15, 1892

Card of Thanks.

Mr. Peter Laverty and family wish to extend their sincere thanks to the many kind friends who so willingly assisted them in their time of trouble, namely: sickness, death and burial of their beloved wife and mother. We desire to express our appreciation of the
kindness of those friends who sent flowers.

Alcona County Review, September 15, 1892

HISTORY OF ONE YEAR.

Chronological History of the Past Year, 1892.

THE DEATH RECORD.

Sept. 8 Mrs. Peter Laverty, Harrisville.

Alcona County Review, January 5, 1893
Cemetery: St. Anne's, Alcona Co.

Laverty, Mary

PERSONAL POINTS.

Miss Mary Laverty, aged 38 years, daughter of Peter Laverty, died last Thursday morning at the home of her brother Alex at South Harrisville. Death resulted from consumption. The funeral services were held at St. Ann's church Monday morning, Rev. Fr. Poulin officiating.

Deceased was a sister of Mrs. Robt. Elliott, Margaret, Thomas and Alex Laverty.

Alcona County Review, April 6, 1899

PERSONAL POINTS.

In behalf of myself and family I desire to thank the friends and neighbors for their many acts of kindness during the illness and death of my beloved daughter.

Peter Laverty

Alcona County Review, April 6, 1899
Cemetery: St. Anne's, Alcona Co.

Laviolette, Victoria [Jeareane]

MRS. ALEXANDER LAVIOLETTE

Departed this life at the residence of her son, Adolphus, Monday, July 4th.

Deceased was born at Regore, Ont., and would have been 60 years old had she lived until July 7th. She came to Michigan in 1881 and settled at Bay City, moving thence to Ausable and then to Greenbush where she has resided since 1885. She was the mother of four daughters and three sons most of whom are married and live in this country. The interment took place yesterday morning in the Catholic cemetery.

The family are very grateful to friends for numerous kind acts.

Alcona County Review, July 8, 1897
Cemetery: St. Anne's, Alcona Co.

Lawrence, David

Haynes Happenings.

Mrs. David Lawrence and child were sent to the county farm on Monday. Her husband to Detroit for 90 days last week.

Alcona County Review, November 21, 1895

Died in Prison.

Justice Beede received word under date of Friday, Feb. 21st, from Joseph Nicholson, Supt. of the Detroit House of Correction, that David Lorence, alias La France, of Haynes township, Alcona county, was seriously ill. The next day Supt. Nicholson wrote again stating that La France died Saturday at 2:15 a.m. and that the burial would take place there. The nature of his disease was not stated, but it is believed here that it was of a contagious character, or the Superintendent would have asked what disposition should be made of the body.

Lorence, or La France, was sent up Nov. 12, 1895, for the larceny of a boat, in default of $39.45 fine and

costs and had completed his sentence.

Lorence's family are county charges, and have been ever since he was sent to Detroit.

Alcona County Review, February 27, 1896

Haynes Happenings.

Haynes, Mar. 3rd, 1896.--The Rev. McBride preached a memorial sermon by request of the friends of David Lawerance who died in the Detroit House of Correction of that dreadful disease, small-pox. The text was "Prepare to Meet Thy God." The sermon was well delivered.

Alcona County Review, March 5, 1896

EVENTS OF ONE WEEK.

David Lorence, alias La France, died of small pox. Several other deaths from the same disease have occurred at the House of Correction.

Alcona County Review, March 5, 1896
Cemetery:

Lawrence, Etta [Carr]

Goes to the Dissecting Table

Mrs. Lawrence, a county charge, who was sent to the county farm from Haynes Twp., was found dead in bed yesterday morning. She was subject to epileptic fits and Coroner Mayo, after inquiring into the facts, deemed an inquest unnecessary. The dead woman was about 36 years of age. She had been married: one of the children of this union was also an epileptic and was sent to the state school sometime ago. The woman seemed to have no friends here who cared enough for her to give her a Christian burial and under the state law the body goes to the university dissecting rooms.

Alcona County Review, September 23, 1897

Haynes Happenings.

Sept. 27, 1897.
Mrs. David Lawrence was interred in Mount Joy Cemetery Sept. 24.

Alcona County Review, September 30, 1897
Cemetery: Mt. Joy, Alcona Co.

Lazarus, E.

The death of E. Lazarus, father of Mrs. W. W. Will, occurred Tuesday morning at the M. E. parsonage. The end was not unexpected for the old gentleman had been growing feebler day after day since the advent of cold weather. He was aged 84 years and 7 months. The funeral takes place at 2 p.m. today.

Alcona County Review, February 20, 1896

Miss Mattie Longstreet arrived from Saginaw Tuesday evening, being called hither by the death of her grandparent, E. Lazarus.

Alcona County Review, February 20, 1896
Cemetery: Springport, Alcona Co.

Lecuyer, {Child}

People We Hear About.

Peter La Cour, section foreman at West Harrisville, buried an infant child this week.

Alcona County Review, July 25, 1890
Cemetery:

Lecuyer, Mary Luella [Hunt]

Death Claims Many Victims.

Mrs. Peter Lecuyer was buried last Sunday in the cemetery west of Harrisville. Service was held in the school house, West Harrisville, Rev. W. E. Marvin officiating.

Alcona County Review, March 26, 1891
Cemetery: West Lawn, Alcona Co.

Lee, Amelia R. [Jorrey]

All Around Alcona County.

Haynes, Nov. 12, 1895.
Geo. H. Lee has erected a beautiful monument to the memory of his wife and children in the cemetery.
[Died December 20, 1884]

Alcona County Review, November 14, 1895
Cemetery: Mt. Joy, Alcona Co.

Lee, Ardela

All Around Alcona County.

Haynes, Nov. 12, 1895.
Geo. H. Lee has erected a beautiful monument to the memory of his wife and children in the cemetery.
[Died March 3, 1874]

Alcona County Review, November 14, 1895
Cemetery: Mt. Joy, Alcona Co.

Lee, Chauncy M.

All Around Alcona County.

Haynes, Nov. 12, 1895.
Geo. H. Lee has erected a beautiful monument to the memory of his wife and children in the cemetery.
[Died December 30, 1884]

Alcona County Review, November 14, 1895
Cemetery: Mt. Joy, Alcona Co.

Lee, Elizabeth [Burton]

LOCAL LACONICS.

Mrs. Erastus Lee, of Alcona, died on Wednesday of consumption.

Alcona County Review, May 8, 1885

Cemetery: Mt. Joy, Alcona Co.

Lee, James

County News and Gossip.

Last Tuesday, at Au Sable, we learn two young men, while skating, accidentally ran into an air-hole and went down under the ice and were drowned. We did not get their names.

Alcona County Review, February 21,1879
Cemetery: Pinecrest, Iosco Co.

Lee, James

LOCAL JOTTINGS.

James Lee, who resided on the North farm, west of Springport, was buried Monday. He was about 45 years of age and leaves a wife and seven children. Mr. Lee originally came from Canada, where he was born, and about one year ago removed from Oscoda to this vicinity. He had been in ill health for more than a year with diabetes, which caused his death.

Alcona County Review, September 30, 1887
Cemetery:

Lee, Louis W.

Rather Sudden.

Sad Death of Louis Lee at Grand Marais.

The sad news of the death of Louis Lee, a bright and popular young man, whose home was in Harrisville, was received here Saturday morning and was a shocking surprise to his relatives and friends who had not heard that he was ill.

The funeral took place Monday at Grand Marais and was in charge of the Odd Fellows to which order he belonged.

The sad facts are these as reported by the Grand Marais Herald.

It is with sincere regret of the deepest nature, that we are forced to record the death of our fellow townsman, Louis W. Lee, which occurred Friday afternoon at 5:30 at the home of his cousin, L. L. Cummings. The cause of his sudden flight was the result of an accident received that occurred to him on Friday, a week ago yesterday.

He was attending to his duties as carriage-man in the Marais Lumber Co.'s mill and while so engaged was struck with the handle of a canthook on the abdomen, causing a rupture of

the peritoneum, causing strangulation of the same. Everything possible was done in a medical way, but without success. Dr. Gould of Munising was summoned to counsel with the attending physician, Dr. Anderson. Their conclusion was that the patient could not live three days in the state he was, and that the only chance to prolong life, with a possibility of recovery, would be by the aid of an operation of laparotomy. The operation was performed Thursday morning, the doctors finding their diagnosis to be correct. The patient revived from the ordeal and up to a short time before death had a good pulse and was in good spirits. But suddenly he was taken with a weakness of the heart, from which he passed quietly away, surrounded by the physician, his cousin and intimate friends.

The deceased was 27 years of age, born and raised at Harrisville, Mich., coming to this city from there years ago. He was a member of the Odd Fellows at this place and a boy that was held in high esteem by all who knew him and loved and cherished by his more intimate friends. He took an active part in church and social circles and was a good-natured fellow. The only surviving relative here is his cousin Lester Cummings.

Alcona County Review, May 12, 1898

PERSONAL POINTS.

Mrs. Emma Martin-Cummings was summoned from Grand Marais again last week on account of a turn for the worse in her father's condition. The death of Louis Lee occurred at her home several hours after she left.

Alcona County Review, May 12, 1898

PERSONAL POINTS.

Lester Cummings has appealed to the probate court of Alger county for letters of administration of the estate of the late Louis Lee. What the estate consists of does not appear.

Alcona County Review, June 23, 1898

Local History of One Year

Chronology of the Principal Events of the Year 1898.

April 7. Death of Louis Lee at Grand Marais.

Alcona County Review, January 5, 1899
Cemetery:

Lee, Mrs.

The Local News.

Mrs. Lee, stewardess on the Metropolis, died very suddenly Tuesday morning just before reaching Harrisville. The cause of death is supposed to have been heart disease. Her home was in Bay City.

Alcona County Review, July 11, 1890

One Year's History.

Record of Local Happenings for the Year 1890.

JULY.

July 9. Mrs. Lee, stewardess on the Metropolis, dies suddenly of heart disease off Harrisville.

Alcona County Review, January 1, 1891
Cemetery:

Lee, Mrs. William [Bratt]

A Long String From Springport.

Springport, Jan. 15, 1895.
Mrs. Wm. Lee, Sr., lies very low at her home near Chas. Briggs, suffering from a severe cold which has weakened her so much that her friends have little hope of her recovery.

Mrs. Hessie Billings of ------ arrived a few days ago to attend her mother, Mrs. Lee, in her sickness.

Alcona County Review, January 17, 1895

South Harrisville.

S. Harrisville, Jan. 21.--Mrs. Lee is much improved this week. Her son Edward arrived Friday night from White Fish Point. He says snow is more plentiful here than there.

Alcona County Review, January 24, 1895

South Harrisville.

South Harrisville, Feb. 18.--Mrs. Lee is still confined to her room. Some say she will not recover.

Alcona County Review, February 21, 1895

South Harrisville.

S. Harrisville, March 4.--Mrs. Wm. Lee, Sr., departed this life early Tuesday morning, after a lingering illness of several weeks. She was 52 years and 6 months old.

Deceased was a Canadian by birth. Since the death of her husband some eight years ago, she has resided at Oscoda. A few months ago, with her youngest son, Beffie, (who is a cripple) and a granddaughter aged 10, she moved here on her farm. She leaves three grown up sons besides Beffie: William is married and lives at Oscoda, Thomas and Edward; also a married daughter, Mrs. D. S. Bilings resides in Duluth.

Her much devoted children mourn not as those who have no hope, their mother having embraced the faith of a Christian and the last few years of her life strove to live very near her God.

Mrs. Bilings has been her mother's faithful attendant in her last illness, and was with her at the time of her death. Her sons have been telegraphed for. Her immediate relatives here are a brother and wife, Mr. and Mrs. Jacob Bratt.

The funeral services were held at the house today (Thursday) at 11 o'clock. Interment at the South Harrisville cemetery.

Alcona County Review, March 7, 1895
Cemetery: Probably Springport, Alcona Co.

Lemon, {Child}

A 9-months old child belonging to a family named Lemon, of Haynes, was buried Sunday. The funeral services were held at the M. E. church.

Alcona County Review, November 10, 1892
Cemetery:

Lemon, Maggie

Haynes Happenings.

April 7, 1896.
A Miss Lemon, a daughter of Oliver Lemon, died suddenly Friday afternoon. She was aged about 16 years.

Alcona County Review, April 9, 1896
Cemetery:

Lensbaum, William F.

Shore Pickings.

Wednesday last, Wm. F. Lensbaum was run over by the cars on the pole railway of the Oscoda Salt & Lumber Company, at Pine River, and killed.

Alcona County Review, September 12, 1879
Cemetery:

Leonard, James

Sudden Death at Camp 8.

Coroner Beede was summoned last Friday to go to Camp 8 to hold an inquest on the body of James Leonard, a woodsman. Leonard it appears had come up to Mud lake Jc. from Oscoda Wednesday morning and was looking for work. He had been drinking and was somewhat under the influence of liquor. In the hotel he fell against the sharp corner of a door jamb with such force as to cut an ugly gash four inches long on the left side of his head. The wound was sewed up by Dr. McCormick and Leonard went on and got a job at Camp 8. He worked an hour Thursday morning but was obliged to return to camp and was sick all day and night. His wants were administered to by his fellow workmen and no serious results were anticipated, but about 10 o'clock Friday morning his dead body was found lying on a platform or stoop before the camp door. Dr. Parr, who retired with the jury to examine the remains, passed the opinion that the cause of death was meningitis, resulting from neglect of the wound in the head, and the jury returned a verdict accordingly.

Leonard's remains were buried at Au Sable on Sunday, under the auspices of the Odd Fellows, of which order he was a member in good standing.

Alcona County Review, August 24, 1893
Cemetery:

LePaige, Oletsime

DUST TO DUST.

Oletsime LePaige, a French-Canadian resident of Haynes township, died last Saturday after a lingering illness originating with la grippe. He was aged about 55 years and leaves a large family of sons and daughters grown to man's and woman's estate to mourn his departure.

Alcona County Review, September 17, 1891
Cemetery:

Lewis, Emma Blanche

REVIEWINGS.

Died: In the village of Harrisville, on the afternoon of July 31st, Emma Blanche, adopted daughter of Guy C. and Maria Lewis; aged 7 years, 10 months and 4 days.

She is gone to the regions where spirits assemble
Around the bright throne of their Father above
Where songs of the angels eternally tremble
On harps overflowing with praise and love.

Alcona County Review, August 1, 1879

REVIEWINGS.

Mr. and Mrs. G. C. Lewis return thanks to all those persons who so kindly assisted them in the care of their adopted little daughter through her sickness, death and burial.

Alcona County Review, August 8, 1879
Cemetery: Springport, Alcona Co.

Lewis, {Female}

The Local News.

A woman named Lewis died in Ward's old camps last week after a lingering illness.

Alcona County Review, January 29, 1891
Cemetery:

Lieb, John

LOCAL JOTTINGS

Jno. Lieb, aged 22 years and unmarried, was killed last week on the Potts logging road in Oscoda county. The remains were taken to Huron county for interment.

Alcona County Review, July 20, 1888
Cemetery:

Lighthart, William

HOME REVIEWINGS.

Wm. Lighthart, aged 19 years, died at Black River last Monday morning from consumption. He was a nephew of Joshua Brown, and a sister [brother] of Miss Minnie Lighthart, who resided with Mr. Brown's family in Harrisville two years ago. Funeral services of the deceased took place on Wednesday, and the remains were deposited in the South Harrisville cemetery.

Alcona County Review, July 22, 1881
Cemetery: Springport, Alcona Co.

Lipscomb, Nelson

Took His Own Life.

A Former Resident of Harrisville Suicides at Tacoma.

Old residents will remember Nelson Lipscomb who resided here some fifteen years or more ago, when he was employed about the old planing mill and in other capacities. Lipscomb removed from Harrisville to Au Sable and about four or five years ago moved west, and took up a residence at Tacoma, Wash., whither he was accompanied by his family, consisting of his wife, three sons and a daughter.

Lipscomb, who had reached the age of 64, had become somewhat

eccentric and melancholy. Early in January he took thirty grains of morphine with suicidal intent, from which he died. After his death letters were found which had been written apparently while his mind was bent upon suicide. One to his favorite son, Frank, concludes with the following language: "I have done the best I could for you all. I might have done worse. Bear in mind I have been sick five years; three years not able to work. If I have not lived to suit all I have kept myself alive in my own way. I have paid over $1200 for insurance myself. If I owe a few dollars in town better let me rest in peace. If you boys see my faults avoid them. I started from nothing, and nothing remains. Your future looks bright. My last wish is for your good.
Your father,
Nelson Lipscomb.

Alcona County Review, January 25, 1894
Cemetery: Tacoma, Pierce Co., WA

Livingstone, Attealla

EVENTS OF ONE WEEK.

The family of Geo. W. Colwell was notified by wire last Thursday of the death of Miss Teal Livingstone, which occurred that day at Portville, N. Y. Deceased had been a faithful friend and servant of the Colwell family for 27 years, and only relinquished her place in that household when compelled to a few months ago by growing infirmities. After leaving Harrisville she was taken to the celebrated specialist, Dr. McLean of Detroit, who pronounced her disease to be cancer of the stomach and that she might live six months, but probably would not survive more than four months. She was not informed then of the nature of the malady, nor of its aggravated nature, out of deference to her own request. She failed rapidly after she reached her relatives at Portville, until death came to relieve her from her sufferings. She was about 60 years of age.

Alcona County Review, August 15, 1895
Cemetery: Chestnut Hill, Cattaraugus Co., NY

Lockwood, James K.

Local Sayings and Doings.

Hon. J. K. Lockwood, of Alpena, well known on this shore for the past twenty odd years as a lumberman,

mill owner, insurance agent, etc., died from a stroke of paralysis at the home of his brother in Put-in-Bay, last Sunday morning. He was one of the most useful citizens Alpena ever had.

Alcona County Review, July 14, 1882
Cemetery: Evergreen, Alpena Co.

Lockwood, William J.

LOCAL JOTTINGS.

W. A. Lockwood, one of the pioneers of Alcona county, died at the county poor house last Sunday at the age of 61. He had been on the shore for 38 years, and became a public charge last spring. The remains were interred Monday at Springport.

Alcona County Review, October 12, 1888
Cemetery: Springport, Alcona Co.

Loney, Abraham

Probably Died from Exposure.

This morning the lifeless remains of Abe Lony, a resident of Haynes township, were found near the roadside near Craven's. He had been missing for two days. He was down to mill Tuesday with a grist. Not returning a search was instituted for him yesterday with this result. He was drinking while in town and a bottle of whiskey was found in his pocket. He probably died from exposure. He lived opposite LaFrance, had a family, and was about 55.

Alcona County Review, November 23, 1893

Up in Haynes.

Something in Dreams.

Haynes, Nov. 27th, 1893.
There was no bottle of whiskey found on the person of Abram Loney. The funeral sermon was preached by the Rev. Mr. Smith on Sunday. The remains were followed to the cemetery by a large concourse of relatives and sympathizing friends. Mrs. Loney begged of her husband not to take any liquor on the day he went to Harrisville, as she had dreamed three nights in succession that he was brought home dead. Is there nothing in dreams? Mrs. Loney is in a delicate state of health at present and she is left with three small children and two sons, who were working in the lumber woods 17 miles from Posen.

Alcona County Review, November 30, 1893

EVENTS OF ONE WEEK.

Coroner Beede held an inquest on the remains of Abe Loney who was found dead last Thursday on a by road near Cravens. No new facts were developed and the jury, composed of Geo. Ritchie, E. Downie, Jos. Elmes, Donald McNeil, Wm. Vennard and Wm. McDonald, returned a verdict in accordance therewith, viz., that death was caused by exposure to cold, rain and snow and from no other cause.

Alcona County Review, November 30, 1893

Paragraphs of Local Interest.

It has been rumored that a damage suit was to be brought against a Harrisville liquor dealer by the heirs of Abram Loney, the Haynes township farmer who was found frozen to death on the morning of Nov. 23, last. Loney was intoxicated when he left Harrisville and that fact was to constitute the basis of the suit; but we understand that the attorney who was working up the case has decided to abandon it.

Alcona County Review, January 18, 1894

Abram Loney's Widow Wants $10,000.

A $10,000 damage suit has been commenced by declaration against Samuel Anderson, of Harrisville, by the widow of Abram Loney. Review readers will remember that on the morning of the 23d day of November, 1893, Loney's remains were found after a long search near the Craven farm; also that it appeared at the inquest that Loney had been in Harrisville two or three days before, where he drank quite freely, so that when he took his departure for home he was considerably intoxicated. Loney's team was found in the woods not far from the highway. Near by was the dead man, who laid on the ground in a drunken stupor during a heavy storm of rain, the result of which was his death from exposure. The purpose of this suit is to fasten the responsibility for Loney's intoxicated condition upon Anderson, who is charged in the declaration with selling him the liquor. It does not appear what evidence the plaintiff possesses. H. K. Gustin is attorney for Mrs. Loney but it is believed he is consulting with experienced Alpena attorneys. It is the first suit of the kind brought in Alcona county, we believe, and its progress will be watched with interest.

Alcona County Review, March 8, 1894

PERSONAL MENTION.

Sam Anderson has retained W. E. Depew to look after his interests in the suit brought against him by Mrs. Loney.

Alcona County Review, March 15, 1894

The Calendar for May.

Full List of Cases to be Disposed of Next Week.

Issues of Fact.

Lizzie Loney vs. Sam Anderson.

Alcona County Review, May 10, 1894

At Court.

Mrs. Abram Loney, widow of the late Abram Loney, deposed and said that she was unable to give security for costs in her $10,000 damage suit against Sam Anderson, but her affidavit read in open court by her attorney, H. K. Gustin, disclosed that she is possessed of a dower interest in 40 acres of land, also a team of horses. Judge Simpson held that she is able to furnish such security and ruled that she should furnish it to the amount of $200 at any time she chose. Her attorney stated that an effort would be made to provide the required security before the close of this term of court, so that trial of the case could be proceeded with.

Alcona County Review, May 17, 1894

Circuit Court Cullings.

The $10,000 damages suit of Mrs. Loney vs. Sam Anderson will be tried at the next term of court, providing plaintiff furnishes $200 security for costs.

Alcona County Review, May 24, 1894

A LIGHT CALENDAR.

Chancery.

The Lizzie Loney $10,000 damage suit versus Samuel Anderson did not get on the calendar, but every preparation had been made by the attorneys on both sides to try the suit at this term, and it will in all probability get before the jury this week.

Alcona County Review, May 21, 1896

PERSONAL MENTION.

The Lizzie Loney damage suit versus Sam Anderson did not come to trial. An amendment to the declaration was desired by plaintiff's attorney; consent was granted on

condition that the case go over the term, so it will now be October at the earliest before this much talked of case gets before a jury.

Alcona County Review, May 28, 1896

The Circuit Court.

But eight cases are noticed on the calendar for trial at the February term of court.
Civil Cases.
Lizzie Loney vs. Samuel Anderson, case.

Alcona County Review, February 4, 1897

The Circuit Court.

Lizzie Loney vs. Samuel Anderson.
A jury was called, but the stentorian voice of Sheriff Edwards calling upon Lizzie to appear in court and prosecute her case remained unanswered and a verdict of not-suit was entered by the Judge.

Alcona County Review, February 18, 1897

STATE OF MICHIGAN.
The Probate Court for the County of Alcona.

At a session of said Court, held at the Probate Office in the City of Harrisville in said County, on the 24th day of May, A. D. 1909.

Present: Hon. Geo. W. Burt, Judge of Probate.

In the matter of the estate of Ella, May, Loney and Laura Loney, Minors.

Elizabeth Loney, Guardian of said Minors, having filed in said court a petition, praying for license to sell the interest of said estate in certain real estate therein described, at private sale.

It is ordered, That the 19th day of June, A. D. 1909, at ten o'clock in the forenoon, at said probate office, be and is hereby appointed for hearing said petition, and that all persons interested in said estate appear before said court, at said time and place, to show cause why a license to sell the interest of said estate in said real estate should not be granted;

It is further ordered, That public notice thereof be given by publication of a copy of this order, for three successive weeks previous to said day of hearing, in the Alcona County Review, a newspaper printed and circulated in said county.

GEO. W. BURT,
Judge of Probate.

Alcona County Review, May 27, 1909
Cemetery: Mt. Joy, Alcona Co.

Long, George

Uncle George Long, who lived alone in his cabin at Indian Town on Pine river, about ten miles from this place, was found dead upon the floor of his cabin by an Indian, yesterday, frozen stiff. As he had not been seen by any person for several weeks, the probabilities are that he has been deceased for some time.--Long was an old man upwards of 80 years, and had lived alone in his cabin at the Indian settlement for many years, securing a livelihood principally from the cultivation of a small parcel of ground. He was an old inhabitant of this neck o'timber, and known for many miles around. Old age was undoubtedly the cause of his death. An inquest will be held over the remains and the same be buried by the county.--*Au Sable News.*

Alcona County Review, February 23, 1883
Cemetery:

Lott, {Girl}

COUNTY JOTTINGS.

The infant daughter of Mr. and Mrs. R. L. Lot, died with the croup, at Black River, Sunday night. The funeral services were held from the residence of George Rutson, in Harrisville, Tuesday forenoon.

Alcona County Review, April 12, 1878
Cemetery:

Loucks, Alman

LOCAL SAYINGS AND DOINGS.

Two little sons of Henry Loucks, aged seven and twelve years respectively, were both drowned in Devil river at Ossineke last Sunday, while in bathing.

Alcona County Review, June 30, 1882
Cemetery:

Loucks, Willard

Two little sons of Henry Loucks, aged seven and twelve years respectively, were both drowned in Devil river at Ossineke last Sunday, while in bathing.

Alcona County Review, June 30, 1882
Cemetery:

Loud, Viletta Jane [Kile]

Mrs. H. M. Load, of Oscoda, died at Jacksonville, Florida, on the morning of the 4th inst. Her remains were brought to Detroit for interment.

Alcona County Review, February 13, 1880
Cemetery: Elmwood, Wayne Co.

Loud, William H.

Wm. H. Loud, a former resident of Oscoda, was killed at Paducah, Ky., recently, by falling from a scaffold. He was the youngest brother of H. M. Loud. The deceased was about 46 years old at the time of his death.

Alcona County Review, April 1, 1887
Cemetery: Pinecrest, Iosco Co.

Lubenow, Adolph

A Black River Tragedy.

Dolph Lubenow, a German shoemaker, who has been in the employ of William Flaws at Black River, was found dead Wednesday morning. He had tied a rope about his neck and fastening the other end securely to the wood box strangled himself by the sheer weight of his body. The rash act was the result, it is said, of domestic infelicity.

A Black River correspondent sends the following additional facts which we condense to save space. Lubenow's wife was Mrs. Benway, mother of a young man killed two weeks ago on Pott's road: Mrs. L. blamed her husband for driving her son away from home. After young Benway's burial, his mother gathered together all the family belongings and moved away. Tuesday Adolph asked permission of his former employer, Wm. Flaws, to sleep in the shop, which was granted. On arrival at shop in morning, latter found door locked on inside. On bursting door open, Lubenow was found dead as above described. The following letter addressed to his wife, was found on the counter:

"Three husbands you now have in the grave with me, A. L. Now who wants to be No. 4. It's now 4 o'clock. God forgive you Annie Lubenow. Good bye Mr. Flaws. From good hearted old Adolph Lubenow."

Alcona County Review, July 11, 1890

The house of Dolph Lubenow at Black River was sold after his burial to satisfy the funeral expenses. The fair widow heard of the sale, however, and complicated matters somewhat by moving in at midnight. This happened three weeks ago and Mrs. L. still holds the fort. The reason the house was sold in this manner seems to be because the widow refused or neglected to bury Dolph's remains, abandoning everything.

Alcona County Review, August 15, 1890

One Year's History.

Record of Local Happenings for the Year 1890.

JULY.

9 Adolph Lubenow, a German shoe maker, suicided at Black River.

Alcona County Review, January 1, 1891
Cemetery:

Luckett, William

NEIGHBORHOOD NOTES.

Wm. Luckett, aged 25, a brakeman was killed on the Au Sable & Northwestern railroad last week. Deaths on this logging railroad are quite a common occurrence.

Alcona County Review, October 4, 1889
Cemetery:

Ludington, Frank B.

OBITUARY.

Ludington.—Died, April 6, 1888, Frank, son of Mr. and Mrs. Robert Ludington.

Once again before the bedside of the dying we must kneel,
Once again the pangs of anguish for a loved one we must feel.
Slowly sinking, slowly parting, like the raindrops on the sand.

Father, give us the strength to bear it, strength to say, "Thy will be done;"
Strength to give, without a murmur, to thy care our darling son.
He has crossed the silent river, gone to that immortal land,
Gone to wear a crown forever, and with angels there to stand.

Yet a little while we linger, ere we too must cross the plain;
Then hand in hand, again united, never more to part again.
Dark the sorrow round us gather, more the anguish in our breast,
Yet the darkest cloud above us has within a silvery vest.

While we mourn the loved departed and we miss them from our sight,
They are mingling with the angels in that land that has no night
Brightest crowns upon their foreheads, sweetest music everywhere
May we turn our thoughts to Heaven when we see the vacant chair.

Frankie Ludington, the 15 year old son of Mr. and Mrs. Robert Ludington died last Friday after a lingering illness. The funeral services were held Sunday afternoon at the Baptist church, the Rev. F. N. Barlow officiating. Robert Ludington, father of the deceased, left only a few months ago for the Pacific slope.

Alcona County Review, April 13, 1888
Cemetery: Springport, Alcona Co.

Ludington, William

County News and Gossip.

A little son of Robert Ludington, one year old, died at Greenbush with the Croup, Wednesday afternoon.

Alcona County Review, January 24, 1879

Died: January 22nd, 1879, little son of Robert Ludington, at Greenbush; aged 1 year, 10 months, and 11 days.

Why God called our little Willie,
Is more than we can tell;
But thank God we have the comfort,
That He doeth all things well.
His little chair is vacant,
His toys are idle now;
But our Willie is in Heaven,
And the angels guard his brow.
How we miss our little darling—
Only parents love can know;
But God called him to his bosom—
And when called we all must go.

Alcona County Review, January 31, 1879
Cemetery: Springport, Alcona Co.

Lumbard, William

Fisherman Drowned.

Wm. Lumbard of Alcona Drowned While Lifting His Nets.

Wm. Lumbard, proprietor of the Union Hotel at Alcona, was drowned last Friday morning.

He arose early as was his custom and went out in a small skiff to lift some nets. He was alone and not until his boat was found on the beach by his son was there any suspicion that he had met with an accident.

His body was found on a submerged reef several hours after he must have lost his life.

Quite a sea was running that morning and it is assumed that while engaged in the act of lifting his nets he must have lost his balance and fell overboard. He was an expert swimmer but he must have become exhausted in the heavy sea, or possibly taken with cramps. He was

seen at work by one person taking in a net with one hand and seemingly baling out the boat with the other hand. That was the last seen of him alive.

When the boat was found it had some water in, though not enough to swamp it, and one of deceased's gill nets, which he had taken up, was in it as he left it.

Coroner Chas. Mayo was notified of the drowning; he repaired at once to the scene, but after a full investigation of the circumstances connected with the death of Mr. Lumbard, so far as they are known, he decided that an inquest was unnecessary and none was held.

He is survived by his wife and seven children, most of the children having reached maturity.

Deceased was a veteran of the civil war, and was bout 48 years of age.

The funeral services were held Sunday and were largely attended. The interment was in the Alcona cemetery.

Alcona County Review, June 16, 1898

HAYNES HAPPENINGS.

Our sincere thanks are due to our friends and the Rev. Mr. Shaffer who kindly officiated, for unremitting kindness and sympathy and assistance during our recent great bereavement. May Heaven bless you and give you friends in the hour of need.

Mrs. Wm. Lumbard and Family.

Alcona County Review, June 16, 1898

Local History of One Year

Chronology of the Principal Events of the Year 1898.

June 10. Wm. Lumbard, fisherman, drowned at Alcona.

Alcona County Review, January 5, 1899

FIRST MONUMENT HAS BEEN RECEIVED

Soldiers' and Sailors' Graves in Alcona County Will Soon be Properly Marked
----

Geo. W. Colwell has just realized the first fruits in his endeavors to get headstones for the graves of soldiers and sailors buried in the cemeteries of Alcona County.

The first stone to arrive is for William Lumbard, unassigned recruit 19th United States Infantry, who died

at Alcona on June 10th, 1898. The stone is of the best American white marble, 39 inches high, 12 inches wide and four inches thick. The top is slightly rounded and the portion that will be above ground when the stone is set is sand rubbed. The name and service record is inscribed within a sunken American shield.

This stone is the first of twenty-eight that will be sent by the government to mark the graves of veterans buried in this county, thanks to the efforts of Mr. Colwell. The stones will be distributed as follows: South Harrisville cemetery 12, West cemetery 4, Catholic cemetery 4, Mt. Joy cemetery 3, Spruce cemetery 4, Curtis cemetery 1.

Alcona County Review, March 6, 1913
Cemetery: Mt. Joy, Alcona Co.

Lyman, Mrs. Jane C.

MRS. JOHN LYMAN.

This estimable lady departed this life at the home of her son Don, in Perry, Oregon, Sunday, Sept. 26, 1896, after an illness of a week. Her death was due in part to the extremities of old age. Mrs. Lyman was born in Potts Co., Pa., Feb. 22, 1824. She came to Michigan in April, 1869 with her husband, the late Dr. Lyman. In 1892 she went west and has since lived with her son. She realized that death was nigh, but it had no terrors for her for she was firm in the Christian faith.

Alcona County Review, October 8, 1896
Cemetery:

Lyman, John C.

Death of Dr. Jno. Lyman.

John Lyman, another of the old pioneers of Alcona county, has gone the way of all flesh, having expired Thursday at 6:45 p. m. after a brief illness. The deceased had not enjoyed good health for a number of years, but he had been able usually to get around and attend to the various small duties incident upon a retired life. Up to Wednesday morning he had apparently been in his usual health. On that day he took to his bed and soon relapsed into an unconscious condition, in which state he remained up to the time of his death. Death is ascribed to a general decay of this vital power.

John Lyman was born in 1819 in Potter Co., Penn., and was therefore at the time of his death, in the sixty-eighth year of his age. He remained in Potter Co. until 1867 where he studied and practiced for a number of years the science of medicine. He settled at Harrisville in 1867, where he has continued to reside with few intermissions up to the time of his death. He practiced medicine here successfully until compelled by ill health to abandon it a number of years ago. The funeral services were held at the Baptist church last Friday afternoon. The deceased leaves a wife and three sons, H. W. Lyman, V. J. Lyman, and Don Lyman.

Alcona County Review, September 16, 1887

Card of Thanks.
I wish to thank the many friends who kindly rendered assistance during the last illness and death of my husband, Jno. Lyman.

Mrs. J. C. Lyman.

Alcona County Review, September 16, 1887
Cemetery:

Lynch, Mrs. Anna

LOCAL JOTTINGS.

Mrs. Lynch, widow of the sheriff whom Blinky Morgan fatally shot, died in Alpena last Saturday. She left four boys the oldest of whom was 14 years of age.

Alcona County Review, April 19, 1889

For Sheriff Lynch's Children.
The Cleveland Plaindealer of the 13th says: Councilman J. T. Logue heard from the Lynch children at Alpena yesterday. He sent a letter some time ago to the postmaster and it was turned over to J. J. Potter. Mr. Potter says that the Lynch children, four in number, are with their aunt, Mrs. T. G. Potter, at Monroe, Mich. They are, Orrington, 14 years old; Charles, 10 years old; Arthur, 7 years old, and George, 6 years old. The only income they receive is $10 per month for the rent of a house. Their mother's funeral expenses have not been paid yet. No administrator of the estate has yet been appointed, though the aunt is the guardian of the children. Mayor Gardner has offered his bond as trustee of the children. It is signed by Tom. L. L. Johnson and J. T. Logue. Mayor Gardner will be appointed trustee to-day and then the solicitor will collect the money offered by the various companies, corporations and commissions at once. The police commission is anxious to pay, and the others are

equally as willing. It is expected that about $4,000 will be collected. Mayor Gardner will take the money to Alpena and deposit it in trust for the children. The claims of others to the rewards will not be recognized, as they never made any attempt to substantiate them. There can be but little question but that the money rightfully belongs to the Lynch children. The council is doing well in forcing a settlement, as outside newspapers are commenting on the city's tardiness.

Alcona County Review, August 23, 1889
Cemetery: Probably Evergreen, Alpena Co.

Lynch, Charles L.

PURELY PERSONAL.
Sheriff Lynch, of Alpena, who was shot in the leg while attempting to arrest the desperado Morgan, last month, died of his injury at the Detroit Sanitarium, where he was taken recently for medical treatment, at 10 o'clock a. m. Wednesday.

Alcona County Review, August 19, 1887

Says He is Innocent.
"Blinkie" Morgan, the notorious character who shot Sheriff Lynch, of Alpena, while the latter was attempting to arrest him, avows his innocence of the crime of murder in the "affair at Alpena," as he calls it in an open letter published in the papers at Ravenna, Ohio. Blinkie says he was sitting quietly at the table with Mrs. Williams and her children engaged in arranging some flowers when three or four men rushed in, knocked him down, choked him, and one of them "jumped upon his stomach." This was really too bad. Sheriff Lynch and his assistants ought to have knocked at the outer door, inquired in a hesitating manner if Blinkie was in, and then, if they were admitted, parleyed with that gentleman, and induced him, if possible, to quietly submit to arrest. What a pleasant affair it would have been. Instead of one funeral in Alpena there would have been four, and it is safe to say that Blinkie would not have been among the number of the slain. If Blinkie escapes the hangman's noose at Revenna he should be brought to Alpena and strung up to the first lamp-post.

Alcona County Review, August 26, 1887

LOCAL JOTTINGS.

Blinkey Morgan was strangled at Columbus, O., August 3d as per programme.

Alcona County Review, August 10, 1888

NEIGHBORHOOD NOTES.

The orphans of Sheriff Lynch, the Alpena officer who received a fatal wound at the time Blinky Morgan was arrested, stand a fair show of getting $4,000, a part of the reward offered for Morgan's capture.

Alcona County Review, August 23, 1889

For Sheriff Lynch's Children.
The Cleveland Plaindealer of the 13th says: Councilman J. T. Logue heard from the Lynch children at Alpena yesterday. He sent a letter some time ago to the postmaster and it was turned over to J. J. Potter. Mr. Potter says that the Lynch children, four in number, are with their aunt, Mrs. T. G. Potter, at Monroe, Mich. They are, Orrington, 14 years old; Charles, 10 years old; Arthur, 7 years old, and George, 6 years old. The only income they receive is $10 per month for the rent of a house. Their mother's funeral expenses have not been paid yet. No administrator of the estate has yet been appointed, though the aunt is the guardian of the children. Mayor Gardner has offered his bond as trustee of the children. It is signed by Tom. L. L. Johnson and J. T. Logue. Mayor Gardner will be appointed trustee to-day and then the solicitor will collect the money offered by the various companies, corporations and commissions at once. The police commission is anxious to pay, and the others are equally as willing. It is expected that about $4,000 will be collected. Mayor Gardner will take the money to Alpena and deposit it in trust for the children. The claims of others to the rewards will not be recognized, as they never made any attempt to substantiate them. There can be but little question but that the money rightfully belongs to the Lynch children. The council is doing well in forcing a settlement, as outside newspapers are commenting on the city's tardiness.

Alcona County Review, August 23, 1889

The Local News.
The lower house of the Ohio legislature voted last week to pay $1,000 to Geo. W. Gardiner, trustee

of the children of Sheriff Lynch, of Alpena, as a part of the reward offered by Gov. Foraker for the capture of Blinkey Morgan.

Alcona County Review, February 28, 1890

Our Neighbors.

The children of the late Sheriff Lynch of Alpena have been paid $2,000, a part of the money offered by the city of Cleveland for the capture of Blinkey Morgan.

Alcona County Review, May 9, 1890
Cemetery: Evergreen, Alpena Co.

Lynch, Della [Craven]
COUNTY REVIEWINGS.

Died.--At Harrisville, April 20, 1880, Della, wife of Stephen Linch, aged 23 years. The deceased was a daughter of Wm. Craven, and is the third of that family that has died within the past year. She has been married about two years, and leaves a child ten months old. The funeral services, preached by Rev. Wm. Donnelly, of Alpena, took place in the M. E. Church, Wednesday afternoon. The bereaved husband and parent have the heart-felt sympathy of the community.

Alcona County Review, April 23, 1880

Resolutions of Harrisville Lodge, I. O. O. F.
Odd Fellows' Hall.
Harrisville, Mich., May 1st, 1880.

At a regular meeting of Harrisville Lodge, No. 218, I. O. O. F., held at this date, it having been communicated that our Brother Stephen Lynch had, in the recent decease of his wife, suffered the greatest bereavement which ever falls to the lot of the pilgrim through this vale of tears; thereupon action was taken resulting in the appointment of a committee to draft resolutions expressive of the profound sentiments of sympathy and condolence felt by the Lodge with the bereaved brother.

The committee reported as follows and the report was unanimously adopted, with instructions to forward a copy of the report to Bro. Lynch and one to the Alcona County Review for publication;

Whereas, it has pleased the All-wise God to call from earth the companion and wife of Brother Stephen Lynch, thus, for the time being, sundering the nearest and

dearest of kindred human ties. Therefore, be it

Resolved, First, that as a band of brothers, we extend to our Brother Lynch our heart felt sympathies, commending him in the hour of his sore trial to the All-Benificent Father in whose ways there is light; in whose favor there is peace, and in whose love there is balm for the wounded heart.

Second, that we assure him of our earnest desire at this time, to extend to him whatever of comfort or cheer fellow mortals, seeking in friendship truth and love to bear one another's burdens, may be able to impart.

Finally, that we remind him that day comes after the night; that in tender sympathy we lift for him the hand that hangs down, and point the eyes, weary with watching and dim with tears, toward the dawning of that radient morning in the light of which they who meet part nevermore.
Committee.

Alcona County Review, May 21, 1880
Cemetery: Probably West Lawn, Alcona Co.

Lynch, {Male}
NEIGHBORHOOD NOTES.

The life of a man named Lynch, killed by freight train last year, was valued at $25,000 by dead man's mother. The circuit court of Arenac county didn't exactly see it in that light. Result, no cause of action.

Alcona County Review, November 23, 1888
Cemetery:

Lynch, Robert Raymond
LOCAL JOTTINGS.

The only child of Mr. and Mrs. Stephen Lynch, aged four weeks, was buried Monday, the services being held in the M. E. church.

Alcona County Review, August 13, 1886

ALCONA ATOMS.

The baby boy of Mr. Steve Lynch died last week.

Alcona County Review, August 13, 1886
Cemetery: West Lawn, Alcona Co.

Lynch, Thomas
NEIGHBORHOOD NOTES.

Thos. Lynch, a woodsman, was killed in Avery's camp, Alpena county by being thrown with great force upon the stump of a small sapling that he had just cut. It penetrated his body several inches.

His death ensued before he could be taken to Alpena.

Alcona County Review, October 4, 1889
Cemetery:

Lyons, Hiram
REVIEWINGS.

Mr. —— Lyons, a resident of Alcona, died, on Wednesday, from the effects of inflammation in the bowels and kidneys. He leaves a family. We did not learn his age.

Alcona County Review, May 30, 1879

ALCONA.
Out Among the Farmers.

Mr. Lyons who died last week (or whom the Review reported as having died, in error) is now living upon and working Charles Larson's farm.

Alcona County Review, June 6, 1879
Cemetery:

Mack, Griswold
LOCAL JOTTINGS.

At 2 o'clock a. m. last Saturday, Griswold Mack, a watchman employed at the mill of the Gratwick, Smith & Fryer Co., of Oscoda, fell from the tramway to the ice below, a distance of 16 feet. Mack struck on his head, the fall crushing his skull and dislocating his neck. He died from his injuries the same morning. Mack left a wife and two children in poor circumstances.

Alcona County Review, April 22, 1887
Cemetery: Foster Township, Sanilac Co.

Madden, Michael S.
EVENTS OF ONE WEEK.

Michael Madden, who went west from Harrisville about six years ago and located at Skamokawa, died recently at the latter place. We have no particulars at hand.

Since the writing of the foregoing Mr. A. Houghton has placed a copy of the Skamokawa paper containing full particulars of Madden's death at our disposal and in another column is printed the greater portion of the article which will be of great local interest.

Alcona County Review, December 6, 1894

MICHAEL MADDEN.

The Skamokawa Eagle of Nov. 29 has the following to say concerning the death of the late Michael Madden:

Michael S. Madden died very suddenly at his residence in this village on Monday, November 26th, 1894. He retired Sunday evening feeling quite unwell, and grew suddenly worse, the end coming at 2 o'clock in the morning. Mr. Madden was born in Friendsville, Pa., and his age was 58 years and 28 days. At the breaking out of the war, or on Aug. 5th, 1863, he enlisted in the 107 Reg. N. Y. Vol. as a private. He served his country nearly three years and was promoted as a Sargeant. He was mustered out June 5th, 1865. After the war he removed to Harrisville, Mich., where he resided for over 20 years. He is a member of Harrisville Lodge No. 218 I. O. of O. F., to which organization he belonged some sixteen years. Mr. Madden was a first class millwright as well as a skillful engineer. He worked for the Colwells for many years in Harrisville and when they came to Skamokawa some seven years ago he followed them here, where he has since resided continuously, with the exception of a short time he was employed in a saw mill at Hillgard, Oregon. Mr. and Mrs. Madden were married June 12, 1859, and they had seven children, three of whom, Mr. Eugene J. of Manistique, Mich., Mr. Frank Durand, Mrs. Milton Haney, of this village, are now living.

The funeral took place from the family residence Tuesday morning. Mr. Madden had many friends and the house could not begin to hold the many who assembled to pay a last sad farewell to their old friend. The local brothers of the I. O. of O. F. took charge of the funeral and the remains were interred in the Middle Valley cemetery. The pall bearers were Elias Cornell, F. I. Burnham, David Cady, I. N. Lott, A. T. Johnston, J. W. Gilmore. A number of beautiful floral pieces were presented by the ladies. Mrs. Madden and her children have the sincere sympathy of the people of this village in their bereavement.

Alcona County Review, December 6, 1894

MICHAEL S. MADDEN.

Whereas, It has pleased Almighty God in his infinite wisdom to remove from our midst our esteemed friend and brother, Michael S. Madden, late a member of Harrisville Lodge No. 218 I.O.O.F.: Therefore be it

Resolved, that while submitting to the will of God, who doeth all things well, we deplore the loss of our absent brother.

Resolved that our charter be draped for 30 days, that a copy of these resolutions be sent to the relatives of the deceased, entered upon the records of our Lodge and published in the Alcona County Review.

Harrisville, Jan. 28, 1895.
H. P. MOORE, Committee.

Alcona County Review, January 31, 1895
Cemetery: Fern Hill, Wahkiakum Co., WA

Madden, Walter

Died—In Harrisville, on the evening of the 19th inst., Walter, son of Michael S. and Julia S. Madden; aged 2 years, 10 months and 7 days.

The funeral services of the deceased were held at the residence of the parents, this (Friday) morning. Verily, the Lord giveth and the Lord taketh away, and happy are they who can say in these afflictions "Blessed be the name of the Lord!" It is hard, yea very hard, to part with these lovely flowers which God has given us, but there comes to the soul sweet consolation when we think they have escaped a thousand snares, and are now eternally safe within the embrace of the Great Father of love. Oh that all might have this confiding trust in the Lord of Glory, and prepare themselves for the great reunion in heaven.

Alcona County Review, February 21, 1879
Cemetery: Springport, Alcona Co.

Magahay, Marcus

The two following paragraphs from the Fort Gratiot Sun of April 2d concern a family well known as recent residents of Harrisville township:

Marcus, the 11 months old son of Mr. and Mrs. David Magahy, Fort street, died on Friday morning of scarlet fever. The funeral was held this afternoon from the house, Rev. D. McFawn officiating.

Bruce, the four year old son of Mr. and Mrs. David Magahy, Fort street, is down with scarlet fever.

Alcona County Review, April 7, 1892
Cemetery: Lakeside, St. Clair Co.

Mahar, James E.

Death of Father Mahar.
Oscoda Press.

Father James E. Mahar, who was in charge of the Catholic congregation of this place a few years, and who was transferred from here to Saginaw, died very suddenly in that city Tuesday night. From the Saginaw Globe of Wednesday the following is taken.

"Father James E. Mahar died last night at 10 o'clock at St. Mary's hospital from heart failure. Fr. Mahar for the past year has been stationed at the hospital as chaplain. Prior to that time he was assistant pastor of St. Mary's church, this year. Fr. Mahar was born near Grand Rapids, this state, 38 years ago and received his early education in the public schools of Grand Rapids, afterwards attending Assumption college, Sandwich, Ontario, where he took a five years classical course. Later he was sent to the Jesuit university, at Louvaine, Belgium. Owing to ill health he was transferred about a year ago to the hospital, where his duties were less onerous and where he might have the constant attention of trained nurses.

Three weeks ago he was called to Petosia, Wisconsin, by the sudden demise of his father, his sole surviving parent. It is not thought that he ever recovered from the shock. Last Sunday morning he sang high mass for Fr. Poulin of the Holy Family church and on his return to the hospital in the afternoon it was noticed that he appeared to be very much fatigued.

"Last night about 9:15 o'clock one of the sisters on duty in the lower corridor of the hospital heard a noise as of someone falling in the room of Fr. Mahar, and she found the priest breathing his last on the sofa. He was attired in his soutan and beretta and had just concluded the saying of his evening prayers. He never spoke again, and before Dr. Ryan, who was summoned, could arrive, he breathed his last.

"Fr. Mahar possessed considerable reputation in the state as a speaker and a polemical writer. He was very popular with his fellow clergyman and a prime favorite with all laymen who knew him."

Alcona County Review, November 18, 1897
Cemetery: Calvary, Saginaw Co.

Malden, William P.

Among Our Exchanges.

Dr. William P. Malden, one of Alpena's most eminent physicians, died last Friday morning after a three weeks' illness from pneumonia and paralysis. He was 49 years old.

Alcona County Review, April 7, 1892
Cemetery:

Malenfaut, George

Probate Order.

State of Michigan.
County of Alcona.

At a session of the Probate Court for the County, held at the Probate office in the village of Harrisville on Friday, the tenth day of July, in the year one thousand eight hundred and eighty-five.

Present--Allen Nevins, Judge of Probate.

In the matter of the estate of George Malenfaut deceased.

On reading and filing the petition, duly filed, of Rev. P. C. Alph Williams, praying for administration of the estate of said deceased be granted to said Rev. P. C. Alph Williams or some other suitable person.

Thereupon it is ordered, that Saturday, the eighth day of August, 1885 next, at ten o'clock in the forenoon, be assigned for the hearing of said petition, and that the heirs at law of said deceased, and all other persons interested in the estate, are required to appear at a session of said Court, then to be holden in the Probate office in the village of Harrisville in said County, and show cause, if any there be, why the prayer of the petitioner should not be granted. And it is further ordered, that said petitioner give notice to the heirs and other persons interested in the estate, of the pendency of said petition, and the hearing thereof, by causing a copy of this order to be published in the Alcona County Review, a newspaper printed and circulated in said county, three successive weeks previous to said day of hearing.

Allen Nevins,
Judge of Probate.

Alcona County Review, July 17, 1885

Probate Order.

State of Michigan.
County of Alcona.

Notice is hereby given, that by an order of the Probate Court for the County of Alcona made on the eighth day of August, A. D. 1885, six months

from that date were allowed for creditors to present their claims against the estate of George Malenfaut, late of said County, deceased, and that all creditors of said deceased are required to present their claims to said Probate Court at the Probate office, in the Village of Harrisville, for examination and allowance, on or before the eighth day of February, 1885, next, and that such claims will be heard before said Court, on Monday, the ninth day of November, 1885 and on Monday, the eighth day of February 1886, next, at ten o'clock in the forenoon of each of those days.

Dated August tenth, A. D. 1885.
Allen Nevins,
Judge of Probate.

Alcona County Review, August 14, 1885
Cemetery:

Manning, George

The Local News.

A heavy timber which was being placed in position at Hawley's new Marquette mill broke last week and three men were seriously injured. Hugh Millen and George Manning— two of the injured men—may die.

Alcona County Review, December 20, 1889

The Local News.

Geo. Manning, one of the men who was injured while working on Hawley's new mill at Marquette, died of his injuries and was buried at Alpena by the members of Alpena Lodge F. & A. M. No. 109, of which he was a member. The deceased was a son-in-law of Jas. Ferguson, a prominent farmer of Harrisville township.

Alcona County Review, January 3, 1890
Cemetery: Evergreen, Alpena Co.

Marcellus, Aaron

Aaron Marcellus Passes Away.

The death of Aaron Marcellus occurred at Saginaw Thursday, the 14th inst., at the residence of his sister, Mrs. E. A. Biggam, with whom he had been stopping for a week. Death was due to pulmonary consumption and was not unexpected, though the end came suddenly, as he was greatly reduced when he went to Saginaw on the 5th inst., and there was no hope then of his ultimate recovery.

The remains were brought back to his late home Saturday night. The

Grand Army comrades at Saginaw took charge of the arrangements prior to shipping the remains home, and the comrades of Wyram Hoyt Post of Harrisville took charge of the arrangements here precedent to burial, deceased having earned an honorable record as a private in the late civil war.

The funeral services were held Sunday at West Harrisville, the Rev. W. P. Tompkins officiating. Interment was in the family lot in the cemetery west of Harrisville, whither the remains were followed by a large concourse of friends of the family.

Alcona County Review, April 21, 1898

Card of Thanks—We wish to express our sincere thanks to friends who so kindly assisted us during our late bereavement.

Mrs. Jessie Marcellus and Family.

Alcona County Review, April 28, 1898

HONORS TO DEAD HEROES.

A magnificent demonstration of the patriotic spirit of the citizens of Alcona county was the observance on Monday of the time honored custom of decorating the graves and commemorating the deeds of valor of the nation's dead heroes.

The roster of soldiers who are buried here is as follows: Harrisville, (West), A. Marcellus, John Pelton, W. W. Douglass: Catholic, Louis Rivard, Geo. Bernizer: South Harrisville, R. Richmond, Chas. Miller, H. J. Aird, A. Noyes, Jas. Johnson.

Alcona County Review, June 2, 1898

Local History of One Year

Chronology of the Principal Events of the Year 1898.

April 14. Death of Aaron Marcellus at Saginaw. Interment at Harrisville.

Alcona County Review, January 5, 1899
Cemetery: West Lawn, Alcona Co.

Marcellus, Anna E.

PERSONAL MENTION.

It is our painful duty this week to record the death of Miss Anna E. Marcellus, an estimable young lady, the eldest living daughter of Mr. and Mrs. A. Marcellus of West Harris-ville. She was a victim of consump-tion and had been gradually fading away for the past six months. The anxious parents did for her all that parental love or money could suggest.

The best medical skill was consulted and the invalid was placed for a time in one of the Detroit hospitals, but all efforts to avert the inevitable end were of no avail and she passed quietly and peacefully away Saturday morning at 9 o'clock. During her entire illness she was confined to her bed but one day—last Friday. The remains were consigned to their last resting place in the family plot in the cemetery west of Harrisville Monday afternoon. The Rev. C. Lewis, rector of St. John's Episcopal church of Au Sable, conducted the funeral services and preached an impressive and appropriate sermon.

The deceased was born Sept. 8, 1873. She was a member of the Episcopal church and lived the life of a consistent Christian.

Alcona County Review, January 12, 1893

Card of Thanks.

To the many kind friends in East and West Harrisville and country around, do we return our sincere and heartfelt thanks for their kindness in our recent great sorrow, especially to those who so kindly came to sing, and also to the ladies of Dalton Hive, L. O. T. M., who furnished beautiful flowers for our loved one.

Mr. A. Marcellus,
Mrs. A. Marcellus,
Miss Clara Marcellus.

Alcona County Review, January 12, 1893

Mrs. George Livingstone of McKinley came down to attend the funeral of Miss Marcellus. Also Thos. and Duncan Duggan from the woods and Miss Anna Duggan was called home from an extended visit she was making among friends.

Alcona County Review, January 12, 1893

West Harrisville.

Received too late for publication last week.

The angel of death, after hovering over the family of Aaron Marcellus for the past three months, made its descent and tore from the bosom of her parents, relatives and friends, Miss Annie Marcellus last Saturday morning. Those who knew Miss Annie bore for her a respect akin to love. Her presence was sunshine even to the saddened and weary hearted. Her nature was both sensitive and sympathetic, she wept with those who wept and rejoiced with those who rejoiced. The people of West Harrisville feel deeply the loss and

their heartfelt sympathy is with the relatives. But in our grief let us always bear in mind that "There is another, a brighter side of life beyond the sky, where sin and sorrow ne'er betide, and loved ones never die."

Alcona County Review, January 19, 1893
Cemetery: West Lawn, Alcona Co.

Marquis, {Child}

Black River Sparks.

Mr. and Mrs. Jos. Markie mourn the loss of their infant child which died April 3rd and was buried at Harrisville R. C. cemetery Sunday, April 5th.

Alcona County Review, April 16, 1896
Cemetery: St. Anne's, Alcona Co.

Marsac, Joseph Francois

COUNTY REVIEWINGS.

Capt. Marsac, of Bay City, the old French trader, died on the 18th. He did not know his age, but was between 90 and 100. He was formerly on the staff of Gen. Cass.

Alcona County Review, June 25, 1880
Cemetery: St. Patrick, Bay Co.

Martin, Charles

Mrs. Lester Cummings, nee Emma Martin, was called home from Grand Marais by the serious illness of her father, reaching here Tuesday.

Alcona County Review, March 3, 1898

PERSONAL POINTS.

Mrs. Lester Cummings, nee Emma Martin, leaves this evening for her home at Grand Marais, after three weeks at home on account of the illness of her father.

Alcona County Review, April 7, 1898

PERSONAL POINTS.

Mrs. Emma Martin-Cummings was summoned from Grand Marais again last week on account of a turn for the worse in her father's condition. The death of Louis Lee occurred at her home several hours after she left.

Alcona County Review, May 12, 1898

The condition of Chas. Martin has been quite alarming again the past week. An iron constitution has enabled him to wage a successful battle with the fell destroyer for a year, and his friends will hope that he will rally again as he has so many

times before when the end has seemed near.

Alcona County Review, July 28, 1898

LOCAL PICK UPS.

Chas. Martin is very low today.

Alcona County Review, August 18, 1898

CHARLES MARTIN.

How rapidly are the ranks of the earlier pioneers of Alcona county being thinned by the ruthless hand of death! The death of Charles Martin on the afternoon of Thursday, August 18th, adds another to the long roll of honored names of those who left the comfortable surroundings of communities far advanced in development and civilizing influences to carve a new destiny and a new abiding place out of the seemingly boundless pine forests of northern Michigan Mr. Martin early became impressed with the agricultural possibilities of this section. He took up a homestead and was more than ordinarily successful. He gave his undivided attention for many years to his farm to the exclusion of everything else and to that as much as to his untiring energy and perseverance must be attributed in large measure his success as a farmer, for the custom of the majority of those who ventured to clear land for farming purposes in the early days was to farm a little, work in the woods a considerable, and between the division of interests and labor little was accomplished in either direction of a lasting nature for the good of the individual or the community at large.

By giving his farm his undivided attention Mr. Martin secured the best results of such work at the time when prices were at the top mark and he was surrounded by an excellent cash market, the best in the world.

As a result of a lifetime of hard and arduous labor he leaves one of the best, if not the best farm, in Alcona county, tidy buildings, good fencing, land of undiminished fertility, orchard, stock and farming machinery.

To untiring industry Mr. Martin combined many other virtues, among them strict integrity. His word was as good as a bond. He was an excellent citizen and commanded universal respect.

The funeral services took place Sunday afternoon from the family residence and were conducted by Rev. W. W. Will. The attendance was very large.

The pall bearers were six life long friends of deceased, and among the earlier pioneers, viz: Geo. H. Blush, John Gray, Wm. C. Gray, W. B. Hogue, Robt. Reed, L. R. Dorr.

Charles Martin was born at Hawthorn Hill, Lincolnshire, England, about the year 1829. He emigrated to America in 1851 and settled in Oakland county. He came to Harrisville in 1853 and engaged in fishing and worked for Mr. Harris. He brought the first horses to this locality Nov. 19, 1864. He was married to Sarah Beever in 1868 and commenced clearing his farm. In 1871 he moved to his farm, which has been his home continuously since. He is survived by his wife and three children, all grown to maturity.

Alcona County Review, August 25, 1898

We wish to express our most heartfelt thanks to our many kind friends and neighbors who rendered us assistance during the long illness and death of our beloved husband and father.

Mrs. Chas. Martin and Children.

Alcona County Review, August 25, 1898

PERSONAL POINTS.

Mrs. Emma Martin Cummings was called home from Grand Marais by her father's death.

Alcona County Review, August 25, 1898

The Late Charles Martin's Will.

The last will and testament of the late Chas. Martin has been admitted to probate and provides for an equitable distribution of the estate to the four surviving heirs. The will was opened by County Clerk Rutson at the family residence and its provisions were read to the heirs last Friday evening.

Robt. Reed is named as executor.

The 80 acres on which the residence stands is left to the widow and son James, to be owned and occupied by them jointly; in case of the death of either title for the entire property is to vest in the survivor. To them is also left a team, mower, binder, plow, drag, wagon, sleigh, cultivator, furniture and goods in the homestead, and half of all other personal except the two best cows and $200 cash.

To his son Walter is left the eighty acres on which he resides, also $200 in cash and half of all other personal not specified above, and a buggy.

To Emma D. Cummings, the daughter, is left the 40 acres east of the old homestead, across the highway; also 2 best cows to be selected by herself.

The old horse "John" is left to the widow to be kept until he dies.

The wheat crop on the land devised to the daughter is to be equally divided between the widow and two sons.

Alcona County Review, September 8, 1898

Local History of One Year

Chronology of the Principal Events of the Year 1898.

August 18. Death of Chas. Martin, pioneer farmer, aged 69.

Alcona County Review, January 5, 1899
Cemetery: Springport, Alcona Co.

Martin, Hugh

REVIEWINGS.

Hugh Martin, a young man known in this vicinity, died last night. We were not acquainted with him personally but hear him spoken of very respectfully.

Alcona County Review, October 10, 1879
Cemetery:

Martin, James

STATE OF MICHIGAN, County of Alcona.

At a session of the Probate Court for said County, held at the Probate office, in the Village of Harrisville on the third day of October, in the year one thousand eight hundred and ninety-eight.

Present, Hon. W. H. Gilpin, Judge of Probate.

In the matter of the estate of James Martin, deceased.

On reading and filing the petition duly verified of James A. Martin, praying that a certain instrument now on file in this Court purporting to be the last will and testament of said deceased, may be admitted to Probate, and that Robert Reed be appointed as Executor of said Will.

Thereupon it is ordered that Friday, the 28th day of October next, at ten o'clock in the forenoon, be assigned for the hearing of said petition, and that the heirs at law of

said deceased and all other persons interested in said estate, are required to appear at a session of the Probate Court, then to be holden at the Probate office, in the Village of Harrisville and show cause, if any there be, why the prayer of the petitioner should not be granted. And it is further ordered that the petitioner give notice to the heirs at law and all persons interested in said estate of the pendency of said petition, and the hearing thereof, by causing a copy of this order to be published in the Alcona County Review, a newspaper printed and circulated in said county three successive weeks previous to said day of hearing.

W. H. Gilpin,
Judge of Probate.

Alcona County Review, October 6, 1898
Cemetery:

Martin, Joseph

A Respected Citizen Gone.

Death has again visited our town, taking away one of our worthy townsmen in the person of Joseph Martin, a gentleman well known here and in Alpena as a lumber jobber. He was operating a large camp here this winter for Alger, Smith & Co.

Mr. Martin felt somewhat ill Thursday and stayed in camp. Friday, feeling a little worse, he went home and continued to sink when Drs. McCormick and Aikens were summoned to his aid, but on their arrival found him beyond medical skill and sinking fast, death claiming him that evening.

Mr. Martin was an active member of the Maccabees, in which order he held $2,000 insurance, payable to his two surviving sons.

The funeral took place Sunday a.m. at St. Gabriel's church, where mass was conducted by Rev. Father Poulian. The funeral was conducted by the Maccabees, who attended in a body. The remains were laid at rest at Harrisville. The pall bearers were Peter Rengie, Clay La Cross, Edward C. Heron, T. Bouchard, James Martin, John Dionnie.

Deceased leaves a wife and two sons to mourn their loss. We extend our sympathy to them in their sad bereavement.

Alcona County Review, January 16, 1896

West Harrisville.

At a special review of Lake Shore Tent 299, Jan. 13th, the following resolutions were unanimously adopted

Wherea,s Death has for the first time entered our Tent taking from our midst our brother and Sir Knight Joseph Martin. Therefore be it

Resolved, That while we bow in humble submission to the will of our Supreme Commander, we cannot help feeling that we have lost a worthy brother and Sir Knight, who always used to be with us, and be it also

Resolved, That we, the members of Lake Shore Tent 299, extend to the widow and family our heartfelt sympathy in their hour of affliction and bereavement

Resolved, That these resolutions be spread upon the records of this Tent and a copy sent to the family of the deceased brother and that it also be published in the Michigan Maccabee and in the Alcona County Review.

Resolved, That our charter by draped in mourning for 90 days.

Black River, Jan. 13, 1896.
Joseph Hoffman, P. C.
Edward Sheanbeck, F. K.
James Johnson, P. C.,
Committee.

Alcona County Review, January 16, 1896

BLACK RIVER IN PRINT.

The saddest local event which has taken place for some time was the death of Mr. Joseph Martin, who died at his home one mile west of town last Friday evening.

Alcona County Review, January 16, 1896

BLACK RIVER IN PRINT.

Mr. and Mrs. Jno. Dubie and Mrs. A. Granelle of Alpena attended the funeral of the late Joseph Martin.

Alcona County Review, January 16, 1896

Black River Sparks.

On Thursday, Jan. 30th a cheque for $2,000 was received from the K. O. T. M. by the guardian of the children of the late Jos. Martin, the amount due for insurance in that order. Great praise is due the Maccabees for their promptness.

Alcona County Review, February 6, 1896
Cemetery: St. Anne's, Alcona Co.

Martin, Willard Stanley
EVENTS OF ONE WEEK.

Mr. and Mrs. Walter Martin mourn the death of their infant son.

The child died Friday last of whooping cough. The funeral services were held at the house Saturday afternoon, the interment taking place at South Harrisville.

Alcona County Review, July 2, 1896
Cemetery: Springport, Alcona Co.

Marvin, Mrs. Henrietta
OUR NEIGHBORS.

From the Monitor.
Died at her home in this city, Saturday morning April 6, at 7:30, of consumption of the bowels, Henrietta, wife of Chas. E. Marvin, in the 36th year of her age.

Alcona County Review, April 11, 1895
Cemetery: Greenwood, Iosco Co.

Maxwell, Mary E. [Moore]
PERSONAL.

Mrs. H. P. Moore was summoned to Tawas yesterday by a telegram announcing the dangerous illness of a relative. A second telegram announced the death of the lady, who was an only sister of Mrs. Moore. The latter was expected to go directly to Tawas from Grand Marais.

Alcona County Review, December 23, 1897

PERSONAL.

H. P. Moore is at home after a season at Grand Marais. He met his wife at Tawas City where they were summoned by his sister's death. Mr. Moore reached there too late for the funeral.

Alcona County Review, December 30, 1897
Cemetery: Greenwood, Iosco Co.

May, Ralph
Sad Fate of a Young Man.

The news reached town Thursday morning that Ralph May, an estimable young farmer of Harrisville township was shot and instantly killed that morning while hunting deer with a party of friends near Sucker creek. His death was caused by the accidental discharge of a gun in the hands of a son of Chas. Briggs. This lamentable accident removes from our midst an exemplary young citizen. He leaves a young wife (formerly Minnie Kibbe) and one child.

Alcona County Review, November 7, 1890

HOW IT HAPPENED.

Particulars of the Accidental Shooting of Ralph May.

The following facts concerning the lamentable death of Ralph May on Sucker Creek, are gleaned from the testimony of Jas. Briggs, which was offered at an inquest held at the house of the deceased's father, on the day following the accident.

"Am 18 years of age. Nov. 6 I and deceased, Albert Kibbe and Edward Myers, were camped near Sucker Creek for purpose of hunting deer. Myself and deceased left camp about daylight of that day. About a mile from camp we started a deer; I fired five or six shots at him and deceased fired two or three. Deceased stepped up on a log to see deer. Deceased was about 20 feet ahead of me and to the left. I stepped up on same log and as I did so I tripped and fell backwards. My gun was across my left arm, my right hand thumb was on the hammer and my forefinger on the trigger. It was a 45-60 Winchester rifle. Next thing I remember I saw Ralph lying on the ground. I ran to him and he seemed to be dead. Could not say for certain that my gun was discharged but when I saw deceased lying on the ground I supposed that my gun went off when I fell and caused the accident."

The inquest was held on petition of five citizens. The jury, consisting of Chas. Martin, Asa Emerson, Robt. Beever, Wm. Beever, Aaron Byse and Frank La Chapelle, returned a verdict in accordance with the above facts, which were substantiated by the remaining members of the hunting party.

The remains were interred in the cemetery at South Harrisville last Sunday. The funeral services were conducted at the M. E. church in the morning, a great concourse of sympathetic friends and neighbors congregating to witness the last sad rites over the dead and show their respect and sympathy for the living. The Rev. L. Hazard's remarks were timely and appropriate.

Alcona County Review, November 14, 1890

OBITUARY.

Ralph, only son of Nelson and Mary May, who was killed last Thursday, was born at Lexington, Mich., Oct. 19th, 1867, and was twenty-three years old at the time of his death. He, with his father, mother and sister, came to Harrisville seven years ago. He was an affectionate son and brother and highly esteemed by all who knew him. He was married to Miss Minnie Kibbe April 14th, 1889. Their short married life proved a very happy one and one child came to bless their home, a little girl now ten months old. This sudden death is an awful blow to them all, yet they sorrow not as those without hope, but know if they are faithful they will meet their loved one where parting will come no more. Many other relatives and friends are left to mourn their great loss.

Our loved one has gone
To a brighter home beyond;
But oh, how sad and lonely
For those who are left to mourn.
But we hope again to meet him,
In that world so bright and fair;
Where all tears have ceased to flow;
Where no sorrow can enter there.

Alcona County Review, November 14, 1890

Card of Thanks.
My kind friends, one and all, will please accept my deep and heartfelt thanks for their assistance during my late bereavement.

Mrs. Ralph May.

Alcona County Review, November 14, 1890

Card of Thanks.
N. H. May and family wish to thank their many kind friends and neighbors who so faithfully assisted them in their bereavement.

Alcona County Review, November 14, 1890

One Year's History.

Record of Local Happenings for the Year 1890.

NOVEMBER.
6 Ralph May shot and instantly killed near Sucker Creek.

Alcona County Review, January 1, 1891
Cemetery: Springport, Alcona Co.

Maynard, Mrs. Louise
Haynes Happenings.

Haynes, Sept. 19, 1894.-- The remains of Mrs. Ed B. Maynard were interred in the Catholic cemetery at Harrisville on the same day [September 14th].
Consumption was the cause of death. She had been ailing for a long time and was a great sufferer from the relentless disease.

Alcona County Review, September 20, 1894
Cemetery: St. Anne's, Alcona Co.

Maynard, Mary
LOCAL JOTTINGS.

A [6] year old daughter of Wm. Maynard who resides in the French settlement in Haynes, was terribly burned last week. She and her little sister were playing with fire when her clothing caught fire with serious results.

Alcona County Review, November 23, 1888

LOCAL JOTTINGS.

The six-years old daughter of Wm. Maynard, a resident of the French settlement in Haynes township, who was so terribly burned a few weeks since by her clothes taking fire while playing with a pile of burning refuse, died Sunday.

Alcona County Review, December 14, 1888
Cemetery:

Mayo, James
LOCAL JOTTINGS.

The Mayo brothers of this place received a dispatch from Cleveland, Ohio, Monday, announcing the death of their brother James of that city. He died suddenly. Mr. George Mayo started Tuesday morning to attend the funeral of the deceased. The deceased is not the brother who resided in Harrisville a year ago this winter, as many suppose. His name is Melburn, and he is now at his native home in England, where he has been some month past.

Alcona County Review, April 24, 1885

LOCAL LACONICS.
The funeral services of Mr. Mayo, who was buried at this place two weeks since, will be held at the M. E. Church, this village, next Sunday evening, Rev. T. B. Leith officiating. The text will be taken from 55 psalm, 23 verse: Cast thy burden upon the Lord and He shall sustain thee. He will never suffer the righteous to be moved.

Alcona County Review, May 8, 1885
Cemetery:

Mayo, James, Sr.
'ROUND ABOUT.

Chas. Mayo has received the sad intelligence that his father has passed over the dark river at the old home in England.

Alcona County Review, August 27, 1891
Cemetery:

Mayott, Frank
HORRIBLE ACCIDENT.

Frank Mayott, of Harrisville, Falls From a Scaffold and is Killed Instantly—Another Man Seriously Injured.

Again it becomes our painful duty to chronicle one of the most terrible accidents that has ever happened within our county, by which Frank Mayott, a highly respected citizen of our thriving village came to his death yesterday (Friday) afternoon. A large number of parties had been secured by Mr. McFarlane, who is erecting the new saw mill building at Black River, to assist in the shingling, among whom were Mr. Mayott, and one Daniel McFarlan, who stood on a certain part of the scaffold adjacent to each other. The work had only just commenced when that part of the scaffold occupied by Messrs. Mayott and McFarlan gave way and precipitated its occupants to the ground below (some 28 feet). Mr. Mayott, who is a large, heavy man, fell head foremost, striking on the mud-sill and crushing in the whole upper portion of his head in a manner that caused the brains to ooze out from several places, killing him instantly. McFarlan, though not killed, was seriously injured, having three ribs broken and sustaining a quite severe wound about the head. It is thought, however that he will survive the accident, and come out all right if no serious internal injuries have been caused.

The news of Mr. Mayott's terrible death, which came to Harrisville by telegraph, spread over the community like wild fire, and the kind hearted ladies of the place flocked to the home of the bereaved wife and children of the deceased from all directions to tender sympathy and condolence.

It was a hard task for Mr. James Brahaney, who had been detailed to break the sad news to Mrs. Mayott, but still harder and more terrible for her to receive and bear up under the same. The poor woman nearly went distracted upon receiving the sudden announcement, and could not be comforted though sympathy came from numerous sources.

Mr. Mayott was a man very much respected in our community because of his industry, sobriety and kind-hearted disposition. He had been gang sawyer in Colwell's mill here for the past two years, and had just gone to Black River to assist in the erection of the new saw mill.

Little did he think, when he left here only a few days ago that he was bidding a last goodbye to wife, children, home and friends. But such is the sad ending of his life, and those of the living will do well to draw a lesson—that life is uncertain and that a preparation for death should always be had in readiness; "For in an hour when ye think not the Son of Man cometh."

The deceased was about 40 years of age, and leaves a wife and three children.

Alcona County Review, November 26, 1880
Cemetery:

McAdam, Joseph Henry

MORE DIPHTHERIA.
Destitution and Disease Rampant in the La Vier Settlement.

On Sunday Health Officer Beede paid another visit to the diphtheria stricken settlement at Mud Lake. Matters there were even worse than on the occasion of his last visit, if that were possible. In the family of Wm. Finger he found five cases of the disease, two girls in a fair way to recover, one boy, Herman, apparently in the last stages of dissolution and two other cases, one a boy and one a girl, the termination of which was uncertain. Previous to going to the settlement he had been informed that the family were in destitute circumstances, owing to long illness and the continuance of the quarantine under which they were placed. To relieve their distress he took along supplies of pork, beef and beans, besides gingham, cotton and factory cloth. Dr. Parr had had charge of the cases but Mr. Beede ordered Dr. Mitchell to visit the settlement also. Sickness was reported in another family, McAdam by name, but he was not able to say whether this was diphtheria or not.

Alcona County Review, January 19, 1893

Diphtheria Claims Another Victim.

Health officer Beede paid the stricken settlement at Mud Lake another official visit Friday last. On this occasion he took a load of provisions and clothing to a family

named McAdam, who were reported as destitute and suffering from diphtheria. Sickness had made its appearance in the family on the occasion of his former visit but he was unable at the time to state the nature of the disease. It proved to be diphtheria, however, and soon all the members of the family were taken down with it. One case, that of a child three years of age, terminated fatally just before the arrival of the officer upon the scene. The family were completely destitute. The man of the house had been sick and out of work and they were driven to the last extremity. Their present wants were relieved.

Alcona County Review, January 26, 1893
Cemetery:

McArthur, Donald

HAYNES TIDBITS.

D. McArthur of Alcona, who died on the 18th was taken home and was buried in the Alcona cemetery.

Alcona County Review, April 2, 1886
Cemetery: Mt. Joy, Alcona Co.

McArthur, Duncan John

Died in the Asylum.

Duncan McArthur Passes Away.

Haynes, Jan. 16th, 1894.
Mrs. Duncan McArthur has been informed by the Asylum authorities that her husband is dead. The remains are expected to arrive here to-night.

Alcona County Review, January 18, 1894

Paragraphs of Local Interest.

Our Haynes correspondent reports the recent death of Duncan McArthur in the asylum at Traverse City. It is a sad ending of a promising life, but not worse than was to be expected from his life of reckless dissipation.

Alcona County Review, January 18, 1894

EVENTS OF ONE WEEK.

The Lakeside Monitor is in error in stating that Duncan McArthur was at one time clerk of Alcona county. He was clerk of Haynes township, though, for a number of terms, and in the early part of that service was highly respected, but latterly his reelection was encompassed by the

free use of whiskey and by the peculiar methods in vogue in northern Michigan eight or ten years ago.

Alcona County Review, January 25, 1894

McArthur's Remains At Rest

Haynes, Jan. 23th, 1894.
The remains of D. J. McArthur arrived home on Wednesday evening, the 17th inst., and were interred on the afternoon of the following day. The remains were followed to the cemetery by numerous relatives and a large concourse of sympathizing friends. The Rev. E. F. Smith conducted the funeral services. The asylum authorities are entitled to considerable credit for the careful manner in which the corpse was laid out and for the trimming of the casket.

Alcona County Review, January 25, 1894
Cemetery: Mt. Joy, Alcona Co.

McArthur, Harold

HAYNES.

Harold, aged 3 ½ years, cause of death brain fever, son of Mr. and Mrs. John McArthur, was interred in our cemetery Sunday.

Alcona County Review, August 3, 1899
Cemetery: Mt. Joy, Alcona Co.

McArthur, Letitia [Hasty]

Obituary.

We learn that on the evening of the 7th inst. Mrs. Letitia McArthur, of Alcona, departed this life. She leaves a husband and one child and many sorrowing friends to mourn her decease. Her Pastor, Rev. N. N. Clark, informs us that he administered the Sacrament of the Lord's Supper a short time before her death, when she manifested a faith that took God, Christ and heaven as her portion. The deceased was a daughter of Robert and Mary Ann Hasty.

Alcona County Review, May 10, 1878
Cemetery: Mt. Joy, Alcona Co.

McArthur, Patrick

HAYNES TID BITS.

Patrick McArthur, an old resident of this place, died at the insane asylum on the 16th. His remains were taken to his home and buried in the Springport cemetery on the 21st.
—Greenbush correspondence.

Alcona County Review, April 2, 1891
Cemetery: Springport, Alcona Co.

McBride, Leah

CALEDONIA.

News has been received here of the death of Rev. McBride's eldest daughter. The family have the sympathy of their friends up here.

Alcona County Review, June 25, 1896
Cemetery: Prob. Romulus Memorial, Wayne Co.

McCain, Abram L.

CRUSHED TO DEATH.

A Passenger Crushed Between the Arundell and the Dock.

A most distressing accident occurred on the steamer Arundell Saturday afternoon as she was backing away from the dock at Point Lookout to continue her trip up the shore. A. L. McLain, of Milford, was standing in the bow of the boat on the lower deck and was watching through the port hole the crowd of people on the dock below. About twenty-five feet from the end of the dock stands a clump of piles, driven to protect the dock from ice in the winter. As the Arundell backed out she brushed past these piles and listing over caught the unfortunate man's head between them and the side of the port hole. His companions had left him but a moment and one of them turned around just in time to see him sink to the floor without a word. A mattress was brought at once and he was tenderly laid upon it, but he was beyond human aid. The blood gushed in a stream from his ears, mouth and nose. One ear was nearly severed. His head was crushed but not otherwise disfigured. After the boat had continued on its course for a time she put about and returned to the Point to secure medical attendance, but he died before reaching the dock. His remains were put off there and sent by rail to his late home. The unfortunate man lived at Milford, Mich., and was on his way to Port Arthur with two companions to look after an interest he had recently acquired in some mining property. He was in good circumstances, aged about 35 and leaves a wife and three children.

Alcona County Review, July 25, 1890

THE ARUNDELL IN TROUBLE.

Libeled for $40,000 for the Life of A. L. McCain, Killed at Point Lookout.

From the Detroit Tribune.

The propeller Arundell has been libeled in the United States Court for the Eastern District of Michigan in the sum of $30,000 for damages for personal injury. The suit is brought by W. H. H. Russell in behalf of Richard P. Bridgeman, administrator of the estate of the late Abram L. McCain, who was accidentally killed on the Arundell July 19, 1890. At that time the boat was plying between Bay City and Tawas City. McCain took passage thereon and paid his fare. While the Arundell was making a landing at Point Lookout, McCain, who stood in the forward gangway, was struck in the head by a pile driven in the water about thirty feet from the dock and killed.

The suit involves the decision of very important points touching contributory negligence by passengers on boats that are common carriers. The libellant will contend that it is the duty of steamboat companies to keep their passengers out of danger, and that the fact of the passenger being where he ought not to be does not bar him from getting redress and indemnity in event of injury. In the United States courts the burden of proof of contributory negligence is upon the defendant, and is a question of fact for the jury to decide.

In the present instance the libellant contends also that only the grossest carelessness can render the passenger on a steamboat open to the charge of contributory negligence by the very nature of the case. The court is asked to say, in effect, that common carriers on the water must keep their passengers in reasonable safety. The decision will have a far reaching effect on shipping interests.

Alcona County Review, February 18, 1892
Cemetery:

McCallum, Anne [Carney]

OBITUARY.

Mrs. Angus McCallum of Caledonia fell asleep on the morning of Tuesday, May 10, at the home of her brother, W. T. Ferguson, Alpena, where she had been staying for the past three weeks that she might have the benefit of regular medical attendance. She was a lady of the most amiable disposition, a kind loving wife, a tender, true-hearted mother, and a consistent friend. She leaves a loving husband, two sons and seven daughters to mourn her loss, all

of whom, with the exception of the eldest daughter, were present when she passed away.

The funeral service was held in the Presbyterian church, Caledonia, and was conducted by the Revs. Thomas Middlemiss, Alpena, and J. Cairns Cram, Grace Church, Saginaw. Rev. Middlemiss preached a plain, practical sermon, emphasizing the fact that the death of the believer was more a matter of joy than of sorrow, as it was simply a passing from this world of sorrow, suffering and pain, to a home of everlasting happiness.

The funeral was very largely attended by friends from far and near, who came to show the high esteem and loving regard in which they held the deceased, and to show true practical sympathy which we all so much appreciate at such a time.

The work Thou gavest me to do, is done;
The life Thou gavest me to live is run.
My work is marred and spoiled,
My life with sin is soiled.
Yet loving father unto Thee I come,
Pleading the merits of the Christ, Thy Son.

No merits have I of my own to plead,
To Thee I come through Him, the sinner's meed.

My work is torn and rent.
My life is bowed and bent.
Yet loving Father unto thee I cry.
Pleading thy mercy, to the cross I fly.

In this my direst hour of need be near,
Hold me by they right hand, I shall not fear;
Renew my work again.
Wash from my life the stain.
My all-in-all I trust in Thee alone.
For with Thy life for mine Thou didst atone.
[J. Cairns Cram.]

Alcona County Review, May 19, 1898

Local History of One Year

Chronology of the Principal Events of the Year 1898.

May 10. Death of Mrs. Angus McCallum of Caledonia.

Alcona County Review, January 5, 1899
Cemetery: Pleasant View, Alcona Co.

McCann, Georgie

County News and Gossip.

Just as we go to press we learn of the death of little Georgie McCann, by diphtheria.

Alcona County Review, April 1, 1881
Cemetery:

McCaul, Alex P.

LOCAL JOTTINGS.

The recent death of Alex. P. McCaul, passenger and ticket agent of the D. A. & A. R. R., is deeply regretted by all. He was a man well liked by the people.

Alcona County Review, November 21, 1884

Note and News Along the Shore

AU SABLE AND OSCODA.

A. P. McCaul, late general passenger agent of the D. B. C. & A. R'y, just prior to his death made a small investment in the Minnesota gold lands, and a few days since his estate was offered and refused $2,500 for the little claim.

Alcona County Review, January 2, 1885
Cemetery:

McCaul, Donald B.

Our Neighbors.

Donald B. McCaul died in Grace hospital, Detroit, yesterday, of pneumonia. He was taken there Friday last. Mr. McCaul started to go to Hale Lake station on the Loon Lake branch, about five miles from camp, for mail and supplies. He reached the station and started to return.

At 3 o'clock p. m. he was overtaken by the great storm. He lost his way and spent the night in a straw stack, about two miles from camp. During the night his feet were partly frozen. He remained there for three days before being discovered.

Alcona County Review, December 13, 1889
Cemetery:

McClatchey, {Child}

The Last Sad Rites

The remains of the late Mrs. Abram McClatchey were laid at rest last Friday morning in the cemetery west of town. The services were held at the M. E. Church. The pastor, Rev. W. Will preached a very impressive sermon, taking as his text Job 10:20-22, prefacing his remarks with the statement that whatever he might say was not intended to apply in any way to the dead but was intended as counsel for the living. The remains were encased in a beautiful casket, and lying on the mother's breast was the babe for which she sacrificed her life. The two hives of lady Maccabees attended in a body, accompanying the remains on foot from the residence to the church; from there they were conveyed by carriages to the cemetery where the Maccabee burial service was performed. There was a very large turnout of citizens.

Alcona County Review, August 12, 1897
Cemetery: West Lawn, Alcona Co.

McClatchey, Clara

Mr. and Mrs. Robert McClatchey mourn the loss of their youngest daughter, Clara, aged 11 years. The child has been a patient sufferer for two months from inflammation of the lungs and passed away in spite of all that medical skill and loving hands could do for her. She was buried Thursday afternoon in the West Harrisville cemetery.

Alcona County Review, February 14, 1890

CARD OF THANKS.

We desire to thank our many kind neighbors for visits and help during the illness of our little Clara. Some most constant helpers were Mrs. Frank Chapelle and family, Mr. and Mrs. John Wood, Mrs. Ed Chapelle and Miss Nevin; and we thank Mrs. Elliott and Mrs. Geo. W. Colwell for a quantity of choice flowers.

We also appreciate the kindness of a large number of neighbors who came so promptly, having very short notice, to attend the funeral; also Mr. Buchanan and Mr. Gilpin, who in the absence of a minister conducted the services.

Mr. and Mrs. Robt. McClatchey.

Alcona County Review, February 21, 1890
Cemetery: West Lawn, Alcona Co.

McClatchey, Elizabeth [Rivard]

A Sudden Death

Mrs. Abram McClatchey, wife of the well known business man, died Wednesday morning at 3 o'clock after a very brief illness. She was taken ill the day before. Dr. Tiffany was summoned but he was powerless to combat the malady that in a few short hours robbed the family of a devoted wife and mother.

Deceased was about 34 years old. Five children survive. She was very domestic in her tastes and was seldom seen on the street. The burial will take place tomorrow at 10 o'clock, from the M. E. church.

She was a Maccabee and carried a policy of $1,000.

Alcona County Review, August 5, 1897

We tender our most heartfelt thanks to the kind friends and neighbors who assisted us in laying to rest our dear wife, and a kind, loving mother, whose last words were, "tell my children good by, I am going, going."

A. McClatchey and Family.

I would add to you, mothers, who are bringing up daughters and know the situation I am in, that the main thought and care of my darling wife was to bring up her daughters to make pure and noble minded women, and any advice you can at times give them to assist me in keeping them as their dear mother has started them will be appreciated by me, watched over by their angel mother and surely rewarded by our Father in Heaven.

A. McClatchey.

Alcona County Review, August 12, 1897

The Last Sad Rites.

The remains of the late Mrs. Abram McClatchey were laid at rest last Friday morning in the cemetery west of town. The services were held at the M. E. Church. The pastor, Rev. W. Will preached a very impressive sermon, taking as his text Job 10:20-22, prefacing his remarks with the statement that whatever he might say was not intended to apply in any way to the dead but was intended as counsel for the living. The remains were encased in a beautiful casket, and lying on the mother's breast was the babe for which she sacrificed her life. The two hives of lady Maccabees attended in a body, accompanying the remains on foot from the residence to the church; from there they were conveyed by carriages to the cemetery where the Maccabee burial service was performed. There was a very large turnout of citizens.

Alcona County Review, August 12, 1897

PERSONAL.

Lester Cummings of Grand Marais was called to Harrisville last week by the death of Mrs. Abram McClatchey, who was his sister.

Alcona County Review, August 12, 1897

Bert McClatchey of Bay City attended the funeral of his brother's wife last Friday.

Alcona County Review, August 12, 1897

In Memoriam.

Whereas, the Great Commander of the Universe in His all-wise providence has seen fit to allow death for the third time to enter our Hive and remove from our midst our beloved sister, Lady Elizabeth McClatchey, therefore be it

Resolved, that while we, her sisters of Alcona Hive No. 295, feel that we must submit to the will of Him "who doeth all things well," yet we do feel that in her removal from among us her husband has lost a loving wife and her children a kind and loving mother, and we an honored and beloved sister.

Be it further resolved, that this Hive extend our heartfelt condolence to Mr. McClatchey and family in this their sad hour of bereavement and may kind Providence shield the motherless children and accompany the husband in his solitude.

Be it further resolved, that as a token of respect to our departed sister the charter of our Hive be draped in mourning for a period of thirty days, and that a copy of these resolutions be handed to the bereaved husband and spread upon the records of this Hive and sent to the Review for publication.

Mary Burnham,
Jennie Ward,
M. Alice Fisher,
Committee.

Alcona County Review, August 19, 1897
Cemetery: West Lawn, Alcona Co.

McClatchey, Clara

Purely Personal.

Burt McClatchey was called to Harrisville from Bay City by the death of his little sister.

Alcona County Review, February 14, 1890
Cemetery: West Lawn, Alcona Co.

McClelland, {Girl}

COUNTY REVIEWINGS.

It becomes our sad duty to announce the death of James McClelland's little baby girl, of three weeks of age, which occurred last Sunday night. The funeral services were held Monday afternoon.

Alcona County Review, August 13, 1880
Cemetery: Probably Springport, Alcona Co.

McClelland, Mary [McKinnon]

HAYNES HAPPENINGS.

Old Mrs. McLellan is very low at present. Also Mrs. Robt. Ritchie.

Alcona County Review, October 13, 1898

MRS MARY McCLELLAND.

This aged and respected lady passed away at the home of her son Douglas in Haynes township Thursday evening. Deceased had been ailing about two years. Cause of death heart failure caused by general dropsy.

Mrs. McLelland was born in Scotland in the town of Benivis in 1828 and would have been 70 years of age the 25th of Oct.

Her husband was a carpenter and was drowned in the Ottawa River in 1862; his canoe was overturned during a storm. The surviving children are Mrs. Isabella Dewar, Alex McLellan, Mrs. Flora McNeil, Miss Lizzie and Dougald McLelland, who were present. Her son John resides in Winnipeg, Manitoba, and a daughter, Mrs. John McKinnon, resides in the state of Washington.

The interment took place Sunday afternoon. The services were held in the school house of district No. 1. Rev. Tompkins conducted the services, assisted by Rev. Long. The undertaker was Chas. Mayo of Harrisville.

Alcona County Review, October 27, 1898

We desire to thank the people who so kindly and generously assisted during the last illness and death of our beloved mother. May God bless them.

Mr. and Mrs. McClelland,
and all deceased's relatives.

Alcona County Review, October 27, 1898
Cemetery: Mt. Joy, Alcona Co.

McClenry, James

Shore Pickings.

James McClenry of Alpena is dead.

Alcona County Review, September 12, 1879
Cemetery:

McConnel, Barney

Barney McConnel, a Montgomery [probably Montmorency] county lumberman, was mistaken for a bear and the contents of a rifle were poured into him by a fellow workman. He died in a few minutes.

Alcona County Review, November 29, 1889
Cemetery:

McCormick, Mrs.

PERSONAL MENTION.

Dr. McCormick was called to Monroe within the week by the death of his mother.

Alcona County Review, August 2, 1894
Cemetery:

McCullough, Samuel

Fatal Accident.

Last Wednesday morning a very sad accident occurred which resulted in the death of Samuel McCullough. The unfortunate young man was walking along side of a wagon near Mudgett's farm, on the way to Pack, Woods & Co.'s camp on the Pine river, when he attempted to take his gun from the wagon in order to go on ahead in search of game. The muzzle of the gun lying toward him, he grasped it and attempted to draw the weapon from the wagon when the hammer was raised by catching on some bags and the gun discharged. The ball took effect in the breast, passing out of the right side and through the right arm, causing almost instantaneous death. Deceased was 28 years of age and leaves a wife and one child near Forester, Sanilac county, who were telegraphed of his death. The funeral took place this afternoon at the Presbyterian church.

Alcona County Review, October 22, 1880
Cemetery: West Lawn, Alcona Co.

McCusky, {Male}

A man named McCusky, an old resident of Gustin township, died Sunday at his late home of consumption, aged about 60 years. His widow and three children survive him. The remains were interred Tuesday in the South Harrisville cemetery. The deceased was by birth and education a member of the Catholic church but strange to relate he changed his faith during his last illness and died firm in the Protestant belief. The Rev. Jos. England officiated.

Alcona County Review, February 7, 1890
Cemetery: Springport, Alcona Co.

McDermaid, Malcolm

Drowned.—A very sad accident happened at Greenbush Monday afternoon last by which the second (ten year old) son of Duncan McDermaid came to his death. The boy was spearing fish from the end of Mudgett's dock, and by some means lost his balance and was precipitated into the water of Lake Huron and drowned before help could reach him. Sad, sad affair and ought to be a warning to all boys.

Alcona County Review, June 25, 1880
Cemetery: Springport, Alcona Co.

McDermaid, Mrs.

Mrs. McDermid, an elderly lady between 80 and 90 years of age, was heard to arise from bed as usual last Monday morning. Not appearing at the breakfast table as soon as she should a search was made and she was found dead on the chamber floor. She had a home with Mr. Stewart who lives on the Collins place four miles south west of Harrisville. She was buried Wednesday, the Rev. P. C. Goldie officiating.

Alcona County Review, March 14, 1890
Cemetery: Probably Springport, Alcona Co.

McDonald, Agnes

COUNTY REVIEWINGS.

A little 3 year old daughter of Alexander McDonald of Greenbush, died this week.

Alcona County Review, May 14, 1880
Cemetery: Probably St. Anne's, Alcona Co.

McDonald, Alex

Greenbush All Right.

Old Mr. McDonald, who has been very sick for some time, is not improving very much.

Alcona County Review, November 23, 1893

EVENTS OF ONE WEEK.

Alex McDonald, aged 75, long a resident of the county, died last week at the home of his son in Greenbush township. The remains were brought to Harrisville Monday for interment in the Catholic cemetery.

Alcona County Review, November 30, 1893
Cemetery: St. Anne's, Alcona Co.

McDonald, Alex Angus

EVENTS OF ONE WEEK.

The remains of another child of R. McDonald of Black River were brought to Harrisville Sunday for interment in the Catholic cemetery.

Alcona County Review, August 30, 1894
Cemetery: St. Anne's, Alcona Co.

McDonald, Angus

Killed at Port Huron.

Sheriff McDonald received the sad intelligence last Friday that his brother, Angus, had been killed at Point Edward, Ont. The deceased was a switchman in the employ of the Grand Trunk. He was run over by an entire train of cars and terribly mangled. Sheriff McDonald left for Port Huron Saturday morning. The dead man was in Harrisville only a short time since, visiting his brother and other relatives.

Alcona County Review, February 26, 1891
Cemetery: Prob. Our Lady of Mercy, Lambton ON

McDonald, Angus J.

Death of Angus J. McDonald.
Angus J. McDonald died at his home in Au Sable yesterday morning about four o'clock, after an illness of some years brought on by blood poisoning.

He was born at Cote St. George, Lavlauge county, P. Q. in 1813. His surviving children are, John McDonald of Fostoria, Ohio, Mrs. Flora McDonald of Cheboygan, Mich., Mrs. E. McDonald of Harrisville, and Mrs. D. R. McDonald of Black River. Mrs. J. C. McDonald nd Duncan McDonald, deceased, were his children.—*Press.*

Alcona County Review, July 22, 1897
Cemetery: Probably St. Anne's, Alcona Co.

McDonald, Angus R.

Killed in Washington.
Dan McDonald of the St. Lawrence House received the sad intelligence this week of the accidental death at Olympia, Wash., of his brother, Angus R. McDonald. Full particulars of the accident were not received but it seems that the unfortunate man was conductor of a train and while engaged in the discharge of his duties he was run over and killed. His remains were interred at Olympia. The dead man was a brother of Dan McDonald of Harrisville, Duncan McDonald of Black River, Mrs. Archie McDonald of Mud Lake, R. R. McDonald and S. A. McDonald of Alpena. His was the first death in a family of 12 children. He was in the employ of Alger, Smith & Co. five years ago, at which time he left for the West. He was 32 years of age and unmarried.

Alcona County Review, October 17, 1890
Cemetery: Pioneer Calvary, Thurston Co., WA

McDonald, Charles

DIPHTHERIA'S HARVEST.

The Dreadful Disease Adds to the Long List of Dead.

Chas. McDonald came home sick with diphtheria last week and died Sunday evening.

Alcona County Review, July 7, 1893
Cemetery:

McDonald, {Child}

West Harrisville
The infant child of Mr. and Mrs. Roey McDonald of Blond's camp died Wednesday night of last week. Its body was taken to Alpena for interment.

Alcona County Review, June 4, 1891

West Harrisville
Mr. and Mrs. Roderick McDonald of Black River, mourn the death of a little child. The remains were brought here on the train yesterday, and the funeral took place at 4 o'clock yesterday afternoon from the residence of Mr. McGillis, on Fletcher street. The remains were interred in the Catholic cemetery.—*Echo.*

Alcona County Review, June 4, 1891
Cemetery: Probably Evergree, Alpena Co.

McDonald, Dan

Again the Oft-told Story.
Dan McDonald, a young unmarried man, aged 22 years, was killed at Archie McDonald's camp Wednesday of this week by a falling tree. The remains were taken to his home in Canada. The unfortunate young man had only just returned from Canada. He was the first man ever killed in Archie McDonald's camp.

Alcona County Review, May 30, 1890

One Year's History.

Record of Local Happenings for the Year 1890.

MAY.
28 Dan McDonald killed by a falling tree in McDonald's camp.

Alcona County Review, January 1, 1891
Cemetery:

McDonald, Daniel

EVENTS OF ONE WEEK.

R. J. McDonald of Black River lost a child Sunday after a short illness from inflammation of the bowels. The remains were brought to

Harrisville Tuesday for interment in the Catholic cemetery.

The parents desire to thank their neighbors at Black River for the kindness shown them during the sickness of their little son.

Alcona County Review, August 9, 1894
Cemetery: St. Anne's, Alcona Co.

McDonald, Daniel

People We Hear About.

Dan McDonald is lying very sick at the residence of Thos. Duggan. Dan has been suffering with rheumatism for a long time and his reluctance to accept the inevitable and go to bed has no doubt greatly aggravated the disease. Dr. Mitchell is giving him medical advice.

Alcona County Review, October 3, 1890

The Local News.

Dan McDonald, who is in Harper's hospital Detroit, will never walk again, it is said. His lower limbs are paralyzed and the attendant physicians express no hope of his recovery. A sad fate, surely.

Alcona County Review, November,7 1890

IN MEMORIAM.

Whereas, By the will of the Divine Ruler of the Universe our esteemed brother, Past Grand Daniel McDonald, has been removed from us

Resolved, That in the death of our brother this Lodge has lost a good member and the community an honest, trustworthy citizen. And that while we mourn his departure and feel we have sustained a loss, yet we bow in humble submission to the will of Him who doeth all things well. And we hereby extend to his friends and relatives our heartfelt sympathy in their hour of deepest affliction.

Resolved, That these resolutions be spread upon the records of our Lodge that a copy be sent to the sorrowing relatives, that they be published in our village paper and that in respect to the memory of our departed brother, our charter be draped in mourning for the space of sixty days.

F. A. Beede,
Chas. Conklin,
Joseph Evans,
Committee.
Harrisville Lodge No. 218 I.O.O.F.

Alcona County Review, December 19, 1890

One Year's History.

Record of Local Happenings for the Year 1890.

NOVEMBER.

November 17. Death of Daniel McDonald at Harper Hospital, Detroit.

Alcona County Review, January 1, 1891
Cemetery:

McDonald, Donald D.

Sudden Death of Dan McDonald

Daniel McDonald dropped dead at his home in the southwestern part of the township just as he was preparing to come to town Monday afternoon. Heart failure is believed to be the cause of death.

Deceased had been a Maccabee, but had allowed his assessments to lapse for sometime before his death.

The funeral was held yesterday afternoon at the residence, the interment taking place at the Catholic cemetery.

Alcona County Review, April 7, 1898

LOCAL PICK UPS.

An object lesson in insurance is furnished by the sudden death of Daniel McDonald this week. Mr. McDonald became a Maccabee on June 5, 1893 and withdrew from the order in October, 1894, having paid in all $16.25. Had he remained in the order his insurance up to the time of his death would have cost him $61.75 and his family would have $1,000 more than they now have, to aid them in the battles of life, which they must now fight without the aid of a husband and father.

Alcona County Review, April 7, 1898

Local History of One Year

Chronology of the Principal Events of the Year 1898.

April 4. Death of Dan McDonald.

Alcona County Review, January 5, 1899
Cemetery: St. Anne's, Alcona Co.

McDonald, Donald R. M.

EVENTS OF ONE WEEK.

The oldest man who ever lived on the shore of Lake Huron, died recently at Lancaster, Ont. Donald R. M. McDonald was born there in 1786. He served in the war of 1812 and the Canadian rebellion of 1837-38. In 1848 he removed to Canton, N.

Y. In 1854 to the Saginaw valley, in 1864 to Harrisville and subsequently to the upper peninsula. He made a living getting out square lumber for the Quebec market.

Alcona County Review, February 18, 1897
Cemetery: Prob. McDonald Family, Glengary ON

McDonald, Elizabeth

Elizabeth McDonald, the 16-years-old daughter of the late Jno. R. McDonald of Greenbush, died last week and was buried Saturday in the Catholic cemetery south of Harrisville. The young lady had been ill but a short time and her death was a great shock to her friends.

Alcona County Review, March 16, 1893
Cemetery: St. Anne's, Alcona Co.

McDonald, Flora

The Local News.

Mr. and Mrs. Dan McDonald mourn the death of one of their little twins, seven months of age. The child was buried Tuesday.

Alcona County Review, November 28, 1890

Your Folks and Our Folks.

R. R. McDonald was called down Tuesday to attend the funeral of his brother's infant child.

Alcona County Review, November 28, 1890
Cemetery:

McDonald, Henrietta [Scott]

DIED.

Henrietta, wife of Hugh McDonald, died at her home in this township, on Friday, June 25th, 1886, aged about 32 years. Mrs. McDonald had been in declining health for a number of years, and her final illness covered a period of nearly a year. The funeral services were held at the M. E. church on Saturday, Rev. T. B. Leith preaching the sermon, and the remains were interred in the Spring-port cemetery. She leaves a husband and one child to mourn their loss.

Alcona County Review, July 2, 1886
Cemetery: Springport, Alcona Co.

McDonald, Hughie

In Memoriam.

Hughie, aged 2 years and 6 months, son of D. A. McDonald of Black River, died August 11. The parents have the sympathy of the whole community.

Lines to memory of little Hughie.

A loved one from us had gone,
A voice we loved is still.

A place is vacant in our home,
Which never can be filled.

We miss him, oh! we miss him.
His face no more we see.
He has gone to join the angels above,
With Jesus forever to be.

We've a loved one now in heaven,
There to welcome us on high.
Oh be ready, do not tarry,
The time is drawing nigh.

He has gone to be with Jesus,
To be there forevermore;
He is dwelling with the angels,
He has crossed the golden shore.

     Mrs. Morris.

Alcona County Review, August 19, 1897

PERSONAL.

Mrs. James Morris was called to Black River last week to the funeral of her brother's child. She returned Monday. Frank Morris attended the funeral also. He was taken sick and did not get home until Monday.

Alcona County Review, August 19, 1897
Cemetery: Springport, Alcona Co.

McDonald, Ida May [Thornton]

South Harrisville.

South Harrisville, Jan. 28.--Mrs. Ronald McDonald died at her home last Friday and was buried in the South Harrisville cemetery Sunday. She leaves three children, a boy of 12 and two girls of 10 and 7 years.

Alcona County Review, January 31, 1895

EVENTS OF ONE WEEK.

The illness of Mrs. Ronald McDonald of Greenbush township terminated fatally last week. Deceased was a daughter of Silas Thornton of Harrisville township.

Alcona County Review, January 31, 1895

Gustin Grist.

Gustin, Jan. 29.--Mrs. Ronald McDonald of Handy is dead.

Alcona County Review, January 31, 1895
Cemetery: Springport, Alcona Co.

McDonald, Jack

ALONG THE SHORE.

Au Sable and Oscoda.

In a saloon brawl at Oscoda Thursday night of last week, Sam Bennett shot and killed Jack McDonald, the ball penetrating the head of McDonald from near the center of the forehead. There is a dispute as to whether it was justifiable homicide or deliberate murder.

Alcona County Review, September 4, 1885
Cemetery:

McDonald, James E.

CIRCUIT COURT NOTES.

"James McDonald," called the clerk of the circuit court Tuesday as a jury was being impaneled in a civil case. "Dead!" was the response from a juryman present. The above named juryman, a resident of Caledonia, was summoned by Sheriff McDonald, but the day after he received this summons came a summons from a higher court.

Alcona County Review, February 15, 1889

Somewhat Personal.

Judge of Probate Ritchie was in town Tuesday and took the initiatory steps to close up the estate of James McDonald, deceased, late a resident of Caledonia.

Alcona County Review, August 13, 1891

STATE OF MICHIGAN,
County of Alcona.

At a session of the Probate Court for said County, held at the Probate office, in the village of Harrisville, on the 11th day of Aug., in the year one thousand eight hundred and ninety-one.

Present, Hon. Geo. S. Ritchie, Judge of Probate.

In the matter of the estate of James McDonald, deceased:

On reading and filing the petition, duly verified, of D. E. McDonald, praying that administration of said estate be granted to E. H. Toland, or some other suitable person:

Thereupon it is ordered that Saturday, the fifth (5) day of September next, at ten o'clock in the forenoon, be assigned for the hearing of said petition, and that the heirs at law of said deceased, and all other persons interested in said estate, are required to appear at a session of said Court, then to be holden at the Probate office, in the village of Harrisville, said County, and show cause, if there be any, why the prayer of the petitioner should not be granted: And it is further ordered, that said petitioner give notice to the persons interested in said estate, of the pendency of said petition, and the hearing thereof, by causing a copy of this order to be published in the Alcona County Review, a newspaper printed and circulated in said county, three successive weeks previous to said day of hearing.

    GEO. S. RITCHIE,
    Judge of Probate.

Alcona County Review, August 13, 1891

STATE OF MICHIGAN,
County of Alcona.

At a session of the Probate Court for said County, held at the Probate office, in the village of Harrisville, on the 2nd day of July, in the year one thousand eight hundred and ninety-two.

Present, Hon. Geo. S. Ritchie, Judge of Probate.

In the Matter of the Estate of James McDonald, deceased.

On reading and filing the petition, duly verified, of E. H. Toland, praying that he may be granted a license to sell the real estate of said deceased for the purpose of paying the debts and expenses of administration of said estate.

Thereupon it is ordered, that Saturday, the sixth day of August, next, at ten o'clock in the forenoon, be assigned for the hearing of said petition, and that the heirs at law of said deceased, and all other persons interested in said estate, are required to appear at a session of said Court, then to be holden in the Probate office, in the Village of Harrisville and show cause, if any there be, why the prayer of the petitioner should not be granted. And it is further ordered, that said petitioner give notice to the persons interested in said estate, of the pendency of said petition, and the hearing thereof, by causing a copy of this order to be published in the Alcona County Review, a newspaper printed and circulated in said county four successive weeks previous to said day of hearing.

    Geo. S. Ritchie,
    Judge of Probate.

Alcona County Review, July 7, 1892

SOMEWHAT PERSONAL.

E. H. Toland of Ossineke was attending a session of the Probate court Saturday. He is administrator of the estate of the late Jas. E.

McDonald of Caledonia, which will soon be closed up.

STATE OF MICHIGAN, County of Alcona.

In the matter of the estate of James McDonald.

Notice is hereby given, that in pursuance of an order granted to the undersigned, Administrator of the estate of said James McDonald, by the honorable Judge of Probate for the County of Alcona, on the Sixth day of August, A. D. 1892, there will be sold at public vendue, to the highest bidder, at the residence of D. E. McDonald, Caledonia Township, in the County of Alcona, in said State, on Saturday, the 29th day of October, A. D. 1892, at 2 o'clock in the afternoon of that day (subject to all incumbrances by mortgage or otherwise existing at the time of the death of said deceased, or at the time of sale), the following described real estate, to-wit: The west half of northeast quarter of section 10, Town 28 North of Range 8 east; the west half of northwest quarter of section 10, Town 28 North of Range 8 East; the east half of northwest quarter of section 10, Town 28 North of Range 8 East.

E. H. TOLAND, Administrator.

Alcona County Review, September 15, 1892
Cemetery:

McDonald, Jennie A. [McDonald]

The death of Mrs. D. A. McDonald, of this place, occurred at the family residence Monday morning at 6 o'clock, from that dread foe of mankind, consumption. Early last summer Mrs. McDonald was attacked by hemorrhage which at the time was thought would result fatally. She rallied partially from this, but as winter approached the disease again presented alarming features, and after six weeks' suffering death came to her relief. Mrs. McDonald was 30 years of age, having been born at Cornwall, Ont., in May, 1857. She was married to D. A. McDonald in October, 1879, since which time she has been a resident of our village where she had during her lifetime made many warm friends who cherish her memory. Besides her husband she leaves two small children to mourn her death. The funeral took place from the Catholic church Tuesday morning, from where

the remains were taken to the depot en route for Glengarry, Ont., for interment.—Monitor.

Alcona County Review, December 23, 1887
Cemetery: Prob. McDonald Family, Glengary ON

McDonald, John

LOCAL JOTTINGS.

A three year old son of Ronald McDonald was buried last Sunday.

Alcona County Review, June 6, 1884
Cemetery:

McDonald, John

Alcona Gatherings.

Miss Flora and Kate McDonald were called home from Alpena on account of their father's illness, Jno. McDonald, who is not expected to live.

Alcona County Review, May 26, 1892

Alcona Gatherings.

Died, at his home in Caledonia, May 27th, 1892, John McDonald, aged 54 years. He leaves a wife and nine children to mourn their loss. The funeral, which was held at the Presbyterian church, was largely attended by sympathizing friends and relatives.

Alcona County Review, June 9, 1892

HISTORY OF ONE YEAR.

Chronological History of the Past Year, 1892.

THE DEATH RECORD.

May 27. John McDonald, Caledonia.

Alcona County Review, January 5, 1893
Cemetery: Pleasant View, Alcona Co.

McDonald, John

PERSONAL MENTION.

Monday morning the remains of John McDonell were brought to Harrisville from Black River for interment in the Catholic cemetery. The young man was a son of Jno. McDonell of Black River. His death occurred Saturday after an illness of 14 days from inflammation of the bowels. A large number of friends and neighbors of deceased's family followed the remains to their last resting place.

The family desire to express their heartfelt appreciation of the many acts of kindness and words of sympathy tendered by their neighbors during the sickness, death

and burial of their beloved son and brother.

Alcona County Review, August 2, 1894

STATE OF MICHIGAN, County of Alcona.

At a session of the Probate Court for said County, held at the Probate office, in the Village of Harrisville on the thirteenth day of October in the year one thousand eight hundred and ninety-six.

Present, C. H. Killmaster, Judge of Probate.

In the matter of the estate of John McDonald.

On reading and filing the petition duly verified of Alexander McDonald, asking that a certain document purporting to be the last will and testament of his deceased father, said document being now in this Court.

Thereupon it is ordered, that Monday, the first day of November next, at ten o'clock in the forenoon, be assigned for the hearing of said petition, and that the heirs at law of said deceased and all other persons interested in said estate, are required to appear at a session of the Probate Court, then to be holden at the Probate office, in the Village of Harrisville and show cause, if any there be, why the prayer of the petitioner should not be granted.

And it is further ordered that the petitioner give notice to the heirs at law and persons interested in the estate of the pendency of said petition, and the hearing thereof, by causing a copy of this order to be published in the Alcona County Review, a newspaper printed and circulating in said county three successive weeks previous to said day of hearing.

C. H. KILLMASTER,
Judge of Probate.

Alcona County Review, October 15, 1896
Cemetery: St. Anne's, Alcona Co.

McDonald, John A.

LOCAL JOTTINGS.

The funeral services over the remains of John A. McDonald were held from the Presbyterian church last Sunday morning.

Alcona County Review, November 6, 1885
Cemetery:

McDonald, John A.

PASSED THE PORTALS.

Died, in Alexian Hospital, Chicago, May 31, aged 21 years and 9 months, John A. McDonald.

———

Word was received in Caledonia on Thursday morning of the death of John A. McDonald in Chicago. Death was due to heart failure, caused by a severe attack of inflammatory rheumatism from which he suffered eight weeks. His family heard from him regularly and no danger was feared until about two weeks ago a letter from a friend stated that a relapse had set in. His brother left immediately for his bedside, and all that kind hearts and loving hands could do was done to make his last hours comfortable. But all help failed and death came Tuesday evening. Johnnie was a young man well and favorably known in Caledonia and his death has cast a gloom over the entire community. Though he had suffered much pain during his long stay in the hospital it had all left by the time his brother reached him. He remained conscious up to the last and talked with his brother and other friends. A minister was by his side, and in talking with him he said he was willing and ready to go if it was God's will, but he still held to the hope that he would get better and come home.

His remains arrived Thursday evening accompanied by his brother and Miss Freda Alstrom of Chicago. The funeral occurred Saturday morning and was conducted by Rev. Middlemiss of Alpena and Rev. Dunham of Ossineke. It was one of the largest ever held in Caledonia; the floral offerings were beautiful among others a beautiful KOTM pillow. After very impressive services in the church all that was mortal of Johnnie McDonald was consigned to the tomb beside his father.

Gently, how gently departed his breath,
No anguish or grief pervaded his breast.
Sweetly, how sweetly he slumbers in death,
Wearing the smile of the pure and the blest.

Alcona County Review, June 9, 1898

We wish through the Review to thank our many kind friends and neighbors for their many kind acts of sympathy during our late bereavement. Especially do we thank the Haynes choir for their services, also to Rev. Dunham and Ossineke friends for beautiful flowers. Such kindness can never be forgotten in a time of trouble.

        Mrs. McDonald and Family.

Alcona County Review, June 9, 1898

Local History of One Year

Chronology of the Principal Events of the Year 1898.

May 31. Death of John McDonald of Caledonia in Alexian Hospital Chicago.

Alcona County Review, January 5, 1899
Cemetery: Pleasant View, Alcona Co.

McDonald, John R.

COUNTY JOTTINGS.

An only son of D. R. McDonald, of Greenbush (7 years of age), died with the diphtheria Wednesday night.

Alcona County Review, November 29, 1878
Cemetery: St. Anne's, Alcona Co.

McDonald, John Roy

Death of Supervisor McDonald.

The death record was increased Monday by the demise of Jno. Roy McDonald, Supervisor of the township of Greenbush, and Chairman of the Board of Supervisors of Alcona county. Mr. McDonald had been working for a short time with his team at Bonney's camp. He was taken ill there a few days ago from an attack of inflammation of the lungs, a malady from which he had suffered at other times. His decline was rapid and his condition became so alarming that his wife was sent for. He breathed his last on Monday.

The deceased had been a resident of Alcona county for many years and had actively participated in all matters of public nature that excited the attention or interest of his fellow citizens. He held various township offices, principal among which was the office of Supervisor of Greenbush township, which he held several terms and the duties of which he discharged with a conscientious regard for the public good. He was at one time one of the Supts. of the Poor for Alcona county. He was not singularly brilliant as a public official, but his honesty of purpose gained for him the respect of his fellows. He it was who began the proceedings to set aside the sale of the old poor farm and the purchase of the new, sincerely believing that an injustice had been done the people. He was a life-long democrat and a member of the Catholic church. He leaves a wife and a family of children, most of whom have arrived at maturity.

The funeral services occurred this morning from the Catholic church and were largely attended.

Alcona County Review, January 19, 1893

EVENTS OF ONE WEEK.

The death of Supervisor John Roy McDonald removes the chairman of the Board of Supervisors of Alcona county by death for the second time within a year. The other death was that of Supervisor Thos. Dean.

Alcona County Review, January 19, 1893

PERSONAL MENTION.

We desire to return our most sincere and heartfelt thanks to all those friends who assisted in any way during the final illness, death and burial of our beloved husband and father, the late John R. McDonald.

        Mrs. John R. McDonald
        and family.

Alcona County Review, January 26, 1893
Cemetery: St. Anne's, Alcona Co.

McDonald, John S.

REVIEWINGS.

John S. McDonald, a young man who had worked in the lumber woods in this county for some time past, died very suddenly at the St. Lawrence House in this village last Sunday, with lung disease. He had no relatives in the state, but was kindly cared for during his sickness, and decently buried by the Catholic people of the village in their cemetery.

Alcona County Review, March 26, 1880
Cemetery: St. Anne's, Alcona Co.

McDonald, Joseph

Au Sable and Oscoda News Items.

A boy and a girl were born to Mr. and Mrs. J. C. McDonald on Monday morning last, each weighing 4 ½ pounds. The little people lived, however, but a short time on this earth--just 24 hours.

Alcona County Review, January 24, 1879
Cemetery: Sacred Heart, Iosco Co.

McDonald, Maggie

COUNTY REVIEWINGS.

In addition to the death of the child reported last week, Alexander McDonald of Greenbush lost a little seven-year old girl, this week.

Alcona County Review, May 21, 1880
Cemetery: Probably St. Anne's, Alcona Co.

McDonald, {Male}
Did He Belong Here?.
The postmaster received a card from F. H. Foote, dated at Viola post office, Mich., stating that a young man named McDonald aged about 20, had been killed there, and it was believed he came from Alcona county.

Alcona County Review, July 29, 1897
Cemetery:

McDonald, Margaret
A child of Mrs. Raynold McDonald [died].

Alcona County Review, January 15, 1886
Cemetery: Probably St. Anne's, Alcona Co.

McDonald, Margaret
GUSTIN.
Dec. 1st.--Mrs. McDonald of Oscoda, who was injured in the run-away last Summer, died yesterday.

Alcona County Review, December 2, 1897
Cemetery:

McDonald, Marguerite [Cameron]
LOCAL PICK UPS.
Mrs. McDonald, sister of Mrs. Dan McDonald of Mikado died at Au Sable Tuesday and will be buried from the Catholic church here tomorrow.

Alcona County Review, March 2, 1899
Cemetery: St. Anne's, Alcona Co.

McDonald, Mary
Au Sable and Oscoda News Items.

A boy and a girl were born to Mr. and Mrs. J. C. McDonald on Monday morning last, each weighing 4 ½ pounds. The little people lived, however, but a short time on this earth--just 24 hours.

Alcona County Review, January 24, 1879
Cemetery: Sacred Heart, Iosco Co.

McDonald, Mary Sarah
COUNTY REVIEWINGS.

Mary, daughter of Daniel D. McDonald, of Harrisville, died on Wednesday the 28th inst., aged 14 years. The remains were interred in the Catholic cemetery Thursday

afternoon. Friends from Au Sable were present at the burial service.

Alcona County Review, July 30, 1880
Cemetery: St. Anne's, Alcona Co.

McDonald, Michael
COUNTY REVIEWINGS.

From the Au Sable *News* we learn that Ernest Whitney, of New Brunswick, Canada, employed by the Oscoda Salt & Lumber company, in Camp 11, on Perry's Creek, Au Sable river, was instantly killed by a hemlock tree, toppled over by a pine, on the 15th inst. Deceased was 20 years old and married. On the same day Michael McDonald, working in Emery Bros.' camp on the South Branch of the Au Sable, had his skull crushed in, a tree falling upon him while he was at his work. Deceased is 35 years old, and is supposed to have friends living in Oswego, N.Y.

Alcona County Review, November 26, 1880
Cemetery:

McDonald, R. A.
ANOTHER ONE KILLED.

R. A. McDonald was the Unfortunate Man.
R. A. McDonald, accompanied by Jas. McDonald, attended the special meeting of the board of supervisors last week for the purpose of petitioning that body in the interest of a new township organization to be called Caledonia. Their mission here accomplished they started to return home Saturday afternoon. They lived in the north half of town 28 north of range 8 east, and the nearest point on the railroad is Roe Lake, where they left the train expecting to walk home from that place. The first named man did not appear to be intoxicated when he left here but the reports that have reached this place state that he was so hopelessly under the influence of liquor that he laid down beside the track unable to proceed further. Engine No. 10, with a load of flats bound for the woods came along. The engineer did not notice McDonald until it was too late to stop the train. The engine passed him safely but the boxes that cover the axes on the flats caught him and dragged one leg under the wheels. This member was severed above the ankle; his collar bone was broken and he was injured internally. He died at 3 o'clock

Sunday morning. The remains were taken to Black River.

The dead man was unmarried and about 45 years of age. He taught school in this township and was chiefly instrumental in getting the new township of Caledonia organized. He kept books a number of years ago for Wm. Conklin at Greenbush, and was possessed of more than ordinary ability.

Alcona County Review, March 23, 1888
Cemetery:

McDonald, Reynold
LOCAL JOTTINGS.

Reynold McDonald, a farmer resident of this township for about 12 years past, died Monday, after a considerable illness; aged about 45 years. He was held in great esteem by the people of his community, as was evidenced by the very large attendance at the obsequies held from the Catholic church Wednesday afternoon. He leaves a wife and 6 children.

Alcona County Review, August 7, 1885
Cemetery: St. Anne's, Alcona Co.

McDonald, William F.
PURELY PERSONAL.

Death of a Shore Pioneer.—Wm. F. McDonald, one of the best known citizens of Cheboygan, died last Monday morning after an illness of several weeks. The funeral was held on Wednesday and was conducted by the G. A. R. Post of Cheboygan, of which he was a member. It was, with one exception, the largest funeral ever held in Cheboygan. The deceased was born in Glengarry, Ont., 54 years ago. He moved to Saginaw in 1863; enlisted in the 27th N. Y. infantry and served till the close of the war. He came to Au Sable in '68 and conducted the old Rockwell hotel for one year, afterwards moving to Greenbush and Harrisville, and to Cheboygan in 1876, where he remained. He was twice married, his first wife and two children dying. He married his second wife, Miss Flora McDonald, at Harrisville. She and four children, all boys, the eldest 13 years of age youngest 3 years, survive him. He has two brothers in Cheboygan, John F. and Ronald, a brother in California, one in Canada, one, Angus F., at Au Sable, and a sister, Mrs. Hugh McDonald, living

in Bay City. He had a very extensive acquaintance along the shore of Lake Huron and many of his friends from this section were present at the funeral, among them being Mr. and Mrs. A. F. and J. C. McDonald of Au Sable.—Saturday Night.

Alcona County Review, August 2, 1889
Cemetery: Calvary, Cheboygan Co.

McDougal, Angus

LOCAL JOTTINGS

Angus McDougall, of Greenbush, died Sunday of a tumor in the stomach. The deceased was 62 years of age and leaves a wife and no children. The funeral services were held Wednesday at the Catholic church in this village.

Alcona County Review, April 13, 1888

Card of Thanks.

We wish to thank our friends and neighbors who rendered such kind services during the last illness and death of Angus McDougall.
Mrs. Angus McDougall.
John A. Kelly.

Alcona County Review, April 13, 1888
Cemetery: Probably St. Anne's, Alcona Co.

McDougal, Mrs. Bell

Mrs. McDougall, of Greenbush township, died yesterday and was buried today in the Catholic cemetery.

Alcona County Review, August 16, 1894
Cemetery: St. Anne's, Alcona Co.

McDougal, John B.

Along the Shore.

John B. McDougall, proprietor of the American House at Alpena, died at his home in that city last Friday. He had been a resident of Alpena for 12 years past.

Alcona County Review, October 7, 1881
Cemetery: Holy Cross, Alpena Co.

McElraney, {Boy}

BLACK RIVER.

Mr. and Mrs. McElraney, of Black River, came to the city on Wednesday to bury their boy babe, which had died a day or two before. Mr. and Mrs. McElraney formerly lived in this city where they have many friends and who sympathize with them in their great loss.—E. Tawas Gazette.

Alcona County Review, February 2, 1899
Cemetery:

McElroy, Guy

Alcona Atoms.

The body of young McElroy, one of the Marine City victims was washed ashore Wednesday.

Alcona County Review, September 10, 1880

Alcona Atoms.

Mr. McElroy, of the Toledo Blade, offered $100 reward for the recovery of the bodies of his son and father-in-law. As before noted, half the reward has been earned.

Alcona County Review, September 10, 1880

COUNTY REVIEWINGS.

The bodies of Dr. C. Pomeroy and Guy McElroy, of Toledo, Ohio, and the body of Jenny Mosser of Alcona, were found by the Life Saving Crew on Wednesday last, the former two near the station, the latter a mile south. The bodies of Dr. Pomeroy and nephew were shipped to their relatives in Toledo.

Alcona County Review, September 10, 1880
Cemetery: Pomeroy, Putnam Co., OH

McFarlane, Daniel

Au Sable Man Killed.

Daniel McFarlane, at one time a resident of Au Sable, was killed at Munising last Wednesday night by the explosion of a boiler in the Loud shingle mill.

The remains were brought to Mikado, where deceased's mother and two sisters, Mrs. Jno. McMaster and Mrs. C. A. Johnson, live. The interment took place at Au Sable on Monday under the auspices of the Maccabee Lodge. Deceased leaves a widow and children.

Alcona County Review, February 2, 1899
Cemetery: Pinecrest, Iosco Co.

McFarlane, {Male}

Jottings Along the Shore.

One day the fore part of last week, two brothers, named McFarlane, in the employ of one of the Alpena lumber camps, were struck by a falling tree, one being quite seriously wounded and the other mortally wounded.

Alcona County Review, March 12, 1880
Cemetery:

McGill, W. P.

OUR STATE.

A reward of $50 is offered by Mrs. W. P. McGill, of Alpena, for the recovery of the body of her husband, who was drowned last January while attempting to pass from the main

land to Middle Island in a skiff. The drowned man has an India ink anchor on one hand, a star on the other, and a cross on his left arm. His height is six feet, and he weighed 180 pounds.

Alcona County Review, May 8, 1885
Cemetery:

McGillis, Ann [Luby]

GREENBUSH ITEMS.

We learn that Mrs. McGillis, mother of John and Duncan McGillis, of this place, is lying seriously ill at the residence of the latter.

Later.—Since writing the above we learn that Mrs. McGillis is dead.

Alcona County Review, March 25, 1887
Cemetery: St. Anne's, Alcona Co.

McGillis, Catherine

LOCAL JOTTINGS.

Mr. and Mrs. Duncan McGillis, of Greenbush, lost their 12 year old daughter, by consumption, last Friday morning. "The Lord giveth, and the Lord taketh away; blessed be the name of the Lord."

Alcona County Review, September 25, 1885
Cemetery:

McGillis, Sarah [McQuaig]

EVENTS OF ONE WEEK.

The remains of Mrs. John McGillis, late of Greenbush, were brought to Harrisville yesterday morning for interment in the Catholic cemetery. Deceased was about 44 years of age and died from consumption.

Alcona County Review, November 7, 1895

Mrs. John McGillis:

The late Mrs. John McGillis who died at her home in Greenbush on Sunday, 3rd. inst., was born in Canada in 1845, and was therefore fifty years of age. Her maiden name was Sarah McQuaig. She was married in 1865 and fifteen years later she and her husband and family moved to Greenbush, where they have since resided.

Deceased had not been well in a long time and about two weeks ago she contracted a severe cold which resulted in inflammation of the lungs. All that medical skill could do was done by the attending physician, Dr. Mitchell, but human agencies proved insufficient to counteract the great call that had been given and had to be answered.

Mrs. McGillis' main characteristic was her great love of home which she always tried to make pleasant and happy and in which she succeeded. She leaves behind her a husband and seven children—six boys and one girl—all but one of whom are grown to man's and woman's estate. The family have the heartfelt sympathy of the whole community; for all realize that that family has lost their shining light—a loving wife and mother.

The remains were interred in the Catholic cemetery at Harrisville, the deceased having been a member of the church all the days of her life.

Alcona County Review, November 14, 1895

We desire to express our sincere thanks to our many friends in Greenbush and vicinity who so kindly gave us their sympathy and assistance in our recent bereavement.

May He who cares for all comfort them if they are ever called upon to pass through a like sad affliction.

Very Thankfully,
John McGillis and Family.

Alcona County Review, November 14, 1895
Cemetery: St. Anne's, Alcona Co.

McGillivary, Hugh

The Local News.

Hugh McGillivary, aged 26 and well known in Alcona county, especially in the woods, was drowned last week in Wolf creek, where he was working on the drive. He was unmarried.

Alcona County Review, May 9, 1890

One Year's History.

Record of Local Happenings for the Year 1890.

MAY.

May 5. Hugh McGilvery aged 26 drowned in Wolf creek.

Alcona County Review, January 1, 1891
Cemetery:

McGrady, Mrs. Bridget

Somewhat Personal.

Mrs. Bridget McGrady died at her home in Sherman Township on Thursday, April 14, aged 58 years. The funeral will be held from the Catholic church here on Saturday, at 10 a.m. The ailment was rheumatism of the heart. Deceased leaves a husband and five children.—E. Tawas Gazette.

The deceased was the mother of Jas. McGrady of Harrisville and had been a sufferer from the above disease for a year or more.

Alcona County Review, April 21, 1892
Cemetery: St. Joseph, Iosco Co.

McGrady, James Peter

PERSONAL MENTION.

Reports from the bed-side of James McGrady are to the effect that he is dangerously ill, and that he cannot recover.

Alcona County Review, May 25, 1893

Called to His Reward.

The final summons came to Jas. McGrady at an early hour Tuesday morning after a protracted illness, during which he suffered intensely. Deceased had been ill all winter and was confined to the house and his bed much of the time. Two weeks ago he seemed to rally somewhat and was so far improved that he walked to the village. But the inevitable relapse seized him and he failed very rapidly until death came to him as a welcome relief. He leaves a wife and three children.

James McGrady was about 35 years of age. He was universally esteemed for his upright character and sterling principles, and his untimely demise is a matter of general regret and sorrow. He was an Odd Fellow and a Maccabee and had $1,000 insurance in the latter order. He was reared a Catholic but was converted to Protestantism a few years ago. He was a life-long Democrat and took a conspicuous part in local politics, although he never sought office.

The funeral services are to be held this afternoon at the M. E. church at 2 o'clock. Harrisville Lodge No. 218, I.O.O.F. and Harrisville Tent No. 18, K.O.T.M., of which he was a member, will have charge of the services and he will be buried with the honors due a member in good standing.

Alcona County Review, June 1, 1893

Card of Thanks.

For myself and family I desire to offer a public expression of our deep gratitude to all whose kindness, sympathy and attention have been a source of comfort during the last sickness, death and burial of our beloved husband and father.

Mrs. K. McGrady.

Alcona County Review, June 8, 1893

EVENTS OF ONE WEEK.

Great Camp warrant No. 757, drawn for the sum of $1,000 in favor of Mrs. James McGrady, beneficiary of the late James McGrady, was received this week by the officers of Harrisville Tent No. 18 K.O.T.M. and the same has been turned over to the widow. Thus another proof is furnished of the stability of this thrifty order and of the great good it is accomplishing in the hour of greatest need.

Alcona County Review, June 29, 1893

Resolutions of Respect.

Whereas, In the wisdom of the Almighty Ruler of the Universe, death has entered our Tent and taken from our midst our esteemed brother, Sir Knight James P. McGrady, therefore be it

Resolved, That the widow and family of said deceased Sir Knight McGrady have lost a kind, and indulgent husband and father, this Tent a good and zealous member and this community an honorable, upright, model citizen. It is also

Resolved, That the members of this Tent, No. 18 K.O.T.M., do hereby extend to the members of the bereaved family, our deep and sincere sympathy in this their hour of grief; and it is further

Resolved, That the charter of our Tent be draped in mourning for the period of sixty days, as a further token of respect for our departed brother; and be it also

Resolved, That these resolutions be spread upon the records of this Tent, and a copy tendered afflicted family; that they be published in the Michigan Maccabee and in the Alcona County Review.

Committee.

Alcona County Review, June 29, 1893
Cemetery: West Lawn, Alcona Co.

McGrady, Catherine A.

LOCAL JOTTINGS.

A year-old child of James McGrady was buried last Monday.

Alcona County Review, August 22, 1884

LOCAL JOTTINGS.

While officiating at the funeral services of James McGrady's child last Monday, B. F. Buchanan was prostrated by the excessive heat of the day and experienced the most severe illness from such cause he has ever known, being obliged to remain at the residence of Wm. Forsythe until near evening before daring to venture out of doors to return home. He is now able to attend to business again, though not entirely recovered. Mr. Buchanan's health is far from the best, and the cool weather of this summer has been most beneficial and enjoyable to him.

Alcona County Review, August 22, 1884
Cemetery: West Lawn, Alcona Co.

McGrath, Patrick

PERSONAL POINTS.

P. McGrath is dangerously ill.

Alcona County Review, February 23, 1899

PERSONAL POINTS.

Miss Maggie McGrath arrived from Detroit Tuesday to be at the bedside of her father, whose recovery at this writing is considered very doubtful.

Alcona County Review, March 2, 1899

Death of P. McGrath.

Just as we go to press we learn that our old townsman and respected citizen, Patrick McGrath, passed away at 10 o'clock this morning. Death was due to the combined attacks of grip and old age. Next week the Review will give a biographical sketch of the deceased.

The funeral services will be held at St. Anne's church at 9 o'clock Saturday morning.

Alcona County Review, March 2, 1899

PATRICK McGRATH, DECEASED.

In the death of Patrick McGrath, Harrisville loses one of its oldest citizens. For more than thirty years he had been a respected member of this community, being occupied as a carpenter, undertaker and finally as proprietor of a general store.

Deceased was an Irishman by birth and next to this he was perhaps proudest of the fact that he was one of Uncle Sam's "Boys"——one of those who fought for the flag in Lincoln's time. He was a member of the ninetieth Ill. Infantry, enlisting from Chicago, and after three years of faithful service received an honorable discharge.

On August 12th, 1867, the year in which he came to Harrisville he married Miss Bridgett Kinsley of Alpena and brought his bride to Harrisville where he had already built

the house in which they have lived ever since.

The only surviving relatives in America are Mrs. McGrath and his daughter, Margaret.

Deceased delighted to be known as the "Irish-American." He had many friends among the commercial men who travel this shore and many of them would not think of leaving Harrisville without first calling on the "Irish American" to exchange jokes, though they were invariably worsted in any trial of wit with "Pat." He was always ready for a joke and was ever ready with a reply. His fund of Irish wit never failed him.

The funeral services were held on Saturday from the Catholic church, of which faith deceased was a devout believer. The G. A. R. veterans of Wyrum Hoyt Post, of which Mr. McGrath was a member, attended the funeral in a body and followed the remains of their departed comrade to their last resting place.

Alcona County Review, March 2, 1899

For the many kindnesses extended to us in our recent bereavement, by our kind and generous friends, we wish to express our sincere obligation and gratitude.

Mrs. P. McGrath and Daughter.

Alcona County Review, March 9, 1899

Resolution of Condolences.

At the regular meeting of Hoyt Post No. 6, Mich. G. A. R., held at Harrisville on March 10, 1899, the following resolutions were passed:

Whereas, Almighty God has seen fit to remove from our ranks our comrades and neighbors Patrick McGrath and Ephriam Waldron, by death;

Resolved, That this Post tender our heartfelt sympathy to the families of the departed comrades, and

Resolved that our post colors and charter be draped in mourning for 30 days.

H. C. Kibbee,
Commander.

Alcona County Review, March 16, 1899

Memorial Day Remembered.

One by one the ranks of the veterans are thinning. The addition since last memorial Day of three graves to the list of those interred in local cemeteries was a present reminder of this fact. They were those of Patrick McGrath, Francis La Chapelle and Epriam Waldron.

Alcona County Review, June 1, 1899

STATE OF MICHIGAN

The Probate Court for the County of Alcona

At a session of said court, held at the probate office, in the City of Harrisville, in said county, on the 13th day of April A. D. 1938.

Present: Hon. George Freer, Judge of Probate.

In the Matter of the Estate of Patrick McGrath, Deceased.

Sam C. Yockey having filed in said court his petition praying that said court adjudicate and determine who were at the time of his death the legal heirs of said deceased and entitled to inherit the real estate of which said deceased died seized,

It is ordered, that the 29th day of April A. D. 1938, at ten o'clock in the forenoon, at said probate office, be and is hereby appointed for hearing said petition;

It is further ordered, that public notice thereof be given by publication of a copy of this order, for three successive weeks previous to said day of hearing, in the Alcona County Review, a newspaper printed and circulated in said county.

GEORGE FREER,
Judge of Probate.

Alcona County Review, April 14, 1938
Cemetery: St. Anne's, Alcona Co.

McGregor, {Child}

CALEDONIA.

Mr. and Mrs. Gregor McGregor mourn the loss of their four days old baby.

Alcona County Review, May 14, 1896
Cemetery:

McGregor, Russell Harwood

LOCAL JOTTINGS.

Peter McGregor, of Black River, buried an infant son last week. The child had been ill for a long time.

Alcona County Review, October 5, 1888

Haynes.

Mr. Peter McGregor has erected a tombstone over his child's grave, one of the most artistic in the cemetery.

Alcona County Review, October 13, 1892
Cemetery: Mt. Joy, Alcona Co.

McGuire, Charles

The Local News.

Chas. McGuire died at Mud Lake Monday evening of a complication of diseases. He is an elder brother of John McGuire, formerly of Alcona, and his remains have been shipped to his former home in Ohio for interment. A wife and grown up family survive him. He had conducted a hotel at Mud Lake for several years, but had discontinued that business recently and was about ready to go back to Ohio when overtaken by his fatal illness.

Alcona County Review, October 1, 1891
Cemetery:

McGuire, Isabella [McLaughlin]

HORRIBLE FATALITY.

Just as we go to press news comes of terrible accident this (Thursday) morning by which Mrs. John McGuire was run over and killed by a special train while she was walking on the railroad track between Handy station and Mikado. The deceased was the much esteemed wife of John McGuire, of Alcona. Particulars have not been received.

Alcona County Review, April 5, 1889

MRS. McGUIRE'S DEATH.

How the Sad Accident Happened.

An immense concourse of people assembled last Sunday at Au Sable to witness the last rites over Mrs. John McGuire and pay their respects to the bereaved family and relatives. A special train left Black River Sunday morning conveying the remains and the relatives and friends whose numbers were augmented at West Harrisville, Mikado and other stations by many others.

As near as can be learned the particulars of the sad accident are as follows: Mrs. McGuire, with her infant child had been visiting at the residence of E. P. Gallagher, of Oscoda, and Wednesday evening started for home stopping over night at her father's home in Handy. In the morning accompanied by her father and brother she started to walk on the track to Mikado a few miles north for the purpose of catching the freight and thus returning home by way of Black River. Just before they reached Mikado they saw a train coming behind them, but they supposed it was the freight, and that it would slack up before it reached them as it always does at that place.

The two men stepped from the track but Mrs. McGuire continued walking on the ties until she was struck by the engine. Her brother seeing her danger grasped her arm with the intention of pulling her to one side, and they were both knocked into the ditch alongside the track. Mrs. McGuire was instantly killed, her back and both legs being broken. Young McLaughlin's arm was bruised but he was not otherwise injured. The only reasonable explanation that can be given why Mrs. McGuire did not leave the tack was that she must have been unaware of the rapidity with which the train was approaching, and as there was a ditch along side the track she endeavored to reach the crossing before leaving the track. The train was a special from Tawas bound for the Mud Lake branch, having on board Superintendent Mike Eastman and family, his brother and wife, from Iowa, W. M. Locke and wife and Road Master James Bolm. No blame attaches to the railroad company.

Mrs. McGuire was the second daughter of postmaster Frank McLaughlin, of Handy. She was married in 1877 to John McGuire, proprietor of the Union Hotel at Alcona. Six children are the fruit of this union, the oldest being a boy of eleven the youngest an infant. It is a cruel blow to the bereaved husband and family; they have the sympathy of the entire community. Mr. McGuire had but just concluded to remove his family to Ohio where he owns a fine farm in Madison county. The sad death of his wife breaks up the bright dreams of future happiness.

Alcona County Review, April 12, 1889
Cemetery:

McIntyre, William T.

EVENTS OF ONE WEEK.

Wm. McIntyre, a son of Mrs. D. McIntyre, an unmarried man 26 years of age, died Sunday morning at the residence of his brother-in-law, Mr. Burt, of Black River. The young man was taken ill in the woods where he was working at Pritchard's camp. He came down to Black River last Wednesday morning to get medical aid and attendance. The first of his indisposition was due as he supposed to aggravated ulcerated teeth. This developed into quinsy, from which he

died Sunday morning. The remains were brought to Harrisville Tuesday morning for interment in the cemetery west of Harrisville. The funeral services were held in the M. E. church, the Rev. W. J. Bailey officiating.

Alcona County Review, January 19, 1893

Mrs. D. McIntyre and family desire to return thanks to all those who rendered timely assistance during the last sickness and death of their beloved son and brother, William McIntyre.

Alcona County Review, January 19, 1893

PERSONAL MENTION.

A. D. McIntyre, of Munising, a former Harrisville boy, was called here last week by the untimely death of his brother.

Alcona County Review, January 26, 1893
Cemetery: West Lawn, Alcona Co.

McKay, Duncan

COUNTY REVIEWINGS.

We have just learned of the death of the grandfather of the Messrs. Duggan Brothers on their mother's side, who had reached the advanced age of over 90 years. We have not learned his name or the circumstances of his death.

Alcona County Review, January 28, 1881
Cemetery: Mt. Joy, Alcona Co.

McKenzie, Anna Belle

ANNA BELLE McKENZIE

A well-known and estimable young lady of Gustin township, died suddenly at her late home at Gustin station, Friday morning, August 20th, after a very brief illness. She was taken with convulsions Thursday morning. Drs. Norton of Killmaster and Wiley of Harrisville were summoned, but the disease was quick in its action and their united skill was of no avail.

Deceased had just completed a term of school at Mud Lake, where she gave perfect satisfaction. She was 21 years of age and was a native of Pennsylvania. The funeral took place Saturday, Rev. F. S. Ford officiating. Interment at South Harrisville.

Alcona County Review, August 26, 1897

I hereby tender my heartfelt thanks to one and all of my neighbors whose aid and sympathy were so acceptable in the sickness, death and burial of my daughter.
A. S. McKenzie.

Alcona County Review, August 26, 1897

Cemetery: Springport, Alcona Co.

McKenzie, Donald

PERSONAL POINTS.

Capt. Henderson goes to Alpena tomorrow to attend the funeral of his friend, Capt. McKenzie, who is to be buried there with Masonic honors.

Alcona County Review, July 7, 1898
Cemetery: Evergreen, Alpena Co.

McKenzie, Catherine [Stewart]

Gustin Grist.

Died, June 12th, 1896, Catherine, wife of A. S. McKenzie.

Deceased was born in Glengarry, Carry, Canada, May 14th, 1845. She was married in Canada in 1868, after which she went to Pennsylvania where she remained until about 12 years ago, when the family removed to Alcona county where they have since resided. She was the mother of 7 children of whom 5 are living, 1 son and 4 daughters.

Funeral services were held at the Catholic church in Harrisville. The remains were interred in the Catholic cemetery. Deceased was a charter member of Van Ettan Hive L. O. T. M. No. 407 of West Greenbush. She was a kind mother, a faithful wife and was loved by all who knew her. The husband and children have the sympathy of all in this vicinity.

Alcona County Review, June 18, 1896

PERSONAL MENTION.

The funeral services at the Catholic church Monday morning were over the remains of Mrs. McKenzie, whose death is reported by our Gustin correspondent.

Alcona County Review, June 18, 1896
Cemetery: St. Anne's, Alcona Co.

McKenzie, Duke

LOCAL JOTTINGS.

Duke McKenzie, book-keeper at Dunlap's camp on Potts' railroad, was struck on the head by a log that was being loaded on a car, a few days since, and almost instantly killed. He was 71 years old, and resided in St. Clair county.

Alcona County Review, December 3, 1886
Cemetery: Pinecrest, Iosco Co.

McKillop, Duncan

LOCAL JOTTINGS.

Duncan McKillop, of Alcona, one of the pioneer residents of the Huron shore, died last week at his late residence in Alcona at a ripe old age. He is remembered by old residents as one of the early residents who derived a profitable business from the fishing interests at South Pointe.

Alcona County Review, January 13, 1888
Cemetery: Mt. Joy, Alcona Co.

McKinnon, Adam

Died—At Ashtabula, Ohio, Oct. 16, Adam McKinnon, beloved son of James and Margaret McKinnon, age 16 years 8 months.

A precious one from us has gone,
A voice we loved is stilled.
A place is vacant in our home,
Which never can be filled.

God in his wisdom has recalled
The boon his love had given;
And though the body slumbers here
The soul is safe in heaven.

[Note: Poem added Nov. 12, 1896]

Alcona County Review, November 5, 1896

We wish to thank the many kind friends and neighbors who so kindly assisted us in our sore bereavement over the loss of our beloved son, Adam.

      Mrs. and Mrs. Jas. McKinnon.
             Caledonia.

Alcona County Review, November 5, 1896
Cemetery: Pleasant View, Alcona Co.

McKinnon, Angus

PINE RIVER'S SECOND VICTIM.

A Twelve Year Old Boy Drowned at Killmaster Dam.

Killmaster, June 29.—Angus McKinnon, the twelve year old son of J. D. McKinnon of this place, was drowned yesterday in the pool below the dam.

The boy had gone fishing about ten o'clock in the morning. After fishing he went in bathing. The two little Dellar boys were with him. At this time the boys both say Angus was going to dress when he fell from a boom and went to the bottom at once and never came up again. After waiting some time to see if he would come to the surface, the boys ran for help. After an hour's search the body was found and was removed to the home of his parents.

On petition an inquest was held at which the testimony of Willie Dellar was taken as to the main facts in the case. Robt. Holcomb, Chas. Glover, Thos. Nolan, L. M. Stockton and F. A. Becker, who were present and assisted in the recovery of the body, were also sworn. Mr. Becker secured the body with a pikepole. The jury's verdict was in accordance with the facts, viz: accidentally drowned.

The funeral was held Tuesday, the Rev. Ford officiating.

This is the second drowning at Killmaster in about the same place, the first having occurred about 16 years ago.

Alcona County Review, July 1, 1897

Mr. and Mrs. J. D. McKinnon desire to express their heartfelt thanks to the kind friends who rendered such acceptable assistance in the hour of their need and sorrow.

Alcona County Review, July 8, 1897
Cemetery:

McKinnon, Sarah

CALEDONIA.

Sarah, the child of John McKinnon, who was burned some time ago, died from the affect Jan. 4, and was interred in the Caledonia cemetery the following day. Rev. McBride conducted the service.

Alcona County Review, January 21, 1897
Cemetery: Pleasant View, Alcona Co.

McLachlan, {Child}

EVENTS OF ONE WEEK.

A child of Peter McLachlan, scaler at Pritchard's camp, was buried in the Catholic cemetery Tuesday. Death resulted from fits to which the child was subject.

Alcona County Review, August 3, 1893

EVENTS OF ONE WEEK.

In the issue of August 3d the Review stated that the child of Peter McLachlan had died of fits "to which it was subject." Dr. Parr writes that the parents desire a correction, inasmuch as the child died of cholera infantum and had never been ill before, much less subject to fits.

Alcona County Review, August 17, 1893
Cemetery: St. Anne's, Alcona Co.

McLain, Anna M.

LOCAL JOTTINGS.

Anna M. McLain, a niece of Hon. J. B. Tuttle, died at East Tawas last Friday night of diphtheria.

Alcona County Review, August 20, 1886
Cemetery:

McLaren, Daniel
HOME REVIEWINGS.

Daniel McLaren of Au Sable was fatally injured Tuesday forenoon by a piece of timber falling upon him from a tramway at Gram's mill. He lived but a few hours. He was a member of the Masonic order and also Royal Templars at Au Sable. He leaves a wife.

Alcona County Review, September 16, 1881
UP AND DOWN THE SHORE.

Speaking of the death and burial of Daniel McLaren, who was killed at Au Sable last week, by a piece of timber falling upon him from John Gram's tram, the News among other things remarks as follows:

"Mr. McLaren leaves a widow who is inconsolable at her sudden and terrible loss, and she is entitled to and has the deepest sympathy of a large circle of mourning friends. The funeral took place Thursday afternoon, in charge of the Royal Templars and Masonic fraternity, he being an honored member of both societies.

We believe the Tyler of the grand lodge has admitted him, and that clothed in a lambskin our brother is squaring his work before the Great Worshipful Master in the East."

Alcona County Review, September 23, 1881
Along the Shore.

Mrs. D. McLaren of Au Sable has received a check for $2,000 from the Royal Templars, the amount due from that association as insurance upon the life of her husband now deceased.

Alcona County Review, October 21, 1881
Cemetery: Pinecrest, Iosco Co.

McLauchlan, Mrs.
We announce the death of Mrs. McLauchlan, who died on the morning of Feb. 24th at Frederick, Mich. Mrs. McLauchlan was 58 years of age and leaves a husband and one son.

Alcona County Review, February 28, 1895
Cemetery:

McLean, Annie [McCrea]
BAD SCORCH AT ALPENA.

----
100 Homes Burned—Three Lives Lost.
A destructive conflagration occurred at Alpena Wednesday afternoon during a gale. A strip three blocks wide was burned on the north side through to the river. Over one hundred houses were burned, also the light-house, the roundhouse of the D. B. C. & A. R. R. and a large amount of lumber at Gilchrist's mill. Three persons were frightfully burned; one has since died and the condition of the others considered hopeless. 1,000 people are homeless.

Alcona County Review, July 13, 1888
ALPENA'S BIG FIRE.

THIRTEEN BLOCKS SWEPT AWAY

And $300,000 Worth of Property Destroyed.
July 12th, 1872, the business portion of the city of Alpena was swept by fire and a loss of $75,000 was incurred. On the sixteenth anniversary of that event, lacking one day, occurred the disastrous fire of last week which swept away all that was combustible in the course of the fire between Morse's mill and the river. Thirteen blocks were completely burned over, and a total loss, as near as can be estimated, of $300,000 was suffered. The fire started in the sawdust pile at Morse's mill and under the influence of a northeast gale it spread like wild fire throughout the frame buildings which a long continued drought had rendered as dry as a tinder-box. It was a populous district, being the home of a large part of the laboring population of Alpena. So rapidly did the fire spread that the inhabitants had barely time to escape, and all efforts to save household goods were futile, so that the three hundred families whose homes were destroyed, were left absolutely destitute. Mayor Klock and the more fortunate citizens of Alpena did gallant service in caring for the homeless people, and steps were at once taken to provide shelter and relieve their temporal wants. At a citizens' meeting held the next day, $5,222 was subscribed, Geo. L. Maltz heading the list with $1,000.

There was one fatality, that of Mrs. Annie McLean, of Buffalo, a widowed lady who was visiting her sister, Mrs. Jno. Kestau. She was so badly burned that she died at midnight at the hospital.

Alcona County Review, July 20, 1888
Cemetery: Evergreen, Alpena Co.

McLennan, Caroline Elizabeth [Kenyon]
Local Sayings and Doings.

We regret to learn that Mrs. C. E. McLennan is dangerously ill at her residence.

Alcona County Review, August 11, 1882
HOME NEWS JOTTINGS.

Died: In Harrisville, Wednesday morning, Nov. 1st, after a lingering sickness, Mrs. Caroline McLennan, favorably known as the landlady of the popular McLennan House in this village. A fuller obituary notice will appear next week.

Alcona County Review, November 3, 1882
Memorial.
Last week it was our painful task to chronicle the death of another of our honored and greatly lamented pioneers of this county, Mrs. Caroline E. McLennan. She was born in Hillsdale, Columbia county, N. Y. Her maiden name was Caroline Elizabeth Kenyon. In the year 1846 she came with M. Holden to the then unorganized county of Alcona, being only about five years of age. At the age of twenty she was married to Wm. Chase, and both took up their residence in the state of Illinois. After a short stay there they returned again to Michigan and after careful prospecting applied themselves to the arduous task of making an opening in the dense forest of Alcona county as their future home. Here she (then Mrs. Chase) passed through all the hardships and privations incident to pioneer life, and right nobly did she act her part for to her good judgment, unceasing labors, rigid economy and indomitable will was largely due the transformation of their wilderness farm to broad acres of hay and grain and corn, as well as the many improvements in and outside of their home.

Some years after the death of Mr. Chase she was united in marriage to James McLennan, with whom she passed through a trying experience.

Among the tasks of toil was the drudgery and corresponding care attendant on a woman's part in a lumber camp life. Mr. M. being engaged in this business more or less for several years, yet notwithstanding the almost insuperable tasks of labor she so faithfully performed, she made these by no means an excuse for neglecting mental improvement. On the contrary she seized and utilized fragments of time which many would have wasted, and succeeded in storing her mind with gleanings from various fields of knowledge, and kept so abreast of the times as to always converse intelligently on the current topics of the day. In order to avail herself of better social, as well as intellectual and moral advantages, she exchanged the old homestead for property in the village of Harrisville, where she at once opened her house to boarders and the traveling public, and although the building she occupied was not intended for the latter purpose, still her amiable spirit, well spread tables, reasonable prices, together with the neat, home-like appearance of all the surroundings, made the McLennan House in a few months the favored stopping place of the better class of the traveling public.

Among Mrs. McLennan's early and intimate friends were persons holding antagonistic views to the Bible, who did not fail to instill into her mind their cherished scepticism. In this relation she read and heard almost every phase of objection to the religion of the Lord Jesus. But amid all the cavellings that met her ear none of them satisfied her convictions permanently, that she was not personally responsible to God for innumerable violations of his sinless law. After months and even years of restless tossing on the cold, dark, portless sea of doubt, she was glad to seek a refuge at last in the clear and quiet waters of the Christian's haven, where the circling "Rock of Eternal Ages" turns every angry wave, and a sense of security possesses the tempest tossed spirit which only those know who enter this heaven-appointed haven.

A short time after, she united with the M. E. church and was a faithful worker in various departments of that organization. Although her sickness was lingering and severe, yet she was patient and resigned to the will of her heavenly father. On the morning of November 1st, 1882, she calmly passed away, being in the fifty-second year of her age. Her funeral took place from the Methodist church the following Friday and was attended by a large concourse of people who had learned from many years' acquaintance to prize Caroline E. McLennan as one of the best of neighbors, a friend of the friendless, and one whose memory is embalmed in many grateful hearts.

Alcona County Review, November 10, 1882
Cemetery: Springport, Alcona Co.

McLeod, {Boy}

LOCAL JOTTINGS.

Conductor McLeod, of railroad, buried a son at Tawas last week.

Alcona County Review, May251, 1888
Cemetery:

McLeod, Catherine [Graham]

LOCAL JOTTINGS.

Mrs. John McLoud died very suddenly at her late home seven miles west of Harrisville, on Monday. She leaves a husband and five small children.

Alcona County Review, December 31, 1886
Cemetery: West Lawn, Alcona Co.

McLeod, Mary [Beaton]

LOCAL PICK UPS.

Mrs. McLeod, aged 65, who has been an invalid for many months, died last evening at the residence of Mrs. Jas. McGrady. Funeral services tomorrow at the M. E. church.

Alcona County Review, December 22, 1898

LOCAL PICK UPS.

We wish to thank the kind neighbors and friends who so willingly and patiently assisted us through the long illness and death of our beloved sister and aunt.

Mrs. McGrady and Family.

Alcona County Review, December 29, 1898
Cemetery: West Lawn, Alcona Co.

McLeod, Seymour D.

Among Our Exchanges.

From the Lakeside Monitor.

Three Au Sable boys named Jerry Murphy, Seymour McLeod and Roeul Valle, were drowned Tuesday afternoon while in swimming on the shore below Penoyar Bros.' docks. The Valle boy got into deep water and the other two were drowned in trying to save him. The bodies were not recovered until they had been in the water over an hour.

The boys were all between 11 and 12 years of age. Jerry Murphy was the son of Eugene Murphy and Seymour McLeod a son of John McLeod.

Alcona County Review, July 21, 1892

The Local News

The remains of a boy named McLeod were buried last week Thursday in the cemetery west of Harrisville, a large procession having come from Au Sable. The lad was one of a number of boys who went in bathing two days previous at Au Sable. One of the lads got beyond his depth and in attempting his rescue three boys were drowned.

Alcona County Review, July 21, 1892
Cemetery: West Lawn, Alcona Co.

McMaster, Robert

THE LOCAL NEWS.

Robt. McMaster aged 25 suicided at Alpena last week by shooting himself.

Alcona County Review, February 21, 1890
Cemetery: Evergreen, Alpena Co.

McMillan, Catherine [McLaren]

MIKADO.

Mrs. D. B. McMillan died at her home, Monday night April 26th, 1897. She had been a long and patient sufferer with that dreaded disease, consumption.

Alcona County Review, April 29, 1897

PERSONAL.

Mrs. D. McMullen died this week at their home in Greenbush township. The deceased was a sufferer from that dread disease, consumption. She leaves a husband and a large family of children to mourn her death.

The funeral services were conducted by Rev. Tompkins at the Greenbush school house yesterday, the interment taking place at the South Harrisville cemetery.

Alcona County Review, April 29, 1897
Cemetery: Springport, Alcona Co.

McMillan, Isabella [Sutherland]

GREENBUSH.

The funeral services of the late Mrs. McMillan were held here Saturday at 10 o'clock.

Alcona County Review, May 4, 1899
Cemetery: Springport, Alcona Co.

McNally, {Boy}

Black River Sparks.

Died at Black River Friday, May 15th, the infant son of Mr. and Mrs. Stanley McNally. The funeral on Sunday, May 17th, at St. Gabriel's church. The little casket was borne by four little boys. The floral offerings were very beautiful, especially a pillow which was presented by the friends of the parents. The remains were interred in the R. C. cemetery at Harrisville. The sympathy of the entire community is extended to the bereaved mother and father.

Alcona County Review, May 21, 1896

PERSONAL MENTION.

The remains of an infant child of Stanley McNally were brought to Harrisville Sunday from Black River for burial.

Alcona County Review, May 21, 1896

Black River Sparks.

Mrs. Stanley McNally thanks her many friends who so kindly assisted her in her recent bereavement, the loss of her infant son.

Alcona County Review, June 4, 1896
Cemetery: St. Anne's, Alcona Co.

McNally, Frederick Henry

Local Sayings and Doings.

Died, at Fort Collins, Colorado, in May last, Fred. H., youngest son of Nicholas McNally, late of Alcona county.

Alcona County Review, June 9, 1882
Cemetery: Bingham Hill, Larimer Co., CO

McNally, {Girl}

PURELY PERSONAL.

Mr. and Mrs. S. J. McNally mourn the death of an infant daughter, born Monday, Oct. 1st.

Alcona County Review, October 5, 1888
Cemetery: Probably St. Anne's, Alcona Co.

McNally, Margaret [McGillis]

PURELY PERSONAL.

Mrs. S. J. McNally has been seriously ill for the past two weeks.

Alcona County Review, October 12, 1888

OBITUARY.

Mrs. S. J. McNally, wife of County Treasurer McNally, died Saturday morning Oct. 13th at 10 o'clock a. m. at her late residence in this village, aged 30 years. The deceased was a daughter of Angus McGillis, a former resident and well known lumberman of Alcona county. She was married to S. J. McNally at West Bay City on the 26th of June, 1876, by the Rev. Fr. Canter. Two daughters aged 9 years and 3 years respectively are left as the fruit of this union. Her death following closely after that of their infant daughter born Oct. 1st, deepens the sorrow of the afflicted family and the sympathy of the entire community is extended to them in this sad bereavement and irreparable loss. The funeral services were held Tuesday from the Catholic church. That edifice was filled to over flowing with friends of the family gathered from all parts of the county and from Au Sable, Alpena and other cities to pay homage to the virtues of the deceased and show their respect for the living. The choir service was rendered by the Au Sable choir. The church was appropriately draped.

Alcona County Review, October 19, 1888

LOCAL JOTTINGS.

The Board of Supervisors met Tuesday morning and adjourned until 2 o'clock p. m. out of respect to County Treasurer McNally.

The Board of Supervisors passed appropriate resolutions of respect and sympathy for County Treasurer McNally in the death of his wife.

Alcona County Review, October 19, 1888

PURELY PERSONAL.

Ranald McGillis and wife, of Alpena, uncle and aunt, Mrs. Angus McGillis, of Hurley, Wis., mother, and Miss Mary McGillis, of late West Bay City, a sister of the Mrs. S. J. McNally were present at the funeral services Tuesday, as were also Angus McDonald and numerous other friends of the family from Alpena and Au Sable.

Alcona County Review, October 19, 1888

SUPERVISOR'S ANNUAL REPORT.

The following resolution was unanimously adopted:

Whereas, An inscrutable Providence has removed from our midst the much esteemed wife of our respected brother officer, Simon J. McNally, treasurer of this county, and in order to manifest our respect to the memory of the deceased, and also our sincere sympathy for our brother officer in his bereavement, therefore,

Resolved, That we do now adjourn until 2 o'clock p. m. for the purpose of attending the funeral.

Alcona County Review, November 9, 1888

PURELY PERSONAL.

The Misses Alice and Mary McGillis, who have been stopping with their brother-in-law, County Treas. McNally, since the death of the latter's wife, have returned to their home in Hurley, Wis. Mr. McNally's two little daughters accompanied them and will remain with their grandparents for an indefinite time.

Alcona County Review, June 14, 1889
Cemetery: St. Anne's, Alcona Co.

McNally, Maria [Ward]

PERSONAL PICKUPS.

Died.—Maria, wife of Geo. McNally, died in this village on Friday last, between the hours of five and six o'clock p. m., aged 22 years, 11 months and 24 days. The funeral services were held in the M. E. church on Sunday, at 11 o'clock a. m., Rev. T. B. Leith preaching the sermon from 1st Cor. chap. 15—53 to 57 v. The house was crowded, many going away. The remains were interred in the Harrisville cemetery. She leaves a husband and three small children, the eldest being but little more than three years of age.

Alcona County Review, July 9, 1886
Cemetery: West Lawn, Alcona Co.

McNally, Norman

Alcona Atoms.

Mr. and Mrs. S. J. McNalley have been called upon to mourn the death of their only child, a nice boy-baby. His death occurred on the 22d ult.

Alcona County Review, August 6, 1880
Cemetery: St. Anne's, Alcona Co.

McNally, Oscar

Local Jottings.

An infant child of Mr. McNally, of Black River, brother of Geo. McNally, died Monday morning of measles.

Alcona County Review, August 24, 1888
Cemetery: West Lawn, Alcona Co.

McNaughton, Mrs. Elizabeth

Greenbush.

A sister of Mrs. McMullen, living 2 miles west of here, died on Wednesday last of consumption. We did not learn the lady's name nor the particulars of her death. The remains were interred in the South Harrisville cemetery on Friday.

Alcona County Review, March 8, 1894
Cemetery: Springport, Alcona Co.

McNeil, Donald

AT DEATH'S DOOR.

Donald McNeil is very low from a stroke of paralysis. He is 79 years of age and it is feared he cannot survive the shock very long.

Mrs. Holmes Witter and husband of McKinley and Mrs. Sara Wolliver of Alpena were notified of the low condition of their father and they hastened to his bed-side to render him assistance in an affectionate manner. All of his children are in the township at present, viz: Mesdames A. Yuill, John McDonald, S. Woliver, H. Witter, D. Mulholland, and Miss Emma McNeil and three sons, Archie, Alex and Donald Jr.

Alcona County Review, July 1, 1897

DONALD MCNEIL.

This aged and respected citizen passed away at his late home in Haynes township at 5:35 Tuesday morning. Deceased had been ill about six weeks; the immediate cause of death was paralysis. He was a patient sufferer and was ready to go, and the end came peacefully in the presence of the surviving members of the family, comprising his wife and nine children.

Mr. McNeil was of the sturdy Scotch race; he was born in Loch Gilphead, Argyleshire, Scotland, July 15, 1818, and was therefore 79 years of age. He removed to Canada in 1842, where six years later he married Emily Baker. Their union was blessed with ten children, all but one of whom are living. The family moved to Alcona county in 1870, and settled in Haynes township.

The surviving children are Mrs. D. Mulholland, Mrs. Mary McDonald, Mrs. Frances Yuill, Mrs. Sarah Witter, Mrs. Solon Woolever, Miss Emma McNeil, Archie, Alexander, and Donald, Jr.

The interment will take place Friday afternoon at 2 o'clock in the Haynes cemetery. The service will be held in the Presbyterian church, of which deceased has been an elder for many years. Rev. Cram of Black River will conduct the services. Undertaker Mayo of Harrisville will direct the funeral.

Alcona County Review, July 29, 1897

Order for Probate of Will.
STATE OF MICHIGAN, County of Alcona.

At a session of the Probate Court for said county, held at the Probate office, in the village of Harrisville, on the 9th day of August in the year one thousand eight hundred and ninety-seven.

Present, Hon. W. H. Gilpin, Judge of Probate.

In the matter of the estate of Donald McNeil.

On reading and filing the petition, duly verified of Emma McNeil, praying that a certain instrument now on file in this court, purporting to be the last will and testament of said deceased, may be admitted to probate, and that Emma McNeil be appointed executrix of said last will and testament.

Thereupon it is ordered, that Saturday, the 4th day of September next, at ten o'clock in the forenoon, be assigned for the hearing of said petition, and that the heirs at law of said deceased, and all other persons interested in said estate, are required to appear at a session of said court, then to be holden at the Probate office, in the village of Harrisville, and show cause, if any there be, why the prayer of the petitioner should not be granted: and it is further ordered that the petitioner give notice to the heirs at law and all other persons interested in said estate, of the pendency of said petition, and the hearing thereof, by causing a copy of this order to be published in the "Alcona County Review," a newspaper printed and circulated in said county, three successive weeks previous to said day of hearing.

W. H. Gilpin,
Judge of Probate.

Alcona County Review, August 12, 1897
Cemetery: Mt. Joy, Alcona Co.

McNeil, Johnny

Johnny McNeil found Dead at Alcona.

A telegram to a coroner was received at this place from Alcona, Wednesday evening announcing that the dead body of a boy had been found near that place, but stating no particulars. Later advices received announce that the boy's name was John McNeil, and that he was found in the woods with a bullet wound in the breast, evidently caused by the accidental discharge of his weapon, which was found pointing towards the young man, the lock being caught in some bushes.

Alcona County Review, December 24, 1886

LOCAL JOTTINGS.

Young McNeil, whose body was found at Alcona, last Wednesday, was buried Friday last. The coroner's jury returned a verdict in accordance with the facts, viz., that it was a case of accidental shooting.

Alcona County Review, December 31, 1886
Cemetery:

McNeil, Thomas William

OUR NEIGHBORS.

Thos. McNeil, aged 24, whose home was at Au Sable, was caught between two logs at Loud's camp last week and died after 15 hours of suffering.

Alcona County Review, June 6, 1895
Cemetery: Pinecrest, Iosco Co.

McNorton, Alexander

ALONG THE SHORE
Au Sable and Oscoda

Alexander McNorton, of Oscoda, was found dead in his bed a week ago Wednesday morning. Whisky was the cause of his death. Deceased was 35 years of age, and was employed as scaler in the O. S. & L. Co.'s mill.

Alcona County Review, July 23, 1880
Cemetery:

McPhee, Duncan

COUNTY JOTTINGS.

Duncan McFee, a young man in the employ of D. B. Mudgett, at Greenbush, died of typhoid fever the fore part of the week. He was taken to Canada for burial.

Alcona County Review, September 6, 1878
Cemetery:

McPherson, Mrs.

ALCONA ATOMS.

(Received too late for last week's issue.)

Mrs. McPherson died on the evening of the 9th inst., aged about

70 years. She was taken with a paralytic stroke on the previous Sunday. She was conscious to the last but could not speak.

Alcona County Review, June 25, 1886
Cemetery:

McQuaig, Andrew

KILLED ON THE RAILROAD.

Conductor McQuaig Run Over by His Train and Killed.

Monday afternoon Andrew McQuaig, a conductor on the log train on the Lake railroad drawn by Engine No. 2, was backing a train of light cars up a skidway on Bonny's branch, when he was precipitated under the wheels. Four cars passed over him, mangling him terribly. He lived half an hour after the tragedy. The dead man lived in Alpena where he leaves a wife and two children.

Alcona County Review, June 15, 1893

Resolutions of Respect To the memory of Brother Andrew McQuaig: Hall of Black River Lodge No. 385 I.O.O.F.

Whereas: It has pleased Him who is too wise to err and too just to be unkind, to remove from the associations of earth to that undiscovered country from which no traveler returns, our beloved Brother Andrew McQuaig, therefore be it

Resolved, That in the death of Brother McQuaig this Lodge has lost an earnest, faithful and worthy member, his family a loving and devoted husband and father, and the community an honest, upright and exemplary citizen.

Resolved, That we as Odd Fellows tender to his sorely bereaved wife and fatherless children, our heart felt sympathy, ever commending them to Him who hath said "My grace is sufficient for thee."

Resolved; As a further token of respect we will cause our hall to be draped in mourning for thirty days.

Resolved: That a copy of these resolutions be spread upon our records, a page of the same being set apart for the purpose and dedicated to the memory of our departed brother. Also that a copy be furnished the family and that they be published in the Alcona County Review and Alpena Argus.

William Flaws,
S. E. McNeil,   Com'tee.

P. C. McGregor.

Adopted at a regular meeting of the Black River Lodge, No. 385 I.O.O.F.

Black River, Mich. June 17, 1893.

Alcona County Review, June 22, 1893

EVENTS OF ONE WEEK.

An excursion will be given on the railroad Sunday from Alpena to Tawas. The proceeds of the excursion are for the benefit of the widow of Conductor McQuaig, who was killed on Bonney's branch June 12.

Alcona County Review, July 27, 1893

ADDITIONAL LOCAL.

A special excursion recently from Alpena to Tawas for the benefit of the widow of Conductor Andrew McQuaig recently killed on the rail road netted the neat sum of $300.

Alcona County Review, August 17, 1893
Cemetery: Evergreen, Alpena Co.

McQuaig, Mrs. Sarah

MIKADO.

March 16, 1897.

Mrs. McQuag died at her son's home last Friday, Mar. 12th, with la grippe. The deceased was 77 years old. The funeral services were held Sunday at Harrisville at the Catholic church.

Alcona County Review, March 18, 1897

EVENTS OF ONE WEEK.

Mrs. McDougall [McQuaig], an elderly lady of Mikado, was buried Sunday in the Catholic cemetery.

Alcona County Review, March 18, 1897
Cemetery: St. Anne's, Alcona Co.

McQuarrie, Malcolm

CALEDONIA.

Malcolm McQuarrie died last Friday evening at the home of his daughter, Mrs. J. McDonald. The old gentleman has been in failing health all winter but just took to his bed on Tuesday. The funeral was held Monday morning, Rev. Austin in attendance.

Alcona County Review, April 20, 1899
Cemetery: Pleasant View, Alcona Co.

McQueen, Georgenia

West Harrisville, Oct. 4.—At Killmaster September 10th union services were held by Rev. S. Boundy for Janean Perry, born at Little Current, Canada, Sept. 12, 1882, died June 19th, 1893, Alcona county, daughter of Ira and Mrs. Perry; and

---

Georgenia McQuean, born at Port Rowan, Canada, Oct. 15th, 1885, died July 2d, 1893, Alcona county, daughter of Mr. and Mrs. James McQuean, having both died of diphtheria.

Alcona County Review, October 5, 1893
Cemetery: Probably West Lawn, Alcona Co.

McQueen, Sarah A. [Perry]

LOCAL JOTTINGS.

Sarah A. McQueen, wife of James W. McQueen, (formerly publisher of Spirit of the Age, Port Rowan, Ont.) died at her home near Killmaster last week of inflammation of the brain. Deceased was 27 years old and leaves a husband and three small children to mourn their loss.

Alcona County Review, September 30, 1887
Cemetery: Probably West Lawn, Alcona Co.

McRae, Edith Madaline [Miller]

Mrs. Duncan McRae, Jr.

It is our sad duty today to record the untimely death of Mrs. Duncan McRae, Jr., formerly Edith Miller, which occurred at 5 o'clock last night, at her late home in Greenbush from childbirth. The child survived the mother's death but a short time. The funeral services will probably be held Saturday from the Harrisville M. E. church.

Alcona County Review, April 30, 1896

The remains of Mrs. Duncan McRae, Jr., nee Edith Miller, were placed at rest Saturday afternoon in the Miller family lot in the beautiful Springport cemetery. They were brought from the family residence at Greenbush to Harrisville and the funeral services were held in the M. E. church, where deceased sang for many years in the choir, and wherein she first declared her attachment to the faith of the Christian. The services were in charge of the Rev. F. S. Ford the spiritual advisor and counselor of deceased. The sermon was well calculated to impress the hearers with the great solemnity of the occasion and was a terrible reminder of the mutability and uncertainty of all things mortal. High tribute was paid to the many virtues of the deceased.

Edith Miller-McRae was born in Boston, March 8, 1871. She came to Harrisville with her parents at the age of 8, and had been a resident of the county almost continuously up to the time of her death. She was married in 1892 to Duncan McRae, Jr. of Greenbush, who survives to mourn his great loss. An infant, the only product of this union, occupied the same casket and rested naturally on its mother's arm. The sight was an affecting one. The floral emblems were profuse and covered the beautiful white casket. The arrangements were under the painstaking care of Chas. Mayo, funeral director.

Alcona County Review, May 7, 1896

PERSONAL MENTION.

Mrs. Spencer Showers of Alpena was in attendance at the funeral of the late Mrs. Duncan McRae, Jr.

Alcona County Review, May 7, 1896

We extend our sincere thanks to our friends for the many acts of kindness and consideration tendered to us during the last sickness and death of our beloved wife and daughter, Edith McRae-Miller.

Duncan McRae, Jr.
Mrs. Chas. Miller.
Greenbush, May 12, 1896.

Alcona County Review, May 14, 1896
Cemetery: Springport, Alcona Co.

McRae, Harold

Mrs. Duncan McRae, Jr.

It is our sad duty today to record the untimely death of Mrs. Duncan McRae, Jr., formerly Edith Miller, which occurred at 5 o'clock last night, at her late home in Greenbush from childbirth. The child survived the mother's death but a short time. The funeral services will probably be held Saturday from the Harrisville M. E. church.

Alcona County Review, April 30, 1896

Edith Miller-McRae was born in Boston, March 8, 1871. She came to Harrisville with her parents at the age of 8, and had been a resident of the county almost continuously up to the time of her death. She was married in 1892 to Duncan McRae, Jr. of Greenbush, who survives to mourn his great loss. An infant, the only product of this union, occupied the same casket and rested naturally on its mother's arm. The sight was an affecting one. The floral emblems were profuse and covered the beautiful white casket. The arrangements were under the painstaking care of Chas. Mayo, funeral director.

Alcona County Review, May 7, 1896
Cemetery: Springport, Alcona Co.

McRae, Isabella [McGougan]

LOCAL JOTTINGS.

Mrs. Duncan McCraye, of Greenbush, died at an early hour Monday morning of cold and inflammation.

Alcona County Review, March 4, 1887

OBITUARY.

Death's cold hand, on Monday morning Feb. 28th, was laid upon the beloved wife of Duncan McRae, of this village, leaving a disconsolate husband and three sons and five daughters to mourn their loss.

————

Mrs. Isabella McRae, daughter of Daniel McGuken, was born in Armagh, Ireland, April 3d, 1845. While she was but a child her parents removed to America. She became acquainted with Mr. McRae in Detroit, and they were there married May 11, 1864, Mr. McRae at that time working in a pail factory. Her father, a boiler maker by trade, resides now in Wyandotte, Mich. Some time after marriage they went to Alpena where Mr. McRae obtained a position as sawyer. From thence they removed to Au Sable, and after residing there some years came to Greenbush, where Mr. McRae has been filer in J. VanBuskirk's mills.

As a wife she was faithful, loving and true; as a parent, fond and indulgent; as a neighbor she was beloved by all, being ever ready to help at any hour those who were ill or needing attention. Her loss will be felt by each and every individual in this community.

Her remains were interred in the Harrisville cemetery, Wednesday, March 2d, when a large number of friends assembled to pay their last respects to the dead.

She's gone—she has left us weeping—
Her sweet face we shall never see more.
And calmly in the cemetery is sleeping--
She has crossed to the beautiful shore.

Alcona County Review, March 11, 1887
Cemetery: Springport, Alcona Co.

McRae, Mary

Died in Canada.

A Clachan, Ont., correspondent of the Glencoe Transcript, writes as follows concerning a young lady who was until a few years ago a resident of Harrisville township:

It is our sad duty this week to record the death of Miss Mary McRae, daughter of John McRae, of this place. Deceased was born in Harrisville, Alcona Co., Mich., removing to this place in 1885, where she grew up to young womanhood loved and admired by all. In school she was always noted for her bright intellect and quick conception. On writing at the high school entrance examination at Wardsville she succeeded in obtaining the highest number of marks in Middlesex county. Going to Dutton she attended the high school for one half day, when she was attacked by la grippe, from which she never recovered. After a lingering illness of 13 months she passed away in the prime of youth at the early age of 19. The remains were interred in the Purcell cemetery, and the large number that followed the remains to their last resting place testified to the esteem in which the departed was held.

Alcona County Review, March 26, 1891
Cemetery: Probably McLean, Elgin Co., ON

McSorley, Bennie

LOCAL JOTTINGS

Bennie McSorley, 13 year old son of Jno. McSorley, an Alpena county farmer, was fatally burned in his father's burning dwelling Sunday morning.

Alcona County Review, August 10, 1888
Cemetery:Probably Evergreen, Alpena Co.

McTamney, Charles

GREENBUSH GETINGS.

The majority of the children of this village are suffering from a severe cough. The Drs. are unable to decide whether it is "whooping cough" or "chin cough."

Drs. Manzer and Mitchell have been called to see Mrs. McTamney's youngest child, and one or both of the above has been called to attend Mrs. Duchermin's infant child.

Alcona County Review, December 11, 1885

GREENBUSH GETINGS.

With sorrow we record the deaths of those infants referred to last week as being so ill.

Alcona County Review, December 18, 1885

GREENBUSH GETINGS.

Died—On Wednesday evening of last week the infant daughter of Mrs. Duchimen, aged 3 months. On Tuesday morning of this week, Mrs.

McTamney's youngest child, aged 7 months.

Alcona County Review, December 18, 1885
Cemetery: St. Anne's, Alcona Co.

McVeagh, James

HOME REVIEWINGS.

The Review learns of the death of an unmarried man, Jas. McVeagh, in the employ of Jas. Beard & Co. at Alcona, which occurred on Wednesday.

Alcona County Review, October 7, 1881
Cemetery:

McVeigh, {Boy}

Haynes Happenings.

An infant child of Mr. and Mrs. Bruce McVeigh was interred in the cemetery Saturday. Cause of death, measles.

Alcona County Review, May 6, 1897
Cemetery: Mt. Joy, Alcona Co.

Medor, Mary V.

A little daughter of Peter Medor was taken suddenly ill with membraneous croup Thursday of last week and died after a few hours of suffering. The child was two years of age and was the pride and pet of the household. It is a sad blow to the bereaved parents.

Alcona County Review, April 6, 1893
Cemetery: St. Anne's, Alcona Co.

Meillure, Levi

CURRAN EVENTS.

An Au Sable man employed at Tong's camp was instantly killed on Friday from the falling of a limb which struck him on the head. He was taken to his home Saturday afternoon.

Alcona County Review, December 14, 1899
Cemetery: Au Sable Township, Iosco Co.

Merchant, Josiah Pease

Died, June 20th, 1894.

At his late home at Corralitos, Cal., Mr. J. P. Merchant, aged seventy-five years. He leaves a wife and four children and many other relatives and friends, to mourn his loss. His children are as follows: Mrs. C. C. Brigg of Harrisville, Mr. W. B. Merchant of Rolla, Mo., Mrs. J. K. Costello of Aurora, Mo. and Mrs. James Johnson, of Corralitos, Cal.

Deceased was the first minister of the gospel to Harrisville, coming here in 1861, when it was a wilderness. Eight years later he moved to Rolla, Mo., where he resided for several

years then moved to Corralitos, Cal., where he died.

His kind, good natured disposition won for him hosts of friends wherever he went. He was a firm, energetic Christian, his faith growing stronger as his body weakened.

"He rests from his labors and his works do follow him."

The deceased was sent here to open up this territory for the Methodist church. It was then practically a wilderness, settlers were few and scattering, mails were carried by dogs and Mr. Merchant used to accompany this primitive mail train on foot to Alpena and Tawas in the discharge of his ministerial duties. He homesteaded the Mudget or present poor farm. He helped to build the present Methodist church in the village and in other ways left the impress of his personality upon this county.

Alcona County Review, July 5, 1894
Cemetery: Pioneer, Santa Cruz Co., CA

Mercier, {Child}

EVENTS OF ONE WEEK.

Nelson Mercier of Mikado lost a child last week.

Alcona County Review, January 26, 1893
Cemetery: Probably Pinecrest, Iosco Co.

Mercier, Mrs. Harriett B. Barlow

Death of Mrs. Nelson Mercier.

Mikado, Dec. 28.
Mrs. Nelson Mercier passed quietly away at her home this morning at 6 o'clock. The deceased will be buried in the Oscoda cemetery Friday morning. Funeral services will be held at the residence of her son, Jas. Barlow of Oscoda.

Alcona County Review, December 29, 1898

MIKADO.

A memoir of Mrs. Nelson Mercier who died on Dec. 28, 1898 and was buried at Oscoda:

Harriett B. Mercier was born in Norwich Eng. 1821. At the age of 17 she married Edwin Barlow of Manchester, Eng. and six children were born to them. In Sept. 1848 they moved to America and settled at Flushing, Genesee county, Michigan, where three more children were born. In May '66 she moved to Au Sable and in '67 she married Nelson Mercier. They moved to their present home in '76. She was the first white woman settler in this township. In

her youth and middle life she was strong and healthy, but in her old age she was an invalid. She had taken to her bed two years before her death.

Four children and a husband are left to mourn her death. Jas. Barlow of Oscoda, Edwin Barlow of Hastings, Mich., N. C. and Belle Smith of Mikado. One son died in the civil war, and one lost an arm, and one was wounded through the stomach.

Mr. Mercier's constant care and devotion to his beloved wife during her long illness has told severely on his health. From a hale and hearty old gentleman he has been reduced to an almost invalid state.

Alcona County Review, February 2, 1899
Cemetery: Pinecrest, Iosco Co

Mercier, William

Fatal Accident at Black River.

Wm. Mercier of Black River, a brakeman on the Mud Lake branch of the D., B. C. & A. R. R., was instantly killed last Thursday about 20 miles from Black River. Mercier was braking on a long timber train, and in attempting to reach the engine from the cars, in some way fell between the tender and the first car. One leg was cut off, two arms broken, and a great gash cut in his head. Death came to his relief in a few minutes.

Mercier was a young man, unmarried, and lived in Black River.

Alcona County Review, September 1, 1892

Another Railroad Fatality.

The remains of Wm. Mercier were hardly buried ere another fatality has been added to the long list of those which have occurred on the logging railroads of Alcona county. Tuesday night as Conductor Joseph Grice was making up his train at McPhee's camp to run into Black River, he was thrown under the wheels and fatally injured. The remains were badly mutilated and death was almost instantaneous. Deceased leaves a wife and one child.

Alcona County Review, September 1, 1892

HISTORY OF ONE YEAR.

Chronological History of the Past Year, 1892.

August.

25. Wm. Mercer killed on a log train at Black River.

Alcona County Review, January 5, 1893

Cemetery: Probably St. Anne's, Alcona Co.

Merritt, {Male}

Curtis.

We are sorry to learn that John Bowser was called to the death-bed of his brother-in-law at Port Huron.

Alcona County Review, October 7, 1897
Cemetery:

Micho, Catherine [O'Neal]

West Harrisville.

Mrs. A. Micho is very ill and will go to St. Mary's Hospital, Detroit. Her many friends wish her a safe return and renewed health.

Alcona County Review, August 2, 1894

EVENTS OF ONE WEEK.

My wife, Catherine Micho, having left my home and protection without due cause or provocation, I hereby notify all persons interested that I will not pay any bills that may be contracted by her.

Alonzo Micho.

Alcona County Review, August 30, 1894

Mrs. A. Micho, who is advertised by her husband as having left his "home and protection," is very seriously ill and is with friends at West Harrisville. No hope of her recovery is offered by physicians.

Alcona County Review, September 6, 1894

West Harrisville.

West Harrisville, Dec. 12.--Mrs. Alonzo Micho died at the home of her daughter, Mrs. Isaac Rose, Tuesday morning after a long and tedious illness from tumorous cancer.

Alcona County Review, December 13, 1894

The funeral services for the late Mrs. Alonzo Micho were held this morning at the Catholic church, the Rev. Fr. Ducette officiating, assisted by the choir of the Au Sable Catholic church.

Alcona County Review, December 13, 1894

Whereas, The Angel of Death has for the second time entered our Hive and taken from our circle our beloved sister, Lady Kate Micho, a member of Dalton Hive No. 143 L. O. T. M.:

Therefore be it

Resolved, That while we humbly submit to the will of our Heavenly Father, we deeply mourn the loss of our departed sister.

Resolved, That our charter be draped for a period of 30 days, that a copy of these resolutions be sent the bereaved family, entered upon the records of our Hive, and published in the Alcona County Review.

West Harrisville, Dec. 11, 1894.

Annie Potts.
Effa D. Genge.
Hannah McMillan.
Committee.

Alcona County Review, December 13, 1894

West Harrisville

Mrs. Isaac Rose and relatives desire to express their gratitude toward their friends for kindness shown during the sickness of her mother and sympathy in their grief.

H. O. Ward.

Alcona County Review, December 20, 1894

The late Mrs. Kate Micho was a native of Canada and was born in 1837.

Her maiden name was O'Neal. At the age of 16 she was married to Edward La Chapelle. They resided in Cleveland, O., for a time and in 1865 came to Harrisville, where deceased resided continuously until her death. Mr. La Chapelle died in 1875 and the next year the subject of this sketch married Alonzo Micho. Six children, three sons and three daughters, survive her.

We have every reason to feel grateful for the many acts and words of kindness and sympathy that were tendered our dear mother, the late Mrs. Catherine Micho, during her long illness. Our especial thanks are due the Lady Maccabees for their kindness and assistance which we will ever hold in grateful remembrance.

Her Sorrowing Children.

Alcona County Review, December 20, 1894

West Harrisville.

The warrant for the end of the late Mrs. Kate Micho was received this morning. There was a great deal of delay because Mr. Micho refused to sign the warrant. Great credit should be given to the Great Hive officers for their promptness and skill in settling all such affairs. Credit should be given where credit is due.

Alcona County Review, March 14, 1895

State of Michigan, County of Alcona, ss.

At a session of the Probate Court for the County of Alcona, holden at the Probate office in the City of Harrisville, on Monday, the 22nd day of October, in the year one thousand nine hundred and six.

Present: Geo. W. Burt, Judge of Probate.

In the matter of the estate of Kate Micho, deceased.

On reading and filing the petition duly verified, of Lorenzo La Chapelle, praying among other things that a certain instrument now on file in this office purporting to be the last will of said deceased, be admitted to probate and that Lorenzo LaChapelle be appointed executor or some other suitable person.

Thereupon it is ordered, That Saturday, the 17 day of November next, at 10 o'clock in the forenoon at said Probate office, be assigned for the hearing of said petition.

And it is further ordered, That a copy of this order to be published in the Alcona County Review, a newspaper printed and circulated in said County of Alcona, for three successive weeks previous to said day of hearing.

GEO. W. BURT, Judge of Probate.

Alcona County Review, October 25, 1906
Cemetery: St. Anne's, Alcona Co.

Micho, Florence

Events of One Week.

Florence Micho was killed at Tawas last Saturday, while at work around the cars.

The remains were brought to West Harrisville and were buried Monday from the Catholic church in this village. Mr. Micho carried a $2,000 in the Maccabees and a large number of the Sir Knights attended the funeral.

Deceased leaves a widow and five small children. [The Review was promised an account of the accident etc. but for some reason it was not handed in. The above is all that could be learned of the sad affair.]

Alcona County Review, March 25, 1897

UNDER THE WHEELS.

From Iosco Co. Gazette.

A shocking fatality occurred on the D. & M. R. R. on Saturday afternoon last. The accommodation train from the Rose City division had arrived in Tawas City, and was switching some logs for the Union Cooperage Co., on the old Hale dock. The brakeman was Florance Micho of this city. He had got off the train to turn the switch, and fell in a swoon or faint in front of the loaded cars, and five of these passed over his body. He was horribly mangled, and killed instantly. The unfortunate man has been employed as brakeman on this train for some time, but he was subject to spells of this kind, and on several previous occasions, we understand, had barely escaped death; and realizing the hazardous position to one thus afflicted, he concluded to quit the work, and a day or two more would have terminated his labor in this capacity.

The remains were brought to the home in this city, where the wife and five children had learned of the awful calamity, and were frantic with grief.

There was no coroner's inquest; the fact of the case being too well authenticated to demand it.

The funeral service, a very short one, was conducted at the house, and on Wednesday the remains were taken to Harrisville for interment.

The deceased was a hard working and industrious man, a kind husband and indulgent father. He was a member of the K. O. T. M., in which he held a policy of insurance of $2,000. His age was about 38 years.

Alcona County Review, April 1, 1897

WEST HARRISVILLE.

March 30.

Mrs. T. J. Hopper of Alpena was in town last week to attend the funeral of her uncle, the late Floren Micho.

Alcona County Review, April 1, 1897

WEST HARRISVILLE.

March 30.

Mrs. Floren Micho was in town today on business. She wishes to thank her friends who so kindly assisted her in her late trouble.

Alcona County Review, April 1, 1897
Cemetery: St. Anne's, Alcona Co.

Micho, Horace

LOCAL JOTTINGS.

Horace Michio, of this township, died on Monday last at the home of his parents of consumption, aged 21 years. The funeral services were held at the Catholic church in this village on Wednesday, Rev. Father Winters coming from Au Sable to conduct the service. This is the second son of the

family who has died from consumption.

Alcona County Review, January 29, 1886
Cemetery: St. Anne's, Alcona Co.

Micho, Lena

PERSONAL MENTION.

Miss Lena Micho is in such a poor state of health that she is compelled to abandon dressmaking permanently. Her machine, a fine antique oak Standard, will be raffled off on Monday, June 5.

Alcona County Review, May 18, 1893

EVENTS OF ONE WEEK.

In the drawing for the sewing machine owned by Lena Micho, the lucky number was held by Chas. Mayo.

Alcona County Review, June 8, 1893

OBITUARY.

The end came very peacefully to Miss Lena Micho Sunday evening, and ere the benediction had been pronounced at the village churches her spirit had taken its flight to that unknown country which lies on the farther shore beyond the ken of human vision. So quietly and peacefully did she pass away that those who were watching by her bedside hardly realized that her sleep was the sleep of death.

It is seldom or never that the public pulse fails to beat with sympathy in the hour of sickness and death, but the circumstances surrounding the last days and hours of this young woman have been particularly sad and have awakened an interest in and sympathy for her which was sincere and general. She long ago realized that the sands of her life were running rapidly, but she had made her peace with her Creator and was ready and anxious to receive the final summons.

The cause of death was quick consumption, her illness dating from last winter. The only relatives present at her bedside were her brother and his wife. Her mother died many years ago and her father and family took their departure two weeks ago for the upper peninsula.

Alcona County Review, June 29, 1893

The only relatives present at her bedside were her brother and his wife. Her mother died many years ago and her father and family took

their departure two weeks ago for the upper Peninsula.

The funeral services took place yesterday morning at the Catholic church.

Alcona County Review, June 29, 1893

We desire to express our thanks to the people of Harrisville whose many acts of kindness eased the suffering and cheered in any way the hours of late lamented sister's long and tedious illness.

F. and David Micho.

Alcona County Review, June 29, 1893

EVENTS OF ONE WEEK.

What was left of the personal property of the late Lena Micho was disposed of by the custodian, Mrs. R. L. Lott, and with the proceeds a suitable tombstone was purchased, which was placed in position at the grave on Thanksgiving day.

Alcona County Review, December 7, 1893
Cemetery: St. Anne's, Alcona Co.

Micho, Peter

LOCAL JOTTINGS.

Peter Micho, son of A. Micho of this township, died on Wednesday of last week from consumption, aged about 21 years. He was buried on Friday in the Catholic cemetery.

Alcona County Review, May 30, 1884
Cemetery: St. Anne's, Alcona Co.

Middleton, Emery

GLENNIE.

Frank Middleton's baby is very sick.

Alcona County Review, November 10, 1898

GLENNIE.

Died, Nov. 7th, Emery Middleton, son of Mr. and Mrs. Frank Middleton. Mr. Middleton's sister Mrs. Taylor and her husband and family from Battle Creek, her mother and father Mr. and Mrs. Watson March and two sisters Misses Blanche and Rona and Mr. Middleton's mother and brothers from South Branch were at the funeral.

Alcona County Review, November 17, 1898
Cemetery: Glennie, Alcona Co.

Miles, Margaret Ella [Jordon]

EVENTS OF ONE WEEK.

Mrs. Matthew Miles, whose maiden name was Ella Jordon, died at her late home in Black River Wednesday, November 25th. She was a former teacher in the pupils schools of Alcona County and was a very estimable young woman. Her untimely death is regretted by a wide circle of friends. The remains were taken to Alpena for interment.

Alcona County Review, December 3, 1896
Cemetery:Holy Cross, Alpena Co.

Millen, {Girl}

OUR EXCHANGES.

From Monday's Echo.

John Millen and John Millen, Jr., left for Spanish River, Georgian Bay, on the tug Frank W. last evening in response to a telegram announcing the drowning of a fourteen year old daughter of Tom Millen. The particulars of the accident are as yet unknown.

Alcona County Review, September 2, 1897
Cemetery:

Millen, Henry L.

BLACK RIVER ITEMS.

Black River, Aug. 9.--Henry Millen, formerly of this place, now residing at St. Ignace, is very sick; the doctors have given up all hopes of his recovery. He has been unwell for about a year and his troubles finally led into that incurable malady, consumption.

Alcona County Review, August 12, 1887

LOCAL JOTTINGS.

Henry L. Millen, son of Thomas Millen, of Manistique, and nephew of Jno. Millen, of Black River, a young man well known in Alcona county, died last week at St. Ignace, of consumption, after a protracted illness. He was 24 years of age at the time of his death. He leaves a young wife.

Alcona County Review, December 30, 1887
Cemetery: Park, Marquette Co.

Millen, John

Home Reviewings.

From A. H. Mather we learn that John Millen, Esq., of Oscoda, father of John Millen, Jr., of Black River, is dangerously ill, and has but little hopes of recovery. He is 93 years of age.

Alcona County Review, June 24, 1881

HOME REVIEWINGS.

John Millen, aged ninety-three yrs., and a soldier of the war of 1812, died in Oscoda Sunday morning. We shall next week publish the interesting discourse delivered at Mr. Millen's funeral by Rev. Mr. Peebles.—*Au Sable News*.

The deceased was the father of John Millen, Jr., of this county, and had resided with his son much of the time in Harrisville. He was a fine old gentleman, and much beloved by all who formed his acquaintance.

Alcona County Review, July 29, 1881

An Eventful Life.

From the sermon of Rev. A. B. Peebles, preached at the recent funeral of John Millen, Esq., (father of John Millen, Jr., this county) at Au Sable, and published in the columns of the News at that place, we copy the following portion of the historical part of the address relative to the deceased.

John Millen was born in Boston, Mass., in the year 1788, making his age in round numbers ninety-three years. His ancestors were New England people, and his own father must have been among the early immigrants to this country. While a young man in Boston he entered upon the trade of a cabinet maker which trade he plied the greater part of his active life. Shortly after learning his trade he entered the army and served through the war of 1812. He entered as a fifer in a company of militia from Philadelphia, known as the Philadelphia Blues. At the close of the war he found his way across into Canada where he spent several years. Here he married a Mrs. Sarah Jones, a widow with three children. Mr. Millen was himself then forty-six years of age. He has five own children all living and present here to-day— Mrs. Chas. Tanner, Mrs. Chas. Fridlander, and Thomas J. Millen of this place, Mrs. S. Bailey of Canada, and John Millen, Jr., of Black River. There are twenty-two grandchildren living and four great-grandchildren. It was during Mr. Millen's residence in Canada that occurred what was known then as the McKenzie war, arising out of some misunderstanding between the British and United States governments. His sympathies were so strongly in favor of his native country that he was taken for a spy. He refused to take the oath of allegiance, but served for a short time in the Canadian army. At one time he secreted in his home a man who was being pursued, and afterward conveyed him across the river to the

American side. He moved from Canada to this country fifteen years ago and settled first in St. Clair. After a stay of three years he moved to this place where he has been a citizen now twelve years. His wife died five years ago last February, her age being 76 ½ years. They made it their home for their last years with their oldest daughter, Mrs. Tanner.

Alcona County Review, August 5, 1881

HOME REVIEWINGS.

A $200 monument is to be erected over the graves of Mr. and Mrs. Jno. Millen, Sen., at Oscoda.

Alcona County Review, September 30, 1881
Cemetery: Pinecrest, Iosco Co.

Millen, Mrs. Nellie

PERSONAL MENTION.

Mrs. John Millen has suffered a change for the worse and her husband went to Ashville, N. C., this week for the purpose of bringing her home.

Alcona County Review, December 27, 1894

PERSONAL MENTION.

Mr. and Mrs. John Millen arrived home last week by special train from Ashville, N. C. Mrs. Millen is quite seriously ill yet, but it is the wish of her many friends that she may soon be restored to the enjoyment of perfect health.

Alcona County Review, January 10, 1895

CROSSED THE DARK RIVER.

The news of the death of Mrs. John Millen which occurred at 1 a. m. Monday at her late residence in Black River, was received with genuine sorrow and deep regret by a wide circle of acquaintances, who loved and admired this gentle lady for her many womanly qualities and for the warm and disinterested friendship she seemed to have for all around her. Her death has been long expected, but her friends feel none the less the bitterness of the parting: all Black River especially has been plunged in deep sorrow and mourning. For many years she was first and foremost in all the social functions of her village and was an honored guest at leading social events up and down the Huron Shore, so that her circle of acquaintance was very wide. She has been a patient sufferer for several years from consumption, but it is only about a year since that the symptoms became so serious as to alarm her. She then went to the vigorous climate of Minnesota and later to the milder climate of Ashville, N. C., but the disease had progressed too far to be stayed by mere climatic influence and it baffled even the skill of the most eminent physicians. She arrived home a few weeks ago and since then her decline was rapid until death claimed her.

Impressive funeral services were held yesterday morning at her late residence and the remains were then taken to Detroit for interment in one of the beautiful city cemeteries.

The funeral services were conducted by the Rev. Middlemiss, of Alpena, assisted by a choir of select voices. The floral tributes were profuse and very choice, consisting of a beautiful wreath of Easter lillies, Roman hyacinths and smilax, a star of roses and Roman hyacinths from the employees at the store, and a large amount besides of lillies, white and pink carnations and roses. The pall bearers were Messrs. Geo. W. Colwell, C. C. Smith, F. J. Hill, W. R. Smith, John Whyte and Peter Churchill. The remains will be placed in a receiving vault in Woodmere cemetery, Detroit, until next summer, when the final interment will be made.

Alcona County Review, February 7, 1895

PERSONAL MENTION.

Mr. and Mrs. Geo. W. Colwell attended the funeral services of the late Mrs. Millen Tuesday morning.

Alcona County Review, February 7, 1895

STATE OF MICHIGAN, County of Alcona.

At a session of the Probate Court for the County of Alcona, held at the Probate office in the village of Harrisville on the First day of April in the year one thousand eight hundred and ninety-five.

Present, C. H. Killmaster, Judge of Probate.

In the matter of the estate of Nellie Millen, deceased:

On reading and filing the petition, of John Millen, praying that administration of said estate may be granted to him or some other suitable person:

It is ordered that Monday, the Sixth day of May next, at 2 o'clock P.M., at the said Probate office be appointed for hearing said petition. And it is further ordered that a copy of this order to be published three successive weeks previous to said day of hearing in the Alcona County Review, a newspaper printed and circulated in said County of Alcona.

C. H. Killmaster,
Judge of Probate.

Alcona County Review, April 4, 1895
Cemetery: Woodmere, Wayne Co.

Miller, Charles H.

Stricken by a Dire Disease.

This community was greatly surprised and shocked upon learning that Chas. Miller a former esteemed citizen of Harrisville had been stricken with paralysis at his home in Greenbush on Saturday evening last. He returned at dusk from Greenbush with a load of lumber. Not coming to the house as soon as he should Mrs. Miller went to investigate and found him lying prone upon the ground, speechless and helpless. He has since been unconscious of his surroundings and there is little hope of his recovery, although he may linger for weeks or months.

Alcona County Review, October 6, 1892

OBITUARY.

The Review had gone to press last week when the news was brought that Chas. Miller had passed away the night previous at his home in Greenbush. No one anticipated that death would result so soon, but it came as a welcome relief to the sufferer from one of the most pitiable of human ailments.

Charles H. Miller was born in the city of Boston in the year 1840. After arriving at maturity he engaged in the manufacture of shoes which trade he followed without intermission until within a few years, when he turned his attention to other pursuits, his recent entrance upon farm life being still fresh in the memory of all.

Mr. Miller enlisted as a private soldier in a Massachusetts regiment at the beginning of the late war, and earned a gallant record for bravery. He had only recently been granted a pension. He was a member of the I. O. O. F. and Masons and of John Earl Post G. A. R. of Au Sable, the three orders being represented at the funeral.

The remains were laid to rest last Saturday morning in the South Harrisville cemetery, whither they were followed by a large concourse of friends.

Deceased came to Detroit in 1873 and to Harrisville six years later. He has not lived here continuously, but during the greater portion of the time since his first arrival he has been an honored and respected citizen of this community.

Alcona County Review, October 13, 1892

In Memorium.

The following resolutions were adopted by Harrisville Lodge No. 218 I. O. O. F. October 12, 1892.

Whereas, An all wise Providence has deemed best to call from our midst our beloved brother Past Grand Charles Miller, one of our oldest and most zealous members in the discharge of his duties, punctilious in his obedience to the laws and regulations of the Order, Therefore be it

Resolved, That we deeply feel and mourn the greatness of our loss. A worthy member, who in the discharge of the various duties assigned him, which were among others the most important, trustworthy and exalted in the order, he displayed a remarkable zeal and aptitude and by such he won the highest respect and esteem of every Odd Fellow who knew him; one who was always ready to work for the advancement of Oddfellowship has been removed from earth and many hearts are made to mourn. And be it further

Resolved, That we extend to the family and relatives of our deceased brother our sincere and heartfelt sympathy in their hour of bereavement, and we further

Resolved, That the charter of our lodge be draped in mourning for thirty days, that a copy of these resolutions be sent to the bereaved family, also spread upon the records of this lodge and published in the Alcona County Review.

F. A. Beede,
C. M. Lund,   Committee.
Geo. Rutson.

Alcona County Review, October 20, 1892

Resolutions of Condolence.

To the Master and Wardens of Alcona Lodge No. 292 F. & A. M.:

Companions—Your committee appointed to prepare resolutions

respecting the death of Brother Charles Miller, beg leave to submit the following and do hereby recommend the adoption of the same.

Inasmuch as it has pleased the Supreme Architect of the universe to remove by death our Brother, Charles Miller, we do therefore humbly and submissively bow to the decree which has removed him from companionship with us, and in token of our regard for him we, his comrades, do hereby adopt the following:

Resolved, That in the death of Brother Charles Miller we recognize the loss of one who as a citizen was upright and honorable, of sterling integrity, kind and generous in all his dealings with his fellows, a kind and indulgent husband and father.

Resolved, That his Lodge extends its sincere sympathy to the bereaved widow and sorrowing children and that an official copy of this memorial be forwarded to them.

Harrisville, Mich., Oct. 18, 1892.
J. Van Buskirk,
C. M. Lund,   Committee
James Anderson.

Alcona County Review, October 27, 1892

HISTORY OF ONE YEAR.

Chronological History of the Past Year, 1892.

October.
1. Chas. Miller stricken with paralysis at Greenbush.

Alcona County Review, January 5, 1893

HISTORY OF ONE YEAR.

Chronological History of the Past Year, 1892.

THE DEATH RECORD.
Oct. 5. Chas. Miller, Greenbush.

Alcona County Review, January 5, 1893

South Harrisville, Oct. 18.
A few improvements of late are noticeable at the S. Harrisville cemetery.

Mrs. Chas. Miller of Greenbush has had a very nice monument erected to the memory of her husband on the family lot.

Alcona County Review, October 19, 1893

HONORS TO DEAD HEROES.

A magnificent demonstration of the patriotic spirit of the citizens of Alcona county was the observance on Monday of the time honored custom of decorating the graves and commemorating the deeds of valor of the nation's dead heroes.

The roster of soldiers who are buried here is as follows: Harrisville, (West), A. Marcellus, John Pelton, W. W. Douglass: Catholic, Louis Rivard, Geo. Bernizer: South Harrisville, R. Richmond, Chas. Miller, H. J. Aird, A. Noyes, Jas. Johnson.

Alcona County Review, June 2, 1898
Cemetery: Springport, Alcona Co.

Miller, {Child}
ALCONA ATOMS.
Mrs. Thomas Miller gave birth to a still-born babe on the 18th. Dr. McCormick requested the assistance of Dr. Mitchell, as it was a very serious case, but their assistance was secured too late, and Mrs. Miller died on Monday evening.

Alcona County Review, January 28, 1887
Cemetery: Mt. Joy, Alcona Co.

Miller, Henry Percy
Our Neighbors.

Haynes, Jan. 13, 1890:—Mr. Henry Miller was buried Monday, the 13 inst. He was born in Brazil and was a soldier in The Seminole war under Gen. Harney. He was 85 years of age. There were ten of his children, seven sons and three daughters, three sons-in-law, and five daughters-in-law present who administered to his wants during his last sickness. His consort survives him after forty seven years of married life. The Rev. Mr. Hazard preached the funeral sermon.

Alcona County Review, January 17, 1890

One Year's History.

Record of Local Happenings for the Year 1890.

JANUARY.
January 10. Henry Miller, aged 85, died at Alcona.

Alcona County Review, January 1, 1891
Cemetery: Mt. Joy, Alcona Co.

Miller, Margaret [Graham]
ALCONA ATOMS.
Mrs. Thomas Miller gave birth to a still-born babe on the 18th. Dr. McCormick requested the assistance of Dr. Mitchell, as it was a very

serious case, but their assistance was secured too late, and Mrs. Miller died on Monday evening.

Alcona County Review, January 28, 1887
Cemetery: Mt. Joy, Alcona Co.

Miller, Maud S.
LOCAL JOTTINGS.

Thomas Miller of Haynes, buried an infant daughter last Sunday, aged five months and ten days. The Rev. Mr. Goldie preached the funeral sermon.

Alcona County Review, August 16, 1889
Cemetery: Mt. Joy, Alcona Co.

Milligan, {Girl}
HAYNES HAPPENINGS.
Mr. and Mrs. Wm. S. Milligan lost their infant child, aged 7 days, from la grippe. Interment took place on the 4th.

Alcona County Review, February 9, 1899
Cemetery: Mt. Joy, Alcona Co.

Milligan, Frank
LOCAL JOTTINGS.
We hear that a three-year-old child of Elison Milligan, of Alcona, died yesterday.

Alcona County Review, December 18, 1885
Cemetery: Probably Mt. Joy, Alcona Co.

Milligan, John
LOCAL JOTTINGS.

The Review, just before going to press, hears that John Milligan, of Alcona township, dropped dead this morning. Heart disease the cause.

Alcona County Review, October 17, 1884
Cemetery: Mt. Joy, Alcona Co.

Milligan, Mary [Macomber]
Haynes Happenings.

Mrs. Wilson Milligan died about 12 o'clock Monday night of paralysis. The funeral will be held today. She was sick only a few weeks. Her age is about 74 years.

Alcona County Review, September 20, 1894
Cemetery: Probably Mt. Joy, Alcona Co.

Milligan, Wilson
Haynes, May 28, 1895.—Wilson Milligan died Monday, the 27, after a sickness of about two years. Standing funeral services will be held in the Presbyterian church by the Rev. Stewart.

Alcona County Review, May 30, 1895
Cemetery: Probably Mt. Joy, Alcona Co.

Mills, Viola

Local News.

Viola Mills, a Bay City 9-years-old, was bitten by a dog six weeks ago. Last Thursday she experienced great difficulty in drinking water and soon after she passed into convulsions, frothing at the mouth. She died Saturday afternoon.

Alcona County Review, July 18, 1895
Cemetery:

Minard, Henry

The Local News

Henry Minard was thrown on a circular saw in Loud's mill last week and cut to pieces.

Alcona County Review, September 17, 1891

The Harrisville Review is respectfully requested not to credit all the accidents of Oscoda to Loud's mill. Henry Minard lost his life at Penoyer's.—Saturday Night.

We stand corrected, brother, but it makes little difference now to the principal actor in the tragedy, viz: poor Minard, whether is was one mill or the other.

Alcona County Review, September 24, 1891
Cemetery:

Minard, William

A TERRIBLE ACCIDENT.

Seven Men Buried Alive Beneath a Mass of Brick.

THE FRIGHTFUL OCCURRENCE AT AU SABLE.

On Monday afternoon the citizens of AuSable and Oscoda were suddenly thrown into a state of excitement and terror, by the announcement of a horrible accident which had occurred at Gram's mill burner, by which five persons lost their lives, seven in all being victims to the terrible calamity. The particulars of the sad occurrence we glean from the Saturday Night extra of Wednesday, as follows:

"There were seven men at work in the burner at Gram's mill. They were Joseph W. Biddle, Thomas Mitchell, George Fulton, John Hardwick, William Miner, George Santerneau, George Gordon. The men were engaged in taking down the brick wall of one of the refuse burners of Gram's mill. A scaffolding had been built inside the burner, and upon the scaffolding the men worked and upon it the brick was also laid as they were

taken from the wall. The men began taking the wall down from the top. They had been working in the burner about a week and had the walls about half down. The brick from the part of the wall already taken down were of course lying on the platforms of the scaffolding above the heads of the workmen. While the men were engaged at work, continuing the tearing down of the wall—with about 20,000 brick, or from 40 to 50 ton's weight, above them, the scaffolding gave way, and in an instant the seven men were buried beneath this immense amount of brick and the lumber and timber of which the scaffolding was made. The alarm was given by Michael Gerrard, who was working but a few feet from the burner. Before an hour had passed there were from 1000 to 1500 men collected at the scene of the accident. The task of uncovering the men was begun as soon as possible after the accident occurred, but under the circumstances it was a very slow job. The bricks, and lumber composing the scaffolding, had all to be thrown out through two small openings—two feet by two and one half—and of course only a small number of them could work at a time. The scaffolding fell about half past four o'clock. At half past seven the first body was reached and taken out. It proved to be that of Joseph Biddle. A short time after young Gordon was taken out alive and seemingly not fatally injured, though at this writing his recovery is doubtful. A few minutes later Fulton and Santerneau were taken out, the former alive and the latter dead. Then the bodies of Mitchell, Miner, and Hardwick were taken out in the order named, it being about nine o'clock, or four and one-half hours after the accident, when the last body was removed. When the scaffolding fell some of the scantlings happened to wedge in such a position that they kept the principal weight of the brick off from Gordon, and he was able to converse at intervals with the men who were removing the brick. The men could also hear groans from one of the other imprisoned victims—probably Fulton, he was the only other one taken out alive. Five of the victims—Biddle, Fulton, Miner, Santerneau and Hardwick—were married men with families. Mr. Hardwick,

familiarly called "Happy Jack," leaves a wife and six children, the oldest a daughter of seventeen. Mr. Biddle leaves a wife and two children, Mr. Miner the same. Mr. Fulton has a wife and three children, and Mr. Santerneau leaves a wife and baby.

Later.—Fulton died Wednesday evening.

Alcona County Review, April 17, 1885

LOCAL JOTTINGS.

Register of Deeds Jamison and Gene Taft spent Monday night at Au Sable, and brought to town early Tuesday morning the news of the killing of the 5 men at Au Sable.

Alcona County Review, April 17, 1885
Cemetery: St. Anne's, Alcona Co.

Mitchell, Elinore

EVENTS OF ONE WEEK.

Elinore, aged one and one-half years, the infant daughter of Dr. and Mrs. D. W. Mitchell, died yesterday from convulsions. The funeral occurs this afternoon from the residence.

Alcona County Review, April 15, 1897
Cemetery: Probably Springport, Alcona Co.

Mitchell, Eugene

EVENTS OF ONE WEEK.

The heavy hand of death was laid upon the family of Dr. D. W. Mitchell on Sunday, and little Eugene, 4 years of age, was ruthlessly torn away from them. The little fellow had been ill for three weeks prior to his death from kidney trouble. The loss is keenly felt by the parents. They have the sympathy of the entire community in their affliction.

Alcona County Review, January 26, 1893
Cemetery: Probably Springport, Alcona Co.

Mitchell, {Girl}

LOCAL PICK UPS.

Mr. and Mrs. Wm. Mitchell last week removed the remains of their little girl, who died 23 years ago, to the family lot at the South Harrisville cemetery.

Alcona County Review, September 7, 1899
Cemetery: Springport, Alcona Co.

Mitchell, John

LOCAL PICK UPS.

Johnnie Mitchell, aged 13 years, son of Mr. and Mrs. Wm. Mitchell, died early Saturday afternoon after several months illness from consumption. The funeral was held Monday afternoon from the Baptist chapel, the interment taking place at the South Harrisville cemetery. Rev. Porterfield preached the funeral sermon.

Alcona County Review, August 31, 1899

PERSONAL POINTS.

Mrs. Wm. Mutch and Arthur Mitchell, of Grand Marais, were present at the funeral of their brother, little Johnnie Mitchell, Monday.

Alcona County Review, August 31, 1899
Cemetery: Springport, Alcona Co.

Mitchell, Morris

DIED IN DISGRACE.

How Morris Mitchell Ended His Career.

John McLeod addresses a letter to the Review dated at Au Sable concerning the fate of a young man who he says taught school in Greenbush and Harrisville six or seven years ago.

"Morris Mitchell's real name was William Bain," says the writer, "your readers will wonder how do I know. I will explain by stating that I made a visit to Canada about two weeks ago, where an old acquaintance of mine told me that Willie Bain told his sister after returning from Michigan that he stayed in my house back of Harrisville three or four days, but did not make himself known to me. His father and mother died near Stratford in Canada when he was very young leaving him and one sister improvided for, without a friend in the world. An uncle of mine who lived in the neighborhood took care of the children and raised and educated them like his own family and started Willie teaching school.

Just as soon as he left the teaching of his benefactor he began to commit those little tricks which made him so famous in Harrisville. He was well known in Canada by the name of the notorious Willie Bain. He was in jail last spring in Toronto and in May last he committed suicide in his cell, thus ending the misspent life of Willie Bain, known to you all as Morris Mitchell.

Alcona County Review, September 19, 1890
Cemetery:

Mitchell, Thomas Richard

A TERRIBLE ACCIDENT.

Seven Men Buried Alive Beneath a Mass of Brick.

THE FRIGHTFUL OCCURRENCE AT AU SABLE.

On Monday afternoon the citizens of AuSable and Oscoda were suddenly thrown into a state of excitement and terror, by the announcement of a horrible accident which had occurred at Gram's mill burner, by which five persons lost their lives, seven in all being victims to the terrible calamity. The particulars of the sad occurrence we glean from the Saturday Night extra of Wednesday, as follows:

"There were seven men at work in the burner at Gram's mill. They were Joseph W. Biddle, Thomas Mitchell, George Fulton, John Hardwick, William Miner, George Santerneau, George Gordon. The men were engaged in taking down the brick wall of one of the refuse burners of Gram's mill. A scaffolding had been built inside the burner, and upon the scaffolding the men worked and upon it the brick was also laid as they were taken from the wall. The men began taking the wall down from the top. They had been working in the burner about a week and had the walls about half down. The brick from the part of the wall already taken down were of course lying on the platforms of the scaffolding above the heads of the workmen. While the men were engaged at work, continuing the tearing down of the wall—with about 20,000 brick, or from 40 to 50 ton's weight, above them, the scaffolding gave way, and in an instant the seven men were buried beneath this immense amount of brick and the lumber and timber of which the scaffolding was made. The alarm was given by Michael Gerrard, who was working but a few feet from the burner. Before an hour had passed there were from 1000 to 1500 men collected at the scene of the accident. The task of uncovering the men was begun as soon as possible after the accident occurred, but under the circumstances it was a very slow job. The bricks, and lumber composing the scaffolding, had all to be thrown out through two small openings—two feet by two and one half—and of course only a small

number of them could work at a time. The scaffolding fell about half past four o'clock. At half past seven the first body was reached and taken out. It proved to be that of Joseph Biddle. A short time after young Gordon was taken out alive and seemingly not fatally injured, though at this writing his recovery is doubtful. A few minutes later Fulton and Santerneau were taken out, the former alive and the latter dead. Then the bodies of Mitchell, Miner, and Hardwick were taken out in the order named, it being about nine o'clock, or four and one-half hours after the accident, when the last body was removed. When the scaffolding fell some of the scantlings happened to wedge in such a position that they kept the principal weight of the brick off from Gordon, and he was able to converse at intervals with the men who were removing the brick. The men could also hear groans from one of the other imprisoned victims—probably Fulton, he was the only other one taken out alive. Five of the victims—Biddle, Fulton, Miner, Santerneau and Hardwick—were married men with families. Mr. Hardwick, familiarly called "Happy Jack," leaves a wife and six children, the oldest a daughter of seventeen. Mr. Biddle leaves a wife and two children, Mr. Miner the same. Mr. Fulton has a wife and three children, and Mr. Santerneau leaves a wife and baby.

Later.—Fulton died Wednesday evening.

Alcona County Review, April 17, 1885

LOCAL JOTTINGS.

Register of Deeds Jamison and Gene Taft spent Monday night at Au Sable, and brought to town early Tuesday morning the news of the killing of the 5 men at Au Sable.

Alcona County Review, April 17, 1885
Cemetery: Pinecrest, Iosco Co.

Molitor, Albert

MURDER WILL OUT.

Wm. Repke Confesses to being one of the Murderers of Albert Molitor in 1875.

The citizens of Presque Isle county are intensely excited over the confession of Wm. Repke to being one of a party of seventeen men who banded themselves together for the purpose of killing Albert Molitor, of Rogers City. He stated that after having kept the secret 16 years his troubled conscience was unbearable to him, and he could stand the remorse and secret no longer. His statement is that seventeen citizens of Presque Isle county, including himself, entered into an oath-bound compact to assassinate Albert Molitor and Frederick Denny Larke. For some reason Larke was not seen on the fatal evening, he states that the killing of the clerk, Sullivan, was a mistake. The shot he received was intended a second one for Molitor.

The story of the murder is as follows: Sixteen years ago the 22nd of this month, Albert Molitor was sitting in his office in Rogers City, looking over his books, when a gun was fired through the window and Molitor dropped with seven buckshot in his side and back. A clerk named Edward Sullivan, who was in the store with Molitor, sprang to his assistance, and received a load of shot in the neck. Both men were mortally wounded. Sullivan lived for about three days, but died as he was being taken to the steamer to be carried home. Molitor lived a couple of weeks, being taken to Harper Hospital, in Detroit, before he died.

The enmity towards Molitor had been growing for some time, but the direct cause of the murder was this: Rogers township originally occupied about one-half of Presque Isle county. Molitor was instrumental in bonding the township to secure sufficient money to build roads to the farms of these same conspirators, as well as other farmers in the surrounding country. Subsequently the county was redistricted, Rogers township being divided up so that the portion then bearing the name of Rogers township was small, even in comparison to the other new townships. Thus this little section was loaded with the bonds on which money was raised to build roads over half of Presque Isle county. Molitor went to the legislature and received a proper apportionment of this debt. It was this that caused feeling against him.

Twelve of the men, including Repke, are in jail at Rogers City. Two of the band are dead; the other three men are in the state and will be arrested and brought to Rogers City

for trial. Henry Clother, a brother-in-law of Molitor, and Judge Shields, of Alpena, are conducting the prosecution, while Frank Emerick and Geo. H. Slator, also of Alpena, have charge of the defense.

Alcona County Review, August 6, 1891

ROGERS CITY'S SENSATION.

Chain of Evidence Tightening about the Murderers.

Edward Molitor, of Detroit, brother of the murdered Albert Molitor, Rogers City, passed up on the Atlantic Sunday to be present at the examination of the murderers which is to take place Tuesday. On the same boat were Sheriff Kuhlman of Presque Isle county who had in charge John and Ferdinand Bruder, whom he had arrested near Mt. Clemens for complicity in the crime. In conversation with Mr. Molitor the Review learned the particulars of the crime as far as known, which is substantially the same as published last week. At the time of the tragedy, sixteen years ago, he went to Rogers City and made an effort to ferret out the murderers, but accomplished so little that when he abandoned his investigations he believed the only chance for discovering the identity of the murderers was through a confession by someone implicated in the crime. Since the crime was committed Wm. Repke, one of the principals, has led a life which has seemed like a perpetual punishment for his misdeeds. His waking and sleeping moments have been as a nightmare. Visions of the dead man ever rising to haunt him and remind him of his part in one of the coldest blooded murders in the annals of crime in Michigan. He carried the secret in this manner and in desperation he gave himself up to the officers and unburdened his mind of the details of the crime, which implicates some of the foremost citizens of Presque Isle county, including Herman Hoeft, a leading inhabitant of Rogers City. Two of the conspirators are dead. Several others of the living have also turned state's evidence. There were 17 men implicated in the plot. Of this number the following have been arrested and are in jail at Rogers City without privilege of bail. Mr. Molitor has retained able counsel and he is

confident that justice will at last be meted out to his brother's slayers. These men are under arrest for complicity in the crime.

Albert Grossman,
Carl Vogler,
Gottlieb Lambert,
Charles Wassengart,
John Bruder,
Ferdinand Bruder,
Henry Jacob,
Herman Henze,
August Furgenfrier,
August Furman.

Alcona County Review, August 13, 1891

FIVE HELD FOR TRIAL!

STATUS OF THE MOLITOR MURDER CASE

Two Men Discharged and Six Released on Bail to Await Examination.

The examination of the thirteen men charged with the murder of Molitor and Sullivan at Rogers City was concluded for the present on Tuesday of last week. Five of the men were held for trial on the charge of murder in the first degree, and they will be confined in jail until after the trial. Their names are:

August Grossman,
Henry Jacobs,
Carl Vogeler,
August Furhman,
Stephen Reiger.

Two of the party were discharged the evidence not being considered strong enough to convict them. They are Fred and Ferdinand Bruder. The other six were released on $500 bail, to appear for examination at a later date, but it is not likely that their cases will be pushed if the five who are to be tried are not convicted. Their names are John Bruder, Charles Weisegart, Gotiob Mende, Wm. Repke, Fred Sargenfrie and Andrew Banks. The latter, however, has been re-arrested and will be examined before another justice, as the prosecution thinks he should be tried with the five named above.

The testimony was very conclusive, and showed that Grossman, Jacobs, Vogeler, Furhman and Reiger, with Barabas who has since died, were the leaders of the conspiracy. Repke also claims that Herman Hoeft was one of the leaders, but the others do not confirm this. Hoeft was out of the country on the night of the murder.

It also appears from the testimony that Jacobs, Grossman, Barabas and Furhman were the men who fired the fatal shots.

A dispatch dated August 15 states that additional evidence which tends to draw the web of conviction closer around the men implicated, is coming to light and their conviction seems certain. The new evidence is damaging to Herman Hoeft, Rogers City's leading merchant, and he may be arrested.

Alcona County Review, August 20, 1891

'ROUND ABOUT.

The circuit court for Presque Isle county convened at Rogers City on Tuesday. The Molitor murder cases are on the calendar and a great legal battle is looked for before they are settled.

Alcona County Review, October 15, 1891

A GREAT CRIME.

The Murderers of Edward Molitor Coming to Justice at Last.

Alpena, Oct. 22.——(Special.)-Wm. Reipke, who made a confession of the Molitor murder at Rogers City, and who was released last week, was rearrested on Tuesday of this week and had his examination before Justice Kaichen yesterday. Several witnesses were sworn. Steven Roger testified that he was present on the night of the murder as was also Reipke and the others whose names have been given before that the two first shots were fired by Grossman and Jacobs and that he was standing within ten feet of them at the time; that Reipke then fired and shot Sullivan. Reipke was bound over for trial and bail was fixed at $5,000 in default of which he was remanded to jail. It is rumored in Rogers City that the charge against the five men for the murder of Molitor will be withdrawn and that new warrants will be issued charging them with the murder of Edw. Sullivan. Sullivan died in this city and for that reason the trial should take place here. Messrs. Shield and McNamara of the prosecution, state that no such course has been decided upon, although this

action may before next January, the time set for the trial.

Alcona County Review, October 29, 1891

'ROUND ABOUT.

The Molitor murder cases in Presque Isle county have gone over to the January term of court.

Alcona County Review, October 29, 1891

AMONG OUR EXCHANGES.

Something like a race war is on in Presque Isle county. The accused murderers of Edward Molitor are Germans, and their trial has been postponed from time to time, and has now gone over to the June term. The murderer of William Hagen is John Idalski, a Pole. He has been promptly tried, convicted and sentenced. The Poles now say that all murderers must be treated alike in Presque Isle county; that the murderers of Molitor, even though they be well-to-do Germans, must be tried, convicted and sentenced, and that if they are not they will take the law into their own hands.

Alcona County Review, January 28, 1892

The Molitor Case.

A dispatch from Lansing says:
Gov. Winans has received a petition, signed by nine out of ten supervisors of Presque Isle county asking that Attorney General Ellis be sent there to prosecute the case of the people against William Ripke, August Grossman and Henry Jacobs for the murder of Albert Molitor. It is charged in the petition that the prosecuting attorney for the county is an habitual drunkard, and therefore unfitted to conduct the prosecution. The hint is also given that he is seemingly averse to making an effort to secure a conviction. The case has been continued without apparent good reason.

Alcona County Review, April 7, 1892

TRANSFERRED TO ALPENA.

The Molitor Murder Case Will be Tried In Alpena County.

The trial of the men charged with implicity in the murder of Edward Molitor, in Presque Isle county some sixteen years ago, was begun in the circuit court for that county last week, Judge Kelley presiding. A large array of legal talent, comprising

Attorneys Emerick, Burnham, Sleator, McNamara and others, were retained on one side or the other of what promises to be one of the most celebrated criminal trials of northern Michigan. Attorney Gen. Ellis was present also to aid in the prosecution. By order of the court a panel of 95 men were summoned to serve as jurors. This list was exhausted in a very brief space of time and the number of jurors and talesmen had reached a total of 255, when it became apparent to the court that it would be impossible to procure a jury in Presque Isle county, as a sufficient number of men could not be found who had not expressed opinions which could not be changed. Judge Kelly thereupon gave an order taking the cases from Presque Isle county and transferring them to Alpena county for trial at the next term of court.

Five and possibly more of Presque Isle county's leading citizens are implicated. The crime was a cold blooded murder and was claimed to have been the outcome of fierce business and political rivalry, which split Presque Isle county into two factions, at the head of one being Edward Molitor, who was a stern, unyielding man, somewhat tyrannical in his dealings with inferiors and opponents. His murder was the result of a carefully planned conspiracy.

Some of the accused, and perhaps all who are now held for the crime, are looked upon with the community's respected eye. They have grown up families which have married and intermarried until they are interwoven into Rogers City society so strongly that a hot, intense and almost anxious feeling pervades the atmosphere of the city as the hours fit into the past.

The people must rely on the confession of one Repka, who is thought so little of as to be without one friend who would go on his bail bond that he might secure his liberty pending his trial, all the others being out on bail. He is christened Judas Iscariot of the men whom the people charge with the killing of Molitor. There are other witnesses to partially corroborate his story, but they do not seem to be so strong in their charges as Repka. The most of them are respected and good citizens. Repka's evidence tends to implicate one Herman Hoeft, the richest man in Presque Isle county, and one Banks, an unpracticing attorney whom Repka says desired to get Molitor out of the way because he was a business rival. But notwithstanding a strong effort on the part of the people to procure satisfactory evidence against those two men, it would seem that little had been accomplished. Hoeft has hosts of friends who are willing to discredit his hand in the whole affair (he being in Detroit, it is claimed on the night of the murder), while again good men in the city are of a contrary mind.

Alcona County Review, June 23, 1892

AMONG OUR EXCHANGES.

The Molitor cases cannot be taken up in Alpena county before the 17th inst. Reason: Atty. Gen. Ellis will assist the prosecution and it will require all his time until after the 17th inst. to convince the delegates to the democratic state convention that he didn't mean it when he told the delegates to the People's Party convention that he owed the democrats nothing, but rather that they were indebted to him, and that he would support Weaver and Reid. Indications are that Ellis has overreached himself and in trying to serve two masters at one and the same time he has worked himself out of a job. As a public officer he has done good work for the state.

Alcona County Review, August 11, 1892

AMONG OUR EXCHANGES.

From the Alpena Pioneer:
The trial of the Molitor murder cases has been postponed until the 30th, to give Attorney General Ellis time to prepare himself for the prosecution.

Alcona County Review, August 18, 1892

SOMEWHAT PERSONAL.

The Molitor murder cases were called for trial Tuesday at Alpena, but an adjournment was taken for another month.

Alcona County Review, September 1, 1892

The Molitor murder cases will be taken up next Tuesday in the Alpena circuit court.

Alcona County Review, November 24, 1892

The Molitor murder cases are occupying the attention of the Alpena circuit court. The prosecution are making a strong case and there is just a possibility that some of the murderers may be brought to justice although it is eighteen years since Molitor was shot at Rogers City.

Alcona County Review, December 8, 1892

AFTER MANY YEARS.

Conviction of Grossman of the Murder of Albert Molitor 17 Years Ago.

From the Pioneer.
Our last week's report of the case included the most important evidence produced by the prosecution, and it is admitted that they made a very strong case. In addition to the testimony of Henry Clothier, Mrs. Edward Molitor, F. D. Larke, and others who knew of the case, and all of which implicated Grossman and the other defendants, the famous confession of Repke was given to the jury in full. This confession was confirmed by the testimony of Stephen Reiger. Ferdinand Bruder, Gottlieb Mende, Frederick Soegenfrie, John Bruder and Carl Weisengart, all of whom admitted that they were with the party which killed Molitor, and strongly implicated the four defendants who are held for trial, namely August Grossman, Henry Jacobs, Carl Vogeler and August Furhman.

The defense began on Thursday, the principal effort being made to establish an alibi for each of the defendants.

Andrew E. Banks testified that he knew nothing of the murder; that the testimony implicating him was false. He was arrested and examined before Justice Harris Aug. 28, 1875, and was discharged. On cross examination he admitted that he was not arrested in 1875, as he had testified; that Molitor had a judgment against him for $200, and that he got farmers together to recover his boots, which were in the possession of the sheriff. Altogether his testimony was very contradictory and he proved a poor witness for the defense.

Herman Hoeft, the wealthy lumberman and merchant of Presque Isle, who has been vaguely charged with complicity in the Molitor murder, was next called. He denied any act, part or knowledge of the affair, and said he was at Detroit for 10 days previous to and during the shooting. Upon cross-examination he admitted he was furnishing the money for the defense, and had neither taken nor asked for security of any kind. He admitted taking a body of men to Crawford's quarry in the spring of 1875 to forcibly take the treasurer's books from Len Crawford. But he claimed to be on friendly terms with Molitor.

Mr. and Mrs. Pauly swore that a sick baby brought them to Grossman's house the night Molitor was shot and they remember of seeing Grossman at home.

On Monday August Grossman was put on the stand in his own defense. He testified that he had lived in Presque Isle since 1870; that he had held some township or county office during almost every year since, but thought he held no office in 1875, the year of the murder; that he knew Molitor in Detroit before coming to Presque Isle county; that he and Molitor were good friends and that he had no enmity toward him; that he was at home the night of the murder; was first told of the murder by Weisengart who told him that they thought in town that the farmers killed Molitor.

On cross-examination he declared that he was with the crowd which demanded the county books from Molitor in 1873. The prosecution tried to show that at that time Grossman said that Molitor ought to be hung, but the judge ruled that out. He admitted also that he was with the crowd which went to Rogers City to recover Bank's boots, and that he wore a belt with a big horse pistol. He also admitted that Molitor had a judgment against him but claimed that it had been paid. He admitted going to Furhman's house to get him up to go with the crowd after Bank's boots. It was shown that he had three offices the year of the murder.

A number of other witnesses were sworn and some former witnesses recalled but nothing of any importance was elicited. The defense rested their case at 6 o'clock.

The testimony having been concluded, the arguments in the case were commenced Wednesday morning by Prosecuting Attorney McNamara for the People. He gave a graphic description of the condition of county affairs in Presque Isle county previous to and at the time of the murder, stating that Grossman and the others in the alleged plot were constant office holders, and were business and political rivals of Molitor. He then reviewed the testimony, pointing out that seven men—Repke, Reiger, Mende, Sergenfrie, Weisengart and the two Bruders—had sworn positively that they took part in the work, and that Grossman and other three defendants were leaders in the awful conspiracy which resulted in the butchering of Albert Molitor and Edward Sullivan. The alibi sought to be established by Grossman was discussed at length, and the testimony in this regard held up in a manner which made it appear very gauzy. He closed with a strong plea for the vindication of the name of northern Michigan, and for the punishment of these murderers, who had too long escaped justice.

Judge Emerick opened the case for the defense. He made a most eloquent plea for justice, bringing forth convincing arguments which were placed before the jury in a manner that evidently made a deep impression.

The large court room was crowded to its upmost capacity Thursday morning to hear the arguments of Sleator and Atkinson for the defense. Business was almost suspended down town, and many could not gain admittance.

Col. Atkinson closed the arguments for the defense, making a clear, strong and able address.

Judge Kelly at once made his charge to the jury. He impressed the jury with the atrocity of the crime which had been committed, but expressly warned them that they were not to find a verdict of guilty unless they were satisfied beyond a reasonable doubt that Grossman was one of the murderers.

The charge was generally conceded to have been exceedingly clear, able and impartial.

The jury were out all night. The first ballot stood 10 for conviction, 2 for acquittal, but an agreement was finally reached and at the opening of court Friday morning the jury returned a verdict of guilty of murder in the first degree.

The other three defendants will be tried in the February term, each separately. Repke and Reiger, who are also under indictment but who have made confessions, will probably plead guilty and throw themselves on the mercy of the court. It is also understood that proceedings will be commenced against Mende, Sorgenfrie, Weisengart and Bruder, the remaining four of the twelve who are alleged to have been in the conspiracy, Barabas and Tuelgetski being dead. Proceedings may also be begun against Andrew E. Banks.

Grossman's attorneys have moved for a new trial and Judge Kelley will hear the motion Dec. 30.

Alcona County Review, December 22, 1892

Public Sympathy for Grossman.

From the Pioneer.

Public sympathy is easily aroused, and sympathy has much to do with crystallizing public sentiment. During the trial of Grossman for the murder of Molitor, public opinion was apparently equally divided as to the guilt or innocence of the accused, and almost all agreed, that if guilty he should be convicted, but that there was little chance of conviction on account of the contradictory character of the testimony. Since the verdict of guilty, however, nine out of ten citizens denounce it as an outrage, the testimony having been so conflicting that Grossman should have been given the benefit of the doubt. Many who believe these men guilty state that it will do no good now to punish them, as they are already law abiding citizens, while it will bring trouble and misery to a large number of people. It is doubtful if a jury could be found in this county now which would convict another of the alleged murderers.

Alcona County Review, December 29, 1892

EVENTS OF ONE WEEK.

It is a singular fact that three adjoining shore counties, Iosco, Alcona and Alpena, have each contributed a life convict to Jackson prison within the past month: Iosco county sent Benson; Alpena county sent Grossman and Alcona county sends Wightman. A pretty trio of murderers.

Alcona County Review, January 19, 1893

SENTENCED FOR LIFE.

August Grossman Sent to Jackson From Alpena.

Circuit court opened in Alpena county last Thursday. August Grossman, who was convicted of complicity in the murder of Albert Molitor, at Rogers City 17 years ago, was brought before the court to receive his sentence.

Attorney Emerick stated that he had been unable to prepare a bill of exceptions. The Judge then asked Mr. Grossman to stand up before him and receive his sentence. Grossman arose with both a determined look and air and folding his hands behind him looked the Judge fairly in the face, body erect, and with the full bearing of a German soldier. Said the Judge: "Mr. Grossman, you have been found guilty of murder in the first degree; have you anything to say why sentence should not be pronounced upon you?" "I am not guilty," said Grossman in a voice strong enough to be heard all over the room, and without even a tremolo or without relaxing a muscle of his face.

Grossman is firm in the conviction that he will not be long in prison. His attorneys will take the case to the Supreme court and it will likely come up at the April term.

The Echo says: "While Grossman has been found guilty of murder in the first degree, yet probably no other man ever stood with the same sentence upon him with as many sympathizing friends as August Grossman. From the first to last he has stood out like a man and guarded the secret to which it is said he was sworn. Even in the face of evident desertion he holds out, and be he guilty or not, he has at least excited the admiration of all who have interested themselves in the case.

Alcona County Review, February 2, 1893

MICHIGAN, MY MICHIGAN.

Alpena: Grossman, the convicted murderer, was taken to Jackson Monday.

Alcona County Review, February 2, 1893

Herman Hoeft, who was represented as having "skipped" the country because of implication and responsibility for the Molitor murder trials, has returned to Rogers City after an absence of several months in the far west.

Alcona County Review, March 16, 1893

The Molitor murder cases were adjourned on Monday until the first day of the May term, on motion of the People's attorneys.

Alcona County Review, April 20, 1893

An important witness for the Molitor murder trials has been discovered in Windsor in the person of A. D. Rodier, who was in the store at Rogers City when Molitor and Sullivan were killed.

Alcona County Review, June 29, 1893

ARE GUILTY!

OF MURDER IN THE FIRST DEGREE FOR KILLING MOLITOR.

Four Rogers City Murderers Have Now Been Brought to Justice.

For a Crime Which Was Committed 18 Years Ago.

Alpena, Mich., July 10.—Vogler, Fuhrman and Jacobs are guilty of the murder of Albert Molitor. The case was given to the jury last Saturday night at 8 o'clock and three hours later a verdict was returned. The prisoners will be sentenced later on.

In all probability the trial of Repke, the self-confessed murderer, will now be taken up. This makes four men convicted, Grossman having been sent to Jackson for life last January.

Albert Molitor, a merchant at Rogers City and a clerk of his named Sullivan, were murdered on the evening of August 23, 1875. There were many theories and suspicions as to who were the murderers, and some of them were pretty close to the truth, but nothing definite was ever learned until Wm. Repke, a farmer living in Moltke township, Presque Isle county, becoming conscious stricken after sixteen years of silence, went to the prosecuting attorney of Presque Isle county at Rogers City during the last days of July in 1892, and confessed that he and sixteen other men, then working in and about Rogers City, entered into a conspiracy to kill Molitor and Frederic Denny Larke, but while they succeeded in shooting Molitor, they made a mistake as to Larke and killed

Sullivan in his stead. Repke gave the names of such of the other murderers as he recollected, as follows:

Albert Grossman, Carl Vogler, Gottlieb Lambert, Charles Wassengart, Fred Bruder, Ferdinand Bruder, Henry Jacob, Herman Menze, August Furgenfrier, August Furhman.

Some of them had moved away and two were dead, but nearly all of those remaining in this section of the county had become prominent and leading citizens, and the confession of Repke accordingly caused a tremendous sensation.

Alpena, Mich.—William Repke, the man who caused the arrest of the Molitor murderers, by turning State's evidence, was placed on trial Tuesday morning.

Alcona County Review, July 13, 1893

AMONG OUR EXCHANGES.

The trial of Repke, one of the Molitor murderers, took place at Alpena last week and resulted in his conviction of murder in the first degree. This makes five in all who have been convicted of this crime. Unless more arrests are made the prosecutions will cease with the trial of Stephen Rieger, which is now in progress.

Alcona County Review, July 20, 1893

CLOSE OF THE MOLITOR CASES.

Rieger Not Guilty, Jacobs, Volger, Fuhrman and Repke Go Up for Life.

The conclusion of the prosecutions in the celebrated Molitor murder cases occurred last week when Stephen Rieger was found not guilty.

The convicted men, Repke, Volger, Fuhrman and Jacobs were taken into court Saturday to receive their sentence. Each one maintained his innocence, when asked if he had anything to say why sentence should not be pronounced upon them. Judge Kelley pronounced sentence in these words: "You will be confined in the State prison at Jackson in solitary confinement for the balance of your natural lives."

Repke was the only one of the four who broke down. As his voluntary divulging of the conspiracy had led to the conviction of the men, it was

generally believed that he would get off with a lighter sentence, but the Court didn't see it that way.

The sheriff started Sunday for Jackson with the prisoners.

Alcona County Review, July 27, 1893

Law Comes High.—According to the bills recently filed with County Clerk Smith, the total cost incurred by Alpena county in prosecuting the Molitor murder cases is 5,882.89. This, however, does not include attorney McNamara's fees for assisting in prosecuting the cases, which amount to $1,650 more. The total amount that Presque Isle county will be obliged to pay since the commencement of the cases is computed to be about $10,000.— Rogers City Advance.

Alcona County Review, August 31, 1893

A Confessed Liar.

Wm. Repke Makes an Astonishing Deposition.

Nearly every Review reader has heard of the celebrated Molitor murder cases, for which during the past two years several prominent citizens of Presque Isle county have been arrested, tried and convicted of the murder of Edward Molitor at Rogers City some 17 years ago. The prosecutions were based upon the confession of Wm. Repke, who was one of the arch conspirators. Repke claimed that he was promised immunity from prosecution as the price of his confession, but instead of going free he too was tried and convicted and is now doing time with the rest in Jackson prison.

A few days ago Repke subscribed to a sworn statement that all the testimony given by him against his confederates was false and untrue in every particular; in other words he confesses himself a moral coward and a despicable liar. It is not likely that it will result in new trials for the others.

Alcona County Review, November 16, 1893

REPKE, THE MURDERER.

Will Have to Serve Out His Life Sentence.

Lansing, Mich., Jan. 5.--Special.-- William Repke was justly sentenced to state prison for life for participation in the conspiracy which resulted in the brutal murder of Edward Molitor in Presque Isle county nearly 20 years ago. The supreme court has so decided.

Repke's counsel held that the circuit court erred in holding that if found guilty it had to be of murder in the first degree. Justice Long declared that the murder was a deliberate and willful one, and the circuit court did right in instructing the jury that Repke was either a murderer in the first degree or an innocent man. This probably seals the fate of the other convicted conspirators, whose cases are still before the court.

Repke is the man who turned state's evidence in the case and made it possible to convict the other five men. He laid in jail two years at Alpena after his arrest, but was given abundance of chances to escape as he had the liberty of the yard and was sent upon errands down town. Repke supposed he would be discharged because of having given evidence in all the other cases.
Alcona County Review, January 17, 1895

The supreme court has taken away the last hope of the murderers of Edward Molitor by affirming the convictions of Grossman, Fuhrman, Jacobs and Voegler.
Alcona County Review, January 24, 1895

Attorneys interested in the case have prepared petitions asking that Grossman and the others convicted of the Molitor murder be pardoned. These petitions are to be circulated in Alpena and Presque Isle counties.
Alcona County Review, May 16, 1895

To Get 'Em Out of Jail.
Petitions for the pardon of the murderers of Edward Molitor have been forwarded to the state pardon board. They are signed by 500 citizens of Presque Isle county, friends and neighbors of the convicts, also by 500 citizens of Alpena county, by prominent citizens of Detroit, by state officials, and others who express a belief that the men now serving life sentences in Jackson prison are not guilty. Repke, the informer, is excepted and his pardon is not asked for.
Alcona County Review, December 19, 1895

Molitor Murderers May Go Free.
The state pardon board has been sitting at Alpena to review the celebrated Molitor murder cases, the five citizens of Presque Isle county who are serving life sentences for that crime having prevailed upon their friends to take active steps for their release. The move seems likely to

succeed so far as Grossman, Vogeler, Jacobs, and Fuhrman are concerned, but Repke, the conscience-smitten informer, will not be recommended for pardon, because he fired the shot that killed Sullivan, Molitor's clerk, and for that crime there was not the same excuse that there might have been for killing Molitor, who has been proven a petty tyrant in his relations with the simple German farmers of Presque Isle.
Alcona County Review, September 3, 1896

EVENTS OF ONE WEEK.

Four of the men convicted four years ago of the murder of Albert Molitor and Edward Sullivan at Rogers City, have been pardoned by Gov. Pingree. They are: August Furhman, Carl Vogeler, August Grossman and Henry Jacobs. Repke, the man who confessed the crime and implicated the others, was not pardoned and will undoubtedly end his days in prison.
Alcona County Review, February 4, 1897

Want Repke Pardoned, Too.
Relatives of Edward Molitor, who was murdered at Rogers City a score of years ago, are interesting themselves to secure the pardon of Repke, the informer, the only man of the convicts remaining in prison, all the others having been pardoned. They urge that Repke is no more guilty than the rest.
Alcona County Review, July 1, 1897

A Pardon for Repke.
A petition emanating from Rogers City, will be presented to Governor Pingree for the pardon of informer Repke, of Molitor murder fame. The petition is signed by the trial judge, R. J. Kelley, and also by a brother of the murdered man. There would seem to be no reason under the sun why Repke, the only convict of the gang to demonstrate the ownership of a conscience tender enough to be worried and tormented by recollections of the crime, should remain in prison to pay the penalty of his confederates' sins, who have long since been excused from durance vile. Had it not been for Repke, his conscience and his confession, justice might have gone on forever unavenged.--Cheboygan Democrat.
Alcona County Review, January 20, 1898
Cemetery: Elmwood, Wayne Co.

Monaghan, Harry Alger
EVENTS IN HAYNES.

James Monaghan buried a ten months old boy on Sunday afternoon in our cemetery. Cause of death, inflammation of the bowels and teething.
Alcona County Review, February 9, 1893

Black River.
OBITUARY.
Harry Alger Monaghan, the ten months old son of Mr. and Mrs. Jas. Monaghan, died on the 3rd inst., after a short illness. The deceased was interred in Alcona cemetery on Sunday last. The services were conducted by Rev. Mr. Smith.
Alcona County Review, February 9, 1893

Black River.
Mr. and Mrs. Jas. Monaghan are deeply grateful for the many acts of kindness rendered by thoughtful Black River friends during the illness and death of their little son. May each of them be spared a like affliction.
Alcona County Review, February 9, 1893

Haynes Happenings.
James Monaghan erected a beautiful headstone at his child's grave.
Alcona County Review, May 24, 1894
Cemetery: Mt. Joy, Alcona Co.

Monaghan, John
Reviewings.

Monday evening last, John Monaghan, employed at the camp of Moses Stafford on the North Branch of Thunder Bay River, Alpena County, was struck by a falling tree and instantly killed.
Alcona County Review, February 6, 1880
Cemetery: Holy Cross, Alpena Co.

Monaghan, John
The Local News.
John Monaghan, of Alpena, felt ill when he arrived in Detroit yesterday, his trouble being heart disease. He walked to St. Mary's hospital and after making arrangements there for treatment he went back to the boat on which he came, got his trunk, and returning to the hospital died in 20 minutes.--News, June 27.
Alcona County Review, July 4, 1890
Cemetery:

Monroe, Allen F.
The Local News

A little son of David Monroe of Greenbush died last week.

Alcona County Review, November 15, 1889
Cemetery: Springport, Alcona Co.

Monroe, David

Obituary.

David Monroe, Sr., father of D. A. Monroe of Greenbush died at the home of his son, Monday, May 20, 1895, at the advanced age of 94 years.

David Monroe was born May 3, 1801 in New York State. In 1826 he was married to Hannah Lafleur. Their union was blessed with eleven children, four sons and seven daughters, nine of whom and his wife survive him. He moved to Michigan in 1866 and has resided in Alcona county 19 years with his son, David. He was a member of the M. E. church and by his request his funeral sermon was preached from the 30th chapter of Job.

Funeral was held at Greenbush Wednesday, Rev. Bailey officiating.

Alcona County Review, May 23, 1895
Cemetery: Probably Springport, Alcona Co.

Moore, Alexander

Jottings Along the Shore.

Last Monday the body of Alexander Moore was found in the river at Alpena. He had been missing about a week, and when last seen was staving drunk.

Alcona County Review, November 28, 1879
Cemetery:

Moore, Mrs. Deborah

ADDITIONAL LOCALS.

Mrs. Jas. Moore, wife of Jas. Moore, of this village, died Tuesday morning after a brief illness from inflammation of the lungs. The deceased was held in high esteem by her neighbors for her womanly qualities; she was a devoted wife and mother, a Christian woman, and the afflicted family have the sympathy of the public in their great loss. The funeral services were held Thursday afternoon.

Alcona County Review, May 4, 1888

LINES
On Mrs. James Moore, who died May 1st, 1888, aged 39 years 3 months and 16 days:

The snow is white—so is her face,
She was the one we held most dear;
No other one can fill her place on earth.

The snow is cold—so are the hands
Which ever did kind, loving deeds;
Her spirit now has fled to lands of light.

The snow is pure—so was her heart,
As angels' in the starry skies;
No thought of evil there had thought or place.

The snow is soft—her accents so;
She spake, and soothed all wrath and strife;
She lived to make this vale below as heaven.

The snow is noiseless; so was she
And feet sped silent on their way;
Distress but nigh, quick she would flee to help.

But as the snow dissolves and flies,
Just as we realize 'tis here,
So she, so young, has gained the skies,
And rest.

Alcona County Review, May 11, 1888

Card of Thanks.
We wish to thank our friends and neighbors who rendered such kind services during the last illness and death of Mrs. James Moore.

James Moore,
Mrs. R. Jones.

Alcona County Review, May 11, 1888
Cemetery:

Moore, Franklin

CHANCERY SALE. In pursuance and by virtue of an order and decree of the circuit court for the county of Alcona in chancery in the state of Michigan, made and entered on the sixteenth day of February A.D. 1897, in a certain cause therein pending wherein

Sullivan M. Cutcheon and Helen M. Moore, surviving executors of the last will and testament of Franklin Moore, deceased, are complainants, vs.

Gilbert Van Buren, Deborah Van Buren, Bernard P. Cowley and Helen C. Cowley, defendants.

Notice is hereby given that I shall sell at public auction to the highest bidder at the front door of the court house in the village of Harrisville and county of Alcona, State of Michigan, (said court house being the place for holding the circuit court for said county), on Tuesday, the 29th day of June, A.D. 1897, at one o'clock in the afternoon all or so much thereof as may be necessary to raise the amount due the said complainants for principal, interest and costs in this cause, of the following parcels of land

situate in the township of Haynes (formerly Alcona) in said county and described as follows, to-wit:

The east half of the northwest quarter and the southwest quarter of the northeast quarter of section thirty-six (36) in town twenty-seven (27) north of range nine (9) east, containing one hundred and twenty [120] acres, more or less.

Dated Harrisville, April 27, 1897.
Fred A. Beede, Circuit Court Commissioner,
Alcona County, Michigan.
Cutcheon, Stellwagen and Fleming,
Solitcitors for Complainants,
Address, Detroit, Mich.

Alcona County Review, June 10, 1897
Cemetery:

Moore, {Child}

LOCAL JOTTINGS.

After a lingering illness of about two weeks, the babe of Mr. and Mrs. H. P. Moore died on Sunday and was buried Tuesday afternoon.

Alcona County Review, September 12, 1884

LOCAL JOTTINGS.

Mr. and Mrs. H. P. Moore desire, through the columns of the Review, to render grateful acknowledgement to their many friends and neighbors of Harrisville for almost unlimited kindness shown them during the sickness, death and burial of their infant child. Such expressions of kindness and sympathy, coming as they did in the hour of need from so many of the townspeople, were doubly appreciated.

Alcona County Review, September 12, 1884
Cemetery:

Moore, James

EVENTS OF ONE WEEK.

James Moore of Black River died Monday at his home after a prolonged illness. The funeral was held Monday from the Black River Catholic church, the burial taking place in the Harrisville cemetery.

Alcona County Review, April 1, 1897

LOCAL PICK UPS.

Amos Bonnville has been appointed administrator of the estate of James Moore, late of Black River.

Alcona County Review, March 17, 1898
Cemetery: St. Anne's, Alcona Co.

Moore, Mrs.

LOCAL JOTTINGS.

H. P. Moore has returned from his trip to Tawas. His visit there was occasioned by the sickness and death of his brother's wife.

Alcona County Review, April 18, 1884
Cemetery:

Moorehead, Fred M.
The Local News.

Fred Moorehead, salesman and manager of the large general store of C. H. Prescott & Sons at Tawas City, was shot and instantly killed on Christmas by the accidental discharge of a gun in the hands of one of his best friends. He and some friends were shooting glass balls when the accident occurred. He leaves a wife and one child in good circumstances. Deceased was but 30 years of age.

Alcona County Review, December 31, 1891
Cemetery:

Moran, Thomas
PERSONAL POINTS.

Thos. Moran has been confined to his bed by illness for two weeks past.

Alcona County Review, April 14, 1898

PERSONAL POINTS.

Thos. Moran is reported to be quite low today. He is suffering from pulmonary trouble.

Alcona County Review, April 21, 1898

Thos. Moran, Deceased.
The serious illness of Thos Moran, which was noted last week, terminated in his death on Friday, the 22d inst. The interment took place Monday morning in the Catholic cemetery.

Deceased was a native of Perce, Gaspe county, Quebec, where he was born April 7, 1843. He came to Harrisville in 1880, and was followed a year later by his family. He has followed the occupation of a woodsman during his residence in Alcona county. His death was due to pleurisy, superinduced, his friends think, by an accident which he sustained sometime ago in the woods.

He is survived by his wife and three children.

Jos. Moran, a brother who lives in Saginaw, and Mr. and Mrs. Wm.

Donahue were the only other relatives present.

Alcona County Review, April 28, 1898

Card of Thanks.
We wish to express our sincere thanks to friends and neighbors who so kindly assisted us during the illness and death of our beloved husband and father.

Mrs. Moran and Family.

Alcona County Review, May 5, 1898

Local History of One Year

Chronology of the Principal Events of the Year 1898.

April 22. Death of Thos. Moran aged 58, at Harrisville.

Alcona County Review, January 5, 1899
Cemetery: St. Anne's, Alcona Co.

Morelle, Emily
EVENTS OF ONE WEEK.

Another case of diphtheria has developed in the family of Phillip Morell, who lives on the Springport road south of Harrisville.

Alcona County Review, June 8, 1893

EVENTS OF ONE WEEK.

The 14-year-old daughter of Phillip Morelle, residing on the South Harrisville road, died Monday morning after a two weeks' illness from what is pronounced by the attending physician to be diphtheria. Two other cases exist in the family also. This family had the disease last summer when it was so epidemic, but they lost no children then.

When the foregoing was written our reporter had not seen Dr. Mitchell, but he states that the patient had recovered from the diphtheria and that he had not thought it necessary to treat her for that disease for 10 days previous to her death. He saw her on Sunday and she appeared to be getting along nicely. Her death Monday morning was very sudden and he expresses an opinion that it was due to neuralgia of the heart. There is but one other case in the family and that one is recovering.

Alcona County Review, October 26, 1893
Cemetery:

Morelle, Phillip
PERSONAL.

Phillip Morelle, honest, inoffensive Phillip Morelle, gave up life's fitful struggle Tuesday morning at 5 o'clock and crossed the dark river. Phillip suffered a paralytic stroke Saturday morning and he did not regain consciousness or rally until his death. He was about 63 years of age and though physically incapacitated for hard work yet he had been engaged in the laborious task of ditching until quite recently and his collapse may have been occasioned by fatigue and exposure.

The funeral occurred this morning and was in charge of D. La Boueff. Services were held at the M. E. church.

Alcona County Review, November 11, 1897
Cemetery: Springport, Alcona Co.

Morgan, Blinkey
PURELY PERSONAL.
Sheriff Lynch, of Alpena, who was shot in the leg while attempting to arrest the desperado Morgan, last month, died of his injury at the Detroit Sanitarium, where he was taken recently for medical treatment, at 10 o'clock a. m. Wednesday.

Alcona County Review, August 19, 1887

Says He is Innocent.
"Blinkie" Morgan, the notorious character who shot Sheriff Lynch, of Alpena, while the latter was attempting to arrest him, avows his innocence of the crime of murder in the "affair at Alpena," as he calls it in an open letter published in the papers at Ravenna, Ohio. Blinkie says he was sitting quietly at the table with Mrs. Williams and her children engaged in arranging some flowers when three or four men rushed in, knocked him down, choked him, and one of them "jumped upon his stomach." This was really too bad. Sheriff Lynch and his assistants ought to have knocked at the outer door, inquired in a hesitating manner if Blinkie was in, and then, if they were admitted, parleyed with that gentleman, and induced him, if possible, to quietly submit to arrest. What a pleasant affair it would have been. Instead of one funeral in Alpena there would have been four, and it is safe to say that Blinkie would not have been among the number of the slain. If Blinkie escapes the hangman's noose at Revenna he

should be brought to Alpena and strung up to the first lamp-post.
Alcona County Review, August 26, 1887

LOCAL JOTTINGS.
Blinkey Morgan was strangled at Columbus, O., August 3d as per programme.
Alcona County Review, August 10, 1887
Cemetery:

Morrill, Bryan V.

Accident at Killmaster

Four Year Old Son of J. C. Morrill Drowned in a Cistern.

The sad intelligence was received here last evening of the drowning of Byron, the four-year-old son of Mr. and Mrs. J. C. Morrill of Killmaster.

The little fellow was missed by his parents and upon search the body was found in a cistern. A physician was called, but the child was beyond human aid.

The body was taken to Yale, Mich. on the morning train, for interment in the family lot.
Alcona County Review, May 25, 1899
Cemetery: Elmwood, St. Clair Co.

Morrill, Howard E.

HOWARD E. MORRELL.
We are sorry to record the death of Howard E. Morrell, son of Mr. Jesse Morrell of Killmaster, who died on Saturday morning, Aug. 14th, of typhoid fever.

Howard was 23 years of age, born at Yale, Mich., a young man of very exemplary character, and much beloved by all who knew him. He was a member of Mineral Water Tent No. 403 K. O. T. M. of Killmaster. On Monday morning a short service was held at the home of Rev. F. S. Ford and the remains were escorted by the Sir Knights and Ladies to the train, thence to Yale for interment. Great sympathy is expressed for the parents.
Alcona County Review, August 19, 1897

KILLMASTER RIPPLES.
J. A. Morrill and family have returned from Yale, where they buried their son, Howard.
Alcona County Review, August 26, 1897

Resolution.
At a regular review of Mineral Water Tent, 403 K. O. T. M., of Killmaster, the following resolutions were adopted:
Resolved, That whereas the Supreme Ruler of the universe in his kind and wise providence has removed from our midst our respected and beloved brother and Sir Knight, Howard E. Morrill.

The parents lose an affectionate son, whose life was full of promise, the community a loving friend, the Tent a faithful member; but we trust that our loss will be his gain.

That we bow in humble submission to Him who doeth all things well; and be it further

Resolved, That our charter be draped for 90 days, that these resolutions be spread upon the records of the Tent, that a copy be sent to the bereft family of the deceased, that they be published in the Alcona County Review, that a copy be sent to the Michigan Maccabee for publication.

Charles Holcomb,
Fred A. Becker,
A. J. Woods,
Committee.
Alcona County Review, September 2, 1897
Cemetery: Elmwood, St. Clair Co.

Morrill, Hulda [Knapp]

Gustin Grist.

Mr. Levi Morrill was in Bay City last week on business. He returned Saturday night only to learn the sad news of his mother's death.
Alcona County Review, March 14, 1895

Gustin Grist.
Mrs. Hulda Morrill died at Killmaster at the residence of her son, Jesse Morrill, March 8, 1895. She was one of the pioneers of Michigan. Born in New York state, Dec. 10th, 1822, she came to this state in March, 1824, and settled in Oakland county where she resided until 1843, when she married Levi Morrill. Six years later she and her husband moved to St. Clair county, where she continued to reside until she came to Alcona county some two years ago with her sons, Levi and Jesse, and a daughter. She has been a member of the Methodist church for nearly 40 years. She leaves five children, two sons and three daughters, to mourn their great loss. Her remains were taken to Yale by the two sons and one daughter for burial beside those of her husband, who preceded her to the better land a little more than three years ago. She died very peacefully. No one but her daughter-in-law was present, who thought she was asleep until time for her to take another dose of medicine and she was found cold in death.

The Rev. Van Horn of West Harrisville preached the funeral sermon at the residence of Jesse Morrill. Those who are left to mourn have the heartfelt sympathy of this community.
Alcona County Review, March 14, 1895
Cemetery: Elmwood, St. Clair Co.

Morris, Albert

LOCAL JOTTINGS.
The little child of Mrs. John Morris is quite ill with spinal fever.
Alcona County Review, January 2, 1885

LOCAL JOTTINGS.
Albert, the younger child of Mrs. John Morris, died last Sunday evening, of spinal fever, after a long and painful illness. Albert was a very bright little boy, but his short life seemed to be full of misfortune. Less than two years ago he was pushed over on the sidewalk by a huge dog and one of his legs fractured. He was aged four years and two months.
Alcona County Review, February 27, 1885
Cemetery: Springport, Alcona Co.

Morris, Charlie G.

COUNTY REVIEWINGS.

Death has again visited the home of Mr. and Mrs. Morris, snatching from their embrace a darling little son, who remained to gladden their home only a few short months. The little one was buried Tuesday afternoon.
Alcona County Review, January 28, 1881

Died on Jan. 23rd Charlie G., son of Mr. and Mrs. J. W. Morris, aged 7 months and 13 days.
Published by request:

Why God called our little Charlie,
Is more than we can tell;
But thank God we have the comfort
That he doeth all things well.

His little crib is vacant now,
His cup is idle too;
But our darling is in heaven,
And the angels guard his brow.

His little day on earth was dear,
His life was full of pain.
Oh, Charlie dear, what means this tear
That asks thee back again.

Friendship and love here done their last,
And now can do no more;
The bitterness of death is past,

And all his suffering oer.

But again we have to meet him,
When the day of life is past,
Then in heaven with joy to greet him,
Where no farewell tear is shed.

Alcona County Review, January 28, 1881

A Card of Thanks.

Mr. and Mrs. J. W. Morris wish to return their sincere thanks to all those friends who so kindly assisted and comforted them during the sickness and death of their little one.

Alcona County Review, January 28, 1881
Cemetery: Springport, Alcona Co.

Morris, John

PERSONAL POINTS.

John Morris Sr. was taken seriously ill Tuesday and is still quite sick.

Alcona County Review, August 31, 1899

JOHN MORRIS, DECEASED.

John Morris, for nearly 30 years a respected resident of Harrisville, passed to the silent majority early Tuesday morning after a two weeks' illness from dysentery.

Deceased was born in England in 1822. His parents came to this country during his infancy, landing in New York. He was left to shift for himself at the tender age of ten. In November, 1870, he came to Harrisville and has resided here ever since. In the early years he acted as fireman at Colwell's mills, both the old and new, and also at the Black River mill.

Deceased was married three times. Of the first union but one child survives, viz: Mrs. Jas. W. Morris, our respected townsman. Mrs. Morris and three young children, Tommy, Dollie and Fannie, are left to mourn the loss of their husband and father.

Funeral today at 2 o'clock p.m. from the Methodist church. Interment at the west cemetery.

Alcona County Review, September 21, 1899
Cemetery: West Lawn, Alcona Co.

Morris, Louis

A fatal accident occurred Monday on the A. S. & N. W. Ry. in which Louis Morris, a train dispatcher, lost his life. Morris was struck by a snow plow attached to an engine, the wheel of which broke allowing it to swing around. He lived until Tuesday night. Only a day or so before a brother of the dead man was shot in the leg in Alpena.

Alcona County Review, February 23, 1893
Cemetery:

Morris, Mrs. Susan L.

Gone!

Just as we go to press we are informed of the sad news of the death of Susan L., wife of Mr. John Morris, of this village, which occurred at noon to-day [Friday]. This is indeed sad news, and falls with startling effect upon the entire community. Mrs. Morris was aged 45 years and 6 months. She had been a resident of this village for a large number of years and had always been identified with every interest tending toward the development of Christianity, morality and temperance, among the people. She was a christian in both practice and experience, [a member of the M. E. church of this village], and might always be found partaking of every means of grace that she might the better serve her great Master, who has now called her home to eternital joy and rest. In this life of hers it may be said: "She has done what she could." The sympathy of the entire community will be extended to the grief-stricken husband and other near relatives left behind.

It is expected that the funeral services of the deceased will be held from the M. E. church Sunday afternoon at 2:00 o'clock.

Alcona County Review, February 4, 1881
Cemetery: Springport, Alcona Co.

Morris, Mrs. Walter

COUNTY REVIEWINGS.

Just as we go to press we learn of the death of Mrs. Walter Morris, of Alcona, which occurred last night.

Alcona County Review, May 28, 1880
Cemetery:

Morrisette, Mrs. Alex

The Deadly Canned Goods.

Last week the family of Alex Morrisette of Au Sable partook of some canned beans for dinner and two of the family including Geo. Sutherland and Mrs. Morrisette became violently ill soon afterwards with every symptom of lead poisoning. Sutherland recovered but the woman became gradually worse until last Monday morning when she died. Her death is attributed to the poisoned beans.

The death of Mrs. Morrisette at Au Sable from lead poisoning suggests a simple precaution against such unfortunate occurrences. Upon opening a can of fruit or vegetables the contents should be immediately removed; exposure to the air for a few minutes only is sufficient to completely impregnate the contents with the deadly poison.

Alcona County Review, May 31, 1889
Cemetery:

Morrison, {Boy}

The Local News

The remains of a boy named Morrison were brought to this village from West Harrisville Monday for burial. He was a son of the late Matt Morrison and had been a confirmed invalid for months.

Alcona County Review, August 25, 1892
Cemetery: Probably Springport, Alcona Co.

Morrison, John

Funeral Services.
(Communicated.)

The funeral services of John Morrison were held at his residence on Saturday last, and although there was a heavy storm a great many friends and sympathizers were present. The remains were interred in the Harrisville burying ground. Rev. T. B. Leath preached from 1st Samuel XX, 18: "And Thou shalt be missed because Thy seat will be empty." The preacher first spoke of the hatred of Saul for David, and as a result of this hatred Johnathan loved David all the more. The bible says Johnathan's love was wonderful, surpassing the love of woman. The interpretation of feeling was complete, and so it was in reference to man and wife who were living in right relations similar to the pure love that bound David and Jonathan. The wilder the storm raged outside the closer their hearts were drawn together. 1st, He will be missed at the table, the bread winner has gone. 2d, He will be missed because his seat will be empty at the fireside in the social circle. 3d, He will be missed because his seat will be empty on board the boat among his fellow sailors. Soon it will be said of everyone of us, our seat is empty. But there is a shining seat which we all may gain among the blood washed throng.

His widow and their children return to Bigden in Canada, where they intend remaining this winter. May the God of consolation and grace keep her children to the end of life.

"Beyond the parting and the meeting,
I shall be soon.
Beyond the farewell and the greeting,
Beyond the pulse's fever beating,
I shall be soon
Love, rest and home!
Sweet home!
Lord, tarry not, but come."

Alcona County Review, November 13, 1885
Cemetery: Probably Springport, Alcona Co.

Morrison, Matthew

LOCAL JOTTINGS.

Matthew Morrison is seriously ill and is confined to his home in this village.

Later.——Morrison died Wednesday morning. The disease that claims him for a victim was the dreaded consumption. He leaves a wife and two children.

Alcona County Review, January 18, 1889
Cemetery: Probably Springport, Alcona Co.

Morton, Herman

Haynes Happenings.

Haynes, Dec. 18.--A child of Lyman Morton took the diphtheria but is reported that he is recovering again.

Alcona County Review, December 20, 1894

Haynes Happenings.
Haynes, Jan. 29th.--Lyman Morton's child died very suddenly Saturday. It was playing in the forenoon and died about 3 o'clock p. m. It had had a slight attack of diphtheria and had recovered. He was 13 months and 11 days old, and it was their first and only child. The parents have the sympathy of the community and your correspondent in their hour of affliction.

Alcona County Review, January 31, 1895

Haynes Happenings.

Lyman Morton's child was two years, one month and eleven days old when he died.
Haynes, Feb. 12th, 1895.

Alcona County Review, February 14, 1895
Cemetery: Mt. Joy, Alcona Co.

Morton, Sarah [Clark]

Haynes Happenings.
Haynes, Aug. 7th

Mrs. Lyman Morton has been under Dr. Mitchell's care for several days; her case was critical but now she is reported as improving.

Alcona County Review, August 8, 1895

Haynes Happenings.
October 8, 1895.
Miss Margaret Clork is not improving. Her sister, Mrs. Lyman Morton, is very poorly. Consumption is thought to be the cause.

Consumption is the most fatal and frequent disease in our township.

Alcona County Review, October 10, 1895

A SAD COINCIDENCE.

Two sisters Die on Succeeding Days and Are Buried in One Grave
----

Haynes, November 12, 1895.
Mrs. Lyman Morton, nee Sarah Clark, passed away quietly on the morning of the 7th at the home of her parents. Her sickness commenced about three months ago, when she gave premature birth to a child, after which she fell into a decline or quick consumption. She was aged 21 years.

Her sister, Miss Maggie Clark, took her departure on the evening of the 8th, at 9 o'clock p.m., aged 19 years, after a lingering illness of three years from that dread disease, consumption.

The mortal remains of both sisters were conveyed to the Presbyterian church about noon Sunday, when the Rev. H. A. Long preached a very effective funeral sermon. The remains were then borne to the cemetery, followed by a large concourse of relatives and sympathizing friends. Both were interred in one grave side by side.

Memory will their vigils keep,
Gathered `round their narrow coffins,
Stand a mourning funeral train;
While for them redeemed too early,
Tears are falling down like rain.
Hopes are crushed and hearts are bleeding,
Drear the fireside now and lone;
They, the best loved and dearest,
Far away to Heaven hath flown.
Long, long will we miss thee, Sarah,
Long watch for Maggie keep;
And through many nights of sorrow,
Memory will thy vigils keep.

The bereft parents and husband of the departed have the sympathy of the whole community in their great sorrow in the loss of their beloved ones.

Quite a number of the deceased's friends and relatives from Black River and West Harrisville were present at the funeral.

Alcona County Review, November 14, 1895
Cemetery: Mt. Joy, Alcona Co.

Morton, Thomas Harvey

Harvey Morton Killed.
Another death was added Monday to the already long list of those who have been killed recently on the D. B. C. & A. R. R. in this vicinity. Harvey Morton, a young man employed as a brakeman on a log train was run over and his head, right arm and left leg severed from the body. The accident occurred on the Mud Lake branch, and was caused by the fracture of a brake chain, which precipitated him from the running train. The embankment being precipitous the unfortunate man slipped under the wheels with the above horrible result. Morton was about 25 years of age and was only recently married.

Alcona County Review, March 16, 1888

ALCONA ATOMS.

Harvey Mourton was buried on the 15th. The funeral service was largely attended; several teams from Harrisville with the friends and neighbors of the bereaved widow attended.

Alcona County Review, March 23, 1888

ORDER OF PUBLICATION.
STATE OF MICHIGAN, County of Alcona.

At a session of the Probate Court for said county, held at the Probate office, in the village of Harrisville, on the twenty-fifth day of September, in the year one thousand eight hundred and eighty-eight. Present, Allen Nevin, Esq., Judge of Probate. In the matter of the
ESTATE OF THOMAS HARVEY MORTON,
deceased. On reading and filing the petition, duly verified, of Lizana Morton, the widow of said deceased, praying that administrator of said estate be granted to her or some other suitable person. Thereupon it is ordered, that Monday, the Twenty-Second Day of October next, at ten o'clock in the forenoon, be assigned for the hearing of said petition, and that the widow and heirs at law of said deceased, and all other persons interested in said estate, are required to appear at a session of said Court, then to be holden in the Probate

office, in the village of Harrisville, and show cause, if any there be, why the prayer of the petitioner should not be granted: And it is further ordered, that said petitioner give notice to the heirs at law and all persons interested in said estate, of the pendency of said petition, and the hearing thereof, by causing a copy of this order to be published in the Alcona County Review, a newspaper printed and circulated in said county, for three successive weeks previous to said day of hearing.

ALLEN NEVIN, Judge of Probate.

Alcona County Review, September 28, 1888

Order of Publication.

STATE OF MICHIGAN, County of Alcona.

At a session of the Probate Court for said county, held at the Probate office in the village of Harrisville, on Tuesday, the 15th day of January, in the year one thousand eight hundred and eighty-nine. Present, George S. Ritchie, Judge of Probate. In the matter of the

ESTATE OF THOMAS HARVEY MORTON,

deceased. On reading and filing the petition, duly verified, of Lizana Morton, the widow, and Mark Morton, the father of said deceased, praying for the administration of said estate, and for the appointment of the said Mark Morton, or some other suitable person, administrator thereof. Thereupon it is ordered, that Saturday, the Sixteenth Day of February, next, at two o'clock in the afternoon, be assigned for the hearing of said petition, and that the widow and heirs at law of said deceased, and all other persons interested in said estate, are required to appear at a session of said Court, then to be holden in the Probate office, in the village of Harrisville, and show cause, if any there be, why the prayer of the petitioner should not be granted: And it is further ordered, that said petitioner give notice of the pendency of said petition, and the hearing thereof, by causing a copy of this order to be published in the Alcona County Review, a newspaper printed and circulated in said county, for four successive weeks previous to said day of hearing.

GEORGE S. RITCHIE,
Judge of Probate.

Alcona County Review, January 18, 1889

LOCAL JOTTINGS.

Mark Morton, administrator of the estate of his son, Harvey Morton, has commenced suit by summons in the circuit court against the Detroit, Bay City & Alpena R. R. company for $25,000 damages. Young Morton was killed on the railroad last year while in the employ of the defendant as brakeman on a logging train. While setting a brake the brake chain broke precipitating Morton under the wheels. The declaration charges the railroad with criminal negligence. Hon. Frank Emerick is attorney for the plaintiff.

Alcona County Review, April 19, 1889

THE COURT RECORD.

Following is the court record for the term of circuit court held last week.

Mark Morton administrator vs. the Detroit, Bay City and Alpena railroad, verdict for plaintiff for $4,000 above costs and charges.

This was a case in which damages were claimed for the death of Harvey Morton, a young man who was killed near Black river last year, while in the employ of the defendant railroad. While engaged in the performance of his duties the brake chain on a log truck broke and he was precipitated under the wheels with fatal results. Negligence was charged against the railroad company for not providing a stronger brake chain.

Alcona County Review, November 8, 1889

BELATED NEWS NOTES.

The Supreme Court has affirmed the judgment of the circuit court of this county, giving the estate of Harvey Morton $4,000 for the death of the latter through negligence on the part of the D., B. C. & A. R. R. It was generally considered a just verdict. Particulars of the case have been published in these columns.

Alcona County Review, June 27, 1890

One Year's History.

Record of Local Happenings for the Year 1890.

JUNE.

June 15. Supreme Court affirmed the decision of the lower court giving the estate of Harvey Morton $4,000

damages against the D. B. C & A. R. R.

Alcona County Review, January 2, 1891

Haynes Happenings.

Mark Morton has erected a beautiful monument in memory of his three children and two grandchildren.

Alcona County Review, May 24, 1894
Cemetery: Mt. Joy, Alcona Co.

Mosser, Jennie

A TERRIBLE DISASTER.

THE OLD RELIABLE GONE.

Burning of the Str. Marine City Off Alcona, Sunday Afternoon Last.

Three Men Burned to Death in the Hold of the Vessel.

Numerous Other Lives Lost.

Heroic Conduct of Capt. Comer and Crew.

Within the history of all marine disasters in this part of the country, none has created equal excitement to that caused by the burning of the steamer Marine City off Alcona, this county, last Sunday afternoon.

It was about 3:30 o'clock. The boat had just previously been into Alcona to take on a cargo of shingles, and was about two miles out from the dock, south-east, when smoke and flames were seen issuing from the hurricane deck about the smoke-stack. The steamer was in command of the first mate, Wm. Smith, at the time. Capt. Comer having "turned in" for his usual nap, and the mate being apprised of the situation, immediately rushed to and informed the captain, who, without stopping to dress rushed forward in his "sleeping clothes" to the scene of flame and from thence to the forward deck, and commenced to issue orders appropriate to an occasion of that kind. The tinder-like condition of the upper works of the boat caused the same to burn with almost lightning rapidity, and hot flames soon began to crowd the panic-stricken passengers to either end of the craft and from thence into the water. The tug Vulcan, which happened to be coming up the lake, and was about two miles east-by-south from the burning steamer, spying the same, applied full steam and put for the scene of the disaster with all possible haste, manning her life-boats and making all possible preparations for the rescue of passengers, on the way. The tug Grayling, which was coming out of Black River with a raft spied the burning steamer about the same time, and hastily cutting loose from her tow, also proceeded to the ill-fated boat to render what assistance she could, having all things ready for successful work when she arrived on the scene. The captains and crews of both these tugs worked in a most successful and untiring manner, and succeeded in rescuing a large majority of the persons aboard the ill-fated steamer. It was a very

FORTUNATE CIRCUMSTANCE

that the tugs Vulcan and Grayling happened to be in the vicinity, otherwise the loss of life must from the nature of things have been terrible. The burning boat was over a mile from shore and the strong east wind made a heavy sea. Very few could ever have reached the shore alive if they had jumped overboard and tried to swim, even with life preservers or floating boards and tables. Therefore it was providential that the tugs happened to be near and equally a fortunate circumstance that the captains of those tugs had a realizing sense of their responsibility in the matter and coolness and courage to do the best possible thing. The conduct of Capt. Thomas Hackett of The Vulcan was especially praiseworthy and has been praised on every hand. He ran up alongside the burning boat and took off the passengers at the risk of his own vessel taking fire. In fact, it was badly scorched and on fire several times. The crew of the tug must have been equally cool and self-possessed to have done their work so well and to have extinguished the fire as it caught upon the upperworks of the tug. No vessel but a tug could have done this work so well. A large steamer would have been unmanagable in the strong wind and heavy sea, and there would have been greater danger of the ignition of her upperworks. But the tug was easily controlled and was able, thanks to Capt. Hackett, to

render most valuable assistance in saving human life.

THE SAVED.

The following is a list of the passengers known to have been saved [only those from Alcona & Alpena area are listed here; the list in the paper is very long]:

Altman, Charles, Alpena.
Beard, F. E., Alcona.
Butterfield, G. T. and wife, Alpena.
Cole, W. B., Rogers City.
Galling, Charles, and two children, Alpena.
Heron, John, Alcona.
Howard, Lafayette, Alcona.
Hudson, Alice, Alcona.
Hueber, Mrs. Chas., Alpena.
Jones, J. N., Alpena.
Keifer, A., Alcona.
Keys, John, Alpena.
Levere, Jules, Alpena.
Matthews, Ella, Alpena.
Matthews, Robert, Alpena.
McLennan, James, Harrisville.
Miller, Joseph, Rogers City.
Moebs, Gus, Alpena.
Perrault, Joseph, Alpena.
Schunk, Charles, Alpena.
Seguin, Isaac, Alpena.
Stockwell, Dr. G. A., Alcona.

THE LOST.

It is impossible to obtain a correct list of the number of persons lost, the trip sheets of the boat, giving the names of the passengers, having been burned, but the best estimate of the clerk, steward and surmising passengers fixes the number between 18 to 20. The following persons are missing and believed to have been drowned:

The father and son of Mrs. McElroy, wife of the editor of the Toledo *Blade*.
Jenny Muzzy, of Alcona.
Richard Schultz, head waiter.
James Griffin, head cook.
Frank Emmet, a musician on the boat, of Port Huron.
Nicholas Watson of Detroit.
Deck passenger, name not known, from Point St. Ignace.
Three persons—formerly deck hands on the steamer Geo. L. Dunlap—unobservedly stowed themselves away among the freight in the hold of the Marine City, with a view to securing free passage to Detroit. One of the party escaped, but thinks his two associates perished in the place of their concealment.

Alcona County Review, September 3, 1880

County Reviewings.

The bodies of Dr. C. Pomeroy and Guy McElroy, of Toledo, Ohio, and the body of Jenny Mosser of Alcona, were found by the Life Saving Crew on Wednesday last, the former two near the station, the latter a mile south. The bodies of Dr. Pomeroy and nephew were shipped to their relatives in Toledo.

Alcona County Review, September 10, 1880
Cemetery: Mt. Joy, Alcona Co.

Mosso, {Male}

EVENTS OF ONE WEEK.

The remains of a young married man named Mosso were brought to Harrisville last Thursday from the vicinity of Killmaster for in interment in the Catholic cemetery. He was about 30 and died of consumption.

Alcona County Review, November 22, 1894
Cemetery: St. Anne's, Alcona Co.

Mosure, Edward

NEIGHBORHOOD NOTES.

Edward Mosure fell off Gratwick, Smith & Fryer's tram at Oscoda and was drowned in the lake. He was aged 22 years' and his home was at Deckerville Sanilac county.

Alcona County Review, August 30, 1889
Cemetery:

Mudgett, Edith May

Obituary.

The terrible destroyer Death has twice visited the home of D. B. Mudgett during the past week, each time coming masked in that dire disease, so surely fatal among its younger victims, cholera-infantum. Sunday morning last the sad news were heard that the infant son had passed away, and while the parents' grief was yet fresh their sorrows were doubled by the death of the little daughter Edith, scarcely two years old. The infant was buried Monday afternoon, with services at the house, and the funeral of Edith will be held to-morrow afternoon at 1 o'clock at the M. E. church, Rev. Mr. McIntosh officiating.

*Baby's left the cradle, for the golden shore
Or the silvery waters, she has flown,
Gone to join the angels—peaceful ever more;
Empty is the cradle, baby's gone.*

Alcona County Review, August 25, 1882

HOME NEWS JOTTINGS.

The funeral services of little Edith Mudgett were postponed from last Saturday to Sunday morning on account of the absence of Mr. Mudgett.

Alcona County Review, September 1, 1882
Cemetery: Springport, Alcona Co.

Mudgett, Florence M.

LOCAL JOTTINGS.

Once again the angel of death has visited the home of Mr. and Mrs. D. B. Mudgett, removing from their midst a lovely little daughter, less than two years of age. The little one had been ailing for some weeks past, and death relieved it of its suffering Tuesday night. While to the parents and others of the household the removal of these precious little lights causes sorrow and grief, and often makes home seem dark and desolate, yet it is the voice of Jesus that calls them to that blissful realm to which any of the storms and blasts cannot enter. With our little ones safe in the arms of the precious Savior, who died to redeem them, what have we to fear?

"Little children, little children,
Who love their Redeemer.
Are His dear ones, are His pure ones,
His loved and His own.
Like the stars in the morning,
His bright crown adorning;
They shall shine in the beauty,
Bright gems for His Crown."

Alcona County Review, October 30, 1885

LOCAL JOTTINGS.

The funeral services of the little daughter of Mr. and Mrs. Mudgett was held from the M. E. church yesterday afternoon.

Alcona County Review, October 30, 1885
Cemetery: Springport, Alcona Co.

Mudgett, Olive [Burt]

Death of Mrs. D. B. Mudgett.

One of the saddest events that it has been our duty to chronicle is the death after a brief illness, at her home near this village, of Mrs. D. B. Mudgett. She passed away Sunday evening, surrounded by her children and friends, but the partner of her joys and sorrows was not present. He had gone only a few short days before on a long trip to points in Tennessee and Virginia to seek a location and prepare for the early removal of

himself and dear ones to a new home in the south. Telegrams carried the sad news to every point where it was thought that Mr. Mudgett might be, but it was not until Tuesday that he was found at Coldwater, Mich., where he had stopped on his homeward way to visit relatives. O, how inscrutable are the ways of Providence. What a desolate home to which to return!

The sympathy of the entire community—such poor sympathy as man can give to man—goes out to the bereaved husband and his family.

Mrs. Mudgett was one of a family of six children—four brothers and one sister. Her maiden name was Olive Burt, and she was born march 7, 1844, at Addison, Stuben Co., N. Y., moving to Michigan in 1868, her husband having reached this state the previous year. She was the mother of seven children, four of whom, two sons and two daughters, survive her. The funeral services were held yesterday at the deceased's late residence, the Rev. C. B. Steele officiating.

Alcona County Review, March 25, 1887

Card of Thanks.

I wish to publicly thank the many friends who were so kind to my family during the last illness and death of my wife.

D. B. Mudgett.

Alcona County Review, April 1, 1887

PROBATE ORDER.

State of Michigan, County of Alcona.

At a session of the Probate Court for said County, held at the Probate Office, in the Village of Harrisville, on the 31st day of March, in the year one thousand eight hundred and eighty-seven. Present, Allen Nevins, Judge of Probate. In the matter of the **ESTATE OF OLIVE MUDGETT, DECEASED.**

On reading and filing the petition, duly verified, of David B. Mudgett, praying that administration of said estate be granted to Edwin Mudgett or some other suitable person.

Thereupon it is ordered, that Saturday, the Twenty-Third Day of April next, at 10 o'clock in the forenoon, be assigned for the hearing of said petition, and that the heirs-at-law of said deceased, and all other persons interested in said estate, are required to appear at a session of said

court, then to be holden in the Probate Court, in the Village of Harrisville, and show cause, if any there be, why the prayer of the petitioner should not be granted; And it is further ordered, that said petitioner give notice to the persons interested in said estate, of the pendency of said petition, and the hearing thereof, by causing a copy of this order to be published in the Alcona County Review, a newspaper printed and circulated in said county, three successive weeks previous to said day of hearing.

Allen Nevins, Judge of Probate.

Alcona County Review, April 1, 1887

ORDER OF HEARING.

State of Michigan, County of Alcona.

At a session of the Probate Court for said county, held at the Probate Office in the village of Harrisville, on the eighteenth day of May, in the year one thousand eight hundred and eighty-seven. Present, Allen Nevins, Judge of Probate. In the matter of the **ESTATE OF OLIVE MUDGETT, DECEASED.**

On reading and filing the petition, duly verified, of Mitchell Prue, praying that an order may be made by this court authorizing and directing Edwin Mudgett Administrator of the estate of said deceased, to convey to said Mitchell Prue the north-west quarter of the south-west quarter of section three; the south half of the south-east quarter of section four; the north half of the north-east quarter of section nine; the west half of the north-west quarter of section ten, all in town 26 north of range 9 east, County of Alcona, State of Michigan. Thereupon it is ordered that Saturday, the Eighteenth Day of June, 1887, next, at ten o'clock in the forenoon, be assigned for the hearing of said petition, and that the heirs at law of said deceased, and all other persons interested in said estate, are required to appear at a session of said court then to be holden at the Probate office, in the village of Harrisville, and show cause if any there be, why the prayer of the petitioner should not be granted. And it is further ordered that said petitioner give notice to the heirs at law, and other persons interested in said estate, of the pendency of said petition, and the hearing thereon, by causing a copy of this order to be published in the Alcona County Review, a newspaper printed and circulated in said county, four successive weeks previous to said day of hearing.

Allen Nevins, Judge of Probate.

Alcona County Review, May 20, 1887

PROBATE ORDER.

State of Michigan, County of Alcona.

Notice is hereby given that by order of the Probate Court for the County of Alcona, made on the 23d day of April, 1887, six months from that date were allowed for creditors to present their claims against the estate of Olive Mudgett, late of said county, deceased and that all creditors of said deceased are required to present their claims to said Probate Court, at the Probate office in the village of Harrisville, for examination and allowance on or before the 24th Day of October, 1887, next, and that such claims will be heard before said Court, on Monday, the 25th day of August, 1887, and on Monday, the 24th day of October, 1887, next, at 10 o'clock in the forenoon of each of those days.

Dated April 23d, 1887.

Allen Nevins, Judge of Probate.

Alcona County Review, July 8, 1887
Cemetery: Springport, Alcona Co.

Mudgett, Raymond

Obituary.

The terrible destroyer Death has twice visited the home of D. B. Mudgett during the past week, each time coming masked in that dire disease, so surely fatal among its younger victims, cholera-infantum. Sunday morning last the sad news were heard that the infant son had passed away, and while the parents' grief was yet fresh their sorrows were doubled by the death of the little daughter Edith, scarcely two years old. The infant was buried Monday afternoon, with services at the house, and the funeral of Edith will be held to-morrow afternoon at 1 o'clock at the M. E. church, Rev. Mr. McIntosh officiating.

Baby's left the cradle, for the golden shore
Or the silvery waters, she has flown,
Gone to join the angels—peaceful ever more;
Empty is the cradle, baby's gone.

Alcona County Review, August 25, 1882
Cemetery: Springport, Alcona Co.

Muellerweiss, Etta

Hunter Savidge Capsized.

The schooner Hunter Savidge, owned by John Mullerwise of Alpena capsized in a sudden squall off Point Aux Barques Sunday afternoon. Mrs. Mullerwise and 6-year old son, the Captain's wife and son and the mate of the boat were lost.

Alcona County Review, August 24, 1899

The schooner Hunter Savidge, which capsized off Point Aux Barques August 19th, has not been found and it is thought the vessel has gone to the bottom, taking with it the bodies of Mrs. Mullerweiss and daughter, of Alpena and Mrs. Capt. Sharpstein.

Alcona County Review, August 31, 1899
Cemetery:

Muellerweiss, Mrs. Mary

Hunter Savidge Capsized.

The schooner Hunter Savidge, owned by John Mullerwise of Alpena capsized in a sudden squall off Point Aux Barques Sunday afternoon. Mrs. Mullerwise and 6-year old son, the Captain's wife and son and the mate of the boat were lost.

Alcona County Review, August 24, 1899

The schooner Hunter Savidge, which capsized off Point Aux Barques August 19th, has not been found and it is thought the vessel has gone to the bottom, taking with it the bodies of Mrs. Mullerweiss and daughter, of Alpena and Mrs. Capt. Sharpstein.

Alcona County Review, August 31, 1899
Cemetery:

Mulhatton, {Male}

A Drowning in Mitchell Township.

A man named Mulhatton, a brother of Pat Mulhatton of Mitchell township, was drowned a few days since. The particulars as reported are as follows: Mulhatton started for his cows; in his way lay a small lake which he started to go around, but Dunc Duggan who was near at hand in a small skiff invited him to get in and he would row him across. Duggan commenced rocking the boat after they got away from shore. The frail craft took in water, filled and went over. Duggan being a good swimmer reached shore in safety, Mulhatton, less fortunate, sank to the bottom to rise no more. Deceased was about 35 years of age and unmarried.

Alcona County Review, August 25, 1892

HISTORY OF ONE YEAR.

Chronological History of the Past Year, 1892.

August.

20. Pat Mulhatton drowned in McCollum Lake.

Alcona County Review, January 5, 1893
Cemetery:

Mulhatton, Patrick

CURRAN.

Pat Mulhatten is very low. He has been very sick for a long time.

Alcona County Review, May 26, 1898

Patrick Mulhatton, a well known citizen of Mitchell township, died Saturday at his late home at the age of 62. The funeral occurred Monday and the burial took place in the cemetery at West Harrisville. Deceased had been in ill health for some time. He was held in high esteem by those who knew him.

Alcona County Review, May 26, 1898

Local History of One Year

Chronology of the Principal Events of the Year 1898.

June 11. Death of Patrick Mulhatton, aged 62, of Mitchell.

Alcona County Review, January 5, 1899
Cemetery: Twin Lakes, Alcona Co.

Mulhatton, Susan McCoy [Elgar]

CURRAN.

Mrs. Susan McCoy died here at 4 o'clock Monday morning.

Alcona County Review, October 13, 1898

DEAD WOMAN'S HOUSE WAS BURNED.

Mrs. Mulhatton, widow of the late Patrick Mulhatton of Mitchell township, died Monday and was buried at West Harrisville Wednesday morning.

The funeral procession left the deceased's late home at a late hour Tuesday night. After that time the dwelling was fired in some way, whether by incendiary or not is not known, but the circumstances point to that. It was entirely destroyed with the contents.

Alcona County Review, October 13, 1898

CURRAN.

Frank Atherton and Miss Bertha McCoy attended the funeral of Mrs. Susan McCoy, formerly Mulhatton.

Alcona County Review, October 20, 1898
Cemetery: Twin Lakes, Alcona Co.

Murphy, Daniel

COUNTY REVIEWINGS.

Fatal Accident.—On Tuesday last a sad accident occurred at Black River which resulted in the death of Daniel Murphy. While Murphy was helping load a car with logs at Frazer's camp, one of the logs rolled back from the car and across his neck, causing instant death. He was a young man of 23 years of age and has friends living in Canada, near Quebec. The remains were interred in the Catholic cemetery in this place Wednesday afternoon.

Alcona County Review, August 8, 1880

Black River Items.

Daniel Murphy was killed Tuesday while loading timber for R. A. Alger & Co., at Frazer's camp.

Alcona County Review, August 8, 1880
Cemetery: St. Anne's, Alcona Co.

Murphy, Jerry E.

Among Our Exchanges.

From the Lakeside Monitor.

Three Au Sable boys named Jerry Murphy, Seymour McLeod and Roeul Valle, were drowned Tuesday afternoon while in swimming on the shore below Penoyar Bros.' docks. The Valle boy got into deep water and the other two were drowned in trying to save him. The bodies were not recovered until they had been in the water over an hour.

The boys were all between 11 and 12 years of age. Jerry Murphy was the son of Eugene Murphy and Seymour McLeod a son of John McLeod.

Alcona County Review, July 21, 1892
Cemetery:Sacred Heart, Iosco Co.

Murphy, Patrick

COUNTY NEWS JOTTINGS.

Mr. P. Murphy, one of the pioneers of Iosco county, died at his residence in Au Sable, yesterday, from the effects of a cancer. He will be buried Sunday afternoon at two o'clock, with Masonic honors.

Alcona County Review, July 13, 1877
Cemetery: Pinecrest, Iosco Co.

Murray, Mrs.

Received Fatal Injuries.

Mrs. Murray, a widow, aged about 76 years, was thrown from her buggy Tuesday of last week and sustained injuries from which she died the next day.

She was a resident of Mikado township and was on her way home from Harrisville, where she had been called on legal business.

Her horse, it is stated, became frightened at a cow coming suddenly from the bushes on the side of the road, and the above fatal results was the outcome.

Alcona County Review, July 14, 1898

Local History of One Year

Chronology of the Principal Events of the Year 1898.

July 5. Mrs. Murray, aged 76, resident of Mikado, thrown from buggy. Injuries fatal.

Alcona County Review, January 5, 1899
Cemetery:

Myers, Charles

County Reviewings.

Marine Disaster.— On Monday evening, the steam barge D. W. Rust, Captain Pringle, collided with the schooner F. B. Berriman, Captain Thomas, about ten miles off Sturgeon Point, near this place. The Berriman was loaded with forty-two thousand bushels of wheat, and sunk in less than fifteen minutes after the collision took place. Andrew Halcrow and Charles Myers were lost. One of the crew, whose name we did not learn, had his leg badly fractured. All but the two parties named were taken on the barge and saved. The Rust, loaded with coal, was considerable injured, and now lies at East Tawas in a sinking condition.

Alcona County Review, May 11, 1877
Cemetery:

Napaire, Louis

Death of Louis Napaire.

At a session of the Probate Court for said County, held at the Probate office, in the village of Harrisville on the 22d day of October, in the year one thousand, eight hundred and ninety-two.

Present, Geo. S. Ritchie, Judge of Probate.

In the Matter of the Estate of Louis Napaire:

On reading and filing the petition, duly verified, of Frank Napaire, praying that he or some other suitable person be granted administration of said estate:

Thereupon it is ordered, that Saturday, the 12th day of November next, at ten o'clock in the forenoon, be assigned for the hearing of said petition, and that the sole heirs at law of said deceased, and all other persons interested in said estate, are required to appear at a session of said Court, then to be holden in the Probate office, in the village of Harrisville and show cause, if any there be, why the prayer of the petitioner should not be granted: And it is further ordered, that said petitioner give notice to the persons interested in said estate, of the pendency of said petition, and the hearing thereof, by causing a copy of this order to be published in the Alcona County Review, a newspaper printed and circulated in said county, 3 successive weeks previous to said day of hearing.

Geo. S. Ritchie,
Judge of Probate.

Alcona County Review, October 27, 1892

HISTORY OF ONE YEAR.

Chronological History of the Past Year, 1892.

May.

27. Louis Napair fatally injured in Black River saw mill.

Alcona County Review, January 5, 1893
Cemetery:

Naylor, Peter

Jottings Along the Shore.

The body of Peter Naylor, of Alpena, who has been missing for three weeks, was found near Towbridge Point, where it was washed Tuesday morning.

Alcona County Review, May 21, 1880
Cemetery:

Neafie, Charles M.

Some of our readers may possibly remember C. M. Neafie, a printer employed in this office a number of years ago. A marked copy of the Citizen, published at Phelps, Ontario Co., N. Y., contains an extended account of Neafie's death at Milwaukee, March 15th after a brief illness from pneumonia. The deceased was 28 years of age. After leaving Harrisville he was employed in Cheboygan, Manistee and at the time of his death in the city of Milwaukee. His parents reside at

Phelps, N. Y. to which place his remains were taken for interment.

Alcona County Review, April 13, 1888
Cemetery: Resthaven, Ontario Co., NY

Nearning, Frank
Killed By the Cars

The Saturday night express train out of Alpena ran into a team at the Bulluck crossing above Ossineke. Frank Nearing, the driver, was instantly killed and badly mangled. Both horses were killed and the sleigh was smashed into kindling wood. Louis Nearing, brother of Frank, was lying asleep in the sleigh when the accident occurred. He escaped unhurt and could tell nothing about the accident. They lived at Ossineke.

Alcona County Review, March 3, 1898
Cemetery:

Nedeau, Hubert
LOCAL JOTTINGS.

G. G. Ferguson and family were called to Alpena, last Thursday, to attend the funeral of Hubert Nedeau, Mrs. Ferguson's father, who died in that city on the 25th ult., aged 69 years.

Alcona County Review, June 4, 1886
Cemetery: Holy Cross, Alpena Co.

Nedeau, Samuel
Your Folks and Our Folks.

Geo. Ferguson and family went to Alpena Saturday to attend the funeral of Samuel Nedeau, brother of Mrs. Ferguson, of this place. Mr. Nedeau is a barber by trade, and has lived in Alpena about fifteen years. He leaves a wife and eight children to mourn their loss.

Alcona County Review, April 9, 1891
Cemetery: Probably Holy Cross, Alpena Co.

Neil, Alice J. [Fick]
LOCAL JOTTINGS.

Died.—At her home in this township, on the 20th inst., of consumption, Mrs. Nicholas Neal, aged 18 years. Mrs. Neal had been in poor health for a long time. The funeral services were held in the Methodist Episcopal church last Saturday, at 11 a.m., Rev. T. B. Leith preaching the sermon from the following text: Psalm 116, 15th verse—"Precious in the sight of the Lord is the death of His saints."

Alcona County Review, May 28, 1886
Cemetery: Springport, Alcona Co.

Neil, {Girl}
MUD LAKE.

Mr. and Mrs. Elmer Neil of Omer buried their three months old daughter. Mrs. Neil was once Jennie Hawes, daughter of Frank and Alice Hawes.

Alcona County Review, August 17, 1899
Cemetery:

Neil, Kate [McDonald]
DUST TO DUST.

A sad event of the past week was the death Monday morning at 10 o'clock of Mrs. Archie Neil, better known until a short time ago as Kate McDonald. Mrs. Neil had been a long and patient sufferer, her illness extending over a period of ten weeks. She was married to Archie Neil the last of May of the present year at the age of 16 and prospects of a long and happy life could not have been brighter. The deceased had a bright and cheerful disposition and was a general favorite among her acquaintants. The funeral services were held yesterday morning at the Methodist church, from which a large concourse of sorrowing friends and relatives followed the remains to their last resting place.

Alcona County Review, September 17, 1891

Somewhat Personal.

The Rev. G. W. Cram was in the village yesterday to officiate at the funeral services of Mrs. Archie Neal.

Alcona County Review, September 17, 1891
Cemetery: Springport, Alcona Co.

Neil, Mrs. Nicholas, Jr.
Among Our Exchanges.

Mrs. Nicholas Neil departed this life at her late home northwest of Harrisville on Tuesday morning after a long illness from consumption. The funeral services were held this morning at the Methodist church. The deceased was a young woman of good education and refined tastes, having pursued the occupation of teaching prior to her marriage. But one child survives her.

Alcona County Review, March 15, 1894

EVENTS OF ONE WEEK.

It was expected that Archie Neil would start up C., McG. & Co.'s shingle mill yesterday, but on account of the death of his brother's wife the start has been postponed for a few days, probably next Monday.

Alcona County Review, March 15, 1894
Cemetery: Probably Springport, Alcona Co.

Neil, Nicholas, Sr.
PERSONAL MENTION.

Nicholas Neil, Sr., is very sick at the home of his daughter, Mrs. Jas. Barber.

Alcona County Review, October 24, 1895

EVENTS OF ONE WEEK.

Nicholas Neil passed away Tuesday at 6 o'clock a.m. at his late home near Harrisville at the advanced age of 77 years. The old gentleman had been in a feeble condition for a long time and death was due to la grippe.

Deceased was a native of county Wexford, Ireland. He came to Canada when five years of age and lived there until about 1884 when he came to Alcona county. He is survived by his wife and eight children, four of whom live in this county, viz: Nicholas and Archie Neil, Mrs. Geo. Edgar and Mrs. James Barber.

The funeral took place this morning, services being held at the M. E. church.

Alcona County Review, November 7, 1895
Cemetery: Probably Springport, Alcona Co.

Nestle, {Boy}
LOCAL JOTTINGS.

An infant son of Wm. Nestle died last Monday.

Alcona County Review, April 23, 1886
Cemetery: Probably Springport, Alcona Co.

Nestle, Caroline [Campau]
FROM ALCONA.

Alcona, December 31st, 1877.
Editor Review: On the 24th of this month we received the sad tidings of the death of Caroline, the beloved wife of Harvey A. Nestle; aged 20 years. She left a little girl 18 months old. Her illness was brief but painful. She died in the peace and love of God, and peaceful be her rest.

Alcona County Review, January 4, 1878
Cemetery: Mt. Joy, Alcona Co.

Nestle, Carrie May [Lee]
Black River.

Mrs. Nestle, daughter of Geo. H. Lee, the well known citizen of Haynes, died last week of inflammation resulting from confinement. She had been married only about a year and her death is a sad blow to her parents, husband and friends.

Alcona County Review, June 9, 1892

Black River.

The funeral of Mrs. Nestle, nee Lee, took place in the Presbyterian church, B. R., on Sunday last. The deceased was interred at Alcona.

Alcona County Review, June 9, 1892

HISTORY OF ONE YEAR.

Chronological History of the Past Year, 1892.

THE DEATH RECORD.

June 3. Mrs. Nestle, Haynes.

Alcona County Review, January 5, 1893

All Around Alcona County.

Haynes, Nov. 12, 1895. Geo. H. Lee has erected a beautiful monument to the memory of his wife and children in the cemetery.

Alcona County Review, November 14, 1895
Cemetery: Mt. Joy, Alcona Co.

Nestle, Claude W.

LOCAL JOTTINGS.

During the past two weeks, cholera-infantum has been having a terrible rage in this community, no less than a dozen small children and babes having died from the same.— This naturally leaves many houses of mourning in our community, and to those of us who are as yet free from the scourge in our own homes, should come forth hearty sympathy and fitting words for the bereaved. Friday last, the scourge took away a little, human flower each from the homes of William Nestle and James Stringer. Tuesday the family of Chas. Larson were bereft of their babe, and Wednesday evening Frank Stevens and wife were called to part with their first-born. Gilbert Landon, one of the Messrs. Byces, and the Ducharms have also each lost a babe, and there are several others in the community apparently nearly at death's door, at the time we go to press. Thus many of the homes in our community are being darkened. May the Lord remove the dark cloud speedily, and give consolation to the sorrowing parents.

Alcona County Review, August 29, 1884

LOCAL JOTTINGS.

Wm. Nestle and wife desire to return thanks to friends and neighbors for their kind assistance and words of sympathy and consolation during the sickness, death and burial of their beloved little son Claud.

Alcona County Review, August 29, 1884
Cemetery: Springport, Alcona Co.

Nestle, Myrtle May

All Around Alcona County.

Haynes, Nov. 12, 1895. Geo. H. Lee has erected a beautiful monument to the memory of his wife and children in the cemetery.

[Died August 18, 1892]

Alcona County Review, November 14, 1895
Cemetery: Mt. Joy, Alcona Co.

Newell, Agnes

A Woman Drowned off Davison's Dock.

An unknown woman of about 25 years of age, supposed to be married, and passing herself off in the village under different names, fell off Davison's dock, it is supposed, Wednesday night, and was drowned. The woman came into the dock office about 9 o'clock in the evening to wait for and take the steamer Metropolis to Au Sable, as she said. After a while she arose to go out, stating that she would like to leave her "satchel" there for a few minutes.

The woman had not been absent but a short time before one loud scream was heard by the parties in the dock-office. All hands immediately rushed out upon the dock and commenced search for the woman, but no traces of her could be discovered. Finally, in about 30 minutes after hearing the noise, a dark object was observed floating upon the surface of the water about three rods to the north of the dock, which proved to be the lifeless body of the woman; but why it should float, as usually is not the case until many days after drowning, is a mystery. C. E. Jamison, who was present, disrobed himself, swam out to and brought the body to the side of the dock, when the same was raised out of the water and placed in the warehouse.

Coroner Geo. W. LaChapelle impaneled a jury and held an inquest over the body, yesterday, when a verdict was rendered to the effect that

deceased came to her death by accidental drowning.

Several of the ladies of the village took charge of the remains and prepared them for burial. They were interred in the village cemetery this morning, Rev. C. Gibbs officiating. No relatives of the deceased could be found, though telegrams were sent in search of the same. It is supposed however that she had a husband living in Port Huron, as a telegram was received from a man named John Beck, of that place, stating that her husband was there, but that he would have nothing to do with her.

Deceased came to Harrisville from Alpena about ten days ago, and had several times been seen upon our streets in an intoxicated condition. She left orders with the Postmaster to forward to Au Sable any letters that might be received here addressed to "Agnes Gussenhart" or "Agnes Ellsworth."

Alcona County Review, September 23, 1881

HOME REVIEWINGS.

A correspondent from Alpena, writing to the Bay City Press, under date of October 3d, says that the woman drowned from the steamboat dock at Harrisville recently, was Mrs. Newell, a former resident of Alpena; also that her husband met with a similar fate in that city about three years ago.

Alcona County Review, October 7, 1881
Cemetery: West Lawn, Alcona Co.

Newell, Charles

In the Columbia River.

A SAIL BOAT CAPSIZES AND THREE WERE DROWNED.

Chas. Newell, a Harrisville Boy, a Victim. Retta Kennedy Escapes.

The Skamokawa (Wash.) Eagle of May 14th contains an account of the drowning of three persons in the deep waters of the Columbia river. The sad catastrophe is of deep interest to many readers of the Review, inasmuch as two members of the ill fated sailing party were formerly residents of the village of Harrisville. They grew up from the cradle here, went to the village school, and left many young friends and relatives here when they went west, who will be deeply interested in their fate.

The Eagle's story in brief is as follows: About 2 o'clock Wednesday (13th) afternoon a happy party composed of Messrs. Frank Peterson, Charles Newell, Rudolph Kraft and Mrs. A. B. Crosby and Miss Retta Kennedy, left in a fish boat for Cathlamet. Frank Peterson was in charge and as he was known to be skillful in handling a boat and the day was fine, no fears were entertained for them. The run to Cathlamet was safely made and the return trip was begun against a head wind. A squally wind was blowing and when about half way back to Skamokawa a sudden squall careened the boat over and she filled with water. Mrs. Crosby lost control of herself at once and though assisted to the bottom of the boat by Kraft she let go and went down. Young Newell could not swim but Peterson could and he tried to help Newell as well as Mrs. Crosby, but in his efforts to do so he was handicapped by a heavy Mackintosh and he was dragged down and all three were drowned.

Miss Kennedy could swim a little and she had presence of mind enough not to get excited. She remembered trying to get away from the boat, reasoning to herself that if the others caught hold of her they might pull her down. Then she tried to float and remembered nothing more until she was restored to consciousness by two fishermen who were trying to bring her back to life into their fish boat.

Not over 400 yards away at the time of the accident was a fish boat containing two men. They reached the scene of the disaster as quickly as possible. An oar was extended to Peterson but he was too exhausted to reach it. Miss Kennedy was rescued as she was going down the last time.

The boat was towed ashore in the vain hope that some of the unfortunates might be under it, but it was empty.

Charley Newell was a son of Henry Newell and Miss Kennedy is the daughter of Ferguson Kennedy. Mr. Newell and Mr. Kennedy are both well known former citizens of Harrisville.

Young Newell was about 24 years of age. He left Harrisville with his parents in 1889.

Skamokawa was plunged in the depths of sorrow over the terrible disaster. The muddy waters of the Columbia were dragged for the bodies, and it was nearly 60 feet deep at the point where the accident occurred. The current was also very swift and the bottom is full of snags, so the work of rescue was pursued under great difficulties and without success up to the time the Eagle went to press.

Alcona County Review, May 28, 1896

The Skamokawa (Wash.) Eagle, of July 23, states that the bodies of Charley Newell and Frank Peterson, who were drowned in the Columbia river on May 12, were found two days before. The body of a young woman drowned at the same time, has not yet been found.

Alcona County Review, July 30, 1896
Cemetery:

Newell, John

Haynes Happenings.
John Newell has been compelled to relinquish teaching our school. Alpena doctors informed him that his left lung is gone. He starts for Florida today with the well wishes of this community and your correspondent for his recovery.

Alcona County Review, October 10, 1895

Haynes Happenings.
John Newell departed last week for North Carolina for the good of his health and I hope the change will prove beneficial and that he may soon recover.

Alcona County Review, October 24, 1895

Haynes, Nov. 4th, 1895.—John Newell has sent for his wife to join him in Ashland N. C. Reported that he is improving and contemplates teaching school there. He has a first grade certificate and a chance for a situation.

Alcona County Review, November 7, 1895

JOHN NEWELL, OF HAYNES, Fooled the Doctors and the Undertaker.
From the Alpena Echo.

Dr. Wilkinson was quietly sitting in his office this afternoon when a well-built, rosy cheeked man strode in and giving the Dr. a slap on the back, yelled, "Hello, Doc! How are you? Just came up to let you have a look at me." The doctor was somewhat nonplused, as he couldn't recognize his visitor, who finally introduced himself as the remains of a consumptive named Newell, of Lodge, a small town down the line,

who had been examined by the doctor last fall and was allowed but a few weeks to live.

The gentleman, who was a school teacher, was advised to give up his position and go into some active business. The doctor gave him some medicine and sent him home never expecting to see him again, but he wrote back that he was feeling better and has continued treatment ever since. The Dr. doesn't claim that his medicine did it, but pronounces the case the most wonderful in his history as a physician.

Mr. Newell underwent an examination this afternoon and was pronounced in the pink of health.

Alcona County Review, March 19, 1896

Haynes Happenings.
John Newell has returned home and is looking better.

Alcona County Review, July 9, 1896

HAYNES HAPPENINGS.
Jan. 10, 1898.--John Newell is reported to be improving. He took a severe cold and has been very poorly for some time.

Alcona County Review, January 13, 1898

Haynes, January 24, '98.
John Newell is very poorly at present.

Alcona County Review, January 27, 1898

LOCAL PICK UPS.

Supervisor Ritchie was circulating a paper here Monday for the benefit of John Newell, whose condition is such that if he ever needed friendly assistance it is just now. The paper was cheerfully and generally signed, and quite a handsome purse was raised.

Alcona County Review, February 10, 1898

HAYNES HAPPENINGS.
John Newell is somewhat better, but still very weak.

Alcona County Review, March 17, 1898

HAYNES HAPPENINGS.
John Newell is not yet able to be around; his courage is good and he hopes for the best.

Alcona County Review, April 14, 1898

HAYNES HAPPENINGS.
April 18.—John Newell's father and mother have come to visit him. Their home is in Canada. Sam Newell, another son, is a member of the life saving crew at Sturgeon Point.

Alcona County Review, April 21, 1898

HAYNES HAPPENINGS.
Death of John Newell.

Haynes, May 3, 1898.

Mr. John Newell passed away very quietly Sunday morning at 7 o'clock. Death was due to consumption. His father and mother were at his bedside besides his own family. Mr. Newell called for his beloved wife and for his father and mother a few minutes before his departure.

He would have been 30 years of age in a few weeks. He was a model young man and his death is a severe loss to the community where he was held in universal respect. By profession he was a school teacher, but had to give up about three years ago on account of ill health.

The funeral services were held Tuesday and were conducted by the Rev. Mr. Middlemiss of Alpena in the First Presbyterian church of Haynes, the internment taking place in Mt. Joy Cemetery.

Alcona County Review, May 5, 1898

Card of Thanks.

We desire to thank the people who so kindly and generously assisted during the last illness and death of John Newell, Jr. May God bless them and the hands that so lovingly contributed to the funeral decorations.

Mrs. John Newell Jr.
and all deceased's relatives.

Alcona County Review, May 5, 1898

PERSONAL POINTS.

The father and mother of Sam Newell returned to Port Huron last week. They were accompanied by Mrs. John Newell and children.

Alcona County Review, May 19, 1898

HAYNES HAPPENINGS.
Aug. 9, 1898.

Mrs. John Newell returned from Canada last week after an extended visit with her deceased husband's parents.

Alcona County Review, August 11, 1898

Local History of One Year

Chronology of the Principal Events of the Year 1898.

May 1. Death of John Newell aged 30 in Haynes.

Alcona County Review, January 5, 1899
Cemetery: Mt. Joy, Alcona Co.

Nicholson, {Girl}

COUNTY JOTTINGS.

The little two years old daughter of Mrs. Rositta Nicholson was taken with the croup, Monday evening, and died early Tuesday morning. The funeral services of the little one were held from the M. E. Church, Wednesday afternoon.

Alcona County Review, March 29, 1878
Cemetery: Springport, Alcona Co.

Nolan, Edward L.

LOCAL JOTTINGS.

The only child of Mr. and Mrs. Jos. Nowlan of Killmaster, a little boy aged 3 years, died on Monday and was buried here on Tuesday.

Alcona County Review, September 24, 1886
Cemetery:

Nolan, Michael T.

LINCOLN.

M. Nolan, who was so dangerously ill last week, is very much improved and will soon be around again. Drs. Eskins, Trask and Tiffany were in attendance.

Alcona County Review, October 5, 1899

Passing of Michael Nolan.

Michael Nolan, one of Lincoln's most prominent citizens and proprietor of the Twin Lake hotel, passed from earth Friday, November 3rd, at 9 o'clock a.m. Death resulted from hemorrhage of the stomach.

Deceased was widely known along this shore, where his social, jovial and generous nature won him a large circle of friends. His wife and two children, Daniel J. and Miss Cora survive to mourn the loss of their husband and father, and to them is extended the sympathy of the citizens of Lincoln.

Michael Nolan was born at Rochester, N. Y., June 12, 1847. He came to Michigan at the age of twenty and located at Saginaw. In '79 he began railroading and accepted a position as train dispatcher of Mich. Cen. R. R., Gladwin Div. and later became road master with headquarters at Pinconning. While there he met and married Miss Alice Quielty of that place. He went to Wisconsin in '83. Returning after two years he became conductor on the D. B. C. & A. R. R. and ran one of the first trains over the road. He next became station agent at W. Harrisville. In '88 he went to the Upper Peninsula, having been engaged as manager for the Iron

Range and Huron Bay R. R. On Nov. 1, 1890, Mr. Nolan purchased the Duggan House, now the Twin Lake House at Lincoln, of which he has been proprietor for nine years.

The funeral services were conducted Monday morning at St. Anne's church by Rev. Fr. Poulin and were attended by a large concourse of sympathizing friends.

Alcona County Review, November 9, 1899

KILLMASTER.

Mrs. C. Fowler attended the funeral of M. Nolan.

Alcona County Review, November 9, 1899

Card of Thanks.

We wish to thank the many friends for their kindness and words of sympathy extended to us during our late bereavement. Also to those who kindly presented the flowers and neighbors and friends who so kindly assisted.

Mrs. M. Nolan and family.

Alcona County Review, November 9, 1899
Cemetery: St. Anne's, Alcona Co.

North, Charlotte [Lee]

LOCAL JOTTINGS.

The young wife of Alford North, Jr., was buried to-day, funeral services being held from the M. E. church.

Alcona County Review, February 13, 1885
Cemetery:

Noyes, Abram

JOINED THE SILENT MAJORITY.

While not unexpected, yet as always will be the case when any citizen as well known and highly respected as the deceased takes his departure to that unknown country, the death of Abram Noyes at his residence last Friday evening shocked the community as only the death of a good citizen can. His death was like his life, calm and peaceful, at peace with all mankind and his Maker.

A gentleman who has been intimately associated with the deceased for twenty years past, remarked after his death, "it is impossible to flatter him in any particular, he was an exemplary citizen, a kind father and husband, honest and fair in all his business dealings, a quiet and unobtrusive yet a devout and sincere Christian gentleman."

Abram Noyes has been intimately identified with the history of Alcona county for over twenty years, coming here shortly after the close of the war. He was a native of the state of Michigan, having first seen the light of day fifty years ago. At the breaking out of the war of the rebellion he was in the regular service, receiving an honorable discharge in 1863, having contracted before that time the disabilities which marked him until his death.

He was in active mercantile business here for a number of years until unfortunate investments in the shingle business brought him face to face with financial disaster. He was several times treasurer of Harrisville township, and held that office at the time of his death.

While on his death bed and fully understanding that he had not long to live the deceased made haste to arrange his business matters. He made his will, and manifested generally a clearness of understanding that was, considering the nearness of his dissolution wonderful to say the least.

He left a widow and four children, all of whom are liberally provided for by a wise investment of the deceased in life insurance.

He was buried Sunday under the auspices of the I. O. O. F. of which order he was an honored member, the Rev. F. N. Barlow delivering the funeral sermon in the Presbyterian church.

Alcona County Review, November 25, 1887

LOCAL JOTTINGS.

Wm. Flawes, of Black River, and others attended the funeral of Abram Noyes last Sunday.

Alcona County Review, November 25, 1887

Card of Thanks.

I wish to thank the many friends who rendered such kind services during the last sickness of my late husband. I wish to thank particularly the members of Harrisville Lodge, I. O. O. F., for their friendly offices, Mr. and Mrs. L. A. Colwell for floral tributes.

Mrs. Abram Noyes.

Alcona County Review, December 2, 1887

LOCAL JOTTINGS.

Mrs. A. Noyes has received a check for $2,000, the amount of insurance carried by her late husband in the benefit fund of the Knights of Honor. This order is to be commended for the promptness with which this loss was settled.

Alcona County Review, December 23, 1887

PROBATE ORDER.
STATE OF MICHIGAN, County of Alcona, ss.

At a session of the Probate Court for said county, held at the Probate Office in the village of Harrisville, on the 19th day of December, in the year one thousand eight hundred and eighty-seven. Present, Allen Nevins, Judge of Probate. In the matter of the

ESTATE OF ABRAM NOYES, DECEASED.

On reading and filing the petition, duly verified, of Clara Noyes praying that a certain instrument now on file in this court, purporting to be the last will and testament of said deceased, be admitted to probate, and that Joseph VanBuskirk, George Rutson and O. H. Smith may be appointed executors thereof.

Thereupon it is ordered that Monday, the 16th Day of January, 1888, next, at ten o'clock in the forenoon, be assigned for the hearing of said petition, and that the heirs at law of said deceased, and all other persons interested in said estate, are required to appear at a session of said court then to be holden at the Probate office, in the village of Harrisville, and show cause if any there be, why the prayer of the petitioner should not be granted. And it is further ordered that said petitioner give notice to the heirs at law, and other persons interested in said estate, of the pendency of said petition, and the hearing thereof, by causing a copy of this order to be published in the Alcona County Review, a newspaper printed and circulated in said county, three successive weeks previous to said day of hearing.

ALLEN NEVINS, Judge of Probate.

Alcona County Review, December 23, 1887

PROBATE ORDER.
State of Michigan, County of Alcona.

At a session of the Probate Court for said county, held at the Probate Office in the village of Harrisville, on the 19th day of December, in the year one thousand eight hundred and eighty-seven. Present, Allen Nevins, Judge of Probate. In the matter of the

ESTATE OF ABRAM NOYES, DECEASED.

On reading and filing the petition, duly verified, of Clara Noyes praying that a certain instrument now on file in this court purporting to be the last will and testament of said deceased, be admitted to probate, and that Joseph VanBuskirk, George Rutson and O. H. Smith may be appointed executors thereof.

Thereupon it is ordered that Monday, the 16th Day of January, 1888, next, at ten o'clock in the forenoon, be assigned for the hearing of said petition, and that the heirs at law of said deceased, and all other persons interested in said estate, are required to appear at a session of said court then to be holden at the Probate office, in the village of Harrisville, and show cause if any there be, why the prayer of the petitioner should not be granted. And it is further ordered that said petitioner give notice to the heirs at law, and other persons interested in said estate, of the pendency of said petition, and the hearing thereof, by causing a copy of this order to be published in the Alcona County Review, a newspaper printed and circulated in said county, three successive weeks previous to said day of hearing.

ALLEN NEVINS, Judge of Probate.

Alcona County Review, January 6, 1888

LOCAL JOTTINGS.

A policy for $3,000 on the life of the late Abram Noyes in the Union Mutual Ins. Co. of Detroit, has been in abeyance ever since the death of the policy holder in the fall of 1887. J. E. Fair has conducted the negotiations for the beneficiaries and this week the company settled by sending a check for the full amount. The objections the company has held to making an earlier settlement of this claim were founded on what might appear good reasons. The total amount of insurance paid on the deceased's life was $7,500.

Alcona County Review, March 8, 1889

STATE OF MICHIGAN,
County of Alcona.

At a session of the Probate Court for said County, held at the Probate office, in the village of Harrisville, on the 11th day of July, in the year one thousand eight hundred and ninety-one.

Present, Hon. Geo. S. Ritchie, Judge of Probate.

In the matter of the estate of Abram Noyes, deceased:

On reading and filing the petition, duly verified, of Clara Silversides, praying that a certain instrument now on file in this Court, purporting to be the last will and testament of said deceased, may be admitted to probate, and that such other and further order and proceedings may be had in the premises as may be required by the statute in such case made and provided.

Thereupon it is ordered that Saturday, the eighth (8) day of August next, at ten o'clock in the forenoon, be assigned for the hearing of said petition, and that the heirs at law of said deceased, and all other persons interested in said estate, are required to appear at a session of said Court, then to be holden at the Probate office, in the village of Harrisville, said County, and show cause, if there be any, why the prayer of the petitioner should not be granted: And it is further ordered, that said petitioner give notice to the persons interested in said estate, of the pendency of said petition, and the hearing thereof, by causing a copy of this order to be published in the Alcona County Review, a newspaper printed and circulated in said county, three successive weeks previous to said day of hearing.

GEO. S. RITCHIE,
Judge of Probate.

Alcona County Review, July 16, 1891

The Local News.

O. H. Smith, guardian of the estates of the minor children of the late Abram Noyes, and attorney for the widow, is taking legal steps to close up the affairs of the several estates.

Alcona County Review, July 23, 1891

HONORS TO DEAD HEROES.

A magnificent demonstration of the patriotic spirit of the citizens of Alcona county was the observance on Monday of the time honored custom of decorating the graves and commemorating the deeds of valor of the nation's dead heroes.

The roster of soldiers who are buried here is as follows: Harrisville, (West), A. Marcellus, John Pelton, W. W. Douglass: Catholic, Louis Rivard, Geo. Bernizer: South Harrisville, R. Richmond, Chas. Miller, H. J. Aird, A. Noyes, Jas. Johnson.

Alcona County Review, June 2, 1898

State of Michigan, County of Alcona. At a session of the Probate Court for said County, held at the probate office, in the village of Harrisville on the 14th day of August in the year one thousand eight hundred and ninety-nine.

Present, Hon. Wm. H. Gilpin, Judge of Probate. In the matter of the estate of Inez M. Noyes a minor. On reading and filing the petition duly verified of O. H. Smith, guardian of said minor, praying among other things that he may be empowered, authorized and licensed to sell at private sale the following real estate of said minor, viz: All that piece of land situate in the township of Gustin, County of Alcona, State of Michigan and described as follows, to-wit: The s e ¼ of the s e ¼ of section (13) in town 26 n r 8 east.

Thereupon it is ordered, That Monday the 11th day of Sept. next at 10 o'clock in the forenoon, be assigned for the hearing of said petition and that the next of kin and all other persons interested in said estate, are required to appear at a session of said court, then to be holden in the probate office in the village of Harrisville and show cause, if any there be why a license should not be granted for the sale of such estate. And it is further ordered that said petitioner give notice to the next of kin and all persons interested in said estate, of the pendency of said petition, and the hearing thereof, by causing a copy of this order to be published in the Alcona County Review, a newspaper printed and circulated in said county three successive weeks previous to said day of hearing.

W. H. Gilpin,
Judge of Probate.

Alcona County Review, August 17, 1899

Doings of the Week
E. J. Hubbard and attorney of Wixom were in attendance at probate court Saturday. They represented Mrs. Hubbard (formerly Inez Noyes)

in the hearing for the final settlement of the Abram Noyes estate.

Alcona County Review, December 5, 1901

Circuit Court Briefs.

The case of the Estate of Mary Esther Noyes-Briggs vs. O. H. Smith, guardian, was put on Tuesday and is still in progress as these pages go to press.

Alcona County Review, July 11, 1907

CIRCUIT COURT BRIEFLETS.

In the matter of the accounting of O. H. Smith, guardian of the estate of Esther Noyes, a verdict was returned in favor of the guardian. This verdict is considered advisory merely to the court. The court has the matter under consideration and may deduct or add to the amount found in guardian's favor.

Alcona County Review, July 18, 1907

Judge Connine has rendered his finding in the matter of the final accounting of the O. H. Smith, guardian for the Esther Noyes estate. In substance it provides that the guardian shall turn over $399.88 in addition to all securities held by him for the estate.

Alcona County Review, September 5, 1907
Cemetery: Springport, Alcona Co.

Noyes, Daniel Henry
Final Summons.

Sudden Death of Daniel H. Noyes on Christmas Night.

This community was greatly shocked Tuesday morning by the news that Daniel H. Noyes, an old resident of Harrisville and Alcona County, had dropped dead upon the floor at the town hall while in attendance at the Christmas dance.

There was an unusually large crowd at the party and the merriment was kept up until a late hour. About two o'clock the lamps began to grow dim and Mr. Noyes had been helping to refill one of them. He held the lighted lamp in his hand and was just raising it to Clerk McClatchey, who was upon a chair to place the lamp in its place, when, without a word, be fell forward upon his face, dead.

Efforts were made to revive him, and Dr. Mitchell was summoned, but all to no avail. He was past human aid. Coronor Hale was called but an inquest was deemed unnecessary.

———

Deceased was a whole-souled, good hearted man and had many friends. He had been ailing for a year or more and was afflicted with heart trouble. On the day of his death he appeared in much better spirits than usual and was jovial, with a "Merry Christmas" for everybody. His sudden death was a shock to all.

While it was well known that he was subject to heart trouble, still the sudden death of her husband was a severe blow to Mrs. Noyes and the family, who have the sympathy of the community.

———

Daniel H. Noyes was born near Port Huron, Michigan on the 28th of Sept. 1840. At an early age he removed to Clawson, Oakland county, where he lived during his boyhood and early manhood. In August, 1862, he enlisted in the Fifth Michigan cavalry and served his country faithfully until the close of the war, when he was honorably discharged. In 1865 he came to Harrisville and with the exception of a few years' residence at Mud Lake, has lived here ever since. Sept., 1868 he married Sarah McLeod. Three children were born to them, all of whom are living, viz: William Noyes of Alpena, Mrs. Carrie Noyes-Thornton of Mud Lake and Frank who lives with his parents.

Deceased leaves three sisters: Mrs. Capt. Beckwith of Chicago; Mrs. Dan McRae of Sidnaw, Mich.; Mrs. Fannie Stevens of Detroit.

The funeral occurs today at 2 o'clock from the Methodist church and is in charge of the Odd Fellows of which order deceased was a member. Ten members of the Black River lodge will be present. The pall bearers were selected from the Odd Fellows and G. A. R. members: Chas. Conklin, Geo. W. Balch, C. M. Lund, Jas. Sovey, Guy Lewis, Geo. W. Young.

Alcona County Review, December 28, 1899

We desire to express our heartfelt thanks to those friends who so kindly assisted us during our bereavement, the death of our beloved husband and father.

Mrs. D. H. Noyes and family.

Alcona County Review, December 28, 1899

Resolutions of Condolence.

Whereas—It has seemed good to the Almighty Ruler of the Universe to remove from our midst our late brother, Daniel H. Noyes; and

Whereas the intimate relations long held by the deceased with the members of Lodge No. 218 of the Independent order of Odd Fellows render it proper that we should place upon record our appreciation of his merits as a man and a brother therefore

Resolved—That we deplore the loss of Brother Noyes with deep feelings of regret softened only by the hope that his spirit is enjoying more perfect happiness in a better world.

Resolved—that we tender to his afflicted relatives our sincere condolence, and our earnest sympathy in their affliction at the loss of one who was a good and loyal citizen, an affectionate husband, a kind and loving father, and an honest man.

Resolved—That our lodge room be hung with emblems of mourning and that our charter be draped for thirty days, as evidence of our sorrow at the loss of our Brother

Resolved—That a copy of the foregoing Resolutions signed by the Noble Grand and certified by the Recording Secretary of our Lodge be transmitted to the wife of our deceased brother.

Alcona County Review, January 4, 1900

MUD LAKE.

The sudden death of our esteemed friend and neighbor, D. H. Noyes, was a shock to his many friends and neighbors in this community. We extend heartfelt sympathy to the bereaved family.

Alcona County Review, January 4, 1900

MUD LAKE.

We desire to express our heartfelt thanks to those friends who so kindly assisted us during our bereavement, the death of our beloved husband and father.

Mrs. D. H. Noyes and family.

Alcona County Review, January 4, 1900

MUD LAKE.

George Hyke has been appointed school assessor to the vacancy caused by death of D. H. Noyes.

Alcona County Review, January 18, 1900

Honored the Nation's Dead.

Despite the threatening weather of Tuesday night and early Wednesday morning, there never was a more perfect day for such an occasion than was yesterday, Memorial Day. When the rain ceased and the clouds lifted, Dame Nature came forth in her best bib and tucker, while Old Sol beamed cheerfully down.

People began to arrive in town quite early and by 10 o'clock the line of march was formed and the procession started for the Catholic and South Harrisville cemeteries. An advance guard of fifty or more bicycles led the way, followed by the veterans, daughters of veterans, U. L. G., schools, citizens, the procession being about a half mile long.

At the cemeteries the graves of the dead heroes were decorated with flags and strewn with flowers and evergreens. At the grave of Daniel Noyes, the last of the veterans of this locality to respond to the final roll call, the veterans gave the impressive grave service of the G. A. R., and at the grave of Francis LaChapelle the Fisher school children sang a song.

Alcona County Review, May 31, 1900

Of Local Interest

Mrs. D. H. Noyes has been granted a pension of 8 per month, dating from January 3, 1900.

Alcona County Review, August 2, 1900
Cemetery: Springport, Alcona Co.

Noyes, William

DUST TO DUST.

Noyes—At Hillgard, September 3, 1891.

Wm. Noyes, aged 61 years.

Wm. Noyes was a native of the state of Michigan and came to Oregon in 1875, where he has since resided. He leaves a wife and two children, besides a large circle of friends to mourn his loss. The funeral will take place at one o'clock this afternoon from the Baptist church.—LaGrande (Ore.) Gazette.

Wm. Noyes was one of the pioneer settlers of Alcona county. He kept the first hotel in Harrisville and was known during his residence here as an upright citizen and energetic business man. He left here early in the 70's for the Pacific coast and has resided there ever since. D. H. Noyes of Mud Lake was a brother of the deceased.

Alcona County Review, September 17, 1891
Cemetery: Grandview, Union County, OR

Oates, Edward Dennis

Three children belonging to Mr. Oates, of Alabaster, died last week of reported scarlet fever. A boy about three years old died on Monday, and his twin sister and a babe both died on Thursday. There were seven sick in the family in all, but the rest, we are glad to learn, are getting well.

Alcona County Review, July 5, 1878
Cemetery: Probably Alabaster Tp., Iosco Co.

Oates, John Thomas

Three children belonging to Mr. Oates, of Alabaster, died last week of reported scarlet fever. A boy about three years old died on Monday, and his twin sister and a babe both died on Thursday. There were seven sick in the family in all, but the rest, we are glad to learn, are getting well.

Alcona County Review, July 5, 1878
Cemetery: Probably Alabaster Tp., Iosco Co.

Oates, Mary Elizabeth

Three children belonging to Mr. Oates, of Alabaster, died last week of reported scarlet fever. A boy about three years old died on Monday, and his twin sister and a babe both died on Thursday. There were seven sick in the family in all, but the rest, we are glad to learn, are getting well.

Alcona County Review, July 5, 1878
Cemetery: Probably Alabaster Tp., Iosco Co.

O'Brien, Mrs. C.
LOCAL JOTTINGS.

Mrs. C. O'Brien, aged 54 years, committed suicide by hanging herself recently, at the residence of her son in Oscoda, while temporarily insane.

Alcona County Review, August 20, 1886
Cemetery:

O'Connor, Kate
Suffocated by Coal Gas.

Miss O'Connor of Killmaster Meets Death at Bay City.

Thos. O'Connor of Killmaster was notified by telegraph Saturday of the death of his daughter, Kate, aged 21, from asphyxiation by gas from a coal stove. The girl was working in the family of a Michigan Central railroad conductor residing at Bay City. The young lady's death occurred Wednesday morning but for some reason her family were not notified until Saturday and Mr. O'Connor was unable to leave for Bay City before Monday.

The Bay City Tribune of the 6th has the following concerning the unfortunate affair.

The family of Wm. T. Hammond, a Michigan Central conductor at 609 North Center street, narrowly escaped death by asphyxiation Wednesday night. As it is, Miss Kate O'Connor, aged 21 years, lies cold in death and Mina, the 12-year-old daughter of Mr. and Mrs. Hammond is in very precarious condition. The accident was caused by gas escaping from a coal stove, which filled the room in which the two victims slept. The stove was put up Wednesday afternoon by Mrs. Hammond and her daughter. The chimney seems to have been stopped up with rubbish, and there was no outlet for the gas to escape. The fire was lighted towards evening and after supper Miss O'Connor complained of smelling gas. An investigation of the chimney was made and a pailful of dirt and bricks removed.

Miss O'Connor and the little Hammond girl used an upstairs bedroom through which a pipe from the coal stove ran. The rest of the family slept below.

At 7:30 yesterday morning, Mrs. Adam Clark, who resides next door noticed that none of the family were moving and went over and knocked at the door. Mrs. Hammond was aroused and complained of a severe headache. Miss O'Connor and Mina could not be aroused. The former was beyond help, and efforts to resuscitate the little girl were not successful until 3 o'clock in the afternoon.

Miss O'Connor was a niece of Mrs. Hammond and has made her home with the family for several years. She was to have been married in about two weeks.

Alcona County Review, November 22, 1894
Cemetery:

O'Donohue, Thomas
THOMAS O'DONOHUE.
This well-known citizen died Tuesday just before noon. His illness from rheumatism had been long and wasting, as he had been confined to the house since last January and for several months has not been able to leave his bed. His suffering was intense and death came as a welcome relief, though the loving hands of his devoted wife and daughter did everything possible for him.

Deceased was born at Percy, lower Canada, Feb. 8, 1832. He followed

the life of a seafaring man until 1881, when he came to Harrisville. Since then he has followed the life of a woodsman and has worked steadily for Alger, Smith & Co., except when incapacitated by illness.

Four children survive, two having died. The survivors are Mrs. Andrew Nevin of Floodwood, Minn., Mrs. Aleck Conture of Manistique, Mich., Michael O'Donohue of Bayfield, Wis., Maggie O'Donohue of Harrisville.

The remains will be buried tomorrow morning in the Catholic cemetery, deceased being a devout Catholic.

The family extend their warm thanks to their neighbors who have been unremitting in their kindness.

Alcona County Review, December 9, 1897
Cemetery: St. Anne's, Alcona Co.

O'Hara, John
A Double Tragedy at Alpena.
A fearful double tragedy occurred at Alpena last week Thursday, resulting in the death of Philip Cross and Jno. O'Hara in the former's saloon. The two men were discovered about 5 o'clock in the afternoon. O'Hara being shot through the body, Cross having received a deadly blow on the head from an axe. Both men have since died. The affair at latest accounts is shrouded in mystery, but the circumstances indicate that a third party did the fearful deed. O'Hara, one of the victims, was once a respected citizen of Harrisville, having in early days worked as a teamster. He then went into the saloon business and has drifted from bad to worse until at the time of his death he was accounted a hard citizen. Cross did not bear the most savory reputation either.

Alcona County Review, November 4, 1887

LOCAL JOTTINGS.

It is now believed at Alpena that O'Hara and Cross must have had some trouble in the latter's saloon, whereupon O'Hara struck Cross with a hatchet, and seeing he had hurt him more severely than he had calculated, he seized a revolver and shot himself.

Alcona County Review, November 11, 1887
Cemetery:

O'Keefe, John D.
Killed in Texas.

Accidental Death of John D. O'Keefe, Well Known Here.

A message was received by Mrs. P. Corcoran Tuesday conveying the sad news of the death of her brother, John O'Keefe, which occurred in Texas near Galveston, the day before.

Particulars were not given, but newspaper dispatches of the same date state that his death was the result of accidental shooting.

At first it was supposed the remains would be brought to Port Huron, his old home, for burial, but a later dispatch stated that the interment had taken place at Galveston.

Mr. O'Keefe is well known in this county, having had charge of the telegraph station at Black River a number of years ago. He was a frequent visitor in Harrisville and was here a year ago.

He had been in Texas for about three years in charge of a telegraph station a few miles out from the city of Galveston.

His untimely death is heard with deep regret as he was held in high esteem by a wide circle of acquaintances.

Alcona County Review, August 4, 1898

PERSONAL POINTS.

John D. O'Keefe, whose death in Texas was noted three weeks ago, was an eye witness to a shooting affray and his life paid the forfeit. He was attracted by the commotion. The principals drew their guns in true Texan style and began shooting at each other. The second shot missed its intended mark and struck Mr. O'Keefe in the forehead with the fatal effect already noted.

Alcona County Review, August 25, 1898

Local History of One Year

Chronology of the Principal Events of the Year 1898.

August 2. News received of accidental death by shooting of John D. O'Keefe near Galveston, Texas.

Alcona County Review, January 5, 1899
Cemetery: Lakeview, Galveston County, TX

Oleson, Peter John

AN OSCODA MURDER.

John Oleson Stabbed and Shot by His Room-mate.

Last week Wednesday cries were heard coming from the G., S. & F. Co.'s docks at Oscoda, and hastily repairing to the spot John Oleson, a Swedish laborer, was found brutally slashed with a razor and with a bullet wound in the right breast. He lived but a few minutes after he was discovered, but before he died he accused his room mate, August Benson, of committing the brutal crime. Benson was found in a saloon and was placed under arrest. He denied all knowledge of the crime, but tell-tale bloodstains were found on his hat and clothing. A coroner's jury returned a verdict that Oleson's death was caused by a pistol shot fired by August Benson.

The motive for the atrocious crime seems to have been furnished by a few dollars which Oleson had saved.

Alcona County Review, November 17, 1892

ANOTHER LIFER.

August Benson Convicted of the Murder of Peter Oleson.

On Nov. 10th last, August Benson, a Swede, murdered Peter Oleson, a fellow countryman and his roommate, at Au Sable. The motive for the heinous crime seems to have been to gain possession of a few paltry dollars which Oleson had on his person.

The trial of Benson was taken up last week in the circuit court and was concluded Thursday evening by the jury bringing in a verdict of guilty of murder in the first degree. Judge Kelly of Alpena, who occupied the bench, at once pronounced sentence which consigns the murderer to Jackson for life at hard labor. C. R. Henry, Benson's attorney, will try to get a new trial for his client. Benson is but 23 years of age. An Au Sable paper says that his physiognomy is bad. "His head," it says, "is largely in front of the ears, with the animal propensities predominating."

Alcona County Review, December 29, 1892

From the Oscoda Press:
It is so seldom that a jury is gotten together in Iosco county capable of rendering a common-sense verdict that the people appreciate one when

they see it. The people appreciated the jury in the Benson case.

Alcona County Review, December 29, 1892

EVENTS OF ONE WEEK.

It is a singular fact that three adjoining shore counties, Iosco, Alcona and Alpena, have each contributed a life convict to Jackson prison within the past month: Iosco county sent Benson; Alpena county sent Grossman and Alcona county sends Wightman. A pretty trio of murderers.

Alcona County Review, January 19, 1893

EVENTS OF ONE WEEK.

Jno. Benson, a lifer sent to Jackson from Iosco county for murdering a swede named Oleson at Oscoda, committed suicide last week by cutting his throat.

Alcona County Review, September 28, 1893
Cemetery:

Oliver, Grace

Caledonia.

Mr. and Mrs. E. Oliver buried their little daughter, 8 months old last week.

Alcona County Review, April 27, 1893
Cemetery: Probably Pleasant View, Alcona Co.

Olmstead, Adeline G.

Order of Hearing.
Dec. 16, 97.
STATE OF MICHIGAN, County of Alcona.

At a session of the Probate Court for said County, held at the Probate office, in the Village of Harrisville, on the tenth day of December in the year one thousand eight hundred and ninety-seven.

Present, Hon. W. H. Gilpin, Judge of Probate.

In the matter of the estate of Adeline G. Olmstead.

On reading and filing the petition duly verified of Peter Churchill, praying that a certain instrument now on file in this court, purporting to be the last will and testament of said deceased, may be admitted to probate and that Peter Churchill be appointed executor of said last will and testament of said deceased.

Thereupon it is ordered, that Monday, the 10th day of January next, at ten o'clock in the forenoon, be assigned for the hearing of said petition, and that the heirs at law of said deceased and all other persons interested in said estate, are required to appear at a session of the Probate Court, then to be holden at the Probate office, in the Village of Harrisville and show cause, if any there be, why the prayer of the petitioner should not be granted.

And it is further ordered that the petitioner give notice to the heirs at law and all persons interested in said estate, of the pendency of said petition, and the hearing thereof, by causing a copy of this order to be published in the Alcona County Review, a newspaper printed and circulating in said county three successive weeks previous to said day of hearing.

W. H. Gilpin,
Judge of Probate.

Alcona County Review, December 23, 1897
Cemetery:

Olson, Peter

Two More Victims.

Two Pewabic Wreckers Lose Their Lives in the Diving Bell.

Geo. G. Campbell and Peter Olson lost their lives Saturday while at work on the wreck of the Pewabic, which lies in deep water off Thunder Bay.

The men went down in the diving bell. Campbell, who was the superintendent of the expedition, telephoned up to the steamer Root for hooks. Communication was then suddenly suspended and an effort to hoist the bell disclosed that it had fouled in the wreck and could not be moved. A heavy sea came on and it was several hours before the bell was finally hoisted and towed into smooth water. A window in the bell was found broken and both men were found dead, of course.

These make a total of four lives lost in the effort to secure the treasure of the Pewabic. Wm. Hike of Buffalo died from exposure in 1865 and Oliver Pelkey became entangled in the wreckage in 1891.

Alcona County Review, June 23, 1898
Cemetery:

O'Meara, Mrs. Bridget

LOCAL JOTTINGS.

Bridget O'Meara, of Greenbush, mother of Mrs. John R. McDonald, was buried Sunday. Mrs. O'Meara was born in Ireland, and at the time of her death was 78 years of age. She

had been a resident of Alcona county 18 years. She was a devout Catholic and a constant attendant at her beloved church. Her last illness covered a period of only ten days, final dissolution being superinduced by old age. The friends of the deceased return sincere thanks to the kind friends for their valued assistance and sympathy.

Alcona County Review, November 18, 1887
Cemetery: St. Anne's, Alcona Co.

O'Neal, Charles M.

HOME REVIEWINGS.

Joseph O'Neal has a very sick little son in his family, who it is hardly expected can survive long. The little fellow has been suffering intensely for seven weeks past. The doctors of the county don't appear to know what ails him.

Alcona County Review, May 20, 1881

HOME REVIEWINGS.

Just as we go to press we learn of the death of the little four year old son of Joseph O'Neal, which occurred this morning. The little one has been afflicted with severe ill-health since the fore part of last November, and has suffered great bodily pain. Death, no doubt, is a sweet relief to the little one, though it causes great grief to the parents.

Alcona County Review, July 1, 1881

In Memory of Little Charlie O'Neal.

Since Charlie died the world seems not so bright
As when it heard his voice of sweetness;
To me tis finished with a serener light,
Though joy is robbed of its completeness,
The flowers that blossom in the field and grove,
The brook that prattles through the wildwood.
Are mellowed by the memory of his love
That perished ere the close of childhood.
And all my thoughts seem purified
By sorrow since my Charlie died.

His little playthings I have laid away;
To him they were a world of pleasure,
And now since with them he has ceased to play,
Each is to me a priceless treasure.
His little shoes, the gipsy hat he wore,
His crimson belt, his pretty dresses.
The hobby horse his dimpled hands no more
Will fondly stroke with love's caresses—
All these, and many more beside,

I've laid away since Charlie died.

The bird still breathes a welcome to the dawn
Beside the window; yet more sadly
It seems to sing to me since Charlie's gone
Who listened to its notes so gladly
In everything within the house I see
I find some sweet and cherished token
That ever speaks most touchingly to me
Of a beloved communion broken.
Yet heaven, where all the just abide,
Seems nearer far since Charlie died.

Fall lightly, softly, winter frost and snow
Upon his grave! Bloom sweetly, flowers
Above his head! Oh, wind, your breezes blow
Sweet with the breath of perfumed bowers!
Charlie lies there! Yet though no more I see
His winsome face nor hear his laughter,
I cannot deem his spirit far from me
Though it abides in the Hereafter.
I seem to hear, while dumb I stand,
His footsteps in the Promised Land.

Alcona County Review, August 26, 1881
Cemetery: Probably St. Anne's, Alcona Co.

O'Neal, Elizabeth [Neil]

Death Claims Many Victims.

On Tuesday morning Mrs. Jas. O'Neal died at her late home in this village of consumption from which she has been a patient sufferer for upwards of two years. The deceased was born in Frankton, Canada, in 1857. She came to Harrisville with her parents 12 years since and the same year married Jas. O'Neal. Her husband and two sons survive her. She was a member of the M. E. church and lived and died a professing christian. Mrs. O'Neal was a devoted wife and mother, and a kind neighbor, and the many relatives and friends who survive her will always bear in grateful remembrance the sterling worth of her christian character. The funeral services were held this morning at the church from whence the remains were followed by a large number to their last resting place at South Harrisville.

Alcona County Review, March 26, 1891

My friends and neighbors will please accept my heartfelt thanks for the many acts of kindness shown my wife during her last illness and death.

Jas. O'Neal.

Alcona County Review, April 2, 1891
Cemetery: Springport, Alcona Co.

O'Neal, {Girl}

EVENTS OF ONE WEEK.

The infant daughter of Jas. O'Neal, a former resident of Harrisville, died on the 9th inst. at Tawas City.

Alcona County Review, September 21, 1893
Cemetery: Springport, Alcona Co.

O'Neal, Mrs. James

The Local News.

Mrs. James O'Neal died of consumption at 2:30 o'clock last Tuesday morning at her home on south Clay street. Her remains were taken to Hillsdale Thursday for interment by the side of those of her husband, the funeral services being held in the Catholic church in that city the same day. Mrs. O'Neal was born in 1828 in Langford, Ireland, and had resided in Coldwater upwards of forty years. Four children survive her.—Coldwater (Mich.) Courier.

The deceased was the wife of a brother of Matthew O'Neal and had many friends and relatives in this county.

Alcona County Review, September 12, 1890
Cemetery: Probably St. Anthony, Hillsdale Co.

O'Neal, Matthew

Matthew O'Neal's condition has taken a turn for the worse again and this morning he is reported quite low.

Alcona County Review, July 16, 1896

PERSONAL MENTION.

Mrs. A. B. Clark, daughter of Matthew O'Neal, arrived from Cleveland Sunday night. Mr. O'Neal's condition is not anywise improved.

Alcona County Review, July 30, 1896

MATTHEW O'NEAL.

The flickering lamp of life which has been feebly burning for many weeks and months at last went out at midday Tuesday, August 11.

The mourning family, separated for many years, were reunited at the bedside to receive the dying blessing of an honored parent and beloved husband.

In the death of Matthew O'Neal this community loses a good citizen, who since 1858 has been identified with the history of the town and county, always taking an active and intelligent part in public affairs, and ever ready to assist a neighbor.

Deceased knew well that the end of his earthly career was at hand and

the arrangements for his funeral were made under his direction, the pall bearers being neighbors of his own selection.

The funeral service was held this morning at the Catholic church and was largely attended.

Deceased was born at Quebec in 1831. He was married in 1852 at Cleveland, Ohio, to Catherine Miller, who survives him. He was a cooper by trade and settled in Harrisville 38 years ago.

Alcona County Review, August 13, 1896

PERSONAL MENTION.

Jos. O'Neal arrived from Tonawanda, N. Y., Saturday to join the other members of the family at the bedside of his father. Wm. O'Neal came down Sunday from the River and James arrived home Monday. The two daughters were already at home and the family was thus reunited for the first time in many years.

Alcona County Review, August 13, 1896

We feel deeply grateful to all who in any way contributed to ease the suffering or to brighten the hours during the long and wasting illness of our dear departed husband and father. Such genuine friendship came from the heart and we appreciate it. Mrs. Catherine O'Neal and Family.

Alcona County Review, August 20, 1896
Cemetery: St. Anne's, Alcona Co.

Orth, Josephine [Klee]

Mrs. Geo. Orth of Au Sable is dead.

Alcona County Review, July 11, 1890
Cemetery: Sacred Heart, Iosco Co.

Orton, Rhoda Effa

Haynes Happenings.

Last Saturday Mr. and Mrs. James Orton buried a daughter aged five months. Cause of death cholera infantum.

Alcona County Review, August 20, 1896
Cemetery: Mt. Joy, Alcona Co.

O'Toole, Felix

PURELY PERSONAL.

Felix O'Toole, one of the best known characters of the pioneer days of this section, was reported in the last issue of the Monitor as nearing his end at his home in Albany, Oregon, at the advanced age of 86 years.

Alcona County Review, August 17, 1888

LOCAL JOTTINGS.

Felix O'Toole, erstwhile "King of Au Sable," died at Albany, Oregon, Sunday, August 12, aged 74 years. The bulk of his fortune, amounting to $43,000, was divided between Fred Blumberg and Geo. P. Warner, both former residents of Au Sable, who were intimately associated with the deceased during his declining years.

Alcona County Review, August 31, 1888

LOCAL JOTTINGS.

Fred Blumberg, the Au Sable lad who fell heir to a comfortable fortune on the death of the late Felix O'Toole, visited his old home last week. He will take his parents to the Pacific coast with him to spend their declining years.

Alcona County Review, November 2, 1888
Cemetery: Masonic, Linn Co. OR

Ouilette, Emma

MUD LAKE JC.

Mr. Willets' little child died on Tuesday. We did not learn the cause.

Alcona County Review, August 27, 1896
Cemetery:

Ouilette, John

EVENTS OF ONE WEEK.

A child was buried from the French settlement on Sunday and another, an 18 months' old boy, died yesterday. The latter belonged to a family named Oulette. Neither died from diphtheria, so far as known.

Alcona County Review, February 2, 1893
Cemetery:

Ouilette, Napoleon

Terrible Accident.

A terrible accident happened on the Black River railroad about noon on Wednesday of this week, by which one Napoleon Ouellette, a brakeman on the road, came to his death. While the train was moving rapidly with a heavy load of long timber, an axle to one of the cars in front of those on which Ouellette was braking suddenly broke, prompting the young man to jump from the train to escape injury. No sooner had he jumped and fell sprawling upon the ground than several pieces of the heavy timber were thrown from the train and rolled down upon him, horribly crushing his body in the vicinity of the abdomen and hips. The unfortunate man lived in intense pain and agony until about 8 o'clock Wednesday evening, when death came to his relief. Ouellette was a Frenchman by birth, and about 25 years of age. He had been in the employ of Alger, Smith & Co. for the past year. His remains were expressed to the home of his friends at Windsor, Ont., for burial, leaving this place on the down boat last evening.

Alcona County Review, August 4, 1882
Cemetery:

Owen, {Male}

PERSONAL MENTION.

Samuel Owen went to New York state this week. We are informed that he received a telegram announcing the sudden demise of his father.

Alcona County Review, December 22, 1892

PERSONAL MENTION.

Samuel Owen returned last week from York State, where he was called last fall by the sudden demise of his father. Mr. Owen chartered a car and brought back with him a team and a quantity of miscellaneous property of value to a farmer. He reports a severe winter in western New York.

Alcona County Review, March 9, 1893
Cemetery:

Pack, Albert

Albert Pack Dead.

Albert Pack, the famous Michigan capitalist, died yesterday at Detroit.

Alcona County Review, June 1, 1899

ALBERT PACK.

Albert Pack was a member of the Michigan House of Representatives when only 22 years old. When he died last Wednesday by joint action of the Senate and the House the flag on the state capital was ordered placed and kept at half mast until after his funeral.

The House adopted the following resolution:

In the death of Mr. Pack the state loses one of its best citizens, who has contributed in no small degree to the development and prosperity of our state; a man of the strictest integrity and untiring industry, he richly deserved the success that crowned his efforts; he was ever mindful of the rights and interests of his fellow men, and the duties and responsibilities devolving upon citizenship in a country governed by the people were never shirked or evaded.

The House of Representatives, of which he was a member during the session of 1865, desire to place upon record the evidence of their appreciation of the noble character of him who has gone from among us and express to those who knew him in the family circle their sincere and heartfelt sympathy.

Alcona County Review, June 8, 1899
Cemetery: Elmwood, Wayne Co.

Pack, Greene

GREENE PACK IS DEAD.

The announcement of the death of Greene Pack of Oscoda was bulletined at the postoffice Monday. His death occurred at the Hotel Imperial, New York, at midnight Sunday, and was due to Bright's disease complicated by a severe attack of the grip.

Mr. Pack was born in Petersboro, N. Y., August 13, 1843. He moved to Lexington at the age of 6. In 1876 he moved to Oscoda and became Vice-President and general manager of the Pack, Woods & Co. corporation. He was very successful financially and leaves a large fortune. He was president of the new street railway company which was granted a franchise in Detroit a few months ago for constructing and operating a street railway system. He was a large stockholder also in the street railways of Toronto. He leaves a widow and one daughter.

Alcona County Review, February 28, 1895

A striking instance of the utter futility of human plans and ambitions is afforded by the untimely death of Greene Pack. Hardly past the period of life known as middle age, yet he had attained a degree of success in a financial way far exceeding the fondest expectations of the great majority of men. He was engaged, even when the grim reaper came "as a thief in the night," in the consummation of plans for the accomplishment of still greater financial successes. He has at his command an ample fortune sufficient to surround him with all the comforts of a luxurious life. If the possession of wealth brings happiness his certainly should have been a happy lot. But death inopportunely steps in and robs him of the power to longer enjoy the sweets of life and robs his family of the comfort and pleasure of his society. He has crossed to that

undiscovered country leaving wealth and family behind, his business plans unfinished. But yesterday vast enterprises hinged upon his determination. Today he lies cold in death's embrace; his friends shed tears of genuine sorrow, extolling his virtues and lamenting his death. Yet tomorrow someone will take up the threads of work where he laid them down and will go on and complete them quite as well as he would have done himself.

Sir Thomas Browne said: "Recon not upon a long life; think every day the last and live always beyond thy account."

And perhaps his injunction is worth heeding.

Alcona County Review, February 28, 1895

EVENTS OF ONE WEEK.

Greene Pack's fortune has been estimated at from one million to two million.

Alcona County Review, March 7, 1895

PERSONAL MENTION.

Arthur Pack has taken up a residence in Oscoda for the purpose of personally superintending the closing up of the estate of the late Greene Pack.

Alcona County Review, November 7, 1895
Cemetery:

Packard, Mary

COUNTY REVIEWINGS.

In our death announcements of last issue we inadvertently omitted to make mention of the death of little Mary, eldest daughter of Marcus and Mary Packard, who died of diphtheria on the morning of the 27th ult. There were other children sick in same family of diphtheria, but we are happy to announce that they have recovered.

Alcona County Review, July 9, 1880
Cemetery:

Paffer, Pansy

EVENTS OF ONE WEEK.

A new case of diphtheria is reported in the family of a man by the name of Paffer, at West Harrisville. Also one in the family of Dune McDonald, living south of Gustin. In the latter case the disease was contracted by one of the boys while working at camp 8.

Alcona County Review, July 20, 1893

EVENTS OF ONE WEEK.

The Paffer child at West Harrisville, reported last week as being down with diphtheria, died Thursday last. Mrs. Paffer, who was also afflicted with the disease, has recovered.

Alcona County Review, July 27, 1893
Cemetery:

Papin, Philiace

LOCAL PICK UPS.

The remains of a young man named Papi were brought to Harrisville Sunday from Black River for burial in the Catholic cemetery. He was aged 21 and died from consumption.

Alcona County Review, April 21, 1898
Cemetery: St. Anne's, Alcona Co.

Parent, August

LOCAL JOTTINGS.

August Parent's clothing caught in the live rollers of the edger in Loud & Sons' saw mill at Au Sable Saturday morning. He was drawn into the saws and horribly mangled. Death was almost instantaneous. He left a wife and six children.

Alcona County Review, June 7, 1889
Cemetery: Sacred Heart, Iosco Co.

Park, John

Death of John Park.

John Park, one of the pioneer residents of Mikado, died at his residence near that village last Friday afternoon, aged about 45 years, of dropsy. The deceased leaves a wife and four children who are provided for by a policy of $2,000 in the Maccabees, which order he joined last year. The deceased was one of those big-hearted, generous, whole-souled men who make friends wherever they go, and hosts of friends mourn his untimely demise. He was buried Sunday according to the rites of the Knights of Maccabees, he being an honored member of Mikado Tent No. 13.

Alcona County Review, October 5, 1888

Card of Thanks.

I take this means of publicly expressing my heartfelt thanks to my friends and neighbors who rendered such kindly offices during my late bereavement.

Mrs. John Park.
Mikado, Oct. 1st.

Alcona County Review, October 5, 1888

Card of Thanks.

I wish to express my thanks to the Knights of Maccabees for the prompt payment of insurance carried by my husband in that order for the amount of $2,000 they have my heartfelt thanks; also Mikado Tent, No. 13. May prosperity attend them always.

Mary Park,
Mikado, Mich., Nov. 7, 1888.

Alcona County Review, November 16, 1888
Cemetery: Springport, Alcona Co.

Partridge, Ina M.

EVENTS OF ONE WEEK.

Mr. and Mrs. Phillip O. Partridge of Mikado lost their little son [daughter], thirteen months old, last week.

Alcona County Review, February 16, 1893

West Harrisville.

The following is mailed as a correct account of the recent death in the family of Phillip O. Partridge of Mikado: Ina M. Partridge, daughter of Mr. and Mrs. Partridge, died Thursday at 6:30 p.m., Feb. 9th. Aged 11 months and 20 days. The disease was membranous croup.

Alcona County Review, March 2, 1893
Cemetery:

Patton, John

EVENTS OF ONE WEEK.

John Patton, an insane man from Alpena county, died Sunday at Saginaw while in charge of the officer and enroute for the Traverse City Asylum.

Alcona County Review, October 22, 1896
Cemetery:

Paul, Allen

ALONG THE SHORE.

AU SABLE AND OSCODA.

On Tuesday morning last, Allen Paul, a jobber at Moore and Tanner's camp about 30 miles up the Au Sable, met with an accident which has since proven fatal to him. He was engaged at rolling logs from a highly piled skidway upon sleighs. A log from the top of the pile suddenly rolled down, and before Paul could get out of the way, one end of same struck him across the forehead, knocking him senseless and producing a fearful wound. Dr. Jeyte of Oscoda, was immediately summoned, and rendered such medical and surgical assistance as the case demanded, and when the doctor left the patient he thought with

proper care would come out all right. The blow from the log caused indenture of the bone from the center of the forehead to the left ear, producing concussion of the brain sufficiently to cause much flowing of blood from the nose, mouth and ears. Monday a physician from Tawas was called, and the patient removed from the camp to his home near by, and yesterday morning he died. He leaves a wife and several children, so we learn.

Alcona County Review, February 10, 1882
Cemetery:

Pearson, AliceA. [Willis]

Purely Personal.

Chas. Conklin and Miss Minnie Chapelle drove to Au Sable Tuesday to attend the funeral of a cousin of the latter.

Alcona County Review, January 24, 1890
Cemetery: Ridge, Sanilac Co.

Pearson, Fred

Purely Personal.

Fred Pearson has suffered a relapse and at last accounts is reported very ill with fever and delirium.

Alcona County Review, December 13, 1889

OBITUARY.

It is our sad duty this week to record the death of Fred Pearson at his home in this village at 2 o'clock on the afternoon of Thursday, December 12. He had been ill with fever for a number of weeks prior to his death, but only the week before he had so far recovered as to be able to get down town several times. His complete recovery seemed to be assured but while visiting at the home of his brother north of this village he was again taken violently ill, this time with inflammation of the bowels of the most aggravated type. He was removed to his late home in this village where he suffered great agony until death relieved him. The deceased had not yet reached his majority. He was endowed with a happy disposition that made friends for him wherever he went and his untimely demise is mourned by a large circle of friends, both young and old. The funeral services were held at his late home last Saturday afternoon, the remains being interred in the South Harrisville cemetery. Six of his companions acted as pall bearers. The floral offerings were pretty, particularly a cross of white calla lillies from Capt. Motly of Alpena. The deceased expected to go west sometime this winter to join his father who is at present at Skamokawa, Washington and to whom the news of his death will be a sad blow.

Alcona County Review, December 20, 1889

Purely Personal.

Capt. Motley of Alpena attended the funeral of Fred Pearson last Saturday.

Alcona County Review, December 20, 1889

Card of Thanks.
We wish to extend our deep and heartfelt thanks to those who assisted in any manner during the last illness and death of our beloved son and brother and may all be spared the grief of a like sad visitation.

Mrs. R. P. Pearson and family.

Alcona County Review, December 20, 1889
Cemetery: Springport, Alcona Co.

Peck, John
LOCAL JOTTINGS.

Jno. Peck, of Killmaster, aged 30, died last week Thursday of consumption after a lingering illness.

Alcona County Review, June 17, 1887
Cemetery:

Pelkie, {Boy}
Curtis.
Jack Pelkie and wife were blest by a fine son a week ago, but sad news came to the father the other day that the child was dead. He was working for J. W. Ferguson and being near Bryant he telephoned for a coffin, which came that night. On his return he found the child living and it is living yet. This is quite a miracle.

Alcona County Review, March 30, 1893

Curtis.
It appeared in the items of last week that Mr. Pelkey's baby lived. Should say it lived near a week. Mr. Pelkey kept the coffin from Saturday till the next Thursday when the father and fond mother, thinking that their darling would live, sent it back to the maker and on Friday the little child departed to the God who gave it. Mr. E. M. Barker took charge of the funeral and the Rev. Mr. Nunn preached a grand sermon. All attended the funeral that could leave

home and their little angel was laid in its mother dust.

Alcona County Review, April 6, 1893
Cemetery:

Pelkie, Oliver
Another Search For Buried Treasure
The fatal termination of the search for the steamer Pewabic last fall will not defer others from attempting to locate the sunken steamer. The Pewabic was sunk in Thunder Bay, off Alpena, some twenty odd years ago, and periodical attempts have been made ever since to secure the valuable cargo which she is supposed to have aboard, but on account of the depth of the water it has been unsuccessful. Another searching expedition is being organized and the Superior Daily Call has the following in relation to it:

"Boiler Inspector M. F. Chalk, of this district, has been offered $1,000, all expenses and an insurance on his life for $14,000 if he will undertake a submarine search for the Pewabic, in which effort Oliver Pelkie lost his life last fall. Besides this, if the vessel is found, Chalk would be given one half the proceeds of the sale of the cargo which includes 555 tons of pure copper it is believed would be over $100,000. Mr. Chalk has been a professional diver ever since he was 16 years of age, but is undecided as to whether to accept the proposal.

Alcona County Review, February 4, 1892
Cemetery:

Pelkier, Henry
ALONG THE SHORE.

The Tawases.
Mr. Henry Pelkier, who was brought from the woods to the Miner House nearly two weeks ago, sick with inflammation of the lungs, as noticed last week, died on Sunday last. His body was taken to his home in Bay City on Monday. Deceased leaves a wife and four children in Bay City.

Alcona County Review, December 23, 1881
Cemetery:

Pelton, John
John Pelton, Veteran.
John Pelton, an aged veteran, died at the home of Daniel Byce last Friday.

Deceased was a member of company I, 27th regiment, Michigan

Inf. volunteers. He had no relatives here, and for the past two or three years has been living at Hubbard Lake, where he had a house and a patch of ground. During the camping season he supplied the campers with green stuff from his garden and made himself generally useful and obliging to visitors at the lake.

He had come out to town on business recently and being too ill to return home, stopped at the home of his friend, Daniel Byce.

The funeral occurred last Saturday, Rev. W. W. Will conducting the service. Members of Wyrum Hoyt Post G. A.R. were among those who paid their respects to the departed veteran.

Alcona County Review, March 24, 1898

Apr. 14.
STATE of Michigan, County of Alcona.

At a session of the Probate Court for said county, held at the Probate office, in the village of Harrisville, on the 11th day of April in the year one thousand eight hundred and ninety-eight.

Present, Hon. Wm. H. Gilpin, Probate Judge.

In the matter of the estate of John Pelton, deceased.

On reading and filing the petition, duly verified, of George Rutson, praying among other things that administration of said estate may be granted to Daniel Byce, or some other suitable person.

Thereupon it is ordered, that Monday, the 9th day of May, next, at 10 o'clock in the forenoon, be assigned for the hearing of said petition, and that the heirs at law of said deceased, and all other persons interested in said estate, are required to appear at a session of said court, then to be holden at the Probate office, in the village of Harrisville, and show cause, if any there be, why the prayer of the petitioner should not be granted: and it is further ordered that said petitioner give notice to the heirs at law and all other persons interested in said estate, of the pendency of said petition, and the hearing thereof, by causing a copy of this order to be published in the "Alcona County Review" a newspaper printed and circulated in said county, three successive weeks previous to said day of hearing.

Wm. H. Gilpin,
Judge of Probate.

Alcona County Review, April 21, 1898

HONORS TO DEAD HEROES.

A magnificent demonstration of the patriotic spirit of the citizens of Alcona county was the observance on Monday of the time honored custom of decorating the graves and commemorating the deeds of valor of the nation's dead heroes.

The grave of John Pelton in the west cemetery, where the first grave service was held, had been neatly trimmed and sodded by Comrades Jos. Sovey and Owen Fox. It is to be marked also by a head stone which the government provides under general law.

The roster of soldiers who are buried here is as follows: Harrisville, (West), A. Marcellus, John Pelton, W. W. Douglass: Catholic, Louis Rivard, Geo. Bernizer: South Harrisville, R. Richmond, Chas. Miller, H. J. Aird, A. Noyes, Jas. Johnson.

Alcona County Review, June 2, 1898

Local History of One Year

Chronology of the Principal Events of the Year 1898.

March 18. Death of John Pelton, a veteran.

Alcona County Review, January 5, 1899
Cemetery: West Lawn, Alcona Co.

Pemberton, Horatio

ALPENA.

Horatio Pemberton, brother of the late confederate general Pemberton, died at Rogers City on the 6th, aged 87 years.

Alcona County Review, February 24, 1882
Cemetery:

Perkins, Guy Clinton

LOCAL JOTTINGS.

Died, at Greenbush, Wednesday, 17 months' old babe of Mr. and Mrs. Owen Perkins.

Alcona County Review, September 4, 1885
Cemetery: Springport, Alcona Co.

Perry, {Child}

DIPHTHERIA'S HARVEST.

The Dreadful Disease Adds to the Long List of Dead.

Another child died in the Perry family in Gustin township Sunday, making the second death. Two more children have the disease.

Alcona County Review, July 7, 1893
Cemetery:

Perry, Jane

EVENTS OF ONE WEEK.

A family named Perry, residing west of Killmaster, lost a boy [girl] last week from diphtheria.

Alcona County Review, June 29, 1893

West Harrisville, Oct. 4.—At Killmaster September 10th union services were held by Rev. S. Boundy for Janean Perry, born at Little Current, Canada, Sept. 12, 1882, died June 19th, 1893, Alcona county, daughter of Ira and Mrs. Perry; and Georgenia McQuean, born at Port Rowan, Canada, Oct. 15th, 1885, died July 2d, 1893, Alcona county, daughter of Mr. and Mrs. James McQuean, having both died of diphtheria.

Alcona County Review, October 5, 1893
Cemetery:

Peterson, Phyllis

PERSONAL MENTION.

Phyllis, the three year old daughter of Jack Peterson, Jr., of West Haven, Mich., died Monday of cholera infantum.

Alcona County Review, August 29, 1895
Cemetery:

Phelps, William Walter

OUR NEIGHBORS.

The will of the late Walter Phelps, of New Jersey, was received here last week for record. The deceased owned a lot of timbered lands in this and adjoining counties. Mr. Phelps was minister to Germany during President Harrison's term.--Cheboygan News.

Alcona County Review, June 20, 1895

EVENTS OF ONE WEEK.

The will of the late William Walter Phelps, Ex-U. S. Minister to Germany, has been placed on record this week in Alcona county by Register Chapelle. Some Alcona county lands belong to the estate. The will was probated in Antrim county and it has been recorded in some 10 Michigan counties already. The will disposes of a vast estate which comprises property in many parts of the world. A half million dollars is bequeathed to a son, $300,000 to a daughter, an annual income of $300 to a coachman, and so on.

Alcona County Review, September 5, 1895
Cemetery:

Phillips, Frank

Leaves Four Children.

East Tawas, Mich., Nov. 25.—Frank Phillips was instantly killed at Emery's mill yesterday afternoon. He was struck over the heart by a piece of board from the edger, the force of the blow knocking him nearly 10 feet. He leaves a wife and four children.

Alcona County Review, December 1, 1892
Cemetery: Greenwood, Iosco Co.

Phillips, Fred

LOCAL JOTTINGS.

Fred Philips of Oscoda, aged 14 years, was drowned in the river there on the 8th inst. He was subject to fits, and was attacked with one when he fell into the water. He had previously had several narrow escapes from drowning from the same cause.

Alcona County Review, September 17, 1886
Cemetery:Pinecrest, Iosco Co.

Pierce, Catherine [Blue]

PERSONAL MENTION.

Hon. C. S. Pierce of the Oscoda Press received the sad intelligence last week of the death of his mother at Belle Branch, Wayne county.

Alcona County Review, November 8, 1894
Cemetery: Redford, Wayne Co.

Pierce, Jerome

COUNTY NEWS JOTTINGS.

Jerome Pierce, of the firm of Jerome Pierce & Co., Buffalo, N. Y., and Black River, this county, is dead. The sad intelligence reaches us, by telegraph, this morning, that he walked off the bridge at Buffalo, last evening. No particulars are given.

Alcona County Review, January 4, 1878
Cemetery: Forest Lawn, Erie Co., NY

Pizer, Fannie [Stock]

PERSONAL MENTION.

Mrs. Jacob Pizer has been critically ill for several days. Sunday night her recovery seemed doubtful, but a slight improvement in her condition was noted the next day and she has improved slowly since. Dr. McCormick was called Monday in consultation with Dr. Mitchell.

Alcona County Review, November 22, 1894

PERSONAL MENTION.

Miss Lizzie Stock arrived by Saturday's express from Detroit to attend her sister, Mrs. J. B. Pizer, during her illness.

Alcona County Review, November 29, 1894

PERSONAL MENTION.

Mrs. Jacob Pizer died at three o'clock a.m. Tuesday morning. The remains were at once prepared for shipment to Detroit and were taken down on the morning express. Deceased was about 27 years of age. Her home was in Detroit and she will be buried there according to the Hebrew rites. Deceased leaves her husband and two small children. She was a member of Alcona Hive of the L. O. T. M. and carried an insurance of $1,000, which goes to her husband. Her death was due to blood poisoning.

Alcona County Review, November 29, 1894

Whereas, Death has for the second time entered our Hive and taken from us our beloved sister, Fannie Pizer, therefore be it

Resolved, That we as members of Alcona Hive No. 295 L.O.T.M. do hereby express our sorrow at the loss of one of our esteemed sisters, and

Resolved, While we bow in submission to the will of our Supreme Ruler, we tender our earnest and heartfelt sympathy to the bereaved family, and that as a token of regard we drape our charter in mourning for a period of 30 days. And be it further

Resolved, That a copy of these resolutions be placed upon the record of our Hive and that they be published in the Alcona County Review and a copy be sent to the family.

Lou E. Lewis,
Ida M. Hogue,   Committee.
Laura B. Graham.

Alcona County Review, December 6, 1894

A draft for $1,000 was received by the officers of Alcona Hive No. 205? L. O. T. M. on Tuesday, which was placed in the hands of Jacob Pizer the following day and is the amount of insurance held in the society on the life of his late wife.

Alcona County Review, January 10, 1895

PERSONAL MENTION.

Jacob Pizer arrived in town last Friday from the east, where he found a temporary home for his children

with relatives. He has not yet decided where to locate.

Alcona County Review, March 14, 1895
Cemetery: Probably Beth Olem, Wayne Co.

Plunkett, Catherine

COUNTY NEWS.

There has been another death this week from diphtheria. Miss Kittie Blanket, sister of Mrs. R. Reed (recently from Deckerville), who had been ill less than a week, died Wednesday evening. She was a bright girl and aged about 13 years. Her sudden decease leaves another vacant chair and lonely household. Be ye also therefore ready "for in an hour when ye think not the Son of Man cometh." Burial takes place to-day at 2:30 p.m.

Alcona County Review, February 11, 1881
Cemetery:

Plunkett, J. T.

The badly decomposed body of a man was found near North Point Tuesday. It is believed to be that of one J. T. Plunkett who jumped overboard from a steambarge opposite Sturgeon Point late last fall.

Alcona County Review, May 18, 1899
Cemetery:

Pomeroy, Calvin Thayer

Alcona Atoms.

Mr. McElroy, of the Toledo Blade, offered $100 reward for the recovery of the bodies of his son and father-in-law. As before noted, half the reward has been earned.

Alcona County Review, September 10, 1880

County Reviewings.

The bodies of Dr. C. Pomeroy and Guy McElroy, of Toledo, Ohio, and the body of Jenny Mosser of Alcona, were found by the Life Saving Crew on Wednesday last, the former two near the station, the latter a mile south. The bodies of Dr. Pomeroy and nephew were shipped to their relatives in Toledo.

Alcona County Review, September 10, 1880
Cemetery: Pomeroy, Putnam County, OH

Porter, Emernett A. [Emerson]

LOCAL JOTTINGS.

Emernett, wife of Wells Porter, of Harrisville, died this morning at 5 o'clock, in the 23d year of her age. She was the only daughter of Mr. and Mrs. Thos. Emerson of this village.

Mrs. Porter was born in New York State, but had spent the greater part of her life here. She was married less than two years since, and proved herself to be a very devoted wife. During several weeks past she had suffered intensely, but bore her great affliction with fortitude and resignation. Besides husband, parents and two brothers, she leaves a young babe.

Alcona County Review, October 17, 1884

LOCAL JOTTINGS.

Wells Porter desires through the Review to express his thanks to the friends and neighbors who so kindly assisted during the illness and death of his wife, hoping that the sad trials through which he has so recently passed may be very far removed from these "friends in need."

Alcona County Review, October 24, 1884
Cemetery: Springport, Alcona Co.

Potter, Emma D. [Mooney]

Local Sayings and Doings.

The wife of Hon. Wm. H. Potter, of Alpena, who died at St. Mary's Hospital in Detroit last Thursday, was buried at her home Sunday afternoon. Mrs. Potter was a lady of fine culture, and a very enthusiastic and effectual worker in the interests of christianity and temperance. She was highly esteemed by all who knew her, many of her acquaintances also living in this place. She was a sister of Mrs. J. W. Glennie, of Au Sable.

Alcona County Review, May 19, 1882
Cemetery: Evergreen, Alcona Co.

Potvin, Julius

Julius Potvin, the proprietor of the Alpena House at Alpena, died two weeks ago.

Alcona County Review, October 13, 1892
Cemetery: Holy Cross, Alpena Co.

Potvin, Mr.

EVENTS OF ONE WEEK.

An old man, a Mr. Potvin, from the French settlement, died last week and was buried Monday morning in the Harrisville Catholic cemetery.

Alcona County Review, April 16, 1896
Cemetery: St. Anne's, Alcona Co.

Pratt, Ralph

Among Our Exchanges

R. E. Pratt of East Tawas, well known along the shore as an

Enthusiastic patron of the turf, dropped dead on the streets of Tawas last week. He leaves a family who will receive $3,000 insurance from the Forresters.

Alcona County Review, March 24, 1892

Alas, for the Milk of Human Kindness.

Ralf Pratt, of East Tawas, died suddenly of the same kind of heart disease that a good many others do. His heart failed to beat. We do not believe in going into ecstacies over a departed bum. So we will drop the matter by stating that Pratt died of "consumption" and probably left as few real friends as it is possible for a man to leave.—Au Sable Monitor.

Alcona County Review, March 31, 1892

The Lakeside Monitor is getting unmercifully scored by its contemporaries for its uncalled for assault upon the memory of the late Ralf Pratt. The dead man might have been a bad man in his way, but there is no creature so low but that he has its redeeming traits, and when the grim reaper steps in and claims the dregs of a miserable existence for his victory, the office of mortals would seem rather to be to draw the cloak of charity about the misdeeds of the departed than to expose them to view in all their hideousness. Human nature is weak at its best. Let him who is without blemish or sin cast the first stone.

Alcona County Review, April 7, 1892

A THORNY ROAD TO TRAVEL.

The Au Sable Monitor Editor in a Peck of Trouble. But He Bids Defiance to His Enemies.

The attack of the Lakeside Monitor on the name of Ralph Pratt, deceased, and subsequently on the democratic candidates for city offices in Au Sable, whom he scourged without mercy and without exception in the issue preceding the last election, culminated in the following resolutions, which are copied from the Times word for word and letter for letter.

CHICKENS COME HOME TO ROOST.

The citizens meet and discuss the best interest of our city and who should live here and who should not.

At a meeting of the citizens of Au Sable held last evening the committee of resolutions handed in the following resolution and recommended its adoption:

Whereas a newspaper in existence in our midst by the name of Lakeside Monitor, edited by one Wesley M. Featherly and

Whereas in the issue of the said paper the editor has grossly insulted and defamed the names and characters of many of our good citizens and

Whereas the citizens have become very indignant regarding the same. We the committee appointed by this meeting do recommend that immediate action be taken at once and that it be

Resolved that we give the said W. M. Featherly due notice to leave this city and county inside of ten days and that it be further

Resolved that should he not obey said notice then we proceed to deal with him as he should be dealt with, viz: He be taken and marched through our streets to the outskirts of the city and then tar and feathered from the crown of his head to the soles of his feet. And be it further

Resolved that the paper now known as Lakeside Monitor must if published in future by any other party or parties, be given another name.

All of which we humbly submit for your approval.

Com. of Resolutions.

Moved and seconded that the resolutions be accepted and adopted and that the Secretary be instructed to have same published in the Au Sable Times and a copy of the same be sent to Wesley M. Featherly.—Carried. Signed on behalf of meeting.

Secretary.

The Saturday Night in its last issue contains the following version of the affair and events subsequent thereto, which account is probably as little colored by prejudice as any obtainable.

A BOYCOTT DECLARED AGAINST THE MONITOR. KING'S OPERA HOUSE PACKED LAST EVENING AT THE INDIGNATION MEETING.

Two or three weeks ago after the death of Ralph E. Pratt of East Tawas, the Lakeside Monitor had an item, nine lines in length, giving an account of Mr. Pratt's death and referring to him as a "departed bum." The item caused indignation all over the county. Those who were acquainted with Mr. Pratt knew that he was not a bum, and those who were not acquainted with him felt that there was no necessity of speaking in such a manner of any dead man. Mr. Pratt belonged to several societies and among the members of these the indignation was greatest.

Last week the Monitor took occasion to rake over the Democratic candidates on the city ticket, and this caused further indignation in Au Sable. In the same issue was an article heaping abuse on one of Oscoda's citizens, Chris. Yockey, just because he happened to be the Democratic candidate for supervisor. Now Mr. Yockey is always and everywhere a gentleman, and there is no man in Oscoda who has a higher reputation for integrity and square dealing. Consequently his many friends are exceedingly angry on account of what the Monitor has said.

Taking all things together the people of Oscoda and Au Sable have become greatly worked up against W. M. Featherly. As a result a meeting of about twenty five leading citizens of both towns was held at the Oscoda Village Hall Wednesday evening, and it was decided at this meeting to call a mass meeting at King's opera house to express the sentiments of the people in regard to the Monitor's course. Posters and bond bills were printed and distributed announcing the meeting.

King's opera house was jammed full last evening, and standing room was at a premium. There were probably a thousand people present. The meeting was called to order by Alex Conenfant. Granger Hill was chosen chairman and A. M. Johnson secretary. The chairman made some remarks explaining the object of the meeting to be to get the sense of the people as to the course pursued by the Lakeside Monitor. Mr. Hill said he was in for anything that would drive Featherly out of town, and that he would abide by the decision of the meeting, even if that decision should be in favor of a coat of tar and feathers for the publisher of the Monitor.

A call was then made for speakers….a motion….appointing a committee to draft a set of resolutions. While the committee was out preparing a set of resolutions A. M. Johnston made a speech. After Mr. Johnston's speech there were loud calls for O. E. McCutcheon, who responded with a sort of political speech, saying little in regard to the subject under consideration. What little he did say was in the nature of a rather mild defense of Mr. Featherly.

The committee on resolutions then reported, recommending the adoption of the following resolutions:

Resolved, That it is the sense of this meeting that a general boycott be declared against W. M. Featherly, editor of the Monitor, and that business men who persist in advertising in the columns of the Monitor be boycotted from this time forth.

Resolved, That a copy of these resolutions be given to The Saturday Night and the Times for publication.

The resolutions were adopted by a rising vote, the vote being unanimously in the affirmative.

After the adoption of the resolutions there were speeches by Jos. Eaton, I. L. Warren and W. L. M. Blakely. Mr. Eaton's speech was a violent denunciation of the Monitor and its publisher. The speeches of Mr. Warren and Mr. Blakely were not so violent as that of Mr. Eaton. The meeting then adjourned.

It is seldom that a man is so universally condemned in the community in which he lives as Featherly is at the present time.

The Monitor evidently thinks it divines the personality of the instigator of the foregoing and the motive for same, and it bids defiance in the following lines which are the only allusions the paper makes to proceedings which it is safe to say are the most pronounced and emphatic ever taken against the publisher of a Michigan paper.

The Monitor's thanks are due to its Granger friend and the Times for efforts to furnish it with free advertising. Our Granger friend does not want the Monitor here, but it does not suit this paper's purpose to please him to any alarming extent, and the sooner the notion is exploded that it is to be run out the less wind will be wasted. It is a hard one to drive as many have found out. If Mr. Granger, or any one else, wants to

make a purchase, we are open to a good bargain, otherwise we stay.

Granger Hill has made a terrible flutter this week in his efforts to attract attention of the people from himself to the Monitor. The community understand the situation all right and it will avail Mr. Hill nothing. It hurts, Mr. Hill; we know it. But where duty calls, etc. The Monitor stands in Mr. Hill's path for preferment he imagines he might secure politically if it was not here. Hit hard Mr. Hill. It will take some hard blows to accomplish your purpose. Blows you are not equal to. A Detroit paper once remarked that like a cat, you could dump the Monitor out of a bag any side up and it would hit on its feet.

Alcona County Review, April 7, 1892
Cemetery: Lakeside, St. Clair Co.

Preston, David

NOTICE.
NOTICE IS HEREBY GIVEN. That under and by virtue of a license granted by the Probate Court for the County of Wayne, State of Michigan, the undersigned will sell at public venue on the 21st Day of January, A. D., 1888, at 12 o'clock M., at the Court House in the County of Alcona, at Harrisville, in said county, all the right, title and interest of David Preston, deceased, in and to all and singular the following described pieces or parcels of land situated in the County of Alcona, State of Michigan, described as follows, to-wit: The south-west quarter of the north-east quarter of section 22 township 27 north, range 8 east, 40 acres; the south-west quarter of the north-west quarter of section 22, township 27 north, range 8 east, 40 acres; the north one-half of the north-west quarter of section 22, township 27 north, range 8 east, 80 acres.

Dated Detroit, Mich., December 9th, 1887.
JANE B. PRESTON.
WILLIAM D. PRESTON.
Executors of Estate of said Deceased.
J. G. Dickenson, Attorney for said Executors.

Alcona County Review, December 9, 1887
Cemetery: Elmwood, Wayne Co.

Prince, George Vanilla

An Alpena Mill Hand Terribly Mangled.
Alpena, Mich., Dec. 5.—George Prince, employed in Pack's mill, fell upon a slab saw this morning and was terribly mangled. He has but little chance for recovery.
Later.—Prince has since died.

Alcona County Review, December 8, 1892
Cemetery: Evergreen, Alpena Co.

Proctor, Maude

EVENTS OF ONE WEEK.

After a long and tedious illness from pulmonary consumption Miss Maude Proctor, until recently a resident of the village of Alcona, has passed away. The funeral services were held at Black River, the Rev. E. F. Smith officiating. The interment took place at Alcona.

Miss Proctor's death occurred at South Rogers last week. The funeral services were held on Sunday at Black River.

Alcona County Review, May 10, 1894

Haynes Happenings.

The remains of Miss Maude Proctor were brought from Black River Sunday, the 6th in the beautiful hearse of D. La Boueff, followed by her relatives and a large number of sympathizing friends, and interred in our cemetery which overlooks the limpid waters of Lake Huron, Sturgeon Pointe Lighthouse Station, Black River Island and part of Thunder bay.

Alcona County Review, May 10, 1894

At Court.

Catherine Proctor was found not guilty of selling liquor without a license. The testimony was similar to that upon which four convictions were secured at the last term of court. Sympathy for defendant in her recent affliction had an influence doubtless on the verdict.

Alcona County Review, May 17, 1894

I wish to thank through the columns of the Review Messrs. Conductors Hackett and McLennan and all the train hands for their kindness; and the many friends in Black River and vicinity for the kind and sympathetic feeling expressed in my late bereavement, the death of my only daughter, Maud. And I especially thank the choir for the great pains taken in practicing appropriate music for the sad occasion.

Mrs. Proctor.

Alcona County Review, May 17, 1894
Cemetery: Mt. Joy, Alcona Co.

Proctor, William J.

Haynes Happenings.

Haynes, Aug. 27.--Wm. J. Proctor was buried on the 24th. The funeral sermon was preached at the residence of the deceased by the Methodist minister of Black River. A very large attendance followed the remains to the grave.

Alcona County Review, August 24, 1888

LOCAL JOTTINGS.

Wm. Proctor, of Alcona, died this week after a long illness.

Alcona County Review, August 31, 1888

Card of Thanks.

I wish to thank my friends and neighbors for their kindness during the last illness and death of my husband.

Mrs. W. I. Proctor.

Alcona County Review, September 7, 1888

Haynes Items.

Mrs. W. I. Proctor has erected a very beautiful monument to the memory of her late consort, of Italian marble at a cost of one hundred dollars, in the public burying grounds. And now it would be in order for the Board of Health to erect a new fence or have the old one repaired, as it is in a very dilapidated condition and is a disgrace to the township, the way it is with the costly monuments and tombstones erected by the relatives of the deceased.

Alcona County Review, May 28, 1891

Haynes Happenings.

Mrs. Robt. Cade has caused to be erected a monument to the memory of her late husband. The design is the same as the one erected to the memory of W. J. Proctor; it has engine and tender No. 20 and D. B. C. & A. R. R. engraved on it.

Alcona County Review, July 30, 1891
Cemetery: Mt. Joy, Alcona Co.

Procunier, Anthony

Paragraphs of Local Interest.

Antoine Procunier, a resident of Gustin township, is suffering untold agony from a rose cancer on his chin, which has eaten away that portion of the face and downward. He is a pitiable sight to behold; has been unable to eat anything for some time and lives chiefly on milk and soft food. He has become very weak but fully realizes his short sojourn on earth. The writer would direct Mr. Procunier's attention to the Lamb of God, which taketh away the sins of the world, St. John 1-29; and as a surety of a rest hereafter read the fourth chapter of Hebrew.

Alcona County Review, February 1, 1894

Greenbush.

We have been informed that Mr. Antoine Procunier is very low.

Alcona County Review, February 22, 1894

OBITUARY.

Anthony Procunier died at his late home in the township of Harrisville, Thursday July 20, 1894, aged 71 years, lacking one month, of malignant cancer.

Deceased was born at Port Royal, Canada, in 1823. In 1848 he married his first wife who was also a native of Port Royal. Eight children were the result of this union, some of whom will be recognized as present residents of Alcona county as follows: Mrs. Robt. Dickson, Peter Procunier, Mrs. Calvin Wilson, Mrs. Frances Bristin, Bruce Procunier, Elizabeth Procunier, Emma Procunier, Dessmus Procunier.

The funeral services were held from deceased's late residence on Saturday, the Rev. W. J. Bailey officiating. A large number of citizens who have known the deceased during the many years of his residence in this county turned out to pay their last respects to the dead and the living.

Alcona County Review, July 26, 1894

Springport and Vicinity.

Antoine Procunier passed away to the great beyond Thursday of last week from the effects of cancer. The funeral was held at the home the following Saturday, from whence the remains were followed to the cemetery by a large concourse of relatives and friends.

Alcona County Review, July 26, 1894

STATE OF MICHIGAN, County of Alcona.

At a session of the Probate Court for said County, held at the Probate office, in the Village of Harrisville, on the eleventh day of August, in the year one thousand eight hundred and ninety-four.

Present, C. H. Killmaster, Judge of Probate.

In the Matter of the Estate of Anthony Procunier:

On reading and filing the petition, duly verified, of Dessmus Procunier praying that a certain instrument now on file in this Court, and purporting to be the last will and testament of said deceased, may be admitted to probate.

Thereupon it is ordered that Saturday, the Fifteenth day of September next, at ten o'clock in the forenoon, be assigned for the hearing of said petition, and that the heirs at law of said deceased, and all other persons interested in said estate, are required to appear at a session of said Court, then to be holden in the Probate office in the Village of Harrisville, and show cause, if any there be, why the prayer of the petitioner should not be granted: And it is further ordered that said petitioner give notice to the persons interested in said estate, of the pendency of said petition, and the hearing thereof, by causing a copy of this order to be published in the Alcona County Review, a newspaper printed and circulated in said county, three successive weeks previous to said day of hearing.

C. H. Killmaster,
Judge of Probate.

Alcona County Review, August 16, 1894

Order of Hearing.

Apr. 21, 98.

STATE OF MICHIGAN, County of Alcona.

At a session of the Probate Court for said County, held at the Probate office, in the Village of Harrisville on the sixteenth day of April in the year one thousand eight hundred and ninety-eight.

Present, Hon. W. H. Gilpin, Judge of Probate.

In the matter of the estate of Anthony Procunier.

On reading and filing the petition duly verified of Dessmus Procunier praying among other things that a certain instrument now on file in this court, purporting to be the last will and testament of said deceased, may be admitted to probate and that administration of said estate may be granted to Lorenzo Frederick, the executor named in said will, or some other suitable person.

Thereupon it is ordered, that Monday, the 16th day of May next, at ten o'clock in the forenoon, be assigned for the hearing of said petition, and that the heirs at law of said deceased and all other persons interested in said estate, are required to appear at a session of the Probate Court, then to be holden at the Probate office, in the Village of Harrisville and show cause, if any there be, why the prayer of the petitioner should not be granted.

And it is further ordered that the petitioner give notice to the heirs at law and all persons interested in said estate, of the pendency of said petition, and the hearing thereof, by causing a copy of this order to be published in the Alcona County Review, a newspaper printed and circulating in said county three successive weeks previous to said day of hearing.

W. H. Gilpin,
Judge of Probate.

Alcona County Review, April 21, 1898
Cemetery: Springport, Alcona Co.

Profit, Mrs. Joseph

NEIGHBORHOOD NOTES.

Mrs. Joseph Profit suicided at Mio last week by cutting her throat with a razor. She was insane from religious excitement.

Alcona County Review, September 13, 1889
Cemetery:

Pulford, Martha H.

Jottings Along the Shore.

A two year old daughter of Wm. Pulford of Alpena has died from the effects of being scalded. Mothers be careful of your kettles of hot water.

Alcona County Review, May 27, 1881
Cemetery:

Purdy, Samuel

Local Sayings and Doings.

Just before going to press the Review learns that Samuel Purdy, aged between 40 and 50 years, died at camp back of Black River yesterday morning.

Alcona County Review, January 13, 1882
Cemetery:

Pyne, {Child}

LOCAL JOTTINGS.

Wm. Pyne buried a five months old child last week.

Alcona County Review, October 4, 1889
Cemetery: Probably Mt. Joy, Alcona Co.

Pyne, Cynthia Ann [Crow]

DIED.

Cynthia Ann, wife of William C. Pyne, at their late home in Haynes township, Sunday night, April 14, 1895, aged 38 years and 9 months.

Mrs. Pyne was born in Ontario on the 10th day of July, 1895 [sic]. Her maiden name was Cynthia Ann Crow. She was married to William C. Pyne June 10th, 1875. Their union was blessed with eleven children, seven sons and four daughters. The father and eight children, six boys and two girls, are left to mourn their loss.

The funeral services were held from the M. E. church Tuesday afternoon, Rev. Bailey officiating. Mr. Pyne and family have the sympathy of the community in their great sorrow.

Alcona County Review, April 18, 1895

Haynes Happenings.

Wm. Pyne has our sympathy in the loss of his wife; also Mr. Beebe in his affliction.

Alcona County Review, April 25, 1895
Cemetery: Mt. Joy, Alcona Co.

Pyne, Charles Forrest

Forrest Pyne Drowned.

Forest Pyne, aged 14, son of Mrs. Jas. Pyne, was drowned in Crystal Lake last Sunday afternoon while in bathing. The boy, who was unable to swim, stepped suddenly into deep water while wading out and before assistance arrived he was drowned. The body was recovered soon after the accident, but all efforts to resuscitate him were futile.

Alcona County Review, July 1, 1887
Cemetery: Springport, Alcona Co.

Pyne, James Fraser

Fatal Accident.

Last Thursday, Fraser Pyne, son of Jas. Pyne, who worked in a lumber camp in R. A. Alger & Co.'s woods, accidentally got one of his legs severely crushed, in the vicinity of the thigh, between a couple of logs. The wound at the time it was dressed, was not considered dangerous, and all anticipated that the young man would get on all right. But it was not long before he began to grow worse, and finally, on Monday, died. Fraser was a young man about 20 years of age, and commanded much friendship among the boys in the lumber woods. His death is a sad blow to the bereaved parents and family, who have the sympathy of the community. The funeral services were held from the M. E. Church, Tuesday afternoon.

Alcona County Review, January 3, 1879

County News and Gossip.

James Fraser Pyne, who died two weeks since, was born March 13, 1858. Aged 20 years, 4 months and 14 days.

Alcona County Review, January 10, 1879

ALCONA.

There have been 9 deaths in the township—two children from diphtheria, two children from causes unknown; one child from whooping cough; one woman from consumption; one man, mortally wounded in Beard & Co's saw-mill; one of the inhabitants of Harrisville by gun shot; and James Pyne's son was mortally wounded in Millen's works, and died at the residence of his father; Mr. Freeman Youngs was mortally wounded on the Black River R. R., and died in Detroit. Mr. D. McArthur also lost his leg by the discharge of a rifle.

Alcona County Review, January 10, 1879
Cemetery: Springport, Alcona Co.

Pyne, Maud

John Pyne and wife lost a 11-months old child this week.

Alcona County Review, July 25, 1890
Cemetery: Probably Springport, Alcona Co.

Quance, William

Gustin Grist.

Gustin, April 2.--Wm. Quance, son-in-law of A. S.Vincent, and who at one time operated a portable saw mill in Harrisville and also in the vicinity of Killmaster, died recently at Beregary, Canada.

Alcona County Review, April 4, 1895
Cemetery:

Quigley, Martha Florence

West Harrisville.

August 21, 1895.
The only daughter of W. Quigley is very ill, as is also the youngest daughter of A. Landon.

Alcona County Review, August 22, 1895

West Harrisville.

August 28, 1895.

Florence, aged 3 yrs. 11 mo., the only daughter of M. Quigley, died last Sunday evening and was buried at the Catholic cemetery Tuesday, August 27. The floral offerings were many and beautiful and thanks are extended by Mr. and Mrs. Quigley to the L.O.T.M. of Harrisville and also to Mrs. B. P. Cowley for beautiful flowers. The bereaved parents have the sympathy of the whole community.

Alcona County Review, August 29, 1895
Cemetery: St. Anne's, Alcona Co.

Quilty, John

Boiled Down for Your Perusal.

The remains of John Quielty were buried this morning in the Catholic cemetery. Deceased was father of Mrs. M. Nolan of West Harrisville, with whom he resided at the time of his death. The cause of death was consumption, from which he has been failing for a year past. He was 57 years old and leaves besides his wife two daughters, Mrs. Nolan and a daughter in Seattle.

We desire to express our sincere thanks to all those sympathizing friends whose many acts of kindness during the sickness and death of our dear departed relative, the late John Quielty, were so timely and so acceptable.
Mrs. John Quielty
Mr. and Mrs. M. Nolan.

Alcona County Review, December 21, 1893
Cemetery: St. Anne's, Alcona Co.

Quinlan, Michael

DROWNED.

Michael Quinlan Voluntarily Jumps Into Lake Huron.

When Michael Quinlan left his home Monday afternoon to come to this village, no one knew or thought for a moment that he would never return to the same alive. Although it was noticed that he had been drinking Monday afternoon and evening, he was not at any time what would be termed drunk. Tuesday morning Eugene Taft, ag't on Union Dock, discovered a coat, pair of pants, shoes and stockings, and hat lying upon a spile, with a bunch of shingles upon them, near the north east corner of the dock, which were identified by members of the family of Quinlan as being his property that he wore away when he left home Monday afternoon. Believing that he had jumped or fallen into the lake, search for his body was made, Wednesday, by dragging the lake bottom in the vicinity of the dock. At about 6 p.m. James Thornton succeeded in catching on to the body with a large grappling hook and brought the same up to the surface. When taken out of the water the body was found clad in woolen shirt and drawers, with the arms carefully folded across the breast, indicating the Quinlan had thus jumped into the lake and submitted voluntarily to the designed ordeal of death without a struggle.

Shortly after finding the body, coroner C. P. Reynolds impaneled a jury, consisting of Geo. Ward, F. A. Beede, Will Reynolds, Ansel Houghton, Chas. Larson, and Geo. Anthony, who inquired into the manner and cause of Quinlan's death. The inquest brought out the fact that he was at the St. Lawrence House Monday night, and left there for Union dock to go off on the boat, as he said; but just before leaving the said hotel he pulled off his coat, and, holding it up before Mike McDonald, who was there, he said "Would you know that coat, Mike, should it be found anywhere to-morrow?" or words to that effect. He was next seen by John Kennedy at Union dock in company with one Alex Strand, who was going off on boat to Sand Beach. He stayed at dock waiting room with Strang until boat came in at 1 a.m., and then Kennedy, being engaged in business with clerk of boat, lost sight of him, and saw him no more. The night was very dark.

After investigation the jury rendered a verdict of suicide by drowning.

The deceased had been a resident of this county for four years past, living in Alcona township until about a year ago, when he removed to a new farm three or more miles west of this village. He was aged about 45 years. Leaves a wife and 8 children.

Alcona County Review, July 10, 1885

LOCAL JOTTINGS.

Michael Quinlan, the drowned man, was buried last Friday.

Alcona County Review, July 17, 1885
Cemetery:

Rajnowski, Joseph

NEIGHBORHOOD NOTES.

The damage suit of Mrs. Rajnowski against the D. B. C. & A. railroad for the loss of her son was tried for the second time in the circuit court this week. On the first trial the plaintiff secured a verdict for $1800, but the case was carried to the supreme court and a new trial ordered. The case took up all of Tuesday and Wednesday and was hotly contested on both sides the jury bringing in a verdict for $1500. The case will be appealed to the supreme court again.—Alpena Pioneer.

Alcona County Review, May 24, 1889
Cemetery:

Ranney, {Boy}

Haynes Happenings.

Haynes, Dec. 11—Mr. Arthur W. Ranney, of Black River, buried an infant in our cemetery on the 6th of December.

Alcona County Review, December 13, 1894
Cemetery: Mt. Joy, Alcona Co.

Read, Allen J.

West Harrisville, March 7.--Mrs. Stewart Clark arrived home after burying her brother at Port Huron.

Alcona County Review, March 7, 1895
Cemetery: Proctor, Macomb Co.

Read, Fred N.

HAWSE TOWNSHIP.

Mrs. Stewart Clark returned home Tuesday night, after a two weeks visit at Mt. Clemens where she was called by the death of her brother, Freddie Reed.

Alcona County Review, June 22, 1899
Cemetery: Proctor, Macomb Co.

Redmon, John

Probate Order.

State of Michigan--County of Alcona--ss. Probate Court for said County.

At a session of the Probate Court for said county, held at the Probate Office in the village of Harrisville on Monday the 5th day of January, A. D. 1880--

Present, R. Z. Roberts, Judge of Probate.

In the matter of the Estate of John Redmon, deceased.

Margaret Redmon and M. D. Hoges, of Pittsburg, in the State of Pennsylvania, having filed in the Probate office certified copies of the letters of administration issued to them by the Register of Wills, &c., in and for the county of Alleghany, in the State of Pennsylvania, granting them administration of all and singular the goods, chattels, rights, credits and estate, which were of John Redmon, late of said county of Alleghany in the State of Pennsylvania, deceased; and having also filed certified copies of their bond in the premises, in the sum of twenty thousand dollars; and having also filed certified copies of the records and proceedings had by them in the Orphans' Court in and for the county of Alleghany, in the State of Pennsylvania, relative to the sale of certain real estate belonging to the Estate of John Redmon, deceased, and situate in Alcona county in the State of Michigan; and said Margaret Redmon and M. D. Hoges having filed in this court their petition for the sale of certain real estate situated within the jurisdiction of this court, for the purpose of paying the debts against said estate; and said papers appearing to be duly authenticated and proper in form: It is hereby ordered that Monday, the 9th day of February next, at nine o'clock A. M., be assigned for the hearing of said petition; and it appearing that all the parties interested in said estate reside without the State of Michigan, it is hereby further ordered that publication be made four weeks successively next previous to said ninth day of February in the Alcona County Review, a newspaper published in said village of Harrisville, notifying the parties named in said petition, and all other parties interested in said estate, to be and appear before this court on said ninth day of February, at nine o'clock A. M., then and there to show cause, if any there be, why the said petition of Margaret Redmon and M. D. Hoges should not be granted.

R. Z. Roberts, Judge of Probate.

Alcona County Review, January 9, 1880
Cemetery: Probably Allegheny, Allegheny Co. PA

Reed, Joseph L.

LOCAL JOTTINGS.

Mr. J. S. Reed, father of Mrs. H. R. Morrison, has been quite sick the past week.

Alcona County Review, March 13, 1885

LOCAL LACONICS.

J. L. Reed, father of Mrs. H. R. Morrison, died at the residence of the latter, in this village, at an early hour Tuesday morning. Deceased was born in Saratoga County, New York, in July of 1814, and was consequently in his seventy-first year. He came to Michigan five years since, and has made his home with Mrs. R. L. Surtees, another daughter, at Brighton, but for a few months past has been visiting here. He leaves a wife and two daughters. Mrs. Morrison and Mrs. Surtees. The remains were taken to Brighton for interment, leaving here on the steamer Alpena yesterday morning.

Alcona County Review, May 29, 1885

LOCAL LACONICS.

Mrs. R. L. Surtees, of Brighton, Mich., sister of Mrs. H. R. Morrison, was in attendance at the sick-bed of their father, at the residence of the latter, during the last few days of his illness.

Alcona County Review, May 29, 1885
Cemetery: Brighton Village, Livingston Co.

Reed, Mrs.

Haynes.

Mrs. Reed, mother-in-law to Mr. Spoon of Alcona township, aged 66 years, was buried on Monday in our public burial grounds.

Alcona County Review, September 1, 1892
Cemetery: Mt. Joy, Alcona Co.

Reeves, James S.

LOCAL JOTTINGS.

Dr. J. S. Reeves, pioneer and one of the oldest members Masonic fraternity in state, died at his home in East Tawas, Wednesday, May 16, aged 76.

Alcona County Review, May 25, 1888
Cemetery: Greenwood, Iosco Co.

Reeves, Jerry

Around the County.

Within the past few days two of the county charges at the poor farm have crossed the dark river. One, Jerry Reeves by name, about 70 years of age, died suddenly, the other, Daniel Cameron, was about 65 and had been failing for a number of months past from consumption and his death was not unexpected. Neither had any friends in this country. There are four charges still at the farm.

Alcona County Review, June 11, 1891

Cemetery:

Regier, Christian

STATE of MICHIGAN.
The Probate Court for the County of Alcona.

At a session of said Court, held at the Probate Office in the city of Harrisville in said county, on the 15th day of April, A. D. 1907.

Present: Geo. W. Burt, Judge of Probate.

In the matter of the estate of Christian Regier, deceased.

Mrs. LeBurney Sampson having filed in said court a petition praying that a certain instrument in writing, purporting to be the last will and testament of said deceased, and now on file in said court be admitted to probate, and that the administration of said estate be granted to Mrs. LeBurney Sampson or to some other suitable person.

It is ordered, That the 13th day of May, A. D. 1907, at ten o'clock in the forenoon, at said probate office, be and is hereby appointed for hearing said petition.

It is further ordered, That public notice thereof be given by publication of a copy of this order, for three successive weeks previous to said day of hearing, in the Alcona County Review, a newspaper printed and circulated in said county.

GEO. W. BURT,
Judge of Probate.

[Note: Died 10/23/1894]

Alcona County Review, April 25, 1907
Cemetery: Saints Peter and Paul, Huron Co.

Reno, John

Killed On the Track.

John Reno, aged about 50, and supposed to be intoxicated, was run over by a train and killed at the sand hill above Black River Monday night.

Alcona County Review, July 7, 1898
Cemetery:

Reynolds, {Boy}

PERSONAL MENTION.

A son was born to Mr. and Mrs. Fred Reynolds Monday morning, but the little innocent's life was destined to be short and it passed away in the evening to the great sorrow of the young parents.

Alcona County Review, April 30, 1896
Cemetery:

Reynolds, Charles P.

A SAD FATALITY.

TRAGIC DEATH OF A PIONEER.

Mysterious Disappearance of C. P. Reynolds.

The Sea Finally Gives Up Its Dead.

This community has not been more shocked over any event that has occurred here in many years than it was last week when it became known that Charles P. Reynolds had met a tragic death under the most deplorable circumstances.

The dead man had been making preparations for some time past to go to the state of Ohio to work territory in the interest of one of the leading nursery concerns of Rochester, N. Y. A life-long study of fruits and horticulture and a deep interest in everything pertaining to the subject led him to look forward to this business venture with a degree of pleasure which was heightened by the hope that removal for a brief period from the vicinity of the lake would relived the distress he experienced by reason of a severe case of nasal catarrh from which he was a great sufferer. His preparations were about completed and he had announced to his friends that he would take the Atlantic last Wednesday for Ohio. He had collected considerable money with which to defray his expenses, and was apparently in the best of spirits for several weeks prior to his death. Tuesday last he was drinking more or less all day and at nightfall he was considerably intoxicated much to the surprise of his friends who say that while he made no pretence to total abstinence yet he seldom, if ever, became intoxicated. He was seen by different persons about 11 o'clock that night; once he was seen on Main-st., apparently on his way home, but when near the residence of county clerk Rutson he seemed undecided which way to go finally turning around and retracing his steps down town. The last time that he was seen alive doubtless was about the hour named when he was seen sitting on the steps of Cowley & Lott's store. A day or two passed and nothing more was seen of him. His disappearance did not cause any great alarm until Friday when his continued absence from the village began to excite the worst fears of those who knew him best. Saturday morning a telephone message was received from Greenbush that the body of a man had been found on the beach a short distance below the dock. A young lad named Danny McCrae had discovered it while patrolling the beach for lumber which usually washes ashore after such a gale as that of last Thursday and Friday. He ran immediately to the mill and notified some men working there of his discovery. They were unable at first to establish the identity of the unfortunate man but when they were informed that Reynolds had disappeared they knew by the clothing that it was he. Justice Beede was notified and he repaired at once to the scene of the ghastly discovery. A jury was impaneled which after hearing what meager testimony there was as to the last seen of him returned a verdict that the deceased came to his death by accidental drowning. The dead man must have fallen into the lake at a point about half way down Cowley and Lott's dock as a hat was found there the next day which was afterwards identified as having belonged to him.

The terrible northeaster that raged all day Thursday and Friday created a terrific undertow down the shore which accounts for the finding of his body so far away from the point at which he went into the water. A deep gash extending from the forehead around over the left ear led to suspicions of foul play but this idea is not generally entertained. A post mortem examination by Dr. Mitchell shows that the gash must have been made before he went into the water, and it is supposed that he must have fallen against one of the heavy timbers of which the dock is built. His watch and chain were gone and but a few cents were found in his pockets.

The remains were brought to the deceased's late home in Harrisville Saturday night and interred Sunday afternoon in the family lot in West Harrisville cemetery. The funeral services were conducted under the auspices of Harrisville Lodge No. 218, I. O. O. F., the Rev. L. Hazard officiating. Although so short a time had elapsed since the news of the deceased's tragic death had become known an immense concourse of citizens gathered about the residence to show by their presence their respect for and sympathy with the bereaved family.

_____

Charles P. Reynolds was born at Penn Yann, Yates county, N. Y., in 1828, and was, therefore, at the time of his death in his sixty-first year. In 1866 he came to Alcona county and entered the employ of Harris Bros. until the sale of their property to Weston, Colwell & Co. by whom he was employed until 1869. In 1867 he was elected town clerk and justice of the peace the latter of which offices he still held at the time of his death. In 1868 he is credited with the organization of a joint stock company which built the first public dock in Harrisville that being the first work done on Cowley & Lott's dock. In 1873 he assisted at the organization of the Alcona County Agricultural Society, in which he at different times held the offices of secretary, director and president; he was indefatigable in his devotion to the interests represented by that society. He held a membership in the State Pomological Society. He was a member of the state board of corrections and charities for Alcona county having received the appointment from the governor in 1880. In 1870 he was elected register of deeds and was re-elected in 1879 when he transcribed the county records. Last fall he was admitted to the bar and received a nomination for prosecuting attorney but was defeated. The deceased was public spirited to a fault and to his disinterested efforts is due many of the substantial benefits enjoyed by this community. He wrote the history of Alcona county which was published by order of the board of supervisors in pamphlet form. He is entitled to credit for planting most of the shade trees in this village including those in and around the court yard. He early introduced improved machinery among our farmers and took a deep interest in the welfare of agricultural interest. The good that he did will live after him. He leaves a wife and three children, two sons and a daughter.

Alcona County Review, June 7, 1889

CARD OF THANKS.

The family of the late C. P. Reynolds desire to express to the dear friends and neighbors who so willingly aided them with their many acts of kindness during their great bereavement their heartfelt thanks, and to the I. O. O. F., who so generously and unselfishly assisted at the obsequies of their late comrade. May God bless you one and all, and in His Infinite mercy spare you the agony suffered by us during the week that is past.

Mrs. C. P. Reynolds.
and Family.

Alcona County Review, June 7, 1889

RESOLUTIONS OF RESPECT.

Whereas, It has pleased Almighty God to remove from our midst our most worthy Brother, Past Grand Charles P. Reynolds, be it therefore

Resolved, that Harrisville Lodge No. 218, I. O. O. F., in Lodge assembled, hereby extend the sympathy and condolence of our Brotherhood to the bereaved family, and

Resolved, that the charter of our Lodge be draped in mourning for sixty days,

Resolved, the a copy of these resolutions be spread on our minutes and published in the Alcona County Review and a copy be sent to the family of our deceased Brother.

F. A. Beede,
Chas. Conklin,
Daniel McDonald,
Committee.

Harrisville, June 5th, 1889.

Alcona County Review, June 7, 1889

A Feeling Tribute to the Memory of Charles P. Reynolds.

Geo. F. Lewis, editor of the Saginawian, Saginaw City, an intimate friend of the late Charles P. Reynolds, speaking editorially of the latter's tragic death, pays the following merited tribute to the memory of his dead friend:

The Saginawian is pained to print from the Alcona Review the sad account of the drowning at Harrisville of C. P. Reynolds, Esq, one of the pioneers of Alcona county and one who has done quite as much as any one man to forward the agricultural interests of Northeastern Michigan. Alcona county can credit to Mr. Reynolds the fact that she has the best system of country roads of any new county in the State; that she

holds an advanced position in farming, fruit-growing and the various divisions of horticulture. Mr. Reynolds, always an earnest worker for the improvement of the soil at home, has ably represented Alcona and the counties north at many of the State Fairs and Institutes, notably those in Saginaw and E. Saginaw; he was the life of Alcona exhibit in the Northern Michigan Department of the State Fair in Detroit in 1879; he has always been an enthusiastic worker in the interest of the Northeastern Agricultural Society and has attended most of that Society's fairs; he was a man of far more than average ability, a thinker, a writer, a competent business man and one whose heart was always right, though hard lines and crushing misfortunes left him but little sunshine in this, to him weary world. "The evil that men do lives after them, the good deeds are often interred with their bones." Of Reynolds it may be said he wrought no evil and his good deeds will live long years as a blessing to her citizens in the advance farm development which was secured to Alcona mainly through his efforts. Peace and pleasant tribute to his memory, for however he may have come short of his hopes and his desserts, no man can gainsay the fact that the world was better for his having lived in it.

Alcona County Review, June 21, 1889
Cemetery: West Lawn, Alcona Co.

Reynolds, Frank

HOME REVIEWINGS.

A young man named Frank Reynolds, a seaman on the steamer Dove and a resident of this city, was instantly killed on the trip down from Alpena yesterday by being caught in the machinery, the main crank striking him on the head and causing instant death. His body will be brought to this city this morning on the Dove.—Saginaw Herald of Tuesday.

Alcona County Review, October 28, 1881

HOME REVIEWINGS.

The jury in the case of Frank Reynolds, killed on the steamer Dove last week, returned a verdict of accidental death.

Alcona County Review, November 4, 1881
Cemetery: Brady Hill, Saginaw Co.

Reynolds, Jesse

REVIEWINGS.

Yesterday morning, C. P. Reynolds received the sad intelligence of the death of his father, Jesse Reynolds, at his home in Penn Yan, N. Y. He was 80 years of age.

Alcona County Review, February 20, 1880
Cemetery:Probably Second Milo, Yates Co., NY

Reynolds, John

A Fatal Accident.

Jno. Reynolds, employed at the H. M. Loud & Son's Camp 8, was run over and instantly killed last Thursday night by a log train. The unfortunate man boarded the train at Loud's Jc. He was warned by the brakeman, Ed Steele, to be cautious as the rough condition of the road made it dangerous. Steel then started toward the rear end of the train, and on looking back a moment later Reynolds was gone. The train was stopped at once and the mangled body of Reynolds was soon discovered. Life was extinct. The deceased was about 50 years old, was a veteran of the late war, and having no known relatives the remains were taken charge of by comrades and buried in the Harrisville cemetery.

Alcona County Review, August 17, 1888
Cemetery: Springport, Alcona Co.

Reynolds, John H.

LOCAL JOTTINGS.

Mr. and Mrs. John Reynolds, of Limeric, buried their 12-year-old son last Saturday.

Alcona County Review, October 2, 1885
Cemetery: Springport, Alcona Co.

Reynolds, Mrs.

West Harrisville.

W. C. Reynolds and wife returned from St. Joe Wednesday evening last week, where they went to attend the funeral of the mother of the former.

Alcona County Review, February 1, 1894
Cemetery:

Reynolds, Pat

PAT RENOLDS DEAD.

Jas. Nevins received a telegram from Port Huron announcing the death of Pat Reynolds, who died in that city Wednesday morning, June 27th. The announcement of Mr. Reynold's death was a surprise and sudden shock to his friends here, although all knew of his long illness.

Word had been received a few days previous saying that it was thought he was then on the road to recovery. Mr. Reynolds contracted a hard cold while returning to camp on election day last spring. He grew worse and went to Alpena hospital for treatment, where he remained until a short time ago when he was taken to the home of relatives in Port Huron.

"Pat" Reynolds was known to almost every resident in this county, having been engaged for many years in lumbering in this and immediate sections. He generally came to Harrisville every spring for a few weeks of rest. He was a man of quiet and kindly manners, loyal to his scores of friends. He was a member in good standing of the Harrisville Lodge, I. O. O. F., which order has looked after his comfort and welfare during his long illness with commendable brotherly love. The deceased was about 45 years of age and unmarried.

Alcona County Review, June 29, 1888
Cemetery: Mt. Hope, St. Clair Co.

Rice, Frank Clarence

County News and Gossip.

Frankie Clarence, younger son of Mr. and Mrs. W. E. Rice of Harrisville, died yesterday morning; aged two years, three months and 17 days. The Review extends the hand of sympathy to the bereaved parents and family, and in this their hour of mourning would commend to their comfort and consolation Him who said: "Suffer little children to come unto me and forbid them not, for of such is the kingdom of heaven."

Alcona County Review, March 18, 1881

County News and Gossip.

The funeral sermon of Frankie Clarence Rice will be delivered at the Presbyterian church next Sabbath morning.

Alcona County Review, March 25, 1881
Cemetery:

Rice, Justin R.

LOCAL JOTTINGS.

Died.—Last Monday, March 30th, Justin R. Rice, aged 37 years. The funeral services took place last Wednesday at the residence of his brother, A. C. Rice, Rev. Lyon officiating.—Alpena Labor Journal.

The deceased, above named, was well known by many Harrisville people, having lived in this place about a year during the residence of his brother here, Capt. W. E. Rice.

Alcona County Review, April 10, 1885
Cemetery: Evergreen, Alpena Co.

Richardson, Charles Wellington

LOCAL PICK UPS.

Charles W. Richardson, a prominent Alpena citizen, died last week.

Alcona County Review, July 13, 1899
Cemetery: Evergreen, Alpena Co.

Richardson, Charles Wellington

THE MAYOR OF ALPENA DEAD.

Charles W. Richardson, mayor of Alpena, died very suddenly at Pittsfield, Maine, last Friday afternoon. Mr. Richardson was a stirring business man, president of the National bank and largely identified with the commercial industries and progress of Alpena. His death is a public calamity and an irretrievable loss to that city. All flags in the city were at half-mast, Saturday, in his honor. He leaves an estate worth $1,000,000.

Alcona County Review, June 25, 1886

Alpena Pioneer: The settlement of the estate of the late C. W. Richardson is attracting considerable attention throughout the State, owing to the large amount of property involved. The heirs contested the will to begin with, and this matter was finally settled by the payment of $120,000 to them. This was expected to settle the whole matter; but it seems Mrs. Richardson had retained Messrs. Kelley, Turnbull and Sleator as counsel. The heirs, however, secured Mr. Moore, of Detroit, for their counsel, and when the settlement was made, gave him $30,000, or one-fourth of the amount, for his services. Mrs. Richardson made the settlement, it is reported, without asking the advice of her attorneys, and they, on the ground that if they had not been retained by her they might have received the big fee paid to Mr. Moore, brought in big bills for retainer fees. Kelley, $20,000; Turnbull, $10,000; and Sleator $8,000. These fees Mrs. Richardson

---

refused to pay, on the ground that they were exorbitant.

Alcona County Review, June 25, 1886

LOCAL JOTTINGS.

The will of the late Chas. W. Richardson, of Alpena, which devises certain lands in this county, has been received at the register's office for record. The will itself is a very concise legal paper.

Alcona County Review, January 14, 1887

The Fees Were Not Exorbitant.

It will be remembered that last fall Mrs. Diana Richardson, of Alpena, in settling up her late husband's estate employed as her attorneys R. J. Kelley, J. D. Turnbull and G. H. Sleator. These attorneys presented bills aggregating $50,000, Kelly's being $30,000 and the others $10,000 each. Mrs. Richardson objected on the ground that the fees were exorbitant, and she skipped to Detroit where a sensation was created when the circumstances leaked out. The matter of the fees has remained in statu quo ever since, but the attorneys have not neglected an opportunity to press their claims. Mrs. Richardson's attorney employed to oppose the triumvirate secured plenty of expert testimony of prominent Detroit lawyers who were willing to "stand to't" that the charges were unreasonable. The other day the other fellows got in their work and such reputable lawyers as Alfred Russell, Don. M. Dickenson, F. A. Baker, H. S. Baker, and Jno. Atkinson testified before Circuit Court Commissioner Joe Weiss that the fees asked were not exorbitant.

Alcona County Review, June 10, 1887

A Good Haul.

In the suit of lawyers R. J. Kelley and J. D. Turnbull, of Alpena, brought to collect attorney's fees from Mrs. C. A. Richardson, which terminated in the Alpena circuit court last week, the jury returned a verdict for the plaintiffs, allowing Turnbull $8,000 and Kelley $20,000. Kelley's claim was for $30,000 and Turnbull's for $10,000 which Mrs. Richardson refused to pay on the grounds that they were exorbitant. Lawyer G. S. Slater also has brought suit to collect $10,000 attorney's fees and the case will be called on at the August term of court.

Alcona County Review, June 24, 1887

THE RICHARDSON WILL CASE.

"Charles W. Richardson, of Alpena county left $1,000,000 behind him when he died in 1886. A will 20 years old was probated giving all his property to his wife, Diana, who was childless. The 15 other heirs paid $40 each into a pool to contest the will. Trouble followed."

This was the beginning of an interesting article which the Journal was compiling from a corpulent bill of complaint which was last night filed in the county clerk's office.

As the word "followed" was written Deputy County Clerk Fenwick came up gobbled the papers and with the remark "That's suppressed" carried them off and gave them to Deputy Clerk Kellog, who put them away.

The Journal however had previously read the bill. It is brought by several of the half-blood heirs, who charge that they hired Charles W. Richardson Jr., as their attorney and empowered him to go ahead and contest the will. He, they say, engaged Moore & Moore, of Detroit, who settled with the widow for $120,000. It is then stated that Moore & Moore induced the heirs to accept smaller shares: that they paid the heirs only about $45,000 and that about $60,000 remains unpaid. The complainants ask that the money be applied where it belongs. Messrs. Charles W. Richardson, Jr., and Moore & Moore are made defendants. The bill was originally brought in Alpena and has been transferred to Detroit.

The Moores are prominent and reputable attorneys.

The answer to the bill has been filed by Moore & Moore in the Alpena circuit court denying the charges in toto. The answer of C. W. Richardson, Jr., is also included, containing specific denials to the charges.—Detroit Journal.

Alcona County Review, April 19, 1889
Cemetery: Woodlawn, Wayne Co.

Richardson, Ida E.

DUST TO DUST.

An infant child of John Richardson died at Black River last week.

Alcona County Review, September 17, 1891
Cemetery: Mt. Joy, Alcona Co.

Richardson, Mrs. Melissa R.

The Local News.

Mrs. John Richardson died at Black River Tuesday morning after a lingering illness from consumption. She was about 35 years of age and leaves five children besides her husband to mourn her untimely death.

Alcona County Review, November 19, 1891

Resolutions of Condolence.

At a Special review of Lake Shore Tent No. 229, K. O. T. M., held at I. O. O. F. Hall, Tuesday evening, Nov. 17th., A. D. 1891, the following Resolutions were adopted:--

Whereas, it has pleased the Supreme Ruler of the universe to remove from this earthly abode the Loving Wife of our worthy Brother, Sir Knight John Richardson, be it

Resolved, That we the members of Lake Shore Tent No. 229, extend to him our heartfelt sympathy in the hour of affliction and bereavement

Resolved, That a copy of these resolutions be sent to our Brother, be spread upon the records of this Tent and a copy of the same be published in the Michigan Maccabee and the Alcona County Review.

SAMUEL E. McNEIL,
JEROME BURT,
ALBERT McDONALD.
Black River, Mich., Nov. 17, 1891

Alcona County Review, November 26, 1891

Card of Thanks.

I wish to thank the friends and neighbors at Black River, through your paper, for their kindness in lending me a helping hand during my wife's affliction, and I can assure you that we appreciated it very much and will ever stand in readiness to help those in distress.

I remain yours,
John Richardson.

Alcona County Review, December 3, 1891
Cemetery: Mt. Joy, Alcona Co.

Richardson, Morry Erwin

Died—At Black River Thursday April 29, Morry Erwin, beloved son of Mr. and Mrs. John Richardson, aged one year and seven months. Cause inflammation of the lungs.

Alcona County Review, May 6, 1897

Card of Thanks.

We very much appreciated the kindness of our friends during the illness and death of our son Morry Erwin, and wish them to accept our sincere thanks.

Mr. and Mrs. John Richardson.

Alcona County Review, May 6, 1897
Cemetery: Mt. Joy, Alcona Co.

Richardson, William

Our Neighbors.

William Richardson, aged 67, came all the way from Iowa to Bay City to visit his brother Alexander. While they were dining together William dropped dead of heart disease.

Alcona County Review, January 31, 1890
Cemetery:

Richmond, Richard A.

HONORS TO DEAD HEROES.

A magnificent demonstration of the patriotic spirit of the citizens of Alcona county was the observance on Monday of the time honored custom of decorating the graves and commemorating the deeds of valor of the nation's dead heroes.

The roster of soldiers who are buried here is as follows: Harrisville, (West), A. Marcellus, John Pelton, W. W. Douglass: Catholic, Louis Rivard, Geo. Bernizer: South Harrisville, R. Richmond, Chas. Miller, H. J. Aird, A. Noyes, Jas. Johnson.

Alcona County Review, June 2, 1898
Cemetery: Springport, Alcona Co.

Rickle, Mrs. Amelia

Mrs. John Rickle died at Killmaster March 19, 1895. She leaves a husband, three small children and a father and mother to mourn their loss. She died very suddenly from heart disease, and was reading the Bible when she died. She was a member of the church and a member of the L. O. T. M., but carried no insurance. The services will be conducted by Rev. Van Horn of West Harrisville, Friday at 11 o'clock at the town hall at Killmaster.

Alcona County Review, March 21, 1895
Cemetery: Probably Springport, Alcona Co.

Riecker, Louis

Horrible Accident!

A BOILER EXPLOSION WRECKS A 5 STORY DETROIT BUILDING.

----

37 Charred and Mangled Bodies Have Been Recovered.

Louis Ricker, an Alcona County Boy, One of the Unfortunates.

The most horrible fatality in the history of Detroit if not in Michigan occurred at 9 o'clock on the morning of Wednesday, Nov. 6th, when a boiler burst in the engine room of the Detroit Evening Journal building completely wrecking the five-story building and burying nearly 50 people in the ruins. 37 dead and mangled corpses were taken out. Incredible as it may seem many persons were carried down with this mass of wreckage, bricks, mortar, machinery and heavy timbers and yet they escaped alive and in a few instances they escaped without a scratch. The terrible accident was attributed to carelessness on the part of the engineer and though injured himself and at present in a hospital he has been arrested and is under constant guard.

The accident is brought home with dreadful force to at least one family in Alcona county, who lost a beloved son and brother. The young man's name was Louis Riecker. His parents reside in the western part of Harrisville township. The dead man was 28 years of age and was unmarried. He was a machinist and was employed in the shop of Dunlap & Co., who had quarters in the building. The remains were sent here Friday morning and were placed at rest in the cemetery west of Harrisville on Sunday. The stricken family have the deepest sympathy of all.

The remains were sadly mutilated and charred and were not exposed to view except to a few most intimate friends.

The wrecked building was occupied by the Journal's press room and mailing department, Hiller's book bindery, a machine shop, etc. The editorial and press rooms of the Journal and the business office of that paper were in an adjoining part of the same building and this very fortunately remained standing although it was badly racked and twisted and was moved off its foundations.

A few minutes after the wreck fire started in the wreckage. The fire department was unable to check it entirely and many imprisoned people were literally roasted to death and

their shrieks and cries were heart-rending.

Alcona County Review, November 14, 1895

Gustin Grist.

Nov. 12, 1895

Louis Ricker's name we see is among those in the terrible explosion in Detroit. He was a resident of Gustin township but unknown to the writer. His friends have the sympathy of this community.

Alcona County Review, November 14, 1895

EVENTS OF ONE WEEK.

Engineer Thompson of the ill-fated Journal building, at Detroit, has been held to the grand jury on a charge of manslaughter. The evidence will be purely circumstantial.

Alcona County Review, November 21, 1895

PERSONAL MENTION.

We most sincerely and heartily thank our friends for the timely sympathy and help which was so welcome in the hour of our recent deep sorrow in the loss of our beloved son and brother, Lewis Riecker.

Mr. and Mrs. Riecker and Family.

Alcona County Review, December 5, 1895
Cemetery: West Lawn, Alcona Co.

Rifenbark, David

Purely Personal.

A small child of Mr. and Mrs. Rhyvenbark, of Greenbush, died Friday, June 13, and was buried the following Sunday in the South Harrisville cemetery.

Alcona County Review, June 20, 1890
Cemetery: Springport, Alcona Co.

Ritchie, Georgia Ann

EVENTS OF ONE WEEK.

A child of Geo. S. Ritchie has been very sick and Dr. McCormick thought recovery doubtful, so word was brought from Haynes on Monday.

Alcona County Review, December 19, 1895

Haynes Happenings.

Haynes, Dec. 23, 1895.

Mr. and Mrs. George S. Ritchie's daughter, Georgean, aged six years last September, was buried last Thursday. Rev. Long preached the funeral sermon. Four young ladies acted as pall bearers and the remains were followed to the cemetery by a large concourse of friends and relatives of the bereft parents, who have the sympathy of the community.

And though your dear one passed away,
And naught be left but lifeless clay,
Yet still her spirit hovers near,
To bless the hearts that loved her
dear.

Alcona County Review, December 26, 1895
Cemetery: Mt. Joy, Alcona Co.

Ritchie, Jane Harriet [Hastings]

HAYNES HAPPENINGS.

Old Mrs. McLellan is very low at present. Also Mrs. Robt. Ritchie.

Alcona County Review, October 13, 1898

HAYNES HAPPENINGS.

Mrs. Robert Ritchie is very low with dropsy at the home of her daughter, Mrs. R. Hastings.

Alcona County Review, November 24, 1898

HAYNES HAPPENINGS.

Wm. Ritchie has come up from Isabella county, as his mother is very low with dropsy and not expected to survive very long.

Alcona County Review, December 1, 1898

PERSONAL POINTS.

Wm. Ritchie, a former resident of the township of Haynes, but now of Isabella county, has been called here by the serious condition of his aged mother who is lying very low at the residence of her daughter, Mrs. Hasty at Henry station. Mr. Ritchie looks particularly well and prosperous. He is well pleased with his present location.

Alcona County Review, December 1, 1898

MRS. ROBERT RITCHIE.

This aged and respected lady passed away very quietly at the home of her daughter, Mrs. Robert Hastings, at Henry Station on Dec. 2d. Deceased has been ailing from advancing years and a complication of diseases which culminated in dropsy.

Deceased was born in Ireland in 1823. She leaves four children to mourn the loss of an upright devoted parent, viz: Mrs. James Johnson, Mrs. Robert Hastings and Geo. S. and Wm. Ritchie. The Rev. Austin preached the funeral sermon and Chas. Mayo of Harrisville, undertaker, conducted the funeral.

The concourse of friends of the family filled the church to overflowing. There was a goodly number from Harrisville, Hawse and West Harrisville. The interment took place Sunday, Dec. 4, in the Haynes Township cemetery.

There were five school teachers present, to-wit: Miss Redhouse, Miss McArthur, Mr. Holmes, Mr. Stuart and Mr. Myers. Also Jos. Yuill and sister, Geo. Ward Sr. and lady, Wm. Gray and lady and others from Harrisville; Alex Savage and others from Mud Lake Jc.

Alcona County Review, December 8, 1898

Local History of One Year

Chronology of the Principal Events of the Year 1898.

December 2. Death of Mr. Robert Ritchie aged 76, at Henry station.

Alcona County Review, January 5, 1899
Cemetery: Mt. Joy, Alcona Co.

Ritchie, Joseph C.

Mrs. Joseph Ritchie, whose husband was killed in December last, is going to her former home in Canada to reside.

Alcona County Review, May 2, 1884

Chas. W. Sherman, agent for the Penn Mutual Life Insurance Company, has been in the town and county the past two weeks in the interest of that company. He settled up the claim of Mrs. Joseph Ritchie in full, the insurance on her late husband's life being $1,000. The Penn Mutual company is giving good satisfaction in these parts, and is working up a large business among our citizens.

Alcona County Review, May 2, 1884

STATE OF MICHIGAN, THE PROBATE COURT FOR THE COUNTY OF ALCONA.

At a session of said Court, held at the Probate Office in the City of Harrisville in said county, on the 23rd day of April, A. D. 1906.

Present: Hon. Geo. W. Burt, Judge of Probate.

In the matter of the estate of Joseph Ritchie, deceased, Mrs. Fred Landon having filed in said court a petition praying that the administration of said estate be granted to George Jack or to some other suitable person.

It is ordered, That the fourteenth day of May, A. D. 1906, at ten o'clock in the forenoon, at said probate office, be and is hereby appointed for hearing said petition;

It is further ordered, That public notice thereof be given by publication of a copy of this order, for three successive weeks previous to said day of hearing, in the Alcona County Review, a newspaper printed and circulated in said county.

GEO. W. BURT,
Judge of Probate.

Alcona County Review, April 26, 1906
Cemetery: Mt. Joy, Alcona Co.

Ritchie, Maud

Haynes Happenings.

Haynes, Feb. 5.—Miss Maud Ritchie died Tuesday, the 29th day of Jan., and was interred on the 31st, which makes four of the diptheria patients who have died.

Alcona County Review, February 7, 1895
Cemetery: Mt. Joy, Alcona Co.

Ritchie, Robert

Robt. Ritchie has been seriously ill at his home near Henry station.

Alcona County Review, December 20, 1894

Haynes Happenings.

Haynes, Dec. 26.--It is reported that Mr. Robert Ritchie is very low and the doctor has no hope of his recovery; his lower limbs are paralyzed.

Alcona County Review, December 27, 1894

Haynes, Jan. 15th, 1895.--Robt. Ritchie is recovering and will pull through according to report.

Alcona County Review, January 17, 1895

ROBERT RITCHIE.

Robert Ritchie passed from this earth Wednesday, March 13, at 5 o'clock a.m. after a long and tedious illness of 14 weeks from paralysis of the spine, thus removing another of the old and respected citizens of Alcona County.

Deceased was a native of Ireland. He was born in the county of Monahan July 12, 1823., and was therefore 72 years and 8 months of age. The date of his removal to America is not stated to the review, but prior to his advent in Alcona county in 1878 he lived in Canada. In 1841 deceased married Jane Hastings and for 54 years, therefore, this couple have shared each other's joys and sorrows. Messrs. George and William Ritchie, Mrs. Sarah Hastings and Mrs. Susie Johnson are surviving children of this union and all are residents of Haynes township.

Mr. Ritchie followed the pursuit of farming. At the time of his death he resided near Henry Station. He was held in the highest esteem by all who know him and was a man of upright character and sterling worth. In politics he was a Republican; by birth and education a strong Presbyterian. The funeral will be held Friday afternoon, leaving Henry at one o'clock and proceeding to the Presbyterian church at Ritchie's corners and thence to the beautiful Alcona cemetery for interment.

Alcona County Review, March 14, 1895

EVENTS OF ONE WEEK.

The funeral of the late Robert Ritchie, which was conducted from the Presbyterian church in Haynes last Friday afternoon, was largely attended. Deceased was an Orangemen of 52 years' standing and Orangemen came from far and near to participate in the last rites over their departed brother, which were conducted according to the ritual of the order.

The funeral sermon was preached by Rev. Dunham.

Robert Ritchie was an Orangeman for 52 years, a Presbyterian for 53 years and had been married for 54 years.

Alcona County Review, March 21, 1895

Haynes Happenings.

The mortal remains of Robert Ritchie were interred in our cemetery on Friday, the 16th, with imposing ceremony under the auspices of the Orange fraternity. A large concourse of relatives and friends followed the remains to their last resting place.

Alcona County Review, March 21, 1895

West Harrisville.

W. Harrisville, Mar. 19.--A large number of the members belonging to L. O. L. Lodge attended the funeral of the late Robert Ritchie. Rev. Dunham preached the funeral sermon.

Alcona County Review, March 21, 1895

Whereas, Almighty God hath deemed best to remove from our midst our esteemed brother, Robert Ritchie, a member of Lake View L. O. L. No. 289, of Mich.

Resolved, That, while we submit to God's will, we deeply deplore the loss of our absent brother.

Resolved further, That the warrant be draped for 60 days and that a copy of these resolutions be published in the Alcona County Review and entered upon the records of our Lodge.

Rec. Sec'y,
Committee.

Alcona County Review, March 28, 1895

Haynes Happenings.

Sept. 24, 1895.
A handsome monument has been erected to the memory of Mr. Robert Ritchie in Mount Joy cemetery.

Alcona County Review, September 26, 1895
Cemetery: Mt. Joy, Alcona Co.

Rivard, Frederick William

PURELY PERSONAL.

Freddie Rivard, son of Louis Rivard died Wednesday after a lingering illness, aged 16 years. The funeral services will be held at the Catholic church to-day, Friday.

Alcona County Review, August 26, 1887
Cemetery: St. Anne's, Alcona Co.

Rivard, Joseph Louis

LOCAL JOTTINGS.

The remains of Joseph Rivard, a young man who was fatally injured in a railroad accident at Black River two weeks ago, were interred last Saturday in the Catholic cemetery at this place. Young Rivard was well known in this place, where he had many friends who admired him for his many excellent qualities and exemplary character. He was braking on a logging train at the time he met with his fatal experience. The forward cars, it seems, ran off the track, the sudden shock precipitating Rivard under the cars where he was crushed and injured internally. He lingered for a week after the accident. The deceased was only 19 years of age at the time of his death.

Alcona County Review, April 15, 1887

Card of Thanks.

The undersigned wish to thank the people of Black River for their kindness during the last sickness and death of our son, Joseph Rivard.

Louis and Jane Rivard.

Alcona County Review, April 15, 1887
Cemetery: St. Anne's, Alcona Co.

Rivard, Louis

Fatally Crushed.

Louis Rivard was fatally crushed under a falling tree at Nevins' camp last Thursday. Both hips were crushed and broken and he was injured internally. Drs. McCormick of Black River, and Campbell, of this place, were summoned but their services were futile and Rivard died the next day. He was aged about fifty and left a wife and two children. A son was killed at Black River last spring on the railroad, and another son died last summer after a lingering illness. The deceased was buried last Sunday from the Catholic church in this village.

Alcona County Review, March 16, 1888

DEATHS.

Rivard.—Louis Rivard, killed at Mud Lake last Thursday. Buried Sunday from the Catholic church in this village, Rev. Fr. Winters officiating.

Alcona County Review, March 16, 1888

PURELY PERSONAL.

Mrs. Louis Rivard, whose husband was recently killed at Mud Lake, has moved on her old farm west of this village.

Alcona County Review, April 6, 1888

HONORS TO DEAD HEROES.

A magnificent demonstration of the patriotic spirit of the citizens of Alcona county was the observance on Monday of the time honored custom of decorating the graves and commemorating the deeds of valor of the nation's dead heroes.

The roster of soldiers who are buried here is as follows: Harrisville, (West), A. Marcellus, John Pelton, W. W. Douglass: Catholic, Louis Rivard, Geo. Bernizer: South Harrisville, R. Richmond, Chas. Miller, H. J. Aird, A. Noyes, Jas. Johnson.

Alcona County Review, June 2, 1898
Cemetery: St. Anne's, Alcona Co.

Rix, Elmer G.

Among Our Exchanges.

Elmer G. Rix, a prominent business man and highly respected citizen of Oscoda, died last week of a complication of diseases. He was a member of the firm of Rix Bros., grocers. He was 38 years of age and leaves a wife and three children well provided for. His death is universally regretted by all who knew him.

Alcona County Review, March 8, 1894
Cemetery: Pinecrest, Iosco Co.

Robbins, Jesse

OBITUARY.

Rev. Jesse Robbins, Methodist preacher of the Greenbush circuit, died at the residence of Mr. Goheen, in Greenbush, Tuesday, April 19th. He was born at Dorchester Station, Ontario, Canada, and came to Michigan about four years ago. He became a member of the Detroit Conference of M. E. churches at its session at East Saginaw, in September, 1884. He came to the Greenbush circuit from Rawsonville. While at Greenbush he has labored hard and by his faithful labors and Christian bearing endeared himself to all; a man more generally respected and beloved has never preached at Greenbush. His last sickness lasted less than two weeks; part of the time he was not rational, but for three days previous to his death his mind was clear. He seemed to feel from the first that he would never recover, and the day of his death expressed himself as in a "straight betwixt two," whether to remain and prosecute the work to which he had given his life, "or to depart and be with Christ, which would be far better." Brother Robbins had abundantly equipped himself, by diligent study and improvement of advantages, for usefulness in the Master's vineyard. Why Providence should take away so pure a young man, standing on the threshold of active life, we cannot say. Surely, he was fitted for life here, and more surely for eternal life hereafter. Although an intense sufferer, he was peaceful through all, and as he felt death approaching felt no dread. His was the death of a Christian warrior in full armor. His life was conspicuous for cheerfulness, diligence and conscientiousness. In all his engagements he was very punctual and his work always had a method and he redeemed the time scrupulously, as a faithful servant of God. He was 32 years of age and unmarried. He leaves three brothers and two sisters to mourn their loss, his parents dying in his youth.

Appropriate services were held at Greenbush, Thursday, the Rev. L. P. Davis, of West Bay City, officiating. The remains were taken by Mr. Peter Robbins, a brother of the deceased, to Dorchester, Canada, for interment. A life of bright promise closes at day-dawn. Knowing the blameless life and triumphant death of our brother, we

"Weep not for a brother deceased,
Our loss is his infinite gain;
A soul out of pain released,
And freed from its bodily chain.
With songs let us follow his flight,
And mount with his spirit above,
Escaped to the mansions of light,
And lodged in the Eden of love."

Alcona County Review, April 22, 1887

KILLMASTER HAPPENINGS.

Killmaster, April 27.--Our people are called to mourn the death of our beloved pastor, the Rev. Mr. Robbins. In the year and a half that he has been among us he has made many warm friends; to know him was to love him; to be in his presence was to feel that there was something really divine in his makeup. He was a faithful sower of the seed, and we expect in the future he will reap a rich harvest, for we believe his influence among the people will result in great good. His daily walk was an example worthy of meditation.

Alcona County Review, April 29, 1887
Cemetery:

Roberts, Katie

PERSONAL MENTION.

The many friends of our former townsman, Hon. R. Z. Roberts, will be pained to learn of the death of his daughter, Katie, which occurred in Lenoir, Tenn., on July 2d, 1896. She had been a great sufferer from that dread disease, consumption, and death came as a happy release to her sufferings.

Alcona County Review, July 9, 1896
Cemetery:

Roberts, Mr.

An aged gentleman named Roberts died yesterday near West Harrisville.

Alcona County Review, March 31, 1892
Cemetery:

Robinson, John

HOME REVIEWINGS.

A young man named Robinson, who came from Carsonville, Sanilac county, was drowned at Oscoda last Saturday afternoon.

Alcona County Review, July 22, 1881
Cemetery:

Rochon, Charles Victor

PERSONAL MENTION.

Two deaths from diphtheria have occurred this week in a family living in Pritchard's old camps in Mitchell.

Alcona County Review, November 2, 1893
Cemetery:

Rochon, Della

PERSONAL MENTION.

Two deaths from diphtheria have occurred this week in a family living in Pritchard's old camps in Mitchell.

Alcona County Review, November 2, 1893
Cemetery:

Roe, Sylvenus A.

SYLVENUS ROE, DECEASED.

Editor Review:—Please allow me space in your paper for a few lines in regard to the late S. A. Roe.

Sylvenus A. Roe died Dec. 24, 1891, of consumption, at the residence of A. J. Montgomery, and by his request was buried in the Middle Valley, close to the grave of the late Mrs. John Ward. The deceased was a member of Harrisville Lodge No. 218 I. O. O. F.; he came to Skamokawa July 4th, 1888, and went to work for Elias Cornel in his logging camp. He afterwards worked in the saw mill for Geo. L. Colwell. About a year ago he caught cold, from the effects of which he never recovered. The funeral service was preached by the Rev. C. A. Luce in the M. E. church in the East Valley Dec. 27. During the discourse there were many eyes in the congregation moistened with tears. The text was in Isaiah, 38th chapter, last part of first verse—"Thus saith the Lord: Set thine house in order, for thou shalt die and not live."

Mr. Roe stopped with Mr. Cornell until about six weeks ago, when he went to visit with Mr. Montgomery and family and the weather being bad, and he so weak it was not advisable for him to leave there, and through the kindness of Mr. and Mrs. Montgomery, where he received the kindest of treatment, he remained there until his death. It will be a satisfaction for his friends to know that he had all the care that a friendship and brotherly love could give. He was an honest upright young man and leaves many friends to mourn his departure. In the spring or as soon as the rainy season is over the Odd Fellows will put a fence around

his grave and erect a tomb stone to mark his last resting place. Yours respectfully,

Dan McLean.
Skamokawa, Wash., Dec. 30, '91.

Alcona County Review, January 14, 1892
Cemetery: Fern Hill, Wahkiakum County, WA

Roney, Thomas

FATAL HOTEL FIRE.

The Miner House at Tawas Burned.
Two of its Inmates Incinerated in the Ruins.

Last week Thursday the Miner House in East Tawas was discovered to be on fire, but not until it had gained such headway that all efforts to check it were of no avail. Jos. Widdifield, the proprietor, and his family had barely time to escape. All the guests were aroused, it was thought, in time to make their escape but E. F. Roney, the barkeeper and a lumberman named Joseph La Clair were missed and an investigation of the ruins after the fire was over revealed the charred remains of the two men. A coroner's jury returned a verdict to the effect that the two men came to their death from suffocation by smoke. The hotel was a total loss with but little insurance.

Alcona County Review, December 13, 1889
Cemetery: Greenwood, Iosco Co.

Rounds, {Female}

LOCAL PICK UPS.

Mr. Rounds of the Echo has received the sad intelligence of the death of his mother, which occurred Sunday. Owing to the serious illness of his only child he could not leave to attend the funeral. Much sympathy is expressed for him.

Alcona County Review, November 10, 1898
Cemetery:

Roundtree, Dennis

Black River Sparks.

Death has again visited Black River and has claimed a worthy citizen in the person of Dennis Roundtree. He died Sunday evening after a lingering illness. The remains were shipped to Port Huron for burial, special services first being held in St. Gabriel's church. Deceased was night foreman in the company's saw mill until his health failed.

Alcona County Review, April 23, 1896

Card of Thanks.

I wish to thank the many friends and neighbors for their kindness during the last illness and death of my beloved husband.

Mrs. D. Roundtree,
Black River, Mich.

Alcona County Review, May 7, 1896

Black River Sparks.

Lines in memory of D. Roundtree, who died at Black River.

Dearest husband thou hast left me,
Never more we'll meet on earth;
But I trust that I will meet you
In that place of peace and rest.

Oh! How very much I miss you.
Miss you daily more and more;
But I know that you're in heaven
Walking on the golden shore.

Husband, dear, our home is lonely
For thy presence loved so well;
But I am contented, knowing
That in Jesus you now dwell.

Young widow cease your weeping.
It is wrong to weep for him;
He has gone to be with Jesus,
In that place that's free from pain.

Do not let your heart be troubled.
Neither let it be dismayed;
Trust in Jesus, Jesus only.
You need never be dismayed.

Alcona County Review, June 4, 1896
Cemetery: Mt. Hope, St. Clair Co.

Rowe, Thomas

Death on the Rail.

Thos. Roe, a brakeman, was accidentally killed by the night log train, Tuesday night, near Pritchard's camp on the Mud Lake branch of the railroad. Justice Reynolds was summoned and requested to hold an inquest, but after investigating the facts and circumstances, he was satisfied that the deceased met his death through his own carelessness, and he did not deem an inquest necessary. The engineer of the train states that Roe was on the engine and started without a lantern for his place on the train. It is supposed that he slipped and fell under the cars. He was missed at the Junction. A search for him was immediately instituted, and

on going back his fellows were horrified to find the ghastly mangled remains of young Roe, the head severed from the body and lying several rods from it, the headless trunk with one arm severed lying across the track. The dead man was about twenty years of age and unmarried, his parents residing at Oscoda. His relatives were notified at once, and his father and an undertaker from Oscoda took charge of the remains.

Alcona County Review, May 27, 1887
Cemetery: Pinecrest, Iosco Co.

Rowe, Vene

The Local News.

Vene Rowe, formerly of Harrisville, died recently in Oregon after a lingering illness of consumption. He was a member of Harrisville lodge No. 218, I. O. O. F. and the expenses of his last sickness and burial are born by them.

Alcona County Review, December 31, 1891
Cemetery:

Rushman, Catherine L.

COUNTY NEWS JOTTINGS.

The four year old daughter of Mr. and Mrs. John Rushman died, Wednesday morning, with the croup.

Alcona County Review, November 23, 1877
Cemetery: Probably St. Anne's, Alcona Co.

Rutson, Mrs. Elizabeth

Purely Personal.

The many friends of Mrs. Geo. Rutson regret to hear that she has been lying very seriously ill at her residence since her return from Bay City.

Alcona County Review, January 31, 1890

Purely Personal.

Mrs. Wm. Dennis of Ovid, Mich., and Mrs. W. I. Tillotson of Oneida, N. Y. have been called to this village by the serious illness of their sister, Mrs. Geo. Rutson.

Alcona County Review, January 31, 1890

Purely Personal.

Mrs. Rutson's condition has not materially changed.

Alcona County Review, February 14, 1890

Mable Rockwell, a trained nurse connected with Harper's Hospital, Detroit, arrived in the village last Saturday and is now in attendance at the bedside of Mrs. Geo. Rutson. That lady's condition is not

materially changed but she is brighter if anything.

Alcona County Review, March 21, 1890

The Local News.

Mrs. Mable Rockwell, the trained nurse from Harpers hospital, Detroit, returned home last week and Mrs. Geo. Ward has resumed her position at the bedside of Mrs. Geo. Rutson.

Alcona County Review, April 18, 1890

People We Hear About.

Mrs. Geo. Rutson, who has been confined to her bed for the last six months, improves very slowly. Mrs. Geo. Ward, who has been in constant attendance during most of her long illness, is taking a much needed rest. Mrs. H. McMaster relieves.

Alcona County Review, July 18, 1890

People We Hear About.

Mrs. Frank Deuell, of Hawkeye, Decatur Co., Kansas, and Mrs. Wm. Dennis, of Ovid, Mich., both sisters of Mrs. Rutson, arrived in the village Monday evening.

Alcona County Review, September 5, 1890

Your Folks and Our Folks.

Mrs. W. I. Tillotson of Oneida, N. Y., Mrs. N. A. Duell of Hawkeye, Kansas, left for their respective homes Tuesday morning after extended visits at the bedside of their sister, Mrs. Geo. Rutson, and other relatives in the village.

Alcona County Review, November 14, 1890

PASSED AWAY.

Rutson.—Elizabeth, beloved wife of George Rutson, at her late home in the village of Harrisville, after a lingering illness.

The deceased was born at Hemlock Lake, N. Y. Here and at other places in that state she passed the earlier years of her life. She was a school teacher, and taught schools in Canada and later in Michigan with marked and gratifying success. For upwards of a quarter of a century her life has been closely identified with the history of what is now Alcona county. She came here when the forests were almost unbroken, when the stately pines lifted their majestic heads towards heaven as if in proud contempt of the human pigmies who were to encompass their destruction. She has witnessed every development of this community, and watched its changing fortunes with a deep interest which can be felt by none but the advance guard, the pioneer citizens.

She was a patient unselfish sufferer, and all through her long illness made frequent inquiries concerning the sick and unfortunate around her. She was first stricken January 24, 1890. The insidious disease, paralysis, gradually sapped the forces of mind and body until at her dissolution she was but a shadow of her former self. The end came peacefully: exclaiming, "I am happier now," her spirit winged its way to the unseen. Besides a wide circle of friends she leaves her husband, her daughter, Mrs. R. L. Lott, and three sisters, Mrs. W. I. Tillotson of Oneida, N. Y.; Mrs. W. W. Dennis of Ovid, Mich. and Mrs. F. Deuell of Hawkeye, Ks.

Her life was marked by a quiet, unostentatious devotion to humanity that manifested itself in innumerable pilgrimages to the homes of the needy and suffering. If there was a bed of sickness or pain, a case of distress or privation, her sympathy was enlisted at once. Delicacies from her table found their way into innumerable homes; flowers from her garden perfumed the atmosphere of many a sick chamber; the cheerful, buoyant, vigorous nature with which she was blessed acted like tonic upon the shattered nerves of a feeble sufferer. This was her religion, the broad and practical kind of Christianity. She was very fond of flowers, being only equaled by her tender love for dumb creatures. With these and her books and her charities she passed her life. Her charities were her own secrets, and her most intimate friends knew nothing of them until the story fell from the lips of the grateful recipient.

The funeral services were held at 10 o'clock a.m. Wednesday at her late residence, the Rev. P. C. Goldie officiating. A large concourse of friends followed the remains to the cemetery at South Harrisville.

It lies around us like a cloud,
The world we can not see.

Alcona County Review, December 19, 1890

Your Folks and Our Folks.
Mrs. Geo. Kimball came down from Alpena Tuesday to attend the funeral of her late friend, Mrs. Geo. Rutson.

Alcona County Review, December 19, 1890

Your Folks and Our Folks.
Mrs. W. W. Dennis of Ovid, sister of the late Mrs. Rutson, and Wm. Rutson and Mrs. Donaldson of Detroit, father and sister of Geo. Rutson, were called to Harrisville this week on account of the death of Mrs. Rutson.

Alcona County Review, December 19, 1890

Your Folks and Our Folks.
Wm. Rutson and Mrs. Donaldson returned to Detroit Monday. Mrs. W. W. Dennis returned to Ovid also the same day.

Alcona County Review, December 19, 1890

Geo. Rutson and Mrs. R. L. Lott desire to express their gratitude to their friends for the many acts of kindness rendered during the long illness of their departed wife and mother.

Alcona County Review, December 19, 1890

IN MEMORIAM.
Whereas, The Omnipotent and Supreme Ruler of the universe has in his Wisdom seen fit to remove from earth, Elizabeth, the estimable and beloved wife of our worthy Brother, Past Grand Geo. Rutson.

Whereas, Although gone from among us, she will not be forgotten as a kind and loving companion, and we cherish her memory as a kind and loving friend. Therefore be it

Resolved that we the members of the Harrisville Lodge No. 218, I. O. O. F. do hereby tender to Brother P. G. Rutson our sincere and heartfelt sympathy, in this his hour of sad bereavement. And be it still further

Resolved that those on whose hearts the blow falls heaviest, we commend to the guidance and care of Him who careth for all, and trust the loss they have sustained will prove a rich gain in spiritual blessings to all. Be it

Resolved that as a token of respect to our brother these resolution be placed on the Records of this Lodge and the same be published in the Alcona County Review, and a copy be sent to our worthy Brother.

F. A. Beede, Sec.

Alcona County Review, December 19, 1890

One Year's History.

Record of Local Happenings for the Year 1890.

DECEMBER.
15 Death of Elizabeth, wife of Co. Clerk, Geo. Rutson.

Alcona County Review, January 1, 1891
Cemetery: Springport, Alcona Co.

Rutson, William

Your Folks and Our Folks.

County Clerk Rutson was called to Detroit Saturday morning last by a telegram announcing the serious illness of his father, Wm. Rutson.

Alcona County Review, January 15, 1891

The Local News.

Wm. Rutson, father of County Clerk Geo. Rutson, died at the home of his daughter in Detroit, Saturday last at the advanced age of 80 years. Mr. Rutson had been a frequent visitor to Harrisville and won the friendship of all who knew him by his gentlemanly and courteous bearing. His last visit here was less than a month prior to his death at the time of the burial of Mrs. Geo. Rutson. He was remarkably well and active for one of his years at that time. The cause of his death was a second attack of La grippe.

Alcona County Review, January 15, 1891
Cemetery:

Ryan, Thomas R.

LOCAL JOTTINGS.

Thos. R. Ryan, at one time steward of the City of Alpena, died in Detroit on the 9th inst., aged 62 years.

Alcona County Review, April 16, 1886
Cemetery:

Safford, Mary [Harwood]

BLACK RIVER.
Maj. C. H. Safford was called to Detroit by a telegram announcing the serious illness of his mother.

Alcona County Review, September 15, 1898

BLACK RIVER.
Major Safford arrived home Saturday but was called to Detroit again by telegram Tuesday morning, his mother's condition being much worse.

Alcona County Review, September 22, 1898

BLACK RIVER.
Word was received here Monday morning of the death of Major Safford's mother.

Of Revolutionary Stock

Mother of Major C. H. Safford Has Passed Away at Detroit.

Mrs. Mary Howard Safford, mother of Major C. H. Safford, the courteous manager of the company store at Black River, died at Detroit Sunday morning at the advanced age of 80 years. Major Safford and three other surviving children were with their aged parent when she entered into eternal rest.

Her early life was spent in Lockport, N. Y. She was a descendant of the Harwood family that settled in Concord, Mass., in 1626, and whose members were prominent actors in the revolution.

She had been a resident of Detroit for 40 years. She was a Presbyterian and in her early life was very active in Christian work.

Alcona County Review, September 29, 1898
Cemetery: Elmwood, Wayne Co.

Sage, Mrs.

LOCAL JOTTINGS.

C. M. Sage, of this office, last week received the sad tidings that his mother was dead. Her death occurred at Bath, Mich., Dec. 19.

Alcona County Review, December 28, 1888
Cemetery:

Sampson, Thomas

Alpena Pioneer: Thos. Sampson, a married man about 54 years of age, while riding horseback a few miles below Ossineke, Monday night, accidently fell from the horse, which kicked him in the back of the head and killed him. He was found about nine o'clock that night lying in the road. Coroner Owens was summoned, and impaneled a jury, who rendered a verdict of death from accident. The deceased was a farmer living near Ossineke.

Alcona County Review, May 7, 1886
Cemetery:

Sanford, Charles

LOCAL LACONICS.

A Mr. Sanford, of Alcona, lost a eleven-year-old child on Wednesday. The cause of its death we did not learn.

Alcona County Review, June 5, 1885
Cemetery:

Santerneau, George

A TERRIBLE ACCIDENT.

Seven Men Buried Alive Beneath a Mass of Brick.

THE FRIGHTFUL OCCURRENCE AT AU SABLE.

On Monday afternoon the citizens of AuSable and Oscoda were suddenly thrown into a state of excitement and terror, by the announcement of a horrible accident which had occurred at Gram's mill burner, by which five persons lost their lives, seven in all being victims to the terrible calamity. The particulars of the sad occurrence we glean from the Saturday Night extra of Wednesday, as follows:

"There were seven men at work in the burner at Gram's mill. They were Joseph W. Biddle, Thomas Mitchell, George Fulton, John Hardwick, William Miner, George Santerneau, George Gordon. The men were engaged in taking down the brick wall of one of the refuse burners of Gram's mill. A scaffolding had been built inside the burner, and upon the scaffolding the men worked and upon it the brick was also laid as they were taken from the wall. The men began taking the wall down from the top. They had been working in the burner about a week and had the walls about half down. The brick from the part of the wall already taken down were of course lying on the platforms of the scaffolding above the heads of the workmen. While the men were engaged at work, continuing the tearing down of the wall—with about 20,000 brick, or from 40 to 50 ton's weight, above them, the scaffolding gave way, and in an instant the seven men were buried beneath this immense amount of brick and the lumber and timber of which the scaffolding was made. The alarm was given by Michael Gerrard, who was working but a few feet from the burner. Before an hour had passed there were from 1000 to 1500 men collected at the scene of the accident. The task of uncovering the men was begun as soon as possible after the accident occurred, but under the circumstances it was a very slow job. The bricks, and lumber composing the scaffolding, had all to be thrown out through two small openings—two feet by two and one

half—and of course only a small number of them could work at a time. The scaffolding fell about half past four o'clock. At half past seven the first body was reached and taken out. It proved to be that of Joseph Biddle. A short time after young Gordon was taken out alive and seemingly not fatally injured, though at this writing his recovery is doubtful. A few minutes later Fulton and Santerneau were taken out, the former alive and the latter dead. Then the bodies of Mitchell, Miner, and Hardwick were taken out in the order named, it being about nine o'clock, or four and one-half hours after the accident, when the last body was removed. When the scaffolding fell some of the scantlings happened to wedge in such a position that they kept the principal weight of the brick off from Gordon, and he was able to converse at intervals with the men who were removing the brick. The men could also hear groans from one of the other imprisoned victims—probably Fulton, he was the only other one taken out alive. Five of the victims—Biddle, Fulton, Miner, Santerneau and Hardwick—were married men with families. Mr. Hardwick, familiarly called "Happy Jack," leaves a wife and six children, the oldest a daughter of seventeen. Mr. Biddle leaves a wife and two children, Mr. Miner the same. Mr. Fulton has a wife and three children, and Mr. Santerneau leaves a wife and baby.

Later.—Fulton died Wednesday evening.

Alcona County Review, April 17, 1885

LOCAL JOTTINGS.

Register of Deeds Jamison and Gene Taft spent Monday night at Au Sable, and brought to town early Tuesday morning the news of the killing of the 5 men at Au Sable.

Alcona County Review, April 17, 1885
Cemetery:

Sawyer, Joseph

Capt. Sawyer Drowned.

It is our sad misfortune to chronicle the death of Capt. Joseph Sawyer, by drowning, which occurred near Rogers City Wednesday morning. Capt. Sawyer, in company with the captain of the life saving station at Forty Mile Point, and one of the station crew, while going from the point to Rogers in a small sail boat, were capsized by the gale, and the two captains drowned. Capt. Sawyer was Supt. of the U. S. life-saving service for the 10th district, and quite well known in this vicinity from his numerous visits here. His residence was in Detroit, and he was off on a tour of inspection at the time of his death.

Alcona County Review, October 22, 1880

County Reviewings.

According to the Presque Isle Advance the body of Capt. Feaben, who was drowned in company with Capt. Sawyer some time ago, was found seven miles above Rogers City. No trace of Capt. Sawyer's body yet, though a vigilant search has been maintained.

Alcona County Review, November 26, 1880

County Reviewings.

Capt. J. K. Kiah will probably be appointed superintendent of the tenth life saving district in place of Captain Joseph Sawyer, who was drowned recently. Capt. Kiah is the only survivor of the crew that was lost at Point aux Barques, April 26th, 1880.-- *Tawas Gazette*.

Alcona County Review, November 26, 1880
Cemetery:

Saxon, Charles

EVENTS OF ONE WEEK.

Chas. Saxon, a resident of this county time "whereof the memory of man runneth not to the contrary" died at his late home Tuesday morning. He had been a county dependent for a number of years and received a regular allowance from the temporary relief fund, although he was possessed of land in Haynes township of considerable value. For a few years past he has been practically helpless and rarely left the house.

Deceased was 69 years of age: His aged wife survives him. Two daughters, Mrs. Rosetta Jones, of Detroit, and Mrs. A. Bondville, of Alcona, are here to attend the last obsequies. A brother and a sister of deceased reside in this state and were notified by wire. The funeral took place this afternoon at 2 o'clock, the interment taking place at South Harrisville.

Alcona County Review, March 7, 1895

Mr. and Mrs. A. J. Fortier, of Alcona are attending the funeral of

Chas. Saxon, Mrs. Fortier's grandfather.

Alcona County Review, March 7, 1895

Card of Thanks.

We wish to thank our kind friends and neighbors for their generous assistance in our great bereavement.

Mrs. A. L. Saxon.

Alcona County Review, March 14, 1895
Cemetery: Springport, Alcona Co.

Sayan, Wilfred

Local Sayings and Doings.

Wilfred Sayan, a boy about 12 years old employed in Comstock's shingle mill, was playing on the logs lying in the river near the mill Tuesday morning, and unfortunately lost his balance, falling into the water. Men at work in the mill saw the accident, but the river being covered with logs at that point assistance could not reach him. Search was at once made for the body which was recovered about noon and taken home. *Alpena Reporter*.

Alcona County Review, August 25, 1882
Cemetery:

Saylor, Edith

EVENTS OF ONE WEEK.

Edith, the youngest child of Mr. and Mrs. Arthur Saylor, died last Friday from spasms. The funeral services were held at the house Sunday afternoon, Rev. Will officiating.

The child was five years of age, but had been almost helpless since babyhood. As is not infrequently the case under such circumstances, this child was the pet of the family, who feel deeply the death of little Edith.

Alcona County Review, March 25, 1897
Cemetery:

Saylor, William David

LOCAL PICK UPS.

The young son of Mr. and Mrs. Edw. Saylor, who has been so seriously sick for 3 weeks past, is slightly better today. The little fellow has been very low and at times his life was despaired of.

Alcona County Review, January 13, 1898

THE GRIM REAPER.

Willie, aged 4 years 6 months, youngest son of Mr. and Mrs. Edward Saylor, died this morning at 4

o'clock. The little fellow has been a patient sufferer for four weeks and death was a welcome release. The funeral will be held Saturday afternoon from the Catholic church.

Alcona County Review, January 20, 1898

LOCAL PICK UPS.

Many hearts were heavy and sad in Harrisville Friday last, Jan. 21. The mortal remains of three persons, one an infant, two in the autumn of life's journey, were borne to their final resting places. The remains of Mrs. Harriet S. Taft were buried in the morning, those of Mrs. Sinclair and the little son of Edw. Saylor at different hours in the afternoon. Services in each case were held at the residences. Three funerals in one day in a town the size of Harrisville is a sad and unusual occurrence.

Alcona County Review, January 27, 1898

We wish to express our most sincere thanks to our many kind neighbors, friends and all those who assisted us during the sickness and death of our dearly beloved little Willie.

Mr. and Mrs. Edgar Saylor.

Alcona County Review, January 27, 1898

WILLIE SAYLOR, DECEASED.

Our darling Willie has left us,
We can never see him more.
He is gone to join the Angels
Upon the golden shore.

He bore his sickness long and brave,
He bore it till the last.
For four long weeks he suffered,
But now in heaven he rests.

Oh, how we all do miss him.
We never will forget his little loving
footsteps.
We often used to hear;
We hope to meet him later in heaven
where he dwells.

Mrs. A. J. Clark.

Alcona County Review, February 3, 1898

Local History of One Year

Chronology of the Principal Events of the Year 1898.

January 19. Deaths: Mrs. Harriett Taft aged 62; Mrs. Sinclair aged 80; Willie Saylor aged 4. Two infants.

Alcona County Review, January 5, 1899
Cemetery: St. Anne's, Alcona Co.

Scarf, Thomas

The greater and more destructive part of the storm that passed over northern Michigan Wednesday, took in a fair portion of the city of Alpena. The wind was forty-eight miles an hour, and the rainfall was over an inch in eight minutes. Thos. Scarf was killed by lightning, and another man's arm was broken. A house, mill, smoke-stack and a number of piles of lumber were blown over a mile. Forty thousand feet of lumber were blown into Thunder Bay. The tornado was not very wide and lasted about 15 minutes.

Alcona County Review, September 12, 1884
Cemetery: Evergreen, Alpena Co.

Scarlett, Adam E.

COUNTY JOTTINGS.

That dreaded disease, diptheria, is raging quite extensively among the children in the southern portion of Alcona township. One of Supervisor A. T. Scarlett's little sons died with the disease Sunday night, and children in the families of Ephriam Waldron, John Hayden and Uriah Emerson are now down with the same. Let all necessary precautions be taken to prevent the further spreading of the disease.

Alcona County Review, October 25, 1878
Cemetery: Springport, Alcona Co.

Scarlett, Lily

IN MEMORIAM.

Lines written by her sister in memory of Lily Scarlett, who died at Duluth, Nov. 21, 1891.

Our loved one from us has departed,
Our home is empty and lone;
Our darling no longer will welcome
Or hasten our footsteps home.

We loved our darling dearly,
But God, in his wisdom and love,
Decided to take her from us,
To his beautiful home above.

To his beautiful home where the angels
Are beckoning and bidding us come;
To his home where dwell souls immortal,
We must look for our darling one.

Our Lily which God had given,
We mourn thee every day;
And well we know that God alone
Our tears can wipe away.
                    --Lavina Scarlett.

Alcona County Review, January 1, 1892
Cemetery:

Scarlett, Robert

Died.—May 4th, Robert, youngest child of Adam T. Scarlett, aged seven weeks.

Alcona County Review, May 7, 1880
Cemetery: Probably Springport, Alcona Co.

Scarlett, Robert, Sr.

Local Sayings and Doings.

The Review learns of the death of the father of the Messrs. Scarlett brothers of this county, which occurred at his home back of Alcona a few days ago. He was a quite aged person, and had been a resident of the county for a long time. We have received no particulars concerning his death, nor learned as to his exact age.

Alcona County Review, January 20, 1882
Cemetery: Probably Springport, Alcona Co.

Schmidt, Charles

Kicked by a Horse.

Chas. Smith, choreman at Pritchard's camp, was found lying on a manure pile at the stables unconscious. It is supposed he was kicked by a horse in the bowels. At last accounts he was still unconscious, and it was feared he would not recover. He is an old employe of the firm.

Alcona County Review, October 1, 1886

Charles Smith, the man who was kicked by a horse, as noted in last week's Review, died from his injuries last Friday night. He was a member of a Milwaukee lodge of I. O. O. F., and the fraternity here took charge of the body. The funeral service was held in the M. E. church Sunday afternoon, Rev. C. B. Steele preaching the funeral sermon. A large delegation from Alcona lodge of Odd Fellows joined with Harrisville lodge in the last sad rites of the order. The body was buried in the west cemetery.

Alcona County Review, October 8, 1886

A Card of Thanks.

Harrisville Lodge No. 218, I. O. O. F., hereby tender a vote of thanks to Mrs. Houghton and Mrs. Tinkey for their kind services and the furnishing of flowers; also to Mr. D. LaBoeuf for gratuitously furnishing teams; all for the occasion of the funeral of our late lamented brother, Charles Schmidt.
                    Chas. Miller, Com.

Alcona County Review, October 8, 1886

NEIGHBORHOOD NOTES.

October 1, 1889, Charles Schmidt, a woodsman employed at Pritchard's camp was kicked by a horse from the effects of which he died. A small sum of money due for labor by Alger, Smith & Company was the extent of his earthly estate. No heirs have appeared to claim it so C. P. Reynolds now seeks administration. What is left, if anything, will be appropriated, for the purchase of a suitable monument. He was buried by the Odd Fellows and the order talks of buying four lots in the Harrisville cemetery for the reception of the remains of members who are buried at the expense of the order.

Alcona County Review, May 24, 1889

Harrisville Township Board.

Moved and supported that Harrisville Lodge, No. 218, I. O. O. F., be granted four lots in the West Harrisville cemetery, said lots comprising one where Chas. Smith now lies and the three next adjoining, said lots to be improved in a neat manner before deed granted. Carried.

Alcona County Review, June 7, 1889

LOCAL JOTTINGS.

F. A. Beede, administrator for the estate of the late Chas. Schmidt, informs the Review that the stone ordered in Port Huron is not for Odd Fellows generally but is to be erected solely in memory of Mr. Schmidt. A $60 monument was ordered.

Alcona County Review, August 2, 1889
Cemetery: West Lawn, Alcona Co.

Schoultz, {Male}

Sentenced for Life.

The Schoultz murder case opened in the Iosco county circuit court, at Tawas, Tuesday, and closed on Wednesday. Wm. B. White was convicted and sentenced Wednesday morning at 11 o'clock. The jury was out forty minutes and returned a verdict of guilty of murder in the first degree. White emphatically declared his innocence of the murder and robbery. He was sentenced to state's prison for life.

Wm. Reynolds after offering a lengthy written statement pleaded guilty to the same charge, being implicated with White. Jacob Katterman defended his own case, and with the others declared his innocence of the murder and robbery.

Both received life sentences, and the three were taken to Jackson yesterday.

The people rejoice over this just conclusion of the horrible affair. Great credit is said to be done Judge Tuttle and Prosecuting Attorney Henry for the speedy and satisfactory manner in which the case was conducted.

Alcona County Review, May 23, 1884
Cemetery:

Schram, {Child}

LOCAL JOTTINGS.

A four years old child of Sam'l Scram was buried last Friday.

Alcona County Review, July 6, 1888
Cemetery:

Schram, Samuel

GREENBUSH GETTINGS.

Samuel Schram, a young man who has been lying ill for some time at Cal Wilson's, died Wednesday morning at 2 a.m. Consumption, we understand, was the disease.

Alcona County Review, February 19, 1886
Cemetery:

Scott, Douglass

PERSONAL MENTION.

Douglass Scott, Alpena city's efficient Chief of Police, died Monday morning after an illness of 17 days. He was born in Detroit in 1842 and was a veteran of the Civil war. He came to Alpena in 1866 and had always been prominently identified with the police interests of that place.

Alcona County Review, July 25, 1895
Cemetery: Evergreen, Alpena Co.

Scott, Dwight

Probate Order.
State of Michigan, County of Alcona, ss.--Probate Court for said County.

At a session of the Probate Court for said county, held at the Probate office in the village of Harrisville, on the 29th day of December, A. D. 1879--

Present, R. Z. Roberts, Judge of Probate.

In the matter of the Estate of Dwight Scott, deceased.

George A. Garretson, of Cleveland, Ohio, having filed in this office certified copies of the letters of administration de bonis non of all

and singular the goods, chattels, rights, credits and estate which were of Dwight Scott, late of Cleveland, Ohio, deceased, and of his bond in the sum of twenty-five thousand dollars filed in pursuance of the order of the Probate Court in and for Cuyahoga County, Ohio, in said court which so appointed him; and said George A. Garretson having also filed, with said other papers, a certificate of the Clerk of said Probate Court duly authenticated, that said Bond on file is good and sufficient for the amount thereof; and said George A. Garretson, as such administrator de bonis non, having filed in this Court his petition for the sale of certain Real Estate situated within the jurisdiction of this Court, for the purpose of paying debts against said estate; and said certificate appearing to be in due form, and the proceedings hitherto appearing to have been legal, it is hereby ordered that Wednesday the 4th day of February, A. D. 1880, at 10 o'clock A. M., be fixed for the hearing of said petitions and it appearing that all the parties interested in said estate reside without the State of Michigan, It is hereby further ordered that publication be made four weeks successively, previous to said 4th day of February, A. D. 1880, in the Alcona County Review, a newspaper published in said village of Harrisville, notifying the parties named in said petition, and all other parties interested in said estate, to be and appear before this Court on said fourth day of February, next at 10 o'clock A. M., then and there to show cause, if any there be, why the said petition of said George A. Garretson, administrator de bonis non, should not be granted, until which period this cause stands adjourned.

R. Z. Roberts, Judge of Probate.

Alcona County Review, January 2, 1880

Probate Sale.
State of Michigan--County of Alcona--ss.

In the Probate Court.

In the matter of the Estate of Dwight Scott, deceased.

Notice is hereby given, that in pursuance of an order granted to the undersigned, administrator de bonis non of the estate of said Dwight Scott, deceased, by the Hon. R. Z. Roberts, Judge of Probate for the

County of Alcona, on the 4th day of February, A. D. 1880, there will be sold at public vendue to the highest bidder, at Harrisville, in the county of Alcona, at the front door of the County Court House in said Harrisville in the State of Michigan, on the 14th day of April, A. D. 1880, at ten o'clock in the forenoon of that day (subject to all claims for taxes against said lands), the following described Real Estate, to wit: The south east quarter of Section twenty-three (23) in Town twenty-six (26) north, of Range three (3) east, in Oscoda County, in the State of Michigan, said county being attached to Alcona County for Judicial purposes. Terms cash on the day of sale.

Harrisville, Mich., February 24, 1880.

Geo. A. Garretson,
Administrator de bonis non of Estate of Dwight Scott, deceased.

Alcona County Review, February 27, 1880
Cemetery:

Scott, Thomas

Found Dead in Bed.

Thomas Scott, for many years in the employ of Alger, Smith & Co., and well known in this vicinity, was found dead in his bed at Black River yesterday (Thursday) morning. Supposed cause of death, heart disease. The deceased was a native of Scotland, and returned there last spring on a visit to relatives. He was unmarried, and has no relatives in this vicinity. Mr. Scott was 57 years of age and had resided in this country 40 years.

Alcona County Review, November 26, 1886

LOCAL JOTTINGS.

The funeral services of Thomas Scott, mention of whose sudden death was made last week, were held in the Presbyterian church in this village last Saturday afternoon, Rev. G. S. Weir, of Black River, preaching the sermon. The body was interred in the Harrisville cemetery.

Alcona County Review, December 3, 1886

ORDER OF HEARING.
State of Michigan, County of Alcona.

At a session of the Probate Court for said county, held at the Probate Office in the village of Harrisville, on the third day of June, in the year one thousand eight hundred and eighty-seven. Present, Allen Nevins, Judge of Probate. In the matter of the

ESTATE OF THOMAS SCOTT, DECEASED.

On reading and filing the petition, duly verified, of Joseph Wedge, praying that Simon J. McNally or some other suitable person be appointed administrator of the estate of said deceased. Thereupon it is ordered that Saturday, the Twentieth Day of August, 1887, next, at ten o'clock in the forenoon, be assigned for the hearing of said petition, and that the heirs at law of said deceased, and all other persons interested in said estate, are required to appear at a session of said court then to be holden at the Probate office, in the village of Harrisville, and show cause if any there be, why the prayer of the petitioner should not be granted. And it is further ordered that said petitioner give notice to the heirs at law, and such other persons interested in said estate, of the pendency of said petition, and the hearing thereof, by causing a copy of this order to be published in the Alcona County Review, a newspaper printed and circulated in said county, four successive weeks previous to said day of hearing.

Allen Nevins, Judge of Probate.

Alcona County Review, June 24, 1887

COMMISSIONERS NOTICE.

State of Michigan, County of Alcona, ss: Probate Court for said county.

ESTATE OF THOMAS SCOTT, DECEASED.

The undersigned having been appointed by the Judge of Probate of said county Commissioners on Claims in the matter of said estate of Thomas Scott deceased, and six months from the 30th day of August, A. D., 1887, having been allowed by said Judge of Probate to all persons holding claims against said estate in which to present their claims to us for examination and adjustment.

Notice is hereby given that we will meet on Tuesday, the 20th day of December, A. D., 1887, and on Monday, the 20th day of February, 1888, at 2 o'clock p. m. of each day, at the office of George Rutson, in the village of Harrisville, in said county, to receive and examine such claims. Dated, October 10th, A. D. 1887.

George Rutson,
C. P. Reynolds.   Commissioners

Alcona County Review, October 14, 1887

PROBATE ORDER.

STATE OF MICHIGAN, County of Alcona.

At a session of the Probate Court for said county, held at the Probate Office in the village of Harrisville, on the tenth day of July, in the year one thousand eight hundred and eighty-eight. Present, Allen Nevins, Judge of Probate. In the matter of the

ESTATE OF THOMAS SCOTT, DECEASED.

On reading and filing the petition, duly verified, of Simon J. McNally, administrator of the estate of said Thomas Scott, deceased, praying that he may be empowered and licensed to sell the real estate of said deceased, situate in the township of Harrisville, County of Alcona, and State of Michigan, known and described as follows: The south-west quarter of section eight, in town twenty-six north of range nine east, for the purpose of paying the debts due against said estate, and the expenses of the administration of said estate.

Thereupon it is ordered that Monday, the Sixth Day of August, 1888, next, at 10 o'clock in the forenoon, be assigned for the hearing of said petition, and that the heirs at law of said deceased, and all other persons interested in said estate, are required to appear at a session of said court then to be holden in the Probate office, in the village of Harrisville, in said county of Alcona, and show cause if any there be, why the prayer of the petitioner should not be granted. And it is further ordered that said petitioner give notice to the heirs at law, and persons interested in said estate, of the pendency of said petition, and the hearing thereof, by causing a copy of this order to be published in the Alcona County Review, a newspaper printed and circulated in said county, three successive weeks previous to said day of hearing.

ALLEN NEVINS, Judge of Probate.

Alcona County Review, July 13, 1888

Notice of Sale of Real Estate.

(First Publication Aug. 10, 1888, No. 19.)

STATE OF MICHIGAN, County of Alcona.

In the matter of the ESTATE OF THOMAS SCOTT, deceased. Notice is hereby given, that in pursuance of an order granted to the undersigned, administrator of the estate of said Thomas Scott, deceased, by the Hon. Judge of Probate for the county of Alcona, on the sixth day of August, A. D. 1888, there will be sold at public vendue, to the highest bidder, at the front door of the Court House, in the village of Harrisville, in the county of Alcona, in said state, on Saturday, the Twenty-second Day of September, A. D. 1888, at eleven o'clock in the forenoon of that day (subject to all encumbrances by mortgage or otherwise existing at the time of the death of said deceased, or at the time of the said sale, and also subject to the right of dower and the homestead rights of the widow of said deceased therein), the following described real estate, to wit: Situate in the township of Harrisville, County of Alcona, and State of Michigan, described as follows: The south-west quarter of section eight, in town twenty-six north of range nine east.

SIMON J. McNALLY,
Administrator of the Estate of Thomas Scott, Deceased.

The above sale is hereby adjourned until the 18th day of December, A. D. 1888, at 2 o'clock in the afternoon.

Dated September 22d, 1888.
SIMON J. McNALLY, Administrator.

Alcona County Review, September 28, 1888

Elizabeth Wedge has petitioned the probate court for an appointment as administrator of the estate of her late husband. She has also petitioned the court to remove Simon J. McNally as administrator of the estate of Thos. Scott, deceased, and for the appointment of B. P. Cowley in his place. Hearing March 18.

Alcona County Review, February 21, 1895

STATE OF MICHIGAN, County of Alcona.

At a session of the Probate Court for said County, held at the Probate office in the Village of Harrisville, on the Sixteenth day of February, in the year one thousand eight hundred and ninety-five.

Present, C. H. Killmaster, Judge of Probate.

In the Matter of the Estate of Thomas Scott:

On reading and filing the petition, duly verified, of Elizabeth Wedge, praying that administration of the said estate may be granted to Bernard P. Cowley Esq. or some other suitable person. Thereupon it is ordered that Monday, the eighteenth day of March next, at ten o'clock in the forenoon, be assigned for the hearing of said petition, and that the heirs at law of said deceased, and all others interested in said estate, are required to appear at a session of said Court, then to be holden in the Probate office, in the Village of Harrisville, and show cause, if any there be, why the prayer of the petitioner should not be granted: And it is further ordered, that said petitioners give notice to the persons interested in said estate, of the pendency of said petition, and the hearing thereof by causing a copy of this order to be published in the Alcona County Review, a newspaper printed and circulated in said county, three successive weeks previous to said day of hearing.

C. H. Killmaster,
Judge of Probate.

Alcona County Review, February 21, 1895

EVENTS OF ONE WEEK.

Judge Killmaster was in town Monday for the hearing in the matter of the estates of Jos. Wedge and Thos. Scott, deceased.

Alcona County Review, March 21, 1895
Cemetery: Probably Springport, Alcona Co.

Scriver, Grace

Coroner Investigated It.

Girl's Peculiar Death at Black River Was From Natural Causes.

A dispatch from Black River to the Detroit dailies stated that Grace Scriver, aged 14, had died from fright at a stranger who called at the house while the girl and a younger brother were alone. The circumstances seemed to warrant an investigation and Coroner Mayo was summoned and the facts elicited were as follows:

The girl was subject to fits; her mother, who is a widow, went to Black River Sunday, leaving the girl and boy alone. Louie Exnord, who lives at Black River, went out in the afternoon to call. Just as he was entering the gate the girl was taken with a fit. He and the boy used what means they could to revive her, but

without result and she died in a short time. Darkness came on and the boy was afraid either to go to the neighbors or to be left alone while Exnord went, so both remained in the house all night and the neighbors were informed in the morning. It was this circumstance that aroused suspicion, but in the light of the facts no blame was attached to anyone by the coroner's jury.

Alcona County Review, August 26, 1897
Cemetery:

Scriver, Henry

BLACK RIVER.

Mr. Scriver, Sr., died at the home of his son George, Sunday, Dec. 30. Funeral services were held at the house Wednesday at 10 o'clock, Rev. Boyce officiating. Interment took place in the west cemetery.

Alcona County Review, January 10, 1901
Cemetery: West Lawn, Alcona Co.

Scroggin, Levi

A notice of the death of Levi Scoggin, father of Mrs. B. F. Buchanan, has been received from Rising Sun, Ind. Deceased was 76 years of age and visited his daughter's family during their residence in Harrisville.

Alcona County Review, April 9, 1896
Cemetery: Union, Ohio Co., IN

Seaman, Arni L.

PERSONAL.

Dr. Seaman, the celebrated Alpena doctor, was found dead in bed one day last week.

Alcona County Review, September 2, 1897
Cemetery: Evergreen, Alpena Co.

Segar, Joseph

County Reviewings.

Drowned.——Joseph Segar, an inmate of the county poor house, who for some months past has been partially insane, was found drowned in Van Buskirk's mill pond last Wednesday morning.

It is supposed that he by some means accidentally fell in the pond the night previous, as he was last seen about the premises late that evening.

Alcona County Review, June 8, 1877
Cemetery:

Selves, Frank

FRANK SELVES.

The remains of Frank Selves, also know as Frank Connors, were

brought to Harrisville from Alpena Monday for burial. Selves had been taking baths at Mt. Clemens for inflammatory rheumatism. He came home against the advice of his physicians, who told him he would run a great risk. Instead of stopping in Alpena as they advised he went to McLaughlin's camp, where his wife was cooking. He was taken sick the next day and continued to decline until Sunday when his death occurred. His father-in-law, Mr. Baldwin of Carson City, and A. L. Gow, his brother-in-law, of Harrisville, were with him at the last and they brought the remains to Harrisville.

The funeral services were held Tuesday afternoon at 2 o'clock at the Baptist church, the interment taking place in the family lot at South Harrisville.

Alcona County Review, March 12, 1896
Cemetery: Springport, Alcona Co.

Sepher, Mrs.

ALCONA ATOMS.

Mr. John Bickle's mother-in-law, Mrs. Sepher, died at his residence last week. Rev. Weir, of Black River, officiated at the funeral ceremonies.

Alcona County Review, September 17, 1886
Cemetery:

Setten, Mrs.

ALCONA ATOMS.

Mrs. Setten, aged 70 years, was buried last week. She had been ailing for several years and liable to pass away at any moment.

Alcona County Review, September 17, 1886
Cemetery:

Sharpstein, John

Hunter Savidge Capsized.

The schooner Hunter Savidge, owned by John Mullerwise of Alpena capsized in a sudden squall off Point Aux Barques Sunday afternoon. Mrs. Mullerwise and 6-year old son, the Captain's wife and son and the mate of the boat were lost.

Alcona County Review, August 24, 1899

The schooner Hunter Savidge, which capsized off Point Aux Barques August 19th, has not been found and it is thought the vessel has gone to the bottom, taking with it the bodies of Mrs. Mullerweiss and daughter, of Alpena and Mrs. Capt. Sharpstein.

Alcona County Review, August 31, 1899

Sharpstein, Mrs. Rosa

Hunter Savidge Capsized.

The schooner Hunter Savidge, owned by John Mullerwise of Alpena capsized in a sudden squall off Point Aux Barques Sunday afternoon. Mrs. Mullerwise and 6-year old son, the Captain's wife and son and the mate of the boat were lost.

Alcona County Review, August 24, 1899

The schooner Hunter Savidge, which capsized off Point Aux Barques August 19th, has not been found and it is thought the vessel has gone to the bottom, taking with it the bodies of Mrs. Mullerweiss and daughter, of Alpena and Mrs. Capt. Sharpstein.

Alcona County Review, August 31, 1899
Cemetery:

Shaver, Captain

ALL ALONG THE SHORE.

Alpena Drift.

From the Pioneer.

News was received here early in the week of the death of Capt. Shaver in Detroit on Monday. Capt. Shaver had been suffering from the effects of two strokes of paralysis received while on the Garden City three weeks ago.

Alcona County Review, June 10, 1887
Cemetery:

Shaver, James W.

LOCAL JOTTINGS.

J. W. Shaver, telegraph operator at Alabaster, fell off the dock at that place last Monday night and was drowned in Lake Huron.

Alcona County Review, September 19, 1884
Cemetery: St. Joseph, Iosco Co.

Shaw, David E.

COUNTY JOTTINGS.

Friday afternoon of last week, the dead body of David E. Shaw, formerly a clerk in the First National Bank of Bay City, was found in the woods below Essexville, near the foot of a large tree. He evidentially had sat down to rest and died while doing so, from what cause is unknown. Beside him was found his hat, cane and a copy of the *Bay City Tribune*.

Alcona County Review, July 19, 1878
Cemetery:

Shea, Dennis Henry

Fatally Injured at Camp 9.

The remains of Dennis Shea were brought to Harrisville Tuesday morning for interment in the Catholic cemetery.

The deceased met with a fatal accident Friday afternoon at Camp 8, where he was engaged in moving loaded cars with the aid of a team. While thus employed Shea got caught between the chain and the car and was so badly crushed that internal injuries resulted, from which he died Sunday morning. He was about 51 years of age and unmarried. He was one of eight brothers, all but one of whom were present to follow the remains to their last resting place.

Alcona County Review, August 4, 1892

Card of Thanks.

We desire to express our appreciation of the many acts of kindness that were rendered our late brother during his last hours and burial.

Shea Bros.

West Harrisville, Mich.

Alcona County Review, August 18, 1892

STATE OF MICHIGAN,
County of Alcona.

At a session of the Probate Court for said County, held at the Probate office, in the village of Harrisville, on the 12th day of August, in the year one thousand eight hundred and ninety-two.

Present, Hon. Geo. S. Ritchie, Judge of Probate.

In the matter of the Estate of Dennis Shea:

On reading and filing the petition, duly verified, of John P. Donahue, praying that a certain instrument now on file in this Court, purporting to be the last will and testament of said deceased, may be admitted to probate and that power of administration of said estate may be granted to Jacob Deadman and Michael Nolan, the executors named in said will.

Thereupon it is ordered, that Saturday, the 10th day of September, next, at ten o'clock in the forenoon, be assigned for the hearing of said petition, and that the heirs at law of said deceased, and all other persons interested in said estate, are required to appear at a session of said Court, then to be holden in the Probate office, in the Village of Harrisville and show cause, if any there be, why the prayer of the petitioner should not be granted: And it is further ordered, that said petitioner give notice to the persons interested in said estate, of the pendency of said petition, and the hearing thereof, by causing a copy of this order to be published in the Alcona County Review, a newspaper printed and circulated in said county, 3 successive weeks previous to said day of hearing.

Geo. S. Ritchie,
Judge of Probate.

Alcona County Review, August 18, 1892

HISTORY OF ONE YEAR.

Chronological History of the Past Year, 1892.

August.

1. Dennis Shea died of injuries sustained at camp 8.

Alcona County Review, January 5, 1893

STATE OF MICHIGAN,
County of Alcona.

At a session of the Probate Court for said county, held at the Probate office in the Village of Harrisville, on the 13th day of January, in the year one thousand nine hundred and two. Present W. H. Gilpin, Judge of Probate. In the matter of the estate of Dennis Henry Shea, deceased: On reading and filing the petition, duly verified, of Mary Donhue, praying among other things, that an instrument now on file in this court purporting to be the last will and testament of Dennis Henry Shea and that said will may be probated and that administration of said estate may be granted to Chas. Conklin or some other suitable person.

Thereupon it is ordered, that Monday, the 10th day of February next, at ten o'clock in the forenoon at said Probate office be assigned for the hearing of said petition.

And it is further ordered, that said petitioner give notice to the heirs at law and all other persons interested by causing a copy of this order to be published in the Alcona County Review, a newspaper printed and circulated in said county three successive weeks previous to said day of hearing.

W. H. Gilpin,
Judge of Probate.

Alcona County Review, January 23, 1902
Cemetery: St. Anne's, Alcona Co.

Sheehan, {Girl}

EVENTS OF ONE WEEK.

The infant child of W. B. Sheehan died Tuesday morning and was buried the same day. Its death was not unexpected, for the child had been sick from its birth.

Alcona County Review, November 1, 1894

EVENTS OF ONE WEEK.

We thank our friends and neighbors and especially the school children, for many kindnesses shown us after the death of our little one.
   Mr. and Mrs. W. B. Sheehan.

Alcona County Review, November 1, 1894
Cemetery:

Shell, Alvina
Caledonia.
Mr. and Mrs. Shell lost a little daughter last week.

Alcona County Review, April 27, 1893
Cemetery:

Shelton, Thomas
STATE OF MICHIGAN, County of Alcona.

At a session of the Probate Court for said County, held at the Probate office, in the Village of Harrisville, on the 19th day of August in the year one thousand eight hundred and ninety-five.

Present, C. H. Killmaster, Judge of Probate.

In the matter of the estate of Thomas Shelton, deceased:

On reading and filing the petition, duly verified, of Catherine L. Peck......Thereupon it is ordered, that Tuesday, the fourteenth day of September next, at one o'clock in the afternoon, be assigned for the hearing of said petition, and that the heirs at law of said deceased, and all others interested in said estate, are required to appear at a session of said Court, then to be holden in the Probate office, in the Village of Harrisville, in said County and show cause, if any there be, why the prayer of the petitioner should not be granted: And it is further ordered, that said petitioner give notice to the persons interested in said estate, of the pendency of said petition, and the hearing thereof by causing a copy of this order to be published in the Alcona County Review, a newspaper printed and circulated in said county, three successive weeks previous to said day of hearing.

  C. H. Killmaster,
  Judge of Probate.
  Henry & Pugh, Attorneys for the petitioner.

Alcona County Review, August 22, 1895
Cemetery:

Shepard, {Girl}
COUNTY JOTTINGS.
A little four year old daughter of Wm. C. Shepard, keeper of the poor farm, died very suddenly, Wednesday last. The little one was only sick about two hours. Cause of death unknown.

Alcona County Review, November 1, 1878
Cemetery: Probably Springport, Alcona Co.

Sherman, Mrs. Edwin
Somewhat Personal.

Mrs. F. J. Hill of Black River was suddenly summoned to Brooklyn, N. Y., Saturday, on account of the death of one of her sisters, Mrs. Edwin Sherman.

Alcona County Review, October 29, 1891
Cemetery: Probably Green-Wood, Kings Co. NY

Shields, John C.
Among Our Exchanges

From the Alpena Pioneer:
Judge J. C. Shields of this city is still very ill at the residence of relatives in Fowlerville. The Lansing *Journal* of Monday says of the case: "Dr. C. N. Hayden was summoned by telegram to Fowlerville Friday by a sudden change in the condition of Judge J. C. Shields. Judge Shields had suffered a relapse and is again very sick, but the physician still has hopes that he will recover."

Alcona County Review, April 28, 1892

Somewhat Personal.
Judge Shields of Alpena died Sunday afternoon at Fowlerville, aged 44 years. He earned his title as judge upon his appointment as chief justice of Arizona Territory by President Cleveland in 1885, which office he only held about six months, the Senate refusing to confirm the appointment.

Alcona County Review, May 5, 1892
Cemetery: Mt. Hope, Ingham Co.

Shorter, {Boy}
ALCONA ITEMS.
H. Shorter of Black River buried an infant in our burial ground last week.

Alcona County Review, March 11, 1887
Cemetery: Probably Mt. Joy, Alcona Co.

Shorter, Horace
Grand Marais Cullings.

Horace Shorter, engineer, died Saturday, Sept. 15. He leaves a wife and two children.

Alcona County Review, September 17, 1896
Cemetery:

Sills, William J.
HOME NEWS JOTTINGS.

One day last week Wm. Sills, employed on Gram's tram at Au Sable, was knocked off the tram by a car load of lumber and killed. Mr. Sills was captain of the Ranger base ball club of that place and highly respected. He leaves a wife and several children.

Alcona County Review, October 27, 1882
Cemetery: Pinecrest, Iosco Co.

Silversides, {Child}
An infant child of Mr. and Mrs. Silversides died last night of congestion of the brain.

Alcona County Review, August 27, 1891

The Local News

We wish to extend our sincere and heartfelt thanks to those kind friends who assisted us in so many ways during the illness and death of our little child.
  Mr. and Mrs. W. Silversides.

Alcona County Review, September 3, 1891
Cemetery: Probably Springport, Alcona Co.

Silversides, Clara Noyes [Henning]
Somewhat Personal.

Mrs. Wm. Silversides went to Detroit Monday to undergo an operation for the removal of tumors which had assumed dangerous proportions.

Alcona County Review, December 17, 1891

Somewhat Personal.

Mrs. Silversides will undergo another operation and possibly two, before returning home.

Alcona County Review, December 31, 1891

THE SICK.
Mrs. Silversides is reported very low at Harper's Hospital, and doubts of her being able to reach Harrisville are expressed.

Alcona County Review, February 4, 1892

Somewhat Personal.

Mrs. Silversides, whose malady and trip to Detroit for surgical aid has been noted in these columns, was brought home last Thursday by her husband and passed away one hour after her arrival at their home, surrounded by her family and friends. She had but one desire when she knew that death was certain and that was to see her children. Her last words were, "Now I am satisfied." The funeral services were held at the M. E. church Saturday, the Rev. W. J. Bailey delivering a timely sermon.

Mrs. Clara Silversides, wife of William Silversides, was born in the city of Detroit on the 12th day of May, 1858, and died at her home in Harrisville Thursday night, February 4, 1892, at 8 o'clock. Two brothers and two sisters are living.

Her maiden name was Clara Henning. She married Abraham Noyes in Harrisville on June 27th 1877. Their union was blessed with four children: Bert, Inez, Cleveland and Esther. Mr. Noyes died Nov. 18th, 1882. She was married to her second husband, Wm. Silversides, on the 3d day of July, 1888. Of this union one child lives to mourn the loss of her mother. A few weeks ago she went to Detroit for treatment, but failed to receive any benefit.

Alcona County Review, February 11, 1892

Card of Thanks.

I sincerely thank the friends who so kindly aided in the late illness and death of my beloved wife.

William Silversides.

Alcona County Review, February 11, 1892

The Local News

The will of the late Mrs. Wm. Silversides has been admitted to probate the application has been made for the appointment of Wm. Silversides as administrator of the estate.

Alcona County Review, February 18, 1892

STATE OF MICHIGAN, County of Alcona.

At a session of the Probate Court for said County, held at the Probate office, in the village of Harrisville, on the 13th day of Feb., in the year one thousand eight hundred and ninety-two.

Present, Hon. Geo. S. Ritchie, Judge of Probate.

In the matter of the Estate of Clara Silversides.

On reading and filing the petition, duly verified, of Wm. Silversides praying that a certain instrument now on file in this Court, purporting

to be the last will and testament of said deceased, may be admitted to probate, and that Wm. Silversides or some other suitable person be appointed administrator of said Estate.

Thereupon it is ordered, that Saturday, the 12th day of March, next, at two o'clock in the afternoon, be assigned for the hearing of said petition, and that the heirs at law of said deceased, and all other persons interested in said estate, are required to appear at a session of said Court, then to be holden in the Probate office, in the Village of Harrisville and show cause, if any there be, why the prayer of the petitioner should not be granted: And it is further ordered, that said petitioner give notice to the persons interested in said estate, of the pendency of said petition, and the hearing thereof, by causing a copy of this order to be published in the Alcona County Review, a newspaper printed and circulated in said county three successive weeks previous to said day of hearing.

Geo. S. Ritchie, Judge.

Alcona County Review, February 18, 1892

The Local News.

Judge Ritchie has appointed Wm. Silversides administrator of the estate of the late Clara Silversides.

Alcona County Review, March 17, 1892

STATE OF MICHIGAN, County of Alcona.

Notice is hereby given, that by an order of the Probate Court for the County of Alcona, made on the 14th day of May, A. D. 1892, six months from that date were allowed for creditors to present their claims against the estate of Clara Silversides, late of said county, deceased, and that all creditors of said deceased are required to present their claims to said Probate Court, at the Probate office in the Village of Harrisville, for examination and allowance, on or before the 14th day of May next, and that such claims will be heard before said Court on Saturday, the 2nd day of July, and on Monday, the 14th day of November next, at 10 o'clock in the forenoon of each of those days.

Dated Harrisville, May 14th, A. D. 1892.

Geo. S. Ritchie, Judge of Probate.

Alcona County Review, May 19, 1892

STATE OF MICHIGAN, County of Alcona.

Notice is hereby given, that by an order of the Probate Court for the County of Alcona, made on the 11th day of June, A. D. 1892, six months from that date were allowed for creditors to present their claims against the estate of Clara Silversides, late of said county, deceased, and that all creditors of said deceased are required to present their claims to said Probate Court, at the Probate office in the Village of Harrisville, for examination and allowance, on or before the 21st day of Dec. next, and that such claims will be heard before said Court on Tuesday the 2nd day of August, and on Wednesday, the 21st day of December next, at 10 o'clock in the forenoon of each of those days.

Dated Harrisville, June 11th, A. D. 1892.

Geo. S. Ritchie, Judge of Probate.

Alcona County Review, June 16, 1892

Notice.

I have charge of the furniture of the late Mrs. Clara Silversides and will sell same to any who may desire to purchase. There are also two cows, a set of one horse sleighs, and one set of heavy, single harness. Any one desiring to see these goods can do so by calling at the house.

Wm. Silversides.

Alcona County Review, August 18, 1892

STATE OF MICHIGAN, COUNTY OF ALCONA.

At a session of the Probate Court for said County, held at the Probate office, in the village of Harrisville, on the 26th day of Oct., in the year one thousand eight hundred and ninety-two.

Present, Hon. Geo. S. Ritchie, Judge of Probate.

In the Matter of the estate of Clara Silversides:

On reading and filing the petition, duly verified, of William Silversides, executor of said estate, praying that he be granted a license to sell the real estate of said Clara Silversides, deceased, for the purpose of paying the debts of said estate and expenses of administration, which real estate is described as follows, to-wit: All the real estate situate in the township of Harrisville, county of Alcona and state of Michigan:

Commencing at the S W corner of the Catholic cemetery, running thence in an easterly course along the south boundary fence of said cemetery and in continuation of said fence 26 rods, thence in a southerly direction on a line parallel with the line of road No. 1, or State road, 23 rods; thence westerly on a line parallel with south boundary fence of said Catholic cemetery 26 rods to E side of road No. 1 or State road; thence in a northerly course along E side of said road No. 1, 23 rods to place of beginning, containing about 3 ¾ acres of land and being a part of the S E 1-4 of S E 1-4 of Sec. 14, T 26 N R 9 E. All that certain piece or parcel of land described as follows: Commencing at the 1/8 post on sec. line between secs 13 and 14, Town 26 N R 9 E, running thence W on said 1/8 line to Catholic cemetery, thence southerly along the E line of the land now owned by Clara Noyes; thence easterly along N line of said land of Clara Noyes to said sec. line between said secs. 13 and 14; thence N on said sec line to place of beginning. Commencing at a point in the center of the road leading from the village of Harrisville to Greenbush 8 chains and 39 lks south of sec. line between secs. 12 and 13, T 27 N R 9 E and south of Main street along which said sec line runs; thence S 31 deg 10 min W along the centre of the Greenbush road 2 chs 32 ½ lks; thence N 76 deg W 7 chs 20 lks; thence N 1 deg E 2 chs 14 lks; thence S 88 deg E 4 chs 80 lks being the S boundary line of lands owned formerly by Boardman and Fairchild; thence 1 deg W along W boundary line of Catholic church property 1 ch 15 lks thence S 66 deg east along S boundary line of said Catholic church property 3 chs 35 1-2 lks to the place of beginning, being part of N W 1-4 of N W 1-4 of Sec 13 T 26 N R 9 E.

Thereupon it is ordered, that Saturday, the 19th day of November next, at ten o'clock in the forenoon, be assigned for the hearing of said petition, and that the heirs at law of said deceased, and all other persons interested in said estate, are required to appear at a session of said Court, then to be holden in the probate office, in the village of Harrisville, and show cause, if any there be, why the prayer of the petitioner should not be granted: And it is further ordered, that said petitioner give

notice to the persons interested in said estate, of the pendency of said petition, and the hearing thereof, by causing a copy of this order to be published in the Alcona County Review, a newspaper printed and circulated in said county, 3 successive weeks previous to said day of hearing.
GEORGE S. RITCHIE,
Judge of Probate.
Alcona County Review, October 27, 1892

HISTORY OF ONE YEAR.

Chronological History of the Past Year, 1892.

THE DEATH RECORD.
Feb. 4. Mrs. Clara Silversides.
Alcona County Review, January 5, 1893

EVENTS OF ONE WEEK.

The real estate of the Clara Silversides estate was sold at auction on Saturday as per advertisement. The property adjoining the Catholic cemetery was knocked down to O. H. Smith for $225. It consists of a house, and five acres of ground. The dwelling in Harrisville village was bid in for Albert Noyes, a minor son of the late Abram Noyes, who holds a first mortgage on the property.
Alcona County Review, January 19, 1893

South Harrisville, Oct. 18.
A few improvements of late are noticeable at the S. Harrisville cemetery.

Wm. H. Anderson has a fine monument placed at the head of his children's graves, also Wm. Silversides to the memory of his wife and Mrs. Fowler of Killmaster in memory of her husband.

Each of the three former have their plots raised and graveled. All show forth the love still cherished for those they have committed to their Creator.
Alcona County Review, October 19, 1893
Cemetery: Springport, Alcona Co.

Silverthorn, Caroline S. [Zwirk]
Another Pioneer Gone.
In the death of Caroline S., beloved wife of Perley Silverthorn, living in Alcona township, which occurred Wednesday morning, the county loses another of its faithful pioneers, who had been a resident in the county for upwards of 27 years. Mrs. Silverthorn was born in Germany in the year 1832, and removed to this

country with her parents in her young girlhood, locating at East Saginaw. In 1855 she became acquainted with and was married to Perley Silverthorn, who was conducting fishing operations in the vicinity of Sturgeon point. Removing immediately to this county after marriage, where she has since resided, truly it may be said of her, "She has done what she could" to advance civilization and contribute to the prosperity of Alcona county. During the past two years she had been confined to her home by sickness, during the last twelve months of which time her condition being that of helplessness, gradually growing weaker and weaker until death came to her relief. She bore her affliction, however, with Christian fortitude and non-complaint, and was prepared to go when the Savior called her to the heavenly rest. She was aged 49 years and 11 months, and leaves a husband and five children to mourn her demise.
Alcona County Review, June 9, 1882

Haynes, Nov. 29.--Mr. Silverthorn has caused to be erected a monument to the memory of his wife and two children which I think is the tastiest in the cemetery.
Alcona County Review, December 1, 1892
Cemetery: Mt. Joy, Alcona Co.

Silverthorn, Helen W. Griswold [Birch]
The Skamokawa, (Wash.) Eagle of the 14th inst., contains an account of the death of Mrs. Helen W. Silverthorn, otherwise Mrs. Griswold, until recently a resident of Haynes Township. Deceased leaves many relatives in this vicinity. She had been in poor health for some time and under her physician's advice she went to Washington about two weeks prior to her death, which occurred on the 9th inst. She was a native of Steuben county, N. Y. and was born in 1833.
Alcona County Review, May 21, 1896
Cemetery:

Silverthorn, Mabel
PURELY PERSONAL.

Mr. and Mrs. Daniel Holst, daughter Clara, and son, Walter, and the Misses Jennie and Mabel Silverthorn, all of East Saginaw, are

guests of A. Silverthorn at Sturgeon Pointe.

Alcona County Review, August 2, 1889

LOCAL JOTTINGS.

Miss Mabel Silverthorn, sister of A. Silverthorn, and daughter of Perley Silverthorn, who arrived this week on a visit to her brother at Sturgeon Pointe, died Tuesday afternoon of inflammation of the lungs, aged 14 years. The young lady had been ill for some time but it was not thought that she was so seriously ill as she appears to have been, and it is supposed that the trip from Saginaw exhausted the little vitality that remained. Her remains were buried Thursday.

Alcona County Review, August 2, 1889

PURELY PERSONAL.

Mr. and Mrs. Wm. Kramer and Miss Jennie Silverthorn, all of East Saginaw, attended the funeral of the latter's sister, Miss Mabel Silverthorn, last week Thursday. Miss Jennie Silverthorn will visit here for a short time before returning to Saginaw.

Alcona County Review, August 9, 1889

Card of Thanks.—We wish to thank our friends who rendered such kind and timely assistance to us during the last illness and death of our child.

P. Silverthorn and Family.

Alcona County Review, August 9, 1889

Mr. Silverthorn has caused to be erected a monument to the memory of his wife and two children which I think is the tastiest in the cemetery.

Alcona County Review, December 1, 1892
Cemetery: Mt. Joy, Alcona Co.

Simons, Mary Jane

Curtis Items.

Mr. and Mrs. Trume Simons have lost their daughter, aged about 2 ½ years. Death entered their home and took the little flower from them, but the Lord giveth and the Lord taketh away, blessed be the name of the Lord.

Curtis, Feb. 11, 1895.

Alcona County Review, February 14, 1895

CURTISVILLE.

April 30, 1903.
Hugh Curley and Truman Simons each had a tombstone placed in his family lot in the cemetery, the former

for his wife and Mr. Simons for his little daughter.

Alcona County Review, April 14, 1902
Cemetery: Curtisville, Alcona Co.

Sims, Adeline [Whiting]

JOTTINGS ALONG THE SHORE.

The wife of Capt. Wm. Sims, keeper of the range lights at Presque Isle, died on Monday of last week.

Alcona County Review, April 22, 1881
Cemetery: Range Light Park, Presque Isle Co.

Sinclair, {Boy}

PERSONAL.

Infant son of Mr. and Mrs. Charles Sinclair died Wednesday, June 9th.

Alcona County Review, June 17, 1897
Cemetery:

Sinclair, Mrs. Katie

THE GRIM REAPER.

Mrs. Sinclair, the aged mother of Mrs. Geo. Ward, Jr., died at the residence of her daughter at noon yesterday, aged 80 years. Death was due to an attack of inflammation of the lungs and the infirmities of age. The funeral services will be held Saturday at 2 o'clock from the house.

Alcona County Review, January 20, 1898

PERSONAL.

Mrs. McDermaid of Grand Marais is expected tomorrow for the funeral of her mother, Mrs. Sinclair.

Alcona County Review, January 20, 1898

LOCAL PICK UPS.

Geo. Ward came down from the woods to attend the funeral of his wife's mother.

Alcona County Review, January 20, 1898

PERSONAL.

Geo. Ward Jr. returned to the woods Monday and expects to remain until spring.

Alcona County Review, January 27, 1898

PERSONAL.

Niel Turner was called down from Presque Isle county by the death of Mrs. Sinclair.

Alcona County Review, January 27, 1898

PERSONAL.

Mrs. Duncan McDermaid, daughter of Mrs. Sinclair, was

summoned from Grand Marais by the death of her mother. She arrived Friday evening last. This week she received a dispatch to return at once on account of sickness in the family at Grand Marais.

Alcona County Review, January 27, 1898

LOCAL PICK UPS.

Many hearts were heavy and sad in Harrisville Friday last, Jan. 21. The mortal remains of three persons, one an infant, two in the autumn of life's journey, were borne to their final resting places. The remains of Mrs. Harriet S. Taft were buried in the morning, those of Mrs. Sinclair and the little son of Edw. Saylor at different hours in the afternoon. Services in each case were held at the residences. Three funerals in one day in a town the size of Harrisville is a sad and unusual occurrence.

Alcona County Review, January 27, 1898

IN MEMORIAM.
MOTHER.

My dear friends and children, I leave you awhile
In this land of probation to labor and toil;
How soon you may follow no mortal can tell,
Prepare then for heaven and all will be well.
I Leave this world without a tear,
Save for the friends I held so dear;
To heal their sorrow, Lord descend
And to the friendless prove a friend.

Alcona County Review, January 27, 1898

Our friends will please accept our sincere thanks for numerous acts of kindness shown us during our late bereavement. We especially thank the Lady Maccabees.

Mrs. Geo. Ward, Jr.

Alcona County Review, January 27, 1898

Local History of One Year

Chronology of the Principal Events of the Year 1898.

January 19. Deaths: Mrs. Harriett Taft aged 62; Mrs. Sinclair aged 80; Willie Saylor aged 4. Two infants.

Alcona County Review, January 5, 1899
Cemetery: Probably Springport, Alcona Co.

Sing, Wah

FROM OUR EXCHANGES.

Wah Sing, Alpena's only Chinese laundryman has committed suicide.

Alcona County Review, August 5, 1897
Cemetery:

Skuse, Anna [McDonald]

The condition of Mrs. Thos. Skuse, who has been ill for some time, is very serious.

Alcona County Review, September 23, 1897

EVENTS OF ONE WEEK.

Mrs. Thos. Skuse, whose serious illness was noted last week, passed away at her late home on Saturday at 2:30 p.m. The cause of death was cancer of the stomach. The interment took place Monday morning in the Catholic cemetery, whither the remains were followed by a large number of the friends and neighbors of the family.

Deceased was a native of Canada and was 55 years of age. Her husband alone survives her, as there are no children.

Mr. Skuse expresses a deep sense of gratitude to the friends for their sympathy and assistance in his bereavement.

Alcona County Review, September 30, 1897

Order of Hearing.
Nov. 11--Dec. 2, 97.
STATE OF MICHIGAN, County of Alcona.

At a session of the Probate Court for said County, held at the Probate office, in the Village of Harrisville, on the ninth day of November in the year one thousand eight hundred and ninety-seven.

Present, Hon. W. H. Gilpin, Judge of Probate.

In the matter of the estate of Annie Skuse, deceased.

On reading and filing the petition duly verified of Thomas Skuse, praying that a certain instrument now on file in this court, purporting to be the last will and testament of said deceased, may be admitted to probate and that Thomas Skuse be appointed executor of said last will and testament.

Thereupon it is ordered, that Monday, the 6th day of December next, at ten o'clock in the forenoon, be assigned for the hearing of said petition, and that the executor ....heirs at law of said deceased and all other persons interested in said estate, are required to appear at a session of the Probate Court, then to be holden at the Probate office, in the Village of Harrisville and show cause, if any there be, why the prayer of the petitioner should not be granted.

And it is further ordered that the petitioner give notice to the heirs at law and all persons interested in said estate, of the pendency of said petition, and the hearing thereof, by causing a copy of this order to be published in the Alcona County Review, a newspaper printed and circulating in said county three successive weeks previous to said day of hearing.

W. H. Gilpin,
Judge of Probate.

Alcona County Review, November 11, 1897
Cemetery: St. Anne's, Alcona Co.

Slaght, Andrew D.

Once more, in the death of Andrew D. Slaght, the community is reminded that in the midst of life we are in death. Here was a man of apparent robust health and vigorous constitution who ten minutes—one minute—before the ruthless hand of death was laid upon him, had every prospect of living many years yet to give comfort and counsel to his family and the benefit of a useful life to the community. How rapidly the ranks of the old pioneers of this county are thinning. One by one they are going to their several rewards. It is a constant reminder to the living to so live that they be found ready to answer the summons and to receive the blessing: "Well done, good and faithful servant; enter thou into the joy of thy Lord."

Alcona County Review, January 9, 1896

Sudden Death of A. D. Slaght.

A. D. Slaght ate a hearty dinner Monday and pushed back from the table and died in his chair without a moment's warning that death was at hand.

His death, like all sudden deaths, was a shock to the community and to his family.

Deceased was, generally speaking, a man of vigorous constitution, although for a few months past he had complained of not feeling like himself.

He was one of Harrisville township's foremost citizens and his death is a public loss.

The funeral occurs today, the services being held at West Harrisville, from whence the remains will be borne to Springport for interment.

Our Gustin correspondent sends up the following data: Deceased was born in Hartford, Canada, in 1835. At age of 12 he removed to Norfolk Co., Can., where he lived until 1880, when he moved to Michigan. He was the father of 10 children, eight of whom are still living. Jobe is in California, Lesley in Seattle and Charles in Simcoe, Ont. Three daughters, Carrie, Maggie and Eva and two sons, Richard and William, and the wife and mother are at home to bear the heavy burden of grief and sorrow. Deceased sympathized with the Baptist belief; he was an Odd Fellow and an Orangeman. Funeral this morning at 10.

Alcona County Review, January 9, 1896

We heartily thank our friends for their kindness and welcome sympathy in the hour of our great sorrow. That their reward may be proportionate to their kindness to us is our earnest wish.

Mrs. Elizabeth Slaght and Family.

Alcona County Review, January 16, 1896
Cemetery: Springport, Alcona Co.

Slaght, Frederick W.

ALPENA DRIFT.

T. W. Slaght, of the photographic firm of Nicholson & Slaght, died at his late home in Alpena, last week. The remains were taken to Flint for burial. The deceased leaves a wife and two children.

Alcona County Review, December 31, 1886
Cemetery: Probably Evergreen, Genesee Co.

Slater, James M.

Haynes Happenings.

April 28, 1896.

The remains of James M. Slater were interred in Mount Joy cemetery today. He was aged 65 years. He was injured years ago by being run over by a run away horse, which left him with St. Vitus dance from which he was a great sufferer. The Rev. Long preached the funeral sermon and the mortal remains were taken to their last resting place in Mayo's beautiful hearse followed by the relatives and friends of the deceased.

Alcona County Review, April 30, 1896
Cemetery: Mt. Joy, Alcona Co.

Slater, James N.

THE GRIM REAPER.

Mr. and Mrs. Slater of Haynes buried an infant child yesterday.

Alcona County Review, January 20, 1898

January 19. Deaths: Mrs. Harriett
Taft aged 62; Mrs. Sinclair aged 80;
Willie Saylor aged 4. Two infants.

Alcona County Review, January 5, 1899
Cemetery: West Lawn, Alcona Co.

Sloan, Mrs. Elizabeth

The Local News.

Mrs. Alex Sloane, wife of a
blacksmith at Black River, was buried
in the cemetery West of town on
Monday. Her death was caused by la
grippe. She leaves three small
children besides her husband. A large
number of friends followed the
remains to the grave from Black
River. The funeral services were
conducted by the Rev. L. Hazard.

Alcona County Review, April 2, 1891
Cemetery: West Lawn, Alcona Co.

Smith, Angus

KILLED BY MISTAKE.

Angus Smith of Harrisville Mistaken for a Bear and Shot by a Comrade.

All Efforts to Save His Life Unavailing—He Died Monday Morning.

Last Saturday our citizens were
somewhat shocked by receiving a
telegram from Otsego Lake, to the
effect that Angus Smith of Harrisville
had been accidentally shot there, and
was lying in a critical condition—no
particulars being given—and
Monday the second dispatch was
received announcing his death. Mr.
Smith was a young man of about 27
years, and was formerly from Canada.
He had been a resident of this county
for a number of years past—being in
the employ of various parties in the
vicinity of Harrisville and
Greenbush—and was familiarly
known and respected by many of our
citizens. We believe he has no
relatives in the county, but he leaves a
large circle of friends to mourn his
untimely decease. The full particulars
of the sad affair, as chronicled in the
Bay City *Daily Tribune* of Tuesday
morning, are as follows:

"On Friday night last Angus Smith
of Harrisville and a Mr. Leonard, of
Detroit, who have been looking over
some land in Otsego county, pitched
their tent in some woods near Otsego
Lake, and being very tired were soon
wrapped in slumber. The night was
very chilly, and early Saturday
morning Mr. Smith awoke, shivering
with cold. He moved outside the tent
without the knowledge of Mr.
Leonard and commenced gathering
together chips for the purpose of
building a fire. All of a sudden Mr.
Leonard was aroused from his sleep,
and peering through the tent door,
observed a dark object moving
around in the darkness, a few paces
from the tent. His first impulse was
that it was a bear and without
waiting for a moment, grasped his
revolver and leveling it at the
supposed bear, fired. The pistol had
been well aimed and the bullet struck
the mark for which it was intended,
entering Smith's abdomen just above
the right hip. The wounded man
uttered a shriek and fell over. Mr.
Leonard was terrified and could not
speak.—Had he made such a
mistake? Yes, it was too true, he had
mistaken Mr. Smith for a bear, and
had driven the fatal bullet deep into
his body.

Mr. Smith was instantly removed
to Brink's Hotel at Otsego Lake,
where every effort was made to make
him comfortable. On Sunday
afternoon he began to show signs of
suffering intense pain, and that
evening a dispatch was sent to this
city summoning Dr. W. E. Vaughan.
A special engine was provided to
convey him thither, but the iron
horse, though under an extra
pressure of steam, arrived too late,
Mr. Smith dying yesterday morning
at one o'clock. The affair creates a
great deal of excitement at Otsego
Lake, and though Mr. Leonard is
censured for carelessness, he is
believed to have done the deed
entirely accidentally."

The remains of Mr. Smith were
interred at Otsego Lake.

Alcona County Review, September 19, 1879

The True Story Concerning the Shooting of Angus Smith of Harrisville.

We extract the following from the
local columns of the Otsego County
Herald of last week:

"A Mr. Leonard, of Detroit, with
two men were engaged in estimating
pine land for the Hon. Wm. Dodge, of
New York. They had pitched their tent
about 10 ½ miles east of Otsego Lake
and commenced their work. The party
consisted of W. B Leonard, of Detroit,
Angus Smith, of Harrisville, and Wm.
Dessereau, of Cheboygan. Dessereau
acted as cook for the party and his
business was to cut the wood and fix
the fires and keep the camp in order,
and prepare the meals for the rest of
the party. It was his special duty to
keep fires at night. Leonard and Smith
had been doing a hard day's work and
returned to camp late at night, ate
their supper and retired as usual.
Leonard on the right, Smith on the
left, and Dessereau in the middle.
Smith awoke during the night and
notwithstanding it was Dessereau's
business to keep the fire, Smith
thought he would not disturb them,
but get up and fix the fire himself. He
was on his hands and knees and with a
piece of bark was scraping the cinders
together. The evening previous the
cook had buried a pail of pork and
beans in the warm cinders to bake.
Leonard hearing the scratching sound
supposing it to be a wild animal,
having met with a similar experience
last June, immediately seized his
revolver and fired in the direction of
the sound. Immediately following the
discharge was heard the cry Oh! Oh!
I'm shot! Leonard said 'for God's
sake Angus is it you?' Smith said 'yes,
how could you make such a mistake?'
Leonard said 'I thought it was a bear;
what were you doing?' He said 'I was
trying to fix the fire.' Leonard then
said, 'Smith, do you blame me?'
Smith said 'no, Leonard, but how
could you make such a mistake?' This
was about 3 o'clock a.m. Dessereau
was at once dispatched to Louk's
camp, four miles distant, for a team,
and when he returned, the wounded
man was taken to Brink's Hotel, at
Otsego Lake. At this time he was able
to walk to the wagon and get into it
without assistance. On arriving at
Otsego Lake Drs. Warner, Robinson
and Gilbert were summoned. The two
former remained with the wounded
man for six hours. Sunday afternoon
Dr. Gilbert notified his friends that he
thought he could not live and after
consultation a special train was
ordered and Drs. Vaugn and Curry, of
Bay City, were brought up to Otsego

Lake. They were too late to render any assistance, as the man had been dead some time when they arrived. They gave their opinion that the best medical skill in the world could not have saved his life.

Mr. Smith remained conscious up to within three hours of his death, and his thoughts were with his brothers and mother; and said to a lady with whom he had lived, 'Tell my mother I loved her.' He exonerated Leonard from all blame in the matter, and gave special directions about the disposal of his property. Mr. Smith has two brothers, one residing in Walton, Ont., and one in East Saginaw. Mr. Leonard has the sympathy of the entire community, and no blame is attached to him by any one cognizant of the facts. He knew Dessereau kept the fires in order and at that time D. was by his side and thought of course the noise was made by some animal; and Leonard acted on that supposition with fatal result. The ball struck Smith just below and little to the right of the spinal column, passed through the pelvis and struck against the inner front of the hip, glanced thence through the neck of the bladder and through the liver towards the chest, causing peritonitus. Everything was done that could be to alleviate his suffering and make him comfortable, but no avail. It is simply a sad and unfortunate affair. On account of decomposition taking place so rapidly, Mr. Leonard, on advice of the physicians, had his remains interred in the Otsego Lake cemetery on Monday afternoon. Smith was well known in Otsego Lake by many persons, who all testify to his good moral character, genial disposition and sober and industrious habits. 'Verily, in the midst of life we are in death.'

Alcona County Review, September 26, 1879

Resolutions of Condolence.

Officers and Brothers of Harrisville Lodge No. 218, I. O. of O. F., your Committee to whom was assigned the duty of reporting resolutions of condolence on the death of our Bro. Angus Smith, beg to report the following:

Whereas, It has come to the knowledge of the Lodge that Bro. Angus Smith was accidentally shot by his companion whilst engaged in his business of examining and locating lands near Petoskey, in this State;

And Whereas, This Lodge has investigated, as best it could, from its remoteness from the place where the sad event occurred, the causes which occasioned this most sorrowful occurrence that has so suddenly deprived it of a respected Brother and companion, which they as brothers were in duty bound to do; those the facts elicited from persons near the place, as reported by the press, those causes are believed to have been accidental, and not the purpose of any one.

Therefore be it resolved, That the Charter of our Lodge be draped in mourning during a period of ninety days, as a memorial of our deceased Brother and of our kindly remembrance of his departed worth as a member of our Lodge so suddenly bereaved.

And be it Further Resolved, That we extend to the relatives of our deceased Brother, our sincere sympathy for their great loss from their family circle, one for whom our warm regards as Brothers, and high esteem as friends, had been pledged for all time of such relationship coupled with our sincere regrets that we were unable as Brothers to extend to our dying companion, in the hour of his greatest extremity, those friendly attentions of our Brotherhood to which he was entitled, by our united pledges, to fulfill all the claims of Friendship, Love and Truth.

Resolved, That these resolutions be recorded upon our Records and published in the Alcona County Review, and a copy thereof sent to the nearest relative of the deceased. Respectfully submitted,
C. P. Reynolds,
Committee on Resolutions.

Alcona County Review, December 26, 1879
Cemetery:

Smith, Arthur

Killed by a Falling Tree.

A young man named Smith, whose first name is reported as Arthur, was killed Wednesday at Dave Nevin's camp by a tree that was blown down in the heavy gale of that day.

Alcona County Review, September 9, 1887
Cemetery:

Smith, Fred

Alcona County Review, September 10, 1886
Cemetery:

Smith, George E.

Your Folks and Our Folks.

Geo. E. Smith, an Au Sable business man, accomplished self destruction last week by the morphine route. The fact that he had taken poison was discovered about two hours after the deadly drug had been swallowed. Dr. Hovis attempted to neutralize the effects of the poison, but all attempts to force antidotes down Smith's throat were successfully resisted by him. He announced his determination to kill himself and if not successful then would accomplish self destruction at another time. He was successful however, and expired the following day. The day before he took the fatal dose he had executed a will in the National hotel leaving all his property to his wife. His estate is valued at $15,000. No reason was given for his act.

Alcona County Review, February 19, 1891
Cemetery:

Smith, Hattie

Miss Hattie Smith, of Mikado, age 20 years, who has been sick for some time with an abcess, died Monday, her funeral taking place Tuesday, after which her remains were interred in the Oscoda cemetery.—Monitor.

Alcona County Review, August 3, 1893
Cemetery: Pinecrest, Iosco Co.

Smith, Henry Herbert

GREENBUSH GETTINGS.

H. H. Smith is sinking fast. Very little hopes are entertained by his physician of his recovery.

Alcona County Review, April 16, 1886

GREENBUSH GETTINGS.

OBITUARY

We regret to report the death, from a disease of a very malignant type, of H. H. Smith, which occurred at 1:30 p.m. on Saturday, April 17, 1886, at the age of 64 years. His body was interred in the Harrisville cemetery, Sunday afternoon, April 18. Henry Herbert Smith was born at Balston Springs, Saratoga Co., N. Y., August, 1822. His father died when deceased was but four years of age leaving a family of children under care of their mother. By the time he had attained his majority he had learned the trade of mill-wright with his brothers, Gideon and Thomas, the latter of whom is now the only surviving member of the family, and employed in Hilbert's car works, Green Island, Albany Co., N. Y., where he at present resides. On the 29th of June, 1867, deceased was united in marriage with Mary J. Huntley, daughter of Gilbert E. and Margaret Huntley, of West Troy, Albany Co., N. Y., now Greenbush, Rensselaer Co., N. Y. The late H. H. Smith was lumber and timber inspector for nearly 40 years, and during the greater part of the time in the employ of Mors & Co., formerly Mors, Weaver & McDougall, of West Troy, Albany and Buffalo, respectively. He was a member of West Troy Fire Department for eighteen years, and during part of the time foreman of the same. His certificate of honorable discharge has been submitted to the writer for examination. Deceased was a resident of Tonawanda, N. Y., for five years and in 1873 came to Greenbush, Alcona Co., Mich., where he built the mill now owned by J. Van Buskirk. He filled the office of town treasurer for two years, and also town clerk for two years, to which latter office he was re-elected April 5th, which day was the last time he was able to leave his house. Deceased was a man of great energy and ability; an educated and industrious citizen and a fond and provident husband. For the last few years he was a great sufferer, but his end was peaceful and he calmly sank to rest.

His loss will be felt by all; but to his disconsolate widow his loss is irreparable, and to her the deepest sympathy of her many friends is extended. The funeral was largely attended by friends from Greenbush, Harrisville and surrounding country.

Alcona County Review, April 23, 1886

LOCAL JOTTINGS.

Greenbush township was to vote for a new township clerk, yesterday, in place of H. H. Smith, deceased; also for justices of the peace to fill vacancies. We could not learn the result in time for this issue of the Review.

Alcona County Review, May 7, 1886
Cemetery: Probably Springport, Alcona Co.

Smith, James
NEIGHBORHOOD NOTES.

Jas. Smith, a river driver aged 20, was drowned on the north branch of the Au Sable river last week.

Alcona County Review, August 16, 1889
Cemetery:

Smith, Lenbly
Our Neighbors.

John Fuller of Pt. Hope didn't know it was loaded and last Wednesday fatally shot his friend Lendley Smith with a 38 caliber revolver.

Alcona County Review, October 25, 1889
Cemetery: Gore Township, Huron Co.

Smith, Margaret Jane [Roash]
A Horrible Accident.

A BLACK RIVER LADY CRUSHED UNDER AN ENGINE.

Tried to Cross the Track on a Wheel ahead of a Moving Engine.

MRS. C. C. SMITH THE VICTIM.

Coroner's Jury Finds That Her Death Was Accidental. No One Blamed.

Mr. and Mrs. C. C. Smith of Black River had arranged to go to Killmaster Saturday for the day. They were to take the morning express to Gustin, then across by wheel. Preparation for a pleasant day.

How horribly their plans were disarranged is now known to a majority of the readers of the Review, and seldom indeed have the sensibilities of the people of this community been so rudely shocked as when the horrid details of the awful death of Mrs. Smith became known.

The passenger train had pulled in at the Black River depot. Mr. Smith was already at the station, and Mrs. Smith, somewhat delayed in her preparations, was speeding along the walk on her wheel to catch the train. Her route lay across a spur track leading to the north pier. A yard engine with long projecting reach such as is found on timber train engines, was backing down upon the crossing at the same moment. One report states that the engineer, Wm. Foster, saw Mrs. Smith approaching and recognizing the danger, slowed down for her to pass; at the same moment she seemed to check her speed as if waiting for the engine to pass. Then as if guided by a common impulse and the relentless hand of fate, both started forward, and in less time that it takes to tell it the awful tragedy was completed: the life of Mrs. Smith was blotted out and her family was robbed forever of the light of her countenance and the benefit of her counsel.

The accident is due to the projecting reach which caught the rear wheel of Mrs. Smith's bicycle throwing her to the ground in front of the moving engine. Mrs. Smith threw up her hands and screamed as she realized her awful position. The engineer reversed his engine, but too late. It was stopped in its own length, but there underneath the ponderous trucks, crushed, mangled and bruised, lay the lifeless form of Mrs. Smith, but a moment before buoyant with life and hope.

Engineer Foster was wholly unmanned by the shocking accident and wept like a child, though innocent of blame.

Black River was thrown into a fever of excitement at once. The news spread like wild-fire and a large crowd quickly gathered while the work of extricating the body was in progress. To do this the engine had to be hoisted.

Mr. Smith was at once apprised of the sad tragedy, and friends did what they could to break the force of the calamity that had fallen upon him with crushing weight.

The body was removed to the family residence and the cruel lacerations were attended to by local physicians.

Death came very quickly to the unfortunate woman and her sufferings were of short duration.

Mrs. Smith was a member of the Catholic church, and the funeral and burial service, which occurred Monday, conformed to the service of that church. The interment was at Harrisville.

Besides her husband, Mrs. Smith leaves two boys aged 3 and 13, and 3 girls of 5, 8 and 11 years respectively.

Mr. Smith attached the blame for the accident to the railroad company through its employees. To fix the responsibility, if any existed, it was decided that an inquest must be held, and accordingly Coroner Chas. Mayo was summoned from Harrisville. A. E. Sharpe, attorney for the D. & M. came up from Tawas on a special to look after the company's interest. A jury was impaneled comprising the following six gentlemen. Robt. Larrett, Wm. Houghton, W. R. Smith, Sam Hill, Henry Clinton and J. Rasch. They viewed the body and then as Mr. Smith desired to retain an attorney, as no one could reach Black River until late in the afternoon, it was decided to adjourn the inquest until Tuesday morning.

THE INQUEST.

The inquest disclosed facts considerably at variance with the foregoing which is the current report. While the projecting reach may have blocked Mrs. Smith's way and would be the direct responsible cause of her death if such was the case, yet the evidence is conclusive that the reach did not catch her wheel, but proves that she dismounted before she could have reached it.

H. K. Gustin appeared for Mr. Smith.

Alice McGregor testified: Was on the opposite side of switch track from direction Mrs. Smith was approaching. Saw her coming on wheel. Heard engine coming and watched to see if she would get off wheel. Got excited, noticed nothing further until I saw her under engine. Did not see when or how engine struck her.

Wm. Foster, engineer of No. 17. I was backing down on north pier; had tank on. When reached crossing the fireman said, "stop her as quick as you can." I put on brakes and reversed engine and stopped here quick as possible. I was on west side engine, did not see Mrs. Smith. Was running about 4 miles an hour. When engine stopped Mrs. Smith was under pilot. Engine had to be jacked up to get her out.

Chas. Neubert, fireman on No. 17. I was ringing bell as we approached crossing. Was facing east, saw Mrs. Smith coming on wheel rapidly, told engineer to stop engine when I saw she intended to cross. She was then about 20 feet from track, and tank of engine was just going on plank in road. She was still on wheel when she passed out of sight behind tank. Did not see when she was struck, did not see her look toward engine, she was going faster than engine. Saw bicycle as engine passed over it.

Ray Beede, aged 12. Saw accident. Was on walk east of track. Mrs. Smith rang bell and passed on wheel. Engine was coming and I thought she would jump off, but she kept on and dismounted on the track on left side of wheel towards engine and was on her feet when she was struck; her feet caught under engine; then I saw her under engine. She was on side of reach toward me; she threw up her hands to catch something and screamed; she nearly caught the chain with one hand. Heard engine bell ringing and saw fireman in window. Reach did not strike bicycle.

Peter La Flame, aged 17, and Peter Lassard, aged 15, also saw the accident and their testimony corroborated that of Beede.

The jury returned a verdict that death was accidental and attached no blame to anyone.

Alcona County Review, June 9, 1898

KILLMASTER RIPPLES.

Killmaster people were very sorry to hear of the tragic death of Mrs. C. C. Smith.

Alcona County Review, June 9, 1898

I would be remiss in my duty if I failed to recognize the kindness and sympathy that have been shown me since the death of my wife. I appreciate it all and thank my friends sincerely.

C. C. Smith.

Alcona County Review, June 16, 1898

STATE OF MICHIGAN, County of Alcona.

At a session of the Probate Court for said county, held at the Probate office, in the

village of Harrisville, on the 25th day of August in the year one thousand eight hundred and ninety-eight.

Present, Hon. Wm. H. Gilpin, Probate Judge.

In the matter of the estate of Margaret Smith.

On reading and filing the petition, duly verified, of Christopher C. Smith, praying that the administration of said estate be granted to Christopher C. Smith or some other suitable person, etc.

Thereupon it is ordered that Saturday the 24th day of September next, at 10 o'clock in the forenoon, be assigned for the hearing of said petition, and that the heirs at law of said deceased, and all other persons interested in said estate, are required to appear at a session of said court, then to be holden at the Probate office, in the village of Harrisville, and show cause, if any there be, why the prayer of the petitioner should not be granted: and it is further ordered that said petitioner give notice to the persons interested in said estate, of the pendency of said petition, and the hearing thereof, by causing a copy of this order to be published in the "Alcona County Review" a newspaper printed and circulated in said county, three successive weeks previous to said day of hearing.

Wm. H. Gilpin,
Judge of Probate.

Alcona County Review, September 1, 1898

Local History of One Year

Chronology of the Principal Events of the Year 1898.

June 4. Horrible death of Mrs. C. C. Smith at Black River. Run down by a switch engine as she was crossing the track on a bicycle.

Alcona County Review, January 5, 1899

The NEWS

The case of C. C. Smith, guardian, vs. the D. & M. R. R. is on for trial today. This is a suit for damages on account of the killing of Mrs. C. C. Smith in 1898. She was run over by a switch engine at Black River.

Alcona County Review, April 9, 1903

$6,000 DAMAGES.

Jury Finds that Amount Against D. & M. R. R. for the killing of Mrs. C. C. Smith.

The trial of the case of Christopher C. Smith, administrator, against the Detroit & Mackinac Railway

Company, occupied three days of the circuit court last week, being given to the jury Saturday afternoon.

Readers of the Review will well remember the accident by which Mrs. Smith lost her life. On June 4, 1898, she and her husband had arranged to spend the day at Killmaster, where Mr. Smith was operating a shingle mill. They were to take the 7:10 passenger train to Gustin and from there wheel across. Mr. Smith was at the depot when it was time for the train to depart, but Mrs. Smith had been delayed and was some distance away on her bicycle when the bell began to ring for the departure of the train. At Mr. Smith's request the conductor held the train and the husband motioned to Mrs. Smith to hurry. Her path was a three foot sidewalk which crossed a spur of the road leading down to the north pier, where the long timber trains dumped their loads into Lake Huron. As Mrs. Smith was hurrying to catch the passenger a switch engine, with a long reach projecting was backing down across the road on this spur. The two met at the point of crossing and the unfortunate woman's life was crushed out underneath the engine. The conditions were such that those standing at the passenger train landing could not see the switch engine, their view being obstructed by the depot.

The defense was that there was contributory negligence on the part of Mrs. Smith; that under the general law in such cases she should have dismounted from her wheel, could have "stopped and looked and listened." If she had done so there would have been no accident. That if the projecting reach caused her to dismount, the railway company was not at fault for that was not an unusual condition; that reaches were a necessity in handling long timber trains and that Mrs. Smith as the wife of a man who had been master mechanic of the road and whose yard was in plain view of the road, was perfectly familiar with these reaches and the way they were handled. That whether or not the reach was there and Mrs. Smith thought she could cross in safety, she had no right to race with death in this way and the railway company was not at fault. That the switch engine bell was

ringing and that every precaution required by law was taken by the defendant in crossing the highway at the time of the accident.

The prosecution claimed in part that the switch engine had no right to cross the highway at all while the passenger train was at the depot, because people were going to and from the depot at that time upon the invitation of the defendant. If it had the right to cross, it had no right to have the long reach projecting and no watchman on the rear of the tank. The reach should have been detached and left with the train. That the engine was going at high rate of speed as shown by the distance it slid on the rails after the application of the brakes. That even if Mrs. Smith had looked in the direction of the engine her view would have been obstructed, in part at least, by a high pile of bolts that was piled near the track south of the highway, and she could not have had a full view of the track until within about 30 feet of the crossing. That the ringing of the bells on both the passenger and switch engine was confusing and deceased had a right to assume that defendant would do nothing to endanger her safe passage to the depot.

The railway company was represented by John Weadock of Bay City and C. R. Henry of Alpena, and Devere Hall of Bay City and H. K. Gustin of Alpena appeared for Mr. Smith.

The case was given to the jury Saturday afternoon and at 8 o'clock Sunday morning they returned a verdict of $6,000 for Smith. Eighty days were given in which to prepare a bill of exceptions and the case will undoubtedly be appealed to the supreme court, or a new trial asked.

This jury was composed of the following persons: Sam Atherton, Wm. Nestle, Wm. Finger, Wm. Miller, Peter Hellig, Alonzo Lyman, Herb Bailey, Otis Lyman, Hugh McQuaig, Geo. R. Lee, Chas. McCallum, R. Hetherington.

Alcona County Review, April 16, 1903

The NEWS
The verdict of the Alcona county circuit court in the case of Chris C. Smith vs. the Detroit & Mackinac railroad, appealed to the supreme court, has been reversed. Smith secured a verdict of $5,000 against the railroad for the death of his wife,

who was run over and killed at Black River by a switch engine. John Weadock of Bay City and C. R. Henry of Alpena were attorneys for the railroad, and Devere Hall and H. K. Gustin appeared for Smith.

Alcona County Review, April 7, 1904
Cemetery: St. Anne's, Alcona Co.

Smith, Martin Snyder
M. S. Smith Dead.
Martin S. Smith, one of Detroit's most prominent business men and citizens, died at his home last Saturday.

Deceased was known in this county chiefly through his connection with the firm of Alger, Smith & Co. of which corporation he was vice president. He was a multi-millionaire and had large business interests outside his connection with the Alger, Smith & Co. corporation. He was a member of the Detroit Commandary.

Alcona County Review, November 2, 1899

BLACK RIVER.
Nov. 1, '99.
All Alger, Smith & Co's. business was suspended Tuesday on account of the death of Martin S. Smith. A. W. Ranney, John White and C. H. Safford left Monday evening to attend the funeral at Detroit.

Alcona County Review, November 2, 1899
Cemetery: Woodmere, Wayne Co.

Smith, May [Anschutz]
PERSONAL MENTION.

Miss Helen Reynolds of Black River attended the funeral of Mrs. E. H. Smith, nee Miss May Anschutz, of East Tawas last week.

Alcona County Review, May 16, 1895
Cemetery: Probably Greenwood, Iosco Co.

Smith, Thompson
LOCAL JOTTINGS.

Thompson Smith, owner of all the property at Duncan City, died at Cheboygan, Tuesday, of a stomach disease. He was the owner of immense tracts of land, much vessel property, some of the most extensive saw mills in the state, and was in fact one of the lumber kings of Michigan. He also had lumber yards at Albany, N. Y., and Toronto, Ont. His wealth is estimated to be between $3,000,000 to $4,000,000, and he leaves a son and daughter.

Alcona County Review, December 12, 1884
Cemetery:

Smith, Truman

Passing of Truman Smith.

Truman Smith, one of the familiar figures along this shore for the past fifteen years, died Saturday morning at Alpena after a long illness. Deceased was born in Onondaga county, New York, in 1819. He resided in St. Clair county for 40 years or more. About the year 1880 he came to Black River, where he engaged in the hotel and stage business.

Alcona County Review, July 16, 1896
Cemetery: Evergreen, Alpena Co.

Smith, W. L.

Died—At the residence of Mr. and Mrs. E. Goheen, of typhoid fever just after midnight of Friday, Sept. 4th, W. L. Smith, late of Alpena, after an illness of three weeks.

Deceased was born at Forest, Ont., where his parents reside. He had been for four months in the employ of J. B. Tackabury, confectioner, and not feeling quite able to work, decided to visit at the home of his aunt, Mrs. E. Goheen. The next day he became quite ill and Dr. McCormick was called, also Dr. Tiffany who pronounced the case typhoid fever. His parents were at once summoned, but despite medical skill and careful and constant nursing he passed quietly from death unto life eternal. During consciousness he expressed his readiness and willingness to go if God should call him hence. He had been a member of the Presbyterian church for some time and passed away with all confidence of his acceptance with God.

He was 23 years and 10 months old and leaves his parents and 3 brothers and 3 sisters to mourn their loss here below.

Alcona County Review, September 10, 1896

We wish to extend our sincere thanks to our friends for their many acts and expressions of kindness and sympathy during the last illness of our beloved Willie and particularly Mr. A. J. McMillan for special favors and to Mr. and Mrs. Murdoch McRae for the care of the children for three weeks.
Mr. and Mrs. C. F. Smith, parents.
Mr. and Mrs. E. Goheen, relatives.

Alcona County Review, September 10, 1896
Cemetery: Twin Lakes, Alcona Co.

Smith, William

THE GREAT STORM.

Probable Loss of the Propeller Oconto. A Terrible Experience.

One of the greatest storms that has prevailed upon the lakes for the past half century, came forth in its wild fury from the northeast last Friday evening, about 5 o'clock, and raged fiercely all night. The air was filled with snow and sleet, and the wind blew at the rate of about 50 miles an hour. The steamer Oconto left Oscoda about an hour before the fierceness of the storm had commenced for Harrisville and Alpena heavily laden with merchandise, horses, etc., for shore people, with also a goodly number of passengers. No clue was had of the steamer from the time she left Oscoda until Monday, and it was feared she had gone down into the lake with all on board, an old sailor said it could not have been possible for her to have "weathered the storm." But Tuesday a dispatch was received from Caseville, on the opposite shore of the Bay, announcing that the steamer was ashore on the east side of Charity Island, about 17 miles from Caseville, that passengers and crew were all safe ashore on the Island.

There was one person in Harrisville who was more than specially anxious about the fate of the Oconto. It was D. C. Emery, whose sister, Margaret Emery of Muskegon, was aboard the same on her return to Harrisville, in answer to a telegram sent to her by her brother from here. One can imagine his feelings and the lengthiness with which the hours appeared to him, as he waited for some news concerning the unfortunate craft and the status of his aged and beloved sister, during Saturday, Sunday and Monday.

From the Bay City Tribune of Wednesday we glean the following:

Four victims of the propeller Oconto disaster reached Bay City last evening, having come by the way of the Pontiac, Oxford, & Port Austin railroad to Clifford and thence to this city over the Port Huron & Northwestern railway. They were J. R. Vanslyke, clerk, James Ross, second mate, both of Detroit, Walter Bostwick, Wheelsman, of Forestville, and N. C. Potts, passenger, of Forestville. They in company with Thomas Cracker, lookout, John Cavanaugh, wheelsman, and Frank Teiper, second engineer all of Detroit, left the Oconto Monday, the three latter going through to their homes in Detroit yesterday. Ascertaining that some of the victims were in Bay City, the Tribune reporter called upon Mr. Vanslyke and Mr. Ross at the Lefever house and held an interview with them regarding the mishap, which is herewith presented, substantially as told by the writer. The Oconto left Oscoda Friday afternoon at 3 o'clock for Alpena. The passenger list numbered twenty-two, nineteen men, two ladies and a child. The boat was in command of Capt. Gregory W. McGregor, a master whose name is familiar to many people of Bay City, Detroit and citizens of the shore towns, and a crew of twenty-four men, all numbering forty-seven person. After a run of about fifteen minutes from Oscoda the wind freshened from the northeast and rapidly increased in velocity, bringing with it a blinding snow storm, and a furious sea that lifted the boat high in the air as each wave struck it. The fury of the storm was so great that it was seen she could not proceed toward Alpena, her destination, so she was brought about and headed for Tawas light, it being intended to seek shelter in Tawas bay. Darkness set in and the light at Tawas was invisible. The gale increased and the snow fell in sheets. The lake became a living sea of foam, and spray fell over the propeller in torrents, and the snow uniting with it, froze solid to every point it touched. The decks, cabin and all upper works were one coating of ice. The bearings were lost and the Oconto was at the mercy of the waves. Everyone on board prepared to meet the death of drowning, and each wore a life preserver that their bodies might wash ashore and thus be returned to their friends. The two larger life boats were swept from the upper deck, the davits being broken short off at the deck. The third and smallest boat was stove in and rendered useless. The sheets of water that rolled over the sides broke in the windows and partially filled the staterooms. So certain did it appear that they must go down that each was furnished with a list of the passengers and crew, so that should any reach shore safely, they could report the number and the names of those drowned.

Wm. Brown, a colored cook whose home was in Cincinnati, was frightened to death and breathed his last in the forecastle shortly before 12 o'clock Friday night.

At 10 minutes past 12 o'clock a light was observed ahead of the propeller. It was only seen occasionally, but often enough so that the course of the steamer could be changed with the assistance of the surf to the south, southeast in order to clear the land ahead. At 20 minutes past twelve, a monster wave picked the Oconto up and in receding left her hard aground on a sandy bottom in six feet of water. The propeller drew twelve feet of water and the reader can imagine the sea that was running to carry her ashore in that depth. As each wave struck her she rose and settled in the sand and soon became fast, while the sea washed over and about her. The hurricane slowly died away and the weather began to grow colder, but the passengers and crew did not suffer, having plenty of fuel and keeping the apartments well warmed. When daylight dawned and the snow ceased falling, it was seen that the land near was big Charity Island in Saginaw bay. They had gone ashore about three quarters of a mile from the island, heading southeast, or nearly in the direction of the Little Charity. The sea was too heavy then to go ashore. The remaining lifeboat was repaired and at the first opportunity was launched, manned and put out for the island, which was reached with great difficulty. Charles McDonald, keeper of the light, his wife and children, gave them a cordial welcome, and it was decided to bring all the persons from the Oconto, which was done by using a skiff obtained from the island. Some of the passengers and crew were given quarters in the light house and others in fish shanties, so that all were comfortable. They have plenty to eat, provisions having been brought from the stranded steamer.

On Sunday the remains of the colored man were brought ashore and given a burial.

Monday morning it was decided to summon assistance, and the seven persons above named volunteered to try and go ashore to Caseville, 11 miles distant. They took the light house sail boat, and made the trip safely, reaching Caseville early in the evening.

Alcona County Review, December 11, 1885

LOCAL JOTTINGS.

Wm. Smith, aged 31, died in Harper's hospital, Detroit, Monday, from injuries received from falling into the hold of the steamer Oconto in November last.

Alcona County Review, May 28, 1886
Cemetery: Probably Woodmere, Wayne Co.

Smith, Willie

EVENTS OF ONE WEEK.

The remains of an infant child of Mr. and Mrs. C. C. Smith were brought here from Black River last Friday morning for burial.

Alcona County Review, December 3, 1896
Cemetery: St. Anne's, Alcona Co.

Smithers, Angie

South Harrisville.

South Harrisville, Jan. 28.--The remains of an only daughter, aged thirteen, of John Smithers, living in District No. 6, were interred at the South Harrisville cemetery last Friday.

Alcona County Review, January 31, 1895
Cemetery: Springport, Alcona Co.

Smithers, William

KILLMASTER.

Nov. 1, '99.
William Smithers died at his home in Gustin after a lingering illness of nearly three years. He leaves a wife and six children who have the sympathy of the entire community.

Alcona County Review, November 2, 1899

KILLMASTER.

Nov. 1, '99.
Mesdames Heath and Graham attended the funeral of William Smithers.

Alcona County Review, November 2, 1899
Cemetery: Springport, Alcona Co.

Snowden, William

PERSONAL MENTION.

Sudden Death of Wm. Snowden.
The startling intelligence comes from Black River today that Wm. Snowden had died very suddenly, but no particulars are at hand.

Alcona County Review, March 23, 1893

The Late William Snowden.

The remains of the late Wm. Snowden of Black River were expressed to Port Huron, where they were met by members of the Masonic lodge of which he was a member, and by them given the interment due the remains of a respected brother and a good citizen. Deceased was about 60 years of age and leaves one daughter only, who resides in San Francisco. The particulars of his death as given to the Review are as follows: He was taken suddenly ill with cramps shortly after eating a hearty supper Wednesday the 22d inst. Dr. Forsythe was summoned but such medical aid as he could render proved unavailing and after two hours of suffering Mr. Snowden passed to his eternal rest. He was a man of sturdy rugged character, honest and upright, strong in his convictions and fearless in his advocacy of anything he believed to be right. He was a Mason and a life-long Republican.

Alcona County Review, March 30, 1893
Cemetery: Lakeside, St. Clair Co.

Snowden, William E. B.

KILLED BY A LOGGING TRAIN.

Conductor William Snowden Meets a Terrible Death Under the Wheels of his Own Train.

Early Wednesday morning William Snowden, of Black River, conductor of a logging train on the D. B. C. & A. R. R., met a horrible death while in the discharge of his duties. It seems that in attempting to step from the forward car to the tender of the engine Snowden missed his footing and fell under the wheels, three heavily loaded log cars passing over him. The train was stopped at once but on reaching the body life was found to be extinct. It is thought death must have been almost instantaneous. The mangled form was tenderly raised and placed aboard the train and taken to the unfortunate man's home at Black River, where he leaves a young wife and two small children, one but a babe in arms. A terrible homecoming of the husband and father.

The deceased, who was but 25 years of age, was the son of Justice Snowden, a well known and respected citizen of Black River.

Conductor Snowden, we understand, had been a valued and trusted employee of the D. B. C. & A. R. R. Co., for about seven years, serving in various capacities, commencing as a brakeman, but gradually arose in the service and two years ago secured the position of conductor. His acquaintances speak of him as a genial, warm-hearted man who enjoyed the friendship and esteem of his associates.

Alcona County Review, February 24, 1888

LOCAL JOTTINGS

Wm. Snowden, the young man who was killed on the railroad last week Wednesday was buried Sunday at Alcona. The deceased was a member of the order of Odd Fellows and a large number of brothers from Harrisville and Alcona joined their Black River brothers to pay their last respects to the memory of the dead.

Alcona County Review, March 2, 1888

Card of Thanks.

To the many friends and neighbors and comrades of the late W. E. B. Snowden, who by their kind and considerate sympathies in the sad hours of bereavement of the wife and little ones of a husband and father and myself in the loss of the deceased, to you all, accept our united heartfelt and sincere gratitude for your valued kindness and never to be forgotten sympathy by you all to us in the sad affliction and trial in the death of the deceased.

Martha Snowdcn,
William Snowden.
Black River, Feb. 27, 1888.

Alcona County Review, March 2, 1888
Cemetery: Mt. Joy, Alcona Co.

Snowden, William Russell
Drowning at Black River.
Russell Snowden, the 11-year-old son of a widow residing at Black River and grandson of the late William Snowden, was drowned Saturday in the lake. While he was fishing off the pier he lost his balance and fell in. Life was extinct when the body was recovered. His remains were buried Monday.

Alcona County Review, May 10, 1894

Haynes Happenings.

Mrs. Wm. Snowden's boy who was drowned at Black River on Saturday was buried here Monday.

Alcona County Review, May 10, 1894

Black River.

From a Special Correspondent:
Black River, May 8.—The funeral of Russell Snowden took place Monday P. M. at the Presbyterian church. Rev. Smith delivered a most able and appropriate address. The school children paid their last respects by marching to the church in a body and placing an abundance of wildwood flowers about the casket. Mrs. Snowden wishes to thank her friends, who have been deeply grieved over the loss of Russell who was a bright, promising boy, on whom his mother looked with pardonable pride expecting that he would some day be of great assistance and a source of comfort to her.

Alcona County Review, May 10, 1894
Cemetery: Mt. Joy, Alcona Co.

Somers, Margaret B. [Wilson]
Mrs. Margaret Somers, a resident of Hawse township, died Tuesday morning and was buried yesterday at the Alcona cemetery. She was aged 41.

The funeral services were conducted by Rev. F. S. Ford and were very largely attended by friends of the family.

Alcona County Review, June 30, 1898

WEST HARRISVILLE.
James Somers and family have the sympathy of the people of this village in their late trouble.

Alcona County Review, July 7, 1898

Local History of One Year

Chronology of the Principal Events of the Year 1898.

June 30. Death of Mrs. Somers, aged 41, of Hawes.

Alcona County Review, January 5, 1899
Cemetery: Mt. Joy, Alcona Co.

Soura, {Child}
THE GRAVE.
Mr. and Mrs. Edward Soura buried a young child last week which had died from the effects of la grippe.

Alcona County Review, February 4, 1892
Cemetery:

Soura, John
LOCAL JOTTINGS.

John Soura died Tuesday evening of inflammation of the lungs at his late home near Harrisville, aged 74 years.

Alcona County Review, January 8, 1887
Cemetery:

Soura, Mary
EVENTS OF ONE WEEK.

Edw. Soura buried an infant Monday which lived only about 36 hours after birth.

Alcona County Review, September 20, 1894
Cemetery:

Sousie, Clarence G.
EVENTS OF ONE WEEK.

An infant child of Geo. Sousie of Black River was buried in the Roman Catholic cemetery here Tuesday.

Alcona County Review, August 20, 1896

Black River Sparks.

Mr. and Mrs. George Sousie thank their many friends who so kindly assisted them in their late bereavement.

Alcona County Review, September 3, 1896
Cemetery: St. Anne's, Alcona Co.

Sousie, Felix
West Harrisville.

Phelix Sousie, one of our esteemed neighbors, is very ill. Mr. Sousie bought a little farm on the edge of Twin Lake a year ago and moved from Black River upon it and has made considerable improvement. He has always been a healthy, robust man. After the fires burned his fences last summer he fenced with barbed wire. On account of losing his fences his cattle strayed away and in hunting them up he overheated his blood; since then he has not seen a well day. Everybody has great respect for Uncle Sousie.

Alcona County Review, November 22, 1894

PERSONAL MENTION.

Phelix Sousie died at his home near West Harrisville on Saturday and the remains were brought to Harrisville Tuesday morning for interment in the Catholic cemetery.

The old gentleman had long been a resident of Alcona county and was universally respected. He was a native of Canada and was born Sept. 25, 1819. He emigrated to the states about 45 years ago and had been a resident of Alcona county for 16 years of that time. Besides his wife he leaves two sons, George and Silas, a stepson, Edw. LeMere, and two daughters, Mrs. Chas. Heron and Mrs. Dan McDermott.

Our heartfelt thanks are due many friends and neighbors who during the last sickness, death and burial of our beloved husband and father, performed acts of kindness and sympathy which we will ever hold in grateful remembrance.

Mrs. Phelix Sousie and Family.

Alcona County Review, November 29, 1894

The probate court was petitioned Saturday for the appointment of Sam'l J. Clark as administrator of the estate of the late Felix Sousie. Hearing Feb. 9th.

Alcona County Review, January 17, 1895

STATE OF MICHIGAN, County of Alcona.

At a session of the Probate Court for said County, held at the Probate office in the Village of Harrisville, on the Twelfth day of January, in the year one thousand eight hundred and ninety-five.

Present, C. H. Killmaster, Judge of Probate.

In the matter of the estate of Phelix Sousie:

On reading and filing the petition, duly verified, of Maria Sousie, praying that Samuel J. Clark or some other suitable person be appointed administrator of the estate of the aforesaid deceased, Felix Sousie. Thereupon it is ordered that Saturday, the ninth day of February next, at ten o'clock in the forenoon, be assigned for the hearing of said petition, and that the heirs at law of said deceased, and all others interested in said estate, are required to appear at a session of said Court, then to be holden in the Probate office, in the Village of Harrisville, and show cause, if any there be, why the prayer of the petitioner should not be granted: And it is further ordered, that said petitioners give notice to the persons interested in said estate, of the pendency of said petition, and the hearing thereof, by causing a copy of this order to be published in the Alcona County Review, a newspaper printed and circulated in said county, three successive weeks previous to said day of hearing.

C. H. Killmaster,

Judge of Probate.

Alcona County Review, January 17, 1895
Cemetery: St. Anne's, Alcona Co.

Sousie, Mary [Higginson]

LOCAL JOTTINGS.

Mrs. Silas Sousie, of Black River, oldest daughter of Mr. and Mrs. Con Hartigan of Harrisville, died at her parent's home near this village Sunday evening of malarial fever after a long illness. The remains were buried Tuesday morning from the Catholic church. They were followed to the grave by a large concourse of friends. She was married four years ago to Silas Sousie. Three children, the youngest but a few weeks old, survive her.

Alcona County Review, September 20, 1889
Cemetery: St. Anne's, Alcona Co.

Sousie, Mary E. [Twite]

PERSONAL.

The remains of Mrs. Geo. Sousie, were brought to Harrisville Monday morning for interment and a very large number of friends of the deceased and the bereaved husband followed the funeral to the last resting place of the deceased.

Mrs. Sousie's maiden name was Mary Twite. She lived in this county most of her life and her lovable qualities endeared her to a large circle of friends.

The husband is left with four small children.

Alcona County Review, January 13, 1898

My heart goes out in gratitude to those who rendered me such timely assistance in the hour of my great sorrow and need. May each and all of them be spared so overwhelming bereavement is my earnest wish.

Geo. Sousie.

Alcona County Review, January 13, 1898

Local History of One Year

Chronology of the Principal Events of the Year 1898.

January 8. Death Mrs. Geo. Sousie, Black River.

Alcona County Review, January 5, 1899
Cemetery: St. Anne's, Alcona Co.

Southgate, {Male}

EVENTS OF ONE WEEK.

Robt. Southgate has received the sad intelligence of his father's recent death in New York. He was unable to attend the funeral.

Alcona County Review, April 13, 1893
Cemetery:

Southgate, Raymond

LOCAL JOTTINGS.

Died, in Harrisville, June 14, 1884, Raymond, only son of Robert and Etta Southgate, aged about 2 years. "Ray," as he was familiarly called, was a bright little fellow and had endeared himself to all those who saw and knew him, especially in the parental home. He was too good and pure for the cold unhallowed climate of earth, so the Good Lord, who doeth all things well, transplanted him to the beautiful flower garden of Heaven, where his innocent spirit voice now mingles with the sweet enchanting choruses of the angels. Death was but the beginning of a brighter and happier life with him. May the bereaved parents receive comfort and consolation from Him who alone is able to give it, even Jesus Christ the righteous.

Alcona County Review, June 20, 1884

A Card of Thanks.

We desire to express our sincere thanks (for which we feel we are indebted) to friends, for their kindness to us during our late affliction. With many thanks we are

Yours, Etc.,

Robt. and Ettie Southgate.

Alcona County Review, June 27, 1884
Cemetery: Springport, Alcona Co.

Southgate, Vidie L.

HOME REVIEWINGS.

How often is it the case in life that one's joy is soon turned into sorrow. Saturday morning last a beautiful ten-pound daughter was born to Mr. and Mrs. Robert Southgate, which remained to gladden their hearts only till Sunday evening when the spirit of the little one returned back to God who gave it. The lovely flower was too tender for the climes of this cold and uneven world and the Good Father has thus transplanted it in His garden of celestial clime and beauty where its bloom shall assume the brightness of eternal glory. "The Lord giveth and the Lord taketh away. Blessed be the name of the Lord."

Alcona County Review, July 1, 1881
Cemetery: Springport, Alcona Co.

Sovey, Kate

COUNTY REVIEWINGS.

As we go to press we learn that the six-years-old daughter of Joseph Sovey has just died from diphtheria.

Alcona County Review, July 2, 1880
Cemetery: Probably West Lawn, Alcona Co.

Specht, Fred

Diphtheria Breaks Out Again.
Diphtheria has broken out in the family of Jos. Specht and three members of the family are down with it. The premises have been placarded and placed under quarantine.

One of the Specht children, aged between 5 and six years, died Tuesday night. Yesterday afternoon two other children were reported as so ill that there was little hope of recovery.

Mr. Herb Bailey is also down with the disease and is reported to be in a critical condition.

The cases in the Specht family are undoubtedly due to the condition of the cellar under the house, which has been flooded with stagnant water and contained a quantity of vegetables in a state of putrefaction.

Alcona County Review, May 25, 1893

EVENTS OF ONE WEEK.

Union funeral services were held last Sunday in the Dean school house for the children of the families of Wm. H. Anderson, Jos. Specht and Jas. Ferguson, who died the past summer from diphtheria. The services were largely attended and the Rev. S. Boundy preached a very feeling and impressive sermon, taking as his text St. Matt. xxiv. 44.

Alcona County Review, September 7, 1893
Cemetery: Springport, Alcona Co.

Specht, Rose

Diphtheria Breaks Out Again.
Diphtheria has broken out in the family of Jos. Specht and three members of the family are down with it. The premises have been placarded and placed under quarantine.

One of the Specht children, aged between 5 and six years, died Tuesday night. Yesterday afternoon two other children were reported as so ill that there was little hope of recovery.

Mr. Herb Bailey is also down with the disease and is reported to be in a critical condition.

The cases in the Specht family are undoubtedly due to the condition of the cellar under the house, which has been flooded with stagnant water and contained a quantity of vegetables in a state of putrefaction.

Alcona County Review, May 25, 1893

EVENTS OF ONE WEEK.
The remaining diphtheria patients in the Specht and Bailey households are in a fair way to recover.

Alcona County Review, June 1, 1893

DIPHTHERIA'S HARVEST.

The Dreadful Disease Adds to the Long List of Dead.

Jos. Specht lost another child, a daughter aged 10 years, on Tuesday. The primary cause of death was diphtheria. The child had the disease several weeks ago and it settled on her lungs, producing quick consumption. The burial was private and at night, the same as with diphtheria patients.

Alcona County Review, July 7, 1893

EVENTS OF ONE WEEK.

Union funeral services were held last Sunday in the Dean school house for the children of the families of Wm. H. Anderson, Jos. Specht and Jas. Ferguson, who died the past summer from diphtheria. The services were largely attended and the Rev. S. Boundy preached a very feeling and impressive sermon, taking as his text St. Matt. xxiv. 44.

Alcona County Review, September 7, 1893
Cemetery: Springport, Alcona Co.

Spencer, Allan H.

Death of A. H. Spencer.
The community was shocked on Monday at the news of the death of A. H. Spencer after a brief illness of nine days, from erysipelas. It was so short a time since he was around on our streets in the full enjoyment of his health, that but few had learned of his illness until the announcement of his demise. Mr. Spencer came to Alcona county about thirteen years ago, and settled on the section where he has since resided. Hard laborious work enabled him to carve a thrifty farm out of the wilderness. He took a special interest in the cultivation of fruits and his plum orchard was both famous and profitable. Mr. Spencer was public spirited and always took an active interest in matters that promised beneficial results to the community. He was an active member of the Agricultural Society, being at one time its President. He held the office of Highway Commissioner of Harrisville township and prior to locating in Alcona county was marshal of Au Sable village. He possessed a rugged character, was strictly moral and temperate in all things. By his death the community loses an honorable and upright citizen who has done his fair share of work in establishing the fact that agricultural pursuits can be successfully prosecuted in Alcona county.

Alcona County Review, January 8, 1891

The Local News.

The business of the late A. H. Spencer and his sons is said to have been done in the name of the deceased, and all of the real estate owned by them was recorded in the same way. He left no written will.

Alcona County Review, January 15, 1891

Whereas, The Omnipotent and Supreme Ruler of the Universe has in His Wisdom seen fit to remove from earth Allen H. Spencer, late President of the Alcona County Agricultural Society, therefore be it

Resolved, That in the death of this good an upright citizen this Society has lost a valued and active member whose services in the past will ever be held in grateful remembrance. That while we sincerely regret his departure, we bow in humble submission to Him who knoweth and doeth all things well. And we hereby extend such sympathy as man can give to man, to his friends and relatives in the hour of their affliction,

Resolved, That these resolutions be spread upon the records of this Society, that they be published in the columns of the local paper and a copy of them transmitted to the family of the deceased.

Geo. E. Gillam, Sec.

Thos. Dean, Pres.

Alcona County Review, January 15, 1891
Cemetery: West Lawn, Alcona Co.

Spencer, Asa

NEIGHBORHOOD NOTES.

Asa Spencer, aged 40 years, Long Rapids, Alpena county, missing since Dec. 15. Suspected he fell off dock at Alpena and was drowned.

Alcona County Review, December 28, 1888

NEIGHBORHOOD NOTES.

Asa Spencer, of Alpena, disappeared last December. His body was found in Thunder Bay Monday.

Alcona County Review, March 22, 1889
Cemetery:

Spencer, Ella E. [Burt]

Mrs. S. H. Spencer, who has for a long time been a patient sufferer from a tumor on the side of her head, and from other ills contracted through its agency, lies very low at her home in this township, and fears are entertained by her friends that her recovery is now beyond hope. On three separate occasions, during the past two years, Mrs. Spencer has endured the painful operation, at the hands of skilled surgeons, of having the tumor removed, but each time it soon reappeared, working out its grim mission.

Alcona County Review, November 12, 1886

LOCAL JOTTINGS.

Dr. Busch, of Cincinnati, Ohio, a specialist, arrived in Harrisville last week, called here to treat Mrs. S. H. Spencer, of this township, for tumor. He returned home last Friday. The Dr. stated that Mrs. Spencer's condition was very bad and her recovery doubtful.

Alcona County Review, December 3, 1886

Died.—At her home in this township, Dec. 3d, Ella E., wife of S. H. Spencer, aged 34 years. Two children and a husband are left to mourn their loss. The funeral services were held at the Spencer school house last Sunday, Rev. F. N. Barlow preaching the sermon. There was a large attendance of sympathizing friends and neighbors. The remains were interred in the west cemetery.

Alcona County Review, December 10, 1886

Card of Thanks.

I wish to return my sincere thanks to friends and neighbors for their kindness and sympathy toward myself and family during our recent sad affliction.

S. H. Spencer.

Alcona County Review, December 10, 1886
Cemetery: West Lawn, Alcona Co.

Spencer, Harriett Newell [Howe]

PASSED FROM EARTH.

Mrs. Harriett Spencer, widow of the late Allen H. Spencer, passed from earth last evening at eight o'clock, after an illness of six months. Since October she has been confined to her bed, and her death has been anticipated for several weeks.

Mrs. Spencer was born at Hertimage, Genessee Co., N. Y., Sept. 1, 1832. In 1840 her parents, Seymour and Hannah Howe, moved to Macomb county, Mich.

Deceased is survived by eight children, all but one of whom are honored residents of Alcona county. She became a resident of Alcona county 20 years ago, coming here from Au Sable with her husband and family. Hers was a sturdy character such as pioneers are made of, of sterling worth and rugged virtue.

The funeral services will be conducted at the residence tomorrow morning at 10 o'clock, burial in the west cemetery.

Alcona County Review, February 3, 1898

Spencer School.

There was no school Friday on account of the funeral of Mrs. Spencer.

Alcona County Review, February 10, 1898

Feb. 17.

STATE OF MICHIGAN, County of Alcona.

At a session of the Probate Court for said county, held at the Probate office, in the village of Harrisville, on the 14th day of February, in the year one thousand eight hundred and ninety-eight.

Present, Hon. Wm. H. Gilpin, Probate Judge.

In the matter of the estate of Harriet Spencer deceased.

On reading and filing the petition, duly verified, of Frank Spencer, praying among other things that administration of said estate may be granted to Lorenzo Frederick, or some other suitable person.

Thereupon it is ordered, that Monday, the 14th day of March, next, at 10 o'clock in the forenoon, be assigned for the hearing of said petition, and that the heirs at law of said deceased, and all other persons interested in said estate, are required to appear at a session of said court, then to be holden at the Probate office, in the village of Harrisville, and show cause, if any there be, why the prayer of the petitioner should not be granted: and it is further

ordered that said petitioner give notice to the heirs at law and all other persons interested in said estate, of the pendency of said petition, and the hearing thereof, by causing a copy of this order to be published in the "Alcona County Review" a newspaper printed and circulated in said county, three successive weeks previous to said day of hearing.

Wm. H. Gilpin,
Judge of Probate.

Alcona County Review, February 17, 1898

LOCAL PICK UPS.

L. Frederick was appointed administrator of the estate of the late Harriett Spencer, by Judge Gilpin on Monday.

Alcona County Review, March 17, 1898

State of Michigan, County of Alcona.

Notice is hereby given, that by an order of the Probate Court for the County of Alcona, made on the 11th day of April A.D. 1898, six months from that date were allowed for creditors to present their claims against the estate of Harriet Spencer deceased late of said County, deceased, and that all creditors of said deceased are required to present their claims to said Probate Court, at the Probate office, in the Village of Harrisville, for examination and allowance, on or before said Court, on Monday, the 20th day of June and on Tuesday, the 11th day of October next, at ten o'clock in the forenoon of each of those days.

Dated April 11th, A.D. 1898.

W. H. Gilpin,
Judge of Probate.

Alcona County Review, April 14, 1898

Local History of One Year

Chronology of the Principal Events of the Year 1898.

February 2. Death of Harriett Spencer aged 66.

Alcona County Review, January 5, 1899

STATE of Michigan, County of Alcona.

At a session of the Probate Court for said County, held at the Probate office, in the village of Harrisville, on the 6th day of February in the year one thousand eight hundred and ninety-nine.

Present, Hon. Wm. H. Gilpin, Probate Judge.

In the matter of the estate of Harriett Spencer deceased.

On reading and filing the petition, duly verified, of Lorenzo Frederick praying that license may be granted to him authorizing him to sell the real estate of said deceased for the purpose of paying indebtedness existing and due against it. Said real estate is described as the southeast quarter of section eighteen (18) in township twenty-six (26) north of range nine (9) east.

Thereupon it is ordered that Monday the 6th day of March next, at ten o'clock in the forenoon, be assigned for the hearing of said petition, and that the heirs at law of said deceased, and all others interested in said estate, are required to appear at a session of said court, then to be holden at the Probate office, in the village of Harrisville, and show cause, if any there be, why the prayer of the petitioner should not be granted: and it is further ordered that said petitioner give notice to the persons interested in said estate, of the pendency of said petition, and the hearing thereof, by causing a copy of this order to be published in the "Alcona County Review" a newspaper printed and circulated in said county, three successive weeks previous to said day of hearing.

Wm. H. Gilpin,
Judge of Probate.

Alcona County Review, February 9, 1899

Probate Court.

L. Frederick, administrator of the estate of the late Harriett Spencer, has been granted license to sell the real property of said estate for the payment of debts existing and due against the estate.

Alcona County Review, March 16, 1899

State of Michigan, County of Alcona.

At a session of the probate court for said county held at the probate office in the village of Harrisville on the 3rd day of April A.D. 1899.

Present, Hon. W. H. Gilpin, Judge of Probate.

In the matter of the estate of Harriet Spencer, deceased: On reading and filing the petition, duly verified, of Lorenzo Frederick, praying that license may be granted to him authorizing him to sell the real estate of said deceased for the

purpose of paying indebtedness existing and due against it. Said real estate is described as follows, to-wit: The southeast quarter of the northeast quarter of section eighteen (18) in township twenty-six (26) north, of range nine (9) east. Also for authority and power to sell all personal property at public or private sale as to him seems advisable for the best interest of said estate to pay said indebtedness.

Thereupon it is ordered that Saturday the 29th day of April next, at ten o'clock in the forenoon be assigned for the hearing of said petition, and that the heirs at law of said deceased and all other persons interested in said estate, are required to appear at a session of said court then to be holden in the probate office in the village of Harrisville and show cause if any there be, why the prayer of the petitioner should not be granted. And it is further ordered that the petitioner give notice to the persons interested in said estate of the pendency of said petition by causing a copy of this order to be published in the Alcona County Review, a newspaper printed and circulated in said county; three successive weeks previous to said day of hearing.

Wm. H. Gilpin,
Judge of Probate.

Alcona County Review, April 6, 1899

LOCAL PICK UPS.

All unpreferred claims against the estate of the late Harriett Spencer will be settled on the basis of 24.06 cents on the dollar. L. Frederick administrator, in conjunction with Judge Gilpin determined the rate on Monday and the claim are now being paid. The aggregate of such claims is $1,278.86.

Alcona County Review, July 27, 1899
Cemetery: West Lawn, Alcona Co.

Spoon, William A.

Haynes Happenings.

Wm. A. Spoon died of cancer of the stomach on May 25th. He was a member of Co. I, 1st N. Y. cavalry.

Alcona County Review, June 3, 1897

STATE OF MICHIGAN, County of Alcona.

At a session of the Probate Court for said County, held at the Probate office, in the Village of Harrisville, on the seventh day of June in the year

one thousand eight hundred and ninety-seven.

Present, W. H. Gilpin, Judge of Probate.

In the matter of the estate of William A. Spoon, deceased.

On reading and filing the petition duly verified of Ellen E. Spoon, praying that a certain instrument now on file in this court, purporting to be the last will and testament of said deceased, may be admitted to probate, and that she, said Ellen E. Spoon, may be appointed executrix of said estate, or some other suitable person as this court may deem best.

Thereupon it is ordered, that Tuesday, the 6th day of July next, at ten o'clock in the forenoon, be assigned for the hearing of said petition, and that the heirs at law of said deceased and all other persons interested in said estate, are required to appear at a session of the Probate Court, then to be holden at the Probate office, in the Village of Harrisville and show cause, if any there be, why the prayer of the petitioner should not be granted.

And it is further ordered that the petitioner give notice to the heirs at law and all persons interested in said estate, of the pendency of said petition, and the hearing thereof, by causing a copy of this order to be published in the Alcona County Review, a newspaper printed and circulating in said county three successive weeks previous to said day of hearing.

W. H. Gilpin,
Judge of Probate.

Alcona County Review, June 10, 1897
Cemetery: Pleasant View, Alcona Co.

Spratt, Alice May

Among Our Exchanges.

Miss Alice Spratt, an esteemed young lady of Alpena, died last week from diphtheria. The case was not properly quarantined and it has resulted in much criticism of officials who were guilty of negligence.

Alcona County Review, June 16, 1892
Cemetery: Evergreen, Alpena Co.

St. Amour, Eugene

DEATH OF EUGENE ST. AMOUR.

He Suddenly Passes Away from Heart Disease.

Our usually quiet village was thrown into a state of considerable excitement at about 2:30 o'clock p.m. on Saturday last, by the announcement of the sudden death of Eugene St. Amour, connected with Mrs. E. Carle in the grocery and hotel business in Harrisville. Lawyer W. E. Depew had just stepped in to the Alcona House to see Mrs. Carle on a business matter, and found Mr. St. Amour lying upon the carpeted floor of the small room in rear of the store. Mr. St. Amour complained that he was not feeling well internally and had just that moment laid down. He rose up, sat upon a chair for a moment or two to talk to Mr. Depew, but immediately after speaking a few words fell off the chair upon the floor in an unconscious state. Mr. Depew started to summon a physician, but had not reached the distance of more than ten rods from the house before the dying man breathed his last. Upon being informed of the death of Mr. St. Amour, Justice C. P. Reynolds immediately impaneled a jury consisting of J. T. Harvie, John Gray, G. W. LaChapelle, Andrew Atchison, Robert Southgate, and J. T. Bissell, and proceeded to hold an inquest over the body of the deceased. The manner of his death seeming to warrant the same, Sunday afternoon an autopsy of the body was held in the presence of the jury, and an examination of the internal organs had, conducted by Drs. D. W. Mitchell of this village, and Frank McCormick of Black River. At the close of the autopsy the inquest was adjourned until this Friday morning, to wait for the decisions and evidence of Drs. Mitchell and McCormick, who gave in the same to the effect that the deceased came to his death, in their opinion, from diseased heart. The lungs bore evidences of congestion, while the liver and kidneys, though much enlarged, appeared to be in a perfectly healthy state. The stomach was entirely empty, not even containing an ounce of liquid, and was free from any disease or unhealthiness. At the conclusion of the evidence produced by Drs. Mitchell and McCormick, who agreed perfectly in their decision that the deceased came to his death from affectation of the heart and lungs, and no traces whatever of poison being found, the jury rendered the following verdict, to wit: "That the deceased came to his death at the Alcona House, Harrisville, Mich., by disease of the heart, on the 23d day of August, 1884."

As yet we have been unable to learn the exact age of Eugene St. Amour, the deceased, but he had seen upwards of 70 odd years. He had often boasted of his good health, stating that he had never been obliged to call a physician to treat him, but death got the upper hand of him at last, as he will all of us sooner or later, and that too, doubtless, when we least expect. The deceased had been a resident of the county for about six years. At one time he was a very wealthy man, but subsequent business reverses took much of his wealth from him, and he had comparatively little of this world's goods at the time of his death. His wife preceded him in death about a year ago. He leaves behind to mourn his departure, a sister, two sons and one daughter, so we are informed. The remains were interred in the cemetery west of the village Monday forenoon.

Alcona County Review, August 29, 1884

EVENTS OF ONE WEEK.

The initial step has been taken to settle up the estate of Eugene St. Amour--better known here as Santamore--who died some twelve years ago in Harrisville.

Alcona County Review, August 30, 1894

STATE OF MICHIGAN, County of Alcona.

At a session of the Probate Court for said County, held at the Probate office in the Village of Harrisville, on the Twenty-third day of August, in the year one thousand eight hundred and ninety-four.

Present, C. H. Killmaster, Judge of Probate.

In the matter of the estate of Eugene St. Amour.

On reading and filing the petition, duly verified, of Francis E. St. Amour, praying that this court determine who are the lawful heirs to the estate of said Eugene St. Amour, deceased. Thereupon it is ordered that Monday, the first day of October, next, at ten o'clock in the forenoon, be assigned for the hearing of said petition, and that the heirs at law of said deceased, and all others interested in said estate, are required to appear at a session of said Court, then to be holden in the Probate office, in the Village of Harrisville, and show cause, if any there be, why the prayer of the petitioner should not be granted: And it is further ordered, that said petitioners give notice to the persons interested in said estate, of the pendency of said petition, and the hearing thereof by causing a copy of this order to be published in the Alcona County Review, a newspaper printed and circulated in said county, three successive weeks previous to said day of hearing.

C. H. Killmaster,
Judge of Probate.

Alcona County Review, August 30, 1894
Cemetery: West Lawn, Alcona Co.

St. Clair, Will

Mud Lake Jots.

We are sorry to hear of the death of Will St. Clair, a very estimable young man, who had many friends here. His two brothers, Howard and Herbert and a sister, Mrs. Sovey, reside here. He died in Chicago very suddenly and was taken to St. Clair for burial.

April 1st., 1895.

Alcona County Review, April 4, 1895
Cemetery:

Stafford, James

Black River.

Infant of Mrs. Stafford died on the 19th. Interred in Harrisville cemetery.

Alcona County Review, February 23, 1893
Cemetery:

Stafford, John Howard

REVIEWINGS.

Death has again entered the family circle of Mrs. Samuel Stafford of this town, this time to lay his icy hand upon the youngest of her flock, a nice boy of seventeen months, who, in just three months, has followed his father to the silent tomb. The bereaved widow and mother again tenders her sincere thanks to her kind neighbors and friends who so kindly assisted her on this melancholy occasion, and remains

Theirs Respectfully,
Mrs. S. Stafford.

Alcona County Review, May 23, 1879
Cemetery: Springport, Alcona Co.

Stafford, Robbie

EVENTS OF ONE WEEK.

Robbie, the 9-year-old son of Mr. and Mrs. Moses Stafford died yesterday from a stroke of paralysis, the result of sickness from measles. The funeral occurs from the Catholic Church at 8 o'clock tomorrow morning.

Alcona County Review, June 3, 1897

Card of Thanks.

I wish to thank my kind friends for their untiring efforts to assist me during the illness and death of my little son. I wish, also, to thank them for the beautiful flowers, especially those which were contributed by his teacher and little schoolmates, which were highly appreciated.

Mrs. M. Stafford and Family.

Alcona County Review, June 10, 1897
Cemetery: Probably St. Anne's, Alcona Co.

Stafford, Samuel E.

Another Pioneer Gone.

The death of our honored townsman, Mr. Samuel Stafford, which occurred at his farm residence five miles west of the village, at about 1 o'clock p.m. on Monday, was of a very sudden order, and the announcement struck our citizens with a surprise almost incomprehensible. Mr. Stafford was a man of good constitution, robust and healthy, and he was the last man whose death the people would have presumed to look for at so early a day. Last Saturday, apparently as well as ever, with the exception of a slight cold, he was engaged all day hauling wood, with tcam, from his farm to Davison's dock. He went home at evening, ate supper, mingled with his family as usual, and retired for the night. About four o'clock in the morning his wife was awakened by him rolling over and over in the bed, and thinking it very strange that he should thus act, spoke to him to ascertain what the matter was. Receiving no answer from her husband save a mumbling of his words, Mrs. Stafford became alarmed and immediately arose from her bed, procured a light, and soon discovered the serious condition of her companion. While he was conscious at the time, his tongue was so palsied that he could not articulate, but expressed himself as suffering great pain in the head. Mrs. Stafford dispatched her little boy for Mr. R.

W. Downer, a near neighbor, who soon arrived and assisted in doing what he could to relieve the sick man. A physician was sent for, who came before noon, and pronounced the affliction of the man congestion of the brain, and said he could not live a great while. The sick man had become unconscious now, but lingered along till 1:10 p.m. the next day (Monday), when he died. Thus suddenly passed away another of the pioneer farmers and respected citizens of Alcona county, in the vigor and prime of manhood.

Samuel Stafford was born in Pennsylvania in 1841, and was 38 years old the 25th day of last January. In the early part of the war he went to Indiana and there enlisted in the One Hundred and First Indiana regiment, and served his country as a soldier. After the war he came to Saginaw, Michigan, and from there to this county, in the fall of 1866. He worked during the winter in the lumber woods, and the following spring purchased land for a farm, five miles west of the village of Harrisville. In the fall of 1868, he was married to Miss Ellen Cady, and moved onto his farm, where he has since resided. He leaves a wife and five children to mourn his loss, who have the sympathy of a large circle of friends.

The obsequies of the deceased were held from the M. E. Church in Harrisville, Thursday afternoon, a very large concourse of people being present.

Alcona County Review, February 21, 1879

A Card.—To those friends who so kindly left their business, and unmindful of the inclemency of the weather, turned out to pay the last tribute of respect to my late husband, and to convey his remains to their last resting place, in my own and in the name of my family I tender my most grateful thanks.

Harrisville, Feb. 26, 1879.
Mrs. Samuel Stafford.

Alcona County Review, February 28, 1879
Cemetery: Springport, Alcona Co.

Starkey, James

COUNTY NEWS JOTTINGS.

On coming down from Alpena yesterday the stage driver found in the road, between Ossineke and Black River, a man frozen and helpless. He had been drinking quite freely the night before, and had laid

out, in the road, from ten to twelve hours. His feet and hands are so badly frozen that amputation of all or a part of such members may be necessary. The stage picked him up and brought him down to Black River.

Alcona County Review, January 25, 1878

COUNTY NEWS JOTTINGS.

The man whom we reported as being found in the road badly frozen, near Ossineke, last week, died, Wednesday afternoon. His name was James Starkey, and his home was in Bangor, this State. Both himself and wife were employed as cooks at Fowler & Merrick's camp, back of Ossineke. The remains of the deceased, followed by the sorrowing wife, passed through Harrisville en route to Bangor, yesterday.

Alcona County Review, February 1, 1878
Cemetery:

Stetcher, Joseph

EVENTS OF ONE WEEK.

A man died last week at Blond's camp. He was a brother-in-law of the foreman, and the remains were shipped by rail Saturday to his home.

Alcona County Review, January 26, 1893

West Harrisville.

Joseph Stetcher, who was employed in Blond's camp, died last Friday. His body was conveyed to Minden City Saturday for burial, accompanied by Frank Blond and wife, who were his brother-in-law and sister.

Alcona County Review, January 26, 1893
Cemetery:

Stevens, Angie

REVIEWINGS.

Miss Angie Stevens, of Greenbush, died of typhoid fever yesterday morning. She was a young lady of about 20 and much respected by all who knew her. Funeral to-day at 2 p.m.

Alcona County Review, October 10, 1879

Angie Stevens.

Editor Review: You say Angie Stevens is dead! Yes, Thursday morning, the 9th inst., is the time when life on earth was ended; but did she then launch forth accompanied by angels and join that "great throng" John saw, "which no man could number, clothed with white robes, and palms in their hands, saying:

salvation to our God which sitteth upon the throne, and unto the Lamb?" If I knew this were so I could drop my pen and anew unite thought to thought around the text, "Have faith in God."

But is she who sang so beautifully, and listened so attentively for three years to the Gospel of Peace proclaimed by the writer, "safe in the arms of Jesus?" Was I faithful in the discharge of my trust? Friends and neighbors did you lead her to the Savior by a well ordered life? Young men and women, some of you have been with Jesus and learned of the new life, have you all done what you could to lead her to rest in heaven?

As the body of Angie rests with sacred dust on the beautiful shore of the Huron, let us meditate.

Now while her willing hands can no longer minister to our wants, and the eye cannot see, neither the ear hear, let us meditate.

As we meditate, let us by faith take Christ for our Savior; live in the glory of His presence, and by life and word do all in our power to lead others to the Joy of pardoned sin here, and the glory of the upper sanctuary hereafter.

N. N. C.

Walled Lake, Oct. 13, 1879.

Alcona County Review, October 17, 1879
Cemetery: Springport, Alcona Co.

Stevens, Clare

LOCAL JOTTINGS.

During the past two weeks, cholera-infantum has been having a terrible rage in this community, no less than a dozen small children and babes having died from the same.— This naturally leaves many houses of mourning in our community, and to those of us who are as yet free from the scourge in our own homes, should come forth hearty sympathy and fitting words for the bereaved. Friday last, the scourge took away a little, human flower each from the homes of William Nestle and James Stringer. Tuesday the family of Chas. Larson were bereft of their babe, and Wednesday evening Frank Stevens and wife were called to part with their first-born. Gilbert Landon, one of the Messrs. Byces, and the Ducharms have also each lost a babe, and there are several others in the community apparently nearly at death's door, at the time we go to

press. Thus many of the homes in our community are being darkened. May the Lord remove the dark cloud speedily, and give consolation to the sorrowing parents.

Alcona County Review, August 29, 1884

LOCAL JOTTINGS.
Mr. and Mrs. Frank Stevens desire through the Review to return thanks to friends for assistance and acts of kindness so freely manifested on the recent sad occasion of the sickness, death and burial of their little son, Clare. They fully appreciate the sympathy and good will of the people thus shown them in their hours of severe trial.

Alcona County Review, September 5, 1884
Cemetery: Springport, Alcona Co.

Stevens, David F.

Local Sayings and Doings.

The Alpena *Argus* says that last Thursday David Stevens was killed by lightning. He was working on a drive on Gilchrist creek, and during a thunder storm took refuge under a tree, where he was struck by the electric fluid.

Alcona County Review, June 23, 1882
Cemetery:

Stevens, John H.

Among Our Exchanges.

John H. Stevens, a prominent citizen of Montmorency county, died Sunday after a brief illness, aged 57.

Alcona County Review, June 23, 1892
Cemetery: Hillman-Rust, Montmorency Co.

Stewart, {Child}

THE GRAVE.
Saturday last Mr. and Mrs. Jno. Stewart buried a nine months old child in the Catholic cemetery. The child died of la grippe.

Alcona County Review, February 4, 1892
Cemetery: St. Anne's, Alcona Co.

Stewart, {Child}

EVENTS OF ONE WEEK.

An infant child of John Stewart was buried in the Catholic cemetery Monday.

Alcona County Review, April 11, 1895
Cemetery: St. Anne's, Alcona Co.

Stewart, Harriet

EVENTS OF ONE WEEK.

Jas. Stewart, who resides near Gustin, lost a 10-year-old daughter Monday morning. The child died of

the prevailing inflammation of the lungs, which seems to affect the old and young folks.

Alcona County Review, March 9, 1893
Cemetery: Probably St. Anne's, Alcona Co.

Stewart, Henry

Black River Sparks.

Died at Black River July 2, 1896, Henry Stewart, after a long illness from Bright's disease. Deceased was the eldest son of Mrs. John Heron, Port Huron, and was born at St. Mary's, Canada, in 1856.

With deepest sorrow and regret the deceased was followed to the D. & M. depot by the largest funeral cortege that has ever taken place in Black River, relatives and friends uniting to show their love and esteem.

Mr. Stewart was of a gentle and retiring disposition and was much respected by all his acquaintances on account of those amiable qualities. Seldom has such universal regret been manifested in this place.

The remains were taken to Port Huron for burial. The pall bearers to the depot were Dan Thompson, James Pritchard, John Nicholson, Robert Larrett, William Mitchell, Sam Hill.

Alcona County Review, July 9, 1896
Cemetery: Probably Lakeside, St. Clair Co.

Stewart, James L.

Gustin Grist.
Oct. 13, 1896.
Mr. and Mrs. James Stewart the loss of an infant son aged 2 months and 4 days. The child died Saturday, Oct. 10, from whooping cough.

Alcona County Review, October 15, 1896
Cemetery:

Stewart, John

LOCAL JOTTINGS.

John Stewart, an old resident of Greenbush township, died Sunday. The remains were buried Tuesday.

Alcona County Review, February 8, 1889
Cemetery: St. Anne's, Alcona Co.

Stewart, John B.

Along the Shore.

General News-Gleanings From the Several Counties.

Au Sable and Oscoda.
A little six-year-old son of Alexander Stewart fell from a log in

Gram's bayou last Thursday afternoon and was drowned.

Alcona County Review, July 2, 1880
Cemetery:

Stewart, Mrs. Mary

EVENTS OF ONE WEEK.

Mrs. Stewart, mother of John and James Stewart, died at her home near Mikado last week at the advanced age of 85 years. The remains were interred in the Catholic cemetery.

Alcona County Review, March 4, 1897

MIKADO.

It was requested that these verses be printed in memory of Mrs. Mary Stewart, who died Feb. 20th, '97.

Farewell, Mother, thou art dead,
In the tomb the body lies;
But thy soul away has fled,
To thy God above the skies.

In the sad and solemn hour,
Still unwav'ring was thy faith;
By the blessed Savior's power,
Thou has triumphed over death.

Till we reach that happy place,
Where immortal spirits dwell,
Till in heaven we see thy face,
Mother, dear, Farewell-Farewell.

Alcona County Review, April 29, 1897
Cemetery: Probably St. Anne's, Alcona Co.

Stickney, Mrs. Mary

HOME REVIEWINGS.

A Mrs. Stickney of Greenbush died last Sunday. She leaves a husband and two children.

Alcona County Review, September 30, 1881
Cemetery:

Stiles, {Child}

Boiled Down for Your Perusal.

When Mrs. Frank Stiles returned to her farm home near Tawas Thursday she found her house in ruins, and all that was left of her two pretty babies were blackened, unrecognizable corpses.

During the afternoon the father was at work on the farm. Mrs. Stiles, thinking everything was secure, ran over to a neighbor's house leaving the children alone. She was gone only a short time and it never entered her head that there was any danger. But there was. The house caught fire and the children could not escape. Before the mother saw the flames the little ones were suffocated and the house was gone. The babes were: one 3 years and one 13 months old.

Alcona County Review, December 21, 1893
Cemetery:

Stiles, {Child}

Boiled Down for Your Perusal.

When Mrs. Frank Stiles returned to her farm home near Tawas Thursday she found her house in ruins, and all that was left of her two pretty babies were blackened, unrecognizable corpses.

During the afternoon the father was at work on the farm. Mrs. Stiles, thinking everything was secure, ran over to a neighbor's house leaving the children alone. She was gone only a short time and it never entered her head that there was any danger. But there was. The house caught fire and the children could not escape. Before the mother saw the flames the little ones were suffocated and the house was gone. The babes were: one 3 years and one 13 months old.

Alcona County Review, December 21, 1893
Cemetery:

Stone, James

COUNTY JOTTINGS.

James Stone, a young man who came to Harrisville some few months ago, to work in G. L. Colwell's mill, died at the residence of Mrs. Jno. Taft, Tuesday afternoon. He was taken ill with typhoid fever some three or four weeks ago, and his case proving a very severe one he died as above noted. His home was at Toronto, Ontario, where he has a mother now living with her second husband. He also has a sister living in Illinois. He was twenty-five years of age. His remains were interred Wednesday, and services in memoriam of the deceased will be held at the M. E. Church next Sunday morning.

Alcona County Review, October 11, 1878
Cemetery:

Storms, {Child}

Local Sayings and Doings.

Mr. and Mrs. Geo. Storms have again been sadly afflicted by the sudden death of their five months old babe, which occurred on Tuesday morning.

Alcona County Review, April 14, 1882
Cemetery:

Storms, Sanford

People We Hear About.

Mr. and Mrs. Geo. Storms mourn the death of an infant son this week. The child died of cholera infantum.

Alcona County Review, August 8, 1890
Cemetery:

Storms, Wilbert

The heavy hand of sorrow has been laid upon Mr. and Mrs. Geo. Storms in the death of their little son, Wilbur. The child was taken ill 10 days previous to his death and the skill of local physicians was completely baffled. The little sufferer passed away Thursday, Aug. 15, at 5 o'clock p.m., the interment taking place Saturday morning. The sorrowing parents have the sympathy of all in their deep bereavement.

————

Mr. Storms and family feel under deep obligations to their friends and neighbors for the many acts of kindness rendered them during their recent bereavement, and they thank them therefore from the depths of grateful hearts.

Alcona County Review, August 22, 1895
Cemetery:

Stout, Ira

COUNTY NEWS AND GOSSIP.

Hon. Ira Stone, an old and much esteemed resident of Alpena, died very suddenly Saturday evening, after a short illness. He was Judge of Probate, Justice of the Peace and member of the City School Board, at the time of his death.

Alcona County Review, December 13, 1878
Cemetery: Evergreen, Alpena Co.

Strange, Charles

Along the Shore.

Alpena.

Friday, Jan. 24, Chas. Strange, who was in the employ of Charles Heuber, accidentally cut his finger with an old axe, neglected the wound, and died on Sunday last. The parents of the deceased reside near Bay City, and the remains were sent to that place for interment.—*Argus.*

Alcona County Review, February 6, 1879
Cemetery:

Stringer, {Child}

LOCAL JOTTINGS.

Mr. and Mrs. E. C. Stringer buried their 3 months' old babe Wednesday.

Alcona County Review, January 23, 1885
Cemetery:

Stringer, {Child}

LOCAL JOTTINGS.

During the past two weeks, cholera-infantum has been having a terrible rage in this community, no less than a dozen small children and babes having died from the same. This naturally leaves many houses of mourning in our community, and to those of us who are as yet free from the scourge in our own homes, should come forth hearty sympathy and fitting words for the bereaved. Friday last, the scourge took away a little, human flower each from the homes of William Nestle and James Stringer. Tuesday the family of Chas. Larson were bereft of their babe, and Wednesday evening Frank Stevens and wife were called to part with their first-born. Gilbert Landon, one of the Messrs. Byces, and the Ducharms have also each lost a babe, and there are several others in the community apparently nearly at death's door, at the time we go to press. Thus many of the homes in our community are being darkened. May the Lord remove the dark cloud speedily, and give consolation to the sorrowing parents.

Alcona County Review, August 29, 1884
Cemetery:

Studer, Michael

LOCAL JOTTINGS.

He died in the Night.—Michael Studer, aged 40, has been employed for some time at Bonney's camp where he officiated in the honorable capacity of chore boy. Last Saturday morning Studer did not make his appearance as usual. He was dead. He had been drinking heavily for some time, so heavily, in fact, that he was incapacitated for work of any description. A couple of days prior to his death he had presented a fellow workman named Tim Currie with a valuable gold time piece. He seemed to have a presentment of death. Justice Beede, accompanied by Sheriff McDonald and H. P. Moore visited the camp at once and held an inquest, a verdict being returned in accordance with the facts. The remains were brought to the county seat and interred in the Potter's field of the West Harrisville cemetery.

Studer had no known relatives. His only estate was a small balance due him by Alger, Smith & Co. Thus quietly and sadly terminates the life of another of the "boys in the woods."

Alcona County Review, August 23, 1889
Cemetery: West Lawn, Alcona Co.

Stuff, Samuel F.

Local Sayings and Doings.

Death of Prof. S. F. Stuff.

Perhaps no sad event which has taken place in this community has cast such a cloud of gloom over a large majority of our citizens as the death of Prof. S. F. Stuff, principal of the Harrisville schools, which occurred at about 5 p. m. on Monday. The Prof. had been ailing for some two or three weeks past, but was not entirely disabled from performing his duties at school until about ten or twelve days prior to his death. During this time he was compelled to remain at his boarding place--the home of County Treasurer Fair and wife, and a large portion of the time was confined to bed. The fore part of last week he seemed to feel much better, but the middle of the week found him growing weaker quite rapidly, indicating in some measure that dissolution might be taking place. The Prof. himself seemed to realize the situation, and remarked to Pastor Weatherwax who visited him on Thursday, that he was sinking. Miss Ellen M. Nethaway, a teacher in the Ovid union schools (a very fine, accomplished young lady) and Prof. Stuff were engaged to be married at the close of the present term of school, and becoming somewhat alarmed at the Prof.'s condition, Mr. Fair telegraphed Miss Nethaway the situation of affairs and that he thought it best for her to come and see him at the earliest possible moment, as danger was possibly near. The arrival of Miss Nethaway last Friday morning seemed to cheer up the Prof. very much, and he indicated a condition much for the better. Even so far had he recovered strength as to be able to sit up in a chair Sunday and Monday, for a large part of the time. Monday evening, a few minutes before 5 o'clock, while in bed, as Mr. Fair came into the room he said to him "I am fainting." While Mrs. Fair and Miss Nethaway remained at the dying Prof.'s bedside, rubbing him

and applying [unreadable]... Mitchell with all possible haste, but before the arrival of the Doctor, the afflicted man was dead, his spirit having taken its departure about 10 minutes from the time when he first complained of being faint. Thus has passed away a representative young man, a generous, kind hearted citizen, educator, benefactor and exemplary Christian gentleman, and in this case as in all others, when such a man dies a whole community mourns.

Alcona County Review, May 12, 1882

Local Sayings and Doings.

Samuel F. Stuff was born in eastern Pennsylvania about the year 1848, and upon the day of his death was therefore 34 years of age. As near as we are able to ascertain from information gained through Mr. J. E. Fair, Mr. Stuff spent the early part of his life on a farm near Upton, Pa. Arriving to young manhood he came west, taking up his abode in Illinois for a year and over, when he formed a co-partnership with a friend and went into the grocery business in Toledo, Ohio. Remaining in this business for a year or more, he finally decided to make school teaching a profession, and entered our State Normal School at Ypsilanti to prepare himself for that work. Being very anxious to complete his studies and store his mind with useful knowledge, he became an exceedingly hard working student at the Normal, often burning the mid-night oil in his search for knowledge, and it is thought that there is where the breaking down of his constitution was first commenced. He remained at the Normal four years, graduating with high honors in the spring of 1880. His attendance at school was followed by a year's teaching at Belville, this state. While at the Normal he became intimately acquainted with J. E. Fair, and when Mr. Fair gave up the Harrisville school to accept a position in the County Treasurer's office, a year ago next month. Mr. Stuff was secured to succeed him, and so far as we have been able to learn he has taught in our village a most excellent school. No sooner had he arrived here to commence school that a place was also found for him in religious work. Being an active Christian man and willing worker, trained in the good work almost from his youth up, he was at once selected to superintend the Presbyterian Sabbath school and teach the young peoples' bible class, which two positions he filled with great credit to himself and great profit to the Sabbath school. He also united with the church by letter, and was immediately thereafter chosen and ordained an Elder in the church.

Personally we shall miss Prof. Stuff greatly. We had learned to love and respect him for his manly, social, moral and Christian virtues, and unswerving fidelity to everything that was good and true. He detested a mean act, but loved good works with all his heart, and by precept and example he strove continually to make mankind better and happier and lead the youth of our community in the path of true virtue. As a Christian professor and practitioner he was zealous for the cause of his Master, always being in his place in the church and Sabbath school services, and never shrinking from performing his whole duty in and out of the church. Indeed, his whole life work in and out of the church bears record to the fact that he was a true disciple of his Lord and Master.

But the good man has gone the way of all the earth; cut down as it were in the most useful part of his life. By his death the cause of education loses one of its tried and true servants, Harrisville one of her honored and respected citizens, Christianity one of its most faithful adherents and zealous leaders, and last but not least a young lady loses a noble, kind-hearted intended life companion and husband. His work has been well done, and the Savior has called him into that sweet rest which remaineth for the people of God.

"Calm on the bosom of thy God,
Fair spirit, rest thee now;
E'en while with us thy footsteps trod
His seal was on thy brow.

"Dust, to its narrow house beneath;
Soul, to its home on high
They that have seen thy look in death
No more may fear to die.

"Lone are the paths and sad the bowers,
Whence thy meek form has gone;

But of a brighter home than this
[unreadable]."
Alcona County Review, May 12, 1882

Local Sayings and Doings.

There will be memorial services by the Sunday school at the Presbyterian church at 1 o'clock, Sunday afternoon, for Prof. S. F. Stuff, the late superintendent of said school. A kind invitation is extended to all.

All good people of Harrisville may justly mourn the death of Prof. S. F. Stuff. He loved the good, the beautiful and the true, and labored zealously for the promotion of character among his pupils and in the village at large. In this he was a benefactor to all.

Alcona County Review, May 12, 1882

Local Sayings and Doings.

The remains of Prof. S. F. Stuff, accompanied by pastor Weatherwax and Miss Nethaway, were taken to Upton, Pa., the home of the Prof., Tuesday morning, for interment. A dispatch received stated that all arrived at destination safely Thursday morning.

Alcona County Review, May 12, 1882

MEMORIAL SERVICES

Held by the Presbyterian Sabbath School in Honor of Prof. S. F. Stuff, their Late Departed Sup't.

At one o'clock Sunday afternoon last, the teachers and pupils of the Presbyterian Sabbath School of Harrisville, met at the Church to pay a tribute of respect to the memory of their departed Superintendent and teacher, Prof. Samuel F. Stuff, by appropriate services. There were also present a large part of the M. E. Sabbath School and many others.

The Bible stand used in the school was covered with dark drapery, and festooned from the four corners with black and white silk ribbon. On the top of the stand rested a very handsome anchor, constructed of moss, evergreens and flowers, letters "S. F. S." being worked in white flowers on the cross-piece. The appearance was very neat.

The services were opened with the anthem written by P. P. Bliss—
"He's Gone!"
Followed by prayer.

Singing—from Jasper and Gold—
"Angels will welcome us home."
ADDRESS.
The following remarks were made by J. K. Fairchild:

Teachers, Pupils and Friends:
We meet here to-day to pay a fitting tribute to the memory of our departed superintendent, teacher and Christian brother. For very many of us the occasion is a sad one--doubly so, because it brings to our remembrance the fact that he whom we have been accustomed to assemble with in this church from Sabbath to Sabbath, and under whose ministrations we have happily sat together as teacher and pupils during many months in the past, shall meet with us on earth no more forever. Under any circumstances it is hard to part with those to whom we have become attached, but more especially does this separation fall heavily upon most of us, because it removes from our midst one whom we loved and revered as a friend and benefactor of more than average kind, and whose goings in and out before us as superintendent, teacher and friend were characterized by noble example and all the qualities of true manhood and pure Christianity. By the Death of Prof. Samuel F. Stuff we have indeed lost a true friend and helper. To be sure, many of us knew but little of the previous history of this young man when he came among us scarcely a year ago, but may we not truthfully say to-day that there are none of us who were not deeply impressed by his noble Christian bearing, good deeds and right living while he moved before us in the various departments of life. As a Christian young man we found him tried and true, and his noble example we all admired. Indeed the beauty of his life was that he daily practiced those virtues which he strove zealously to teach others to observe. There was no counterfeit about the life of Prof. Stuff; all was genuine. He was the same true, unselfish, kind hearted Christian man every day--in the church, the school room, upon the street, or wherever you met him, and he greeted all alike with a smile and a kind word. In the church he was a most valuable helper. He never shrank from duty, but performed his

part in the services of the sanctuary with a willing, earnest heart. No cross, apparently, was too heavy for him to bear. He loved the service of his Divine Master, and could submit to any legitimate work so long as it was for Christ's sake, and the encouragement and bettering of fellow humanity. In the weekly prayer and social meetings of the church when ill health did not forbid he was always present and in his place, regardless almost of the condition of the weather, and his voice in prayer and song was always heard. Likewise also was his presence in the Sunday school. He never failed to be there, unless prevented by sickness, and his constant presence and labors in the school were not without good fruitage. In his words of instruction he sought continually to impress you, pupils, with the great benefit and advantage of a pure Christian life, and urged upon you the immediate adoption and pursuance of such a living. Ever remember his kind words so lovingly and earnestly spoken in your interests, and forget not those cardinal virtues which he urged you ever to keep in remembrance and practice in your daily walks of life. In his counseling with you, teachers, his great desire and constant aim was to impress you more fully with the grandeur and high importance of your work and to encourage you to continue the active study of God's holy word that you might become better enabled to impart therefrom saving instruction to those of the young under your religious care and training. Forget not his solicitations in this great labor zealously that in the work of the Lord may prosper in your hands. In the day school Prof. Stuff's life was characterized by principles of earnest work akin to those common with him in church and in the Sabbath school; and we may say that his zeal in the interests of education was to a large extent unmeasured. Night in large part, as well as day, he labored hard to assist his pupils in their difficult studies, and to promote the highest possible success of the school at large; and indeed the school prospered materially under his direction and management as principal. As a citizen the Prof. was conceded to be a true man by all who made his

slightest acquaintance. His fidelity to principle and matters of general right, whatever might oppose, stamping him as a friend and benefactor to the race. But--teacher, pupil, friend, citizen--he will be with us no more. This bright star from the constellation of grand humanity has fallen, never again to be seen by mortal eye, or to illumine the pathway of earthly brother, companion or friend. Apparently in the most useful part of his life-work has the good man been taken away, and perhaps some of us wonder at this early, sudden decease. But to an All-wise Providence only is the key to this mystery held. Let us trust in Him with the same obedient, confiding trust as did our late friend and brother, ever remembering that "He doeth all things well," and in His own time he shall reveal to our understanding the full import of this mystery, and also prove the glory which he has in keeping for those who are faithful and true to the end of mortal existence.

RESOLUTIONS.

The following resolutions were read and presented by Mr. Geo. W. Colwell and unanimously adopted:

Whereas The Great Father of mankind has permitted the grim harvester Death to invade our circle and remove therefrom our late beloved superintendent, Prof. S. F. Stuff. And

Whereas, It seems proper and fitting that we make some acknowledgement of the sentiments of esteem in which we held him while living, and of our regret for his untimely death; therefore, be it

Resolved, That in the death of our late companion and brother we have lost a wise counselor, a patient monitor, a Conscientious and pains-taking teacher, a moral and upright Christian gentleman, one whose examples and precepts were always upon the side of truth and right.

That we deeply sympathize with the relatives of our deceased friend in their doubly sad affliction, but do not grieve as those without hope, bully recognizing that he was prepared to enter into the life everlasting.

That in the memory of his life and death we shall do well to keep in mind the nobleness of his aspirations, his unselfish labor for others, and if we can but live up to that high

standard which he maintained while with us, we shall find it well with us in the end.

Resolved, That this brief heartfelt testimonial of our regard be spread upon the records and furnished the "Review" for publication, and that a copy be transmitted to the aged mother of the deceased and to Miss Ella Nethaway, of Ovid, Mich.

The services were closed by singing from Jasper and Gold--

"Angels will welcome us home."

Alcona County Review, May 19, 1882

Local Sayings and Doings.

Rev. F. W. Weatherwax returned this morning from his sad journey to Upton, Pa., with the remains of Prof. Stuff.

Alcona County Review, May 19, 1882

Local Sayings and Doings.

Last Sunday evening Rev. F. W. Weatherwax preached a sermon in honor of the late Prof. Stuff.

Alcona County Review, May 26, 1882

To-day the Harrisville village school closes for the year. The work of the year has been well done by both teachers and a large part of the pupils. Though affliction has come upon the school by the sudden taking away of the able, faithful and beloved principal, Prof. S. F. Stuff, yet the work, under the principle management of Miss Mae Colwell, has gone on in a manner commendable to both teacher and pupils. Miss Colwell is a good teacher, especially in her chosen department, and her faithfulness and success shown in the work here under adverse circumstances is worthy of high commendation. Miss Satie Tait has performed the duties of assistant teacher in the school for four weeks past, very acceptably.

Alcona County Review, June 30, 1882
Cemetery: Cedar Hill, Franklin Co., Pennsylvania

Sukekurn, Charles E.

Our Neighbors.

Chas. E. Sukekurn, druggist at Potts, Oscoda county, has died from la grippe.

Alcona County Review, January 31, 1890
Cemetery:

Sullivan, Edward

MURDER WILL OUT.

Wm. Repke Confesses to being one of the Murderers of Albert Molitor in 1875.

The citizens of Presque Isle county are intensely excited over the confession of Wm. Repke to being one of a party of seventeen men who banded themselves together for the purpose of killing Albert Molitor, of Rogers City. He stated that after having kept the secret 16 years his troubled conscience was unbearable to him, and he could stand the remorse and secret no longer. His statement is that seventeen citizens of Presque Isle county, including himself, entered into an oath-bound compact to assassinate Albert Molitor and Frederick Denny Larke. For some reason Larke was not seen on the fatal evening, he states that the killing of the clerk, Sullivan, was a mistake. The shot he received was intended a second one for Molitor.

The story of the murder is as follows: Sixteen years ago the 22nd of this month, Albert Molitor was sitting in his office in Rogers City, looking over his books, when a gun was fired through the window and Molitor dropped with seven buckshot in his side and back. A clerk named Edward Sullivan, who was in the store with Molitor, sprang to his assistance, and received a load of shot in the neck. Both men were mortally wounded. Sullivan lived for about three days, but died as he was being taken to the steamer to be carried home. Molitor lived a couple of weeks, being taken to Harper Hospital, in Detroit, before he died.

The enmity towards Molitor had been growing for some time, but the direct cause of the murder was this: Rogers township originally occupied about one-half of Presque Isle county. Molitor was instrumental in bonding the township to secure sufficient money to build roads to the farms of these same conspirators, as well as other farmers in the surrounding country. Subsequently the county was redistricted, Rogers township being divided up so that the portion then bearing the name of Rogers township was small, even in comparison to the other new townships. Thus this little section was loaded with the bonds on which money was raised to build roads over half of Presque Isle

county. Molitor went to the legislature and received a proper apportionment of this debt. It was this that caused feeling against him.

Twelve of the men, including Repke, are in jail at Rogers City. Two of the band are dead; the other three men are in the state and will be arrested and brought to Rogers City for trial. Henry Clother, a brother-in-law of Molitor, and Judge Shields, of Alpena, are conducting the prosecution, while Frank Emerick and Geo. H. Slator, also of Alpena, have charge of the defense.

Alcona County Review, August 6, 1891

A GREAT CRIME.

The Murderers of Edward Molitor Coming to Justice at Last.

Alpena, Oct. 22.——(Special.)-Wm. Reipke, who made a confession of the Molitor murder at Rogers City, and who was released last week, was rearrested on Tuesday of this week and had his examination before Justice Kaichen yesterday. Several witnesses were sworn. Steven Roger testified that he was present on the night of the murder as was also Reipke and the others whose names have been given before that the two first shots were fired by Grossman and Jacobs and that he was standing within ten feet of them at the time; that Reipke then fired and shot Sullivan. Reipke was bound over for trial and bail was fixed at $5,000 in default of which he was remanded to jail. It is rumored in Rogers City that the charge against the five men for the murder of Molitor will be withdrawn and that new warrants will be issued charging them with the murder of Edw. Sullivan. Sullivan died in this city and for that reason the trial should take place here. Messrs. Shield and McNamara of the prosecution, state that no such course has been decided upon, although this action may before next January, the time set for the trial.

Alcona County Review, October 29, 1891

'ROUND ABOUT.

The Molitor murder cases in Presque Isle county have gone over to the January term of court.

Alcona County Review, October 29, 1891

AFTER MANY YEARS.

Conviction of Grossman of the Murder of Albert Molitor 17 Years Ago.

From the Pioneer.

Our last week's report of the case included the most important evidence produced by the prosecution, and it is admitted that they made a very strong case. In addition to the testimony of Henry Clothier, Mrs. Edward Molitor, F. D. Larke, and others who knew of the case, and all of which implicated Grossman and the other defendants, the famous confession of Repke was given to the jury in full. This confession was confirmed by the testimony of Stephen Reiger. Ferdinand Bruder, Gottlieb Mende, Frederick Soegenfrie, John Bruder and Carl Weisengart, all of whom admitted that they were with the party which killed Molitor, and strongly implicated the four defendants who are held for trial, namely August Grossman, Henry Jacobs, Carl Vogeler and August Furhman.

The defense began on Thursday, the principal effort being made to establish an alibi for each of the defendants.

Andrew E. Banks testified that he knew nothing of the murder; that the testimony implicating him was false. He was arrested and examined before Justice Harris Aug. 28, 1875, and was discharged. On cross examination he admitted that he was not arrested in 1875, as he had testified; that Molitor had a judgment against him for $200, and that he got farmers together to recover his boots, which were in the possession of the sheriff. Altogether his testimony was very contradictory and he proved a poor witness for the defense.

Herman Hoeft, the wealthy lumberman and merchant of Presque Isle, who has been vaguely charged with complicity in the Molitor murder, was next called. He denied any act, part or knowledge of the affair, and said he was at Detroit for 10 days previous to and during the shooting. Upon cross-examination he admitted he was furnishing the money for the defense, and had neither taken nor asked for security of any kind. He admitted taking a body of men to Crawford's quarry in the spring of 1875 to forcibly take the treasurer's books from Len Crawford. But he claimed to be on friendly terms with Molitor.

Mr. and Mrs. Pauly swore that a sick baby brought them to Grossman's house the night Molitor was shot and they remember of seeing Grossman at home.

On Monday August Grossman was put on the stand in his own defense. He testified that he had lived in Presque Isle since 1870; that he had held some township or county office during almost every year since, but thought he held no office in 1875, the year of the murder; that he knew Molitor in Detroit before coming to Presque Isle county; that he and Molitor were good friends and that he had no enmity toward him; that he was at home the night of the murder; was first told of the murder by Weisengart who told him that they thought in town that the farmers killed Molitor.

On cross-examination he declared that he was with the crowd which demanded the county books from Molitor in 1873. The prosecution tried to show that at that time Grossman said that Molitor ought to be hung, but the judge ruled that out. He admitted also that he was with the crowd which went to Rogers City to recover Bank's boots, and that he wore a belt with a big horse pistol. He also admitted that Molitor had a judgment against him but claimed that it had been paid. He admitted going to Furhman's house to get him up to go with the crowd after Bank's boots. It was shown that he had three offices the year of the murder.

A number of other witnesses were sworn and some former witnesses recalled but nothing of any importance was elicited. The defense rested their case at 6 o'clock.

The testimony having been concluded, the arguments in the case were commenced Wednesday morning by Prosecuting Attorney McNamara for the People. He gave a graphic description of the condition of county affairs in Presque Isle county previous to and at the time of the murder, stating that Grossman and the others in the alleged plot were constant office holders, and were business and political rivals of

Molitor. He then reviewed the testimony, pointing out that seven men—Repke, Reiger, Mende, Sergenfrie, Weisengart and the two Bruders—had sworn positively that they took part in the work, and that Grossman and other three defendants were leaders in the awful conspiracy which resulted in the butchering of Albert Molitor and Edward Sullivan. The alibi sought to be established by Grossman was discussed at length, and the testimony in this regard held up in a manner which made it appear very gauzy. He closed with a strong plea for the vindication of the name of northern Michigan, and for the punishment of these murderers, who had too long escaped justice.

Judge Emerick opened the case for the defense. He made a most eloquent plea for justice, bringing forth convincing arguments which were placed before the jury in a manner that evidently made a deep impression.

The large court room was crowded to its upmost capacity Thursday morning to hear the arguments of Sleator and Atkinson for the defense. Business was almost suspended down town, and many could not gain admittance.

Col. Atkinson closed the arguments for the defense, making a clear, strong and able address.

Judge Kelly at once made his charge to the jury. He impressed the jury with the atrocity of the crime which had been committed, but expressly warned them that they were not to find a verdict of guilty unless they were satisfied beyond a reasonable doubt that Grossman was one of the murderers.

The charge was generally conceded to have been exceedingly clear, able and impartial.

The jury were out all night. The first ballot stood 10 for conviction, 2 for acquittal, but an agreement was finally reached and at the opening of court Friday morning the jury returned a verdict of guilty of murder in the first degree.

The other three defendants will be tried in the February term, each separately. Repke and Reiger, who are also under indictment but who have made confessions, will probably plead guilty and throw themselves on the mercy of the court. It is also

understood that proceedings will be commenced against Mende, Sorgenfrie, Weisengart and Bruder, the remaining four of the twelve who are alleged to have been in the conspiracy, Barabas and Tuelgetski being dead. Proceedings may also be begun against Andrew E. Banks.

Grossman's attorneys have moved for a new trial and Judge Kelley will hear the motion Dec. 30.

Alcona County Review, December 22, 1892

EVENTS OF ONE WEEK.

It is a singular fact that three adjoining shore counties, Iosco, Alcona and Alpena, have each contributed a life convict to Jackson prison within the past month: Iosco county sent Benson; Alpena county sent Grossman and Alcona county sends Wightman. A pretty trio of murderers.

Alcona County Review, January 19, 1893

ARE GUILTY!

OF MURDER IN THE FIRST DEGREE FOR KILLING MOLITOR.

Four Rogers City Murderers Have Now Been Brought to Justice.

For a Crime Which Was Committed 18 Years Ago.

Alpena, Mich., July 10.—Vogler, Fuhrman and Jacobs are guilty of the murder of Albert Molitor. The case was given to the jury last Saturday night at 8 o'clock and three hours later a verdict was returned. The prisoners will be sentenced later on.

In all probability the trial of Repke, the self-confessed murderer, will now be taken up. This makes four men convicted, Grossman having been sent to Jackson for life last January.

Albert Molitor, a merchant at Rogers City and a clerk of his named Sullivan, were murdered on the evening of August 23, 1875. There were many theories and suspicions as to who were the murderers, and some of them were pretty close to the truth, but nothing definite was ever learned until Wm. Repke, a farmer living in Moltke township, Presque Isle county, becoming conscious stricken after sixteen years of silence, went to the prosecuting attorney of Presque Isle county at Rogers City during the last days of July in 1892, and confessed that he and sixteen other men, then working in and about Rogers City, entered into a conspiracy to kill Molitor and Frederic Denny Larke, but while they succeeded in shooting Molitor, they made a mistake as to Larke and killed Sullivan in his stead. Repke gave the names of such of the other murderers as he recollected, as follows:

Albert Grossman, Carl Vogler, Gottlieb Lambert, Charles Wassengart, Fred Bruder, Ferdinand Bruder, Henry Jacob, Herman Menze, August Furgenfrier, August Furhman.

Some of them had moved away and two were dead, but nearly all of those remaining in this section of the county had become prominent and leading citizens, and the confession of Repke accordingly caused a tremendous sensation.

Alpena, Mich.—William Repke, the man who caused the arrest of the Molitor murderers, by turning State's evidence, was placed on trial Tuesday morning.

Alcona County Review, July 13, 1893

CLOSE OF THE MOLITOR CASES.

Rieger Not Guilty, Jacobs, Volger, Fuhrman and Repke Go Up for Life.

The conclusion of the prosecutions in the celebrated Molitor murder cases occurred last week when Stephen Rieger was found not guilty.

The convicted men, Repke, Volger, Fuhrman and Jacobs were taken into court Saturday to receive their sentence. Each one maintained his innocence, when asked if he had anything to say why sentence should not be pronounced upon them. Judge Kelley pronounced sentence in these words: "You will be confined in the State prison at Jackson in solitary confinement for the balance of your natural lives."

Repke was the only one of the four who broke down. As his voluntary divulging of the conspiracy had led to the conviction of the men, it was generally believed that he would get

off with a lighter sentence, but the Court didn't see it that way.

The sheriff started Sunday for Jackson with the prisoners.

Alcona County Review, July 27, 1893

A Confessed Liar.

Wm. Repke Makes an Astonishing Deposition.

Nearly every Review reader has heard of the celebrated Molitor murder cases, for which during the past two years several prominent citizens of Presque Isle county have been arrested, tried and convicted of the murder of Edward Molitor at Rogers City some 17 years ago. The prosecutions were based upon the confession of Wm. Repke, who was one of the arch conspirators. Repke claimed that he was promised immunity from prosecution as the price of his confession, but instead of going free he too was tried and convicted and is now doing time with the rest in Jackson prison.

A few days ago Repke subscribed to a sworn statement that all the testimony given by him against his confederates was false and untrue in every particular; in other words he confesses himself a moral coward and a despicable liar. It is not likely that it will result in new trials for the others.

Alcona County Review, November 16, 1893
Cemetery:

Sutherland, George

PURELY PERSONAL.

Mrs. P. C. Goldie was called to Oil Springs, Ont., last Saturday, a telegram received the day before announcing the death of her father at that place.

Alcona County Review, March 2, 1888

PURELY PERSONAL.

Mrs. P. C. Goldie has returned from Oil Springs, Ont., where she went to attend the funeral of her father.

Alcona County Review, March 9, 1888
Cemetery: Oil Springs, Lambton Co. ON

Suydam, Elmira

Probate Order.

STATE OF MICHIGAN. County of Alcona.

At a session of the Probate Court for the county of Alcona, holden at the Probate Office in the village of Harrisville, on Monday the fifth day

of February, in the year one thousand eight hundred and eighty-three.

Present, B. P. Cowley, Judge of Probate.

In the matter of the estate of Elmira Suydam, deceased. On reading and filing a duly certified copy of the last will and testament of Elmira Suydam, deceased, together with due proof of the probate thereof before the Serrogate of Essex county, of the state of New Jersey, the same having been produced by persons claiming to be interested in said will, Thereupon it is ordered, that Monday the twelfth day of March next, at ten o'clock in the forenoon, be assigned for the hearing of said petition, and that all persons interested in said estate, are required to appear at a session of said Court, then to be holden at the Probate Office, in the Court House in Harrisville, and show cause, if any there be, why the prayer of the petitioners should not be granted. And it is further ordered, that said petitioners give notice to the persons interested in said estate, of the pendency of said petition, and the hearing thereof, by causing a copy of this order to be published in the Alcona County Review, a newspaper printed and circulated in said county of Alcona for four successive weeks previous to said day of hearing.

B. P. Cowley,
Judge of Probate.

Alcona County Review, January 31, 1890
Cemetery:

Swindlehurst, William J.

A little son of Wm. Swindlehurst was buried Sunday. The child died of summer complaint.

Alcona County Review, August 5, 1897
Cemetery:

Switzer, {Boy}

HAYNES.

July 30.—Martin Switzer lost a boy last Thursday, aged 3 years. The symptoms seemed to be worms; he was seized with choking and died in twenty minutes. He was buried Friday afternoon.

Alcona County Review, August 2, 1889
Cemetery: Mt. Joy, Alcona Co.

Switzer, {Male}

COUNTY JOTTINGS.

Harry Shwitzer received the sad intelligence yesterday of the death of his father, who resided in Poland.

Alcona County Review, August 2, 1889
Cemetery:

Tacie, John

LOCAL JOTTINGS.

A man, name not learned, was run over near Black River, Wednesday, and both legs were crushed.

Alcona County Review, August 24, 1888

It Was A Fatal Accident.

The man reported as having been injured near Black River last week was John Tacie, of Alpena. He was walking to Black River on the railroad track when a log train came along. It stopped and he boarded it, expecting to ride to the village. The train had not gone far before he fell under the wheels. Both legs were cut off. It was an hour before he was discovered lying by the track. As soon as possible after he was discovered he was taken to Black River where Dr. McCormick did all for him that it was possible to do. He was placed on the Alpena log train, and his relatives were notified to meet him, but he died just after the train left Ossineke. He was 27 years old and unmarried.

Alcona County Review, August 31, 1888
Cemetery:

Taft, Harriett S. [Witter]

PERSONAL.

Eugene Taft came up Monday from Detroit to visit his mother and old associates. Mrs. Taft is in poor health and is confined to bed.

Alcona County Review, October 21, 1897

PERSONAL.

Eugene Taft returned Tuesday morning to Detroit. He was accompanied by his mother, who goes for the purpose of receiving treatment in one of the hospitals of that city.

Alcona County Review, October 28, 1897

HARRIETT S. TAFT.

This old and respected citizen died at her home in the village at 6:30 o'clock last evening, after years of illness and suffering. Her sickness extended over a period of about six years, sometimes being confined to her bed and at other times able to be about her household duties. In October last she went to a Detroit hospital, but received no benefits from her treatment there. Since her return home about three weeks ago she has been confined to her bed a greater part of the time. Tuesday night she took a sudden turn for the worse and last evening the end came.

Thus endeth the life of a worthy woman, who has had her full share of life's trials and has fought well the fight.

Harriett S. Witter was born in New York state on August 11, 1835, and was therefore 62 years and 5 months old at the time of her death. She was married to John Taft in 1858. Thirty years ago they came to Harrisville. In June, 1878, Mr. Taft died, leaving his widow the care of seven children, six of whom are still living to mourn the departure of a beloved mother. The children are Mrs. F. E. Stevens and Mrs. C. E. Jameson, of Montesano, Wash., Eugene J. Taft of Detroit, Lester W. Taft of Grand Marais, and the Misses Matie and Lyda Taft of Harrisville.

The funeral services will be held at the residence Saturday morning at 10 o'clock. It was the wish of the deceased that a private funeral be held, with none but the family and immediate friends in attendance.

Eugene Taft came up from Detroit this morning, L. W. Taft is expected from Grand Marais tomorrow.

Alcona County Review, January 20, 1898

LOCAL PICK UPS.

Many hearts were heavy and sad in Harrisville Friday last, Jan. 21. The mortal remains of three persons, one an infant, two in the autumn of life's journey, were borne to their final resting places. The remains of Mrs. Harriet S. Taft were buried in the morning, those of Mrs. Sinclair and the little son of Edw. Saylor at different hours in the afternoon. Services in each case were held at the residences. Three funerals in one day in a town the size of Harrisville is a sad and unusual occurrence.

Alcona County Review, January 27, 1898

LOCAL PICK UPS.

The estate of the late Mrs. Taft was equitably partitioned among the heirs, her six children, prior to her death, and a warranty deed for each one's portion was signed, sealed and delivered, avoiding all future complications.

Alcona County Review, January 27, 1898

PERSONAL.

Holmes Witter of McKinley and Mr. and Mrs. Otis Witter of Au Sable were here to attend the funeral of their sister, Mrs. Taft.

Alcona County Review, January 27, 1898

PERSONAL.

Eugene Taft returned Tuesday to Detroit. Lester leaves this evening for Grand Marais.

Alcona County Review, January 27, 1898

Local History of One Year

Chronology of the Principal Events of the Year 1898.

January 19. Deaths: Mrs. Harriett Taft aged 62; Mrs. Sinclair aged 80; Willie Saylor aged 4. Two infants.

Alcona County Review, January 5, 1899
Cemetery: Springport, Alcona Co.

Taft, John

A SAD ACCIDENT.
By Which Our Worthy Townsman, Mr. John Taft, Came to His Death.

It is with painful regret that we are called upon to announce the decease of our worthy and respected pioneer citizen, Mr. John Taft, who came to his death through the agency of a terrible accident which happened to him last Saturday evening about five o'clock.

It is perhaps well-known by our readers that Mr. Taft had contracted with Messrs. R. A. Alger & Co. to build several miles of railway at Black River, and that he had built his camps four miles back of that village, and was prosecuting the job. At a watering-place about one-half mile from the camps, it seems Mr. Taft and one of his men had made what is termed a "deer lick." When on their way to this place, with guns in hand, Saturday evening, and nearing the spot, Mr. Taft stepped upon a log to inspect the "situation" and see if any deer were visible, and here he met with an accident, the particulars of which we will now give: While upon the log, Mr. Taft's rifle accidentally slipped from his hand and fell upon the log, he catching the same by the muzzle with the left hand simultaneously. In its fall the rifle was discharged, the ball penetrating Mr. Taft's left arm at the lower extremity of the wrist, and passing up the same came out immediately below the elbow and entered the arm again below the muscles. It then pursued its upward course and finally lodged in the shoulder joint. The whole arm was completely shattered from hand to shoulder. By the aid of his companion huntsman, Mr. Taft succeeded in walking back to the camp, when Dr. D. W. Mitchell and Mrs. Taft were dispatched for. Upon examination of the arm the doctor came to the conclusion that it would have to be amputated, to make it possible to save the patient's life, and accordingly Dr. W. P. Maiden, of Alpena, was sent for, who arrived on Sunday, and, assisted by Dr. Mitchell, amputated the arm at the shoulder joint. It was thought at first that the patient would survive the operation, and get well, but Monday afternoon came only to reveal the fact that life was rapidly wasting away, and at five o'clock Monday evening he died.

The decease was born at Lindley Town, in the State of New York, on the 15th day of May, 1837, and consequently was forty-one years and eighteen days old on the day of his death. He removed with his family from New York State to Harrisville in 1867, eleven years ago, where he purchased a home and where also he has since resided. He was an exemplary temperance man, and a prominent member of the Red Ribbon Club and Independent Order of Good Templars of Harrisville. He was a man who had a great many warm friends, and but few, if any enemies. In fact, none knew John Taft but to honor and respect him, and his death is a public calamity, as well as a terrible blow to his family.

The funeral services of the deceased were held from the M. E. Church, Tuesday afternoon, under the auspices of the Masonic Order, of which fraternity he was a member and prominent officer.--The Independent Order of Good Templars, of which also he was a member, were out in full regalia. The sermon preached by the pastor, Rev. N. N. Clark, was a very appropriate one, and was based upon the following words, which were among the last uttered by the deceased: "Has not a man the right to pray for his own soul?"

The attendance upon the funeral services of the deceased was very large, nearly every person in the community turning out to pay their last respects to the beloved neighbor and citizen.

Thus has passed away one of Harrisville's most worthy pioneer citizens.

Alcona County Review, June 7, 1878

COUNTY JOTTINGS.

On account of the funeral services, and in honor of our worthy townsman, Mr. John Taft, deceased, the schools in the township were closed and all the mills shut down.

Alcona County Review, June 7, 1878

In Memoriam.

At a regular communication of Alcona Lodge, No. 292, F. and A. M., held at Harrisville, Michigan, June 12, 1878, the following resolutions relative to the death of Brother John Taft were unanimously adopted:

Whereas, It has pleased the great architect of the Universe, in the dispension of his divine providence, to call from our midst our worthy Brother, John Taft, and

Whereas, the Masonic ties which have bound us in friendship are severed, no more to be reunited until the day when the grave shall yield up its dead; therefore

Resolved, that in the death of our Brother, John Taft, we recognize that wisdom which, while it removes from our midst an esteemed Brother, from the domestic circle a kind husband and father, from society a valuable citizen, a warm friend and good neighbor, admonishes us not only of the uncertainties of life, but of the many sterling virtues which he exhibited in his daily intercourse with the world, and in his devotion to the principles of his profession as a man and a Mason. Therefore

Resolved, That we deeply sympathize with the bereaved family and friends of our deceased Brother, and pray for them that consolation the world can neither give nor take away. Therefore

Resolved, That as a tribute of respect to the memory of our deceased Brother, this Lodge where the badge of mourning for the next thirty days. And

Resolved, That a copy of these resolutions be entered upon the minutes of this Lodge, and a copy presented to the family of our deceased Brother, and a copy furnished the Michigan Free Mason and Alcona County Review for publication.

F. O. Gullifer,

L. H. Higgins, Com.
D. McGregor,

Alcona County Review, June 21, 1878
Cemetery: Springport, Alcona Co.

Taft, Nellie

REVIEWINGS.

Nellie, the youngest daughter of Mrs. Harriet S. Taft, died Sunday evening last; aged 2 years, 3 months and 10 days. Mrs. Taft is certainly having her full measure of affliction. She should have the warm sympathy of our citizens.

Alcona County Review, July 11, 1879

Card of Thanks.--Permit me through your paper, Mr. Editor, to thank many friends for their kindness during the sickness and death of our little Nellie. The repeated kind acts of C. P. Reynolds, Esq., and others, in hours of sorrow, have done much to throw sunlight in a lonely path. Resting assured that Nellie is a jewel in the care of my Savior, I am yours in hope,

Mrs. Harriet S. Taft.

Alcona County Review, July 11, 1879
Cemetery: Springport, Alcona Co.

Tageson, John

The Local News.

H. P. Moore was called to Kimball's camp Thursday morning by a telegram to the affect that a man had been killed there. No particulars were learned further than that his name was Jno. Tagurison.

Alcona County Review, December 27, 1889

SAD ACCIDENT.

News reached this place Thursday morning of the sad death of Jno. Tagerson, at Kimball's camp. He with his fellow workmen were cutting down a Norway tree. He not thinking of a tree falling his way didn't get out in time, the tree struck him in back of the neck causing such injuries that he lived about 20 minutes. His companions speak very highly of him as a straight forward young man and it cast a gloom over the boys as they went back to their work after the holidays. A brother employed at Pritchard's camp took his remains to Bad Axe, his former home.

Alcona County Review, January 3, 1890

One Year's History.

Record of Local Happenings for the Year 1890.

JANUARY.

2 John Tagerson killed in Kimball's camp.

Alcona County Review, January 1, 1891
Cemetery: Verona Township, Huron Co.

Tall, Effie

Curtis.

Curtis, May 23, 1892.

Sad news to all: Miss Effie Tall was called from earth on Sunday, May 15, to try the realities of the other world. Her death was very sudden. Saturday night she was in apparent good health and full of life and spirits and at bed-time she selected her clothing to wear to Sabbath school, but little realized that they were to be her funeral garments. But God giveth and God taketh away. Blessed be the name of the Lord. At about five o'clock Sunday morning she died, only a short period of 7 or 8 hours from her enjoyment of her usual health, till Death's cold arms took her away from her mother's arms who loved her so tenderly. She was about 18 years of age, and was thus cut off in the fullness of her youth and beauty; but man's days are as grass; as flowers of the fields so he flourisheth for the wind passeth over it and it is gone. This beloved one has many friends to mourn the loss of one so fair. The Rev. A. R. Snetsigner preached the funeral sermon at her home at Mr. Lot Simond's. Then the remains were conducted to their last resting place by the largest number of people ever in attendance at a funeral in Curtis.

Alcona County Review, May 26, 1892

HISTORY OF ONE YEAR.

Chronological History of the Past Year, 1892.

THE DEATH RECORD.

May 15. Effie Tall of Curtis.

Alcona County Review, January 5, 1893
Cemetery:

Talmadge, Raymond S.?

Local Sayings and Doings.

By telegram last evening from Rev. C. H. Talmage, at Dundee, to Dr. Freeman, his father-in-law, it is learned that the oldest child is much worse, and calling Dr. Freeman to Dundee at once. The Doctor left on the 10:40 train last evening. The family of Mr. Talmadge is sadly af-
[the next line is missing]
it being the youngest child that died on Monday, and not the eldest, as reported. The oldest is now dangerously ill with diphtheria accompanied by croup.—*Saginaw Daily Herald*, Dec. 16.

It will be remembered that the Rev. Talmadge, above referred, was pastor of the M. E. church of Harrisville two years ago.

Alcona County Review, December 23, 1881
Cemetery:

Tarsney, Mary A. [Murray]

Hon. T. E. Tarsney was called home to Saginaw last week by the dangerous illness of his mother, who died on Tuesday, aged 76.

Alcona County Review, March 5, 1886
Cemetery: Calvary, Saginaw Co.

Tate, Mrs. Elizabeth

SPRINGPORT AND VICINITY.

Mrs. Tate, mother of Mrs. Wm. Donahue, is reported quite ill.

Alcona County Review, February 4, 1897

PERSONAL.

Mr. Jno. Sayers of Lansing, and Mrs. Worden of Mason, have arrived in the village on a visit to their mother, Mrs. Tate, who is in very feeble health.

Alcona County Review, May 27, 1897

Another Pioneer Gone.

The death of Mrs. Tate occurred at the home of her daughter, Mrs. Wm. Donahue last Friday afternoon, after a long illness.

Deceased was born in Queens County, Ireland, in the year 1815, and had therefore reached the advanced age of 82 years at the time of her death. She came to America at the age of 12 years, and has been a resident of Alcona County for 36 years. She was twice married. Four children survive her, viz: Mrs. Wm. Donahue of Harrisville; Jos. Sayers of Grand Rapids, Minn.; Mrs. C. Worden of Mason, Mich., and John Sayers of Lansing, Mich.

The funeral was held Monday morning from the Catholic church.

Alcona County Review, June 10, 1897

Card of Thanks.—We desire to express our thanks to the many kind friends who assisted us during the illness and death of our beloved mother. We desire to especially thank those who contributed flowers, and the choir for the sweet music furnished at the church.

Children of Mrs. Tate.

Alcona County Review, June 10, 1897
Cemetery: St. Anne's, Alcona Co.

Tate, Peter

The Local News.

Mr. Tait, who lacked but three years of being a centenarian, died on Tuesday of this week after a long illness. He had been a resident of the county for upwards of a quarter of a century. Funeral services were held this morning. We expected to give particulars concerning this worthy gentleman's life but they have not reached us as we close the forms.

Alcona County Review, April 23, 1891

Wm. Donahue wishes to express for himself and wife their gratitude to those who offered their kind assistance during the recent illness and death of Mr. Tait.

Alcona County Review, April 30, 1891
Cemetery: St. Anne's, Alcona Co.

Taylor, Walter

A Somewhat Mysterious Fatality.

Au Sable Monitor: Thursday afternoon, about two o'clock, Walter Taylor, a teamster who lived with his family near the Burke property, in the lower end of Au Sable, started from Pack, Woods & Co.'s store for Pott's Headquarters camp with a load of supplies for Hamilton & O'Brien at that point. This was the last seen of Taylor until about 8 o'clock Thursday night, when a young man named Jas. Brooks, coming from camp, run across the body of Taylor lying in the road, while his team appeared to be hitched a short distance away. Brooks shook Taylor, supposing he was asleep, and asked him if he had not slept long enough. Failing in waking him Brooks came on to town, and thought but little more of the matter until the next morning, when he with a companion started back, thinking perhaps something was wrong. In the meantime Joseph Beadle had come across Taylor's body while driving up to his father's place early Friday morning. Mr. Beadle immediately gave the alarm and a messenger was sent for Coroner Chevarier who brought the remains to town and an inquest was held at the residence of the deceased Friday afternoon. From the evidence it appears that Mr. Taylor was subject to cramps and frequently became helpless. In the absence of any bruises on the person sufficient to cause death, the jury determined that death was caused from something else than injuries received by the wagon passing over one arm and his shoulder, causing slight bruises. They inclined to the belief that being taken in a fit, Taylor had fallen off from the wagon and being stunned by the wagon running over him, had died from the combined effects of the fit, the injuries and exposure. No traces that Taylor was intoxicated at the time the accident occurred were found.

Mr. Taylor was born at Ottawa, Ont., in March, 1856. He was married and had four children. He bore a good name among his acquaintances. Besides his immediate family he leaves a brother, John Taylor, with whom he was engaged in the woods during the past winter.

Alcona County Review, May 7, 1886
Cemetery:

Teeple, Chester

Haynes Happenings.

Aug. 10, 1896.

Mr. and Mrs. Fred O. Teeple lost their baby boy of cholera infantum after a sickness of 24 hours, aged 5 months and 2 days. The Rev. McBride preached a funeral sermon on Saturday. The remains were followed to our beautiful cemetery by a goodly number of relatives and friends of the bereft parents.

Alcona County Review, August 13, 1896
Cemetery: Mt. Joy, Alcona Co.

Teeple, Clifford

ALCONA ATOMS.

Frederick Teeple and wife were called to Alpena last week to attend the funeral of his sister who was buried on Sunday, August 1st. Unhappily for them their little boy died on the same day. He was a fine child about five months old. The funeral took place to-day, Tuesday, the Rev. Mr. Wier officiating.

Alcona County Review, August 6, 1886

LOCAL JOTTINGS.

A little son of Fred and Eliza Teeple, of Alcona, died last Sunday.

The funeral service was held Tuesday, at the residence.

Alcona County Review, August 6, 1886

Resolutions of Condolence.

At a regular convocation of Black River Commandery, No. 53, Black Knights of Malta, the following resolutions were presented and unanimously passed:

Whereas, Our worthy companion, Frederick Teeple, has been afflicted by the death of his child, Clifford Teeple,

Resolved, That we extend to our companion and his family our sincere sympathy, and trust that God may mercifully apply the balm of Gilead to their wounded and stricken hearts, and that this affliction, which for a time seemeth grievous, may be so overruled that the sorrow which may endure for a night shall give place to joy in the resurrection morning.

Resolved, That a copy of these resolutions be furnished to the afflicted family, and that they be printed in the Harrisville Review.

IN MEMORY OF CLIFFORD TEEPLE.

We have lost our darling Clifford,
Oh! how hard it is to part
With our darling little treasure,
Whom we loved with all our heart.

Yes, we loved him, and our heart strings
Seem to break with tears of woe;
But we know our Father called him,
And we had to let him go.

Let him go;
Hard it is those words to say;
But remember, fondest mother,
He is so happy all the day.

In that home that knows no sorrow,
All is happiness and peace;
There he's waiting for his mamma,
When on earth your troubles cease.

Donald Fraser,
Wm. Flawes,   Committee
Wm. M Bence

Alcona County Review, August 13, 1886

There has been some artistic and costly tombstones erected in Mount Joy cemetery this spring in memory of Mr. Bridgeman, a son and daughter of A. Yuill, Peter McGregor, Jas. E. Fleming and Geo. Jack erected one to the memory of his children Fred, Mary and Charles and F. O.

Teeple to his son, Clifton [Clifford]. There are a number who take pride in keeping their lots in good order but the majority of the graves and lots are neglected, which don't speak well for the relatives. Sunken graves and toppling tombstones speak louder than words.

Alcona County Review, July 2, 1903
Cemetery: Mt. Joy, Alcona Co.

Tefft, A. C.

LOCAL JOTTINGS.

We learn from the Alpena Labor Journal that Bro. A. C. Tefft, of the Pioneer, is dangerously ill; that physicians have given up all hopes of his recovery. We are sorry to hear this sad news.

Alcona County Review, January 15, 1886

Death of Editor Tefft of Alpena.

It is with feelings of deep regret and sorrow that we receive the sad news of the death of our friend and contemporary in journalism, Mr. A. C. Tefft, editor and proprietor of the Alpena Pioneer, which occurred at this home, in Alpena, Friday evening last, after an illness of about two weeks. The writer first met and became acquainted with Mr. Tefft in the summer of 1878, (when he was in attendance at a political convention held in Harrisville) which acquaintance ripened into greater intimacy in the three years following, as we often met and conversed with him during 1879, 1880 and 1881, more particularly the latter year. Mr. Tefft was a man of unusually kind disposition, and would go as far out of his way to accommodate a friend as any man we ever met; and from what we personally knew of him in this regard we do not believe any legitimate act of kindness was ever asked at his hand that he did not grant it, if within his power. He was a man of good scholarship, a very pleasant and entertaining conversationalist, and had done a large amount of good in very many ways. As an editor, he was acknowledged as being competent and able, and his power thus wielded through the columns of his paper, had much to do in moulding the religious, moral, social, and political interests of Alpena county. He was the pioneer journalist of the shore, having come into possession of the Pioneer about 16 years ago. He became a resident of Alpena 20 years ago, and spent the first few years of his residence there as county surveyor, and kept books for Campbell, Potter & Co., also Mason, Luce & Co. He leaves a wife and two children, all of whom he was permitted to have about his bedside at the closing hours of his life. But the earthly pilgrimage of this good man is now ended, and we hope and trust the soul of Brother Tefft is forever with the Lord. The Review extends sympathy to the sorrowing wife and children.

Alcona County Review, January 22, 1886
Cemetery:

Thebault, Pascale

Monday Pascale Tebault, a relative of Peter Medor, of this village, was caught between the ends of the logs while coupling cars at Loud's camp 8, and his head was crushed to a jelly, causing almost instant death. He was unmarried.

Alcona County Review, November 9, 1888
Cemetery:

Thibadeau, Alice M. [O'Donahue]

Death Claims Many Victims.

Thos. O'Donahue brought the sad intelligence to the village Sunday that his daughter, Mrs. Eli Tibbido, had died that morning at McDonald's camp after a lingering illness from consumption. The deceased was about 24 years of age and leaves her husband and three children to mourn her untimely departure.

The remains were brought to Harrisville and buried in the Catholic cemetery. A large concourse of relatives and friends followed the remains to the grave.

Alcona County Review, March 26, 1891
Cemetery: St. Anne's, Alcona Co.

Thompson, Mrs. Alexianna

OBITUARY.

Died at the residence of her son-in-law, Mr. Archie Dewar, on Sunday, April 13, 1890, at 3 o'clock in the morning, Mrs. Alexianna Thompson passed away to eternal rest, having reached the age of seventy-seven years. Mrs. Thompson was born in Glengary county, Ontario, and lived all but the last three years of her life in that place. Three years ago she moved to this place. She had ten children four of whom survive her, one of whom is single and three married. Mrs. Allen

McMillen, Mrs. Alexander Sloan, Mrs. Archie Dewar and Annie, her single daughter in Glengary, Canada. She was ever a patient and affectionate mother and a tender hearted Christian and she leaves many sorrowing friends.

Alcona County Review, April 18, 1890

Card of Thanks.

Card of Thanks.

We extend our heart felt thanks to our kind friends and neighbors who shared our sorrow and assisted us in our late bereavement in burying our dear mother. I hope they will accept of our sincere thanks for their unspeakable kindness.

Archie Dewar.

Alcona County Review, May 2, 1890
Cemetery: West Lawn, Alcona Co.

Thompson, Cinderella [Caverly]

LOCAL JOTTINGS.

Mrs. John Thompson, of Alpena, sister-in-law of Mrs. Jas. Morris, died of consumption, Aug. 15th.

Alcona County Review, August 29, 1884
Cemetery:

Thompson, David

Mysterious Death.

Many of our citizens will no doubt remember a quite large, stout built, middle-aged man named David Thompson, who worked at the carpenters trade in this county last summer, who was frequently given to the immoderate use of intoxicating drinks. If we remember rightly he superintended the building of a barn for C. C. Briggs, and worked for various other parties in this township. However, it appears from the following clipping from a certain Canada paper, that he has sustained a mysterious death near Zurich, Ontario. The item is clipped from the *Western Advertiser and Liberal:*

Zurich, Ont., April 15.--The inquest on the body found yesterday was held by Drs. Stanbury and Buchanan. The body appeared to have been in the water since last fall, and was of a stout built, dark complexioned man about forty years of age. Papers found in his pocket show his name, David Thompson of Harrisville, Mich. There were also two prescriptions of Dr. J. V. White, of Oscoda, two bills of lumber, two grocery bills dated Nov. 5, a pocket knife, a small flask full of brandy, and

a tobacco holder found on him. They body will be buried today.

The following letter was received by Postmaster Colwell of this place:

Zurich, April 15, 1882.

Postmaster, Harrisville, Mich.:

Sir--The body of a man was found in the lake about four miles from here yesterday, and judging from papers found on him I am led to believe his name was David Thompson, of Harrisville or Oscoda. Two prescriptions were found among the papers written by Dr. J. V. White, M. D., of Oscoda, to be filled by Mr. Hicks, druggist, of Harrisville. Lumber, store and other bills were also found.

Should you know any friends of such a party you can tell them that they can have a description and any particulars they may desire by addressing me. I examined the body and had it buried near here today.

Geo. Buchanan, M. D.,
Reeve of Hay,
Zurich P. O., Ont.

We hardly think the deceased had any relatives living in this county. We know of none, however.

Alcona County Review, April 28, 1882
Cemetery:

Thompson, Kate [LaPier]

Word was received yesterday that Mrs. Kate Thompson, sister of Mrs. Geo. W. Young, was dead at Tawas. There were no particulars.

Alcona County Review, December 7, 1899

Mrs. Kate Thompson's Death.

The following facts in connection with the death of Mrs. Kate Thompson, sister of Mrs. Geo. W. Young, have been received from C. L. Benjamin the undertaker who had charge of the funeral:

"Saginaw, Mich., Dec. 12, 1899.

"My dear Mrs. Miller:—
Answering yours of Dec. 8. Mrs. Thompson came here from Mt. Pleasant sometime last summer and for a while was nurse at the Poor Farm taking care of the insane patients. She came to Saginaw a few weeks ago and at the time of her death was at Fosters, about 12 miles from here, taking care of some children who had lost their mother. She had a stroke of apoplexy Monday, Dec. 4th, and died the next day. I brought her here and she was buried here on Thursday afternoon, Dec. 7. Everything was done for her that could be and she was buried very nicely.

"Her daughter, Miss Lottie, is at present at Mt. Pleasant but will return here after New Years, and go to school. Yours Truly,

Charles L. Benjamin."

Alcona County Review, December 21, 1899
Cemetery: Oakwood, Saginaw Co.

Thompson, Max

ALONG THE SHORE.

Au Sable and Oscoda.

A Swede by the name of Max Thompson, was killed at Pack & Woods' mill last week, by being struck on the head with a large stick of timber which rolled off a car.

Alcona County Review, September 4, 1885
Cemetery:

Thompson, Rebecca [Crippen]

Two Centenarians Dead.

Mrs. Rebecca Thompson of Wilson township, Alpena county, died last week at the extreme old age of 102 ½ years.

Alcona County Review, March 2, 1899
Cemetery: Wilson Township, Alpena Co.

Thorner, Hattie

Haynes Happenings.

Received too late for Publication last week.

Haynes, Sept. 13th, 1894.--Miss Hattie Thorner died very suddenly at Black River yesterday. Cause of death pleurisy.

Alcona County Review, September 20, 1894

EVENTS OF ONE WEEK.

The remains of Miss Hattie Thorner, daughter of a Haynes township citizen, were buried in Alcona cemetery last Saturday. The young lady died at Black River suddenly a few days before and under sad circumstances. She was making preparations to be married and was at Black River making purchases for her wedding outfit, she was taken suddenly ill with pleurisy and died in a few hours, before her friends could be summoned to her bedside. She was 18 years of age.

Alcona County Review, September 20, 1894

Haynes Happenings.

Haynes, Sept. 19, 1894.--Miss Hattie Thorner was interred in our cemetery on the 14th, the remains were conveyed from Black River in D. La Boueff's hearse and were followed by a very large concourse of sympathizing friends and relatives.

Alcona County Review, September 20, 1894

In Memory of Hattie Thorner.

(By her brother George.)

A precious soul from us has fled,
A voice we loved is still;
A place is vacant in our hearts
That never can be filled.

The messenger came so suddenly
To call our sister home,
To dwell in peace with Christ above,
With angels 'round the throne.

Call me not back, dear mother,
For my suffering now is o'er;
My Heavenly Father called me
To dwell with him forever more.

When you leave this world of changes
And you leave this world of care,
You will find your loving Hattie
In our Father's mansions fair.

Dearest Hattie, thou hast left us;
Death is conquered, life is won;
Though we miss your lovely form,
Father, still thy will be done.

Physicians tried their utmost skill,
Their skill was all in vain,
For Christ had said gently:
"Hattie, thou must be born again."

She bore her sickness with great patience
And was never seen to frown,
She always had a pleasant smile
For those who gathered 'round.

Grieve not, dear father, for your Hattie,
And mother, cease to mourn;
For your daughter now is happy
And will never more return.

When you all shall cross the rolling river,
And stand before God's throne,
May you find your loving Hattie
With the Angelic throng.

Miss Thorner was aged 18 years, one month and 30 days.

Mr. and Mrs. Wm. Thorner wish to thank the citizens of Black River who rendered so much kindness to them and their daughter during her sickness; also to their many friends of Haynes township. To each and all of them we extend our sincere thanks.

Mr. and Mrs. Wm. Thorner.

Alcona County Review, October 4, 1894

Haynes, May 28, 1895.--Charles Atkinson has erected a very neat headstone in memory of Miss Hattie Thorner in our cemetery.

Alcona County Review, May 30, 1895
Cemetery: Mt. Joy, Alcona Co.

Thornton, Caroline A. [Moore]

EVENTS OF ONE WEEK.

Mrs. Silas Thornton, aged about 74, joined the silent majority Saturday after an illness covering about 10 days. Softening of the brain was the malady which resulted in her death. The funeral services were held Monday in the Fisher school house and a large number of friends of the family gathered to pay their respects to the living and dead and witness the last sad rites over the remains, which were placed at rest in the South Harrisville cemetery. Rev. F. P. Dunham preached an excellent sermon.

Alcona County Review, November 8, 1894

Words cannot express the deep feeling of gratitude I have toward those neighbors and friends who in the hour of my heavy sorrow offered words of comfort and performed innumerable deeds of kindness. I thank them all from the bottom of a grateful heart.

Silas Thornton, Sr.

Alcona County Review, November 15, 1894

EVENTS OF ONE WEEK.

The late Mrs. Silas Thornton, Sr., was 65 years of age and was a native of New Brunswick. She was married to Silas Thornton in Canada at the age of 21 and their wedded life therefore covered a period approaching half a century.

Alcona County Review, November 15, 1894
Cemetery: Springport, Alcona Co.

Thornton, George

LOCAL JOTTINGS.

Jas. Thornton and wife lost a child by diptheria the first of the week.

Alcona County Review, January 30, 1885
Cemetery: Springport, Alcona Co.

Tibbitts, Elmer M.

LOCAL JOTTINGS.

Just as we go to press we learn that a young man named Smith employed on the night log train as brakesman on the Black River railroad, was run over last night and killed. His body was horribly mangled. His home was at Alpena.

Alcona County Review, January 2, 1885

LOCAL JOTTINGS.

The Review was in error last week in giving the name of Smith to the young man killed on the Black River railroad. Elsewhere we copy from the Alpena Argus a full account of the terrible accident, together with the obsequies had in that city last Sunday.

Alcona County Review, January 9, 1885

Terrible Accident.

Elmer M. Tibbitts was killed on the Black River railway last Thursday. He was employed as a brakeman and had occupied his position but three days. About the time of the accident the train was going down grade with a load of logs and several of the cars had broken loose from the engine. The engineer signaled "down brakes," and Tibbitts and another brakeman went to work to apply the brakes—they being on that part of the train that had broken loose from the engine. When the train had been got together, it was found that Tibbitts was missing. A search was made and after going back a short distance, the remains of Tibbitts were found strewed along the track. His body was terribly mangled having been run over by several heavily loaded cars. The head was nearly severed from the body, parts of both arms and legs were cut off, and the body frightfully mutilated. Nearly every bone in the body was broken and several severe wounds were found on the heads and face. The remains were gathered and afterwards sewn together. E. A. Furbush, of this city was a relative, and on being informed of the disaster immediately went to Black River and then brought the remains to this city. As the deceased was a member of the Guards, he was buried with military honors. His comrades to the number of about thirty, in parade dress, with draped banner and muffled drums, marched to the residence of E. A. Furbush, where the body was, about two o'clock Sunday last, and then escorted the remains to the Baptist church where the funeral services were held, after which they proceeded with the funeral procession to the cemetery.—Alpena Argus.

Alcona County Review, January 9, 1885

Cemetery: Evergreen, Alpena Co.

Titus, George W.

The remains of Geo. W. Titus, a well known citizen of Black River, were brought to Harrisville Sunday last for interment in the cemetery west of Harrisville. Services were held in the Baptist chapel, the Rev. W. J. Bailey officiating.

The deceased was born at Vienna, Nova Scotia, May 3rd, 1825. At the age of 3 he with his father, Isaac Titus, moved to Verne, Canada, where he spent his youth. At the age of twenty he engaged in the marine service. He met with much favor from his employers and after a few years was promoted to a captainship. He followed a seafaring life until 6 years ago. He was married in May, 1865, to Elizabeth J. Light and by her had Ada L., Melbourn W. and Nellie J., all of whom survive to mourn the loss of a kind husband and father. He moved to Black River in 1886 where he lived until his death.

Alcona County Review, May 26, 1892

Card of Thanks.—We wish to extend to our many sympathetic friends and neighbors sincere thanks for the many kindnesses shown us during the sickness and death of our beloved husband and father, Geo. W. Titus. May they be spared a like affliction is our earnest prayer.

Mrs. G. W. Titus and Family,
Black River, Mich., June 20.

Alcona County Review, June 23, 1892

SOMEWHAT PERSONAL.

Mrs. Geo. W. Titus of Black River has taken the steps necessary to secure possession of the estate of her late husband.

Alcona County Review, July 7, 1892

HISTORY OF ONE YEAR.

Chronological History of the Past Year, 1892.

THE DEATH RECORD.

May 22. Geo. Titus, Black River.

Alcona County Review, January 5, 1893
Cemetery: West Lawn, Alcona Co.

Tolmie, John W.

TIME HONORED PEDAGOGUE.

Passed Away Yesterday in John W. Tolmie.

Bay City Tribune, Apr. 8.

John W. Tolmie, 1413 Columbus avenue, died Wednesday night of fatty degeneration of the heart. He had been teaching at McKinley and came here Tuesday very low.

Mr. Tolmie was 59 years of age and had been a school teacher for 38 years, 32 of which were spent as a pedagogue in Norfolk county Ontario. He came to Bay City six years ago in order to give his children better school advantages. Two daughters graduated from the high school and one now teaches in the city schools. The deceased was an ardent Methodist, joining the church at the age of sixteen years. He was a Mason and a member of the A. O. U. W. The funeral will be held at 2:30 this afternoon from the house and there will be a Masonic burial.

The subject of the above sketch has many friends in Harrisville and Alcona County, having resided here with his family for several years. His life work was school teaching and he has taught in the schools of this county for upwards of eight years, and during the greater part of that time was a member of the county board of school examiners.

The passing of Mr. Tolmie will be learned with sincere regret by a large circle of friends here who will sympathize with the bereaved family.

Alcona County Review, April 15, 1897
Cemetery:

Tooker, Susan [Hinchman]

Correspondence

Black River, Feb. 17.--Mrs. F. J. Hill has returned from Brooklyn, N. Y., where she was summoned by a telegram announcing the death of her mother, Mrs. Tooker, who had many acquaintances in this vicinity.

Alcona County Review, February 25, 1892
Cemetery: Green-wood, Kings Co., NY

Tovey, Mrs. Johanna

Death of an Aged Lady.

Mrs. Johanna Tovey, the aged mother of Michael and Jas. Tovey of Harrisville, passed away Saturday morning last and was buried Monday morning in the Catholic cemetery according to the rites of that denomination, of which she had been a devout and consistent member throughout her life. The deceased was a native of Ireland and was upwards of 86 years of age. Up to within a few weeks she possessed unusual vigor for one of such great age. Her husband, who is several years her senior, survives her.

Deceased was born at Waterford, Ire., in 1807. She was married in 1827. In 1848 she moved with her husband and family to Canada where she lived until 1883 when she came to Harrisville with her oldest son. Her death is deeply felt by her venerable husband and five children, four of whom reside in Harrisville, viz., the two sons above mentioned and Mrs. Jas. Martin and Mrs. Peter Collins.

Alcona County Review, February 9, 1893

Card of Thanks.

We wish to thank our friends and neighbors for the kind assistance they rendered us during the sickness and death of our beloved wife and mother.

RICHARD TOVEY
and Family.

Alcona County Review, February 9, 1893
Cemetery: St. Anne's, Alcona Co.

Tovey, Mary Agnes [Shirley]

PERSONAL POINTS.

Mrs. Jas. Tovey went to Detroit last week accompanied by her husband, for the purpose of taking treatment at St. Mary's hospital for a malignant cancer that has progressed to an alarming extent.

Mrs. Tovey received no encouragement from the hospital authorities and has returned home.

Alcona County Review, June 30, 1898

LOCAL PICK UPS.

Mrs. Jas. Tovey, who has been a great sufferer from cancer, was released by death from further suffering Sunday morning.

The interment took place on the afternoon of the following day in the catholic cemetery, a large number of sympathizing friends following the remains to their last resting place. Deceased was 41 years of age and was a native of Ontario. Her husband and a large family of children are left to mourn their irreparable loss.

Alcona County Review, August 18, 1898

We wish to express our most heartfelt thanks to the many kind friends and neighbors who rendered us such assistance in the long, painful illness and death of our beloved wife and sister, also to those who contributed such beautiful flowers.

May God reward them all and in his mercy grant they may be spared such suffering as it was her lot to endure.

James Tovey.
Mrs. O'Brien.
Mrs. Cuyler.

Alcona County Review, August 18, 1898

Local History of One Year

Chronology of the Principal Events of the Year 1898.

August 14. Death of Mrs. Jas. Tovey aged 41.

Alcona County Review, January 5, 1899
Cemetery: St. Anne's, Alcona Co.

Tovey, Richard

DIED AGED 100 YEARS.

Mr. Richard Tovey, the aged father of Michael and Jas. Tovey, of Harrisville, departed from this life last Thursday evening and was buried Sunday morning in the Catholic cemetery according to the rites of that denomination, of which he had been a devout member throughout his life. His death was not unexpected but nevertheless it brought deep sorrow to his surviving relatives and friends.

The deceased was born at Kilkenny, Ireland, in 1794. He was married in 1827. In 1848 he moved with his wife and family to Canada, where he lived until 1883, when he came to Harrisville with his oldest son. He leaves three sons and two daughters to mourn his loss.

Alcona County Review, January 17, 1895

Card of Thanks.--We wish to thank our many friends and neighbors for the kind assistance they rendered us during the illness and death of our beloved father.

Mr. Jas. Tovey.
Mr. Michael Tovey.
Mrs. Peter Collins.
Mrs. Jas. Martin.

Alcona County Review, January 17, 1895
Cemetery: St. Anne's, Alcona Co.

Tower, Eli

LOCAL JOTTINGS.

Eli Tower is afflicted with continued poor health.

Alcona County Review, June 20, 1884

LOCAL JOTTINGS.

Eli Tower, whose health is failing very fast, expects to be able to go to

the sea shore the fore part of next week where he hopes to regain his strength. Mr. Tower has been unable to do scarcely any work for the past six months.

Alcona County Review, July 11, 1884

LOCAL JOTTINGS.

Eli Tower desires the Review to return thanks, for him, to the citizens of Harrisville, Greenbush and South Harrisville for generous contribution toward defraying the expenses of his trip to Massachusetts, in search of health.

Alcona County Review, July 18, 1884

LOCAL JOTTINGS.

Eli Tower departed Sunday morning for the sea shore in Massachusetts, hoping by the trip and change of climate to be materially benefitted in health. He went per steamer city of Cleveland far as Detroit. The Review hopes Mr. T. may soon return a well man.

Alcona County Review, July 18, 1884

LOCAL JOTTINGS.

The Review regrets exceedingly to hear of the death of Eli Tower, late of this village, which occurred in Massachusetts week ago last Wednesday. Mr. Tower was afflicted with consumption, and went east to the sea shore with the hope that he might possibly regain his health by the change; but the dread disease had progressed too far and consequently the change availed him nothing. Mr. Tower had been a resident of Harrisville for several years past and commanded a large circle of friends. He was honest, industrious, a man perfectly trustworthy in any position to which he was called. He leaves a devoted wife and two daughters, residents of Harrisville, to mourn his decease. They should command the tender sympathy of our townspeople.

Alcona County Review, October 10, 1884
Cemetery:

Townsand, Mr.

POTTS PARAGRAPHS.

Potts' Headquarters, Dec. 24.-- Died, on the 23d, at D. A. McDonald's camp, of pleurisy, Mr. Townsand, of Brockway Center, aged 24 years. He was sick four days. Remains passed down to Au Sable to-day.

Trask, Charles S.

West Harrisville.

The infant son of Peter Trask died last Friday eve. Mr. and Mrs. Trask have the sympathy of the whole community.

Alcona County Review, June 17, 1897
Cemetery:

Trask, {Girl}

WEST HARRISVILLE GOSSIP.

The death of the infant daughter of Mr. and Mrs. Geo. Trask occurred last evening. The family have the sympathy of the entire community.

Alcona County Review, January 19, 1899

HAWSE TOWNSHIP.

Much sympathy is expressed for Mr. and Mrs. Geo. Trask in the death of their baby, notice of which was in last week's issue.

Alcona County Review, January 26, 1899
Cemetery: Probably West Lawn, Alcona Co.

Trask, Henry

LOCAL JOTTINGS.

Engineer Henry Trask, killed in the railroad accident which occurred near his home, Horrnelsville, N. Y., last Saturday, was an uncle of Wm. and D. E. Storms, of this village. Many others in this place doubtless made the acquaintance of Mr. Trask during his visit with his relatives here last fall.

Alcona County Review, June 22, 1888
Cemetery: Probably Sheridan, Chatauqua Co., NY

Trask, Samuel Levi

WEST HARRISVILLE GOSSIP.

Mr. Trask, a respected citizen of West Harrisville, aged 69 years, died at his home early Monday morning, from peritonitis. He was sick only five days.

Deceased was father of a family of ten children, nine of whom are living. Most of the children were present at the funeral, which was held on Tuesday afternoon, Rev. Geo. Nixon officiating. The Ladies of West Harrisville rendered very appropriate music.

Alcona County Review, May 4, 1899

STATE OF MICHIGAN
County of Alcona

At a session of the Probate Court for County of Alcona, held at the Probate office in the Village of Harrisville, on Monday the 28th day of Sept. in the year one thousand nine hundred and three. Present, Hon. W. H. Gilpin, Judge of Probate. In the matter of the Estate of Samuel Trask and Anna Trask deceased.

On reading and filing the petition duly verified, of Wm. B. Trask praying among other things that an administrator be appointed and that administration of said estate may be granted to O. H. Smith or some other suitable person.

Thereupon it is ordered, that Monday, the 26th day of October, A. D. 1903 at 10 o'clock in the forenoon, be assigned for the hearing of said petition.

And it is further ordered, that said Petitioner give notice to the heirs at law and all persons interested by causing a copy of this order to be published in the Alcona County Review, a newspaper printed and circulated in said County of Alcona, for three successive weeks previous to said day of hearing,

W. H. Gilpin,
Judge of Probate.

Alcona County Review, October 1, 1903

STATE OF MICHIGAN
County of Alcona

Estate of Samuel Trask and Anna Trask, deceased.

The undersigned having been appointed by the judge of Probate of said County, Commissioners on Claims in the matter of said estate and six months from the 26th day of October A. D. 1903, having been allowed by said Judge of Probate to all persons holding claims against said estate, in which to present their claims to us for examination and adjustment.

Notice is hereby given, that we will meet on Monday, the 7th day of December, A. D. 1903, and on Tuesday, the 26th day of April, A. D. 1904, at ten o'clock of each day, at Court House in the Village of Harrisville in said County, to receive and examine such claims.

Dated 31st day of October A. D. 1903.

Robt. Southgate, Commissioners.
Howard C. Kibbee.

Alcona County Review, November 5, 1903

Auction

There will be sold at public auction, on the 26th day of May, 1904, at two o'clock in the afternoon of that date, at the farm of the late Samuel Trask by the administrator of said estate the following goods and chattels:

1 heavy wagon; 1 spring tooth drag; 1 wooden roller; 2 scythes and snathes; 1 brush hook; 2 hoes; 2 potato forks; 1 shovel plow; 1 spike tooth harrow; 4 sheep, and 4 of their increase subject to lease of 2 years; 2 boom chains; 2 draft chains; 1 cant hook; one cross cut saw; 1 long handled shovel; 2 spades; 6 pieces of chain; 1 swamp hook with grab hook; 2 pick axes; 1 wagon lock shoe; 1 stove thimble; 1 long swamp hook with ring; 1 pulley block; 1 pair wagon arms; 1 fork without handle; 2 plows; 1 iron plow beam; 1 hay rack; 1 pair steelyards; 1 corn planter; 1 ox yoke; 2 single blocks; 1 adze; and some miscellaneous articles, too small to mention. Also a team of horses.

Terms of sale, cash, or good secured notes on all sums over five dollars for short time.

If other parties wish to sell anything at this sale, they are at liberty to do so, after this sale is over.

O. H. Smith,
Administrator.

Alcona County Review, May 19, 1904
Cemetery: Twin Lakes, Alcona Co.

Treat, Mrs. Charles

HOME REVIEWINGS.

The wife of Mr. Chas. Treat, one of the pioneers of this township, died at her home on Wednesday night at 11:30; aged 58 years. The deceased had been in ill-health for several months past, and her death though coming suddenly was not unexpected. She was a kind-hearted wife and lady, and will be greatly missed by relatives and neighbors.

Alcona County Review, August 5, 1881
Cemetery:

Trombley, Peter

One More Unfortunate.

Another fatality occurred at Black River last week by which a young man, Peter Trombley, lost his life. He was engaged in the discharge of his duty unloading long timber at the banking ground. The chain which binds the load had become fastened and it became necessary to cut it with a coal chisel. As soon as the timbers were loosened he was knocked down, falling face downward. Before he could get out of the way one of the sticks fell upon him, striking him across the back. His back was broken and he was injured internally. He was about 25 years of age, unmarried and had no friends in this country. The remains were taken to Alpena and buried Saturday.

Alcona County Review, August 20, 1891
Cemetery:

Turner, Mrs. Elizabeth
HOME REVIEWINGS.

Mrs. Elizabeth Turner, mother of Mr. E. H. Turner, our hardware merchant, died at the home of the latter in Harrisville last Saturday night. Mrs. T. has been an invalid for the past five years, and at intervals during this time was partially deranged in mind. She was born near London, England, in 1804, and was therefore 77 years of age.

Alcona County Review, June 17, 1881
Cemetery:

Turner, Mr.
Curtis.
Received too late for last issue.
Mr. Turner, second boss on the A. S. & N. W. R. R. died suddenly on the 14th. He worked all day on the 13th but when he came to his boarding house at night he took sick. A doctor was summoned but he only lived 24 hours till death gave him relief. It has been remarked by many how sudden he died and also the shortness of time they kept him: his death was Saturday night at about 5 o'clock and he was buried Sunday afternoon. There was a large funeral for a man who had no relations here. Mr. E. M. Barker appeared to take charge of the funeral.

Alcona County Review, January 26, 1893
Cemetery:

Twite, Charles Edward
LOCAL JOTTINGS

Chas. Twite died at the home of his daughter in Black River Saturday morning June 9, at the ripe old age of 70 years. Mr. Twite was one of the old pioneers of this section. He had been a sufferer for a number of years from asthma which was the immediate cause of his death. The funeral services were held Sunday afternoon from the Methodist church, the Rev. C. B. Steele officiating. The deceased left a wife and nine children.

Alcona County Review, June 15, 1888

Cemetery: Springport, Alcona Co.

Twite, William
Black River Sparks.

In a letter received by Walter Yokom on Feb. 1st, from Mrs. Twite of Denver, Col., we learn that William, who has been suffering from consumption for some time, is now confined to his bed and there are no hopes for his recovery.

Alcona County Review, January 30, 1896

Black River Sparks.

Mr. Wm. Twite left here some time ago for Denver, Col., for his health. It was thought he had bronchial trouble, but after arriving in Denver it soon developed into the dreaded disease, consumption, and he failed rapidly. The sad news was received here by telegram that he passed away on April 9th. He was a member of the K. O. T. M. and his remains were laid to rest under the auspices of that order.

Mr. Twite was a gentleman well known in this vicinity and has many relatives living in Alcona county, by whom the news of his death was received with sadness. Mr. Twite was yet a young man, only 38 years old at his death. We extend our sympathy to all the bereaved ones in their sad loss of such a good husband and townsman.

Alcona County Review, April 23, 1896
Cemetery: Fairmount, Denver Co., CO

Tye, Marshall
A TERRIBLE DEATH.

Thursday morning an accident occurred on Potts' railroad, of which no one can give an account of how it happened, but which resulted in the death of a brakeman, Marshal Tye, and the derailing of the car. Tye had just started out on his first trip as brakesman, and the train had not been started long before the accident occurred. He was brought down to Chevrier's undertaking establishment Thursday afternoon, to be sent to his home in Croswell, Sanilac county, where his parents reside. He was a young man, just past his 21st year, and unmarried. He leaves two sisters here, Mrs. Dan Little and Mrs. Manzer Raymond. The body was not mangled much, one of the singular things of the

accident, his right arm being broken just above the wrist, the right leg broken just above the knee and the left one broken below the knee.—*Au Sable Monitor*.

Alcona County Review, June 11, 1886
Cemetery:

Vallee, Raouel
Among Our Exchanges
From the Lakeside Monitor.
Three Au Sable boys named Jerry Murphy, Seymour McLeod and Roeul Valle, were drowned Tuesday afternoon while in swimming on the shore below Penoyar Bros.' docks. The Valle boy got into deep water and the other two were drowned in trying to save him. The bodies were not recovered until they had been in the water over an hour.

The boys were all between 11 and 12 years of age. Jerry Murphy was the son of Eugene Murphy and Seymour McLeod a son of John McLeod.

Alcona County Review, July 21, 1892
Cemetery:Sacred Heart, Iosco Co.

Vallie, Moses
From The Press, Oscoda.
Mose Valley, who had been in Detroit for some time doctoring for kidney trouble started to come home Saturday. He was, however, unable to stand the fatigue of travel and died on the train between here and Alger. He was buried Tuesday from the Catholic church under the auspices of the Knights of St. John, of which society he was a member. He was also a Maccabee.

Alcona County Review, February 23, 1893
Cemetery:Sacred Heart, Iosco Co.

Van Alstine, Martha [Johnson]
Haynes.
Mrs. Van Alstine is in a very dangerous condition. She had a relapse. Drs. McCormick and Mitchell were in attendance on Monday. Her case is doubtful.

Alcona County Review, April 13, 1893

Haynes.

Sad Death of Mrs. Van Alstine.
Mrs. William Van Alstine died at 2 o'clock on the morning of the 13th. She leaves a family of seven children, the eldest a girl of fifteen summers, the youngest a babe a few weeks old. Her remains were followed to the cemetery by numerous relatives and a large concourse of sympathizing friends on Saturday afternoon. The

Rev. Mr. Long preached the funeral sermon.

This is one of the saddest cases which has ever happened in Haynes. Her husband was killed on the 24th day of October, 1892, while oiling a threshing machine. A few days after her babe was born she got up to attend to it as the rest of the family were asleep. She caught cold and had a relapse. Dr. McCormick was called to attend her. He had no hopes of her recovery as she became violently insane and as her vitality was very low she soon became of victim to the fatal disease.

Alcona County Review, April 20, 1893
Cemetery: Mt. Joy, Alcona Co.

Van Alstine, William H.

FATALLY INJURED.

Wm. Van Alstine Meets a Horrible Death in Haynes.

Last Monday morning a horse power threshing machine, owned by J. M. Fettis, was in operation at Archie Campbell's in Haynes township. Wm. H. Van Alstine was assisting and while engaged in oiling the gearing near the separator his overcoat became entangled in the tumbling rod and in an instant he was whirled around the shaft, his head striking a block of wood with sickening force, crushing his skull. He was carried around a second time. The machinery was stopped as soon as possible when it was found that besides the fatal blow he had received on the skull, his arm was broken and he was otherwise frightfully injured. He did not rally but lived for an hour and a half after the accident.

Deceased had been a resident of the township for many years and was a respected citizen, being a member in good standing of the local lodge of Odd Fellows. He leaves a wife and a family of several small children in rather poor circumstances.

Alcona County Review, October 27, 1892

IN MEMORIUM.
The following resolutions were adopted by Alcona Lodge No. 322 I. O. O. F., Nov. 5th, 1892:

Whereas, An all-wise Providence has deemed best to call from our midst our beloved Brother, P. G. William Vanalstine, one of our oldest and most zealous members in the discharge of his duties, punctilious in

his obedience to the laws and regulations of the Order, therefore be it

Resolved, That we deeply feel and mourn the greatness of our loss; a worthy member, who in the discharge of the various duties assigned him, which were among others the most important, trustworthy and exalted in the Order, he displayed a remarkable zeal and aptitude and by such he won the highest respect and esteem of every Oddfellow who knew him; one who was always ready to work for the advancement of Oddfellowship, has been removed from earth and many hearts are made to mourn. And be it further

Resolved, That we extend to the family and relations of our deceased brother our sincere and heartfelt sympathy in the hour of bereavement, and be it further

Resolved, That the charter of our Lodge be draped in mourning for thirty days, that a copy of these resolutions be sent to the bereaved family, also spread upon the records of this Lodge and published in the Alcona County Review.

John Greenfield,
J. E. Fleming,   Committee.
Geo. H. Lee.

Alcona County Review, November 10, 1892

HISTORY OF ONE YEAR.

Chronological History of the Past Year, 1892.

October.
24. Wm. H. Vanalstine fatally injured in a threshing machine in Haynes.

Alcona County Review, January 5, 1893

HISTORY OF ONE YEAR.

Chronological History of the Past Year, 1892.

THE DEATH RECORD.
Oct. 24. Wm. H. VanAlstine, Haynes.

Alcona County Review, January 5, 1893
Cemetery: Mt. Joy, Alcona Co.

Van Buren, Gilbert

GILBERT VAN BEUREN.

The mortal remains of this old citizen were laid away at South Harrisville Saturday. He died two days previously at his late residence

in Haynes township, where he had long been confined to his bed with a complication of diseases due in a measure to the infirmities of advancing age.

Mr. Van Beuren was one of the historic characters of the county, and came here in a very early day and engaged in fishing. Then the pine trees, tall, majestic and straight rifted, came down to the very water's edge, and were principally valued by the fishermen because they made excellent barrel staves.

Mr. Van Beuren was a native of New York and came to this locality as early as 1847. He engaged in fishing under S. M. Holden, the first actual settler of Alcona county, who established himself in 1846 at Springport, then known from the topography of the land as the "High Banks of the Au Sable." After a time Mr. Van Beuren began fishing for himself at Greenbush and later at "the Cove" at Alcona. Then he engaged in agriculture and hunted and trapped on the side, and "for six months at one time," it is related of him in the History of the Shore, "he never slept in a bed."

The history of such a man must have been full of exciting incidents and romantic adventure, such as constitute, however, the daily life of every person who courts the hardships and dangers and privations of a pioneer life.

Deceased was not a successful man as the world uses the term. We do not hear that he was ever a prominent actor in the political history and development of the county, but he leaves behind him an unsullied name, which is better than riches.

"Gil" claimed relationship to Martin Van Beuren, eighth President of the United States.

Alcona County Review, November 25, 1897

We desire to thank our neighbors and friends for their kindness and sympathy during the illness and death of our beloved husband and father. May God reward them as they deserve.

Mrs. Van Buren and Daughter.

Alcona County Review, December 2, 1897
Cemetery: Springport, Alcona Co.

Van Buskirk, Harmon

LOCAL PICK UPS.
Clio, Mich., March 5.— (Special)—H. Van Buskirk, a highly respected pioneer of this section, died

to-day of old age, aged 72. Deceased has been a merchant of Pine Run for thirty years and was one of the first store-keepers of that once thriving village.

The subject of the above dispatch was an only brother of Mr. J. Van Buskirk of this place. Mr. Van Buskirk's health would not permit of his attending the funeral, which occurred yesterday at Pine Run.

Alcona County Review, March 9, 1899
Cemetery: Pine Run, Genesee Co.

Van Dyke, Fannie E.

REVIEWINGS.

Just as we go to press, we learn of the death of Fannie, second daughter of Rev. D. VanDyke, of consumption; aged 13 years. She died at 3 p.m. to-day. On account of the death no Presbyterian services will be held at the Court House on Sunday.

Alcona County Review, June 6, 1879

Obsequies Of Fannie VanDyke.

The funeral services of Fannie, deceased daughter (aged 13 years) of Rev. D. and Mrs. L. VanDyke, held at the home residence, last Sabbath morning, were conducted by Rev. A. McKinnon (Presbyterian), of Oscoda, assisted by Rev. N. N. Clark, (Methodist) of this place. A large circle of our citizens were present to sympathize with the bereaved parents and sisters, and assist them in paying the last tribute of respect to the departed dead. The short address of Elder McKinnon was highly appropriate to the occasion, and his allusions to the manner of Fannie's death were affecting. She knew that she was going to die, had realized this for a long time, and when the hour finally came, she kissed and bid parents and sisters good bye, with her own little fingers wiped the tears from their eyes, and calling up on the dear Jesus come quickly, her loving, trusting spirit took its flight up to the celestial city of immortal glory. Thus she died in the triumph of the Christian's faith, realizing that death was but the transmission from sorrowing earth to the realms of immortal bliss. O, what a glorious change! Who would not feel to say: "Let me die the death of the righteous, let my last end be like his."

Alcona County Review, June 13, 1879

Card of Thanks.

To the Editor:

Dear Sir: We beg leave to express, through your paper, our unfeigned gratitude and thanks to the people of Harrisville, in view of their great kindness to us during our recent bereavement. We were made to feel that we were not strangers in a strange land, but in the midst of a circle of kind hearts, taking the places of the friends we have left behind us. For this timely sympathy, we can only look up to our common Father, and invoke his richest blessings upon you all.

D. and L. VanDyke.

Alcona County Review, June 13, 1879

HOME REVIEWINGS.

Rev. D. VanDyke has placed a handsome marble monument over the grave of his daughter Fannie, in South Harrisville cemetery, this week. It was manufactured at the Bay City marble works.

Alcona County Review, July 1, 1881
Cemetery: Springport, Alcona Co.

Van Horn, Clara [Marcellus]

MRS. SCOTT VAN HORN.

The following account of the death of Mrs. Scott Van Horn, nee Miss Clara Marcellus, is sent in by our West Harrisville correspondent.

Mrs. Van Horn was nearly as well known here as at West Harrisville, and a large circle of friends will read with deep regret of her early death. The Review extends its sincere sympathy to the bereaved family.

It is our sad duty this week to announce the death of our former neighbor, school teacher and society leader, Mrs. Scott Van Horn, who died after several months sickness of typhoid fever, at Tuscola.

Mrs. Van Horn was loved and admired by all who knew her. She leaves besides her husband, Rev. Scott Van Horn of Tuscola, two children, Waldo aged 2 years 4 months and Floyd Blair aged 9 months. She also leaves her mother, one brother, Chris, who is in Detroit, and sister, Jessie, who is home.

The remains were brought up on the evening train Monday and taken to the family residence. The funeral was held Tuesday in the Baptist church, of which the deceased was a member, Rev. Porterfield conducting the services. The remains were

interred at the family lot in the west cemetery. The floral offerings were beautiful. Two pillars of flowers from the B Y P. U. at Tuscola and numerous other floral pieces from friends.

Mrs. Van Horn was formerly Miss Clara Marcellus; was twenty three years old, a devout Christian and attractive in manners and appearance. She was a daughter of Mr. and Mrs. A. Marcellus, early settlers of this village. Her father preceded her in death by a year.

She leaves a wide circle of friends who will always remember her as a true friend, sympathizing neighbor and a pleasant companion.

Alcona County Review, June 8, 1899

WEST HARRISVILLE GOSSIP.

Mrs. N. J. Oliver of Black River attended the funeral of Mrs. S. Van Horn.

Alcona County Review, June 8, 1899

KILLMASTER.

Our tenderest and sincerest sympathy is extended to our former pastor, Mr. Van Horn in his sad bereavement.

Alcona County Review, June 8, 1899

WEST HARRISVILLE GOSSIP.

Rev. Scott Van Horn leaves Thursday for his home in Tuscola. Mrs. A. Marcellus and daughter Jessie will accompany him home and remain there permanently.

Alcona County Review, June 15, 1899
Cemetery: West Lawn, Alcona Co.

Vance, Mrs. John [Crozer]

Mrs. John Vance died at the home of her sister, Mrs. Gallagher, on Monday. The immediate cause of death was consumption. The interment took place in the west cemetery yesterday morning.

Alcona County Review, April 21, 1898
Cemetery: West Lawn, Alcona Co.

Varelius, Adolph

Jottings Along the Shore.

Adolph Varelius, a Swede, 28 years of age, was drowned in Pack, Woods & Co.'s bayou, Oscoda, Saturday afternoon. He leaves a wife and two children.

Alcona County Review, July 8, 1881
Cemetery:

Vaughn, Maudie

Au Sable and Oscoda Items.

A 3-year-old daughter of W. W. Vaughn, of Roscommon, formerly of Oscoda, fell into a barrel of water last week and was drowned.

Alcona County Review, May 14, 1886
Cemetery: Roscommon Village, Roscommon Co.

Vennard, John

Black River Sparks.

John Vennard who passed through here on his way to Haynes from Grand Marais, being quite ill, died at his home Tuesday p.m. Our sympathy is extended to his dear parents and family.

Alcona County Review, August 27, 1896

Haynes Happenings.
Sept. 1st, 1896.
The remains of Mr. John Vennard were interred in Mount Joy Cemetery on Thursday, the 27th, with imposing ceremonies by the Orange fraternity of Alcona county. A large concourse of relatives and friends followed the remains to their last resting place. Deceased was 24 years of age and the cause of death originated from catarrh and bleeding of the gums.

Alcona County Review, September 3, 1896

JOHN VENNARD.
John Vennard, eldest son of Mr. and Mrs. Wm. Vennard, died at his home in Haynes Aug. 25, after an illness of about four weeks. At the time he was taken sick he was cooking in Green's camp at Grand Marais, where he had been since May. He was attended by two physicians of that place, also by Dr. Wier of Au Sable, but in spite of all could be done he kept growing worse. His father was summoned to Grand Marais August 14th. Arrangements were made to bring him home and they arrived home on the 20th. Dr. Wiley was summoned on Sunday and upon seeing him stated that he could not recover. His last hours were quiet and peaceful. He passed away on Tuesday at about 10:30 o'clock a.m. The direct cause of death is unknown.

The funeral took place Thursday p.m. from the I. O. O. F. Hall under the auspices of the Loyal Orange association. Elder David Smith of Whittemore preached the funeral sermon. The remains were interred in Mount Joy cemetery. He leaves a large circle of friends and relatives to mourn his death. The parents and friends have the sympathy of the community in the loss of their dear

son. We feel that there has gone from our midst a well respected, much loved citizen and companion, and although we fain would keep him we must bow to the diving wisdom of the most high and say, "Thy will, O God, be done."

Alcona County Review, September 3, 1896

WEST HARRISVILLE.
At the regular meeting of the Loyal Orange Lodge No. 287 held Sept. 18th, the following Resolutions were unanimously adopted.

Resolved, That whereas it has pleased Almighty God in his wise providence to remove from our midst our loved brother, the late John Vennard, our Lodge loses one of its most ardent and loyal members, the bereft parents a loving and dutiful son, the community a good natured friend and neighbor.

Resolved, That we will keep green the memory of one whose wise counsel and loving words are no longer heard in our meetings. That while we deplore our loss, we bow in humble submission to the will of Him who doeth all things well, and be it further

Resolved, That our charter be draped for a period of 90 days. That a copy of these Resolutions be sent to the bereft family, that they be spread upon the records of the Lodge and that they be published in the Alcona County Review.

E. Goheen,
A. Smith,
F. S. Ford, Committee.
West Harrisville, Sept 21st, 1896.

Alcona County Review, September 24, 1896
Cemetery: Mt. Joy, Alcona Co.

Vincent, Mrs. Sarah Hannah

Obituary.
The following obituary, clipped from a York state paper, which will be of interest to many citizens of Harrisville, has been handed the editor of the Review for publication:

Died, at Greeley, Colorado, June 1?th, 1881, Hannah, wife of Mr. James Vincent, aged 33 years, 5 months, and 7 days. Mrs. V. was a sister of Mrs. L. J. Brown, of this village. She lived during nearly her whole life in this vicinity, and was well known, loved and respected by all, who deeply sympathize with her relatives and friends, and also with her husband and two little children left to mourn for her.

"Asleep in Jesus! Far from thee

Thy kindred and their graves may be;
But thine is still a blessed sleep,
From which none ever wake to weep."

Alcona County Review, August 12, 1881
Cemetery: Linn Grove, Weld Co. CO

Voisine, Joseph

OUR STATE.

An old and respected citizen of Bay City, named Joseph Voisner, was buried Monday.

Alcona County Review, May 1, 1885
Cemetery: Calvary, Bay Co.

Wagner, George C.

ALL ALONG THE SHORE.

Oscoda and Au Sable Notes.
From the Saturday Night.
Wednesday evening about 7 o'clock, George Wagner, the 11-year old son of John Wagner, of the Vienna bakery, Au Sable, while playing on a boom log in the river near his father's shop, fell into the water and was drowned. A couple of small boys who were with him at the time at once notified his father, but by the time he got there there was no trace of the boy. A party at once began dragging the river for the body, but did not find it. The river has since been dragged from the place where he fell in to the mouth, and torpedoes have been exploded with the hopes of raising the body, but all to no purpose, as it has not yet been recovered. As the current in the river is pretty swift it is likely that the body has been carried out into the lake. Mr. and Mrs. Wagner have the sympathy of the community in the loss of their only son.

Alcona County Review, June 10, 1887
Cemetery: Pinecrest, Iosco Co.

Wahbedahgan, {Male}

EVENTS OF ONE WEEK.

**** Wahbedahgan, an aborigine resident of the Indian settlement at Mikado, died last week aged 107 years.

Alcona County Review, April 30, 1896
Cemetery: Chippewa Indian, Iosco Co.

Waldron, Charles

PERSONAL.

Chas. Waldron, the second son of Mr. and Mrs. Ephriam Waldron, died at the home of his parents on

Tuesday of this week from diphtheria.

The young man, who was about 20 years of age, lived with his parents and was to them all that a dutiful son should be. The afflicted family have the sympathy of the community.

Alcona County Review, April 29, 1897
Cemetery: Springport, Alcona Co.

Waldron, {Child}

COUNTY JOTTINGS.

That dreaded disease, diptheria, is raging quite extensively among the children in the southern portion of Alcona township. One of Supervisor A. T. Scarlett's little sons died with the disease Sunday night, and children in the families of Ephriam Waldron, John Hayden and Uriah Emerson are now down with the same. Let all necessary precautions be taken to prevent the further spreading of the disease.

Alcona County Review, October 25, 1878
Cemetery: Springport, Alcona Co.

Waldron, Ephriam

Local News.

Ephriam Waldron of the Silverthorn district suffered a stroke of apoplexy last week and has been in a critical condition since. He is not any better today.

Alcona County Review, March 2, 1899

The Sick.

Ephriam Waldron in very low today. It is not thought that he can recover.

Alcona County Review, March 9, 1899

Death of Ephriam Waldron.

Ephriam Waldron died at his home north of this village on Thursday evening last. The deceased suffered a stroke of apoplexy two weeks prior to his death from which he did not regain consciousness for more than a few seconds at a time and death was a welcome relief from his sufferings.

Mr. Waldron was born in the state of New York in 1834; he came to Michigan and Alcona county in 1877 and has resided here ever since. He served in the civil war. Besides a widow he leaves a family of six children, four of whom are at home, one in Canada and one at Syracuse, N. Y.

The funeral services were held at the Methodist church on Saturday afternoon; interment at the South Harrisville cemetery. Wyrum Hoyt

Post G. A. R. of which deceased was a member, attended the funeral in a body.

Alcona County Review, March 16, 1899

We wish to extend our heartfelt thanks to the friends who so kindly aided us during the illness and death of our beloved husband and father. May God reward them for all they have done.

Mrs. E. Waldron and Family.

Alcona County Review, March 16, 1899

Resolution of Condolences.

At the regular meeting of Hoyt Post No. 6, Mich. G. A. R., held at Harrisville on March 10, 1899, the following resolutions were passed:

Whereas, Almighty God has seen fit to remove from our ranks our comrades and neighbors Patrick McGrath and Ephriam Waldron, by death;

Resolved, That this Post tender our heartfelt sympathy to the families of the departed comrades, and

Resolved that our post colors and charter by draped in mourning for 30 days.

H. C. Kibbee,
Commander.

Alcona County Review, March 16, 1899

Memorial Day Remembered.

One by one the ranks of the veterans are thinning. The addition since last memorial Day of three graves to the list of those interred in local cemeteries was a present reminder of this fact. They were those of Patrick McGrath, Francis La Chapelle and Epriam Waldron.

Alcona County Review, June 1, 1899

Of Local Interest.

Mrs. E. Waldron has been granted a pension of $12 per month, also two minor children $2 per month. The pensions date from March 1898.

Alcona County Review, May 10, 1900
Cemetery: Springport, Alcona Co.

Walker, Sarah Adelaide [O'Dell]

LOCAL JOTTINGS.

A telegram received Thursday morning announces the death in Washington Ter. of Mrs. Jno. Walker. The remains will be brought here for burial.

Alcona County Review, February 8, 1889

LOCAL JOTTINGS.

The remains of Mrs. John Walker were expected to arrive in Harrisville Thursday evening. Date of the funeral will be decided on the arrival of Mr. Walker and Allen Nevins, who accompany the remains. It will probably be held Saturday or Sunday at the latest.

Alcona County Review, February 15, 1889

LOCAL JOTTINGS.

The remains of Mrs. John Walker, accompanied by the deceased's husband and Allen Nevins, reached Harrisville Thursday evening of last week. They were interred the following day in the South Harrisville cemetery. The deceased and her husband left Harrisville for the Pacific slope early in January. Mrs. Walker contracted a severe cold on the journey which resulted in typhoid pneumonia and death. She died in Astoria, Oregon. The deceased left no children.

Alcona County Review, February 22, 1889

Card of Thanks.—I wish to thank my friends for their kindness during my recent bereavement.

John Walker.

Alcona County Review, February 22, 1889
Cemetery: Springport, Alcona Co.

Walker, James

Card of Thanks.

Mrs. Sarah Walker, mother of James Walker, deceased, called on us yesterday and wished us to tender her heartfelt thanks, through the columns of the Review, to all those who so kindly cared for her boy during his late sickness. The venerable lady feels the blow keenly, and as we conversed with her we could not but think of how "Rachael wept, and would not be comforted, because her children were not." The grief stricken mother has the sympathy of the whole community.

Alcona County Review, November 1, 1878
Cemetery:

Walker, James

Jottings Along the Shore.

A sad accident occurred at Alpena Tuesday morning last which resulted in the death of James Walker, a mason. Walker was working on the ground in a refuse burner, when a piece of iron weighing several hundred pounds fell from the hands of workmen twenty feet above, striking the ground on its edge and tipping over, crushing Walker up against the side of the burner. He was released as quickly as possible and taken to his home where he died at noon of same day. He leaves a wife and two children.

Alcona County Review, May 7, 1880
Cemetery:

Walker, John
EVENTS OF ONE WEEK.

John, better known as "Jack" Walker, died Sunday night at the county house, aged about 44 years, after a long and tedious illness from pulmonary consumption. Deceased had been a resident of this county for many years and in his younger days was a very steady and promising young man. He had been married but his wife died about six years ago. He has well-to-do relatives in Canada but he preferred not to notify them of his physical condition, and he died therefore, unattended by any relative. Under the law of this state the body would have been sent to the dissecting room at Ann Arbor, unless claimed by friends. Rather than permit this a sum of money sufficient for the purpose was raised Monday among our citizens and all that was mortal of Jack Walker was given a respectable burial in the lot beside the grave of his late wife. The funeral services were held at the M. E. church and were well attended by friends of the deceased.

Alcona County Review, October 4, 1894
Cemetery:

Walker, Reuben J.
HOME REVIEWINGS.

The only child of Mr. and Mrs. John Walker, a son of five months, died on Saturday last of bloody flux, after an illness of several days, and sorrow now reigns within their house. May the bereaved parents look unto Him who is able to comfort them in this sorrowing period of life. Christ alone is able to give the heart needed consolation.

Alcona County Review, August 26, 1881
Cemetery: Springport, Alcona Co.

Walker, Samuel
OUR NEIGHBORS.

News Jottings Along the Shore.
A Canadian named Samuel Walker, employed at one of Ramund's camps in Alpena county,

was killed by a falling tree on Thursday of last week. The blow smashed in the entire top of the head, death resulting instantaneously.

Alcona County Review, December 24, 1880
Cemetery:

Walker, William
Shore News and Gossip.

Died at Alpena last Tuesday— Capt. Wm. Walker, of the tug Fisher.

Alcona County Review, July 25, 1884
Cemetery: Sanilac, Sanilac Co.

Wallace, Frank
Death Claims Many Victims.
J. Wallace, of Au Sable, brought the remains of one of his children to the South Harrisville cemetery Sunday.

Alcona County Review, March 26, 1891
Cemetery: Springport, Alcona Co.

Ward, {Boy}
The 15-year old son of Henry Ward was drowned at Oscoda Monday.

Alcona County Review, June 29, 1899
Cemetery:

Ward, Mrs. Charles [Wheeler]
PERSONAL MENTION.

Mrs. Chas. Ward, a daughter of Isaac Wheeler, died last week at the home of her parents and was buried Sunday afternoon. The funeral services were held in the Harrisville M. E. church, the regular pastor officiating. Deceased died of consumption which she contracted nearly a year ago.

Alcona County Review, August 31, 1893
Cemetery:

Ward, Charlotte [Sanderson]
Obituary.
Died, in Harrisville, Dec. 24, Charlotte, wife of Robert Ward, in the 74th year of her age.

The deceased was the mother of George and Charles Ward, of this township, and came here from York county, N. B., with her husband, nearly four years ago to reside with the former. Shortly after arriving here she was taken ill and confined to her bed for nine months, after which she recovered sufficiently to be up about the house for a time. Later she was taken ill again with Asthma and Dropsy, and for seven months was forced, by the nature of affliction, to sit in her chair continuously night and day. During a few weeks prior to her last sickness which resulted in

death so suddenly, she was able to be moved about and do knitting, but her condition soon grew worse again, and the aged and infirm body finally yielded to the summons of the death messenger, and the spirit of mother Ward took its flight to the celestial shores. Mother Ward was born in Yorkshire, England, and married to Robert Ward, who still survives her, in 1830. A few years afterward she removed with her husband to York county, New Brunswick, where the twain resided, until removal to this place, and raised a family of 13 children, 10 of whom are now living. With reference to the religious life of the deceased, she was reared in the faith of the Church of England, but on removing to New Brunswick her sympathies became allied to the Episcopal Methodists, with whom she has since worshiped. She died in the triumph of a Christian's faith, having fought a good fight. Truly it may be said of her, "she hath done what she could."

Alcona County Review, December 29, 1882
Cemetery: Springport, Alcona Co.

Ward, Howard O.
Mud Lake Jots.
How I shall miss the signature of H. O. Ward. His face was the second one I met at W. Harrisville, and a kind one it was. It seems the depot will not be just the same now. The hearty hand shake and the genial laugh—we need lots of more just such men as George Howard. Though Heaven is his gain our world is better off for his having been among us.

Alcona County Review, January 24, 1895
Haynes Happenings.
I was grieved to learn of the death of your valued correspondent, H. O. Ward.

Alcona County Review, January 24, 1895
Cemetery:

Ward, Robert
PERSONAL MENTION.

"Grandfather" Ward, father of our respected townsman, Geo. Ward, Sr., is lying very ill at his son's residence and it is thought that he can live only a short time. If he survives until December 20th he will be 85 years old.

Alcona County Review, November 16, 1893
OBITUARY.
Robert Ward died Friday, June 4th, 1894, at 5 minutes after 4

o'clock p.m. aged 85 years, 6 months and 13 days.

The deceased was born Nov. 20th, 1808 in Yorkshire, England. In the fall of 1833 he married Sharlot Sanderson who was his companion in life until Dec. 1882, when death claimed her. They had five sons and five daughters, seven of whom still survive. In the fall of 1843 the family emigrated to St. Johns, New Brunswick. Deceased came to this county in 1878 since which time he has lived with his son George. Deceased was admitted to membership in the Methodist Episcopal church while yet a young man and he maintained a sterling consistent Christian character to the end. He was well known to the older residents of Alcona county as a patriotic and upright citizen.

The funeral services took place at 2 p.m. Sunday at the church, the Rev. Bailey paying a fitting tribute to the virtues of the deceased and offering an exposition of the belief which is the comfort of the dying and the hope of the living Christian.

The interment took place at South Harrisville whither the remains were followed by a very large procession.

Alcona County Review, June 7, 1894

Card of Thanks.—We desire to express our sincere thanks to all those kind friends and neighbors whose welcome assistance or presence during the illness, death and burial of our dear father, the late Robert Ward, we deeply appreciate.

Mr. and Mrs. Geo. Ward Sr.

Alcona County Review, June 7, 1894
Cemetery: Springport, Alcona Co.

Waters, Alexander

REVIEWINGS.

Alexander Waters, a young man, of West Bay City, died Sunday evening of lock jaw as the result of stepping upon a rusty nail ten or twelve days ago.

Alcona County Review, February 13, 1880
Cemetery:

Waters, Carl

EVENTS OF ONE WEEK.

A child of J. L. Waters at Greenbush is reported very ill today.

Alcona County Review, February 23, 1893

GREENBUSH.

The infant son of Mr. and Mrs. J. L. Waters died last Thursday after an illness of one week. The remains were

buried on Saturday in the Springport cemetery. The many friends of Mr. and Mrs. Waters tender them their most sincere sympathy in this, their bereavement.

Alcona County Review, March 2, 1893

DEATH'S HARVEST.

The infant son of Mr. and Mrs. J. L. Waters of Greenbush died Friday morning last from cold and inflammation. The burial took place Saturday at the South Harrisville cemetery.

Alcona County Review, March 2, 1893

Card of Thanks.—Our deepest and most heartfelt thanks are due to those of our friends whose timely assistance and sympathy contributed in a measure to soften the sorrow occasioned by the untimely death of our little son. May each and all of them be spared a like affliction.

Mr. and Mrs. J. L. Waters.

Alcona County Review, March 2, 1893
Cemetery: Springport, Alcona Co.

Watrous, Mary [Smith]

Jottings Along the Shore.

The wife of Dr. E. H. Watrous, dentist, of Alpena died on Thursday afternoon last.

Alcona County Review, May 27, 1881
Cemetery: Evergreen, Alpena Co.

Weatherwax, {Male}

Local Sayings and Doings.

Rev. F. W. Weatherwax received a telegram from Cassleton, N. Y., Wednesday morning, announcing the sudden death of an elder brother. The dispatch was received just a few hours too late to allow the Elder to take the down boat, thereby making it impossible for him to reach the home of the deceased in time to attend the obsequies.

Alcona County Review, July 14, 1882
Cemetery:

Webb, {Boy}

HAYNES HAPPENINGS.

Haynes, Nov. 9th, 1897.
Mr. and Mrs. Webb recently buried a child, aged 2 months, which died of whooping cough.

Alcona County Review, November 18, 1897
Cemetery: Mt. Joy, Alcona Co.

Webster, Abigail C. [Barker]

GLENNIE.

Mrs. John Webster passed away last Thursday at her late home. The remains were placed in their long resting place on Saturday and were followed to the grave by a large number of sorrowing relatives and friends. Deceased was a patient sufferer and her untimely death is a matter of general regret in the community. Her husband, who was too ill to attend the funeral, and six sons survive her. Undertaker Gagnier of Oscoda conducted the service in the absence of a regular minister.

Alcona County Review, October 6, 1898

We return our heartfelt thanks to our friends for many kindnesses rendered us during the sickness, death and burial of our beloved wife and mother.

John Webster and Family.

Alcona County Review, October 13, 1898

Local History of One Year

Chronology of the Principal Events of the Year 1898.

SEPTEMBER

28. Death of Mrs. John Webster of Curtis.

Alcona County Review, January 5, 1899
Cemetery: Glennie, Alcona Co.

Wedge, {Boy}

West Harrisville.

The Review.—The little son of Mrs. Jos. Wedge, whose age is about ten years, and who has suffered from hip disease for five years, died at his home in this village last Saturday night, and was buried south of Harrisville last Monday.

Another chair is vacant,
And other hearts made sore,
But there is consolation,
They can meet and part no more.

Alcona County Review, August 25, 1892
Cemetery:

Wedge, Joseph

PERSONAL MENTION.

Jos. Wedge, who until recently resided at West Harrisville, died suddenly at Pritchard's camp yesterday morning from heart disease.

Alcona County Review, October 11, 1894

EVENTS OF ONE WEEK.

Mrs. Jos. Wedge, relict of the late Jos. Wedge, has received a $1,000 warrant from the order of the

Maccabees for the amount of insurance held on the life of her husband. Wedge was a member of the Mud Lake Tent.

Alcona County Review, December 13, 1894

Elizabeth Wedge has petitioned the probate court for an appointment as administrator of the estate of her late husband. She has also petitioned the court to remove Simon J. McNally as administrator of the estate of Thos. Scott, deceased, and for the appointment of B. P. Cowley in his place. Hearing March 18.

Alcona County Review, February 21, 1895

STATE OF MICHIGAN, County of Alcona.

At a session of the Probate Court for said County, held at the Probate office, in the Village of Harrisville, on the Sixteenth day of February, in the year one thousand eight hundred and ninety-five.

Present, C. H. Killmaster, Judge of Probate.

In the matter of the estate of Joseph Wedge, deceased:

On reading and filing the petition, duly verified, of Elizabeth Wedge, widow and heir at law of said deceased, praying that the said petitioner, or some other suitable person, be appointed to administer the estate of the aforesaid deceased Joseph Wedge. Thereupon it is ordered, that Monday, the eighteenth day of March next, at two o'clock in the afternoon, be assigned for the hearing of said petition, and that the heirs at law of said deceased, and all other persons interested in said estate, are required to appear at a session of said Court then to be holden in the Probate office, in the Village of Harrisville, and show cause, if any there be, why the prayer of the petitioner should not be granted: And it is further ordered, that said petitioner give notice to the persons interested in said estate, of the pendency of said petition, and the hearing thereof, by causing a copy of this order to be published in the Alcona County Review, a newspaper printed and circulated in said county, three successive weeks previous to said day of hearing.

C. H. Killmaster,
Judge of Probate.

Alcona County Review, February 21, 1895

EVENTS OF ONE WEEK.

Judge Killmaster was in town Monday for the hearing in the matter of the estates of Jos. Wedge and Thos. Scott, deceased.

Alcona County Review, March 21, 1895

Haynes, May 28, 1895.—Mrs. Joseph Wedge will erect a monument to the memory of her husband, tomorrow.

Alcona County Review, May 30, 1895

Haynes Happenings.

Mrs. Joseph Wedge has erected one of the handsomest monuments in the cemetery to the memory of her husband.

Alcona County Review, June 13, 1895
Cemetery: Mt. Joy, Alcona Co.

Weeks, W. A.

Prof. W. A. Weeks, who taught the Harrisville school a number of years ago, died this week at Ypsilanti where he had held the position of Greek and Latin instructor at the State normal. He was aged 36 and leaves a wife and daughter.

Alcona County Review, March 10, 1892
Cemetery:

Weir, Dr. David H.

Dr. Weir Is Dead.

Dr. Weir, the well-known Oscoda physician who has practiced considerably in this county, died rather suddenly last week in the Bay View hospital at Grand Marais, of which he was proprietor, after an illness lasting but four days. He and a party of friends went fishing on the previous Saturday. He contracted a severe cold, which resulted in an acute attack of Bright's disease. Nothing serious was suspected until last Friday morning, when he sank into a comatose condition and died that night at 12:30. He was a native of London, Ontario, and the remains were taken there for burial. he was about 50 years old and leaves a wife, but no family. He had but recently settled in Grand Marais, but he had a large medical practice.

Alcona County Review, September 9, 1897
Cemetery:

Weir, Hiram

Hiram Weir, for 8 years foreman of the Oscoda Boom Co. disappeared August 10. Last Saturday his lifeless body was found at Fish Point, 8 miles south. He left a wife, two children and $7,000 life insurance.

Alcona County Review, August 22, 1890
Cemetery: Pinecrest, Iosco Co.

Weittzer, George

Among Our Exchanges.

From the Alpena Echo:

Geo. Weittzer, aged 40 years, a farmer living back of Alcona, but who had been here for medical treatment, died yesterday (Friday) in his chair at the saloon of Charles Selouka on Dock street, where he had been stopping. Mr. Weittzer was a member of the Black Knights of Malta Order and one of the members of that order had been here attending him. He owns a farm of forty acres in Haynes. The remains were shipped to Alcona today by Shannon.

Alcona County Review, May 26, 1892

STATE OF MICHIGAN, County of Alcona.

At a session of the Probate Court for said County, held at the Probate office, in the village of Harrisville, on the 10th day of June, in the year one thousand eight hundred and ninety-three.

Present, Geo. S. Ritchie, Judge of Probate.

In the matter of the Estate of George Webitzer:

On reading and filing the petition, duly verified, of Isadore Otto, praying that letters of administration be granted unto said James Carson or some other suitable person.

Thereupon it is ordered, that Saturday, the Eighth day of July next, at ten o'clock in the forenoon, be assigned for the hearing of said petition, and that the lawful heirs at law of said deceased, and all other persons interested in said estate, are required to appear at a session of said Court, then to be holden in the Probate office, in the village of Harrisville and show cause, if any there be, why the prayer of the petitioner should not be granted. And it is further ordered, that said petitioner give notice to the persons interested in said estate, of the pendency of said petition, and the hearing thereof, by causing a copy of this order to be published in the Alcona County Review, a newspaper printed and circulated in said county, 3 successive weeks previous to said day of hearing.

C. H. Killmaster,
Judge of Probate.

Alcona County Review, June 8, 1893

**STATE OF MICHIGAN,
County of Alcona.**

At a session of the Probate Court for said County, held at the Probate office, in the Village of Harrisville, on the Fourth day of November, in the year one thousand eight hundred and ninety-three.

Present, C. H. Killmaster, Judge of Probate.

In the matter of the Estate of George Newetzer:

On reading and filing the petition, duly verified, of Isadore Otto, praying that letters of administration be granted unto James Carson or some other suitable person: Thereupon it is ordered that Saturday, the second day of December next, at ten o'clock in the forenoon, be assigned for the hearing of said petition, and that the lawful heirs at law of said deceased, and all other persons interested in said estate, are required to appear at a session of said Court, then to be holden in the Probate office, in the Village of Harrisville, and show cause, if any there be, why the prayer of the petitioner should not be granted: And it is further ordered, that said petitioner give notice to the heirs and all other persons interested in said estate, of the pendency of said petition and the hearing thereof, by causing a copy of this order to be published in the Alcona County Review, a newspaper printed and circulated in said county, three successive weeks previous to said day of hearing.

C. H. Killmaster, Judge of Probate.

Alcona County Review, November 9, 1893

STATE OF MICHIGAN, COUNTY OF ALCONA.

At a session of the Probate Court for said County, held at the Probate office, in the Village of Harrisville, on the seventh day of April, in the year one thousand eight hundred and ninety-four.

Present, C. H. Killmaster, Judge of Probate.

In the Matter of the Estate of George Webitzer:

On reading and filing the petition, duly verified, of James Carson, asking that a license may be granted to him to sell the Real Estate, to-wit: the southeast quarter of the southwest quarter of section five in Town Twenty-seven north Range Nine East, of which the said George Webitzer died well seized and

possessed, for the purpose of paying debts.

Thereupon it is ordered, that Monday, the Seventh day of May next, at ten o'clock in the forenoon, be assigned for the hearing of said petition, and that the heirs at law of said deceased, and all other persons interested in said estate, are required to appear at a session of said Court, then to be holden in the Probate office, in the Village of Harrisville, and show cause, if any there be, why the prayer of the petitioner should not be granted:

And it is further ordered, that said petitioner give notice to the persons interested in said estate, of the pendency of said petition, and the hearing thereof, by causing a copy of this order to be published in the Alcona County Review, a newspaper printed and circulated in said county, three successive weeks previous to said day of hearing.

C. H. Killmaster, Judge of Probate.

Alcona County Review, April 12, 1894
Cemetery: Mt. Joy, Alcona Co.

Welch, {Boy}

Oscoda County Mail Items.
On Tuesday Mr. Joseph Welch's youngest son died of diphtheria.

Alcona County Review, January 27, 1882
Cemetery:

Welsh, Fredrick W.

Fred Welsh, an Oscoda liquor dealer, committed suicide Sunday evening by cutting his throat with a pen-knife. He had $8,000 insurance besides considerable property and therefore leaves his widow and children in good circumstances.

Alcona County Review, July 1, 1897
Cemetery: Pinecrest, Iosco Co.

Wesson, Ernest

From Wednesday's Alpena Argus we learn that a 16-year-old lad named Ernest Wesson, employed about the lath machine of W. H. & E. K. Potter's mill, met with a sad accident Monday afternoon last, from which he has since died. He was pushing the sawdust from under the lath saws with a lath when the stick struck one of the saws and was thrown back against him with such force that the end of the lath was driven some three or four inches into the abdomen, severing one of the intestines and lacerating others.

Alcona County Review, August 12, 1881
Cemetery:

Westman, {Child}

ALONG THE SHORE.

THE TAWASES.
Four children of the family of Christ. Westman, living at the head of Tawas Lake, have all been sick with scarlet fever. Two of them died Tuesday, and the others are now slowly recovering.

Alcona County Review, January 6, 1882
Cemetery:

Westman, {Child}

ALONG THE SHORE.

THE TAWASES.
Four children of the family of Christ. Westman, living at the head of Tawas Lake, have all been sick with scarlet fever. Two of them died Tuesday, and the others are now slowly recovering.

Alcona County Review, January 6, 1882
Cemetery:

Weston, Abijah

LOCAL PICK UPS.

Abijah Weston, one of the first to engage in lumbering at Harrisville many years ago, died a few days ago at Buffalo at the advanced age of 90.

Alcona County Review, June 9, 1898
Cemetery: West High Street, Steuben Co., NY

Wheeler, Henry Lewis

Just as we go to press we learn that Henry Wheeler, a son of Sherman Wheeler, of Alabaster, was drowned this forenoon about 10 o'clock. He was fishing on the shore of the lake, and is supposed to have had a fit, as he was drowned in very shallow water. The funeral will take place tomorrow at 1 o'clock. These are all the particulars we could learn.

Alcona County Review, July 5, 1878
Cemetery: Alabaster Township, Iosco Co.

Wheeler, William C.

LOCAL JOTTINGS.

The younger son of Richard Wheeler was buried last Sunday.—We were wholly unacquainted with the young man.

Alcona County Review, October 17, 1884
Cemetery: West Lawn, Alcona Co.

White, George J.

AMONG OUR EXCHANGES.

A man named Geo. White, who, according to Alpena papers, once lived at Killmaster, committed suicide at Alpena by shooting himself through the head. Domestic troubles was the cause.

Alcona County Review, January 14, 1897
Cemetery: Evergreen, Alpena Co.

White, Harriet Holbrook

Jottings Along the Shore.
Robert White of East Tawas has lost his five-months-old baby.

Alcona County Review, August 19, 1881
Cemetery: Greenwood, Iosco Co.

White, John

Jno. White, a substantial farmer who resides in the Limerick settlement near Mikado, was last seen alive at Oscoda last Thursday while on his way to the depot to take the train north for home. The train had gone before his arrival at the depot, and his friends are fearful that he must have succumbed to the terrible storm that raged on that night. A search has been instituted and is being vigorously prosecuted.

Alcona County Review, January 20, 1888

Jno. White, the Limerick farmer who was reported as missing last week, has not been found at latest accounts (Thursday morning) and nothing new has developed to throw any light on his whereabouts. The Au Sable papers state that White filled up on poor whiskey before he left that village, and, as was stated in this paper last week, the last seen of him was when he was on his way to take the 5 o'clock train for home.

Alcona County Review, January 20, 1888

LOCAL JOTTINGS

Eliza White, the wife of Jno. White, the Limerick farmer who mysteriously disappeared at Oscoda a few weeks since, acting on the supposition that her husband is dead, applies to the probate court of this county for the administration of her husband's estate. The whereabouts of White is still an unsolved mystery.

Alcona County Review, February 17, 1888

PROBATE ORDER.
STATE OF MICHIGAN, County of Alcona.

At a session of the Probate Court for said county, held at the Probate Office in the village of Harrisville, on the 14th day of February, in the year one thousand eight hundred and eighty-eight. Present, Allen Nevins, Judge of Probate. In the matter of the

ESTATE OF JOHN WHITE, DECEASED.

On reading and filing the petition, duly verified, of Eliza White, praying that she may be appointed administratrix of the estate of said John White, deceased.

Thereupon it is ordered that Saturday, the Tenth Day of March, 1888, next, at ten o'clock in the forenoon, be assigned for the hearing of said petition, and that the heirs at law of said deceased, and all other persons interested in said estate, are required to appear at a session of said court then to be holden at the Probate office, in the village of Harrisville, and show cause if any there be, why the prayer of the petitioner should not be granted. And it is further ordered that said petitioner give notice to the heirs at law, and other persons interested in said estate, of the pendency of said petition, and the hearing thereof, by causing a copy of this order to be published in the Alcona County Review, a newspaper printed and circulated in said county, three successive weeks previous to said day of hearing.

ALLEN NEVINS, Judge of Probate.

Henry & Cornville, Attorneys for Petitioner.

Alcona County Review, February 17, 1888

LOCAL JOTTINGS.
With the disappearance of the snow it was expected that the body of Jno. White, the Limerick farmer, would be found. Search has failed to discover it, however, and all hope in that direction has been abandoned. Meantime Mrs. White has applied to the probate court of this county for administration of her husband's estate.

Alcona County Review, April 20, 1888

LOCAL JOTTINGS

Mrs. White, whose husband John White disappeared one night last January during a terrible snow storm, recently wrote to a Grand Rapids lady who can read the past, present and future with perfect ease, and received a reply stating that her husband had been murdered by an enemy, and his body buried in a shanty. Up to date neither the shanty nor the body has been found.—Saturday Night.

Alcona County Review, June 15, 1888

WHITE IS STILL MISSING.

His Place of Burial Located by a Medium—But Diligent Search and Much Digging Fail to Bring him Forth.

One night last January John White, a farmer from near Handy, twelve miles up the railroad, disappeared, and no trace of him has since been found. On the day of his disappearance White came to town, transacted some business and indulged in a little "tangle foot." When near train time—5 o'clock in the evening—he started for the depot, which is about three-quarters of a mile out of town. When he arrived there the train had gone and he started back for town. This was the last seen of him, and it was supposed that he had either lost his way in the storm and frozen to death or had fallen off the Boom Co.'s bridge into the river. After the snow disappeared in the spring no trace of the body was yet seen, so the river theory was held as the manner of his disappearance.

As announced in last week's issue, Mrs. White recently wrote to a Grand Rapids medium, simply telling her she has lost her husband. In return she received a letter stating that White had been murdered by an enemy and his body hid under a house. The letter went on and described accurately a man who had cooked in White's camp a year ago last winter, named Stephen Carrier. Carrier's wife was in camp at the time and it is said that both Mrs. White and Carrier were jealous of the other two. This spring Carrier and his wife moved to Dakota.

Tuesday Mrs. White came to town and proceeded to look for the remains of her husband, directing her search to the house formerly occupied by Carrier, and now the home of Pierre Blaise. The house is on the lake shore, at the foot of Adams avenue, back of the last house on the north side of the street. Entrance to it is obtained by an alley.

The house is built on the side of a hill, and under the end toward the lake there is a space of six or seven feet between the ground and the first floor. This is enclosed and it is used as a store room. The ground under that portion of the house, to the depth of three or four feet, was dug up, as was also the ground under a shed in the rear of the house, but no trace of the body was found.

Mrs. White left on the evening train for home, but is not yet satisfied, and says she will return and have the digging resumed till the body is found, or she is convinced that it is not there.—Saturday Night.

Alcona County Review, June 15, 1888

NO LONGER A MYSTERY!

AFTER MANY DAYS OF WAITING THE RIVER GIVES UP IT'S DEAD.

The Body of John White is Found Floating in the Au Sable River.

From the Oscoda Saturday Night.

The excitement and interest created last week by the search for the body of John White of Handy, who disappeared last January, and whom it was claimed by a Grand Rapids medium, was murdered and buried under a house, was strangely supplemented this week by the finding of his body—not in any such place as was described by the medium, however.

Last Monday morning David Colden was going to perform some work for Wilcox & Richards, but they not being ready for him he borrowed a pike pole and went to the river, a little below Wilcox & Richards' hardware store, to catch some drift wood which he saw coming down. He had worked but a moment when an object lodged against a piece of drift which had fastened itself to the bank caught his eye. He dropped his pole and ran to the street for aid which was speedily found. Returning, the object was drawn to the shore and proved to be the badly decayed body of a man. Coroner Marvin was summoned and took charge of the body. The news of the discovery spread rapidly and the scene of the finding of the body and the premises of undertaker Chevrier, where the remains were taken, were thronged with people, urged on by morbid curiosity. Those who looked once at the remains hardly cared to look again, the sight being too horrible for description. Were it not for the clothing which was still on his person the body could not have been identified. As it was there was little

doubt but that it was the body of John White. Mrs. White was immediately sent for and when she arrived identified the articles found on his person. These were $2.95 in change, some papers, a compass, a handkerchief, a pipe, some harness snaps and a tobacco pouch made by Mrs. White. She also identified his overcoat and under clothing, leaving little doubt as to the identity of the body. The remains were buried Monday. There is but little doubt now that White, upon finding himself too late to catch the train started up the railroad track and when he reached the railroad bridge fell off into the river. He must have become fastened to some object under water and there remained until in some manner the body became loosened and drifted to the place where it was discovered.

In accordance with the above facts the coroner's jury brought in a verdict of accidental drowning. So ends all doubt as to the fate of John White.

Alcona County Review, June 29, 1888

State of Michigan, County of Alcona.

Notice is hereby given, that by an order of the Probate Court for the County of Alcona, made on the 1st day of August A.D. 1898, six months from that date were allowed for creditors to present their claims against the estate of John White, late of said county, deceased, and that all creditors of said deceased are required to present their claims to said Probate Court at the Probate office in the Village of Harrisville for examination and allowance on or before the 1st day of February next, and that such claims will be heard before said Court on Monday, the 17th day of October and on Wednesday, the 1st day of February next, at ten o'clock in the forenoon of each of those days.

Dated Aug. 15th, A.D. 1898.

W. H. Gilpin, Judge of Probate.

Alcona County Review, August 18, 1898

LOCAL PICK UPS.

The final hearing of claims in the John White (of Mikado) estate was held in the probate court Monday. Wm. Strouthers, son of Mrs. White (or Murray) and administrator of the estate, paid all claims allowed by the court and was given a deed of the Mikado property. Mr. Strouthers deeded the property to his wife.

Alcona County Review, February 9, 1899
Cemetery: Pinecrest, Iosco Co.

White, Robert

Death of Robert White.—Robert White, one of the best known citizens of the Huron shore, dropped dead Monday night in Mowrey's jewelry store, East Tawas, while talking with some friends. The deceased was a former resident of Alcona county and was prominently identified with its early history, being one of the first justices of the peace elected after the organization of Harrisville township in 1860. Deceased was 60 years old, leaves a wife and six years old son. He left but little property.

Alcona County Review, February 22, 1889
Cemetery: Greenwood, Iosco Co.

Whitney, Ernest

COUNTY REVIEWINGS.

From the Au Sable *News* we learn that Ernest Whitney, of New Brunswick, Canada, employed by the Oscoda Salt & Lumber company, in Camp 11, on Perry's Creek, Au Sable river, was instantly killed by a hemlock tree, toppled over by a pine, on the 15th inst. Deceased was 20 years old and married. On the same day Michael McDonald, working in Emery Bros.' camp on the South Branch of the Au Sable, had his skull crushed in, a tree falling upon him while he was at his work. Deceased is 35 years old, and is supposed to have friends living in Oswego, N.Y.

Alcona County Review, November 26, 1880
Cemetery:Au Sable Township, Iosco Co.

Whittaker, Ella M. [Cummings]

PERSONAL MENTION.

Mrs. Frank Whittaker, formerly Miss Ella M. Cummings, and well known here died at their home in Detroit Friday, Oct. 16, inst. of pulmonary consumption.

Alcona County Review, October 22, 1896
Cemetery:

Whittemore, William B.

LOCAL JOTTINGS.

Wm. B. Whittemore, a pioneer of the Tawases, well known to many of our citizens, died last week.

Alcona County Review, September 27, 1889
Cemetery: Probably Greenwood, Iosco Co.

Widdifield, Josephine

NEIGHBORHOOD NOTES.

Josephine Widdifield, the 6 years-old daughter of the well-known life insurance agent, died at their home in Tawas last week.

Alcona County Review, January 1, 1885
Cemetery:

Widdifield, Maggie [Milligan]

AMONG OUR EXCHANGES.

Mrs. J. B. Widdifield died at East Tawas last week.

Alcona County Review, April 28, 1892
Cemetery: Greenwood, Iosco Co.

Wiley, {Child}

PERSONAL POINTS.

Friends of Mr. and Mrs. Dr. F. C. Wiley of Pinnebog, will learn with sadness of the death of their infant child. Mrs. Wiley has been very low, but is now well on the way to recovery.

Alcona County Review, August 3, 1899
Cemetery:

Williams, Herbert M.

ALL ALONG THE SHORE

ALPENA DRIFT.

From the Pioneer.
The funeral of little Bert Williams, son of C. E. Williams, took place last Wednesday. The boy was drowned while gallantly trying to rescue another boy.

Alcona County Review, July 29, 1887
Cemetery: Evergreen, Alpena Co.

Williams, John W.

People We Hear About.

Mr. and Mrs. A. R. Williams, of West Harrisville, mourn the loss of their little son, 10 months old. The child died Sunday evening from inflammation of the brain.

Alcona County Review, July 25, 1890

Card of Thanks.

We wish to publicly thank our friends and neighbors who rendered such timely assistance during the illness and death of our little son.
Mr. and Mrs. A. R. Williams.

Alcona County Review, July 25, 1890
Cemetery: West Lawn, Alcona Co.

Williams, Mrs.

LOCAL JOTTINGS

Mrs. Williams, of Mikado, upwards of 80 years of age, died Wednesday.

Alcona County Review, July 20, 1888
Cemetery:

Wilmot, R. S.

While boat riding with Miss Sarah Currie on the lake at Au Sable, R. S. Wilmot was stricken with apoplexy and died in a few hours.

Alcona County Review, July 25, 1890
Cemetery:

Wilson, Albert

West Harrisville, March 7.--Chas. Wilson and wife were called away to attend a funeral of their brother and sister at Lapeer, both of whom died at the same time.

Alcona County Review, March 7, 1895
Cemetery:

Wilson, Alexander

NEIGHBORHOOD NOTES.

Alex Wilson an Oscoda veteran was run over and killed at Potts by a log train Tuesday. He was under the influence of liquor.

Alcona County Review, August 30, 1889
Cemetery: Sacred Heart, Iosco Co.

Wilson, Calvin

Purely Personal.

Calvin Wilson has been so seriously ill that grave doubts of his recovery were entertained by those who watched anxiously at his bedside.

Alcona County Review, December 20, 1889

Purely Personal.

Calvin Wilson, that sturdy old pioneer who bade his friends good by a few weeks ago expecting to get a summons to cross over Jordan at almost any moment, conquered the dropsy that threatened his life and is "worth a dozen dead men yet" as the saying is. "Cal" drove over to Harrisville a few days ago.

Alcona County Review, February 21, 1890

Calvin Wilson is reported very ill again and grave doubts of his recovery are felt.
Since writing the above it becomes our sad duty to state that Mr. Wilson has passed away. He died Tuesday and his remains were buried Thursday from his late residence.

Alcona County Review, October 24, 1890

The Local News.

Judge of Probate Ritchie held court Saturday and issued an order admitting to probate the last will and testament of the late Calvin Wilson.

Alcona County Review, December 26, 1890

PROBATE ORDER.

State of Michigan,
County of Alcona.
At a session of the Probate Court for said county, held at the Probate office in the village of Harrisville, on the 20th day of December, in the year one thousand eight hundred and ninety.
Present, Geo. H. Ritchie, Judge of Probate.
In the matter of the estate of Calvin Wilson.
On reading and filing the petition, duly verified, of Sarah Wilson, praying that a certain instrument now on file in this Court, purporting to be the last will and testament of said deceased, may be admitted to Probate, and that she or some other suitable person be appointed executor of said estate.
Thereupon it is ordered, that Saturday, the twenty-fifth day of January next, at ten o'clock in the forenoon, be assigned for the hearing of said petition, and that the heirs at law of said deceased, and all other persons interested in said estate, are required to appear at a session of said court, then to be holden at the Probate office, in the village of Harrisville, and show cause, if any there be, why the prayer of the petitioner should not be granted: And it is further ordered, that said petitioner give notice to all persons interested in said estate, of the pendency of said petition, and the hearing thereof, by causing a copy of this order to be published in the Alcona County Review, a newspaper printed and circulated in said county, four successive weeks previous to said day of hearing.
GEO. S. RITCHIE.
Judge of Probate.

Alcona County Review, December 26, 1890

One Year's History.

Record of Local Happenings for the Year 1890.

OCTOBER.

21 Death of Calvin Wilson.

Alcona County Review, January 1, 1891

The Local News.

The will of Calvin Wilson was probated last Saturday.

Alcona County Review, January 29, 1891
Cemetery: Springport, Alcona Co.

Wilson, Calvin, Jr.

REVIEWINGS.

Calvin Wilson, of Greenbush, buried a five weeks' old babe, yesterday.

Alcona County Review, May 30, 1879
Cemetery: Springport, Alcona Co.

Wilson, Claude J.

County News and Gossip.

Isaac Wilson and youngest daughter have gone to Otsego Lake to look after Mr. Wilson's son, Dewit, and his family, all of whom are badly afflicted with the Diphtheria. One child, the eldest in the family has died of the disease.

Alcona County Review, January 3, 1879
Cemetery:

Wilson, Graeme M.

COUNTY NEWS JOTTINGS.

Graeme Wilson, Prosecuting Attorney of Bay County, committed suicide at his room in the Campbell House, Bay City, on Tuesday morning, by cutting his throat with a razor. No cause known why he committed the rash act.

Alcona County Review, July 13, 1877
Cemetery:Pine Ridge, Bay Co.

Wilson, Mrs. Jane

Mrs. Alex. Wilson, an Au Sable widow, died last week from blood poisoning. She ran a rusty nail into her foot sometime ago which became very serious from neglect and amputation did not suffice to save her life.

Alcona County Review, September 20, 1894
Cemetery: Probably Sacred Heart, Iosco Co.

Wilson, Mrs. [Leith]

LOCAL JOTTINGS.

Word was received by Rev. T. B. Leith, Thursday morning, of the death of his sister, Mrs. Wilson, aged 42 years, at Collingwood, Ontario. She leaves a husband and ten children.

Alcona County Review, May 28, 1886
Cemetery:

Wilson, Olive Independence

Olive Independence Wilson.

Memorial services, in honor of Olive Independence Wilson, deceased, daughter of Isaac and Sarah Wilson, of Harrisville, first white child born on the west shore of Lake Huron, will be held at the M. E. Church, in Harrisville, next Sabbath morning. The deceased was born on the 4th of July, 1846, and died a few years thereafter at Tawas City. At the time of the death of this child there was no such thing as neighbors to sympathize with the sorrowing parents, and Mr. and Mrs. Wilson were therefore compelled to prepare it for burial themselves. The incident is one that seldom occurs even in pioneer life. The remains of the deceased were removed from Tawas and interred in the South Harrisville cemetery about two weeks ago. Hence the memorial services next Sabbath morning.

Alcona County Review, July 5, 1878

COUNTY JOTTINGS.

The sermon in memory of Olive Independence Wilson, deceased, first white child born on the Shore, preached at the M. E. church last Sabbath morning, was one of Elder Clark's best productions, and commanded much earnest attention.

Alcona County Review, July 12, 1878
Cemetery: Springport, Alcona Co.

Wilson, Phebe [Dibble]

Isaac Wilson was the son of Peter Wilson and Phebe Dibble, his widow, who died June 1, 1886, at Plainfield, Kent Co., at the advanced age of 107 years. Her father, Peter Dibble, died at Colchester, Delaware Co., N. Y., at the age of 108 years. Mr. Wilson is 78 years old and one of the last of Alcona county's pioneers, and is still hale and hearty.

Alcona County Review, September 10, 1886
Cemetery:

Wilson, Sarah

West Harrisville, March 7.--Chas. Wilson and wife were called away to attend a funeral of their brother and sister at Lapeer, both of whom died at the same time.

Alcona County Review, March 7, 1895
Cemetery: Probably Attica Township, Lapeer Co.

Wilson, Sarah R. Frances [Miller]

MRS. ISAAC WILSON

Just as she was preparing to retire for the night Saturday, Mrs. Isaac Wilson gave a gasp and passed away. She had been enjoying extraordinarily good health all winter and was in her usual health apparently up to the last moment. She had been visiting throughout the day with friends and was sprightly and vivacious as ever, and there was not the slightest indication that the sands of her useful and eventful life had so nearly run out.

Mrs. Wilson was a native of Rhode Island where she was born 71 years ago in December. Her husband, who survives her, was a native of New York. They came to Michigan in the early 40's and on the first day of August, 1845, they landed at Devil River, now Ossineke, from the schooner Baltic and were the first actual white settlers on the Huron coast between Bay City and Alpena. The emigrants were Mr. and Mrs. Wilson, their son Charles, 17 months age, and some workmen for the saw mill, the pioneer saw mill of the coast, which had been built by Birch and Aldridge of Detroit and which Mr. Wilson was to superintend.

There was a fishing station of Thunder Bay Island but aside from the few people there the infant settlement at Devil River comprised the total white population of northern Michigan.

The lives of the early settlers were full of hardships and privations as might be imagined, and in these early experiences Mrs. Wilson bore an honorable and distinguished part. In Christian spirit and fortitude, fertility of resources, and unselfishness, she was rich, and the isolated situation made frequent demands upon her skill as a nurse and a mixer of healing draughts. On one occasion the deceased was sent for to go to the aid of a sick woman, the nearest neighbor, distant 60 miles, at another point on the coast. The trip had to be made by water in an open fish boat. It was late in the season, the weather was treacherous and the perilous trip was made in the teeth of a gale of so severe a nature that the boatmen as a matter of precaution and safety lashed Mrs. Wilson to the mast. The trip was successfully made and the sick woman survived to bless the ministering angel who braved such dangers and hardships to relieve the sufferings of a fellow being.

On July 4th, 1846, a child was born to Mr. and Mrs. Wilson at Devil River, to whom was given the name of Olive Independence Wilson. This was the first white child born in northeastern Michigan. Olive died before reaching maturity.

The winter of 1845-6 was a severe one; snow covered the earth from early in November until May. On April 23d, 1846, it was five feet deep on the level. All the supplies for man and beast had to be hauled on hand sleds by men on snow shoes. At Christmas the Wilsons came down to Springport to visit S. M. Holden, the first actual settler of Alcona county, who had a fishing station on the high banks. The supply of provisions was short during the winter but a kind providence brought them through and their larder was replenished from a boat which arrived from Detroit at the first opportunity in the spring.

In November, 1846, the Wilsons migrated to Saginaw and later to Tawas and in 1856 became residents of what is now Alcona county. They settled at Springport near the Holden homestead. A hewed log house was built, land was cleared, and a crop of rye was raised which was the first grain raised in Alcona county.

Later they purchased the Holden homestead, on which they have resided continuously ever since.

Mrs. Wilson was a hale and hearty type of womanhood, of a cheerful disposition and rare intelligence. Her early married life inured her to hardships and privations that moulded a character of sterling worth. She placed an implicit reliance on the promises and hopes of the Christian faith and it is not too much to say that she was fully prepared to answer the final summons. To the last day of her life, however, she took a lively interest in the current events of the world.

She is survived by five children, viz: Chas. Wilson of St. Ignace, Mrs. Wm. Hooper of Denver, Colo., Mrs. Albert Kirsten of McKinley, Mrs. R. W. Downer, Greenbush, DeWitt Wilson, Harrisville. The aged partner of her joys and sorrows also survives. Mr. Wilson is 86 years of age and is still in the unimpaired possession of his faculties.

The funeral services were held Tuesday afternoon at 2 o'clock at the late home of the deceased. The interment took place at South Harrisville. The funeral obsequies were conducted by Rev. W. W. Will of the Methodist church, to which

denomination Mrs. Wilson faithfully adhered.

Mrs. Wilson was born at Greenwich, R. I., 1826. Had she lived until April 3, she would have completed 57 years of married life. They were married on the day of President Wm. Henry Harrison's death.

Alcona County Review, March 10, 1898

PERSONAL POINTS.
Card of Thanks.—We desire to sincerely thank our many friends and neighbors for their kindness and sympathy during the death and burial of our beloved wife and mother.
Isaac Wilson and Children.

Alcona County Review, March 17, 1898

Local History of One Year

Chronology of the Principal Events of the Year 1898.

March 5. Sudden death of Mrs. Isaac Wilson aged 71. She and her husband first actual white settlers of Huron shore, settling at Devil River near Ossineke in August 1845.

Alcona County Review, January 5, 1899
Cemetery: Springport, Alcona Co.

Wilson, Thomas A.
Haynes Happenings.

Aug. 16th.—The remains of Mr. Wilson, aged 73 years, were interred last Sunday afternoon. He was the father-in-law of Messrs. John and William Greenfield and John Cook and the father of Mrs. Margaret Somers who died June 28. Two of his sons were present. His remains were followed to the grave by a large concourse of sympathizing friends. Mr. Wilson had been ailing for several years.

Alcona County Review, August 18, 1898

Local History of One Year

Chronology of the Principal Events of the Year 1898.

August 12. Death of--Wilson of Haynes aged 73.

Alcona County Review, January 5, 1899
Cemetery: Mt. Joy, Alcona Co.

Weimer, Inath
Haynes
Mr. Wimer of Black River has also caused to be erected a very neat tombstone over his daughter's grave in our cemetery.

Alcona County Review, October 13, 1892
Cemetery: Mt. Joy, Alcona Co.

Winter, Earle
EVENTS OF ONE WEEK.

One of the famous Winter triplets born last summer at Au Sable is dead.

Alcona County Review, December 27, 1894
Cemetery:

Withey, {Child}
EVENTS OF ONE WEEK.

An infant child belonging to Mrs. Ellen Withey of Black River, formerly of Harrisville, died last week and was buried in the South Harrisville cemetery Saturday.

Alcona County Review, February 23, 1893

Card of Thanks.
We wish to thank our friends and neighbors who so kindly assisted us in our recent bereavement. May God's richest blessing be their portion.
Mrs. E. Withey and Family.

Alcona County Review, February 23, 1893
Cemetery: Springport, Alcona Co.

Witter, Sarah [Purdy]
Died.
On the 27th inst., at the residence of her son-in-law, John Taft, Harrisville, Sarah P. Witter; aged 69 years and 10 months.

The deceased was born in Oswego, N. Y., in November, 1808. About eight years ago, in company with her husband, Lester Witter, who died some three years ago, she removed from Stuben Co., N. Y. and came to Harrisville, where her husband purchased a small farm and they two resided till Mr. W.'s death. The deceased leaves six grown up children--Mrs. Harriet Taft, Mrs. Helen Griswold, Otis and Holmes Witter, Harrisville; D. H. Witter, Manistique, Mich., and David P. Witter, Colorado--all of them share the sympathy of a large circle of friends.

Alcona County Review, September 28, 1877
Cemetery: Springport, Alcona Co.

Wood, Hannah [Niles]
HOME NEWS JOTTINGS.
The Review regrets to learn of the serious illness of the venerable Mrs. Hannah Wood, mother of John Wood and Abram Noyes. She is badly afflicted with inflammatory rheumatism.

Alcona County Review, December 29, 1882

Obituary.

Died—In Harrisville, Mich., January 6, 1883, Mrs. Hannah Wood aged nearly 75 years.

The subject of this memoir was born at North Danville, Vermont, March 16, 1808. Her maiden name was Niles. She was united in marriage to Abram Noyes in the year 1830, and shortly after removed with husband to Michigan and settled in Detroit. In the year 1843 Mr. Noyes died, and two years after she was married to John Wood, with whom she removed from Detroit to Royal Oak. In the year 1860 Mr. Wood also died and ten years after she came to Harrisville where she lived until her death.

At an early age the subject of religion became, to her mind, the all absorbing theme, leading to entire consecration of herself to God, and His cause. Shortly after her conversion she united with the Free-Will Baptists, and after moving to Detroit she joined the Methodist Episcopal church, of which she remained a faithful member until she was called to the church triumphant. Although Sister Wood's last illness was brief and her death sudden, to many, yet the messenger found "her house in order." As dissolution drew near she called her children around her and gave them her last counsel in earnest, loving words. Assured them that the religion that sustained her amid all the cares and trials and bereavements that she had experienced, amply supported her spirit in the last ordeal. Her funeral took place from the M. E. church, on Sunday afternoon, the pastor preaching an appropriate discourse to a large audience, from the words, "Blessed are the dead who die in the Lord, etc.," Rev. 14, 13.

Four children, Abram Noyes of this village, Nancy McClatchy (children of the first marriage), Mrs. F. Chapelle, and John Wood, (children of the second marriage) live to mourn the loss of a mother that they all passionately loved. J. H. M.

Alcona County Review, January 12, 1883
Cemetery: Springport, Alcona Co.

Woods, George
ALONG THE SHORE.

There were two drownings at Oscoda last week—Geo. Woods, aged 17 years, in Van Ettan Lake, and a seven-year-old boy in Potts bayous.

Alcona County Review, June 19, 1885
Cemetery:

Woodward, Edward

Edward Woodward, aged 22, was taken with cramps while in bathing in the Alpena river Tuesday and was drowned.

Alcona County Review, June 8, 1893
Cemetery:

Wyman, Wallace
EVENTS OF ONE WEEK.

Last week the remains of a human being were found in a swamp near Hubbard Lake, which prove to be those of Wallace Wyman, a 13-year-old boy who in the month of February, 1887, was sent from a camp on the Lower South to visit his uncle. That was the last seen of him and he undoubtedly froze to death.

Alcona County Review, September 28, 1893
Cemetery:

Young, Curtis

Died, in Harrisville, Monday morning, June 21st, Curtis, son of G. W. and Mary Young, aged about two years.

This is the second son that has been snatched from the fold of this family by death within the past two weeks, both dying of the diphtheria. Sad, sad it is to part with those we love at long intervals between each other's death, but sadder still is it for father and mother to part with two lovely, promising little boys in so short a period. Truly, Mr. and Mrs. Young, in this their sad affliction, should receive the heart-felt sympathy of the entire community.

Alcona County Review, June 25, 1880

Presbyterian Appointments.--The funeral sermon of Curtis, infant son of G. W. and Mary Young, will be preached in the Presbyterian Church next Sabbath morning at 10:30 o'clock.

Alcona County Review, June 25, 1880
Cemetery: Springport, Alcona Co.

Young, Ella
REVIEWINGS.

The death of Miss Ella Young, daughter of John B. Young, Esq., of Greenbush, from diphtheria, which occurred at the County Farm last Friday evening, has occasioned much sorrow on the part of the people in that vicinity. Miss Young was a young lady much respected and loved by all who knew her, and in her death society loses one of its charms. Her faith in Christ was firm and unswerving to the last, and in His loving arms she thus fell asleep.

Alcona County Review, December 26, 1879
Cemetery: Springport, Alcona Co.

Young, John
COUNTY REVIEWINGS.

A terrible accident occurred in J. C. Gram's mill at Au Sable, last Tuesday which resulted in the almost instant death of a young man named John Young, who was employed as tail sawyer on the carriage. The saw had just passed through the log and the carriage was being reversed for another cut, when the unfortunate young man turned round and fell backward on the saw. The right leg and arm were severed from the body, and he was thrown across the mill by the force of the saw, which caused almost instant death. Deceased was about 20 years of age, and leaves friends in Ottawa, Ont.

Alcona County Review, November 12, 1880
Cemetery:

Young, John B.
John B. Young.

John B. Young died at his home in Greenbush on the morning of Sunday, Jan. 31st.

Deceased had been a sufferer from asthma and heart trouble for years, but did not take to his bed until about two months ago, since which time he steadily failed until Sunday morning, when death released him from his sufferings.

John B. Young was a native of the state of Maine. He was married in Barrie, Ont., in 1853, to Isabella Hamilton. He had a family of eight children, six of whom and his widow survive him. Mr. Young came to Alcona county in 1879, and engaged in lumbering. He has held several offices in his township and has held the office of justice of the peace since 1870.

The surviving children are Mrs. Wm. Kell and Mrs. Wm. Jenkins of Harrisville, Mrs. W. H. Sanborn and Ernest Young, of Greenbush; Charles

Young of Oregon, and Wm. Young of Victoria, B. C.

The funeral services were conducted by the Rev. F. S. Ford at the Greenbush church on Tuesday. The remains were interred at South Harrisville.

Alcona County Review, February 4, 1897

MIKADO.

Several from here attended the funeral of the late Jno. B. Young.

Alcona County Review, February 4, 1897

Card of Thanks.

I desire to thank the many friends and neighbors, who so kindly assisted us during the last sickness and death of my departed husband.

Greenbush, Feb. 9th, 1897.

Mrs. J. B. Young.

Alcona County Review, February 11, 1897
Cemetery: Springport, Alcona Co.

Young, Martin B.

COUNTY REVIEWINGS.

The funeral discourse of Martin B. Young, infant son of Mr. and Mrs. G. W. Young, will be delivered in the Presbyterian church, next Sabbath at 0:30 a.m., by the pastor, Rev. D. Van Dyke.

Alcona County Review, June 11, 1880
Cemetery: Springport, Alcona Co.

Young, Robert

Local News.

Robert Youngs of Mikado, died Monday at the home of D. D. Bruce, where he made his home. Deceased was 63 years of age and a Maccabee. The funeral was held yesterday, Rev. W. W. Will officiating.

Alcona County Review, October 12, 1899

Card of Thanks.

I wish through the medium of your paper, to express my heart-felt thanks to the friends of Mikado and surrounding country for the kindness shown me in my bereavement, in the loss of my father, and especially I thank Mr. and Mrs. D. D. Bruce for their sympathy and kindness shown me.

MAGGIE J. YOUNG.

Alcona County Review, October 26, 1899
Cemetery: Springport, Alcona Co.

Youngs, Freeman

ALCONA.

Dear Editor:—Herewith I send you a condensed report of the principal events which have transpired in the township of Alcona during the year A. D., 1878.

To my knowledge there have been 30 births, 18 girls and 12 boys. If there have been any more let the midwives speak up. There have been 9 deaths in the township—two children from diphtheria, two children from causes unknown; one child from whooping cough; one woman from consumption; one man, mortally wounded in Beard & Co's saw-mill; one of the inhabitants of Harrisville by gun shot; and James Pyne's son was mortally wounded in Millen's works, and died at the residence of his father; Mr. Freeman Youngs was mortally wounded on the Black River R. R., and died in Detroit. Mr. D. McArthur also lost his leg by the discharge of a rifle.

Alcona County Review, January 10, 1879
Cemetery:

Yuill, Joseph

Haynes Happenings.

Haynes, April 10.—Mr. and Mrs. A. Yuill have a very sick child at present. Dr. Mitchell is the attending physician.

Alcona County Review, April 12, 1894

Haynes Happenings.

Haynes, April 18.—Alex Yuill's child died on the morning of the 16th and was buried on the 17th. It was a boy aged about 11 months. Mr. Yuill is not feeling very well himself at present owing to a very severe attack of the grip.

Alcona County Review, April 19, 1894
Cemetery: Mt. Joy, Alcona Co.

Yuill, Mary [Paris]

Mrs. Mary Yuill died at the home of her son, Joseph last Friday morning. Deceased had resided in this county about 10 years and was beloved by all who knew her.

Mary Paris was born in Scotland Dec. 15, 1814 and was therefore over 84 years of age when she died. She was the daughter of a parish school teacher. After the death of her father she came to America with her mother and the other members of the family. The mother died as they landed in Quebec. Deceased was married to Joseph Yuill, who died some 40 years ago leaving her with a family of eight children, seven of whom are still living. She came to Michigan about 10 years ago to spend her remaining days with her two youngest children, Miss Margaret and Joseph. She had

been a member of the Presbyterian church for 60 years.

The surviving children in this county are Joseph and Alex and Miss Margaret Yuill, all respected citizens. The other children live in Canada.

The funeral occurred Sunday afternoon at the home of Jos. Yuill, Rev. W. W. Will preaching the sermon. A large number of friends and neighbors attended the funeral and followed the remains to the cemetery.

Alcona County Review, March 30, 1899

We desire to thank the friends and neighbors for their many acts of kindness during the sickness and death of our beloved parent.

Children of Mrs. Yuill.

Alcona County Review, March 30, 1899

LOCAL PICK UPS.

We omitted to state last week that Rev. Mr. Austin of the Black River Presbyterian church assisted at the funeral services of the late Mrs. Mary Yuill.

Alcona County Review, April 6, 1899
Cemetery: West Lawn, Alcona Co.

?, {Child}

Reviewings.

A man and wife, accompanied by a small child, drove into Caro from the north, last week Thursday, and upon their arrival discovered that the child was frozen to death.-- *Tuscola Pioneer.*

Alcona County Review, March 14, 1879
Cemetery:

?, {Child}

The body of a fully developed infant was recently found floating in a box on the bayou at Au Sable. It is stated on the quiet that a number of very prominent people are interested in the matter, and therefore a Herculean effort has been made to hush it up.

Alcona County Review, July 21, 1892
Cemetery:

?, {Child}

EVENTS OF ONE WEEK.

A child was buried from the French settlement on Sunday and another, an 18 months' old boy, died yesterday. The latter belonged to a family named Oulette. Neither died from diphtheria, so far as known.

Alcona County Review, February 2, 1893
Cemetery:

?, {Child}

LOCAL PARAGRAPHS.

The remains of a child were brought down from the French settlement Tuesday for burial in the Catholic cemetery.

Alcona County Review, October 25, 1894
Cemetery: St. Anne's, Alcona Co.

?, {Child}

EVENTS OF ONE WEEK.

A child was born in this village last Friday whose advent into this vale of sin and sorrow has been a matter of anxiety to more than one person besides the girl's mother. Fortunately for all concerned the child died on Monday.

Alcona County Review, June 20, 1895
Cemetery:

?, {Child}

The remains of a child were brought to Harrisville from Black River Sunday for interment.

Alcona County Review, April 9, 1896
Cemetery: St. Anne's, Alcona Co.

?, {Female}

COUNTY JOTTINGS.

Prof. Grout informs us that his wife, who left Harrisville last Saturday, arrived at the home of her parents in St. Clair just in time to attend the funeral of a sister.

Alcona County Review, June 21, 1878
Cemetery:

?, {Female}

Au Sable and Oscoda News Items.

The funeral of the mother of Indian John took place on the 7th at the M. E. Church, the friends desiring that their relative should have Christian burial. She was 68 years old at the time of her death, and her funeral was very largely attended. The Indians present were very much bowed down with grief, and a lady present at the time says she never attended a more affecting and impressive funeral service.

Alcona County Review, January 24, 1879
Cemetery:

?, {Female}

Curtis, Jan. 6, '90.--Mrs. Quay went to Au Sable to spend the Holidays and was called away to Forrester by the death of her younger sister. She has not returned yet.

Alcona County Review, January 10, 1890

Cemetery:

?, {Female}

Purely Personal.

P. McGrady was called to Alabaster last week by the death of a sister.

Alcona County Review, February 21, 1890
Cemetery:

?, {Female}

Purely Personal.

Mrs. H. R. Morrison was called to Brighton, Mich., last Saturday by a telegram announcing the death of her mother. She went down on the Flora the same day.

Alcona County Review, May 16, 1890
Cemetery:

?, {Female}

Around the County.

Haynes, April 29, '91.
The mother of Mrs. McGregor died in Alpena on Monday morning of paralysis.

Alcona County Review, April 30, 1891
Cemetery:

?, {Female}

Somewhat Personal.

The Rev. W. J. Bailey was called to Detroit last week by the death of a sister, the wife of a brother minister, who had been changed at last conference from Romeo to Menominee.

Alcona County Review, December 17, 1891
Cemetery:

?, {Female}

West Harrisville.

Mrs. Wm. Apsey, her daughter, brother and Mrs. Foster, left Thursday for Peck, Mich., to attend the funeral of a sister.

Alcona County Review, April 20, 1893

West Harrisville.

Received last week too late for publication.
West Harrisville, April 20, '93.—Mrs. Wm. Apsey was called to attend the funeral of her sister, who died very suddenly.

Alcona County Review, April 20, 1893
Cemetery:

?, {Female}

A Variety of Interesting Happenings at West Harrisville.

West Harrisville, Aug. 22.—Mrs. Jas. A. Simpson left with her husband and brother last week to attend the funeral of her mother in Sarnia, Ont.

Alcona County Review, August 24, 1893
Cemetery:

?, {Female}

CALEDONIA.

Mrs. James McDonald left for St. Charles last week to attend the funeral of her mother.

Alcona County Review, June 18, 1896
Cemetery:

?, {Female}

EVENTS OF ONE WEEK.

Chas. Conklin went down to Fostoria yesterday in response to an urgent request from an aunt whose husband died a few days ago.

Alcona County Review, December 3, 1896
Cemetery:

?, {Female}

PERSONAL.

Mrs. W. P. Tompkins, who has been from home four weeks, is expected to return this week. Her brother's wife, who had been down with that fatal disease consumption since last spring, passed away on Monday morning at 3:30, leaving a husband and five small boys to mourn a mother's loss.

Alcona County Review, November 18, 1897
Cemetery:

?, {Female}

GREENBUSH.

Mrs. D. McGillis went to Canada to see her mother who was very low, but she was too late.

Alcona County Review, March 16, 1899
Cemetery:

?, {Male}

LOCAL JOTTINGS.

John Shehan, belonging to Laughley McColloch's crew, while driving logs on Black River the 4th of last May, fell off a log, and, being unable to swim, was drowned. The Democrat mentioned the occurrence at the time. The body was found the 2d of June. Dr. Beach, the coroner of Indian River, was notified, a jury impaneled and an inquest held. The body was identified and a verdict rendered of "accidental drowning." The mother of the deceased, who resides in Canada, was written to notifying her of the death of her son, and an answer was received two weeks ago by Dr. Beach from the mother saying: "My son returned home the day before I received your letter." Here is a mystery that we should like to see cleared up, and if any one can account for it let them send word to us and we will publish their statements.—Cheboygan Dem.

Alcona County Review, August 22, 1884
Cemetery:

?, {Male}

LOCAL JOTTINGS.

An Indian, name unknown, was found in the woods near Corcoran's camp in the southwestern part of this township, yesterday morning, with his hands badly frozen and himself in a dying condition. He was taken to camp and expired in a very few moments. It is rumored that two Harrisville parties, making a trip out to Mason's camp the day before, met said Indian in the road, both going out and returning, and stopped and treated him very generously to Harrisville whisky, which is warranted to kill within 40 rods. Nuff ced!

Alcona County Review, February 27, 1885

The Dead Indian Again.

Copying our item of two weeks ago, concerning the dead Indian found near Corcoran's camp and the rumored co-incident of two Harrisville parties and Indian, "Jay Eye See," a correspondent of the Au Sable Saturday Night from this place remarks as follows:

"Now, Bro. Fairchild don't you think you were a little too previous when you published that article? At an inquest held by the coroner over the body of this Indian, nothing was found implicating any Harrisville parties whatever."

Naw! we were not "a little too previous." No charged *fact* was expressed by us in the article referred to. It was simply given as a matter of *rumor*, no names mentioned, construed from statements made by the parties themselves to others prior to the finding of the Indian. The Review did not implicate anybody; the parties implicated themselves by too much talk about the affair publicly. One of the party, to *silence* the Review, we suppose, and cause us to regret our editorial note of the affair, has ordered his paper and

advertisement discontinued. But that *will not* silence the Review; we are not made of that kind of stuff. The hasty action of this individual will be a thousand times more regretted by himself than the writer. Our duty is plain, when men contribute directly or indirectly to the injury of others, by the violation of law, or even otherwise, and cannot be suppressed—though we are always willing to make amends when we may have done another undeserved injury. We do not affirm that these parties had anything to do with the death of said Indian, nor do we say they really did give him or any other Indian a drop of intoxicants. We have published only what is purported they told others before the Indian was found. But when he withdrew his advertisement from the Review, one of the party "let the cat out of the bag," as our readers will readily discover who he is by the absence of said advertisement in our columns.

"With malice toward none, with charity for all, with firmness in the right," the Review will continue to do its duty, irregardless of men or measures. Stick a pin here!

Alcona County Review, March 13, 1885
Cemetery:

?, {Male}

LOCAL JOTTINGS.

Oscoda, Nov. 16.--Capt. Berunier of the schooner Imperial reports at this port to-day that on Saturday last he struck a gale off Thunder bay and hoisted a flag of distress while three miles from the life saving station from 1 to 5 p. m. but got no assistance. In the meantime one man was washed overboard and drowned, 100,000 feet of lumber washed away and the boat sprung a leak. The lumber was from Ed. Spense, Hammond bay, to John Spense, Detroit.

Alcona County Review, November 20, 1885
Cemetery:

?, {Male}

OUR ALPENA LETTER.

A German whose name we have been unable to learn, dropped dead very suddenly from heart disease in the office of Dr. Howell to-day.

Alcona County Review, April 16, 1886
Cemetery:

?, {Male}

FOUND DEAD!

Curtis, Feb. 5.—An unknown man apparently about 30 years old, was found dead near the Twin Trees, 18 miles up the Au Sable river, by D. McCollum, Friday afternoon, Feb. 3. the dead man was seen passing Beadle's in the afternoon of the previous day. Coroner C. E. Marvin was notified and the body taken to Oscoda where a post mortem will be held.

Alcona County Review, February 10, 1888
Cemetery:

?, {Male}

A TERRIBLE DEATH!

An Unknown Man Killed on the Railroad.

Cut to pieces by a Log Train.
From the Saturday Night.

About 9 o'clock Tuesday evening a log train from the Mud Lake branch brought in a load of logs to Pack Woods & Co's banking ground near their mill. After unloading the train started out again, and when near the State road crossing the engineer saw a man lying on the track apparently asleep. Of course it was impossible to stop the train before reaching him, and the unfortunate victim was run over by the entire train, and his remains scattered in all directions. His head, one arm and one foot were cut off, and the body otherwise badly cut up.

Coroner Morin was immediately notified and started with assistants to take charge of the remains which were brought down to his undertaker establishment.

The dead man was identified as a fireman who had been employed on the propeller Dean Richmond, and who left the boat Tuesday for some unknown reason, but as the boat left for Chicago that evening his name could not be ascertained.

During the afternoon and evening he had been drinking. About 7 o'clock he started to go to the seven-mile hill to work on the railroad grading. He was much the worse of liquor when last seen leaving town and undoubtedly lay down to sleep unconscious of the dangerous position which he selected. The remains were interred by Coroner Morin Tuesday evening.

Alcona County Review, June 14, 1889
Cemetery:

?, {Male}

NEIGHBORHOOD NOTES.

Wess Lanktree, book-keeper and general "push" of the lumbering firm of Dease & Graham, drove into town yesterday with an unusually broad and pleasant smile on his countenance, over which an expression of contentment is wont to play. Upon being asked the cause of all this blithesome spirit, he remarked, on the Q T that a rich uncle in England had just died leaving $4,000,000. There are many who will rejoice at this stroke of good fortune.—Tawas Herald.

Alcona County Review, February 15, 1889
Cemetery:

?, {Male}

The Revolver Was Loaded.

While in Au Sable Monday Geo. W. Chapelle says the remains of a man were brought down from Potts. He was shot by a woman and lived long enough to recite the details of his tragical death. The woman picked up the revolver with the remark, "Is it loaded?" addressed to the man she killed. "No" he replied. "Are you sure?" she asked. "Yes, you may be sure of it." Thereupon she proceeded to snap the revolver. At the fourth or fifth chamber it proved to be loaded, and the ball passed through the palm of her hand, and entered his abdomen causing death in a few hours. Before his death he exonerated the woman from all blame. Mr. L. did not learn the names of the parties, but inferred the accident took place in a saloon.

Alcona County Review, January 8, 1891
Cemetery:

?, {Male}

DUST TO DUST.

A lad 14 years of age was buried near Gustin last Friday. The cause of death was consumption.

Alcona County Review, September 17, 1891
Cemetery:

?, {Male}

An unknown man was seen to disappear through the ice on Thunder Bay last Saturday.

Alcona County Review, March 17, 1892
Cemetery:

?, {Male}

A German, aged about 60 years was buried last Friday from Mikado. He was the father of Mrs. Kramer.

Alcona County Review, July 14, 1892
Cemetery:

?, {Male}

Mrs. Ira Minard received news last week that her father died leaving her a neat sum in her own name. They contemplate selling out and seeking greener fields.

Alcona County Review, March 23, 1893
Cemetery:

?, {Male}

The body of an unknown man, aged about 40 years, was found floating in the lake at Oscoda on the 20th inst.

Alcona County Review, July 27, 1893
Cemetery:

?, {Male}

Curtis Tid Bits.

Curtis, March 19.—Mrs. Vaughn has returned from Caro, where she was attending her father's funeral. She will receive $2,000 from his estate. It is better to be born lucky than rich.

Alcona County Review, March 22, 1894
Cemetery:

?, {Male}

EVENTS OF ONE WEEK.

The remains of a young French-Canadian, aged about 22 years, were brought to Harrisville Sunday morning for interment in the Catholic cemetery. The name of deceased was not learned but he resided in the vicinity of Black River.

Alcona County Review, May 17, 1894
Cemetery: St. Anne's, Alcona Co.

?, {Male}

EVENTS OF ONE WEEK.

The remains of a young Frenchman, a citizen of Black River, were buried in the Harrisville Catholic cemetery Tuesday morning.

Alcona County Review, April 9, 1896
Cemetery: St. Anne's, Alcona Co.

?, {Male}

Haynes Happenings.

Report says that Mrs. Carr lost her second dear hubby and buried him on the farm of Joseph Bond out near Puget Sound. She has written to a citizen of Hawes Township for money

to bring him back. I would say, let him stay where she is.

Alcona County Review, June 10, 1897
Cemetery:

?, {Male}

Killed Another Man.

The night express bound up last night is reported to have killed a man near Pinconning who was walking on the track.

Alcona County Review, March 3, 1898
Cemetery:

?, {Male}

MIKADO.

Mr. and Mrs. Maharg of Alpena came down to attend their brother-in-law's funeral.

Alcona County Review, April 7, 1898
Cemetery:

?, {?}

The Local News.

Another of the county charges died at the poor farm this week.

Alcona County Review, May 9, 1890
Cemetery:

?, {?}

Members of the family of Mrs. J. McGrady were called to Tawas last week, to attend the funeral of a relative.

Alcona County Review, July 27, 1893
Cemetery:

?, {?}

Rev. Middlemiss left this afternoon for Black River to officiate at a funeral.—Alpena Echo, Feb. 12.

Alcona County Review, February 15, 1894
Cemetery:

?, {?}

PERSONAL MENTION.

Miss Lizzie McGrady was called to Tawas the first of the week by the death of a relative.

Alcona County Review, December 27, 1894

?, {?}

PERSONAL POINTS.

Mary Evans returned Tuesday from Bay City, where she had been to attend the funeral of a relative.

Alcona County Review, April 20, 1899
Cemetery:

INDEX

Barber, Isabella, 61
Barber, James, 45
Barber, James E., 2
Barber, John B., 2
Barber, Lyle Ross, 2
Barber, Margaret M., 2
Barber, Mary E., 2
Barber, Nicholas N., 45
Barber, Peter, 146
Barber, William R., 147
Barclay, Mrs. Eliza, 147
Barker, Abigail C., 423
Barkley, Mrs. E. A., 147
Barley, Archie, 45
Barley, Mrs. Anna, 147
Barlow, Edwin, 147
Barlow, Harriett B.. *see Mercier, Mrs. Harriett B.*
Barlow, Helen May, 76
Barlow, Isabelle E., 128
Barlow, Mrs. Elizabeth J., 147
Barmby, Marion, 79
Barnes, J. M., 46
Barnum, Delilah, 2
Baror, Henry, 46
Baror, Maud, 3
Baror, Maud Lula, 117
Barret, Mary, 97
Barrett, Robert, 148
Barringer, {Female}, 433
Bartley, Alexander, 148
Bartley, Mrs. Rose L., 148
Barton, Annie, 155
Basher, Charles, 46
Basher, Frank, 3
Bassett, Delia, 103
Batten, Amy Mae, 3
Batten, Grace Beulah, 3
Batten, Ida, 3
Batten, John M., 3
Batton, Frederick A., 148
Baucus, Frank, 148
Baxter, Stephen, 149
Bayley, Frances, 118
Bayne, Christina, 89
Beach, John, 149
Beach, Rhoda J., 149
Beadle, Joseph, 149
Beadore, Frank, 149
Beam, Thomas, 150
Beams, Benjamin, 150
Beard, Fred, 150
Beard, Harold F., 3
Beard, Ida, 150
Beard, James, 150, 151
Beard, James H., 3
Beaton, Daniel, 46
Beaton, Gertrude A., 3
Beaton, Henry, 46
Beaton, Jessie Marie, 3
Beaton, John Murray, 3
Beaton, Mary, 313
Beaumont, Charles Aruth, 3, 151
Becker, Frederick Austin, 46
Becker, George Henry, 151
Becker, Sarah E., 105
Beckman, Agnes, 101

Beebe, Emma, 54
Beebe, James, 151
Beebe, Mrs. Hannah, 151
Beech, Bessie May, 72
Beede, Charles H., 3
Beede, Fred Alger, 3, 46
Beede, Glenn Allison, 3
Beede, Mornelva, 3
Beede, Ray L., 3
Beegle, Charles, 46
Beever, Charlotte Emma, 48
Beever, Esther, 151
Beever, Esther Etta, 3
Beever, Evaline, 109
Beever, George B., 46
Beever, Harold H., 3
Beever, Jennie, 50
Beever, Raymond, 3
Beever, Robert Russell, 3
Beever, Rose, 114
Beever, Ruth, 4, 152
Bejin, Joseph Stanley, 152
Belair, {Girl}, 4
Belknap, Etta, 274
Bell, {Boy}, 4
Bell, Alice S., 237
Bell, Jacob J., 152
Bell, James, 46
Bell, Jane Sarah, 152
Bell, Manley A., 47
Bell, Martin J., 4, 152
Bellmore, Victoria, 45
Benaire, William, 152
Bennaway, Francis, 152
Bennett, {Male}, 152
Bennett, J. F., 47
Benway, Eunice Ann, 81
Benway, Silas, 152
Berkhart, Annie May, 114
Bernard, Joseph, 47
Bernhizer, George H., 152
Berry, William H., 153
Bertrand, Frank, 153
Bessinger, George, 47
Best, Arthur, 47
Betts, Bessie, 46
Betz, Frank J., 153
Betz, George, 153
Bickell, W. R., 47
Bickle, George J., 47
Biddle, Joseph W., 153
Bigelow, James Harvey, 154
Biggam, Thomas, 154
Billings, Lucille, 4
Billings, Samuel Olen, 47
Birch, Helen W., 383
Birch, Ransom, 154
Biron, Joseph, 48
Birtch, Dresden E., 48
Bissell, {Boy}, 4, 154
Bissell, {Male}, 154
Bissell, Evelyn, 47
Bissell, Jerome T., 154
Bissell, Maria, 154
Bissonette, Anna B., 4
Bissonette, Margaret, 155
Bittner, Herbert Paul, 155

Blackburn, Hannah, 155
Blackwell, Bert, 48
Blair, Jane, 155
Blake, Charlotte Ann, 48
Blakely, Abram Randolph, 155
Blakeney, {Boy}, 4
Blakeney, Earl D., 48
Blanchard, Arthur H., 48
Blanchard, Hannah, 155
Blanchard, Hannah, 155
Blanchard, Norman, 155
Bloodgood, Jennie, 52
Bloomingdale, Catherine, 155
Bloomingdale, Courtney, 156
Bloomingdale, Harriet, 98
Bloomingdale, Stephen, 156
Blue, Catherine, 356
Blumberg, Nettie, 67
Blush, Harriet [Miller], 156
Boardman, Eunice, 4
Boardman, Nattie, 79
Bock, Anna, 156
Bock, Catherine, 156
Bock, John, Jr., 156
Bock, John, Sr., 156
Bock, Josephine, 156
Bock, Sylvester C., 157
Bock, William, 156
Boddy, Edward E., 48
Boddy, Rachael, 119
Body, Female, 132
Boice, {Boy}, 4
Bollet, {Male}, 157
Bolster, William, 48
Bolton, Robert, 49
Bonaher, George, 157
Bonan, Carrie, 50
Bond, {Boy}, 4
Bond, {Female}, 121
Bond, {Girl}, 4
Bond, Elijah H., 157
Bond, Josh, 121
Bond, Joshua, 49
Bond, Justus, 4
Bond, Mary, 157
Bond, Mrs. Eliza, 122
Bond, William, Jr., 121
Bond, William, Sr., 158
Bonnard, Victor, 4
Bonner, Thomas P., 49
Bonneville, Mrs. Joseph, 160
Bonville, Louisa, 43, 63, 223
Boothroyd, William H., 160
Boquest, Frank, 160
Bothwell, James, 160
Boudreau, Selena, 86
Bouford, {Girl}, 4
Boulieu, Clarissa, 57
Boutyette, Charles, 160
Bowser, Fred M., 122
Bowser, Frederick N., 49
Bowser, Maud B., 122
Boyce, Carrie, 104
Boyer, John, 49
Brabant, Jennie S., 117
Brabant, Mrs. Elizabeth, 122
Brabant, Richard, 122

Curley, {Boy}, 189
Curley, Susie May, 96
Curran, Philip, 57
Currie, John, 57
Currie, William D., 57
Curriveau, David, 9, 189
Curriveau, Max Joseph, 9
Curriveau, Ralph, Jr., 190
Curry, Mrs. Alex, 190
Curtis, Jane Sarah, 152
Curtis, Nancy E., 116
Curtis, Peter, 57
Curtis, Richard E., 58
Cutting, Annie, 44
Cutting, John, 190
Cutting, Mary, 57
Cuyler, Elmer James, 190
Cuyler, George Alonzo, 58
Cuyler, Hazen Shirley, 9
Cyr, Mable, 110

D

Dafoe, Eleanor, 101
Dafoe, Phillip, 190
Daily, John, 190
Dalton, Pursie, 48
Davelay, Alexander Louis, 58
Davis, James, 190
Davis, Lewis P., 191
Davis, Mrs. George, 191
Davison, Crozier, 191
Davison, Mrs., 123
Davison, Mrs. William, 192
Davison, William, 123
Dayton, James O., 58
Deacon, Clyde, 9
Deacon, Delormy, 58
Deacon, Edith, 113
Deacon, Ethel, 58
Deacon, Evadne Leburney, 98
Deacon, Laburnia, 101
Deacon, Mrs. Archibald, 192
Deacon, Mrs. Mary E., 123
Deacon, Washington H., 123
Deacon, William H., 192
Dean, Annie, 49
Dean, Birdie, 193
Dean, David, 193
Dean, Thomas, 193
Dease, Charles Johnson Watts, 194
Dease, Ollie, 68
Decarie, Marie, 9
DeCarie, Oliver Edward, 58
DeCoste, William, 58
DeForest, Eliza, 101
DeForest, Elizabeth Maud, 71
DeForrest, Maggie, 97
Dege, Ernest, 58
Dege, Ernest J., 194
Dege, William, 9
DeKett, George, 58
DeKett, Minnie, 105
DeKlyne, Leonard E., 194
Deklyne, Mrs. Ella, 123

DeKlyne, William, 194
Deklyne, William P., 123
Delahanty, Pat, 194
Deland, Mrs., 194
Delano, Hiram H., 194
DeLavolette, Alexander, 195
Dellar, Hattie, 9
Dellar, James, 195
Delorme, Joseph, 195
Demarro, Willie, 195
Demott, Charlotte M., 195
Dennis, Lorena M. [Brown], 195
Dennis, Mrs. Alex, 195
Depew, William E., 195
Derby, Arthur W., 58
Derby, Edwin, 59
Derby, Leonard Edwin, 196
Derochie, William, 196
DeRosia, Lewis, 196
DeRosia, Louis, Sr., 59
DeRosia, Roena C., 196
DeRosier, Louis, 123
DeRosier, Mrs. Mary, 123
Detrick, Thomas, 197
Deucharme, Mary, 94
Devault, Mr., 59
Devlin, Martha, 55
Dewar, Benjamin, 9
Dewar, Catherine, 71
Dewar, Daniel, 59
Dewar, Flora, 107
Dewar, John, 197
Dewar, Mary, 100
Dewar, Mrs., 197
Dewar, Mrs. Sarah, 197
Dewar, Roderick, 9
Dewer, Christina, 85
Dewey, Gladys, 9
Dewey, John S., 59
Dewey, Lynn Dana, 9
Dewey, Monica E., 9, 197
Dewitt, Charles, 197
DeWitt, Julian F., 197
Deyermond, Henry, 197
di Cenda, Emil R., 123
di Cenda, Mrs. Emma, 123
Diamond, Kate, 110
Dibble, Phebe, 429
Dickenson, Hiram Alexander, 197
Dickerson, John, 59
Dickinson, Annie R., 112
Dickinson, James A., 59
Dickinson, Mrs., 198
Diem, Rose B., 86
Dietz, Cornelius, 198
Dietz, William, 198
Dimmick, Joseph, 198
Dingwell, Mrs. Mary, 123
Dingwell, William, 123
Dixon, {Boy}, 9
Dixon, Maud B., 122
Dixon, Maude, 49
Dobson, Harry R., 9
Dobson, Pearl, 9
Dobson, Robert, 59, 198
Dodge, Benjamin, 59

Dodge, Frank, 59
Dolson, John, 198
Donahue, Annie, 250
Donahue, Elizabeth, 241
Donahue, Katie, 91
Donahue, Lizzie, 67
Donnelly, William, 198
Donohoe, Tommie, 198
Donohue, Thomas, 349
Dorr, Jennette, 198
Dougherty, Anna, 9
Doughty, Clara, 76
Doughty, Hannah E., 116
Douglas, {Boy}, 9
Douglas, Ethel E., 10
Douglas, Margaret E., 10
Douglas, William Lester, 59
Douglass, William Wallace, 199
Dove, Cynthia Ellen, 49
Downer, {Girl}, 10
Downer, Albert C., 199
Downer, Aurelia F., 10
Downer, Frederick W., 60
Downer, Isaac Jefferson, 60
Downer, Olive I., 10
Downie, Edward, 60
Downie, Herbert Dewey, 10
Downie, James R., 10
Downie, Mrs. Catherine, 200
Downing, Mrs. Rose Etta, 116
Drake, Janie, 112
Drefka, Max, 200
Drennon, William W., 60
Dreyer, Charity, 10
Dreyer, Faith, 10
Dreyer, Hope, 10
Druer, {Child}, 200
Dube, Michael, 200
Duby, Tom, 200
Ducharme, {Child}, 200
Ducharme, Vina, 72
Duchemin, Floy G., 200
Duchemin, William, 200
Dudgeon, Mrs. Margaret, 201
Duff, Ralph M., 60
Duffey, {Male}, 201
Duggan, Daniel, 60
Duggan, John, 60, 201
Duggan, Maria, 48
Duggan, Thomas, 60
Dunbar, John, 60
Dunbar, John, Sr., 201
Duncan, James Stuart, 201
Duncan, Jennie M., 111
Duncan, Nellie, 76
Duncan, Robert, 60, 201
Dunham, {Child}, 201
Dunham, {Girl}, 10
Dunham, Lizzie, 55
Dunlop, Ethel Amelia, 64
Dunn, Dan, 201
Dunn, Mary A., 201
Dunn, Rose A., 43
Dunn, Ruth Agnes, 113
Dunton, Alton C., 201
Dupont, {Girl}, 202

Durfee, Mary Wightman, 202
Durfee, Nettie M., 102
Durkee, {Child}, 202
Durkee, {Girl}, 10
Durkee, Charlotte L., 59
Durkee, George W., 60
Durkee, Gilbert James, 202
Dwyer, Kathrine, 71
Dyer, Clara, 10
Dyer, Honor, 10
Dyer, Mrs. Hattie N., 202
Dyer, W. R., 60

E

Eager, {Male}, 61
Earl, George E., 61
Earle, {Girl}, 10
Eastman, Emma, 66
Edgar, {Boy}, 203
Edgar, Andrew K., 203
Edgar, Annabell, 10
Edgar, Eliza, 203
Edgar, George, 61, 203
Edgar, John D., 61
Edgar, Lewella, 96
Edgar, Loyle, 203
Edgar, Margaret, 204
Edgar, William, 61
Edmundson, Margaret Ann, 60
Edwards, Anne, 204
Edwards, Bertie., 204
Edwards, Charles H., 11
Edwards, Freeman W., 11
Edwards, Hazel Fern, 11
Edwards, James F., 11
Edwards, Wilbert L., 204
Edwards, William, 61
Effingham, Lorena, 209
Effrick, Albert F., 61
Effrick, Christina, 204
Effrick, Ernest, 11
Effrick, Milo G., 11
Eilbert, Emma, 53, 123
Elgar, Susan, 340
Ellico, Harry Russell, 204
Elliott, William N., 205
Ellis, Charles, 61
Ellis, Charles B., 205
Ellis, Chauncey, 61
Ellis, Sarah J., 205
Elmer, Frank J., 61
Elmer, Ida M., 71
Elmer, Josephine, 11
Elmer, Milo, 61
Elmer, Nora, 11
Elmer, Ralph, 11
Elmes, Catherine Jane, 69
Elmes, Sarah, 57
Elmes, Susanna, 106
Emerson, Arthur B., 11
Emerson, Asa, 205
Emerson, Aurelia T., 212
Emerson, Clyde, 11
Emerson, Curtis, 61
Emerson, Emernett A., 357
Emerson, Fred, 61

Emerson, Gertie, 73
Emerson, Goldie, 206
Emerson, Ina, 11
Emerson, James E., 62
Emerson, Jared, 206
Emerson, John, 11
Emerson, Lorena, 209
Emerson, Murriel, 11
Emerson, Nancy, 209
Emerson, Nancy Estella, 206
Emerson, Nina, 11, 209
Emerson, Orilla T., 62
Emerson, Thomas, 11
Emerson, Velma, 11
Emerson, Waldo, 11
Emery, Hiram A., 209
Emmel, {Child}, 210
Emmel, {Girl}, 11
Emmel, Fanny, 210
Emmel, Mabel, 47
Emmel, Oscar, 62
Emmorey, David C., 62, 210
Emmorey, Emma, 211
Eneuf, Mary, 75
Erb, Catherine, 71
Erb, Henry, 212
Erb, Johnny, 212
Erskine, James, 212
Esmond, Lorinda, 212
Etta, 274
Evans, Joseph, 62, 212
Evans, Lizzie, 68
Evans, Mary E., 11
Evarts, David, 212
Everingham, Aurelia T., 212
Evingham, {Boy}, 11
Evingham, Mrs. Sarah, 213
Evingham, Sarah, 213
Evringham, Philip H., 62
Evringham, William Henry, 62
Ewar, Duncan, 62

F

Fadden, Sarah S., 213
Fair, {Boy}, 11
Fair, Mabel, 12
Fairchild, {Female}, 213
Fairchild, Clarence, 213
Fairchild, George, 213
Fairchild, Henry, 213
Fairchild, Nina May, 213
Fairchild, Timothy, 214
Farrington, Mrs. Mary, 214
Fassett, James, 62
Feaban, George, 214
Fecteau, Marie Eliza, 214
Fecto, Amanda, 79
Fecto, Mary, 78
Fenilon, Daniel, 214
Ferguson, Arthur G., 215
Ferguson, Donald, 12, 215
Ferguson, Eliza Jane, 44
Ferguson, Henry Melvin, 215
Ferguson, John, 62
Ferguson, Lavina, 222
Ferguson, Margaret Matilda, 61

Ferguson, Melinda E., 78
Ferguson, Rebecca, 115
Ferguson, Wallace C., 215
Ferris, Albert, 12
Ferris, Annie L., 216
Ferris, Frank A., 12
Ferris, Nellie S., 94
Ferris, Percy, 12
Ferris, W. B., 215
Fettes, Agnes, 52
Fettes, Charles Murray, 12
Fettes, Sarah Anne, 46
Fettes, William, 62
Fick, Alice Irene, 91
Fick, Alice J., 342
Fick, Francis, 215
Fick, Lizana J., 90
Filkins, Roena C., 59
Finch, Annie L., 216
Finch, Bertie, 216
Finch, William H., 62
Finger, Herman T., 216
Finger, Julia V. S., 217
Fish, Thomas A., 63
Fisher, Anna, 234
Fisher, Bertie, 12
Fisher, Eva Pearl, 12
Fisher, Guy, 12, 217
Fisher, Hogue, 63
Fisher, John W., 63
Fisher, Joseph, Jr., 63
Fisher, Joseph, Sr., 217
Fisher, Martha, 67
Fisher, Mary A., 12
Fisher, Sara Maria, 12
Fisher, Satie, 50
Fisher, Sherman, 12, 217
Fiske, Louis R., 63
Fiske, Luella J., 88
Fitz, Mrs. Lena, 124
Fitz, William, 123
Fitzmaurice, Tillie, 124
Fitzmaurice, William B., 124
Fitzpatrick, Michael, 218
Fitzpatrick, Mrs. Mary A., 218
Fitzpatrick, Viola, 12
Flanagan, Bertha M., 12
Flanders, Mont, 218
Flawes, William, 63
Flaws, Jessie Lulu, 218
Fleck, {Boy}, 12
Fleck, {Girl}, 12
Fleck, Charles Addison, 218
Fleck, Joseph, 63
Fleming, Abram, 218
Fleming, Annabel, 68
Fleming, Charles, 12
Fleming, Hattie S., 13
Fleming, Maggie Belle, 218
Fleming, William, 13
Fleming, Willie, 218
Fleury, Hattie S., 13
Flint, Moses, 219
Foley, Anna, 219
Foley, Charles, 219
Foley, Michael, 219
Fonger, {Girl}, 13, 219

(Maiden names in italics)

Forbes, Jennie, 97
Forbes, Mary Ellen, 84
Forcleau, {Boy}, 13
Ford, Mildred M., 13
Forrest, James E., 219
Forrest, William Edwin, 219
Forsyth, Sarah, 92
Forsythe, George Henry, 63
Forsythe, Henry, 219
Forsythe, John T., 222
Forsythe, Lavina, 222
Forsythe, Myrtle, 13
Forsythe, Rachael Ann, 65
Fortier, {Boy}, 13, 223
Fortier, {Child}, 223
Fortier, {Girl}, 13
Fortier, A. J., 63
Fortier, Louisa, 223
Foster, {Boy}, 224
Foster, Ella B., 224
Foster, James, 63
Foster, Minnie, 131
Foster, Mrs. Mary Ann, 224
Foster, Oveld, 13, 224
Foster, Robert N., 63
Fowler, Charles, 63
Fowler, George, 224
Fowler, Kate, 224
Fowler, Lyle, 13
Fowler, Nettie, 117
Fowler, William, 224
Fox, Bub, 225
Fox, Maud A., 110
Fox, Mrs. Sarah A., 225
Fralic, Stella B., 80
Frank, {Boy}, 225
Franklin, Adella M., 225
Franklin, Charles O., 64
Franklin, Edna, 13
Franklin, Leonard, 13
Fraser, Clementine, 13
Fraser, Donald, 64, 124
Fraser, Ella, 78
Fraser, Ellen, 124
Fraser, Esther, 13
Fraser, Jennie, 66
Fraser, Jessie, 92
Fraser, John, 13
Fraser, John A., 64, 225
Fraser, Lawrence W., 13
Fraser, Maud, 13
Fraser, Myrtle, 13
Fraser, William, 226
Frasier, {Male}, 227
Frasier, Alice M.. *see McNally, Alice M.*
Frasier, Mary, 227
Frederick, {Child}, 228
Frederick, Barton, 227
Frederick, Harrison S., 13
Frederick, Herman, 14
Frederick, Howard, 14
Frederick, Margaret L., 56
Frederick, Myrtle E., 14
Frederick, Stanley, 228
Freer, {Boy}, 228
Freer, {Girl}, 14

Freer, Andrew J., 64
Freer, Ann M., 83
Freer, George G., 64
Freer, Jewel, 14
Freer, John S., 64
Freer, Joseph, 14
Freer, Julia, 67, 86, 96
Freer, Katie, 14
Freer, Marion, 14
Freer, Orrin, 14
Freer, Voil, 14, 228
Freer, William Sherman, 64
French, Almira C. [Chapelle], 228
Friedlander, Charles Millen, 64
Friedman, Annie, 96
Fry, William, 228
Fuller, Claude, 14
Fullerton, Alma M., 84
Fullerton, Harvey, 229
Fullerton, Henry J., 64
Fullerton, Henry John, 229
Fullerton, John Stephen, 229
Fullerton, Robert John, 14, 230
Fulsher, Joseph, 64
Fulton, George, 230
Fulton, Minnie, 80

G

Gage, {Boy}, 14
Gagne, Zorilla, 231
Gallagher, Emma J., 78
Gallagher, Hattie, 231
Gallagher, James William, 231
Gannon, Mrs., 231
Gardiner, {Boy}, 14
Gardiner, Daniel D., 231
Gardiner, Harry, 64
Gardiner, Mrs. Christina, 124
Gardiner, William C., 124
Gardner, {Boy}, 14
Gardner, Llewellyn, 64
Gardner, Mrs. Annie, 232
Garland, Edward, 234
Gaulait, Theodore, 234
Gauthier, Angeline, 78
Gauthier, Joseph, 234
Gaymer, Anna, 234
Geer, Nettie, 72
Genge, Alice H., 84
Genge, Eliza, 234
Genge, Herbert, 234
Genge, John, 65
Genge, Martha, 77
Genge, Mary H., 51
Genge, Mrs. Nettie Elizabeth, 235
Genge, Nathaniel, 234
Genge, Roy, 14, 235
Genge, William Lee, 14
Gerlatt, R. B., 65
Gibbs, Montgomery, 235
Gibson, Josephia, 84, 126
Gilbert, Roena C., 196
Gillam, {Girl}, 15
Gillam, Bruce Rupert, 14, 235

Gillam, Earl, 14
Gillam, Florence Luella, 235
Gillam, George E., 65
Gillard, Reuben Clare, 15
Gillett, Frances, 79, 131
Gillis, Dan, 236
Gilpin, Lillian Margaret, 92
Gilpin, Norman, 236
Ginn, Anna, 167
Gircke, Dora, 86
Girvin, Samuel, 15
Glendennie, John, 236
Glennie, Elizabeth, 80
Glennie, John W., 236
Glode, James, 65
Glosienke, Alexander, 237
Glover, Amanda, 61
Glover, William John, 65
Goddard, Charles, 237
Godfrey, Alice S., 237
Goff, George, 66
Goheen, Ezra, 66
Goheen, Ray, 15
Goheen, Ward J., 15
Goldie, Georgeana M., 237
Golling, Agnes, 237
Golling, Jacob, 237
Gonyea, {Male}, 237
Gonyea, Jerry Albertis, 237
Good, Emma, 64
Good, Hattie, 110
Good, Jennette, 105
Good, Josephus E., 66
Good, Mrs. Mary J., 97
Good, William Darius, 15, 238
Goodell, Alfred, 238
Goodell, Mrs. Mary Sapphira, 87
Goodfellow, Agnes, 238
Goodfellow, Mary, 58
Goodfellow, Robert, 66
Goodsell, C. William, 66
Goodwin, Harvey, 66
Goodwin, Myrtle, 238
Gorbutt, T. H., 66
Gordon, Charlotte, 238
Goshman, Lewis, 238
Gougiou, John, 66
Gould, Lulu Jane, 238
Gould, Mary E., 15
Gould, Mrs. Mary, 239
Gould, Rilla Ann, 239
Goupell, Sophia, 118
Gow, Alexander L., 67
Gow, Harold R., 15
Gow, Logan, 15
Graham, Catherine, 313
Graham, Lucy, 67
Graham, Margaret, 323
Graham, William C., 239
Gram, {Girl}, 15, 239
Grantham, Joseph H., 239
Graves, Amandus, 239
Gray, {Male}, 240
Gray, Albert, 67
Gray, John, 239
Gray, Mrs. Mary, 241

Gray, Rachel, 15
Gray, William, 67
Green, {Male}, 241
Green, Birdie M., 15
Green, Edward M., 67
Green, Elizabeth, 241
Green, Ernest Valentine, 15
Green, Fred L., 15
Green, Harry, 241
Green, John, 67
Green, Myra, 241
Green, Percy, 15
Green, Will, 67
Green, William, 15
Green, William, 241
Green, Willie, 241
Greenfield, {Boy}, 241
Greenfield, {Girl}, 15
Greenfield, Margaret May, 15
Greenman, Charles, 241
Gregory, Ramsey, 242
Grice, Joseph, 242
Griswold, Carrie Adeline, 62
Griswold, Francis Hosmer, 67
Griswold, Freddie, 242
Griswold, Harvey C., 242
Griswold, Hattie, 242
Griswold, Helen W. \t, 383
Griswold, Jennie, 242
Griswold, Melvina, 96
Groom, Willie, 242
Groves, John M., 67
Guimond, Marie Eliza, 214
Gullickson, Thora M., 242
Gullifer, {Child}, 15
Gullifer, Eliphas, 242
Gullifer, Freeman O., 124
Gullifer, Harriett, 124
Gullifer, Mildred, 51
Gullifer, Sarah, 242
Gullifer, Thomas, 243
Gunther, Mary, 16
Gurd, {Girl}, 16
Gurnsay, John, 243
Gustin, H. K., 67
Gustin, Maria, 154
Gustin, Richard P., 243
Gustin, Ruth Huntington, 244

H

Habersham, Emma, 55
Hackett, Percy, 67
Hackett, Ralph, 244
Hagen, William, 244
Haggett, William H., 67
Hailey, Lottie, 16
Haining, Mrs. Addie, 244
Halcrow, Andrew, 244
Hale, {Boy}, 16
Hale, Bessie E., 244
Hale, Claude, 16
Hale, Eunice, 245
Hale, Jessie Eunice, 85
Hale, Myrtle May, 16
Hale, William D., 67
Haley, George W., 68

Haley, Rebecca, 68
Hall, Elizabeth, 97
Hall, Fredrick C., 245
Hall, Harry, 245
Hall, Hattie, 116
Hall, Lagrand, 16
Hall, Lulu E., 79
Hall, Margaret J., 84
Hall, Minnie B., 89
Hall, Mrs. H. E., 245
Hall, Mrs. Lydia, 245
Hall, Thomas, 245
Hall, William, 68
Halverson, Olof, 245
Hamilton, Alexander B., 68
Hamilton, Dell, 245
Hamilton, Flora, 51
Hamilton, George, 68
Hamilton, George, Sr., 245
Hamilton, Hattie, 110
Hamilton, Henrietta, 55
Hamilton, James, 68
Hammond, James, 247
Handy, T. P., 68
Hankinson, Joseph T., 247
Hannah, Jacob, 247
Hardwick, John, 247
Hare, Nicholas, 248
Harrington, {Groom}, 68
Harris, Ben, 68
Harris, Jennette, 198
Harris, Raymond, 16
Harris, William, 248
Harrison, Calista M., 248
Harrison, Georgia, 248
Harrison, Maud, 76
Harshaw, Mary E., 76
Hart, Celina, 78
Hart, Edith, 80
Hart, Joseph Aalbert, 248
Hart, Julia, 50
Hart, Mary, 52
Hart, Selina, 51
Hartigan, Howard J., 248
Hartigan, Matthew, 16, 68
Hartion, Mary Ellen, 107
Hartman, August, 248
Harvey, Mary J., 101
Harwood, Mary, 373
Hastings, {Boy}, 16
Hastings, Anna Jane, 16
Hastings, Anne Jane, 100
Hastings, Eliza, 110
Hastings, Evelina, 16, 248
Hastings, George, 68
Hastings, Jane Harriet, 368
Hastings, Joseph Alexander, 69
Hastings, Joseph Ellsworth, 16
Hastings, Lavina S., 16
Hastings, Lloyd, 249
Hastings, Martha, 89
Hastings, Mary, 16
Hastings, Minnie, 44
Hastings, Robert, 249
Hastings, Robert E., 16
Hastings, Robert Thomas, 69
Hastings, Sarah J., 205

Hastings, Shirley Laselles, 16
Hastings, Stella Belle, 16
Hastings, Warren Erwin, 16
Hastings, William John, 69
Hasty, Letitia, 297
Hasty, Sarah, 61
Haviland, Elnore, 90
Hawkins, {Boy}, 249
Hawkins, Adella, 75
Hawkins, Harriet, 249
Hawkins, Harry B., 17
Hawkins, Jennie, 17
Hawkins, Luther, 249
Hawkins, Stephen, 69
Hawse, {Girl}, 250
Hawse, Ella, 81
Hawse, Floyd J., 17
Hawse, Francis, 250
Hawse, Frank, 124
Hawse, Mrs. Agnes Catherine, 124
Hay, P., 69
Hayden, {Child}, 250
Hayden, Annie, 250
Hayden, Daniel, 69
Hayden, John, 250
Hayden, Mrs. Mary, 250
Hayes, {Male}, 250
Hayes, George Albert?, 17
Hayes, John Hartwell, 69
Hayes, William, 250
Haynes, Elijah R., 250
Haynes, Georgie, 77
Hazen, Charles, 125
Hazen, James, 252
Hazen, Mrs. Mary, 125
Healy, Welcome, 69
Hebener, Daniel Dewey, 17, 252
Hecox, Iva Maud, 85
Hedroig, Friederika D., 104
Heilig, James Nolan, 17
Heinold, Christian, 69
Henderson, {Groom}, 69
Henderson, James, 252
Henderson, James E., 70
Henderson, May E., 17
Henderson, Minnie M., 252
Henderson, Mrs. Libbie, 70
Henderson, Norman J., 17
Henderson, Samuel, 253
Hendricks, William, 253
Hendrie, Annie, 253
Hendrie, Joanna, 129
Hendrie, Johanna, 109
Hendrie, John, 253
Henning, Clara, 93, 105, 381
Henry, Bertha, 81
Henry, John, 254
Hensey, Nellie Prudence, 45
Henson, William, 254
Heron, {Girl}, 17
Heron, Charles, 70
Heron, George Colburn, 255
Heron, Henry, 255
Heron, John Bailey, 255
Heron, John W., 70
Heron, Mary Blanchard, 17
Heron, Priscilla Alden, 255

Herron, {Boy}, 17
Herron, Jennie Electra, 58
Hershey, John, 255
Hetherington, Sarah E., 109
Heumann, {Boy}, 17
Heumann, Clara, 17
Heumann, Clara Louise, 255
Heumann, Frank Faust, 255
Heumann, Fred G., 125
Heumann, George, 255
Heumann, Minnie, 76
Heumann, Mrs. Fred G., 125
Heuston, Martha, 60
Hewett, John, 70
Hickey, John, 70
Hicks, Mary Ann, 73
Higgins, Florence A., 17
Higginson, Mary, 394
Hike, Elizabeth, 104
Hike, William, 255
Hiler, Joseph, 256
Hill, Abram, 256
Hill, Belle, 71
Hill, Benjamin, 70
Hill, Catherine, 64
Hill, Ezra N., 256
Hill, Fitz James, 70
Hill, Floyd R., 17
Hill, Fred, 17
Hill, Greeley, 70
Hill, Harriett, 124
Hill, Helen Genevieve, 56
Hill, Milton Abram, 256
Hill, Milton Adrian, 17
Hill, Mrs., 256
Hill, Mrs. Mary A., 60
Hill, Samuel, 17
Hill, Will, 256
Hill, William, 256
Hillman, Annie M., 263
Hinchman, Susan, 414
Hinckley, Mary, 257
Hoard, Eugene Temple, 258
Hodges, Ella, 115
Hogan, James J., 71
Hogan, Matt, 258
Hogue, Josephine, 17
Hogue, Mattie B., 80
Hogue, Wilder B., 71
Hohenstein, Alida, 58
Hohenstine, Truth W., 258
Holbrook, Mary A., 116
Holcomb, {Male}, 258
Holcomb, Mary Jane, 258
Holden, Carrie, 259
Holden, Carrie J., 86
Holden, Eliza, 110
Holden, Lewis, 259
Holmes, Alice M., 18
Holmes, Beatrice M., 259
Holmes, Ellsworth G., 71
Holmes, Eva L., 259
Holmes, Frank C., 71
Holmes, Herbert F., 18, 259
Hompstead, Elizabeth Jane, 259
Hompstead, Emma, 259

Hompstead, George, 71
Hompstead, Mrs., 259
Hompstead, Samuel, 71
Hood, {Girl}, 260
Hood, Agnes B., 81
Hood, Charles, 260
Hood, Jetta B., 97
Hood, Margaret A., 52
Hood, Robert, 260
Hooley, Anna, 219
Hooper, Guy S., 18
Hooper, Lewis W., 260
Hooper, Rosalie E., 183
Hoover, Eli, 260
Hopkins, Fred, 71
Hopkins, Harvy, 71
Hopper, Thomas J., 71
Hornby, Alice M., 18
Hornby, Charles W., 71
Hornby, Minnie, 18
Horton, {Girl}, 18
Hortwick, Eliza, 92
Hotchkiss, Charles, 260
Houghton, {Girl}, 18
Houghton, Ansel, 126
Houghton, Charles William, 71
Houghton, Edwin, 18
Houghton, Eliza, 260
Houghton, Jehial, 260
Houghton, Mrs. Elizabeth, 126
Houston, Peter, 260
Howard, {Child}, 261
Howard, E. G., 261
Howard, Flavia, 261
Howard, George F., 72
Howard, George Francis, 261
Howard, Henry, 262
Howe, Harriett Newell, 396
Howe, William, 72
Howitson, Albert, 18
Howitson, Alfred, 18
Howitson, William S., 72
Hoyt, Frankie A., 262
Hubert, Fred, 72
Hubert, Sarah Delia, 262
Hudson, Lydia A., 89
Hudson, Mary Sophia, 62
Huffman, Annie, 72
Huffman, Joseph, 72
Hugill, Frances, 55
Hugill, Harriett, 280
Hugill, Henry, 72
Hugill, Mary Ellen, 92
Hugill, Mrs. William, 263
Hulbert, Montville, 263
Hull, George, 72
Hull, James Robert, 18
Hull, Lesbia H., 70
Hulme, Ida, 101
Hulme, James, 72
Hunt, A. Jackson, 263
Hunt, Annie M., 263
Hunt, James E., 263
Hunt, John, 264
Hunt, Mary Luella, 78, 283
Hunter, John, 264

Hunter, Mrs. W. J., 264
Hunter, W. H., 264
Huntley, Calista M., 248
Huot, Joseph, 72
Hurd, William, 265
Hyke, Arthur Wellington, 18
Hyke, Elizabeth, 51
Hyke, George A., 72
Hyke, George Warren, 18

I

Illman, Justina, 61
Illman, Louisa, 84
Ingraham, Roena C., 59
Irons, Mrs. Mary, 265
Irwin, George Wilfred, 72

J

Jack, Charles, 265
Jack, Florence Belle, 54
Jack, George, 72
Jack, James, 72
Jack, Mary, 265
Jackson, Chester E., 18
Jacob, Bertha, 118
Jacobs, Sarah, 169
Jacobson, Margaret, 155
Jacques, Mrs. Margareth, 265
Jacques, Pierre, 265
James, Ephraim, 73
James, Sarah A., 265
Jameson, Earl C., 18
Jameson, Eula V., 18
Jameson, Harriet Roma, 18
Janes, Jane, 177
Janson, Matilda, 78
Jantz, {Child}, 266
Jantz, Howard, 18
Jantz, May, 18
Jantz, Nichols, 19
Jantz, Pearl, 19
Jaquet, Paul, 266
Jarvis, Hattie, 49
Jeareane, Victoria, 282
Jeffers, Emmor, 266
Jeffries, Elizabeth, 266
Jeffries, May, 267
Jehn, Mary, 53
Jenkins, {Boy}, 19
Jenkins, Martha J., 267
Jenkins, William, 73, 267
Johnson, {Boy}, 19
Johnson, Annie, 19, 66
Johnson, Canute A., 73
Johnson, Elizabeth E., 267
Johnson, Fannie, 111
Johnson, James M., 267
Johnson, John, 19
Johnson, Laura, 55
Johnson, Margaret, 107
Johnson, Martha, 417
Johnson, Minnie Elizabeth, 268

(Maiden names in italics)

Lynch, Robert, 24
Lynch, Robert Raymond, 290
Lynch, Stephen, 81
Lynch, Thomas, 290
Lynham, Harriet E., 97
Lyon, McCormick, 126
Lyon, Mrs. Sarah A., 126
Lyon, Mrs. Sarah Ann, 73
Lyons, Hiram, 290
Lytle, Francis Ida, 53
Lytle, Minnie M., 252

M

Mack, Griswold, 290
Macomb, John, 81
Macomber, Mary, 323
Madden, Earl C., 24
Madden, Edna, 119
Madden, Frank D., 81
Madden, Lewis A., 81
Madden, Michael S., 290
Madden, Walter, 291
Magahay, David Charles, 82
Magahay, Marcus, 291
Mahar, James E., 291
Malden, William P., 291
Malenfaut, George, 292
Malotte, Jennie, 72
Manette, Lia, 103
Manlove, Stephen P., 82
Mann, Samuel K., 82
Manning, Edward B., 82
Manning, George, 292
Manning, Melinda E., 78
Manson, John, 82
Marble N., 82
Marble, Ralph N., 24
Marcellus, Aaron, 292
Marcellus, Anna E., 292
Marcellus, Clara, 113, 419
Marchefski, Ignatius, 82
Marquis, {Child}, 293
Marsac, Joseph Francois, 293
Marsh, Ella M., 105
Marsh, Etta Jane, 88
Marshall, Frank, 24
Marshall, Julia Elizabeth, 24
Martin, Annie, 73
Martin, Charles, 293
Martin, Charles C., 24
Martin, Emma A., 57
Martin, Frank, 126
Martin, Grace Belle, 24
Martin, Hugh, 294
Martin, Hurburt, 24
Martin, James, 294
Martin, Joanna M., 90
Martin, Joseph, 294
Martin, Mary, 86
Martin, Minnie, 63
Martin, Mrs. Lillian, 126
Martin, Walter B., 83
Martin, Willard Stanley, 295
Marvin, Mrs. Henrietta, 295
Mason, Ellen, 47
Mason, Flora, 90

Mason, Victoria, 67
Mather, Albert H., 83
Mather, Henry O., 24
Mather, Increase, 83
Maxwell, Mary E., 295
May, Minnie G., 70
May, Ralph, 83, 295
Maynard, Charlie A., 24
Maynard, Josephine, 97
Maynard, Mary, 296
Maynard, Mary L., 48
Maynard, Mrs. Louise, 296
Mayo, James, 296
Mayo, James, Sr., 296
Mayott, Frank, 296
McAdam, Joseph Henry, 297
McAdams, Elizabeth, 85
McArthur, {Boy}, 24
McArthur, Catherine Jane, 114
McArthur, Donald, 297
McArthur, Duncan John, 297
McArthur, Duncan Robert, 24
McArthur, George J., 24
McArthur, Harold, 297
McArthur, Hattie, 112
McArthur, John G., 83
McArthur, Letitia, 297
McArthur, Margaret, 85
McArthur, Mary, 62
McArthur, Patrick, 297
McBride, Leah, 297
McCain, Abram L., 298
McCallum, Anne, 298
McCambridge, Michael, 83
McCann, Georgie, 298
McCary, John, 83
McCaul, Alex P., 299
McCaul, Donald B., 299
McCauley, Mary, 87
McClain, {Girl}, 24
McClatchey, {Child}, 25, 299
McClatchey, Abram, 83
McClatchey, Bert, 84
McClatchey, Charles, 24
McClatchey, Clara, 299, 300
McClatchey, Earl E., 25
McClatchey, Elizabeth, 299
McClatchey, Nancy, 44
McClatchey, Nellie, 25
McClatchey, Rena, 25
McClellan, Dougal, 84
McClelland, {Girl}, 300
McClelland, Lillian, 56
McClelland, Margaret, 90
McClelland, Mary, 300
McClenry, James, 300
McClymont, Minnie, 66
McCollum, Georgena, 25
McConnel, Barney, 300
McConnell, Guy, 25
McConnell, Harwood, 25
McConnell, Varnum, 84
McCormick, {Boy}, 25
McCormick, Earl, 25
McCormick, Francis P., 84
McCormick, George C., 84
McCormick, Mrs., 300

McCoy, Clarence, 25
McCoy, John, 84
McCoy, Susan. *See Susan Mulhatton*
McCrae, Agnes Catherine, 108
McCrea, Annie, 312
McCullough, Mary Jane, 86
McCullough, Samuel, 300
McCusky, {Male}, 300
McDermaid, Daniel, 84
McDermaid, Malcolm, 300
McDermaid, Mrs., 301
McDonald, {Boy}, 25
McDonald, {Child}, 301
McDonald, {Girl}, 25
McDonald, {Male}, 306
McDonald, Agnes, 301
McDonald, Albert, 84, 126
McDonald, Alex, 301
McDonald, Alex Angus, 301
McDonald, Angus, 84, 301
McDonald, Angus J., 301
McDonald, Angus R., 301
McDonald, Anna, 385
McDonald, Annie, 105
McDonald, Archibald, 84
McDonald, Archie, 85
McDonald, Arthur D., 85
McDonald, Catherine, 84, 105
McDonald, Charles, 301
McDonald, Christine, 68
McDonald, Dan, 301
McDonald, Dan E., 85
McDonald, Daniel, 85, 301, 302
McDonald, Donald, 85
McDonald, Donald D., 302
McDonald, Donald R. M., 302
McDonald, Dora, 96
McDonald, Dougal, 126
McDonald, Elizabeth, 94, 302
McDonald, Flora, 79, 302
McDonald, George L., 25
McDonald, Henrietta, 302
McDonald, Hugh H., 85
McDonald, Hughie, 302
McDonald, Ida May, 303
McDonald, Jack, 303
McDonald, James E., 303
McDonald, Jennie A., 304
McDonald, John, 85, 304
McDonald, John A., 304
McDonald, John J., 85
McDonald, John R., 305
McDonald, John Roy, 305
McDonald, John S., 305
McDonald, Joseph, 305
McDonald, Josephia, 126
McDonald, Kate, 91, 342
McDonald, Katherine, 43
McDonald, Lizzie, 105
McDonald, Maggie, 305
McDonald, Margaret, 306
McDonald, Marguerite, 306
McDonald, Mary, 85, 86, 227, 306
McDonald, Mary Ann, 87
McDonald, Mary Loraine, 25
McDonald, Mary Sarah, 306
McDonald, Michael, 306

Parks, {Girl}, 31
Parks, Jennie, 45
Parks, Joseph, 95
Parreau, Mena, 77
Parrow, Henry, 96
Parrow, Julia, 67
Partridge, Ina, 31
Partridge, Ina M., 354
Partridge, Pearl, 31
Partridge, Philip O., 96
Paterson, Ralph, 96
Patterson, {Boy}, 32
Patterson, George, 96
Patterson, Lois E., 74
Patton, John, 354
Paul, Allen, 354
Paul, Julia, 129
Peacock, {Girl}, 32
Pearson, Alice A., 354
Pearson, Anna Louisa, 47
Pearson, Armand, 32
Pearson, Fred, 354
Pearson, Mabelle L., 32
Pearson, Minnie, 79
Peck, John, 355
Peck, Miner, 96
Pelkie, {Boy}, 32, 355
Pelkie, Oliver, 355
Pelkier, Henry, 355
Pelton, John, 355
Pemberton, Horatio, 356
Pepper, Solomon, 96
Perkins, Guy Clinton, 356
Perkins, Jessie A., 60
Perry, {Child}, 356
Perry, Byron, 96
Perry, Jane, 356
Perry, Nellie Dora, 54
Perry, Sarah A., 316
Peterson, {Boy}, 32
Peterson, Charlotte Elizabeth, 83
Peterson, Phyllis, 356
Peterson, Sarah Myrtle, 75
Phelps, Myron, 96
Phelps, William Walter, 356
Phillips, Frank, 356
Phillips, Frank A., 96
Phillips, Fred, 356
Phillips, George E., 96
Philp, {Boy}, 32
Philp, William, 96
Pierce, Catherine, 356
Pierce, Jerome, 356
Pierson, {Girl, 32
Pierson, John, 96
Pierson, Wayne, 32
Pierson, William, 32
Pizer, Fannie, 356
Pizer, Julius, 96
Pizer, Mildred, 32
Plunkett, Catherine, 155, 357
Plunkett, J. T., 357
Pomeroy, Calvin Thayer, 357
Porter, Alma, 32
Porter, Emernett A., 357
Potter, Arthur, 97
Potter, Emerson, 97

Potter, Emma D., 357
Potts, Gladys, 32
Potts, Grace I., 32
Potvin, Julius, 357
Potvin, Mr., 357
Poultny, James C., 97
Pratt, Harriet, 32
Pratt, Ralph, 357
Prell, Blanch, 50
Preston, David, 359
Preston, Henry, 97
Price, Emma, 259
Prince, George Vanilla, 359
Pringle, Catherine M., 45
Pritchard, James Roberts, 97
Pritchard, Jennie, 32
Proctor, {Boy}, 32
Proctor, Maude, 359
Proctor, William F., 97
Proctor, William J., 360
Procunier, Anthony, 97, 360
Procunier, Beatrice, 44
Procunier, Carrie, 85
Procunier, Dessmus, 97
Profit, Mrs. Joseph, 361
Provencher, Napolean, 97
Pulford, Martha H., 361
Purdy, Samuel, 361
Purdy, Sarah, 430
Putman, Mary, 32
Pyne, {Child}, 361
Pyne, Charles Forrest, 361
Pyne, Cynthia Ann, 361
Pyne, Ella, 67
Pyne, Ellen J., 63
Pyne, George, 97
Pyne, Horatio Albert, 32
Pyne, James Fraser, 361
Pyne, Maud, 361
Pyne, Meda, 68
Pyne, Victoria B., 32
Pyne, William C., 97

Q

Quance, William, 361
Quesnell, Hermidas, 97
Quigley, Elizabeth, 96
Quigley, Francis Patrick, 33
Quigley, Martha Florence, 361
Quilty, John, 362
Quinlan, Michael, 362
Quinlan, Thomas J., 98

R

Raciat, Joseph, 98
Rajnowski, Joseph, 362
Ralston, Hattie, 108
Ralston, Ida May, 54
Ranney, {Boy}, 362
Ranney, {Girl}, 33
Ranney, Arthur W., 98
Read, Allen J., 362
Read, Fred N., 362
Read, Ina, 45

Read, Nelson H., 98
Rebelle, Aurelia, 62
Redmon, John, 362
Reed, Joseph L., 363
Reed, Linna, 95
Reed, Matt, 98
Reed, Mrs., 363
Reefer, Ada, 65
Reeves, Emma, 211
Reeves, James S., 363
Reeves, Jerry, 363
Regier, Christ, 98
Regier, Christian, 363
Regier, Laburnia, 101
Renis, Theresa Grace, 81
Rennell, Andrew, 98
Reno, John, 363
Repke, Frederick, 132
Repkey, Mrs., 132
Reynolds, {Boy}, 33, 363
Reynolds, {Girl}, 33
Reynolds, {Groom}, 98
Reynolds, Charles P., 363
Reynolds, Frank, 365
Reynolds, Frederick C., 98
Reynolds, Helen, 111
Reynolds, Jennie E., 52
Reynolds, Jesse, 365
Reynolds, John, 365
Reynolds, John H., 365
Reynolds, Mrs., 365
Reynolds, Pat, 365
Reynolds, Paul F., 33
Reynolds, Thomas W., 99
Rhinehart, Barbara, 46
Rice, Earl Blaine, 33
Rice, Earle R., 100
Rice, Frank Clarence, 33, 366
Rice, Jessie, 131
Rice, Justin R., 366
Rice, Minnie, 118
Rice, Viola, 88
Richards, Lewis H., 100
Richardson, Carl, 33
Richardson, Charles Wellington, 366
Richardson, Flora, 90
Richardson, Ida E., 367
Richardson, John S. R., 100
Richardson, Morry Erwin, 367
Richardson, Mrs. Melissa R., 367
Richardson, William, 367
Richmond, Mrs. Margaretta, 60
Richmond, Richard A., 367
Richter, James, 128
Richter, Mrs. Claudia, 128
Richway, Mary Agnes, 101
Richway, Selena, 86
Ricker, Louisa S., 107
Rickle, John, 100
Rickle, Mrs. Amelia, 367
Riecker, Louis, 367
Rifenbark, {Boy}, 33
Rifenbark, David, 368
Ritchie, Betrum W., 33
Ritchie, Edna S., 33
Ritchie, Ellen, 124
Ritchie, Ellen D., 64

(Maiden names in italics)

Simons, Mary Jane, 384
Simons, Richard, 35
Simons, William, 105
Simpson, William, 105
Sims, Adeline, 384
Sinclair {Boy}, 35
Sinclair Jennie, 115
Sinclair, {Boy}, 384
Sinclair, Anna M., 61
Sinclair, Mary A., 81
Sinclair, Mrs. Katie, 384
Sing, Wah, 385
Sinton, {Girl}, 35
Sinton, Ida M., 35
Sinton, Isabella, 54
Sinton, Mary Jane, 114
Sisson, Charlotte Elizabeth, 83
Sisson, Laura A., 98
Sissons, Frank, 105
Skuse, Anna, 385
Skuse, Charles, 35
Skuse, Eliza, 35
Skuse, Esther, 35
Skuse, Fanny, 35
Skuse, Thomas, 105
Skuse, William H., 105
Slaght, Andrew D., 385
Slaght, Frederick W., 385
Slaght, Richard, 105
Slater, Arthur, 105
Slater, Everett, 35
Slater, Frances Jane, 60
Slater, Glenn, 35
Slater, James M., 385
Slater, James N., 386
Slater, Sadie, 35
Slater, Walter, 105
Sloan, Alexander, 106
Sloan, Malcolm A., 128
Sloan, Mrs. Elizabeth, 386
Sloan, Mrs. Ellen, 62
Sloan, Mrs. Esther Jane, 128
Sloan, Samuel, 106
Sly, {Girl}, 36
Small, J. W., 106
Smiley, {Girl}, 36
Smith, {Boy}, 36
Smith, Alva J., 128
Smith, Angus, 386
Smith, Angus W., 106
Smith, Anna Belle, 89
Smith, Arthur, 387
Smith, Arvilla Evangelina, 43
Smith, Clark Harold, 36
Smith, Eliza, 260
Smith, Ella, 106
Smith, Fred, 387
Smith, Fred H., 106
Smith, George E., 387
Smith, Gladys Gertrude, 36
Smith, Hattie, 387
Smith, Helen Flora, 36
Smith, Henry Herbert, 387
Smith, Howard, 36
Smith, Isabelle E., 128
Smith, James, 388
Smith, Joseph, 106

Smith, Jude A., 106
Smith, Lenbly, 388
Smith, Lizzie, 58
Smith, Margaret Jane, 388
Smith, Martin Snyder, 390
Smith, Mary, 423
Smith, Mary E., 115
Smith, Maude J., 36
Smith, May, 390
Smith, Percy, 36
Smith, Satie, 78
Smith, Thompson, 390
Smith, Truman, 391
Smith, W. L., 391
Smith, William, 391
Smith, Willie, 392
Smithers, Angie, 392
Smithers, John H., 106
Smithers, William, 106, 392
Snell, Francis M., 108
Snooks, Mrs. Mary, 69
Snowden, William, 36, 392
Snowden, William E. B., 392
Snowden, William Russell, 393
Snowdon, William E., 106
Snyder, Male, 132
Socient, Napoleon, 106
Somers, Anne Cordelia, 51
Somers, Clifford, 36
Somers, Frank, 106
Somers, Margaret B., 393
Somers, Minnie, 102
Somers, Selena A., 79
Soura, {Child}, 393
Soura, Edward, 107
Soura, John, 393
Soura, Mary, 393
Sousie, {Boy}, 36
Sousie, Clara, 70
Sousie, Clarence G., 393
Sousie, Felix, 393
Sousie, George, 107
Sousie, Mary, 394
Sousie, Mary E., 394
Sousie, Sarah, 84
Sousie, Silas, 107
Southern, Jennie L., 117
Southgate, {Boy}, 36
Southgate, {Male}, 394
Southgate, Jennie H., 36
Southgate, Nellie M., 36, 107
Southgate, Raymond, 394
Southgate, Vidie L., 36, 394
Sovey, Clair O., 37
Sovey, Herbert, 37
Sovey, John F., 107
Sovey, Kate, 395
Sovey, Linna Elizabeth, 64
Sovey, Mabel, 64
Spain, Elmer R., 107
Sparr, Joseph, 37
Specht, Fred, 395
Specht, Joseph H., 37
Specht, Mary A., 44
Specht, Raymond, 37
Specht, Rose, 395
Spencer, Allan H., 395

Spencer, Asa, 396
Spencer, Ella, 37
Spencer, Ella E., 396
Spencer, Ernest E., 107
Spencer, Frank H., 107
Spencer, Hannah C., 64
Spencer, Harriett Newell, 396
Spencer, John A., 107
Spencer, Lincoln Edward, 107
Spencer, Mary E., 89
Spencer, Minnie L., 92
Spencer, Rhoda J., 95
Spencer, Seymour H., 107
Spoon, William A., 397
Spratt, Alice May, 397
Spratt, Lizzie, 71
Springstead, Isabelle Joan, 66
Springstead, Kezia, 270
St. Amour, Eugene, 398
St. Clair, Phoebe E., 107
St. Clair, Will, 398
St. Laurent, George Victor, 107
St. Peter, Fred, 107
Staats, Carrie M., 109
Stafford, Alice, 59
Stafford, Ella, 84
Stafford, James, 398
Stafford, John Howard, 398
Stafford, Mrs. Eleanor M., 118
Stafford, Robbie, 399
Stafford, Samuel E., 399
Starkey, James, 399
Stecker, {Boy}, 37
Steele, {Boy}, 37
Steele, Lois E., 37
Steere, Edwin M., 107
Steffes, Josephine, 189
Stephens, Cora, 85
Sterritt, {Boy}, 37
Stetcher, Joseph, 399
Stevens, Angie, 399
Stevens, Arbor C., 108
Stevens, Clara, 37
Stevens, Clare, 400
Stevens, David F., 400
Stevens, George T., 108
Stevens, John H., 400
Stewart, {Boy}, 37
Stewart, {Child}, 400
Stewart, Catharine, 311
Stewart, Charlotta, 98
Stewart, Duncan, 108
Stewart, Earl, 37
Stewart, Ethel, 37
Stewart, Harriet, 400
Stewart, Henry, 400
Stewart, James L., 400
Stewart, John, 400
Stewart, John B., 400
Stewart, Mrs. Mary, 401
Sthall, Frances, 105
Stickney, Mrs. Mary, 401
Stiles, {Child}, 401
Stinchcomb, Henry J., 108
Stinchcombe, Gervin Lucean, 37
Stinchcombe, Guy, 37
Stinchcombe, Margaret, 37

Witter, Harriett S., 408
Witter, Sarah [Purdy], 430
Wolf, Mary, 50
Woo, Rosa Maud, 41
Woo, Willie C., 118
Wood, Arthur D., 118
Wood, Emma R., 96
Wood, Hannah, 430
Wood, John, 118
Woods, {Bride}, 90
Woods, George, 431
Woods, Idsa, 123
Woods, Rilla, 45
Woodward, Edward, 431
Wyman, Wallace, 431

Y

Yalomstein, Fanny, 117
Yearn, Louis F., 118
Yockey, Fred H., 119
Yokom, Olive Mary, 88, 127
Young, Clio, 74
Young, Curtis, 431
Young, Ella, 431
Young, Ernest, 119
Young, John, 431
Young, John B., 431
Young, Martha J., 73, 267
Young, Martin B., 432
Young, Mrs., 131
Young, Robert, 432

Young, Sophronia, 102
Young, William, 119
Youngs, Freeman, 432
Yuill, Ethel, 41
Yuill, Jennie R., 41
Yuill, Joseph, 42, 432
Yuill, Leota Ruth, 42
Yuill, Mary, 432
Yuill, Viola, 42
Yuill, William, 42

Z

Zorn, A. William, 119
Zwirk, Caroline S., 383

www.ingramcontent.com/pod-product-compliance
Lightning Source LLC
Chambersburg PA
CBHW081143270326
41930CB00014B/3013